The Descendants of JOHANN PETER Klinger AND CATHARINA Steinbruch

FOURTH EDITION

Max E. Klinger

Mechanicsburg, PA USA

Published by Sunbury Press, Inc.
Mechanicsburg, Pennsylvania

www.sunburypress.com

Copyright © 2006, 2009, 2012, 2017 by Max E. Klinger.
Cover Copyright © 2017 by Sunbury Press, Inc.

Sunbury Press supports copyright. Copyright fuels creativity, encourages diverse voices, promotes free speech, and creates a vibrant culture. Thank you for buying an authorized edition of this book and for complying with copyright laws by not reproducing, scanning, or distributing any part of it in any form without permission. You are supporting writers and allowing Sunbury Press to continue to publish books for every reader. For information contact Sunbury Press, Inc., Subsidiary Rights Dept., PO Box 548, Mechanicsburg, PA 17007 USA or legal@sunburypress.com.

For information about special discounts for bulk purchases, please contact Sunbury Press Orders Dept. at (855) 338-8359 or orders@sunburypress.com.

To request one of our authors for speaking engagements or book signings, please contact Sunbury Press Publicity Dept. at publicity@sunburypress.com.

ISBN: 978-1-62006-769-7 (Hard cover)
ISBN: 978-1-62006-768-0 (Trade Paperback)

Library of Congress Control Number: 2017948380

FOURTH SUNBURY PRESS EDITION: July 2017

Product of the United States of America
0 1 1 2 3 5 8 13 21 34 55

Cover design by Alice Buchman
Cover photos by Lawrence Knorr

Continue the Enlightenment!

Contents

I.	Klinger Coat of Arms	1
II.	Ancestry and Origins of Peter Klinger	3
III.	The Klingers in Pennsylvania	13
IV.	Peter Klinger and Catharina Steinbruch	21
V.	Photographs	35
VI.	Descendants of Peter Klinger and Catharina Steinbruch	49
	1. Catharine Klinger, b._____, d. before 1858	49
	2. Johann Philip Klinger, b. 20 Apr 1792, d. 12 Nov 1857	49
	3. Eve Elizabeth Klinger, b. 16 Jan 1794, d. 18 Jan 1870	132
	4. Johann Peter Klinger, b. 2 Jan 1796, d. 4 Jan 1879	209
	5. Johann George Klinger, b. 7 Jan 1798, d. 16 Sep 1880	310
	6. Johannes Klinger, b. 18 Mar 1802, d. 11 Oct 1873	372
	7. Alexander Klinger, b. 28 May 1805, d. 2 May 1876	398
	8. Hanna Klinger, b. 21 Oct 1807, d. 27 Apr 1885	420
	9. Johann Adam Klinger, b. 18 Feb 1810, d. 15 Apr 1885	426
	10. Jacob S. Klinger, b. 29 Jan 1813, d. 23 Jan 1883	431
	11. Daniel Klinger, b. 28 Jan 1816, d. 2 Mar 1899	448

Index to the Genealogical Listings 499

I. Klinger Coat of Arms

The Klinger Coat of Arms shown above is a grayscale photographic copy, made by the author, of a painting by George Malick (1924 – 1993), an artist who lived in Hegins, PA. The painting was completed around 1976 for Carlos and Marion Klinger, who were then living in Chambersburg, PA. The painting is now in the possession of the author.

The painting was a copy of the coat of arms that was painted on glass, that then was in the possession of Carl H. Klinger, of Sacramento, PA. In 1948, Oliver C. Klinger, of Bayonne, New Jersey, printed a pamphlet in German entitled, "History of the Klinger Family," by Curt R. Vincentz, who was then deceased, formerly of Hanover, Germany. Included in the pamphlet was a reprint of the Coat of Arms with the following explanation, apparently written by Oliver Klinger:

> *For the benefit of the Klinger family, I am printing herewith the Klinger Coat of Arms, which you will note is dated 1524. I have the original in my possession, which is printed on old glass. I obtained this from a friend, Kurt [sic] Vincentz, of Hanover, Germany. He obtained it in Heidelberg, near the birthplace of Johann Philip Klinger, who came from Paffenbeerfurth [sic], and who arrived in this country in 1749 [sic], and settled near Klingerstown, Pa.*

The legend encircling the coat of arms is often translated as:

"A Good Sharp Sword – May It Bring You Much Honor."

II. Ancestry and Origins of Peter Klinger

Peter Klinger's father, Johann Philip Klinger ("Philip"), was born on July 11, 1723 in Pfaffen-Beerfurth, Germany. Pfaffen-Beerfurth was located in a mountainous geographical region known as the "Odenwald," meaning Oden's or Wotan's Forest. In Norse mythology, the name "Oden" or "Odin" is associated with the chief god. "Wotan" is the German equivalent. Today the Odenwald region covers portions of three German states – Hessen (Hesse), Bayern (Bavaria), and Baden-Württemberg, although the largest part of the region lies within the modern state of Hesse, and is situated in the southwestern portion of Hesse, between the Rhine River valley to the west and the Main River valley to the east. A portion of the Odenwald region is part of a natural park called "Naturpark Bergstrasse Odenwald." The Odenwald itself covers an area roughly 50 miles by 25 miles.

Google® Earth Image of the area around Reichelsheim and Pfaffen-Beerfurth (reprinted with permission).

Pfaffen-Beerfurth lay on the west side of the Gersprenz River, while Kirch-Beerfurth was on the east side of the river. Beginning around the year 1550, these two parts of Beerfurth were referred to as Unter (Lower) and Ober (Upper) Beerfurth, but from about 1650 onward, they were known as Pfaffen-Beerfurth and Kirch-Beerfurth. In 1970, during a period of land reform, the two parts, along with the neighboring communities of Gerssprenz and Bockenrod, united to become "Beerfurth." Since 1972, the village of Beerfurth administratively has been part of the town or municipality (Gemeinde) of Reichelsheim. According to information at http://www.reichelsheim.de/, Beerfurth today has a population of approximately 1,120 residents.

When the village of Beerfurth was founded is not clear. According to http://www.reichelsheim.de/, the first documented reference to the village was in 1321 as "Berenforte," and later as "Beerfurth." It has been suggested that the village became divided because in 1454, half of the village was pawned, and then in 1478, two brothers who owned a portion of the village sold their share of the village to a church body in Heidelberg. After that, the village was divided. A German gepgraphy book published in London in English in 1762 notes that Pfaffen-Beerfurth "with respect to its ground-jurisdiction and government, [belongs] to the foundation of the Holy-Ghost at Heidelberg."

Reichelsheim, a traditional village only a few kilometers southwest of Pfaffen-Beerfurth, was also the traditional center of the Protestant parish for the region. The following image, a closer view of the Google® Earth satellite imagery shown on the previous page, shows both villages.

Google® Earth Image of Pfaffen-Beerfurth, on the left, and Kirch-Beerfurth, on the right (reprinted with permission).

It is often written that the name "Beerfurth" derives from the name "Berenforte" or "Bernfurt" meaning "boar-ford" – a place where boar (or wild pigs) could ford the Gersprenz River. Pfaffen-Beerfurth lies roughly midway between Frankfurt am Main, to the north, and Heidelberg, to the south. It is about 50 kilometers (30 miles) south-southeast of the city of Frankfurt am Main and about 35 to 40 kilometers (22 to 25 miles) northeast of Heidelberg.

Photograph by Jacky Abromitis

Contemporary road sign for Beerfurth

Today, Beerfurth is a village within the *Gemeinde* of Reichelsheim. A *"Gemeinde"* is the the smallest administrative division of local government having corporate status and powers of self-government. It can be translated as "borough," "community," or "municipality." The Gemeinde of Reichelsheim is part of the Odenwaldkreis. *"Kreis"* is a larger division of local government akin to a District. The largest division of local government is a *"Land,"* which can be translated as "State." Beerfurth is part of the State of Hesse.

Photographs by Jacky Abromitis

Contemporary photos of insignia for the former villages

Some sources indicate that at various times throughout recorded history, the area around Pfaffen-Beerfurth was part of the Rheinish Palatinate (Pfalz) region. For example, historical maps of Germany after the Peace of Westphalia, which in 1648 ended the Thirty-Years' War, show that much of the area south of Frankfurt, between the Main and the Rhine rivers, was part of the Rheinish Palatinate. Unfortunately, the history of German political divisions, especially before the Holy Roman Empire was finally dissolved in 1806, is exceedingly complex.

Before 1871, Germany was not the unified country we think of today. Following the Peace of Westphalia in 1648, "Germany," as part of the Holy Roman Empire, consisted of a conglomeration of many governmental units of varying sizes, importance, and powers. These "states," both secular and ecclesiastical, had leaders of varying descriptions, including kings, counts, dukes, landgraviates, and archbishops, to name but a few. Only a few of these governmental units were direct members of the Holy Roman Empire, while many more owed their authority and jurisdiction to one of these larger units. Many of these so-called states, particularly the smaller ones, were treated more like family property than sovereign states, and their boundaries and owners changed frequently. As noted above, ownership of the village of Beerfurth was transferred several times in the 15th Century.

Historical maps from around 1635 and as late as 1789 show that the area around Reichelsheim was part of Grafschaft Erbach (County Erbach), under the control of the Count of Erbach. The Count of Erbach held control over the area under a feudal arrangement called a "fief" with the Elector Palatine. A book published in London in 1762, which was a translation of a German book by A. F. Busching, says that "The county of Erbach is for the most part a fief of the Elector-palatine, and on the raising of the house of Erbach to the dignity of Counts [which occurred in 1532], the feudal-rights were expressly reserved to that of the Elector [Palatine]." In simplistic terms, the Elector Palatine created the County of Erbach, and the Count of Erbach held title under a feudal arrangement with the Elector Palatine, so called because he was one of the relatively few officials entitled to vote on the election of the Holy Roman Emperor.

The connection between Pfaffen-Beerfurth and the County of Erbach is evidenced by the photograph of a sign in Pfaffen-Beerfurth in 2005, reprinted on the following page, which, loosely translated, says: "Market Town Pfaffenbeerfurth, District (or County) of Erbach, Court District of Michelstadt."

A sign, photographed in 2005, in what was formerly Pfaffen-Beerfurth, says, "Market Town Pfaffenbeerfurth, District (or County) of Erbach, Court District of Michelstadt."

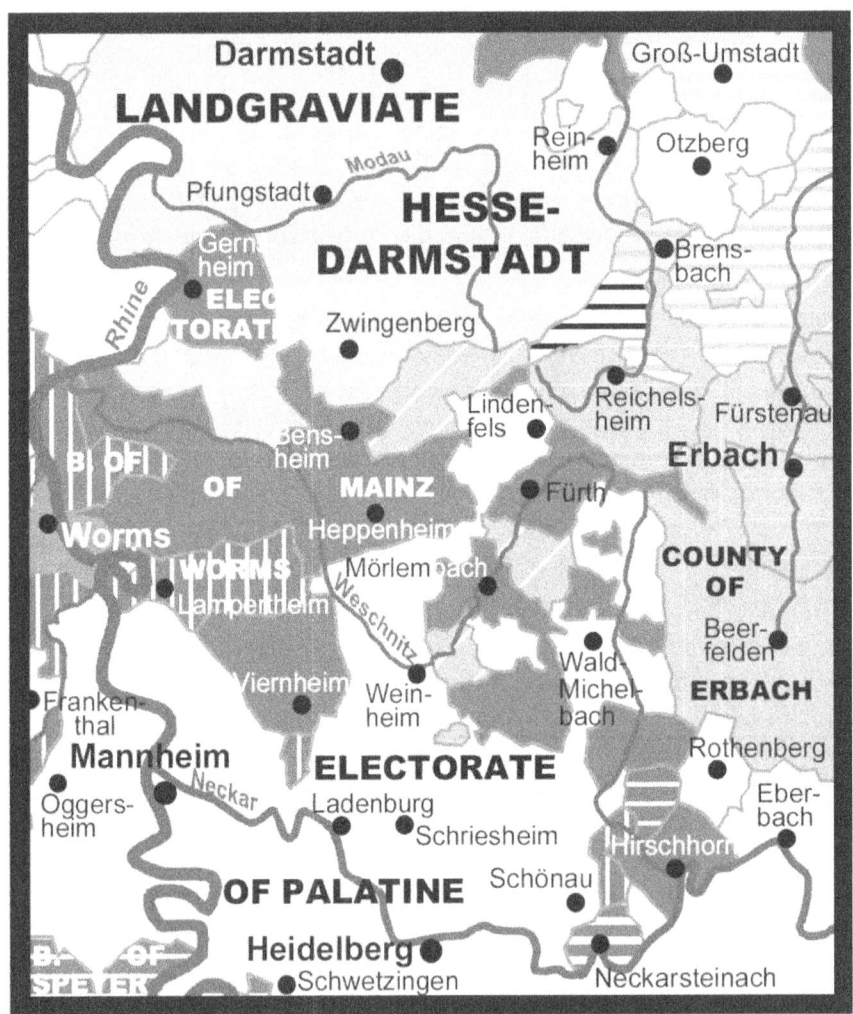

Map showing portion of Germany in 1789, prepared by Thomas Höckmann and reprinted with permission.

The map on the previous page shows the western portion of the County of Erbach in 1789, along with the surrounding territories. The light-colored cross-hatched area just east of the town of Reichelsheim was an area that was under the joint control of Erbach and the Rheinish Palatinate, which is consistent with the feudal arrangement discussed above. The map shows that Reichelsheim was part of the County of Erbach at the time. Pfaffen-Beerfurth lay just a few kilometers east of Reichelsheim.

A detail from a 1647 map of the County of Erbach, available on the Library of Congress website, includes the area around Reichelsheim (spelled "Reicholsheim" on the map) just below the center of the map, with Pfaffen-Beerfurth (spelled "Pfaffenberfurt") just above and to east (right) of it.

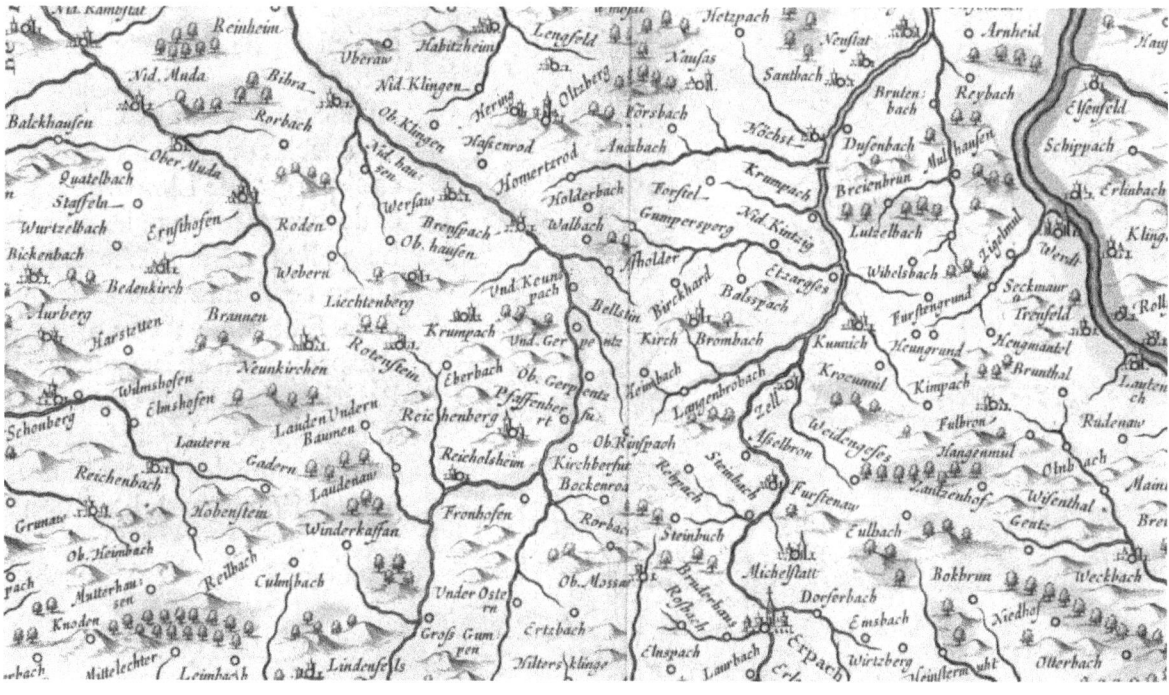

A portion of a 1647 map, originally published in Amsterdam, of the County of Erbach, available on the Library of Congress website, https://www.loc.gov/resource/g3200m.gct00035/?sp=67.

The Palatinate itself spanned the Rhine River, with the bulk of the territory on the left, or west, side of the Rhine. Near the end of the 18th Century, most of the Palatinate west of the Rhine came under French control. In 1806, after the hereditary line of Palatinate rulers died out, much of the Palatinate on the right, or east, bank of the Rhine was divided between Hesse–Darmstadt and Baden. At that time, the area around Reichelsheim, along with County of Erbach, became part of Hesse-Darmstadt. Today, the area is part of the German State of Hesse.

In the first half of the 16th Century, much of what is now Hesse was under the control of Philip I, called "Philip the Magnanimous" (1509-1567), who was Landgrav of Hesse. After Philip's death, his Hessian lands were divided among four heirs, with the largest two portions being Hesse-Kassel and Hesse-Darmstadt. Following some consolidation with smaller states, Hesse-Kassel to the north and Hesse-Darmstadt to the south comprised most of what is now the State of Hesse.

Photograph by Lawrence Knorr

A house in the former Pfaffen-Beerfurth believed to have been a home of Philip Klinger's family before he emigrated to America in 1751. The street address for this house is 10 Marktplatz.

Photograph by Lawrence Knorr

Another view of the house in what was previously Pfaffen-Beerfurth believed to have been a home of Philip Klinger's family before emigrating to America in 1751.

Photo by Lawrence Knorr

The center of the town of Pfaffen-Beerfurth in 2005.

The century or so before four members of the Klinger family left Pfaffen-Beerfurth beginning in 1749 was a tumultuous period. The history of the nearby village of Reichelsheim illustrates this period. According to http://www.reichelsheim.de/, the village had a population of about 120 inhabitants at the start of the Thirty Years' War in 1618. As Wikipeadia notes, this was a war that began between various Protestant and Catholic states in the fragmented Holy Roman Empire after the election of Frederick II, as Holy Roman Emperor. Frederick sought to impose religious uniformity (*i.e.,* Catholicism) on the people of the Holy Roman Empire. Triggered by a revolt in the predominantly Protestant Kingdom of Bohemia (an area comprising much of what is today the Czech Republic), the conflict spread to Germany. As the various factions sought the support of outside powers, and neighboring states sought to protect their interests, Sweden, Spain, France, and the Dutch Republic all got involved. By its end, the Thirty Years' War was one of the longest and most destructive of the European religious wars. By some estimates, it resulted in as many as eight million casualties.

Reichelsheim's website, http://www.reichelsheim.de/, indicates that the Thirty Years' War created a long period of terror for the residents of the village, who on a number of occasions had to seek refuge in the nearby castle of Schloss Reichenberg. In 1623, nearly two-thirds of the houses in the village were destroyed and virtually all of the village's historical records in the town hall were burned. At the start of the Thirty Years' War, Reichelsheim's population had been around 160, but it was greatly reduced by the war, and the resulting epidemics, hunger, and emigration. After the war, it grew again to about 120, aided by immigrants from Switzerland.

According to a number of sources, the Klinger name first appears in Pfaffen-Beerfurth records as early as 1426. Similarly, a number of sources trace the ancestry of Peter Klinger and his father Philip back to Georg Klinger, a mayor of Beerfurth, who was born around 1610, probably in Pfaffen-Beerfurth, and died around 1694. This ancestry is as follows:

Ancestors of Peter Klinger

--- 1st Generation ---

1. Johann Peter Klinger was born on 3 Nov 1773, Reading, Berks County, PA. He married Catharina Steinbruch, daughter of Adam Steinbrecher and Anna Margaretha Hoffman, circa 1791, Lykens Township, Dauphin County, PA. He died on 10 Aug 1858, Lykens Township, Dauphin County, PA, at age 84. He was buried at Klinger's Church, Erdman, Dauphin County, PA.

--- 2nd Generation ---

2. Johann Philip Klinger was born on 11 Jul 1723, Pfaffen-Beerfurth, Hesse, Germany. He married Anna Elizabeth Heist on 22 Oct 1744, Reichelsheim. He married Eva Elizabeth Beilstein, daughter of John Jacob Beilstein and Anna Elizabeth Rettich, on 21 May 1754, Neunkirchen, Germany. He died on 30 Sep 1811, Schuylkill County, PA, at age 88. He was buried at Klinger's Church, Erdman, Dauphin County, PA.

3. Eva Elizabeth Beilstein was born on 27 May 1730, Brandau, Germany. She was baptized on 29 May 1730. She married Johann Philip Klinger, son of Johannes Klinger and Agatha Heist, on 21 May 1754, Neunkirchen, Germany. She died circa 1815, Lykens Township, Dauphin County, PA.

--- 3rd Generation ---

4. Johannes Klinger was born on 18 Nov 1694, Pfaffen-Beerfurth, Germany. He married Agatha Heist, daughter of Johann Leonhard Heist and Anna Rosina Meister, on 6 Nov 1720, Reichelsheim, Germany. He died on 22 Sep 1774, Pfaffen-Beerfurth, Germany, at age 79.

5. Agatha Heist was born on 2 Apr 1699, Pfaffen-Beerfurth, Germany. She married Johannes Klinger, son of Johann Georg Klinger and Elizabeth Göttman, on 6 Nov 1720, Reichelsheim, Germany. She died on 10 Apr 1780, Pfaffen-Beerfurth, Germany, at age 81.

6. John Jacob Beilstein was born in 1696. He married Anna Elizabeth Rettich, daughter of John Martin Rettich and Otilla (--?--), on 22 Jun 1723.

7. Anna Elizabeth Rettich was born in 1705, Brandau, Germany. She married John Jacob Beilstein, son of George Beilstein and Eva Kohl, on 22 Jun 1723.

--- 4th Generation ---

8. Johann Georg Klinger was born on 6 May 1655, Pfaffen-Beerfurth, Germany. He married Elizabeth Göttman, daughter of Philip Gottman, on 5 May 1680, Reichelsheim, Germany. He died on 25 Mar 1693/94, Kirch-Beerfurth, Germany, at age 38. He was buried on 28 Mar 1694.

9. Elizabeth Göttman was born in 1663, Kirch-Beerfurth, Germany. She married Johann Georg Klinger, son of Georg Klinger and Christina (--?--), on 5 May 1680, Reichelsheim, Germany. She married Hans Johann Simon Ripper, son of Adam Ripper and Anna (--?--), on 3 Jan 1698/99, Reichelsheim, Germany. She died on 4 May 1743, Beerfurth, Germany. She was buried in 1743, at Kirch-Beerfurth, Germany.

10. Johann Leonhard Heist was born on 22 Jan 1672/73, Pfaffen-Beerfurth, Germany. He married Anna Rosina Meister, daughter of Georg Meister and Euphrasina (--?--), on 19 Feb 1695/96. He died on 12 Mar 1737/38, Pfaffen-Beerfurth, Germany, at age 65.

11. Anna Rosina Meister was born on 16 Feb 1673/74, Pfaffen-Beerfurth, Germany. She married Johann Leonhard Heist, son of Hans Johannes Heist and Kunigunda Groh, on 19 Feb 1695/96. She died on 29 Oct 1746, at age 72.

12. George Beilstein was born in 1661. He married Eva Kohl in 1695, Neunkirchen, Germany. He died on 9 Jan 1736/37, Lutzelbach, Germany.

13. Eva Kohl married George Beilstein, son of Johann Balthasar Beilstein, in 1695, Neunkirchen, Germany.

14. John Martin Rettich was born circa 1661. He married Otilla (--?--) on 11 Aug 1723. He died before 1761.

15. Otilla (--?--) was born circa 1663. She married John Martin Rettich on 11 Aug 1723. She died before 1763.

--- 5th Generation ---

16. Georg Klinger was born circa 1610 in Pfaffen-Beerfurth, Germany. He married Christina (--?--) on 21 August 1640 in Pfaffen-Beerfurth. He died before 1694 in Pfaffen-Beerfurth, Germany.

17. Christina (--?--) was born in 1614, Beerfurth, Germany. She married Georg Klinger on 21 August 1640 in Pfaffen-Beerfurth. She died on 31 Oct 1695, Pfaffen-Beerfurth, Germany. She was buried on 1 Nov 1695, at Pfaffen-Beerfurth, Germany.

18. Philip Gottman.

20. Hans Johannes Heist married Kunigunda Groh, daughter of Heinrich Groh and Elizabetha (--?--). He was born in 1644, Pfaffen-Beerfurth, Germany. He died on 14 Nov 1709, Reichelsheim, Germany.

21. Kunigunda Groh married Hans Johannes Heist, son of Conrad Cuntz Heist and Margaretha (--?--). She was born in 1646, Hessen, Germany. She died on 26 Apr 1702, Hessen, Germany.

22. Georg Meister married Euphrasina (--?--).

23. Euphrasina (--?--) married Georg Meister.

24. Johann Balthasar Beilstein was born circa 1641, Herchennode, Germany.

A pedigree chart summarizing this ancestry is shown on the next page.

Peter Klinger Pedigree

Chart of
Johann Peter Klinger

1 JOHANN PETER KLINGER
b. 3 Nov 1773
m. circa 1791
d. 10 Aug 1858

CATHARINA STEINBRUCH
SPOUSE
b. 3 May 1774
d. 21 Sep 1845

2 JOHANN PHILIP KLINGER
b. 11 Jul 1723
m. 21 May 1754
d. 30 Sep 1811

3 EVA ELIZABETH BEILSTEIN
b. 27 May 1730
d. circa 1815

4 JOHANNES KLINGER
b. 18 Nov 1694
m. 6 Nov 1720
d. 22 Sep 1774

5 AGATHA HEIST
b. 2 Apr 1699
d. 10 Apr 1780

6 JOHN JACOB BEILSTEIN
b. 1696
m. 22 Jun 1723
d.

7 ANNA ELIZABETH RETTICH
b. 1705
d.

8 JOHANN GEORG KLINGER
b. 6 May 1655, d. 25 Mar 1693/94

9 ELIZABETH GÖTTMAN
b. 1663, d. 4 May 1743

10 JOHANN LEONHARD HEIST
b. 22 Jan 1672/73, d. 12 Mar 1737/38

11 ANNA ROSINA MEISTER
b. 16 Feb 1673/74, d. 29 Oct 1746

12 GEORGE BEILSTEIN
b. 1661, d. 9 Jan 1736/37

13 EVA KOHL
b.

14 JOHN MARTIN RETTICH
b. circa 1661, d. before 1761

15 OTILLA (--?--)
b. circa 1663, d. before 1763

16 GEORG KLINGER
b. circa 1610, d. before 1694

17 CHRISTINA (--?--)
b. 1614, d. 31 Oct 1695

18 PHILIP GOTTMAN
b.

19

20 HANS JOHANNES HEIST
b. 1644, d. 14 Nov 1709

21 KUNIGUNDA GROH
b. 1646, d. 26 Apr 1702

22 GEORG MEISTER
b.

23 EUPHRASINA (--?--)
b.

24 JOHANN BALTHASAR BEILSTEIN
b. circa 1641

25

26

27

28

29

30

31

Some researchers argue that Peter Klinger's great-great-grandfather Georg Klinger (number 16 in the foregoing list), a mayor of Pfaffen-Beerfurth, may have been born around 1618 in the German town of Rielingshausen, identifying him with a child named Georg or Georgius, born to an Eberhard and Ursula Klinger, part of a line of Klingers in Rielingshausen, Württemberg (now part of Baden-Württemberg). Rielingshausen is about 20 to 25 km (about 12 to 15 miles) northeast of Stuttgart and about 90 km (about 56 miles) south of Beerfurth. These sources usually trace Georg Klinger's ancestry to a Jacob Klinger, born in Rielingshausen, in about 1520.

None of these sources, however, offer any primary documentary evidence to prove that the Georg Klinger who died in Pfaffen-Beerfurth was the same person as the Georg Klinger who was born in Rielingshausen. While there is much speculation about such a connection, that connection, at least in this writer's opinion, has not been proven. It must also be remembered that, at that time, Rielingshausen, in Württemberg, was effectively in an entirely different country or kingdom from Pfaffen-Beerfurth. Also, at that time, people were not so mobile as they are today.

Other sources, including several researchers in Germany, contend that Georg and Christina Klinger were in fact born in Pfaffen-Beerfurth. There is evidence of a line of Klingers in the Pfaffen-Beerfurth area that included a Peter Klinger (in 1557), Leonhard Klinger (in 1610), and his son Hans (in 1619). There are also records of a Claus Klinger, who had a farm in Pfaffen-Beerfurth in 1483. In addition, there appears to be written evidence of Klingers in Pfaffen-Beerfurth as early as 1426.

Some of these German researchers, including Bianka Klinger, believe that Georg Klinger was the son of Hans Klinger, who was the son of Leonhard and Appolonia Klinger. Leonhard's father was Peter Klinger, and his grandfather was Claus Klinger.

Another German researcher named Gerd Klinger belives that Georg Klinger was the son of Leonhard Klinger, born around 1590, in Pfaffen-Beerfurth and that Leonhard's father was Leonhard Klinger, born in 1540 who married Apollonia (--?--) in Reichelsheim. Under this theory Leonhard was the son of Peter, born in 1501, and Peter's father was Hans Klinger, born about 1480, the son of Claus Klinger, born about 1450. At present, unfortunately, Georg Klinger's ancestry remains an unsettled question.

Photograph of the historic "Klinger Mill" near Pfaffen-Beerfurth, Germany, provided by Elsie K. Eaves. There is evidence that the mill was owned by members of the Klinger family in 1557, 1610, and 1619. "Wiesenmühle" translates as "Meadow Mill."

III. The Klingers in Pennsylvania

Between 1749 and 1751, three Klinger brothers (Alexander, Johann Philip, and Johann Peter) and a cousin (Johannes) emigrated, with their families, to Pennsylvania from Pfaffen-Beerfurth, Germany. Alexander Klinger and his wife Elizabeth, along with a number of relatives, arrived in Philadelphia on September 2, 1749 aboard the Ship "Albany." He settled near Reading, PA, where he was later joined by his brother Johann Philip Klinger ("Philip").

Philip Klinger and his wife Anna, along with a third brother, Johann Peter Klinger ("Peter") and his family, sailed to America on the Ship "Neptune," which arrived in Philadelphia in September, 1751, but Anna died aboard the "Neptune," apparently around the time the ship arrived in Philadelphia, on September 23 or 24, 1751. She was buried in the cemetery of Trinity Church, Philadelphia, PA.

While both Alexander and Philip settled in Reading, their brother Peter Klinger settled in Exeter Township, Berks County, about 10 miles southeast of Reading. Their cousin Johannes settled in Chester County, PA. Philip later returned to Germany where, on May 21, 1754, he married Eva Elizabeth Beilstein, daughter of Johann Jacob and Anna Elisabeth (Martin) Beilstein of Brandau, Hesse. Philip and Eva sailed for America on board the "Neptune," which landed in Philadelphia on September 30, 1754.

Early evidence of Alexander and Philip's presence in Reading includes several references in the early records of Trinity Lutheran Church, Reading. On June 17, 1753, at a service at which the Church's first building was dedicated, Alexander was installed as a deacon of the Church. Both Philip and Alexander served as sponsors for a baptism on March 5, 1758, at Trinity Lutheran Church, when "Philip Klinger," along with Alexander and his wife Anna Elizabeth Klinger, were sponsors for the baptism of Alexander Philip Eisenbeiss.

Morton Montgomery's *History of Berks County* (published in 1886) lists Philip, Alexander, and Peter Klinger as the first patentees of three lots in Reading which was laid out in 1748. The first lots were sold in 1751, and the three Klingers, apparently, purchased their lots in 1753. Philip purchased Lot number 203, while Alexander purchased the adjacent Lot number 204. Peter purchased Lot number 349. Lots 203 and 204 were located on the north and south sides of East Penn Street, between what were then Lord Street and Vigor Street. Today these are 10th and 11th Streets, respectively. In 1763, the three brothers each acquired an additional lot (Philip, Lot 176, Alexander, Lot 207, and Peter, Lot 222).

Philip, Alexander, and Peter Klinger were included on a 1759 List of Taxables in Berks County. According to Montgomery's *History of Berks County* (1886), this was the earliest tax assessment list for Berks County, which was organized in 1752. A 1767 Berks County Tax List included both Alexander and his brother Philip, who were listed as "Taverners." Alexander was shown in "Reading Town" as owning two houses, with two lots, and one cow. Philip, also listed in Reading Town, had two houses, two lots, and one cow.

A 1768 Tax List for Berks County listed Philip as a "taverner" who owned one house and one lot. His brother Alexander was also listed as a taverner, owning two houses and one and one-half lots.

Philip and his family moved west to an area that now lies at the intersection of three counties – Northumberland, Dauphin, and Schuylkill. Schuylkill County was not formed until 1811, with most of its territory coming from Berks County. This area is shown on the following map:

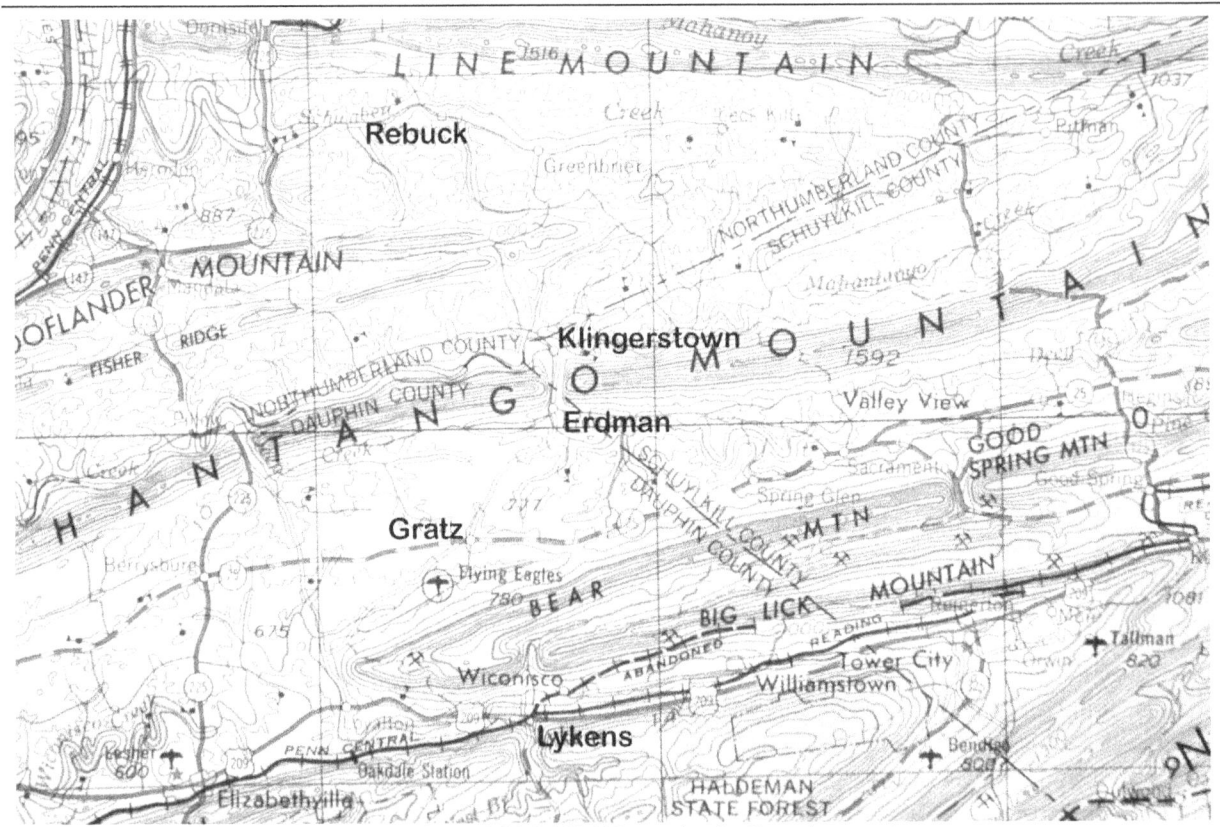
Portion of the USGS 1:250,000 map for the Harrisburg region.

The foregoing map covers portions of Mifflin, Lykens, Washington, Wiconisco, and Williams Townships in Dauphin County, Jordan, Washington, and Upper Mahanoy Townships in Northumberland County, and Upper Mahantango, Hubley, Porter, and Hegins Townships in Schuylkill County. Many of Peter and Catharina Klinger's immediate descendents lived in the area covered by this map. Many of the town names shown on this map, including Erdman, Klingerstown, Hegins, Valley View, Sacramento, Spring Glen, Gratz, Elizabethville, Lykens, Williamstown, and Wiconisco are frequently mentioned in the genealogical listings that follow.

Between 1771 and 1796, Philip obtained warrants for a number of contiguous tracts of land, covering more than 1,100 acres along Pine Creek to the south of the Klingerstown Gap in the Mahantango Mountain. These tracts were patented between 1793 and 1796. At roughly 1,100 or 1,200 acres, Philip's land would have covered slightly less than 2 square miles. Philip's land included four named parcels known as "Springfield," "Union," "Mount Holly," and "Salem," located generally east of the Klingerstown Gap and between Pine Creek and the Mahantango Mountain. Alexander also acquired land in roughly the same area, generally north of the Mahantango Mountain and east of present-day Klingerstown, which lies about a half mile north of the gap, where Pine Creek flows through the mountain. Klingerstown, which was founded in 1807, lies in the extreme northwest corner of Schuylkill County. Erdman, in Dauphin County, lies just south of the gap.

On January 8, 1771, Philip received a warrant for a tract of land called "Springfield," for which he received a patent on November 6, 1793. A portion of this tract was conveyed to Philip and Elizabeth's son Alexander and his wife Magdalena, and a 1-acre portion of that was conveyed to Klinger's Church on September 18, 1801. Philip patented two other tracts, "Union" and "John," in 1796, and portions of these were transferred to Philip's son Philip and his wife Catherine on January 8, 1810. The Union tract was about 360 acres.

Philip acquired another tract called "Kling-well" or "Klingerwell" on June 17, 1788. This tract had originally been acquired by Jacob Fisher on August 20, 1762, and was later transferred to John Harman, from whom Philip acquired the land. On May 25, 1800, Philip conveyed this tract to his son Peter, to whom a warrant and patent were issued in 1810. Philip acquired interests in another tract, called "Mount Holly," by patent from the Commonwealth of Pennsylvania on September 9, 1796. Philip and Elizabeth conveyed this tract, or portions thereof, to Peter Klinger on November 6, 1797.

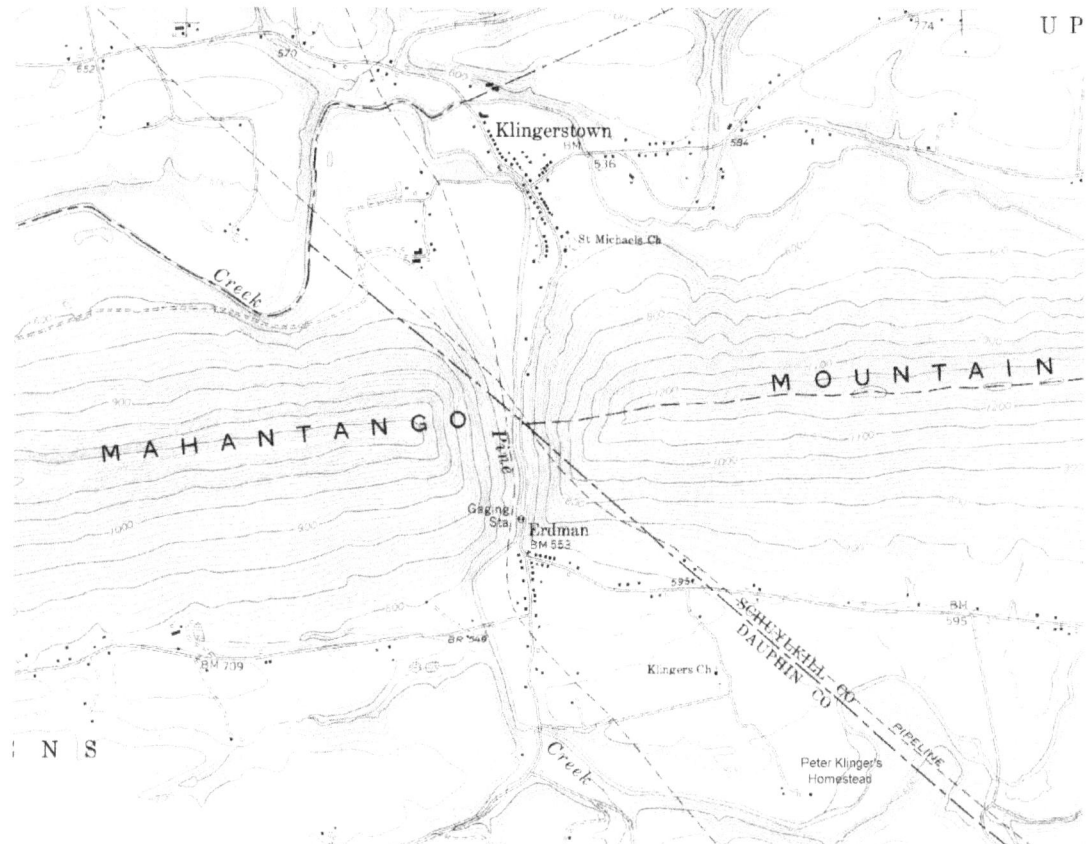

A portion of the USGS 1:24,000 map for the Klingerstown quadrangle.

The map above is a portion of the USGS 7.5-minute topographical map for the "Klingerstown" quadrangle showing the Klingerstown Gap in the Mahantango Mountain, formed where the Pine Creek flows through the mountain, and the towns of Klingerstown, in Schuylkill County, on the north side of the gap, and Erdman, in Dauphin County, just south of the gap. The distance from Klingerstown to Erdman is just over one mile. The Mahantango Creek flows on the north side of the Mahantango Mountain and, west of the gap, forms the southern boundary line of Northumberland County, while the Dauphin County-Schuylkill County line runs from the southeast to the northwest, meeting the Northumberland County line at the Mahantango Creek, just northwest of the gap. Klinger's Church is shown southeast of Erdman. Peter Klinger's homestead was just south and east of the hill on which the Klinger's Church sits. The area in Dauphin County, south of the Mahantango Mountain, is known as the "Lykens Valley."

Philip's homestead was almost certainly in present day Dauphin County, between the village of Erdman and Klinger's Church, which sits south and east of Erdman. Philip's original home was probably on the north side of the hill on which Klinger's Church is now located. Philip's original homestead may have been at or near the place shown in the photograph below, which sits at the base of the hill on which the Church stands, along the south side of the road from Erdman to Fearnot. According to some sources, the house shown on the photo on the next page was built on the old foundation of Philip's home. Philip's son Alexander, who donated the land for Klinger's Church, lived on this property after Philip's death. In recent years, the property was owned by Edwin Klinger.

House owned by Edwin Klinger

It is likely that Philip's land extended into what is now Schuylkill County, erected in 1811, the boundary of which lies only about one-quarter mile east of Klinger's Church. Philip's land, being mostly on the south side of the Mahantango Mountain, probably did not extend as far north as Klingerstown.

The "Klingerstown Gap" in the Mahantango Mountain, as viewed from the north or the Klingerstown side.

It is not clear precisely when Philip and his family moved to the Lykens Valley area in eastern Dauphin County. Records of the Lykens Valley Lower Church (St. David's Reformed Church) in Killinger, PA, include a reference to a "Philip Klinger" as sponsor at the baptism of John Philip Rauschkolb, in June 1779. Although it is not clear which "Philip Klinger" this is, it appears likely that at least some of the Klingers had migrated from Berks County by 1779. Other sources suggest that Philip's family settled in the Klingerstown-Erdman area as early as 1769 or 1770, but other writers suggest that Philip and Alexander moved to the area "about 1790."

Philip's name does not appear on the Berks County 1779 register of property in Reading, although his brother Alexander's does. Similarly, on the 1780 Berks County Tax Lists, Alexander's name appears, but Philip's does not. These lists suggest that Philip and his family had probably moved to the Klingerstown-Erdman area some time before 1779.

A photograph of Klinger's Church, probably dating from the 1950's.

Both Philip's and Alexander's names are missing from the 1781 and 1784 Tax Lists in Berks County, but Alexander's name appears on the 1785 Berks County lists, while Philip's does not. The name of a "Philip Clinger" appears on the Supply Tax List for 1779 in the "Wisconisco District" of Lancaster County (now part of Dauphin County). Dauphin County was not formed until 1785. Philip is shown as owning 100 acres of land, three horses, and three cattle. The 1790 United States Census for Dauphin County lists two Philip "Clingers," most likely the immigrant Philip and his son Philip, who was born in 1765.

Both Philip and Alexander served in the Berks County Militia during the Revolutionary War. It appears that they served at various times between about 1777 and 1781. Schuylkill County was not formed until 1811, much of its territory coming from Berks County.

Philip expressed his desire to set aside land for a church, a cemetery, and a school. While no school was ever built, in 1801 Philip's son Alexander deeded land for the construction of a church, which came to be known as "Klinger's Church." The original church building was razed in 1894, and the current Church was dedicated in 1895. Peter Klinger's grandson Emanuel Klinger (#11.6 in the genealogical listings below), son of Daniel Klinger and Mary Ann Schoffstall, was head carpenter for the construction of the church.

Contemporary photograph of Zion (Klinger's) Church, looking across the cemetery on the south side of the Church. The front (right side) part of the building was constructed in 1894 and 1895, while the back portion (on the left side), which houses educational and fellowship rooms, was completed in 1982.

The first baptism in the published record at Klinger's Church was dated September 16, 1787. It was for one of Philip's grandsons, "Johen George," son of Philip's son George and his wife Elizabeth (Brosius). It is probable that the congregation was actually started sometime before that date and most likely met in Philip's home which was just north of where the Church now stands.

In her book, *The Klingers from the Odenwald, Hesse, Germany ca. 1610-1989*, pp. 319-20, Mary Klinger says that Philip divided his land into four parts for four of his sons – Philip, Peter, Alexander, and George. She says that Philip lived on one section of his father's original holding, located "right across Pine

Creek where it makes its bend to flow through the Klingerstown Gap. . . , west of his brother Alexander, who had inherited from his father, John Philip's homestead." Peter had the section "south of Klinger's Church," while George "had the eastern section of Philip's estate." There is, however, evidence that Philip and Elizabeth conveyed a number of parcel of land to their sons before Philip's death in 1811, so it is not clear how much of this property was actually "inherited," as Mary Klinger suggests.

The younger Philip Klinger built a home close to the south side of the Klingerstown Gap. Reportedly the home was originally a log structure, built perhaps as early as 1798. The house, as shown in the recent photograph below, has been enlarged and modernized. It is easily visible from the highway that passes beside Pine Creek and through the Klingerstown Gap. It is possible that both the elder Philip and his son Philip lived on this property.

The homestead of Philip Klinger, son of the immigrant Philip Klinger and Eva Elizabeth Beilstein, on the south side of the Klingerstown Gap, visible from the road between Erdman and Klingerstown.

Philip Klinger died September 30, 1811, in Lykens Township, Dauphin County, PA , and was buried in the cemetery at Klinger's Church. His tombstone is the eleventh stone in the seventh row of the cemetery. There does not appear to be any record at Klinger's Church of the death or burial of Philip's wife, Eva Elizabeth.

Philip Klinger's tombstone at Klinger's Church, Erdman, PA.

IV. Peter Klinger and Catharina Steinbruch

Johann Peter Klinger, commonly known as "Peter," was the youngest son of Johann Philip and Eva Elizabeth (Beilstein) Klinger. Philip, along with two brothers, Alexander and Johann Peter, had emigrated from Pfaffen-Beerfurth, Germany, to America between 1749 and 1751.

Philip Klinger and Eva Elisabeth (Beilstein) Klinger had eight children: (1) Elisabeth (born March 10, 1756), who married Johann Conrad Weiser, grandson of the noted Indian agent and interpreter of the same name; (2) Johann Philip (born 25 April 1758, died in 1759); (3) Christina (born May 10, 1760, died in 1760); (4) Johann George (born May 13, 1761), who married Elizabeth Brosius; (5) Christina (born June 30, 1764, died December 11, 1768); (6) Johann Philip (born December 11, 1765), who married Anna Maria Loeffler; (7) Johann Alexander (born February 16, 1767), who married Magdalena Haag; and (8) Johann Peter (born November 3, 1773), who married Catharina Steinbruch (or Steinbrecher), daughter of Adam Steinbrecher and Anna Margaretha Hoffman.

Peter was likely born in Reading, PA, when his father Philip was 50 years old, although there appears to be no baptismal record for him at Trinity Lutheran Church in Reading, where a number of his siblings were baptized. It is possible, however, that Peter was born around the time or after the family moved to the Lykens Valley. At the baptism of Peter and Catharina's first child, Philip, at Klinger's Church, May 6, 1792, the sponsors were "Philip Klinger and w. Eva Elisabeth, grandparents," thereby confirming that Peter was in fact the son of Philip and Eve or Eva Elisabeth Beilstein. Philip and Eva Elisabeth, as "grandparents," were also sponsors for the baptism of Peter and Catharina's daughter Eva Elisabeth, on February 16, 1794.

At the time of the 1790 Census, when apparently most of Philip and Eva Elizabeth's older children had already married, Philip's household consisted of two males 16 and over and one female. Probably the other male in the household would have been Peter, who would have been 16 as of August 2, 1790, the effective date of the Census.

Peter married Catharina Steinbruch, daughter of Adam Steinbrecher and Anna Margaretha Hoffman, around 1791 in Lykens Township, Dauphin County, PA. The 1800 US Census for Upper Paxton Township, Dauphin County, PA, lists Peter Klinger's household as follows: 3 Males under 10; 1 Male between 26 and 45 [Peter]; 2 Females under 10; and 1 Female between 26 and 45 [Catharina]. Based on this list, the three males under 10 were likely Philip, Peter, and George, while one of the two females under 10 was likely Peter and Catharina's daughter Eve Elizabeth. It is not clear who may have been the second female under 10.

The 1810 US Census for Upper Paxton Township, Dauphin County, PA, contains a listing for a household of "Peter Glinger," which is likely that of Peter Klinger. That household consisted of the following: 2 Males under 10; 3 Males between 10 and 15; 1 Male between 15 and 25; 1 Male over 45; 1 Female under 10; 1 Female between 10 and 16; 2 Females between 15 and 25; 1 Female between 25 and 44. On the Census Date, August 6, 1810, Peter would have been 36 years old, but no male in the 26 to 45 range is listed. Apparently, Peter was wrongly listed as being in the 45 and over category. This household listing suggests that the two males under 10 were Johannes and Alexander, while the female under 10 would likely have been Hanna. The male between 10 and 15 could have been either George or Peter, while the male between 15 and 25 was likely Philip. The female between 10 and 16 could have been Eve Elizabeth. It is not clear who were the two females between 15 and 25. Catharina was likely the female between 25 and 44. Adam, who was five months old on the Census Date, may have been omitted.

The 1820 Census lists the household of Peter "Glinger," which is also likely Peter Klinger's. There is no other listing for a Peter Klinger, and the "Peter Glinger" household is listed very close in proximity to the listings for a number of other Klingers, including descendants of the immigrant Philip. The Census lists the following household: 3 males under the age of 10 (probably Daniel, Jacob, and Adam); 1 male between 10 and 16 (probably Alexander); 2 males between 18 and 26 (probably Johannes and George); 1 male over 45 (Peter); 0 females under 10; 1 female between 10 and 16 (probably Hanna); 1 female between 16 and 26 (possibly Eve Elizabeth); 1 female over 45 (Catharina). The household composition shown in the census closely fits the children believed to be those of Peter and Catharine. It is likely that by 1820, the eldest sons, Philip and Peter, had already left home.

By the time of the 1830 Census, Peter Klinger's household was listed as consisting of: 1 Male between 10 and 15 [Daniel?]; 1 Male between 15 and 20; 1 Male between 20 and 30; 1 Male between 50 and 60 [Peter], and 1 Female between 50 and 60 [Catharina]. The 1850 Census lists the following household (all born in Pennsylvania): Peter Klinger, age 77, male, Farmer, 1200 (value of property); Daniel Klinger, 36, male; Mary Ann, 29, female; Susanna Klinger, 9 female; John, 7, male; Samuel, 5, male; Catherine, 11/12, female. Thus in 1850, after the death of Peter's wife Catharina in 1845, Peter's son Daniel and his family (wife Mary Ann Schoffstall along with 4 children) were living in his household.

Mary Klinger's article in the Journal of Johannes Schwalm Historical Association (1987) says Peter operated a farm "east" of Sacramento, PA, which is in present-day Schuylkill County. This appears to be inaccurate. Mary Klinger's book, *The Klingers from the Odenwald, Hesse, Germany ca. 1610-1989*, p. 363 (1989), says he was a "farmer and grist mill operator" who "lived most of his life in Lykens Twp., around the present day Erdman." By some accounts, Peter inherited the southern portion of his father's land, which is mostly in Dauphin County, and lived on a homestead just south of Klinger's Church, as shown on the map on page 17 and the satellite image on the next page. In any event, to the extent that Peter's land lay in Schuylkill County, it would have been west, not east, of Sacramento.

The satellite image reprinted on the following page shows the area surrounding Erdman, PA. The wooded area at the top of the image is the Mahantango Mountain. Route 1024, labeled the "Fearnot Road," runs east and west along the base of the Mahantango Mountain from Erdmann to Fearnot, which is off the image to the right, or to the east. Route 1013, labeled the "Erdman Road," is the road from Gratz to Erdman, running from south to north through the western (left) part of the image. This is also the main street through Erdman, and it then passes through the Klingerstown Gap, north of Erdman, and eventually reaches Klingerstown, which is just to the north of this image.

Klinger's Church is shown south and east of the village of Erdman. The Church Cemetery is the dark area immediately below (to the south of) the Church building. Peter Klinger's homestead, is farther south and slightly east of Klinger's Church. The road running to Peter Klinger's homestead is labeled "Swamp Road."

The approximate site of Peter Klinger's mill is shown just west of Route 1013 and just north of the Luxemburg Road at the southern end of the village of Erdman. The straight white line running from the lower right hand corner of the image diagonally northwest (upward and to the left) is the Dauphin County-Schuylkill County line. The area to the right (east) of the line is in Schuylkill County, while the area to the left (west) of the line is in Dauphin County.

Google® Earth Image (taken April, 2004) showing the area south of Erdman, Dauphin County, PA. Pine Creek runs along the south (bottom) edge of the image before turning northerly on the western (left) side of the image (reprinted with permission).

Enlarged portion of the previous Google® Earth Image showing Zion (Klinger's) Church and Peter Klinger's Homestead (reprinted with permission).

Peter's homestead, including the frame house and accompanying buildings, is visible from Klinger's Church. The image reprinted below represents the view of Peter's homestead from the cemetery at Klinger's Church.

Peter Klinger's homestead south of Klinger's Church, as seen from the church cemetery.

The Gratz Historical Society's book *History of Lykens Township,* volume 2, indicates that much of the land in the village of Erdman came from various tracts originally surveyed to the Klinger family, but a large portion of it was part of a tract patented by the Commonwealth to Peter Klinger on April 30, 1874, with buildings and improvements.

On August 24, 1844, Peter sold six different parcels of property to his son Jacob S. Klinger. Tract 1 was the property called "Kling-well," original acquired by Peter from his father Philip in 1800. Tract 2 was part of several tracts, one of which was the Spread Eagle tract that had originally been acquired by Philip's brother Alexander Klinger and that after several intervening transactions was purchased by Peter on October 3, 1806. Tract 3 was part of two of Philip's original grants, "Salem" and "Union," which Philip and Elizabeth conveyed to Peter on September 5, 1804. Tracts 4 and 5 were tracts originally acquired by Peter by warrants in 1814 and 1815 and later patented from the Commonwealth by Peter in 1840. Tract 6 came from Philip's original 1796 patent for Mount Holly which Philip had conveyed to Peter on November 11, 1797.

Peter Klinger's homestead, as photographed a some years ago by Carlos G. Klinger.

According to the Gratz Historical Society's book *History of Lykens Township,* volume 2, p. 476, the land comprising Peter's homestead came from four different land grants (including Union and Springfield) that were patented to Philip Klinger as well as land patented to Peter in 1841. This property was sold to Peter's son Daniel on August 24, 1855. After Daniel's death on 1899, his executors sold the 70-acre, 14-perch property to Francis and Harriet Klinger on April 2, 1900, the same day on which Francis and Harriet sold the property to Daniel's son Daniel. A perch is 160th of an acre. Following the death of Daniel Jr. in 1919, his widow Sevilla (Shaffer) and heirs sold the property to Harry Daniel Klinger, Daniel and Sevilla's son. He owned the property for about 11 years, before selling 64 acres and 15 perches of the property to Oscar and Mabel Kessler, on March 21, 1931. They sold it to Homer and Violet (Schmeltz) Kessler on October 26, 1946, who in turn sold it to the present owners, Darwin A. and Shirley Erdman on May 14, 1965.

As Mary Klinger notes, Peter dammed the Pine Creek in Erdman and built a mill there. The Gratz Historical Society's book *History of Lykens Township,* volume 2, says that Peter built his mill around 1817, and that he transferred to the mill to his son George P. Klinger by 1855.

Although there is no portion of the mill now standing, its approximate location was just north of the Luxemburg Road (State Route 4002) on the east side of Pine Creek, as shown by the satellite image below. The mill was a short distance downstream from the stone bridge on Luxemburg Road.

Google® Earth Image showing the approximate location of Peter Klinger's Mill in relation to the village of Erdman and the Luxemburg Road (reprinted with permission).

In the image printed above, Pine Creek flows from south (bottom) to north (top) on the left hand side of the image. The creek flows beneath a stone arch bridge on Luxemburg Road. Pictures of the bridge appear below and on the next page. Peter Klinger's Mill apparently sat in the open area just to the east (right) of Pine Creek north of (above) the Luxemburg Road, while the dam was located south of (below) the bridge. As is shown in the photograph below, the mill race ran through a small arch in the stone bridge on the east (right) side of the creek. There are two large arches on the west (right) side of the bridge, while the smaller arch through which the mill race passed is shown on the left, although it is somewhat obscured by the vegetation in this image. The mill race now provides a second channel for Pine Creek.

The stone bridge on Luxemburg Road over the Pine Creek, viewed from the north. The photograph on the next page better shows the small, third arch (on the left), through which the mill race flowed.

The photograph below shows the small arch through which the mill race passed. This is the arch on the left side of the previous photograph.

A hand drawn map, made by Mike Kessler and reprinted in the *Klingerstown Bi-Centennial Album* (p. 303), depicting Erdman in the 1920s and 1930s, shows the ruins of an "old mill" just north of the Luxemburg Bridge. It also shows a "grist mill dam built by Peter Klinger" somewhat south of the bridge, with the mill race running along the east side of Pine Creek and passing under the bridge. Thus the grist mill itself must have been destroyed before the 1920s. The map also shows the Peter Klinger homestead, listing it as the "Harry Klinger Farm."

It is believed that one of the mill stones for Peter Klinger's mill is owned by Glenn and Deb Heim of Rough and Ready, PA. They incorporated it into their stone patio. This is shown in the photograph on the next page that was taken during the summer of 2007.

One of the Millstones from Peter Klinger's mill.

Peter Klinger died on August 10, 1858, and is buried alongside his wife Catharina at Klinger's Church Cemetery, Erdman, Dauphin County, PA. Catharina died on September 21, 1845. Photographs of Peter and Catharina's tombstones at Klinger's Church Cemetery, as they appeared a few years ago, are reprinted on the next two pages.

Peter Klinger's tombstone at Zion (Klinger's) Church, Erdman, PA.

Catharina Steinbruch Klinger's tombstone at Klinger's Church, Erdman, PA.

After Peter's death, his land was surveyed by Daniel Hoffman for the heirs. A rough sketch of that survey, as reprinted from Mary Klinger, *The Klingers from the Odenwald, Hesse, Germany ca. 1610-1989*, p. 363, was as follows:

Peter and Catharina had eleven children, all of whom survived to adulthood and married, although little is known about their daughter Catharine:

1. Catharine Klinger, d. before 1858.

2. Johann Philip Klinger, b. 20 Apr 1792, d. 12 Nov 1857;

3. Eve Elizabeth Klinger, b. 16 Jan 1794, d. 18 Jan 1870;

4. Johann Peter Klinger, b. 2 Jan 1796, d. 4 Jan 1879;

5. Johann George Klinger, b. 7 Jan 1798, d. 16 Sep 1880;

6. Johannes Klinger, b. 18 Mar 1802, d. 11 Oct 1873;

7. Alexander Klinger, b. 28 May 1805, d. 2 May 1876;

8. Hanna Klinger, b. 21 Oct 1807, d. before 1907;

9. Johann Adam Klinger, b. 18 Feb 1810, d. 15 Apr 1885;

10. Jacob S. Klinger, b. 29 Jan 1813, d. 23 Jan 1883; and

11. Daniel Klinger, b. 28 Jan 1816, d. 2 Mar 1899.

The following compilation of the descendants of Peter and Catharina Klinger is intended to gather together listings for as many descendants as can be reasonably identified. This edition includes about 10,650 direct descendants across 10 generations.

These listings derive from a large number of sources. Mary Klinger's 1989 book, *Klingers from the Odenwald, Hesse, Germany,* pages 363 – 433, formed the initial basis for the listings, but that information was supplemented with independent research and with information provided by numerous other researchers and other descendants of Peter Klinger, without whose generous help this publication would not have been possible.

Because of the number of family listings, however, some of this information has not been independently verified by the author. While the following listings have benefitted enormously from such contributions, this author is solely responsible for any errors or omissions in the listings.

The listings of Peter and Catharina's descendants employ the d'Aboville numbering system, in which each child in each generation is given a number comprising one or more digits. Except in the first generation (the children of Peter Klinger and Catharina Steinbruch), each number has two or more component numbers separated by periods. The periods correspond to separate generations. Each child in a given family is numbered sequentially and each person's d'Aboville number represents that child's number attached to the number for that child's parent. Thus, the child numbered "11.2.3," for example, means third child born to person number "11.2," which in turn means the second child born to person number "11." In this instance, the first number refers to the number given to each of Peter and Catharine's eleven children. For example, Daniel Klinger is child number 11 in this system, so the numbers of all of Daniel Klinger's descendants begin with "11." Likewise, Daniel's eight children bear the numbers "11.1" through "11.8" respectively. Similarly, all of the descendants of Daniel's Klinger's second child Johannes will have numbers beginning with "11.2."

The d'Aboville numbers facilitate keeping track of relationships. For example, all siblings will have the same number except for the last digit. All persons with common grandparents listed here will have the same number except for the last two digits.

Many of the genealogical details given in the following listings, especially residence, occupation, and family composition, are derived from the decennial US Census records. The Census listings for 1880 and 1900 through 1940 (the latest Census that is available to the public), particularly, contain a wealth of family detail. Unfortunately, these records, which are all handwritten, also contain many mistakes as well as widely varying, and sometimes indecipherable, spellings for individual names. The information taken from the Census data given in the following genealogical listings, except where noted, generally preserve the spellings given in the original Census records, although in some cases the original spellings are uncertain or difficult to transcribe. Thus the spellings used in descriptions of the information taken from the Census records often vary from the names given in the main genealogical listings.

V. Photographs to Accompany the Genealogical Listings

Photo provided by Otto and Joan (Klinger) Crumroy

Forrest Eugene Klinger (#2.7.1.6.2) at work for the Southamptom School District.

Photo provided by Otto and Joan (Klinger) Crumroy

Forrest Eugene Klinger (#2.7.1.6.2) and a student in front of Eugene Klinger Junior High (now Middle) School in Southampton, Bucks County, PA.

Photo provided by Otto and Joan (Klinger) Crumroy

Jasper A. Klinger (#2.7.1.8) and his wife Vesta (Long) Klinger.

Photo provided by Otto and Joan (Klinger) Crumroy

Harry Clarence Klinger (#2.7.1.6) and Harriet Mae (Rhodes) Klinger.

Peter Klinger (Jr.) (#4) son of Peter and Catharine Steinburch Klinger.

Photograph provided by Elsie K. Eaves.

*The family of Elmira Klinger (# 5.3.1) and Jonathan C. Williard. Jonathan and daughter Catherine are in the back row.
In the middle row are the infant Moses, Elmira, and daughter Dorsey (Dorothy), while Mary and Emma are in the front.*

Birth and baptismal certificate (Taufschein) for Peter and Catharina's son Johann Adam Klinger (# 9).

A Currier and Ives baptismal certificate for Lincoln Calvin Carl (# 9.4.1), son of Caroline Klinger (# 9.4) and Jeremiah Carl.

Photographed by Nikki Edwards

The metal sign that hung outside the law office of Lincoln Calvin Carl (# 9.4.1) in Williamstown, PA.

Tombstone of Daniel Klinger (# 11) at Zion (Klinger's) Church Erdman, PA.

Tombstone for Daniel Klinger's (# 11) wife Mary Ann Schoffstall's at Klinger's Church, Erdman, PA.

Death Certificate for Johannes Klinger (#11.2), 1918.

Death Certificate for Daniel Klinger (#11.5), 1919.

Daniel Klinger (Jr.) (# 11.5) and Sevilla (Shaffer) Klinger and five of their children, Summer 1915.
Front row (left to right): Daniel Klinger, Jr; Sevilla (Shaffer) Klinger.
Back row (left to right): Milton C. Klinger (# 11.5.1); Carrie A. Klinger (# 11.5.2); William O. Klinger (# 11.5.5);
Emma L. Klinger (# 10.5.3); Harry D. Klinger (# 11.5.4).

Tombstone of Daniel Klinger (Jr.) (# 11.5) and Sevilla (Shaffer) Klinger, Klinger's Church Cemetery, Erdman, Dauphin County, PA.

Tombstone of Milton Klinger (# 11.5.1) and Sarah E. (Schwalm) Klinger at (Zion) Klinger's Church, Erdman, PA.

Daniel Klinger (# 10.5) Jr. Family, Summer 1915, at Peter Klinger's homestead, near Klinger's Church, Erdman, PA.
Back Row, Left to Right: Carrie Ellen (Klinger) Zimmerman (1897-1924); Harry Klinger (1883-1940); Sally (Engle) Klinger (1885-1939); John Daniels (1875-1969); Carrie (Klinger) Daniels (1878-1938); William Elias Klinger (1881-1959); Emma L. Klinger (1881-1947); William Oscar Klinger (1885-1962); Ida (Tobias) Klinger (1886-1963); Milton Klinger (1877-1918) holding Ira (1915-1993); Sarah Ellen (Schwalm) Klinger (1874-1947).
Middle Row, Left to Right: Frederick Klinger (1901-1920); Winnie Daniels (1899-1981); Daisy A. (Klinger) Koppenhaver (1902-1967); Harry Daniels; Clarence Klinger (1899-1960); Daniel Klinger, Jr. (1852-1919); Sevilla (Shaffer) Klinger (1857-1923); Guy Klinger (1895-1961); Carlos Klinger (1899-1920).
Front Row, Left to Right: Mary Klinger (1908-1975); Alma (Klinger) Oxenrider (1907-1974); Floyd Klinger (1912-1986); Vera (Klinger) Martz (1906-1997); Sevilla (Klinger) Schmeltz (1909-1997); Darwin Daniels (1904-1953); Roy Milton Klinger (1906-1990).

Photo by Carlos G. Klinger

Descendants of Daniel Klinger (# 11.5) Jr. and Sevilla (Shaffer) Klinger, Hegins Park, Schuylkill County, PA, at family reunion in the mid-1950's.
Front row (left to right): Floyd A. Klinger (1912-1986); Guy E. Klinger (1895-1961); William O. Klinger (1885-1962); Roy M. Klinger (1906-1990); Ira C. Klinger (1915-1993)
Back row (left to right): Sarah Sevilla Klinger 1909-1997) (married Frank G. Schmeltz); Vera M. Klinger (1906-1997) (married Gurney Martz); Daisy A. Klinger (1902-1967) (married Jeremiah I. Koppenhaver); Mary S. Klinger (1908-1975) (married Harlan A. Klinger); Alma Klinger (1910-1974) (married Earl M. Oxenrider).

Photograph by Carlos G. Klinger

1955 Reunion of the Descendants of Daniel Klinger, Jr., and Sevilla Shaffer, Hegins Park, Hegins, Schuylkill County, PA. Left to right. Front row: Mary (Mrs. Carl) Martz; Gurney Martz; Vera Klinger Martz; Miriam Koppenhaver; Max E. Klinger; Helen L. (Mrs. Guy) Klinger; Guy E. Klinger; (--?--); Glen Schmeltz; (--?--); Ted Reinoehl.

Second row: Harlan Martz; Virginia Lenig Martz; Roy Klinger; Doris (Mrs. Roy) Klinger; Jennette Klinger Sherwood; Mary L. (Mrs. Ira) Klinger; Ira C. Klinger; Frank Schmeltz; Sevilla K. Schmeltz, holding Lois Schmeltz.

Third row: (--?--) Oxenrider; (--?--); Earl Oxenrider; Marion Klinger; Bob Appleby; Joanne Klinger Appleby; Mary (Mrs. Harlan) Klinger; Carol (Mrs. Carl) Klinger; Alma Klinger Oxenrider; to far right: George Reinoehl.

Fourth row: (standing) (--?--) Deibler; Daisy Koppenhaver; Laura (Mrs. Floyd) Klinger; Floyd Klinger; Ida Klinger; Dorothy Reinoehl.

Fifth row: (--?--) holding child; (--?--); William Klinger; William Mattern.

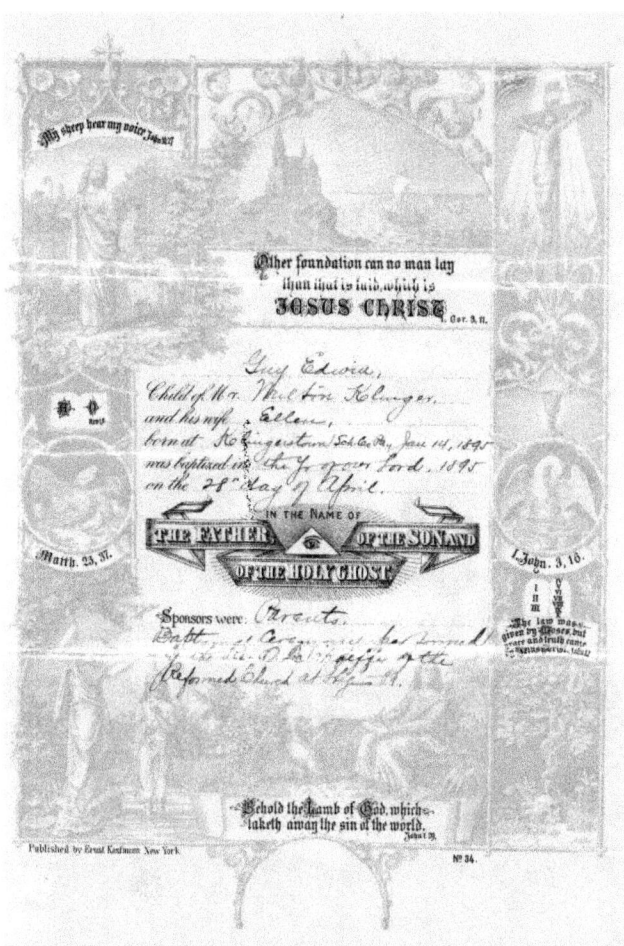

Baptismal Certificate for Guy Edwin Klinger (# 11.5.1.1.), dated 28 April 1895.

*Guy E. Klinger (# 11.5.1.1.), Wagoner, Supply Company, 314th Infantry,
79th Division, at Camp Meade, 1917, before sailing for France.*

Carlos G. Klinger (#11.5.1.1.2), 1943

Photo provided by Jackie Abromitis

The family of Emanuel Klinger (#11.6) and Christiana Schadel, c. 1924
Front Row (L to R): Meda Mamie (Klinger) Knorr (#11.6.13); Clara (Klinger) Scheib (#11.6.4); Charles Daniel Klinger (#11.6.2); Emanuel Klinger (#11.6); Christiana (Schadel) Klinger; Mary Alice (Klinger) Schwalm (#11.6.1); Catherine (Klinger) Rebuck (#11.6.3).
Back Row (L to R): Henry Wilson Klinger (#11.6.7); Eston Isaiah Klinger (#11.6.12); Ira Jacob Klinger (#11.6.11); Alice Christiana (Klinger) Bensinger (#11.6.5); John Alexander Alvin Klinger (#11.6.9).

Death Certificate for Emanuel Klinger (#11.6)

Death Certificate for Mary Ann (Klinger) Glantz (#11.7), 1911.

Death Certificate for Sarah Louisa (Klinger) Knohr (#11.8), 1924.

The Descendants of Johann Peter Klinger and Catharina Steinbruch

JOHANN PETER KLINGER also went by the name of **PETER**. He was born on 3 November 1773, Reading, Berks County, PA. There does not appear to be any baptismal record for Peter in Reading, PA, where most of his siblings were baptized. On the baptism of his first child, Philip, at Klinger's Church, 6 May 1792, the sponsors were "Philip Klinger and w. Eva Elisabeth, grandparents." (Zion (Klinger's) Church History, part II, p. 10, thereby confirming that Peter was in fact the son of Philip and Eve or Eva Elisabeth Beilstein. Philip and Eva Elisabeth, as "grandparents" were also sponsors for the baptism of Peter and Catharine's daughter Eva Elisabeth, on 16 Feb 1794. (Id., p. 13.). He married **CATHARINA STEINBRUCH**, daughter of **ADAM STEINBRECHER** and **ANNA MARGARETHA HOFFMAN**, circa 1791, Lykens Township, Dauphin County, PA. He died on 10 August 1858, Lykens Township, Dauphin County, PA, at age 84. He was buried at Zion (Klinger's) Church, Erdman, Lykens Township, Dauphin County, PA.

1 CATHERINE KLINGER married **JOHN REIFSCHNEIDER**. She died before 1858, PA. According to some sources, Catherine was mentioned in Peter's will, but apparently was deceased at that time. Apart from such references, there is virtually no information about Catherine. Some researchers appear to conflate this Catherine Klinger with the daughter of Peter Klinger (Jr.) and Catharine Wiest named Eva Catharina, who was baptized at Klinger's Church July 20, 1820 and who married Abraham Schwenk. Eva Catherine lived until 1887. The 1820 Census lists no female in the householde under the age of 10, suggesting that Peter and Catharina (Steinbruch) had no daughter then living born after 1810.

1.1 DANIEL REIFSNYDER

1.2 JACOB REIFSNYDER

2 JOHANN PHILIP KLINGER was born on 20 April 1792, Lykens Township, Dauphin County, PA. He was baptized on 6 May 1792, Zion (Klinger's) Church, Erdman, Lykens Township, Dauphin County, PA. He married **CATHARINA (--?--)** circa 1810. He married **CATHARINE YEAGER** circa 1828, Lykens Township, Dauphin County, PA. He died on 12 November 1857, Lykens Township, Dauphin County, PA, at age 65. He was buried at Zion (Klinger's) Church Cemetery, Erdman, Lykens Township, Dauphin County, PA.

2.1 JOHN A. KLINGER is also referred to as **JOHANNES** in some sources. He was born on 23 March 1811. He was baptized on 14 April 1811, Zion (Klinger's) Church, Erdman, Lykens Township, Dauphin County, PA. He married **SUSANNAH ROMBERGER**, daughter of **HEINRICH ROMBERGER** and **ELIZABETH HOFFMAN**. John served in the Civil War as a private in Company A, 50th Pennsylvania Infantry, from 1861 to 1863. He died on 16 December 1872, Elizabethville, Dauphin County, PA, at age 61. He was buried at Salem Lutheran and Reformed Church Cemetery, Elizabethville, Dauphin County, PA. Records of St. John's Lutheran Church in Lykens, PA, indicate that John and Susannah had 14 children, only 7 of whom were living at the time of Susanna's death in 1891.

2.1.1 ELIZABETH KLINGER also went by the name of **BETTY**. She was born in 1833. Some sources record that she was born circa 1836. She married **ANDREW JACKSON WILLIAMS**. She died in 1886. She was buried at Oak Hill Cemetery, Millersburg, Dauphin County, PA.

2.1.1.1 JOHN WESLEY WILLIAMS was born on 18 August 1857, Millersburg, Dauphin County, PA. He married **LOUISA GAMBER**. He died on 9 July 1912, Sunbury, Northumberland County, PA, at age 54. He was buried on 12 July 1912, at Pomfret Manor Cemetery, Sunbury, Northumberland County, PA.

2.1.1.1.1 MARY ELIZABETH WILLIAMS was born on 25 June 1880, Tower City, Schuylkill County, PA. She married **EDWIN THEODORE HARNER**, son of **CORNELIUS E. HARNER** and **ELIZA KIMMEL**. She died on 20 January 1941, Sunbury, Northumberland County, PA, at age 60.

2.1.1.1.1.1 RAYMOND EDWARD CHARLES HARNER was born on 28 August 1906. He married **THEONA EVELYN THOMPSON**. He died on 24 February 1978, Orange County, FL, at age 71. He was buried at Pomfret Manor Cemetery, Sunbury, Northumberland County, PA.

2.1.1.1.1.1.1 CORRNINE M. HARNER was born circa 1929.

2.1.1.1.1.1.2 RAYMOND EDWIN CHARLES HARNER was born on 6 February 1936, Danville, Montour County, PA. He died on 14 February 1936, Danville, Montour County, PA. He was buried at Pomfret Manor Cemetery, Sunbury, Northumberland County, PA.

2.1.1.1.1.1.3 JUDITH R. HARNER was born circa 1937.

2.1.1.1.1.2 EVELYN L. HARNER was born on 15 August 1913. She died on 30 October 1966, at age 53. She was buried at Pomfret Manor Cemetery, Sunbury, Northumberland County, PA.

2.1.1.1.1.3 EDWARD T. HARNER was born on 23 January 1918, Sunbury, Northumberland County, PA. He died on 25 January 1918, Sunbury, Northumberland County, PA. He was buried at Pomfret Manor Cemetery, Sunbury, Northumberland County, PA.

2.1.1.1.2 BESSIE ANN WILLIAMS was born on 20 September 1881, Tower City, Schuylkill County, PA. She married MILTON CLAIR WILLARD, son of DANIEL C. WILLARD and EVA M. (--?--), on 24 December 1901, Northumberland County, PA. She died on 16 May 1931, Sunbury, Northumberland County, PA, at age 49. She was buried on 19 May 1931, at Pomfret Manor Cemetery, Sunbury, Northumberland County, PA.

2.1.1.1.3 LOVINA MAE WILLIAMS is also referred to as LAVINA MAY WILLIAMS in some sources. She was born in May 1884, Tower City, Schuylkill County, PA. She married GEORGE WHALEN, son of FREDERICK WHALEN and LYDIA (--?--), circa 1902. She died on 1 April 1938, Danville State Hospital, Mahoning Township, Montour County, PA, at age 53. She was buried on 4 April 1938, at Pomfret Manor Cemetery, Sunbury, Northumberland County, PA.

2.1.1.1.3.1 HELEN MAE WHALEN was born on 19 June 1903, Sunbury, Northumberland County, PA. She married DAVID CHASE ICKES, son of TURIE S. ICKES and BESSIE BAIR, on 26 November 1925, Newport, Perry County, PA. She died on 10 April 1953, Sunbury, Northumberland County, PA, at age 49. She was buried on 13 April 1953, at Pomfret Manor Cemetery, Sunbury, Northumberland County, PA.

2.1.1.1.3.1.1 RIDGELY HELEN ICKES was born on 30 April 1928, Newport, Perry County, PA. She married MARLIN GEORGE LENIG on 3 July 1946, Sunbury, Northumberland County, PA. She died on 21 June 2010, Colonial Park, Dauphin County, PA, at age 82. She was buried on 24 June 2010, at Woodlawn Memorial Gardens, Harrisburg, Dauphin County, PA.

2.1.1.1.3.1.1.1 CAROL LENIG married RONALD KERSHNER.

2.1.1.1.3.1.1.2 WALTER D. LENIG married RHONDA (--?--).

2.1.1.1.3.1.1.3 MICHAEL E. LENIG

2.1.1.1.3.2 WALTER LUTHER WHALEN was born on 15 January 1906, Sunbury, Northumberland County, PA. He died on 5 September 1906, Sunbury, Northumberland County, PA. He was buried on 7 September 1906, at Riverview Cemetery, Northumberland, Northumberland County, PA.

2.1.1.1.3.3 WILLIARD WHALEN is also referred to as WILLARD L. WHELAN in some sources. He was born circa 1912.

2.1.1.1.4 GEORGE HOWARD WILLIAMS was born on 18 November 1886, Tower City, Schuylkill County, PA. He married ABIGAIL ISORAH HINE. He died on 25 October 1956, Conshohocken, Montgomery County, PA, at age 69. He was buried on 28 October 1956, at Millville Cemetery, Millville, Columbia County, PA.

2.1.1.1.5 CARRIE ELLEN WILLIAMS was born on 30 July 1889, Tower City, Schuylkill County, PA. She married HARRY F. CONRAD. Carrie's death certificate indicates that prior to her demise, she was living in Cuyahoga Falls, OH. She died on 12 August 1931, Mary Packer Hospital, Sunbury, Northumberland County, PA, at age 42. She was buried on 15 August 1931, at Pomfret Manor Cemetery, Sunbury, Northumberland County, PA.

2.1.1.1.5.1 CHARLES CONRAD was born circa 1909.

2.1.1.1.6 RUTH A. WILLIAMS was born on 25 November 1893, Sunbury, Northumberland County, PA. She married WILLIAM F. EICHHOLTZ, son of JACOB ELY EICHHOLTZ and ROSA SHEFFLEY. She died on 5 January 1953, Sunbury, Northumberland County, PA, at age 59. She was buried on 8 January 1953, at Pomfret Manor Cemetery, Sunbury, Northumberland County, PA.

2.1.1.2 GEORGE W. WILLIAMS was born on 4 September 1858, Dauphin County, PA. He married MARY CATHERINE POWLEY, daughter of MICHAEL POWLEY and ELIZABETH MEASE, circa 1884. He married LILLIAN C. MILLER, daughter of DANIEL MILLER and ELIZABETH (--?--). He died on 2 October 1932, Harrisburg Hospital, Harrisburg, Dauphin County, PA, at age 74. He was buried on 6 October 1932, at Oak Hill Cemetery, Millersburg, Dauphin County, PA.

2.1.1.3 ANDREW L. WILLIAMS was born on 18 April 1861, Millersburg, Dauphin County, PA. He married **REBECCA SEILER.** He died on 1 May 1935, Mahoning Township, Montour County, PA, at age 74. He was buried on 4 May 1935, at Oak Hill Cemetery, Millersburg, Dauphin County, PA.

2.1.2 JOHN KLINGER was born on 28 June 1838, Lykens Township, Dauphin County, PA. He married **ELIZABETH BENJAMIN.** He married **SARAH A. BUFFINGTON,** daughter of **JOHANNES BUFFINGTON** and **CHRISTIANA FRANCE,** circa 1865. He died on 5 February 1913, Wiconisco, Dauphin County, PA, at age 74. He was buried on 7 February 1913, at Calvary United Methodist Cemetery, Wiconisco, Dauphin County, PA.

2.1.2.1 EMMA JANE KLINGER also went by the name of **JENNIE.** She was born circa November 1859. Some sources record that she was born in December 1859, Dauphin County, PA. She married **DANIEL W. BOHNER**, son of **DAVID BOHNER** and **CATHARINE YEAGER,** in 1879, Ogle County, IL. She died on 27 March 1933, Omaha, Douglas County, NE. She was buried at Westlawn-Hillcrest Memorial Park, Omaha, Douglas County, NE.

2.1.2.1.1 HARRY HOWARD BOHNER was born on 1 August 1881, Carroll County, IL. He died on 14 November 1952, Omaha, Douglas County, NE, at age 71. He was buried at Westlawn-Hillcrest Memorial Park, Omaha, Douglas County, NE.

2.1.2.2 MARY CATHERINE KLINGER also went by the name of **KATE.** She was born on 22 November 1861. She married **JOHN F. ZIMMERMAN,** son of **SAMUEL ZIMMERMAN** and **LOURETTA SHOOP,** circa 1877. She died on 1 June 1916, Dauphin County, PA, at age 54. She was buried at Straws Cemetery, Enders, Dauphin County, PA.

2.1.2.2.1 SADIE M. ZIMMERMAN was born on 13 March 1879. She married **WILLIAM L. WOLFE,** son of **ADAM H. WOLFE** and **MELINDA (--?--),** on 7 October 1899, Tower City, Schuylkill County, PA. She married **ALBERT G. DUBBS,** son of **JEFFERSON DUBBS** and **EMMA BROWN,** before 1920. She died on 20 November 1934, Ashland, Schuylkill County, PA, at age 55. She was buried on 23 November 1934, at Greenwood Cemetery, Tower City, Schuylkill County, PA.

2.1.2.2.1.1 NORMAN HENRY WOLFE was born on 12 April 1900, Tower City, Schuylkill County, PA. He married **BESSIE MAY EBERHART,** daughter of **MELVIN EBERHART** and **ANNETTE PIERCE,** on 29 June 1923, Monroe County, MI. He married **FLORENCE MAE RUTHERFORD,** daughter of **CHARLES RUTHERFORD** and **THERESA DAVIS,** on 18 April 1931, Ashland County, OH. He died on 5 November 1960, Licking Memorial Hospital, Newark, Licking County, OH, at age 60. He was buried at Newark Memorial Gardens, Newark, Licking County, OH.

2.1.2.2.1.2 WALTER W. WOLFE was born on 28 May 1903, Schuylkill County, PA. He married **RUBY V. LUBOLD,** daughter of **RILEY LUBOLD** and **ALICE ESTELLE ENGLE.** He died on 25 August 1984, at age 81. He was buried at Greenwood Cemetery, Tower City, Schuylkill County, PA.

2.1.2.2.1.2.1 WILLIAM WALTER WOLFE was born on 29 June 1925, Tower City, Schuylkill County, PA. He married **CHRISTINE SOPHIE BAUER,** daughter of **JACOB BAUER** and **MARY HAMBURGER,** on 27 July 1946, Lebanon County, PA. He died on 11 January 1998, Shamokin, Northumberland County, PA, at age 72. He was buried at Manheim Fairview Cemetery, Manheim, Lancaster County, PA.

2.1.2.2.1.2.2 DORIS M. WOLFE was born on 20 August 1926, Tower City, Schuylkill County, PA. She married **HERMAN HEILMAN.** She died on 10 January 2013, Lebanon, Lebanon County, PA, at age 86. She was buried at Covenant Greenwood Cemetery, Ebenezer, Lebanon County, PA.

2.1.2.2.1.2.2.1 CHERYL HEILMAN married **WILLIAM RUHLE.**

2.1.2.2.1.2.2.2 LONNIE HEILMAN

2.1.2.2.1.2.2.3 TODD HEILMAN

2.1.2.2.1.2.2.4 CYNTHIA A. HEILMAN was born on 2 June 1950, Lebanon, Lebanon County, PA. She married **RANDALL WARREN KOPP** circa 1972. She died on 2 July 2014, Lebanon, Lebanon County, PA, at age 64. She was buried at Indiantown Gap National Cemetery, Annville, Lebanon County, PA.

2.1.2.2.1.2.2.4.1 TONYA M. KOPP married **PAUL GADEL.**

2.1.2.2.1.2.2.4.1.1 CAITLIN GADEL

2.1.2.2.1.2.2.4.1.2 DAVID GADEL

2.1.2.2.1.2.2.4.2 SANDRA R. KOPP

2.1.2.2.1.2.2.4.3 RANDI N. KOPP

2.1.2.2.1.2.3 DALE R. WOLFE was born on 9 September 1927, Tower City, Schuylkill County, PA. He married ADA T. TONINI, daughter of JOHN TONINI and EVA PADALION, on 7 September 1946, Cornwall, Lebanon County, PA. He married KATHRYN E. SUMMY, daughter of ELMER KEENER SUMMY and ROSA GARMAN, circa 1951. He died on 6 January 2010, Manheim, Lancaster County, PA, at age 82.

2.1.2.2.1.2.3.1 GLENDA L. WOLFE married JACK GLANTZ.

2.1.2.2.1.2.4 ALICE ESTELLA WOLFE was born on 9 February 1932, Tower City, Schuylkill County, PA. She married WILLIAM SMITH. She died in February 1981. She was buried at White Chapel Memorial Gardens, Springfield, Greene County, MO.

2.1.2.2.1.2.5 DEWEY WOLFE was born after 1940.

2.1.2.2.1.3 MARY EMMA DUBBS was born on 31 October 1920, Tower City, Schuylkill County, PA. She married GUY TOBIAS ECKLER, son of HARRY R. ECKLER and AMY R. TOBIAS, on 1 June 1940, Manassas, VA. She died in November 1991, at age 71.

2.1.2.2.2 HENRY FRANKLIN ZIMMERMAN was born on 18 September 1880. He married ANNIE SARAH ROWE, daughter of ALBERT THEODORE ROW and IDA (--?--), on 12 August 1905, Lykens, Dauphin County, PA. He died by self-inflicted gunshot wound on 9 December 1906, Jackson Township, Dauphin County, PA, at age 26. He was buried on 13 December 1906, at Calvary United Methodist Cemetery, Wiconisco, Dauphin County, PA.

2.1.2.2.3 BERTIE ZIMMERMAN was born on 6 May 1882. She died on 16 September 1882. She was buried at Straws Cemetery, Enders, Dauphin County, PA.

2.1.2.2.4 IDA SEVILLA ZIMMERMAN was born on 3 May 1884, Dauphin County, PA. She married CHARLES MONROE WOLFGANG, son of GEORGE WOLFGANG and MARY FETEROLF. She died on 5 April 1959, Elizabethville, Dauphin County, PA, at age 74. She was buried on 8 April 1959, at Straws Cemetery, Enders, Dauphin County, PA.

2.1.2.2.4.1 HELEN MAE WOLFGANG was born in 1903, Millersburg, Dauphin County, PA. She married MARK CURTIN SHOOP on 25 December 1921, Dauphin County, PA. She died on 26 April 1965, Elizabethville, Dauphin County, PA. She was buried at Union Church Cemetery, Enterline, Dauphin County, PA.

2.1.2.2.4.1.1 LENA ELIZABETH SHOOP was born on 8 March 1922, Halifax, Dauphin County, PA. She married JOHN LEROY STONEROAD, son of LEWIS L. STONEROAD and MARY WERTZ, on 24 March 1943, Harrisburg, Dauphin County, PA. She died on 17 September 2001, Millersburg, Dauphin County, PA, at age 79. She was buried at Union Church Cemetery, Enterline, Dauphin County, PA.

2.1.2.2.4.1.2 KARL DEAN SHOOP was born on 24 June 1923, Halifax, Dauphin County, PA. He married MARY MARGUERITE ELLEN WARFEL, daughter of ARTHUR C. WARFEL and OLIVE M. LUBOLD, on 22 August 1942, Dauphin County, PA. He died on 28 October 1993, Harrisburg, Dauphin County, PA, at age 70. He was buried at Riverview Memorial Gardens, Halifax, Dauphin County, PA.

2.1.2.2.4.2 CHARLES EDWARD WOLFGANG was born on 21 May 1907, Washington Township, Dauphin County, PA. He married FLORENCE M. DOTTERER, daughter of LEVI DOTTERER and MANAVILLA MILLER, on 29 March 1930, Allentown, Lehigh County, PA. He died in June 1976, at age 69.

2.1.2.2.4.3 VIOLET GLADYS WOLFGANG was born on 6 November 1913, Elizabethville, Dauphin County, PA. She married LEWIS EDWARD SPANGLER on 16 September 1935. She died on 15 January 2006, Harrisburg, Dauphin County, PA, at age 92. She was buried at Fairview Cemetery, Enders, Dauphin County, PA.

2.1.2.2.4.4 WARREN CARL WOLFGANG was born on 5 March 1921, Halifax, Dauphin County, PA. He died on 17 April 1977, Elizabethville, Dauphin County, PA, at age 56. He was buried at Straws Cemetery, Enders, Dauphin County, PA.

2.1.2.2.5 AMANDA R. ZIMMERMAN was born on 1 March 1886, Dauphin County, PA. She married ALFRED I. GISE, son of GEORGE M. GISE and ELLEN (--?--), on 2 February 1907,

Carsonville, Dauphin County, PA. She married **JAMES LENTZ**. She died on 7 January 1960, Harrisburg, Dauphin County, PA, at age 73. She was buried on 11 January 1960, at Straws Cemetery, Harrisburg, Dauphin County, PA.

2.1.2.2.5.1 RICHARD WILLIAM GISE was born on 26 March 1907, Lykens, Dauphin County, PA.

2.1.2.2.5.2 VIRGINIA E. LENTZ was born circa 1912.

2.1.2.2.5.3 PEARL I. LENTZ was born on 24 November 1914, Elizabethville, Dauphin County, PA. She married **JOHN W. BIXLER**, son of **GARVIN SYLVESTER BIXLER** and **MARY ELIZABETH RUMBERGER**. She died on 28 February 2011, Schuylkill Medical Center-South Jackson Street, Pottsville, Schuylkill County, PA, at age 96. She was buried at Grace Methodist Church Cemetery, Muir, Schuylkill County, PA.

2.1.2.2.5.3.1 JEAN MARIE BIXLER was born on 12 July 1935, Muir, Schuylkill County, PA. She married **CLAIR L. BRESSLER** circa 1955. She died on 29 October 2009, Lancaster General Hospital, Lancaster, Lancaster County, PA, at age 74. She was buried on 2 November 2009, at Grace Methodist Church Cemetery, Muir, Schuylkill County, PA.

2.1.2.2.5.3.1.1 THOMAS L. BRESSLER

2.1.2.2.5.3.1.2 TIMOTHY S. BRESSLER married **DAWN (--?--)**.

2.1.2.2.6 SOLLY ZIMMERMAN was born on 18 August 1889. He died circa 7 April 1890. He was buried at Straws Cemetery, Enders, Dauphin County, PA.

2.1.2.2.7 NATHAN SAMUEL ZIMMERMAN was born on 14 June 1891, Dauphin County, PA. He married **ANNA L. KINDERMAN**, daughter of **CHARLES KINDERMAN** and **LENA KOHLER**, on 17 February 1914, Harrisburg, Dauphin County, PA. He died on 14 August 1945, Harrisburg, Dauphin County, PA, at age 54. He was buried at East Harrisburg Cemetery, Harrisburg, Dauphin County, PA.

2.1.2.2.7.1 VERNA M. ZIMMERMAN was born on 1 June 1914. She married **JOSEPH LOUIS JOHANIDES**. She died on 13 October 2002, Elizabethtown, Lancaster County, PA, at age 88. She was buried at Indiantown Gap National Cemetery, Annville, Lebanon County, PA.

2.1.2.2.7.2 PAUL FRANKLIN ZIMMERMAN was born on 1 August 1917, Harrisburg, Dauphin County, PA. He died on 22 March 1977, at age 59. He was buried at East Harrisburg Cemetery, Harrisburg, Dauphin County, PA.

2.1.2.2.8 JENNIE G. ZIMMERMAN was born on 15 November 1893. She married **PHILIP JOHN ETZWEILER**, son of **DAVID H. ETZWEILER** and **EMMA SULTZBAUGH**, on 23 October 1912, Harrisburg, Dauphin County, PA. She died on 21 February 1975, at age 81. She was buried at Halifax United Methodist Church Cemetery, Halifax, Dauphin County, PA.

2.1.2.2.8.1 DARWIN P. ETZWEILER was born on 6 April 1914, Halifax, Dauphin County, PA. He married **MARY LOUISE KOPPENHAVER**, daughter of **SAMUEL W. KOPPENHAVER** and **ANNA RUTTER**, on 24 November 1934, Halifax, Dauphin County, PA. He died on 26 August 1972, at age 58. He was buried at Halifax United Methodist Church Cemetery, Halifax, Dauphin County, PA.

2.1.2.2.8.1.1 WILLIAM ETZWEILER was born circa 1935.

2.1.2.2.8.2 KERMIT LEON ETZWEILER was born on 26 January 1920, Halifax, Dauphin County, PA. He married **REGENA ELIZABETH WILHELM**, daughter of **CHARLES WILHELM** and **RUTH HARRISON**, on 24 June 1939, Harrisburg, Dauphin County, PA. He died on 19 December 1996, Harrisburg, Dauphin County, PA, at age 76. He was buried at Halifax United Methodist Church Cemetery, Halifax, Dauphin County, PA.

2.1.2.2.8.2.1 INFANT SON ETZWEILER was born on 9 September 1939, Polyclinic Hospital, Harrisburg, Dauphin County, PA. He died on 9 September 1939, Polyclinic Hospital, Harrisburg, Dauphin County, PA. He was buried on 11 September 1939, at Halifax United Methodist Church Cemetery, Halifax, Dauphin County, PA.

2.1.2.2.9 INFANT ZIMMERMAN was born on 17 June 1895. He died on 17 June 1895. He was buried at Straws Cemetery, Enders, Dauphin County, PA.

2.1.2.2.10 BEULAH M. ZIMMERMAN was born on 1 August 1896, Dauphin County, PA. She married **WADE MORRISON DAVIS**, son of **JOHN C. DAVIS** and **SARA HANNA MORRISON**. She died on 20 December 1934, Harrisburg, Dauphin County, PA, at age 38. She was buried at Snyders Cemetery, New Bloomfield, Perry County, PA.

2.1.2.2.10.1 SARAH JEAN DAVIS was born on 25 December 1919, Harrisburg, Dauphin County, PA. She married CHARLES PAUL KREISER, son of SAMUEL KREISER and EMMA R. SCHROY. She died on 21 October 1986, at age 66. She was buried at Snyders Church Cemetery, New Bloomfield, Perry County, PA.

2.1.2.2.10.1.1 DELENORE W. KREISER was born on 19 June 1938.

2.1.2.2.10.2 EVELYN MAE DAVIS was born on 17 December 1922, Harrisburg, Dauphin County, PA. She married NORMAN R. GLINSKI. She died on 15 August 1997, Lewisburg, Union County, PA, at age 74. She was buried at Chapman Community Chapel Cemetery, Chapman, Snyder County, PA.

2.1.2.2.10.3 MELVIN MORRISON DAVIS was born on 22 October 1924, Harrisburg, Dauphin County, PA. He married IDA JANE MYERS. He died on 23 April 2007, Liverpool, Perry County, PA, at age 82. He was buried at Snyders Church Cemetery, New Bloomfield, Perry County, PA.

2.1.2.2.10.3.1 DONALD D. DAVIS married JO (--?--).

2.1.2.2.10.3.2 MEL M. DAVIS

2.1.2.2.10.4 EDRIS BETTY DAVIS was born on 21 March 1928, Harrisburg, Dauphin County, PA. She married EUGENE ROBERT GILL, son of JOSEPH A. GILL and MINNIE GUYER, on 22 July 1947, Arlington, VA. She married ROBERT MORRIS, son of DAVID H. MORRIS and ELLEN H. JOSS. She died on 4 May 1996, Liverpool, Perry County, PA, at age 68. She was buried at Snyders Church Cemetery, New Bloomfield, Perry County, PA.

2.1.2.2.11 PEARL I. ZIMMERMAN was born on 20 October 1899, Dauphin County, PA. She married CLARK C. MILLER, son of HENRY A. MILLER and HANNAH P. (--?--), circa 1915. She died on 1 August 1955, Elizabethville, Dauphin County, PA, at age 55. She was buried on 5 August 1955, at Maple Grove Cemetery, Elizabethville, Dauphin County, PA.

2.1.2.2.11.1 LORENE K. MILLER was born on 22 April 1917, Dauphin County, PA. She married CLAIR R. ZIMMERMAN, son of RAYMOND P. ZIMMERMAN and ANNA SCHOFFSTALL, on 23 May 1936, Dauphin County, PA. She died on 5 November 1989, Millersburg, Dauphin County, PA, at age 72. She was buried at Maple Grove Cemetery, Elizabethville, Dauphin County, PA.

2.1.2.2.11.1.1 MARILYN M. ZIMMERMAN married HARRY SEIBERT.

2.1.2.2.11.1.1.1 KEITH SEIBERT

2.1.2.2.11.1.1.2 BRIAN SEIBERT

2.1.2.2.11.1.2 SANDRA A. ZIMMERMAN married GALEN LENTZ.

2.1.2.2.11.1.2.1 GLEN LENTZ

2.1.2.2.11.1.2.2 RYAN LENTZ

2.1.2.2.11.2 MARGARET MAGRARITA MILLER was born circa 1924. She married ROBERT MILTON ROSS, son of RAYMOND M. ROSS and HELEN OAKES, on 1 January 1946, Harrisburg, Dauphin County, PA.

2.1.2.2.11.3 KATHLEEN M. MILLER was born circa 1926.

2.1.2.2.12 CATHERINE E. ZIMMERMAN also went by the name of KATIE. She was born on 4 May 1903, Dauphin County, PA. She married CYRUS EPHRAIM MARKS, son of GEORGE MARKS and ELIZABETH UHLER. She died on 24 May 1937, Pottsville, Schuylkill County, PA, at age 34. She was buried at Straws Cemetery, Enders, Dauphin County, PA.

2.1.2.2.12.1 MILDRED C. MARKS was born on 19 February 1923, Tower City, Schuylkill County, PA. She died on 15 September 1997, at age 74. She was buried at Straws Cemetery, Enders, Dauphin County, PA.

2.1.2.3 ROSA MINERVA KLINGER was born on 6 January 1866, Millersburg, Dauphin County, PA. She married JOSEPH LAWLEY circa 1881. She died on 18 July 1942, Lykens, Dauphin County, PA, at age 76. She was buried on 21 July 1942, at Odd Fellows Cemetery, Lykens, Dauphin County, PA.

2.1.2.3.1 WILLIAM CHARLES LAWLEY was born on 11 January 1882, Lykens, Dauphin County, PA. He married SARAH JANE WEHRY, daughter of WASHINGTON WEHRY and PHOEBE GRAEFF, on 9 September 1900, Shamokin, Northumberland County, PA. He died on 23 August 1951, Sunbury, Northumberland County, PA, at age 69. He was buried on 27 August 1951, at Odd Fellows Cemetery, Shamokin, Northumberland County, PA.

2.1.2.3.1.1 IRENE V. LAWLEY was born circa 1902. She married **CLAYTON RICHARD SAVIDGE** circa 1920.

2.1.2.3.1.1.1 WILLIAM ISAAC SAVIDGE was born on 11 November 1920, Shamokin, Northumberland County, PA. He died on 3 December 1920, Coal Township, Northumberland County, PA. He was buried on 5 December 1920, at Odd Fellows Cemetery, Shamokin, Northumberland County, PA.

2.1.2.3.1.1.2 THOMAS C. SAVIDGE was born on 14 November 1921, Shamokin, Northumberland County, PA. He died on 12 March 1922, Coal Township, Northumberland County, PA. He was buried on 15 March 1922, at Odd Fellows Cemetery, Shamokin, Northumberland County, PA.

2.1.2.3.1.1.3 CHARLES SAVIDGE was born circa 1922.

2.1.2.3.1.1.4 ROBERT E. SAVIDGE was buried at Odd Fellows Cemetery, Shamokin, Northumberland County, PA. He was born on 22 September 1924, Coal Township, Northumberland County, PA. He died on 25 April 1928, Coal Township, Northumberland County, PA, at age 3.

2.1.2.3.1.1.5 SARAH LORRAINE SAVIDGE was born on 11 July 1926, Shamokin, Northumberland County, PA. She married **GEORGE JACKSON CALL**. She died on 2 December 1997, at age 71. She was buried at Beverly National Cemetery, Beverly, Burlington County, NJ.

2.1.2.3.2 OSCAR EDWARD LAWLEY was born on 15 December 1883, Lykens, Dauphin County, PA. He married **SULA C. LAUDENSLAGER** circa 1904. He died on 11 December 1953, Lykens, Dauphin County, PA, at age 69. He was buried on 15 December 1953, at Calvary United Methodist Cemetery, Wiconisco, Dauphin County, PA.

2.1.2.3.2.1 ROLAND LAWLEY was born on 20 May 1905. He married **EVA C. (--?--)**. He died on 6 March 1970, Los Angeles County, CA, at age 64.

2.1.2.3.2.1.1 DOROTHY LAWLEY was born circa 1928.

2.1.2.3.2.2 SHIRLEY VIOLA R. LAWLEY was born on 28 February 1910, Lykens, Dauphin County, PA. She married **JOHN F. FORTENBAUGH**, son of **JOHN FORTENBAUGH** and **KATHRYN B. FLYNN**, on 6 December 1928, Dauphin County, PA. She married **JAMES PHILIP BECK**, son of **JOHN BECK** and **ELIZABETH BOYER**, on 8 February 1946, Dauphin County, PA. She died on 10 October 1995, Camp Hill, Cumberland County, PA, at age 85. She was buried at Shoops Cemetery, Harrisburg, Dauphin County, PA.

2.1.2.3.2.3 OSCAR E. LAWLEY JR. was born on 4 December 1911, Lykens, Dauphin County, PA. He married **ELSIE M. HERB**, daughter of **DAVID HERB** and **FLORENCE STRAYER**, on 25 November 1933, Dauphin County, PA. He and **ELSIE M. HERB** were divorced before 28 November 1957. He died on 28 November 1957, Polyclinic Hospital, Harrisburg, Dauphin County, PA, at age 45. He was buried on 2 December 1957, at Shoops Garden of Rest, Harrisburg, Dauphin County, PA.

2.1.2.3.2.3.1 NANCY LAWLEY was born circa 1935.

2.1.2.3.2.4 CARL DAVID LAWLEY was born on 16 November 1921, Lykens, Dauphin County, PA. He married **SHIRLEY SYLVIA RUDISILL**, daughter of **ALBERT M RUDISILL** and **EVA M. (--?--)**, on 7 November 1940, Gettysburg, Adams County, PA.

2.1.2.3.2.4.1 THOMAS EDWARD LAWLEY was born on 16 November 1947, Keystone Hospital, Lemoyne, Dauphin County, PA.

2.1.2.3.3 ANNE MABEL LAWLEY was born on 4 May 1885. She married **GURNEY ISRAEL WILLIARD**, son of **GEORGE D. WILLIARD** and **AMANDA MILLER**, on 5 September 1903, Lykens, Dauphin County, PA. She married **HARRY F. HOLWIG**, son of **HENRY HOLWIG** and **JENNIE JONES**, on 15 February 1938, Harrisburg, Dauphin County, PA. She died on 15 October 1941, Lykens, Dauphin County, PA, at age 56. She was buried on 19 October 1941, at Patriotic Order Sons of America Cemetery, Lykens, Dauphin County, PA.

2.1.2.3.3.1 LEROY JAMES WILLIARD was born on 11 February 1904. He died on 13 November 1911, Lykens, Dauphin County, PA, at age 7. He was buried on 14 November 1911, at Patriotic Order Sons of America Cemetery, Lykens, Dauphin County, PA.

2.1.2.3.4 ARTHUR WELLINGTON LAWLEY was born on 9 August 1888, Lykens, Dauphin County, PA, (an unknown value). He was buried on 8 April 1929, at Lykens, Dauphin County, PA. He died on 5 April 1939, Harrisburg State Hospital, Susquehanna Township, Dauphin County, PA, at age 50.

2.1.2.3.5 LUCY ROSIA LAWLEY was born on 14 August 1891. She married **WALTER LOGAN SALLADA**, son of **HENRY SALLADA** and **HENRIETTA COPENHAVER,** on 21 February 1906, Lykens, Dauphin County, PA. She married **SAMUEL RAYMOND THOMAS.** She died on 13 May 1950, Wiconisco, Dauphin County, PA, at age 58. She was buried at Calvary United Methodist Cemetery, Wiconisco, Dauphin County, PA.

2.1.2.3.5.1 HENRY SALLADA

2.1.2.3.5.2 VELMA ALVERTA SALLADA was born on 6 April 1907, Williamstown, Dauphin County, PA. She died on 26 November 1958, Lebanon, Lebanon County, PA, at age 51.

2.1.2.3.5.3 HARRY SALLADA was born circa 1911.

2.1.2.3.5.4 HAROLD V. SALLADA was born on 17 November 1913. He married **EDITH ELDA MORGAN**, daughter of **DAVID O. MORGAN** and **FRANCIS (--?--).** He died on 24 December 1983, at age 70. He was buried at Kochenderfer's Cemetery, Lebanon, Lebanon County, PA.

2.1.2.3.5.4.1 DEAN SALLADA married **JOAN (--?--).**

2.1.2.3.5.4.2 DAVID HAROLD SALLADA was born on 2 November 1937, Northumberland County, PA. He married **MARIAN ETZWEILER.** He died on 10 March 2011, Schuylkill County, PA, at age 73. He was buried on 16 March 2011, at Most Blessed Trinity Cemetery, Tremont, Schuylkill County, PA.

2.1.2.3.5.4.2.1 LORI SALLADA married **(--?--) CARL.**

2.1.2.3.5.4.3 NANCY SALLADA is also referred to as **NANCYLEE** in some sources. She was born circa 1939. She married **EMERSON CAIN.**

2.1.2.3.5.5 FLORENCE HENRIETTA SALLADA was born on 14 September 1917, Williamstown, Dauphin County, PA. She married **ELWOOD B. KEEN**, son of **JAMES B. KEEN** and **MAUDE P. MESSNER**, on 26 February 1938, Harrisburg, Dauphin County, PA. She died on 26 April 1992, Harrisburg, Dauphin County, PA, at age 74.

2.1.2.3.5.5.1 JANICE M. KEEN married **(--?--) WHITCOMB.** She was born circa 1938.

2.1.2.3.6 ADAM L. LAWLEY was born on 20 August 1903, Lykens, Dauphin County, PA, (an unknown value). He married **EMMA CATHERINE WREN**, daughter of **IRA A. WREN** and **IDA M. STALL,** on 1 January 1945, Dauphin County, PA. He died in January 1982, at age 78. He was buried at Fairview Cemetery, Williamstown, Dauphin County, PA.

2.1.2.4 WILLIAM R. KLINGER is also referred to as **WILLIAM H. KLINGER** in some sources. He was born on 25 May 1869. Some sources record that he was born in August 1868, in Pennsylvania. He married **EMMA ERDMAN**, daughter of **MAGDALINA (--?--),** circa 1888. He died on 31 March 1909, at age 40. He was buried at Calvary Cemetery, Wiconisco, Dauphin County, PA.

2.1.2.4.1 CLARENCE KLINGER is also referred to as **CLARENCE ROMBERGER** in some sources. He was born in February 1888.

2.1.2.4.2 EVA N. KLINGER was born in February 1900.

2.1.2.5 ANNIE E. KLINGER was born in December 1873. She married **MONROE HARVEY HOLWIG**, son of **LEVI D. HOLWIG** and **MARY ELLA HECKERT**, on 4 January 1895, Lykens, Dauphin County, PA. She died on 23 September 1931, Harrisburg, Dauphin County, PA, at age 57. She was buried on 26 September 1931, at Calvary United Methodist Church Cemetery, Wiconisco, Dauphin County, PA.

2.1.2.5.1 MYRTLE E. HOLWIG was born in November 1895. She married **GEORGE KNELL.** She and **GEORGE KNELL** were divorced. She died on 8 February 1929, North Whitehall, Lehigh County, PA, at age 33, from injuries sustained in an automobile accident in which her brother-in-law Theodore Bowen also died. She was buried at Calvary United Methodist Church Cemetery, Wiconisco, Dauphin County, PA.

2.1.2.5.1.1 MARGARET E. KNELL was born on 2 January 1916, Pottsville, Schuylkill County, PA. She married **GEORGE F. EASH (--?--),** son of **JAMES F. EASH** and **MARY J.**

GUYER, in May 1936. Margaret and George had no children. She died on 3 April 1989, at age 73. She was buried at Calvary United Methodist Church Cemetery, Wiconisco, Dauphin County, PA.

2.1.2.5.2 MARGARET E. HOLWIG was born on 23 April 1897, in Pennsylvania. She married **THEODORE SHELLY BOWEN**, son of **JAMES R. BOWEN** and **CATHERINE D. SHELLY,** on 19 July 1917, Pottsville, Schuylkill County, PA. She died on 21 June 1925, Sacred Heart Hospital, Allentown, Lehigh County, PA, at age 28. She was buried on 24 June 1925, at Charles Baber Cemetery, Pottsville, Schuylkill County, PA. At the time of her passing, Margaret and Theodore lived at 743 Turner Street, Allentown, PA.

2.1.2.5.2.1 MYRTLE ELLEN BOWEN was born on 5 May 1918, Pottstown, Montgomery County, PA. She married **LAWRENCE EDGAR HUMMEL SR.**, son of **WILLIAM HENRY HUMMEL** and **SAVILLA JANE LEHR,** on 8 October 1931, Hagerstown, Washington County, MD. She died on 18 August 1984, Oxnard, Ventura County, CA, at age 66. She was buried at Ivy Lawn Memorial Park, Ventura, Ventura County, CA.

2.1.2.5.2.1.1 LAWRENCE EDGAR HUMMEL JR. was born on 22 August 1933, Tower City, Schuylkill County, PA. He married **VIRGINIA LEE SMIDDY**, daughter of **WILLIAM J. SMIDDY** and **JOSEPHINE C. BIGOS,** in September 1954, Harris County, TX. He and **VIRGINIA LEE SMIDDY** were divorced on 27 June 1969. He married **DORIS ALMA MARTIN** on 28 June 1969, Hollywood, CA. Lawrence and Doris adopted two children.

2.1.2.5.2.1.1.1 VALERIE ELAINE HUMMEL was born on 5 May 1955, El Paso, TX. She married **RICHARD WILLIAM ERICKSON** on 10 March 1979, La Habra, CA. She and **RICHARD WILLIAM ERICKSON** were divorced on 16 September 1983 Pomona, CA. She married **STEVEN WILBUR KING** on 28 November 1987, Colorado Springs, CO. Valerie was the source of much information on the descendants of Annie E. Klinger.

2.1.2.5.2.1.1.1.1 SHAUNA MARIE ERICKSON was born on 9 January 1982, Fullerton, CA. She married **GARY JONATHAN NELSON**, son of **MATTHEW JONATHAN NELSON** and **DEA DENELLE PATTON,** on 26 January 2014, Auburn, Placer County, CA.

2.1.2.5.2.1.1.2 TERESA MARIE HUMMEL was born on 18 August 1956, El Paso, TX. She married **BRADLEY LANDIS** on 21 June 1992, Los Angeles, CA.

2.1.2.5.2.1.1.2.1 JASON AARON LANDIS was born on 16 January 1993, Los Angeles, CA.

2.1.2.5.2.1.1.2.2 JONAH ELIJAH LANDIS was born on 9 December 1995, Los Angeles, CA.

2.1.2.5.2.1.1.2.3 JULIA ALEXANDRA LANDIS was born on 6 June 1998, Los Angeles, CA.

2.1.2.5.2.1.1.2.4 JERAMY NOAH LANDIS was born on 12 May 2000, Los Angeles, CA.

2.1.2.5.2.1.1.3 KATHRYN ANN HUMMEL was born on 5 December 1960, Salina, KS. She married **ELDON RAGAN** on 12 May 2012, Colorado Springs, CO.

2.1.2.5.2.1.2 LAMAR EDWARD HUMMEL was born on 30 September 1938, Tower City, Schuylkill County, PA. He married **BOBBIE JEAN MCKINNEY** on 27 April 1964, Herrington Methodist Church, Paris, KY. He and **BOBBIE JEAN MCKINNEY** were divorced.

2.1.2.5.2.1.2.1 HOLLIE LYNN HUMMEL was born on 9 January 1968, Lexington, KY. She married **KURT W. BRYANT** on 16 July 2011, Glendale, CA.

2.1.2.5.2.1.2.2 ANTHONY WALLACE HUMMEL was born on 30 June 1970, Paris, KY. He married **DANA ROGERS** on 21 May 2004, St. Andrew State Park, Panama City, FL.

2.1.2.5.2.1.2.2.1 ALYSSA KATE HUMMEL was born on 25 September 2005, Baptist West Hospital, Knoxville, TN.

2.1.2.5.2.1.3 BARBARA HUMMEL was born on 31 July 1944, Pottsville Hospital, Pottsville, Schuylkill County, PA. She was stillborn.

2.1.2.5.2.1.4 LINDA ELAINE HUMMEL was born on 4 January 1948, Lykens, Dauphin County, PA. She married **GARY LYN WHETSTONE** in June 1968, Schuylkill Haven, Schuylkill County, PA. She and **GARY LYN WHETSTONE** were divorced on 23 November 1971 Harrisburg, Dauphin County, PA. She married **RICHARD EUGENE DUCLOS** in December 1971, Harrisburg, Dauphin County, PA. She and **RICHARD EUGENE DUCLOS** were divorced on 13 May 1981.

> **2.1.2.5.2.1.4.1 JACQUELINE FLORENCE WHETSTONE** is also referred to as **JACQUELINE FLORENCE WHETSTONE DUCLOS** in some sources because she was adopted by Richard DuClos. She was born on 22 January 1969, Pottsville, Schuylkill County, PA. She married **CHARLES FREDRICK SWANEPOEL** on 17 March 1990, Thousand Oaks, CA.
>
>> **2.1.2.5.2.1.4.1.1 BIANCA SWANEPOEL** was born on 18 May 1993, Tarzana, CA.
>
> **2.1.2.5.2.1.4.2 JENNIFER ELAINE DUCLOS** was born on 24 October 1972, Omaha, NE.
>
>> **2.1.2.5.2.1.4.2.1 NICHOLAS BRYAN CHRISTOPHER HUBER** was born on 15 May 1990, Northridge, CA.

2.1.2.5.2.1.5 ROBERT EUGENE HUMMEL was born on 18 April 1949, Pottsville, Schuylkill County, PA. He married **CAROL ANN CLINE** on 10 June 1975, Los Angeles, CA.

> **2.1.2.5.2.1.5.1 AARON ROBERT HUMMEL** was born on 6 February 1977, Burbank, CA. He married **ALINA R. TURNER** on 14 November 2009, Villa Park, CA.
>
>> **2.1.2.5.2.1.5.1.1 KINGSTON SCOTT HUMMEL** was born on 15 July 2009, West Hills, CA.
>
> **2.1.2.5.2.1.5.2 MANDY YATES HUMMEL** was born on 7 October 1978, West Hills, CA.
>
> **2.1.2.5.2.1.5.3 KEVIN IAN HUMMEL** was born on 12 August 1982, North Hills, CA. He married **MARINA FILIPPELI** on 21 March 2011, Culver City, CA.
>
>> **2.1.2.5.2.1.5.3.1 JOAQUIN FILIPPELI HUMMEL** was born on 11 July 2011, Beverly Hills, CA.

2.1.2.5.2.2 MARGARET ELIZABETH BOWEN was born on 13 December 1923, Allentown, Lehigh County, PA. She married **CALVIN GIFFORD KLINGER**, son of **CLARENCE MARK KLINGER** and **MAUDE IRENE KESSLER,** on 10 September 1941, Barry United Brethren Church, Schuylkill County, PA. She married **JAMES CENTRELLA**. She died on 11 December 1998, at age 74. She was buried at Blue Ridge Memorial Gardens, Harrisburg, Dauphin County, PA.

> **2.1.2.5.2.2.1 MARGARET ELIZABETH KLINGER** was born on 13 October 1942, Tower City, Schuylkill County, PA. She married **ROBERT J. MILLS**, son of **ROBERT J. MILLS** and **ANITA M. (--?--),** on 28 July 1962. She and **ROBERT J. MILLS** were divorced in 1988. She married **GLEN E. ALBERT**.
>
>> **2.1.2.5.2.2.1.1 ROBERT J. MILLS JR.** was born on 28 December 1962, Harrisburg, Dauphin County, PA. He married **CYNTHIA LEA ARCHIBALD** on 20 August 1986.
>
>> **2.1.2.5.2.2.1.2 SHARON MARIE MILLS** was born on 23 November 1968, Harrisburg, Dauphin County, PA.
>
>> **2.1.2.5.2.2.1.3 J. ROBERT MILLS** was born on 13 December 1970, Camp Hill, Cumberland County, PA.
>
> **2.1.2.5.2.2.2 CALVIN GIFFORD KLINGER JR.** was born on 1 December 1943, Lykens, Dauphin County, PA. He married **CORRINE EILEEN MILLER** on 1 December 1962. He married **GERALDINE COLELLA**, daughter of **ALBERT COLELLA** and **CATHERINE GIANNONE**.
>
>> **2.1.2.5.2.2.2.1 CHRISTINE E. KLINGER** was born on 10 May 1963, Harrisburg, Dauphin County, PA. She married **JERRY ARMSTRONG JR.**, son of **JERRY ARMSTRONG,** on 12 February 1983.

2.1.2.5.2.2.3 THEODORE MARK KLINGER was born on 30 November 1946, Minersville, Schuylkill County, PA. He married GERALDINE STUMP, daughter of JOHN STUMP and MARGARET MCKINNEY, on 31 December 1966, Middletown, Dauphin County, PA.

> **2.1.2.5.2.2.3.1** VENUS CRYSTIN TARA KLINGER was born on 22 June 1967, Harrisburg, Dauphin County, PA.
>
> **2.1.2.5.2.2.3.2** SHANELL DAWN LYNN KLINGER was born on 8 June 1973, Harrisburg, Dauphin County, PA.
>
> **2.1.2.5.2.2.3.3** AMBER TYE CETESS KLINGER was born on 12 May 1982, Harrisburg, Dauphin County, PA.

2.1.2.5.2.2.4 ELLEN ANN KLINGER was born on 8 August 1957, Hershey, Dauphin County, PA. She married RONALD L. SHULTZ, son of SHERWOOD LEE SHULTZ and RUTH ANN BONAWITZ, on 18 August 1973. She married (--?--) BOYD.

> **2.1.2.5.2.2.4.1** TONY LEE SHULTZ was born on 23 April 1974, Harrisburg Osteopathic Hospital, Harrisburg, Dauphin County, PA.
>
> **2.1.2.5.2.2.4.2** MICHAEL LEE SHULTZ was born on 11 October 1977, Allentown Hospital, Allentown, Lehigh County, PA.

2.1.2.5.2.2.5 GENE RAY KLINGER was born on 13 December 1959, Hershey, Dauphin County, PA. He married MARGARET HOOVER, daughter of DALE EDWARD HOOVER and JOANE LORETTA REIGLE, on 14 February 1981.

> **2.1.2.5.2.2.5.1** JUSTIN ROBERT KLINGER was born on 27 June 1981, Harrisburg Osteopathic Hospital, Harrisburg, Dauphin County, PA.
>
> **2.1.2.5.2.2.5.2** LYNSAY MICHELE KLINGER was born on 28 May 1986, Harrisburg Hospital, Harrisburg, Dauphin County, PA.

2.1.2.5.2.2.6 PATTILYNN LOUISE KLINGER was born on 12 November 1951, Ashland, Schuylkill County, PA. She married ROBERT HUDSON, son of JOHN A. HUDSON and EDNA V. OLDT, on 3 December 1971. She married JAMES ORA MULLENHOUR, son of JOHN CORBIN MULLENHOUR and RUTH DELMA HERRING, on 31 December 1982, in Ohio.

> **2.1.2.5.2.2.6.1** JEFFREY ALLAN HUDSON was born on 20 April 1972, Harrisburg, Dauphin County, PA. He married KERI NICHOLE POWERS on 29 May 1999, Newport News, VA.
>
>> **2.1.2.5.2.2.6.1.1** MOIRA ELIZABETH HUDSON was born on 1 November 2000, Hillsboro, Washington County, OR.
>>
>> **2.1.2.5.2.2.6.1.2** CORA ROAN HUDSON was born on 23 March 2002, Hillsboro, Washington County, OR.
>>
>> **2.1.2.5.2.2.6.1.3** AELA MURPHY HUDSON was born on 2 February 2009, Fredericksburg, VA.

2.1.2.6 JOHN WESLEY KLINGER was born on 14 March 1876. He died on 23 December 1925, Harrisburg State Hospital, Harrisburg, Dauphin County, PA, at age 49. John was a coal miner.

2.1.2.7 HARRY FRANKLIN KLINGER was born on 26 March 1880. He married CORA MAE (--?--) circa 1906. He died on 8 January 1919, Millersburg, Dauphin County, PA, at age 38.

> **2.1.2.7.1** MILTON HARVEY KLINGER was born circa 1905.
>
> **2.1.2.7.2** MYRTLE KLINGER was born circa 1907.
>
> **2.1.2.7.3** MARGARET KLINGER was born circa 1907.
>
> **2.1.2.7.4** PRISCILLA KLINGER was born circa 1913.

2.1.2.8 ALBERT GARFIELD KLINGER was born on 18 May 1884, Lykens, Dauphin County, PA.

2.1.3 PHILIP KLINGER is also referred to as PHILIP RUMBERGER in some sources. He was born on 21 July 1840, Dauphin County, PA. Philip was a musician who served with the 190th NY Infantry during the Civil War. He married MARY AMANDA RUSHON on 18 October 1863, Pennsylvania. He married MARY M. UNDERWOOD, daughter of ERI UNDERWOOD and MARGARET C. AMMERMAN, circa 1868. He married MARY MAGDALENE FAUBER. He married ELLA COULSON. He died on 22 April 1918, Michigan Soldiers Home, Grand Rapids Township, Kent County, MI, at age 77. He was buried on 24 April 1918, at Grand Rapids Veterans Home Cemetery, Grand Rapids, Kent County, MI.

2.1.3.1 JOHN A. KLINGER was born on 7 July 1866, Lykens, Dauphin County, PA. He married **ELIZABETH WAGNER**. He died on 26 November 1939, at age 73. He was buried at Middletown Cemetery, Middletown, Dauphin County, PA.

2.1.3.1.1 JOHN EARLE KLINGER was born on 5 November 1893, Middletown, Dauphin County, PA. He married **VIRGINIA MARY HERSHEY**. He died on 27 October 1964, Arlington, Tarrant County, TX, at age 70. He was buried at Hershey Cemetery, Hershey, Dauphin County, PA.

2.1.3.1.1.1 JOHN EARLE KLINGER JR. was born on 11 January 1923, Camden, Camden County, NJ. He married **WANDA MARIE MOORE**, daughter of **RAY MOORE** and **NETTIE BEA ARCHER**. He died on 18 February 1986, Tarrant County, TX, at age 63. He was buried at Johnson Station Cemetery, Arlington, Tarrant County, TX.

2.1.3.1.1.1.1 JOHN KLINGER

2.1.3.1.1.1.2 GARY KLINGER married **ADELE** (--?--).

2.1.3.1.1.1.3 PHILIP KLINGER

2.1.3.1.1.1.4 KRISTI KLINGER

2.1.3.2 HERBERT ROMBYER is also referred to as **BERT ROMLYER** in some sources. He was born on 21 July 1869, Jackson, Jackson County, MI. He married **LILLIE SNYDER**, daughter of **CHARLES H. SNYDER** and **CAROLINE EDMONDS**, on 24 November 1891, Jackson, Jackson County, MI. He died on 2 May 1949, Jackson, Jackson County, MI, at age 79. He was buried at Woodland Cemetery, Jackson, Jackson County, MI.

2.1.3.2.1 HAZEL MAY ROMBYER was born on 16 September 1893, Jackson, Jackson County, MI. She married **ALFRED OWEN UPDIKE**, son of **ALFRED UPDIKE** and **EMMA LIGHT**, on 8 April 1914, Jackson, Jackson County, MI. She died in January 1960, Jackson, Jackson County, MI, at age 66. She was buried at Woodland Cemetery, Jackson, Jackson County, MI.

2.1.3.2.1.1 EARLE EUGENE UPDIKE was born on 28 March 1918, Jackson, Jackson County, MI. He married **JOSEPHINE MARGARET LAMMERS**. He died on 16 January 1998, Jackson, Jackson County, MI, at age 79. He was buried at Woodland Cemetery, Jackson, Jackson County, MI.

2.1.3.2.1.2 MARY LOUISE UPDIKE was born on 7 September 1922, Jackson, Jackson County, MI. She married **HAROLD EUGENE SCHULTZ**. She died on 12 October 2002, at age 80. She was buried at Woodland Cemetery, Jackson, Jackson County, MI.

2.1.3.2.2 JESSIE ROMBYER was born on 14 February 1899, Michigan. She married **EVERETT DEWEY RUSSELL**, son of **BERT RUSSELL** and **EMMA EASTERLING**, on 21 August 1921, Jackson, Jackson County, MI. She died on 19 November 1942, Jackson, Jackson County, MI, at age 43. She was buried at Woodland Cemetery, Jackson, Jackson County, MI.

2.1.3.2.2.1 LA JANE RUSSELL was born circa 1922.

2.1.3.2.2.2 MAX DEAN RUSSELL was born on 12 July 1923, Jackson, Jackson County, MI. He married **MADELINE R. MILLER**, daughter of **EDWARD J. MILLER** and **FLORENCE DUSSELL**, on 6 November 1946, Leslie, Ingham County, MI. He died on 10 November 2000, Port Saint Lucie, St. Lucie County, FL, at age 77. He was buried at Woodland Cemetery, Jackson, Jackson County, MI.

2.1.3.2.2.3 EVERETT HARVEY RUSSELL was born on 10 March 1930, Jackson, Jackson County, MI. He married **MARIE G. BEAUDOIN**, daughter of **JEROME R. BEAUDOIN** and **LILLIAN M. KENNEDY**, on 12 May 1950, Jackson, Jackson County, MI. He died on 20 December 1998, at age 68. He was buried at Oak Grove Cemetery, Napoleon, Jackson County, MI.

2.1.3.2.3 CHARLES H. ROMBYER was born on 25 August 1902. He married **IDA BRINKERHUFF**, daughter of **FRANK BRINKERHUFF** and **AMELIA STANTZENBERGER**, on 3 October 1925, Jackson, Jackson County, MI. He was buried on 16 May 1975, at Jackson, Jackson County, MI.

2.1.3.2.3.1 ROBERT J. ROMBYER

2.1.3.2.3.2 THOMAS CHARLES ROMBYER was born on 17 September 1926, Jackson County, MI. He married **CORNELIA PAULINA AVERY** circa 1945. He died on 2 November 2003, Jackson, Jackson County, MI, at age 77. He was buried on 9 November 2013, at Roseland Memorial Gardens, Jackson, Jackson County, MI.

2.1.3.2.3.2.1 FREDERICK ROMBYER married **JANET** (--?--).

2.1.3.2.3.2.1.1 **FREDERICK ROMBYER II** married **AMY (--?--)**.

2.1.3.2.3.2.2 **CANDICE ROMBYER** married **(--?--) LITTLE**. She married **RANDALL CARLSON** after 2010.

2.1.3.2.3.2.2.1 **RACHEL LITTLE** married **DENNIS DAY**.

2.1.3.2.3.2.3 **THOMAS G. ROMBYER** was born on 14 February 1947, Jackson, Jackson County, MI. He married **PATRICIA (--?--)**. He died on 28 January 2010, The Villages, Lake County, FL, at age 62.

2.1.3.2.3.2.3.1 **GARY ROMBYER** married **JESSICA (--?--)**.

2.1.3.2.3.2.3.2 **PATRICK ROMBYER** married **HELENA (--?--)**.

2.1.3.2.4 **WILFORD W. ROMBYER** was born on 27 May 1905, Jackson County, MI. He married **ELLA WETHERELL**, daughter of **ALFONSO WETHERELL** and **MAY SHAFER**, on 3 September 1927, Jackson, Jackson County, MI. He died on 24 July 1992, Clarklake, Jackson County, MI, at age 87. He was buried at Woodland Cemetery, Jackson, Jackson County, MI.

2.1.3.2.4.1 **DANIEL WESLEY ROMBYER** was born on 24 May 1945, Manistee, Manistee County, MI. He died on 10 September 2004, Spring Arbor, Jackson County, MI, at age 59. He was buried at Woodland Cemetery, Jackson, Jackson County, MI.

2.1.4 **DANIEL KLINGER** was born in 1842. Daniel enlisted in Company A, Pennsylvania 50th Infantry Regiment on 09 Sep 1861. According to Registers of Pennsylvania Volunteers, available online at the Pennsylvania Historical and Museum Commission's website, Daniel "died of disease" while in service. Histories of the Regiment indicate that the regiment had been at the Battle of Fredericksburg, December 12-15, 1862, then at Falmouth, Virginia, until February 12, after which it moved to Newport News, VA, February 12-14, thence to Kentucky March 21-26. It was on duty at Paris, Ky., until April 27, after which it eventually joined the siege of Vicksburg. Daniel apparently died while the regiment was in Kentucky. He died on 28 April 1863. He was buried at Lexington National Cemetery, Lexington, Fayette County, KY.

2.1.5 **JOSEPH KLINGER** was born on 24 November 1844, Dauphin County, PA. He married **SARAH J. (--?--)**. He died on 10 December 1897, at age 53.

2.1.5.1 **EMMA KLINGER** was born circa 1868.

2.1.5.2 **LILLIE KLINGER** was born circa 1874.

2.1.5.3 **WILLIAM KLINGER** also went by the name of **WILLIE**. He was born circa 1874.

2.1.6 **CHARLES EDWIN KLINGER** was born in April 1853. He married **MALINDA JANE DANIELS**, daughter of **BENNEVELL F. DANIELS** and **MARY M. ADAMS**, circa 1873. He died on 14 November 1916, Harrisburg, Dauphin County, PA, at age 63. He was buried at Paxtang Cemetery, Paxtang, Dauphin County, PA.

2.1.6.1 **CHARLES EDWIN KLINGER JR.** was born on 8 April 1874, Philadelphia, Philadelphia County, PA. He married **EMMA LONG KINTER**, daughter of **ANDREW G. KINTER** and **ELIZABETH HUSS**, on 5 January 1899. He died on 6 October 1927, Harrisburg, Dauphin County, PA, at age 53. He was buried at Paxtang Cemetery, Paxtang, Dauphin County, PA.

2.1.6.1.1 **ETHEL LAURA KLINGER** was born on 17 January 1900, Harrisburg, Dauphin County, PA. She married **HARRY CALVIN HEIDER**, son of **HARRY HEIDER** and **LILLIE CATHERINE HANN**, on 11 March 1919, Harrisburg, Dauphin County, PA. She and **HARRY CALVIN HEIDER** were divorced in 1922 Dauphin County, PA, on grounds of desertion. She married **CHARLES EDGAR STEPHENS**, son of **JESSE K. STEPHENS** and **BERTHA M. OWENS**, on 1 April 1923, Harrisburg, Dauphin County, PA. She died on 24 March 1972, at age 72. She was buried at Westminster Memorial Gardens, Carlisle, Cumberland.

2.1.6.1.1.1 **CHARLES E. STEPHENS JR.** was born circa May 1926.

2.1.6.1.1.2 **PAUL A. STEPHENS** was born on 22 May 1928, Camp Hill, Cumberland County, PA. He married **DELORES K. DANNER**. He died on 18 January 2013, Manor Care, Carlisle, Cumberland County, PA, at age 84. According to a newspaper obituary, Paul lived in Carlisle, PA. Before retirement, he was employed for 28 years by L.B. Smith Heavy Equipment Division.

2.1.6.1.1.2.1 **ROGER L. STEPHENS** married **JEANNE (--?--)**. Roger lives in Carlisle, PA.

2.1.6.1.1.3 **VERNON E. STEPHENS** was born circa 1930. Vernon lives in Shippensburg, PA.

2.1.6.1.1.4 **WILLIAM A. STEPHENS** was born circa 1933.

2.1.6.1.1.5 **ROBERT Q. STEPHENS** was born circa 1936. Bob lives in Mechanicsburg, PA.

2.1.6.1.2 EDWIN CHARLES KLINGER was born on 12 August 1902, Harrisburg, Dauphin County, PA. He married IRENE MARY WRIGHTSTONE, daughter of EDWIN UNDERWOOD WRIGHTSTONE and HATTIE AMELIA ARNOLD, on 29 April 1926, Annville, Lebanon County, PA. He died on 16 August 1985, Mechanicsburg, Cumberland County, PA, at age 83. He was buried at Rolling Green Memorial Park, Camp Hill, Cumberland County, PA.

> **2.1.6.1.2.1** RUSSELL EDWIN KLINGER was born on 25 September 1926, Dauphin County, PA. He married JOYCE BEMILLER. He married RUTH ELAINE GENERAL, daughter of FRANK ALBERT GENERAL and VIOLET MALLOY, on 1 April 1966, Frederick County, VA. He died on 17 March 2007, Hershey Medical Center, Derry Township, Dauphin County, PA, at age 80. Russell worked at the Naval Defense Supply Command in Mechanicsburg, PA.
>
> **2.1.6.1.2.2** DOROTHY IRENE KLINGER was born on 28 November 1928, Shiremanstown, Cumberland County, PA. She married ROBERT HARVEY GRAHAM, son of CALVIN STOEY GRAHAM and RUTH ETTA BARR, on 5 November 1948, Mechanicsburg, Cumberland County, PA. She died on 27 November 2001, Camp Hill, Cumberland County, PA, at age 72. She was buried on 2 December 2001, at Dillsburg Cemetery, Dillsburg, York County, PA.
>
>> **2.1.6.1.2.2.1** JOAN AILEEN GRAHAM
>>
>> **2.1.6.1.2.2.2** ROSEMARY ANN GRAHAM
>>
>> **2.1.6.1.2.2.3** ROBERT CALVIN GRAHAM. Robert maintains a website with much information on the descendants of Charles E. Klinger at http://taylorgrahamlibrary.net/.
>>
>> **2.1.6.1.2.2.4** DEBORAH LOUISE GRAHAM
>
> **2.1.6.1.2.3** CHARLES RICHARD KLINGER was born on 29 November 1930, Mechanicsburg, Cumberland County, PA. He married LOLA J. GUISE, daughter of EMORY GUISE and EDITH LOBAUGH, in 1961, Holy Trinity Lutheran Church, York Springs, Adams County, PA. He died on 20 March 1979, Mercy Hospital, Philadelphia, Philadelphia County, PA, at age 48.
>
>> **2.1.6.1.2.3.1** JAY W. KLINGER
>>
>> **2.1.6.1.2.3.2** DONNA J. KLINGER
>
> **2.1.6.1.2.4** BETTY ETHEL KLINGER was born on 18 December 1932, Cumberland County, PA. She married JOHN JOSEPH HOOVEN II on 28 February 1953, Hagerstown, Washington County, MD.
>
>> **2.1.6.1.2.4.1** JOHN JOSEPH HOOVEN III was born on 26 August 1953. He married KATHLEEN MILLER. He married KAREN AUSTRIA.
>>
>>> **2.1.6.1.2.4.1.1** VALERIE A. HOOVEN was born on 18 January 1984.
>>
>> **2.1.6.1.2.4.2** LINDA JO HOOVEN was born on 1 June 1955. She married JOHN W. COOK on 23 August 1985.

2.1.6.1.3 HELEN M. KLINGER was born on 11 August 1905, Harrisburg, Dauphin County, PA. She died on 13 August 1927, Pennsylvania State Sanatorium, South Mountain, Franklin County, PA, at age 22 of tuberculosis. She was buried at Paxtang Cemetery, Paxtang, Dauphin County, PA.

2.1.6.1.4 ALMA R. KLINGER was born on 19 December 1908. She married JACOB KRAHLING, son of HENRY KRAHLING and CATHERINE ROBINSTINE. She died on 23 March 1994, Renova Center, Lower Allen Township, Dauphin County, PA, at age 85. She was buried at Paxtang Cemetery, Paxtang, Dauphin County, PA.

> **2.1.6.1.4.1** JACOB HENRY KRAHLING was born on 23 October 1935. He died on 18 June 1985, at age 49.
>
> **2.1.6.1.4.2** EMMA KATHERINE KRAHLING was born on 15 December 1939, Harrisburg, Dauphin County, PA. She married DONALD CRUMLICH, son of ELEANOR (--?--). She married ALAN BLACK. She died on 21 July 2015, Harrisburg Hospital, Harrisburg, Dauphin County, PA, at age 75.
>
>> **2.1.6.1.4.2.1** SCOTT L. CRUMLICH
>>
>> **2.1.6.1.4.2.2** LORRI K. CRUMLICH married TIMOTHY CISCO.
>>
>> **2.1.6.1.4.2.3** DONALD CRUMLICH
>>
>> **2.1.6.1.4.2.4** EDWARD L. CRUMLICH married CHRISTINA (--?--).

2.1.6.1.4.2.5 TODD A. CRUMLICH was born on 18 April 1963, Harrisburg, Dauphin County, PA. He married **RAE ANN WISMAN.** He died on 13 August 2014, at age 51.

2.1.6.1.5 PANSEY I. KLINGER was born on 30 May 1912, Harrisburg, Dauphin County, PA. She married **ELMER E. DORER**, son of **RALPH DORER** and **HELEN SMITH,** on 2 November 1940, Harrisburg, Dauphin County, PA. She died on 20 January 2004, Spring Creek Rehabilitation and Health Center, Harrisburg, Dauphin County, PA, at age 91. She was buried at Paxtang Cemetery, Paxtang, Dauphin County, PA.

2.1.6.1.5.1 RICHARD E. DORER was born after 1940.

2.1.6.1.5.2 JAMES E. DORER was born after 1940.

2.1.6.1.6 CLARENCE W. KLINGER was born on 7 December 1914, Harrisburg, Dauphin County, PA. He married **HELEN I. SNYDER**, daughter of **JOHN A. SNYDER** and **JENNIE M. WERT**. He died in June 1970, at age 55. He was buried at Woodlawn Memorial Gardens, Harrisburg, Dauphin County, PA.

2.1.6.1.6.1 ROBERT WAYNE KLINGER was born on 24 December 1936, Harrisburg, Dauphin County, PA. He married **JEAN TROUT** circa 1960. He died on 19 September 2015, Vibra Life, Mechanicsburg, Cumberland County, PA, at age 78. According to a newspaper obituary, Robert was a retired Communications Specialist with the Commonwealth of PA Office of Attorney General, Harrisburg and served eight years in the U.S. Naval Reserves.

Bob received the 2010 John H. McCormick Educational Outreach Award given by the Central PA Engineers Week Council (CPEWC), and served as president of CPEWC where he was a strong advocate for their educational outreach program. He was buried on 24 September 2015, at Hilltop Cemetery, Lewisberry, York County, PA.

2.1.6.1.6.1.1 SUZANNE MARIE KLINGER died before 2015.

2.1.6.1.6.1.2 DOUGLAS ROBERT KLINGER

2.1.6.1.6.2 THOMAS KLINGER

2.1.6.1.6.3 RONALD KLINGER

2.1.6.1.6.4 DAVID KLINGER

2.1.6.2 IDA PEARL KLINGER was born on 2 May 1876, Dauphin County, PA. She married **HARRY W. KAUFFMAN** on 14 April 1896, Camden, Camden County, NJ. She died on 17 July 1937, Harrisburg, Dauphin County, PA, at age 61.

2.1.6.2.1 HOWARD KAUFFMAN was born in March 1898.

2.1.6.2.2 ESTHER M. KAUFFMAN was born circa 1901.

2.1.6.2.3 HARRY EDWARD KAUFFMAN was born circa 1902.

2.1.6.2.4 ADA F. KAUFFMAN was born in 1906. She married **JOSEPH D. COLEMAN** circa 1927. She died in 1983. She was buried at Hummelstown Cemetery, Hummelstown, Dauphin County, PA.

2.1.6.2.4.1 JAMES G. COLEMAN was born on 3 June 1937, Harrisburg, Dauphin County, PA. He married **MARGARET E. (--?--)** in 1945. He died on 27 April 2010, Hummelstown, Dauphin County, PA, at age 72. He was buried on 1 May 2010, at Hummelstown Cemetery, Hummelstown, Dauphin County, PA.

2.1.6.2.4.1.1 CHARLES R. COLEMAN

2.1.6.2.4.1.2 JAMES D. COLEMAN

2.1.6.2.4.1.3 JOSEPH G. COLEMAN

2.1.6.2.4.1.4 MARY E. COLEMAN

2.1.6.2.5 ALICE M. KAUFFMAN was born on 22 April 1909. Some sources record that she was born in June 1910. She married **GEORGE R. MUMPER** on 4 August 1933, Lebanon County, PA. She died on 5 April 1977, Pompano Beach, Broward County, FL, at age 67.

2.1.6.2.5.1 PATRICIA A. MUMPER was born on 16 November 1939. Patricia never married. She died on 17 June 1992, New Cumberland, Cumberland County, PA, at age 52. She was buried at Camp Hill Cemetery, Camp Hill, Cumberland County, PA.

2.1.6.3 WILLIAM ELMER KLINGER was born on 12 January 1879. He married **SERILDA PEARL HOUSE**, daughter of **JOHN ROBERT HOUSE** and **SARAH ELIZABETH SMITH.** He married **MARY**

CATHERINE COOK, daughter of CLEASON COOK and ANNA BARBARA SHAMBAUGH, circa 1931. He died on 5 January 1944, Harrisburg, Dauphin County, PA, at age 64. He was buried at Paxtang Cemetery, Paxtang, Dauphin County, PA.

2.1.6.3.1 GLENN ROBERT KLINGER was born on 8 November 1905, Harrisburg, Dauphin County, PA. He married SARAH ELIZABETH HOFFMAN, daughter of JOHN C. HOFFMAN and MARY E. STERRETT. He died in September 1970, Carlisle, Cumberland County, PA, at age 64. He was buried at Westminster Memorial Gardens, Carlisle, Cumberland County, PA.

2.1.6.3.1.1 MARY KLINGER married (--?--) SHUMATE.

2.1.6.3.1.2 LOIS KLINGER married (--?--) EVANS.

2.1.6.3.1.3 FRANK G. KLINGER

2.1.6.3.1.4 GLADYS KLINGER married (--?--) CARDER.

2.1.6.3.1.5 SARAH GLENNETTE KLINGER was born on 22 May 1933, Harrisburg, Dauphin County, PA. She married ALBERT B. COCHRAN. She died on 10 October 2010, Carlisle, Cumberland County, PA, at age 77. She was buried at Blue Ridge Memorial Gardens, Harrisburg, Dauphin County, PA.

2.1.6.3.1.5.1 LINDA S. COCHRAN married (--?--) KUHARIC.

2.1.6.3.1.5.2 MARIANNE COCHRAN married (--?--) WHITE.

2.1.6.3.1.5.3 ALBERT BROYLES COCHRAN JR. was born on 26 October 1949. He died on 24 July 1976, Camp Hill, Cumberland County, PA, at age 26. He was buried at Blue Ridge Memorial Gardens, Harrisburg, Dauphin County, PA.

2.1.6.3.1.6 JOHN ROBERT KLINGER was born on 25 June 1935. He died on 26 December 1935, Harrisburg, Dauphin County, PA.

2.1.6.3.2 ELIZABETH MAY KLINGER was born on 12 February 1908, Dauphin County, PA. She married WILLIAM J. ARNOLD, son of JACOB ARNOLD and ANNA BELL JONES, on 26 February 1925, Liverpool, Perry County, PA. She died on 31 July 1971, at age 63. She was buried at Red Hill Cemetery, Newport, Perry County, PA.

2.1.6.3.3 ANNA R. KLINGER is also referred to as ANNA ZIMMERMAN KLINGER in some sources. She was born on 18 March 1911, Perry County, PA. She married LUTHER L. BLACK, son of IKE P. BLACK and LULA RING, on 21 March 1929, Harrisburg, Dauphin County, PA. She died on 26 June 1958, Polyclinic Hospital, Harrisburg, Dauphin County, PA, at age 47. She was buried at Oak Hill Cemetery, Millersburg, Dauphin County, PA.

2.1.6.3.3.1 ROBERT BLACK

2.1.6.3.3.2 LOIS M. BLACK was born on 13 September 1929, Minersville, Schuylkill County, PA. She married ROBERT P. KROSTER. She died on 20 February 2008, Susquehanna Village, Millersburg, Dauphin County, PA, at age 78. She was buried on 29 February 2008, at Indiantown Gap National Cemetery, Annville, Lebanon County`, PA.

2.1.6.3.3.2.1 SALLY KROSTER married MICHAEL GOTTSHALL before 2008. She married DAVID BOWERSOX.

2.1.6.3.3.2.2 LINDA KROSTER married RANDY LEONARD.

2.1.6.3.3.2.2.1 MATTHEW LEONARD

2.1.6.3.3.2.2.2 ERIN LEONARD

2.1.6.3.3.2.3 KATHY KROSTER married MICK MUMMA.

2.1.6.3.3.2.3.1 TRAVIS MUMMA

2.1.6.3.3.2.3.2 DYLAN MUMMA

2.1.6.3.3.2.4 ROBERT KROSTER JR. married CINDY (--?--).

2.1.6.3.3.2.4.1 BRANDON KROSTER

2.1.6.3.3.2.4.2 CODY KROSTER

2.1.6.3.3.2.4.3 KYLE KROSTER

2.1.6.4 ALBERT JEFFERSON KLINGER was born on 5 November 1883, Philadelphia, Philadelphia County, PA. He married ANNIE R. (--?--) circa 1908. He died in May 1970, at age 86. He was buried at Paxtang Cemetery, Paxtang, Dauphin County, PA.

2.1.6.4.1 IDA KLINGER was born in March 1910.

2.1.6.4.2 ALBERT KLINGER was born in 1914. He died in 1914. He was buried at Paxtang Cemetery, Paxtang, Dauphin County, PA.

2.1.6.5 HARRY VICTOR KLINGER was born on 16 February 1886, Harrisburg, Dauphin County, PA. He married **KATHRYN MATILDA KINTER**, daughter of **ANDREW G. KINTER** and **ELIZABETH HUSS,** on 18 May 1916, Harrisburg, Dauphin County, PA. He died on 28 June 1958, Dauphin County, PA, at age 72. He was buried at Paxtang Cemetery, Paxtang, Dauphin County, PA.

2.1.6.5.1 BEATRICE IRENE KLINGER was born on 21 May 1919, Harrisburg, Dauphin County, PA. Some sources record that she was born on 21 May 1918. Beatrice never married. She died on 6 December 2006, South Mountain, Franklin County, PA, at age 87.

2.1.6.6 JAMES FRANKLIN KLINGER was born on 25 March 1889. He married **ROSE E. (--?--)** before 1920. He died on 15 April 1965, at age 76. He was buried at Middletown Cemetery, Middletown, Dauphin County, PA.

2.1.6.6.1 WILMER F. KLINGER was born on 4 November 1916. He died in June 1980, at age 63.

2.1.6.6.2 RALPH H. KLINGER was born on 27 August 1918. He died on 22 October 1994, at age 76. He was buried at Indiantown Gap National Cemetery, Annville, Lebanon County, PA.

2.1.6.6.3 WILLIAM H. KLINGER was born circa 1920.

2.1.7 JONAS KLINGER is also referred to as **JAMES** in some sources. He was born on 1 April 1856. He married **SARAH ANN MUCHER**, daughter of **JOHN MUCHER** and **LENA RUDISILL**. He died circa 1889.

2.1.7.1 MICHAEL KLINGER was born in February 1865. He married **VIOLET LAMBERSON** on 18 October 1892, Bradford County, PA. He died before 1910. Michael's wife listed was listed as a widow in the 1910 Census.

2.1.7.1.1 ELWOOD MICHAEL KLINGER was born on 16 October 1890. He married **HELEN DUBY**. He died in October 1966. He was buried at Calvary Cemetery, Mount Carbon, Schuylkill County, PA.

2.1.7.1.1.1 ROBERT JOSEPH KLINGER was born on 9 August 1915, Pottsville, Schuylkill County, PA. He married **ROSINE ELIZABETH HUGHES**. He died on 12 August 1997, Lawnton, Dauphin County, PA, at age 82. He was buried at Holy Cross Cemetery, Harrisburg, Dauphin County, PA.

2.1.7.1.2 ROSA KAROLINE KLINGER was born on 20 January 1894. She was baptized on 9 September 1894, St. Paul's Lutheran Church, Philadelphia, Philadelphia County, PA.

2.1.7.2 EDWIN KLINGER was born circa 1876.

2.1.7.3 ADAM MONROE KLINGER was born on 11 March 1877. He married **EVA M. TREON**, daughter of **JOHN HENRY TREON** and **JOSEPHINE GIMBEL,** on 25 May 1903, Shamokin, Northumberland County, PA. He and **EVA M. TREON** were divorced before 1920. He died on 4 January 1925, Shamokin, Northumberland County, PA, at age 47. He was buried on 8 January 1925, at Odd Fellows Cemetery, Shamokin, Northumberland County, PA.

2.1.7.3.1 EVA MAY KLINGER was born circa 1907.

2.1.7.3.2 MARY ELEANOR KLINGER was born on 10 November 1910. She married **JOHN C. LONG**. She died on 22 April 1989, at age 78. She was buried at Milford Community Cemetery New, Milford, Kent County, DE.

2.1.7.3.3 GILBERT A. KLINGER was born on 7 December 1912. He married **EVELYN SINKEY**, daughter of **EMERY B. SINKEY** and **MARTHA E. SHIELDS**. He married **DOROTHY L. HARTWELL** on 29 December 1954, Monterey County, CA. He died on 8 April 1962, at age 49. He was buried at Cypress Lawn Memorial Park, Colma, San Mateo County, CA.

2.1.7.3.3.1 MARTHA EVA KLINGER was born on 29 June 1934, Monterey County, CA. She married **(--?--) LOGAN**. She died on 13 April 2004, at age 69.

2.1.7.3.3.2 KENNETH RONALD KLINGER was born on 4 May 1936, Monterey County, CA.

2.1.7.3.3.3 WANDA MAE KLINGER was born on 14 August 1939, Salinas, Monterey County, CA. She married **(--?--) SMITH**. She died on 8 February 1992, at age 52.

2.1.7.3.4 GALEN CHESTER KLINGER was born on 15 March 1914, Shamokin, Northumberland County, PA. He died on 31 May 1991, at age 77. He was buried at Limerick Garden of Memories, Limerick, Montgomery County, PA.

2.1.7.4 ELIZA KLINGER was born circa December 1879.

2.1.7.5 Susan Klinger was born circa December 1879.

2.1.7.6 Edith Julian Klinger is also referred to as **Edith May Klinger** in some sources. She was born on 22 February 1883. She was baptized on 12 May 1883, St. John's Lutheran Church, Lykens, Dauphin County, PA. She married **Charles Monroe Koons**, son of **Michael Koons** and **Ann Durr**, on 13 September 1902, Northumberland County, PA. She married **(--?--) Thomas** before 1920. She died on 3 June 1952, Coal Township, Northumberland County, PA, at age 69. She was buried on 6 June 1952, at Odd Fellows Cemetery, Shamokin, Northumberland County, PA.

2.1.7.7 Robert Walter Klinger was born on 6 May 1884. He died on 16 October 1915, Shamokin, Northumberland County, PA, at age 31. He was buried on 20 October 1915, at Odd Fellows Cemetery, Shamokin, Northumberland County, PA.

2.1.7.8 Clayton Daniel Klinger was born on 29 June 1886, Harrisburg, Dauphin County, PA. He died on 17 June 1965, Houston, Harris County, TX, at age 78. He was buried at Forest Park Cemetery, Houston, Harris County, TX.

2.1.7.9 Charles Klinger was born on 7 September 1888, Lykens, Dauphin County, PA. He married **Maude Irene Weikel**. He married **Maude Schreffler**, daughter of **John Schreffler** and **Martha Richards**, in 1922, Philadelphia, Philadelphia County, PA. He died on 27 July 1959, Philadelphia, Philadelphia County, PA, at age 70. He was buried on 31 July 1959, at Oakland Cemetery, Philadelphia, Philadelphia County, PA.

> **2.1.7.9.1 Melvin C. Klinger** was born on 7 September 1912. He died on 23 May 1935, Coal Township, Northumberland County, PA, at age 22. He was buried on 27 May 1935, at Odd Fellows Cemetery, Shamokin, Northumberland County, PA.
>
> **2.1.7.9.2 Lilly Klinger** was born circa 1914.
>
> **2.1.7.9.3 Lester Walter Klinger** was born on 30 April 1916, Shamokin, Northumberland County, PA. He married **Meriel Lois Whitaker**. He died on 18 March 2000, at age 83. He was buried at Biloxi National Cemetery, Biloxi, Harrison County, MS.
>
> **2.1.7.9.4 Martha A. Klinger** was born on 9 February 1922, Shamokin, Northumberland County, PA. She married **James McDermott**. She died on 11 August 2000, Pottstown, Montgomery County, PA, at age 78. She was buried at Friedens Union Church Cemetery, Sumneytown, Montgomery County, PA.
>
>> **2.1.7.9.4.1 Marsha McDermott** was born in 1949. She died in 1975. She was buried at Friedens Union Church Cemetery, Sumneytown, Montgomery County, PA.
>
> **2.1.7.9.5 Charlotte Betty Klinger** was born on 24 February 1923, Shamokin, Northumberland County, PA. She married **Joseph Walter Zagnojny**, son of **Theodore Zagnojny** and **Cecelia Breskius**, on 2 July 1952, Northampton County, VA. She died on 15 December 2013, at age 90.

2.1.8 Lydia Ann Klinger was born circa 1858.

2.2 Lydia Klinger was born on 18 July 1813. She was baptized on 1 August 1813, Zion (Klinger's) Church, Erdman, Lykens Township, Dauphin County, PA. She married **George Hoffman**, son of **John George Hoffman** and **Rebecca Kunsman**. She died on 2 October 1858, at age 45.

> **2.2.1 David Hoffman**
>
> **2.2.2 Emanuel Hoffman**
>
> **2.2.3 Daniel Hoffman** was born before 1836.
>
> **2.2.4 John Hoffman** was born before 1836.

2.3 Catharine Klinger was born on 15 February 1815. Some sources record that she was born on 19 February 1815. She married **John Masser**, son of **Johannes Masser** and **Maria Margaretha Fick**. She died on 13 July 1847, at age 32. Some sources record that she died on 13 January 1847, but it is doubtful whether this is correct. She was buried at Howerter's Church, now St. James Lutheran Church, Pitman, Schuylkill County, PA.

> **2.3.1 Moses Masser**
>
> **2.3.2 Manassas Masser**
>
> **2.3.3 Gine Masser** was born on 18 June 1834. She died on 18 June 1834.
>
> **2.3.4 Elias Masser** was born on 20 May 1836. He was baptized on 26 June 1836, Howerter's Church, now St. James Lutheran Church, Pitman, Eldred Township, Schuylkill County, PA.

2.3.5 JOHANN MASSER is also referred to as JOHN MASSER in some sources. He was born on 10 March 1844. He died on 12 December 1845, at age 1.

2.3.6 HENRY MASSER is also referred to as HEINRICH in some sources. He was born on 20 November 1846. He died on 6 July 1847.

2.4 SUSANNAH KLINGER is also referred to as SUSANNA in some sources. She was born on 27 January 1817. She was baptized on 14 April 1817, Zion (Klinger's) Church, Erdman, Lykens Township, Dauphin County, PA. She married SAMUEL SCHOFFSTALL, son of JOHN SCHOFFSTALL and MARY MAGDALENA HOOVER. She died on 1 March 1885, at age 68. She was buried at Gratz, Dauphin County, PA.

2.4.1 SUSANNAH SCHOFFSTALL was born circa 1841.

2.4.2 ELIZABETH SCHOFFSTALL was born in 1843.

2.4.3 CATHERINE SCHOFFSTALL was born in 1844.

2.4.4 ANN ELIZABETH SCHOFFSTALL was born in September 1847. She married JOHN ADAM SALTZER. She died on 22 September 1918.

2.4.5 AMANDA SCHOFFSTALL was born in May 1849. She died on 7 February 1925, at age 75.

2.4.6 ADAM SCHOFFSTALL is also referred to as ADAM SHOFFSTALL in some sources. He was born on 7 January 1853. He married POLLY SCHWALM, daughter of FREDERICK STEIN SCHWALM and ELIZABETH SCHERDEL, circa 1874. He died on 9 December 1922, at age 69. He was buried at Simeon Church Cemetery, Gratz, Dauphin County, PA.

2.4.6.1 WILLIAM SCHOFFSTALL

2.4.6.2 HARRY SCHOFFSTALL died young.

2.4.6.3 CHARLES SHOFFSTALL was born in 1874. He married KATE SCHMELTZ.

2.4.6.3.1 MINNIE SHOFFSTALL married JIMMY WILLIAMSON.

2.4.6.3.1.1 ELVIN WILLIAMSON was born circa 1912. He married MABEL DEETER. He died on 2 December 1988, Maple Farms Nursing Home, Akron, PA. He was buried at Lincoln Cemetery, Ephrata, PA.

2.4.6.3.1.1.1 JANICE WILLIAMSON married BARTON HENLY.

2.4.6.3.1.1.1.1 SUSAN HENLY

2.4.6.3.1.1.1.2 SARA HENLY

2.4.6.3.1.1.2 JAMES WILLIAMSON married ISOBEL (--?--).

2.4.6.3.1.1.2.1 JAMES A. WILLIAMSON

2.4.6.3.1.2 ALFRED A. WILLIAMSON was born circa 1921. He married PAULINE M. BROSIOUS, daughter of EDGAR BROSIOUS and MABEL (--?--). Prior to his death, he lived at 1504 West Maple Street, Valley View, Hegins Township, Schuylkill County, PA. He died on 28 May 1992, Charles Cole Memorial Hospital, Coudersport, PA.

2.4.6.3.1.2.1 RICHARD H. WILLIAMSON married DONNA HEPLER.

2.4.6.3.1.2.1.1 DENISE WILLIAMSON married JEFFREY SEAMAN.

2.4.6.3.1.2.1.1.1 ZACHARY C. SEAMAN

2.4.6.3.1.2.1.1.2 JEREMY J. SEAMAN

2.4.6.3.1.3 C. LEONARD WILLIAMSON also went by the name of PETE. He was born on 22 March 1928, Valley View, Hegins Township, Schuylkill County, PA. He married SHIRLEY CLOUSER circa 1966. Pete was a self-employed coal miner and former employee of Kocher Coal Co., Valley View, PA. Prior to his death, he lived at 11 North Vista Road, Valley View, Hegins Township, Schuylkill County, PA. He died on 1 March 2003, Good Samaritan Regional Medical Center, Pottsville, Schuylkill County, PA, at age 74. He was buried at St. Andrew's Church Cemetery, Valley View, Hegins Township, Schuylkill County, PA.

2.4.6.4 MARY A. SCHOFFSTALL was born on 5 February 1877. She married WILLIAM E. BROSIUS circa 1892, Jordan Township, Northumberland County, PA. She died in 1928.

2.4.6.4.1 CHARLES A. BROSIUS was born in July 1893, Pennsylvania.

2.4.6.4.2 JAY ADAM BROSIUS was born in June 1895, Pennsylvania.

2.4.6.4.3 HARRY W. BROSIUS was born in October 1896, Pennsylvania. He died between 1900 and 1910.

2.4.6.5 EMMA E. SCHOFFSTALL was born in May 1881. She married CHARLES MONROE KLINGER, son of PETER KLINGER and MARGARET ANNA MUENCH, on 1 January 1898, Reformed Church, Pillow, Northumberland County, PA. She died in 1934.

2.4.6.5.1 KATIE BEULAH KLINGER was born on 17 November 1901. She married REUBEN HARRIS MUTH, son of HENRY D. MUTH and LULU HERALD, on 23 March 1918. She died in March 1987, at age 85. Prior to her death, Katie was living in the vicinity of Gratz, Dauphin County, PA. She was buried at Simeon Church Cemetery, Gratz, Dauphin County, PA.

2.4.6.5.1.1 CHARLES E. MUTH was born on 10 July 1918. He married ALTA PHILLIPS, daughter of OSCAR PHILLIPS and MARGARET E. STRAYER. He died on 11 January 1985, at age 66.

2.4.6.5.1.1.1 CHARLES MUTH

2.4.6.5.1.1.2 DONNA MUTH married RANDY KRATZER, son of WILLIAM M. KRATZER and MAE C. E. DEPPEN.

2.4.6.5.1.1.2.1 MEGAN KRATZER

2.4.6.5.1.2 MARY LOUISA MUTH was born on 19 January 1922, Lykens Township, Dauphin County, PA. She married HAROLD H. BECHTEL. She died on 23 October 2009, Holy Spirit Hospital, Camp Hill, Cumberland County, PA, at age 87.

2.4.6.5.1.2.1 LARRY E. BECHTEL married JANET (--?--). Larry lives in Berrysburg, PA.

2.4.6.5.1.2.2 DONALD R. BECHTEL married DONNA (--?--). Donald lives in Elizabethville, PA.

2.4.6.5.1.2.3 MICHAEL T. BECHTEL

2.4.6.5.1.2.4 HAROLD K. BECHTEL was born on 8 October 1941. He died on 8 January 2003, at age 61.

2.4.6.5.2 CHARLES E. KLINGER was born in 1918, Pennsylvania.

2.4.6.6 JOHN ADAM SCHOFFSTALL was born in September 1890. He married LILLIE ANN WILLIER, daughter of RUFUS F. WILLIER and ANNIE LAURA RABUCK, in 1911. He died in 1958.

2.4.6.6.1 ALBERT SCHOFFSTALL. Albert lives in York, PA.

2.4.6.6.2 CHARLES H. SCHOFFSTALL. Charles lives in Harrisburg, PA.

2.4.6.6.3 HANNAH D. SCHOFFSTALL was born on 5 July 1913. She married JOHN SHIFFER. She died in December 1977, at age 64.

2.4.6.6.4 EVA S. SCHOFFSTALL was born in 1915. She married BLAIR A. WIEST, son of RUFUS LEON WIEST and KATIE ALICE SCHMELTZ. She died in 1951, Lykens Township, Dauphin County, PA. She was buried at Zion (Klinger's) Church Cemetery, Erdman, Dauphin County, PA.

2.4.6.6.4.1 MARLIN E. WIEST was born on 10 July 1936, Lykens Township, Dauphin Co., PA. He married MARCIA MILDRED MORRIS circa 1953.

2.4.6.6.4.1.1 KATHY JEAN WIEST was born on 4 April 1955, Harrisburg Hospital, Harrisburg, Dauphin Co., PA. She married MARK LUTHER HOFFMAN on 20 April 1974, Zion (Klinger's) Lutheran Church, Erdman, Dauphin Co., PA.

2.4.6.6.4.1.1.1 SCOTT BRIAN HOFFMAN was born on 7 September 1974, Dauphin Co., PA. He married BRONWEN ELAINE SWAB circa 1998.

2.4.6.6.4.1.1.2 NICHOLAS RYAN HOFFMAN was born on 31 July 1979, Dauphin Co., PA.

2.4.6.6.4.1.2 MARLIN E. WIEST JR. was born on 1 July 1958, Harrisburg Hospital, Harrisburg, Dauphin Co., PA. He married DEBRA SUE WILLIARD, daughter of ALVIN RAY WILLIARD and SARAH ARLENE WILLIARD, on 3 September 1987, Zion (Klinger's) Lutheran Church, Erdman, Dauphin Co., PA.

2.4.6.6.4.1.2.1 KYLE WIEST was born on 27 September 1987, Dauphin Co., PA.

2.4.6.6.4.1.3 BRADLEY F. WIEST was born on 6 May 1960, Dauphin Co., PA.

2.4.6.6.4.1.4 SHEILA ANN WIEST was born on 28 May 1965, Dauphin Co., PA.

2.4.6.6.4.2 GRACE MERVINE WIEST

2.4.6.6.4.3 (--?--) WIEST was born in July 1940, Dauphin County, PA. She died on 20 July 1940, Dauphin County, PA.

2.4.6.6.4.4 BARBARA ANN WIEST was born circa 1946, Dauphin County, PA. She died on 23 September 1946, Dauphin County, PA.

2.4.6.6.5 JOHN A. SCHOFFSTALL JR. was born on 22 April 1917, Gratz, Dauphin County, PA. He married **MARGARET HOPPLE**. He died on 22 January 2007, Friendly Nursing Home, Pitman, Schuylkill County, PA, at age 89. According to a newspaper obituary, John was a retired manager and co-owner of Schoffstall's General Store in Gratz. He was also an ambulance driver. He was buried on 26 January 2007, at Gratz Union Cemetery, Gratz, Dauphin County, PA.

2.4.6.6.5.1 LINDA SCHOFFSTALL married (--?--) **WENRICH**.

2.4.6.6.5.2 GERALD SCHOFFSTALL

2.4.6.6.6 EDNA SCHOFFSTALL was born on 29 May 1920. She married **ARTHUR LUBOLD**. She died on 16 January 2004, at age 83.

2.4.6.6.7 STANLEY H. SCHOFFSTALL also went by the name of **BUD**. He was born on 5 September 1924, Gratz, Dauphin County, PA. He married **JANETTE L. BRUCE**. He was buried on 5 March 2009, at Union Cemetery, Duncannon, Perry County, PA. He died on 2 September 2009, Holy Spirit Hospital, Camp Hill, Cumberland County, PA, at age 84. According to a newspaper obituary, Stanley lived in Duncannon, PA. He retired from Motor Truck Equipment Co and was also a musician having played with Al Shade & The Short Mountain Boys, The Outsiders and The Pine Knots.

2.4.6.6.8 ALBERTA E. SCHOFFSTALL was born in 1934. She married **GLENN HUBERT LEITZEL**, son of **CLARENCE ELMER LEITZEL** and **MARY VIRGINIA SNODY**. Alberta lives in Dallastown, PA.

2.4.6.6.8.1 RODNEY D. LEITZEL was born on 4 January 1954, Danville, Montour County, PA. He married **JOLEEN SMITH**. He died on 5 October 2015, Spring Garden Township, York County, PA, at age 61.

2.4.6.6.8.1.1 RYAN LEITZEL

2.4.6.6.8.2 GLENDA LEITZEL was born on 5 May 1955.

2.4.6.6.8.3 BRENDA LEITZEL was born on 9 November 1958. She married (--?--) **FIRESTONE**.

2.4.6.6.8.3.1 AMANDA FIRESTONE

2.4.6.6.9 SARA JANE SCHOFFSTALL was born in 1938. She married **EARL JURY**. Sara lives in Gratz, PA.

2.4.7 ELIAS SCHOFFSTALL was born on 3 June 1857. He married **CATHERINE E. BUFFINGTON** circa 1883. He married **EMMA JANE DUTTRY**, daughter of **ELIAS DUTTRY** and **SARAH M. (--?--)**, circa 1905. He died on 27 October 1912, at age 55.

2.4.7.1 CHARLES A. SCHOFFSTALL was born circa 1907, Pennsylvania.

2.4.7.2 MAUDIE E. SCHOFFSTALL was born circa 1908, Pennsylvania.

2.4.7.3 LEROY SCHOFFSTALL was born circa 1910, Pennsylvania.

2.4.8 LYDIA ANN SCHOFFSTALL also went by the name of **ANNIE**. She was born in April 1862. She married **CHARLES M. THOMAS** circa 1888. She died in 1919.

2.5 SALOME KLINGER is also referred to as **SARAH AND SALMI** in some sources. She was born on 1 June 1819. She married **JONAS HARTMAN**.

2.6 SOLOMON KLINGER is also referred to as **SALOMON** in some sources. He was born on 8 March 1820. He was baptized on 9 April 1820, Zion (Klinger's) Church, Erdman, Lykens Township, Dauphin County, PA. He married **ANNA MARGARETHA BIEGSLER** in 1839, Pennsylvania. He married **CATHARINE REHRER** after 16 September 1854. He died on 10 August 1893, at age 73. He was buried at St. Jacob's Cemetery, Pine Grove, Schuylkill County, PA.

2.6.1 ANNA CATHERINE KLINGER is also referred to as **KATE AND EMMA** in some sources. She was born on 19 August 1841, Schuylkill County, PA. She was baptized on 24 October 1841, St. Peter's Lutheran Church, Pine Grove, Schuylkill County, PA. She married **REUBEN BARTO**, son of **ISAAC JACOB BARTO** and **ELIZABETH ESHELMAN**, on 20 September 1857, Schuylkill County, PA. She died on 9 September 1901, Pine Grove, PA, at age 60. She was buried at St. John's Lutheran Cemetery, Pine Grove, Schuylkill County, PA.

2.6.1.1 **EDWIN K. BARTO** is also referred to as **EDWARD** in some sources. He was born in 1858. He married **KATE C. (--?--)** circa 1880. Some sources suggest that he and **KATE C. (--?--)** were married circa 1893. He died in 1943, Pine Grove, PA. He was buried at St. John's Lutheran Cemetery, Pine Grove, Schuylkill County, PA.

2.6.1.1.1 **HAZEL E. BARTO** was born circa 1892, Pennsylvania.

2.6.1.1.2 **FLORENCE BARTO** was born in 1899, Pennsylvania.

2.6.1.1.3 **LILLIAN BARTO** was born in 1902, Pennsylvania.

2.6.1.1.4 **ANNA B. BARTO** was born in 1908, Pennsylvania. She married **WILLIAM F. MILLER** circa 1926.

2.6.1.1.5 **ROSS F. BARTO** was born in 1911, Pennsylvania.

2.6.1.1.6 **WILLIAM F. BARTO** was born in 1913, Pennsylvania.

2.6.1.2 **JOHN WILSON BARTO** was born on 8 April 1860. He married **ALMA REBECCA HUBLEY**, daughter of **JONATHAN HUBLEY** and **SARAH (--?--)**, circa 1880. He died in 1928.

2.6.1.2.1 **WARREN R. BARTO** was born in February 1881. He married **MABEL ELIZABETH MOYER** circa 1908. He married **JULIA E. FIDLER SHAFFNER** before 1920. He died in 1929.

2.6.1.2.1.1 **HENRY WILSON BARTO** was born on 1 April 1908. He married **RUTH ELIZABETH THOMPSON.** He died in March 1973, at age 64.

2.6.1.2.1.1.1 **JOSEPH WARREN BARTO** was born on 11 March 1931, Philadelphia, Philadelphia County, PA. He married **LEONA RUDY.** He died on 27 March 2016, Schoentown, Schuylkill County, PA, at age 85. He was buried on 31 March 2016, at Saint Casimir's Cemetery, Saint Clair, Schuylkill County, PA.

2.6.1.2.1.1.2 **HENRY WILSON BARTO** was born on 3 September 1932. He married **MELBA SMITH.** He married **NANCY TOMACYK.** He died on 30 October 1996, at age 64.

2.6.1.2.1.1.2.1 **BRIAN KEITH BARTO**

2.6.1.2.1.1.2.2 **HENRY WILSON BARTO**

2.6.1.2.1.1.2.3 **MICHAEL ARTHUR BARTO**

2.6.1.2.1.1.2.4 **ROBERT JOSEPH BARTO**

2.6.1.2.1.1.3 **RUTH ELLENA BARTO** was born on 14 January 1947. She married **JOHN BUEHLER.**

2.6.1.2.1.2 **WARREN MOYER BARTO** was born on 8 June 1909. He married **JULIA QUIDACHAY.** He died on 20 November 1982, at age 73.

2.6.1.2.1.2.1 **WARREN BARTO** married **THERESA (--?--).**

2.6.1.2.1.2.1.1 **AGNES BARTO**

2.6.1.2.1.2.1.2 **DOMINIC BARTO**

2.6.1.2.1.2.1.3 **JOE BARTO**

2.6.1.2.1.2.1.4 **JOHN BARTO**

2.6.1.2.1.2.1.5 **JULIE BARTO**

2.6.1.2.1.2.1.6 **KATHLEEN BARTO**

2.6.1.2.1.2.1.7 **MARIE BARTO**

2.6.1.2.1.2.1.8 **MIKE BARTO**

2.6.1.2.1.2.1.9 **TERESA BARTO**

2.6.1.2.1.2.1.10 **WARREN BARTO**

2.6.1.2.1.2.1.11 **NICK BARTO** was born in December 1989.

2.6.1.2.1.2.2 **JULIA BARTO** was born on 25 December 1947. She married **VICENTE CRUZ LEON GUERRERO.** She married **THOMAS PANGELINAN.**

2.6.1.2.1.2.2.1 **ELOISE STEPHANIE BARTO LEON GUERRERO SEMAN** was born on 21 December 1967.

2.6.1.2.1.2.2.1.1 **TIMOTHY JAMES BARTO LEON GUERRERO** was born on 5 January 1987.

2.6.1.2.1.2.2.1.2 **JOYLIE IBAI CHISATO** was born on 2 November 1993.

2.6.1.2.1.2.2.1.3 ERIC VINCENT CHISATO was born on 4 March 1996.

2.6.1.2.1.2.2.1.4 MILTON MOODY was born on 16 December 2000.

2.6.1.2.1.2.2.2 VICENTE LEON GUERRERO was born on 27 July 1970. He married MARILYN ADA AQUINO.

2.6.1.2.1.2.2.2.1 EVAN MICHAEL SQUINO LEON GUERRERO was born on 29 June 1994.

2.6.1.2.1.2.2.3 JOY CHRISTINE LEON GUERRERO was born on 30 December 1974. She married MICHAEL SCOTT SAN NICOLAS.

2.6.1.2.1.2.2.3.1 MIKAYLA LIANN LEON GUERRERO SAN NICOLAS was born on 14 April 1994.

2.6.1.2.1.2.2.3.2 CHRISTIAN MICHAEL LEON GUERRERO SAN NICOLAS was born on 19 December 2002.

2.6.1.2.1.2.2.4 CHRISTOPHER JASON BARTO LEON GUERRERO was born on 8 September 1976.

2.6.1.2.1.2.2.5 ADAM VINCENT LEON GUERRERO was born on 13 November 1978.

2.6.1.2.1.2.3 VIRGINIA BARTO is also referred to as GINNY in some sources. She was born on 18 May 1949. She married KARL TUDELA REYES.

2.6.1.2.1.2.3.1 KARL TUDELA REYES was born on 9 November 1972.

2.6.1.2.1.2.3.2 RHETA INEZ BARTO REYES was born on 6 April 1975. She married ALEX ESTRADA ANGELES.

2.6.1.2.1.2.3.3 REINHOLD REID REYES was born on 23 May 1978.

2.6.1.2.1.2.3.4 SEAN SPENCER REYES was born on 21 April 1980.

2.6.1.2.1.2.4 CONCEPCION Q. BARTO is also referred to as CONNIE in some sources. She was born on 4 October 1950. She married KENNETH W. COWARD.

2.6.1.2.1.2.4.1 DAWNA KAY COWARD was born on 8 July 1973. She married (--?--) TUDELA.

2.6.1.2.1.2.4.1.1 CHRISTOPHER JAMES COWARD TUDELA

2.6.1.2.1.2.4.2 KENNETH W. COWARD JR. was born on 1 November 1980.

2.6.1.2.1.2.4.3 JULIA A. COWARD was born on 9 March 1982.

2.6.1.2.1.2.5 EVELYN ELIZABETH BARTO was born on 19 July 1954. She married ROBERT KERR.

2.6.1.2.1.2.5.1 ALEX KERR

2.6.1.2.1.2.5.2 NICOLE KERR was born on 22 August 1977.

2.6.1.2.1.2.6 HARRY GEORGE BARTO was born on 29 July 1957. He married BETTYE DAVIS.

2.6.1.2.1.2.6.1 JULIANNA DAVIS BARTO was born on 13 December 1993.

2.6.1.2.1.2.7 JOSEPH BARTO was born on 26 September 1962.

2.6.1.2.1.2.8 MICHAEL BARTO was born on 26 September 1964.

2.6.1.2.1.3 ROBERT WILLIAM BARTO was born on 22 July 1915, Mt. Zion, PA. He married GERTRUDE REYNOLDS. He died on 17 February 1982, Bedford Heights, Ohio, at age 66.

2.6.1.2.1.3.1 LONA AMON BARTO was born on 11 June 1942, Everett, PA. She married THOMAS BRYANT WILSON on 22 August 1970, Meridian, MS.

2.6.1.2.1.3.2 VAN ADRIAN BARTO was born on 24 June 1944, Corry, PA. He married JANICE CATALANO. He married KATHLEEN SAVAGE HOEHNEN.

2.6.1.2.1.3.2.1 CORI PATRICIA BARTO was born on 26 January 1976, Mayfield Heights, OH. She married MYRLE ELBERT SIEGER on 2 July 2001.

2.6.1.2.1.3.2.2 DANA ELIZABETH BARTO was born on 12 June 1980, Mayfield Heights, OH.

2.6.1.2.2 EFFIE L. BARTO was born in September 1882. She died on 27 August 1884, at age 1.

2.6.1.2.3 HARRY W. BARTO was born in March 1885. He married EVA M. (--?--) after 1920. He died in 1939.

2.6.1.2.4 NORMAN BARTO was born on 18 January 1887. He died on 28 September 1888, at age 1.

2.6.1.2.5 ANNA PAULINE BARTO was born in February 1889. She married EDWARD ROBB. She died in 1958.

2.6.1.2.6 ROBERT E. BARTO was born in October 1890. He married EMILIE MOORE. He died in 1960.

> **2.6.1.2.6.1** SARAH BARTO
>
> **2.6.1.2.6.2** ROBERT M. BARTO was born in 1919.

2.6.1.2.7 HILDA S. BARTO was born in May 1894. She married HARRY Z. GENSEMER, son of GEORGE W. GENSEMER, circa 1915. She died in 1977.

> **2.6.1.2.7.1** ELLA MARGARET GENSEMER was born in 1917. She married ROBERT G. GRAY.
>
>> **2.6.1.2.7.1.1** ROBERT GRAY
>
> **2.6.1.2.7.2** GEORGE JOHN GENSEMER is also referred to as JACK in some sources. He was born in 1923. He died in 1983.
>
> **2.6.1.2.7.3** HARRY Z. GENSEMER also went by the name of RED. He was born in 1925. He married SARAH (--?--).
>
>> **2.6.1.2.7.3.1** CATHERINE GENSEMER
>>
>> **2.6.1.2.7.3.2** HARRY J. GENSEMER married JENNIFER B. (--?--). He is also referred to as JACK in some sources.
>>
>>> **2.6.1.2.7.3.2.1** ALEXANDRA GENSEMER
>>>
>>> **2.6.1.2.7.3.2.2** HARRY GENSEMER

2.6.1.2.8 JOHN WILLIS BARTO was born on 8 June 1896. He died on 14 October 1972, at age 76.

2.6.1.2.9 MARION R. BARTO was born in 1903. She married PAUL ROSS.

> **2.6.1.2.9.1** ANDREW BARTO ROSS

2.6.1.3 SUSAN ELIZABETH BARTO was born on 25 November 1863. She married MORGAN L. PARRY on 4 March 1881.

> **2.6.1.3.1** ANNA PEARL PARRY was born in 1886.

2.6.2 PERCIVAL KLINGER was born in March 1842. He was baptized on 15 January 1843, St. Peter's Lutheran Church, Pine Grove, Schuylkill County, PA. He married SUSANNA EMERICH. He died in 1899. He was buried at St. Jacob's Evangelical Lutheran Church Cemetery, Pine Grove, Schuylkill County, PA.

2.6.2.1 PENROSE KLINGER is also referred to as PENRO in some sources. He was born on 25 December 1864. He was baptized on 7 May 1865, St. Jacob's Evangelical Lutheran Church, Pine Grove, Schuylkill County, PA. He married AMANDA CAROLINA (--?--). He died on 5 January 1936, at age 71. He was buried at St. Jacob's Evangelical Lutheran Church Cemetery, Pine Grove, Schuylkill County, PA.

> **2.6.2.1.1** ROY P. KLINGER was born circa 1900, Pennsylvania. He married GUSSIE M. (--?--) circa 1921.
>
>> **2.6.2.1.1.1** DELPHINE M. KLINGER was born circa 1928, Pennsylvania.

2.6.2.2 CARRIE ELIZABETH KLINGER also went by the name of LIZZIE. She was born on 23 December 1866. She was baptized on 10 March 1868, St. Jacob's Evangelical Lutheran Church, Pine Grove, Schuylkill County, PA. She married ANDREW UMBENHAUR circa 1885.

> **2.6.2.2.1** HARRY UMBENHAUR was born in November 1885, Pennsylvania.
>
> **2.6.2.2.2** MABEL UMBENHAUR was born in June 1888, Pennsylvania.

2.6.3 ELIAS KLINGER is also referred to as ELI in some sources. He was born on 2 December 1844, Schuylkill County, PA. Some sources record that he was born in 1845. He was baptized on 5 May 1845, St. Peter's Lutheran Church, Pine Grove, Schuylkill County, PA. According to the History of Pennsylvania Volunteers, Elias enlisted in Company B, Pennsylvania 93rd Infantry Regiment as a private. He mustered out on 27 July 1865 at Washington, DC. He married EMMA WARNER, daughter of JOHN WARNER and ELIZABETH (--?--), circa 1868. He died on 3 April 1932, at age 87. He was buried at Church of God Cemetery, Suedberg, Schuylkill County, PA.

2.6.3.1 ADELIA KLINGER was born on 12 January 1868, Outwood, Schuylkill County, PA. She was baptized on 28 June 1868, St. Jacob's Evangelical Lutheran Church, Pine Grove, Schuylkill County, PA. Some sources record that she was born in June 1869. She married **ADAM LONG**, son of **ADAM LANG** and **MARY SHOLLY,** circa 1890. She died on 3 November 1926, Union Township, Lebanon County, PA, at age 58. She was buried on 7 November 1926, at Outwood Lutheran Church, Pine Grove, Schuylkill County, PA.

    2.6.3.1.1 MARY ELLEN LONG was born on 18 April 1890. She was baptized on 23 August 1891, Sattazahns Evangelical Lutheran Church, Union Township, Lebanon County, PA. She married **CLINTON W. MINNICH**, son of **FRANK MINNICH** and **CATHERINE F. DAGATA**. She died in May 1977, at age 87. She was buried at Outwood Lutheran Church Cemetery, Pine Grove, Schuylkill County, PA.

        2.6.3.1.1.1 CLARENCE RICHARD MINNICH was born on 5 May 1911, Outwood, Schuylkill County, PA. He married **DOROTHY FRANCES CULLATHER**, daughter of **PETER JAMES CULLATHER** and **JULIA MARIA BRENNAN**, before 1940. He married **ELSIE ANNA HUMMEL**, daughter of **FREDERICK HUMMEL** and **ANNA KATHRYN SCHUH**, on 5 April 1980, Richmond, VA. He died on 13 February 1988, Ephrata, Lancaster County, PA, at age 76. He was buried at Cedar Hill Cemetery, Ephrata, Lancaster County, PA.

            2.6.3.1.1.1.1 ELLEN MINNICH married **JOHN RUPP**.

            2.6.3.1.1.1.2 ADA MATILDA MINNICH was born on 8 February 1914. She was baptized on 11 March 1914, Jacobs Evangelical Lutheran Church, Pine Grove, Schuylkill County, PA. Some sources record that she was born on 8 February 1913. She married **FREDERICK SAMUEL SCHWARTZ**, son of **CHARLES SCHWARTZ** and **CARRIE OWENS**, after 1930. She died on 1 January 2004, at age 89. She was buried at Outwood Lutheran Church Cemetery, Pine Grove, Schuylkill County, PA.

                2.6.3.1.1.1.2.1 FLOYD SCHWARTZ was born circa 1938.

        2.6.3.1.1.2 GUY WILLIAM MINNICH was born on 8 January 1916. He died on 7 February 1917, Pine Grove, Schuylkill County, PA, at age 1.

        2.6.3.1.1.3 GRACE MINNICH was born on 18 December 1918. She died on 17 December 1920, Union Township, Lebanon County, PA, at age 1.

    2.6.3.1.2 SARAH E. LONG was born in November 1893.

    2.6.3.1.3 MABEL ADELIA LONG was born on 18 December 1903, Lebanon County, PA. Some sources record that she was born on 5 December 1905. She married **WARREN HENRY FAKE**, son of **ELMER NORMAN FAKE** and **ANNA LOUISA DITZLER**. She died on 5 February 1973, Ephrata, Lancaster County, PA, at age 69. She was buried at Cedar Hill Cemetery, Ephrata, Lancaster County, PA.

        2.6.3.1.3.1 MARGARET A. FAKE was born on 13 August 1928, Schuylkill County, PA. She married **GUY ENCK**. She married **LEE EDWARD ANDERS**.

        2.6.3.1.3.2 ELAINE G. FAKE was born circa 1931.

        2.6.3.1.3.3 ETHEL FAKE was born circa 1935.

        2.6.3.1.3.4 JOAN E. FAKE was born circa 1936. She married **MELVIN R. SWEIGART**.

    2.6.3.1.4 EVA M. LONG was born circa 1906, Pennsylvania.

2.6.3.2 SARAH CATHERINE KLINGER is also referred to as **SALLIE KLINGER** in some sources. She was born on 29 January 1870, Schuylkill County, PA. She was baptized on 16 October 1870, St. Jacob's Evangelical Lutheran Church, Pine Grove, Schuylkill County, PA. She married **MORRIS SWALM**, son of **GEORGE SWALM** and **MATILDA WISE**, circa 1895. She died on 13 February 1942, Pine Grove, Schuylkill County, PA, at age 72. She was buried at Church of God Cemetery, Pine Grove, Schuylkill County, PA.

    2.6.3.2.1 LUELLA SWALM was born on 6 April 1896, Pine Grove, Schuylkill County, PA. She married **REUBEN T. NEWCOMER**, son of **THEODORE NEWCOMER** and **EMMA C. TOBIAS**. She died on 3 February 1996, at age 99. She was buried at Suedberg Church of God Cemetery, Suedberg, Schuylkill County, PA.

        2.6.3.2.1.1 MORRIS NEWCOMER was born circa 1919.

        2.6.3.2.1.2 RAY NEWCOMER was born circa 1920.

2.6.3.2.1.3 WILBERT NEWCOMER was born on 30 September 1925, Suedberg, Schuylkill County, PA. He married MILDRED ROEDER, daughter of RUFUS ROEDER and KATIE STEINBRUNN. He died on 16 July 1996, Pottsville, Schuylkill County, PA, at age 70. He was buried at Schuylkill Memorial Park, Schuylkill Haven, Schuylkill County, PA.

> **2.6.3.2.1.3.1** CYNTHIA NEWCOMER married WAYNE YEAGER.
>> **2.6.3.2.1.3.1.1** BRIAN YEAGER married BRIGETTE (--?--).
>>> **2.6.3.2.1.3.1.1.1** MADISON YEAGER
>>> **2.6.3.2.1.3.1.1.2** CARISSA YEAGER
>> **2.6.3.2.1.3.1.2** KRISTA YEAGER married SANDOW LASZLO.
>>> **2.6.3.2.1.3.1.2.1** ZOEY LASZLO

2.6.3.2.2 GEORGE SWALM was born circa 1898.

2.6.3.2.3 RAY SWALM is also referred to as RAY SCHWALM in some sources. He was born on 7 November 1900. He married IVY MINERVA OLT, daughter of EDWIN OLT and EMMA (--?--). He died in January 1987, at age 86. He was buried at Suedberg Church of God Cemetery, Suedberg, Schuylkill County, PA.

> **2.6.3.2.3.1** EARL MORRIS SCHWALM was born on 9 April 1925, Suedberg, Schuylkill County, PA. He married ALMA M. (--?--). He died on 25 September 1996, at age 71. He was buried at Grand View Memorial Park, Annville, Lebanon County, PA.

> **2.6.3.2.3.2** ALLEN ROBERT SWALM was born on 19 May 1930, Suedberg, Schuylkill County, PA. He married FRANCES L. (--?--). He died on 27 August 1994, at age 64. He was buried at Grand View Memorial Park, Annville, Lebanon County, PA.

> **2.6.3.2.3.3** ANNA MAE SWALM was born circa 1931.

2.6.3.2.4 KATIE SWALM was born on 20 February 1903. She married FRED DEICHERT. She died in October 1973, Pine Grove, Schuylkill County, PA, at age 70. She was buried at Suedberg Church of God Cemetery, Suedberg, Schuylkill County, PA.

> **2.6.3.2.4.1** HOWARD IRVIN DEICHERT was born on 27 August 1923, Pine Grove, Schuylkill County, PA. He died on 22 December 2007, at age 84.

> **2.6.3.2.4.2** LLOYD CLAIR DEICHERT was born on 1 May 1925, Pine Grove, Schuylkill County, PA.

> **2.6.3.2.4.3** IVY ANNA DEICHERT was born on 25 April 1929, Suedberg, Schuylkill County, PA. She married LESTER E. HAUER, son of GEORGE D. HAUER and LILLIE HIESTER. She died on 15 June 2007, York Hospital, York, York County, PA, at age 78. She was buried on 19 June 2007, at Hamlin Cemetery, Hamlin, Lebanon County, PA.

>> **2.6.3.2.4.3.1** LESTER E. HAUER JR. married DOLORES (--?--).
>>> **2.6.3.2.4.3.1.1** CHRISTOPHER HAUER
>>> **2.6.3.2.4.3.1.2** JASON HAUER
>> **2.6.3.2.4.3.2** SUSAN L. HAUER married DONALD POTTS.
>>> **2.6.3.2.4.3.2.1** KATIE POTTS
>>> **2.6.3.2.4.3.2.2** RYAN POTTS

2.6.3.2.5 MINERVA SWALM was born on 19 May 1908, Pine Grove, Schuylkill County, PA. She married CHARLES ALLEN DITZLER, son of IRVIN WILSON DITZLER and GERTRUDE BOLTZ, on 7 January 1928, Suedberg Church of God, Suedberg, Schuylkill County, PA. She died in June 1986, at age 78. She was buried at Suedberg Church of God, Suedberg, Schuylkill County, PA.

> **2.6.3.2.5.1** JAMES MORRIS DITZLER was born on 7 February 1933, Schuylkill County, PA. He died in August 1981, at age 48. He was buried at Suedberg Church of God, Suedberg, Schuylkill County, PA.

2.6.3.3 WILSON KLINGER was born on 12 April 1872. He was baptized on 28 February 1873, St. Jacob's Evangelical Lutheran Church, Pine Grove, Schuylkill County, PA. He married FLORENCE ELLIOTT in 1893. He died in February 1962, Suedberg, Schuylkill County, PA, at age 89. He was buried at Suedberg Church of God Cemetery, Suedberg, Schuylkill County, PA.

> **2.6.3.3.1** MARY EMMA KLINGER was born on 9 March 1893. She married EARL E. SCHLARB. She died on 30 December 1973, Los Angeles County, CA, at age 80.

2.6.3.3.1.1 MARY ELIZABETH SCHLARB was born on 21 September 1915. She married **LEON CHARLES FARRELL**. She died on 8 November 1990, Los Angeles County, CA, at age 75.

2.6.3.3.2 RALPH ELIAS KLINGER was born on 7 May 1894, Suedberg, Schuylkill County, PA. He married **NELLIE M. STRUBHAR** circa 1918. He died on 7 April 1960, at age 65. He was buried at Church of God Cemetery, Suedberg, Schuylkill County, PA.

2.6.3.3.2.1 HARVEY WILSON KLINGER was born on 12 April 1918, Pine Grove, Schuylkill County, PA. He was baptized on 25 December 1927, Jacob's Evangelical Lutheran Church, Pine Grove, Schuylkill County, PA. He married **EVA MILLER**, daughter of **ABRAHAM MILLER** and **KATIE HEINBACH,** after 1940. Harvey served in the US Army from 22 Jan 1941 to 5 Nov 1945. He died on 7 April 2002, Lebanon, Lebanon County, PA, at age 83. He was buried at Indiantown Gap National Cemetery, Annville, Lebanon County, PA.

2.6.3.3.2.1.1 CLIFFORD H. KLINGER

2.6.3.3.2.1.2 DONALD H. KLINGER

2.6.3.3.2.2 HARVENA KLINGER is also referred to as **HARVENIA** in some sources. She was born on 26 December 1919, Suedberg, Schuylkill County, PA. She married **RUSSELL A. FELTY**, son of **LEVI HENRY FELTY** and **ELIZA MARIA BOHR,** after 1939. She died on 7 August 2012, Pine Grove, Schuylkill County, PA, at age 92, at her home. According to a newspaper obituary, Harvena was a graduate of Pine Grove High School. She was survived by four grandchildren: Robert, Elizabeth, Russell and Jennifer; and two great-grandchildren, Abigail and Brynn. She was buried at Outwood Lutheran Church Cemetery, Pine Grove, Schuylkill County, PA.

2.6.3.3.2.2.1 MARY ANN FELTY was born after 1940.

2.6.3.3.2.3 RUSSEL CHARLES KLINGER was born on 2 August 1921, Suedberg, Schuylkill County, PA. He was baptized on 25 December 1927, Jacob's Evangelical Lutheran, Pine Grove, Schuylkill County, PA. He married **HELEN LEHR** circa 1940. He died on 31 August 2012, Thornwald Home, Carlisle, Cumberland County, PA, at age 91. According to a newspaper obituary, Russel, who lived in Chambers Hill, PA, retired from the Reading Railroad and was an Army Air Corp veteran of World War ll. He was buried at Paxtang Cemetery, Paxtang, Dauphin County, PA.

2.6.3.3.2.3.1 JEAN KLINGER married **JOSEPH UPDIKE**.

2.6.3.3.2.3.1.1 DEBRA UPDIKE married **BRAD EPLEY**. Debra lives in Frederick, MD.

2.6.3.3.2.3.1.1.1 ZACHARY EPLEY

2.6.3.3.2.3.1.1.2 ALEXANDER EPLEY

2.6.3.3.2.3.1.2 CHRISTINE UPDIKE married **MATTHEW ENGLISH.** Christine lives in Palmyra, PA.

2.6.3.3.2.3.1.2.1 ABIGAILE ENGLISH

2.6.3.3.2.3.1.2.2 MASON ENGLISH

2.6.3.3.2.4 LUTHER RALPH KLINGER was born on 3 March 1924, Suedberg, Schuylkill County, PA. He was baptized on 25 December 1927, Jacob's Evangelical Lutheran, Pine Grove, Schuylkill County, PA. Luther served in the US Army from 11 Dec 1942 to 14 Jan 1946. He married **ARLENE BINKLEY** circa 1947. He died on 12 February 1999, Good Samaritan Hospital, Lebanon, Lebanon County, PA, at age 74. Some sources record that he died on 19 February 1999. He was buried at Indiantown Gap National Cemetery, Annville, Lebanon County, PA.

2.6.3.3.2.4.1 GARY KLINGER

2.6.3.3.2.4.2 LUTHER L. KLINGER

2.6.3.3.2.4.3 KEVIN KLINGER

2.6.3.3.2.4.4 DEAN KLINGER

2.6.3.3.2.4.5 JANICE KLINGER married (--?--) **MINNICH**.

2.6.3.3.2.4.6 APRIL KLINGER married (--?--) **REIBOLD**.

2.6.3.3.2.5 WAYNE ARTHUR KLINGER was born on 10 February 1929, Suedberg, Schuylkill County, PA. He was baptized on 18 February 1931, Jacob's Evangelical Lutheran Church, Pine Grove, Schuylkill County, PA. He married **ANNA BELLE L. STICKLER**, daughter of **JOHN STICKLER** and **ALICE OBER,** on 19 March 1949, Suedberg, Schuylkill County, PA. Wayne served in the US Army from 19 Aug 1950 to 1 May 1952. He married **FRANCES MAE PRITZ,** daughter of **FRANK JOSEPH PRITZ** and **CATHERINE MARY VOGEL,** on 5 May 1986, Winchester, VA. He died on 17 September 2002, Akron, Summit County, OH, at age 73.

2.6.3.3.3 CLARENCE FRANKLIN KLINGER was born on 23 March 1896, Pennsylvania. He married **MARY M. SWOPE** in 1918. He died in August 1954, at age 58.

2.6.3.3.4 MARGARETTE KLINGER was born in June 1897.

2.6.3.3.5 MARTHA E. KLINGER was born on 23 March 1899, Pennsylvania. She married **JAMES HERBERT AMBLER.** She died in February 1972, at age 72.

   2.6.3.3.5.1 JAMES H. AMBLER was born in 1922.

   2.6.3.3.5.2 JANE FLORENCE AMBLER was born in 1924. She married **ROY JAMES LOTZ JR.**

2.6.3.4 MARY ANN KLINGER was born on 11 August 1874, Schuylkill County, PA. She was baptized on 5 December 1875, St. Jacob's Evangelical Lutheran Church, Pine Grove, Schuylkill County, PA. She married **HARVEY FAKE**, son of **AMOS FAKE** and **CATHARINA ELIZABETH DEAVEN,** circa 1896. She died on 11 December 1948, St. Joseph's Hospital, Reading, Berks County, PA, at age 74. She was buried at Laureldale Cemetery, Tuckerton, Berks County, PA.

   2.6.3.4.1 STELLA M. FAKE was born on 26 October 1897, Green Point, Lebanon County, PA. She married **PAUL NYE.** She died in July 1987, at age 89.

     2.6.3.4.1.1 PAUL HARVEY NYE was born on 4 November 1923, Lebanon, Lebanon County, PA. He married **BARBARA A. (--?--).** He died on 22 December 2006, at age 83. He was buried at Indiantown Gap National Cemetery, Annville, Lebanon County, PA.

   2.6.3.4.2 EARL ELIAS FAKE was born on 27 March 1899, Green Point, Lebanon County, PA. He married **RUTH HOFFMAN.** He died on 26 October 1970, Reading, Berks County, PA, at age 71. He was buried at Laureldale Cemetery, Tuckerton, Berks County, PA.

     2.6.3.4.2.1 KENNETH HARVEY FAKE was born on 24 August 1931. He was baptized on 22 February 1948, Christ Episcopal Church, Reading, Berks County, PA.

     2.6.3.4.2.2 EARL ELIAS FAKE JR. was born on 4 December 1932, Reading, Berks County, PA. He was baptized on 22 February 1948, Christ Episcopal Church, Reading, Berks County, PA. He died on 15 August 1996, at age 63. He was buried at Yocom Cemetery, Grill, Berks County, PA.

     2.6.3.4.2.3 BARRY HOFFMAN FAKE was born on 17 January 1940. He was baptized on 22 February 1948, Christ Episcopal Church, Reading, Berks County, PA. He married **JUDITH ANN MICKANIS.** He and **JUDITH ANN MICKANIS** were divorced on 18 March 1994 Manassas, VA. He married **SUSAN MAE MARINO** on 28 October 1994, Manassas, VA.

   2.6.3.4.3 CLARENCE A. FAKE was born on 2 March 1901, Green Point, Lebanon County, PA. He married **RUTH ELIZABETH HEILMAN**, daughter of **SAMUEL W. HEILMAN** and **ELIZABETH FANNIE KETTERING.** He died on 10 August 1986, at age 85. He was buried at Grand View Memorial Park, Annville, Lebanon County, PA.

     2.6.3.4.3.1 ROBERT C. FAKE was born on 1 January 1925, Green Point, Lebanon County, PA. He married **GRACE I. HEFFELFINGER** on 8 December 1943. He died on 20 March 2010, Good Samaritan Hospital, Lebanon, Lebanon County, PA, at age 85. According to a newspaper obituary, Robert, who lived in Lebanon, PA, served in the U.S. Marines during WW II and in the U.S. Air Force during the Korean Conflict. He was employed at Bethlehem Steel, Lebanon, for 37 1/2 years, retiring in 1983. He was buried on 24 March 2010, at Indiantown Gap National Cemetery, Annville, Lebanon County, PA.

        2.6.3.4.3.1.1 ANN L. FAKE married **DANIEL KLOHR.**

        2.6.3.4.3.1.2 LINDA G. FAKE married **(--?--) HASSON.**

        2.6.3.4.3.1.3 MARIE E. FAKE married **RONNIE THOMPSON.**

        2.6.3.4.3.1.4 HELEN R. FAKE married **(--?--) LONG.**

        2.6.3.4.3.1.5 SHARON G. FAKE married **WILLIAM STORCK.**

2.6.3.4.3.1.6 LOIS E. FAKE married JAMES MARSHALL.

2.6.3.4.3.1.7 NANCY E. FAKE married MARK BASSELIGIA.

2.6.3.4.3.2 MARY LOUISE FAKE was born on 8 May 1928.

2.6.3.4.3.3 DALE C. FAKE was born on 7 June 1938. He married SHIRLEY A. SMITH. He died on 22 March 1996, at age 57. He was buried at Forest Hill Cemetery, Haines City, Polk County, FL.

2.6.3.4.4 PAUL ALBERT FAKE was born on 26 July 1906, Green Point, Lebanon County, PA. Some sources record that he was born on 26 June 1906. He married EVELYN G. MARKS. He married MILDRED ERB BOEHRINGER, daughter of MARTIN LUTHER BOEHRINGER and MAMIE ERB. He died on 7 July 1977, at age 70. He was buried at St. Mark's Evangelical Lutheran Church Cemetery, East Earl, Lancaster County, PA.

2.6.3.4.4.1 MARY FAKE was born circa 1935.

2.6.3.4.5 AMOS IRA FAKE was born on 18 October 1908, Green Point, Lebanon County, PA. He married HELEN T. DUNKELBERGER. He died on 29 December 1992, at age 84. He was buried at Yocom Cemetery, Grill, Berks County, PA.

2.6.3.4.5.1 NANCY JANE FAKE was born on 18 April 1932, Reading, Berks County, PA. She died on 18 April 1932, Reading, Berks County, PA.

2.6.3.4.5.2 JACQUELINE FAKE was born circa 1934.

2.6.3.4.5.3 JOAN FAKE was born circa 1935.

2.6.3.4.5.4 RICHARD FAKE was born circa 1938.

2.6.3.4.6 IRENE MILDRED FAKE was born on 6 March 1911, Green Point, Lebanon County, PA. She married HORACE ROTZ. She died on 30 December 1999, at age 88. She was buried at Laureldale Cemetery, Tuckerton, Berks County, PA.

2.6.3.4.6.1 GENE D. ROTZ was born in 1935, Reading, Berks County, PA. He died on 14 January 1962, Philadelphia, Philadelphia County, PA. He was buried at Laureldale Cemetery, Tuckerton, Berks County, PA.

2.6.3.4.7 ETHEL FAKE was born on 27 August 1914, Reading, Berks County, PA. She married ROY C. JOHNSON. She died on 27 December 2016, Lourdes Hospital, Vestal, Broome County, NY, at age 102. She was buried at Vestal Park Cemetery, Vestal, Broome County, NY.

2.6.3.5 HARRY HARVEY KLINGER was born on 29 April 1876, Pine Grove Township, Schuylkill County, PA. He was baptized on 1 February 1877, St. Jacob's Evangelical Lutheran Church, Pine Grove, Schuylkill County, PA. Some sources record that he was born on 29 April 1875. He married MABEL L. LOOSE on 11 November 1905. He died on 15 March 1953, Union Township, Lebanon County, PA, at age 76. He was buried on 19 March 1953, at Church of God Cemetery, Suedberg, Schuylkill County, PA.

2.6.3.5.1 EARLA EMMA KLINGER was born on 8 April 1907, Green Point, Lebanon County, PA. She died on 2 July 1963, Wernersville, Berks County, PA, at age 56. She was buried on 6 July 1963, at Church of God Cemetery, Suedberg, Schuylkill County, PA. Never married.

2.6.3.5.2 LYDIA A. KLINGER was born in 1908, Lebanon County, PA. She married JAMES IRVIN TRUMBO, son of MILTON TRUMBO and MARY BERGER. She was buried at Mount Lebanon Cemetery, Lebanon, Lebanon County, PA. She died on 6 May 1997, Tremont, Schuylkill County, PA.

2.6.3.5.2.1 AMY TRUMBO married JAMES HARMAN.

2.6.3.5.2.2 MAYANNA M. TRUMBO is also referred to as MAE in some sources. She was born circa 1928. She married LESTER STAMM.

2.6.3.5.3 BESSIE ALICE KLINGER was born on 11 April 1910. She married LESTER T. RHOAD, son of JACOB L. RHOAD and IDA ELIZABETH SEAMAN. She died on 31 January 1986, Harrisburg, Dauphin County, PA, at age 75. She was buried at Zion Lutheran Church Cemetery, East Hanover Township, Lebanon County, PA.

2.6.3.5.4 HERMAN PAUL KLINGER was born on 22 December 1913. He married PEARL GRACE KRAUSE. He died on 6 May 1959, RD 2, Pine Grove, Schuylkill County, PA, at age 45.

2.6.3.5.4.1 JOAN M. KLINGER

2.6.3.5.4.2 JUNE E. KLINGER

2.6.3.5.4.3 KAREN J. KLINGER

2.6.3.5.4.4 LARRY P. KLINGER

2.6.3.5.4.5 JUDY PEARL KLINGER was born on 21 July 1948, Schuylkill County, PA. She died on 17 December 2006, Pine Grove, Schuylkill County, PA, at age 58.

2.6.3.5.4.6 GARY LEE KLINGER was born on 13 February 1954. He died on 28 June 1974, at age 20.

2.6.3.5.5 IRENE M. KLINGER was born on 16 January 1916, Union City, Lebanon County, PA. She married HARRY C. BECKER. She died in August 1982, Downers Grove, DuPage County, IL, at age 66.

2.6.3.5.6 SARAH C. KLINGER was born on 23 September 1918, Union Township, Lebanon County, PA. She married NORMAN W. EBEY, son of CHARLES GARFIELD EBEY and ELIZABETH L. (--?--). She died on 22 May 2002, Pine Grove, Schuylkill County, PA, at age 83. She was buried at St. Joh 's Lutheran Church Cemetery, Pine Grove, Schuylkill County, PA.

2.6.3.5.7 CARRIE KLINGER was born circa 1922.

2.6.3.6 KATE E. KLINGER is also referred to as ELLA KATIE KLINGER in some sources. She was born on 20 August 1878. She married ALFRED JACOB WOLFE circa 1897. She died on 13 December 1970, Jonestown, Lebanon County, PA, at age 92. She was buried at Pleasant Hill Chapel Cemetery, Green Point, Lebanon County, PA.

2.6.3.6.1 CLARENCE ELIAS WOLFE is also referred to as W. CLARENCE WOLFE in some sources. He was born on 21 December 1899. He married HARRIET C. ZIMMERMAN. Census records suggest that he and a CARRIE S. MILLER were married circa 1919. He died on 27 October 1945, at age 45.

2.6.3.6.1.1 ALLEN C. WOLFE also went by the name of GALLY. He was born on 26 August 1919, Pine Grove, Schuylkill County, PA. He married CATHERINE L. SCANLAN, daughter of JOSEPH SCANLAN and HARRIET BARR, circa 1941. He died on 19 October 2013, Seton Manor, Orwigsburg., Schuylkill County, PA, at age 94. According to a newspaper obituary, Allen served in the US Army from Jan. 21, 1944 to Feb. 14, 1946, when he was discharged to accept federal employment in the European Theater. Later, he was a self-employed truck driver for more than 50 years and lived in Pine Grove, PA. He was buried on 24 October 2013, at St. John's Lutheran Cemetery, Pine Grove, Schuylkill County, PA.

2.6.3.6.1.1.1 JEAN WOLFE married BRUCE HOOVER. Jean lives in Cressona, PA.

2.6.3.6.1.1.2 BARBARA WOLFE married CARL HUNTZINGER. Barbara lives in Pine Grove, PA.

2.6.3.6.1.2 MARIAN J. WOLFE was born circa 1922. She married (--?--) SWINEHART. She died before 2013.

2.6.3.6.1.3 VIOLET WOLFE was born circa 1926. She married (--?--) HOPKINS. Violet lives in Rineville, KY.

2.6.3.7 GEORGE KLINGER was born on 6 July 1880, Outwood, Schuylkill County, PA. Some sources record that he was born circa June 1879. He married ELANORA OLDT circa 1902. He died in February 1966, Pine Grove, Schuylkill County, PA, at age 85. He was buried at Church of God Cemetery, Suedberg, Schuylkill County, PA.

2.6.3.7.1 PAUL E. KLINGER was born on 17 November 1903. He married ANNIE E. REINHART on 7 March 1925, Jacobs Lutheran Evangelical Church, Pine Grove, Schuylkill County, PA. He died on 7 June 1998, at age 94. He was buried at Schuylkill Memorial Park, Schuylkill Haven, Schuylkill County, PA.

2.6.3.7.1.1 ANNA E. KLINGER married (--?--) ADAM.

2.6.3.7.1.2 CLARENCE G. KLINGER was born on 21 May 1925, Pine Grove, Schuylkill County, PA. He married SANDRA L. DEISHER on 18 December 1965. He died on 14 February 2017, Kutztown Manor, Kutztown, Berks County, PA, at age 91. He was buried on 20 February 2017, at Schuylkill Memorial Park, Schuylkill Haven, Schuylkill County, PA.

2.6.3.7.1.2.1 BRUCE KLINGER married PATRICIA (--?--).

2.6.3.7.1.2.2 BRIAN KLINGER married MING ZU.

2.6.3.7.1.3 GUY G. KLINGER was born on 6 May 1927, Auburn, Schuylkill County, PA. He married **KATHLEEN ILLIG**, daughter of **HARRY P. ILLIG** and **ELSIE M. KREITZER.** He died on 14 August 2012, Sanatoga Center, Pottstown, Montgomery County, PA, at age 85. He was buried at Union Cemetery, Womelsdorf, Berks County, PA.

2.6.3.7.1.4 EUGENE GEORGE KLINGER was born on 8 March 1932. He was baptized on 14 November 1937, Jacobs Lutheran Evangelical Church, Pine Grove, Schuylkill County, PA. Some sources record that he was born on 5 March 1932. He married **ALMA A. PHILLIPS** on 23 May 1953. He died on 25 February 2010, Berks County, PA, at age 77.

> **2.6.3.7.1.4.1 LONNIE E. KLINGER**
>
> **2.6.3.7.1.4.2 STEVEN E. KLINGER** married **DEBORAH A. (--?--).**
>
> **2.6.3.7.1.4.3 CHRIS E. KLINGER** was born on 6 October 1962, West Reading, Berks County, PA. He married **CAROLYN E. SCHNEIDER.** He died on 25 October 2014, Golden Living Center, Exeter Township, Berks County, PA, at age 52. He was buried at St. Mary's Parish Cemetery, Hamburg, Berks County, PA.
>
>> **2.6.3.7.1.4.3.1 SHANNA C. KLINGER**
>>
>> **2.6.3.7.1.4.3.2 BRENNA A. KLINGER**

2.6.3.7.2 HARVEY KLINGER was born on 20 March 1906. He married **ALVERTA M. DEICHERT**, daughter of **RALPH N. DEICHERT** and **JENNIE E. KURTZ.** He died on 31 May 1978, at age 72. He was buried at Church of God Cemetery, Suedberg, Schuylkill County, PA.

> **2.6.3.7.2.1 JOAN KLINGER** married (--?--) **HALL.**
>
> **2.6.3.7.2.2 BETTY F. KLINGER** was born on 1 May 1927, Pine Grove, Schuylkill County, PA. She married **RALPH AARON PHILLIPPY**, son of **ISAAC G. PHILLIPPY** and **EDNA WIKEL.** She was buried on 23 July 2014, at Outwood Lutheran Church Cemetery, Pine Grove, Schuylkill County, PA.
>
>> **2.6.3.7.2.2.1 DIANE PHILLIPPY** married **JAMES THORNTON.**
>>
>> **2.6.3.7.2.2.2 KANDICE PHILLIPPY** married **DAVID GASSERT.**
>>
>> **2.6.3.7.2.2.3 DAVID PHILLIPPY** married **DEBRA (--?--).**
>>
>> **2.6.3.7.2.2.4 JEFFREY LEE PHILLIPPY** was born on 30 September 1954, Lebanon, Lebanon County, PA. He married **SANDY NEIDLINGER.** He died on 27 May 2013, Penn State Milton S. Hershey Medical Center, Hershey, Dauphin County, PA, at age 58. According to a newspaper obituary, Jeffrey served in the military during the Vietnam era and was employed as a commercial refrigeration mechanic. He lived in Pine Grove, PA. He was buried on 31 May 2013, at Outwood Lutheran Church Cemetery, Pine Grove, Schuylkill County, PA.
>>
>>> **2.6.3.7.2.2.4.1 HILLERY PHILLIPPY** married (--?--) **KELLER.**
>>>
>>> **2.6.3.7.2.2.4.2 CRAIG JAMES PHILLIPPY**
>>>
>>> **2.6.3.7.2.2.4.3 ANGELA PHILLIPPY**
>>>
>>> **2.6.3.7.2.2.4.4 JEFFREY LEE PHILLIPPY JR.**
>
> **2.6.3.7.2.3 JAMES E. KLINGER** was born in 1929. He married **OPHELIA F. (--?--).** He died in 1968. He was buried at Grand View Memorial Park, Annville, Lebanon County, PA.
>
> **2.6.3.7.2.4 NANCY L. KLINGER** was born on 24 December 1935. She died on 22 March 1936. She was buried at Outwood Lutheran Church Cemetery, Pine Grove, Schuylkill County, PA.

2.6.3.7.3 JENNIE KLINGER was born on 25 November 1909. She married **EARL S. MEASE.** She died on 22 April 1989, at age 79. She was buried at Suedberg Church of God Cemetery, Suedberg, Schuylkill County, PA.

> **2.6.3.7.3.1 MARVIN E. MEASE** was born on 26 March 1927, Pine Grove, Schuylkill County, PA. He married **JEAN MARIE WARNER**, daughter of **SAMUEL WARNER** and **MARY ELLEN KEMMERLING.** He died on 18 March 2002, Fredericksburg, Lebanon County, PA, at age 74. He was buried on 21 March 2002, at Indiantown Gap National Cemetery, Annville, Lebanon County, PA.
>
>> **2.6.3.7.3.1.1 RODNEY E. MEASE**
>>
>> **2.6.3.7.3.1.2 ROGER E. MEASE** married **JERILYNN (--?--).**

2.6.3.7.4 IRA G. KLINGER was born on 29 January 1912. He married **MILDRED E. CHRIST**. He died on 3 June 1983, at age 71. He was buried at Suedberg Church of God Cemetery, Suedberg, Schuylkill County, PA.

2.6.3.7.4.1 EVELYN ALBERTA KLINGER was born on 18 October 1931, Pine Grove, Schuylkill County, PA. She married **EDWARD H. BASHORE**, son of **HERBERT BASHORE** and **EMMA KLAHR**. She died on 16 April 2007, at age 75. She was buried at Little Swatara Church of the Brethren Cemetery, Bethel, Berks County, PA.

2.6.3.7.4.1.1 EDWARD L. BASHORE married **DONNA J. (--?--)**.

2.6.3.7.4.1.2 AUDREY A. BASHORE married **(--?--) BROWN**.

2.6.3.7.4.1.3 CHARLENE M. BASHORE married **(--?--) MUCKEL**.

2.6.3.7.4.1.3.1 CORY MUCKEL

2.6.3.7.4.1.4 WENDA M. BASHORE married **(--?--) DINATALE**.

2.6.3.7.4.1.4.1 MARIO DINATALE

2.6.3.7.4.1.4.2 NINO DINATALE

2.6.3.8 LUCY A. KLINGER was born on 9 November 1881, Pennsylvania. She married **HOWARD S. JONES** after 1900. She died on 24 March 1976, Pine Grove, Schuylkill County, PA, at age 94.

2.6.3.8.1 ARCHIE JONES is also referred to as **ARCHIE KLINGER** in some sources. He was born circa 1903.

2.6.3.8.2 EDWARD L. JONES was born circa 1905.

2.6.4 JOHANNES KLINGER is also referred to as **JOHN** in some sources. He was born on 15 January 1847, Pine Grove, Schuylkill County, PA. He was baptized on 1 August 1847, St. Jacob's Evangelical Lutheran Church, Pine Grove, Pine Grove Township, Schuylkill County, PA. Some sources record that he was born on 15 January 1848. He married **SARAH ZIMMERMAN** circa 1871. He died on 14 September 1922, at age 75. He was buried at Suedberg Church of God Cemetery, Suedberg, Schuylkill County, PA.

2.6.4.1 SUSANNA KLINGER was born on 4 March 1872. She was baptized on 28 April 1872, St. Jacob's Evangelical Lutheran Church, Pine Grove, Schuylkill County, PA.

2.6.4.2 ELLA REBECCA KLINGER was born on 10 June 1876. She was baptized on 9 September 1876, St. Jacob's Evangelical Lutheran Church, Pine Grove, Schuylkill County, PA. She married **(--?--) YINGST**. She died on 1 May 1950, at age 73. She was buried at Suedberg Church of God Cemetery, Suedberg, Schuylkill County, PA.

2.6.5 SAMUEL KLINGER was born circa 1849. He died before 1860.

2.6.6 LAVINA KLINGER was born on 3 November 1849, Pine Grove, Schuylkill County, PA. She was baptized on 16 April 1850, St. Jacob's Evangelical Lutheran Church, Pine Grove, Schuylkill County, PA.

2.6.7 ISAAC KLINGER was born on 3 August 1851, Pine Grove, Schuylkill County, PA. He was baptized on 9 November 1851, St. Jacob's Evangelical Lutheran Church, Pine Grove, Schuylkill County, PA. He married **LOUISA (--?--)** circa 1872. He died in 1935. He was buried at Suedberg Church of God Cemetery, Pine Grove Township, Schuylkill County, PA.

2.6.7.1 LILLIE R. KLINGER was born on 7 June 1878. She married **(--?--) FELTY**. She died on 31 August 1960, at age 82. She was buried at Outwood Lutheran Church Cemetery, Pine Grove Township, Schuylkill County, PA.

2.6.7.2 STELLA KLINGER was born in December 1887, Pennsylvania.

2.6.7.2.1 ELLEN NEAL is also referred to as **ELLA** in some sources. He was born circa 1903. The 1910 and 1920 Census listings for Isaac and Louisa Klinger include a granddaughter Ellen or Ella Neal. It is likely, although not certain, that Ellen or Ella was a child of their daughter Stella who perhaps died earlier.

2.6.7.3 ROY W. KLINGER was born on 25 May 1890, Pennsylvania. He married **MAMIE M. (--?--)** circa 1909. Prior to his death, Roy was living in the vicinity of Pine Grove, Schuylkill County, PA. He died in May 1974. He was buried at Suedberg Church of God Cemetery, Pine Grove Township, Schuylkill County, PA.

2.6.7.3.1 CHARLES W. KLINGER was born circa March 1910.

2.6.7.3.2 BEATRICE M. KLINGER was born circa 1911.

2.6.7.3.3 IVIE R. KLINGER was born circa 1917.

2.6.7.3.4 HOWARD J. KLINGER was born circa 1924. He married **MARIAN BROWN**, daughter of **RICHARD F. BROWN** and **MABEL HAIN**, circa 1949.

    2.6.7.3.4.1 DEAN H. KLINGER. Dean lives in Pine Grove, Schuylkill County, PA.

    2.6.7.3.4.2 LISA KLINGER. Lisa lives in Idaho Falls, ID.

2.6.7.3.5 LILLIE M. KLINGER was born circa 1926.

2.6.7.3.6 JIMMY I. KLINGER was born in February 1929.

2.6.8 EMMANUEL KLINGER. Some sources list a child named "Emanuel," but this may be a duplication for Aaron Klinger. He was born in 1860, Pine Grove, PA.

2.6.9 AARON A. KLINGER is also referred to as **ADAM** in some sources. He was born on 9 July 1860, Pine Grove, Schuylkill County, PA. He was baptized on 15 September 1860, St. Jacob's Evangelical Lutheran Church, Pine Grove, Schuylkill County, PA. Some sources record that he was born Lists his mother as Catherine Brensinger (who was actually his wife). on 9 July 1867. He married **CATHERINE BRENSINGER** circa 1878. He died on 13 June 1914, North Manheim Township, Schuylkill County, PA, at age 53. He was buried on 16 June 1914, at Church of God Cemetery, Suedberg, Schuylkill County, PA.

2.6.9.1 GEORGE KLINGER was buried at Church of God Cemetery, Suedberg, Schuylkill County, PA.

2.6.9.2 CARRIE REBECCA KLINGER was born on 28 November 1879, Pennsylvania. She married **HARRY MATTERNAS** in 1897. She married **LYMAN E. AUNGST**. She died in February 1979, at age 99.

    2.6.9.2.1 ELLA V. MATTERNAS was born on 29 October 1897. She married **JAMES SAMUEL RAGER** before 1920. She died in June 1976, at age 78.

    2.6.9.2.2 ANNA MARGARET MATTERNAS was born in September 1899. She married **CLAUDE E. AUNGST**. She died in January 1963, at age 63.

    2.6.9.2.3 MARY MATTERNAS was born in 1901.

    2.6.9.2.4 JOHN MATTERNAS was born on 29 January 1903. He married **MARIE REBECCA REAM**. He died in July 1974, at age 71.

    2.6.9.2.5 SALLIE C. MATTERNAS was born in 1906. She married **RICHARD BOLINGER JOHNSON**.

2.6.9.3 CHARLES HENRY KLINGER was born on 28 July 1881. He was baptized on 20 December 1881, St. Jacob's Evangelical Lutheran Church, Pine Grove, Schuylkill County, PA. He married **MARY SOPHIA SCHNECK** on 16 March 1906. He died in October 1971, at age 90. He was buried at St. Jacob's Evangelical Lutheran Church Cemetery, Pine Grove, Schuylkill County, PA.

    2.6.9.3.1 EVA RENA KLINGER was born on 29 December 1906. She married **GEORGE E. MILLER**. She died on 25 February 2005, at age 98.

        2.6.9.3.1.1 VINCENT C. MILLER was born circa 1927. He married **VELVA RUBY HOKE** on 18 January 1947, Schuylkill Haven, Schuylkill County, PA.

        2.6.9.3.1.2 DOLORES MILLER was born circa 1930.

        2.6.9.3.1.3 GEORGE MILLER was born circa 1934.

    2.6.9.3.2 HANNAH M. KLINGER was born on 23 August 1909, Schuylkill County, PA. She died on 18 February 1975, West Reading, Berks County, PA, at age 65.

2.6.9.4 VALERIA KLINGER was born on 9 November 1883, Schuylkill County, PA. She died circa 1900. She was buried at Church of God Cemetery, Suedberg, Schuylkill County, PA.

2.6.9.5 ELISE KLINGER was born on 8 December 1885, Schuylkill County, PA. She died on 20 December 1891, Schuylkill County, PA, at age 6. She was buried on 24 December 1891, at Church of God Cemetery, Suedberg, Schuylkill County, PA.

2.6.9.6 EDWARD KLINGER was born on 30 March 1887, Pine Grove, Schuylkill County, PA. Some sources record that he was born in March 1888, Pennsylvania. He married **LOTTIE M. WOLFE** on 18 August 1910, Pine Grove, Schuylkill County, PA. He died in 1968. He was buried at Church of God Cemetery, Suedberg, Schuylkill County, PA.

2.6.9.7 AGNES KLINGER was born on 29 December 1890, Pine Grove Township, Schuylkill County, PA. She married **HARRY WILLIAM MANN**. She died on 23 October 1961, A.C. Milliken Hospital, Pottsville, Schuylkill County, PA, at age 70. She was buried on 27 October 1961, at St. Peter's Cemetery, Pine Grove, Schuylkill County, PA.

2.6.9.8 SAMUEL ELIAS KLINGER was born on 12 January 1894, Pine Grove, Schuylkill County, PA. He married **CELIA I. DAUBERT** on 28 February 1914, Suedberg, Schuylkill County, PA. He died on 11 April 1958, Lebanon, Lebanon County, PA, at age 64. He was buried at Saint John's Lutheran Church Cemetery, Pine Grove, Schuylkill County, PA.

    2.6.9.8.1 CLARK L. KLINGER was born in 1917. He died in 1939. He was buried at Saint John's Lutheran Church Cemetery, Pine Grove, Schuylkill County, PA.

    2.6.9.8.2 ELVIN ELIAS KLINGER was born on 10 April 1923, Pine Grove, Schuylkill County, PA. He married **ROMA L. TOBIAS**. He died on 7 September 2007, Tremont, Schuylkill County, PA, at age 84. He was buried at Saint John's Lutheran Church Cemetery, Pine Grove, Schuylkill County, PA.

2.6.9.9 ELMER KLINGER was born on 7 March 1897, Pine Grove, Schuylkill County, PA. Some sources record that he was born in March 1898, Pennsylvania. Elmer was a seaman in the US Navy during World Wat I. He married **IVY I. WHITE**. He died in 1939. He died on 23 December 1939, Pine Grove, Schuylkill County, PA, at age 42. He was buried at Church of God Cemetery, Suedberg, Schuylkill County, PA.

    2.6.9.9.1 BETTY I. KLINGER was born in 1925, Pine Grove, Schuylkill County, PA. She married **MERRITT EMORY HEIN**. She died on 19 February 2017, Cornerstone Living Nursing Home, New Tripoli, Lehigh County, PA. She was buried on 23 February 2017, at Bethlehem Memorial Park, Bethlehem, Northampton County, PA.

        2.6.9.9.1.1 CHRISTINE HEIN married (--?--) **REICHARD**.

            2.6.9.9.1.1.1 RICHARD REICHARD

            2.6.9.9.1.1.2 ANDREW REICHARD

        2.6.9.9.1.2 THOMAS HEIN

        2.6.9.9.1.3 JANE HEIN married (--?--) **PIERCE**.

        2.6.9.9.1.4 LINDA DIANE HEIN was born on 5 February 1952, Austria. She married **SCOTT A. PULLEY** on 1 April 1995. She died on 27 October 2014, at age 62. She was buried at Bethlehem Memorial Park, Bethlehem, Northampton County, PA.

            2.6.9.9.1.4.1 JOHN PULLEY

            2.6.9.9.1.4.2 NICOLE PULLEY

    2.6.9.9.2 CHARLES E. KLINGER was born on 4 November 1926, Schuylkill County, PA. He married **MARGUERITE L. KIDWELL**, daughter of **EARL KIDWELL** and **ELSIE SCHWARTZ**. He died on 15 February 1989, Lake County Memorial Hospital - West, Mentor, Lake County, OH, at age 62. He was buried at Western Reserve Memorial Gardens, Chesterland, Geauga County, OH.

        2.6.9.9.2.1 SHARON KLINGER married **ROBERT BOTTIGGI**.

        2.6.9.9.2.2 KEITH KLINGER married **LEE MERCER**.

        2.6.9.9.2.3 STEPHEN KLINGER married **BETTY** (--?--).

    2.6.9.9.3 ARLENE E. KLINGER was born on 26 July 1928, Pine Grove, Schuylkill County, PA. She married **ELVIN WILLIAM FIDLER**, son of **WILLIAM FIDLER** and **BERTHA E. SCHNECK**, circa 1950. She died on 8 August 2014, Rest Haven Nursing Home, Schuylkill Haven, Schuylkill County, PA, at age 86.

        2.6.9.9.3.1 CAROL FIDLER married **JOHN HALDEMAN**.

        2.6.9.9.3.2 GARY FIDLER

    2.6.9.9.4 ANNA MAE KLINGER was born circa 1931. She married **STEWART SMITH**.

    2.6.9.9.5 EUGENE R. KLINGER was born on 18 February 1935, Pine Grove, Schuylkill County, PA. He married **NANCY LOU FRANTZ**. He died on 1 September 2005, Mentor Way Nursing Center, Mentor, OH, at age 70.

        2.6.9.9.5.1 LAURIE JEAN KLINGER married (--?--) **WIEST**.

        2.6.9.9.5.2 CINDY LOU KLINGER married (--?--) **DIETER**.

        2.6.9.9.5.3 JEFFREY KLINGER

    2.6.9.9.6 JANET MARIE KLINGER was born in 1938. She married **NORMAN D. TARMAN**. She married **RONALD FELTY**. She died in February 1969. She was buried at Saint John's Lutheran Church Cemetery, Pine Grove, Schuylkill County, PA.

2.6.9.10 ALICE SARA KLINGER was born on 6 February 1904, Schuylkill County, PA. She married CALVIN RICHARD NEAL. She died on 25 August 1995, at age 91. She was buried at Saint John's Lutheran Church Cemetery, Pine Grove, Schuylkill County, PA.

2.6.9.10.1 ROSANNA E. NEAL was born circa 1927.

2.7 ELIAS KLINGER was born on 23 March 1822. He was baptized on 5 May 1822, Zion (Klinger's) Church, Erdman, Lykens Township, Dauphin County, PA. He married LOUISIANNA TROUTMAN, daughter of ABRAHAM TROUTMAN and ELIZABETH REGINA TSCHOPP. He married ELIZABETH BUSH. He died on 30 January 1889, at age 66. He was buried at Grandview Cemetery, Pillow, Dauphin County, PA. Mary Klinger, Klingers from the Odenwald, Hesse, Germany, p. 365, contains a rather confusing discussion of Elias's family. In describing burial locations in a cemetery south of Pillow [apparently the Grandview Cemetery], she writes:

"In the same cemetery is buried, on a different lot, Elias Klinger, d. 30-1-1889, age 66-10-7 and Elizabeth (wife, d. 17-8-1889, age 51-11-1); his second wife, being Elizabeth Bush. On his one side lies Lidia A. Chilton, nee Klinger, 1869-1931, and on the other side lies Israel (son of Elias, 1878-1879); J. Arthur 1880- & Mabel E. 1884-1957." The text goes on to list the children, apparently, of Elias and Elizabeth Bush as follows: "Emanuel of Georgetown [Dalmatia]; David of Washington, D.C.; Art of Washington, D.C.; Lucia m. ____ Seaman of Uniontown [Pillow]; Mrs. John Bingman."

2.7.1 EMANUEL T. KLINGER is also referred to as EMANUAL in some sources. He was born on 24 October 1843. He was baptized on 7 January 1844, St. David's Lutheran and Reformed Church, Hebe, Jordan Township, Northumberland County, PA. He married LOVINA RADEL, daughter of MICHAEL RADEL and MARIA CATHERINE BONAWITZ, circa 1868. He died on 21 January 1917, Dalmatia, Northumberland County, PA, at age 73. He was buried at Trinity Evangelical Reformed Cemetery, Dalmatia, Northumberland County, PA. According to a newspaper obituary, Emanuel was a resident of Dalmatia for many years. He died after complications from a fall in his stable a few days earlier at which time he broke a rib and suffered other injuries. The Herndon News reported that Emanuel had served in the Civil War from beginning to end in Company B, 9th Regiment, 1st Pennsylvania Volunteers and he was a member of the Dalmatia G.A.R. Post.

2.7.1.1 MARY LAURA KLINGER was born in 1867, Pennsylvania. She married ISAAC LAHR, son of ISAAC LAHR and ELIZABETH MICHAEL, circa 1887. She died in 1928. She was buried at Trinity Evangelical Reformed Church Cemetery, Dalmatia, Northumberland County, PA.

2.7.1.1.1 MARGARET F. LAHR was born circa 1903.

2.7.1.2 SARAH ADELLA KLINGER was born in October 1869, Pennsylvania. She married HENRY S. BUBB, son of BENNEVILLE M. BUBB and SUSAN SEACHRIST, circa 1892. She died in 1939. She was buried at Trinity Evangelical Reformed Church Cemetery, Dalmatia, Northumberland County, PA.

2.7.1.2.1 MYRTLE M. BUBB was born circa 1893.

2.7.1.2.2 ANNIE BUBB was born in August 1898. She died on 16 February 1904, at age 5. She was buried at Trinity Evangelical Reformed Church Cemetery, Dalmatia, Northumberland County, PA.

2.7.1.2.3 MARK H. BUBB was born circa 1902. He married IRENE L. (--?--) circa 1923.

2.7.1.2.3.1 ESTHER G. BUBB was born circa 1924.

2.7.1.2.3.2 RICHARD S. BUBB was born circa January 1930.

2.7.1.3 GORDON E. M. KLINGER was born on 23 February 1873, Pennsylvania. He married MARGARET BLANCHE OGDEN, daughter of TOLBERT D. OGDEN and MARY E. (--?--), on 18 June 1902. At the time of their marriage, Gordon was living in Dalmatia, while Blanche was living in Clearfield. At the time of his father's death in 1917, Gordon was living in Baltimore, MD. The Social Security Death index contains a listing for a "Gorden Klinger," SSN: 212-03-4040, whose last residence was at zip code 49931, Houghton, Michigan. "Gorden" was born 23 Jul 1873 and died Feb 1970. His social security number was issued in Maryland before 1951, suggesting that this Gorden may have been the son of Emanuel Klinger. He died in February 1970.

2.7.1.3.1 MARY ELIZABETH KLINGER was born on 4 August 1911, Baltimore, Baltimore County, MD. She married (--?--) BREDEKAMP after 1940. She died on 24 February 2002, at age 90. Mary was apparently living in Michigan before she died.

2.7.1.4 ISAAC JAY KLINGER is also referred to as JAY in some sources. He was born on 17 March 1876, Pennsylvania. Isaac enlisted in the US Army on 28 November 1898. His enlistment record indicates that he was 22 years and 8 months old, he had dark brown hair, blue eyes, and dark complexion, and was 5' 9 1/2" tall. His occupation was listed as "farmer," while his hometown was

Georgetown (now Dalmatia), PA. He served with the 10th Infantry Division, Company B for 3 years and was discharged November 28, 1901 from Fort McKenzie, WY, at the expiration of his service. His record contains the notation "excellent." He married **JENNETTE KERSTETTER**, daughter of **JOHN KERSTETTER** and **LOUISA WITMER,** on 23 August 1902, by the Rev. Geiger. He died on 2 February 1920, at age 43. He was buried at Zion (Stone Valley) Lutheran and Reformed Church Cemetery, Hickory Corners, Lower Mahanoy Township, Northumberland County, PA.

2.7.1.4.1 EARLE D. KLINGER was born in 1903, Pennsylvania.

2.7.1.4.2 ANNA L. KLINGER was born on 2 August 1907. Some sources record that she was born in 1905, Pennsylvania. She married **RALPH M. LAHR**, son of **JACOB LAHR** and **SARAH C. DOWNEY,** on 21 February 1925. She died in September 1983. She was buried at Trinity Evangelical Reformed Cemetery, Dalmatia, Northumberland County, PA.

2.7.1.4.2.1 KERMIT R. LAHR was born on 16 March 1926. He married **JUNE (--?--)**. He died on 16 October 1992, at age 66.

2.7.1.4.2.1.1 JOE LAHR married **JACKIE (--?--)**.

2.7.1.4.2.2 HILDA IRENE LAHR was born on 30 July 1927, Dalmatia, Northumberland County, PA. She married **(--?--) YERGER**. She died on 5 April 2011, Hershey Medical Center, Hershey, Dauphin County, PA, at age 83. According to a newspaper obituary, Hilda, who lived in Middletown, PA, was a seamstress for the former RoughWear of Middletown and retired from Orwego of Mechanicsburg.

2.7.1.4.2.2.1 DONALD YERGER married **BARBARA (--?--)**. Donald lives in Mechanicsburg, PA.

2.7.1.4.2.2.1.1 PHILIP YERGER

2.7.1.4.2.2.1.2 ANDREW YERGER married **SARAH (--?--)**.

2.7.1.4.2.2.1.2.1 WYATT YERGER

2.7.1.4.2.2.2 CINDY YERGER married **JOHN BROMMER**. Cindy is a minister who lives in Middletown, PA.

2.7.1.4.2.2.2.1 MICHAEL BROMMER

2.7.1.5 ISRAEL KLINGER was born in 1878. He died in 1879. He was buried at Grandview Cemetery, Pillow, Dauphin County, PA. There is a conflict among the sources concerning the parentage of Israel. Some sources suggest that he was the son of Elias Klinger and Elizabeth Bush, while others suggest that he was the son of Elias's son Emanuel Klinger and Lavina Radel. Israel is buried close to Elias Klinger in the Grandview Cemetery in Pillow in Dauphin County, close to where Elias lived, while Emanuel lived in Lower Mahanoy Township of Northumberland County, in the vicinity of Dalmatia. A letter written by Forrest Eugene Klinger, to his daughter Joan, concerning a visit to the cemetery, states: "[i]n the Klinger plot in Pillow ... is ... my Dad's infant brother, Israel, 1878-79. I was amused to see that the small gravestone on the latter grave read "Israel, son of E. and Lovina Klinger."

2.7.1.6 HARRY CLARENCE KLINGER was born on 1 September 1880, Dalmatia, Northumberland County, PA. He married **HARRIET MAE RHOADS**, daughter of **HENRY LANDIS RHOADS** and **FRANCIS ANN SUMMERSON,** on 25 December 1902. He died on 18 March 1947, Williamsport, Lycoming County, PA, at age 66. He was buried at Montoursville Cemetery, Montoursville, Lycoming County, PA. After living in Renovo, Harry and his family moved to Williamsport. Harry held various service-type jobs including: a Metropolitan Insurance Agent, fireman in a gas works just down the street from their home, one year as school teacher in Rough and Ready, PA, a railroad telegraph operator, grocery store clerk, foreman of the mail room and proof reader for the Williamsport Grit Publishing Company. He also operated a bakery route at one time. His wife worked in the bakery as well as managed the home.

2.7.1.6.1 ELEANOR KLINGER was born in 1903. She died in 1903.

2.7.1.6.2 FORREST EUGENE KLINGER SR. went by the name of **EUGENE OR GENE**. He was born on 18 February 1905, Renovo, Clinton County, PA. He married **ETHEL ROSS ANDERSON**, daughter of **MATTHEW M. ANDERSON** and **ELLA JOSEPHINE ROSS**, on 26 November 1930, Glenside, Montgomery County, PA. He married **JEAN IRENE LACHMAN** on 10 November 1962, Churchville, Bucks County, PA. He died on 3 September 1997, Meadowbrook, Montgomery County, PA, at age 92 of congestive heart failure. Eugene's ashes were interred at Memorial Garden, North and Southampton Reformed Church, Churchville, Bucks County, PA. After graduating from Williamsport High School, Gene graduated in 1927 from Dickinson College, in

Carlisle, PA, and began a lifetime of service in education and to the community. First, he began teaching social studies and coaching track at Lower Moreland High School in 1927. He then moved to Southampton in Bucks County, PA, and became supervising principal of the Upper Southampton Schools. During World War II, he served on the Ration Board and was also known to drive the school bus and stoke the coal fired boilers. In 1954 he was appointed assistant superintendent in charge of business administration and held this position until his retirement in 1963. In 1965 the new "Eugene Klinger Junior High School" was dedicated in his honor. In 1967 he was named Southampton Distinguished Citizen.

2.7.1.6.2.1 **JOAN ROSS KLINGER** was born on 11 December 1931, Montgomery County, PA. She married **OTTO FREDERICK CRUMROY JR.**, son of **OTTO FREDERICK CRUMROY SR** and **RUTH IRENE BLOOD,** on 16 August 1958, Churchville, Bucks County, PA. Joan initially taught art in the elementary schools in the Langhorne-Middleton School District, Langhorne, Pennsylvania, then later moved to a high school, Mount Clemens, Michigan. After her marriage, she taught part-time in Department of Defense schools in Tokyo, Japan. In the early 1970's Joan became interested in creating textiles for a church sanctuary and eventually went back to school earning a Master of Theological Studies at Perkins School of Theology at Southern Methodist University.

2.7.1.6.2.1.1 **BRENDA ROSS CRUMROY** was born on 5 May 1959, Harrison Township, Macomb County, MI. She married **DANIEL EDWARD REIN** on 9 April 1983, Randolph AFB, Universal City, Bexar County, TX.

2.7.1.6.2.1.1.1 **JEFFREY MICHAEL REIN** was born on 9 September 1988, Suffolk, England.

2.7.1.6.2.1.1.2 **KATHERINE ROSS REIN** was born on 29 June 1992, Bexar County, TX.

2.7.1.6.2.1.2 **JENIFER RUTH CRUMROY** was born on 5 May 1959, Harrison Township, Macomb County, MI. She married **JAMES EDWARD MORGAN** on 3 July 1982, King County, WA.

2.7.1.6.2.1.2.1 **JAMES BURTON MORGAN** was Financial Adviser with Edward Jones. He was born on 8 March 1987, Tarrant County, TX.

2.7.1.6.2.1.2.2 **RACHEL ELIZABETH MORGAN** was born on 2 January 1990, Tarrant County, TX.

2.7.1.6.2.1.3 **KIMBERLY ANN CRUMROY** was born on 3 January 1964, St Clair, IL. She married **LLOYD KEITH HINTON** on 20 June 1987, Dallas County, TX.

2.7.1.6.2.1.3.1 **KRISTY NICOLE HINTON** was born on 14 March 1993, Dallas County, TX.

2.7.1.6.2.2 **BARBARA JEAN KLINGER** was born on 13 May 1936, Montgomery County, PA. She married **KENNETH RICHARD NELSON** in June 1960, Churchville, Bucks County, PA.

2.7.1.6.2.2.1 **JEFFREY DAVID NELSON** was born on 16 February 1963, Bucks County, PA. He married **ANN MARIE ROMANCZYK** on 30 September 1995, Putnam County, NY.

2.7.1.6.2.2.1.1 **GRAHAM FORREST NELSON** was born on 26 June 1998.

2.7.1.6.2.2.2 **TIMOTHY SCOTT NELSON** was born on 7 August 1965, Bucks County, PA. He married **JULIE ANNE GIGLIO** on 22 May 1993, Rockland County, NY.

2.7.1.6.2.2.2.1 **JOSEPH KENNETH NELSON** was born on 18 July 1997, Fairfield, CT.

2.7.1.6.2.2.2.2 **RACHEL ANNE NELSON** was born on 25 October 1999, Fairfield, CT.

2.7.1.6.2.2.2.3 **REBECCA ANNE NELSON** was born on 9 February 2004, Fairfield, CT.

2.7.1.6.2.2.3 **PATRICIA SUE NELSON** was born on 22 July 1968, Schenectady, NY. She married **OLE GRONBORG** on 29 July 2006, Schenectady, NY.

2.7.1.6.2.3 **FOREST EUGENE KLINGER JR.** also went by the name of **CHIP OR GENE.** He was born on 20 June 1940, Montgomery County, PA. He married **FREDA CATHERINE SCHEMBERG** on 28 June 1969, Feasterville, Bucks County, PA. He died on 13 April 1987, Bucks County, PA, at age 46. Chip grew up in Southampton and was his high school class valedictorian and later earned a bachelor's degree at Haverford College and a Masters at the

University of North Carolina. He served as an intelligence officer in the US Air Force and the National Guard, earning the rank of Lt. Colonel. His life was cut short by colon cancer.

2.7.1.6.2.3.1 KARL ROSS KLINGER was born on 20 February 1970, Meadowbrook, Montgomery County, PA. He married **JANE FRANCES DECHANTAL MICALLEF** on 3 June 1995, New Castle, DE.

2.7.1.6.2.3.1.1 AMELIA ANNE KLINGER was born on 29 March 2003, New Castle, DE.

2.7.1.6.2.3.1.2 NOELLE CATHERINE KLINGER was born on 29 January 2007, New Castle, DE.

2.7.1.6.2.3.1.3 FORREST GERALD KLINGER was born on 3 July 2009, New Castle, DE.

2.7.1.6.2.3.2 KAREN LYNNE KLINGER was born on 20 June 1973, Berks County, PA. She married **MICHAEL SCOTT KAUFFMAN** on 2 October 1999, Montgomery County, PA.

2.7.1.6.2.3.2.1 JEFFREY MICHAEL KAUFFMAN was born on 19 July 2004, Montgomery County, PA.

2.7.1.6.2.3.2.2 HANNAH ROSE KAUFFMAN was born on 11 October 2007, Montgomery County, PA.

2.7.1.6.2.3.3 KURT EUGENE KLINGER was born on 9 March 1979, Meadowbrook, Montgomery County, PA.

2.7.1.6.3 ETHEL ELLEN KLINGER is also referred to as **ELLEN ETHEL KLINGER** in some sources. She went by the name of **ELLEN.** She was born on 5 October 1909, Williamsport, Lycoming County, PA. She married **CHARLES C. WRIGHT** on 25 June 1933, Williamsport, Lycoming County, PA. She died on 26 April 2000, Williamsport, Lycoming County, PA, at age 90. She was buried on 28 April 2000, at Wildwood Cemetery, Williamsport, Lycoming County, PA. Ellen lived her entire life in Williamsport, or nearby in Montoursville and out on the Loyalsock Creek. Ellen's husband, George, had been a police officer and was on disability because of an injury suffered while on duty. Always busy, she had various jobs and was employed by the former Kresge's Department Store for 25 years. An excellent cook, she ran a coffee shop in Williamsport and later another out on "The Sock." They lived out on the Loyalsock Creek until her husband died, and then she moved into Montoursville.

2.7.1.6.3.1 NANCY KAY WRIGHT was born on 15 August 1934, Lycoming County, PA. She married **JAMES ROBERT ESHBACH** on 5 February 1955.

2.7.1.6.3.1.1 CHERYL ANN ESHBACH was born on 24 May 1956, Lycoming County, PA. She married **JOSE ANTONIO SERRA** on 16 June 1979.

2.7.1.6.3.1.1.1 REBECCA ANN SERRA was born on 14 July 1982, Dade County, FL.

2.7.1.6.3.1.1.2 MICHAEL JOSEPH SERRA was born on 7 July 1986, Lycoming County, PA.

2.7.1.6.3.1.1.3 MATTHEW JAMES SERRA was born on 16 January 1989, Lycoming County, PA.

2.7.1.6.3.1.2 BECKY LOU ESHBACH was born on 8 October 1962, Los Angeles, CA. She married **CHARLES EDGAR REEDER** on 1 October 1981.

2.7.1.6.3.1.2.1 CARL JAMES REEDER was born on 22 April 1982, Lycoming County, PA. He married **NICOLE EDELIA MEDINA.**

2.7.1.6.3.1.2.1.1 JOSIAH PHILLIP REEDER was born on 27 June 2007.

2.7.1.6.3.1.2.1.2 FAITH ELIZABETH REEDER was born in 2009.

2.7.1.6.3.1.2.2 MANDY MARIE REEDER was born on 26 December 1984, Lycoming County, PA. She married **SHAWN LEROY DOWNEY** on 10 April 2010, Lycoming County, PA.

2.7.1.6.3.1.2.3 DANIEL THOMAS REEDER was born on 9 February 1987, Lycoming County, PA.

2.7.1.6.3.1.3 JAMES DOUGLAS ESHBACH was born on 18 September 1964, Lycoming County, PA. He married **JANET MARIE WILLIAMS.** He and **JANET MARIE WILLIAMS** were divorced.

2.7.1.6.3.1.3.1 KYLE JAMES ESHBACH was born on 21 June 1991, Lycoming County, PA.

2.7.1.6.3.1.3.2 TAYLER MARIE ESHBACH was born on 8 March 1995, Lycoming County, PA.

2.7.1.7 BERTHA E. KLINGER is also referred to as **BIRTHA** in some sources. She was born in July 1884. She married **JAMES EDWIN WIRT**, son of **WILLIAM WIRT** and **ELIZABETH (--?--)**, circa 1903.

2.7.1.7.1 LUTHER C. WIRT is also referred to as **CHAUNCEY L. KLINGER** in some sources. He was born on 24 March 1904. He died on 14 August 1979, at age 75. He was buried at West Side Cemetery, Monroe Township, Snyder County, PA.

2.7.1.7.2 TOLBERT G. WIRT was born on 22 January 1907, in Pennsylvania. He died on 13 January 1997, at age 89.

2.7.1.7.3 VIOLET L. E. WIRT was born on 15 June 1909, in Pennsylvania. She married **THEODORE R. CONRAD**, son of **HOWARD O. CONRAD** and **MARIE K. (--?--)**, circa 1917. She died on 22 April 1997, at age 87.

2.7.1.7.3.1 THEODORE ROOSEVELT CONRAD JR. was born on 9 November 1926, Sunbury, Northumberland County, PA. He died on 28 April 2001, at age 74. He was buried at Pomfret Manor Cemetery, Sunbury, Northumberland County, PA.

2.7.1.7.3.2 MAXINE J. CONRAD was born circa July 1928, in Pennsylvania.

2.7.1.7.3.3 ARLENE F. CONRAD was born circa January 1930, in Pennsylvania.

2.7.1.8 JASPER ANTHONY KLINGER was born on 16 August 1886, Dalmatia, Northumberland County, PA. He was baptized on 26 September 1886, Trinity Evangelical Lutheran Church, Dalmatia, Northumberland County, PA. He married **VESTA LONG**, daughter of **JOHN ADAM LONG** and **EMMA JANE TROUTMAN**, on 25 December 1911. The marriage was performed by the Rev. J.W. Weetz. He died on 4 November 1957, Dalmatia, Northumberland County, PA, at age 71. He was buried on 7 November 1957, at Trinity Evangelical Reformed Cemetery, Dalmatia, Lower Mahanoy Township, Northumberland County, PA.

2.7.1.9 LUTHER G. KLINGER is also referred to as **GUY W. KLINGER** in some sources. He was born in April 1890, Pennsylvania. He married **FEENEY E. CABLE** on 1 June 1912. He married **MARY C. REEDER** circa 1917. An obituary for Luther's son Guy lists his mother's name as "Mary C. Reeder," but the 1920 and 1930 Census records list her name as "Esther R." (Reeder) Klinger. He died on 20 September 1922, Northumberland, Northumberland County, PA, at age 32, of anemia. He was buried at Riverview Cemetery, Northumberland, Northumberland County, PA.

2.7.1.9.1 GUY W. KLINGER was born on 10 August 1919, Northumberland, Northumberland County, PA. He married **MABLE E. HASSINGER**, daughter of **JOHN ALLEN HASSINGER** and **MABEL GRACE FULTZ**, on 15 September 1940, Clay County, FL. He died on 14 April 2010, Community Hospital, Sunbury, Northumberland County, PA, at age 90. He was buried at Riverview Cemetery, Northumberland, Northumberland County, PA.

2.7.1.9.1.1 JOHN R. KLINGER married **RUTH ANN (--?--)**.

2.7.1.9.1.2 TIMOTHY A. KLINGER

2.7.1.9.1.3 DEBRA A. KLINGER married **GEORGE LEHMAN**.

2.7.1.9.2 CARL RAYMOND KLINGER was born on 10 December 1920, Sunbury, Northumberland County, PA. He married **LAURA MAE BICKHART**, daughter of **WILLIAM S. BICKHART** and **MARGARET H. REICHENBACH**, on 5 June 1941, Granville County, NC. He died on 31 December 2002, Port Trevorton, Snyder County, PA, at age 82. He was buried at Paradise United Methodist Cemetery, Snyder County, PA.

2.7.1.9.2.1 CRAIG R. KLINGER married **ESTHER (--?--)**.

2.7.1.9.2.2 DAVID L. KLINGER married **KATHRYN (--?--)**.

2.7.1.9.2.3 KATINA S. KLINGER married **DANIEL HECKERT**.

2.7.1.9.2.4 CAROL J. KLINGER married **DAVE KEISTER**.

2.7.1.9.2.5 WILLIAM R. KLINGER was born on 26 September 1943, Glen Ridge, NJ. He married **SHARON SCOTT** circa 1975. He died on 17 September 2016, Holy Spirit Hospital, Camp Hill, Cumberland County, PA, at age 72. He was buried on 22 September 2016, at Cumberland Valley Memorial Gardens, Carlisle, Cumberland County, PA.

2.7.1.9.2.5.1 PAULA KLINGER married **ROBERT SGRIGNOLI**.

2.7.1.9.2.5.2 KEVIN ERNEST KLINGER

2.7.1.9.2.5.3 JACQUELINE KLINGER married **RAY CRISSMAN**.

2.7.1.9.2.5.4 ANGIE KLINGER married **DENE LEONARD**.

2.7.2 AMANDA KLINGER was born circa 1845.

2.7.3 JOHN ADAM KLINGER was born on 28 April 1849. He was baptized on 30 June 1849, St. David's Lutheran and Reformed Church, Hebe, Jordan Township, Northumberland County, PA.

2.7.4 CATHERINE ANNA KLINGER is also referred to as **KATE** in some sources. She was born on 15 September 1850. She was baptized on 1 December 1850, St. David's Lutheran and Reformed Church, Hebe, Jordan Township, Northumberland County, PA. She married **(--?--) BOWMAN**. She married **JOHN W. BINGAMAN**, son of **JOHN BINGAMAN** and **SUSANNA (--?--)**, circa 1887. She died in 1935. She was buried at Union Cemetery, Pillow, Jordan Township, Northumberland County, PA.

2.7.4.1 JOHN HENRY BINGAMAN was born in May 1889, in Pennsylvania. He married **ALICE E. PHILLIPS**, daughter of **JOHN JACOB PHILLIPS** and **MAGDALENA WITMER**, circa 1915. In 1944, 4 of John and Alice's sons, and one son-in-law, were serving in the armed forces. Sons Fred and John were in the US Navy, while Owen and Byron were in the Army and Army Air Corp respectively. Son-in-law Raymond Rowe was in the Army stationed in England. In 1947 John and Alice purchased a piece of property in Gratz and built a house on it. They lived there for many years. Eventually they sold part of the land to their son Byron and eventually sold the house to their son Clarence. John was a tinsmith and had a shop on the lot for a number of years. John and Alice had an ice cream store nearby. Eventually, Clarence, also known as Chuck, followed in his father's footsteps and became a tinsmith and plumber. John and Clarence installed many of the standing seam tin roofs in the Gratz area. He died in 1961. He was buried at Simeon Cemetery, Gratz, Dauphin County, PA.

2.7.4.1.1 KATHRYN MINERVA BINGAMAN is also referred to as **CATHERINE BINGAMAN** in some sources. She was born on 17 June 1915, in Pennsylvania. She married **ANDREW EHRINGER**. She died on 4 June 1985, at age 69.

2.7.4.1.1.1 SHIRLEY LORRAINE EHRINGER was born in 1936. She married **STEWART A. WIRE JR.**

2.7.4.1.1.2 PATRICIA EHRINGER was born in 1939. She married **PHILLIP FURHMAN III**.

2.7.4.1.2 OWEN E. BINGAMAN was born on 21 November 1918, Pillow, Dauphin County, PA. He died on 23 November 1986, Gratz, Dauphin County, PA, at age 68. He was unmarried.

2.7.4.1.3 FRED ROBERT BINGAMAN was born on 20 December 1919. Some sources record that he was born in Pennsylvania in 1916. He died on 29 May 1989, at age 69.

2.7.4.1.4 BYRON HENRY BINGAMAN was born on 27 March 1921. He married **HELEN LETTICH**. He died on 30 September 1987, at age 66.

2.7.4.1.4.1 RONALD BINGAMAN married **(--?--) RITZ**.

2.7.4.1.4.2 BEVERLY BINGAMAN married **BARRY PETERS**.

2.7.4.1.4.3 GLORIA BINGAMAN married **DREW STEVENS**.

2.7.4.1.5 CELIA IRENE BINGAMAN was born on 5 July 1923, Gratz, Dauphin County, PA. She married **RAYMOND HENRY ROWE** on 6 August 1943, United Brethren Parsonage, Lykens, Dauphin County, PA. She died on 1 February 1999, Lykens, Dauphin County, PA, at age 75. She was buried at Simeon United Lutheran Church Cemetery, Gratz, Dauphin County, PA.

2.7.4.1.5.1 RAYMOND JOHN ROWE married **XANDRA KOPPENHAVER**. He was born in 1944.

2.7.4.1.5.2 SUSANNE LOUISE ROWE is also referred to as **SUSANNE LOUISE ROWE** in some sources. She was born on 29 October 1947, Dauphin County, PA. She married **ROBERT ALBERT WOLFE**, son of **ROBERT ALLEN WOLFE** and **BETTY J. EBERT**, on 22 August 1969.

2.7.4.1.6 JOHN JACOB BINGAMAN was born on 7 May 1925. He was unmarried. He died on 28 March 1991, Gratz, Dauphin County, PA, at age 65. He was buried at Simeon United Lutheran Church Cemetery, Gratz, Dauphin County, PA.

2.7.4.1.7 CLARENCE FRANKLIN BINGAMAN was born on 8 October 1926. He married **MARY A. SHADLE**.

2.7.4.1.7.1 ROBERT ALLEN BINGAMAN was born in 1949. He married **ALANE MOYER**. Robert is a minister.

  2.7.4.1.7.2 JANE LOUISE BINGAMAN married TERRY LEE LAHR. She was born in 1951.

  2.7.4.1.7.3 MARY ANN BINGAMAN was born in 1957. She married RANDOLPH SNYDER.

  2.7.4.1.7.4 BELLANN BINGAMAN was born in 1964. She married ANTHONY KLINGER.

  2.7.4.1.7.5 ALAN FRANKLIN BINGAMAN was born in 1968. He married SARAH E. SAUERS.

2.7.4.1.8 DONALD EUGENE BINGAMAN was born on 20 December 1927. He married HELEN STUTZMAN.

  2.7.4.1.8.1 VALERIE BINGAMAN was born in 1951. She married ROBBIE SCHELL SR.

  2.7.4.1.8.2 KEITH BINGAMAN was born in 1955. He married BRENDA SUE WILLIARD.

  2.7.4.1.8.3 GAIL BINGAMAN was born in 1957. She married KENNETH SNYDER.

  2.7.4.1.8.4 LARRY BINGAMAN was born in 1958. He married EUNICE HEIMBAUGH.

  2.7.4.1.8.5 KENNETH BINGAMAN was born in 1967. He married WENDY LEE TROUTMAN.

2.7.4.1.9 BETTY LORRAINE BINGAMAN was born on 24 August 1929, Pillow, Dauphin County, PA. She married FRANKLIN DANIEL BIXLER on 18 May 1946, Lutheran Parsonage, Elizabethville, Dauphin County, PA. She married RUSSELL RUE SCHADLE, son of RAY WOODROW WILSON SHADLE and EVA MAY KLINGER, on 29 August 1959, Simeon Union Church, Gratz, Dauphin County, PA. She died on 13 December 2013, Community General Osteopathic Hospital, Harrisburg, Dauphin County, PA, at age 84.

  2.7.4.1.9.1 VIRGINIA DIANNE BIXLER was born in 1946. She married WILMER GUEST.

  2.7.4.1.9.2 FRANKLIN DANIEL BIXLER JR. was born in 1950.

  2.7.4.1.9.3 TIMOTHY JAMES BIXLER was born on 23 March 1950.

  2.7.4.1.9.4 ALICE MAE SHADLE is also referred to as ALICE MAY SHADLE in some sources. She was born on 5 March 1960.

  2.7.4.1.9.5 JOHN RUSSELL SHADLE is also referred to as JOHN RUSSELL RUE SHADLE in some sources. He was born on 3 July 1963. He married KAREN KULP.

2.7.4.1.10 RICHARD ARLEN BINGAMAN was born on 27 December 1931. He is unmarried.

2.7.4.1.11 JAMES MONROE BINGAMAN was born on 28 November 1936. He married APRIL GAIL HOFFMAN. James lives near Elizabethville, PA.

2.7.5 MARY M. KLINGER was born on 31 May 1853. She died on 2 July 1854, at age 1. She was buried at Grandview Cemetery, Pillow, Dauphin County, PA.

2.7.6 WILLIAM H. KLINGER was born on 8 November 1854. He married ANNA B. MILLER on 19 August 1882. He died on 4 April 1937, Prairie Township, Kosciusko County, IN, at age 82. He was buried at Stony Point Cemetery, Clunette, Kosciusko County, IN.

2.7.7 LOUSIAN KLINGER is also referred to as LUCY in some sources. She was born circa 1857. It is unclear whether Emanuel's daughter "Louisan," listed in the 1860 Census as 3 years old at the time, is the same person as the daughter Lucy or Louisa Ann listed in the 1870 and 1880 Censuses. All three were listed with birth dates of around 1858. These may all be references to the same person.

2.7.8 LUCIA KLINGER is also referred to as LUCY in some sources. She was born circa 1859. Some sources record that she was born in 1850. She married (--?--) SEAMAN. She died in 1929. The 1900 Census for Uniontown (Pillow), Dauphin County, PA, lists a Lucy A. Seaman, born January 1859, as wife in a household headed by Jeremiah Seaman, born August 1866. They were married circa 1893 had 2 children, Charles, born July 1895, and Mary, born February 1899. In 1910, "Jerry" and Lucy were lodging in a household headed by a widow Sarah Moyer, age 75. According to the Census, Jerry and Lucy had given birth to 1 child. The 1920 Census apparently lists this couple as "Jerry" and "Lizzie" Seaman. In 1930, "Jerry" was widowed and living on Market Street in Pillow. This is consistent with the evidence suggesting that Lucy died in 1929. These listings appear to be for the only Lucy or Lucia Seaman in the Uniontown (Pillow) area. The Census records generally suggest that she was born in 1859. While this is not consistent with the burial listing for a Lucy A. Seaman (1850 - 1929) at Grandview Cemetery in Pillow, it appears to be more consistent with the birth dates of the other children of Elias Klinger. She may have been buried at Grandview Cemetery, Pillow, Dauphin County, PA. There is a burial listing at the Grandview Cemetery in Pillow for a "Lucy A. Seaman," born in 1850 and died in 1929. It is possible that this is the daughter of Elias Klinger. This may be the same person as Emanuel's daughter Louisan listed in the 1860 Census.

2.7.9 DAVID B. KLINGER was born in October 1860. He married MARY J. (--?--) circa 1885. He may have been buried at Union Cemetery, Pillow, Jordan Township, Dauphin County, PA. The published listings for the Union Cemetery in Pillow include a "David B. Klinger" (1860 - 1953) and his wife "M. Jane" (1864 - 1919). The birth dates and the death date of Mary Jane are consistent with the Census records. In addition, the cemetery listings include listings for what appear to be David's two daughters, Maude and Blanche. According to Otto and Joan (Klinger) Crumroy, David Klinger did research on his branch of the Klinger family tree. He did so in cooperation with Earl Klinger, who had been on the faculty of Purdue University and collected considerable information about the Klinger family. David Klinger worked in Washington D.C., Department of Interior, and later, Pensions. In the 1970's Forrest Eugene Klinger, Sr. went to Pillow and Klingerstown looking for family history and discovered that his Uncle J. Arthur Klinger was still alive. Forrest Eugene wrote to J. Arthur with a number of questions about the family history. J. Arthur answered his questions and sent him the material that Earl Klinger and David Klinger had gathered. Later, Forrest Eugene Klinger, Sr. passed the data on to Joan Ross Klinger Crumroy, his oldest child.

> **2.7.9.1 MAUDE A. KLINGER** was born in October 1885, in Pennsylvania. She died in 1953. She was buried at Union Cemetery, Pillow, Jordan Township, Dauphin County, PA.
>
> **2.7.9.2 BLANCHE O. KLINGER** was born in February 1894, in the District of Columbia. She died in 1933. She was buried at Union Cemetery, Pillow, Jordan Township, Dauphin County, PA.

2.7.10 MARTHA E. KLINGER was born on 19 September 1865. She died on 15 March 1873, at age 7. She was buried at Grandview Cemetery, Pillow, Dauphin County, PA.

2.7.11 LIDIA A. KLINGER was born in 1869. She married (--?--) **CHILTON**. She died in 1931. She was buried at Grandview Cemetery, Pillow, Dauphin County, PA.

2.7.12 JAMES ARTHUR KLINGER is also referred to as **ARTHUR J. KLINGER** in some sources. He was born in October 1880. He married **MABEL E. SNYDER** circa 1905. He may have been buried at Grandview Cemetery, Pillow, Dauphin County, PA. One listing of burials at the Grandview Cemetery includes a "J. Arthur Klinger, 1880 - ____." It is not clear whether Arthur was in fact buried in this cemetery, although the description of the cemetery layout by Mary Klinger suggests that he was buried there with his wife Mabel.

> **2.7.12.1 MILDRED M. KLINGER** was born on 21 May 1911, in the District of Columbia. She married **HARRY WALTER KLINGER**, son of **SAM BRADY KLINGER** and **MARY ELIZABETH WILLIARD**. She died in 1981. She was buried at Mellinger Mennonite Cemetery, Lancaster, Lancaster County, PA.
>
>> **2.7.12.1.1 JAMES H. KLINGER** was born circa 1935, Harrisburg, Dauphin County, PA. He married **MARILYN BRODHECKER** circa 1957. He died on 15 February 2015, The Mennonite Home, Lancaster, Lancaster County, PA. He was buried at Landis Valley Mennonite Cemetery, Lancaster, Lancaster County, PA.
>>
>>> **2.7.12.1.1.1 ROBERT KLINGER** married **DARLA DIVET**.
>>>
>>> **2.7.12.1.1.2 NANCY ANN KLINGER** married **THOMAS LAWRENCE**.
>>
>> **2.7.12.1.2 MARTHA JEAN KLINGER** was born circa 1938. She married **PAUL GISH**.

2.8 CHARLES KLINGER is also referred to as **PHILIP CARL KLINGER** in some sources. He was born on 15 September 1824. He was baptized on 17 October 1824, Zion (Klinger's) Church, Erdman, Lykens Township, Dauphin County, PA. He married **LIDIA MILLER**. The 1850 Census lists Charles as a "miller" in Mifflin Township, Dauphin County, age 26, with a wife Lydia, age 31. Their children were listed as Emanuel 8; Frederick 6; Amelia 5; and Elias 1. Charles and Lydia sold their farm in Dauphin County, PA, on March 16, 1865, and then moved to Indiana, where they purchased a farm in Kosciusko County, IN. He died on 17 November 1887, Kosciusko County, IN, at age 63. He was buried at Row 2, # 18, Stony Point Cemetery, Prairie Township, Kosciusko County, IN. According to Bruce Hall, in his will, Charles left all his property, income from that property, and personal assets to his wife Lydia, once his funeral expenditures and any debts are paid. At that time, his real estate was valued at $5000 and his personal estate at $100. His will stipulates that after his wife's death, his estate is to be divided among his four sons and three daughters. His youngest son, John A. Klinger, preceded him in death and was not mentioned in the will. He instructed his children to sell everything as soon as practically possible and divide the proceeds equally among them. He also inserted a clause in his will that any of his heirs that would cause problems in the speedy settling of his estate would receive only $10 for his share. He also requested that his children "erect a respectful monument, something like my son John's, for him and his wife, paying for the same out of the residuary estate.

> **2.8.1 EMANUEL KLINGER** was born on 23 May 1843. He married **SARAH GINTER**, daughter of **JOHN GINTER** and (--?--) **MOYER**, on 17 November 1863. He died on 21 July 1908, at age 65. He was buried at Stony Point Cemetery, Clunette, Kosciusko County, IN.

2.8.1.1 ELMER ELSWORTH KLINGER was born on 27 December 1865, PA. He married **JOANNA JOHNSON**, daughter of **JOHN JOHNSON**, on 19 February 1891, Kosciusko County, IN. He died on 27 March 1947, Warsaw, Kosciusko County, IN, at age 81. He was buried at Stony Point Cemetery, Clunette, Kosciusko County, IN.

2.8.1.2 CLINTON CHARLES KLINGER was born on 4 November 1868, Washington Township, Dauphin County, PA. Some sources record that he was born in August 1869. He married **ARTIMISSIA EPLER**, daughter of **WILLIAM EPLER** and **AMANDA HOPPIS**, on 8 December 1892, Kosciusko County, IN. He died on 17 July 1961, Eureka, Humboldt County, CA, at age 92. He was buried at Ocean View Cemetery, Eureka, Humboldt County, CA.

> **2.8.1.2.1 SARAH ESTELLA KLINGER** was born on 4 April 1894, Harrison Township, Kosciusko County, IN. She was born on 4 April 1893, IN. She married **DEBELT DAVID SCHRIEVER** on 3 May 1918, Stillwater, MN. She married **WILLIAM LYSTAD BERG** on 11 May 1921, Duluth, MN. Some sources suggest that she and **WILLIAM LYSTAD BERG** were married circa 1921 Eureka, Humboldt County, CA. She died on 22 April 1952, Eureka, Humboldt County, CA, at age 59. She was buried at Ocean View Cemetery, Eureka, Humboldt County, CA.
>
> > **2.8.1.2.1.1 BERT DAVID SCHRIEVER** married **JUNE DUEL**. He and **JUNE DUEL** were divorced. He married **ROBERTA (--?--)**. He is also referred to as **BERT DAVID BERG** in some sources. He was born on 11 February 1919, IN. He died on 20 February 1979, Eureka, Humboldt County, CA, at age 60. He was buried at Ocean View Cemetery, Eureka, Humboldt County, CA.
> >
> > > **2.8.1.2.1.1.1 BERT BERG**
> >
> > **2.8.1.2.1.2 JAMES WILLIAM BERG** was born on 6 May 1922, Webster, Burnett County, WI. He married **HELEN MARIAN ARDEL ANDERSON** on 23 January 1949, Eureka, Humboldt County, CA. He died on 19 July 2002, Eureka, Humboldt County, CA, at age 80.
> >
> > > **2.8.1.2.1.2.1 SHARON A. BERG** was born on 5 July 1950. She married **TIMOTHY P. CISSNA**.
> > >
> > > **2.8.1.2.1.2.2 JAMES WILLIAM BERG JR.** was born on 5 July 1950, Eureka, Humboldt County, CA. He died on 6 July 1950, Eureka, Humboldt County, CA.
> > >
> > > **2.8.1.2.1.2.3 SHARON ANN BERG** was born on 5 July 1950, Eureka, Humboldt County, CA. She married **TIMOTHY PAUL CISSNA** on 19 March 1972, Eureka, Humboldt County, CA.
> > >
> > > > **2.8.1.2.1.2.3.1 KEVIN JAMES CISSNA** was born on 24 February 1980, Eureka, Humboldt County, CA.
> > >
> > > **2.8.1.2.1.2.4 BONNIE D. BERG** was born on 9 March 1952. She married **JAMES E. MANLEY**.
> > >
> > > **2.8.1.2.1.2.5 BONNIE DIANNE BERG** was born on 9 March 1952, Eureka, Humboldt County, CA. She married **JAMES ERNEST MANLEY**. She and **JAMES ERNEST MANLEY** were divorced. She married **PATRICK MICHAEL RAHM** on 21 June 1979, Multnomah County, OR.
> > >
> > > > **2.8.1.2.1.2.5.1 DANIEL PATRICK RAHM** was born on 24 June 1982, Portland, Multnomah County, OR.
> > > >
> > > > **2.8.1.2.1.2.5.2 KIRSTEN ALICIA RAHM** was born on 27 August 1989, Portland, Multnomah County, OR.
>
> **2.8.1.2.2 BELVA E. KLINGER** was born on 24 September 1896, Atwood, Kosciusko County, IN. She married **PHILIP G. LARSON**. She died in January 1989, Arizona at age 92.
>
> > **2.8.1.2.2.1 PHILLIP G. LARSON JR.**
> >
> > **2.8.1.2.2.2 ROBERT LARSON**
> >
> > **2.8.1.2.2.3 ELOISE LARSON** married **(--?--) KRAMER**.

2.8.1.3 HARRY WILSON KLINGER was born on 5 February 1875, Lykens, Wiconisco Township, Dauphin County, PA. He married **VIOLA E. TREESH** on 25 March 1900, Kosciusko County, IN. He died in October 1946, Kosciusko County, IN, at age 71. He was buried at Stoney Point Cemetery, Atwood, Kosciusko County, IN.

2.8.1.3.1 IVAN R. KLINGER was born on 24 January 1902. He married **THELMA BARNUM** circa 1930. He married **BERNICE WOOFTER BENNETT** on 6 July 1959. He died on 8 March 1978, at age 76. He was buried at Stony Point Cemetery, Clunette, Kosciusko County, IN.

2.8.1.3.1.1 HARRY JACK KLINGER was born on 11 November 1930. He married **JEAN GODFRIED** circa 1950.

2.8.1.3.1.1.1 HARRY KLINGER

2.8.2 FREDERICK KLINGER was born on 6 May 1844, Berrysburg, Dauphin County, PA. Frederik served as a musician with the 177th Regiment of the Pennsylvania Infantry during the Civil War. He married **ELISABETH BITTIKOFER** circa 1866. He died on 6 October 1907, at age 63. He was buried at Stony Point Cemetery, Clunette, Kosciusko County, IN.

2.8.2.1 CHARLES FREDERICK KLINGER was born on 27 August 1867, Prairie Township, Kosciusko County, IN. He married **ANNETTA ELTON ANGLIN** circa 1893. He died on 11 November 1937, Prairie Township, Kosciusko County, IN, at age 70. He was buried at Stony Point Cemetery, Clunette, Kosciusko County, IN.

2.8.2.1.1 JOHN F. KLINGER was born in September 1893, Indiana. He died in 1944.

2.8.2.1.2 EDITH C. KLINGER was born on 27 October 1894, Indiana. She died on 26 June 1982, at age 87. She was buried at Stony Point Cemetery, Clunette, Kosciusko County, IN.

2.8.2.1.3 EARL LLOYD KLINGER was born on 2 April 1898, in Indiana. He married **MARY COSETTE WRIGHT** circa 1926. He died on 4 March 1995, at age 96. At the time of his death, Earl was living in West Lafayette, IN. He retired as a professor at Purdue University.

2.8.2.1.3.1 CHARLES W. KLINGER was born on 29 July 1927. He married **NORMA JO STATTON**, daughter of **GEORGE RAYMOND STATTON** and **SARAH ETTA BURNS,** circa 1953.

2.8.2.1.3.1.1 JACQUELINE KLINGER married (--?--) **SOWATSKY**.

2.8.2.1.3.1.2 KATHERINE KLINGER married (--?--) **ROULEAU**.

2.8.2.1.3.1.3 JAMES KLINGER

2.8.2.1.3.1.4 DOUGLAS KLINGER

2.8.2.1.3.2 RUTH ANN KLINGER was born on 19 July 1933. She married **HALBERT SMITH**.

2.8.2.1.3.2.1 JENNIFER SMITH

2.8.2.1.3.2.2 CAROLYN SMITH

2.8.2.1.3.3 PHILIP W. KLINGER was born on 13 December 1935. He married **BETTY MIKEL**.

2.8.2.1.3.3.1 MICHAEL KLINGER

2.8.2.1.3.3.2 SUSAN KLINGER

2.8.2.1.3.3.3 LISA KLINGER

2.8.2.1.3.3.4 CYNTHIA KLINGER

2.8.2.1.4 HOWARD R. KLINGER was born on 23 September 1901. He married **MILDRED A. BICKEL**. He died on 30 March 1987, at age 85. He was buried at Stony Point Cemetery, Clunette, Kosciusko County, IN.

2.8.2.1.4.1 DEWAYNE KLINGER married **EVIE** (--?--). He was born circa 1936, Indiana. DeWayne lives in Mineral Springs, OH.

2.8.2.1.4.2 GEORGE E. KLINGER was born on 3 April 1938, Kosciusko County, IN. He married **MARTHA** (--?--) **DRUDGE** on 6 June 1965. According to a newspaper obituary, George was an accountant in Warsaw, IN, and owned Klinger Accounting since 1972. He was also a farmer since 1996. He died on 19 December 2013, Lutheran Hospital, Fort Wayne, IN, at age 75. He was buried at Oakwood Cemetery, Warsaw, Kosciusko County, IN.

2.8.2.1.4.2.1 BRIAN R. KLINGER. Brian lives in Etna Green, IN.

2.8.2.1.4.2.2 VICKI L. KLINGER. Vicki lives in Etna Green, IN.

2.8.2.1.4.3 MARVIN KLINGER was born circa 1940, Indiana. Marvin lives in Marion, IN.

2.8.2.1.4.4 WILLIAM KLINGER married **DEBBY** (--?--). He was born after 1940. Bill lives in Seymour, IN.

2.8.2.1.5 HENRY KLINGER was born in 1904.

2.8.2.1.6 INEZ MAE KLINGER was born on 14 September 1907, Kosciusko County, IN. She married **JESSE MELVIN PFEIFER**. She died on 24 August 1994, Warsaw, Kosciusko County, IN, at age 86.

2.8.2.1.7 AMY KLINGER was born in 1911.

2.8.3 AMELIA KLINGER was born on 26 February 1846, Dauphin County, PA. She married **JOHN C. WOLF** circa 1867. She died on 9 September 1920, Kosciusko County, IN, at age 74. She was buried in 1921, at Stony Point Cemetery, Clunette, Dauphin County, IN.

2.8.3.1 ELLA WOLF was born on 23 August 1867. She married **CHARLES DANIEL ROMBERGER**, son of **WILLIAM ROMBERGER** and **SUSANNAH KLINGER**. She died on 20 September 1896, at age 29.

2.8.3.1.1 LULU ROMBERGER was born on 11 February 1888, Indiana. She died on 11 December 1960, at age 72.

2.8.3.1.2 GERTRUDE ROMBERGER was born on 1 June 1892, Indiana. She died on 12 October 1935, at age 43.

2.8.3.2 EVA WOLF was born on 10 June 1872. She married **CYRUS MINER**. She died on 15 January 1906, at age 33.

2.8.3.2.1 ALON D. MINER was born on 13 November 1895. He died on 4 September 1898, at age 2.

2.8.3.2.2 DEWEY MINER was born on 14 May 1898. He married **VIRGINIA R. SCOTT**. He died on 9 February 1983, at age 84.

2.8.4 ELIAS KLINGER was born on 16 March 1849. He married **MARY ELLEN WRIGHT** circa 1873. He married **HENRIETTA SIBERT**. He died on 28 March 1926, Harrison Township, Kosciusko County, IN, at age 77.

2.8.4.1 NETTIE MAY KLINGER was born on 27 August 1875, Kosciusko County, IN. She married **JOHN CINNINGER** circa 1896. She died on 5 August 1957, at age 81. She was buried at Oakwood Cemetery, Warsaw, Kosciusko County, IN.

2.8.4.1.1 RUTH M. CINNINGER was born on 10 June 1897. She died on 3 August 1898, at age 1. She was buried at Oakwood Cemetery, Warsaw, Kosciusko County, IN.

2.8.4.1.2 DONALD J. CINNINGER was born in March 1899, Indiana. Some sources record that he was born on 8 March 1900. He married **ESTHER ROWLAND** circa 1922.

2.8.4.1.2.1 JOAN E. CINNINGER is also referred to as **JOE ANN** in some sources. She was born on 7 November 1925.

2.8.4.1.2.2 BARBARA LOU CINNINGER was born on 10 April 1929.

2.8.4.1.2.3 HAL EUGENE CINNINGER was born on 3 August 1933.

2.8.4.1.3 LEROY O. CINNINGER was born on 25 September 1901. He married **CELESTIA JOHNSON**. He married **BLANCHE YEITER**. He died on 19 July 1973, at age 71.

2.8.4.1.3.1 BETTY ANN CINNINGER was born on 7 October 1930.

2.8.4.1.4 ROBERT E. CINNINGER was born on 25 September 1901. He married **DUELLA DANIELSON**. He died on 11 February 1986, at age 84.

2.8.4.1.4.1 MARY ELLEN CINNINGER was born on 28 July 1923.

2.8.4.1.4.2 VERNA DEAN CINNINGER was born on 8 November 1924.

2.8.4.1.4.3 JOHN E. CINNINGER was born on 9 March 1925.

2.8.4.1.4.4 JAMES D. CINNINGER was born on 28 February 1929.

2.8.4.1.5 CHARLES P. CINNINGER is also referred to as **BUN** in some sources. He was born on 21 December 1906. He married **ALICE (--?--) BAYLOR**.

2.8.4.1.6 MARY R. CINNINGER was born on 13 January 1908. She died on 3 September 1908.

2.8.4.1.7 LEE H. CINNINGER was born on 9 September 1909. He died circa 18 June 1910.

2.8.4.1.8 EDWARD A. CINNINGER was born on 23 January 1913. He married **IRENE (--?--)**.

2.8.4.2 EDWARD ELLSWORTH KLINGER was born on 30 January 1877. He married **ANNA A. (--?--)** circa 1897. He married **LUCRETIA HARRIS**. He married **WINIFRED BIVIN**. He married **DOLLIE MILLER**. Some sources list various additional wives for Edward, including Dollie Miller, Lucretia Harris, and Winifred Bivin, but according to the Census records, from 1900 through 1930, his wife was named "Anna A." It is not clear if the listings for these other wives are correct.

2.8.4.2.1 PAULINE KLINGER was born on 24 July 1901.

2.8.4.2.2 JOHN PRESTON KLINGER was born on 12 June 1904. He married VENNETTA JOHNSON circa 1927. He died in July 1979, at age 75.

2.8.4.2.2.1 ROGER P. KLINGER was born on 26 February 1929, Indiana.

2.8.4.2.3 DOROTHY KLINGER was born on 17 March 1913. She married JOSEPH BAUMGARTNER. She married ERNEST VIERS. She died on 30 May 2000, Tampa, Hillsborough County, FL, at age 87.

2.8.4.2.3.1 JAMES VIERS married KATHY (--?--).

2.8.4.2.3.1.1 JAMES VIERS

2.8.4.3 HARRY CALVIN KLINGER was born on 13 February 1881, Kosciusko County, IN. He died on 31 October 1902, Kosciusko County, IN, at age 21. He was buried at Oakwood Cemetery, Warsaw, Kosciusko County, IN.

2.8.4.4 CHARLES RAY KLINGER was born on 14 January 1883.

2.8.4.5 VIOLA MYRTLE KLINGER was born on 25 March 1884, Kosciusko County, IN. She married OWEN EDWARD KEEFER. She and OWEN EDWARD KEEFER were divorced. She married ERNEST EARL MCFARREN. She married FESTUS G. HOOS. She died on 14 December 1953, FL at age 69. She was buried at Oakwood Cemetery, Warsaw, Kosciusko County, IN.

2.8.4.5.1 EMMETT EARL KEEFER was born on 28 July 1908, Indianapolis, Marion County, IN. He married FRANCES FAY BROWN, daughter of ERNEST V. BROWN and EMMA FLORENCE GOODRICH. He died on 28 December 1978, Plymouth, Marshall County, IN, at age 70. He was buried in 1979, at Stony Point Cemetery, Clunette, Kosciusko County, IN.

2.8.4.6 ALBERT EARL KLINGER is also referred to as ALBERT E. CLINGER in some sources. He was born on 7 March 1888. He married MABEL E. DASHER circa 1915. He died on 30 July 1957, at age 69.

2.8.4.6.1 JEAN ALBERTA KLINGER was born circa 1914. She married JOHN NORRIS ZIEGLER.

2.8.4.7 GRACE MARIE KLINGER was born on 12 June 1890. She married JOHN NORRIS circa 1909. She died on 3 October 1964, Kosciusko County, IN, at age 74. She was buried at Oakwood Cemetery, Warsaw, Kosciusko County, IN.

2.8.4.7.1 CLARENCE ALBERT NORRIS was born on 15 November 1909, Kosciusko County, IN. He married ARLETTA G. STAHL. He died on 22 November 1985, Warsaw, Kosciusko County, IN, at age 76. He was buried at Oakwood Cemetery, Warsaw, Kosciusko County, IN.

2.8.4.7.2 EARL EDWIN NORRIS was born on 17 October 1911, Kosciusko County, IN. He married MARY BELLE STACKHOUSE, daughter of JAMES STACKHOUSE and FLORENCE (--?--). He died on 22 July 1992, Kosciusko County, IN, at age 80. He was buried at Oakwood Cemetery, Warsaw, Kosciusko County, IN.

2.8.4.7.2.1 BETTY JEAN NORRIS was born on 23 May 1933, Warsaw, Kosciusko County, IN. She married JAMES EDWARD PHILLIPS.

2.8.4.7.2.1.1 STEPHEN ALLEN PHILLIPS was born on 17 September 1953, Fairborn, Greene County, OH. He married RACHAEL OGLESBEE.

2.8.4.7.2.1.1.1 ELIZABETH RENAE PHILLIPS was born on 16 August 1979, South Bend, St. Joseph County, IN.

2.8.4.7.2.1.1.2 CHRISTINA MICHELLE PHILLIPS was born on 17 May 1982, Plymouth, Marshall County, IN.

2.8.4.7.2.1.1.3 DAVID CAMERON PHILLIPS was born on 15 April 1985, Plymouth, Marshall County, IN.

2.8.4.7.2.1.2 BRAD EUGENE PHILLIPS was born on 7 December 1956, Bloomington, Monroe County, IN. He married MARY KAY MCGUIRE.

2.8.4.7.2.1.2.1 CHRISTOPHER RYAN PHILLIPS was born on 13 July 1981, Lexington, Fayette County, KY.

2.8.4.7.2.1.2.2 JULIA ANN PHILLIPS was born on 23 August 1983, Lexington, Fayette County, KY.

2.8.4.7.2.1.2.3 SARAH ELIZABETH PHILLIPS was born on 10 December 1985, Lexington, Fayette County, KY.

2.8.4.7.3 HELEN BERNICE NORRIS was born on 15 June 1914, Kosciusko County, IN. She married **RALPH F. BOGGS.** She died on 27 April 1991, Pierceton, Kosciusko County, IN, at age 76. She was buried at Oakwood Cemetery, Warsaw, Kosciusko County, IN.

2.8.4.7.3.1 MARY ELLEN BOGGS was born circa 20 September 1934, Kosciusko County, IN. She married **WILLIAM STILLSON.**

2.8.4.7.3.1.1 SUSAN STILLSON married **(--?--) SHEPHERD.**

2.8.4.7.3.1.2 SANDY STILLSON

2.8.4.7.3.2 JOHN HAMILTON BOGGS was born on 28 June 1936, Kosciusko County, IN. He married **PEGGY DRUDGE AIRGOOD.** He died on 16 January 2001, Wabash County, IN, at age 64. He was buried at Eel River Ulrey Memorial Cemetery, Silver Lake, Kosciusko County, IN.

2.8.4.7.3.3 DONALD DEAN BOGGS was born on 12 October 1940, Warsaw, Kosciusko County, IN. He married **CAROLYN COLLIER.**

2.8.4.7.3.3.1 ROGER ALLAN BOGGS was born on 1 January 1960, Fort Belvoir, Fairfax County, VA. He married **KELLY ANN GEARHART.**

2.8.4.7.3.3.1.1 STEPHANIE MICHELLE BOGGS was born on 29 April 1986, Warsaw, Kosciusko County, IN.

2.8.4.7.3.3.1.2 CASEY ALAN BOGGS was born on 25 October 1988, Warsaw, Kosciusko County, IN.

2.8.4.7.3.3.2 TONY LEE BOGGS was born on 10 January 1962, Columbia City, Whitley County, IN. He married **BERNADENE KAY CAMDEN.**

2.8.4.7.3.3.2.1 BRYAN TOLIVER BOGGS was born on 9 August 1988, Warsaw, Kosciusko County, IN.

2.8.4.7.3.3.2.2 KURT THOMAS BOGGS was born on 6 January 1992, Warsaw, Kosciusko County, IN.

2.8.4.7.3.3.3 JEFFREY JAY BOGGS was born on 4 May 1966, Columbia City, Whitley County, IN.

2.8.4.7.3.3.4 DAVID DEAN BOGGS was born on 23 November 1969, Columbia City, Whitley County, IN.

2.8.4.7.3.4 KENNETH BOGGS was born in 1942. He married **FRIEDA (--?--).**

2.8.4.7.4 NELLIE NORRIS was born on 5 July 1917, Kosciusko County, IN. She died on 13 March 1926, Kosciusko County, IN, at age 8. She was buried at Oakwood Cemetery, Warsaw, Kosciusko County, IN.

2.8.4.7.5 RUTH MAXINE NORRIS was born on 12 December 1919, Atwood, Kosciusko County, IN. She married **LORRAINE VERLING WARNER** on 25 January 1939, Sidney, Kosciusko County, IN.

2.8.4.7.5.1 JACK EUGENE WARNER was born on 3 April 1940, Warsaw, Kosciusko County, IN. He married **FLORA SANTOS MANGUEIRA** on 20 January 1963, Spring Creek Church of the Brethren, Sidney, Kosciusko County, IN.

2.8.4.7.5.1.1 BENTON MARCOS MANGUEIRA-WARNER was born on 13 January 1966, Tarma, Peru. He married **SHERI SUE HAMLIN** on 21 October 1989, Ganta, Liberia.

2.8.4.7.5.1.1.1 ALEXANDRA GRACE MANGUEIRA was born on 22 October 1993, Ft. Meyers, Lee County, FL.

2.8.4.7.5.1.1.2 HUNTER HAMLIN MANGUEIRA was born on 28 March 1995, Atlanta, Fulton County, GA.

2.8.4.7.5.1.2 BRIAN CARLOS MANGUEIRA WARNER was born on 22 September 1968, Tarma, Peru. He married **BARBARA LOUISE BRADBURY** on 5 August 1989, Warsaw, Kosciusko County, IN.

2.8.4.7.5.1.2.1 JUAN MARCOS WARNER was born on 25 July 1989, Dallas, Dallas County, TX.

2.8.4.7.5.1.2.2 MARSAIL CARLOS WARNER was born on 12 February 1991, Dallas, Dallas County, TX.

2.8.4.7.5.1.2.3 ELISABETH LOUISE WARNER is also referred to as **LISA** in some sources. She was born on 12 June 1996.

2.8.4.7.5.2 REX JAY WARNER was born on 23 July 1942, Warsaw, Kosciusko County, IN. He married **AVONELLE LUCILLE COOK** on 2 September 1962, Claypool, Kosciusko County, IN.

2.8.4.7.5.2.1 BONITA JO WARNER was born on 2 May 1963, Lafayette, Tippecanoe County, IN. She married **DAVID SMITH** on 2 July 1983, West Lafayette, Tippecanoe County, IN.

2.8.4.7.5.2.1.1 RACHEL CATHERINE SMITH was born on 1 May 1987, Lexington, Fayette County, Ky.

2.8.4.7.5.2.1.2 DANIEL SMITH was born on 8 February 1990.

2.8.4.7.5.2.2 DEBRA WARNER was born on 13 December 1965.

2.8.4.7.5.2.3 ANGELA MARIE WARNER was born on 30 May 1970, Vincennes, Knox County, IN. She married **BRADLEY ROLLAR ALLEN** on 1 August 1992, West Lafayette, Tippecanoe County, IN.

2.8.4.7.5.2.3.1 ALEXIS NICOLE ALLEN was born on 30 May 1994, Indianapolis, Marion County, IN.

2.8.4.7.5.2.3.2 BRADAN ROLLER ALLEN was born on 17 August 1998, Indianapolis, Marion County, IN.

2.8.4.7.5.3 DEAN PAUL WARNER was born on 24 February 1944, Warsaw, Kosciusko County, IN. He married **RUTH ARLENE SNYDER** on 27 December 1964, Spring Creek Church of the Brethren, Sidney, Kosciusko County, IN.

2.8.4.7.5.3.1 KEVIN LEE WARNER was born on 28 January 1969, Quito, Ecuador. He married **LAURA WADE CONN** on 23 May 1992.

2.8.4.7.5.3.1.1 ERIN KATHERINE WARNER was born on 31 March 1996, Lexington, Fayette County, Ky.

2.8.4.7.5.3.1.2 ELISSA WADE WARNER was born on 19 April 1999, Lexington, Fayette County, Ky.

2.8.4.7.5.3.2 TIMOTHY ALAN WARNER was born on 10 March 1972, Columbus, Franklin County, OH. He married **JENNIFER NICOLE GRANT** on 22 May 1997.

2.8.4.7.6 MARY CATHERINE NORRIS was born on 23 December 1921, Atwood, Kosciusko County, IN. She married **ROBERT H. SNEP** on 8 January 1941, IN. She died on 6 November 1966, Kosciusko County, IN, at age 44. She was buried at Oaklawn Cemetery, North Manchester, Wabash County, IN.

2.8.4.7.6.1 WILLIAM SNEP married **ANITA (--?--)**.

2.8.4.7.6.1.1 PHILLIP SNEP married **BRENDA (--?--)**.

2.8.4.7.6.1.2 DOUGLAS SNEP

2.8.4.7.6.2 LARRY SNEP

2.8.4.7.6.2.1 GREGORY SNEP married **TRACY (--?--)**.

2.8.4.7.6.2.2 PAMELA SNEP

2.8.4.7.6.3 JANICE MARIE SNEP married **DANIEL SELL**.

2.8.4.7.6.3.1 MICHAEL SELL

2.8.4.7.6.3.2 MATTHEW SELL

2.8.4.7.6.3.3 JENNIFER SELL

2.8.4.7.6.4 JANET SUE SNEP is also referred to as **SUZIE** in some sources.

2.8.4.8 MARY RUBY KLINGER also went by the name of **RUBY**. She was born on 12 September 1899, Indiana. She married **RUSSELL CAUFFMAN**, son of **ALBERT M. CAUFFMAN** and **MARY C. (--?--)**, on 30 October 1918, Kosciusko County, IN. She died on 26 April 1996, IN at age 96.

2.8.4.8.1 LOUISE CAUFFMAN is also referred to as **WILMA L.** in some sources. She was born on 6 March 1922. She married **ROBERT PARTRIDGE**.

2.8.4.8.1.1 JUDY PARTRIDGE

2.8.4.8.1.2 MICHAEL PARTRIDGE

2.8.4.8.2 MARY EVELYN CAUFFMAN was born on 5 November 1925. She married **KENNETH KNIGHT**.

2.8.4.8.2.1 SAMUEL KNIGHT

2.8.5 EMMA KLINGER is also referred to as **EMALINE** in some sources. She was born on 24 February 1851, Pennsylvania. She married **FREDERICK A. SIBERT** on 12 August 1871, Kosciusko County, IN. She died in June 1911, at age 60.

2.8.5.1 IDA MAY SIBERT was born on 2 September 1872, Kosciusko County, IN. She died on 12 February 1878, Kosciusko County, IN, at age 5.

2.8.5.2 CALVIN E. SIBERT was born on 28 July 1874, Indiana. He married **MAUD ALICE NORTHRUP**, daughter of **ERIE NORTHRUP** and **JOSEPHINE (--?--)**, circa 1901.

2.8.5.2.1 EMERSON C. SIBERT was born on 25 April 1901, Nebraska.

2.8.5.2.2 GLADYS SIBERT was born on 2 September 1904, Nebraska.

2.8.5.2.3 EARIE SIBERT was born on 20 May 1907. He was born before 1910.

2.8.5.2.4 ROY F. SIBERT was born on 15 August 1908, Nebraska.

2.8.5.2.5 OREY H. SIBERT was born on 10 November 1913.

2.8.5.3 CHARLES F. SIBERT was born on 22 November 1878, Indiana. He married **LELA TIBBITTS** circa 1909.

2.8.5.3.1 LUCILLE F. SIBERT was born on 28 January 1913, Nebraska. She married **WILLIAM HANNON** after 1930.

2.8.5.3.1.1 CHARLES W. HANNON was born on 7 May 1935.

2.8.5.3.2 CHARLES B. SIBERT also went by the name of **BRUCE**. He was born on 7 March 1915, Nebraska.

2.8.5.3.3 JEAN M. SIBERT was born on 10 April 1917, Nebraska.

2.8.5.3.4 ELIZABETH ANNE SIBERT was born on 23 March 1920, Nebraska.

2.8.5.4 RENA SIBERT was born on 22 August 1882, Iowa. She married **JAMES ELMER RICHMOND** circa 1898.

2.8.5.4.1 VERNA RICHMOND was born on 16 June 1899, Nebraska. She married **CLAUD DOWNHOUR**.

2.8.5.4.1.1 FRANK F. DOWNHOUR was born on 13 July 1918. He died on 16 July 1918.

2.8.5.4.1.2 ALICE J. DOWNHOUR was born on 14 October 1921, Montana.

2.8.5.4.1.3 RONALD R. DOWNHOUR was born on 1 November 1923, Montana.

2.8.5.4.1.4 JEAN F. DOWNHOUR was born on 7 May 1930.

2.8.5.4.2 MARIE RICHMOND was born on 22 April 1902, South Dakota. She married **AUGUSTUS SCHUCK** circa 1924.

2.8.5.4.3 HARRY C. RICHMOND was born on 11 March 1905, South Dakota. He married **ELSIE B. ASEMAN** circa 1925.

2.8.5.4.3.1 PATRICIA ANN RICHMOND was born on 2 February 1929, Montana.

2.8.5.4.4 A.C. RICHMOND was born on 17 August 1907, South Dakota.

2.8.5.4.5 GLADYS RICHMOND was born on 19 November 1910, South Dakota.

2.8.5.4.6 MYRLE RICHMOND is also referred to as **MERLE** in some sources. He was born on 20 February 1913, South Dakota. He married **ANN HILL**.

2.8.5.4.6.1 HAZEL L. RICHMOND was born on 1 December 1934.

2.8.5.5 LULU SIBERT is also referred to as **LULA** in some sources. She was born on 10 November 1888. She married **FLOYD ERNEST KEITH**.

2.8.5.5.1 GEORGE S. KEITH was born on 4 January 1914, New York.

2.8.5.5.2 EMMA B. KEITH was born on 3 June 1916, New York.

2.8.5.5.3 ERNEST F. KEITH is also referred to as **FLOYD E.** in some sources. He was born on 7 May 1918, New York.

2.8.5.5.4 MARJORIE L. KEITH was born on 8 November 1919, Florida.

2.8.5.5.5 ARCHIBALD KEITH was born on 24 February 1924, Illinois.

2.8.5.5.6 LULU M. "BESSIE" KEITH is also referred to as **LULA MAY** in some sources. She was born on 26 May 1926, Illinois.

2.8.5.6 FREDERICK A. SIBERT was born on 2 January 1893. He married **RAE JACOBS**.

2.8.5.6.1 IRVING SIBERT was born on 1 June 1921.

2.8.5.6.2 JOHN SIBERT was born on 14 December 1926.

2.8.6 CHARLES MONROE KLINGER was born on 24 January 1855, PA. He married **MARTHA E. BENNETT** on 23 December 1875, Kosciusko County, IN. He died on 31 July 1905, at age 50.

2.8.6.1 ARTHUR KLINGER was born on 12 March 1878. He married **EFFIE BOWMAN** on 30 September 1900, Kosciusko County, IN.

2.8.6.2 FREDERICK KLINGER was born on 9 January 1881. He married **MARGARET KELLY** on 7 September 1901, Kosciusko County, IN.

2.8.6.2.1 WILMA E. KLINGER was born on 14 February 1907.

2.8.6.3 EVA KLINGER was born on 15 November 1883. She married **JOHN OLIVER EPPLER** on 4 May 1899, Kosciusko County, IN.

2.8.6.3.1 THELMA M. EPPLER was born on 26 March 1912. She married **ARTHUR MCCLURE** circa 1929.

2.8.6.3.1.1 DONALD L. MCCLURE was born on 10 December 1930. He married **ELLEN JOSEPHINE FERGUSON** on 20 December 1957.

2.8.6.3.1.1.1 ALLEN LEE MCCLURE was born on 15 October 1959.

2.8.6.3.1.1.2 DONNA JO MCCLURE was born on 8 June 1961.

2.8.6.3.1.2 KENNETH MCCLURE was born on 30 July 1935. He married **MARY ANN PALATINUS**.

2.8.6.3.1.2.1 DEBRA SUE MCCLURE was born on 31 January 1957.

2.8.6.3.1.2.2 MARCIA ANN MCCLURE was born circa 17 March 1960.

2.8.6.3.2 ETHEL E. EPPLER was born on 4 March 1916. She married **CLAYTON WRIGHT** circa 1933. She married **HARLEY E. HOLDERMAN** on 3 September 1935.

2.8.6.3.2.1 RAYMOND WRIGHT married **DELORES (--?--)** in 1956.

2.8.6.3.2.1.1 COLLEEN WRIGHT was born on 30 December 1960.

2.8.6.3.2.1.2 TINA MARIE WRIGHT was born circa 14 March 1962.

2.8.6.4 CHARLES E. KLINGER was born on 1 March 1885, Prairie Township, Kosciusko County, IN. He married **ESTELLA CARTWRIGHT** on 20 October 1903, Kosciusko County, IN. He married **MARY JACOBS HARRINGTON**, daughter of **JOHN HARRINGTON**, on 28 October 1916, St. Joseph, Berrien County, MI. He married **CLARA L CASSLER**, daughter of **LOUIS CASSLER** and **HANNAH (--?--)**, on 19 March 1921, St. Joseph, Berrien County, MI. He died on 26 April 1934, South Bend, St. Joseph County, IN, at age 49. He was buried on 28 April 1934, at Union Cemetery, Warsaw, Kosciusko County, IN.

2.8.6.4.1 EVA L. KLINGER was born on 8 August 1904.

2.8.6.4.2 CHARLES MONROE KLINGER was born on 12 February 1917. He married **THELMA MAE MAXWELL**, daughter of **CLAUDE G. MAXWELL** and **LELAH A. CULLISION**. He died on 4 August 1962, St. Joseph Hospital, South Bend, St. Joseph County, IN, at age 45. He was buried on 7 August 1962, at Fairview Cemetery, Mishawaka, St. Joseph County, IN.

2.8.6.4.2.1 MARY ANN KLINGER was born on 18 September 1959. She married **(--?--) CLINEHENS**. She and **(--?--) CLINEHENS** were divorced on 3 April 1989. She married **GREGORY MICHAEL KRAKOSKE** on 15 December 1990, Mishawaka, St. Joseph County, IN.

2.8.6.4.3 JOSEPH FRANCIS KLINGER was born on 22 March 1920, South Bend, St. Joseph County, IN. He married **MARGARET CAMPBELL** circa 1943. He married **LOUISE B. BOWERS**, daughter of **HARRY BOWERS** and **CORA PLUMMER**, on 14 February 1947, St. Paul's Lutheran Church, South Bend, St. Joseph County, IN. He died on 8 July 1989, Memorial Hospital, South Bend, St. Joseph County, IN, at age 69. He was buried on 10 July 1989, at Highland Cemetery, South Bend, St. Joseph County, IN.

2.8.6.4.3.1 CHARLES RONALD KLINGER was born on 14 September 1944. He married **SHAN (--?--).** Ronald lives in Odessa, TX.

2.8.6.4.3.2 ARTHUR MONROE KLINGER was born on 2 October 1947. He married **JENNY (--?--).**

2.8.6.4.3.3 JANICE MARY KLINGER was born on 3 July 1956. She married **ERNIE RETEK.**

2.8.6.5 IDA KLINGER was born on 11 July 1888. She married **CLARENCE ROBINSON** on 11 July 1907, Kosciusko County, IN. She married **JOHN MCPHERSON** after 1920. She died on 13 February 1943, at age 54.

2.8.6.5.1 HOWARD W. ROBINSON was born on 13 February 1909. He married **PAULINE DURHAM.**

2.8.6.5.2 ARTHUR J. ROBINSON was born on 11 June 1911. He married **FENETA R. TRUITT** in October 1940. He married **HELEN ANN HANEZ** on 1 May 1948.

2.8.6.5.2.1 CURTIS JOEL ROBINSON was born on 12 December 1951.

2.8.6.6 WALTER KLINGER was born on 10 October 1891, Kosciusko County, IN. He died on 11 October 1891, Kosciusko County, IN.

2.8.7 ELOMA KLINGER is also referred to as **ALOMA** in some sources. She was born on 5 March 1858, Pennsylvania. She married **EMANUEL RUCH** on 28 December 1876, Kosciusko County, IN. She died on 16 September 1928, at age 70.

2.8.7.1 MYRTLE RUCH was born on 24 March 1881. She died on 29 August 1939, at age 58.

2.8.7.2 CLARA RUCH was born on 12 June 1888. She died on 1 August 1939, at age 51.

2.8.8 JOHN A. KLINGER was born on 2 September 1860, Dauphin County, PA. He died on 17 February 1884, Kosciusko County, IN, at age 23. He was buried at Stony Point Cemetery, Clunette, Kosciusko County, IN.

2.9 ELIZABETH KLINGER was born on 13 October 1825. She was baptized on 11 January 1826, Zion (Klinger's) Church, Erdman, Lykens Township, Dauphin County, PA. She married **NICOLAUS MERTZ**, son of **HEINRICH MERTZ** and **SOPHIA (--?--).** She died before 1858.

2.10 SAMUEL KLINGER was born on 23 October 1826. He married **MARY SHAFFER**, daughter of **FRANCIS SHAFFER** and **EVA MARIA TROUTMAN,** on 25 December 1858, Rev. Elias Miller, officiating. According to Mary Klinger, "Samuel and Mary lived most of their married life in Uniontown (Pillow). Samuel served in the Civil War from 30-10-1862 to 1-6-1865, and at least part of that time was present for duty in Virginia. In July 1890 he applied for and received a pension. After Samuel's death, Mary lived with their dau. Agnes in the same town." He died on 14 October 1897, at age 70. He was buried at Union Cemetery, northeast of, Pillow, Northumberland County, PA.

2.10.1 EMMA J. KLINGER was born in April 1854. She married **ELIAS C. MILLER** in 1873, Pillow, Dauphin County, PA. Mary Klinger says that Emma lived in Williamstown and operated a produce store. She died in 1929. She was buried at Williamstown, PA.

2.10.1.1 MORRIS W. MILLER was born circa 1874, Pennsylvania.

2.10.1.2 STELLA MILLER was born circa 1876, Pennsylvania.

2.10.1.3 JENNIE M. MILLER was born in February 1877, Pennsylvania.

2.10.1.4 MARY MILLER was born circa 1879, Pennsylvania.

2.10.1.5 EDNA L. MILLER was born in March 1881, Pennsylvania.

2.10.1.6 HARRY E. MILLER was born circa 1884, Pennsylvania.

2.10.1.7 CLAYTON R. MILLER was born in July 1886, Pennsylvania. He died in 1939. He was buried at Williamstown, PA.

2.10.1.8 AMY M. MILLER was born in December 1889, Pennsylvania. She married **JAMES T. GRAHAM** circa 1909. She died before 1930.

2.10.1.8.1 EMMA N. GRAHAM was born circa 1913, Pennsylvania.

2.10.1.8.2 AMY M. GRAHAM was born circa 1918, Pennsylvania.

2.10.2 BENJAMIN F. KLINGER was born on 21 April 1860. He married **JANE (--?--)** circa 1891. He died on 19 February 1942, at age 81. He was buried at Pillow, Dauphin County, PA.

2.10.2.1 EMMA L. KLINGER was born in August 1892. She married **(--?--) MCCLEELLAN.**

2.10.2.2 EVA O. KLINGER was unmarried. She was born in December 1895.

2.10.3 AGNES KLINGER was born on 1 January 1862. According to some sources, Agnes lived on the Shaffer homestead in Pillow, Dauphin County, PA. She married **DAVID ZERBE** in November 1902. She died on 16 July 1926, at age 64. She was buried at Pillow, Dauphin County, PA.

2.10.3.1 JEREMIAH ALBERT FEGLEY was born on 21 August 1863, According to some sources, Jeremiah was adopted by Agnes Klinger. He married **CATHERINE MOYER.** He died in 1949.

2.10.3.2 KATHARINE RADEL was born circa 1908, Pennsylvania. The 1920 Census lists a "Catherine Zerbe" as the daughter of Agnes Klinger and David Zerbe. According to Mary Klinger, Katharine was the daughter of James Radel and was adopted by Agnes Klinger. She married **JAMES TSCHOPP.**

2.11 JESTINA KLINGER is also referred to as **JOSTIA** in some sources. She was born on 3 March 1830. She was baptized on 18 April 1830, Zion (Klinger's) Church, Erdman, Lykens Township, Dauphin County, PA. She died before 1859.

2.12 LEAH KLINGER was born on 20 March 1832. She was baptized on 24 May 1835, Zion (Klinger's) Church, Erdman, Lykens Township, Dauphin County, PA. She died before 1859.

2.13 EVE ELIZABETH KLINGER was born on 4 March 1834.

2.14 HANNAH KLINGER was born on 20 March 1835. She was baptized on 24 May 1835, Zion (Klinger's) Church, Erdman, Lykens Township, Dauphin County, PA.

2.15 PHILIP KLINGER was born on 7 November 1836. He married **PHOEBY ANN KOCH** on 18 December 1855, St. John's Lutheran Church, Berrysburg, Mifflin Township, Dauphin County, PA.

2.15.1 (--?--) KLINGER married **WILLIAM BAINBRIDGE.**

2.15.2 SARAH KLINGER married **(--?--) HERNER.**

2.15.3 FIETTA KLINGER married **DANIEL HERB.**

2.15.4 WILLIAM HENRY KLINGER was baptized, Zion (Klinger's) Church, Erdman, Lykens Township, Dauphin County, PA. He was born on 4 July 1859.

2.15.5 PRESCILLA KLINGER was born on 2 March 1862. She was baptized on 18 May 1862, Zion (Klinger's) Church, Erdman, Lykens Township, Dauphin County, PA. She married **WILLIAM D. DAVIS** circa 1878. Mary Klinger notes that Prescilla and William lived on the south side of Klingerstown, PA. She died on 28 August 1929, Dauphin County, PA, at age 67. She was buried at Zion (Klinger's) Church Cemetery, Erdman, Lykens Township, Dauphin County, PA.

2.15.5.1 CHARLES CLINTON DAVIS was born on 10 August 1879, Dauphin County, PA. He was baptized on 19 October 1879, Zion (Klinger's) Church, Erdman, Lykens Township, Dauphin County, PA. He married **HANNAH STROHECKER** circa 1900. He died in 1944, Dauphin County, PA. He was buried at Zion (Klinger's) Church, Erdman, Lykens Township, Dauphin County, PA.

2.15.5.1.1 MOSES WILLIAM DAVIS was born on 1 November 1901. He was baptized on 23 November 1901, Zion (Klinger's) Church, Erdman, Lykens Township, Dauphin County, PA.

2.15.5.1.2 HOWARD E. DAVIS was born circa 1905, Pennsylvania.

2.15.5.1.3 RUSSELL DAVIS was born circa 1913, Pennsylvania.

2.15.5.2 WILLIAM ALBERT DAVIS is also referred to as **ALBERT W. DAVIS** in some sources. He was born on 7 October 1881, Dauphin County, PA. He was baptized on 1 January 1882, Zion (Klinger's) Church, Erdman, Lykens Township, Dauphin County, PA. He married **BEULAH WIEST**, daughter of **JOHN BAUM WIEST** and **HANNAH WIEST STROHECKER,** on 1 July 1905, Zion (Klinger's) Church, Erdman, Lykens Township, Dauphin County, PA. He died on 26 April 1967, Dauphin County, PA, at age 85. He was buried at Zion (Klinger's) Church Cemetery, Erdman, Lykens Township, Dauphin County, PA.

2.15.5.2.1 DWIGHT DAVIS

2.15.5.2.2 REGINALD DAVIS was born circa 1906, Pennsylvania.

2.15.5.2.3 DELPHIN D. DAVIS was born in 1907. He married **HELEN E. (--?--).** He died Klingerstown, Schuylkill County, PA.

2.15.5.2.4 LEROY ELWELL DAVIS was born on 5 June 1912, Dauphin County, PA. He was baptized on 28 October 1916, Zion (Klinger's) Church, Erdman, Lykens Township, Dauphin County, PA. He died in 1976, Lykens Township, Dauphin County, PA. He was buried at Zion (Klinger's) Church Cemetery, Erdman, Lykens Township, Dauphin County, PA.

2.15.5.2.5 DARWIN D. DAVIS was born circa 1910. Some sources record that he was born on 26 February 1920, Schuylkill County, PA. He died on 1 March 1921, Dauphin County, PA, at age 1.

He was buried at Zion (Klinger's) Church Cemetery, Erdman, Lykens Township, Dauphin County, PA.

2.15.5.3 EMMA JANE DAVIS was born on 28 December 1883. She was baptized on 20 April 1884, Zion (Klinger's) Church, Erdman, Lykens Township, Dauphin County, PA. She married **HENRY W. ENGLE** on 4 March 1905, Zion (Klinger's) Church, Erdman, Lykens Township, Dauphin County, PA.

2.15.5.4 CORA MAY DAVIS was born on 24 January 1886. She was baptized on 1 May 1886, Zion (Klinger's) Church, Erdman, Lykens Township, Dauphin County, PA. She died on 14 February 1895, at age 9.

2.15.5.5 CATHERINE ANNORA DAVIS was born on 28 April 1888. She was baptized on 20 July 1888, Zion (Klinger's) Church, Erdman, Lykens Township, Dauphin County, PA. She died on 11 February 1895, at age 6.

2.15.5.6 PHILIP WALTER DAVIS is also referred to as **WALTER H. DAVIS** in some sources. He was born on 14 August 1890. He was baptized on 9 November 1890, Zion (Klinger's) Church, Erdman, Lykens Township, Dauphin County, PA. He married **BARBARA ELURA ERDMAN**, daughter of **JACOB JOSEPH ERDMAN** and **CHRISTIANA KLINGER,** on 13 April 1912, St. Michael's Church, Klingerstown, Schuylkill County, PA. He died on 11 August 1965, at age 74. He was buried at Zion (Klinger's) Church, Erdman, Lykens Township, Dauphin County, PA.

2.15.5.6.1 WELLIE C. DAVIS was born on 15 December 1915. He died on 3 March 1916. He was buried at Zion (Klinger's) Church Cemetery, Erdman, Lykens Township, Dauphin County, PA.

2.15.5.6.2 EVA GRACE DAVIS was born on 29 September 1918, Klingerstown, Schuylkill County, PA. She was baptized on 9 November 1918, St. Michael's Church, Klingerstown, Schuylkill County, PA. She married **CHARLES E. KISSINGER**. She died on 22 December 2006, Tremont Health and Rehabilitation Center, Tremont, Schuylkill County, PA, at age 88. According to a newspaper obituary, Eva was a hair dresser and owned a beauty shop in Klingerstown for more than 50 years. She was buried at Union Cemetery, Gratz, Dauphin County, PA.

2.15.5.6.2.1 ROY KISSINGER married **ALICE WETZEL**.

2.15.5.6.2.1.1 ANDREW KISSINGER

2.15.5.6.2.1.2 KATHRYN KISSINGER married **(--?--) SNOWE**.

2.15.5.6.3 ELISE ELURA DAVIS was born on 16 May 1930. She married **(--?--) BURRELL**.

2.15.5.7 SALLIE PHEBE PRECILLA DAVIS was born on 12 October 1892. She was baptized on 12 February 1893, Zion (Klinger's) Church, Erdman, Lykens Township, Dauphin County, PA. She died on 6 February 1895, at age 2.

2.15.5.8 BELTON RAYMOND DAVIS was born on 8 May 1895, Rough and Ready, Schuylkill County, PA. He was baptized on 16 June 1895, Zion (Klinger's) Church, Erdman, Lykens Township, Dauphin County, PA. He married **MAZIE S. FETTEROLF**. He married **KATIE L. FETTER** circa 1926. He died in 1987. He was buried at Zion (Klinger's) Church, Erdman, Lykens Township, Dauphin County, PA.

2.15.5.8.1 LEON JAY DAVIS was born on 1 October 1916. He was baptized on 28 October 1916. He married **ANNA PRISCILLA HOFFMAN** on 18 May 1940, Zion (Klinger's) Church, Erdman, Lykens Township, Dauphin County, PA.

2.15.5.8.2 LAWRENCE ELWOOD DAVIS was born on 19 May 1933. He was baptized on 27 June 1933, Zion (Klinger's) Church, Erdman, Lykens Township, Dauphin County, PA.

2.15.5.9 HARRY AUSTIN DAVIS also went by the name of **AUSTIN**. He was born on 12 October 1897, Dauphin County, PA. He was baptized on 27 January 1898, Zion (Klinger's) Church, Erdman, Lykens Township, Dauphin County, PA. He married **HATTIE SCHLEGEL** circa 1920. Austin operated an insurance agency in Klingerstown, PA. He died on 19 March 1989, at age 91. He was buried at St. Michael's Church Cemetery, Klingerstown, Schuylkill County, PA.

2.15.5.9.1 BRYANT AUSTIN DAVIS was born on 18 January 1920, Dauphin County, PA. He was baptized on 23 May 1920, Zion (Klinger's) Church, Erdman, Lykens Township, Dauphin County, PA. He died on 19 May 1921, at age 1.

2.15.5.9.2 MELVIN H. DAVIS was born in 1922. He died in 1942, in plane crash while a sergeant in the US Air Force.

2.15.5.9.3 WILLARD STANLY DAVIS was born on 17 May 1924. He was baptized on 8 October 1924, St. Michael's Church, Klingerstown, Schuylkill County, PA.

2.15.5.9.4 ALMA JEAN DAVIS was born on 13 September 1927. She was baptized on 11 December 1927, St. Michael's Church, Klingerstown, Schuylkill County, PA. She married **GILBERT EUGENE TROUTMAN**, son of **JOY ABRAHAM TROUTMAN** and **ELSIE V. TROUTMAN,** on 30 January 1943. Alma lives in Klingerstown, Schuylkill County, PA.

2.15.5.9.4.1 JAMES ALLEN TROUTMAN was born on 27 July 1943. He was baptized on 7 October 1943, St. Michael's Church, Klingerstown, Schuylkill County, PA. He married **MYRA (--?--)** circa 1966. In 2008, James was living in Klingerstown, Schuylkill County, PA.

2.15.5.9.4.2 JUDITH ANN TROUTMAN was born on 20 November 1946. She was baptized on 12 March 1947, St. Michael's Church, Klingerstown, Schuylkill County, PA. She married **GARY LEE SHADE**, son of **LAWRENCE ELVIN SHADE** and **LENA LUELLA MORGAN,** circa 1968. In 2008, Judy was living in Klingerstown, Schuylkill County, PA.

2.15.5.9.4.2.1 CHRIS SHADE was born circa 1970, Schuylkill County, PA. She married **DENNIS SCHWALM** circa 1994.

2.15.5.9.4.3 DALE TROUTMAN was born on 9 April 1948, Schuylkill County, PA. He was baptized on 23 October 1948, St. Michael's Church, Klingerstown, Schuylkill County, PA. He married **YVONNE (--?--)** circa 1971. In 2008, Dale was living in Klingerstown, Schuylkill County, PA.

2.15.5.9.4.4 SHEILA JEAN TROUTMAN was born on 3 January 1950, Klingerstown, Schuylkill County, PA. She was baptized on 25 March 1950, St. Michael's Church, Klingerstown, Schuylkill County, PA. In 2008, Sheila was living in Holiday, FL.

2.15.5.9.4.5 KAYE LOUISE TROUTMAN is also referred to as **KAY** in some sources. She was born on 29 June 1951, Klingerstown, Schuylkill County, PA. She was baptized on 28 October 1951, St. Michael's Church, Klingerstown, Schuylkill County, PA. She married **MICHAEL B. WHARTON** on 28 July 1973, St. Michael's Lutheran Church, Klingerstown, Schuylkill County, PA. In 2008, Kay was living in York Haven, PA.

2.15.5.9.4.6 VICKIE TROUTMAN was born on 1 April 1954, Schuylkill County, PA. She married **JERRY NARLOCK** circa 1977. In 2008, Vickie was living in Box Elder, SD.

2.15.5.9.4.6.1 JARED NARLOCK was born circa 1980. He married **NICKIE (--?--)** circa 2003.

2.15.5.9.4.6.2 BRANDON NARLOCK was born circa 1982.

2.15.5.9.4.7 ELAINE MARIE TROUTMAN was born on 12 July 1959, Klingerstown, Schuylkill County, PA. Some sources record that she was born on 12 July 1959, Sunbury, Northumberland Co., PA. She was baptized on 20 September 1959, St. Michael's Church, Klingerstown, Schuylkill County, PA. She married **JAMES MONROE ARTZ** on 20 August 1988, St. Michael's Lutheran Church, Klingerstown, Schuylkill County, PA.

2.15.5.9.4.7.1 TYLER ARTZ was born circa 1990, PA.

2.15.5.9.5 SHIRLEY CARINE DAVIS was born on 31 July 1929. She was baptized on 24 November 1929, St. Michael's Church, Klingerstown, Schuylkill County, PA. She died on 23 May 1934, at age 4. She was buried at Zion (Klinger's) Church, Erdman, Lykens Township, Dauphin County, PA. Some sources list Shirley Davis as married to a Paul Shiffer, but since she apparently died at the age of 5, this is probably incorrect. As further confirmation of this, there are baptismal records at St. Michael's Church in Klingerstown for a Paul T. Shiffer and a Norma Davis.

2.15.5.10 EVA A. DAVIS was born in 1901. She married **HOWARD MONROE ARTZ**. She died on 4 January 1980, St. Luke's Hospital, Maumee, Lucas County, OH.

2.15.5.10.1 HELEN ARTZ was born circa 1920.

2.15.5.10.2 PHYLLIS ARTZ was born circa 1928.

2.15.5.10.3 BEVERLYANN ARTZ was born circa 1938.

2.15.5.11 CARLOS DAVIS is also referred to as **IKE OR CHARLES EDMOND** in some sources. He was born on 20 September 1902. He was baptized on 7 October 1902, Zion (Klinger's) Church, Erdman, Lykens Township, Dauphin County, PA. Carlos, known as "Ike", operated a Sunoco gas station and store in Klingerstown, Schuylkill County. He died on 16 October 1986, at age 84.

2.15.5.12 LOLA MARIE DAVIS was born on 20 June 1905. She was baptized on 22 October 1905, Zion (Klinger's) Church, Erdman, Lykens Township, Dauphin County, PA. She married **DANIEL WEBSTER ARTZ**, son of **HENRY K. ARTZ** and **CHRISTIANA C. MANN**. She died on 3 September 1995,

Valley View, Schuylkill County, PA, at age 90. She was buried at Saint Pauls United Church of Christ Cemetery, Sacramento, Schuylkill County, PA.

2.15.5.12.1 MARIE M. ARTZ was born circa 1922.

2.15.5.12.2 FAYNE HENRY ARTZ was born on 24 August 1926, Valley View, Schuylkill County, PA. He was buried on 15 March 1931, at Saint Pauls United Church of Christ Cemetery, Sacramento, Schuylkill County, PA. He died on 11 May 1931, in an auto accident Schuylkill County, PA, at age 4.

2.15.6 PHILLIP KLINGER was born on 1 April 1868, Dauphin County, PA. Some sources record that he was born in May 1873, Pennsylvania. He married **MARY DIANA TSCHOPP**, daughter of **ABSALOM TSCHOPP** and **ELIZABETH WITMER**, circa 1889. Some sources suggest that he and **ELIZABETH IDA TSCHOPP** were married circa 1902. He married **ELIZABETH IDA TSCHOPP**, daughter of **ABSALOM TSCHOPP** and **ELIZABETH WITMER**, after 1910, but apparently they lived as husband and wife beginning around 1904. He died on 27 January 1950, at his home on North Street, Wiconisco, Dauphin County, PA, at age 81. He was buried on 31 January 1950, at Calvary United Methodist Cemetery, Wiconisco, Dauphin County, PA. According to a newspaper obituary, Phillip retired from the America Briquet Company in Lykens, PA. He was survived by seventeen children, including ten daughters and seven sons, as well as 72 grandchildren and a number of great-grandchildren.

2.15.6.1 MAUD ELNORA KLINGER also went by the name of **MAUDE ELIZABETH**. She was born on 21 April 1892. Some sources record that she was born in April 1891. She was baptized on 17 March 1896, Zion (Klinger's) Church, Erdman, Lykens Township, Dauphin County, PA. Troy Schreiber indicates that Maud and Walter never married and that they separated sometime after 1920. She married **FREDERICK FENZEL SR.** circa 1922. She died on 4 March 1975, Harrisburg, Dauphin County, PA, at age 82. She was buried at Calvary United Methodist Church Cemetery, Wiconisco, Dauphin County, PA.

2.15.6.1.1 ROYCE E. BUFFINGTON is also referred to as **ROY E.** in some sources. He was born in 1909. Roy apparently moved to California.

2.15.6.1.2 ELLEN MARIE DIETRICH also went by the name of **TILLIE**. She was born on 25 September 1911. Ellen was for a time raised by Lloyd and Maud Buffington, and some sources list Ellen "Tillie" Dietrich as "Tillie Buffington." She married **CARLOS RAYMOND SCHEIB**, son of **FRANCIS WASHINGTON SCHEIB** and **SALOME ELLEN WELKER**, Valley View, Schuylkill County, PA. She died on 10 December 2004, Polk Assisted Living, Millersburg, Dauphin County, PA, at age 93. She was buried on 14 December 2004, at Union Cemetery, Pillow, Dauphin County, PA.

2.15.6.1.2.1 RONALD ELWOOD SCHEIB was born on 24 April 1935. He married **LARAE LYNN KESSLER.** .

2.15.6.1.2.1.1 VICKIE SCHEIB was born in November 1960.

2.15.6.1.2.1.2 WENDY SCHEIB was born in February 1964.

2.15.6.1.2.2 PATRICIA LOU SCHEIB was born on 24 September 1937. She married **ROBERT L. LEITZEL**, son of **ALBERT LEITZEL** and **STELLA PAUL.** .

2.15.6.1.2.2.1 DIANE ELAINE LEITZEL was born on 4 November 1957. She married **JAMES KITSON**.

2.15.6.1.2.2.2 SANDRA LEE LEITZEL was born on 14 November 1959. She married **THOMAS ERDMAN**.

2.15.6.1.2.2.2.1 ASHLEE ELIZABETH ERDMAN was born on 9 September 1986.

2.15.6.1.2.2.3 MICHAEL ROBERT LEITZEL was born on 9 September 1961. He married **DANIELLE KEEFER**. He married **KAREN OTTENGIER**.

2.15.6.1.2.2.3.1 KODY MICHAEL LEITZEL was born on 8 April 1988.

2.15.6.1.3 FREDERICK ALVIN FENZEL was born on 18 December 1923. He married **ETHEL JANE CROSSON**. He died on 10 May 2005, Lykens, Dauphin County, PA, at age 81.

2.15.6.1.3.1 KAREN DIANE FENZEL was born on 17 February 1952. She married **LARRY LEE WINGARD**.

2.15.6.1.3.2 DEBRA KAY FENZEL was born on 10 September 1954. She married **JEFFREY STEVEN BIGGERS**.

2.15.6.2 GERTRUDE ISABELLA KLINGER also went by the name of **GERTRUDE ISABELLE**. She was born on 9 July 1894, Upper Paxton Township, Dauphin County, PA. Some sources record that she was born in July 1893, Pennsylvania. She was baptized on 17 March 1896, Zion (Klinger's) Church, Erdman, Lykens Township, Dauphin County, PA. She married **Charles Allen Lenker Sr.**, son of **Clayton Johnathan Lenker** and **Ebbie Jane Koppenheffer,** circa 1912. She died on 5 January 1977, Halifax, Dauphin County, PA, at age 82.

2.15.6.2.1 Herbert Charles Lenker was born on 1 June 1913, Upper Paxton Township, Dauphin County, PA. He married **Beulah Mae Snody**, daughter of **James Snody** and **Cora Schrawder**, on 24 December 1934. He married **Josephine Hardesty Schlegel** on 3 October 1946. He died on 26 December 1996, Harrisburg, Dauphin County, PA, at age 83.

2.15.6.2.1.1 Harvey James Lenker was born on 11 September 1935. He married **Rose A. Chubb**. He died on 14 January 2006, Halifax, Dauphin County, PA, at age 70.

2.15.6.2.1.2 Pearl Marie Lenker was born on 10 February 1937. She married **Alvin Howard Dietrich**. She died on 28 March 2007, Halifax, Dauphin County, PA, at age 70.

2.15.6.2.1.2.1 Alvin Howard Dietrich Jr. was born on 20 July 1955. He married **Connie Sands**.

2.15.6.2.1.2.2 Debby Kaye Dietrich was born on 26 June 1957. She married **Barry K. Whary**.

2.15.6.2.1.2.3 Nancy Darlene Dietrich was born on 19 April 1961. She married **Kyle Yoder**.

2.15.6.2.1.2.4 Judy Ann Dietrich married **Warren D. Pottiger**. She was born on 9 April 1964.

2.15.6.2.1.2.5 Trudy Ann Dietrich was born on 9 April 1964. She married **Craig S. Kessler**.

2.15.6.2.1.3 William Robert Lenker was born in 1940. He married **Nancy L. Bowles**.

2.15.6.2.1.4 Steven Craig Lenker was born in March 1949.

2.15.6.2.2 Pauline Elizabeth Lenker was born on 3 January 1915. She married **Harry W. Forney**, son of **John Henry Forney** and **Sarah Jane Umholtz**. Pauline and Harry had no children. She died on 3 October 1952, of leukemia, Millersburg, Dauphin County, PA, at age 37.

2.15.6.2.3 Mildred Marie Lenker was born on 12 July 1916. She married **Clarence Roush**. She died on 10 July 1999, Halifax, Dauphin County, PA, at age 82.

2.15.6.2.3.1 (--?--) Roush was born stillborn.

2.15.6.2.4 Alverta Mae Lenker was born on 29 July 1918, Dauphin County, PA. She married **Floyd Allen Miller** on 24 December 1935. She died on 15 May 1983, Halifax, Dauphin County, PA, at age 64.

2.15.6.2.4.1 Carl James Miller was born on 29 March 1937. He married **June Marie Smeltz**.

2.15.6.2.4.1.1 Ricky Allen Miller was born on 4 January 1956.

2.15.6.2.4.1.2 Dawn Louise Miller was born on 14 January 1957. She married **Michael Gromley**. She and **Michael Gromley** were divorced. She married **Wayne Herb**.

2.15.6.2.4.1.2.1 Jeremy Herb

2.15.6.2.4.1.3 Michael Lee Miller was born on 1 July 1959. He married **Joann (--?--)**. He and **Joann (--?--)** were divorced. He married **Denise Wilkinson**.

2.15.6.2.4.1.3.1 April Miller

2.15.6.2.4.1.3.2 Karen Miller

2.15.6.2.4.1.3.3 Michael Lee Miller Jr.

2.15.6.2.4.1.4 Teresa Ann Miller was born on 11 September 1960. She married **Ralph Ohmacht**.

2.15.6.2.4.1.4.1 Adam Ohmacht

2.15.6.2.4.1.4.2 Christopher Ohmacht

2.15.6.2.4.1.4.3 Dana Ohmacht

2.15.6.2.4.2 **JANET MARIE MILLER** was born on 16 January 1941. She married **RALPH LEROY SCHOLL**. She and **RALPH LEROY SCHOLL** were divorced. She married **LAWRENCE SUNG**.

    2.15.6.2.4.2.1 **DERWIN L. SCHOLL**

    2.15.6.2.4.2.2 **DIERDRE SCHOLL**

2.15.6.2.4.3 **SANDRA ANN MILLER** was born on 7 January 1942, Halifax, Dauphin County, PA. She married **RALPH LEROY SCHOLL**. She died on 27 November 2012, Mechanicsburg, Cumberland County, PA, at age 70, at her daughter's residence. She was buried on 3 December 2012, at Grubb's Church Cemetery, Chapman, Snyder County, PA. According to a newspaper obituary, Sandra was a retired seamstress.

    2.15.6.2.4.3.1 **DWAYNE L MILLER.** Dwayne lives in Sunbury, PA.

    2.15.6.2.4.3.2 **DEIRDRE SCHOLL** married **(--?--) HANSEN.** Deirdre lives in Mechanicsburg, PA.

    2.15.6.2.4.3.3 **DERWIN SCHOLL.** Derwin lives in Northumberland, PA.

2.15.6.2.4.4 **LINDA JEAN MILLER** was born on 15 August 1943. She married **OSCAR M. WEAVER**. She died in May 1979, at age 35.

    2.15.6.2.4.4.1 **CHESTER W. WEAVER**

    2.15.6.2.4.4.2 **LINDA J. WEAVER**

2.15.6.2.4.5 **RONALD LEE MILLER** was born on 18 May 1946, Halifax, Dauphin County, PA. He married **PATRICIA A. CARR**. He died on 26 September 2012, Halifax, Dauphin County, PA, at age 66. at his home on Armstrong Valley Road. According to a newspaper obituary, Ronald who lived in Halifax, PA, was a veteran of the US Marines Reserves and was retired from Bethlehem Steel. He was buried on 1 October 2012, at Reigels Bible Fellowship Cemetery, Millersburg, Dauphin County, PA.

    2.15.6.2.4.5.1 **GINA MILLER** married **(--?--) CARL.**

    2.15.6.2.4.5.2 **SONYA MILLER** married **RAYMOND LEACH**, son of **JOEL M. LEACH** and **PHYLLIS MAE LENKER**.

    2.15.6.2.4.5.3 **RHONDA MILLER** married **(--?--) FOX.**

2.15.6.2.4.6 **RALPH LEROY MILLER** was born on 16 January 1949. He married **ANNA M. SMELTZ**. He died on 19 April 1996, at age 47.

    2.15.6.2.4.6.1 **DALE L. MILLER**

    2.15.6.2.4.6.2 **DAVID L. MILLER**

    2.15.6.2.4.6.3 **DEAN L. MILLER**

    2.15.6.2.4.6.4 **DEBBIE A. MILLER**

2.15.6.2.4.7 **GARY FLOYD MILLER** was born on 9 March 1950. He married **CAROL WERT**.

    2.15.6.2.4.7.1 **CORRINA MARIE MILLER** was born on 17 April 1974. She married **MITCHELL WILLIARD**.

    2.15.6.2.4.7.2 **ANGELICA NICOLE MILLER** was born on 11 June 1986.

2.15.6.2.4.8 **JUANITA SUE MILLER** was born on 1 August 1952. She married **RICHARD SNYDER**. She and **RICHARD SNYDER** were divorced.

2.15.6.2.4.9 **TAMMY JO MILLER** was born on 22 February 1961.

2.15.6.2.5 **ALBERT RAY LENKER** was born on 23 October 1920, Lenkerville, Dauphin County, Dauphin County. He married **ERMA IRENE TEETER**. He died on 7 November 2002, Susquehanna Village, Dauphin County, Dauphin County, at age 82.

    2.15.6.2.5.1 **GREGORY ABE LENKER** was born in 1951. He died on 17 October 1967, in an automobile accident.

2.15.6.2.6 **RAYMOND FREDERICK LENKER** was born on 29 October 1922. He married **JUNE DELAINE ORNER**. He died on 17 October 1994, Halifax, Dauphin County, PA, at age 71.

    2.15.6.2.6.1 **JANICE ELAINE LENKER** was born on 21 September 1948. She married **CLAIR L. SHOOP**.

2.15.6.2.6.2 PHYLLIS MAE LENKER was born on 3 April 1953. She married JOEL M. LEACH. She and JOEL M. LEACH were divorced.

2.15.6.2.6.2.1 RAYMOND LEACH married SONYA MILLER, daughter of RONALD LEE MILLER and PATRICIA A. CARR.

2.15.6.2.7 DOROTHY VIRGINIA LENKER was born on 3 March 1924. She married FLOYD HARPER UNDERKOFFLER.

2.15.6.2.7.1 DONNA LEE UNDERKOFFLER was born on 13 February 1947. She married BARRY L. STONE SR.

2.15.6.2.7.1.1 BARRY LEE STONE JR. was born on 24 September 1969.

2.15.6.2.7.1.2 MELISSA LEE STONE was born on 26 October 1971.

2.15.6.2.7.2 RODNEY FLOYD UNDERKOFFLER was born on 2 June 1952. He married DARLEE MAURER.

2.15.6.2.7.2.1 CHRISTOPHER ALAN UNDERKOFFLER was born on 13 August 1973.

2.15.6.2.7.2.2 SHANNON RODNEY UNDERKOFFLER was born in July 1977.

2.15.6.2.7.3 PATTY JO UNDERKOFFLER was born on 17 March 1956. She married KENNETH ADAMS.

2.15.6.2.7.3.1 KENT ALLEN ADAMS

2.15.6.2.7.3.2 LINDSAY JO ADAMS

2.15.6.2.8 ALLEN FRANKLIN LENKER was born on 8 April 1926. He married SARA JANE KLINGER, daughter of HOMER EDWIN KLINGER and KATIE ELLEN MATTER. He died on 19 September 1975, at age 49. He was buried at Riverview Memorial Gardens, Halifax, Dauphin County, PA.

2.15.6.2.8.1 DAVID ALLEN LENKER was born on 24 August 1950. He married CARLEA M. LEPPERT. He and CARLEA M. LEPPERT were divorced. He married DEE SCHULER.

2.15.6.2.8.1.1 LINETTE LENKER

2.15.6.2.8.1.2 NATHANIEL LENKER

2.15.6.2.8.1.3 SARAH LENKER

2.15.6.2.8.2 JOAN MARIE LENKER was born on 14 November 1954. She married LARRY A. CHUBB.

2.15.6.2.8.2.1 MATTHEW ALLEN CHUBB was born on 17 August 1978.

2.15.6.2.9 CHARLES ALLEN LENKER JR. was born on 15 February 1929. He married WILMA LEODA CRESWELL. He died on 2 June 1978, at home, Millersburg, Dauphin County, PA, at age 49. He was buried at Riverview Memorial Gardens, Halifax, Dauphin County, PA.

2.15.6.2.9.1 MACK NELSON CRESSWELL. Charles adopted Mack after his marriage to Mack's mother Wilma.

2.15.6.2.9.2 ADAM SPENCER LENKER was born on 15 August 1964.

2.15.6.2.9.3 CHARLES ALLEN LENKER III was born on 17 April 1950. He married SHARYN ANNE LESHKO.

2.15.6.2.9.3.1 CHARLES NICHOLAS LENKER was born on 3 May 1971.

2.15.6.2.9.4 ARLENE LORAINE LENKER was born on 10 December 1953. She married JOSEPH DOYLE.

2.15.6.2.9.4.1 JAIME DOYLE

2.15.6.2.9.4.2 JAN DOYLE

2.15.6.2.10 VERNA JANE LENKER was born on 3 May 1934. She married GEORGE ALVIN SNYDER.

2.15.6.2.10.1 DENNIS EUGENE SNYDER was born on 7 October 1952.

2.15.6.2.10.2 TIMOTHY GEORGE SNYDER was born on 20 September 1954.

2.15.6.2.10.3 JEFFREY ALVIN SNYDER was born on 7 September 1956.

2.15.6.2.10.4 PATRICIA JANE SNYDER was born on 19 October 1960.

2.15.6.2.11 CLAYTON PHILIP LENKER was born on 6 June 1935, Millersburg, Dauphin County, PA. He married **SHIRLEY FAE SCHOLL**, daughter of **HENRY L. SCHOLL** and **ROSA SCHRAWDER**. He died on 20 October 2012, the Manor at Susquehanna Village, Millersburg, Dauphin County, PA, at age 77. He was buried on 24 October 2012, at Riverview Memorial Gardens, Halifax, Dauphin County, PA.

> **2.15.6.2.11.1 RANDY LEE LENKER** was born on 13 February 1954. He married **AROM THAREESUT**. He and **AROM THAREESUT** were divorced. He died on 23 September 2010, Community General Osteopathic Hospital, Harrisburg, Dauphin County, PA, at age 56. According to a newspaper obituary, Randy was a veteran of the Air Force, serving during the Vietnam War. Later, he worked as a truck driver for Verdelli Farms, Harrisburg.
>
>> **2.15.6.2.11.1.1 BRUCE L. LENKER**
>>
>> **2.15.6.2.11.1.2 JACLYN F. LENKER**
>
> **2.15.6.2.11.2 TONY LEE LENKER** was born on 25 March 1959. He married **JAN ALEXANDER**. He died on 20 April 1999, Nyssa, OR, at age 40. He was buried on 28 April 1999, at Riverview Memorial Gardens, Halifax, Dauphin County, PA.
>
>> **2.15.6.2.11.2.1 EVANGELINA LENKER**
>>
>> **2.15.6.2.11.2.2 DANIELLE LENKER**
>
> **2.15.6.2.11.3 CURTIS LEE LENKER** was born on 29 January 1963. He married **MARY SCHUERKAMP**.
>
> **2.15.6.2.11.4 RUBY IRENE LENKER** was born on 27 November 1966. She married **RICKY STROUP**. She and **RICKY STROUP** were divorced. She married **ROBERT LAMB**. She and **ROBERT LAMB** were divorced. She married **KEVIN YEAGER**. She and **KEVIN YEAGER** were divorced. She married **LAWRENCE PHELAN**.
>
>> **2.15.6.2.11.4.1 AMANDA STROUP**
>>
>> **2.15.6.2.11.4.2 KEVIN YEAGER JR.**
>>
>> **2.15.6.2.11.4.3 BRANDON YEAGER**
>>
>> **2.15.6.2.11.4.4 JENNIFER YEAGER**
>>
>> **2.15.6.2.11.4.5 RACHELLE YEAGER**
>>
>> **2.15.6.2.11.4.6 HEATHER PHELAN**

2.15.6.2.12 BERNICE JUNE LENKER was born on 9 February 1937, Lenkerville, Dauphin County, PA. She married **ROY THOMAS MITCHELL PATTON** circa 1959. She died on 16 April 2017, Millersburg, Dauphin County, PA, at age 80. She was buried on 21 April 2017, at Riverview Memorial Gardens, Halifax, Dauphin County, PA.

> **2.15.6.2.12.1 CHRISTINE A. PATTON** married **MICHAEL A. EGGLESTON**.
>
>> **2.15.6.2.12.1.1 JOSHUA EGGLESTON** married **ASHLEY (--?--)**.
>>
>>> **2.15.6.2.12.1.1.1 HEATHER EGGLESTON** married **ANDREW BLASCOVICK**. She married **ERIC BENDER**.
>>>
>>>> **2.15.6.2.12.1.1.1.1 CALEB BENDER**

2.15.6.3 BELTON GARFIELD KLINGER was born on 16 March 1897. Some sources record that he was born on 16 March 1899. He was baptized on 19 November 1905, Zion (Klinger's) Church, Erdman, Lykens Township, Dauphin County, PA. He married **MARTHA GERTRUDE GONDER**, daughter of **CHARLES OMAR GONDER** and **MABEL HANNAH LEITZEL**, circa 1921. He died on 15 May 1970, Millersburg, Dauphin County, PA, at age 71. He was buried at Oak Hill Cemetery, Millersburg, Dauphin County, PA.

> **2.15.6.3.1 BELTON EUGENE KLINGER** was born on 16 August 1921, Pennsylvania. He married **VIOLET ELIZABETH MONGOLD**, daughter of **JOHN CALVIN MONGOLD** and **PEARL E. LANTZ**. He married **MARGUERITE ARLENE SNYDER**, daughter of **MOSES SNYDER** and **ESTHER WELKER**. He died on 3 January 2001, Millersburg, Dauphin County, PA, at age 79.
>
>> **2.15.6.3.1.1 GAYLE YVONNE KLINGER** was born on 27 June 1949. She married **ROGER KOONS**. She married **LARRY NEVIN LOHR**.
>>
>>> **2.15.6.3.1.1.1 DWAYNE LEE KOONS** was born on 4 May 1969.

2.15.6.3.1.1.2 JOELLE RENE KOONS was born on 10 February 1976. She married **MICHAEL SHOOP**.

    2.15.6.3.1.1.2.1 ALEXIS SHOOP

    2.15.6.3.1.1.2.2 EMMA SHOOP

    2.15.6.3.1.1.2.3 FELICIA SHOOP

2.15.6.3.1.1.3 MATTHEW EDWARD KOONS was born circa February 1994.

2.15.6.3.1.2 DALE EUGENE KLINGER was born on 16 November 1953. He married **JOY (--?--)**.

    2.15.6.3.1.2.1 LEANN KLINGER

    2.15.6.3.1.2.2 JADEE KLINGER

    2.15.6.3.1.2.3 TOBY KLINGER

    2.15.6.3.1.2.4 MICAH KLINGER

2.15.6.3.2 RALPH LESTER KLINGER SR. was born on 4 November 1935. He married **MARY ESTHER STROUP**. He and **MARY ESTHER STROUP** were divorced. He died on 16 December 1996, Hickory, Catawba County, NC, at age 61. He was buried at Oak Hill Cemetery, Millersburg, Dauphin County, PA.

2.15.6.3.2.1 TRACY MARIE KLINGER was born on 24 October 1954. She married **DAVID EUGENE ROADCAP**. She and **DAVID EUGENE ROADCAP** were divorced.

    2.15.6.3.2.1.1 HEATHER MARIE ROADCAP was born on 30 November 1977. She married **MICHAEL NYE**.

2.15.6.3.2.2 DEBIE JO KLINGER was born on 29 June 1956. She married **EDWARD NOBLIT JR.**

    2.15.6.3.2.2.1 JESSICA MAE NOBLIT was born on 14 May 1991.

    2.15.6.3.2.2.2 JENNIFER MARIE NOBLIT was born on 28 October 1992.

    2.15.6.3.2.2.3 FRANK EUGENE KLINGER was born on 8 January 1973, Harrisburg, Dauphin Co., PA. Frank's father was Frank Eugene Stroup. He married **ERIQUE ADRIENNE BYERLY**, daughter of **RANDOLPH IRA BYERLY** and **EMMA JEAN MOORE**, on 14 August 1993, Millersburg, Dauphin Co., PA.

        2.15.6.3.2.2.3.1 GRACE REBECCA KLINGER was born on 26 January 1998, Dauphin Co., PA. She was born on 26 January 1998.

        2.15.6.3.2.2.3.2 GRANT ANDREW KLINGER was born on 25 March 2000, Harrisburg Hospital, Harrisburg, Dauphin Co., PA.

        2.15.6.3.2.2.3.3 OWEN MICHAEL KLINGER was born on 22 February 2004.

        2.15.6.3.2.2.3.4 LANDON SCOTT KLINGER was born on 20 March 2006.

2.15.6.3.2.3 RALPH LESTER KLINGER JR. was born on 2 February 1958. He married **JILL GILMORE**.

    2.15.6.3.2.3.1 BILLIE JO KLINGER

    2.15.6.3.2.3.2 CHERIE KLINGER

    2.15.6.3.2.3.3 NICOLE KLINGER

    2.15.6.3.2.3.4 SONYA KLINGER

2.15.6.3.2.4 KATHY KAY KLINGER was born on 20 March 1959. She married **RONALD MILLER**.

    2.15.6.3.2.4.1 SCOTT LEROY MILLER

    2.15.6.3.2.4.2 STACY LYNN BARRY was born after 1972. She married **(--?--) CARR**. Stacy lives in Halifax, PA.

2.15.6.3.2.5 RANDY EUGENE KLINGER was born on 5 August 1960.

    2.15.6.3.2.5.1 RANDY EUGENE KLINGER JR.

2.15.6.4 LILLIE ERRENA KLINGER is also referred to as **IRENE S. AND LILLIE IRENE** in some sources. She was born on 20 December 1900. She was baptized on 19 November 1905, Zion (Klinger's) Church, Erdman, Lykens Township, Dauphin County, PA. She married **MARK UMEHOLTZ**

SCHREIBER, son of **BENJAMIN O. SCHREIBER** and **CORA S. UMHOLTZ,** circa 1919. She died on 14 March 1987, Tower City, Schuylkill County, PA, at age 86.

2.15.6.4.1 WILLIAM H. SCHREIBER also went by the name of **BILL**. He was born on 28 August 1918, Pennsylvania. He married **DELORES BUFFINGTON**. He married **SARAH ELIZABETH EBERT**. He died on 6 January 1980, Harrisburg, Dauphin County, PA, at age 61.

2.15.6.4.1.1 DEBRA SCHREIBER

2.15.6.4.1.2 WILLIAM SCHREIBER JR.

2.15.6.4.2 DOROTHY MAE SCHREIBER was born on 1 September 1919. She married **DANIEL ABRAHAM BARRY**. She died on 26 September 2008, at her home on Armstrong Valley Road, near Halifax, Dauphin County, PA, at age 89. She was buried on 30 September 2008, at Riverview Memorial Gardens, Halifax, Dauphin County, PA.

2.15.6.4.2.1 ROY EDWARD BARRY also went by the name of **FROSTY**. He was born on 10 April 1935, Fisherville, Dauphin County, PA. He married **EVELYN JUENO CORSNITZ**. According to family sources, Roy's only biological child was his daughter Sandra. He died on 30 April 2009, Harrisburg Hospital, Harrisburg, Dauphin County, PA, at age 74. According to a newspaper obituary, Roy lived on Peters Mountain Road, near Halifax, PA, and was the retired owner of Barry's Masonry. He was buried on 5 May 2009, at Riverview Memorial Gardens, Halifax, Dauphin County, PA.

2.15.6.4.2.1.1 DONNA BARRY married **JERRY DALEY**. Donna lives in Millersburg, PA.

2.15.6.4.2.1.2 JUDY BARRY married **RICHARD HUMMEL**. Judy lives in Ocean Pines, MD.

2.15.6.4.2.1.3 JEAN BARRY married **JEFF FEGLEY**. Jean lives in Millersburg, PA.

2.15.6.4.2.1.4 SANDRA LEE BARRY was born on 23 March 1961. She married **MICHAEL A. OXENDINE**. Sandra lives in Lykens, PA.

2.15.6.4.2.1.4.1 MARC A. OXENDINE was born on 31 December 1984.

2.15.6.4.2.1.4.2 MATTHEW A. OXENDINE was born on 15 July 1988.

2.15.6.4.2.2 ANNA MAE BARRY was born on 28 June 1938, Halifax, Dauphin County, PA. She married **JOHN CARL WILLIARD**. Anna lives in Halifax, Dauphin County, PA. She died on 6 July 2015, Dauphin County, PA, at age 77. She was buried on 10 July 2015, at Long's Cemetery, Halifax, Dauphin County, PA.

2.15.6.4.2.3 CARL EUGENE BARRY was born on 5 April 1940. He married **LOLA CALLOWAY**. He and **LOLA CALLOWAY** were divorced. Carl lives in Halifax, Dauphin County, PA.

2.15.6.4.2.3.1 BETTY BARRY

2.15.6.4.2.3.2 JOHN BARRY

2.15.6.4.2.4 RAY RICHARD BARRY SR. was born on 24 July 1943, Halifax, Dauphin County, PA. He married **ARLENE MAURER**. He and **ARLENE MAURER** were divorced. He died on 30 November 2013, Tremont Health and Rehabilitation Center, Tremont, Schuylkill County, PA, at age 70. According to a newspaper obituary, Ray was an U.S. Army veteran and retired as a self-employed mason. He also worked as a driver with S&L Spindles, Millersburg.

2.15.6.4.2.4.1 SAMANTHA LEE BARRY was born on 7 June 1966. She married **(--?--) SHIPLEY**. Samantha lives in Lykens, PA.

2.15.6.4.2.4.2 RAY RICHARD BARRY JR. was born on 16 September 1967. Ray lives in Lykens, PA.

2.15.6.4.2.4.2.1 MAE BARRY was born on 25 February 1992.

2.15.6.4.2.4.3 MARIANNE C. BARRY is also referred to as **MARYANN** in some sources. She was born on 11 March 1971. She married **(--?--) HARMAN**. Marianne lives in Lykens, PA.

2.15.6.4.2.4.4 STACY LYNN BARRY (see above)

2.15.6.4.2.5 MARLIN EUGENE BARRY was born on 26 October 1945. He married **LORETTA SIMS**. He married **DARLENE KAY MILLER**. Marlin lives in Elizabethville, Dauphin County, PA.

2.15.6.4.2.5.1 DIANE LYNN BARRY was born on 12 May 1968.

2.15.6.4.2.5.2 DANIEL EDWARD BARRY was born on 20 January 1970.

2.15.6.4.2.5.3 HEIDI LYNN MILLER was born on 18 January 1977.

2.15.6.4.2.6 ELSIE MARIE BARRY was born on 5 November 1946. She married ELWOOD PATTON. She married WILLIAM W. WELCOMER. Elsie lives in Gratz, Dauphin County, PA.

- **2.15.6.4.2.6.1** TAMMY BARRY
- **2.15.6.4.2.6.2** PAUL PATTON
- **2.15.6.4.2.6.3** RICHARD PATTON
- **2.15.6.4.2.6.4** TONY PATTON
- **2.15.6.4.2.6.5** SHERRY WELCOMER

2.15.6.4.2.7 DARLENE LEE BARRY was born on 16 December 1951. She married ROGER LEE SOSTAR. Darlene lives in Halifax, Dauphin County, PA.

- **2.15.6.4.2.7.1** ROGER LEE SOSTAR JR. was born on 1 February 1972.
- **2.15.6.4.2.7.2** JEFFREY MICHAEL SOSTAR was born on 21 March 1973.

2.15.6.4.3 MARK OTIS SCHREIBER also went by the name of LANDY. He was born on 11 January 1921. Mark was a Marine sniper during the World War II and apparently suffered for the rest of his life as a result of the traumatic experiences. He never married. He died on 18 September 1986, Wiconisco, Dauphin County, PA, at age 65.

2.15.6.4.4 CHARLES E. SCHREIBER also went by the name of CHOW. He was born on 26 March 1922. He married VERA E. MCDONALD. He died on 4 December 1968, at age 46.

- **2.15.6.4.4.1** MYRTLE IRENE SCHREIBER
- **2.15.6.4.4.2** MARSHALL IRVING SCHREIBER was born in February 1967.

2.15.6.4.5 ETHEL IRENE SCHREIBER also went by the name of ETZ. She was born on 30 March 1923. She married COLEMAN JANDLE. She died on 29 March 1996, Fontana, San Bernardino County, CA, at age 72.

- **2.15.6.4.5.1** COLEMAN NANDOR JANDLE JR. was born in August 1947.
- **2.15.6.4.5.2** ROBERT J. JANDLE was born in 1950.
- **2.15.6.4.5.3** BARBARA JANE JANDLE was born in September 1952. She married (--?--) KLEIN.
- **2.15.6.4.5.4** ALVERA C. JANDLE was born in April 1955.
- **2.15.6.4.5.5** RICHARD R. JANDLE was born on 17 April 1959. He died on 29 January 1993, Fontana, San Bernardino County, CA, at age 33.
- **2.15.6.4.5.6** CALVIN C. JANDLE was born in 1961.

2.15.6.4.6 JOHN ALBERT SCHREIBER was born in 1924, Pennsylvania. He married MARY ELIZABETH POORE. He died on 2 July 1952. He was buried at Fairview Cemetery, Coatesville, Chester County, PA.

- **2.15.6.4.6.1** KENNETH M. SCHREIBER was born on 5 July 1943.
- **2.15.6.4.6.2** MARY E. SCHREIBER
- **2.15.6.4.6.3** JOHN ALBERT SCHREIBER JR. was born in 1946.
- **2.15.6.4.6.4** HARVEY MARK SCHREIBER was born in August 1948.
- **2.15.6.4.6.5** WILLIAM SCHREIBER was born in 1952.

2.15.6.4.7 EDITH ANN SCHREIBER also went by the name of CHUTT. She was born on 5 March 1927, Pennsylvania. Edith worked at the Libro Shirt Factory in Lykens, Dauphin County, PA.

- **2.15.6.4.7.1** TERRY LEE SCHREIBER was born on 27 June 1950.

2.15.6.4.8 CORA JANE SCHREIBER was born on 20 February 1929. She married JEREMIAH SNYDER RUPP JR.

- **2.15.6.4.8.1** GLORIA JEAN RUPP was born on 10 March 1948. She married CHARLES H. BROWN.
- **2.15.6.4.8.2** CARL DAVID RUPP was born on 7 August 1952. He married JOAN HOLENA.
- **2.15.6.4.8.3** BARBARA RUPP was born circa 10 May 1955. She died circa 4 July 1971, in a car accident.

2.15.6.4.9 RAY MELVIN SCHREIBER also went by the name of **DOPE**. He was born on 11 April 1931, Millersburg, Dauphin County, PA. He married **KATHLEEN STAHL** on 16 November 1957, Hagerstown, Washington County, MD. He married **PATRICIA A. FINSTERBUSH**. According to a newspaper obituary, Ray lived in Harrisburg, PA, and was retired from Ritter Bros. construction. He was a veteran of the US Army serving during the Korean War. He was buried at Indiantown Gap National Cemetery, Annville, Lebanon County, PA.

    2.15.6.4.9.1 KIM SCHREIBER was born on 30 June 1951. Kim lives in Idaho.

    2.15.6.4.9.2 KATHRINE LOUISE SCHREIBER was born on 26 December 1979. She married **MUHAMMED SFAXI**. Kathryn lives in Mt. Holly Springs, PA.

    2.15.6.4.9.3 RAY MELVIN SCHREIBER JR. was born on 3 May 1981. Ray lives in Halifax, PA.

2.15.6.4.10 LORETTA MARIE SCHREIBER also went by the name of **RETZ**. She was born on 22 February 1934, Millersburg, Dauphin County, PA. She married **ROY EMMANUEL TROXELL**. Loretta and Roy had no children. She died on 14 May 2008, at home, 914 Isle of Q Road, Millersburg, Dauphin County, PA, at age 74. She was buried on 19 May 2008, at Zion Lutheran Church Cemetery, Rife, Dauphin County, PA.

2.15.6.4.11 MYRTLE JEAN SCHREIBER also went by the name of **MYRT**. She was born on 20 February 1936. She married **KERMIT BINGAMIN**. She married **GERALD C. FULKROAD SR.** She died in October 1987, Rife, Dauphin County, PA, at age 51.

    2.15.6.4.11.1 ERNEST LEROY SCHREIBER was born circa 1 March 1954. He married **JEAN MARIE REINER**, daughter of **JAMES LAMAR REINER SR.** and **MARGARET MARIE KLINGER**. He married **GAIL L. ENDERS**.

        2.15.6.4.11.1.1 CANDACE MARIE SCHREIBER was born on 24 June 1971.

        2.15.6.4.11.1.2 BRENDA JEAN SCHREIBER was born on 2 September 1972.

        2.15.6.4.11.1.3 LYNN SCHREIBER

        2.15.6.4.11.1.4 MARK SCHREIBER

    2.15.6.4.11.2 SANDRA DEE BINGAMIN was born in 1960.

    2.15.6.4.11.3 GERALD CONRAD FULKROAD JR.

    2.15.6.4.11.4 HENRY ADAM FULKROAD

    2.15.6.4.11.5 TINA LOUISE FULKROAD

2.15.6.4.12 CALVIN CARLOS SCHREIBER was born on 15 May 1940, Rife, Dauphin County, PA. He married **AMANDA JEAN STENCE**, daughter of **JOHN CHARLES STENCE** and **GRACE HELEN PAUL**. Calvin lives in Millersburg, PA.

    2.15.6.4.12.1 TAMMY BARRY (see above)

    2.15.6.4.12.2 KEITH CARLOS SCHREIBER was born on 1 July 1966, Harrisburg, Dauphin County, PA. He married **SAMANTHA HOKE**. He and **SAMANTHA HOKE** were divorced.

        2.15.6.4.12.2.1 TABITHA AMANDA SCHREIBER was born on 5 February 1996.

    2.15.6.4.12.3 EDDIE WAYNE SCHREIBER was born on 23 October 1967. He married **ZEBRILLA SNYDER**.

        2.15.6.4.12.3.1 HAILEE JOELLE SCHREIBER

    2.15.6.4.12.4 TROY ALLEN SCHREIBER was born on 19 January 1985, Harrisburg, Dauphin County, PA. Troy, who lives in Millersburg, PA, provided much information on the descendants of Phillip Klinger and his two wives -- Mary and Elizabeth Tschopp.

2.15.6.4.13 ROBERT FREDERICK SCHREIBER was born on 7 November 1942. He married **JUDY MAE BOWERMAN**. Robert lives in Newport, PA.

    2.15.6.4.13.1 CAROL JEAN SCHREIBER

    2.15.6.4.13.2 ROBERT J. SCHREIBER was born on 26 September 1965. He died on 29 November 2004, Newport, Perry County, PA, at age 39.

2.15.6.5 HATTIE CATHERINE KLINGER was born on 17 July 1903, Dauphin County, PA. She married **THOMAS LESTER PICKUP**, son of **WILLIAM PICKUP** and **ELIZA EDWARDS**, circa 1919. She died on 19 March 1965, Harrisburg Hospital, Harrisburg, Dauphin County, PA, at age 61. According to a newspaper obituary, Hattie was living in Millersburg, R.D., before her death. She was buried at Wiconisco Cemetery, Wiconisco, Dauphin County, PA.

2.15.6.5.1 ROBERT B. PICKUP was born in 1919, Pennsylvania. In 1965, Robert was living in Oregon. He died after 1965.

2.15.6.5.2 WILLIAM P. PICKUP was born on 17 December 1922. He married **SOPHIE A. FLORICK**. He died in February 1985, at age 62.

2.15.6.5.2.1 ANNE T. PICKUP was born in July 1944.

2.15.6.5.2.2 WILLIAM P. PICKUP JR. was born in 1946.

2.15.6.5.2.3 MICHAEL J. PICKUP was born in 1947.

2.15.6.5.3 BLANCHE PICKUP was born circa December 1924. She died before 1945.

2.15.6.5.4 BETTY E. PICKUP was born on 5 October 1926. She married **GEORGE ROMBERGER**. She and **GEORGE ROMBERGER** were divorced. She married **CLYDE WILSON**. She died on 18 November 2001, Mesa, Maricopa County, AZ, at age 75.

2.15.6.5.4.1 DONALD ROMBERGER

2.15.6.5.5 RUTH MARIE PICKUP was born on 5 March 1928. She married **RAYMOND ALBERT HUMMEL**, son of **WILLIAM HENRY HUMMEL** and **SAVILLA JANE LEHR**. She and **RAYMOND ALBERT HUMMEL** were divorced. She died on 16 September 1992, Tower City, Schuylkill County, PA, at age 64.

2.15.6.5.5.1 KAREN RUTH HUMMEL was born on 12 July 1947, Tower City, Schuylkill County, PA. She married **ROBERT CLARK**, son of **DONALD R. CLARK** and **MAXINE CRANE**, on 4 May 1968.

2.15.6.5.5.1.1 TAMARA LESLIE CLARK was born on 3 April 1971, Mesa, Maricopa County, AZ. She married **SEAN EMBURY**. She married **ROBERT BARTLETT**.

2.15.6.5.5.1.1.1 MIKAYLA MARIE EMBURY was born on 18 August 1993, Mesa, Maricopa County, AZ.

2.15.6.5.5.1.1.2 KYLEE CHEYENNE CLARK was born on 27 May 1995, Mesa, Maricopa County, AZ.

2.15.6.5.5.1.1.3 ALANNA LESLIE BARTLETT was born on 27 May 2005, Mesa, Maricopa County, AZ.

2.15.6.5.5.1.1.4 TRYTHENA MAXINE BARTLETT was born on 31 July 2005, Mesa, Maricopa County, AZ.

2.15.6.5.5.1.1.5 JAYDEN AARON BARTLETT was born on 19 October 2009, Mesa, Maricopa County, AZ.

2.15.6.5.5.1.1.6 JORDAN AUSTIN BARTLETT was born on 19 October 2009, Mesa, Maricopa County, AZ.

2.15.6.5.5.1.2 MILESSA MICHELE CLARK was born on 13 December 1973, Mesa, Maricopa County, AZ. She married **ROBERT WARREN JR.**

2.15.6.5.5.1.2.1 LIAM CLARK WARREN was born on 13 March 2007, Denver, CO.

2.15.6.5.5.1.2.2 ELLIOT ROBERT WARREN was born on 22 August 2008, Denver, CO.

2.15.6.5.6 THOMAS EUGENE PICKUP was born on 29 March 1929. He married **VERA MAE HERTZEL**. He married **GWENDOLYN LEONE (--?--)**. He died on 21 March 1997, Augusta, Richmond County, GA, at age 67.

2.15.6.5.6.1 THOMAS EUGENE PICKUP JR. was born on 1 August 1948. He married **DENISE GRIMM**.

2.15.6.5.6.1.1 JENNIFER PICKUP

2.15.6.5.6.1.2 THOMAS EUGENE PICKUP III

2.15.6.5.6.2 CHARLENE CAROLINE PICKUP was born on 31 October 1951. She married **WOODROW G. MORGAN**.

2.15.6.5.6.2.1 TODD MORGAN

2.15.6.5.6.2.2 TONYA MORGAN

2.15.6.5.6.3 MICHAEL RICHARD PICKUP was born on 13 February 1954. He married **SUZETTE KLINGER**.

    2.15.6.5.6.3.1 AMANDA PICKUP

    2.15.6.5.6.3.2 AMBER PICKUP

2.15.6.5.6.4 JERRY PICKUP

2.15.6.5.6.5 LUCINDA PICKUP married **RICHARD D. HOFFMAN**.

2.15.6.5.7 CHARLES J. PICKUP was born on 4 October 1932, Dauphin County, PA. He married **JEAN C. THOMPSON**, daughter of **JOHN H. THOMPSON** and **MAE CHRISTINE GRIM**, circa 1948. He died on 24 February 2002, Dauphin County, PA, at age 69. He was buried at Calvary United Methodist Cemetery, Wiconisco, Dauphin County, PA.

    2.15.6.5.7.1 CATHY PICKUP

    2.15.6.5.7.2 DEBRA SUE PICKUP

2.15.6.6 MITCHELL R. KLINGER was born on 29 August 1905, Dauphin County, PA. He married **JENNIE LOUISA MOFFET**, daughter of **ROBERT MOFFET JR.** and **ANNA ORR**. He and **JENNIE LOUISA MOFFET** were divorced on 18 November 1931. He married **MARION V. SULTZBAUGH**, daughter of **HENRY ISAAC SULTZBAUGH** and **MABEL ALICE MILLER**, on 13 July 1949, Richmond, VA. He died on 13 December 1964, Baltimore, Baltimore County, MD, at age 59. He was buried at Calvary United Methodist Cemetery, Wiconisco, Dauphin County, PA.

    2.15.6.6.1 ROBERT MITCHEL KLINGER was born on 26 October 1925, Elizabethville, Dauphin County, PA. He married **SONJA MARGARET JOHNOM** on 26 March 1946, Pierce County, WA. He died on 16 October 2003, Puyallup, Pierce County, WA, at age 77. He was buried at Fir Lane Memorial Park, Spanaway, Pierce County, WA.

2.15.6.7 PHILLIP WILLIAM ABSALOM KLINGER was born on 24 January 1908, Dauphin County, PA. He married **LEONA SARAH GAYNOR**. He married **JUNE ELIZABETH EBERSOLE**, daughter of **RALPH EBERSOLE** and **JOSEPHINE DISNEY**. He died on 11 January 1983, Polyclinic Hospital, Harrisburg, Dauphin County, PA, at age 74. He was buried on 14 January 1983, at Calvary United Methodist Cemetery, Wiconisco, Dauphin County, PA.

    2.15.6.7.1 ELEANOR PHYLLIS KLINGER was born on 29 April 1933, Lykens, Dauphin County, PA. She married **HOMER D. STERNBERGER** in 1950. She died on 26 September 2014, Good Samaritan Hospital, Lebanon, Lebanon County, PA, at age 81. She was buried on 1 October 2014, at Indiantown Gap National Cemetery, Annville, Lebanon County, PA.

        2.15.6.7.1.1 DOUGLAS A. STERNBERGER

        2.15.6.7.1.2 JAMES E. STERNBERGER married **BETSEY (--?--)**.

        2.15.6.7.1.3 KIM STERNBERGER married **(--?--) HENNESSY**.

        2.15.6.7.1.4 LORI J. STERNBERGER

        2.15.6.7.1.5 MICHAEL D. STERNBERGER married **DAWN (--?--)**.

    2.15.6.7.2 RONALD EUGENE KLINGER was born on 24 August 1934. He married **PATRICIA MCCORMICK**. He died on 21 April 2015, at age 80.

        2.15.6.7.2.1 ALLISON KLINGER

        2.15.6.7.2.2 GLENN KLINGER

        2.15.6.7.2.3 JANICE KLINGER

        2.15.6.7.2.4 MARK KLINGER

    2.15.6.7.3 PRISCILLA MAE KLINGER was born on 16 July 1935. She married **JOHN JOSEPH WRUBEL JR.**

        2.15.6.7.3.1 CAROL ANN WRUBEL

        2.15.6.7.3.2 DAVID ALAN WRUBEL

        2.15.6.7.3.3 JAMES ANDREW WRUBEL

        2.15.6.7.3.4 JOHN JOSEPH WRUBEL III

        2.15.6.7.3.5 MICHAEL ANTHONY WRUBEL

        2.15.6.7.3.6 MICHELLE MARIA WRUBEL

        2.15.6.7.3.7 WILLIAM THOMAS WRUBEL

2.15.6.7.4 EDITH JANE KLINGER was born on 24 September 1937. She married ROBERT WILLIAM SHOOP.

    2.15.6.7.4.1 REBECCA JANE SHOOP married RICHARD T. MCGEE.

2.15.6.7.5 MARY CATHERINE KLINGER was born on 2 October 1938. She married PAUL DONALD HOFFMAN. She and PAUL DONALD HOFFMAN were divorced.

    2.15.6.7.5.1 SHERRY ANN HOFFMAN

    2.15.6.7.5.2 DALE JOHN HOFFMAN

    2.15.6.7.5.3 DAWN AELYN HOFFMAN

    2.15.6.7.5.4 RENEE COLEEN HOFFMAN

2.15.6.7.6 PHILLIP WILLIAM KLINGER was born on 4 January 1941. He married NANCY MESSNER. He married HELEN (--?--).

    2.15.6.7.6.1 ADAM KLINGER

    2.15.6.7.6.2 NICOLE KLINGER

    2.15.6.7.6.3 PHILLIP KLINGER

    2.15.6.7.6.4 ZOANN KLINGER

2.15.6.7.7 GEORGE DALE KLINGER also went by the name of PORK. He was born on 31 May 1942. He married SHIRLEY (--?--). He married CHERYL (--?--). George lives in Nebraska.

2.15.6.7.8 GEORGINA DELPHINE KLINGER also went by the name of SUE. She was born on 31 May 1942, Lykens, Dauphin County, PA. She married JUNIOR HOOVER. She and JUNIOR HOOVER were divorced. She died on 9 March 2009, Hershey Medical Center, Hershey, Dauphin County, PA, at age 66.

    2.15.6.7.8.1 SANDRA LEE HOOVER married (--?--) VUOLO.

    2.15.6.7.8.2 MERREDITH DOREEN HOOVER

2.15.6.7.9 LARRY JOSEPH KLINGER was born on 28 February 1944. He died on 15 December 1993, at age 49. He was buried at Atlantic County Veterans Cemetery, Estell Manor, Atlantic County, NJ.

2.15.6.7.10 DONNA LEE KLINGER was born on 9 March 1946. She married CHARLES R. ENGLISH.

2.15.6.7.11 ANTHONY PHILLIP KLINGER was born on 27 February 1964. He married BELLANN BINGAMIN.

    2.15.6.7.11.1 BRENTON ANTHONY KLINGER was born on 29 November 1985.

    2.15.6.7.11.2 CHRISTIAN PHILLIP KLINGER was born on 21 October 1993.

2.15.6.8 STANLEY LOUIS KLINGER was born on 18 April 1910, Lykens, Dauphin County, PA. Stanley never married. He died on 11 April 1983, Polyclinic Hospital, Harrisburg, Dauphin County, PA, at age 72. He was buried on 15 April 1983, at Calvary United Methodist Cemetery, Wiconisco, Dauphin County, PA.

2.15.6.9 ELIZABETH SARAH KLINGER was born on 15 July 1913, Lykens, Dauphin County, PA. She married JOHN MARLIN SCHORR. She married ALBERT F. RAHO JR. She died on 4 February 2009, Tremont Health & Rehabilitation Center, Tremont, Schuylkill County, PA, at age 95. According to a newspaper obituary, Elizabeth lived in Tower City, Schuylkill County, PA and retired as a seamstress from the garment industry. She was buried on 7 February 2009, at Greenwood Cemetery, Tower City, Schuylkill County, PA.

    2.15.6.9.1 JOHN FREDERICK SCHORR JR. was born on 26 March 1930. He married BARBARA PAUL. He died in September 1986, at age 56.

        2.15.6.9.1.1 RANDY LEE SCHORR

        2.15.6.9.1.2 DENISE SCHORR

        2.15.6.9.1.3 KEVIN EUGENE SCHORR

        2.15.6.9.1.4 KIM JOHN SCHORR

        2.15.6.9.1.5 TODD SCHORR

        2.15.6.9.1.6 MELANIE SCHORR

2.15.6.9.2 GLORIA-DEAN ELIZABETH SCHORR was born on 15 December 1931. She married JOHN LEROY NOLEN.

> **2.15.6.9.2.1** BELINDA SUZANNE NOLEN was born on 18 January 1952.
>
> **2.15.6.9.2.2** JOHN RODNEY NOLEN was born on 13 February 1954.
>
> **2.15.6.9.2.3** BRADLEY LEE NOLEN was born on 2 May 1955.

2.15.6.9.3 ALBERT EUGENE RAHO also went by the name of JIT. He was born on 20 April 1935. He married NANCY KAY EVANS.

2.15.6.9.4 MITCHELL LESTER RAHO SR. was born on 16 November 1944. He married BONITA LAING.

> **2.15.6.9.4.1** JANINE MARIE RAHO
>
> **2.15.6.9.4.2** MITCHELL LESTER RAHO JR.

2.15.6.10 JAMES ROBERT KLINGER was born on 14 October 1915, Pennsylvania. He married MARGARET IRENE MILLER. He and MARGARET IRENE MILLER were divorced. He married MARY L. MOYER. He died on 13 December 1992, at age 77.

> **2.15.6.10.1** JAMES EUGENE KLINGER was born on 12 February 1938. He married BARBARA A. ADAMS. In 2008, James was living in Newport, PA.
>
> > **2.15.6.10.1.1** HEATH ALLEN KLINGER
> >
> > **2.15.6.10.1.2** JAMES EUGENE KLINGER JR.
>
> **2.15.6.10.2** MARGARET MARIE KLINGER also went by the name of PEGGY. She was born on 22 March 1939. She married JAMES LAMAR REINER SR. She and JAMES LAMAR REINER SR. were divorced. She married JAMES EDGAR CHUBB. In 2008, Margaret was living in Millersburg, PA.
>
> > **2.15.6.10.2.1** MICHAEL EUGENE KLINGER is also referred to as DONALD LEE ELLENBERGER in some sources. He was born on 9 April 1953. Michael was later adopted and changed his name to Donald Lee Ellenberger. He died on 12 February 2002, at age 48.
> >
> > **2.15.6.10.2.2** JEAN MARIE REINER was born on 14 September 1955. She married ERNEST LEROY SCHREIBER, son of MYRTLE JEAN SCHREIBER.
> >
> > > **2.15.6.10.2.2.1** CANDACE MARIE SCHREIBER (see above)
> > >
> > > **2.15.6.10.2.2.2** BRENDA JEAN SCHREIBER (see above)
> > >
> > > **2.15.6.10.2.2.3** SARAH JO ANN MCCREARY was born on 7 January 1976.
> > >
> > > **2.15.6.10.2.2.4** MICHAEL PAUL MCCREARY was born on 11 August 1977.
> >
> > **2.15.6.10.2.3** JAMES LAMAR REINER JR. was born on 18 February 1957. He married MARTHA KERRS.
> >
> > **2.15.6.10.2.4** JOHN JOSEPH REINER was born on 24 October 1958. He died on 16 March 1970, at age 11.
>
> **2.15.6.10.3** ROBERT LEROY KLINGER SR. was born on 4 December 1941. He married BONNIE (--?--). He and BONNIE (--?--) were divorced. He married EVELYN KOONS. He died on 15 November 2008, Rapid City Regional Hospital, Rapid City, SD, at age 66.
>
> > **2.15.6.10.3.1** ROBERT LEROY KLINGER JR. In 2008, Robert was living in Portland, OR.
> >
> > **2.15.6.10.3.2** WILLIAM KLINGER. In 2008, William was living in Rapid City, SD.
>
> **2.15.6.10.4** MARY LOUISE KLINGER was born on 9 April 1943. She married WILLIAM CLARENCE LENKER SR., son of THOMAS LENKER and RUTH STUTZMAN, circa 1960. In 2008, Mary was living in Williamstown, PA.
>
> > **2.15.6.10.4.1** APRIL DAWN LENKER was born on 2 October 1961. She married (--?--) CINQMARS.
> >
> > **2.15.6.10.4.2** WILLIAM CLARENCE LENKER JR. was born on 28 January 1966. He married RICKANN (--?--).
> >
> > > **2.15.6.10.4.2.1** THOMAS EDWARD LENKER
> >
> > **2.15.6.10.4.3** MELISSA ANN LENKER was born on 9 January 1970. She married HAL KEISTER. She married PETER BOHR.
> >
> > > **2.15.6.10.4.3.1** HOWIE ERIC KEISTER
> > >
> > > **2.15.6.10.4.3.2** COLBY JAMES BOHR

2.15.6.10.5 JUDITH ANN KLINGER was born on 11 January 1947. She married JAMES M. FETTERHOFF. She and JAMES M. FETTERHOFF were divorced. In 2008, Judith was living in New Mexico.

2.15.6.10.5.1 ASHLEY FITE

2.15.6.10.5.2 CHRISTINE FETTERHOFF

2.15.6.10.5.3 JAMES M. FETTERHOFF JR.

2.15.6.10.5.4 LORIE ANN FETTERHOFF married JERRY LYNN UNGER.

2.15.6.10.5.5 SHERRY FETTERHOFF

2.15.6.10.6 DARWIN D. MOYER. Darwin was adopted.

2.15.6.11 HENRY WADSWORTH KLINGER was born on 20 October 1917, Lykens, Dauphin County, PA. He married HELEN A. KIEHL. He married MABEL LAURA ROMBERGER, daughter of GEORGE ROMBERGER and GERTRUDE (--?--), circa 1942. He died on 14 July 2003, Harrisburg Hospital, Harrisburg, Dauphin County, PA, at age 85. According to a newspaper obituary, Henry was an Army veteran of World War II. He was buried at Calvary United Methodist Cemetery, Wiconisco, Dauphin County, PA.

2.15.6.11.1 SANDRA JOYCE KLINGER was born on 7 August 1942. She married RICHARD GORDON CONANT.

2.15.6.11.1.1 JOYCE DIANE CONANT married STEPHEN HARKEY.

2.15.6.11.1.2 DENISE MARGARET CONANT married GABRIEL VERA.

2.15.6.11.1.3 CAROL LYNN CONANT married DAVID CLANCY.

2.15.6.11.2 HENRY ROBERT KLINGER was born on 2 May 1944. He married DIANE RUTH REIBSANE on 27 April 1968, Methodist Church, Tower City, Schuylkill County, PA.

2.15.6.11.2.1 ROBERT ANTHONY KLINGER married PHYLLIS SNYDER. He was born on 2 June 1969.

2.15.6.11.2.1.1 ANTHONY ROBERT KLINGER

2.15.6.11.2.1.2 ROBYN KLINGER

2.15.6.11.2.2 VICTORIA DIANE KLINGER was born on 4 October 1973. She married RICHARD FREDERICK.

2.15.6.11.2.2.1 LLARS FREDERICK

2.15.6.11.2.3 CHRISTOPHER NORMAN KLINGER was born on 16 December 1974.

2.15.6.12 MYRTLE MARIE KLINGER was born on 27 October 1919, Dauphin County, PA. She married LEO JOSEPH RODICHOK circa 1936. She married CLARENCE SHINDLER. She died on 31 December 1997, Pottsville Hospital, Pottsville, Schuylkill County, PA, at age 78. According to a newspaper obituary, Myrtle was a seamstress in the garment industry. She was buried on 3 January 1998, at Sacred Heart of Jesus Cemetery, Williamstown, Dauphin County, PA.

2.15.6.12.1 BERNARD LEO RODICHOK was born on 22 October 1938, Tower City, Schuylkill County, PA. He married JEAN M. SCHEIB, daughter of HOMER WILLIAM SCHEIB and MARY JUSTINA SHAFFER, after 1964, PA. He died on 12 June 1969, Good Samaritan Hospital, Pottsville, Schuylkill County, PA, at age 30. He was buried on 16 June 1969, at Simeon Union Cemetery, Gratz, Dauphin County, PA. Bernard worked for American Heat Reclaiming Company in Lykens, Dauphin County, PA.

2.15.6.12.1.1 DAVID MICHAEL RODICHOK was born in June 1966, PA.

2.15.6.12.1.2 THOMAS C. RODICHOK was born in 1969.

2.15.6.12.2 MICHAEL GEORGE RODICHOK was born on 16 July 1943, Sheridan, Schuylkill County, PA. He married MARIE SHADLE circa 1965. He died on 25 February 2015, The Manor at Susquehanna Village, Millersburg, Dauphin County, PA, at age 71. According to a newspaper obituary, Michael an Army veteran of the Vietnam War. He retired as a maintenance leader from Tyco, Lickdale, and was also the owner of the former Mike's TV and Radio Shack, Tower City. He was an avid musician, a member of Liberty Hose Company Band, of Lykens, the Tremont Community Band, and After Hours Band. He was buried on 28 February 2015, at Greenwood Cemetery, Tower City, Schuylkill County, PA.

2.15.6.12.2.1 CHAD MICHAEL RODICHOK was born on 15 March 1967. He married ERIN LEUSCHNER.

2.15.6.12.2.1.1 IAN MICHAEL RODICHOK was born on 27 May 1989.

2.15.6.12.2.1.2 MADISON MARGARET RODICHOK was born on 27 November 1992.

2.15.6.12.3 WALTER TERRY RODICHOK was born on 30 July 1945. He married SUEANN BETTINGER. He and SUEANN BETTINGER were divorced. He died on 24 July 1991, at age 45.

2.15.6.12.3.1 GWENDOLYN RODICHOK

2.15.6.12.3.2 JOSEPH RODICHOK

2.15.6.12.3.3 STEVEN RODICHOK

2.15.6.12.4 GARY DAVID RODICHOK was born in November 1954. He married ELEANOR YEAGER. He and ELEANOR YEAGER were divorced.

2.15.6.12.4.1 BARBARA RODICHOK

2.15.6.12.4.2 JODI RODICHOK

2.15.6.13 MARTHA PRISCILLA KLINGER was born on 10 March 1922, Lykens, Dauphin County, PA. She married JOHN F. DIAKOW circa 1935. She died on 17 August 1997, Millersburg, Dauphin County, PA, at age 75. According to a newspaper obituary, Martha attended the First Baptist Church in Lykens and was in the choir.

2.15.6.13.1 MARSHA E. DIAKOW was born in November 1947. She married (--?--) KLINGER. She and (--?--) KLINGER were divorced.

2.15.6.13.1.1 JENNIFER E. KLINGER

2.15.6.13.2 JOHN F. DIAKOW JR. was born on 30 May 1950. He married BARBARA ANN LEBO, daughter of RALPH EDWIN LEBO JR. and BETTY R. MILLER, circa 1976. He and BARBARA ANN LEBO were divorced. He married JODEE (--?--).

2.15.6.13.2.1 RACHEL A. DIAKOW

2.15.6.13.2.2 NATHAN J. DIAKOW was born circa 1977. He died on 2 November 1995.

2.15.6.13.2.3 ELIZABETH L. DIAKOW

2.15.6.13.2.4 GABRIELLE E. DIAKOW

2.15.6.14 MARGARET SAVILLA KLINGER was born on 10 March 1922. She married RAYMOND LAMAR RESSLER SR. She died on 6 August 2005, Community General Osteopathic Hospital, Harrisburg, Dauphin County, PA, at age 83. She was buried on 10 August 2005, at Calvary United Methodist Cemetery, Wiconisco, Dauphin County, PA. According to a newspaper obituary, Margaret retired as a seamstress from the former Wiconisco Dress Co.

2.15.6.14.1 LOUELLA JANE RESSLER was born on 12 October 1939. She married HAROLD BENDER. She married CLIFFORD PORTER. She married VERNON DOCKEY. She married GERALD STOVER.

2.15.6.14.2 PEGGY ANN RESSLER was born on 5 August 1942. She married LEO DONALD SCHMICK. She married EDGAR T. MARCH JR.

2.15.6.14.3 WAYNE DELMAR RESSLER was born on 1 June 1944. He married LINDA KULP.

2.15.6.14.4 LINDA LOU RESSLER was born on 16 November 1946. She died in January 1947.

2.15.6.14.5 LAMAR RAYMOND RESSLER JR. was born on 22 January 1948. He married NANCY L. UNGER.

2.15.6.14.6 TERRY LEE RESSLER was born on 11 August 1950. He married KAREN STROUP. He and KAREN STROUP were divorced. He married DEBRA L. HOFFMAN, daughter of WILLARD HOFFMAN and LAVERNE JEAN LONTZ.

2.15.6.14.7 DONDI ELVIS RESSLER was born on 2 July 1956. He married DEBORAH KAY WIEST.

2.15.6.14.8 SHANE HUGH RESSLER married SANDRA L. CLAY. He was born on 21 April 1958.

2.15.6.15 GEORGE EUGENE KLINGER was born on 18 December 1923, Dauphin County, PA. He married VIOLET M. KAHLER. George served in the US Army during World War II. He died on 16 April 1998, Dauphin County, PA, at age 74. He was buried at Calvary United Methodist Cemetery, Wiconisco, Dauphin County, PA.

2.15.6.15.1 JEAN ELIZABETH KLINGER was born on 1 April 1950. She married **GERALD M. RESSLER SR.** circa 1965. She married **LAWRENCE FORRESTER**. She died on 14 January 2009, at age 58. According to a newspaper obituary, Jean was living in Selinsgrove, PA, at the time of her death. She was buried on 21 January 2009, at Calvary United Methodist Church Cemetery, Wiconisco, Dauphin County, PA.

2.15.6.15.1.1 KEVIN RESSLER. Kevin lives in Wiconisco, PA.

2.15.6.15.1.2 KIMBERLY RESSLER. Kimberly lives in Millersburg, PA.

2.15.6.15.1.3 GERALD M. RESSLER JR. was born on 12 July 1966, Dauphin County, PA. He married **DEBBIE S. (--?--)**. He died on 21 August 2004, in an accident at age 38.

2.15.6.15.1.3.1 MANDY RESSLER

2.15.6.15.1.3.2 MADDIE RESSLER

2.15.6.15.1.3.3 SADIE RESSLER

2.15.6.15.1.3.4 TANAR RESSLER

2.15.6.15.2 BONNIE MARIE KLINGER was born on 2 February 1961. She married **RANDY BECK**. She married **RALPH JONES**. She married **OMAR CONTENTO**. Bonnie lives in Tucson, AZ.

2.15.6.15.2.1 JASON BECK

2.15.6.16 MILDRED JANE KLINGER was born on 10 June 1925, Pennsylvania. She married **DONALD OLSEN SR.** She married **MICHAEL GRIFFIN**.

2.15.6.16.1 LORAINE OLSEN

2.15.6.16.2 LARRY OLSEN

2.15.6.16.3 DONALD OLSEN JR.

2.15.6.17 EVELYN KATHLEEN KLINGER was born on 2 July 1927, Lykens, Dauphin County, PA. She married **GEORGE MILLER**. She married **EDMUND T. HUNTER**. She died on 27 August 2011, Hershey, Dauphin County, PA, at age 84.

2.15.6.17.1 DENNIS MILLER

2.15.6.17.2 KATHARINE MILLER

2.15.6.17.3 KAREN MILLER

2.15.6.17.4 KENNETH MILLER died before 2008.

2.15.6.17.5 KEITH E. HUNTER was born in 1968. He died in 1969, in infancy. He was buried at Calvary United Methodist Church Cemetery, Wiconisco, Dauphin County, PA.

2.16 PETER KLINGER was born on 20 November 1838. He married **MARGARET ANNA MUENCH**, daughter of **JACOB DEWALD MUENCH** and **SALOME MEYER**, on 7 March 1861, Lykens Township, Dauphin County, PA. Some sources suggest that he and **MARGARET ANNA MUENCH** were married in 1860, Pillow, Dauphin County, PA. He died on 27 May 1915, at age 76. He was buried at Grandview Cemetery, Pillow, Dauphin County, PA. His estate was probated on 7 June 1915 while his will was dated 8 August 1910.

2.16.1 FRANCIS W. KLINGER is also referred to as **FRANCIS V.** in some sources. He was born in June 1862, Pennsylvania. He married **MARY LILLIE BEAN** circa 1885.

2.16.1.1 CHARLES E. KLINGER also went by the name of **ED**. He was born in November 1885, Pennsylvania.

2.16.1.2 ELMER F. KLINGER was born in August 1888, Pennsylvania.

2.16.1.3 MORRIS H. KLINGER was born in November 1890, Pennsylvania.

2.16.1.4 MARY E. KLINGER was born in May 1892, Pennsylvania.

2.16.1.5 PETER F. KLINGER was born in May 1895, Pennsylvania.

2.16.1.6 MABEL R. KLINGER was born in July 1897, Pennsylvania.

2.16.2 FIETTA E. KLINGER was born on 16 January 1863. She married **JOHN SNYDER** circa 1885. She died in 1932. She was buried at St. Peter's (Hoffman's) Union Church Cemetery, Lykens Township, Dauphin County, PA.

2.16.2.1 CHARLES SNYDER

2.16.2.2 ANNIE SNYDER was born on 5 July 1881. She was baptized on 22 October 1881, St. Peter's (Hoffman's) Union Church, Lykens Township, Dauphin County, PA.

2.16.2.3 HENRY EDWARD SNYDER was born on 14 April 1883, 15 6 1883. He was baptized on 18 April 1883, St. Peter's (Hoffman's) Union Church, Lykens Township, Dauphin County, PA. He died on 15 June 1883. He was buried at St. Peter's (Hoffman's) Union Church Cemetery, Lykens Township, Dauphin County, PA.

2.16.2.4 CLARA ELIZABETH SNYDER was born on 14 April 1883. She was baptized on 18 April 1883, St. Peter's (Hoffman's) Union Church, Lykens Township, Dauphin County, PA. She died on 14 June 1883. She was buried at St. Peter's (Hoffman's) Union Church Cemetery, Lykens Township, Dauphin County, PA.

2.16.2.5 HARRY SNYDER was born in October 1884.

2.16.2.6 DANIEL SNYDER was born in January 1887.

2.16.2.7 EDNA SNYDER is also referred to as **ETNA** in some sources. She was baptized on 12 March 1889, Simeon's Reformed Church, Gratz, Dauphin County, PA. She was born on 26 March 1889.

2.16.2.8 JOHN SNYDER was born in November 1895.

2.16.3 ANNIE SEVILLA KLINGER was born on 13 February 1865. She married **DANIEL KEBOCH**, son of **HENRY KEBOCH** and **REBECCA DEIBLER**, circa 1885. She died on 21 August 1925, at age 60. She was buried at St. John's Lutheran Church Cemetery, Berrysburg, Dauphin County, PA.

2.16.3.1 CORA KEBOCH is also referred to as **CORA EDNA KEBAUGH** in some sources. She married **DANIEL DOCKEY**, son of **BENJAMIN F. DOCKEY** and **MARY A. LENKER**.

2.16.3.1.1 EVELYN FAY DOCKEY was born on 12 November 1908, Dauphin County, PA. She married **MARK FRANKLIN WISE**, son of **BENJAMIN FRANKLIN WEISS** and **MAGGIE R. KLINGER**. She died on 16 July 1995, Dauphin County, PA, at age 86. She was buried at Maple Grove Cemetery, Elizabethville, Dauphin County, PA.

2.16.3.2 SALLIE KEBOCH was born circa 1890. She married **WILLIAM GOTTSCHALL** circa 1910.

2.16.4 SARAH A. KLINGER also went by the name of **SALLIE**. She was born in September 1868, Pennsylvania. She married **LEWIS C. HOFFMAN** circa 1888.

2.16.4.1 FAY HOFFMAN married **LANDON HOOVER**.

2.16.4.2 CATHERINE E. HOFFMAN also went by the name of **KATIE**. She was born in February 1888, Pennsylvania. She married **CALVIN L. ENGLE**, son of **DANIEL ENGLE** and **EMMA BORDNER**, circa 1906.

2.16.4.2.1 MILDRED P. ENGLE was born circa 1908, Pennsylvania.

2.16.4.2.2 EARL E. ENGLE was born in 1910, Pennsylvania.

2.16.4.2.2.1 GERALDINE E. ENGLE was born circa October 1929, Pennsylvania.

2.16.4.2.3 MARLIN D. ENGLE was born in 1915, Pennsylvania.

2.16.4.2.4 SARAH J. ENGLE was born circa November 1917, Pennsylvania.

2.16.4.2.5 LAURENCE C. ENGLE was born circa 1922, Pennsylvania.

2.16.4.2.6 ROBERT LEWIS ENGLE was born on 17 March 1931.

2.16.4.3 EDWARD C. HOFFMAN was born in 1891, Pennsylvania. He married **CARRIE MAY UMHOLTZ**. He died in 1927. He was buried at Simeon Church Cemetery, Gratz, Dauphin County, PA.

2.16.4.3.1 ROY HOFFMAN was born circa 1914, Pennsylvania.

2.16.4.4 THOMAS ALVIN HOFFMAN was born on 20 December 1892. He was baptized on 20 March 1893, Simeon's Reformed Church, Gratz, Dauphin County, PA. He died on 18 October 1943, at age 50.

2.16.5 KATIE KLINGER is also referred to as **CATHARINE** in some sources. She was born on 19 March 1871. She married **CHARLES LEHMAN** circa 1891.

2.16.5.1 MAGGIE E. LEHMAN was born in October 1891, Pennsylvania. She married **HARVEY J. FRANK** circa 1909.

2.16.5.1.1 EDNA FRANK was born in 1910, Pennsylvania.

2.16.5.2 CHARLES W. LEHMAN was born circa 1902, Pennsylvania.

2.16.6 CORA KLINGER was born on 28 January 1875, Pennsylvania. Some sources record that she was born circa 1872. She married **MICHAEL BOHNER**, son of **MICHAEL D. BOHNER** and **CATHERINE RUBENDALL**, circa 1895.

2.16.6.1 Dorah Bohner

2.16.6.2 Robert Bohner

2.16.6.3 Laura R. Bohner was born in October 1894, Pennsylvania.

2.16.6.4 Mamie C. Bohner was born in April 1898, Pennsylvania.

2.16.7 George W. Klinger is also referred to as **George Franklin Klinger** in some sources. He was born on 12 September 1876. He married **Lizzie Bohner** on 25 December 1906, Hebe, Northumberland County, PA.

2.16.8 Maude E. Klinger was born in November 1877. She married **Milton O. Buffington** circa 1906. She died on 3 May 1952, Millersburg, Dauphin County, PA, at age 74. She was buried at Maple Grove Cemetery, Elizabethville, Dauphin County, PA.

2.16.8.1 Laura Irene Buffington was born on 2 April 1906, Dauphin County, PA. She married **Amos Robert Rothermel**, son of **Manasses W. Rothermel** and **Susan Jane Bixler**. She married (--?--) **Schucker** after 1945. She died on 6 May 1989, Valley View, Schuylkill County, PA, at age 83. She was buried at St. Michael's Cemetery, Klingerstown, Schuylkill County, PA.

2.16.8.1.1 Stanley Rothermel was born on 27 November 1925, Lykens RD, Dauphin County, PA. He married **Katie Fetterolf** on 28 September 1946. He died on 12 March 2015, Peter Brecker Community, Harleysville, PA, at age 89. He was buried at Saint Michaels Lutheran Church Cemetery, Klingerstown, Schuylkill County, PA.

2.16.8.1.1.1 Rhonda Rothermel

2.16.8.1.1.2 Susan Rothermel married (--?--) **Baker**.

2.16.8.1.1.3 Kristine Rothermel married (--?--) **Perry**.

2.16.8.1.1.3.1 Jonathan Perry

2.16.8.1.1.3.2 Shawn Perry

2.16.8.1.1.4 Randall Charles Rothermel was born on 20 April 1949. He died on 23 April 1949. He was buried at Saint Michaels Lutheran Church Cemetery, Klingerstown, Schuylkill County, PA.

2.16.8.1.2 Arlene Rothermel was born circa 1926.

2.16.8.1.3 Mildred Marie Rothermel was born circa 1929.

2.16.8.2 John Robert Buffington married **Viola May Paul**, daughter of **John Alfred Paul** and **Stella Wiest**. He was born on 26 April 1907, Pennsylvania. He married **Viola May Paul**, daughter of **John Alfred Paul** and **Stella Wiest**. He died on 26 September 1959, Gratz, Dauphin County, PA, at age 52.

2.16.8.2.1 Janice Buffington

2.16.8.3 Helen M. Buffington was born circa 1912, Pennsylvania.

2.16.8.4 Edwin E. Buffington is also referred to as **Edwin B. Buffington** in some sources. He was born on 4 December 1912, Pennsylvania. He married **Sallie Schwalm**, daughter of **Rufus M. Schwalm** and **Flora Adams**, on 6 August 1938, Simeon Lutheran Church, Gratz, Dauphin County, PA. Prior to his death, Edwin was living in the vicinity of Elizabethville, Dauphin County, PA. He died on 7 December 1998, at age 86.

2.16.8.4.1 Jean Buffington was born on 13 January 1939. She was baptized on 5 March 1939, Simeon Lutheran Church, Gratz, Dauphin County, PA. She married **Fred Weaver**.

2.16.8.4.1.1 Angela Weaver

2.16.8.4.1.2 Marlene Weaver

2.16.8.4.2 Elma Elaine Buffington was born on 12 June 1940. She was baptized on 4 August 1940, Simeon Lutheran Church, Gratz, Dauphin County, PA. She married **Dale Umholtz**.

2.16.8.4.2.1 Kirby Umholtz

2.16.8.4.2.2 Christine Umholtz

2.16.8.4.2.3 Michael Umholtz

2.16.8.4.2.4 Eric Umholtz

2.16.8.4.3 Ronald Edwin Buffington was born on 22 February 1943. He was baptized on 3 April 1943, Simeon Lutheran Church, Gratz, Dauphin County, PA. He married **Karen Kingery**.

2.16.8.4.3.1 RONALD BUFFINGTON

2.16.8.4.3.2 LORELEA BUFFINGTON

2.16.8.4.4 DENNIS ELVIN BUFFINGTON was born on 11 August 1944. He was baptized on 29 December 1944, Simeon Lutheran Church, Gratz, Dauphin County, PA. He married **ANNA CARAL**.

2.16.8.4.4.1 KRISTIN BUFFINGTON

2.16.8.4.4.2 MELANIE BUFFINGTON

2.16.8.5 GILBERT J. BUFFINGTON was born circa 1914, Pennsylvania.

2.16.8.6 HANNAH S. BUFFINGTON was born circa 1916, Pennsylvania.

2.16.8.7 MARLIN LEROY BUFFINGTON was born on 23 January 1920, RD, Lykens, Dauphin County, PA. He married **PEARL GERALDINE HOWARD**, daughter of **ISAAC LEROY HOWARD** and **HATTIE IRENE KLINGER**. Prior to his death, Marlin was living in the vicinity of Halifax, Dauphin County, PA. He died on 9 July 1993, at age 73.

2.16.8.7.1 LEONARD BUFFINGTON was born on 20 November 1946, PA. He died on 3 March 1968, Halifax, Dauphin County, PA, at age 21.

2.16.8.7.2 JEFFREY BUFFINGTON was born on 4 October 1948, Elizabethville, Dauphin County, PA. He married **SHARON LEE HOLLOWAY**. He married **DELORES KRAMER** on 2 March 1973, Halifax, Dauphin County, PA.

2.16.8.7.2.1 JEFFREY LYNN BUFFINGTON

2.16.8.7.2.2 JENNIFER LYNN BUFFINGTON

2.16.8.7.3 CRAIG BUFFINGTON was born on 22 July 1955. He married **DENISE MARIE ALLEN**.

2.16.8.7.4 KEITH ALAN BUFFINGTON was born on 10 December 1957. He married **DANE LEE STROHECKER**.

2.16.8.7.4.1 ELIJAH ALAN BUFFINGTON

2.16.8.7.5 TINA BUFFINGTON was born on 13 June 1959.

2.16.8.7.5.1 CHAD AARON BUFFINGTON

2.16.8.8 FAYE M. BUFFINGTON was born on 15 May 1924, Lykens, Dauphin County, PA. She married (--?--) **SPOTTS**. She died on 14 November 2006, The Manor at Susquehanna Village, Millersburg, Dauphin County, PA, at age 82. According to a newspaper obituary, Faye worked as a cake decorator at the SuperThrift in Linglestown, PA. She was buried on 17 November 2006, at Riverview Memorial Gardens, Halifax, Dauphin County, PA.

2.16.8.8.1 DIANNE M. SPOTTS married **DAVID B. BUFFINGTON**.

2.16.8.8.1.1 RANDY D. BUFFINGTON married **ANN M.** (--?--). Randy and his family were living in Virginia Beach, VA, in 2007.

2.16.8.8.1.1.1 TAYLOR BUFFINGTON

2.16.8.8.1.1.2 ABIGAIL BUFFINGTON

2.16.8.8.1.2 KELLY A. BUFFINGTON married **JOHN S. MORRIS**. Kelly and her family were living in Harrisburg, PA, in 2007.

2.16.8.8.1.2.1 CODY MORRIS

2.16.8.8.2 DONNA SPOTTS married **JAMES KONYAR**.

2.16.8.8.2.1 JAMES KONYAR JR.

2.16.8.8.3 TERRY SPOTTS

2.16.8.9 BLAIR LAMAR BUFFINGTON was born on 23 August 1932, Gratz, Dauphin County, PA. Some sources record that he was born on 24 August 1932. He was baptized on 1 January 1933, Simeon Lutheran Church, Gratz, Dauphin County, PA. He married **LYNORE K. HOUTZ** circa 1960. Prior to his death, Blair was living on Wiconisco Avenue in Tower City, Schuylkill County, PA. He died on 11 January 2008, ManorCare, Lebanon, Lebanon County, PA, at age 75. According to a newspaper obituary, Blair served in the U.S. Army during the Korean War for 6 years, during which time he was a paratrooper and a cook. Later, he worked for H.B. Reese Candy Company for more than 30 years. He was buried on 16 January 2008, at Greenwood Cemetery, Tower City, Schuylkill County, PA.

2.16.8.9.1 ROXANNE BUFFINGTON married **BILL JONES**.

   2.16.8.9.1.1 Daniel Jones

  2.16.8.9.2 Cheryl Buffington married **(--?--) Carl**.

  2.16.8.9.3 Lynette Buffington married **(--?--) Klinger**. She also went by the name of **Tiger**.

   2.16.8.9.3.1 Heather Klinger

2.16.9 Charles Monroe Klinger was born on 9 July 1878. He married **Emma E. Schoffstall**, daughter of **Adam Schoffstall** and **Polly Schwalm,** on 1 January 1898, Reformed Church, Pillow, Northumberland County, PA. He died in 1956. He was buried at Simeon Church Cemetery, Gratz, Dauphin County, PA.

 2.16.9.1 Katie Beulah Klinger (see above)

  2.16.9.1.1 Charles E. Muth (see above)

   2.16.9.1.1.1 Charles Muth (see above)

   2.16.9.1.1.2 Donna Muth (see above)

    2.16.9.1.1.2.1 Megan Kratzer (see above)

  2.16.9.1.2 Mary Louisa Muth (see above)

   2.16.9.1.2.1 Larry E. Bechtel (see above)

   2.16.9.1.2.2 Donald R. Bechtel (see above)

   2.16.9.1.2.3 Michael T. Bechtel (see above)

   2.16.9.1.2.4 Harold K. Bechtel (see above)

 2.16.9.2 Charles E. Klinger (see above)

2.17 Phoebe Klinger was born in 1839.

2.18 William Henry Klinger was born in 1842.

2.19 Jacob E. Klinger was born on 3 April 1843, Hubley Township, Schuylkill County, PA. He married **Sarah A. Reed**. Jacob was a private in Company D, Pennsylvania 172nd Volunteers. He was mustered out on 1 Aug 1863 at Harrisburg, PA. He died on 11 May 1899, Harrisburg, Dauphin County, PA, at age 56.

 2.19.1 Sevilla Agnes Klinger was born on 30 July 1865. She married **John Killian Clauser** on 27 May 1883, St. Paul's Lutheran Church, Tower City, Schuylkill County, PA. She died on 14 March 1922, Philadelphia, Philadelphia County, PA, at age 56. She was buried on 18 March 1922, at Mount Peace Cemetery, Philadelphia, Philadelphia County, PA.

  2.19.1.1 Charles Austin Clauser Sr. was born on 9 October 1883, Tower City, Schuylkill County, PA. He married **Elizabeth Bertha Brehmer**. He married **Maud Ethel Harris** after 1914. He died on 22 November 1955, Philadelphia, Philadelphia County, PA, at age 72.

   2.19.1.1.1 Charles Austin Clauser Jr. was born on 26 April 1911, Philadelphia, Philadelphia County, PA. He died in August 1977, at age 66.

  2.19.1.2 Carrie Edna Clauser was born on 3 March 1885, Shamokin, Northumberland County, PA. She married **Albert J. Hartley** in 1926, Philadelphia, Philadelphia County, PA. She died on 18 March 1952, Philadelphia, Philadelphia County, PA, at age 67.

  2.19.1.3 Sadie Mae Clauser was born on 10 May 1887. She married **Samuel E. McKinney Jr.** circa 1908. She died in September 1983, at age 96. She was buried at Ivy Hill Cemetery, Philadelphia, Philadelphia County, PA.

  2.19.1.4 Mary Clauser was born on 22 May 1890. She died on 5 October 1890. She was buried at Shamokin Cemetery, Shamokin, Northumberland County, PA.

 2.19.2 Abraham Klinger was born on 4 April 1867, Shamokin, Northumberland County, PA. According to some sources, Abraham was born in Dauphin County, PA. He married **Mary Elizabeth Snyder**, daughter of **William Snyder,** on 9 May 1885. He died on 23 March 1950, Bellefonte, Centre County, PA, at age 82.

  2.19.2.1 Sallie Mae Klinger was born on 8 August 1888. She died on 15 August 1903, at age 15.

  2.19.2.2 Charles Franklin Klinger was born on 5 February 1891. He married **Grace L. McDermott**. He died on 21 December 1949, West Deer Township, Allegheny County, PA, at age 58. He was buried at East Union Church Cemetery, Cheswick, Allegheny County, PA.

   2.19.2.2.1 Elizabeth Klinger died before 2009.

2.19.2.2.2 LORETTA FRANCES KLINGER was born on 10 June 1912, Clinton County, PA. She married RICHARD CLAIR RYDBOM SR. circa 1928. She married GEORGE SERVERN. She died on 14 September 2005, Gulfport, Harrison County, MS, at age 93.

> **2.19.2.2.2.1** RICHARD CLAIR RYDBOM JR. was born circa 1928. He married BETTY J. BURGESS, daughter of HARRY BURGESS and KATHERINE (--?--), on 31 July 1948, Alleghany County, NC.
>
> **2.19.2.2.2.2** REA NAOMI RYDBOM was born circa 1930. She married HENRY EDWARD BOWEN.
>
> **2.19.2.2.2.3** ADORA DELIGHT RYDBOM was born on 1 June 1931, Allegheny County, PA. She married CHESTER MELTON STOUT. She died on 18 November 2010, Summit County, OH, at age 79.
>
> **2.19.2.2.2.4** CALVIN BERNARD RYDBOM was born on 14 September 1935. He married GLADYS L. (--?--).
>
> **2.19.2.2.2.5** ROBERT JAMES RYDBOM was born on 14 February 1936, Allegheny County, PA. He married KAYE FRINKLEY on 7 December 1957. He died on 17 September 2013, Palmyra Township, Portage County, OH, at age 77. He was buried at Grandview Memorial Park, Ravenna, Portage County, OH.
>
>> **2.19.2.2.2.5.1** KIM RYDBOM married LOUELLA (--?--).
>>
>> **2.19.2.2.2.5.2** JULIE RYDBOM married WILLIAM CROOP.
>>
>>> **2.19.2.2.2.5.2.1** COLLIN CROOP
>>>
>>> **2.19.2.2.2.5.2.2** JENSON CROOP
>
> **2.19.2.2.2.6** ELLEN RUTH RYDBOM was born in 1937. She married ROBERT RANKIN.
>
> **2.19.2.2.2.7** AUDREY DALE RYDBOM was born in 1940. She married DONALD M. SCHAUER.
>
> **2.19.2.2.2.8** LARRY BLAIN RYDBOM was born on 14 September 1941, Allegheny County, PA. He died on 22 January 1942, Pittsburgh, Allegheny County, PA. He was buried at Mount Airy Cemetery, Natrona Heights, Allegheny County, PA.
>
> **2.19.2.2.2.9** LORETTA MARIE RYDBOM was born on 14 September 1942. She married (--?--) SMITH.
>
> **2.19.2.2.2.10** CHARLES ANDREW RYDBOM was born on 31 October 1944, Harris County, TX. He married CAROLYN DIANE REIST on 10 June 1973. He and CAROLYN DIANE REIST were divorced on 21 April 2004 Harris County, TX.
>
> **2.19.2.2.2.11** DAVID DOUGLAS KOESEL was born in 1946. He married BRENDA DARLENE TUCKER.
>
> **2.19.2.2.2.12** GEORGIA SERVERN married CHARLES WALTMAN.

2.19.2.2.3 MARGARET M. KLINGER was born on 13 February 1917, Lockport, Clinton County, PA. She married JACOB WALTER. She married WILLIAM MERLE ELDER after 1972. She died on 8 April 2009, Consulate Care Center, Cheswick, Allegheny County, PA, at age 92. She was buried at Lakewood Memorial Gardens, Dorseyville, Allegheny County, PA.

2.19.2.2.4 JEAN CHARLOTTE KLINGER was born in 1919. She married (--?--) HAINES. She died in 2003.

2.19.2.2.5 CHARLES FRANKLIN KLINGER JR. was born on 3 January 1923, Bitumen, Clinton County, PA. He married MARY JOAN ALLEN on 18 August 1952, Alleghany County, NC. He died on 16 November 1988, at age 65. He was buried at Lakewood Memorial Gardens, Dorseyville, Allegheny County, PA.

2.19.2.2.6 LUCILLE M. KLINGER was born in 1924. She married LOUIS J. SCHREIBER. She married FRANK S. DAWSON, son of ALFRED DAWSON and MARGARET CULP, after 1996. She and FRANK S. DAWSON were divorced before 2008.

> **2.19.2.2.6.1** LOUIS C. SCHREIBER was born on 5 June 1947, Pittsburgh, Allegheny County, PA. He married LINDA L. NICHOLAUS. He died on 3 June 2008, West Deer Township, Allegheny County, PA, at age 60. He was buried on 7 June 2008, at Mount Airy Cemetery, Natrona Heights, Allegheny County, PA.

2.19.2.2.6.2 **Terry D. Schreiber** was born on 31 October 1950, Pittsburgh, Allegheny County, PA. She married **Tony Guerrieri** circa 1971. She died on 9 August 2005, West Deer Township, Allegheny County, PA, at age 54.

2.19.2.2.6.2.1 **Robert A. Guerrieri Jr.** married **Lisa** (--?--).

2.19.2.2.6.2.1.1 **Zak Guerrieri**

2.19.2.2.6.2.1.2 **Cole Guerrieri**

2.19.2.2.6.2.2 **Stacey L. Guerrieri** married (--?--) **Lindgren**.

2.19.2.2.6.2.2.1 **Tyler Lindgren**

2.19.2.2.6.2.2.2 **Logan Lindgren**

2.19.2.2.7 **Louis Donald Klinger** was born on 4 October 1925, Bitumen, Clinton County, PA. He married **Mary Elsie Oswald** in 1950. He died on 23 October 2002, UPMC Passavant Hospital, McCandless, Allegheny County, PA, at age 77. He was buried at Saint Marys of the Assumption Cemetery, Glenshaw, Allegheny County, PA.

2.19.2.2.8 **Richard C. Klinger** was born on 12 February 1928. He married **Marlene R. Seel**, daughter of **Albert Seel** and **Marie Huffmon**.

2.19.2.2.8.1 **Marianne Klinger** was born in 1962. She married **Gary Latuszewski**.

2.19.2.2.9 **Carl Allen Klinger** was born on 1 December 1929, Bairdford, Allegheny County, PA. He married **Hattie P.** (--?--). He died on 29 March 1989, at age 59.

2.19.2.3 **William Edward Klinger** was born on 25 September 1893, Dupont, Luzerne County, PA. According to some sources, William was born in Dauphin County, PA. He married **Julia R. Dearmitt** on 20 December 1920, Trinity United Methodist Church, Bellefonte, Centre County, PA. He died on 26 February 1929, Spring Township, Centre County, PA, at age 35. He was buried at Union Cemetery, Bellefonte, Centre County, PA.

2.19.2.3.1 **Pauline M. Klinger** was born on 1 December 1921, Centre County, PA. She died on 1 March 1923, Spring Township, Centre County, PA, at age 1. She was buried at Union Cemetery, Bellefonte, Centre County, PA.

2.19.2.3.2 **Roy Edward Klinger** was born on 12 March 1924, Spring Township, Centre County, PA. He married **Mary E. Woodring** on 28 November 1953. He died on 12 September 1992, State College, Centre County, PA, at age 68.

2.19.2.3.2.1 **Brenda Klinger**

2.19.2.3.2.2 **B. Hope Klinger**

2.19.2.3.2.3 **Edward Klinger**

2.19.2.3.2.4 **Braden Klinger**

2.19.2.3.2.5 **Scott Klinger**

2.19.2.3.2.6 **Timothy Klinger**

2.19.2.3.3 **Dorothy Alice Klinger** was born in 1928, Centre County, PA. She married **Paul Edward McClaskey** on 9 February 1946, Pleasant Gap, Centre County, PA.

2.19.2.4 **Infant Klinger** was born on 27 June 1896, Shamokin, Northumberland County, PA. He died on 27 June 1896, Shamokin, Northumberland County, PA. He was buried at Shamokin Cemetery, Shamokin, Northumberland County, PA.

2.19.2.5 **Getrude Alice Klinger** was born on 1 July 1898, Shamokin, Northumberland County, PA. She married **Homer Joseph Young** before 1921. She died on 18 January 1983, at age 84. She was buried at Union Cemetery, Bellefonte, Centre County, PA.

2.19.2.5.1 **Richard Allen Young** was born on 12 November 1922, Bellefonte, Centre County, PA. He married **Margaret Mae Dashem**, daughter of **Elmer Dashem** and **Maude Horner**, on 13 July 1946. He died on 29 May 2010, at age 87. He was buried at Emanuel Union Cemetery, Tusseyville, Centre County, PA.

2.19.2.5.1.1 **Ronald R. Young** married **Connie** (--?--).

2.19.2.5.1.1.1 **April Young** married **Hasan Mohamed**.

2.19.2.5.1.1.2 **Todd Young** married **Amber** (--?--).

2.19.2.5.1.1.2.1 **Connor Young**

2.19.2.5.1.2 ANN E. YOUNG was born on 21 July 1949, Bellefonte, Centre County, PA. She died on 24 December 2014, Hearthside Nursing and Rehabilitation Center, State College, Centre County, PA, at age 65. She was buried on 31 December 2014, at Emanuel Union Cemetery, Tusseyville, Centre County, PA.

2.19.2.5.2 HOMER JOSEPH YOUNG JR. was born on 9 April 1927, Bellefonte, Centre County, PA. He died on 18 January 1928, Bellefonte, Centre County, PA. He was buried on 20 January 1928, at Sunnyside Cemetery, Bellefonte, Centre County, PA.

2.19.2.6 INFANT KLINGER was born on 29 July 1898, Shamokin, Northumberland County, PA. He died on 30 July 1898, Shamokin, Northumberland County, PA. He was buried at Shamokin Cemetery, Shamokin, Northumberland County, PA.

2.19.2.7 FRANK M. KLINGER was born on 14 February 1904. He died on 25 February 1904. He was buried at Shamokin Cemetery, Shamokin, Northumberland County, PA.

2.19.2.8 ALLEN HENRY KLINGER was born on 23 June 1905, Mill Hall, Clinton County, PA. He married ANNA MAY MARIA DEARMENT. He died on 27 May 1947, Potter Township, Centre County, PA, at age 41. He was buried on 29 May 1947, at Potter Township, Centre County, PA.

2.19.2.8.1 JOYCE KLINGER was born circa 1932.

2.19.2.8.2 DENN A. KLINGER was born circa 1936.

2.19.3 HARVEY EDWARD KLINGER was born on 2 November 1869, Clark's Valley, Dauphin County, PA. He married MARY CARL, daughter of JOHN CARL and HANNAH WEARY, circa 1890. He died on 20 May 1930, Gregg Township, Centre County, PA, at age 60. He was buried at Odd Fellows Cemetery, Shamokin, Northumberland County, PA.

2.19.3.1 GUERNEY EDWARD KLINGER was born on 10 April 1892, Clark's Valley, Dauphin County, PA. He married CARRIE MAE CASSATT, daughter of WILLIAM CASSATT and HANNAH LEWIS, on 23 March 1920, Sunbury, Northumberland County, PA. He married MARY TABITHA FILER, daughter of GEORGE FILER and MARY A. POWELL, on 1 February 1952, Shamokin, Northumberland County, PA. He died on 27 November 1957, Shamokin State Hospital, Coal Township, Northumberland County, PA, at age 65. He was buried on 30 November 1957, at Odd Fellows Cemetery, Shamokin, Northumberland County, PA.

2.19.3.1.1 CHARLOTTE KLINGER married (--?--) VETOVICH. She died before 2005.

2.19.3.1.2 MARY KATHLENE KLINGER was born on 27 October 1921, Shamokin, Northumberland County, PA. She married GEORGE E. MARTIN. She died on 11 January 2005, Hospice of Lancaster County, Lancaster, Lancaster County, PA, at age 83.

2.19.3.1.2.1 GEORGE E. MARTIN married DONNA M. (--?--).

2.19.3.1.2.2 CHERYL L. MARTIN married KENNETH C. HERSHEY.

2.19.3.1.2.3 MARLENE ELAINE MARTIN was born on 4 August 1950, Lancaster, Lancaster County, PA. She married (--?--) STOUT. She married (--?--) REESE. She died on 1 June 2001, at age 50.

2.19.3.1.3 DOROTHY MAE KLINGER was born on 7 December 1922, Shamokin, Northumberland County, PA. She married (--?--) BUBERNACK. She died on 19 March 2003, at age 80. She was buried at Shamokin Cemetery, Shamokin, Northumberland County, PA.

2.19.3.1.4 ELIZABETH THELMA KLINGER was born on 18 February 1925, Shamokin, Northumberland County, PA. She married JOSEPH GEORGE THOMAS SR. She died on 5 February 2008, Lancaster, Lancaster County, PA, at age 82.

2.19.3.1.4.1 JOSEPH GEORGE THOMAS JR.

2.19.3.1.4.2 BETTY JANE THOMAS

2.19.3.1.4.3 CHARLES E. THOMAS

2.19.3.1.4.4 KATHALENE ANN THOMAS was born on 4 August 1952, Columbia, Lancaster County, PA. She married (--?--) DOLBY. She married (--?--) HURLBURT. She died on 14 August 2000, at age 48.

2.19.3.2 MURREL RAYMOND KLINGER was born on 19 December 1895, Shamokin, Northumberland County, PA. He married ANNA C. (--?--). He died in December 1982.

2.19.3.2.1 RAYMOND MURREL KLINGER was born on 28 May 1923, Trevorton, Northumberland County, PA. He married **LORRAINE E. (--?--)**. He died in January 1983, at age 59. He was buried at Glen Haven Memorial Park, Glen Burnie, Anne Arundel County, MD.

2.19.4 ULYAS GRAND KLINGER was born on 20 March 1872. He died on 11 January 1873.

2.19.5 FLORA A. KLINGER was born in 1874.

2.19.6 IRVIN KLINGER was born on 15 August 1876, Schuylkill County, PA. He died on 27 August 1937, Coal Township, Northumberland County, PA, at age 61.

2.19.7 HY. F. KLINGER was born in October 1879.

2.19.8 GUERNEY KLINGER was born in 1881.

2.20 JONAS KLINGER was born in April 1845. He married **MARIA WOLFE** circa 1872. He died on 26 February 1911, at age 65. He was buried at Zion (Klinger's) Church, Erdman, Lykens Township, Dauphin County, PA.

2.20.1 ELMER MICHAEL KLINGER is also referred to as **MICHAEL E. KLINGER** in some sources. He was born on 19 September 1874, Northumberland County, PA. Some sources record that he was born Different sources list Elmer's birth date variously, ranging between 1874 and 1878. The Zion (Klinger's) Church burial records suggest a birth date of 30 September 1874, while the cemetery listings give a date of 1876. The Census records give a range of birth dates from about 1876 through September 1878. Still other sources give a birth date of 9 September 1876. circa 1877, Pennsylvania. Several sources identify an "Elmer" Klinger, born circa 1876, as a son of Jonas and Maria (Wolf) Klinger. The 1880 Census for Lykens Township, Dauphin County, lists Jonas and Maria's children as "Michael E." Klinger (born c. 1877) and Clara A. Klinger (born c. 1879). While there appear to be no further records of "Michael E." Klinger, an "Elmer" or "Elmer M." Klinger, born Sep. 1878, appears in subsequent Census listings for Lykens Township. The Census listings for Jonas and Maria consistently indicate that they had only 2 children, and only one of them survived past 1900. These facts suggest that Michael E. Klinger, identified in the 1880 Census, is the person later listed as Elmer Klinger. He married **MARY CATHERINE ENGLE**, daughter of **ISAAC ENGLE** and **ISABELLE RUSSELL,** circa 1894. Some sources give Catherine's maiden name as "Engle." He died on 30 September 1954, Erdman, Dauphin County, PA. He was buried on 5 October 1954, at Zion (Klinger's) Church Cemetery, Erdman, Dauphin County, PA.

2.20.1.1 JENNIE I. KLINGER was born on 21 February 1896, Lykens Township, Dauphin County, PA. She married **FRANCIS SAMUEL DEIBERT**, son of **GEORGE E. DEIBERT** and **SARA A. (--?--)**. She died on 26 July 1970, Pottsville, Schuylkill County, PA, at age 74. She was buried on 5 August 1970, at Zion (Klinger's) Church Cemetery, Erdman, Dauphin County, PA.

2.20.1.1.1 CLARENCE R. DEIBERT was born on 17 January 1913. He died on 25 February 1997, at age 84.

2.20.1.1.2 HELEN I. DEIBERT was born on 8 April 1915. She married **(--?--) DUNKLE**. She married **ROY S. DUNKLE**, son of **SOLON R. DUNKLE** and **FRONIE T. SCHREINER**. She died in August 1983, at age 68. She was buried at Saint Pauls United Church of Christ Cemetery, Sacramento, Schuylkill County, PA.

2.20.1.1.3 LEROY DEIBERT was born on 31 May 1917. He married **PAULINE SCHAFFER**. He died in August 1967, at age 50. He was buried at Zion Lutheran Church Cemetery, Rife, Dauphin County, PA.

2.20.1.1.4 JOSEPH C. DEIBERT was born on 20 September 1923, Valley View, Schuylkill County, PA. He married **JEAN L. BIXLER** circa 1946. He died on 31 October 2014, Tremont Health and Rehabilitation Center, Tremont, Schuylkill County, PA, at age 91. According to a newspaper obituary, Joseph was a truck driver for the former M & G Convoy Co. prior to his retirement. He was buried on 3 November 2014, at St. Andrew's Cemetery, Valley View, Schuylkill County, PA.

2.20.1.1.4.1 JAY C. DEIBERT

2.20.1.1.4.1.1 JOSEPH DEIBERT

2.20.1.1.4.1.2 TIFFANY DEIBERT married **(--?--) LENKER.**

2.20.1.1.4.2 GUY T. DEIBERT was born in 1956, Valley View, Schuylkill County, PA. He married **LORI YOUSE** in 2001. He died on 6 June 2014, Schuylkill Medical Center-East Norwegian Street., Pottsville, Schuylkill County, PA. According to a newspaper obituary, Guy was an Army veteran and a truck driver for Stine Trucking in Branchdale.

2.20.1.1.4.2.1 CHRYSTAL DEIBERT

2.20.1.1.4.2.2 JOSEPH DEIBERT married AMANDA (--?--).

2.20.1.2 VERNA MAE KLINGER was born on 28 January 1898. She married ESTON EMANUEL KLINGER, son of GEORGE M. KLINGER and JULIANN KOPPENHAVER, on 30 May 1914, Frieden's Reformed Church, Hegins, Schuylkill County, PA. She died on 6 April 1977, at age 79. She was buried on 9 June 1977, at Zion (Klinger's) Church Cemetery, Erdman, Lykens Township, Dauphin County, PA.

2.20.1.2.1 JOHN ELWOOD KLINGER was born on 19 July 1916. He was baptized on 8 October 1916, Zion (Klinger's) Church, Erdman, Lykens Township, Dauphin County, PA. He married ALVERTA NELSON. He died in 1957. He was buried at Zion (Klinger's) Church Cemetery, Erdman, Dauphin County, PA.

2.20.1.2.1.1 VIOLET KLINGER married (--?--) KOHR. She died before 2012.

2.20.1.2.1.2 ALMA E. KLINGER married (--?--) UPDEGROVE.

2.20.1.2.1.3 KENNETH F. KLINGER was born on 27 August 1941. He married JUDITH I. RITZMAN. He died on 30 December 2011, Lebanon VA Medical Center, Lebanon, Lebanon County, PA, at age 70. According to a newspaper obituary, Kenneth, who lived in Orwin, Schuylkill County, PA, was a 1959 graduate of Porter Tower High School and an Army Veteran. He worked for TRW and then retired from AMP Inc, and later from Wegmans Distribution Center. He was buried on 5 January 2012, at Indiantown Gap National Cemetery, Annville, Lebanon County, PA.

2.20.1.2.2 BLANCHE IRENE KLINGER was born on 4 August 1918, Erdman, Lykens Township, Dauphin County, PA. She married ALLEN E. SCHEIB, son of OSCAR E. SCHEIB and CARRIE M. (--?--), on 25 August 1934, St. Andrew's United Methodist Church, Valley View, Schuylkill County, PA. She died on 1 December 2007, The Manor at Susquehanna Village, Millersburg, Dauphin County, PA, at age 89. According to a newspaper obituary, Blanche lived in Valley View, Schuylkill County, PA, where she was a seamstress for garment factories in the area. She was also an avid quilt maker. She was buried on 5 December 2007, at Zion (Klinger's) Church Cemetery, Erdman, Lykens Township, Dauphin County, PA.

2.20.1.2.2.1 MILDRED MARIE SCHEIB was born on 8 April 1935. She was baptized on 21 July 1935, St. Andrew's United Methodist Church, Valley View, Schuylkill County, PA. She married (--?--) SHEPLEY.

2.20.1.2.2.2 JOHNNY ALLEN OSCAR SCHEIB was born on 10 July 1947. He was baptized on 6 September 1947, St. Andrew's United Methodist Church, Valley View, Schuylkill County, PA.

2.20.1.2.3 WILLIAM GUY KLINGER was born on 13 December 1923. He was baptized on 12 April 1924, Zion (Klinger's) Church, Erdman, Lykens Township, Dauphin County, PA. He married WRELA V. (--?--). He died on 2 October 1970, at age 46. He was buried on 7 October 1970, at Zion (Klinger's) Church Cemetery, Erdman, Lykens Township, Dauphin County, PA.

2.20.1.2.4 THOMAS LEROY KLINGER was born on 26 June 1926, Erdman, Dauphin County, PA. Some sources record that he was born on 25 June 1926. He was baptized on 10 August 1926, Frieden's Reformed Church, Hegins, Schuylkill County, PA. He married DOROTHY ARLENE SHIPMAN on 11 September 1948, Zion (Klinger's) Church, Erdman, Dauphin County, PA. He married BETTY A. FESIG, daughter of GEORGE FESIG and BESSIE SILKS. He died on 23 May 1997, Polyclinic Hospital, Harrisburg, Dauphin County, PA, at age 70. He was buried on 28 May 1997, at St. James' Cemetery, Carsonville, Dauphin County, PA.

2.20.1.2.4.1 RICHARD KLINGER

2.20.1.2.4.2 VIRGINIA KLINGER married (--?--) KISSINGER.

2.20.1.2.4.3 KATHRYN SUSAN MAE KLINGER was born on 12 February 1949, Dauphin County, PA.

2.20.1.2.4.4 JANET RENEE KLINGER was born on 9 January 1950, Dauphin County, PA. She married CHARLES J. BAX JR.

2.20.1.2.4.5 BRENDA LEE KLINGER was born on 30 December 1950, Dauphin County, PA. She married (--?--) LENKER.

2.20.1.2.4.6 VICKIE JEAN KLINGER was born on 11 August 1952, Dauphin County, PA. She married ROBERT EUGENE CHUBB. She married EUGENE HARRY MACE, son of HARRY MACE and MYRLE KEENEY, circa 1979.

2.20.1.2.4.6.1 STACY M. CHUBB married JOHN LITCHFIELD.

2.20.1.2.4.6.2 BRIAN K. CHUBB was born on 27 July 1970, Harrisburg, Dauphin County, PA. He died on 7 January 2010, Harrisburg Hospital, Harrisburg, Dauphin County, PA, at age 39. He was buried at Oak Hill Cemetery, Millersburg, Dauphin County, PA.

2.20.1.2.4.6.2.1 BROOKE CHUBB

2.20.1.2.4.6.2.2 MOLLY CHUBB married (--?--) DIETRICH.

2.20.1.2.4.6.2.3 FELISHA CHUBB

2.20.1.2.4.6.2.4 MAKAYLA CHUBB

2.20.1.2.4.6.2.5 CODIE ALLEN CHUBB was born in 1991. He died in 2011. He was buried at Calvary United Methodist Church Cemetery, Wiconisco, Dauphin County, PA.

2.20.1.2.4.6.3 SONYA L. CHUBB was born on 9 May 1973. She married JOHN PARKER on 15 September 2001.

2.20.1.2.4.7 JACQUELINE L. KLINGER was born in 1959. She married HARRY G. KOONS. She married KENNETH L. DEPPEN.

2.20.1.2.5 BETTY MAY KLINGER was born on 25 October 1927. She was baptized on 29 November 1927, Frieden's Reformed Church, Hegins, Schuylkill County, PA. She married EMERY E. ERDMAN, son of FARUS RILEY ERDMAN and MACIE M. ENGLE. She died on 21 February 1996, at age 68.

2.20.1.2.6 SELIN HERMAN KLINGER is also referred to as CEYLON in some sources. He was born on 28 February 1929, Erdman, Dauphin County, PA. He was baptized on 18 May 1929, Frieden's Reformed Church, Hegins, Schuylkill County, PA. He died on 9 April 2011, Community Hospital, Sunbury, Northumberland County, PA, at age 82. According to a newspaper obituary, Selin lived in Erdman, Dauphin County, PA. He was buried on 14 April 2011, at Zion (Klinger's) Church Cemetery, Erdman, Dauphin County, PA.

2.20.1.2.7 GEORGE ELMER KLINGER was born on 1 February 1936. He was baptized on 1 March 1936, Zion (Klinger's) Church, Erdman, Lykens Township, Dauphin County, PA. He died on 20 October 2003, Pennsylvania at age 67.

2.20.1.3 CHARLES R. KLINGER was born on 6 October 1900. He married BEULAH M. HAIN circa 1922. He died on 9 June 1956, Geisinger Hospital, Danville, Montour County, PA, at age 55. He was buried on 13 June 1956, at Zion (Klinger's) Church Cemetery, Erdman, Dauphin County, PA. At the time of his death, Charles was living in Erdman, PA.

2.20.1.3.1 CATHERINE EMMA KLINGER was born on 6 August 1924. She was baptized on 2 November 1924, Frieden's Reformed Church, Hegins, Schuylkill County, PA. She married HAROLD GRANT KISSINGER on 11 May 1946, Reformed Parsonage, Lykens, Dauphin County, PA. Prior to her death, Catherine was living in Elizabethtown, Lancaster County, PA. She died on 4 July 1997, Polyclinic Hospital, Harrisburg, Dauphin County, PA, at age 72. She was buried on 8 July 1997, at Zion (Klinger's) Church Cemetery, Erdman, Dauphin County, PA.

2.20.1.3.1.1 DONALD LEE KISSINGER married SUSAN (--?--).

2.20.1.3.1.2 RONALD KISSINGER married TINA (--?--).

2.20.1.3.1.3 MARILYN D. KISSINGER was born on 8 November 1952, Polyclinic Hospital, Harrisburg, Dauphin County, PA. She married (--?--) NEY. She married RODGER YOUNG on 29 August 1988, Coatesville, PA. She died on 16 March 2011, Geisinger Medical Center, Danville, Montour County, PA, at age 58. According to a newspaper obituary, Marilynn, lived in Lancaster County for much of her life before moving to Mount Carmel, Northumberland County, where she lived for about 15 years. She worked as a production worker for Charles Chips.

2.20.1.3.1.3.1 DONNY NEY married TRACY (--?--).

2.20.1.3.1.3.2 JEREMIAH J. NEY married ANGELA (--?--).

2.20.1.3.1.3.3 ASHLEY NEY

2.20.1.3.2 FLOYD ELMER KLINGER was born on 31 December 1925, Lykens, Dauphin County, PA. He was baptized on 21 February 1926, Frieden's Reformed Church, Hegins, Schuylkill County, PA. He married **DOROTHY CLARA SMITH**, daughter of **CHARLES SMITH** and **CARRIE IRENE OXENRIDER**, on 18 January 1947. He died on 12 September 2010, Holy Spirit Hospital, Camp Hill, Cumberland County, PA, at age 84. According to a newspaper obituary, Floyd was a veteran of the US Army during World War II. He was a retired truck driver for the US Postal Service, and prior to that he drove for Big Yank Shirt Factory, Millersburg. He also drove coach and school buses. He was buried on 15 September 2010, at Riverview Memorial Gardens, Halifax, Dauphin County, PA.

    2.20.1.3.2.1 MAE KLINGER married **LEROY ARTHUR SHADE**, son of **ALBERT LEROY SHADE** and **SULA MAY JOHNS**, on 25 May 1970.

        2.20.1.3.2.1.1 JEFFREY SHADE married **SHELBY (--?--)**.

        2.20.1.3.2.1.2 JULIE MARIE SHADE married **SCOTT DEPPEN**.

2.20.1.3.3 BETTY JUNE KLINGER was born on 17 July 1927. She was baptized on 17 August 1927, Frieden's Reformed Church, Hegins, Schuylkill County, PA. She married **ERNEST C. ERDMAN**, son of **HERMAN W. ERDMAN** and **JENNIE E. MATTERN**. She died on 13 February 2014, Harrisburg Hospital, Harrisburg, Dauphin County, PA, at age 86. According to a newspaper obituary, Betty, who lived in Erdman, PA, was employed at Muskin Shoe Factory and picked grapes at Romberger's Vineyard, and for the largest part of her life was a homemaker. She was buried on 18 February 2014, at Zion (Klinger's) Lutheran Church Cemetery, Erdman, Dauphin County, PA.

    2.20.1.3.3.1 LAMAR E. ERDMAN married **KAREN (--?--)**. Lamar lives in Sacramento, PA.

    2.20.1.3.3.2 RANDY L. ERDMAN married **JANE (--?--)**. Randy lives in Ashland, PA.

    2.20.1.3.3.3 SHARON ERDMAN married **LEONARD L. STROHECKER JR.** Sharon lives in Erdman, PA.

2.20.1.3.4 CHARLES DAVID KLINGER was born on 3 November 1929. He was baptized on 8 December 1929, Frieden's Reformed Church, Hegins, Schuylkill County, PA. Charles lives in Erdman, PA.

2.20.1.3.5 ISABEL GLADYS KLINGER was born on 31 August 1931. She was baptized on 22 October 1931, Frieden's Reformed Church, Hegins, Schuylkill County, PA. She married **WILLARD EARL OXENRIDER**, son of **EARL MONROE OXENRIDER** and **ALMA MARIE KLINGER**, on 24 December 1949. She died on 21 May 1996, at age 64.

    2.20.1.3.5.1 DEBRA ANN OXENRIDER was born on 7 November 1955. She was baptized on 3 December 1955, Salem (Herb's) Church, Rough and Ready, Schuylkill County, PA. She married **RICHARD ERDMAN**.

        2.20.1.3.5.1.1 CHRISTIE MARIE ERDMAN was born on 20 November 1975.

        2.20.1.3.5.1.2 STACEY LYNN ERDMAN was born on 24 October 1979.

    2.20.1.3.5.2 BILLIE EARL OXENRIDER was born on 30 November 1961. He was baptized on 21 January 1962, Salem (Herb's) Church, Rough and Ready, Schuylkill County, PA. He married **ANN CARL** on 28 April 1978, Weishample, PA.

        2.20.1.3.5.2.1 LYNNETTE ANN OXENRIDER was born on 8 August 1979.

        2.20.1.3.5.2.2 JASON EARL OXENRIDER was born on 26 January 1981.

2.20.1.4 LUTHER E. KLINGER was born in 1904. He married **HELEN A. ENGLE** circa 1925. He died in 1989. He was buried at Zion (Klinger's) Lutheran Church Cemetery, Erdman, Dauphin County, PA.

    2.20.1.4.1 ERNEST LUTHER KLINGER was born on 26 July 1925, Klingerstown, Schuylkill County, PA. He was baptized on 4 October 1925, Frieden's Reformed Church, Hegins, Schuylkill County, PA. He married **ALMA MAE ROTHERMEL**, daughter of **CHARLES EDWIN ROTHERMEL** and **MARY CARDELLA SHAFFER**, circa 1946. He died on 30 October 2011, at age 86. According to a newspaper obituary, Ernest attended Kessler's School and Hubley Township School. Ernie was self-employed working as a plumber, electrician, farmer and also ran a barber shop with his father. He was always self-employed and either worked alone or with his father his entire life.

    He was a member of Zion Lutheran (Klinger's) Church and served on the church council. He was proud to have been responsible for placing the Archangel Gabriel on the church steeple. He served on the Lykens Township Planning Committee and served on the Gratz Fair Board for close to 60 years. He was also proud to be the leader of Boy Scout Troop 152 of Erdman for many years and also the Gratz Boy Scout Troop for a number of years.

In December of 1989 he lived out his dream by completing and moving into his log home and was proud to have taken care of the grass mowing and upkeep until 3 years ago. He was buried on 4 November 2011, at Riverview Memorial Gardens, Halifax, Dauphin County, PA.

 2.20.1.4.1.1 MARY C. KLINGER married (--?--) LEITZEL. Mary lives in Mechanicsburg, PA.

  2.20.1.4.1.1.1 MICHAEL E. LEITZEL

   2.20.1.4.1.1.1.1 SETH M. LEITZEL

   2.20.1.4.1.1.1.2 JOHN P. LEITZEL

   2.20.1.4.1.1.1.3 SARAH A. LEITZEL

 2.20.1.4.1.2 STEPHEN E. KLINGER. Stephen lives in Lykens, PA.

2.20.1.4.2 PAULINE MARIE KLINGER was born on 26 September 1927. She was baptized on 29 November 1927, Frieden's Reformed Church, Hegins, Schuylkill County, PA. She married **CHARLES ELSWORTH HERB**, son of **EDWIN LEE HERB** and **IDA MINERVA REBUCK**. She died in October 1964, at age 37.

 2.20.1.4.2.1 EDWIN L. HERB. Edwin was raised by his uncle Ernest Klinger and aunt Alma Klinger.

 2.20.1.4.2.2 ROY PAUL HERB was born on 6 July 1961. He was baptized on 30 March 1967, Zion (Klinger's) Lutheran Church, Erdman, Dauphin County, PA.

2.20.1.4.3 ROBERT RAYMOND KLINGER was born on 17 August 1931, Erdman, Lykens Township, Dauphin County, PA. He was baptized on 22 October 1931, Frieden's Reformed Church, Hegins, Schuylkill County, PA. He married **ELSIE BROWN** circa 1952. He died on 18 February 2004, at home, Sunbury Street, Dalmatia, Northumberland County, PA, at age 72. He was buried on 23 February 2005, at Riverview Memorial Gardens, Halifax, Dauphin County, PA.

 2.20.1.4.3.1 KENNETH KLINGER

 2.20.1.4.3.2 KELVIN KLINGER

 2.20.1.4.3.3 KRISTA KLINGER

 2.20.1.4.3.4 KANDY KLINGER married **STEVEN WILBERT CONRAD JR.**, son of **STEVEN WILBERT CONRAD SR.** and **MARGARET IRENE SHINGARA**.

2.20.1.4.4 SHIRLEY KLINGER was born circa 1936. She married **ROY MARVIN KAHLER**, son of **NORMAN KAHLER** and **MILDRED SOPHIA KAHLER**, on 4 May 1957.

 2.20.1.4.4.1 GARY KAHLER married **PATTI (--?--)**.

 2.20.1.4.4.2 ELAINE KAHLER married **TERRANCE MACON**.

 2.20.1.4.4.3 LISA KAHLER married (--?--) REITZ.

2.20.1.5 STANLEY ROOSEVELT KLINGER was born on 29 September 1908. He married **KATIE IRENE RAMBERGER**, daughter of **DANIEL EDGAR RAMBERGER** and **MARY EVA SNYDER**, on 12 May 1928, Frieden's Reformed Church, Hegins, Schuylkill County, PA. He died on 9 August 1995, at age 86. He was buried at St. Michael's Lutheran Church Cemetery, Klingerstown, Schuylkill County, PA.

 2.20.1.5.1 DONALD A. KLINGER. Don lives in Klingerstown, PA.

 2.20.1.5.2 RONALD L. KLINGER. Ronald lives in Palmyra, PA.

 2.20.1.5.3 MARIAN ROMAINE KLINGER was born on 27 February 1928, Klingerstown, Schuylkill County, PA. She was baptized on 9 June 1928, Frieden's Reformed Church, Hegins, Schuylkill County, PA. She married **MARLIN LEROY SCHREFFLER**, son of **SAMUEL SCHREFFLER** and **KATIE JEMIMA DONMOYER**. She died on 4 March 2011, Harrisburg Hospital, Harrisburg, Dauphin County, PA, at age 83. According to a newspaper obituary, Marian worked for the former Ned Rich and Gorden Peters, in Elizabethville, where she also resided. She was buried at Maple Grove Cemetery, Elizabethville, Dauphin County, PA.

  2.20.1.5.3.1 RICHARD SCHREFFLER married **SUE (--?--)**. Richard lives in Palmyra, PA.

  2.20.1.5.3.2 MICHAEL SCHREFFLER. Michael lives in College Park, MD.

  2.20.1.5.3.3 SUSAN SCHREFFLER married **STEVE TROUTMAN**. Susan lives in Elizabethville, PA.

 2.20.1.5.4 DENNIS EUGENE KLINGER was born circa 1929. Dennis lives in Herndon, PA.

2.20.1.5.5 STANLEY HOWARD KLINGER was born on 30 March 1930, Klingerstown, Schuylkill County, PA. He was baptized on 22 June 1930, Frieden's Reformed Church, Hegins, Schuylkill County, PA. He married **VIOLA C. DOCKEY** on 28 August 1954. He died on 5 September 2009, at his home on Rumshton Road, Lykens, Dauphin County, PA, at age 79. According to a newspaper obituary, Stanley, who lived near Lykens, Dauphin County, PA, graduated from the former Hegins Township High School and was a Marine Corps veteran serving in the Korean War. In 1992, he retired as a meat cutter from Troutman Brothers, Inc., in Klingerstown. He was buried on 19 September 2009, at St. Michael's Lutheran Church Cemetery, Klingerstown, Schuylkill County, PA.

> **2.20.1.5.5.1 DALE KLINGER** was born on 21 March 1955. He married **CAROL ANN ROADCAP**, daughter of **WARD ROADCAP** and **ELEANOR (--?--)**, in December 1977. Dale lives in Gratz, PA.
>
>> **2.20.1.5.5.1.1 ADAM KLINGER**
>>
>>> **2.20.1.5.5.1.1.1 IAIN KLINGER** was born in 2011.
>>>
>>> **2.20.1.5.5.1.1.2 EMERSON KLINGER** was born in 2013.
>
> **2.20.1.5.5.2 DAVID STANLEY KLINGER** was born on 6 January 1958. He married **BARBARA (--?--)**.
>
>> **2.20.1.5.5.2.1 ASHLEY KLINGER**

2.20.1.5.6 RANDALL KLINGER was born in 1931. He died in 1961.

2.20.1.5.7 ROY EDGAR KLINGER was born on 28 February 1932. He was baptized on 24 April 1932, Frieden's Reformed Church, Hegins, Schuylkill County, PA. He married **ANZONETTA JANE HOFFNER**, daughter of **RUSSELL HOFFNER** and **ELIZABETH NEWCOMER**, circa 1958. He died on 2 May 2013, at age 81. He was buried at Indiantown Gap National Cemetery, Annville, Lebanon County, PA.

> **2.20.1.5.7.1 DANIEL KLINGER** married **TRISH (--?--)**. Daniel lives in Camp Hill, PA.
>
>> **2.20.1.5.7.1.1 ANDREW KLINGER**
>>
>> **2.20.1.5.7.1.2 JOSEPH KLINGER**

2.20.1.5.8 WILLIAM ELMER KLINGER was born on 16 December 1933. He was baptized on 6 May 1934, St, Michael's Church, Klingerstown, Schuylkill County, PA. William lives in Klingerstown, PA.

2.20.1.5.9 DEAN ELLWOOD KLINGER was born on 16 March 1936. He was baptized on 7 August 1936, Frieden's Reformed Church, Hegins, Schuylkill County, PA. He married **BETTY L. (--?--)**. He died on 31 May 1991, at age 55.

> **2.20.1.5.9.1 TERRY KLINGER**
>
> **2.20.1.5.9.2 DEAN KLINGER JR.**
>
> **2.20.1.5.9.3 TAMMY KLINGER**
>
> **2.20.1.5.9.4 DIANE KLINGER**

2.20.1.5.10 RUTH ANN KLINGER was born on 12 May 1939. She was baptized on 6 August 1942, Frieden's Reformed Church, Hegins, Schuylkill County, PA. She married **MARK RICHARD SIMS**, son of **HENRY SIMS** and **HELEN DEWALT**, on 31 May 1958. Ruth Ann lives in Lykens Township, Dauphin County, PA.

> **2.20.1.5.10.1 ALAN SIMS.** Alan lives in Lykens, PA.
>
> **2.20.1.5.10.2 BRIAN SIMS** married **DEANNA (--?--)**. Brian lives in Klingerstown, PA.
>
> **2.20.1.5.10.3 DOREEN SIMS** married **(--?--) DOCKEY**. Doreen lives in Harrisburg, PA.
>
> **2.20.1.5.10.4 CAROLYN SUE SIMS** was born on 30 January 1962, Harrisburg, Dauphin County, PA. She married **RODNEY C. FENSTERMACHER**, son of **GILBERT FENSTERMACHER** and **CORDELIA (--?--)**, circa 1991. Carolyn lives in Lykens, PA. She was buried on 2 January 2016, at St. Peter's (Hoffman's) United Church of Christ Cemetery, Lykens, Dauphin County, PA.

2.20.1.5.11 CAROL JEAN KLINGER was born on 21 May 1941. She was baptized on 6 August 1942, Frieden's Reformed Church, Hegins, Schuylkill County, PA. She married **DARVIN ELMER TROUTMAN**, son of **HARVEY E. TROUTMAN** and **CARRIE VIOLET KRATZER**. Carol lives in Klingerstown, PA.

2.20.1.5.11.1 KEITH ALLEN TROUTMAN

2.20.1.5.12 GLENN LAMAR KLINGER was born on 24 January 1944. He was baptized on 10 March 1945, Frieden's Reformed Church, Hegins, Schuylkill County, PA. He died in 1991.

2.20.1.6 ROY S. KLINGER was born on 12 October 1910, Lykens, Dauphin County, PA. He married EVA M. REED, daughter of WILLIAM REED and LILLIE BROWN, on 6 February 1943, Frieden's Reformed Church, Hegins, Schuylkill County, PA. He died on 23 April 1973, Lykens, Dauphin County, PA, at age 62. He was buried at Zion (Klinger's) Lutheran Church Cemetery, Erdman, Dauphin County, PA.

2.20.2 CLARA MALA KLINGER is also referred to as CLARA A. in some sources. She was born on 9 July 1878. She was baptized on 31 August 1878, Zion (Klinger's) Church, Erdman, Lykens Township, Dauphin County, PA. She died before 1900.

3 EVE ELIZABETH KLINGER is also referred to as EVA KLINGER in some sources. She was born on 16 January 1794, Lykens Township, Dauphin County, PA. She was baptized on 16 February 1794, Zion (Klinger's) Church, Erdman, Lykens Township, Dauphin County, PA. She married SAMUEL WIEST, son of JACOB WIEST and BARBARA FEICK. Samuel was a farmer, cattleman, butcher, and logger, who lived on a 500 acre farm. In later years, he retired to a home located about one-half mile west of Klingerstown. She died on 18 January 1870, PA at age 76. She was buried at Zion (Klinger's) Church Cemetery, Erdman, Lykens Township, Dauphin County, PA.

3.1 BARBARA WIEST was born on 30 May 1814, Jordan Township, Northumberland County, PA. According to the Deppen Family History ("Counting Kindred"), Barbara Wiest and Abraham Deppen had a child, Henry W. Deppen, before each one married other persons. She married DANIEL B. SNYDER. She died on 2 June 1886, at age 72. She was buried at St. David's Lutheran and Reformed Church, Hebe, Jordan Township, Northumberland County, PA.

3.1.1 HENRY W. DEPPEN was born on 16 September 1833, Jordan Township, Northumberland County, PA. He married AMANDA LETTIG in 1857. He died on 20 October 1902, at age 69. He was buried at St. David's Lutheran and Reformed Church, Hebe, Jordan Township, Northumberland County, PA.

3.1.1.1 ELIZABETH DEPPEN was born on 29 May 1858, Jordan Township, Northumberland County, PA. She married WILLIAM KOPENHAVER. She died in April 1905, at age 46. She was buried at Pottsville, Schuylkill County, PA.

3.1.1.1.1 CHARLES KOPENHAVER married GRACE WEAHY. He died before 1940, CA.

3.1.1.1.2 WILLIAM KOPENHAVER married ALICE MESSNER. He died before 1940.

3.1.1.1.2.1 MARIAN KOPENHAVER

3.1.1.1.2.2 HELEN KOPENHAVER

3.1.1.1.2.3 SARAH KOPENHAVER

3.1.1.1.2.4 GRACE KOPENHAVER

3.1.1.1.3 HARRY W. KOPENHAVER married FLORENCE ENDY. He lived in Newport, VA.

3.1.1.1.3.1 MARGARET KOPENHAVER

3.1.1.1.3.2 WALTER KOPENHAVER

3.1.1.1.3.3 WARREN KOPENHAVER

3.1.1.1.3.4 EMILY E. KOPENHAVER died before 1940.

3.1.1.1.3.5 ELIZABETH KOPENHAVER was born on 29 October 1919.

3.1.1.1.4 RUFUS KOPENHAVER was born on 13 May 1877. He married MATHILDA HEPLER. He married LOUISE GRUBE. He lived in New Ringgold, PA.

3.1.1.1.4.1 JARED KOPENHAVER was born on 2 May 1914. He married JEAN ANDREA (--?--). He lived in Brooklyn, NY.

3.1.1.1.4.2 IVAN KOPENHAVER was born in December 1916. He married JOSEPHINE GUTHIE. He lived in Tamaqua, PA.

3.1.1.1.4.3 ETHEL KOPENHAVER was born on 22 September 1917. She married HARVEY LECHLENLEITER.

3.1.1.1.4.3.1 NAOMI LECHLENLEITER was born on 5 August 1935.

3.1.1.1.4.4 OLVEN KOPENHAVER was born on 2 September 1919. She married WILLIAM F. BAILEY. She lived in New Ringgold, PA.

3.1.1.1.5 HARVEY KOPENHAVER was born circa 1879, Pennsylvania. He married **KATE PEIFFER**. He died before 1940.

> **3.1.1.1.5.1 CHARLES KOPENHAVER**
>
> **3.1.1.1.5.2 HARVEY KOPENHAVER JR.**

3.1.1.1.6 MINNIE KOPENHAVER was born on 1 April 1884. She married **FRANK BINDLEY** circa 1902. She lived in New Ringgold, PA. She died on 7 November 1937, at age 53.

> **3.1.1.1.6.1 FRANKLIN BINDLEY** was born on 26 February 1902.
>
> **3.1.1.1.6.2 LEROY BINDLEY** was born on 16 February 1906. He married **CATHERINE MOLTZ**.
>
>> **3.1.1.1.6.2.1 VIRGINIA BINDLEY** was born on 15 May 1932.
>>
>> **3.1.1.1.6.2.2 ARTICE BINDLEY** was born on 25 May 1936.
>
> **3.1.1.1.6.3 CHARLES BINDLEY** was born on 19 August 1912.
>
> **3.1.1.1.6.4 CATHERINE BINDLEY** was born on 19 July 1917.
>
> **3.1.1.1.6.5 DELBERT BINDLEY** was born on 8 July 1920.

3.1.1.2 WILLIAM DEPPEN was born on 21 December 1859. He married **KATIE WENTZEL** circa 1880. He died in 1931. He was buried at Hebe, Northumberland County, PA.

> **3.1.1.2.1 CHARLES W. DEPPEN** was born on 4 March 1881. He married **SARAH FRANCES BROSIOUS** circa 1908. He lived in Shamokin, PA.
>
>> **3.1.1.2.1.1 EMORY ALVIN DEPPEN** was born on 27 April 1898. He died in September 1898.
>>
>> **3.1.1.2.1.2 HARLAN F. DEPPEN** was born on 8 January 1902. He married **BESSIE SCHROEDER**. He lived in New Cumberland, PA.
>>
>>> **3.1.1.2.1.2.1 ROBERT DEPPEN** was born on 16 January 1927.
>
> **3.1.1.2.2 FANNY DEPPEN** was born on 7 August 1882. She married **JOHN H. BOHNER** circa 1901. She lived in Hebe, PA.
>
>> **3.1.1.2.2.1 BOYD BOHNER** was born on 29 May 1903. He married **VIOLET B. LEITZEL**.
>>
>>> **3.1.1.2.2.1.1 ARABELLA V. BOHNER** was born on 26 September 1924.
>>>
>>> **3.1.1.2.2.1.2 WILLIAM L. BOHNER** was born on 25 August 1926.
>>>
>>> **3.1.1.2.2.1.3 DEAN A. BOHNER** was born on 3 December 1929.
>
> **3.1.1.2.3 MINNIE DEPPEN** was born on 21 October 1884. She married **OSCAR SCHLEGEL**. She lived in Hebe, PA.
>
>> **3.1.1.2.3.1 WILLIAM SCHLEGEL** married **MABEL HOLLENBACH**. He was born on 22 June 1902.
>>
>>> **3.1.1.2.3.1.1 MARIAN SCHLEGEL** was born on 2 May 1928.
>>
>> **3.1.1.2.3.2 ANNA SCHLEGEL** married **ADAM REED**. She was born on 31 March 1905.
>
> **3.1.1.2.4 KATIE DEPPEN** was born on 23 January 1888. She married **FRANK SCHAEFFER** circa 1916. She lived in Hebe, PA.
>
>> **3.1.1.2.4.1 FERN SCHAEFFER** was born on 22 December 1916.
>>
>> **3.1.1.2.4.2 MABEL SCHAEFFER** was born on 4 February 1919. She married **NATHAN ADAMS**. She lived in Hebe, PA.
>>
>>> **3.1.1.2.4.2.1 LEONA ADAMS** was born on 8 August 1934.
>>>
>>> **3.1.1.2.4.2.2 SHIRLEY ADAMS** was born on 17 December 1935.
>>
>> **3.1.1.2.4.3 ERMA SCHAEFFER** was born on 31 August 1921.
>>
>> **3.1.1.2.4.4 RAY SCHAEFFER** was born on 21 November 1924.
>>
>> **3.1.1.2.4.5 MILDRED SCHAEFFER** was born on 13 February 1926.
>>
>> **3.1.1.2.4.6 ANNABELLE SCHAEFFER** was born on 5 May 1928.

3.1.1.3 THOMAS LINKOLN DEPPEN was born on 1 April 1861. He died on 23 December 1861.

3.1.1.4 SARAH DEPPEN was born on 24 January 1863. She married **CHARLES LUDWIG** circa 1881. She died in 1924.

> **3.1.1.4.1 WILLIAM LUDWIG** lived in Bristol, PA.

3.1.1.4.2 CARRIE LUDWIG was born circa 1882, Pennsylvania. She married **(--?--)** SWANGLER circa 1907. She later lived in Bristol, PA.

3.1.1.4.2.1 RUTH SWANGLER was born circa 1906.

3.1.1.4.3 THOMAS LUDWIG was born circa 1885. He died before 1940.

3.1.1.4.4 MABEL LUDWIG was born circa 1891, Pennsylvania. She lived in Centralia, PA.

3.1.1.4.5 ARTHUR LUDWIG was born circa 1894, Pennsylvania. He lived in Mount Carmel.

3.1.1.4.6 SARAH LUDWIG was born circa 1897.

3.1.1.4.7 WALTON LUDWIG was born circa 1897.

3.1.1.4.8 FLOSSIE LUDWIG was born circa 1898, Pennsylvania. She lived in Bristol, PA.

3.1.1.4.9 JOHN LUDWIG was born circa 1901, Pennsylvania. He lived in Bristol, PA.

3.1.1.4.10 MARIE LUDWIG was born circa 1904, Pennsylvania.

3.1.1.5 H. JOHNSON DEPPEN is also referred to as JOHN H. AND HENRY J. DEPPEN in some sources. He was born on 9 January 1865. He married CATHERINE A. TROUTMAN, daughter of SIMON TROUTMAN and SARAH SCHADEL, on 27 September 1884. He lived in Hebe, PA. He died on 24 June 1939, at age 74. He was buried at St. David's Lutheran and Reformed Church, Hebe, Jordan Township, Northumberland County, PA.

3.1.1.5.1 ALLEN SIMON DEPPEN was born on 12 February 1889. He was baptized on 10 March 1889, St. David's Lutheran and Reformed Church, Hebe, Jordan Township, Northumberland County, PA. He married LYDIA JANE BOHNER, daughter of WILLIAM T. BOHNER and ELIZABETH TROUTMAN. He died on 28 January 1932, at age 42. He lived in Hebe, PA.

3.1.1.5.1.1 MILDRED DEPPEN died before 2012.

3.1.1.5.1.2 RAY JONATHAN DEPPEN was born on 20 October 1912, Hebe, Jordan Township, Northumberland County, PA. He was baptized on 5 January 1913, St. David's Lutheran and Reformed Church, Hebe, Northumberland County, PA. He married MAE ELEANOR KESSLER, daughter of SINARY RAYMOND KESSLER and LOLA ALBERTA ZERBE, on 23 December 1933, Lutheran Parish, Urban, Northumberland County, PA. He lived in Gratz, PA. He died on 24 March 1997, Susquehanna Village, Millersburg, Dauphin County, PA, at age 84. According to a newspaper obituary, Ray was a retired farmer who formerly had lived in Lykens.

3.1.1.5.1.2.1 RAY JONATHAN DEPPEN JR. is also referred to as RAY JONATHON DEPPEN JR. in some sources. He was born on 14 August 1934, Erdman Hotel, Erdman, Lykens Township, Dauphin County, PA. He married JEAN MARIE HOOVER, daughter of HAROLD HOOVER and ELVA HOFFNER.

3.1.1.5.1.2.1.1 LYNN ALAN DEPPEN was born on 15 September 1957.

3.1.1.5.1.2.1.2 MARY ELIZABETH DEPPEN is also referred to as MARY LIZABETH DEPPEN in some sources. She was born on 23 December 1959, Lykens, Dauphin County, PA. She died on 27 August 1974, Reading Hospital, Reading, PA, at age 14.

3.1.1.5.1.2.1.3 THOMAS RAY DEPPEN was born on 21 August 1966, Harrisburg, Dauphin County, PA.

3.1.1.5.1.2.2 DELORES LaMAE DEPPEN was born on 7 August 1938, Gratz, Dauphin County, PA. She married CARL ROADCAP on 23 November 1963, Harrisburg, Dauphin County, PA.

3.1.1.5.1.2.2.1 DAWN ROADCAP was born on 26 June 1965, Harrisburg Hospital, Harrisburg, Dauphin County, PA.

3.1.1.5.1.2.2.2 KEVIN R. ROADCAP was born on 22 February 1967, Harrisburg Hospital, Harrisburg, Dauphin County, PA.

3.1.1.5.1.3 WILLIAM LLOYD DEPPEN was born on 4 December 1918, Hebe, Northumberland County, PA. He married MIRIAM IRENE KRATZER, daughter of PAUL RUSSELL KRATZER and LULA MARIE HOFFMAN, on 27 November 1941. He died on 3 February 2000, VA Medical Center, Lebanon County, PA, at age 81. He was buried at St. David's Cemetery, Hebe, Northumberland County, PA.

3.1.1.5.1.3.1 DAVID MICHAEL DEPPEN was born on 22 February 1949. He married DEBRA DENISE STARR, daughter of LEE PERCY STARR and ROSE MARIE PAUL, on 12

November 1971, Urban, Northumberland County, PA. He married **KELLY RIFE** after 1983.

3.1.1.5.1.3.1.1 HEIDI MARIE DEPPEN was born on 8 June 1971, Harrisburg Hospital, Harrisburg, Dauphin County, PA. She married **BRENT RUSSELL BUFFINGTON**, son of **GARY RUSSELL BUFFINGTON** and **ELLEN REBA WIEST**, on 6 October 2001, Gratz, Dauphin County, PA.

3.1.1.5.1.3.1.1.1 BROCK WILLIAM BUFFINGTON was born on 30 April 2004. He was baptized on 8 August 2004, Simeon Church, Gratz, Dauphin County, PA.

3.1.1.5.1.3.1.1.2 BRADEN JAMES BUFFINGTON was born on 27 April 2006. He was baptized on 6 August 2006, First Evangelical Lutheran Church, Chambersburg, Franklin County, PA.

3.1.1.5.1.3.1.1.3 BRYCE RUSSELL BUFFINGTON was born on 15 September 2008, Chambersburg Hospital, Chambersburg, Franklin County, PA.

3.1.1.5.1.3.1.2 ANTHONY MICHAEL DEPPEN was born on 26 July 1974, Harrisburg Hospital, Harrisburg, Dauphin County, PA. He married **JULIE BIDEN**.

3.1.1.5.1.3.1.3 ANDREW LEE DEPPEN was born on 26 September 1975, Harrisburg Hospital, Harrisburg, Dauphin County, PA.

3.1.1.5.1.4 MAE C. E. DEPPEN was born on 10 May 1924, Hebe, Northumberland County, PA. She married **WILLIAM M. KRATZER**. According to a newspaper obituary, Mae lived in Hebe, PA. She died on 27 December 2012, at age 88. She was buried at St. David's Lutheran and Reformed Church Cemetery, Hebe, Northumberland County, PA.

3.1.1.5.1.4.1 LANA KRATZER married **ROBERT FORSE**.

3.1.1.5.1.4.1.1 WILLIAM FORSE

3.1.1.5.1.4.2 CATHY KRATZER married (--?--) **SORRELL**.

3.1.1.5.1.4.3 RANDY KRATZER married **DONNA MUTH**, daughter of **CHARLES E. MUTH** and **ALTA PHILLIPS**.

3.1.1.5.1.4.3.1 MEGAN KRATZER (see above)

3.1.1.6 EMMA JANE DEPPEN was born on 10 May 1867. She married **CHARLES HENRY SCHWALM**, son of **DANIEL S. SCHWALM** and **MARY ANN WHEARY**, circa 1883. She died on 20 December 1931, at age 64.

3.1.1.6.1 HOLDEN E. SCHWALM is also referred to as **HALDEN** in some sources. He was born on 17 October 1884. He married **MARY A. OMHOLTZ** circa 1907. He died on 2 February 1934, at age 49. He lived in Millersburg, PA.

3.1.1.6.1.1 HOMER C. SCHWALM was born circa 1907.

3.1.1.6.1.2 ELVIN R. SCHWALM is also referred to as **EDWIN AND ELDIN** in some sources. He was born circa 1908.

3.1.1.6.2 ADA SCHWALM was born in December 1885. She married **ELIAS ARTZ**. She lived in Millersburg, PA.

3.1.1.6.2.1 LAWRENCE ARTZ married **HANNAH KIMMEL**.

3.1.1.6.2.1.1 ERNEST R. ARTZ. In August, 2007, Ernest was living in Schuylkill Haven, Schuylkill County, PA.

3.1.1.6.2.1.2 LINDA ARTZ married (--?--) **ROBINSON**. In August, 2007, Linda was living in Florida.

3.1.1.6.2.1.3 MAHLON R. ARTZ also went by the name of **STETS**. He was born on 16 September 1930, Spring Glen, Hubley Township, Schuylkill County, PA. He married **DOROTHY B. KUENTZLER** circa 1952. He died on 4 August 2007, Community Hospice House, Merrimack, NH, at age 76. According to a newspaper obituary, Mahlon was living in Nashua, NH, prior to his death. A graduate of Pottsville High School, he went on to earn a bachelor's degree in electrical engineering from Penn State University and a master's degree in electrical engineering from Northeastern University. After serving in the Navy Seabees, Mahlon worked for Lockheed Sanders, from which he retired as senior principal engineer. He was granted a patent for the solid state electronic compass, which he developed for the US Navy. He was buried on 8 August 2007, at New Hampshire Veteran's Cemetery, Boscawen, NH.

>**3.1.1.6.2.1.3.1 JEFFREY M. ARTZ.** In August, 2007, Jeffery was living in Los Angeles, CA.

>**3.1.1.6.2.1.3.2 LAWRENCE A. ARTZ** married **MARIANNE (--?--).** In August, 2007, Lawrence and his family were living in Nashua, NH.

>>**3.1.1.6.2.1.3.2.1 DANIEL ARTZ**

>>**3.1.1.6.2.1.3.2.2 MATTHEW ARTZ**

>>**3.1.1.6.2.1.3.2.3 JONATHAN ARTZ**

>>**3.1.1.6.2.1.3.2.4 KATIE ARTZ**

>**3.1.1.6.2.1.3.3 CYNTHIA S. ARTZ** married **JAMES KELLY.** In August, 2007, Cynthia and her family were living in Nashua, NH.

>>**3.1.1.6.2.1.3.3.1 STEPHEN KELLY**

>>**3.1.1.6.2.1.3.3.2 CHRISTINA KELLY**

>**3.1.1.6.2.1.3.4 STEPHANIE K. ARTZ** married **MARK HOWELL.** In August, 2007, Stephanie and her family were living in New York, NY.

3.1.1.6.2.2 CLARENCE ARTZ

>**3.1.1.6.2.2.1 LAMAR ARTZ**

3.1.1.6.2.3 RAYMOND ARTZ married **VERNA BROWN.**

>**3.1.1.6.2.3.1 RAYMOND ARTZ JR.**

>**3.1.1.6.2.3.2 EDWIN ARTZ**

3.1.1.6.2.4 WALTER ARTZ married **ELSIE WILLIAMS.** He married **CATHERINE CONRAD.**

>**3.1.1.6.2.4.1 LAURA ARTZ**

3.1.1.6.2.5 LESTER ARTZ

3.1.1.6.2.6 ESTON C. ARTZ was born on 27 May 1910. He married **MAE E. DUNLEVY,** daughter of **WILLIAM DUNLEVY** and **NORA UMHOLTZ.** He died in May 1970.

>**3.1.1.6.2.6.1 MARK L. ARTZ** married **PHYLLIS (--?--).**

>**3.1.1.6.2.6.2 WARREN E. ARTZ** married **JOSEPHINE (--?--).**

3.1.1.6.3 ELSIE SCHWALM was born in October 1887. She married **BEN KOPPENHAVER.** She lived in Spring Glen, Schuylkill County, PA.

>**3.1.1.6.3.1 HOWARD KOPENHAVER** died before 1940.

3.1.1.6.4 MINNIE M. SCHWALM was born in March 1889. She married **EDWIN S. KLINGER,** son of **SAMUEL KLINGER** and **MARY COLEMAN,** circa 1906. In 1940, Minnie and Edwin were living in Sacramento, Schuylkill County.

>**3.1.1.6.4.1 VERNA KLINGER** was born on 29 May 1908. She died circa 1909. She was buried at Fearnot Cemetery, Fearnot, Schuylkill County, PA.

>**3.1.1.6.4.2 ALLEN E. KLINGER** was born circa 1910.

>**3.1.1.6.4.3 MABEL V. KLINGER** was born circa 1911. She married **ALLEN WAGNER.**

>>**3.1.1.6.4.3.1 MAY WAGNER**

3.1.1.6.5 CARRIE E. SCHWALM was born circa 1884. Some sources record that she was born in January 1877, but this date, given in the 1900 Census, appears to be incorrect, because her mother Emma was only 10 years old in 1877. Some sources record that she was born on 3 May 1879 but this date, given in Deppen Family History, appears to be questionable. According to the 1900 Census, Carrie's parents had been married 17 years and their eldest daughter "Callie" had been born May 1883. This means that Emma was only 16 when she married Henry in about 1883. For Carrie to have been born in 1879, her mother Emma would have been only about 12 or 13 years old at the time. Subsequent Census records support a birth date of around 1883 or 1884. Some sources record that she was born in 1889, but this date, which appears in the Gratz History, is inconsistent with most other sources, except that the 1930 Census says that Carrie was 20 years old at the time of her marriage, which according to the 1900 Census occurred about 1899. She married **CLARENCE U. KRATZER** circa 1899. In 1940, Carrie was living in Gratz, Dauphin County, PA.

3.1.1.6.5.1 VERNA S. KRATZER was born on 29 November 1904. She married **ALLEN SCHOFSTAHL.** She died in 1924.

3.1.1.6.5.1.1 JEAN SCHOFSTAHL was born on 17 October 1920.

3.1.1.6.5.2 ALBERT ROOSEVELT KRATZER was born on 26 August 1906. He married **VIOLET STARR.** He married **DORA REINERT.** He lived in Herndon, PA. He died on 21 January 1992, at age 85.

3.1.1.6.5.3 BLANCHE MARGARET KRATZER was born on 20 May 1908. Some sources record that she was born on 20 May 1907. She married **WILLIAM P. TROUTMAN.** She lived in Reading, PA.

3.1.1.6.5.3.1 CHARLOTTE TROUTMAN was born on 8 February 1926.

3.1.1.6.5.3.2 ANNA TROUTMAN was born on 8 January 1927.

3.1.1.6.5.3.3 WILLIAM TROUTMAN JR. was born on 15 February 1931.

3.1.1.6.5.4 GUY LIVINGSTON KRATZER was born on 24 April 1911. He married **KATHRYN H. MILLER.** He died in March 1994, at age 82.

3.1.1.6.5.4.1 GUY M. KRATZER

3.1.1.6.5.5 RALPH HENRY KRATZER was born on 17 July 1921. He married **UNA E. BURNS.** He lived in Gratz, PA. Ralph was a blacksmith in Gratz, Dauphin County, PA. He died on 12 May 1964, CA at age 42.

3.1.1.6.5.5.1 CHRIS KRATZER

3.1.1.6.6 EMMA A. SCHWALM was born in August 1890. She married **HARRY A. HEPLER.** In 1940, Emma and Harry were residing in Pleasantville, NJ.

3.1.1.6.6.1 IDA S. HEPLER was born circa 1910. She married **JOHN JOSEPHSON** after 1930. In 1940, Ida and John Josephson were living in Absecon, NJ.

3.1.1.6.6.1.1 MARVIN JOSEPHSON

3.1.1.6.6.1.2 FRED JOSEPHSON

3.1.1.6.6.1.3 WAYNE JOSEPHSON

3.1.1.6.6.1.4 RUTH JOSEPHSON

3.1.1.6.6.2 AUSTIN HEPLER was born circa 1913. He married **MARY JOSEPHSON.** In 1940, Austin was living in Linwood, NJ.

3.1.1.6.6.2.1 NANCY HEPLER

3.1.1.6.6.2.2 MARY GRACE HEPLER

3.1.1.6.7 MABEL V. SCHWALM was born in November 1893. She married **HARRY E. OTTO** circa 1913. In 1940, Mabel and Harry were living in Hegins, Schuylkill County, PA.

3.1.1.6.7.1 AARON HENRY OTTO was born on 10 February 1915.

3.1.1.6.7.2 CLARENCE OTTO was born on 23 December 1923.

3.1.1.6.8 JENNIE M. SCHWALM was born in June 1895. She married **NOLEN E. MILLER** circa 1916. She lived in Spring Glen, Schuylkill County, PA.

3.1.1.6.8.1 JAMES D. MILLER was born circa 1912.

3.1.1.6.9 IDA ESTA SCHWALM was born circa 7 July 1898, Hubley Township, Schuylkill County, PA. She married **IRA CALMON KOPPENHAVER**, son of **CALVIN OSCAR KOPPENHAVER** and **SARAH L. HEBERLING,** on 10 May 1919, St. Andrew's Church, Valley View, Schuylkill County, PA. She died on 2 October 1936, Spring Glen, Schuylkill County, PA. She was buried on 7 October 1936, at U.B. Cemetery, Spring Glen, Schuylkill County, PA.

3.1.1.6.9.1 RUBY CATHLEEN KOPPENHAVER married (--?--) **REPPERT.** She was born on 30 November 1919. She died before 2008.

3.1.1.6.9.2 IRA ELVIN KOPPENHAVER was born on 6 January 1921. He died before 2008.

3.1.1.6.9.3 WARREN LORAINE KOPPENHAVER was born on 4 April 1922. He died before 2008.

3.1.1.6.9.4 CALVIN CHARLES KOPPENHAVER was born on 23 October 1924. He married MILDRED S. (--?--). He died on 27 June 2006, Kinkora Pythian Home, Duncannon, Perry County, PA, at age 81. According to a newspaper obituary, Calvin was retired from Speece's Dairy and was a member of Dauphin/Middle Paxton Fire Company and of American Legion Post #1001. He was a Marine Veteran of World War II. He was buried on 5 July 2006, at Indiantown Gap National Cemetery, Annville, Lebanon County, PA.

    3.1.1.6.9.4.1 DAVID C. KOPPENHAVER

    3.1.1.6.9.4.2 FRED J. KOPPENHAVER

3.1.1.6.9.5 ERNEST HENRY KOPPENHAVER was born on 23 December 1925, Spring Glen, Schuylkill County, PA. He married FREEDA MAE STENCE, daughter of JOHN STENCE and BESSIE KEITER. He died on 8 October 1980, at age 54. He was buried on 12 October 1980, at United Methodist Cemetery, Spring Glen, Schuylkill County, PA.

3.1.1.6.9.6 ARLENE MAY KOPPENHAVER was born on 27 March 1927, Spring Glen, Schuylkill County, PA. She married ROMAIN N. WISE, son of CHARLES MARLIN WISE and KATIE JULIAN LENKER. She died on 12 March 1988, Harrisburg, Dauphin County, PA, at age 60. She was buried at Maple Grove Cemetery, Elizabethville, Dauphin County, PA.

3.1.1.6.9.7 DANIEL MARTIN KOPPENHAVER was born on 28 August 1927. He died before 2008.

3.1.1.6.9.8 ANNA LUCILLE KOPPENHAVER was born on 27 December 1929, Spring Glen, Schuylkill County, PA. She married JOHN WARD JR. She died on 16 August 2008, at her home, Harrisburg, Dauphin County, PA, at age 78. According to a newspaper obituary, Anna lived in Harrisburg, PA, and prior to retirement she worked as a central supply technician with the Polyclinic Hospital in Harrisburg. She was buried at Woodlawn Memorial Gardens.

    3.1.1.6.9.8.1 LESLIEANN WARD married STEVEN REHM. Leslieann lives in Harrisburg, PA.

        3.1.1.6.9.8.1.1 STEPHANIE REHM

        3.1.1.6.9.8.1.2 KIMBERLY REHM

    3.1.1.6.9.8.2 DIANE WARD married MICHAEL CALHOUN. Diane lives in Dover, PA.

3.1.1.6.9.9 CEYLON LAMAR KOPPENHAVER is also referred to as SELIN KOPENHAVER in some sources. He was born on 11 January 1931. He married ELEANOR E. BOYER. He died on 9 August 2016, Seaton Manor, Orwigsburg, Schuylkill County, PA, at age 85. He was buried on 12 August 2016, at St. Michael's Church Cemetery, Tilden Township, Berks County, PA.

    3.1.1.6.9.9.1 DONNA L. KOPPENHAVER married DONALD E. HOSHAUER.

        3.1.1.6.9.9.1.1 HEIDI HOSHAUER married CHAD ZIEGLER.

            3.1.1.6.9.9.1.1.1 CHASE ZIEGLER died before 9 August 2016.

        3.1.1.6.9.9.1.2 HEATHER HOSHAUER married MARK KESSLER.

        3.1.1.6.9.9.1.3 D.J. HOSHAUER married BECKY (--?--).

3.1.1.6.9.10 MARY NAOMI KOPPENHAVER was born on 28 March 1932, Spring Glen, Schuylkill County, PA. She married MARVIN G. ARTZ, son of RALPH ARTHUR ARTZ and KATHRYN LOVINA LESHER. She died on 18 August 1996, at age 64.

3.1.1.7 SAMUEL GRANT DEPPEN was born on 10 August 1870. Some sources record that he was born circa 1872. He married EMMA SCHLEGEL circa 1883. Some sources suggest that he and EMMA SCHLEGEL were married circa 1892. In 1940, Samuel lived in Hershey, PA.

    3.1.1.7.1 CLARENCE RAY DEPPEN was born on 3 November 1891. He married ARNIE SMELTZ. He died on 11 May 1918, at age 26.

        3.1.1.7.1.1 MIRIAM DEPPEN married HAROLD BRANDT.

        3.1.1.7.1.2 MAY DEPPEN

        3.1.1.7.1.3 ARVEL DEPPEN married MARGARET (--?--).

    3.1.1.7.2 HARVEY DEPPEN was born on 3 November 1891. He married BLANCHE HEPNER. He lived in Pillow, PA.

        3.1.1.7.2.1 BEATRICE DEPPEN married ELMER SHADE. She lived in Berrysburg, PA.

        3.1.1.7.2.2 ELWOOD DEPPEN

3.1.1.7.2.3 Forrest Deppen

3.1.1.7.2.4 Charles Deppen

3.1.1.7.2.5 William Deppen

3.1.1.7.2.6 James Deppen

3.1.1.7.2.7 Harold Deppen was born in 1919. He died in 1939.

3.1.1.7.3 Arvel Grant Deppen was born on 3 January 1893. He married **Helen Yeick**. He lived in Palmyra, PA.

3.1.1.7.3.1 Ernest G. Deppen was born on 16 April 1923. He married **Lorraine (--?--)**. Ernest lived in Warner Robins, GA. He died on 30 September 1986, at age 63. He was buried at Andersonville National Historical Site, Andersonville, GA.

3.1.1.7.3.2 Richard Deppen was born on 26 August 1925.

3.1.1.7.3.3 Arvel Deppen Jr. was born on 25 August 1933.

3.1.1.7.4 Hattie Deppen was born on 27 September 1894. She died on 9 October 1899, at age 5.

3.1.1.7.5 Samuel Harry Deppen was born on 11 February 1897. He married **Irene Kent** circa 1920. In 1940, Samuel was living in Duncannon, PA.

3.1.1.7.5.1 Charles G. Deppen was born circa 1921.

3.1.1.7.5.2 Anna Deppen is also referred to as **Annie B.** in some sources. She was born circa 1922.

3.1.1.7.5.3 William K. Deppen was born circa 1924.

3.1.1.7.5.4 Helen R. Deppen was born circa 1927.

3.1.1.7.6 Charles Ralph Deppen was born on 9 March 1899. He married **Eva Kerstetter** circa 1920. In 1940, Charles (Ralph) was living in Annville, PA.

3.1.1.7.6.1 Millard Deppen. The listing for "Millard" given in some sources could be a duplicate for Willard.

3.1.1.7.6.2 Pearl Deppen was born circa 1922.

3.1.1.7.6.3 Betty Deppen was born circa 1927.

3.1.1.7.6.4 Willard Deppen was born circa 1928.

3.1.1.7.7 William Henry Deppen was born on 8 July 1901. He married **Viola Boyer**. He lived in Philadelphia, PA.

3.1.1.7.8 Anna Helen Deppen was born on 21 February 1904. She married **Charles R. Dell** circa 1921. In 1940, Anna lived in Hershey, PA.

3.1.1.7.8.1 Doris Dell

3.1.1.7.8.2 Carolyn Dell

3.1.1.7.8.3 May E. Dell was born circa 1921.

3.1.1.7.8.4 Robert W. Dell was born circa 1926.

3.1.1.7.8.5 William S. Dell was born circa 1927.

3.1.1.7.8.6 Donald L. Dell was born circa 1929.

3.1.1.7.9 Blanche Deppen was born on 13 February 1908. She married **Orville King**. She lived in Hershey, PA.

3.1.1.7.10 Eva Jane Deppen was born on 10 January 1909.

3.1.1.7.11 Floyd Edgar Deppen was born on 23 February 1910. He married **Elva Keckler** after 1930. In 1940, Floyd was living in Hershey, PA.

3.1.1.7.12 Roy Edwin Deppen was born on 15 August 1913. He died on 25 August 1913.

3.1.1.7.13 Melvin Oscar Deppen was born on 29 November 1914. He died on 11 March 1915.

3.1.1.7.14 Mary Fay Deppen was born on 8 April 1916. She married **Stewart Hess** after 1 April 1930. She lived in Hershey, PA.

3.1.1.7.14.1 Jacqueline Hess was born on 26 November 1931.

3.1.1.8 AMANDA SINORA DEPPEN is also referred to as **SALARAH AND SELARAH** in some sources. She was born on 9 August 1874. She married **WILSON ELLSWORTH KNORR**, son of **ISAAC C. KNORR** and **ELIZABETH FETTEROLF,** in 1891. In 1940, Amanda was living in Pleasantville , NJ.

> **3.1.1.8.1 GURNIE KNORR** is also referred to as **GUERNEY E.** in some sources. He was born on 23 November 1892, Pillow, Dauphin County, PA. Some sources record that he was born on 23 November 1894. He married **JOSEPHINE KOLVA** on 9 September 1913. In 1940, Gurnie lived in Lykens, Dauphin County, PA. He died on 3 February 1964, Lykens, Dauphin County, PA, at age 69.
>
> > **3.1.1.8.1.1 IRENE KNORR** was born on 15 June 1916. Some sources record that she was born circa 1918. She married **(--?--) ALVORD**.
> >
> > **3.1.1.8.1.2 JAMES B. KNORR** is also referred to as **JAMES H.** in some sources. He was born on 11 November 1921. Some sources record that he was born circa 1920.
> >
> > **3.1.1.8.1.3 MARGARET KNORR** died before 1940.
> >
> > **3.1.1.8.1.4 WALTER LEROY KNORR** was born on 20 August 1925. Some sources record that he was born circa 1916.
> >
> > **3.1.1.8.1.5 RAYMOND G. KNORR** was born on 30 June 1927. Some sources record that he was born circa 1914.
> >
> > **3.1.1.8.1.6 DOLLY KNORR** was born on 26 April 1930. Some sources record that she was born circa 1924. She married **(--?--) WHITMORE**.
> >
> > **3.1.1.8.1.7 INA LOU KNORR** was born on 8 November 1934. Some sources record that she was born circa 1922. She married **(--?--) MCNALIS**.
>
> **3.1.1.8.2 SULA G. KNORR** is also referred to as **SULA C.** in some sources. She was born in March 1896. She died on 20 August 1896. She was buried at St. Michael's Lutheran Church Cemetery, Klingerstown, Schuylkill County, PA.
>
> **3.1.1.8.3 AMANDA S. KNORR** was born circa 29 October 1896. She died on 10 December 1896. She was buried at St. Michael's Lutheran Church Cemetery, Klingerstown, Schuylkill County, PA.
>
> **3.1.1.8.4 STELLA KNORR** was born on 9 January 1898. She married **RICHARD YATES**. She lived in Atlantic City, NJ.
>
> > **3.1.1.8.4.1 RICHARD YATES JR.**
>
> **3.1.1.8.5 ROSE REGINA KNORR** also went by the name of **ROSIE**. She was born on 4 March 1904. Some sources record that she was born on 27 March 1904, Klingerstown, Schuylkill County, PA. She married **FORREST HERB KEISER**. In 1940, Rosie lived in Lykens, Dauphin County, PA. She married **CLARENCE HOFFMAN**.
>
> > **3.1.1.8.5.1 ARLENE KEISER**
> >
> > **3.1.1.8.5.2 ELAINE KEISER**
> >
> > **3.1.1.8.5.3 FORREST KEISER JR.**
> >
> > **3.1.1.8.5.4 WILBERT KEISER**
>
> **3.1.1.8.6 LUTHER R. KNORR** was born on 10 July 1906. He died on 15 September 1908, at age 2. He was buried at St. Michael's Lutheran Church Cemetery, Klingerstown, Schuylkill County, PA. Some sources list a "Wilson R. Knorr" with the same birth and death dates as Luther R.
>
> **3.1.1.8.7 BOYD KNORR** was born in 1909, Pennsylvania. Some sources record that he was born on 29 June 1906. He lived in Atlantic City, NJ.
>
> **3.1.1.8.8 MABEL KNORR** was born in 1912. She married **HARRY EPHRAIM WITMER**. She died on 17 October 1963, Lykens, Dauphin County, PA.
>
> > **3.1.1.8.8.1 MARY FLORENCE WITMER**
> >
> > **3.1.1.8.8.2 BETTY J. WITMER** was born on 28 April 1936, Lykens, Dauphin County, PA. She married **JAMES C. BUGGY**. She died on 20 August 2009, The Manor at Susquehanna Village, Millersburg, Dauphin County, PA, at age 73. According to a newspaper obituary, Betty lived in Lykens and was retired from Reiff & Nestor Co., a machine tool manufacturer in Lykens. She was buried on 25 August 2009, at Sacred Heart of Jesus Cemetery, Williamstown, Dauphin County, PA.
> >
> > > **3.1.1.8.8.2.1 JAMES C. BUGGY.** James lives in Halifax, PA.

3.1.1.8.8.2.2 WILLIAM M. BUGGY. William lives in Hong Kong.

3.1.1.8.8.2.3 JEROME P. BUGGY. Jerome lives in Middletown, PA.

3.1.1.8.8.2.4 KENNETH J. BUGGY. Kenneth lives in Hummelstown, PA.

3.1.1.8.8.2.5 LISA M. BUGGY married (--?--) **BARRY.** Lisa lives in Reading, PA.

3.1.1.8.8.2.6 ANN E. BUGGY married (--?--) **WIEST.** Ann lives in Tower City, PA.

3.1.1.8.9 KERMIT KNORR was born on 21 March 1914. He lived in Atlantic City, NJ.

3.1.1.8.10 ALLEN KNORR was born circa 1913, Pennsylvania. Some sources record that he was born in July 1910. He lived in Wiconisco, PA.

3.1.1.9 CHARLES J. DEPPEN was born on 28 December 1876, Jordan Township, Northumberland County, PA. He married **RACHEL ELLEN GEISE** circa 1893. He died in 1937.

3.1.1.9.1 SULA M. DEPPEN is also referred to as **ZULA AND SULA T. DEPPEN** in some sources. She was born on 16 July 1893. She married **CHARLES A. BOHNER**, son of **WILLIAM T. BOHNER** and **ELIZABETH TROUTMAN**, in 1909, Hebe, Jordan Township, Northumberland County, PA. She died on 26 June 1932, at age 38.

3.1.1.9.1.1 IRENE C. BOHNER was born on 11 November 1910. She married **GEORGE PINKERTON.**

3.1.1.9.1.2 MARION M. BOHNER is also referred to as **MARIAN** in some sources. She was born on 18 September 1912. She married **ALLEN CLOUGH.**

3.1.1.9.1.3 GUY EMERSON BOHNER was born on 9 March 1916. He married **THEDA MAE CAMPBELL** on 17 November 1934. He died on 23 December 1993, Tower City, Schuylkill County, PA, at age 77.

3.1.1.9.1.3.1 WILLIAM C. BOHNER was born on 8 October 1937.

3.1.1.9.1.3.2 YVONNE LEAH BOHNER was born on 28 March 1941, Pottsville, Schuylkill County, PA. She married **JOHN ARTHUR MINNICH**, son of **ARTHUR F. MINNICH** and **MARY E. MOLKO,** on 16 November 1957, Lykens, Dauphin County, PA.

3.1.1.9.1.3.2.1 DEBRA LOUISE MINNICH was born on 18 June 1958, Lykens, Dauphin County, PA. She married **JAMES VINCENT KANDYBOWSKI** on 18 June 1977.

3.1.1.9.1.3.2.2 LORI JEAN MINNICH was born on 12 September 1960, Takoma Park, MD. She married **JAMES ALBERT DEITER** on 8 December 1979, Muir, Schuylkill County, PA.

3.1.1.9.1.3.2.2.1 JAMES ALBERT DEITER III was born on 19 April 1980, Pottsville, Schuylkill County, PA.

3.1.1.9.1.3.2.2.1.1 JAMES RONALD DEITER was born on 7 April 1995, Williamstown, Dauphin County, PA.

3.1.1.9.1.3.2.2.2 CHRISTINE MARIE DEITER was born on 23 March 1988, Harrisburg, Dauphin County, PA.

3.1.1.9.1.3.3 SARAH E. BOHNER was born on 4 September 1943.

3.1.1.9.1.3.4 GUY DAVID BOHNER was born on 14 April 1954.

3.1.1.9.1.4 LEAH E. BOHNER was born circa 1919.

3.1.1.9.1.5 LEE W. BOHNER was born circa 1920.

3.1.1.9.1.6 OWEN E. BOHNER was born circa 1923.

3.1.1.9.1.7 FLORA L. BOHNER was born circa 1925.

3.1.1.9.1.8 CHARLES ROBERT BOHNER was born on 20 November 1926.

3.1.1.9.1.8.1 JEAN K. BOHNER was born on 23 July 1949.

3.1.1.9.1.8.2 ROBERT T. BOHNER was born on 6 June 1952.

3.1.1.9.1.8.3 DONALD K. BOHNER was born on 21 February 1957.

3.1.1.9.2 MARY DEPPEN was born on 7 January 1895. Some sources record that she was born in June 1897. She married **HARRY TROUTMAN**. She lived in Shamokin, PA.

3.1.1.9.2.1 DAISY TROUTMAN was born on 2 September 1910.

3.1.1.9.2.2 CLAIR TROUTMAN was born on 19 January 1913. He married **JOSEPHINE BUTCHINSKI.**

    3.1.1.9.2.2.1 DONALD TROUTMAN was born on 16 March 1934.

3.1.1.9.2.3 WILLIAM TROUTMAN was born on 21 October 1915.

3.1.1.9.2.4 EDNA TROUTMAN was born on 31 October 1919.

3.1.1.9.3 STELLA DEPPEN was born in June 1897. She married **JOSEPH MOORE.** She lived in Ocean Grove, NJ. She died before 1940, Bradley Beach, NJ.

    3.1.1.9.3.1 RAE MOORE was born on 19 June 1919, Jordan Township, Northumberland County, PA.

    3.1.1.9.3.2 JOSEPH MOORE JR. was born on 30 September 1922, Jordan Township, Northumberland County, PA.

    3.1.1.9.3.3 RUTH MOORE was born on 5 March 1924, Jordan Township, Northumberland County, PA.

3.1.1.9.4 ARTHUR DEPPEN was born on 13 November 1899. He married **ANNA DEWALT.** He lived in Shamokin, PA.

    3.1.1.9.4.1 MARY DEPPEN was born on 28 September 1918.

    3.1.1.9.4.2 BEATRICE DEPPEN was born in July 1921.

    3.1.1.9.4.3 PEARL REBECCA DEPPEN was born in 1923.

3.1.1.10 DANIEL A. DEPPEN was born on 6 January 1879. He married **HARRIET TROUTMAN,** daughter of **HENRY LESHER TROUTMAN** and **ANGELINE TOBIAS,** circa 1900.

    3.1.1.10.1 FLORENCE EDNA DEPPEN was born on 30 July 1901. She was baptized on 8 September 1901, St. David's Lutheran and Reformed Church, Hebe, Northumberland County, PA. Some sources record that she was born on 30 July 1900. She married **BURLINGTON LEE LEITZEL,** son of **SAMUEL AMMON LEITZEL** and **ALICE BERTIE TROUTMAN,** circa 1915. In later years, Florence lived in Dornsife, Northumberland County, PA. She died on 20 January 1940, Washington Township, Northumberland County, PA, at age 38. She was buried at Wesleyan Church Cemetery, Washington Township, Northumberland County, PA.

        3.1.1.10.1.1 DAISY D. LEITZEL is also referred to as **DAISY V. LEITZEL** in some sources. She was born in 1916. She married **JOHN KREISHER.** Daisy lived in Philadelphia.

        3.1.1.10.1.2 LEONARD LEITZEL was born circa 1918.

        3.1.1.10.1.3 RALPH D. LEITZEL was born on 19 June 1920. He married **ROSIE J. LENTZ.** He died on 31 October 1967, at age 47. He was buried at Wesleyan Church Cemetery, Washington Township, Northumberland County, PA.

        3.1.1.10.1.4 FORREST LEITZEL was born in 1922.

    3.1.1.10.2 EVA DEPPEN was born on 18 September 1903. She married **OSCAR BOWER.** She lived in Klingerstown, PA.

        3.1.1.10.2.1 LEAH BOWER was born on 24 December 1926.

    3.1.1.10.3 PEARL DEPPEN was born on 6 May 1905. She married **FRANK RENNER.** She lived in Ashland, PA.

        3.1.1.10.3.1 MYRALINE RENNER was born in 1925.

        3.1.1.10.3.2 DANIEL RENNER was born in 1927.

    3.1.1.10.4 ELMER DEPPEN was born on 7 October 1910. He married **ELSIE BUSH.** He lived in Ashland, PA.

    3.1.1.10.5 ALBERT DEPPEN was born on 13 August 1912. He lived in Locust Gap, PA.

3.1.1.11 C. ARTHUR DEPPEN was born on 8 September 1882. He died in 1891.

3.1.1.12 HARVEY DEPPEN was born in 1884. He died in 1884.

3.1.2 WILHELM SNYDER was born on 16 July 1838. He was baptized on 9 September 1838, St. David's Lutheran and Reformed Church, Hebe, Jordan Township, Northumberland County, PA.

3.1.3 MARIA SNYDER was born on 28 June 1843. She was baptized on 1 October 1843, St. David's Lutheran and Reformed Church, Hebe, Jordan Township, Northumberland County, PA.

3.1.4 FRANNY SNYDER was born on 23 May 1845. She was baptized on 13 July 1845, St. David's Lutheran and Reformed Church, Hebe, Jordan Township, Northumberland County, PA. She married **EDWARD CLARK**, son of **SAMUEL B. CLARK** and **CATHERINE WIEST**. She married **DANIEL W. SHAFFER**, son of **MICHAEL SHAFFER** and **ELIZABETH WERT**, circa 1868. She died on 16 August 1906, at age 61. She was buried at St, David's Church Cemetery, Hebe, Jordan Township, Northumberland County, PA.

    3.1.4.1 BARBARA ALICE CLARK was born on 26 January 1862. She was baptized on 5 March 1862, St. David's Lutheran and Reformed Church, Hebe, Jordan Township, Northumberland County, PA. She died on 17 August 1907, Jordan Township, Northumberland County, PA, at age 45.

    3.1.4.2 CATHERINE ELIZABETH CLARK is also referred to as **CASSY ELIZABETH CLARK** in some sources. She was born on 19 August 1864. She married **EMANUEL ADAMS**. She died in 1943, Lower Mahanoy Township, Northumberland County, PA.

        3.1.4.2.1 CHARLES B. ADAMS was born on 19 July 1884, Lower Mahanoy Township, Northumberland County, PA. He died on 30 December 1903, at age 19. He was buried at Evangelical (Bingeman's) Church Cemetery, County Line, Lower Mahanoy Township, Northumberland County, PA.

        3.1.4.2.2 MILTON S. ADAMS was born in 1895, Lower Mahanoy Township, Northumberland County, PA. He married **ELIZABETH M. SHOWERS**. He died on 30 March 1964. He was buried at Evangelical (Bingeman's) Church Cemetery, County Line, Lower Mahanoy Township, Northumberland County, PA.

        3.1.4.2.3 JAMES ADAMS married **CARRIE M. FORNEY**. He was born Lower Mahanoy Township, Northumberland County, PA. He died on 15 August 1964. He was buried at Evangelical (Bingeman's) Church Cemetery, County Line, Lower Mahanoy Township, Northumberland County, PA.

            3.1.4.2.3.1 WARREN ADAMS was born on 20 October 1917. He died on 17 January 1920, at age 2. He was buried at Evangelical (Bingeman's) Church Cemetery, County Line, Lower Mahanoy Township, Northumberland County, PA.

            3.1.4.2.3.2 RUTH F. ADAMS was born on 26 September 1921, Lower Mahanoy Township, Northumberland County, PA. She married **JOHN J. WERT**. She died on 23 May 1967, at age 45. She was buried at Evangelical (Bingeman's) Church Cemetery, County Line, Lower Mahanoy Township, Northumberland County, PA.

        3.1.4.2.4 SADIE O. ADAMS was born in 1900. She died in 1902. She was buried at Evangelical (Bingeman's) Church Cemetery, County Line, Lower Mahanoy Township, Northumberland County, PA.

        3.1.4.2.5 HARRY L. ADAMS was born on 21 May 1902. He married **MIRIAM L. BATDORF**. He died on 17 December 1977, at age 75. He was buried at Evangelical (Bingeman's) Church Cemetery, County Line, Lower Mahanoy Township, Northumberland County, PA.

    3.1.4.3 WILLIAM ELSWORTH SHAFFER was born on 19 September 1869, Jordan Township, Northumberland County, PA. He married **MARY JANE LEITZEL**, daughter of **DAVID BYERLY LEITZEL** and **MARIA ANNA TROUTMAN**, on 19 June 1890, St. David's Lutheran and Reformed Church, Hebe, Jordan Township, Northumberland County, PA. He died on 30 March 1950, Shamokin, Northumberland County, PA, at age 80.

        3.1.4.3.1 SADIE I. SHAFFER was born on 20 September 1892, Hebe, Jordan Township, Northumberland County, PA. She died in October 1896, Hebe, Jordan Township, Northumberland County, PA, at age 4.

        3.1.4.3.2 WINNIE ALVA SHAFFER was born on 5 January 1894, Pottsville, Schuylkill County, PA. She died on 30 April 1972, Shamokin, Northumberland County, PA, at age 78.

        3.1.4.3.3 KIMBER CLEAVER SHAFFER was born on 30 January 1901, Shamokin, Northumberland County, PA. He married **ADAHA DOROTHY PALMER** on 2 December 1921, Hagerstown, Washington County, MD. He died on 10 February 1972, Danville, Montour County, PA, at age 71. He was buried at St. Peter's Reformed (Blue) Church, Ralpho Township, Northumberland County, PA.

            3.1.4.3.3.1 FRANCIS PALMER SHAFFER was born on 20 August 1922, Mount Carmel, Northumberland County, PA. He married **ANNABELLE NEWBERRY** on 31 December 1955, Sunbury, Northumberland County, PA. He died on 23 September 1986, Kelso, WA, at age 64.

3.1.4.3.3.1.1 MARGARET RUTH SHAFFER was born on 29 May 1959, North Plainfield, NJ. She married TODD ALAN YOUNG on 30 June 1984.

>**3.1.4.3.3.1.1.1** EMILY MARGARET YOUNG was born on 8 February 1985.

>**3.1.4.3.3.1.1.2** BENJAMIN TODD YOUNG was born on 17 February 1987.

3.1.4.3.3.1.2 RICHARD KIMBER SHAFFER was born on 30 April 1961.

3.1.4.3.3.1.3 LINDA I. SHAFFER was born on 17 June 1967, El Dorado County, CA.

3.1.4.3.3.1.4 LOIS J. SHAFFER was born on 26 November 1968, Alameda County, CA.

3.1.4.3.3.2 JANE ANNE SHAFFER was born on 17 November 1930, Shamokin, Northumberland County, PA. She married WILLIAM CHARLES ARBOGAST, son of (--?--) ARBOGAST and VERDA FLEMING, on 14 February 1959, Pottstown, Montgomery County, PA.

>**3.1.4.3.3.2.1** WILLIAM CHARLES ARBOGAST JR. was born on 3 September 1953. He married DONNA LEIGH HENDERSON on 21 May 1977, Mechanicsburg, Cumberland County, PA. He married CYNTHIA ANN HAWK on 28 July 2001, Mechanicsburg, Cumberland County, PA.

>>**3.1.4.3.3.2.1.1** SETH WILLIAM ARBOGAST was born on 20 May 1983.

>>**3.1.4.3.3.2.1.2** SHEA KIMBERLY ARBOGAST was born on 9 April 1986.

>>**3.1.4.3.3.2.1.3** KATHANNE ARBOGAST was born on 22 June 1988.

>**3.1.4.3.3.2.2** KATHLEEN JO ARBOGAST was born on 19 May 1957. She married TIMOTHY CHARLES WINTER on 30 June 1979, Mechanicsburg, Cumberland County, PA.

>>**3.1.4.3.3.2.2.1** MATTHEW WILLIAM WINTER was born on 31 July 1980.

>>**3.1.4.3.3.2.2.2** LEANNE WINTER was born on 26 September 1982.

>**3.1.4.3.3.2.3** ROBERT MARK ARBOGAST was born on 11 July 1961. He married PATRICIA ANN BRANSTED on 4 May 1985, Burlington, WI. He married TRACI GUSLER on 17 December 1994, Mechanicsburg, Cumberland County, PA.

>>**3.1.4.3.3.2.3.1** COURTNEY LYNN ARBOGAST was born on 6 July 1986, Travis AFB, Fairfield, CA.

3.1.4.3.3.3 WILLIAM ALBERT SHAFFER was born on 10 September 1936, Shamokin, Northumberland County, PA. He married FRANCES MARLENE MARCHESKIE on 20 June 1959, Pottstown, Montgomery County, PA.

>**3.1.4.3.3.3.1** MARK WILLIAM SHAFFER was born on 29 June 1962, Potsdam, St. Lawrence County, NY. He married LISA MARIE ST. JACQUES on 17 November 1984, St. Theresa's Catholic Church, South Hadley, MA.

>>**3.1.4.3.3.3.1.1** CHERYL ANNE SHAFFER was born on 27 January 1986, Holyoke, MA.

>>**3.1.4.3.3.3.1.2** MARTIN ANTHONY SHAFFER was born on 14 April 1989, Holyoke, MA.

>**3.1.4.3.3.3.2** MICHAEL FRANCIS SHAFFER was born on 8 September 1964, Potsdam, St. Lawrence County, NY. He married DOREEN LISA HEMM on 7 May 1988, Long Meadow, MA.

>>**3.1.4.3.3.3.2.1** AMANDA MARIE SHAFFER was born on 15 November 1990.

>>**3.1.4.3.3.3.2.2** CHRISTINE LISA SHAFFER was born on 17 May 1993.

3.1.4.3.3.4 WINNIE ELIZABETH SHAFFER was born on 16 February 1943, Shamokin, Northumberland County, PA. She married BRUCE TRAVIS HALL, son of JOSEPH CHAMPION HALL and SARA LEAH WIEST, on 1 September 1962, Grace Lutheran Church, Shamokin, Northumberland County, PA.

>**3.1.4.3.3.4.1** VALERIE LEIGH HALL was born on 13 September 1963, Centre County Hospital, Bellefonte, Centre County, PA. She married LARRY ERIK ARKLEY, son of JOHN K. ARKLEY and SHIRLEY (--?--), on 4 April 1981, Annapolis, Anne Arundel County, MD. She and LARRY ERIK ARKLEY were divorced in 1989. She married RICHARD WILLIAM STILLWELL, son of HAROLD WILLIAM STILLWELL and

ERNESTINE MISCKA, on 12 March 1990, Las Vegas, NV. She married ROBERT BROWN on 24 August 1996, Memphis, TN.

    3.1.4.3.3.4.1.1 JEREMY ERIK ARKLEY was born on 27 October 1983, Ewa Beach, HI.

    3.1.4.3.3.4.1.2 JARON TRAVIS ARKLEY was born on 23 October 1984, Ewa Beach, HI. He died on 25 November 1984, Ewa Beach, HI.

3.1.4.3.3.4.2 BONNIE JOY HALL was born on 25 February 1966, Centre County Hospital, Bellefonte, Centre County, PA. She married TROY DOUGLAS LINGELBACH, son of LEROY ERNEST LINGELBACH JR. and SHIRLEY BARTON RAVER, on 14 January 1989, Annapolis, MD.

    3.1.4.3.3.4.2.1 ANDREW ZACHARY LINGELBACH was born on 11 March 1992, Towson, MD.

    3.1.4.3.3.4.2.2 JACOB RYAN LINGELBACH was born on 3 February 2000, Baltimore, MD.

3.1.4.3.3.4.3 HOLLY LYNN HALL was born on 14 November 1969, Centre County Hospital, State College, Centre County, PA. She married ERIC DANIEL HOUGHTON, son of LOUIS HOUGHTON and BARBARA FEE, on 15 February 1992, Annapolis, Anne Arundel County, MD.

    3.1.4.3.3.4.3.1 JOSEPH CARL HOUGHTON was born on 13 April 1993, Annapolis, Anne Arundel County, MD.

    3.1.4.3.3.4.3.2 MELISSA LEE HOUGHTON was born on 14 April 1996, Annapolis, Anne Arundel County, MD.

    3.1.4.3.3.4.3.3 JENNIFER ELIZABETH HOUGHTON was born on 22 July 1998, Annapolis, Anne Arundel County, MD.

    3.1.4.3.3.4.3.4 LOUIS REUBEN HOUGHTON was born on 30 December 1999, Annapolis, Anne Arundel County, MD.

    3.1.4.3.3.4.3.5 JAMES MADISON HOUGHTON was born on 23 February 2002, Annapolis, Anne Arundel County, MD.

3.1.4.3.3.4.4 SHARI JEANNE HALL was born on 9 January 1973, Centre County Hospital, State College, Centre County, PA. She married JOSEPH CHRISTOPHER JONES on 1 June 1996, Sandy Point State Park, Annapolis, MD.

    3.1.4.3.3.4.4.1 SARAH ELIZABETH JONES was born on 30 September 2002, Calvert County, MD.

    3.1.4.3.3.4.4.2 LAURA GRACE JONES

3.1.4.3.3.5 KIMBER CLEAVER SHAFFER was born on 31 December 1943, Shamokin, Northumberland County, PA. He married ANITA DOBSON on 12 August 1967, St. Anthony's Church, Ranshaw, Coal Township, Northumberland County, PA. He died on 12 July 1981, Shamokin, Northumberland County, PA, at age 37.

    3.1.4.3.3.5.1 DAVID KIMBER SHAFFER was born on 21 September 1971. He married SARA ELAINE CHEANEY on 20 October 2001.

    3.1.4.3.3.5.2 BRIAN EDWARD SHAFFER was born on 20 February 1975.

    3.1.4.3.3.5.3 CHRISTOPHER LAWTON SHAFFER was born on 12 October 1978.

3.1.4.4 DANIEL MORRIS SHAFFER was born on 20 May 1871. He was baptized on 9 July 1871, St. David's Lutheran and Reformed Church, Hebe, Jordan Township, Northumberland County, PA. He married SALLY KATHRYN SHOTT.

3.1.4.5 PHRENE ELMIRA SHAFFER was born on 27 June 1875. She was baptized on 29 August 1875, St. David's Lutheran and Reformed Church, Hebe, Jordan Township, Northumberland County, PA. She died on 20 April 1956, at age 80.

    3.1.4.5.1 MINNIE SHADE was born on 1 January 1893. She married MERRILL E. RUCH. She died on 31 May 1981, at age 88. She died on 31 May 1981, at age 88. She was buried at IOOF Cemetery, Shamokin, Northumberland County, PA.

3.1.4.5.1.1 INFANT RUCH was born on 26 May 1930, Shamokin, Northumberland County, PA. He/she died on 2 June 1930, Shamokin, Northumberland County, PA. He/she was buried at IOOF Cemetery, Shamokin, Northumberland County, PA.

3.1.4.5.2 LULU MAY SHADE is also referred to as **LURA MAY** in some sources. She was born on 12 June 1895. She was born on 12 June 1895. She was baptized on 11 August 1895, Zion (Klinger's) Church, Erdman, Lykens Township, Dauphin County, PA.

3.1.4.6 FRANCIS SHAFFER was born on 6 April 1879, Lower Mahanoy Township, Northumberland County, PA. He was baptized on 1 June 1879, St. David's Lutheran and Reformed Church, Hebe, Jordan Township, Northumberland County, PA. He married **CAROLYN MOORE**. He died on 19 September 1939, at age 60.

3.1.5 DANIEL WIEST SNYDER was born on 19 February 1848, Jordan Township, Northumberland County, PA. He died on 16 September 1908, Hebe, Jordan Township, Northumberland County, PA, at age 60.

3.1.6 BARBARA SNYDER is also referred to as **ELLEN JANE SNYDER** in some sources. She was born in 1850, Dauphin County, PA. She married **HARRISON WILLIARD**, son of **WILLIAM WILLIARD** and **SEBILLA CARL,** circa 1868. She died on 27 March 1920, Gratz, Dauphin Co., PA. She was buried at Simeon United Lutheran Church Cemetery, Gratz, Dauphin Co., PA.

3.1.6.1 SAMUEL MORRIS WILLIARD married **IDA MAY HEITZMAN**. He was born on 22 June 1876, Dauphin County, PA. He died on 3 October 1953, Klingerstown, Schuylkill County, PA, at age 77. He was buried at St. Michael's Lutheran Church Cemetery, Klingerstown, Schuylkill County, PA.

3.1.6.1.1 ALLEN H. WILLARD was born on 2 June 1910, Klingerstown, Schuylkill County, PA. He was baptized on 20 October 1910, St. Michael's Lutheran Church, Klingerstown, Schuylkill County, PA. He married **MABEL G. ROTHERMEL**, daughter of **MANASSES W. ROTHERMEL** and **SUSAN JANE BIXLER,** circa 1928. He married **CATHERINE E. HARTZELL** after 1954. He died on 11 June 1991, at age 81. He was buried at Grand View Memorial Park, Annville, Lebanon County, PA.

3.1.6.1.1.1 PEARL N. WILLARD was born on 17 September 1928. She died on 19 January 1929, Hubley Township, Schuylkill County, PA. She was buried on 22 January 1929, at St. Michael's Lutheran Church Cemetery, Klingerstown, Schuylkill County, PA.

3.1.6.1.1.2 SAMUEL M. WILLARD was born on 5 January 1930, Lykens, Dauphin County, PA. He married **BETTY J. LINGLE** on 27 November 1952. Samuel lives in Chambersburg, PA. He died on 3 March 2016, Chambersburg, Franklin County, PA, at age 86.

3.1.6.1.1.2.1 WYNN ALAN WILLARD married **PATRICIA (--?--)**.

3.1.6.1.1.2.1.1 MARSHALL WYNN WILLARD

3.1.6.1.1.2.1.2 SHERIDAN SAMUEL WILLARD

3.1.6.1.1.2.1.3 ASHTON ALAN WILLARD

3.1.6.1.1.2.2 LORI ANN WILLARD was born on 28 May 1962. She died on 15 November 1991, at age 29. She was buried at Hershey Cemetery, Hershey, Dauphin County, PA.

3.1.6.1.1.3 SHIRLEY MAE WILLARD was born on 19 September 1937, Valley View, Schuylkill County, PA. She married **PAUL G. PAPONETTI**. She died on 26 August 2009, Carolyn Croxton Slane Residence, Harrisburg, Dauphin County, PA, at age 71. According to a newspaper obituary, Shirley lived in Palmyra, PA, and had retired from Ohio Casualty Insurance Company, in Harrisburg. She was buried at Hershey Cemetery, Derry Township, Dauphin County, PA.

3.1.6.1.1.3.1 LISA R. PAPONETTI married **KEVIN Q. LUU**.

3.1.6.1.1.3.1.1 KATIA P. LUU

3.1.6.1.1.4 DELORES VERA WILLARD was born on 21 September 1939. She married **RICHARD LYMAN**.

3.1.6.2 BARBARA SEDORA WILLIARD was born on 30 April 1877, Lykens Township, Dauphin Co., PA. She married **ALEXANDER W. KLINGER**, son of **DAVID S. KLINGER** and **BARBARA MERKEL WIEST**. She died on 15 June 1948, Lykens Township, Dauphin Co, PA, at age 71. She was buried on 19 June 1948, at St. Michael's Church Cemetery, Klingerstown, Schuylkill County, PA.

3.1.6.2.1 INFANT SON KLINGER was born circa 1901, Klingerstown, Schuylkill County, PA. He died on 24 August 1901, Klingerstown, Schuylkill County, PA. He was buried after 24 August 1901, at St. Michael's Church Cemetery, Klingerstown, Schuylkill County, PA.

3.1.6.2.2 ALICE REGINA KLINGER was born on 1 April 1903, Klingerstown, Schuylkill County, PA. She married an unknown person on 10 June 1922, Simeon Lutheran Church, Gratz, Dauphin Co., PA. She died in 1968.

3.1.6.2.3 MAUDE MAE KLINGER was born in 1898, Klingerstown, Schuylkill County, PA. She married **WILLIAM A. WIEST**, son of **SYLVESTER SCHADEL WIEST** and **ISABELLA S. LESHER**, in 1915, Klingerstown, Schuylkill County, PA. She died in 1960, Klingerstown, Schuylkill County, PA.

> **3.1.6.2.3.1 DAISY MARIE WIEST** married **JOHN MILLER**. She was born in 1915, Klingerstown, Schuylkill County, PA.
>
>> **3.1.6.2.3.1.1 ALICE MILLER**
>>
>> **3.1.6.2.3.1.2 JOHN MILLER** married **ROSEANN DUNLEVY**.
>>
>> **3.1.6.2.3.1.3 BARBARA I. MILLER** was born on 16 August 1942, PA. She married **WAYNE LEMAR SITLINGER**, son of **EMORY ISAIAH SITLINGER** and **HENRIETTA WEISS**, circa 1963, PA. She married **JOHN D. MORGAN SR.** Valley View, Schuylkill County, PA.
>>
>>> **3.1.6.2.3.1.3.1 JOHN D. MORGAN JR.**
>>>
>>> **3.1.6.2.3.1.3.2 JEFFREY MILLER MORGAN** was born circa 1965.
>
> **3.1.6.2.3.2 TILLIE IRENE WIEST** was born on 11 June 1916, Klingerstown, Schuylkill County, PA. She married **CLARENCE R. WILLIARD**. She died on 5 July 2002, Klingerstown, Schuylkill County, PA, at age 86.
>
>> **3.1.6.2.3.2.1 ARLENE M. WILLIARD** married **MARK MACE**.
>>
>> **3.1.6.2.3.2.2 RAY A. WILLIARD** was born Klingerstown, Schuylkill County, PA. He married **ELEANOR (--?--)**.
>>
>> **3.1.6.2.3.2.3 JAMES L. WILLIARD** was born on 21 June 1935, Klingerstown, Schuylkill County, PA. He married **KAY (--?--)**. He died on 31 October 2004, at age 69.
>>
>> **3.1.6.2.3.2.4 LEE L. WILLIARD** was born on 26 November 1947, Klingerstown, Schuylkill County, PA. He married **FAITH HAAS** on 17 May 1986. He died on 18 February 2008, Evangelical Community Hospital, Lewisburg, Union County, PA, at age 60. He was buried on 21 February 2008, at St. Michael's Lutheran and Reformed Church Cemetery, Klingerstown, Schuylkill County, PA.
>>
>>> **3.1.6.2.3.2.4.1 CINDY WILLIARD** married **RICH BEILHARZ**.
>>>
>>>> **3.1.6.2.3.2.4.1.1 AMY BEILHARZ**
>>>>
>>>> **3.1.6.2.3.2.4.1.2 MISSY BEILHARZ**
>>>
>>> **3.1.6.2.3.2.4.2 ANDY WILLIARD** married **SHANE (--?--)**.
>>>
>>> **3.1.6.2.3.2.4.3 TERRY WILLIARD** married **MARLA (--?--)**.
>>>
>>> **3.1.6.2.3.2.4.4 JERRY WILLIARD** married **HEATHER (--?--)**.
>>>
>>> **3.1.6.2.3.2.4.5 DOUGLAS KLINGER** married **TRISHA (--?--)**.
>>>
>>> **3.1.6.2.3.2.4.6 ANDY KLINGER** married **KILEY (--?--)**.
>
> **3.1.6.2.3.3 CHARLES LEROY WIEST** was born on 12 January 1919, Klingerstown, Schuylkill County, PA. He died on 16 March 1978, Klingerstown, Schuylkill County, PA, at age 59.
>
> **3.1.6.2.3.4 HARRY ALVIN WIEST** married **HELEN ADAMS**. He was born in 1922, Klingerstown, Schuylkill County, PA.
>
>> **3.1.6.2.3.4.1 CAROL WIEST**
>>
>> **3.1.6.2.3.4.2 ROJEAN WIEST**
>
> **3.1.6.2.3.5 JOHN JACOB WIEST** was born on 20 June 1924, Klingerstown, Schuylkill County, PA. He died on 20 June 1924, Klingerstown, Schuylkill County, PA.
>
> **3.1.6.2.3.6 SHIRLEY ARLENE WIEST** was born in 1930, Klingerstown, Schuylkill County, PA. She died in 1931, Klingerstown, Schuylkill County, PA.
>
> **3.1.6.2.3.7 BILLY LAMAR WIEST** married **RUBY ERDMAN**. He was born on 11 August 1932, Klingerstown, Schuylkill County, PA.

3.1.6.2.3.8 JAMES ALLEN WIEST married **(--?--) ENTERLINE.** He was born on 23 March 1934, Klingerstown, Schuylkill County, PA.

3.1.6.2.4 TILLIE SEDORA KLINGER was born in 1905. She was born on 21 April 1905, Klingerstown, Schuylkill County, PA. She was baptized on 16 July 1905, St. Michael's Church, Klingerstown, Schuylkill County, PA. She married **RAYMOND EDWARD HARTMAN,** son of **EDWIN HARTMAN** and **JENNIE LOUISA WELKER,** on 25 July 1925, Simeon Lutheran Church, Gratz, Dauphin County, PA. She was buried in 1994, at Simeon United Lutheran Church Cemetery, Gratz, Dauphin Co., PA. She died in 1994, Dauphin County, PA.

3.1.6.2.4.1 EDDIE ALEXANDER HARTMAN was born on 10 February 1926. He was born on 10 February 1926, Dauphin Co., PA. He was baptized on 21 March 1926, Simeon Lutheran Church, Gratz, Dauphin Co., PA. He was baptized on 21 March 1926, Simeon Lutheran Church, Gratz, Dauphin County, PA. He married **MARGARET EDITH BIXLER.** He married **MARGARET EDITH BIXLER** circa 1948, PA.

3.1.6.2.4.1.1 VICKI HARTMAN married **LARRY WELKER.**

3.1.6.2.4.1.1.1 LARRY WELKER JR.

3.1.6.2.4.1.1.2 TRACY WELKER

3.1.6.2.4.1.2 JAN HARTMAN married **RONALD MALICK.** She and **RONALD MALICK** were divorced.

3.1.6.2.4.1.2.1 SHANNON MALICK

3.1.6.2.4.1.2.2 GARRETT MALICK

3.1.6.2.4.1.3 ANN HARTMAN married **GARY DUNKELBERGER.**

3.1.6.2.4.1.4 VICKI RAE HARTMAN was born before February 1952, Dauphin Co., PA. She married **LARRY C. WELKER SR.** circa 1974, PA.

3.1.6.2.4.1.4.1 LARRY C. WELKER JR. was born circa 1976, Dauphin Co., PA.

3.1.6.2.4.1.4.2 TRACY WELKER was born circa 1978, Dauphin Co., PA.

3.1.6.2.4.1.5 SUZETTE CAROL HARTMAN was born on 28 June 1954, Dauphin Co., PA. She was baptized on 28 November 1954, Simeon Reformed Church, Gratz, Dauphin Co., PA. She married **GLENN LEITZEL** circa 1976, PA.

3.1.6.2.4.1.5.1 STEPHEN LEITZEL is also referred to as **STEPHEN LEITZEL** in some sources. He was born circa 1978, PA.

3.1.6.2.4.1.6 JAN LOUISE HARTMAN was born on 13 October 1959, Dauphin Co., PA. She married **RONALD CRAIG MALICK** circa 1975.

3.1.6.2.4.1.6.1 SHANNON MARIE MALICK was born on 6 February 1977. She married **JASON AVERY BUCHANON** circa 1996.

3.1.6.2.4.1.6.1.1 JADEN AVERY MALICK BUCHANON was born on 8 July 1998.

3.1.6.2.4.1.6.1.2 ASHTON BERKLEY BUCHANON was born on 17 May 2000.

3.1.6.2.4.1.6.2 GARRETT MALICK was born on 13 October 1981.

3.1.6.2.4.1.6.3 MORGAN MALICK was born circa 1983.

3.1.6.2.4.1.7 ANN MARIE HARTMAN was born on 8 November 1960, Dauphin Co., PA. She married **GARY MAYNARD DUNKELBERGER** circa 1992.

3.1.6.2.4.2 RICHARD RAYMOND HARTMAN was born on 17 May 1928, Lykens, Dauphin County, PA. He was baptized on 5 August 1928, Simeon Lutheran Church, Gratz, Dauphin County, PA. He married **IRENE I. LAUDENSLAGER** on 26 June 1954, Simeon Reformed Church, Gratz, Dauphin Co., PA.

3.1.6.2.4.2.1 RICHARD RAYMOND HARTMAN JR. was born on 2 September 1955, Geisinger Medical Center, Danville, Montour Co., PA. He was baptized on 11 December 1955, Simeon Reformed Church, Gratz, Dauphin Co., PA.

3.1.6.2.4.2.2 SHELLEY LYNN HARTMAN was born on 6 August 1956, Lentz Hospital, Lykens, Dauphin Co., PA. She died on 22 March 2008, Harrisburg, Dauphin Co., PA, at age 51. She was buried after 22 March 2008, at Gratz Union Church Cemetery, Gratz, Dauphin Co., PA.

3.1.6.2.4.2.3 RODNEY C. HARTMAN was born either 14 January 1958 or 2 April 1958, Geisinger Medical Center, Danville, Montour Co., PA.

3.1.6.2.4.2.4 EDDIE HARTMAN was born on 13 April 1959, Geisinger Medical Center, Danville, Montour Co., PA.

3.1.6.2.4.3 SHIRLEY RUTH HARTMAN was born on 31 October 1930, Dauphin County, PA. She was baptized on 23 May 1931, Simeon Lutheran Church, Gratz, Dauphin County, PA. She married **DR. FREDERICK M. WILKINS** on 25 August 1954, Salem Reformed Church, Elizabethville, Dauphin County, PA. She died on 27 June 1989, at age 58. She was buried at Simeon United Lutheran Church Cemetery, Gratz, Dauphin County, PA.

3.1.6.2.4.3.1 KIMBERLY ANNE WILKINS was born on 12 August 1955, PA.

3.1.6.2.4.4 BENJAMIN FRANKLIN HARTMAN was born on 11 September 1935, Dauphin County, PA. He was baptized on 3 May 1936, Simeon Lutheran Church, Gratz, Dauphin County, PA. He died on 11 October 1936, Dauphin County, PA, at age 1. He was buried on 14 October 1936, at Simeon United Lutheran Church Cemetery, Gratz, Dauphin Co., PA.

3.1.6.2.4.5 RAYMOND PAUL HARTMAN JR. was born on 27 September 1937, Lykens Township, Dauphin County, PA. He was baptized on 6 March 1938, Simeon Lutheran Church, Gratz, Dauphin County, PA. He married **VIOLET KESSLER**, daughter of **MARK WILLIAM KESSLER** and **MARGARET IRENE ERDMAN,** on 30 June 1956, Simeon Lutheran Church, Gratz, Dauphin County, PA.

3.1.6.2.4.5.1 MICHAEL C. HARTMAN was born on 20 December 1956, Harrisburg, Dauphin County, PA. He was born either 20 December 1956 or 30 November 1956, Harrisburg, Dauphin Co., PA. He married **SHARON HARTWIG** on 15 February 1975, Gratz, Dauphin Co., PA.

3.1.6.2.4.5.1.1 DIANE MARIE HARTMAN was born on 23 July 1975, Dauphin Co., PA.

3.1.6.2.4.5.1.2 MICHELLE LYNN HARTMAN was born on 22 March 1979, Dauphin Co., PA.

3.1.6.2.4.5.1.3 GREG ALAN HARTMAN was born on 11 October 1981, Dauphin Co., PA. He died on 22 January 1993, Harrisburg, Dauphin Co., PA, at age 11. He was buried after 22 January 1993, at Simeon United Lutheran Church Cemetery, Gratz, Dauphin Co., PA.

3.1.6.2.4.5.1.4 DIANE MARIE HARTMAN was born on 23 July 1975, Elizabethville, Dauphin County, PA.

3.1.6.2.4.5.1.5 MICHELLE LYNN HARTMAN was born on 22 March 1979, Gratz, Dauphin County, PA.

3.1.6.2.4.5.1.6 GREG ALAN HARTMAN was born on 11 October 1981, Freedom, Beaver County, PA.

3.1.6.2.4.5.2 LORI A. HARTMAN was born on 5 April 1961, Harrisburg, Dauphin County, PA. She married **JEFFREY SCHMITT.**

3.1.6.2.4.5.2.1 LAURA SCHMITT was born circa 1986.

3.1.6.2.4.5.3 JENNIFER SUE HARTMAN was born on 20 December 1970, Harrisburg, Dauphin County, PA. She married **DOUGLAS HARVEY SCHULTZ** on 30 July 1994, Simeon Lutheran Church, Gratz, Dauphin Co., PA.

3.1.7 SAMUEL WIEST SNYDER was born on 13 June 1853. He married **SARAH BENSINGER.** He died on 6 April 1904, at age 50.

3.1.8 JOHN WIEST SNYDER was born on 26 September 1855. He married **CATHARINE (--?--)**. He died on 6 June 1913, at age 57. He was buried at St. David's Lutheran and Reformed Church Cemetery, Hebe, Jordan Township, Northumberland County, PA.

3.1.8.1 WASHTELL SNYDER was born on 11 September 1890. She died on 11 October 1892, at age 2.

3.1.8.2 (--?--) SNYDER was born on 23 October 1892. She died on 23 October 1892. She was buried at St. David's Lutheran and Reformed Church Cemetery, Hebe, Jordan Township, Northumberland County, PA.

3.1.9 (--?--) SNYDER died on 23 October 1892, in infancy.

3.2 CATHERINE WIEST is also referred to as **CATHARINA WIEST** in some sources. She was born on 17 January 1816, Klingerstown, Schuylkill County, PA. She married **SAMUEL B. CLARK**, son of **JOHANNES R. CLARK** and **ANNA MARIA BAUMAN**. She died on 29 March 1868, at age 52. She was buried at St. David's Lutheran and Reformed Church Cemetery, Hebe, Jordan Township, Northumberland County, PA.

3.2.1 ELIZABETH CLARK was born on 25 April 1835. She died on 17 February 1861, at age 25.

3.2.2 ANNA MARY CLARK is also referred to as **POLLY** in some sources. She was born on 4 April 1837. She married **DAVID BOWERMAN**. She died in 1908.

3.2.3 SAMUEL W. CLARK was born on 17 November 1844, Klingerstown, Schuylkill County, PA. He married **JOHANNA WIEST**, daughter of **MOSES MERKEL WIEST** and **MARIA SCHADEL**. He died on 27 April 1905, Klingerstown, Schuylkill County, PA, at age 60. He was buried at St. Michael's Lutheran and Reformed Church Cemetery, Klingerstown, Schuylkill County, PA.

3.2.3.1 ELMIRA CLARK was born on 16 March 1866. She married **ISAIAH KLINGER ROMBERGER**, son of **WILLIAM ROMBERGER** and **SUSANNAH KLINGER**, circa 1884. Elmira Clark and her husband Isaiah Romberger owned the general store in Klingerstown, Schuylkill County, PA. She died on 14 May 1926, at age 60. She was buried at St. Michael's Church, Klingerstown, Schuylkill County, PA.

3.2.3.1.1 BERTHA VIOLA ROMBERGER was born on 4 June 1885. She was baptized on 19 July 1885, Zion (Klinger's) Lutheran Church, Erdman, Dauphin County, PA. She married **LUTHER CALVIN HAVICE** circa 1901. She died on 31 July 1931, at age 46.

3.2.3.1.1.1 (--?--) HAVICE died on 4 January 1908. Some sources record that she died on 10 April 1906. She was buried at St. Michael's Lutheran and Reformed Church Cemetery, Klingerstown, Schuylkill County, PA.

3.2.3.1.1.2 ELMIRA F. HAVICE is also referred to as **ELAMIRA OR ELAMINA** in some sources. She was born on 2 February 1911. She married **FRED E. WILLIAMS**, son of **WILLIAM WILLIAMSON** and **MARY (--?--)**, circa 1925. Prior to her death, Elmira was living in the vicinity of Herndon, Northumberland County, PA. She died in November 1984, at age 73.

3.2.3.1.1.2.1 LUTHER C. WILLIAMS was born in 1927, Pennsylvania.

3.2.3.1.1.2.2 BERTHA C. WILLIAMS was born circa 1930, Pennsylvania.

3.2.3.1.2 SAMUEL WALTER ROMBERGER was born on 30 March 1888. He was baptized on 13 May 1888, Zion (Klinger's) Lutheran Church, Erdman, Dauphin County, PA. He died on 25 November 1895, at age 7. He was buried at St. Michael's Lutheran and Reformed Church Cemetery, Klingerstown, Schuylkill County, PA.

3.2.3.1.3 THOMAS CLARK ROMBERGER was born on 10 July 1891. He was confirmed on 28 October 1906 St. Michael's Church, Klingerstown, Schuylkill County, PA. He married **MINNIE MAY KLINGER**, daughter of **JOHN S. KLINGER** and **SARAH DIETZ**, circa 1910. He died on 1 December 1945, at age 54. He was buried at St. Michael's Church Cemetery, Klingerstown, Schuylkill County, PA.

3.2.3.1.3.1 JOHN ISAIAH ROMBERGER was born on 12 August 1912, Hubley Township, Schuylkill County, PA. He was baptized on 22 September 1912, St. Michael's Church, Klingerstown, Schuylkill County, PA. He married **EMMA MAURER**, daughter of **FRANCIS HERB MAURER** and **IDA GOTTSCHALL OCHS**. He died on 13 November 1989, Polyclinic Hospital, Harrisburg, PA, at age 77. He was buried on 16 November 1989, at Zion (Klinger's) Lutheran Church Cemetery, Erdman, Dauphin County, PA.

3.2.3.1.3.1.1 GENE THOMAS ROMBERGER was born on 31 May 1935, Hegins, Schuylkill County, PA. He married **MABEL GILBERT** on 14 June 1958, Sacramento, PA. He died on 15 June 2005, at age 70.

3.2.3.1.3.1.1.1 GARY GENE ROMBERGER was born on 30 January 1959, Lebanon, Lebanon County, PA. He married **SHERRY ANN GREEN** on 3 June 1978, Camp Hill, Cumberland County, PA.

3.2.3.1.3.1.1.1.1 AMY MARIE ROMBERGER was born on 8 February 1981, Manassas, VA.

3.2.3.1.3.1.1.1.2 BRIAN ADAM ROMBERGER was born on 11 December 1983, Manassas, VA.

3.2.3.1.3.1.1.2 JOHN RALPH ROMBERGER was born on 7 December 1960.

3.2.3.1.3.1.1.3 LORI ANN ROMBERGER was born on 23 September 1962. She married **STEVEN GREEN** on 6 September 1980.

3.2.3.1.3.1.1.3.1 VALERIE GREEN was born on 18 November 1981.

3.2.3.1.3.1.2 CARL FRANCIS ROMBERGER was born on 10 November 1937. He married **CAROLYN MARY STRAUB** on 9 April 1960, Valley View, Schuylkill County, PA.

3.2.3.1.3.1.2.1 COLLEEN ANN ROMBERGER was born on 13 October 1960. She married **GREGORY ALLEN SEIBEL** on 25 April 1981.

3.2.3.1.3.1.2.1.1 HEATHER ANN SEIBEL was born on 31 March 1982, Camp Hill, Cumberland County, PA.

3.2.3.1.3.1.2.1.2 CARLEE LYNN SEIBEL was born on 12 February 1988, Carlisle, PA.

3.2.3.1.3.1.2.2 RANDY LEE ROMBERGER was born on 6 May 1965.

3.2.3.1.3.1.3 ROBERT LAMAR ROMBERGER was born on 18 May 1939, Valley View, Schuylkill County, PA. He married **JUDY PERRY** on 4 April 1960, possibly in KS.

3.2.3.1.3.1.3.1 JODY ANN ROMBERGER was born on 12 November 1964.

3.2.3.1.3.1.3.2 TINA ROMBERGER was born on 28 March 1967. She married **CHRIS FEELEY**.

3.2.3.1.3.2 MAE ELMIRA ROMBERGER was born on 20 August 1914. She married **GEORGE JOHN GERHART**. She died in February 1978, at age 63. Prior to her death, Mae was living in the vicinity of Orwigsburg, Schuylkill County, PA.

3.2.3.1.3.3 ROY ELWOOD ROMBERGER was born on 13 February 1920, Sacramento, Schuylkill County, PA. He married **HILDA I. WOLFE**. He died on 29 July 2003, Community Hospital, Sunbury, Northumberland County, PA, at age 83. He was buried on 2 August 2003, at Fairview Cemetery, Williamstown, PA.

3.2.3.1.3.3.1 RONALD T. ROMBERGER lived in Tower City, Schuylkill County, PA.

3.2.3.1.3.3.2 LARRY E. ROMBERGER. Larry is the owner of Southwest Bingo Supply in Cheyenne, WY, where he lives.

3.2.3.1.3.3.3 TERRY LEE ROMBERGER was born on 15 March 1942, Pillow, Dauphin County, PA. He married **ANNE M. KRAMER** circa 1964. He died on 2 April 2008, at his home on 342 Market Street, Williamstown, Dauphin County, PA, at age 66. According to a newspaper obituary, Terry worked for Medco in Lykens, Dauphin County, PA, for 38 years. He was buried on 5 April 2008, at Sacred Heart of Jesus Catholic Church Cemetery, Williamstown, Dauphin County, PA.

3.2.3.1.3.3.3.1 KAREN A. ROMBERGER married (--?--) **PENDAL**. Karen lives in Williamstown, PA.

3.2.3.1.3.3.3.1.1 KATELYNN PENDAL

3.2.3.1.3.3.3.2 DIANE M. ROMBERGER married **GEORGE ANCHEFF**. Diane lives in Williamstown, PA.

3.2.3.1.3.3.3.2.1 BOBBY ANCHEFF

3.2.3.1.3.3.3.2.2 BEN ANCHEFF

3.2.3.1.3.3.3.2.3 OLIVIA ANCHEFF

3.2.3.1.3.3.3.3 LEEANN ROMBERGER married **DAN KLINGER**. LeeAnn lives in Newark, DE.

3.2.3.1.3.3.3.3.1 CAROLINE KLINGER

3.2.3.1.3.3.3.3.2 OWEN KLINGER

3.2.3.1.3.3.4 ROBERT W. ROMBERGER was born on 26 April 1946. He died on 14 December 1970, at age 24. He was buried at Fairview Cemetery, Williamstown, Dauphin County, PA.

3.2.3.1.3.4 CURTIS RAY ROMBERGER was born on 8 February 1922. He died on 21 April 1923, at age 1. He was buried at St. Michael's Lutheran and Reformed Church Cemetery, Klingerstown, Schuylkill County, PA.

3.2.3.1.3.5 EARL THOMAS ROMBERGER was born on 7 September 1926. He married **MARIE CLARA GLEM.** He died in August 1981, at age 54. Prior to his death, Earl was living in the vicinity of Colorado Springs, El Paso County, CO.

3.2.3.1.3.5.1 THOMAS STACE ROMBERGER was born on 14 September 1951.

3.2.3.1.3.5.2 GARY MICHAEL ROMBERGER was born on 23 March 1955.

3.2.3.1.3.6 RUSSELL ROLAND ROMBERGER was born on 3 September 1928. He married **JEAN RENEE SCHEIB.**

3.2.3.1.3.7 ALMA JEAN ROMBERGER was born on 12 September 1930. She married **PETER N. SPIRKO.** She died on 5 May 1950, at age 19.

3.2.3.1.3.8 MARY LOU ROMBERGER was born on 25 August 1933. She married **JOHN JOSEPH KANAVAL.**

3.2.3.1.3.9 MARION MARIE ROMBERGER was born on 27 January 1936. She married **WILLIAM LECK SANTAK.**

3.2.3.1.4 CHARLES ROMBERGER was born on 24 October 1894. He died on 19 December 1895, at age 1. He was buried at St. Michael's Church, Klingerstown, Schuylkill County, PA.

3.2.3.1.5 HARRY CLARK ROMBERGER was born on 26 September 1897. He was baptized on 24 December 1897, St. Michael's Lutheran Church, Klingerstown, Schuylkill County, PA. He married **MYRTLE MAE KUNTZELMAN,** daughter of **WILSON E. KUNTZELMAN** and **EMMA (--?--),** on 21 November 1921, St. Michael's Lutheran Church, Klingerstown, Schuylkill County, PA. Some sources suggest that he and **MYRTLE MAE KUNTZELMAN** were married on 26 November 1919. He died on 6 November 1953, at age 56. He was buried at St. Michael's Church Cemetery, Klingerstown, Schuylkill County, PA.

3.2.3.1.5.1 HELEN MAE ROMBERGER was born on 10 June 1922. She was baptized on 30 July 1922, St. Michael's Church, Klingerstown, Schuylkill County, PA. She married **CARLOS DANIEL KOPPENHAVER,** son of **ANDREW CLEVELAND KOPPENHAVER** and **KATIE A. STRAUB.** Helen and her husband Carlos Koppenhaver operated a general store in Klingerstown, Schuylkill County. The store, which was the original general store in Klingerstown, was established by H.C. Romberger, Helen's father, and was later known as "Koppy's Store."

3.2.3.1.5.1.1 DAVID HARRY KOPPENHAVER was born on 27 April 1948, Schuylkill County, PA. He was baptized on 30 May 1948, St. Michael's Church, Klingerstown, Schuylkill County, PA. He married **RACHAEL E. BLOCH,** daughter of **KENNETH A. BLOCH** and **PHYLLIS P. MILLER,** on 17 June 1972.

3.2.3.1.5.1.1.1 KARA KAY KOPPENHAVER was born on 26 June 1979, Schuylkill County, PA.

3.2.3.1.5.1.1.2 KRISTEN KYLEE KOPPENHAVER was born on 16 February 1985, Schuylkill County, PA.

3.2.3.1.5.1.2 MARY ALICE KOPPENHAVER was born on 24 February 1952. She married **MELVIN NORMAN FIELD JR.** on 23 July 1977.

3.2.3.1.5.1.2.1 CASEY ALLISON FIELD was born on 14 November 1981.

3.2.3.1.5.1.2.2 LINDSEY RAGAN FIELD was born on 19 February 1985.

3.2.3.1.5.1.3 REBECCA KAY KOPPENHAVER was born on 18 June 1958. She married **ROBERT WARREN KLINE** on 12 July 1980.

3.2.3.1.5.1.3.1 KURT ROBERT KLINE was born on 19 September 1985.

3.2.3.1.5.1.3.2 DREW CARLOS KLINE was born on 23 April 1990.

3.2.3.1.5.1.4 JANE MARIE KOPPENHAVER was born on 10 February 1964. She was baptized on 12 April 1964, St. Michael's Lutheran Church, Klingerstown, Schuylkill County, PA. She married **JOHN MICHAEL WEIGEL** on 1 August 1987, Klingerstown, Schuylkill County, PA.

3.2.3.1.5.1.4.1 DANIEL THOMAS WEIGEL was born on 10 July 1992.

3.2.3.1.5.1.4.2 LEAH MARIE GENEVIEVE WEIGEL was born on 27 February 1995.

3.2.3.1.6 STANLEY CLARK ROMBERGER was born on 14 January 1901. He married **VERNA MAE KLINGER,** daughter of **ELSWORTH KLINGER** and **IDA C. KNORR,** on 4 October 1919. According to the recollections of his son Roland, Stanley was a huckster who initially used mules and wagons to travel to places like Minersville, Pottsville, Shamokin and Mount Carmel to sell animals, eggs, and produce that he got from local farmers. Later he acquired a Model T truck to use on his routes. He died on 20 September 1957, at age 56. He was buried at St. Michael's Church, Klingerstown, Schuylkill County, PA.

3.2.3.1.6.1 QUENTIN STANLEY ROMBERGER was born on 22 March 1920, Klingerstown, Schuylkill County, PA. He married **JEAN ELIZABETH SMITH**, daughter of **CHARLES SMITH** and **CARRIE IRENE OXENRIDER**, on 18 May 1946, St. Michael's Lutheran Church, Klingerstown, Schuylkill County, PA. He died on 24 June 1991, at age 71. He was buried at St. Michael's Lutheran and Reformed Church Cemetery, Klingerstown, Schuylkill County, PA.

3.2.3.1.6.1.1 DIANNE LEA ROMBERGER was born on 13 June 1947. She was baptized on 7 August 1947, St. Michael's Lutheran Church, Klingerstown, Schuylkill County, PA. She married **GEORGE GALLAGHER** in 1967.

3.2.3.1.6.1.1.1 SHARON GALLAGHER was born on 1 August 1968.

3.2.3.1.6.1.1.2 SCOTTIE GALLAGHER was born in 1973.

3.2.3.1.6.1.1.3 STEPHANIE GALLAGHER was born on 10 July 1975.

3.2.3.1.6.1.2 DONNA LEE ROMBERGER was born on 15 July 1953. She was baptized on 26 September 1953, St. Michael's Lutheran Church, Klingerstown, Schuylkill County, PA.

3.2.3.1.6.1.2.1 BRIAN ROMBERGER was born in 1975.

3.2.3.1.6.2 ROLAND RUSSEL ROMBERGER was born on 20 April 1923. He was baptized on 30 July 1923, St. Michael's Lutheran Church, Klingerstown, Schuylkill County, PA. He married **MARY KATHRYN WOLFGANG**, daughter of **GEORGE WOLFGANG** and **ELIZABETH ROTHERMEL**, on 19 September 1942, St. Michael's Lutheran Church, Klingerstown, Schuylkill County, PA. He died on 15 April 2009, at his home on Klingerstown Road, Herndon, Northumberland County, PA, at age 85. According to a newspaper obituary, Roland was a 1940 graduate of the former Dalmatia High School and a World War II veteran, having served in the Army in Northern Africa, Italy, Southern France and the Rhineland. He was awarded the Purple Heart. After his service, he was a farmer, a former employee at the Olmstead Air Force Base at Middletown, and later employed by TRW at Harrisburg, from which he retired in 1985. He was buried on 18 April 2009, at St. Michael's Lutheran Church Cemetery, Klingerstown, Schuylkill County, PA.

3.2.3.1.6.2.1 ROLAND JAMES ROMBERGER was born on 27 July 1946. He was baptized on 1 September 1946, St. Michael's Lutheran Church, Klingerstown, Schuylkill County, PA.

3.2.3.1.6.2.2 JOYCE ELIZABETH ROMBERGER was born on 12 February 1948. She was baptized on 6 May 1948, St. Michael's Lutheran Church, Klingerstown, Schuylkill County, PA. She married **JEFFREY LOVE.**

3.2.3.1.6.2.2.1 GILLIAN LOVE

3.2.3.1.6.2.3 BEVERLY VERNA ROMBERGER was born on 12 August 1950. She was baptized on 12 November 1950, St. Michael's Lutheran Church, Klingerstown, Schuylkill County, PA. She married **FRANK HARNER**. Beverly is Professor of Speech Communications at Susquehanna University, Selinsgrove, PA.

3.2.3.1.6.2.3.1 JESSE HARNER is also referred to as **JESSICA** in some sources.

3.2.3.1.6.2.3.2 JAKE ROMBERGER HARNER was baptized on 18 February 1973, St. Michael's Lutheran Church, Klingerstown, Schuylkill County, PA. He was born on 31 May 1986.

3.2.3.1.6.2.4 GAIL ANN ROMBERGER was born on 6 November 1953. She was baptized on 10 December 1953, St. Michael's Lutheran Church, Klingerstown, Schuylkill County, PA. She married **BRIAN NONNECKE.**

3.2.3.1.6.2.4.1 ERIC NONNECKE

3.2.3.1.6.2.5 R‍ENEE M‍ARY R‍OMBERGER was born on 25 March 1959. She was baptized on 10 June 1959, St. Michael's Lutheran Church, Klingerstown, Schuylkill County, PA. She married K‍EVIN B‍REEN.

3.2.3.1.6.2.5.1 P‍ETER B‍REEN

3.2.3.1.6.2.5.2 S‍COTT B‍REEN

3.2.3.1.6.3 M‍ARION A‍NNA R‍OMBERGER was born on 26 December 1929, 1 mile west of, Klingerstown, Schuylkill County, PA. She was baptized on 16 February 1930, St. Michael's Lutheran Church, Klingerstown, Schuylkill County, PA. She married E‍ARL G‍EORGE T‍ROUTMAN, son of G‍EORGE M‍ONROE T‍ROUTMAN and M‍ARY S‍ARAH R‍EBUCK, on 10 April 1948, Lutheran Parsonage, Leck Kill, PA. She died on 13 May 2005, Klingerstown, Schuylkill County, PA, at age 75. According to a newspaper obituary, Marion resided at RR1 Herndon, Northumberland County, PA. When she was young, Marion helped with the picking and packing of the onions for her father's produce business. After graduating from Lower Mahanoy Township High School in Dalmatia, where she was a basketball star, Marion worked in the toy department of Creative Play-Things in Herndon, that made wooden toys and rubber figure sets for school distribution. Marion had an avid interest in local history and genealogy. She was buried on 17 May 2005, at St. Michael's Lutheran Cemetery, Klingerstown, Schuylkill County, PA.

3.2.3.1.6.3.1 S‍TEVEN E‍ARL T‍ROUTMAN was born on 4 May 1952. He was baptized on 25 May 1952, St. Michael's Lutheran Church, Klingerstown, Schuylkill County, PA. He married J‍OAN E‍LIZABETH M‍ASSER on 21 June 1975. Steve and his family live near Klingerstown, Schuylkill County, where he is co-owner of Troutman Brothers Butcher Shop. He is also a local historian, author, and compiler of the Trautman/Troutman Family History as well as a contributor to the recently published Klingerstown Bicentennial Album.

3.2.3.1.6.3.1.1 M‍ICHAEL T‍ROUTMAN was born on 12 January 1978.

3.2.3.1.6.3.1.2 V‍ALERIE T‍ROUTMAN was born on 23 September 1980.

3.2.3.1.6.3.2 G‍LENN L‍AMAR T‍ROUTMAN was born on 27 May 1954. He was baptized on 16 July 1954, St. Michael's Lutheran Church, Klingerstown, Schuylkill County, PA. He married M‍ARILYN K. H‍OFFMAN on 26 June 1976. He married D‍ONNA M. K‍LINGER. In 2005, Glenn was living in Sunbury, PA.

3.2.3.1.6.3.2.1 H‍EATHER L‍YNNE T‍ROUTMAN was born on 8 June 1978.

3.2.3.1.6.3.2.2 M‍ATTHEW J‍AMES T‍ROUTMAN was born on 14 February 1982.

3.2.3.1.6.3.2.3 H‍ILLARY A‍PRIL T‍ROUTMAN was born on 20 April 1985.

3.2.3.1.6.3.3 R‍UBY M‍ARY T‍ROUTMAN was born on 20 September 1955. She was baptized on 6 November 1955, St. Michael's Lutheran Church, Klingerstown, Schuylkill County, PA. She married J‍OSEPH C. M‍ICHETTI J‍R. on 31 August 1974. In 2005, Ruby was living at RR 1, Herndon, Northumberland County, PA.

3.2.3.1.6.3.3.1 A‍NTONIO D‍AVID M‍ICHETTI was born on 9 March 1979.

3.2.3.1.6.3.3.2 R‍OSALYNDA M‍ARY M‍ICHETTI was born on 4 August 1980.

3.2.3.1.6.3.3.3 A‍NGELINA M‍AE M‍ICHETTI was born on 25 December 1981. She was baptized on 10 April 1982, St. Michael's Lutheran Church, Klingerstown, Schuylkill County, PA.

3.2.3.1.6.3.3.4 M‍ARIA M‍ELINDA M‍ICHETTI is also referred to as M‍ARIA M‍ALINA in some sources. She was born on 27 January 1983. She was baptized on 22 May 1983, St. Michael's Lutheran Church, Klingerstown, Schuylkill County, PA.

3.2.3.1.6.3.3.5 Y‍OLANDA M‍ARION M‍ICHETTI was born on 4 August 1984. She was baptized on 22 December 1984, St. Michael's Lutheran Church, Klingerstown, Schuylkill County, PA.

3.2.3.1.6.4 L‍EE L‍AMAR R‍OMBERGER was born on 14 February 1932. He was baptized on 13 March 1932, St. Michael's Lutheran Church, Klingerstown, Schuylkill County, PA. He married J‍ENNIE K‍EITER.

3.2.3.1.6.4.1 D‍ALE L‍EE R‍OMBERGER was born on 2 October 1952. He died on 17 January 1994, at age 41.

3.2.3.1.6.4.2 JANE MARIE ROMBERGER was born on 20 September 1954.

3.2.3.1.6.5 ROY ALBERT ROMBERGER is also referred to as **ROY ROBERT** in some sources. He was born on 2 June 1934. He was baptized on 29 July 1934, St. Michael's Lutheran Church, Klingerstown, Schuylkill County, PA. He married **BARBARA LEE ROMBERGER**.

3.2.3.1.6.5.1 ROBIN LEE ROMBERGER was born on 21 February 1959.

3.2.3.1.6.6 MARK MARTIN ROMBERGER is also referred to as **MARK MARLIN** in some sources. He was born on 2 July 1939. He was baptized on 23 July 1939, St. Michael's Lutheran Church, Klingerstown, Schuylkill County, PA. He married **SANDRA HUNTSINGER**.

3.2.3.1.6.6.1 MICHAEL IRVIN ROMBERGER was born on 3 December 1968.

3.2.3.1.6.7 BARBARA MARIE ROMBERGER was born on 1 October 1941. She was baptized on 18 October 1941, St. Michael's Lutheran Church, Klingerstown, Schuylkill County, PA. She married **LARRY PAUL KOPPENHAVER**, son of **PAUL ALBERT KOPPENHAVER** and **MARY IRENE MARTZ**, on 18 November 1961, St. Michael's Lutheran Church, Klingerstown, Schuylkill County, PA.

3.2.3.1.6.7.1 VICKI LEE KOPPENHAVER was born on 3 April 1963. She married **DAVID ROMBERGER**.

3.2.3.1.6.7.1.1 ZANE DAVID ROMBERGER was born on 6 November 1997, Lancaster General Hospital, Lancaster, Lancaster County, PA.

3.2.3.1.6.7.2 KELLY SUE KOPPENHAVER was born on 19 March 1969.

3.2.3.1.7 STELLA JOANNA ROMBERGER is also referred to as **ESTELLA ROMBERGER** in some sources. She was born on 2 November 1906. She was baptized on 23 December 1906, St. Michael's Lutheran Church, Klingerstown, Schuylkill County, PA. She married **CLARENCE E. HORNBERGER** on 15 June 1929, St. Michael's Lutheran Church, Klingerstown, Schuylkill County, PA. She died on 28 December 1929, at age 23.

3.2.3.1.8 ALLEN CLARK ROMBERGER is also referred to as **ALLAN** in some sources. He was born on 15 April 1909. He was baptized on 30 April 1909, St. Michael's Lutheran Church, Klingerstown, Schuylkill County, PA. He married **ALVENA MAE STRAUB**, daughter of **EDGAR W. STRAUB** and **ESTELLA L. STROHECKER**, on 20 November 1926, St. Michael's Lutheran Church, Klingerstown, Schuylkill County, PA. He died on 25 November 1992, at age 83. He was buried at St. Michael's Church, Klingerstown, Schuylkill County, PA.

3.2.3.1.8.1 ALLEN ISAIAH ROMBERGER also went by the name of **DUTCH**. He was born on 26 May 1927. He was baptized on 24 July 1927, St. Michael's Lutheran Church, Klingerstown, Schuylkill County, PA. He married **MARGIANNE GAMERAL**. He died on 26 May 1983, at age 56. He was buried at St. Michael's Church, Klingerstown, Schuylkill County, PA.

3.2.3.1.8.1.1 KRISTENE LEA ROMBERGER is also referred to as **KRISTINE** in some sources. She was born on 31 October 1953.

3.2.3.1.8.1.2 MICHAEL ALLEN ROMBERGER was born on 2 November 1954. He was baptized on 5 December 1954, St. Michael's Lutheran Church, Klingerstown, Schuylkill County, PA.

3.2.3.1.8.1.3 CLARK ALLEN ROMBERGER was born on 18 May 1966. He was baptized on 10 July 1966, St. Michael's Lutheran Church, Klingerstown, Schuylkill County, PA.

3.2.3.1.8.2 ALICE LORRAINE ROMBERGER was born on 13 January 1934. She was baptized on 11 March 1934, St. Michael's Lutheran Church, Klingerstown, Schuylkill County, PA. She married **JACK RUSSELL WILLIARD**, son of **DARWIN RANDOLF WILLIARD** and **LEONA MAE MITCHELL**, in 1953.

3.2.3.1.8.2.1 ANN MARIE WILLIARD was born on 15 August 1953. She was baptized on 13 September 1953, St. Michael's Lutheran Church, Klingerstown, Schuylkill County, PA. She married **MICHAEL MATTER**.

3.2.3.1.8.2.2 JACK RUSSELL WILLIARD JR. was born on 31 July 1955, Harrisburg, Dauphin County, PA. He was baptized on 11 September 1955, St. Michael's Lutheran Church, Klingerstown, Schuylkill County, PA. Some sources record that he was born on 3 July 1955. He married **MARY ANN (--?--)** circa 1978. He married **KRISTINA KAY MINNICH** in 1985. He married **WANDA MOYER**. He died on 13 May 2016, Mount

Nittany Medical Center, State College, Centre County, PA, at age 60. He was buried at Christ Lutheran Church Columbarium, Hilton Head Island, Beaufort County, SC.

3.2.3.1.8.2.2.1 LUKE WILLIARD was born on 24 March 1980.

3.2.3.1.8.2.2.2 ZACH HERSHEL WILLIARD was born on 24 December 1985. He died on 12 March 1987, at age 1. He was buried at St. Michael's Lutheran Church Cemetery, Klingerstown, Schuylkill County, PA.

3.2.3.1.8.2.3 JEFFREY ALLEN WILLIARD was born on 24 April 1957. He was baptized on 29 December 1957, St. Michael's Lutheran Church, Klingerstown, Schuylkill County, PA. He married **KAREN (--?--)**.

3.2.3.1.9 HELEN SUSANNAH ROMBERGER was born on 15 October 1911. She was baptized on 17 December 1911, St. Michael's Lutheran Church, Klingerstown, Schuylkill County, PA. She married **RUE OTIS ERDMAN**, son of **OTIS OLIVER ERDMAN** and **EDNA BOWMAN,** on 23 November 1935, St. Michael's Lutheran Church, Klingerstown, Schuylkill County, PA. She died on 7 December 1972, at age 61. She was buried at St. Michael's Church, Klingerstown, Schuylkill County, PA.

3.2.3.1.9.1 LARUE HELEN ERDMAN was born on 10 March 1938. She was baptized on 17 April 1938, St. Michael's Lutheran Church, Klingerstown, Schuylkill County, PA. She married **ROBERT M. MACHAMER**, son of **ROLAND MACHAMER** and **ELSIE HUMMEL,** circa 1963.

3.2.3.1.9.1.1 ROBERT MACHAMER JR.

3.2.3.1.9.2 STELLA HELEN ERDMAN was born on 26 August 1942. She was baptized on 28 September 1942, St. Michael's Lutheran Church, Klingerstown, Schuylkill County, PA. She married **DENNIS K. BINGAMAN**, son of **CHARLES BINGAMAN** and **MYRTLE HOFFMAN,** on 4 August 1968. Stella lives in Dalmatia, Northumberland County, PA.

3.2.3.1.9.3 SANDRA HELEN ERDMAN was born on 6 June 1948. She was baptized on 11 July 1948, St. Michael's Lutheran Church, Klingerstown, Schuylkill County, PA. She married **ALAN LONG.** Sandra and her husband live in Milton, Northumberland County, PA.

3.2.3.1.9.4 RUE OTIS ERDMAN JR. was born on 17 December 1951. He was baptized on 4 January 1952, St. Michael's Lutheran Church, Klingerstown, Schuylkill County, PA.

3.2.4 EDWARD CLARK was born circa 1842. Some sources record that he was born circa 1845. He married **FRANNY SNYDER**, daughter of **DANIEL B. SNYDER** and **BARBARA WIEST.** He died circa 1864.

3.2.4.1 BARBARA ALICE CLARK (see above)

3.2.4.2 CATHERINE ELIZABETH CLARK (see above)

3.2.4.2.1 CHARLES B. ADAMS (see above)

3.2.4.2.2 MILTON S. ADAMS (see above)

3.2.4.2.3 JAMES ADAMS (see above)

3.2.4.2.3.1 WARREN ADAMS (see above)

3.2.4.2.3.2 RUTH F. ADAMS (see above)

3.2.4.2.4 SADIE O. ADAMS (see above)

3.2.4.2.5 HARRY L. ADAMS (see above)

3.2.5 HIRAM CLARK was born circa 1846. He died circa 1864, in action during the Civil War.

3.2.6 THOMAS CLARK was born on 9 March 1852, Hebe, Jordan Township, Northumberland County, PA. He died on 18 August 1868, Hebe, Jordan Township, Northumberland County, PA, at age 16.

3.2.7 JOHN CLARK was born circa 1848. Some sources record that he was born circa 1853, Hebe, Jordan Township, Northumberland County, PA.

3.2.8 FRANKLIN W. CLARK was born on 27 November 1854, Hebe, Jordan Township, Northumberland County, PA. He married **CATHERINE (--?--)**.

3.2.9 ESTHER CLARK was born circa 1856. She married **DAVID BOWMAN**.

3.3 MARIA WIEST also went by the name of **MARY AND POLLY**. She was born on 27 July 1818. She married **PETER S. REBUCK**, son of **JOHANNES CONRAD REBOCK** and **JULIANNA REITZ,** on 15 March 1840. She died on 27 May 1888, Klingerstown, Schuylkill County, PA, at age 69. She was buried at Zion (Klinger's) Church, Erdman, Lykens Township, Dauphin County, PA.

3.3.1 SAMUEL REBUCK was born circa 1840.

3.3.2 KATHERINE REBUCK is also referred to as **CATHERINE** in some sources. She was born on 7 January 1843. She married **E. WETZEL**. She died on 5 June 1914, at age 71. She was buried at St. Michael's Church Cemetery, Klingerstown, Schuylkill County, PA.

3.3.3 POLLY REBUCK is also referred to as **MARY** in some sources. She was born on 1 November 1844. She married **HENRY GESSNER**. She died on 11 August 1909, at age 64. She was buried at St. David's Lutheran and Reformed Church Cemetery, Hebe, Northumberland County, PA.

3.3.3.1 MARY GESSNER was born on 20 June 1878, Mandata, Northumberland County, PA. She married **JOEL RICHARD MAURER**, son of **PETER MAURER** and **ELIZA REBUCK**, on 10 April 1897, St. David's Lutheran and Reformed Church, Hebe, Northumberland County, PA. She died on 28 December 1934, Elizabethville, Dauphin County, PA, at age 56. She was buried on 31 December 1934, at Salem Lutheran Church Cemetery, Killinger, Dauphin County, PA.

3.3.3.1.1 MAUDE MAY MAURER was born on 24 July 1897. She was baptized on 12 September 1897, St. David's Lutheran and Reformed Church, Hebe, Northumberland County, PA. She married **CARLOS RAY BROSIUS**, son of **MAURICE E. BROSIUS** and **CATHERINE ELIZABETH WIEST**, before 1920. She died in 1971. She was buried at Salem Lutheran Church Cemetery, Killinger, Dauphin County, PA.

3.3.3.1.1.1 MARY C. BROSIUS was born on 26 October 1915, Millersburg, Dauphin County, PA. She married **LEROY D. DEIBLER**. She died on 9 July 2011, Manor at Susquehanna Village, Millersburg, Dauphin County, PA, at age 95.

3.3.3.1.1.1.1 SANDRA E. DEIBLER married **KARL K. BOBB**.

3.3.3.1.1.1.1.1 STEVEN C. BOBB

3.3.3.1.1.1.1.2 KENNETH E. BOBB

3.3.3.1.1.1.2 KARL E. DEIBLER was born on 11 November 1937, Millersburg, Dauphin County, PA. He died on 4 December 2009, Millersburg, Dauphin County, PA, at age 72. He was buried on 12 December 2009, at Salem Lutheran Church Cemetery, Killinger, Dauphin County, PA.

3.3.3.1.1.1.2.1 SCOTT DEIBLER

3.3.3.1.1.1.2.2 SHARI DEIBLER married **DANIEL KNOUSE**.

3.3.3.1.1.2 ELEANOR BROSIUS married **(--?--) BEAVER**. She was born circa 1916. She died before 25 December 2016.

3.3.3.1.1.3 MELVIN R. BROSIUS was born in 1920. He died in 1961. He was buried at Salem Lutheran Church Cemetery, Killinger, Dauphin County, PA.

3.3.3.1.1.4 FERN M. BROSIUS was born circa 1923. She married **(--?--) MCCORMICK**. She died before 9 July 2011.

3.3.3.1.1.5 JOHN PERSHING BROSIUS was born on 28 October 1926, Berrysburg, Dauphin County, PA. Some sources record that he was born on 28 October 1927. He married **BETTY (--?--)**. He died on 29 July 2004, at age 77. He was buried at Salem Lutheran Church Cemetery, Killinger, Dauphin County, PA.

3.3.3.1.1.6 BALIR E. BROSIUS was born on 23 May 1930, Berrysburg, Dauphin County, PA. He married **JUNE M. BOYER** circa 1955. He died on 25 December 2016, Millersburg, Dauphin County, PA, at age 86. He was buried on 30 December 2016, at Zion Lutheran Church Cemetery, Rife, Dauphin County, PA.

3.3.3.1.1.6.1 DAVID BROSIUS married **DEE (--?--)**.

3.3.3.1.1.6.2 KIRBY BROSIUS married **JAN (--?--)**.

3.3.3.1.2 SADIE ALVENA MAURER was born on 9 December 1898. She was baptized on 26 February 1899, St. David's Lutheran and Reformed Church, Hebe, Northumberland County, PA. She married **CHARLES WALTER HAIN**, son of **JOHN W. HAIN**, before 1920. She died in November 1968, at age 69.

3.3.3.1.2.1 NORMAN JAY HAIN was born on 23 April 1923, Elizabethville, Dauphin County, PA. He married **MARY ELLEN TROUTMAN**, daughter of **HARRY N. TROUTMAN** and **MARY A. MUMMA**, circa 1940. He died on 24 November 2004, Susquehanna Lutheran Village,

Millersburg, Dauphin County, PA, at age 81. He was buried on 27 November 2004, at Maple Grove Cemetery Mausoleum, Elizabethville, Dauphin County, PA.

3.3.3.1.2.1.1 **THOMAS N. HAIN** married **LLOYAL ANN FREEMAN.** He lived in Elizabethville, Dauphin County, PA.

3.3.3.1.2.1.2 **MARTHA JANE HAIN** married **JAY FULKROD.** She lived in Elizabethville, Dauphin County, PA.

3.3.3.1.3 **DAVID WALTER MAURER** was born on 24 October 1901. He was baptized on 23 January 1902, St. David's Lutheran and Reformed Church, Hebe, Northumberland County, PA.

3.3.4 **HANNAH REBUCK** is also referred to as **HANNAH RABUCK** in some sources. She was born on 4 April 1847. Some sources record that she died on 26 January 1849 PA and that Hannah was buried at St. David's Church, Hebe, Northumberland County, but neither the Genealogists Guide to Burials in Northumberland County, PA, nor the published church records list to Hannah as being buried there. In addition, Hannah is listed in the 1850 Census as part of Peter and Maria Rebuck's family. Hannah is also listed in the 1860 Census. She died after 1860.

3.3.5 **JOHN ROBERT REBUCK** was born on 18 November 1849. He died on 14 September 1859, Klingerstown, Schuylkill County, PA, at age 9.

3.3.6 **HARRIET REBUCK** was born on 18 November 1849. Some sources record that she was born on 18 November 1850. She married **JOSIAH LAHR**. She died on 27 February 1929, Hebe, Northumberland County, PA, at age 78.

3.3.6.1 **SUSAN MCCLATA LAHR** was born in 1871. She married **WILLIAM ELLSWORTH TROUTMAN**, son of **WILLIAM K. TROUTMAN** and **LYDIA LEITZEL,** on 25 December 1886. She died on 17 April 1958.

3.3.6.1.1 **GRANT L. TROUTMAN** was born on 12 June 1888. He married **HANNA E. (--?--).** He died in 1973. He was buried at Union Cemetery, Pillow, Northumberland County, PA.

3.3.6.1.2 **CLARENCE R. TROUTMAN** was born on 30 November 1889. He married **SALLIE E. (--?--).** He died on 14 January 1944, at age 54. He was buried at St. David's Lutheran and Reformed Church Cemetery, Hebe, Jordan Township, Northumberland County, PA.

3.3.6.1.2.1 **(--?--) TROUTMAN** died on 21 August 1916. She was buried at St. David's Lutheran and Reformed Church Cemetery, Hebe, Jordan Township, Northumberland County, PA.

3.3.6.1.2.2 **(--?--) TROUTMAN** was born on 1 April 1918. He died on 2 April 1918. He was buried at St. David's Lutheran and Reformed Church Cemetery, Hebe, Jordan Township, Northumberland County, PA.

3.3.6.1.3 **EARL EUGENE TROUTMAN** was born on 25 September 1891. He married **MARY L. LEITZEL**, daughter of **GEORGE ADAM TROUTMAN LEITZEL** and **CATHERINE ALICE SNYDER,** circa 1915. He died on 11 December 1949, at age 58. He was buried at St. David's Lutheran and Reformed Church Cemetery, Hebe, Jordan Township, Northumberland County, PA.

3.3.6.1.3.1 **LEAR ELWYN TROUTMAN** was born on 3 March 1916. He married **VIOLET ELIZABETH REED.** He died on 22 October 1970, at age 54.

3.3.6.1.3.1.1 **NARDELLE ELIZABETH TROUTMAN** was born on 20 March 1938. She married **JAMES CLIFFORD LEITZEL.**

3.3.6.1.3.1.1.1 **CANDITH YVONNE LEITZEL** was born on 4 December 1958. She married **BILL HOLTZER** circa 1977. She married **CRAIG HILL** after 1978.

3.3.6.1.3.1.2 **TERRY LEAR TROUTMAN** was born on 6 July 1940. He married **VIOLET WITMER** circa 1957.

3.3.6.1.3.1.2.1 **DEBORAH ANN TROUTMAN** was born in 1957. She died in 1957.

3.3.6.1.3.1.2.2 **KEVIN JEFFREY TROUTMAN** was born on 11 April 1958. He married **BONNIE ELAINE FEIDT.**

3.3.6.1.3.1.2.3 **SHERI LYNN TROUTMAN** was born on 11 September 1960.

3.3.6.1.3.1.2.4 **WENDY LYNN TROUTMAN** married **DAVID CALVIN MONGOLD.** She was born on 8 November 1961.

3.3.6.1.3.1.2.5 **DOUGLAS TROUTMAN** was born on 24 February 1964.

3.3.6.1.3.1.3 DONNA LEE TROUTMAN was born on 22 December 1942. She married **LARRY ALFRED KAUFMAN**.

    3.3.6.1.3.1.3.1 SCOTT DOUGLAS KAUFMAN was born on 29 December 1961.

    3.3.6.1.3.1.3.2 KIRBY ALAN KAUFMAN was born on 11 April 1964.

    3.3.6.1.3.1.3.3 DAVID MICHAEL KAUFMAN was born on 8 July 1969.

    3.3.6.1.3.1.3.4 LEAR ANTHONY KAUFMAN was born on 18 January 1971.

3.3.6.1.3.1.4 BRENDA RAE TROUTMAN was born on 2 April 1944. She married **DENNIS EUGENE MILLER**.

    3.3.6.1.3.1.4.1 DENNIS EUGENE MILLER JR. was born on 15 September 1961.

    3.3.6.1.3.1.4.2 TODD ANTHONY MILLER was born on 16 July 1965.

3.3.6.1.3.2 OWEN DONALD TROUTMAN was born on 28 May 1919. He married **MAY CRISTINA KLINGER**. He died on 21 June 1977, at age 58. He was buried at Union Cemetery, Pillow, Northumberland County, PA.

    3.3.6.1.3.2.1 ELAINE CARRIE TROUTMAN was born on 10 June 1938. She married **PARK GENE WIEST**, son of **LUTHER A. WIEST** and **KATHRYN RAMBERGER**.

        3.3.6.1.3.2.1.1 RICKY GENE WIEST was born on 25 July 1958, Alexandria, VA. He married **CHRISTINE ELIZABETH SHUMAKER**.

        3.3.6.1.3.2.1.2 VICKY KAY WIEST was born on 5 August 1959. She married **MICHAEL LEE OTT**.

        3.3.6.1.3.2.1.3 LISA ANN WIEST was born on 8 May 1963.

3.3.6.1.3.3 PAULINE CATHERINE TROUTMAN was born on 21 August 1922, Hebe, Northumberland County, PA. She married **NEILO JOSEPH TOCKET**, son of **VAN TOCKET** and **JOHANNA ZANETTE**, on 12 April 1947. Some sources suggest that she and **NEILO JOSEPH TOCKET** were married circa 1946. She died on 21 June 2009, the Bridges at Bent Creek Assisted Living Center, Mechanicsburg, Cumberland County, PA, at age 86. According to a newspaper obituary, Pauline lived in Mechanicsburg, PA. She retired as a secretary from Arthur Myers Esq., and from CCNB Banks. She was buried on 25 June 2009, at Indiantown Gap National Cemetery, Annville, Lebanon County, PA.

    3.3.6.1.3.3.1 GREGORY VON TOCKET was born on 30 September 1947, Bethlehem, Lehigh County, PA. He married **SHARON E. MILLER**. He died on 17 August 2011, Lewisberry, York County, PA, at age 63.

        3.3.6.1.3.3.1.1 DANIELLE NADINE TOCKET was born on 16 June 1976. She married **MATTHEW MOSER**.

            3.3.6.1.3.3.1.1.1 JACOB MOSER

            3.3.6.1.3.3.1.1.2 MITCHELL MOSER

            3.3.6.1.3.3.1.1.3 NATHAN MOSER

        3.3.6.1.3.3.1.2 HEATHER O'NEAL TOCKET was born on 18 March 1978. She married **JEREMIAS RAMOS**.

            3.3.6.1.3.3.1.2.1 JULIAN RAMOS

    3.3.6.1.3.3.2 CYNTHIA ANN TOCKET was born on 27 December 1948. She married **ROY JAY SHEELY** on 16 April 1966. She married **LYNN A. KEELEY**.

        3.3.6.1.3.3.2.1 KENNETH BRIAN SHEELY was born on 1 November 1966. He married **KRISTEN LYNN THOMSON**.

            3.3.6.1.3.3.2.1.1 DEREK THOMSON SHEELY was born on 14 April 1989.

            3.3.6.1.3.3.2.1.2 KEYTON SIERRA SHEELY was born on 26 April 1993.

        3.3.6.1.3.3.2.2 BARBARA ANN SHEELY was born on 21 February 1968. She married **MICHAEL J. KAUFMAN** on 19 May 1990.

            3.3.6.1.3.3.2.2.1 KAITY KAUFMAN was born on 17 April 1994.

            3.3.6.1.3.3.2.2.2 MICHAELA MARIE KAUFMAN was born on 12 February 1997.

        3.3.6.1.3.3.2.3 TIMOTHY ANDREW SHEELY was born on 9 September 1970.

3.3.6.1.3.3.3 SUSAN LYNN TOCKET was born on 24 May 1950. She married **ROBERT WILLIAM FLEMING**. She married **WILLIAM HENRY RICHTER**.

    3.3.6.1.3.3.3.1 ANDREA LYNN FLEMING was born on 7 January 1973.

    3.3.6.1.3.3.3.2 KRISTINA RENE FLEMING was born on 29 July 1984.

3.3.6.1.3.3.4 JEFFREY EARL TOCKET was born on 12 May 1954. He married **VICKI LEE PATTON**. He married **NICOLE LOMANO**.

3.3.6.1.3.4 MARY K. TROUTMAN was born in 1927. She died in 1929.

3.3.6.1.3.5 MARK KENT TROUTMAN was born on 28 November 1927. He died on 29 January 1929, at age 1.

3.3.6.1.3.6 DORIS SHIRLEY TROUTMAN was born on 7 April 1933. She married **LESTER ARTHUR JOHNS**.

    3.3.6.1.3.6.1 DIANE LOUISE JOHNS was born on 14 December 1957.

    3.3.6.1.3.6.2 LESTER ARTHUR JOHNS JR. was born on 29 January 1959.

3.3.6.1.4 WILLIAM F. TROUTMAN was born on 31 December 1892.

3.3.6.1.5 AMMON J. TROUTMAN was born on 29 June 1894.

3.3.6.1.6 EVA J. TROUTMAN is also referred to as **EVA G.** in some sources. She was born on 30 May 1896.

3.3.6.1.7 NETTIE T. TROUTMAN was born on 4 June 1898. She died on 29 September 1915, at age 17.

3.3.6.1.8 ROSCOE ROY TROUTMAN was born on 30 June 1900. In 1917, Roscoe was living in Pillow, PA, and working at the Alvord Reamer Works in Millersburg, PA. He married **BLANCHE M. BOYER**, daughter of **JACOB A. BOYER** and **ANNA CELESTE HOY**, circa 1921. He died in February 1977, at age 76. He was buried at St. David's Lutheran and Reformed Church Cemetery, Hebe, Jordan Township, Northumberland County, PA.

3.3.6.1.8.1 GRACE M. TROUTMAN was born on 2 July 1922, Northumberland County, PA. She married **JOHN F. SHAFFER JR.** She died on 22 August 2012, Hospice Residence, Harrisburg, Dauphin County, PA, at age 90. According to a newspaper obituary, Grace lived in Hebe, Northumberland County, PA. She was employed by Muskin Shoe Co., Millersburg, and Mon-Mar, Gratz, from where she retired. She was buried on 26 August 2012, at St. David's Lutheran and Reformed Church Cemetery, Hebe, Northumberland County, PA.

    3.3.6.1.8.1.1 GARY SHAFFER

    3.3.6.1.8.1.2 RICK SHAFFER

    3.3.6.1.8.1.3 WENDY SHAFFER married (--?--) **CLOUGH**.

    3.3.6.1.8.1.4 LISA SHAFFER married (--?--) **SPECHT**.

3.3.6.1.8.2 ROY K. TROUTMAN was born in 1923. He died in 1929. He was buried at St. David's Lutheran and Reformed Church Cemetery, Hebe, Northumberland County, PA.

3.3.6.1.8.3 BETTY L. TROUTMAN was born circa May 1927. She married (--?--) **BOHNER**.

3.3.6.1.8.4 ELEANOR E. TROUTMAN was born on 16 December 1930. She married (--?--) **SCHAFFNER**. She died on 11 June 1997, at age 66.

3.3.6.1.8.5 JOAN TROUTMAN was born circa 1935. She married (--?--) **PEAY**.

3.3.6.1.9 RUTH FAYE TROUTMAN was born on 12 May 1902. She married **ALLEN RAY SCHLEGAL** on 31 December 1919. She died on 29 November 1985, at age 83.

3.3.6.1.10 PAUL LEO TROUTMAN was born on 2 November 1906. He died in 1935. He was buried at St. David's Lutheran and Reformed Church Cemetery, Hebe, Northumberland County, PA. Paul was a minister.

3.3.6.2 PETER LAHR was born on 25 December 1872. He died in 1877.

3.3.6.3 DANIEL F. LAHR was born on 18 June 1876. He died on 17 April 1883, at age 6.

3.3.6.4 MONROE I. LAHR was born on 28 August 1878. He married **MAYME J. KILLHEFFER** on 29 September 1900. He died on 21 June 1954, at age 75. He was buried at St. David's Lutheran and Reformed Church, Hebe, Jordan Township, Northumberland County, PA.

3.3.6.5 JOHN J. LAHR was born on 20 October 1878. He died on 20 March 1881, at age 2.

3.3.6.6 **HANNAH R. LAHR** was born on 21 December 1880. She died on 19 May 1882, at age 1.

3.3.6.7 **EMMA S. LAHR** was born on 23 February 1883. She married **H. S. WINKELMAN.** She died on 27 July 1906, at age 23. She was buried at St. David's Lutheran and Reformed Church Cemetery, Hebe, Jordan Township, Northumberland County, PA.

3.3.6.8 **VICTOR W. LAHR** was born on 27 November 1885. He died on 3 November 1891, at age 5.

3.3.6.9 **FRANCIS G. LAHR** was born on 18 April 1888. He died on 28 December 1910, at age 22. He was buried at St. David's Lutheran and Reformed Church Cemetery, Hebe, Jordan Township, Northumberland County, PA.

3.3.6.10 **MAUD LAHR** was born on 28 November 1892. She died on 27 March 1894, at age 1.

3.3.7 **JACOB W. REBUCK** was born on 7 June 1853. He married **SUSAN SHAFFER.** He died on 28 January 1909, at age 55.

3.3.7.1 **MABEL REBUCK**

3.3.7.2 **PETER REBUCK** died in 1938, Belvedere, Ill.

3.3.7.3 **IRA REBUCK** was born on 22 May 1891. He married **LIZZIE M. KNORR.** He died on 12 May 1991, at age 99.

3.3.7.3.1 **LEWIS E. REBUCK** was born on 11 April 1918. Some sources record that he was born on 11 March 1918. He died on 16 September 1918. He was buried at Salem Church Cemetery, Rough and Ready, Upper Mahantango Township, Schuylkill County, PA.

3.3.8 **FRANKLING REBUCK** was born on 26 February 1854. He died on 9 May 1865, Klingerstown, Schuylkill County, PA, at age 11. He was buried at Zion (Klinger's) Church, Erdman, Lykens Township, Dauphin County, PA.

3.3.9 **ALFIS E. REBUCK** was born circa 31 January 1856. He died on 17 April 1923. He was buried at Klinger's Church, Erdman, Dauphin County, PA.

3.3.10 **EVE ELIZABETH REBUCK** was born circa 1852. She was born circa 1858. She married **JACOB WIEST** in 1867.

3.4 **JOHN KLINGER WIEST** was born on 14 January 1821, Jordan Township, PA. He married **LUCETTA BEISEL.** Although John was born after his family migrated from Berks County, he was known as "Oley John" and his family as the "Oley Wiests." He farmed 150 acres on the Mahantongo Creek, Schuylkill County. He was the first member of his family to venture west and went to California around the time of Gold Rush of 1849, before later returning to Klingerstown. According to some sources he made a "fortune" in the gold fields. All of his adult children, except Elizabeth and Daniel, later settled in Oregon and Washington. He died on 20 April 1877, at age 56. He was buried at Zion (Klinger's) Church, Erdman, Lykens Township, Dauphin County, PA.

3.4.1 **JACOB BEISEL WIEST** was born on 8 November 1844, Jordan Township, PA. He married **MARY ANN OXENREIDER**, daughter of **MICHAEL HENRY OCHSENRIDER,** on 29 March 1884. He married **IDA SCHAFFER** on 27 June 1895. Jacob kept daily diaries which are the source of much of the information about the life of the Wiests in the Pacific Northwest. Although they are written in a combination of Pennsylvania Dutch and very poor English, Mary Stapleton -- who has transcribed the years 1884-1901 -- reports that they are a delight to read.

According to the Wiest Family History, Jacob and his brother, William, went to California in 1868, and thence to Portland, OR, in 1872, where they engaged in the logging business. At that time, logging was conducted with oxen, with men working 14 hours per day for wages of about $1.50.

In time Jacob Beisel Wiest founded the Wiest Logging Company which, at one time, had extensive operations in the Pacific Northwest.

According to Mary Stapleton, as relayed by Bruce Hall, Jacob Beisel " Jake" Wiest was born in Hebe, Northumberland Co., PA, on November 8, 1844. He left Pennsylvania in 1871, probably by train, to go to California and then north by steamer to Portland, OR. There, he purchased timber and established logging operations in the Stella WA. area, with his brothers Sam, Dan, John, and William. Sam, Dan, William, and Jake eventually bought out John's interest in the business. Later, Sam, who lost a leg in a logging accident, sold his share of the business and moved to Portland. Dan also sold his share, and returned to Pennsylvania.

In 1901, Jake and William sold their operation to Chapman Bros. Logging. However, Jake remained in the lumber business, buying and selling timber rights, for the rest of his life -- even after moving to Skamokawa, Wahkiakum County, WA, and taking up the life of a farmer.

Jacob Beisel Wiest died November 21, 1919, in Skamokawa, WA, of acute dilation of the heart complicated by diabetes mellitus. He died on 19 November 1919, Stella, Cowlitz County, WA, at age 75.

3.4.1.1 GORDON GRANT WIEST was born on 11 April 1885. He married ELENOR WADDELL. He died on 6 April 1953, Skamokawa, Wahkiakum County, WA, at age 67.

3.4.1.1.1 GORDON GRANT WIEST was born on 28 January 1918, Skamokawa, Wahkiakum County, WA. He married OPAL CHARLENE MCNALLEY on 22 October 1941, Cathlamet, Wahkiakum County, WA. He died on 9 May 1957, Skamokawa, Wahkiakum County, WA, at age 39.

3.4.1.1.1.1 GLEN GORDON WIEST also went by the name of BUTCH. He was born on 6 September 1946, WA. He married VICKI HARSHAM.

3.4.1.1.1.1.1 GORDON GRANT WIEST was born on 28 October 1978, Seattle, King County, WA.

3.4.1.1.1.1.2 LINDSEY ALENE WIEST was born on 30 January 1984, Seattle, King County, WA.

3.4.1.1.1.2 JENNIE LYNN WIEST was born on 22 August 1950, WA.

3.4.1.1.2 ARLEE ILA WIEST was born on 4 October 1919, Skamokawa, Wahkiakum County, WA. She married ALFRED ADOLPH BRANDT on 25 December 1940, Skamokawa, Wahkiakum County, WA. She died on 12 December 1954, Renton, King County, WA, at age 35.

3.4.1.1.2.1 ALFRED ARLIE BRANDT was born on 20 May 1943. He married SUSAN (--?--).

3.4.1.1.2.1.1 ARLEE BRANDT

3.4.1.1.2.1.2 NEIL BRANDT

3.4.1.1.3 WILMA MAXINE WIEST was born on 16 December 1922, Skamokawa, Wahkiakum County, WA. She married WINTHROP RAY WILBUR on 31 December 1941, Skamokawa, Wahkiakum County, WA. She died on 22 April 1993, Seattle, King County, WA, at age 70.

3.4.1.1.3.1 BETTY JO WILBUR was born on 11 January 1943, Skamokawa, Wahkiakum County, WA. She died on 28 January 1995, Las Vegas, NV, at age 52.

3.4.1.1.3.2 MARLA RAE WILBUR was born in April 1948.

3.4.1.1.4 BETTY MARGRETTA WIEST was born on 30 June 1924, Skamokawa, Wahkiakum County, WA. She married JAMES EDMUND LORANGER on 5 January 1952, Seattle, King County, WA.

3.4.1.1.4.1 PAULA RENEE LORANGER was born on 3 March 1953, Seattle, King County, WA. She married HAROLD STEPHEN MILLER on 10 September 1972, Seattle, King County, WA.

3.4.1.1.4.1.1 PAMELA ANN MILLER was born on 6 July 1973, Seattle, King County, WA.

3.4.1.1.4.1.2 CARL STEPHEN MILLER was born on 28 January 1975, Seattle, King County, WA.

3.4.1.1.4.2 MICHELE ANN LORANGER was born on 2 March 1954, Seattle, King County, WA. She married STAN WAGENHALS on 22 October 1983, Seattle, King County, WA.

3.4.1.1.4.2.1 OWEN HUNTER WAGENHALS was born on 5 August 1984, Seattle, King County, WA.

3.4.1.1.4.2.2 ERIC SAYERS WAGENHALS was born on 9 June 1985, Seattle, King County, WA.

3.4.1.1.4.2.3 ANNA KATHLEEN WAGENHALS was born on 6 December 1986, Seattle, King County, WA.

3.4.1.1.4.3 ROBERT JAMES LORANGER was born on 6 March 1955, Seattle, King County, WA. He married DAWN BABETTE FANDRICH on 7 June 1975, Seattle, King County, WA.

3.4.1.1.4.3.1 CHRISTOPHER ROBERT LORANGER was born on 23 July 1976, Seattle, King County, WA.

3.4.1.1.4.3.2 HEIDI DAWN LORANGER was born on 2 August 1977, Seattle, King County, WA.

3.4.1.1.4.4 JEFFRY ALLEN LORANGER was born on 5 June 1959, Seattle, King County, WA. He married **CAROL ANN HURST** on 10 May 1986, Seattle, King County, WA.

3.4.1.1.5 JACOB BEISEL WIEST was born on 25 May 1926, Skamokawa, Wahkiakum County, WA. He married **DIANE CAVANAUGH** on 7 August 1953, Puget Island, Wahkiakum County, WA. He died on 5 January 1990, Seattle, King County, WA, at age 63.

> **3.4.1.1.5.1 JAMES KENNETH WIEST** is also referred to as **JANES** in some sources. He was born on 17 March 1954, WA.

> **3.4.1.1.5.2 DEBORAH ELAINE WIEST** was born on 25 February 1955, WA. She married **JAMES P. FAY**.

>> **3.4.1.1.5.2.1 TAYLOR HAMILTON FAY** was born on 26 April 1982.

> **3.4.1.1.5.3 RONALD ALLEN WIEST** was born on 27 February 1957, WA. He married **CINDY J. STRATTON**.

>> **3.4.1.1.5.3.1 ROLAND ALLEN WIEST JR.** was born on 1 October 1974.

> **3.4.1.1.5.4 ROGER HAMILTON WIEST** was born on 27 December 1958, WA. He married **LORRAINE WRIGHT**.

>> **3.4.1.1.5.4.1 NICHOLAS JACOB WIEST** was born on 30 September 1979.

>> **3.4.1.1.5.4.2 TUCKER ADAM WIEST** was born on 1 October 1982.

> **3.4.1.1.5.5 LORI JANE WIEST** was born on 7 October 1962, WA. She married **ROBERT A. MADEO**.

>> **3.4.1.1.5.5.1 SAMANTHA CHRISTINE MADEO** was born on 11 September 1988.

3.4.1.2 JENNIE MAE WIEST was born on 27 June 1886. She married **THOMAS THOMPSON JR.** on 3 December 1902, Skamokawa, Wahkiakum County, WA. She died on 17 December 1975, Beaverton, Washington County, OR, at age 89.

> **3.4.1.2.1 VIOLET CHARLOTTE THOMPSON** was born on 8 April 1904, Astoria, Clatsop County, OR. She died on 18 May 1910, Skamokawa, Wahkiakum County, WA, at age 6.

> **3.4.1.2.2 LAURA MAE THOMPSON** was born on 9 September 1911, Astoria, Clatsop County, OR. She married **JAY GUY MILLER** on 19 August 1934, Skamokawa, Wahkiakum County, WA. She died on 15 February 1987, Longview, Cowlitz County, WA, at age 75.

>> **3.4.1.2.2.1 LESLIE JO MILLER** was born on 21 July 1944, Pasco, Franklin County, WA. She married **JAMES GOLDSMITH** on 11 June 1966, Kelso, Cowlitz County, WA.

>>> **3.4.1.2.2.1.1 ELIZABETH KAREN GOLDSMITH** was born on 14 December 1968. She married **PHILIP DREW FENTER** on 28 November 1992.

>>>> **3.4.1.2.2.1.1.1 LYNSEY KANOELANI FENTER** was born on 1 March 1997, HI.

>>>> **3.4.1.2.2.1.1.2 DREW MICHAEL FENTER** was born on 2 November 2000.

>>> **3.4.1.2.2.1.2 CHERYL LYNN GOLDSMITH** was born on 5 August 1973. She married **STASINOS STAVRIANEAS** on 18 December 1977.

>>>> **3.4.1.2.2.1.2.1 AMALEAH OLEGA STAVRIANEAS** is also referred to as **LEAH** in some sources. She was born on 9 October 2000, Salem, Marion County, OR.

> **3.4.1.2.3 EUNICE WIEST THOMPSON** was born on 11 March 1913, Astoria, Clatsop County, OR. She married **DAVID FILER HEAD** on 17 October 1931, Kelso, Cowlitz County, WA. She died on 13 October 1976, The Dalles, Wasco County, OR, at age 63.

>> **3.4.1.2.3.1 THOMAS WILKIE HEAD** was born on 28 January 1936, Skamokawa, Wahkiakum County, WA. He married **GWENDOLYN SUE STANDIFER** on 12 December 1955, Vancouver, Clark County, WA. He married **MARY LOU JOHNSTON** circa 1969, AZ.

>>> **3.4.1.2.3.1.1 MICHAEL SCOTT HEAD** was born on 12 July 1956, The Dalles, Wasco County, OR. He married **JAN MUSGROVE** on 4 June 1983, Eugene, Lane County, OR.

>>>> **3.4.1.2.3.1.1.1 MOLLY ELFERS** was born on 13 November 1986.

>>>> **3.4.1.2.3.1.1.2 PETER ELFERS** was born on 13 February 1990.

>>> **3.4.1.2.3.1.2 TAMMI SUE HEAD** was born on 24 June 1957, The Dalles, Wasco County, OR. She married **JOSEPH TICER** Beaverton, Washington County, OR.

>>>> **3.4.1.2.3.1.2.1 MEGAN TICER** was born on 6 June 1985.

3.4.1.2.3.1.2.2 CASAUNDRA JOLENE TICER was born on 29 March 1987.

3.4.1.2.3.1.3 LISA LYNN HEAD was born on 27 March 1961, Hillsboro, Washington County, OR. She married THOMAS SCOTT EWING on 29 April 1995, Beaverton, Washington County, OR.

3.4.1.2.3.1.3.1 THOMAS MCKINLEY EWING was born on 23 December 1998, Port Trevorton, Snyder County, PA.

3.4.1.2.3.1.3.2 BLAIR ROBERT EWING was born on 15 December 2000, Port Trevorton, Snyder County, PA.

3.4.1.2.3.1.4 THOMAS WILLIAM HEAD was born on 4 April 1970, Phoenix, Maricopa County, AZ.

3.4.1.2.3.2 DANIEL ROBERT HEAD was born on 5 November 1938, Longview, Cowlitz County, WA. He married MERIDITH SUE WALLACE in December 1958, Goldendale, Skamania County, WA. He died on 23 February 2001, Spokane, Spokane County, WA, at age 62.

3.4.1.2.3.2.1 DAVID DANIEL HEAD was born on 2 June 1960, The Dalles, Wasco County, OR. He married TAMMY LAUDERBACH.

3.4.1.2.3.2.1.1 KAITLAN MARIE HEAD was born on 9 October 1996, Carthage, Jefferson County, NY.

3.4.1.2.3.2.1.2 CARSON ELIZABETH HEAD was born on 7 January 2000, Carthage, Jefferson County, NY.

3.4.1.2.3.2.2 TIMOTHY PATRICK HEAD was born on 26 September 1961, The Dalles, Wasco County, OR. He married TAMMY ALLEX.

3.4.1.2.3.2.2.1 TREVOR NELSON HEAD was born on 5 July 1989, Spokane, Spokane County, WA.

3.4.1.2.3.2.2.2 TORI LYNN HEAD was born on 9 September 1990, Spokane, Spokane County, WA.

3.4.1.2.3.3 SHARON JUNE HEAD was born on 9 June 1942, Cathlamet, Wahkiakum County, WA. She married RONALD MERTON STEIN on 10 November 1963, The Dalles, Wasco County, OR. She married WILLIAM COOK circa 1970, WA. She married JAMES (--?--) after 1973, The Dalles, Wasco County, OR.

3.4.1.2.3.3.1 JAY MERTON STEIN was born on 10 October 1964, Orange County, CA.

3.4.1.2.3.3.1.1 CHRISTOPHER STEIN

3.4.1.2.3.3.1.2 PATTON STEIN

3.4.1.2.3.3.1.3 NICHOLAS STEIN

3.4.1.2.3.3.2 JENNIE LEE STEIN was born on 5 May 1968, Pensacola, Escambia County, FL.

3.4.1.2.3.3.2.1 ASHLEY (--?--)

3.4.1.2.3.3.3 RANDY COOK was born on 27 June 1972, Moses Lake, Grant County, WA. He died in August 2000, ID at age 28.

3.4.1.2.4 JUNE ORA THOMPSON was born on 28 June 1919, Skamokawa, Wahkiakum County, WA. She married RAYMOND HENRY EGSTAD on 26 August 1944, Bremerton, Kitsap County, WA. She died on 5 May 1998, Woodland, Cowlitz County, WA, at age 78.

3.4.1.2.4.1 RUTH ANN EGSTAD was born on 19 June 1947, Longview, Cowlitz County, WA. She married DONALD WENDT on 26 June 1976, Woodland, Cowlitz County, WA.

3.4.1.2.5 MARY BELLE THOMPSON was born on 14 July 1927, Skamokawa, Wahkiakum County, WA. She married THOMAS GARDNER STAPLETON on 1 August 1959, The Dalles, Wasco County, OR.

3.4.1.2.5.1 BETH ANN STAPLETON was born on 29 May 1960, Grants Pass, Josephine County, OR. She married GREGORY GEORGE LAVEY on 20 June 1987, Beaverton, Washington County, OR.

3.4.1.2.5.1.1 CAITLIN ELIZABETH LAVEY was born on 13 March 1994.

3.4.1.2.5.1.2 ROBERT THOMAS LAVEY was born on 2 December 1996.

3.4.1.2.5.2 JOHN THOMAS STAPLETON was born on 5 June 1962, Oregon City, Clackamas County, OR. He married **KRISTEN KINCADE** on 19 December 1998.

3.4.1.2.5.3 DANIEL BENTON STAPLETON was born on 26 June 1963, Oregon City, Clackamas County, OR. He married **PAMALA ANN FRANKLIN** on 31 August 2002, Oaks Pioneer Church, Portland, Multnomah County, OR.

3.4.1.3 MAYBELLE AGNES WIEST is also referred to as **DORA BELLA** in some sources. She was born on 22 January 1905, Skamokawa, Wahkiakum County, WA. She married **ROBERT G. SMYTH** on 28 June 1921, Skamokawa, Wahkiakum County, WA. She died on 24 August 1979, at age 74. She was buried at Fern Hill Cemetery, Skamokawa, Skamokawa County, WA.

3.4.1.3.1 PATRICIA SMYTH was born on 3 February 1925, Skamokawa, Wahkiakum County, WA. She married **REGINALD NETTLES** circa 1943. She married **RAY IWAMOTO** after 1945.

3.4.1.3.1.1 CRAIG NETTLES was born in July 1944.

3.4.1.3.1.2 RAYMOND IWAMOTO

3.4.1.3.1.3 ROBERT IWAMOTO

3.4.2 MARIA WIEST was born on 22 April 1845. Some sources record that she was born in 1843. She died on 3 February 1851, at age 5. According to some sources she was buried at Zion (Klinger's) Church, Erdman, Lykens Township, Dauphin County, PA, but the Klinger's Church History cemetery listing does not include her.

3.4.3 SAMUEL BEISEL WIEST was born on 13 December 1845, Hebe, Jordan Township, Northumberland County, PA. He married **HARRIET BROWN**. According to a newspaper obituary, Samuel was the founder of the town of Stella, Washington and one of the first loggers of the Pacific northwest. He enlisted in the Union Army at the age of 17 and fought in many important Civil War battles, serving in the 50th Pennsylvania Volunteer Infantry. He suffered severe wounds at the Battle of the Wilderness and at Spotsylvania Courthouse. After the end of the Civil War, he traveled to the Pacific coast, sailing from San Francisco for Portland on the first trip of the "City of Chester" and reaching Astoria, Oregon, six days later. With his two brothers, Jacob and William, he started the first logging operations of any consequence in the northwest. He retired after an accident in which he lost one of his legs, and after that made his home in Portland. Samuel died at his home, 1090 Hawthorne Avenue, in Portland. He died on 15 October 1922, Portland, Multnomah County, OR, at age 76. He was buried at Rose City Cemetery, Portland, Multnomah County, OR.

3.4.3.1 MARY JANE WIEST married **CHARLES SCOTT PIPER** on 17 February 1918, Vancouver, WA.

3.4.3.2 FAIRY WIEST was born circa 1882. She died in 1914.

3.4.4 WILLIAM BEISEL WIEST was born on 18 May 1848, Jordan Township, Northumberland County, PA. Some sources record that he was born on 18 October 1855. He married **ELMIRA PAUL**. He died on 20 January 1929, Portland, Multnomah County, OR, at age 80. According to a newspaper obituary, William journeyed to San Francisco in 1878 with his four brothers and in the same year started logging operations at Oak Point, Washington, on the Columbia River. He later moved to Stella, Washington, where he continued in the logging business. He ceased active participation in logging when he joined the East Side Mill & Lumber Company of Portland, Oregon. William died at his home at 403 East Forty-first Street North, Portland, following a short illness caused by pneumonia. He was the last of five brothers who came to the Pacific northwest in 1878.

3.4.4.1 FRANCIS WIEST was born on 19 May 1874. He married **MAUDE HILL**. He died on 2 February 1922, Portland, Multnomah County, OR, at age 47.

3.4.4.1.1 JOHN FRANCIS WIEST

3.4.4.1.2 DAUGHTER WIEST

3.4.4.1.3 JOHN WIEST

3.4.4.1.4 CLYDE WIEST was born on 31 January 1901, Portland, Multnomah County, OR. He died on 12 October 1963, Portland, Multnomah County, OR, at age 62.

3.4.4.1.5 CLIFFORD WIEST was born on 23 May 1903, Portland, Multnomah County, OR. He died on 9 February 1922, with his father in a logging accident, Portland, Multnomah County, OR, at age 18.

3.4.4.1.6 VERNON FRANCIS WIEST was born on 15 April 1909, Portland, Multnomah County, OR. He married **FRANCES A. (--?--)**. He died on 7 February 1935, Portland, Multnomah County, OR, at age 25.

3.4.4.2 JOHN A. WIEST also went by the name of **DIAMOND JACK**. He was born in January 1876. He married **MARTHA (--?--)** before 1914. He married **HELEN LEWIS** circa 1915. He died on 20 September 1963, at age 87. He was buried at Greenwood Hills Cemetery, Portland, Multnomah County, OR.

    3.4.4.2.1 VIVIAN WIEST was born in 1916, Canada. She married **JACK J. HUNTLEY**.

        3.4.4.2.1.1 HELEN HUNTLEY

        3.4.4.2.1.2 LOUELLA HUNTLEY

3.4.4.3 SEVILLA WIEST was born on 29 November 1878. She married **JOHN BAUM WIEST**, son of **TOBIAS BAUM WIEST** and **MARY ANN BAUM**. She died on 16 December 1945, at age 67. She was buried at Greenwood Hills Cemetery, Portland, Multnomah County, OR.

3.4.4.4 CYRUS WIEST was born on 22 January 1883, Stella, Cowlitz County, WA. He married **NETTIE SHERMAN**. He died on 24 December 1964, at age 81.

3.4.5 DANIEL WIEST was born on 18 May 1848, Jordan Township, Northumberland County, PA. He married **(--?--) KLINGER**. He married **MARY BAUM WIEST**, daughter of **SAMUEL MERKEL WIEST** and **ESTHER BAUM**. He died circa 1927, near Loyalton, Big Run, PA. According to Mary Klinger, Daniel went to Oregon and worked in the logging business, but he later returned to Pennsylvania and operated a hotel in Big Run, near Loyalton.

    3.4.5.1 WILLIAM MORRIS WIEST was born on 1 July 1870, Klingerstown, Schuylkill County, PA. He died on 26 February 1904, Klingerstown, Schuylkill County, PA, at age 33.

3.4.6 ELIZABETH WIEST was born on 3 August 1849, Jordan Township, Northumberland County, PA. She married **JACOB WEIST STROHECKER**, son of **WILLIAM STROHECKER** and **SARAH WIEST,** on 7 January 1870. She died on 13 December 1924, Hebe, Jordan Township, Northumberland County, PA, at age 75. She was buried at St. David's Lutheran and Reformed Church, Hebe, Jordan Township, Northumberland County, PA.

    3.4.6.1 MARY STROHECKER married **HARRY BOYER**.

    3.4.6.2 JOHN WEIST STROHECKER was born circa 17 June 1870. He died on 22 May 1915. He was buried at St. David's Lutheran and Reformed Church, Hebe, Jordan Township, Northumberland County, PA.

        3.4.6.2.1 GRACE STROHECKER

        3.4.6.2.2 SULA STROHECKER married **RAY WIEST**.

    3.4.6.3 CASSIE STROHECKER is also referred to as **CATIE** in some sources. She was born circa 1872. She married **FRANK HOFFMAN**.

        3.4.6.3.1 JACOB HOFFMAN

        3.4.6.3.2 WESLEY HOFFMAN

        3.4.6.3.3 (--?--) HOFFMAN married **PAUL LEITZEL**.

3.4.7 JOHN BEISEL WIEST was born on 13 December 1850, Jordan Township, PA. He married **SARAH N. HERRING**. John originally farmed the land located at the extreme southeast corner of Jordan , Township, Northumberland County, adjoining Schuylkill County on the Mahantongo Creek. In 1878 he moved to Oregon and joined the logging business with his brothers. He died on 10 April 1897, drowned in Columbia River, Portland, Multnomah County, OR, at age 46.

    3.4.7.1 SARAH ALICE WIEST married **JACK GILLETTE**.

    3.4.7.2 AUGUSTUS MONROVIA WIEST married **VELMA CAMAISH** in 1924. He died Oregon. He married **MARGARET MCKENZIE**. Augustus lived in Portland, Oregon, where he was a timber operator for the Wiest and Thomas Logging Co.

    3.4.7.3 CLARA CATHERINE WIEST was born Stella, Cowlitz County, WA. She died Portland, Multnomah County, OR.

    3.4.7.4 IDA WIEST was born on 12 February 1873. She married **WILLIAM H. WILLIAMSON** on 26 October 1888. She died in May 1943, at age 70.

        3.4.7.4.1 LESTER SHERLOCK WILLIAMSON married **ANNA (--?--)**.

        3.4.7.4.2 GEORGE OLIVER WILLIAMSON died in logging accident at age 17.

        3.4.7.4.3 LOU ELSIE GERALDINE WILLIAMSON married **J.D. PARTRICK**.

        3.4.7.4.4 WILLIAM WILLIAMSON JR. married **ROSINA ESTHER HIRTE** on 14 June 1941, Vancouver, Clark County, WA. He died on 31 May 1968.

3.4.7.4.4.1 HEDWIG WILLIAMSON was born on 26 July 1943. She married **LARRY WALDRIN** on 12 April 1965.

3.4.7.4.4.2 ERIK PAUL WILLIAMSON was born on 17 March 1945, Longview, Cowlitz County, WA.

3.4.7.4.4.3 HARVEY WILLIAMSON was born on 2 August 1950, Longview, Cowlitz County, WA.

3.4.7.4.4.4 OLIVER WILLIAMSON was born on 22 July 1954, Longview, Cowlitz County, WA. He died on 29 January 1972, at age 17.

3.4.7.4.5 ESTES J. WILLIAMSON married **ETHEL OYSTER**.

3.4.7.4.5.1 VIRGINIA WILLIAMSON

3.4.7.4.6 J. RAYMOND WILLIAMSON married **BELLE BROCK**.

3.4.7.4.6.1 NANCY WILLIAMSON was born in 1927.

3.4.7.5 SAMUEL MAURICE WIEST was born on 12 February 1874. He married **MARTHA BRAZEL**. He died on 1 May 1920, in an auto accident near Portland, Multnomah County, OR, at age 46.

3.4.7.6 GEORGE ORIN WIEST was born in October 1879, Stella, Cowlitz County, WA. He married **ELIZABETH WIEST**. He died California.

3.4.7.7 DORA BELLE WIEST was born in February 1888. She married **(--?--) BUTLER**. She died in 1917, Arkansas. Dora (Wiest) Butler died leaving two young daughters: Delores, who was raised by her uncle and aunt, Jack and Alice Gillette, in Longview, OR, and Maxine who was raised by another uncle and aunt, Bill and Ida Williamson, in Stella, WA.

3.4.7.7.1 DELORES BUTLER was born in 1909.

3.4.7.7.2 MAXINE EDNA BUTLER was born in December 1914, AR. She married **(--?--) MCCLAREN**.

3.4.7.7.2.1 RICHARD MCCLAREN

3.4.8 CATHARINE WIEST was born on 13 April 1852. She married **ABRAHAM MAURER**, son of **MANASSAS MAURER** and **ELIZABETH KOHLMAN**. She died in September 1919, at age 67.

3.4.8.1 JOSEPH MAURER married **MABEL MILLER**.

3.4.8.1.1 HAL MAURER was adopted.

3.4.8.2 MORRIS MAURER was born in November 1872, Klingerstown, Schuylkill County, PA. He married **MINNIE PALMER** in WA. He died in Washington or Oregon.

3.4.8.2.1 EMMA MAURER is also referred to as **EMMA MOWERY** in some sources. She was born in September 1897.

3.4.8.2.2 ERNEST MAURER is also referred to as **ERNEST MOWERY** in some sources. He was born in August 1898.

3.4.8.3 IDA CELARA MAURER was born on 18 February 1875, Klingerstown, Schuylkill County, PA. She was baptized on 24 March 1875, Zion (Klinger's) Church, Erdman, Lykens Township, Dauphin County, PA. She married **ALVIN JOSEPH ADAM POFFENBERGER**, son of **ADAM R. PAFFENBERGER** and **ELLA AMANDA WIEST**, on 28 December 1892, Kalama, Cowlitz County, WA. She died on 27 November 1941, Chinook, Pacific County, WA, at age 66.

3.4.8.3.1 HATTIE POFFENBERGER was born Portland, Multnomah County, OR. She married **JOHN SCHULER**. She was born Portland, Multnomah County, OR. She is also referred to as **HATTIE POFFENBERGER** in some sources.

3.4.8.3.2 ROY ALVIN POFFENBERGER was born in 1893, Stella, Cowlitz County, WA. He married **ANNA (--?--)**.

3.4.8.3.3 FLORA JENNIE MAY POFFENBERGER was born in 1895, Stella, Cowlitz County, WA. She married **FREDERICK J. HISSEY**, son of **FREDERICK T. HISSEY**, circa 1917, Portland, Multnomah County, OR. She died on 14 December 1918, Portland, Multnomah County, OR. Flora and her baby daughter died in the influenza epidemic of 1918. Her husband, a sergeant in the US Army, was stationed in France at the time and was unable to return home for the funeral.

3.4.8.3.3.1 INFANT DAUGHTER HISSEY was born in 1918, Portland, Multnomah County, OR. She died in 1918, Portland, Multnomah County, OR.

3.4.8.3.4 ROBY EARL POFFENBERGER was born on 26 November 1896, Stella, Cowlitz County, WA. He married **HAZEL MARGRETA CARLSON** on 17 September 1921. He died on 30 August 1971, Portland, Multnomah County, OR, at age 74.

3.4.8.3.4.1 JUNE MADELINE POFFENBERGER was born on 8 December 1925, Portland, Multnomah County, OR. She married **GUNNER NILSSON** on 2 July 1950.

3.4.8.3.4.1.1 LISA BRITT NILSSON was born in 1957, Oregon.

3.4.8.4 HARRY MAURER was born in July 1878. He married **DORIS MARY PETERS**. He and **DORIS MARY PETERS** were divorced. He married **LILY (--?--)**. He died WA.

3.4.8.4.1 FREDERICK MAURER is also referred to as **FREDERICK MOWERY** in some sources.

3.4.8.4.2 ARCHIE MAURER is also referred to as **ARCHIE MOWERY** in some sources.

3.4.9 AMELIA WIEST was born on 18 November 1854. She married **GABRIEL PAUL** Centralia, WA. She died on 19 April 1919, Kelso, Cowlitz County, WA, at age 64.

3.4.9.1 TIMOTHY POWELL

3.4.9.2 SEVILLA POWELL married **TEED GRAY**.

3.4.9.2.1 PAUL GRAY was born in Washington. He married **(--?--) SAWYER**. Paul lived in Hawaii.

3.4.9.2.2 JEAN GRAY was born in Washington. She married **NORMAN PARKS** Kelso, Cowlitz County, WA. Jean lived and worked in Longview, WA.

3.4.9.3 FRANCES POWELL married **(--?--) JOHNS**.

3.4.9.3.1 VIVIAN JOHNS

3.4.9.3.2 BESS JOHNS

3.4.9.4 FRANCIS POWELL was born on 3 June 1871.

3.4.10 ISABELLA WIEST was born on 5 August 1857. She married **LAER JEAN WIEST**, son of **JACOB MERKEL WIEST** and **SUSANNAH SCHMELTZ**. She died on 19 September 1938, Stella, Cowlitz County, WA, at age 81.

3.4.10.1 SAMUEL WIEST was born on 2 August 1875. He died on 8 May 1883, Stella, Cowlitz County, WA, at age 7.

3.4.10.2 AUGUSTUS WIEST was born on 2 April 1877, Stella, Cowlitz County, WA. He died on 6 May 1883, Stella, Cowlitz County, WA, at age 6.

3.4.10.3 CHARLES WIEST was born on 10 July 1882, Stella, Cowlitz County, WA. He married **NELLIE SHERMAN**. He died on 1 January 1943, Stella, Cowlitz County, WA, at age 60.

3.4.10.3.1 RAYMOND WIEST married **DONNA WALTZ**.

3.4.10.4 WALTER WIEST was born on 27 November 1884, Stella, Cowlitz County, WA. He died on 12 January 1886, Stella, Cowlitz County, WA, at age 1.

3.4.11 SEVILLA WIEST is also referred to as **FAYETTE OR FEYETTA WIEST** in some sources. She was born on 4 January 1859. She died on 30 October 1862, at age 3. She was buried at Zion (Klinger's) Church, Erdman, Lykens Township, Dauphin County, PA.

3.5 HANNAH WIEST was born on 10 December 1823. She married **ISAAC MONROE ROTHERMEL**, son of **ABRAHAM M. ROTHERMEL** and **CATHARINE YEAGER**, circa 1 January 1842. She died on 7 September 1887, Klingerstown, Schuylkill County, PA, at age 63. She was buried at Zion (Klinger's) Church Cemetery, Erdman, Lykens Township, Dauphin County, PA.

3.5.1 ANDREW ROTHERMEL married **SARAH ZARTMAN**. He died after 1923.

3.5.1.1 GEORGE LINTON ROTHERMEL was born on 15 August 1863.

3.5.1.2 LILLIE IDA ROTHERMEL was born on 10 April 1865. She married **CHARLES C. BINGAMAN** on 9 December 1883.

3.5.1.2.1 CLARENCE H. BINGAMAN was born in 1884. He died in 1888. He was buried at Trinity Evangelical Reformed Cemetery, Dalmatia, Northumberland County, PA.

3.5.1.2.2 CLINTON CLEAVER BINGAMAN was born circa 1885. He married **EFFIE FEGLEY**.

3.5.1.3 ANNIE B. ROTHERMEL was born on 12 January 1868. She married **FRANK ZERBE**. She died on 10 September 1952, at age 84.

3.5.1.4 CHARLES ELLSWORTH ROTHERMEL was born on 22 April 1869. He married **SARAH ELIZABETH FENSTERMACHER** on 3 February 1889.

3.5.1.4.1 ARLIE MAY ROTHERMEL was born on 23 August 1889.

3.5.2 WILLIAM WILSON ROTHERMEL was born on 2 May 1842. He was baptized on 1 August 1842, Zion (Klinger's) Lutheran and Reformed Church, Erdman, Dauphin County, PA. He married **SARA A. SHAFFER**, daughter of **DANIEL W. SHAFFER** and **ANNA MARIA BOHNER,** on 30 December 1865. According to Bruce Hall, William lived on his parents' farm until, at the age of 19, he enlisted in the Union Army during the Civil War as a member of Company P, 50th Regiment, Pennsylvania Volunteer Infantry. When his initial 3-year term of enlistment expired, he reenlisted for another three years at Blain's Cross Road in eastern Tennessee. He attained the rank of sergeant and Right General Guide. In addition to traveling all over the South, he also saw service in Ohio, Indiana, and Illinois, seeing action in 32 engagements as a member of Sherman's army, including: Bull Run, Fredericksburg, Antietam, South Mountain, Vicksburg, and Jackson. He also participated in the siege of Knoxville and operations at Petersburg. Shortly after he returned to Northumberland County, PA, at the close of the war, he began farming in Hubley , Township, Schuylkill Co., PA, where he was a tenant for nine years. In 1877, he acquired a tract of 22 acres in Jordan Township, Northumberland County, PA, which he cultivated until the time of his retirement. In addition to farming, he was a carpenter. He died on 18 May 1922, at age 80. According to some sources he was buried at St. Michael's Evangelical Lutheran Church, Klingerstown, Schuylkill County, PA. He was buried at St. David's Lutheran and Reformed Church Cemetery, Hebe, Jordan Township, Northumberland County, PA.

3.5.2.1 EMMA ROTHERMEL was born in 1867. She married **JOHN SALTZER.**

3.5.2.2 MANASSES S. ROTHERMEL was born in 1870. He married **KATE A. KISSINGER**, daughter of **DANIEL KISSINGER** and **MARY KLINGER,** circa 1892. He died in 1947. He was buried at St. Michael's Church Cemetery, Klingerstown, Schuylkill County, PA. He died on 4 January 1929,, but this appears to be incorrect.

3.5.2.2.1 BLANCHE MARIE ROTHERMOL was baptized, Zion (Klinger's) Church, Erdman, Lykens Township, Dauphin County, PA. She was born on 22 April 1909. She was baptized on 5 September 1909, St. Michael's Lutheran and Reformed Church, Klingerstown, Schuylkill County, PA. She married **HARRY NATHAN FETTER** circa 1931.

3.5.2.2.1.1 LAMAR CURTIS FETTER was born on 2 June 1927. He was baptized on 12 June 1927, St. Michael's Lutheran and Reformed Church, Klingerstown, Schuylkill County, PA.

3.5.2.2.1.2 JOAN BLANCHE FETTER is also referred to as **JEAN BLANCHE FETTER** in some sources. She was born on 26 August 1928. She was baptized on 16 September 1928, St. Michael's Lutheran and Reformed Church, Klingerstown, Schuylkill County, PA.

3.5.2.2.1.3 EVELYN ELAINE FETTER was born on 28 May 1933. She was baptized on 1 July 1934, St. Michael's Lutheran and Reformed Church, Klingerstown, Schuylkill County, PA.

3.5.2.2.1.4 CAROL ANN FETTER was born on 6 June 1937. She was baptized on 17 April 1938, St. Michael's Lutheran and Reformed Church, Klingerstown, Schuylkill County, PA.

3.5.2.2.2 AUSTIN D. ROTHERMEL was born on 2 October 1894. He married **FRONIE E. WOLFGANG.** He died on 31 July 1969, at age 74. He was buried at St. Michael's Church Cemetery, Klingerstown, Schuylkill County, PA.

3.5.2.2.3 FLORENCE MAY ROTHERMEL was born on 19 March 1904. She was baptized on 17 April 1904, St. Michael's Lutheran and Reformed Church, Klingerstown, Schuylkill County, PA. She married **IRA HOFFMAN** circa 1920. She died on 11 May 1997, Community General Osteopathic Hospital, Harrisburg, Dauphin County, PA, at age 93.

3.5.2.2.3.1 DOTTIE KATIE HOFFMAN was born on 13 June 1921. She was baptized on 3 July 1921, St. Michael's Lutheran and Reformed Church, Klingerstown, Schuylkill County, PA. She married **ALBANUS COLEMAN.**

3.5.2.2.3.2 BETTY FLORENCE HOFFMAN was born circa 1923. She married **PAUL RAYMOND REED**, son of **WILLIAM GARFIELD REED** and **STELLA CATHERINE SCHMELTZ,** on 25 May 1938.

3.5.2.2.3.2.1 DRUCILLA MARJORIE REED

3.5.2.2.3.3 CLEO B. HOFFMAN was born in 1926. She died in 1926.

3.5.2.2.3.4 BOBBY HOFFMAN was born circa February 1928.

3.5.2.2.3.5 RHODA MARILYN HOFFMAN was born after 1929. She married **WILLIAM LAMAR ERDMAN,** son of **HARRY LEE ERDMAN** and **EDNA MAMIE WILLIARD,** circa 1950.

3.5.2.2.3.5.1 DAVID LYNN ERDMAN

3.5.2.2.3.5.2 RICKY A. ERDMAN

3.5.2.2.3.6 JACOB LEROY HOFFMAN was born on 10 June 1930. He was baptized on 6 July 1930, St. Michael's Lutheran and Reformed Church, Klingerstown, Schuylkill County, PA. He married **VIOLET ARLENE ERDMAN** circa 1949.

3.5.2.2.3.7 RODNEY I. HOFFMAN was born in 1941. He died in December 1941.

3.5.2.3 POLLY ROTHERMEL was born in 1874. She married **CHARLES BROWN.**

3.5.2.4 MONROE ROTHERMEL was born circa 1880.

3.5.2.5 JENNIE SARAH ROTHERMAL was born on 14 November 1888, RD, Klingerstown, Schuylkill County, PA. She married **GORDON EDWIN KLINGER,** son of **FRANCIS KLINGER** and **HARRIET TROUTMAN,** on 9 September 1905, Simeon Lutheran Church, Gratz, Dauphin County, PA. She died on 14 March 1978, Lykens Township, Dauphin County, PA, at age 89.

3.5.2.5.1 ADA MAY KLINGER was born on 24 August 1906, Schuylkill County, PA. She married **ALLEN HENRY WOLFE,** son of **JACOB MILTON WOLFE** and **MARY LIZA HARNER,** on 26 February 1925, Valley View, Schuylkill County, PA. She died on 19 October 2003, Lykens, Dauphin County, PA, at age 97. She was buried on 23 October 2003, at Simeon United Lutheran Church Cemetery, Gratz, Dauphin County, PA.

3.5.2.5.1.1 ROBERT ALLEN WOLFE was born on 1 August 1925, Lykens Township, Dauphin County, PA. He married **BETTY J. EBERT** on 7 October 1944, Valley View, Schuylkill County, PA.

3.5.2.5.1.1.1 BRUCE ALLEN WOLFE was born on 28 March 1945, Dauphin County, PA. He married **EVA MACKIEWICZ** on 12 September 1981.

3.5.2.5.1.1.1.1 WOJTEK MACKIEWICZ WOLFE was born on 21 April 1973.

3.5.2.5.1.1.2 LARRY ERROL WOLFE was born on 19 March 1946, Dauphin County, PA. He died on 7 January 1973, at age 26. He married **SHIRLEY WERTZ** on 7 January 1973.

3.5.2.5.1.1.2.1 SIMON LARRY WOLFE was born on 7 July 1971, Dauphin County, PA.

3.5.2.5.1.1.2.1.1 CHASE EVERY WOLFE was born on 24 December 2005.

3.5.2.5.1.1.3 SANDRA LEE WOLFE was born on 7 November 1947, Dauphin County, PA.

3.5.2.5.1.1.4 ROBERT ALBERT WOLFE was born on 2 February 1949, Dauphin County, PA. He married **SUSANNE LOUISE ROWE,** daughter of **RAYMOND HENRY ROWE** and **CELIA IRENE BINGAMAN,** on 22 August 1969.

3.5.2.5.1.1.5 JUNE WOLFE was born on 23 June 1950, Lykens Township, Dauphin County, PA. She married **FREDERICK WARREN WILLARD,** son of **WARREN W. WILLARD** and **MARIE A. WALBORN,** on 4 April 1970.

3.5.2.5.1.1.5.1 DANIEL R. WILLARD was born on 15 September 1970, Dauphin County, PA.

3.5.2.5.1.1.5.2 JENNIFER WILLARD was born on 22 December 1976, Dauphin County, PA. She married **(--?--) MILLER.**

3.5.2.5.1.1.5.2.1 PAIGE ELIZABETH MILLER was born on 25 November 2005.

3.5.2.5.1.2 VIOLET ISMAY WOLFE was born on 23 May 1930. She married **THOMAS H. SNYDER,** son of **CLAYTON SNYDER** and **TAMIE CAROLINE SHADE,** on 24 May 1947, Evangelical United Brethren Church, Valley View, Schuylkill County, PA.

3.5.2.5.1.3 BILLY ELIAS WOLFE was born on 26 February 1932, Lykens Township, Dauphin County, PA. He married **ELEANOR M. BLYLER,** daughter of **ELMER BLYLER** and **ALBERTA OCHS,** on 13 July 1960, Valley View, Schuylkill County, PA. He died on 14 August 1995, Danville, Montour County, PA, at age 63.

3.5.2.5.1.3.1 BRENDA LEE WOLFE was born on 3 August 1962, Valley View, Schuylkill County, PA.

3.5.2.5.1.3.2 GLEN ALAN WOLFE was born on 17 March 1965, Valley View, Schuylkill County, PA.

3.5.2.5.1.3.3 MARK ELMER WOLFE was born on 24 March 1971, Valley View, Schuylkill County, PA.

3.5.2.5.1.4 TWILA NAOMI WOLFE was born on 22 September 1933, RD, Lykens, Dauphin County, PA. She married EUGENE GEISTWITE, son of LOUELLA GEISTWITE, on 24 February 1951, Valley View, Schuylkill County, PA.

3.5.2.5.1.4.1 LINDA LOU GEISTWITE was buried at Gratz Cemetery. She was born on 24 September 1951. She died on 26 September 1951.

3.5.2.5.1.4.2 RANDOLPH ALAN GEISTWITE was born on 10 August 1955, Gratz, Dauphin County, PA.

3.5.2.5.1.4.3 DAVID GORDON GEISTWITE was born on 9 May 1966, Gratz, Dauphin County, PA.

3.5.2.5.1.4.4 HEIDI MAY GEISTWITE was born on 21 December 1970, Gratz, Dauphin County, PA.

3.5.2.5.1.5 MILLIE MARIE WOLFE married PAUL LEFFLER, son of LINCOLN LEFFLER and ELLEN BOHNER. She was born on 15 September 1940, Lykens Township, Dauphin County, PA.

3.5.2.5.1.5.1 LORI ANN LEFFLER was born on 29 August 1958, Gratz, Dauphin County, PA.

3.5.2.5.1.5.2 BRIAN PAUL LEFFLER was born on 25 March 1969, Gratz, Dauphin County, PA.

3.5.2.5.1.6 CAROL ELAINE WOLFE was born on 18 July 1942, RD, Lykens, Dauphin County, PA. She married DENNIS NEY, son of CLAIR NEY and RUTH STRAUB, on 21 May 1960, Fearnot EUB Church, Fearnot, Schuylkill County, PA.

3.5.2.5.1.6.1 ANDREW ALLEN NEY was born on 23 September 1970, RD, Lykens, Dauphin County, PA.

3.5.2.5.2 ELMA MARIE KLINGER was born on 10 October 1908, Lykens Township, Dauphin County, PA. She died on 20 November 1913, Lykens Township, Dauphin County, PA, at age 5. She was buried at Simeon Union Cemetery, Gratz, Dauphin County, PA.

3.5.2.5.3 NAOMI IRENE KLINGER was born on 3 May 1922, Lykens Township, Dauphin County, PA. She was baptized on 2 July 1922, Simeon Lutheran Church, Gratz, Dauphin County, PA. She married WILLIAM D. STRAUB.

3.5.2.5.3.1 TERRY GORDON STRAUB was born on 18 August 1946. He died on 22 May 1967, in an ambush while serving with the US Army in Vietnam at age 20. He was buried at Simeon United Lutheran Church Cemetery, Gratz, Dauphin County, PA.

3.5.2.5.3.2 WENDY M. STRAUB was born on 7 May 1951, Lykens Township, Dauphin County, PA. She married CLARENCE J. SHOOP, son of WILLIAM J. SHOOP and MARY TRAVITZ, on 2 March 1968, Gratz, Dauphin County, PA. She and CLARENCE J. SHOOP were divorced in January 1974. She married JAMES MARVIN GEIST, son of MARVIN E. GEIST and BETTY DUNKELBERGER, circa 1999.

3.5.2.5.3.2.1 C. JAMES SHOOP was born on 19 August 1968.

3.5.2.5.3.2.2 KIMBERLEE ANN SHOOP was born on 1 September 1969. She married (--?--) DREISBACH.

3.5.2.5.3.2.3 PATRICK TODD SHOOP was born on 9 November 1971, Harrisburg, Dauphin County, PA. He married BONNIE (--?--).

3.5.2.6 MINNIE ROTHERMEL was born in June 1892. She married HARVEY SMITH.

3.5.3 JESTINA ROTHERMEL was born on 25 January 1847, Northumberland County, PA. She married JOHN WEISER, son of JOHN JACOB WEISER and ELIZABETH DEIBLER, on 29 November 1868, Jordan Township, Northumberland County, PA. She died on 16 June 1925, Pillow, Dauphin County, PA, at age 78. She was buried at Grandview Cemetery, Pillow, Dauphin County, PA.

3.5.3.1 (--?--) WEISER was born on 17 January 1868. Some sources record that he was born on 23 January 1868. He died on 26 January 1868. He was buried at Zion (Klinger's) Church, Erdman, Lykens Township, Dauphin County, PA.

3.5.3.2 MARY E. WEISER was born on 13 January 1872, Pillow, Dauphin County, PA. She died on 18 December 1946, Pillow, Dauphin County, PA, at age 74. She was buried at Pillow, Dauphin County, PA. She was unmarried.

3.5.3.3 WILLIAM ISAAC WEISER was born on 6 December 1875, Pillow, Dauphin County, PA. He died on 26 October 1881, Pillow, Dauphin County, PA, at age 5. He was buried at Grandview Cemetery, Pillow, Dauphin County, PA.

3.5.3.4 JACOB MONROE WEISER was born on 22 May 1877, Pillow, Dauphin County, PA. He married **ALICE CORA HOKE** on 4 April 1901. Jacob was a storekeeper in Harrisburg, Pillow, and Berrysburg. He died on 1 September 1951, Harrisburg, Dauphin County, PA, at age 74. He was buried at Harrisburg, Dauphin County, PA.

3.5.3.4.1 MARTHA WEISER was born on 8 March 1902, Pillow, Dauphin County, PA. She married **WILLIAM HAROLD WASSON** on 10 December 1923. She and **WILLIAM HAROLD WASSON** were divorced in 1925. She married **CLETUS BOMGARDNER** on 22 December 1934. She and **CLETUS BOMGARDNER** were divorced in 1944. She married **NEWTON REESE** on 14 May 1954. She died on 11 June 1990, Harrisburg, Dauphin County, PA, at age 88. She was buried at Harrisburg, Dauphin County, PA.

3.5.3.4.1.1 WILLIAM HAROLD WASSON JR. was born on 29 October 1924, Harrisburg, Dauphin County, PA. He married **JEAN KLOCK** on 22 June 1946, Harrisburg, Dauphin County, PA. William served in World War II in the Air Force. After graduating from Lehigh University he was a chemical engineer in New York and New Jersey. He died on 10 December 1983, New Providence, NJ, at age 59.

3.5.3.4.1.1.1 TERRY LEE WASSON was born on 4 August 1947, Harrisburg, Dauphin County, PA. He married **NANCY LEE MACPHERSON** on 10 June 1972, Medford, MA. After serving in the US Navy, Terry went to work for the CIA in McLean, VA. In 1997, he was residing in Stafford, VA.

3.5.3.4.1.1.1.1 ERIKA LEE WASSON was born on 21 May 1974, New Delhi, India.

3.5.3.4.1.1.1.2 HEATHER MARIE WASSON was born on 1 March 1976, Manassas, VA.

3.5.3.4.1.1.1.3 DANIEL WEBSTER WASSON was born on 8 July 1983, Manassas, VA.

3.5.3.4.1.1.2 DONALD WILLIAM WASSON was born on 24 December 1951, Haddon Heights, NJ. He married **PATRICIA REINHARD** on 12 July 1975, New Providence, NJ.

3.5.3.4.1.1.2.1 JEFFREY SCOTT WASSON was born on 20 April 1981, Media, Delaware County, PA.

3.5.3.4.1.1.2.2 JULIE MEREDITH WASSON was born on 18 November 1984, Media, Delaware County, PA.

3.5.3.4.1.1.3 KAREN MARIE WASSON was born on 9 March 1953, Haddon Heights, NJ. She married **SALVATORE DELANO** on 13 April 1974, New Providence, NJ. As of 1997, Karen was a legal secretary living in Florham Park, NJ.

3.5.3.4.1.1.3.1 JENNIFER LYNN DELANO was born on 31 March 1979, Florham Park, NJ.

3.5.3.4.1.1.3.2 STEPHANIE ANN DELANO was born on 13 October 1980, Florham Park, NJ.

3.5.3.4.1.1.4 DIANE LOUISE WASSON was born on 26 September 1955, Haddon Heights, NJ. She married **MARK A. VIGLIOTTI** on 12 August 1978, New Providence, NJ. In 1997, Diane was a math teacher in Westminster, MD.

3.5.3.4.1.1.4.1 BETH ANN VIGLIOTTI was born on 17 June 1981, Westminster, MD.

3.5.3.4.1.1.4.2 LAURA MARIE VIGLIOTTI was born on 28 April 1984, Westminster, MD.

3.5.3.4.1.1.4.3 SARAH LOUISE VIGLIOTTI was born on 25 February 1987, Westminster, MD.

3.5.3.4.1.1.4.4 RACHEL LYNN VIGLIOTTI was born on 25 October 1988, Westminster, MD.

3.5.3.4.2 JOHN ALBERT WEISER was born on 31 December 1905, Elizabethville, Dauphin County, PA. He married EDNA RHEN in 1929. He died on 30 May 1996, Brooklyn, NY, at age 90. He was buried at Harrisburg, Dauphin County, PA.

3.5.3.4.3 WILSON MONROE WEISER was born on 12 November 1912, Harrisburg, Dauphin County, PA. He was unmarried.

3.5.3.5 HANNAH JENNIE WEISER was born on 22 March 1885, Pillow, Dauphin County, PA. She married HARRY ABRAHAM MILLER on 29 February 1908, Pillow, Dauphin County, PA. She died on 22 June 1957, Pillow, Dauphin County, PA, at age 72. She was buried at Grandview Cemetery, Pillow, Dauphin County, PA.

3.5.3.5.1 JESTINE ELNORA MILLER was born on 20 September 1908, Pillow, Dauphin County, PA. She was unmarried. She died on 19 November 1971, Pillow, Dauphin County, PA, at age 63. She was buried at Pillow, Dauphin County, PA.

3.5.3.5.2 HANNAH ELIZABETH MILLER was born on 4 January 1910, Pillow, Dauphin County, PA. She married GRANT BUFFINGTON on 10 October 1948, Washington, DC. She died on 10 June 1986, Shamokin, Northumberland County, PA, at age 76. She was buried at Pillow, Dauphin County, PA.

3.5.3.5.2.1 ROY BUFFINGTON was born on 3 September 1932, Pillow, Dauphin County, PA. He married MARQUEEN LATSHA on 10 November 1956, Red Cross, Northumberland County, PA.

3.5.3.5.2.1.1 DOUGLAS HAROLD BUFFINGTON was born on 7 September 1960, Harrisburg, Dauphin County, PA. He married LOU ANN SEILER on 15 August 1987, Millersburg, Dauphin County, PA.

3.5.3.5.2.1.1.1 KEVIN ROY BUFFINGTON was born on 29 September 1990, Harrisburg, Dauphin County, PA.

3.5.3.5.2.1.1.2 DANIEL HAROLD BUFFINGTON was born on 16 February 1994, Harrisburg, Dauphin County, PA.

3.5.3.5.2.1.2 STEPHANIE JAN BUFFINGTON was born on 29 October 1963, Harrisburg, Dauphin County, PA. She married RYAN DAVID WILFONG on 25 September 1993, Elizabethville, Dauphin County, PA.

3.5.3.5.3 MARY ALICE MILLER was born on 6 April 1914, Pillow, Dauphin County, PA. She died on 1 April 1979, Millersburg, Dauphin County, PA, at age 64.

3.5.3.5.4 (--?--) MILLER was born on 6 October 1915, Pillow, Dauphin County, PA. He died in 1915, Pillow, Dauphin County, PA. He was buried at Grandview Cemetery, Pillow, Dauphin County, PA.

3.5.3.5.5 LULU ELLEN MILLER was born on 27 October 1916, Pillow, Dauphin County, PA. She married HENRY FRANKLIN KOPPENHAVER on 28 September 1940, Elizabethville, Dauphin County, PA.

3.5.3.5.5.1 GLORIA RENEE MILLER was born on 10 June 1938, Pillow, Dauphin County, PA. She married BOBBY ALBERT HOFFMAN on 29 June 1957, Pillow, Dauphin County, PA. She married FRANTZ REED SIGAFOOS on 7 June 1973, Zerbe Township, Northumberland County, PA.

3.5.3.5.5.1.1 TINA ELLEN HOFFMAN was born on 29 June 1960, Harrisburg, Dauphin County, PA. She married JAMES WILSON JR. on 7 June 1980, Sunbury, Northumberland County, PA.

3.5.3.5.5.1.1.1 MATTHEW JAMES WILSON was born on 13 January 1982, Havre de Grace, MD.

3.5.3.5.5.1.1.2 MEGAN RENEE WILSON was born on 18 October 1985, Lebanon, Lebanon County, PA.

3.5.3.5.5.2 WILLIAM HARRY KOPPENHAVER was born on 30 November 1941, Gratz, Dauphin County, PA. He married MARTHA ELAINE SCHAFFER on 15 August 1964, Berrysburg, Dauphin County, PA.

3.5.3.5.5.2.1 MICHAEL PATRICK KOPPENHAVER was born on 18 August 1965, Harrisburg, Dauphin County, PA. He married LYNNE ELIZABETH SMITH on 20 January 1990, Virginia Beach, VA.

3.5.3.5.5.2.1.1 PATRICK RYAN KOPPENHAVER was born on 24 August 1990, Virginia Beach, VA.

3.5.3.5.5.2.1.2 PHILIP MICHAEL KOPPENHAVER was born on 27 April 1993, Virginia Beach, VA.

3.5.3.5.5.2.2 CAROL ANN KOPPENHAVER was born on 11 March 1972, Danville, Montour County, PA. She married RAYMOND MARTIN BARNES on 7 October 1995, Danville, Montour County, PA.

3.5.3.5.5.3 LORRAINE ESTHER KOPPENHAVER was born on 9 March 1944, Gratz, Dauphin County, PA. She married JAMES CHARLES SCHADLE, son of RAY WOODROW WILSON SHADLE and EVA MAY KLINGER, on 15 April 1961, Erdman, Dauphin County, PA. She and JAMES CHARLES SCHADLE were divorced in 1974. She married MAHLON WARFEL JR. on 24 May 1975, Rife, Dauphin County, PA.

3.5.3.5.5.3.1 LYNN CHARLES SHADLE is also referred to as LYNN CHARLES SCHADLE in some sources. He was born on 11 September 1961, Pottsville, Schuylkill County, PA. He married DIANE LEE ALLEN DOHERTY on 22 June 1985, Gratz, Dauphin County, PA.

3.5.3.5.5.3.2 STEVEN JAMES SHADLE is also referred to as STEVEN JAMES SCHADLE in some sources. He was born on 27 July 1962, Pottsville, Schuylkill County, PA. He married an unknown person on 5 May 1986.

3.5.3.5.5.3.2.1 STEVEN REID SHADLE is also referred to as STEVEN REID SCHADLE in some sources. He was born on 15 May 1992, Harrisburg, Dauphin County, PA.

3.5.3.5.5.3.3 REBECCA SUE SHADLE is also referred to as REBECCA SUE SCHADLE in some sources. She was born on 15 June 1970, Pottsville, Schuylkill County, PA. She married EDWARD GEORGE MENTZER on 16 April 1994.

3.5.3.5.5.3.3.1 ALEXIS NICOLE MENTZER was born on 10 September 1993, Harrisburg, Dauphin County, PA.

3.5.3.5.5.3.4 ANITA NICHOLE WARFEL was born on 22 May 1978, Sunbury, Northumberland County, PA.

3.5.3.5.6 JOHN HARRY ABRAHAM MILLER was born on 19 December 1920, Pillow, Dauphin County, PA. He married ANITA PAUL on 27 November 1946, Elizabethville, Dauphin County, PA. He died on 16 March 1990, Gratz, Dauphin County, PA, at age 69. He was buried at Gratz, Dauphin County, PA.

3.5.3.5.6.1 CATHIE MAE MILLER was born on 22 September 1959. She married STEVEN LAMAR WILKINSON on 17 August 1985, Gratz, Dauphin County, PA.

3.5.3.5.6.1.1 TIMOTHY JACOB WILKINSON was born on 18 January 1988, Danville, Montour County, PA.

3.5.3.5.6.1.2 TIFFANY ANN WILKINSON was born on 18 January 1988, Danville, Montour County, PA.

3.5.3.5.7 HAROLD LEROY MILLER was born on 24 October 1925, Pillow, Dauphin County, PA. He died on 14 January 1945, in the Battle of the Bulge, Luxembourg, at age 19.

3.5.4 LUCY ANN ROTHERMEL was born on 15 January 1849. She married NICHOLAS ADAMS on 28 January 1866. She died in 1928.

3.5.4.1 HANNAH SIVILLA ADAMS was born on 6 October 1866. She married JEREMIAH KLECKNER PAUL, son of ELI PAUL and SUSAN SHIVE, on 1 January 1882. She died on 6 May 1910, Gloucester City, Camden County, NJ, at age 43.

3.5.4.1.1 BERTHA PAUL was born on 10 October 1882. She married OTTMER NEISWENDER on 19 July 1902, Camden, Camden County, NJ. She died on 10 August 1949, at age 66.

3.5.4.1.2 STILES KLECKNER PAUL was born on 15 August 1884. He married FLORENCE ELNORA MCCREADY. He died in 1935.

3.5.4.1.3 FESTUS PAUL was born on 15 February 1887. She married GEORGE HUSTED. She died on 31 October 1915, Gloucester City, Camden County, NJ, at age 28.

3.5.4.1.3.1 EDYTH HUSTED

3.5.4.1.3.2 ANTOINETTE HUSTED

3.5.4.1.4 AMY S. PAUL was born on 8 January 1888. She married SAMUEL ADDISON. She died on 14 February 1918, Gloucester City, Camden County, NJ, at age 30.

3.5.4.1.4.1 PAUL ADDISON was born in 1907.

3.5.4.1.5 ELIZABETH PAUL was born on 12 February 1889. She married GEORGE EDMUND CARR on 1 September 1910. She died on 26 October 1972, Worcester, Worcester County, MA, at age 83.

3.5.4.1.5.1 EDMUND GEORGE CARR was born on 5 March 1911. He married MARION ANNA WHITNEY on 10 October 1934, St. Albans, Queens County, NY. He married MARIE THIBEAULT on 13 April 1989, Hampton Falls, Rockingham County, NH. He died on 23 February 2001, Worcester, Worcester County, MA, at age 89.

3.5.4.1.5.1.1 RICHARD EDMUND CARR

3.5.4.1.5.1.2 EMMA BARBARA CARR

3.5.4.1.5.1.3 ROGER GEORGE CARR

3.5.4.1.5.1.4 CAROLE ELIZABETH CARR

3.5.4.1.5.1.5 SHIRLEY ANN CARR

3.5.4.1.5.1.6 SHARON ESTELLE CARR married GLENN RICHARD BARNETT on 5 September 1969, Trenton, Mercer County, NJ.

3.5.4.1.5.1.7 GARY ROBERT CARR

3.5.4.1.5.2 WINSTON PAUL CARR was born on 3 March 1913. He married RITA JOSEPHINE HAND on 17 September 1935, Brooklyn, Kings County, NY. He died on 16 April 1978, Deer Park, Suffolk County, NY, at age 65.

3.5.4.1.5.2.1 MARGARET CATHERINE CARR

3.5.4.1.5.2.2 PATRICIA CARR

3.5.4.1.5.2.3 JOAN CARR

3.5.4.1.5.2.4 LINDA MARY CARR

3.5.4.2 ROLANDUS ADAMS is also referred to as LORANZA ADAMS in some sources. He was born on 28 July 1868. He married KATIE R. (--?--) on 4 October 1887, Old Evangelical parsonage, Williamstown, Dauphin County, PA. He died in 1955.

3.5.4.2.1 CHARLES N. ADAMS was born on 29 February 1888.

3.5.4.2.2 HARRY F. ADAMS was born on 11 March 1890.

3.5.4.2.3 LUCY A. ADAMS was born on 15 January 1892.

3.5.4.2.4 VERNA M. ADAMS was born on 3 February 1894.

3.5.4.2.5 ELMER J. ADAMS was born circa December 1896. He married MARY (--?--).

3.5.4.2.5.1 HAROLD ADAMS was born in 1917.

3.5.4.2.5.2 HELEN ADAMS was born in 1918.

3.5.4.2.6 ROY H. ADAMS was born on 14 April 1897. He died in July 1973, at age 76.

3.5.4.2.7 RUSSELL N. ADAMS was born on 12 July 1900.

3.5.4.2.8 FLORENCE A. ADAMS was born on 7 November 1902.

3.5.4.2.9 RAYMOND C. ADAMS was born on 3 July 1905. He died in March 1982, at age 76.

3.5.4.2.10 CLARENCE MARLIN ADAMS was born on 23 December 1908. He died on 9 March 1998, Lebanon County, PA, at age 89.

3.5.4.3 ISAAC MONROE ADAMS was born on 19 June 1870. He married CARRIE WITMER. He died on 22 February 1915, at age 44.

3.5.4.4 ANNA ELIZABETH ADAMS is also referred to as EMMA in some sources. She was born on 2 January 1873. She married (--?--) MORRIS. She died in April 1922, at age 49.

3.5.4.4.1 WILLIAM MORRIS

3.5.4.5 CHARLES MILTON ADAMS was born on 9 February 1875. He married CARRIE M. (--?--) circa 1900.

3.5.4.5.1 ANNE E. ADAMS was born in 1903.

3.5.4.5.2 FLOYD M. ADAMS was born in 1910.

3.5.4.5.3 MIRIAM ADAMS was born in 1912.

3.5.4.5.4 ALAN ADAMS was born in 1913.

3.5.4.5.5 MARK L. ADAMS was born in 1916.

3.5.4.5.6 W. KAY ADAMS was born in 1919.

3.5.4.5.7 LEE L. ADAMS was born circa 1924.

3.5.4.6 WILLIAM VICTOR ADAMS was born on 2 August 1876. He married ANNIE M. (--?--). He married FLORENCE (--?--).

3.5.4.6.1 PAUL ADAMS is also referred to as JEREMIAH K. P. ADAMS in some sources. He was born circa 1902.

3.5.4.6.2 BEULAH M. ADAMS was born circa 1903.

3.5.4.6.3 NICHOLAS S. ADAMS was born circa 1904.

3.5.4.6.4 JOHN Q. ADAMS was born circa 1906.

3.5.4.6.5 GEORGE W. ADAMS was born in 1906.

3.5.4.6.6 MONROE I. ADAMS was born circa 1908. He married FRANCES BROSIUS after 1930. He died in 1957.

3.5.4.6.6.1 ROY ADAMS

3.5.4.6.6.2 LILLIAN ADAMS married (--?--) REINERT.

3.5.4.6.6.3 JEANNE ADAMS

3.5.4.6.6.4 KENNETH ADAMS

3.5.4.6.6.5 HAROLD ADAMS

3.5.4.6.6.6 GUY ADAMS

3.5.4.6.6.7 MILDRED E. ADAMS. Some sources record that she was born in 1907, but that seems impossible. She married PHILLIP K. FRANK. She died on 14 March 1956.

3.5.4.6.6.7.1 DOROTHY A. FRANK

3.5.4.6.6.7.2 GARY A. FRANK

3.5.4.6.7 HOWARD ADAMS was born circa 1911.

3.5.4.6.8 ALBERT ADAMS was born circa 1911.

3.5.4.6.9 MARGARET ADAMS was born circa 1915.

3.5.4.6.10 LUCY ADAMS was born circa 1916.

3.5.4.6.11 ROBERT ADAMS was born circa 1923.

3.5.4.7 SARAH ELLEN ADAMS was born on 21 December 1878.

3.5.4.8 NICHOLAS EDWIN ADAMS is also referred to as EDWARD N. ADAMS in some sources. He was born on 26 May 1880.

3.5.4.9 JOHN QUINCY ADAMS was born on 9 June 1882.

3.5.4.10 LUCY MAY ADAMS was born on 31 May 1885. She married (--?--) DIEBLER. She died on 14 October 1921, at age 36.

3.5.4.11 CLAYTON FRANKLIN ADAMS was born on 9 December 1890. He married ANNY A. (--?--).

3.5.4.11.1 FRANCIS G. ADAMS was born in 1914.

3.5.4.11.2 FRANK E. ADAMS was born in 1916.

3.5.4.11.3 KENNETH W. ADAMS was born circa 1921.

3.5.4.11.4 ESTHER J. ADAMS was born in 1922.

3.5.4.11.5 ELIZABETH M. ADAMS was born circa 1925.

3.5.5 AMOS W. ROTHERMEL is also referred to as AMOS ROTHERMOL in some sources. He was born circa 1844. He was born circa 1845. Some sources record that he was born circa 1850. He married MARIA ELISABETH KLINGER, daughter of JACOB S. KLINGER and LOUISA ALSPACH, Klingerstown, Schuylkill County, PA. He died on 11 January 1907, Minersville, Schuylkill County, PA. He was buried at Zion (Klinger's) Church, Erdman, Lykens Township, Dauphin County, PA.

3.5.5.1 ELWIN ROTHERMOL was born circa 1866, Pennsylvania.

3.5.5.2 THEODORE ROTHERMOL was born circa 1868, Pennsylvania.

3.5.5.3 MACLADA ROTHERMEL is also referred to as MECLADA ROTHERMOL in some sources. She was born circa 1871, Klingerstown, Schuylkill County, PA. She married WILLIAM J. MORRIS circa 1893.

    3.5.5.3.1 AMOS MORRIS is also referred to as EMANS in some sources. He was born in May 1893.

    3.5.5.3.2 BEATRICE MORRIS was born in 1896.

    3.5.5.3.3 LOUIS MORRIS was born circa 1898.

3.5.5.4 MILTON ROTHERMEL is also referred to as MILTON ROTHERMOL in some sources. He was born on 9 June 1873, Klingerstown, Schuylkill County, PA. He married EDITH CARDELLA BUECK on 29 December 1895.

    3.5.5.4.1 NORMAN LESTER ROTHERMEL was born on 25 April 1910, Primrose, Schuylkill County, PA.

    3.5.5.4.2 DOROTHY PEARL ROTHERMEL is also referred to as DORTHEA in some sources. She was born circa 1913.

    3.5.5.4.3 HERBERT MILTON ROTHERMEL was born circa 1916.

    3.5.5.4.4 RUSSELL H. ROTHERMEL was born circa 1920.

3.5.5.5 EDWIN ROTHERMEL is also referred to as EDWIN ROTHERMOL in some sources. He was born on 18 June 1874, Klingerstown, Schuylkill County, PA. He married MARGARET STEVENSON on 15 June 1904.

    3.5.5.5.1 EDWIN FRANCIS ROTHERMEL was born circa 1906.

    3.5.5.5.2 GLADYS MARGARET ROTHERMEL was born circa 1908. She married RUSSEL RIDGE circa 1928.

3.5.5.6 JOHN ROTHERMOL was born circa 1876, Pennsylvania.

3.5.5.7 CHARLES K. ROTHERMEL was born on 13 March 1876, Mt. Pleasant, Schuylkill County, PA. He married BESSIE ATHEY VERA CRONE, daughter of JOHN CRONE and LIZZIE ATHEY, on 10 November 1904, Minersville, Schuylkill County, PA.

    3.5.5.7.1 CHARLES ROTHERMEL was born on 7 April 1905, Minersville, Schuylkill County, PA. He died on 17 April 1905, Minersville, Schuylkill County, PA.

    3.5.5.7.2 HARRY BURTON ROTHERMEL was born circa 1920.

    3.5.5.7.3 GLORIA ROTHERMEL was born circa 1923.

3.5.5.8 JAMES ROTHERMEL was born on 26 December 1879. He died on 13 October 1883, at age 3. He was buried at Zion (Klinger's) Church, Erdman, Lykens Township, Dauphin County, PA.

3.5.5.9 INFANT ROTHERMOL was born circa January 1880, Pennsylvania.

3.5.5.10 LUCY ROTHERMEL is also referred to as LUCY ROTHERMOL in some sources. She was born in 1877. Some sources record that she was born circa 1881, Minersville, Schuylkill County, PA.

3.5.5.11 CLAUDE L. ROTHERMEL was born on 10 October 1883, New Castle, Luzerne County, PA. He married HELEN JONES on 26 May 1906.

    3.5.5.11.1 MARY ROTHERMEL was born in 1907.

    3.5.5.11.2 MARTHA ROTHERMEL is also referred to as MARGARET in some sources. She was born circa 1915.

    3.5.5.11.3 HELEN ROTHERMEL was born circa 1921.

3.5.6 EVE ELIZABETH ROTHERMEL was born on 14 December 1850. She died on 16 December 1852, at age 2.

3.5.7 CHARLES A. ROTHERMEL was born in 1853. He married ELIZABETH KLINGER.

    3.5.7.1 ELIZABETH ROTHERMEL

    3.5.7.2 CLAUDE F. ROTHERMEL was born on 18 October 1883. He married HELEN JONES. He died on 15 August 1958, at age 74.

        3.5.7.2.1 MARY OLIVE ROTHERMEL married (--?--) FITZPATRICK. She died in 1953.

3.5.7.2.2 MARGARET JONES ROTHERMEL married WILBUR ULMER.

3.5.7.2.3 HELEN ROTHERMEL married WILLIAM J. BUSH.

3.5.8 CATHARINE ROTHERMEL is also referred to as CARLINA in some sources. She was born on 5 January 1853. She was baptized on 1 May 1853, Zion (Klinger's) Lutheran and Reformed Church, Erdman, Dauphin County, PA. She died on 25 September 1854, at age 1. She was buried at Zion (Klinger's) Church Cemetery, Erdman, Lykens Township, Dauphin County, PA.

3.5.9 LAZARUS W. ROTHERMEL is also referred to as LAZARETH ROTHERMOL in some sources. He was born on 15 April 1855, Pennsylvania. He was baptized on 3 June 1855, Zion (Klinger's) Lutheran and Reformed Church, Erdman, Dauphin County, PA. He married EMMA L. BUSH circa 1881. He died in 1934, Klingerstown, Schuylkill County, PA. He was buried at St. David's Lutheran and Reformed Church Cemetery, Hebe, Jordan Township, Northumberland County, PA.

3.5.9.1 JANE ROTHERMEL is also referred to as JENNIE AND JANIE in some sources. She was born on 15 June 1882. She was baptized on 30 July 1882, Zion (Klinger's) Church, Erdman, Lykens Township, Dauphin County, PA. She died on 15 August 1892, at age 10. She was buried at St. David's Lutheran and Reformed Church Cemetery, Hebe, Jordan Township, Northumberland County, PA.

3.5.9.2 JESTIE B. ROTHERMEL was born on 27 February 1884. She was baptized on 19 April 1884, Zion (Klinger's) Church, Erdman, Lykens Township, Dauphin County, PA. She married JAMES RUNKLE. She died on 11 May 1959, at age 75.

3.5.9.2.1 CHESTER GUY RUNKLE was born on 22 April 1904. He was baptized on 12 June 1904, St. David's Lutheran and Reformed Church, Hebe, Northumberland County, PA.

3.5.9.3 ALICE ELIZABETH ROTHERMEL was born on 8 November 1885. She was baptized on 7 March 1886, Zion (Klinger's) Church, Erdman, Lykens Township, Dauphin County, PA. She married JACOB SCHADEL WIEST, son of MOSES MERKEL WIEST and MARIA SCHADEL, circa 1901. She died on 13 January 1970, at age 84.

3.5.9.3.1 ESTELLA ALICE WIEST was born on 29 October 1903, Portland, Multnomah County, OR. She married O.K. KINDOOM.

3.5.9.3.2 ALBERT JACOB WIEST was born on 1 January 1908, Portland, Multnomah County, OR. He married DOROTHY M. ROBINSON circa 1930. He died circa 1994, Portland, Multnomah County, OR.

3.5.9.3.2.1 RONALD E. WIEST was born on 17 August 1932. He married MARIE GRASSET.

3.5.9.3.2.1.1 PHOEBE J. WIEST was born on 26 March 1954. She married DONALD WITHAM.

3.5.9.3.2.1.2 RHONDA L. WIEST was born on 28 July 1955. She married DALE M. HEADDRESS.

3.5.9.3.2.1.3 ANDY B. WIEST was born on 10 February 1958. He married JUDY A. HERN.

3.5.9.3.2.1.4 SHANNA M. WIEST was born on 27 February 1961.

3.5.9.3.3 HALLIE MARIE WIEST was born on 8 March 1910. She married JOHN MUNK.

3.5.9.3.3.1 BARBARA MUNK was born on 2 April 1931. She married HENRY T. ROCHE.

3.5.9.3.3.1.1 TERESA ROCHE was born on 6 November 1952. She married MICHAEL WARD.

3.5.9.3.3.1.1.1 ERIC J. WARD was born on 27 January 1977.

3.5.9.3.3.1.1.2 ALAN J. WARD was born on 19 November 1979.

3.5.9.3.3.1.1.3 BRIAN J. WARD was born on 25 February 1982.

3.5.9.3.3.1.2 SUSAN L. ROCHE was born on 22 September 1954. She married JAMES P. HOLL.

3.5.9.3.3.1.2.1 DANIEL A. HOLL was born on 11 October 1984.

3.5.9.3.3.1.3 LAURA A. ROCHE was born on 7 August 1957. She married JAN LUKENS. She married JEFF GARBUTT.

3.5.9.3.3.1.4 TIMOTHY J. ROCHE was born on 10 February 1962.

3.5.9.3.4 ALTA MOLLIE WIEST was born on 22 June 1912. She married KENNETH J. ROBINSON.

3.5.9.3.4.1 KENNETH C. ROBINSON was born on 21 April 1938, in Washington.

3.5.9.3.4.2 NANCY K. ROBINSON was born on 1 July 1942, in Washington. She married **DONALD R. JAMISON**.

3.5.9.3.4.2.1 DAVID A. JAMISON was born on 27 March 1963. He married **SUSAN M. BRAGET**.

3.5.9.3.4.2.1.1 APRIL M. JAMISON was born on 28 February 1982.

3.5.9.3.4.2.1.2 SHAWNA M. JAMISON was born on 26 March 1986.

3.5.9.3.4.2.2 STEVEN T. JAMISON was born on 12 March 1965.

3.5.9.3.4.2.3 TINA M. JAMISON was born on 24 March 1968. She married **BRIAN LUND**.

3.5.9.3.5 CLARE ELIZABETH WIEST was born on 29 October 1914.

3.5.9.4 CHARLES HENRY ROTHERMEL was born on 17 November 1887. He was baptized on 4 March 1888, Zion (Klinger's) Church, Erdman, Lykens Township, Dauphin County, PA. He died on 13 August 1889, at age 1. He was buried at St. David's Lutheran and Reformed Church Cemetery, Hebe, Jordan Township, Northumberland County, PA.

3.5.9.5 IDA M. ROTHERMEL was born on 4 October 1889. She married **CHARLES JAY PHILLIPS**. She died on 10 April 1984, at age 94. She was buried at St. Michael's Church Cemetery, Klingerstown, Schuylkill County, PA.

3.5.9.6 JOHN L. ROTHERMEL was born on 14 September 1891. He married **KATIE GESSNER**. He married **BERTHA E. KRISSINGER**. He died on 6 July 1979, at age 87.

3.5.9.6.1 BLANCHE ANNA ROTHERMEL was born on 27 February 1914. She was baptized on 14 April 1914, St. David's Lutheran and Reformed Church, Hebe, Northumberland County, PA.

3.5.9.7 EMMA BERTHA ROTHERMEL was born on 2 August 1894. She married **JAMES SCHADEL**. She died on 16 March 1966, at age 71. She was buried at St. David's Lutheran and Reformed Church Cemetery, Hebe, Jordan Township, Northumberland County, PA.

3.5.9.7.1 RAY WOODROW WILSON SCHADEL was born on 18 May 1913. He was baptized on 22 June 1913, St. David's Lutheran and Reformed Church, Hebe, Northumberland County, PA. Some sources record that he was born on 15 May 1917, Klingerstown, Schuylkill County, PA. He died on 3 November 1941, at age 24.

3.5.9.7.2 GUY AMBROSE SCHADEL was born on 17 June 1917, Klingerstown, Schuylkill County, PA. He married **BERTHA ELIZABETH STROHECKER** on 11 May 1946, Jordan Township, Northumberland County, PA. He died on 24 October 1996, Plano, TX, at age 79.

3.5.9.8 SAMUEL EDGAR ROTHERMEL was born on 29 July 1895. He married **MARY WALTERS**. He married **GOLDIE A. REBUCK** on 15 January 1916. He died on 2 April 1971, at age 75. He was buried at Emanuel Wesleyan Cemetery, Gratz, Dauphin County, PA.

3.5.9.8.1 PAUL RAYMOND ROTHERMEL was born on 29 May 1915. He married **ARLENE R. BOHNER**, daughter of **ELIJAH BOHNER** and **AMELIA C. LAHR**, on 12 October 1940. He died on 16 May 1968, at age 52. He was buried at Northumberland Memorial Park, Stonnington, Northumberland County, PA.

3.5.9.8.1.1 JOAN ROTHERMEL married **JIM SNYDER**.

3.5.9.8.1.2 STEVE ROTHERMEL married **JANET (--?--)**.

3.5.9.8.1.3 BRYANT ROTHERMEL married **LINDA (--?--)**.

3.5.9.8.1.4 LARRY ROTHERMEL married **LUCILLE (--?--)**.

3.5.9.8.1.5 CARL RAYMOND ROTHERMEL was born on 10 July 1942, Harrisburg, Dauphin County, PA. He married **CONNIE (--?--)**. He died on 17 February 2003, Dalmatia, Northumberland County, PA, at age 60. He was buried at Salem Lutheran Church Cemetery, Killinger, Dauphin County, PA.

3.5.9.8.2 LLOYD K. ROTHERMEL was born on 13 February 1921, Klingerstown, Schuylkill County, PA. He married **EDITH E. (--?--)**. He died on 2 January 1959, Polyclinic Hospital, Harrisburg, Dauphin County, PA, at age 37. He was buried at Emmanuel Wesleyan Church Cemetery, Gratz, Dauphin County, PA.

3.5.9.8.3 ROXEY A. ROTHERMEL was born on 14 November 1924, Jackson Township, Northumberland County, PA. She married **PAUL A. GESSNER**, son of **WILLIAM GESSNER** and **JENNIE WERT**, on 25 December 1945. She died on 21 October 2014, Sunbury, Northumberland County, PA, at age 89. She was buried on 29 October 2014, at Emmanuel Wesleyan Church

Cemetery, Gratz, Dauphin County, Luzerne County. According to a newspaper obituary, Roxey who lived near Herndon, PA, worked as a seamstress in Millersburg, PA, before retiring in 1986.

 3.5.9.8.3.1 RENEE J. GESSNER married **JOHN S. SHIKO**.

  3.5.9.8.3.1.1 CARL CRILEY

  3.5.9.8.3.1.2 CALVIN CRILEY

  3.5.9.8.3.1.3 ANTHONY CRILEY

3.5.9.8.4 SHIRLEY ROTHERMEL was born circa 1929. She married **(--?--) HARMAN**. She died before 2014.

3.5.9.9 EVA M. ROTHERMEL was born on 17 August 1897, Klingerstown, Schuylkill County, PA. She married **IRA JACOB KLINGER**, son of **EMANUEL KLINGER** and **CHRISTIANA SCHADEL**, on 8 April 1916, Zion (Klinger's) Church, Erdman, Lykens Township, Dauphin County, PA. She was buried at Valley View, Schuylkill County, PA. She died on 1 March 1963, Valley View, Schuylkill County, PA, at age 65.

 3.5.9.9.1 MARY EMMA KLINGER was born on 11 February 1927, Lamberton, Schuylkill County, PA. According to some sources, Mary may have been adopted by Ira and Eva and that her original surname may have been "Moyer." Mary was not part of Ira and Eva's household at the time of the 1930 Census, when she would have been about 3 years old, but was listed as their daughter in the 1940 Census. She married **ALVIN H. STEHR**. She died on 18 February 2009, Penn State Milton S. Hershey Medical Center, Hershey, Dauphin County, PA, at age 82. She was buried at Trinity Lutheran Church Cemetery, Valley View, Schuylkill County, PA.

  3.5.9.9.1.1 TERRY L. STEHR married **CAROL (--?--)**.

  3.5.9.9.1.2 CRAIG R. STEHR married **LINDA (--?--)**.

  3.5.9.9.1.3 SUSAN K. STEHR

3.5.9.10 HARRY NORMAN ROTHERMEL was born on 17 October 1899. He married **MATTIE CARL**. He died on 28 January 1983, Klingerstown, Schuylkill County, PA, at age 83. He was buried at Salem Church Cemetery, Rough and Ready, Schuylkill County, PA.

 3.5.9.10.1 NORMAN RICHARD ROTHERMEL also went by the name of **DICK**. He was born on 23 February 1929, Klingerstown, Schuylkill County, PA. He married **NANCY HOFFMAN** on 15 August 1952. He died on 19 December 2011, at age 82. According to a newspaper obituary, Norman was self-employed as a dairy farmer and later worked as a coal hoister for Summit Anthracite and Tracey Coal. Formerly, he was an Upper Mahantongo Township supervisor and also served with the Hubley Township Police. Norman was the owner of the Peter Knorr farm on Vista Road near Rough & Ready, Schuylkill County, PA.

  3.5.9.10.1.1 RICHARD S. ROTHERMEL was born on 1 June 1952. He married **JUDY (--?--)**.

  3.5.9.10.1.2 KENNETH D. ROTHERMEL was born on 23 April 1953.

  3.5.9.10.1.3 RANDY C. ROTHERMEL was born on 9 October 1954. He married **CINDY (--?--)**.

  3.5.9.10.1.4 GAIL I. ROTHERMEL was born on 3 November 1956. She married **GARY LAUDENSLAGER**, son of **FRED LAUDENSLAGER** and **MAE ENDERS**.

   3.5.9.10.1.4.1 GARY LEE LAUDENSLAGER was born on 21 February 1975. He married **MELISSA SHAFFER**. He died on 16 July 1998, at age 23.

  3.5.9.10.1.5 CATHERINE G. ROTHERMEL was born on 25 July 1959. She married **(--?--) HERB**.

  3.5.9.10.1.6 MICHAEL J. ROTHERMEL was born on 31 December 1961. He married **KANDI (--?--)**.

  3.5.9.10.1.7 TIMOTHY L. ROTHERMEL was born on 10 November 1966.

3.5.9.11 MAZIE M. ROTHERMEL was born on 10 August 1901. She married **JOHN E. WILLARD**.

3.5.9.12 MINNIE E. ROTHERMEL was born on 3 October 1903. She married **GEORGE BIXLER**.

3.5.9.13 ELMA ETHEL ROTHERMEL was born on 14 August 1905. She married **HOMER WIEST**, son of **SAMUEL BAUM WIEST** and **SARAH JENNIE SNYDER**, before 1923. She married **ALLEN G. WARFIELD**, son of **RUDY C. WARFIELD** and **MINNIE J. (--?--)**, circa 1924. She married **TYSON COLEMAN**. Prior to her death, Ethel was living in the vicinity of Klingerstown, Schuylkill County, PA. She died in June 1978, at age 72.

3.5.9.13.1 DARWIN CLAIR WIEST is also referred to as **DARWIN WARFIELD** in some sources. He was born on 8 April 1923, Klingerstown, Schuylkill County, PA. He married **ANNA LOIS LESHER** on 18 July 1953, St. Michael's Church, Klingerstown, Upper Mahantango Township, Schuylkill County, PA.

3.5.9.13.1.1 PATRICIA LOUISE WIEST was born on 14 June 1954, Geisinger Hospital, Danville, Montour County, PA. She was baptized on 15 August 1954, St. Michael's Lutheran and Reformed Church, Klingerstown, Schuylkill County, PA.

3.5.9.13.1.2 BETTY JANE WIEST was born on 2 December 1956, Geisinger Hospital, Danville, Montour County, PA. She was baptized on 27 January 1957, St. Michael's Church, Klingerstown, Schuylkill County, PA. She married **STEVEN DENNIS SCHEIB**, son of **ROBERT BENJAMIN SCHEIB** and **PHYLLIS EVA MAE PAUL**, on 9 July 1977, PA. She married **SCOTT E. MINARICH** after 1986.

3.5.9.13.1.2.1 JENNIFER ANN SCHEIB was born on 11 November 1981, Schuylkill County, PA. She was baptized on 10 April 1982, St. Michael's Church, Klingerstown, Schuylkill County, PA.

3.5.9.13.1.2.2 MICHAEL B. SCHEIB was born on 20 June 1986, Schuylkill County, PA.

3.5.9.13.1.3 DAVID LYNN WIEST was born on 17 October 1962, Geisinger Hospital, Danville, Montour County, PA. He was baptized on 1 June 1963, St. Michael's Lutheran and Reformed Church, Klingerstown, Schuylkill County, PA.

3.5.9.13.2 ALTON M. WARFIELD was born circa February 1926.

3.5.10 MANASSES W. ROTHERMEL was born on 24 September 1857. He married **EVA ELIZABETH WENTZEL**. According to some sources, Manasses and his first wife Eva Elizabeth, had 8 children, all of whom died in infancy. Three of them are buried at Zion (Klinger's) Church, Erdman, Dauphin County, PA. He married **SUSAN JANE BIXLER**, daughter of **JOHN BIXLER** and **SALLIE BAUM**, circa 1898. He died on 4 January 1929, Klingerstown, Schuylkill County, PA, at age 71. He was buried at St. Michael's Lutheran and Reformed Cemetery, Klingerstown, Schuylkill County, PA.

3.5.10.1 INFANT SON ROTHERMEL was born on 7 October 1880. She died circa 1880. She was buried at Zion (Klinger's) Church, Erdman, Lykens Township, Dauphin County, PA.

3.5.10.2 INFANT SON ROTHERMEL was born on 30 January 1884. He died circa 1884. He was buried at Zion (Klinger's) Church, Erdman, Lykens Township, Dauphin County, PA.

3.5.10.3 INFANT DAUGHTER ROTHERMEL was born on 5 October 1885. She died on 5 October 1885. She was buried at Zion (Klinger's) Church, Erdman, Lykens Township, Dauphin County, PA.

3.5.10.4 INFANT SON ROTHERMEL was born on 20 December 1892.

3.5.10.5 AMOS ROBERT ROTHERMEL is also referred to as **ROBERT AMOS ROTHERMEL** in some sources. He was born on 3 March 1899, Jordan Township, Northumberland County. He married **LAURA IRENE BUFFINGTON**, daughter of **MILTON O. BUFFINGTON** and **MAUDE E. KLINGER**. He married **CARTIE WOLFGANG** on 4 February 1943. He died on 7 July 1944, Lykens Township, Dauphin County, PA, at age 45. He was buried on 10 July 1944, at St. Michael's Lutheran and Reformed Cemetery, Klingerstown, Schuylkill County, PA. Robert Amos was a farmer in Lykens Township, Dauphin County, PA, northeast of Gratz, and also worked as an anthracite miner in Williamstown, PA.

3.5.10.5.1 STANLEY ROTHERMEL (see above)

3.5.10.5.1.1 RHONDA ROTHERMEL (see above)

3.5.10.5.1.2 SUSAN ROTHERMEL (see above)

3.5.10.5.1.3 KRISTINE ROTHERMEL (see above)

3.5.10.5.1.3.1 JONATHAN PERRY (see above)

3.5.10.5.1.3.2 SHAWN PERRY (see above)

3.5.10.5.1.4 RANDALL CHARLES ROTHERMEL (see above)

3.5.10.5.2 ARLENE ROTHERMEL (see above)

3.5.10.5.3 MILDRED MARIE ROTHERMEL (see above)

3.5.10.6 RUTH B. ROTHERMEL was born on 24 November 1900. She married **GEORGE E. SNYDER**. She died in 1965.

3.5.10.7 MABEL G. ROTHERMEL was born on 30 December 1904. She married **ALLEN H. WILLARD**, son of **SAMUEL MORRIS WILLIARD** and **IDA MAY HEITZMAN,** circa 1928. She died on 19 March 1954, at age 49. She was buried at St. Michael's Lutheran Church Cemetery, Klingerstown, Schuylkill County, PA.

- **3.5.10.7.1 PEARL N. WILLARD** (see above)
- **3.5.10.7.2 SAMUEL M. WILLARD** (see above)
    - **3.5.10.7.2.1 WYNN ALAN WILLARD** (see above)
        - **3.5.10.7.2.1.1 MARSHALL WYNN WILLARD** (see above)
        - **3.5.10.7.2.1.2 SHERIDAN SAMUEL WILLARD** (see above)
        - **3.5.10.7.2.1.3 ASHTON ALAN WILLARD** (see above)
    - **3.5.10.7.2.2 LORI ANN WILLARD** (see above)
- **3.5.10.7.3 SHIRLEY MAE WILLARD** (see above)
    - **3.5.10.7.3.1 LISA R. PAPONETTI** (see above)
        - **3.5.10.7.3.1.1 KATIA P. LUU** (see above)
- **3.5.10.7.4 DELORES VERA WILLARD** (see above)

3.5.10.8 JOHN E. ROTHERMEL was born on 11 February 1907. He married **SARAH E. WOLF** circa 1927. He married **GERTRUDE HEPLER** circa 1940. He died on 3 September 1974, at age 67. He was buried at St. Michael's Lutheran and Reformed Cemetery, Klingerstown, Schuylkill County, PA. Prior to his death, John was living in Lykens, Dauphin County, PA.

- **3.5.10.8.1 EDWIN E. ROTHERMEL** was born circa 1928.
- **3.5.10.8.2 JEAN M. ROTHERMEL** was born in 1929.
- **3.5.10.8.3 JOHN E. ROTHERMEL** was born on 5 December 1940.

3.5.10.9 MANASSES ROTHERMEL was born in 1909. He married **SARA WOLF**. He died on 19 August 1958.

3.5.11 EZRAM E. ROTHERMEL is also referred to as **EAROM ROTHERMEL** in some sources. He was born on 24 February 1860. He was baptized on 22 April 1860, Zion (Klinger's) Lutheran and Reformed Church, Erdman, Dauphin County, PA. He married **SARAH HODGKINS.** He died on 14 November 1933, at age 73.

3.5.12 MONROE W. ROTHERMEL is also referred to as **ISAAC MONRO** in some sources. He was born on 8 March 1862. He married **ELIZABETH SCHMELTZ** circa 1887. He died on 28 December 1923, at age 61. He was buried at St. David's Lutheran and Reformed Church Cemetery, Hebe, Jordan Township, Northumberland County, PA.

3.5.12.1 CHARLES EDWIN ROTHERMEL was born on 4 April 1887. He married **MARY CARDELLA SHAFFER**, daughter of **ELIAS ZERBE SHAFFER** and **SARAH ELIZABETH HOAST,** circa 1910. He died on 26 January 1957, at age 69. He was buried at Zion (Klinger's) Church Cemetery, Erdman, Lykens Township, Dauphin County, PA.

3.5.12.1.1 MILDRED E. ROTHERMEL was born circa 1914. She married **IRA I. SCHWALM**, son of **ALBERT PETER SCHWALM** and **BARBARA A. CLARK.** She died on 3 July 1992, Rothermel Personal Care Home, Hegins, Schuylkill County, PA. She was buried at Zion (Klinger's) Church Cemetery, Erdman, Lykens Township, Dauphin County, PA.

- **3.5.12.1.1.1 MARK SCHWALM** married **JEAN BIXLER.**
    - **3.5.12.1.1.1.1 ANGELA SCHWALM**
- **3.5.12.1.1.2 ROY SCHWALM** married **CATHY SULLIVAN.**
- **3.5.12.1.1.3 PAUL I. SCHWALM** was born on 4 March 1935, Lykens Township, Dauphin County, PA. He married **NANCY MARION HARNER.** He married **LORRAINE M. KESSLER** circa 1998. He died on 9 December 2016, Lehigh Valley Hospital - East Norwegian, Pottsville, Schuylkill County, PA, at age 81. He was buried on 14 December 2016, at Saint Andrews United Methodist Church Cemetery, Valley View, Schuylkill County, PA.
    - **3.5.12.1.1.3.1 JASON M. SCHWALM** married **AMANDA MICHELLE BOWMAN**, daughter of **DAN BOWMAN** and **DONNA (--?--),** on 6 September 2003, St. Andrew's United Methodist Church, Valley View, Schuylkill County, PA.
        - **3.5.12.1.1.3.1.1 MADYSON MICHELLE SCHWALM** was born on 8 November 2006, Pottsville Hospital, Pottsville, Schuylkill County, PA.

3.5.12.1.1.3.2 **DENNIS I. SCHWALM** married **CHRISTINE E. SHADE**, daughter of **GARY SHADE** and **JUDY (--?--)**, on 27 August 1994, St. Michael's Lutheran Church, Klingerstown, Schuylkill County, PA.

3.5.12.1.1.3.3 **TERRY SCHWALM** married **AMY STIELY**. He lived in Hegins, Schuylkill County, PA.

    3.5.12.1.1.3.3.1 **EMILY BETH SCHWALM** was born on 26 May 1998.

    3.5.12.1.1.3.3.2 **DAWSON PAUL SCHWALM** was born on 8 July 2000.

3.5.12.1.1.3.4 **SCOTT PAUL SCHWALM** was born on 22 July 1957. He married **DELINDA LEE FLOOK** circa 1986, United Methodist Church, New Cumberland, PA.

    3.5.12.1.1.3.4.1 **SARAH ELIZABETH SCHWALM** was born on 24 February 1993, Harrisburg Hospital, Harrisburg, Dauphin County, PA.

3.5.12.1.2 **NEVIN CHARLES ROTHERMEL** was born on 4 December 1916, Lykens Township, Dauphin Co., PA. He married **ELSIE LAVINA SCHEIB**, daughter of **LEWIS ANDREW SCHEIB** and **KATIE LOVINA HARTMAN**, on 19 June 1937, Gratz, Dauphin Co., PA. He died on 15 June 2006, R.R. 1, Dornsife, Northumberland County, PA, at age 89. He was buried at Zion (Klinger's) Lutheran Church Cemetery, Erdman, Dauphin County, PA.

3.5.12.1.2.1 **ELEANOR ELIZABETH ROTHERMEL** was born on 20 February 1939, Pillow, Dauphin Co., PA. She died on 26 March 1941, Geisinger Hospital, Danville, Montour Co., PA, at age 2. She was buried on 29 March 1941, at Zion (Klinger's) Lutheran Church Cemetery, Erdman, Dauphin Co., PA.

3.5.12.1.2.2 **DENNIS NEVIN ROTHERMEL** was born on 27 June 1942, Pillow, Dauphin Co., PA. He married **SANDRA JOAN HERRING** on 30 May 1962.

    3.5.12.1.2.2.1 **TODD DENNIS ROTHERMEL** was born on 7 January 1963, Geisinger Hospital, Danville, Montour Co., PA. He married **STACEY JAE WALTER** on 2 August 1986, Emmaus, PA.

        3.5.12.1.2.2.1.1 **ALYSSA LIAN ROTHERMEL** was born on 4 February 1990, FL.

        3.5.12.1.2.2.1.2 **ANDREW TODD ROTHERMEL** was born on 17 April 1992, Albuquerque, Bernalillo Co., NM.

    3.5.12.1.2.2.2 **TARA LYNN ROTHERMEL** was born on 28 June 1971, Allentown Hospital, Allentown, PA. She married **SCOTT DAVID DRUCKMILLER** on 18 September 1993, Reading, Berks County, PA.

        3.5.12.1.2.2.2.1 **TY SCOTT DRUCKMILLER** was born on 28 May 1997, St. Luke's Hospital, Bethlehem, PA.

        3.5.12.1.2.2.2.2 **DANE SCOTT DRUCKMILLER** was born on 9 August 2000, St. Luke's Hospital, Bethlehem, PA.

3.5.12.1.2.3 **MARLIN JAMES ROTHERMEL** was born on 13 June 1947, Pillow, Dauphin Co., PA. He married **JOAN ARLENE HEIM** on 19 December 1970.

    3.5.12.1.2.3.1 **TY MARLIN ROTHERMEL** was born on 13 February 1974, Dauphin Co., PA. He was baptized on 31 March 1974, Zion (Klinger's) Lutheran Church, Erdman, Dauphin Co., PA.

    3.5.12.1.2.3.2 **GENA ELEANOR ROTHERMEL** was born on 28 July 1976, Dauphin Co., PA. She was baptized on 19 September 1976, Zion (Klinger's) Lutheran Church, Erdman, Dauphin Co., PA.

3.5.12.1.2.4 **SUZANNE ELIZABETH ROTHERMEL** was born on 16 August 1949, Danville, Montour Co., PA. She married **GARY LEE SNYDER** on 28 October 1967, Zion (Klinger's) Lutheran Church, Erdman, Dauphin Co., PA. She married **ROBERT L. SNYDER** after 1973, Zion (Klinger's) Lutheran Church, Erdman, Dauphin Co., PA.

    3.5.12.1.2.4.1 **SPENCE RODNEY SNYDER** was born on 16 July 1969, Danville, Montour Co., PA. He married **SHANNON LEE NEITZ** on 15 December 1990.

    3.5.12.1.2.4.2 **NICOLE JILL SNYDER** was born on 25 May 1972, Danville, Montour Co., PA. She married **KENNETH JOHN HEIM** on 5 September 1996, St. John's Lutheran Church, Leck Hill, Northumberland Co., PA.

3.5.12.1.3 ALMA MAE ROTHERMEL was born on 3 March 1925, Erdman, Dauphin County, PA. She married **ERNEST LUTHER KLINGER**, son of **LUTHER E. KLINGER** and **HELEN A. ENGLE**, circa 1946. She died on 10 May 2014, Harrisburg Hospital, Harrisburg, Dauphin County, PA, at age 89. She was buried on 14 May 2014, at Riverview Memorial Gardens, Halifax, Dauphin County, PA. According to a newspaper obituary, Alma was employed as a seamstress at DorMar Manufacturing, Gratz, and after retiring, she transported Amish to various places and appointments. For many years, Alma took part in the entertainment for the Pennsylvania Dutch Fersommling and taught Pennsylvania Dutch classes.

    3.5.12.1.3.1 MARY C. KLINGER (see above)

        3.5.12.1.3.1.1 MICHAEL E. LEITZEL (see above)

            3.5.12.1.3.1.1.1 SETH M. LEITZEL (see above)

            3.5.12.1.3.1.1.2 JOHN P. LEITZEL (see above)

            3.5.12.1.3.1.1.3 SARAH A. LEITZEL (see above)

    3.5.12.1.3.2 STEPHEN E. KLINGER (see above)

3.5.12.1.4 GUY WILLIAM ROTHERMEL was born on 18 May 1930, Lykens, Dauphin County, PA. He was baptized on 18 May 1930, Zion (Klinger's) Church, Erdman, Lykens Township, Dauphin County, PA. He married **FRANCES GRACE BAIR** on 29 August 1970. He died on 29 March 2014, Winfield, Union County, PA, at age 83. He was buried on 1 April 2014, at Shreiner's Cemetery, Shamokin Dam, Perry County, PA.

    3.5.12.1.4.1 KATHY ROTHERMEL married (--?--) **SHUR**.

    3.5.12.1.4.2 GUY W. ROTHERMEL JR. was born on 13 September 1965, Dauphin County, PA. He was baptized on 10 December 1965, Zion (Klinger's) Lutheran Church, Erdman, Dauphin County, PA. He married **KATHRYN SMITH**, daughter of **JACQUE LAMAR SMITH** and **JEANNETTE MARIE UPDEGRAVE**.

        3.5.12.1.4.2.1 DWIGHT ROTHERMEL was born on 1 October 1982.

3.5.12.2 ALLEN SAMUEL ROTHERMEL was born on 10 September 1895. He married **FLORENCE MAY SCHWALM**, daughter of **ANDREW J. SCHWALM** and **ROSA KEHRES**. He died on 7 March 1966, at age 70. He was buried at Himmel Church Cemetery, Rebuck, Northumberland County, PA.

    3.5.12.2.1 ROY ROTHERMEL was born on 30 March 1919. He died on 7 November 1926, at age 7. He was buried at Himmel Church Cemetery, Rebuck, Northumberland County, PA.

3.5.12.3 HANNAH JANE ROTHERMEL was born on 5 January 1899. She married **NALDY LEITZEL**, son of **GEORGE ADAM TROUTMAN LEITZEL** and **CATHERINE ALICE SNYDER**, on 27 December 1917. She died on 21 February 1973, at age 74. She was buried at Simeon Church Cemetery, Gratz, Dauphin County, PA.

    3.5.12.3.1 GUY MONROE LEITZEL was born on 3 August 1918. He was born on 3 August 1918, Lykens, Dauphin Co., PA. He married **BETTY LUCILLE KOPPENHAVER**, daughter of **CLARENCE ROBERT KOPPENHAVER**, on 21 November 1942, Church Parsonage, Elizabethville, Dauphin Co., PA. He died on 29 December 2003, at age 85. Prior to his death, Guy lived in Lemoyne, PA.

        3.5.12.3.1.1 RUTH ANN LEITZEL was born on 22 June 1946, Dauphin Co., PA. She was baptized on 18 August 1946, Simeon Reformed Church, Elizabethville, Dauphin Co., PA. She married **DONALD WAYNE ALLEN** on 20 June 1969, PA.

            3.5.12.3.1.1.1 TERRY MICHAEL ALLEN was born on 27 February 1969, PA. He married **TINA BURNS** on 5 March 1994, PA.

                3.5.12.3.1.1.1.1 ELIZABETH CHRISTINE ALLEN was born on 8 April 1994, PA.

            3.5.12.3.1.1.2 LISA ANN ALLEN was born on 29 November 1972.

        3.5.12.3.1.2 GLORIA JEAN LEITZEL was born on 18 April 1949, Dauphin Co., PA. She was baptized on 12 June 1949, Simeon Lutheran Church, Gratz, Dauphin Co., PA. She married **THOMAS LEININGER BOYER SR.** on 28 March 1969, PA.

            3.5.12.3.1.2.1 MICHELLE LYNN BOYER was born on 16 February 1969.

            3.5.12.3.1.2.2 THOMAS LEININGER BOYER JR. was born on 2 August 1969, Dauphin Co., PA.

            3.5.12.3.1.2.3 MICHELLE LYNN BOYER was born on 16 February 1973, Dauphin Co., PA.

3.5.12.3.1.3 BRENDA JOYCE LEITZEL was born on 8 October 1950, Dauphin Co., PA. She was baptized on 19 November 1950, Simeon Reformed Church, Gratz, Dauphin Co., PA. She married **RONALD GEORGE KIMMEL** on 10 October 1979, PA.

3.5.12.3.1.3.1 ERIN NICOLE KIMMEL was born on 16 July 1983, Dauphin Co., PA.

3.5.12.3.1.3.2 GREGORY SCOTT KIMMEL was born on 24 June 1984, Dauphin Co., PA.

3.5.12.3.2 LEE MELVIN LEITZEL was born on 16 September 1923. He married **DORIS VIRGINIA MAUSSER** circa 1948. He married **ANNA JANE WITMER** after 1960.

3.5.12.3.2.1 CHRISTINE ELIZABETH LEITZEL was born on 27 October 1949.

3.5.12.3.2.2 THOMAS LEE LEITZEL was born on 11 January 1952.

3.5.12.3.2.3 TIMOTHY PAUL LEITZEL was born on 23 May 1958.

3.5.12.3.3 ANNA LORRAINE LEITZEL was born on 21 December 1929. She married **JAMES HENRY LENKER**.

3.5.12.3.3.1 RICHARD EUGENE LENKER was born on 28 June 1952. He married **DEANNA LYNN RAMSEY** circa 1980.

3.5.12.3.3.1.1 ERIN LORRAINE LENKER was born on 31 August 1982.

3.5.12.3.3.2 JAMES ALLEN LENKER was born on 28 April 1956. He married **PATRICIA ANN MILLER** circa 1980.

3.5.12.3.3.2.1 BRIAN SCOTT LENKER was born on 29 January 1981.

3.5.12.3.3.2.2 ASHLEY LYNN LENKER was born on 24 December 1983.

3.5.13 ABRAHAM W. ROTHERMEL was born on 8 March 1864. He married **ELIZABETH ELLEN HOFFMAN** circa 1887. He died on 31 July 1950, Klingerstown, Schuylkill County, PA, at age 86. He was buried at Zion (Klinger's) Church, Erdman, Lykens Township, Dauphin County, PA.

3.5.13.1 INFANT SON ROTHERMEL was born on 4 June 1888, Klingerstown, Schuylkill County, PA. He died Klingerstown, Schuylkill County, PA,, in infancy. He was buried at Zion (Klinger's) Church Cemetery, Erdman, Lykens Township, Dauphin County, PA.

3.5.13.2 INFANT DAUGHTER ROTHERMEL was born on 4 June 1888, Klingerstown, Schuylkill County, PA. She died in infancy. She was buried at Zion (Klinger's) Church Cemetery, Erdman, Lykens Township, Dauphin County, PA.

3.5.13.3 INFANT SON ROTHERMEL was born on 20 December 1892, Klingerstown, Schuylkill County, PA. He died in 1892, Klingerstown, Schuylkill County, PA. He was buried at Zion (Klinger's) Church Cemetery, Erdman, Lykens Township, Dauphin County, PA.

3.5.13.4 JAY WILLIAM ROTHERMEL is also referred to as **JOSEPH W.** in some sources. He was born on 20 December 1892, Klingerstown, Schuylkill County, PA. He married **CORA V. KEISER**. He died on 2 January 1949, at age 56. He was buried at Zion (Klinger's) Church Cemetery, Erdman, Lykens Township, Dauphin County, PA.

3.5.13.5 MAE H. E. ROTHERMEL was born on 1 November 1901, Klingerstown, Schuylkill County, PA. She married **ALVIN KLOUSER**. She died on 11 January 1966, Klingerstown, Schuylkill County, PA, at age 64. Funeral held at Klinger's Church, Erdman, Dauphin County, PA, 15 Jan 1966.

3.5.14 HANNAH ROTHERMEL was born on 19 October 1866. She married **AMMON I. HOUCK** circa 1887. She died on 13 February 1929, at age 62. She was buried at Jacob's (Howerter's) Church Cemetery, Pitman, Eldred Township, Schuylkill County, PA.

3.5.14.1 INFANT HOUCK was born on 27 October 1887. He/she died on 28 October 1887.

3.5.14.2 JENNIE MABEL HOUCK was born in May 1893. She married **WILLIAM FREEMAN SCHREFFLER** on 28 November 1914, Pitman, Eldred Township, Schuylkill County, PA. She died on 26 September 1972, at age 79.

3.5.14.3 ANNIE DELLA HOUCK was born in May 1893. She married **GEORGE E. PAUL** circa 1916. She died in November 1937, at age 44.

3.5.14.3.1 GEORGE A. PAUL was born circa 1917.

3.5.14.3.2 HARLAN F. PAUL was born circa 1922.

3.5.14.4 MAZIE E. HOUCK was born on 28 May 1895. She died on 14 January 1912, Pitman, Eldred Township, Schuylkill County, PA, at age 16.

3.5.15 ISAAC MONROE ROTHERMEL is also referred to as **MONROE ROTHERMOL** in some sources. He was born on 28 August 1874. He was baptized on 7 November 1874, Zion (Klinger's) Church, Erdman, Lykens Township, Dauphin County, PA.

3.6 JACOB KLINGER WIEST was born on 23 June 1826, Jordan Township, Northumberland County, PA. He married **ELIZABETH TROUTMAN**, daughter of **PETER TROUTMAN** and **ELIZABETH BODDEIGER**. The Genealogical & Biographical Annals of Northumberland County (1911) says that: "Jacob K. Wiest, son of Samuel and grandson of Jacob, was born Jan. 14, 1821, in Jordan township, Northumberland county, and died April 20, 1877. He was a farmer in Jordan township, owning a tract of 120 acres, and during the winter time following butchering and selling meat. He was also engaged in droving, and in buying and selling cattle, to some extent. For eight years before his death he lived retired, making his home in Uniontown, where he owned a house and where he died. He and his wife, Elizabeth (Trautman) daughter of Peter Trautman (whose wife's name was Potteiger), are buried at Klingers Church; she was struck dead by lightning, while walking through the kitchen. Their children were Harry, John T., Amelia (married Reuben Shade), Frank, Samuel, E. T., Catharine (married Edward Witmer, of Allentown, Pa.), Monroe (of Allentown, Pa.), Jacob (deceased), Preston and William." He died on 23 October 1878, Klingerstown, Schuylkill County, PA, at age 52. He was buried at Zion (Klinger's) Church, Erdman, Lykens Township, Dauphin County, PA.

3.6.1 HARRY TROUTMAN WIEST was born on 24 November 1844. He married **CATHERINE SCHMELTZ**, daughter of **DANIEL SCHMELTZ** and **ANNA MARIA MILLER**. He died on 1 April 1917, at age 72. He was buried at Zion (Klinger's) Church, Erdman, Lykens Township, Dauphin County, PA.

3.6.1.1 NATHANIEL ANDREW WIEST was born on 25 June 1868. He married **EMMA VESTA SCHWALM**, daughter of **FREDERICK STEIN SCHWALM** and **SARAH ANN RUBENDALL**, circa 1894. Nathaniel Andrew Wiest owned and operated a farm located about two miles east of Klingerstown. There is a photograph of Emma and Nathaniel's family in the Journal of Johannes Schwalm Historical Association, vol. 2, no. 4, p. 89 (1984). He died on 17 January 1941, PA at age 72. He was buried on 22 January 1941, at Zion (Klinger's) Church, Erdman, Lykens Township, Dauphin County, PA.

3.6.1.1.1 MINNIE EDNA WIEST was born on 27 January 1896. Some sources record that she was born on 22 January 1895. She married **GURNEY ARTHUR STARR**, son of **OSCAR ADAM STARR** and **ELIZABETH SOPHRONIA KNORR**, circa 1914. She died on 13 June 1966, at age 70.

3.6.1.1.1.1 RUSSELL WOODROW STARR was born on 30 December 1915, Klingerstown, Schuylkill County, PA. He married **MABEL HANNA REINER**. He lived in R.D. # 1, Klingerstown, Schuylkill County, PA. He died on 7 December 1994, Tremont Nursing Center, Tremont, Schuylkill County, PA, at age 78. He was buried at Salem Cemetery, Klingerstown, Schuylkill County, PA.

3.6.1.1.1.1.1 BEVERLY N. STARR was born on 9 November 1938. She married **BOYD L. WEDDE**. She died on 13 April 1979, at age 40. She was buried at St. Johns United Church of Christ Cemetery, Ashland, Schuylkill County, PA.

3.6.1.1.1.1.1.1 RANDAL ALLEN WEDDE was born on 26 November 1957.

3.6.1.1.1.1.1.2 BEVERLY SUE WEDDE was born on 7 July 1959.

3.6.1.1.1.1.1.3 PEGGY ANN WEDDE was born on 28 November 1965.

3.6.1.1.1.1.2 MARIE STARR was born on 30 November 1941. She married **LARRY MILLER**. She died on 1 March 1979, at age 37.

3.6.1.1.1.1.3 DENNIS E. STARR married (--?--) **HEPNER**. He was born on 20 September 1945.

3.6.1.1.1.1.3.1 TROY STARR married **GEORGINA MARIE STAUFFER**, daughter of **THOMAS RAY STAUFFER** and **SHARON LOUISE MASSER**.

3.6.1.1.1.1.3.1.1 MORGANNE STARR

3.6.1.1.1.1.3.1.2 TYLER STARR

3.6.1.1.1.1.4 CHRISTINE STARR was born on 19 March 1961. She married (--?--) **GESSNER** in 1970.

3.6.1.1.1.2 BLANCHE IRENE STARR was born on 6 May 1918, Klingerstown, Schuylkill County, PA. She married **JOHN ELIAS OXENRIDER**, son of **FRANCIS GORDON OXENRIDER** and **SARAH FALCK**, on 16 April 1938. She died on 22 June 1972, Herndon, Jackson Township, Northumberland County, PA, at age 54, when her home was caught in a landslide caused by Tropical Storm Agnes. According to newspaper reports, she was killed inside her home, which collapsed under the force of the landslide. Her husband John was seriously injured. She was buried at St. John's Reformed Church Cemetery, Leck Kill, Northumberland County, PA.

3.6.1.1.1.2.1 WILLIAM RUSSELL OXENRIDER is also referred to as **WILLIAM A. OXENRIDER** in some sources. He was born on 8 October 1938, PA. He married **JOANN (--?--)**.

3.6.1.1.1.2.1.1 WILLIAM E. OXENRIDER JR.

3.6.1.1.1.2.1.2 JOHNNY LYNN OXENRIDER

3.6.1.1.1.2.1.3 CHRISTOPHER LEE OXENRIDER

3.6.1.1.1.2.2 FLORENCE IRENE OXENRIDER was born on 14 February 1941, PA. She was baptized on 23 March 1941, Salem (Herb's) Lutheran & Reformed Church, Rough & Ready, Schuylkill County, PA. She married **LEE DALE DOCKEY**, son of **PAUL G. DOCKEY** and **SYLVIA LAURA RADEL**, circa 1957.

3.6.1.1.1.2.2.1 YVONNE I. DOCKEY was born on 6 March 1959, PA. She married **RODNEY ROY ROMBERGER**.

3.6.1.1.1.2.2.1.1 RYAN R. ROMBERGER was born on 15 August 1983, Dauphin Co., PA.

3.6.1.1.1.2.2.1.2 KYLE L. ROMBERGER was born on 15 August 1985, Dauphin Co., PA.

3.6.1.1.1.3 ALMA MARIE STARR was born on 20 February 1920. She married **MARLIN JEFFERSON SCHREFFLER**.

3.6.1.1.1.3.1 MAYNARD E. SCHREFFLER was born on 23 July 1939.

3.6.1.1.1.3.2 JANICE SCHREFFLER was born on 13 January 1943. She married **(--?--) DEFACIS**.

3.6.1.1.1.3.3 LARRY STEVEN SCHREFFLER was born on 14 April 1945, Dillsburg, York County, PA. He married **BARBARA REIDINGER**. He died on 13 January 2013, Dillsburg, York County, PA, at age 67.

3.6.1.1.1.3.3.1 CURTIS SCHREFFLER married **URSULA (--?--)**.

3.6.1.1.1.3.3.1.1 AUSTIN SCHREFFLER

3.6.1.1.1.3.3.1.2 LEAH SCHREFFLER

3.6.1.1.1.3.3.1.3 SHYLA SCHREFFLER

3.6.1.1.1.3.3.1.4 LESLIE SCHREFFLER

3.6.1.1.1.3.3.2 JULIE SCHREFFLER married **ERNIE ELLER**.

3.6.1.1.1.3.3.2.1 KYRSTEN ELLER

3.6.1.1.1.3.3.2.2 DUNCAN ELLER

3.6.1.1.1.3.4 MARLIN RANDY SCHREFFLER was born on 14 December 1952. He married **LINDA MIELKE** on 8 April 1972.

3.6.1.1.1.3.4.1 JASON F. SCHREFFLER married **AMY J. WALT**.

3.6.1.1.1.3.4.1.1 ASHLEY NICOLE SCHREFFLER

3.6.1.1.1.3.4.2 JUSTIN SCHREFFLER

3.6.1.1.1.4 EARL WELLINGTON STARR was born on 6 November 1922. He was baptized on 24 December 1922, Salem (Herb's) Lutheran and Reformed Church, Rough and Ready, Schuylkill County, PA. He married **MARY H. LAUDENSLAGER**, daughter of **JOSEPH DANIEL LAUDENSLAGER** and **LAURA ALVERNA WIEST**. He died on 27 September 2002, at his home on North Center Street Gratz, Dauphin County, PA, at age 79. He was buried at Gratz Union Cemetery, Gratz, Dauphin County, PA.

3.6.1.1.1.4.1 CAROLYN LOUISE STARR is also referred to as **CAROL** in some sources. She was born on 13 February 1942, Lykens Township, Dauphin Co., PA. She married **ROY EDWIN BARRY**, son of **JOHN EARL BARRY** and **CORA MAE TROUTMAN**, on 14 August 1958, St. Peter's (Hoffman's) Church in Lykens Township, Dauphin Co., PA. She married **(--?--) BARRY**.

3.6.1.1.1.4.1.1 EDWIN ROY BARRY was born on 21 December 1958, Polyclinic Hospital, Harrisburg, Dauphin Co., PA. He married **WANDA MARBERGER** on 19 August 1981.

3.6.1.1.1.4.1.2 SCOTT EARL BARRY was born on 22 February 1961, Polyclinic Hospital, Harrisburg, Dauphin Co., PA. He married **HOLLY MARIE LEISER** on 18 May 1985.

3.6.1.1.1.4.1.2.1 MEAGAN HOLLY BARRY was born on 4 September 1986, PA.

3.6.1.1.1.4.1.2.2 FAITH ELIZABETH BARRY was born on 26 April 1989, PA.

3.6.1.1.1.4.1.2.3 RACHEL LOUISE BARRY was born on 26 April 1989, PA.

3.6.1.1.1.4.2 DARLENE KAY STARR was born on 12 July 1949, Klingerstown, Schuylkill County, PA. She married **GARY HARNER** circa 1967. She married **GALEN PAUL HOFFMAN JR.** on 21 June 1969. She died on 10 August 1997, at age 48. She died on 10 August 1997, Valley View, Schuylkill County, PA, at age 48. She was buried on 13 August 1997, at Simeon United Lutheran Church Cemetery, Gratz, Dauphin Co., PA.

3.6.1.1.1.4.2.1 GALEN PAUL HOFFMAN III was born on 24 February 1970, Pottsville Hospital, Pottsville, Schuylkill County, PA.

3.6.1.1.1.4.2.1.1 KYLE PAUL HOFFMAN was born in 1993.

3.6.1.1.1.4.2.2 GRETA JANE HOFFMAN was born on 23 February 1972, Pottsville Hospital, Pottsville, Schuylkill County, PA. She married **JOSEPH CONRAD** circa 1994.

3.6.1.1.1.4.2.2.1 ALSTON CONRAD was born circa 1996.

3.6.1.1.1.4.2.2.2 REILY CONRAD was born circa 1998.

3.6.1.1.1.4.2.3 KEITH BRADLEY HOFFMAN was born on 7 February 1976, Pottsville Hospital, Pottsville, Schuylkill County, PA.

3.6.1.1.1.4.3 SHIRLEY IRENE STARR was born on 8 November 1950, Klingerstown, Schuylkill County, PA. She married **CHARLES B. HAIN**, son of **CHARLES EDGAR HAIN** and **ANNIE MARIE SHIRO,** on 28 March 1969. She died on 25 June 1990, at age 39. She died on 25 June 1990, Gratz, Dauphin Co., PA, at age 39. She was buried after 25 June 1990, at Simeon United Lutheran Church Cemetery, Gratz, Dauphin Co., PA.

3.6.1.1.1.4.3.1 STACEY MARIE HAIN was born on 11 September 1969, Dauphin Co., PA. She married (--?--) **DOWNEY** circa 1991.

3.6.1.1.1.4.3.2 KYLIE ANNIE HAIN was born on 31 January 1979, Dauphin Co., PA. She married **STEPHEN P. BOYER** circa 1997.

3.6.1.1.1.4.3.2.1 PATRICK STEPHEN BOYER was born on 25 December 1999, Dauphin Co., PA.

3.6.1.1.1.4.3.3 BRYANT CHARLES HAIN was born on 24 October 1980, Dauphin Co., PA.

3.6.1.1.1.5 NEVIN WILLARD STARR was born on 10 June 1926, Klingerstown, Schuylkill County, PA. He was baptized on 18 July 1926, Salem (Herb's) Lutheran & Reformed Church, Rough and Ready, Schuylkill County, PA. He married **PEGGY LOU SWAB.** Nevin Starr was a carpenter in Trevorton, Zerbe Township, Northumberland County, PA. Other sources list him as a retired trucker. Prior to his death, Nevin lived in the vicinity of Elizabethville, Dauphin County, PA. He died on 16 February 1995, Polyclinic Medical Center, Harrisburg, Dauphin County, PA, at age 68. He was buried at Maple Grove Cemetery, Elizabethville, Dauphin County, PA. Some sources list additional children (Darlene, Carolus, and Linwood) for Nevin and Peggy Lou Starr, but this is questionable.

3.6.1.1.1.5.1 GARY FRANKLIN STARR was born on 1 January 1949. Some sources record that he was born on 21 January 1950, Elizabethville, Dauphin Co., PA. He married **PEGGY SNYDER** circa 1968. He married **CYNTHIA MARIE STROUP** on 14 June 1975.

3.6.1.1.1.5.1.1 BRANDI MARIE STARR was born on 24 July 1969, Pottsville, Schuylkill County, PA.

3.6.1.1.1.5.1.2 CHRISTOPHER STARR was born circa 1971, Schuylkill County, PA.

3.6.1.1.1.6 RUBY EDNA STARR was born on 23 August 1928. She married LAWRENCE HENRY SCHWALM, son of JOHN ALFRED SCHWALM and MARGARET ALICE KLINGER. She married LOUIS E. WOOD, son of CHARLES WOOD and DORA PEARSON, circa 1994.

3.6.1.1.1.6.1 SONJA SCHWALM. Some sources omit Sonja from the listing of the children of Ruby Edna Starr and Lawrence Schwalm.

3.6.1.1.1.6.2 REBECCA J. SCHWALM is also referred to as REBECCA J. STARR in some sources. She was born on 10 March 1943, Rebuck, Northumberland County, PA. She married JAMES W. CLARK, son of CALVIN A. CLARK and MAZIE C. SCHADEL. She died on 5 April 2005, at home, Elizabethville, Dauphin County, PA, at age 62. According to a newspaper obituary, Rebecca was a machine trainer at the Brubaker Tool Co., Millersburg, Dauphin County, PA. She was buried on 9 April 2005, at Riverview Memorial Gardens, Halifax, Dauphin County, PA.

3.6.1.1.1.6.2.1 LISA K. CLARK was born on 26 October 1965, Harrisburg, Dauphin County, PA. She married KEVIN L. STRAUB, son of MARLIN N. STRAUB and DARLEE MICKA. She lived in 178 Market Street, Berrysburg, Dauphin County, PA. She died on 13 November 2004, at the home of her parents, Mifflin Township, Dauphin County, PA, at age 39. She was buried at Riverview Memorial Gardens, Halifax, Dauphin County, PA.

3.6.1.1.1.6.2.1.1 NOLAN CLARK STRAUB was born on 9 May 1993, Harrisburg Hospital, Harrisburg, Dauphin County, PA.

3.6.1.1.1.6.2.1.2 NICHOLAS C. STRAUB was born on 3 December 1999, Pinnacle Health Harrisburg Hospital, Harrisburg, Dauphin County, PA.

3.6.1.1.1.6.3 GLEN HENRY SCHWALM was born on 27 January 1945, Rebuck, Northumberland County, PA. Some sources record that he was born on 10 March 1945. He married MARY E. MAUSER on 16 April 1965, Salem United Church of Christ, Elizabethville, Dauphin County, PA. He married DEBRA MARIE WELKER circa 1997. He died on 10 February 2000, Osteopathic Hospital, Harrisburg, Dauphin County, PA, at age 55.

3.6.1.1.1.6.3.1 TANIA LEE SCHWALM was born on 29 July 1965, Dauphin County, PA. She was baptized on 10 October 1965, Salem United Church of Christ, Elizabethville, Dauphin County, PA. She married TIMOTHY LEE MAURER, son of BRUCE ELWOOD MAURER and YVONNE RIEGEL, circa 1983.

3.6.1.1.1.6.3.1.1 STEVEN MAURER was born on 7 May 1985, Dauphin County, PA.

3.6.1.1.1.6.3.2 GLEN H. SCHWALM was born on 22 September 1966, Dauphin County, PA. He married LORIE ANN MAUS on 14 February 1987.

3.6.1.1.1.6.3.2.1 TRAVIS RYAN SCHWALM was born on 11 August 1994. He was baptized on 26 February 1995, Salem United Church of Christ, Elizabethville, Dauphin County, PA.

3.6.1.1.1.6.3.2.2 KELSEY RAE SCHWALM was born on 9 August 1996, Holy Spirit Hospital, East Pennsboro Township, Dauphin County, PA. She was baptized on 8 December 1996, Salem United Church of Christ, Elizabethville, Dauphin County, PA.

3.6.1.1.2 NEVIN ANDREW WIEST was born on 3 September 1897. He married LORETTA MAE KOCK, daughter of HOWARD KOCK and FLORA HEISER. He died on 6 March 1982, Shamokin State General Hospital, Shamokin, Northumberland County, PA, at age 84. He was buried on 9 March 1982, at Odd Fellows Cemetery, Shamokin, Northumberland County, PA.

3.6.1.1.2.1 DARLENE ADELINE WIEST was born on 3 April 1929, Trevorton, Zerbe Township, Northumberland County, PA. She married ROBERT HANKEN. She died on 20 August 2006, Staten Island, Richmond County, NY, at age 77.

3.6.1.1.2.1.1 DANIEL HANKEN was born on 12 January 1953.

3.6.1.1.2.1.2 MELISSA HANKEN was born on 27 May 1957.

3.6.1.1.2.1.3 JULIA HANKEN was born on 1 August 1961. She married (--?--) GABRIEL.

3.6.1.1.2.1.4 LAURIE HANKEN was born on 9 December 1967. She married (--?--) TORRES.

3.6.1.1.2.2 LINWOOD NEVIN WIEST was born on 23 July 1931, Trevorton, Zerbe Township, Northumberland County, PA. He married AUDREY M. ANDREWS in 1953. He died on 1 May 1991, at his home on Trevorton Road Shamokin, Northumberland County, PA, at age 59. He was buried at Odd Fellows Cemetery, Shamokin, Northumberland County, PA.

3.6.1.1.2.2.1 ANDREW WIEST was born on 1 May 1965.

3.6.1.1.2.2.2 JENNIFER WIEST was born on 30 March 1968.

3.6.1.1.2.3 CARLOS HOWARD WIEST was born on 24 October 1932, Trevorton, Zerbe Township, Northumberland County, PA. He married LOIS NICKERSON. He married BEATRICE S. DIX on 20 November 1965, Orange County, CA. Carlos lives in Anaheim, CA.

3.6.1.1.2.3.1 JEFFREY WIEST was born on 6 September 1954.

3.6.1.1.2.3.2 CYNTHIA WIEST was born on 22 August 1955. She married (--?--) GRAINEY.

3.6.1.1.2.3.3 DENNIS WIEST was born on 23 October 1957.

3.6.1.1.2.3.4 WENDY WIEST was born on 2 August 1959.

3.6.1.1.2.3.5 GREGORY WIEST was born on 25 January 1962.

3.6.1.1.2.3.6 DAWN WIEST was born on 5 September 1966. She married (--?--) HAMILL.

3.6.1.1.2.3.7 KEVIN WIEST was born on 27 December 1971.

3.6.1.1.2.4 MARDELL S. WIEST was born on 11 May 1934, Trevorton, Zerbe Township, Northumberland County, PA. She married JACOB R. WALZ JR. on 6 June 1953. She died on 15 June 2001, Manor Care Health Services, Sunbury, Northumberland County, PA, at age 67. She was buried at Northumberland Memorial Park, Stonington, Northumberland County, PA.

3.6.1.1.2.4.1 JEAN WALZ was born on 27 May 1954. She married CHARLES RITZMAN.

3.6.1.1.2.4.1.1 BRADLEY RITZMAN

3.6.1.1.2.4.2 PEGGY WALZ was born on 18 July 1958. She married TIMOTHY LAGERMAN.

3.6.1.1.2.4.2.1 TIMOTHY LAGERMAN II

3.6.1.1.2.4.2.2 DANIEL LAGERMAN

3.6.1.1.2.4.2.3 DAVID LAGERMAN

3.6.1.1.2.4.2.4 SARAH LAGERMAN

3.6.1.1.2.5 MASON N. WIEST was born on 5 August 1935, Trevorton, Zerbe Township, Northumberland County, PA. He married FRANCIS ANSKIS.

3.6.1.1.2.5.1 DARLENE WIEST was born on 12 August 1956. She married (--?--) BRANNON.

3.6.1.1.2.5.2 CAROL WIEST was born on 17 June 1962. She married (--?--) DAWES.

3.6.1.1.2.5.3 DAVID WIEST was born on 10 June 1964.

3.6.1.1.2.5.4 TAMMY WIEST married (--?--) MILLER. She was born on 26 July 1968.

3.6.1.1.2.6 ANNETTA MAE WIEST is also referred to as ENNETTE M. WIEST in some sources. She was born on 14 November 1937, Trevorton, Zerbe Township, Northumberland County, PA. She died in 1953, in a drowning accident at Saylor's Lake, near Saylorsburg, Monroe County, PA. She was buried at I.O.O.F. (Odd Fellow's) Cemetery, Shamokin, Northumberland County, PA.

3.6.1.1.2.7 BRIENT ARDEN WIEST was born on 3 July 1938, Trevorton, Zerbe Township, Northumberland County, PA. He married LOUISE TENTROMANO on 23 August 1958. Brient and his wife Louise, along with their three children and 5 grandchildren (Tony, Tyler, Cory, Brooke, and Olivia) celebrated their 50th wedding anniversary on August 23, 2008. Brient lives in Trevorton, PA.

3.6.1.1.2.7.1 BRIAN DAVID WIEST was born on 13 July 1960. He married VICTORIA (--?--).

3.6.1.1.2.7.2 ANTHONY WIEST was born on 14 April 1962. He married **LINDA (--?--)**.

3.6.1.1.2.7.3 MELANIE WIEST was born on 18 November 1963. She married **(--?--) HAAS**.

3.6.1.1.2.8 BERNITA JANE WIEST was born on 12 October 1939, Trevorton, Zerbe Township, Northumberland County, PA. Some sources record that she was born on 12 October 1931. She married **J. ROBERT KLOCK**. She married **JOHN W. MCCARTHY** on 5 August 1978. She lived in 122 Fairview Avenue, Sunbury, Northumberland County, PA. She died on 23 October 2000, Sunbury Community Hospital, Sunbury, Northumberland County, PA, at age 61. Some sources record that she died on 23 December 2000 Sunbury Community Hospital, Sunbury, Northumberland County, PA. She was buried at Pomfret Manor Cemetery, Sunbury, Northumberland County, PA.

3.6.1.1.2.8.1 DARLA KLOCK was born on 15 March 1958. She married **NATHAN REIGLE**.

3.6.1.1.2.8.2 BRUCE KLOCK was born on 22 October 1959. He married **SHERRY (--?--)**.

3.6.1.1.2.8.3 ROBERT KLOCK JR. was born on 22 August 1964. He married **PATRICIA (--?--)**.

3.6.1.1.2.8.4 TERRY MCCARTHY

3.6.1.1.2.8.5 NANCY MCCARTHY married **JEFF SHAWVER**.

3.6.1.1.2.8.6 ANN LOUISE MCCARTHY

3.6.1.1.2.9 NEVIN ANDREW WIEST JR. was born on 28 April 1943, Trevorton, Zerbe Township, Northumberland County, PA. He married **JOYCE (--?--)** on 25 November 1989, Broward County, FL. He died on 28 September 2002, Broward Medical Center, Deerfield Beach, Broward County, FL, at age 59. According to a newspaper obituary, after attending school in Trevorton, PA, Nevin was self-employed in Hanover, PA, refinishing and selling antique furniture. In the 1970's, he moved to Florida where he worked for Boca Resort and Club in Boca Raton, FL. He was married twice but had no children.

3.6.1.1.2.10 GLORIA JEAN WIEST. Gloria Jean lives in Trevorton, PA. She was born on 8 February 1945, Trevorton, Zerbe Township, Northumberland County, PA. She married **FRANKLIN BARTHOLOMEW**. She married **RICHARD AZINGER**. She married **WILLIAM PERSING**.

3.6.1.1.2.10.1 RICHARD BARTHOLOMEW was born on 16 May 1965.

3.6.1.1.2.10.2 VINCENT AZINGER was born on 30 April 1973.

3.6.1.1.2.11 CAROLYN M. WIEST was born on 20 June 1946, Trevorton, Northumberland County, PA. She married **RAYMOND R. HEATH**. She married **PHIL SIPERKO** on 25 November 1989. She died on 4 March 2010, Shamokin Area Community Hospital, Shamokin, Northumberland County, PA, at age 63. According to a newspaper obituary, Carolyn lived in Coal Township, Northumberland County, PA, for more than 40 years.

After graduating from Trevorton High School and McCann School of Business, she worked as an office clerk for Weis Markets, Sunbury.

3.6.1.1.2.11.1 BRENDA HEATH was born on 2 July 1965. She married **STEPHEN HUFF**.

3.6.1.1.2.11.1.1 GRACE JIEYUN HUFF

3.6.1.1.2.11.2 JEFFREY HEATH was born on 26 June 1969. He married **TRACEY (--?--)**.

3.6.1.1.2.11.3 MICHAEL SIPERKO married **KELLY (--?--)**. Michael was a step-son.

3.6.1.1.2.11.4 MICHELLE SIPERKO married **SHAWN WARG**. Michelle was a step-daughter.

3.6.1.1.3 MAISIE JEMIMA WIEST is also referred to as **MAIZIE** in some sources. She was born on 19 May 1900, Lykens Township, Dauphin County, PA. She married **JAMES M. MILLER**, son of **JAMES MILLER** and **LIZZIE (--?--)**, on 10 August 1918, Leck Kill, Northumberland County, PA. She died on 16 March 1974, Pottsville Hospital, Pottsville, Schuylkill County, PA, at age 73. She was buried on 20 March 1974, at Salem United Church of Christ Cemetery, Rough and Ready, Schuylkill County, PA.

3.6.1.1.3.1 FLORENCE MILLER was born on 16 February 1919. She died on 22 February 1919.

3.6.1.1.3.2 Darwin Eugene Miller was born on 6 October 1922, Klingerstown, Schuylkill County, PA. He was baptized on 20 October 1922, Salem (Herb's) Lutheran and Reformed Church, Rough and Ready, Schuylkill County, PA. He married **Theresa F. Webry**. He was buried on 15 February 1974, at Trinity Lutheran Church Cemetery, Valley View, Schuylkill County, PA. He died on 11 February 1975, Geisinger Medical Center, Danville, Montour County, PA, at age 52.

> **3.6.1.1.3.2.1 Craig Miller** was born on 15 October 1948. He married **Linda Mae Spotts** on 16 June 1973.
>
>> **3.6.1.1.3.2.1.1 Brian Miller** was born circa 1975, Norristown, Montgomery County, PA.
>>
>> **3.6.1.1.3.2.1.2 Brent Miller** was born circa 1975.
>>
>> **3.6.1.1.3.2.1.3 Brooke Miller** was born circa 1977.
>
> **3.6.1.1.3.2.2 Peggy Miller** was born on 7 April 1954. She married **Roy Klinger**.

3.6.1.1.3.3 Barbara Ann Miller was born on 24 March 1939. She married **Richard Bowman**.

> **3.6.1.1.3.3.1 Debra Bowman** was born on 26 May 1958. She married **(--?--) Dwyer**.
>
> **3.6.1.1.3.3.2 Richard Bowman II** was born on 25 May 1960.
>
> **3.6.1.1.3.3.3 Linda Bowman** was born on 28 December 1963.

3.6.1.1.4 Infant Son Wiest was born in April 1902. He died on 10 April 1902.

3.6.1.1.5 Kathryn Mae Wiest also went by the name of **Katie**. She was born on 22 February 1905. She married **William Allen Deibert**, son of **George Edward Wiest Deibert** and **S. Alice (--?--)**. She died on 10 January 1980, Susquehanna Lutheran Village, Millersburg, Dauphin County, PA, at age 74. She was buried on 12 January 1980, at Zion (Klinger's) Lutheran Church Cemetery, Erdman, Dauphin County, PA.

> **3.6.1.1.5.1 George Nathaniel Deibert** was born on 3 March 1929, RR 1, Klingerstown, Schuylkill County, PA. He married **Arlene Ellen Blyler**, daughter of **Daniel Blyler** and **Dorothy Carl**, circa 1951. He died on 7 November 2002, Milton Hershey Medical Center, Hershey, Derry Township, Dauphin County, PA, at age 73. He was buried on 11 November 2002, at Zion (Klinger's) Church, Erdman, Lykens Township, Dauphin County, PA.
>
>> **3.6.1.1.5.1.1 Michael George Deibert** was born on 8 June 1958. He married **Alissa Harner** on 28 February 1981, Zion (Klinger's) Church, Erdman, Lykens Township, Dauphin County, PA. He married **Jacqueline L. Kimmel**, daughter of **Robert Kimmel** and **Janell (--?--)**, on 11 June 1988, St. John's Lutheran Church, Ashland, PA.
>>
>>> **3.6.1.1.5.1.1.1 Lauran Ashley Deibert** was born on 14 December 1994.
>>>
>>> **3.6.1.1.5.1.1.2 Jessica Alexis Deibert** was born on 14 December 1994.
>>>
>>> **3.6.1.1.5.1.1.3 Kori Nicole Deibert** was born on 4 November 1997, Reading Hospital, Reading, Berks County, PA.

3.6.1.1.6 Clarence Edwin Wiest also went by the name of **Clippy Wiest**. He was born on 26 January 1907. Some sources record that he was born on 26 January 1908, Klingerstown, Schuylkill County, PA. He married **Irene Katherine Reed**, daughter of **John S. Reed** and **Vertie J. Geist**, on 24 December 1934, Lykens, Dauphin County, PA. He died on 4 February 1992, Community Hospital, Sunbury, Northumberland County, PA, at age 85. He was buried on 8 February 1992, at Zion (Klinger's) Church Cemetery, Erdman, Lykens Township, Dauphin County, PA.

> **3.6.1.1.6.1 Larona A. Wiest** is also referred to as **Leona** in some sources. She was born on 27 April 1936. She married **Lamar R. Klinger**, son of **Ralph Raymond Klinger** and **Hilda S. Mattern**, on 27 August 1955, Salem (Herb's) Church, Rough and Ready, Schuylkill County, PA. She married **H. Charles Smink**, son of **Henry Smink** and **Mary Knerr**, circa 1979, Pitman RD, Schuylkill County, PA.
>
>> **3.6.1.1.6.1.1 Charlene Kay Klinger** was born on 9 September 1956, Sunbury, Northumberland County, PA. She was baptized on 7 October 1956, Salem (Herb's) Church, Sunbury, Northumberland County, PA. She married **Homer E. Woodring Jr.**, son of **Homer E. Woodring Sr.** and **Marion E. Woodring**, circa 1984.

3.6.1.1.6.1.1.1 SARAH ELIZABETH WOODRING was born on 13 July 1986, Northumberland Co., PA.

3.6.1.1.6.1.1.2 EMILY WOODRING was born in 1988, Northumberland Co., PA.

3.6.1.1.6.1.2 BONITA EILEEN KLINGER also went by the name of **BONNIE**. She was born on 24 August 1958. She was baptized on 21 September 1958, Salem (Herb's) Church, Rough and Ready, Schuylkill County, PA. She married **JAMES SNYDER**.

3.6.1.1.6.1.2.1 ASHLEY JAMES SNYDER married **ALISSA KEHLER** on 5 October 2002, St. John's Lutheran Church, Leck Kill, Northumberland County, PA.

3.6.1.1.6.1.2.1.1 ALEXANDRA GRACE SNYDER was born on 5 October 2005.

3.6.1.1.6.1.2.2 ALEXIS LAMAR SNYDER

3.6.1.1.6.1.3 BRIAN LAMAR KLINGER is also referred to as **BRYAN KLINGER** in some sources. He was born on 2 September 1962, Danville, Montour County, PA. He was baptized on 30 September 1962, Salem (Herb's) Church, Rough and Ready, Schuylkill County, PA. He married **SHEILA HERB**, daughter of **ANTHONY HERB** and **GLADYS** (--?--).

3.6.1.1.6.1.3.1 TRISHIA NICOLE KLINGER was born on 13 July 1987. She was baptized on 27 September 1987, St. Michael's Lutheran Church, Klingerstown, Schuylkill County, PA.

3.6.1.1.6.1.3.2 ALYSSA MARIE KLINGER was born on 14 August 1990, Harrisburg Hospital, Harrisburg, Dauphin County, PA. She was baptized on 11 September 1990, St. Michael's Lutheran Church, Klingerstown, Schuylkill County, PA.

3.6.1.1.6.1.4 TODD LAMAR KLINGER was born on 14 December 1969, Danville, Montour County, PA. He was baptized on 25 January 1970, Salem (Herb's) Church, Rough and Ready, Schuylkill County, PA. He married **BETTY ELLEN WEHRY**, daughter of **LLOYD E. WEHRY** and **DORICE A. KEHLER,** on 19 July 1997, Himmel's Church, Rebuck, Northumberland County, PA.

3.6.1.1.6.1.4.1 DELANEY KATHERINE KLINGER was born on 21 November 2001, Hershey Medical Center, Dauphin County, PA.

3.6.1.1.6.1.4.2 RHETT CHARLES KLINGER was born on 9 October 2003, Geisinger Medical Center, Danville, Montour County, PA.

3.6.1.1.7 ANNA IRENE WIEST was born on 6 May 1912, at Klingerstown RD. She married **GUY L. BIXLER**. She died on 27 August 1977, Mechanicsburg Rehabilitation Center, Mechanicsburg, Cumberland County, PA, at age 65. She was buried on 30 August 1977, at St. Andrew's Church Cemetery, Valley View, Schuylkill County, PA.

3.6.1.1.7.1 RONALD BIXLER was born on 17 August 1940. He married **SANDRA ROSENSTAEL**.

3.6.1.1.7.1.1 JENNIFER BIXLER was born on 2 April 1974. She married (--?--) **TELESCA**.

3.6.1.1.7.1.2 MATTHEW BIXLER was born on 22 February 1977.

3.6.1.1.7.2 DARLENE BIXLER was born on 23 October 1943. She married **DENNIS SHEARER**.

3.6.1.1.7.2.1 TEENA SHEARER was born on 9 January 1966.

3.6.1.1.7.2.2 DENNIS SHEARER JR. was born on 6 January 1971.

3.6.1.1.8 MABEL SEVILLA WIEST was born on 30 October 1914, Mahantango Township, Schuylkill County, PA. She married **HENRY ALBERT SNYDER**, son of **HARVEY CLARENCE SNYDER** and **ROSA SEVILLA MATTERN**. Prior to her death, Mabel lived at 46 West Bond Street, Elizabethville, Dauphin County, PA. She died on 30 July 1999, Susquehanna Lutheran Village, Millersburg, Dauphin County, PA, at age 84. She was buried at Maple Grove Cemetery, Elizabethville, Dauphin County, PA.

3.6.1.1.8.1 RALPH L. SNYDER was born on 2 July 1933. He married **SHIRLEY GUNDERMAN**.

3.6.1.1.8.1.1 JILL SNYDER was born on 12 June 1957. She married (--?--) **MOTTER**.

3.6.1.1.8.1.2 LORI SNYDER was born on 2 April 1960. She married (--?--) **KIEFFER**.

3.6.1.1.8.1.3 TRACY SNYDER was born on 5 July 1961. She married (--?--) **SUDER**.

3.6.1.1.8.2 LORRAINE B. SNYDER was born on 17 February 1938, Elizabethville, Dauphin County, PA. She died on 18 December 2014, Hershey Medical Center, Dauphin County, PA, at age 76. According to a newspaper obituary, Lorraine, known as "Toots," lived in Elizabethville, PA, and retired after 35 years as a secretary with the PA Dept. of Environmental Protection, Harrisburg. She was buried on 23 December 2014, at Maple Grove Cemetery, Elizabethville, Dauphin County, PA.

3.6.1.1.8.3 LEONARD D. SNYDER was born after 1940. He married **WANDA JOAN KLINE**, daughter of **RAY KLINE** and **REBECCA (--?--)**. He married **NANCY TROUTMAN**.

3.6.1.1.8.3.1 MARJORIE SNYDER was born on 15 June 1966. She married **(--?--) FELTON**.

3.6.1.1.8.3.2 JENNIFER SNYDER was born on 14 March 1969. She married **(--?--) STINSON**.

3.6.1.1.8.3.3 NATHAN SNYDER was born on 1 November 1970.

3.6.1.1.9 EVA BEATRICE WIEST was born on 26 February 1922, Schuylkill County, PA. She married **RUSSEL D. PAUL**, son of **JOHN ADAM PAUL** and **FLOSSIE E. GEIST,** on 25 June 1938, Leck Kill, Northumberland County, PA. She died on 27 February 1995, Hershey Medical Center, Dauphin County, PA, at age 73. She was buried on 3 March 1995, at Salem Church Cemetery, Rough and Ready, Upper Mahantango Township, Schuylkill County, PA.

3.6.1.1.9.1 ROY D. PAUL was born circa 1938. He married **MARLENE REBUCK**, daughter of **RUSSELL REBUCK** and **ALMA (--?--)**, on 2 April 1960, Herndon, Northumberland County, PA. Roy and Marlene live in Klingerstown, PA. He retired from Troutman Brothers in Klingerstown, while she is retired from Shelbi Industries, Pillow, PA.

3.6.1.1.9.1.1 DEBBRA PAUL was born on 29 August 1960. She married **BRUCE WEAVER**.

3.6.1.1.9.2 ELEANOR MARIE PAUL was born on 8 September 1946, Schuylkill County, PA. She married **HAROLD JEROME LENKER**, son of **LEE EARLINGTON LENKER** and **SARAH E. MECKLEY,** on 9 November 1968, Klingerstown, Schuylkill County, PA.

3.6.1.1.9.2.1 CHRIS HAROLD LENKER was born on 15 March 1969, Schuylkill County, PA. He married **MELISSA JO BRAY**, daughter of **THOMAS BRAY** and **JUNE (--?--),** on 17 March 2001. He lived in Klingerstown, Schuylkill County, PA.

3.6.1.1.9.2.1.1 TYLER LEE LENKER was born on 21 April 2003.

3.6.1.1.9.2.2 CURT DAVID LENKER was born on 20 February 1973, Schuylkill County, PA. He married **JOY LYNNE LESHER** on 11 November 2006, Christ Evangelical and Reformed Church, Leck Kill, Northumberland County, PA.

3.6.1.1.9.2.3 MINDY MARIE LENKER was born on 5 April 1983, Schuylkill County, PA. She married **ARLIN WEIKEL**, son of **WILLIAM WEIKEL** and **KAREN KROHN**, circa 2005.

3.6.1.2 CHARLES MONROE WIEST was born on 14 September 1870, Northumberland County, PA. He married **MARY AMELIA CLARK**, daughter of **JOHN S. CLARK** and **SOPHIE ROMBERGER**, circa 1898. Some sources suggest that he and **MARY AMELIA CLARK** were married in 1892. He died on 6 January 1958, Hubley Township, Schuylkill County, PA, at age 87. He was buried on 9 January 1958, at Salem (Herb's) United Church of Christ Cemetery, Rough and Ready, Schuylkill County, PA.

3.6.1.2.1 CARRIE M. WIEST was born on 6 March 1898. She married **WILMER J. BROWN**, son of **JOSEPH BROWN** and **LYDIA (--?--)**, circa 1922. She died on 27 December 1962, Leck Kill, Northumberland County, PA, at age 64. She was buried on 31 December 1962, at Salem Church Cemetery, Rough and Ready, Schuylkill County, PA.

3.6.1.2.2 GABRIELLA WIEST was born on 26 July 1899, Schuylkill County, PA. She married **GURNEY WEBSTER SCHMELTZ**, son of **SAMUEL A. SCHMELTZ** and **EMMA JANE FETTEROLF**. She died on 27 October 1972, Schuylkill County, PA, at age 73. She was buried at St. Paul's United Church of Christ Cemetery, Sacramento, Schuylkill County, PA.

3.6.1.2.3 JEMIMA AMELIA WIEST was born on 18 January 1900. She married **CHARLES ELIAS REBUCK**, son of **ELIAS F. REBUCK** and **SARAH SNYDER**. Before her death, Jemima was living in Orwigsburg, Schuylkill County, PA. She died on 27 September 1984, Pottsville, Schuylkill

County, PA, at age 84. She was buried at Salem (Herb's) United Church of Christ Cemetery, Rough and Ready, Schuylkill County, PA.

3.6.1.2.3.1 EARNEST G. REBUCK was born circa 1921. Ernest lives at RR1 Klingerstown, PA.

3.6.1.2.3.2 ALMA MARGARET REBUCK was born on 12 January 1926, Leck Kill, Northumberland County, PA. She married **IRVIN E. REITZ**, son of **LEWIS E. REITZ** and **IDA M. GOTTSHALL**, on 26 June 1948. She died on 13 November 2007, Holy Spirit Hospital, Camp Hill, Cumberland County, PA, at age 81. According to a newspaper obituary, Alma graduated in 1946 from the Geisinger School of Nursing. She was a registered nurse at various hospitals and nursing facilities and was last employed at Bethany Village, Mechanicsburg. She lived in Camp Hill. She was buried on 17 November 2007, at Salem (Herb's) Church Cemetery, Rough and Ready, Schuylkill County, PA.

3.6.1.2.3.2.1 JANET REITZ married **CHARLES COE**. Janet and her husband live in Macungie, Lehigh County, PA.

3.6.1.2.3.2.1.1 JENNIFER COE married **(--?--) LENTZ**.

3.6.1.2.3.2.1.2 HEATHER COE

3.6.1.2.3.2.1.3 AMBER COE

3.6.1.2.3.2.2 DENNIS REITZ. Dennis lives in Camp Hill, Cumberland County, PA.

3.6.1.2.3.2.3 EILEEN REITZ married **REV. ALLAN SONES**. Eileen and her husband live in Mechanicsburg, Cumberland County, PA.

3.6.1.2.3.2.3.1 ANDREA SONES died in 1987.

3.6.1.2.3.2.3.2 KRISTIN SONES

3.6.1.2.3.2.3.3 KAITLIN SONES

3.6.1.2.3.2.3.4 NICOLE SONES

3.6.1.2.3.3 CHARLES E. REBUCK JR. was born circa 1929. Charles lives at RR1 Klingerstown, PA.

3.6.1.2.3.4 ESTHER MIRIAM REBUCK was born on 20 November 1937, Klingerstown, Schuylkill County, PA. She married **(--?--) SPECK**. She died on 15 February 1991, at age 53.

3.6.1.2.4 DANIEL OSCAR WIEST was born on 24 November 1902, Rough and Ready, Schuylkill County, PA. He was baptized on 7 February 1903, Salem (Herb's) Church, Rough and Ready, Schuylkill County, PA. He died on 16 May 1903, Schuylkill County, PA. He was buried at Salem (Herb's) Church, Rough and Ready, Schuylkill County, PA.

3.6.1.2.5 JOHN ALVIN WIEST was born on 10 January 1904, Schuylkill County, PA. He died on 5 April 1924, in a mine accident Porter Township, Schuylkill County, PA, at age 20. He was buried on 9 April 1924, at Salem Church Cemetery, Rough and Ready, Schuylkill County, PA.

3.6.1.2.6 GERTRUDE SOPHIA WIEST was born on 21 May 1907, Rough and Ready, Schuylkill County, PA. She was baptized on 11 August 1907, Salem (Herb's) Church, Rough and Ready, Schuylkill County, PA. She married **ERNEST MILTON KISSINGER**, son of **DANIEL MILTON KISSINGER** and **HANNAH MARY ETTE DEIBERT**. She died in December 1981, at age 74. She was buried at St. Paul's United Church of Christ Cemetery, Sacramento, Schuylkill County, PA.

3.6.1.2.6.1 EDITH HANNAH KISSINGER was born on 10 September 1926, Spring Glen, Schuylkill County, PA. She married **HERMAN HENRY KLINGER**, son of **JOHN ALEXANDER ALVIN KLINGER** and **LILLIAN ONEDA TROUTMAN**. She died on 13 October 2009, The Manor at Susquehanna Village, Millersburg, Dauphin County, PA, at age 83. According to a newspaper obituary, Edith lived in Spring Glen, PA, and retired from Puritan Fashions, Millersburg. She was buried on 16 October 2009, at St. Paul's Church Cemetery, Sacramento, Schuylkill County, PA.

3.6.1.2.6.1.1 DOROTHY EDITH KLINGER was born on 23 December 1945, Dauphin County, PA. She married **ELVIN C. BLYLER**, son of **ELMER C. BLYLER** and **ALBERTA M. OCHS**, circa 1960. She lived in. Dorothy lives in Spring Glen, PA.

3.6.1.2.6.1.1.1 DANIEL E. BLYLER was born on 28 November 1962, Schuylkill County, PA. He married **CAROL L. LAHR**, daughter of **RAYMOND W. LAHR** and **MARTHA MARIE KISSINGER**, on 21 November 1992.

3.6.1.2.6.1.1.1.1 SARA BLYLER was born on 29 January 1997, Dauphin Co., PA.

3.6.1.2.6.1.1.2 ANN MARIE BLYLER was born on 12 April 1967, Schuylkill County, PA.

3.6.1.2.6.1.1.3 CAROLE A. BLYLER was born on 29 September 1969, Schuylkill County, PA.

3.6.1.2.6.1.1.4 KAY M. BLYLER was born circa 1971, Schuylkill County, PA.

3.6.1.2.6.1.2 LINDA MARIE KLINGER was born on 19 September 1954. She married IRVIN P. MOYER circa 1975. She married IVAN MORGAN. Linda lives in Lewisberry, PA.

3.6.1.2.6.2 WILLARD MILTON KISSINGER was born on 13 September 1928. He married EMMA CAROLINE CHUBB. Prior to his death, Willard lived in the vicinity of Lykens, Dauphin County, PA. He died on 28 May 1974, Dauphin County, PA, at age 45. He was buried at Riverview Memorial Gardens, Halifax, Dauphin County, PA.

3.6.1.2.6.2.1 EDITH KISSINGER

3.6.1.2.6.2.2 MARY LOU KISSINGER was born on 8 July 1948. She married CARL REINER circa 1971. She died on 15 March 2012, Geisinger Medical Center, Danville, Montour County, PA, at age 63. She was buried at Riverview Memorial Gardens, Halifax, Dauphin County, PA.

3.6.1.2.6.2.2.1 CATHY REINER married (--?--) HOOVER.

3.6.1.2.6.2.2.2 WILLY REINER

3.6.1.2.6.3 ARLENE MARY KISSINGER was born on 20 August 1930, Spring Glen, Schuylkill County, PA. Some sources record that she was born on 30 May 1934. She married MARLIN FEGER. She married ELWOOD E. LUCAS. She died on 20 October 2007, Friendly Nursing Home, Pitman, Schuylkill County, PA, at age 77. According to a newspaper obituary, prior to her death, Arlene lived at 32 E Market Street, Gratz, Dauphin County. She previously had worked as a seamstress for the former Philmark Manufacturing Company of Gratz, and retired as manager of the Gratz VFW Post. She was buried on 24 October 2007, at St. Matthew's (Coleman's) United Church of Christ Cemetery, Dauphin County, PA.

3.6.1.2.6.3.1 BRENDA KAY FEGER was born on 2 October 1953. She married MARK LONG.

3.6.1.2.6.3.1.1 ALISON J. LONG was born circa 1978, Dauphin County, PA.

3.6.1.2.6.3.2 DENNIS LEROY FEGER was born on 19 November 1957. He married PATRICIA (--?--).

3.6.1.2.6.3.2.1 KIRK A. FEGER married BECKY WENRICH.

3.6.1.2.6.3.2.2 SHAUN A. FEGER

3.6.1.2.6.4 LEROY CHARLES KISSINGER was born on 18 April 1932, Spring Glen, Schuylkill County, PA. He was born on 18 April 1932, Lykens Township, Dauphin Co., PA. He married CAROL J. LEITZEL circa July 1955, St. David's Lutheran & Reformed Church, Hebe, Northumberland Co., PA. He died on 30 March 2011, Dauphin County, PA, at age 78. He was buried on 3 April 2011, at Riverview Memorial Gardens, Halifax, Dauphin County, PA.

3.6.1.2.6.4.1 WANDA ANN KISSINGER was born on 11 January 1957, Lentz Hospital, Lykens, Dauphin Co., PA.

3.6.1.2.6.4.2 ERNEST LAMAR KISSINGER was born on 11 July 1958, Dauphin Co., PA. He married DAWN LATSHA on 22 April 1978, Millersburg, Dauphin Co., PA. He married SALLY (--?--) after 1982.

3.6.1.2.6.4.2.1 TRISHA KISSINGER was born circa 1980, Dauphin Co., PA. She married ANDREW HEPNER circa 1995.

3.6.1.2.6.4.2.1.1 CODY CHARLES HEPNER was born on 7 October 1997.

3.6.1.2.6.4.2.1.2 (--?--) HEPNER was born on 20 October 2000.

3.6.1.2.6.4.3 SCOTT PAUL KISSINGER was born on 1 March 1961, Dauphin Co., PA.

3.6.1.2.6.4.4 PAMELA ANN KISSINGER was born on 6 September 1962, Dauphin Co., PA. She married RANDY L. ARNOLD circa 1985.

3.6.1.2.6.4.5 TODD ALBERT KISSINGER was born on 6 June 1965, Dauphin Co., PA.

3.6.1.2.6.4.6 LEROY CHARLES KISSINGER JR. was born on 7 January 1956, Lentz Hospital, Lykens, Dauphin Co., PA. He married ELIZABETH BOYD circa 1978.

3.6.1.2.6.5 ANNA MAE KISSINGER was born on 30 May 1934. She married WHELAN ELLIS WENRICH, son of ELLIS CLARENCE WENRICH and MARY MARTHA BOWMAN. Anna lives in Spring Glen, PA.

3.6.1.2.6.5.1 LYNN L. WENRICH

3.6.1.2.6.5.2 LORI A. WENRICH married (--?--) BELACK.

3.6.1.2.6.5.3 TAMMY S. WENRICH

3.6.1.2.6.5.4 DAVID ELLIS WENRICH was born on 23 October 1952, Lykens, Dauphin County, PA. He married ROXANNE M. BECKER circa 1971. He died on 6 July 2006, at age 53, as a result of an auto accident in Mount Carmel Township, Northumberland County, PA.

3.6.1.2.6.5.4.1 DAVID E. WENRICH JR. married AMANDA L. (--?--).

3.6.1.2.6.5.4.2 DAWN R. WENRICH

3.6.1.2.6.5.4.3 AMANDA J. WENRICH

3.6.1.2.6.5.5 RANDY ERNEST WENRICH was born on 1 May 1954, Lykens, Dauphin County, PA. He married MARGARET MARIE SCHEIB circa 1976. On 2 July 2012, from injuries suffered in a motor vehicle accident in Lykens Township, Dauphin County, PA.

3.6.1.2.6.5.5.1 RANDY E. WENRICH JR.

3.6.1.2.6.5.5.2 HILARY M. WENRICH

3.6.1.2.6.5.6 RICHARD LEE WENRICH was born on 12 May 1955, Dauphin County, PA. He married TAMMY JANE WILLIARD, daughter of ALVIN RAY WILLIARD and SARAH ARLENE WILLIARD, on 24 June 1978, Zion (Klinger's) Lutheran Church, Erdman, Dauphin Co., PA.

3.6.1.2.6.5.6.1 JENNIFER ROSE WENRICH was born on 9 October 1978, PA. She was baptized on 12 November 1978, Zion (Klinger's) Lutheran Church, Erdman, Dauphin Co., PA.

3.6.1.2.6.5.6.2 JESSICA ANN WENRICH was born on 2 June 1981, PA. She was baptized on 27 September 1981, Zion (Klinger's) Lutheran Church, Erdman, Dauphin Co., PA.

3.6.1.2.6.5.7 WHELAN ELLIS WENRICH was born on 8 August 1956.

3.6.1.2.6.6 RUTH GERTIE KISSINGER was born on 6 October 1935, Spring Glen, Schuylkill County, PA. She married LESTER SCHMELTZ, son of WILLIAM ROY SCHMELTZ and VERNA MAY WAGNER. She died on 6 January 2014, The Manor at Susquehanna Village, Millersburg, Dauphin County, PA, at age 78. She was buried at St. Paul's United Church of Christ Cemetery, Sacramento, Schuylkill County, PA.

3.6.1.2.6.6.1 BRUCE LAMAR SCHMELTZ was born on 16 August 1954, Dauphin County, PA. He married DAWN LINDA MATTERN on 14 September 1974, St. John's Lutheran Church, Leck Kill, Northumberland Co., PA. He married DEBRA HENTZ after 1979.

3.6.1.2.6.6.1.1 JASON LAMAR SMELTZ was born on 9 December 1976, Danville, Montour Co., PA.

3.6.1.2.6.6.1.2 JEREMY LESTER SMELTZ was born on 23 November 1979, Danville, Montour County, PA. He died on 21 July 1993>, <in a farm accident>. He was buried at St. Peter's (Schwalm's) United Methodist Church Cemetery, Fearnot, Schuylkill County, PA.

3.6.1.2.6.6.2 DEBRA ANN SCHMELTZ was born on 1 March 1957, Dauphin Co., PA. She married ARLEN SMUCKER circa 1980. She married ROBERT SNYDER after 1985.

3.6.1.2.6.6.3 DIANE MARIE SCHMELTZ was born on 14 June 1959, Dauphin Co., PA. She married RANDY WOLFGANG, son of ALFRED WOLFGANG and BETTY JOAN SCHADE, circa 1978.

3.6.1.2.6.6.3.1 ADAM L. WOLFGANG was born on 24 September 1980.

3.6.1.2.6.6.3.2 REBEKAH SUE WOLFGANG was born on 8 August 1987, Pottsville, Schuylkill County, PA.

3.6.1.2.6.7 ELWOOD ERNEST KISSINGER was born on 8 April 1938, Spring Glen, Schuylkill County, PA. He married JEAN E. KESSLER, daughter of JOHN EARL KESSLER and RUBY ARLENE SCHULTZ, on 12 December 1959, Zion (Klinger's) Church, Erdman, Lykens Township, Dauphin County, PA. He died on 2 May 2001, at age 63. He was buried on 7 May 2001, at Riverview Memorial Gardens, Halifax, Dauphin County, PA.

3.6.1.2.6.7.1 MIKE KISSINGER

3.6.1.2.6.7.2 KIMBERLY SUE KISSINGER was born on 7 November 1963, Dauphin County, PA. She married JON PAUL HENRY ADAMS, son of PAUL JOHN HENRY ADAMS and CARRIE IRENE HARRIS.

3.6.1.2.6.7.2.1 JONENE ADAMS

3.6.1.2.6.7.3 LARRY E. KISSINGER was born on 2 January 1968, Dauphin County, PA. He married PENNY (--?--).

3.6.1.2.6.7.3.1 GABRIELLE KISSINGER

3.6.1.2.6.7.3.2 TRISTAN KISSINGER

3.6.1.2.7 GUY W. WIEST was born in 1910. He died in 1990. He was buried at Salem Church Cemetery, Rough and Ready, Schuylkill County, PA.

3.6.1.3 EMMA WIEST was born on 17 October 1871, Northumberland County, PA. She married ALVIN S. ERDMAN, son of JACOB W. ERDMAN and CATHARINE SEITZ, circa 1885. She died on 2 May 1945, Mahantongo Township, Schuylkill County, PA, at age 73. She was buried on 5 May 1945, at Salem (Herb's) United Church of Christ Cemetery, Rough and Ready, Schuylkill County, PA.

3.6.1.3.1 WILLIAM RALPH ERDMAN was born on 9 August 1891, Klingerstown, Schuylkill County, PA. He died on 14 August 1957, Pottsville, Schuylkill County, PA, at age 66. He was buried on 17 August 1957, at Salem (Herb's) United Church of Christ Cemetery, Rough and Ready, Schuylkill County, PA. He was never married.

3.6.1.4 HENRY MORRIS WIEST was born on 9 September 1874, Northumberland County, PA. He married MARY JANE WIEST Pennsylvania. He died in February 1948, at age 73.

3.6.1.4.1 ALICE CLARA WIEST was born on 16 January 1896, Ashland, Schuylkill County, PA. She married HENRY IRVIN WETZEL, son of SAMUEL WETZEL and CLARA GOTSHALL, in 1911.

3.6.1.4.1.1 JOSEPHINE RETTA WETZEL was born circa 1912. She married HARRY LYNCH.

3.6.1.4.1.2 HENRY IRVIN WETZEL JR. is also referred to as HENRY E WETZEL JR. in some sources. He was born on 26 March 1915, Ashland, Schuylkill County, PA. He married MARY (--?--). He married VIRGINIA TOPHONEY. He died in February 1982, Ashland, Schuylkill County, PA, at age 66. He was buried at Brock Cemetery, Ashland, Schuylkill County, PA.

3.6.1.4.1.2.1 RONALD WETZEL was born on 5 April 1932, Ashland, Schuylkill County, PA. He married JEWEL (--?--). He died on 26 April 1975, Ashland, Schuylkill County, PA, at age 43. He was buried on 30 April 1975, at Brock Cemetery, Ashland, Schuylkill County, PA.

3.6.1.4.1.2.2 RICHARD WETZEL was born circa 1934.

3.6.1.4.1.2.3 RAYMOND WILLIAM WETZEL was born on 27 July 1951, Ashland, Schuylkill County, PA. He married PATRICIA ALVAREZ on 24 May 1991, Miami-Dade County, FL. He died on 3 June 2004, Cooper City, Broward County, FL, at age 52.

3.6.1.4.1.2.3.1 RAYMOND W. WETZEL JR.

3.6.1.4.1.2.3.2 MICAH G. WETZEL married LEIGHANNE (--?--).

3.6.1.4.1.2.3.2.1 MICAH G. WETZEL II

3.6.1.4.1.2.3.3 DOMINIC F. WETZEL

3.6.1.4.1.2.3.4 REGINA WETZEL married (--?--) BEATO.

3.6.1.4.1.2.3.4.1 JULIAN BEATO

3.6.1.4.1.2.4 CAROL ANN WETZEL married GUY MERVINE.

3.6.1.4.1.2.5 REGINA WETZEL married RON AKELAITIS.

3.6.1.4.1.2.6 HENRY WETZEL III married **EVELYN (--?--)**.

3.6.1.4.1.3 CARLOS IRA WETZEL was born on 24 August 1918, Ashland, Schuylkill County, PA. He was born on 24 August 1918, Ashland, Schuylkill County, PA. He married **VIRGINIA M. WELKER**, daughter of **HARRY CLAYTON WELKER** and **FLORENCE MAE FERTIG**. He died on 17 October 1987, Veterans Administration Hospital, Wilkes-Barre, Luzerne County, PA, at age 69. He was buried at Brock Cemetery, Ashland, Schuylkill County, PA.

3.6.1.4.1.3.1 RONALD E. WETZEL was born on 5 April 1932, Ashland, Schuylkill County, PA. He married **JEWEL A. EDMONDSON**. From 1953 to 1961, Ronald served in the US Army. He died on 26 April 1975, Ashland, Schuylkill County, PA, at age 43. He was buried on 30 April 1975, at Brock Cemetery, Ashland, Schuylkill County, PA.

3.6.1.4.1.3.2 GERALD C. WETZEL was born on 21 December 1937, Lavelle, Schuylkill County, PA. Some sources record that he was born on 23 December 1937. He married **DONNA HUBLER**. He married **RUTH ANN BEACHER**. He died on 25 July 1989, at age 51. He was buried at Christ Church Cemetery, Fountain Springs, Schuylkill County, PA.

3.6.1.4.1.3.2.1 GAIL WETZEL married **JOHN MOORE**.

3.6.1.4.1.3.2.2 CHERYL WETZEL married **ANDREW PETROWSKY**.

3.6.1.4.1.3.2.3 CINDY WETZEL married **RICHARD PRICE**.

3.6.1.4.1.3.2.4 DAWN WETZEL married **DENNIS PACZKOWSKI**.

3.6.1.4.1.3.2.5 WENDY WETZEL married **ALBERT MCCAIN**.

3.6.1.4.1.3.2.6 GERALD C. WETZEL JR. was born on 23 December 1964. He died on 23 October 2006, Northumberland County, PA, at age 41. He was buried at Barry Immanuel Evangelical Congregation Cemetery, Lavelle, Schuylkill County, PA.

3.6.1.4.1.3.2.6.1 GERALD C. WETZEL III

3.6.1.4.1.3.2.6.2 KRISTA WETZEL

3.6.1.4.1.3.3 DONALD G. WETZEL was born on 12 April 1940, Lavelle, Schuylkill County, PA. He married **NADJA HORWATH** on 10 July 1961, Northumberland County, PA.

3.6.1.4.1.3.3.1 BRENDA WETZEL

3.6.1.4.1.3.3.2 DEBBIE WETZEL

3.6.1.4.1.4 PAUL WETZEL was born circa 1920.

3.6.1.4.1.5 ROSELLA M. WETZEL is also referred to as **ROSE** in some sources. She was born on 8 May 1922. She married **ROBERT C. HORBACH**. She died on 21 February 2009, at age 86. She was buried at Christ Church Cemetery, Fountain Springs, Schuylkill County, PA.

3.6.1.4.1.5.1 CANAL HORBACH was born circa 1928.

3.6.1.4.1.6 JEAN R. WETZEL was born on 15 September 1923, Ashland, Schuylkill County, PA. She married **THOMAS P. MCGINLEY** on 22 February 1944. She died on 17 February 1973, Ashland Hospital, Ashland, Schuylkill County, PA, at age 49. She was buried on 21 February 1973, at Saint Ignatius Cemetery, Centralia, Columbia County, PA.

3.6.1.4.1.6.1 REGINA MCGINLEY married **DANIEL SLOTTERBACK**.

3.6.1.4.1.6.2 LISA MCGINLEY

3.6.1.4.1.6.3 ALICE MCGINLEY

3.6.1.4.1.7 JANET WETZEL was born circa 1927.

3.6.1.4.1.8 RALPH S. WETZEL was born on 22 April 1928, Ashland, Schuylkill County, PA. He married **GEORGINE M. ROSTI** circa 1951. He died on 6 April 1997, Levittown, Bucks County, PA, at age 68. He was buried on 10 April 1997, at Resurrection Cemetery, Bensalem, Bucks County, PA.

3.6.1.4.1.8.1 RALPH S. WETZEL JR. married **LINDA JONES**.

3.6.1.4.1.8.1.1 MATTHEW WETZEL

3.6.1.4.1.8.1.2 KRISTY WETZEL

3.6.1.4.1.8.2 SANDRA WETZEL married **(--?--) ENNIS**. She married **ALAN LOMBARDI**.

3.6.1.4.1.8.2.1 JARED ENNIS

3.6.1.4.1.9 MARY JANE WETZEL was born on 3 May 1933, Ashland, Schuylkill County, PA. She married **JOSEPH SELINSKY**. She died on 29 October 1998, at age 65.

3.6.1.4.1.10 WILLIAM WETZEL was born circa 1934.

3.6.1.4.1.11 DAVID LAWRENCE WETZEL was born on 18 March 1939. He married **CAROLE L. KLINGER** on 3 October 1959. He died on 5 October 1999, North Penn Hospital, Hatfield Township, Montgomery County, PA, at age 60.

    3.6.1.4.1.11.1 DEBORAH WETZEL married **ROBERT IRICK**.

    3.6.1.4.1.11.2 DENISE WETZEL married **JOSEPH BRACKIN**.

    3.6.1.4.1.11.3 DAVID L. WETZEL JR. married **DIANE (--?--)**.

3.6.1.4.2 HARRY JAY WIEST was born on 16 April 1897, Klingerstown, Schuylkill County, PA. Some sources record that he was born on 16 April 1898, Ashland, Schuylkill County, PA. He married **VIOLA ESSLER** after 1920. He died in a mine accident on 19 May 1948, Branch Township, Schuylkill County, PA, at age 51. He was buried on 24 May 1948, at Schuylkill Memorial Park, Schuylkill Haven, Schuylkill County, PA.

    3.6.1.4.2.1 HENRY F. WIEST was born on 16 May 1923, Pottsville, Schuylkill County, PA. He married **NAOMI M. FESSLER**. He married **JEAN F. BROWN**. He died on 11 July 2011, Lehigh Valley Medical Center, Allentown, Lehigh County, PA, at age 88. He was buried at Schuylkill Memorial Park, Schuylkill Haven, Schuylkill County, PA.

    3.6.1.4.2.2 KATHERINE WIEST was born circa 1925. She married **(--?--) MCCLINTOCK**. She died before 2011.

    3.6.1.4.2.3 VIOLET WIEST was born circa 1932. She married **(--?--) BOWERS**. She died before 2012.

    3.6.1.4.2.4 NORMAN JAY WIEST was born on 17 June 1936, Pottsville, Schuylkill County, PA. He died on 23 August 1998, at age 62. He was buried at Cressona Cemetery, Cressona, Schuylkill County, PA.

    3.6.1.4.2.5 EMMA JANE WIEST was born circa 1938.

3.6.1.4.3 CARLOS RAY WIEST was born on 22 April 1897, Ashland, Schuylkill County, PA. He died in 1918, in influenza epidemic.

3.6.1.4.4 IRA VICTOR WIEST was born on 25 February 1899, Ashland, Schuylkill County, PA. He died on 18 May 1918, in ammunition factory explosion, Oakdale, Dauphin County, PA, at age 19.

3.6.1.4.5 MAURICE WILLIAM WIEST was born on 12 August 1901, Ashland, Schuylkill County, PA. He died in 1921, Pennsylvania.

3.6.1.4.6 JOHN ADAM WIEST was born on 8 March 1903, Ashland, Schuylkill County, PA. He died on 15 January 1921, Minnesota at age 17. John died while serving in the U.S. Medical Corps.

3.6.1.4.7 RICHARD DANIEL WIEST was born on 10 January 1904, Ashland, Schuylkill County, PA. He died in 1937, Pennsylvania.

3.6.1.4.8 ESTON EDWARD WIEST was born on 9 December 1907, Ashland, Schuylkill County, PA. He died on 5 July 1910, in accident while playing with fireworks, Ashland, Schuylkill County, PA, at age 2.

3.6.1.4.9 ARTHUR BOYD WIEST was born circa 1908, Ashland, Schuylkill County, PA. He died on 24 November 1909.

3.6.1.4.10 SAMUEL ELMER WIEST was born on 9 June 1912, Ashland, Schuylkill County, PA.

3.6.1.4.11 ELSIE MAY WIEST was born on 22 May 1916, Ashland, Schuylkill County, PA.

3.6.1.5 JOHN WIEST was born on 16 December 1878. He married **STELLA SCHLEGEL**, daughter of **JAMES D. SCHLEGEL** and **LIZZIE ALICE PEIFFER,** after 1910. He died in 1964.

    3.6.1.5.1 SHIRLEY CATHARINE WIEST married **(--?--) SCHEIB**.

    3.6.1.5.2 JOHN WIEST died before 28 September 2006.

    3.6.1.5.3 SON WIEST

    3.6.1.5.4 HELEN M. WIEST was born circa 1921. She married **(--?--) STEIN**. She died before 28 September 2006.

    3.6.1.5.5 VIOLET M. WIEST was born circa 1924. She married **(--?--) SMELTZ**.

3.6.1.5.6 BRYANT HARRY WIEST was born on 7 February 1926, Klingerstown, Schuylkill County, PA. He married **ANNA HOFFMAN** on 26 January 1959. He died on 28 September 2006, Klingerstown, Schuylkill County, PA, at age 80. He was buried on 2 October 2006, at Salem United Church of Christ Cemetery, Rough and Ready, Schuylkill County, PA.

> **3.6.1.5.6.1 BONNIE WIEST** married (--?--) **SCHADEL**.
>> **3.6.1.5.6.1.1 JUSTIN SCHADEL**
>> **3.6.1.5.6.1.2 ADAM SCHADEL**
>
> **3.6.1.5.6.2 SHEILA WIEST** married (--?--) **STRAUB**.
>
> **3.6.1.5.6.3 HEIDI WIEST** married (--?--) **RITTER**.
>
> **3.6.1.5.6.4 JAMES WIEST**
>> **3.6.1.5.6.4.1 NOLAN WIEST**

3.6.1.5.7 JUNE EMMA WIEST was born on 22 August 1930, Klingerstown, Schuylkill County, PA. She died in November 1977, at age 47.

3.6.1.6 CATHERINE V. WIEST was born on 2 July 1886, Schuylkill County, PA. Some sources record that she was born on 3 July 1886. She married **CHARLES F. FERTIG**. She died on 11 March 1921, at age 34. She was buried at Zion (Klinger's) Church, Erdman, Lykens Township, Dauphin County, PA.

> **3.6.1.6.1 JOHN FERTIG**
>
> **3.6.1.6.2 GUERNEY W. FERTIG** was born on 5 May 1905, Dauphin County, PA. He died on 26 October 1918, Klingerstown, Schuylkill County, PA, at age 13.
>
> **3.6.1.6.3 NORMAN FERTIG** was born on 17 December 1908, Dauphin County, PA. He died on 18 December 1908, Dauphin County, PA.
>
> **3.6.1.6.4 FLORENCE M. FERTIG** was born on 13 July 1913, Schuylkill County, PA. She married **LEON RAY KLINGER**, son of **CALVIN CHARLES KLINGER** and **JENNIE M. ERDMAN**, circa 1929. She married **ARTHUR PENSYL** circa 1938.
>> **3.6.1.6.4.1 LENA KLINGER** was born circa 1929. She married **DAVID HERR**.
>>
>> **3.6.1.6.4.2 BERTRAM L. KLINGER** was born on 1 July 1931, Klingerstown, Schuylkill County, PA. He married **JEANNE WARY**, daughter of **STANLEY WARY**, in 1951, St. John's United Church of Christ, Shamokin, Northumberland County, PA. He died on 13 July 2013, Elysburg, Northumberland County, PA, at age 82.
>>> **3.6.1.6.4.2.1 CYNTHIA KLINGER** married **ROBERT MIRILLO**.
>>>> **3.6.1.6.4.2.1.1 RICHARD MIRILLO**
>>>
>>> **3.6.1.6.4.2.2 KATHY KLINGER** married **ROBERT KUFTA**.
>>>
>>> **3.6.1.6.4.2.3 KAREN KLINGER** married **ROBERT MACKEY**.
>>>
>>> **3.6.1.6.4.2.4 LAURIE KLINGER** married **JONATHAN CLARK**.
>>>> **3.6.1.6.4.2.4.1 EMMA CLARK**
>>
>> **3.6.1.6.4.3 GARY LEE PENSYL** was born on 2 October 1954, Shamokin, Northumberland County, PA. He married **DOLORES W. SPADE**. He died on 20 July 2011, Sunbury, Northumberland County, PA, at age 56. He died before 13 July 2013.

3.6.2 JOHN TROUTMAN WIEST was born on 4 October 1846, Jordan Township, Northumberland County, PA. He married **CATHERINE HEIM**, daughter of **SAMUEL HEIM** and **CATHERINE BATTORF**, in 1867. The Genealogical & Biographical Annals of Northumberland County (1911) says:

"John T. Wiest, son of Jacob K., has long been a substantial citizen of Jordan township, Northumberland county. His present home is at Hebe. He was born in the township Oct. 4, 1846, was reared on the farm, and worked for his parents until he attained his majority. For about five years following he worked at Klingerstown in the employ of Jacob M. and Tobias M. Wiest, merchants at that place, driving their huckster team to Pottsville as often as twice a week. From Klingerstown Mr. Wiest moved to Hebe, Northumberland county, where he lived for six years, engaged in cattle droving, and then settled on his father's farm of 120 acres near that place, which he bought. After a year's ownership of that property, however, he sold it at a profit to John Trautman, and moved to another place in Jordan township, which he bought, consisting of seventy acres near Uniontown. He cultivated this place for seventeen years, at the end of that time moving back to Hebe, where he owned a house and where he remained for three years before moving to the farm he has since occupied. This place is also close to Hebe, and consists of 125 acres, which he and his son Irwin owned for a time in partnership, Mr. Wiest finally purchasing his son's interest. This was at one time the Henry Bowman homestead. It is a fine piece of property, fertile and well located, and Mr. Wiest has cultivated it profitably for a number of years. He built the present barn on the place in the nineties. He is an industrious man and an excellent manager, and his fellow citizens have so approved of his integrity and ability that they have chosen him to serve in several public offices. He was treasurer of Jordan township for eight years, school director seven years and supervisor one year. He has also been prominent in church affairs as trustee and treasurer of the Hebe Church known as David's Church, of which he and his family are Reformed members. He has also served the church as deacon and elder, having been one of its prominent workers for years.

"In 1867 Mr. Wiest married Catharine Heim, daughter of Samuel and Catharine (Battorf) Heim, of Washington township, Northumberland county, born Feb. 24, 1848; Mrs. Wiest died Oct. 12, 1908, and is buried in the Wiest family plot at Hebe, where a fine monument marks her grave. To Mr. and Mrs. Wiest were born four children Irwin H., mentioned below; Nolan H.; Catharine who married Maurice Brosius and they are farming people in Jordan township (their children are Mabel, Carlos, Frederick, Harold and John); and John E., who died when four years, four months old." He died on 16 August 1919, Hebe, Jordan Township, Northumberland County, PA, at age 72. He was buried at St. David's Lutheran and Reformed Church, Hebe, Jordan Township, Northumberland County, PA.

3.6.2.1 WILLIAM IRVIN HEIM WIEST was born on 21 October 1868, Pillow, PA. He married **ELIZABETH TROUTMAN** on 25 February 1888, Northumberland County, PA. William owned and operated a 24-acre farm that was formerly the Henry Miller homestead. He died on 24 May 1938, Pillow, Dauphin County, PA, at age 69. He was buried at Union Cemetery, Pillow, Dauphin County, PA.

3.6.2.1.1 NORA WIEST was born Hebe, Jordan Township, Northumberland County, PA.

3.6.2.1.2 MAUDE M. WIEST was born on 7 July 1888, Northumberland County, PA. She married **GURNEY V. MAURER** circa 1910. She died in 1944, Hebe, Jordan Township, Northumberland County, PA. She was buried at St. David's Cemetery, Hebe, Jordan Township, Northumberland County, PA.

3.6.2.1.2.1 DOROTHY M. MAURER was born circa 1912.

3.6.2.1.2.2 WILLIAM V. MAURER was born circa 1917.

3.6.2.1.3 CARRIE WIEST was born on 28 March 1889, Hebe, Jordan Township, Northumberland County, PA. She died on 27 December 1903, Hebe, Jordan Township, Northumberland County, PA, at age 14. She was buried at Union Cemetery, Pillow, Dauphin County, PA.

3.6.2.2 NOLAN HEIM WIEST was born on 1 April 1870, Northumberland County, PA. He married **EMMA L. DEPPEN**, daughter of **ALEXANDER DEPPEN** and **CATHERINE STEPP**, circa 1895. Nolan H. Wiest was a merchant in Red Cross, PA. He died on 14 July 1950, Jackson Township, Northumberland County, PA, at age 80. He was buried at St. Peter's (Kreb's) Cemetery, Red Cross, Jackson Township, Northumberland County, PA.

3.6.2.2.1 RUTH C. WIEST was born on 21 February 1897, Jackson Township, Northumberland County, PA. She died on 29 November 1908, Jackson Township, Northumberland County, PA, at age 11.

3.6.2.2.2 ROY WIEST was born on 15 July 1900, Jackson Township, Northumberland County, PA. He died on 22 October 1918, Jackson Township, Northumberland County, PA, at age 18.

3.6.2.2.3 MAY E. WIEST was born on 20 August 1906, Jackson Township, Northumberland County, PA. She died on 19 April 1958, Jackson Township, Northumberland County, PA, at age 51.

3.6.2.3 CATHERINE ELIZABETH WIEST was born on 22 October 1874, Northumberland County, PA. She was baptized on 21 December 1874, St. David's Lutheran and Reformed Church, Hebe, Jordan Township, Northumberland County, PA. She married **MAURICE E. BROSIUS**, son of **MICHAEL BROSIUS** and **CATHARINE BUSH**. She died in 1957, Hebe, Jordan Township, Northumberland County, PA. She was buried at St. David's Lutheran and Reformed Church Cemetery, Hebe, Jordan Township, Northumberland County, PA.

3.6.2.3.1 JOHN BROSIUS

3.6.2.3.2 FRED BROSIUS

3.6.2.3.3 HAROLD BROSIUS

3.6.2.3.4 MABEL BROSIUS

3.6.2.3.5 CARLOS RAY BROSIUS was born on 12 November 1895, Northumberland County, PA. He married **MAUDE MAY MAURER**, daughter of **JOEL RICHARD MAURER** and **MARY GESSNER**, before 1920. He died in December 1975, Millersburg, Dauphin County, PA, at age 80. He was buried at Salem Lutheran Church Cemetery, Killinger, Dauphin County, PA.

    3.6.2.3.5.1 MARY C. BROSIUS (see above)

        3.6.2.3.5.1.1 SANDRA E. DEIBLER (see above)

            3.6.2.3.5.1.1.1 STEVEN C. BOBB (see above)

            3.6.2.3.5.1.1.2 KENNETH E. BOBB (see above)

        3.6.2.3.5.1.2 KARL E. DEIBLER (see above)

            3.6.2.3.5.1.2.1 SCOTT DEIBLER (see above)

            3.6.2.3.5.1.2.2 SHARI DEIBLER (see above)

    3.6.2.3.5.2 ELEANOR BROSIUS (see above)

    3.6.2.3.5.3 MELVIN R. BROSIUS (see above)

    3.6.2.3.5.4 FERN M. BROSIUS (see above)

    3.6.2.3.5.5 JOHN PERSHING BROSIUS (see above)

    3.6.2.3.5.6 BALIR E. BROSIUS (see above)

        3.6.2.3.5.6.1 DAVID BROSIUS (see above)

        3.6.2.3.5.6.2 KIRBY BROSIUS (see above)

3.6.2.4 JOHN EDWARD WIEST was born on 17 July 1882, Hebe, Jordan Township, Northumberland County, PA. He died on 24 November 1883, Hebe, Jordan Township, Northumberland County, PA, at age 1. He was buried at St. David's Cemetery, Hebe, Jordan Township, Northumberland County, PA.

3.6.2.5 MABEL C. WIEST was born in 1894, Northumberland County, PA. She married **CHAUNCY E. BOYER**. She died in 1972, Jordan Township, Northumberland County, PA. She was buried at St. David's Lutheran and Reformed Church Cemetery, Hebe, Jordan Township, Northumberland County, PA.

    3.6.2.5.1 MARK P. BOYER was born on 16 December 1911, Hebe, Jordan Township, Northumberland County, PA. He died on 23 February 1913, Hebe, Jordan Township, Northumberland County, PA, at age 1.

    3.6.2.5.2 GRANDEE BOYER was born on 6 October 1915, Hebe, Jordan Township, Northumberland County, PA. She died on 8 January 1916, Hebe, Jordan Township, Northumberland County, PA.

3.6.3 AMELIA JANE TROUTMAN WIEST was born on 23 September 1849, Klingerstown, Schuylkill County, PA. She married **REUBEN H. SHADE**, son of **JOHN SHADE** and **HANNAH HOFFA**, circa 1867, Klingerstown, Schuylkill County, PA. She died on 23 January 1918, Klingerstown, Schuylkill County, PA, at age 68. She was buried at Zion (Klinger's) Church Cemetery, Erdman, Lykens Township, Dauphin County, PA.

    3.6.3.1 DANIEL ANDREW SHADE is also referred to as **NATHANIEL A.** in some sources. He was born on 18 May 1869, Klingerstown, Schuylkill County, PA. He died on 28 December 1877, Klingerstown, Schuylkill County, PA, at age 8. He was buried at Zion (Klinger's) Church Cemetery, Erdman, Lykens Township, Dauphin County, PA.

    3.6.3.2 JONATHAN MONROE SHADE was born on 21 June 1871, Klingerstown, Schuylkill County, PA. He died on 19 August 1888, Klingerstown, Schuylkill County, PA, at age 17. He was buried at Zion (Klinger's) Church Cemetery, Erdman, Lykens Township, Dauphin County, PA.

    3.6.3.3 OSCAR M. SHADE was born on 26 December 1873. He married **PHRENE ELMIRA SHAFFER** circa 1892. He died on 18 December 1954, Shamokin, Northumberland County, PA, at age 80. He was buried at Odd Fellows Cemetery, Shamokin, Coal Township, Northumberland County, PA.

        3.6.3.3.1 MINNIE SHADE (see above)

            3.6.3.3.1.1 INFANT RUCH (see above)

        3.6.3.3.2 LULU MAY SHADE (see above)

    3.6.3.4 HANNAH ELIZABETH SHADE was born on 10 July 1878, Klingerstown, Schuylkill County, PA. She was baptized on 25 August 1878, Zion (Klinger's) Church, Erdman, Lykens Township,

Dauphin County, PA. She married **CHARLES OSCAR MILTON HERB**, son of **SAMUEL C. HERB** and **MARY A. SCHWALM,** on 25 March 1899. She died on 24 August 1961, Valley View, Schuylkill County, PA, at age 83. She was buried on 28 August 1961, at Greenwood Cemetery, Tower City, Schuylkill County, PA.

    3.6.3.4.1 **WARREN OSCAR HERB** was born on 27 June 1901. He was baptized on 2 February 1902, St. Andrew's United Methodist Church, Valley View, Schuylkill County, PA. He married **HELEN GRACE REEDY** on 14 May 1921.

        3.6.3.4.1.1 **BETTY IRENE HERB** was born on 30 May 1923, Tower City, Schuylkill County, PA. She married **MARK LOUIS REIGHTLER** on 21 July 1949. She died on 14 August 2002, Good Samaritan Regional Medical Center, Pottsville, Schuylkill County, PA, at age 79.

            3.6.3.4.1.1.1 **WARREN THOMAS REIGHTLER** was born on 5 April 1951, Pottsville, Schuylkill County, PA. He married **KAREN G. (--?--)**. He died on 27 May 2002, at age 51.

    3.6.3.4.2 **EVA MAE HERB** was born on 6 October 1911. She married **LEO ELVIN UNDERKOFFLER**, son of **ELVIN LAWRENCE UNDERKOFFLER** and **BESSIE FIETTA REEDY,** on 16 May 1936, St. Andrew's Evangelical United Brethren Church, Valley View, Schuylkill County, PA. She died on 24 November 1986, 318 East Main St., Valley View, Hegins Township, Schuylkill County, PA, at age 75. She was buried at St. Andrew's United Methodist Church Cemetery, Valley View, Schuylkill County, PA.

        3.6.3.4.2.1 **KARL LEO UNDERKOFFLER** was born on 21 February 1937, Wayne Hospital, Pottsville, Schuylkill County, PA. He died on 23 April 1937. He was buried on 25 April 1937, at St. Andrew's United Methodist Church Cemetery, Valley View, Schuylkill County, PA.

3.6.3.5 **EDNA STELLA MAY SHADE** was born on 13 June 1885, Klingerstown, Schuylkill County, PA. She was baptized on 23 August 1885, Zion (Klinger's) Church, Erdman, Lykens Township, Dauphin County, PA. She married **RATHMUS MILLER**, son of **WILLIAM MILLER** and **JANE (--?--)**, circa 1901.

    3.6.3.5.1 **WILLIAM R. MILLER** was born circa 1901. He died before 2009.

    3.6.3.5.2 **DAISY MILLER** was born on 25 September 1904, Schuylkill County, PA. She married **NORMAN LETTICH**. Prior to her death, Daisy was living in the vicinity of Sacramento, Schuylkill County, PA. She died in March 1987, at age 82.

    3.6.3.5.3 **ROSE JANE MILLER** is also referred to as **ROSIE AND ROSA** in some sources. She was born on 29 October 1906, Hubley Township, Schuylkill County, PA. She married **ALLEN ZERBE**, son of **ELIZABETH (--?--),** circa 1925. She died on 14 January 2008, Polk Personal Care Center, Millersburg, Dauphin County, PA, at age 101. According to a newspaper obituary, Rosa lived in Sacramento, Schuylkill County, PA. She was buried on 19 January 2008, at St. Andrew's United Methodist Church Cemetery, Sacramento, Schuylkill County, PA.

        3.6.3.5.3.1 **JOHN I. ZERBE** also went by the name of **IRVIN**. He was born circa 1926, Pennsylvania.

        3.6.3.5.3.2 **ELSIE E. ZERBE** is also referred to as **ELISE** in some sources. She was born in 1929. She married **(--?--) BROWN**. She died before 14 January 2008.

    3.6.3.5.4 **EDNA VIOLET MILLER** was born on 1 November 1911, Fearnot, Schuylkill County, PA. She married **IVAN WAYNE ARTZ**, son of **IRVIN ARTZ** and **JENNY CYLVESTA COLEMAN**. She died on 17 February 2009, Schuylkill Medical Center-South Jackson Street, Pottsville, Schuylkill County, PA, at age 97. She was buried on 21 February 2009, at St. Mark's Church Cemetery, Spring Glen, Schuylkill County, PA.

        3.6.3.5.4.1 **VERA VIOLET ARTZ** was born on 15 February 1928, Fearnot, Schuylkill County, PA. She married **IVAN R. COLEMAN**. She died on 9 March 2016, McGraw Center for Caring, Jacksonville, Duval County, PA, at age 88. She was buried on 21 March 2016, at Indiantown Gap National Cemetery, Annville, Lebanon County, PA.

            3.6.3.5.4.1.1 **STEPHEN COLEMAN** married **GLORIA (--?--)**.

            3.6.3.5.4.1.2 **GAIL COLEMAN** married **JAMES BACKFISCH.**

        3.6.3.5.4.2 **WAYNE I. ARTZ** was born on 31 October 1930, Fearnot, Schuylkill County, PA. He married **RUTH M. HUNTZINGER** circa 1951. He died on 25 February 2017, Penn State Milton S. Hershey Medical Center, Hershey, Dauphin County, PA, at age 86. He was buried on 4 March 2017, at St. Mark's Cemetery, Spring Glen, Schuylkill County, PA.

3.6.3.5.4.2.1 JAMES W. ARTZ married DEBORAH (--?--).

3.6.3.5.4.2.1.1 PAMELA B. ARTZ married ALVIN SWEIGART.

3.6.3.5.4.2.1.1.1 KELTEN B. SWEIGART

3.6.3.5.4.2.1.2 SHAWN J. ARTZ

3.6.3.5.4.2.1.2.1 FAITH E. ARTZ

3.6.3.5.4.3 ELWOOD EUGENE ARTZ was born on 4 February 1934, Spring Glen, Schuylkill County, PA. He died on 26 August 1996, at age 62.

3.6.3.5.4.4 IRVIN RATHMUS ARTZ was born on 17 May 1939, Spring Glen, Schuylkill County, PA. He died on 4 November 2000, at age 61.

3.6.3.5.5 SEVILLA MILLER was born Schuylkill County, PA. She married WILLIAM RISSINGER. Some sources list Sevilla as a daughter of Edna Shade Miller, but this may be an erroneous reference to Edna's sister Sevilla. There is no Sevilla Miller listed in Census records among the children of Edna Shade and Rathmus Miller.

3.6.3.5.6 FOX MILLER married JENNIE KLINGER.

3.6.3.6 SEVILLA PROMELIA SHADE was born on 12 July 1888, Klingerstown, Schuylkill County, PA. She was baptized on 8 October 1888, Zion (Klinger's) Church, Erdman, Lykens Township, Dauphin County, PA. She married WILLIAM REISSINGER Klingerstown, Schuylkill County, PA. She died in January 1976, Manchester, York County, PA, at age 87.

3.6.4 FRANK TROUTMAN WIEST was born on 24 September 1851, Jordan Township, Northumberland County, PA. He married AMELIA A. OSSMAN, daughter of BENNEVILLE OSSMAN and HANNA BECK, on 4 November 1877, Dauphin County, PA. Frank Troutman Wiest was a butcher in Pillow. He died on 12 April 1925, Dauphin County, PA, at age 73. He was buried at Grandview Cemetery, Pillow, Dauphin County, PA.

3.6.4.1 CARRIE S. WIEST was born on 26 February 1878, Dauphin County, PA. She married JAMES M. GOTTSHALL. She died on 30 November 1923, Pillow, Dauphin County, PA, at age 45. She was buried at Grandview Cemetery, Pillow, Mifflin Township, Dauphin County, PA.

3.6.4.1.1 EARL W. GOTTSHALL married MARY E. (--?--). He was born in 1902, Pillow, Dauphin County, PA. He died in 1963, Pillow, Dauphin County, PA.

3.6.4.1.2 CARL GOTTSHALL married MILDRED A. (--?--). He was born in 1909, Pillow, Dauphin County, PA. He died in 1963, Pillow, Dauphin County, PA.

3.6.4.2 M. DILLIE WIEST married HARRY V. RUNK. She was born in 1879. She died in 1922, Pillow, Dauphin County, PA.

3.6.4.2.1 MYRTLE RUNK was born Pillow, Dauphin County, PA.

3.6.4.3 JACOB A. WIEST was born in June 1881, Pillow, Dauphin County, PA. Jacob married and relocated to Allentown, Lehigh County, PA. He died in 1947, PA.

3.6.4.3.1 VIOLET WIEST was born Allentown, Lehigh County, PA.

3.6.4.4 EMMA J. WIEST was born in August 1883, Pillow, Dauphin County, PA. She married ROY RAMSEY.

3.6.4.5 GUERNEY WIEST was born on 7 December 1884, Pillow, Dauphin County, PA. He married DERESA STELLA LEITZEL, daughter of SAMUEL LEITZEL, in 1916, Northumberland County, PA. He died on 14 February 1945, at age 60. Guerney was a butcher by trade and made his home in Lykens, Dauphin County, PA.

3.6.4.5.1 EVELYN L. WIEST was born in 1918, Lykens Township, Dauphin County, PA. She married JOHN SCHNEIDER. There is some conflict in the sources about three children, sometimes listed as children of Guerney and Deresa Wiest. These children are: Eleanor, Lester, and Mildred L. Some sources (e.g., Bruce Hall) list them as children of Guerney and Deresa, while other sources, including Mary Klinger (p. 373) list them, as children of Evelyn L. Wiest and John Schneider and grandchildren of Guerney and Deresa. Mary Klinger's listing, however, gives dates of birth for the children that are impossible, as the mother Evelyn would have been less than 5 years old.

3.6.4.5.1.1 ELEANOR SCHNEIDER was born in 1919.

3.6.4.5.1.2 LESTER SCHNEIDER married MELBA COX. He was born in 1921.

3.6.4.5.1.3 MILDRED L. SCHNEIDER married **WALTER SIERER**. She was born on 28 February 1922.

3.6.4.5.1.3.1 WALTER SIERER JR.

3.6.4.6 MABEL M. WIEST was born on 21 February 1887, Pillow, Dauphin County, PA. She died on 12 October 1887, Pillow, Dauphin County, PA. She was buried at Grandview Cemetery, Pillow, Mifflin Township, Dauphin County, PA.

3.6.4.7 FLORENCE WIEST is also referred to as **FLOSSIE T. WIEST** in some sources. She was born in November 1888, Pillow, Dauphin County, PA. She married **DANIEL SNYDER**.

3.6.4.7.1 JOHN SNYDER

3.6.4.8 FRANK TROUTMAN WIEST JR. is also referred to as **FRANK L. WIEST** in some sources. He was born in July 1897, Pillow, Dauphin County, PA. He married **CORA SNYDER**. He married **SARAH ELIZABETH LENKER**, daughter of **MICHAEL L. LENKER** and **CECELIA REBUCK**, circa 1951. Frank T. Wiest Jr. was a wholesaler in Pillow, Dauphin County, PA.

3.6.4.8.1 ROBERT L. WIEST was born on 12 September 1921, Pillow, Dauphin County, PA. He married **MARGARET MATSKO**. He died on 24 November 2005, Harrisburg Hospital, Harrisburg, Dauphin County, PA, at age 84. He was buried on 29 November 2005, at Calvary United Methodist Cemetery, Wiconisco, Dauphin County, PA.

3.6.4.8.2 RUTH WIEST was born in 1926, Pillow, Dauphin County, PA. She married **RICHARD GRANT LEMON**, son of **MARCUS DEAN LEMON** and **SARAH ELIZABETH LENKER**, on 24 February 1951, Conestoga, PA.

3.6.4.8.2.1 CONNIE LOU LEMON was born on 20 January 1954.

3.6.4.8.2.2 AMBER DAWN LEMON was born on 18 December 1960.

3.6.4.9 ETHEL A. WIEST was born on 12 January 1898, Pillow, Dauphin County, PA. She died on 18 October 1898, Pillow, Dauphin County, PA. She was buried at Grandview Cemetery, Pillow, Mifflin Township, Dauphin County, PA.

3.6.5 EDWARD TROUTMAN WIEST was born on 18 February 1854, Jordan Township, Northumberland County, PA. He married **EDITH MUSSER**, daughter of **HENRY MUSSER** and **ANETTA NOBLET**, on 28 March 1880. Some sources suggest that he and **EDITH MUSSER** were married circa 1878. In his early adulthood, Edward Troutman Wiest was a butcher and hotelman. Later he was a merchant at Malta. He died in 1927, Malta, Northumberland County, PA. He was buried at Union Cemetery, Pillow, Jordan Township, Northumberland County, PA.

3.6.5.1 CHARLES WIEST was born in 1873. Some sources list Charles as a son of Edward T. and Edith (Musser) Wiest, but that is questionable. According to the 1900 Census, Edith was the mother of three children, Elizabeth, Stella, and Edward. Similarly, the 1910 Census list's Edith, who was then 49 years old, as the mother of 3 children, all of who were then living. The 1910 Census, however, indicates that Edith was Edward T. Wiest's second wife, suggesting that Charles was born to Edward T. Wiest's first wife. He married **LEAH BYERLY** on 13 January 1904.

3.6.5.2 ELIZABETH WIEST was born in August 1881. She married **LANE RESSER**.

3.6.5.3 STELLA MAY WIEST was born in May 1886.

3.6.5.4 EDWARD H. WIEST is also referred to as **EDWARD J. WIEST** in some sources. He was born on 18 September 1889. He married **BEULAH HARRIS**, daughter of **WALTER HARRIS** and **LUCINDA SCHAEFFER**, circa 1908.

3.6.5.4.1 GERTRUDE M. WIEST was born on 31 October 1908. She died on 15 November 1908. She was buried at Grandview Cemetery, Pillow, Mifflin Township, Dauphin County, PA.

3.6.6 SAMUEL TRAUTMAN WIEST was born in March 1857, Northumberland County, PA. Some sources record that he was born circa 1856. He married **ELLEN HEPNER**, daughter of **SAMUEL S. HEPNER** and **ANGELINE KEPPLER**, circa 1880. He died in 1928, Pillow, Dauphin County, PA. He was buried at Grandview Cemetery, Pillow, Mifflin Township, Dauphin County, PA.

3.6.6.1 LAURA MAE WIEST was born on 18 May 1880. She married **BEN C. SNYDER**. She died on 4 July 1898, Pillow, Dauphin County, PA, at age 18. She was buried at Pillow, Dauphin County, PA.

3.6.6.2 STELLA WIEST was born circa 1911. She married **CLARENCE I. LENKER**, son of **JEREMIAH W. LENKER** and **EVA JANE SPOTTS**, circa 1927. She died before 7 August 2007.

3.6.6.2.1 JANET LENKER married **(--?--) BARNHARDT**. In August, 2007, Janet was living in Tower City, Schuylkill County, PA.

3.6.6.2.2 GERALD ROBERT LENKER is also referred to as **ROBERT LENKER** in some sources. He was born on 7 June 1927, Pillow, Dauphin County, PA. He married **FEARL KATHLEEN HOWARD**, daughter of **ISAAC LEROY HOWARD** and **HATTIE IRENE KLINGER**. He died on 26 May 1991, at age 63.

3.6.6.2.2.1 SANDRA KATHLEEN LENKER was born on 11 September 1948, Harrisburg, Dauphin County, PA. She married **GEORGE PARKER LYNCH**. She married **(--?--) LAMENZA**. Sandra lives in Southbury, CT.

3.6.6.2.2.2 DEBRA ROBERTA LENKER was born on 5 September 1956, Pillow, Dauphin County, PA. She married **MICHAEL ALAN MAGILTON**. She died on 10 February 1988, Harrisburg, Dauphin County, PA, at age 31.

3.6.6.2.3 JUNE A. LENKER was born on 26 June 1932, Pillow, Dauphin County, PA. She married **MYRON E. RILAND**. She died on 5 August 2007, at home, 563 Lebo Street, Millersburg, Dauphin County, PA, at age 75. According to a newspaper obituary, June and her husband, who lived in Millersburg, Dauphin County, PA, owned the former Maydale Greenhouse as well previously working at Seal Glove and the former Johnson-Bailee shoe factory. She was buried on 9 August 2007, at St. John's Lutheran Church Cemetery, Berrysburg, Dauphin County, PA.

3.6.6.2.3.1 DEAN RILAND married **REBECCA (--?--)**. In August, 2007, Dean and his family were living in Millersburg, Dauphin County, PA.

3.6.6.2.3.1.1 MATTHEW RILAND

3.6.6.2.3.1.2 TODD RILAND

3.6.6.2.3.2 RENA RILAND married **(--?--) SCHOMPER**. In August, 2007, Rena was living in Millersburg, Dauphin County, PA.

3.6.6.2.3.2.1 TIMOTHY SCHOMPER

3.6.6.2.3.2.1.1 TYLER SCHOMPER

3.6.6.2.3.2.1.2 KYLIE SCHOMPER

3.6.7 JACOB TRAUTMAN WIEST was born on 6 April 1857. Some sources record that he was born circa 1859. He married **ADELINE WEAVER**.

3.6.7.1 NORA WIEST married **(--?--) LAW**.

3.6.8 WILLIAM OSCAR TROUTMAN WIEST was born on 28 January 1859. He married **ELIZABETH TROUTMAN**. He married **ANNA DREIBELBIS BROSIUS**. After William's first wife, Elizabeth died at a relatively young age, he married Anna Dreibelbiss. They lived in Wiconisco, Dauphin County, PA. He died on 16 June 1887, at age 28.

3.6.8.1 MARGARET WIEST

3.6.8.2 GEORGE WIEST was born in 1882. He died in 1956.

3.6.9 CATHERINE TRAUTMAN WIEST was born on 19 September 1861. She married **GEORGE EDWIN WITMER**, son of **DANIEL WITMER** and **REBECCA REHRER**, circa 1878. She died on 7 June 1940, at age 78. She was buried at Grandview Cemetery, Allentown, Lehigh County, PA.

3.6.9.1 (--?--) WITMER died before 1900.

3.6.9.2 JACOB DANIEL WITMER was born on 12 September 1881. He married **MINNIE MAY WETZEL**. He married **EDITH MAE (--?--)**. He died on 25 December 1964, at age 83. He was buried at Grandview Cemetery, Allentown, Lehigh County, PA.

3.6.9.3 LIZZIE S. WITMER was born in October 1883.

3.6.9.4 MORRIS R. WITMER was born on 17 December 1887. Some sources record that he was born in December 1886. He married **EMMA KEISER**. He died on 20 September 1955, at age 67. He was buried at Grandview Cemetery, Allentown, Lehigh County, PA.

3.6.9.5 JENNIE A. WITMER was born in February 1890. She married **CHARLES SWEITZER** circa 1910.

3.6.9.6 CARRIE E. WITMER was born in April 1892.

3.6.10 MONROE TRAUTMAN WIEST was born on 9 January 1863. He married **ELIZABETH LAHR**, daughter of **HENRY LAHR** and **CATHERINE WOLF**. He married **KATIE R. (--?--)** circa 1903. He died Allentown, Lehigh County, PA.

3.6.10.1 MARY FLORENCE WIEST married ED RAU.

3.6.10.2 ETTA TRAPHINA WIEST married STEWART HARRIER.

3.6.10.3 CLARA KATIE ELIZABETH WIEST married CHARLES CARR.

3.6.10.4 MABEL EDITH WIEST married ED WILL.

3.6.10.5 WILLIAM OSCAR WIEST. William lived in Pillow, Dauphin County, PA. He was born on 29 May 1882. He married OLIVA A. SNYDER.

3.6.10.5.1 MAYE WIEST is also referred to as ERMA M. AND MAY E. U. WIEST in some sources. She was born circa 1903, Pillow, Dauphin County, PA. She married DANIEL BELTON HOKE circa 1920. She died before 2014.

3.6.10.5.1.1 NORWOOD QUENTIN HOKE was born on 29 May 1921, Pillow, Dauphin County, PA. He married JEAN I. (--?--). He died on 28 October 1975, Pillow, Dauphin County, PA, at age 54. He was buried at Maple Grove Cemetery, Elizabethville, Dauphin County, PA.

3.6.10.5.1.1.1 LYNN L. HOKE was born in 1952. He died in 1970. He was buried at Maple Grove Cemetery, Elizabethville, Dauphin County, PA.

3.6.10.5.1.2 CORRINE OLIVE SENORA HOKE was born on 22 April 1925, Pillow, Dauphin County, PA. She married JAMES M. SCHADE SR. She died on 15 May 2005, Lebanon County, PA, at age 80. She was buried at Grandview Cemetery, Pillow, Dauphin County, PA.

3.6.10.5.1.2.1 DON B. SCHADE

3.6.10.5.1.2.2 JAMES M. SCHADE JR.

3.6.10.5.1.3 ERMA J. HOKE was born on 6 June 1929, Pillow, Northumberland County, PA. She married NEIL SCHLEGEL. She died on 29 January 2014, The Manor at Susquehanna Village, Millersburg, Dauphin County, PA, at age 84. According to a newspaper obituary, Erma was employed by local factories and retired from Kocher's IGA in Elizabethville. She was buried at Grandview Cemetery, Pillow, PA.

3.6.10.5.2 RAYMOND W. WIEST was born on 22 July 1906. He married PAULINE SCHOFFSTALL. Raymond was a school teacher in Pillow, Dauphin County, PA.

3.6.10.5.2.1 CARLEY L. WIEST was born on 24 June 1927, Star Route, Gratz, Dauphin County, PA. She married PAUL W. ENDERS circa 1955. She died on 16 January 2014, Susquehanna Village, Millersburg, Dauphin County, PA, at age 86. According to a newspaper obituary, Carley graduated from the Elizabethville High School, Class of 1945 and attended Susquehanna University and the Central Pennsylvania Business School. She worked for The Bureau of Highway Safety. She was buried on 21 January 2014, at Fairview Enders Cemetery, Enders, Dauphin County, PA.

3.6.10.5.2.1.1 RAYMOND ENDERS married LINDA (--?--).

3.6.10.5.2.1.2 DOUGLAS ENDERS married DONNA (--?--).

3.6.10.5.2.1.3 MARK ENDERS married JOANNE (--?--).

3.6.10.5.3 MILTON MONROE WIEST was born on 20 July 1911, Pillow, Dauphin County, PA. He married EDNA M. WHISTLER. He died on 27 June 2001, Pillow, Dauphin County, PA, at age 89. He was buried at Grandview Cemetery, Pillow, Dauphin County, PA.

3.6.10.5.3.1 MILTON MONROE WIEST JR.

3.6.10.5.3.2 DAWN E. WIEST married (--?--) KEOUGH.

3.6.10.5.4 EUGENE WIEST was born on 16 April 1918.

3.6.10.6 MONROE WIEST was born on 17 March 1886.

3.6.10.7 RALPH WIEST was born circa 1898.

3.6.10.8 LAURA M. WIEST was born circa 1899. She married HOWARD DENNIS.

3.6.11 PRESTON TROUTMAN WIEST was born on 18 April 1865. He married MARY A. WOLF in 1884. He died on 16 March 1916, Pillow, Dauphin County, PA, at age 50. He was buried at Grandview Cemetery, Pillow, Dauphin County, PA.

3.6.11.1 JENNIE E. WIEST was born on 31 October 1886. She died on 3 September 1888, at age 1.

3.6.11.2 BEULAH A. WIEST was born on 28 March 1889. She died on 26 September 1890, Pillow, Dauphin County, PA, at age 1.

3.7 JESTINA WIEST was born on 9 August 1828. She married WILLIAM SHERTEL, son of GEORGE SHERTEL. She died on 6 February 1872, at age 43.

3.7.1 EVE SHERTEL married WILLIAM BOYER.

3.7.2 MARY SCHARTEL also went by the name of POLLY. She is also referred to as MARY SHERTEL in some sources. She was born circa 1854, Klingerstown, Schuylkill County, PA. She married JOHN T. BOYER.

3.7.2.1 CARRIE BOYER married CYRUS T. LEITZEL. She was born in 1876. She died in 1959, PA.

3.7.2.1.1 BESSIE J. LEITZEL was born after 1895.

3.7.2.2 ELURA BOYER was born on 14 October 1883, PA. She married DAVID RICHARD WIEST, son of SYLVESTER SCHADEL WIEST and ISABELLA S. LESHER. She died on 11 August 1935, of chronic nephritis and diabetes mellitus, Portland, Multnomah County, OR, at age 51. She was buried at Rose City Cemetery, Portland, Multnomah County, OR.

3.7.2.2.1 ROY WIEST was born Klingerstown, Schuylkill County, PA.

3.7.2.2.2 ALMON L. WIEST was born on 20 June 1901, Klingerstown, Schuylkill County, PA. He married GERTRUDE (--?--). He died in November 1980, Portland, Multnomah County, OR, at age 79.

3.7.2.2.3 CLARENCE AUSTIN WIEST was born in 1904, Klingerstown, Schuylkill County, PA. He married MARGARET (--?--). He died on 21 January 1960, Clackamas, Clackamas County, OR.

3.7.2.2.3.1 SHIRLEY WIEST married (--?--) WHIPPLE.

3.7.2.2.3.1.1 PETER WHIPPLE

3.7.2.2.4 EVELYN WIEST was born in 1907, Portland, Multnomah County, OR. She married (--?--) CALLAHAN.

3.7.3 AMELIA SHERTEL was born circa 1856. She married (--?--) MEHRWEIN.

3.7.4 ELIZABETH SHERTEL was born circa 1859.

3.7.5 CASSE SHERTEL was born on 21 July 1861. She died on 27 February 1862. She was buried at Zion (Klinger's) Church, Erdman, Lykens Township, Dauphin County, PA.

4 JOHANN PETER KLINGER was born on 2 January 1796, Lykens Township, Dauphin County, PA. He was baptized on 3 April 1796, Zion (Klinger's) Church, Erdman, Lykens Township, Dauphin County, PA. He married CATHARINE WIEST, daughter of JACOB WIEST and BARBARA FEICK, circa 1816, Lykens Township, Dauphin County, PA. He married ANNA HOLDERMAN circa 1867. He left a will with a codicil prepared on 30 November 1878. The original will provided that his farm or plantation was bequeathed to his wife Anna for her life along with such of Peter's personal property as she desired, provided that she "must take good care of it, keep the fences in good repair, and pay the taxes." After her death, assuming that she survived him, all of Peter's property was to be sold and the proceeds divided among his children. Personal property that Anna brought to the marriage to be given to her children. The codicil ordered that the farm or plantation be sold within one year after Peter's death and 2/3 of the proceeds divided among Peter's children, with 1/3 treated as a dower for Anna the interest on which was to be paid to Anna yearly so long as she lived. After her death, that portion of the proceeds was to be divided among Peter's children. It also provided that Anna was to receive all of the furniture "that she brought to me, and one cow, whichever she wants, two hogs, the cooking stove, iron kettle, butter churn, small clock, ten bushels of wheat, ten bushels of corn, ten bushels of oats. She shall have as much firewood as she needs to be taken from such timber as lies down until the farm is sold." He died on 4 January 1879, Dauphin County, PA, at age 83. He was buried at St. Paul's Church, Sacramento, Schuylkill County, PA. His estate was probated on 10 May 1882. His estate was probated on 15 December 1900.

4.1 MARIA KLINGER was born on 22 September 1818. She was baptized on 29 October 1818, Zion (Klinger's) Lutheran and Reformed Church, Erdman, Dauphin County, PA.

4.2 EVA CATHARINA KLINGER was born on 29 May 1820, Sacramento, Schuylkill County, PA. She was baptized on 2 July 1820, Zion (Klinger's) Lutheran and Reformed Church, Erdman, Dauphin County, PA. She married ABRAHAM S. SCHWENK circa 1840. She died on 10 November 1887, Philadelphia, Philadelphia County, PA, at age 67. She was buried at Lewisburg Cemetery, Lewisburg, Union County, PA.

4.2.1 MARY E. SCHWENK

4.2.2 LILLIAN SCHWENK

4.2.3 FREDERICK K. SCHWENK

4.2.4 SAMUEL K. SCHWENK was born on 8 May 1842. He married **EMMA MAI MARCONNIER** on 24 December 1879, Arch Street Presbyterian Church, Philadelphia, PA. He died on 10 April 1915, at age 72. He died on 17 April 1915, at age 72.

4.2.5 AARON SCHWENK married **ELIZABETH BARNHART.** He was born circa 1844, Klingerstown, Schuylkill County, PA.

4.2.6 ABRAHAM K. SCHWENK was born on 16 March 1847. He was baptized on 16 May 1847, St. Paul's (Artz's) Lutheran and Reformed Church, Sacramento, Schuylkill County, PA.

4.2.7 DANIEL K. SCHWENK was born on 12 August 1848. He was baptized on 29 October 1848, St. Paul's (Artz's) Lutheran and Reformed Church, Sacramento, Schuylkill County, PA. He died on 16 June 1850, at age 1. He was buried at St. Paul's (Artz's) Lutheran and Reformed Church Cemetery, Sacramento, Schuylkill County, PA.

4.2.8 ALMIRA K. SCHWENK was born in 1850.

4.2.9 JOHN E. K. SCHWENK was born on 24 August 1854.

4.2.10 PETER N. K. SCHWENK married **MARY R. SCHEPP.** He was born on 24 August 1854. He died in 1934.

    4.2.10.1 PETER N. K. SCHWENK JR. married **MARIE HAURDEL.**

        4.2.10.1.1 JEANNETTE SCHWENK

        4.2.10.1.2 PETER SCHWENK III

        4.2.10.1.3 DANIEL SCHWENK

4.2.11 GEORGE SCHWENK was born on 20 October 1856. He died on 24 August 1859, at age 2.

4.2.12 JACOB SCHWENK was born on 27 September 1858. He died on 20 August 1859.

4.3 DANIEL KLINGER was born on 27 June 1823. He died circa 3 March 1837. He was buried at St. Paul's (Artz's) Lutheran and Reformed Church Cemetery, Sacramento, Schuylkill County, PA.

4.4 ISRAEL KLINGER was born on 7 March 1826. Some sources record that he was born on 7 February 1826. He married **CAROLINA SCHWALM**, daughter of **FREDERICK SCHWALM** and **CATHARINA STEIN.** He married **LYDIA A. WETZEL**, daughter of **PETER WETZEL** and **MARY MAGDALENA SCHNEIDER,** on 29 August 1891. He died on 21 October 1900, at age 74. He was buried at Church of God Cemetery, Valley View, Hegins Township, Schuylkill County, PA.

4.4.1 CATHARINE KLINGER died on 14 February 1848. She was buried at Jacob's (Howerter's) Church Cemetery, Line Mountain, Northumberland County, PA.

4.4.2 MARY SAVILLA KLINGER was buried at Jacob's (Howerter's) Evangelical Lutheran and Reformed Church Cemetery, Line Mountain, Northumberland County, PA. Cemetery records indicate that two of Israel and Carolina's daughters, Mary Savilla and Catharine, are buried there with no dates given, presumably indicating that they died in infancy.

4.4.3 JUSTINA KLINGER was born on 15 April 1847. She married **AMOS RUMBERGER**, son of **JOHN ROMBERGER** and **HANNAH HOFFMAN.** She died on 29 May 1909, Porter Township, Schuylkill County, PA, at age 62. She was buried on 1 June 1909, at (Hepler's) Church of God Cemetery, Valley View, Schuylkill County, PA.

    4.4.3.1 GEORGE M. RUMBERGER was born on 16 January 1865. He died on 13 July 1932, Porter Township, Schuylkill County, PA, at age 67. He was buried on 16 July 1932, at Saint John's Lutheran Church Cemetery, Pine Grove, Schuylkill County, PA.

    4.4.3.2 ELIZABETH ANNA RUMBERGER was born on 8 January 1867, Valley View, Schuylkill County, PA. She married **THOMAS J. PARRY**, son of **WILLIAM PARRY** and **ELIZABETH LEWIS,** circa 1886. She died on 23 January 1940, Pine Grove, Schuylkill County, PA, at age 73. She was buried on 26 June 1940, at Saint John's Lutheran Church Cemetery, Pine Grove, Schuylkill County, PA.

        4.4.3.2.1 AGNES M. PARRY was born on 21 April 1888, Keffers, Schuylkill County, PA. Some sources record that she was born in April 1887. She married **PIERCE ELMER NOLL**, son of **DAVID NOLL** and **KATE OWENS.** She died on 23 July 1960, Pottsville, Schuylkill County, PA, at age 72. She was buried at Saint John's Lutheran Church Cemetery, Pine Grove, Schuylkill County, PA.

            4.4.3.2.1.1 ESTHER IRENE NOLL was born on 9 February 1916, Pine Grove, Schuylkill County, PA. She was baptized on 23 July 1916, St. Peter's United Church of Christ, Pine Grove, Schuylkill County, PA. She married **MELVIN S. DANIELS**, son of **STANFORD N. DANIELS** and **VERDIE S. KLINGER.** She died on 12 December 1988, at age 72. She died on 12

December 1988, at age 72. She was buried at Saint John's Lutheran Church Cemetery, Pine Grove, Schuylkill County, PA.

4.4.3.2.1.1.1 ROBERT MELVIN DANIELS was born on 26 June 1936, Tremont, Schuylkill County, PA. He died on 11 August 2003, at age 67.

4.4.3.2.1.1.1.1 JEFFREY DANIELS

4.4.3.2.1.2 RUTH ELIZABETH NOLL was born on 23 March 1918, Pine Grove, Schuylkill County, PA. She was baptized on 30 June 1918, St. Peter's United Church of Christ, Pine Grove, Schuylkill County, PA. She married **THEODORE DONMOYER**, son of **MONROE EDWARD DONMOYER** and **MARY OWENS**. She died on 9 March 1998, at age 79. She was buried at Saint John's Lutheran Church Cemetery, Pine Grove, Schuylkill County, PA.

4.4.3.2.1.2.1 SHIRLEY BETTY DONMOYER was born on 10 November 1936, Tremont, Schuylkill County, PA. She died on 25 March 1937, Pine Grove, Schuylkill County, PA. She was buried at Saint John's Lutheran Church Cemetery, Pine Grove, Schuylkill County, PA.

4.4.3.2.2 JENNIE ESTHER PARRY was born on 18 November 1890, Lebanon County, PA. She married **FRANK TRAUTMAN**, son of **WILLIAM TRAUTMAN** and **MARY KRALL,** before 1920. She died on 9 November 1964, Lebanon, Lebanon County, PA, at age 73. She was buried on 12 November 1964, at Cedar Hill Cemetery, Fredericksburg, Lebanon County, PA.

4.4.3.2.2.1 FRANKLIN JUNIOR TRAUTMAN was born on 12 May 1921, Lebanon County, PA. He married **MAZIE FURMAN**, daughter of **LOT FURMAN** and **MABEL KRALL.** He died on 2 February 1998, Orange County, FL, at age 76. He was buried at Cedar Hill Cemetery, Fredericksburg, Lebanon County, PA.

4.4.3.2.3 WILLIAM ROY PARRY was born on 8 March 1893, Joliett, Schuylkill County, PA. He married **CLARA W. INGRAM** in 1920, Philadelphia, Philadelphia County, PA. He died in November 1982, at age 89. He was buried at Arlington Cemetery, Drexel Hill, Delaware County, PA.

4.4.3.2.3.1 SUE PARRY was born circa 1930.

4.4.3.2.4 HELEN I. PARRY was born on 8 August 1895, Keffers, Schuylkill County, PA. She married **JOHN WILSON KLICK**, son of **GEORGE KLICK** and **SALLY KOBLE.** She married **THOMAS F. FESSLER**, son of **HARLAN FESSLER** and **SARAH WORKMAN**. She died on 27 March 1981, at age 85. She was buried at Saint John's Lutheran Church Cemetery, Pine Grove, Schuylkill County, PA.

4.4.3.2.5 PEARL JOSEPHINE PARRY was born on 29 April 1897, Schuylkill County, PA. She married **RAYMOND LEWIS RUNKLE**, son of **FRANKLIN C. RUNKLE** and **MINNIE (--?--)**, after 1920. She died in June 1976, at age 79. She was buried at Saint John's Lutheran Church Cemetery, Pine Grove, Schuylkill County, PA.

4.4.3.2.6 HERMAN HARRY PARRY was born on 18 April 1901, Keffers, Schuylkill County, PA. He died on 29 March 1917, Pine Grove, Schuylkill County, PA, at age 15. He was buried at Saint John's Lutheran Church Cemetery, Pine Grove, Schuylkill County, PA.

4.4.3.2.7 GEORGE T. PARRY was born on 23 March 1906. He married **MARIETTA L. LOOSE**, daughter of **MAX C. LOOSE** and **EMMA HAAK**. He died on 3 November 1992, Cumberland County Nursing Home, Middlesex Township, Cumberland County, PA, at age 86. He was buried at Mechanicsburg Cemetery, Mechanicsburg, Cumberland County, PA.

4.4.3.2.7.1 G. THOMAS PARRY

4.4.3.2.7.2 MARILOW PARRY married (--?--) **SPAETH**.

4.4.3.3 DANIEL RUMBERGER was born in September 1873. He died on 3 May 1935, Schuylkill County Almshouse Hospital, North Manheim Township, Schuylkill County, PA, at age 61. He was buried on 6 May 1935, at Valley View, Schuylkill County, PA. Daniel was single at the time of his death.

4.4.3.4 CHARLES F. RUMBERGER was born on 11 March 1875, Joliett, Schuylkill County, PA. He married **MARY A. KIMMEL**, daughter of **EDWARD KIMMEL** and **LUCY GRAEGER**, circa 1898. He died on 27 January 1944, Keffers, Schuylkill County, PA, at age 68. He was buried on 30 January 1944, at Saint John's Lutheran Church Cemetery, Pine Grove, Schuylkill County, PA.

4.4.3.4.1 HELEN I. RUMBERGER was born on 8 January 1899, Schuylkill County, PA. She married (--?--) **UPDEGROVE.** She died on 8 December 1921, Porter Township, Schuylkill County, PA, at age 22. She was buried on 12 December 1921, at Saint John's Lutheran Church Cemetery, Pine Grove, Schuylkill County, PA.

4.4.3.4.2 MABEL RUMBERGER was born on 29 October 1900, Keffers, Schuylkill County, PA. She married **DR. MICHAEL JOSEPH MCCARTHY**, son of **DENNIS MCCARTHY** and **WINIFRED MCGRATH,** circa 1926. She died on 15 October 1987, at age 86. She was buried at Saint Mary's Cemetery, Troy, Rensselaer County, NY.

> **4.4.3.4.2.1 MARY MCCARTHY** was born circa 1926. She married (--?--) **DOLAN.**
>
> **4.4.3.4.2.2 ANN MARIE MCCARTHY** was born on 26 July 1929, Philadelphia, Philadelphia County, PA. She married (--?--) **WYLAND.** She died on 13 August 2008, Van Rensselaer Manor, Troy, Rensselaer County, NY, at age 79. She was buried on 16 August 2008, at Saint Mary's Cemetery, Troy, Rensselaer County, NY.
>
>> **4.4.3.4.2.2.1 WILLIAM C. WYLAND** married **KATHRYN** (--?--).
>>
>> **4.4.3.4.2.2.2 PATRICIA A. WYLAND** married **JOSEPH QUILLIAN.**
>>
>>> **4.4.3.4.2.2.2.1 BRENDAN QUILLIAN**
>>>
>>> **4.4.3.4.2.2.2.2 COLIN QUILLIAN**
>>>
>>> **4.4.3.4.2.2.2.3 HALLEY QUILLIAN**
>>
>> **4.4.3.4.2.2.3 CHRISTOPHER M. WYLAND**

4.4.3.4.3 HARRY KIMMEL RUMBERGER was born on 25 October 1902, Keffers, Schuylkill County, PA. He married **GRACE MAMIE REINER**, daughter of **WILLIAM FRANK REINER** and **HANNAH MAYME YOHE,** after 1940. He died on 7 March 1970, Tower City, Schuylkill County, PA, at age 67. He was buried at Greenwood Cemetery, Tower City, Schuylkill County, PA.

4.4.3.4.4 CLARENCE C. RUMBERGER was born on 19 August 1907, Porter Township, Schuylkill County, PA. He married **CARRIE E. MILLER**, daughter of **EDWARD MILLER** and **FLORA CRONE.** He died on 25 June 1983, Pottsville, Schuylkill County, PA, at age 75. He was buried at Saint John's Lutheran Church Cemetery, Pine Grove, Schuylkill County, PA.

> **4.4.3.4.4.1 CHARLES EDWARD RUMBERGER** married **ETHEL KATHLEEN REED.** He was born on 18 October 1929, Joliett, Schuylkill County, PA. He died on 8 July 1999, at age 69. He was buried at Saint John's Lutheran Church Cemetery, Pine Grove, Schuylkill County, PA.
>
> **4.4.3.4.4.2 CLARENCE A. RUMBERGER** was born on 18 January 1933, Keffers, Schuylkill County, PA. He married **PAMELA Y. NUNLEY.** He died on 15 February 1991, Pottsville, Schuylkill County, PA, at age 58. He was buried at Greenwood Cemetery, Tower City, Schuylkill County, PA.
>
> **4.4.3.4.4.3 ROBERT D. RUMBERGER** was born in 1938.

4.4.3.4.5 KENNETH W. RUMBERGER is also referred to as **KENNETH W. ROMBERGER** in some sources. He was born on 14 June 1910, Joliett, Schuylkill County, PA. He married **HELEN G. MCGOVERN.** He died in March 1981, at age 70. He was buried at Saint Mary Star of the Sea Cemetery, Llewellyn, Schuylkill County, PA.

> **4.4.3.4.5.1 KENNETH M. RUMBERGER** is also referred to as **KENETH M. ROMBERGER** in some sources. He was born on 21 March 1947, Pottsville, Schuylkill County, PA. He died on 26 April 1954, Minersville, Schuylkill County, PA, at age 7. He was buried on 29 April 1954, at Saint Vincent de Paul Cemetery #1, Minersville, Schuylkill County, PA.

4.4.3.5 WILLIAM FRANCIS RUMBERGER was born on 27 August 1877, Schuylkill County, PA. He married **MATILDA M. JONES**, daughter of **JOHN JONES** and **CATHERINE SCHUCKER,** circa 1904. He died on 31 January 1954, Pottsville, Schuylkill County, PA, at age 76. He was buried on 4 February 1954, at Greenwood Cemetery, Tower City, Schuylkill County, PA.

4.4.3.6 HARRY EZRA RUMBERGER was born on 21 November 1880. He married **BEATRICE MAE WHINNEY** in 1926, Philadelphia, Philadelphia County, PA. He died on 11 January 1943, Philadelphia, Philadelphia County, PA, at age 62. He was buried on 15 January 1943, at Northwood Cemetery, Philadelphia, Philadelphia County, PA.

> **4.4.3.6.1 ANNE JUSTINE RUMBERGER** was born on 31 July 1931, Philadelphia, Philadelphia County, PA. She married (--?--) **TROISI.** She died on 3 April 2000, at age 68.

4.4.3.7 MARY JANE C. RUMBERGER also went by the name of **JENNIE C. RUMBERGER**. She was born on 19 June 1884, Keffers, Schuylkill County, PA. She married **THOMAS WARD FESSLER**, son of **JEREMIAH FESSLER** and **CAROLINE KANTNER**, circa 1908. She died on 5 July 1956, Cornwall Methodist Church Home, Cornwall, Lebanon County, PA, at age 72. She was buried on 7 July 1956, at Forest Hills Memorial Park, Huntingdon Valley, Montgomery County, PA.

4.4.4 MARIA CATHARINE KLINGER was born on 2 December 1847. She is also referred to as **MARY** in some sources. She married **JOHN H. DEITER**, son of **SOLOMON DIETER** and **ANNA HOLDIMAN**, circa 1864. She died on 25 July 1922, Hegins Township, Schuylkill County, PA, at age 74. She was buried on 28 July 1922, at Church of God Cemetery, Valley View, Schuylkill County, PA.

4.4.4.1 IDA DEITER was born on 17 December 1864. She married **HARRY ELLSWORTH SANDS**. She died on 15 November 1907, at age 42. She was buried at Church of God Cemetery, Valley View, Schuylkill County, PA.

4.4.4.2 ELLEN JANE DEITER was born in March 1868. She married **WILLIAM SCHLEGEL**. She died in 1935. She was buried at Greenwood Cemetery, Allentown, Lehigh County, PA.

4.4.4.2.1 IRVIN SCHLEGEL was born in March 1885.

4.4.4.2.2 BEULAH MAUD SCHLEGEL was born on 18 November 1886. She married **HARRY ALEXANDER ELTRINGHAM**. She died on 4 April 1938, Allentown, Lehigh County, PA, at age 51. She was buried at Greenwood Cemetery, Allentown, Lehigh County, PA.

4.4.4.2.3 LILLIAN SCHLEGEL was born in February 1891. She married **(--?--) LAMB**.

4.4.4.2.4 PERDIE MINERVA SCHLEGEL was born in 1892. She married **EARL HEIMBACH**. She died in 1950. She was buried at Greenwood Cemetery, Allentown, Lehigh County, PA.

4.4.4.2.4.1 WILLIAM E. HEIMBACH

4.4.4.2.5 ELMER L. SCHLEGEL was born in 1894. He died in April 1929. He was buried at Greenwood Cemetery, Allentown, Lehigh County, PA.

4.4.4.3 SAMUEL K. DEITER was born on 17 May 1870. Although his death certificate and some other sources say that he was born on 17 May 1872, that date is impossibly close to the birth date of his twin siblings, Fred and Elizabeth. He married **CORA TAMEY HUNTZINGER**, daughter of **HENRY HUNTZINGER** and **AMANDA ERDMAN**. He died on 21 July 1937, Frailey Township, Schuylkill County, PA, at age 67. He was buried at Palmyra Cemetery, Palmyra, Lebanon County, PA.

4.4.4.3.1 MABEL TOLEDO DEITER was born on 19 January 1890, Sacramento, Schuylkill County, PA. She married **HENRY GEORGE BARRY**. She died on 15 August 1946, Pottsville, Schuylkill County, PA, at age 56. She was buried at Donaldson Community Cemetery, Donaldson, Schuylkill County, PA.

4.4.4.3.1.1 IRENE E. BARRY was born on 14 September 1908, Tower City, Schuylkill County, PA. She married **JOHN KREIDER LANDIS**, son of **JOHN M. LANDIS** and **LILLIE E. HARTZ**, on 6 October 1928, Lebanon County, PA. She died on 7 July 1961, Palmyra, Lebanon County, PA, at age 52. She was buried on 10 July 1961, at Gravel Hill Cemetery, Palmyra, Lebanon County, PA.

4.4.4.3.1.1.1 JOHN KREIDER LANDIS JR. was born on 8 May 1929, Hershey, Dauphin County, PA. He married **MARY L. (--?--)**. He died on 13 January 2004, Holy Spirit Hospital, Camp Hill, Cumberland County, PA, at age 74. He was buried at Gravel Hill Cemetery, Palmyra, Lebanon County, PA.

4.4.4.3.1.1.1.1 JOHN M. LANDIS married **SUSAN (--?--)**.

4.4.4.3.1.1.1.2 ROBERT C. LANDIS married **LOIS (--?--)**.

4.4.4.3.1.1.1.3 JUDY LANDIS married **RICHARD ZEIDERS**.

4.4.4.3.1.1.2 IRENE E. LANDIS was born on 18 May 1930, South Londonderry Township, Lebanon County, PA. She died on 19 May 1930, Hershey Hospital, Hershey, Dauphin County, PA. She was buried on 19 May 1930, at Gravel Hill Cemetery, Palmyra, Lebanon County, PA.

4.4.4.3.1.1.3 HENRY B. LANDIS was born on 19 July 1937. He married **JACQUELINE M. (--?--)**. He died on 16 March 1998, Hershey, Dauphin County, PA, at age 60. He was buried on 20 March 1998, at Gravel Hill Cemetery, Palmyra, Lebanon County, PA.

4.4.4.3.1.1.3.1 BRIAN S. LANDIS

4.4.4.3.1.1.3.2 MARK E. LANDIS

4.4.4.3.1.1.3.3 KARL H. LANDIS

4.4.4.3.1.1.3.4 LINDA I. LANDIS married PEARSON (--?--).

4.4.4.3.1.2 ELMER CHARLES BARRY was born on 27 March 1910, Tower City, Schuylkill County, PA. He married HILDA VIOLA UPDEGROVE, daughter of IRA UPDEGROVE and SADIE DRUM. He died on 31 January 1940, Frailey Township, Schuylkill County, PA, at age 29. He was buried on 4 February 1940, at Greenwood Cemetery, Tower City, Schuylkill County, PA.

4.4.4.3.1.2.1 CARL R. BARRY was born circa 1932.

4.4.4.3.1.2.2 MARIAN A. BARRY was born circa 1936.

4.4.4.3.1.3 MARGARET MAE BARRY was born on 26 December 1911, Schuylkill County, PA. She married BENJAMIN F. NEY, son of HARVEY NEY and JENNIE BENSINGER. She died in June 1975, Manheim, Lancaster County, PA, at age 63. She was buried at Donaldson Community Cemetery, Donaldson, Schuylkill County, PA.

4.4.4.3.1.3.1 SHIRLEY J. NEY was born circa 1932.

4.4.4.3.1.3.2 BENJAMIN F. NEY JR. was born circa 1934.

4.4.4.3.1.3.3 DELORIS MABLE NEY was born on 29 June 1938, Donaldson, Schuylkill County, PA. She died on 31 January 1997, at age 58. She married (--?--) SUTER on 31 January 1997. She was buried at Donaldson Community Cemetery, Donaldson, Schuylkill County, PA.

4.4.4.3.1.3.4 CATHERINE NEY was born on 18 July 1942, Donaldson, Schuylkill County, PA. She died on 18 July 1942, Frailey Township, Schuylkill County, PA. She was buried at Donaldson, Schuylkill County, PA.

4.4.4.3.1.4 JOHN HENRY BARRY was born on 19 September 1914, Donaldson, Schuylkill County, PA. He married FLORENCE WORMER. He died on 12 July 1992, Tremont, Schuylkill County, PA, at age 77. He was buried at Donaldson Community Cemetery, Donaldson, Schuylkill County, PA.

4.4.4.3.1.5 CLYDE SIDNEY BARRY was born on 28 July 1916. He married BETTY J. HATTER. He died on 6 September 1979, at age 63. He was buried at Donaldson Community Cemetery, Donaldson, Schuylkill County, PA.

4.4.4.3.1.5.1 CLYDE R. BARRY was born on 28 May 1940, Pottsville Hospital, Pottsville, Schuylkill County, PA. He died on 15 November 1941, Pottsville Hospital, Pottsville, Schuylkill County, PA, at age 1. He was buried at Donaldson Community Cemetery, Donaldson, Schuylkill County, PA.

4.4.4.3.1.6 CHARLES SAMUEL BARRY was born on 7 August 1918, Schuylkill County, PA. He married MILDRED K. GROSS, daughter of JOHN GROSS and AMELIA KOHLER. He died in December 1972, Schuylkill County, PA, at age 54. He was buried at Calvary United Methodist Cemetery, Wiconisco, Dauphin County, PA.

4.4.4.3.1.6.1 ALLEN CHARLES BARRY was born on 22 April 1943, Pottsville, Schuylkill County, PA. He married TINA M. BOPP. He died on 27 October 2015, Health and Rehabilitation Center, Tremont, Schuylkill County, PA, at age 72.

4.4.4.3.1.7 GUY RAYMOND BARRY was born on 21 July 1920, Donaldson, Schuylkill County, PA. He married DORIS SIDNEY HEPLER, daughter of OSCAR HEPLER and ANNIE DINGER, circa 1941. He died on 26 May 1993, at age 72. He was buried at Donaldson Community Cemetery, Donaldson, Schuylkill County, PA.

4.4.4.3.1.8 ALLEN WILLIAM BARRY was born on 11 May 1922, Donaldson, Schuylkill County, PA. He married RUTH PAUL. He died on 5 May 2002, at age 79.

4.4.4.3.1.9 ARTHUR LEVI BARRY was born on 3 July 1924, Donaldson, Schuylkill County, PA. He married IRENE G. ATHEY, daughter of CLIFFORD ATHEY and MAE KOPPENHAVER. He died on 27 June 1999, Tremont, Schuylkill County, PA, at age 74. He was buried at Donaldson Community Cemetery, Donaldson, Schuylkill County, PA.

4.4.4.3.1.9.1 MICHAEL K. BARRY was born in 1956. He died in 1975. He was buried at Donaldson Community Cemetery, Donaldson, Schuylkill County, PA.

4.4.4.3.1.10 CATHERINE LORRAINE BARRY is also referred to as **KATHRYN** in some sources. She was born on 7 May 1926. She married **WARREN DANIEL REED.** She died in May 1970.

4.4.4.3.1.11 HELEN FLORENCE BARRY was born on 28 May 1928, Donaldson, Schuylkill County, PA. She died on 8 May 1929, Frailey Township, Schuylkill County, PA. She was buried on 11 May 1929, at Donaldson Community Cemetery, Donaldson, Schuylkill County, PA.

4.4.4.3.1.12 DOROTHY J. BARRY was born circa 1930.

4.4.4.3.1.13 ROBERT E. BARRY was born on 23 May 1934, Donaldson, Schuylkill County, PA. He married **HELEN MAE SNYDER**, daughter of **MILLARD SNYDER** and **MARGARET SNYDER.** He died on 22 October 2012, Somerset, Somerset County, PA, at age 78. He was buried at Donaldson Community Cemetery, Donaldson, Schuylkill County, PA.

    4.4.4.3.1.13.1 ROBERT BARRY

        4.4.4.3.1.13.1.1 ROBERT BARRY JR.

    4.4.4.3.1.13.2 DALE BARRY

    4.4.4.3.1.13.3 KAREN BARRY married **SHAWN PRICE.**

        4.4.4.3.1.13.3.1 CODY PRICE

4.4.4.3.2 BESSIE M. DEITER was born on 5 December 1891, Schuylkill County, PA. She married **DANIEL M. FETTERHOFF.** Some sources record that she was born on 2 December 1902. She died on 19 June 1947, Lebanon, Lebanon County, PA, at age 55. She was buried on 23 June 1947, at Palmyra Cemetery, Palmyra, Lebanon County, PA.

    4.4.4.3.2.1 LAWRENCE D. FETTERHOFF was born on 25 February 1912, Tower City, Schuylkill County, PA. He married **MARIAN L. (--?--).** He died on 20 February 1963, Harrisburg, Dauphin County, PA, at age 50. He was buried on 23 February 1963, at Palmyra Cemetery, Palmyra, Lebanon County, PA.

    4.4.4.3.2.2 MILDRED MAE FETTERHOFF was born on 25 October 1914. She married **HUGH RALPH BUCKS** on 12 March 1935. She died on 16 November 2000, at age 86. She was buried at Palmyra Cemetery, Palmyra, Lebanon County, PA.

    4.4.4.3.2.3 PAUL MILTON FETTERHOFF was born on 5 April 1917, Palmyra, Lebanon County, PA. He was baptized on 13 September 1924, Lutheran Church, Palmyra, Lebanon County, PA. He married **KATHLEEN JANE PATRICK**, daughter of **OLIVER PATRICK** and **KATHRYN RHODES**, on 27 July 1940, Albin, Frederick County, VA. He married **CATHERINE CIALINI**, daughter of **GUERNO CIALINI** and **MARY CANFORD,** on 5 March 1948, Martinsburg, Berkeley County, WV. He died on 10 November 1965, at age 48. He was buried at Palmyra Cemetery, Palmyra, Lebanon County, PA.

        4.4.4.3.2.3.1 DONNE E. FETTERHOFF married **SEBASTIAN PETRINO.**

            4.4.4.3.2.3.1.1 TRACI PETRINO

            4.4.4.3.2.3.1.2 MICHAEL PETRINO

    4.4.4.3.2.4 HAROLD WILLIAM FETTERHOFF was born on 15 September 1921, Palmyra, Lebanon County, PA. He was baptized on 13 September 1924, Lutheran Church, Palmyra, Lebanon County, PA. He married **MARGARET MARIE ROSSI**, daughter of **CONSTANTINO ROSSI** and **MARIA COCCIA**, on 16 July 1948, Dauphin County, PA. He died on 19 January 1997, at age 75.

    4.4.4.3.2.5 CHARLOTTE ANN FETTERHOFF was born on 18 July 1924, Palmyra, Lebanon County, PA. She married **PAUL HENRY KEENER**, son of **JOHN KEENER** and **STELLA WESTENBERGER**, on 28 November 1942, Palmyra, Lebanon County, PA. She died on 23 October 1998, at age 74. She was buried on 26 October 1998, at Palmyra Cemetery, Palmyra, Lebanon County, PA.

        4.4.4.3.2.5.1 PAMELA A. KEENER married **ROBERT KREISER.**

            4.4.4.3.2.5.1.1 SHELLY KREISER

        4.4.4.3.2.5.2 DENNIS P. KEENER married **MARIAN (--?--).**

    4.4.4.3.2.6 CLIFFORD DAVID FETTERHOFF was born on 22 August 1928. He married **IRENE M. LEFRANCOIS**, daughter of **WILLIAM LEFRANCOIS** and **JEANETTE BELAND.** He died on

28 February 1975, at age 46. He was buried at Palmyra Cemetery, Palmyra, Lebanon County, PA.

4.4.4.3.3 JOHN HENRY DEITER was born on 7 May 1893, Sacramento, Schuylkill County, PA. He married MYRTLE AMY RITZMAN, daughter of WILLIAM RITZMAN and SARAH KOPPENHAVER. He died on 26 August 1955, Tremont, Schuylkill County, PA, at age 62. He was buried on 30 August 1955, at Greenwood Cemetery, Tower City, Schuylkill County, PA.

4.4.4.3.3.1 FLORENCE AGNES DEITER was born on 17 August 1913. She was baptized on 12 December 1913, St. Paul's Lutheran Church, Tower City, Schuylkill County, PA. She married CLYDE L. MILLER. She died in 1971.

4.4.4.3.3.1.1 CLYDE L. MILLER JR. was born circa 1933.

4.4.4.3.3.1.2 JOAN M. MILLER was born circa 1936.

4.4.4.3.3.2 MERLE CORRINE DEITER is also referred to as MYRLE in some sources. She was born on 4 October 1915, Tower City, Schuylkill County, PA. She married EDGAR T. MORGAN, son of JOHN MORGAN and MARY ECKLER. She died on 8 May 1959, Tower City, Schuylkill County, PA, at age 43. She was buried on 11 May 1959, at Greenwood Cemetery, Tower City, Schuylkill County, PA.

4.4.4.3.3.3 PEARL IRENE DEITER was born on 4 October 1915, Tower City, Schuylkill County, PA. She married WILLIAM R. AUNGST. She died on 9 November 2007, at age 92. She was buried at Greenwood Cemetery, Tower City, Schuylkill County, PA.

4.4.4.3.3.4 FREDA MAE DEITER was born on 21 February 1917. She died on 27 January 1965, at age 47.

4.4.4.3.3.5 MYRTLE ELEANOR DEITER was born on 17 December 1919, Tower City, Schuylkill County, PA. She married RAYMOND L. KIMMEL, son of HENRY KIMMEL and ANN FOCHT, circa 1938. She died on 10 March 2016, Donaldson, Schuylkill County, PA, at age 96. She was buried on 14 March 2016, at Donaldson Community Cemetery, Donaldson, Schuylkill County, PA.

4.4.4.3.3.5.1 ELEANOR JEAN KIMMEL married (--?--) CARL.

4.4.4.3.3.5.2 BARBARA KIMMEL married RAYMOND WHITTAKER.

4.4.4.3.3.5.3 KATHERINE KIMMEL married JOHN KOHR.

4.4.4.3.3.6 JOHN H. DEITER was born on 1 April 1928, Tower City, Schuylkill County, PA. He married FLO-ELLA C. MOYER, daughter of HAROLD MOYER and MELBA HAND. He died on 27 January 2013, Health and Rehabilitation Center, Tremont, Schuylkill County, PA, at age 84. He was buried at Greenwood Cemetery, Tower City, Schuylkill County, PA.

4.4.4.3.3.7 ROBERT D. DEITER was born on 21 January 1932. He married ANNA MAE WENRICH. He died on 28 November 2003, Tower City, Schuylkill County, PA, at age 71. He was buried at Saint John's Lutheran Church Cemetery, Pine Grove, Schuylkill County, PA.

4.4.4.3.3.7.1 DENNIS DEITER

4.4.4.3.3.7.2 BRENDA DEITER married (--?--) EMBERG.

4.4.4.3.3.7.3 DIANE DEITER married (--?--) MACHAMER.

4.4.4.3.3.8 DALE W. DEITER was born on 19 November 1934, Tower City, Schuylkill County, PA. He married GLADYS V. PERHACH. He died on 7 December 2010, Tower City, Schuylkill County, PA, at age 76. He was buried on 11 December 2010, at Greenwood Cemetery, Tower City, Schuylkill County, PA.

4.4.4.3.3.8.1 JOHN D. DEITER married KIM (--?--).

4.4.4.3.3.8.1.1 TODD DEITER

4.4.4.3.3.8.1.2 STEPHEN DEITER

4.4.4.3.4 LOTTIE C. DEITER was born in June 1895. She married RAY H. MILLER, son of WILLIAM EDWARD MILLER and SUSAN ADALINE HESS. She died in 1983. She was buried at Grand View Memorial Park, Annville, Lebanon County, PA.

4.4.4.3.4.1 E. GUY MILLER was born in 1916. He died before 7 June 2007.

4.4.4.3.4.2 ARLENE SUZANNE MILLER is also referred to as ARLENE SUSAN MILLER in some sources. She was born on 22 March 1916, Tower City, Schuylkill County, PA. She was baptized on 10 September 1916, St. Paul's Lutheran Church, Tower City, Schuylkill County,

PA. She married **HAROLD F. GINGRICH**, son of **CLAYTON C. GINGRICH** and **GRACE M. TICE**, on 9 November 1939, Tower City, Schuylkill County, PA. She married **MARK D. SHEARER** circa 1986. She died on 7 June 2007, Milton Hershey Medical Center, Hershey, Dauphin County, PA, at age 91. She was buried on 12 June 2007, at Salem United Church of Christ Cemetery, Campbelltown, Lebanon County, PA.

> **4.4.4.3.4.2.1 CALVIN B. GINGRICH** married **MAUREE (--?--)**.

> **4.4.4.3.4.2.2 ALDUS E. GINGRICH**

4.4.4.3.4.3 INEZ M. MILLER was born circa 1919. She married **CECIL WOODROW CLINE**, son of **GOLDIE CLINE** and **NAOMI E. BRUNK**, on 22 January 1938, Palmyra, Lebanon County, PA.

> **4.4.4.3.4.3.1 RODNEY J. CLINE**

> **4.4.4.3.4.3.2 WILLIAM E. CLINE** was born on 24 April 1939. He died on 11 February 1994, at age 54. He was buried at Gravel Hill Cemetery, Palmyra, Lebanon County, PA.

> **4.4.4.3.4.3.3 DAVID C. CLINE** was born on 20 July 1941. He died on 21 January 2005, Hershey, Dauphin County, PA, at age 63. He was buried at Gravel Hill Cemetery, Palmyra, Lebanon County, PA.

4.4.4.3.4.4 FRANCES MILLER was born in 1933. She married **DONALD LEON VANCE**, son of **CHARLES GLENN VANCE** and **NEDRA MAXINE HOPPES**. She died on 30 September 1990, Palmyra, Lebanon County, PA. She was buried at Grand View Memorial Park, Annville, Lebanon County, PA.

4.4.4.3.5 MYRTLE I. DEITER was born on 24 November 1896. She married **LEVI R. KAPP**, son of **HARRY KAPP** and **LUCY NYE**, on 25 December 1920, Palmyra, Lebanon County, PA. She died in July 1979, at age 82.

> **4.4.4.3.5.1 ALLEN LEVI KAPP** was born on 15 April 1921, Palmyra, Lebanon County, PA. He married **MARY J. WILSON**, daughter of **JOHN A. WILSON** and **JEWEL MOSELEY**, on 4 July 1951, Montgomery County, AL. He died on 4 June 2004, at age 83. He was buried at Delaware Veterans Memorial Cemetery, Millsboro, Sussex County, DE.

> **4.4.4.3.5.2 ARTHUR HARRY KAPP** was born on 29 December 1922, Palmyra, Lebanon County, PA. He married **MYRTLE M. HOOVER**, daughter of **AUGUSTUS G. HOOVER** and **LOTTIE M. MOYER**, on 9 September 1945, Palmyra, Lebanon County, PA. He died on 2 March 1996, at age 73.

> **4.4.4.3.5.3 DORIS J. KAPP** was born circa 1925. She married **ARTHUR HIEPLER** on 16 January 1948.

> **4.4.4.3.5.4 LUCILLE I. KAPP** was born circa 1927. She married **ROBERT W. SHOWERS**, son of **EUGENE W. SHOWERS** and **SALLIE MILLER**, on 18 July 1946, Palmyra, Lebanon County, PA.

> **4.4.4.3.5.5 JEAN ROMAINE KAPP** is also referred to as **GRACE R. KAPP** in some sources. She was born on 5 January 1930, Palmyra, Lebanon County, PA. She married **(--?--) BAKER**. She died on 15 November 2005, at age 75.

> **4.4.4.3.6 ALLEN WILLIAM DEITER** was born on 8 October 1903. He married **MIRIAM ARMINTA EVANS**, daughter of **MARK M. EVANS** and **STELLA M. SNYDER**, on 1 November 1924, Palmyra, Lebanon County, PA. He died on 13 August 1966, at age 62. He was buried at Gravel Hill Cemetery, Palmyra, Lebanon County, PA.

4.4.4.4 FRED DEITER is also referred to as **FREDERIC** in some sources. He was born on 2 April 1872, Hegins Township, Schuylkill County, PA. He died on 14 October 1940, Schuylkill Haven, Schuylkill County, PA, at age 68. He was buried at Church of God Cemetery, Valley View, Schuylkill County, PA.

4.4.4.5 ELIZABETH K. DEITER also went by the name of **LIZZIE**. She was born on 2 April 1873, Schuylkill County, PA. She married **FELIX H. KLINGER**, son of **ELIAS KLINGER** and **REBECCA HEPLER**. She died on 21 April 1932, Lebanon, Lebanon County, PA, at age 59. She was buried at Church of God Cemetery, Valley View, Schuylkill County, PA.

4.4.4.6 CHARLES K. DEITER is also referred to as **CHARLES K. DIETER** in some sources. He was born on 31 March 1877, Hegins Township, Schuylkill County, PA. He married **EDITH TERESA BOWMAN**, daughter of **JOHN A. BOWMAN** and **SARAH A. ROMBERGER**, on 26 March 1901, Saint Paul's (Artz's)

Lutheran and Reformed Church, Sacramento, Schuylkill County, PA. He died on 29 June 1935, Valley View, Schuylkill County, PA, at age 58. He was buried on 3 July 1935, at Saint Andrews United Methodist Church Cemetery, Valley View, Schuylkill County, PA.

4.4.4.6.1 WILLA MERLE DEITER was born on 5 July 1902. She was baptized on 17 August 1902, Saint Paul's (Artz's) Lutheran and Reformed Church, Sacramento, Schuylkill County, PA. She married **WILLIAM DEWALD**. She died before 11 August 2008.

4.4.4.6.2 HILDA RHEA MINERVA DEITER was born on 25 January 1904. She was baptized on 13 May 1904, Saint Paul's (Artz's) Lutheran and Reformed Church, Sacramento, Schuylkill County, PA. She married **ROY HENRY REINOEHL**, son of **GEORGE REINOEHL** and **SAVILLA SCHNELL**. She married **HARVEY DANIEL MORGAN**, son of **CURTIS MORGAN** and **EMMA BAHNEY**, on 23 June 1928. She married **JOHN STEIN** circa 1940. She died in September 1973, at age 69.

4.4.4.6.2.1 GEORGE CHARLES REINOEHL was born on 15 December 1920, Tower City, Schuylkill County, PA. He married **DOROTHY MARY KOPPENHAVER**, daughter of **JEREMIAH I. KOPPENHAVER** and **DAISY ALVENA KLINGER,** on 24 September 1943, Dauphin County, PA. George was a long time insurance agent, retiring in 1986 from the Roy W. Paul Insurance, after working there since 1979. Earlier he had worked for the Davis Agency and the Washington National Insurance Company. During World War II, served as cook on USS Concord. He died on 11 December 1988, Spring Glen, Schuylkill County, PA, at age 67. He was buried at Saint Mathew's (Coleman's) Church, Lykens Township, Dauphin County, PA.

4.4.4.6.2.1.1 TED JOHN REINOEHL was born on 20 March 1947, Ashland, PA. He was baptized on 6 May 1947, Saint Mathew's (Coleman's) Church, Lykens Township, Dauphin County, PA. He was confirmed on 26 March 1961 Saint Mathew's (Coleman's) Church, Lykens Township, Dauphin County, PA. He married **MARIE ANN LUDWIG**, daughter of **LESTER HERBERT LUDWIG** and **LUCILLE MARY LUBOLD,** on 15 April 1978.

4.4.4.6.2.1.2 LYNN GEORGE REINOEHL was born on 26 January 1953, Lykens Maternity Home, Lykens, Dauphin County, PA. He was baptized on 31 March 1953, Saint Mathew's (Coleman's) Church, Lykens Township, Dauphin County, PA. Some sources record that he was born on 26 January 1950. He married **BARBARA J. (--?--).**

4.4.4.6.2.2 ROBERT ROY REINOEHL was born on 25 September 1924, Tower City, Schuylkill County, PA. He married **ALICE MARIE MCDONOUGH** on 9 March 1948, Trinity Lutheran Church, Valley View, Schuylkill County, PA. He died on 27 August 1997, at age 72.

4.4.4.6.2.3 MARK DANIEL MORGAN was born on 22 November 1929, Valley View, Schuylkill County, PA. He died on 20 February 2002, Reading Hospital, Reading, Berks County, PA, at age 72.

4.4.4.6.3 MARGUERITE CORDELLA DEITER was born on 6 October 1916, Valley View, Schuylkill County, PA. She married **WILLIAM WALTER DIETRICH** on 29 June 1935, Trinity Lutheran Church, Valley View, Schuylkill County, PA. She died on 11 August 2008, at age 91. She was buried on 14 August 2008, at Calvary United Methodist Church Cemetery, Wiconisco, Dauphin County, PA.

4.4.4.6.3.1 PAUL JOHN HURATIAK is also referred to as **PAUL J. DIETRICH** in some sources. He was born on 16 October 1931, Valley View, Schuylkill County, PA. He married **GLORIA ROMAINE COLES**, daughter of **GEORGE THOMAS COLES** and **ANNA LAURA ORR**. He died on 19 April 2004, Harrisburg Hospital, Harrisburg, Dauphin County, PA, at age 72. He was buried at Calvary United Methodist Cemetery, Wiconisco, Dauphin County, PA.

4.4.4.6.3.2 MARY CAROL DIETRICH married **ALECK TIMKO**.

4.4.4.6.3.2.1 CHRISTA ANN TIMKO was born on 30 June 1968, Harrisburg Hospital, Harrisburg, Dauphin County, PA. She married **STEPHEN E. ULSH**. She died on 18 April 2003, Elizabethville, Dauphin County, PA, at age 34. She was buried at Maple Grove Cemetery, Elizabethville, Dauphin County, PA.

4.4.4.6.3.2.1.1 NATHANIEL ULSH

4.4.4.6.3.2.1.2 MADISON ULSH

4.4.4.6.3.3 PHYLLIS KAREN DIETRICH

4.4.4.6.3.4 WILLIAM CHARLES DIETRICH was born circa 1936.

4.4.4.6.3.4.1 BRYAN KEITH DIETRICH

4.4.4.6.3.5 MARLENE JEANETTE DIETRICH was born circa 1938, Valley View, Schuylkill County, PA.

4.4.4.6.3.6 JAMES LAMAR DIETRICH was born on 5 September 1941, Valley View, Schuylkill County, PA. He died on 12 August 1997, at age 55. He was buried at Calvary United Methodist Church Cemetery, Wiconisco, Dauphin County, PA.

4.4.4.6.3.6.1 ROBERT WILLY DIETRICH

4.4.4.7 CATHERINE ESTELLA DEITER was born on 4 August 1880, Schuylkill County, PA. She married ELMER E. ARTZ in November 1900, Elizabethville, Dauphin County, PA. She died on 22 November 1938, Valley View, Schuylkill County, PA, at age 58. She was buried on 26 November 1938, at Church of God Cemetery, Valley View, Schuylkill County, PA.

4.4.4.7.1 FLORENCE ALMA ARTZ was born on 24 May 1901, Valley View, Schuylkill County, PA. She died on 11 May 1914, Valley View, Schuylkill County, PA, at age 12. She was buried on 14 May 1914, at Church of God Cemetery, Valley View, Schuylkill County, PA.

4.4.4.8 HARRY K. DEITER was born on 25 November 1885, Sacramento, Schuylkill County, PA. He married BEULAH SAVILLA HEPLER, daughter of CHARLES HEPLER and IDA BUSH, on 1 August 1908, Friedens Reformed Church, Hegins, Schuylkill County, PA. He died on 12 January 1956, at age 70. He was buried at Covenant Greenwood Cemetery, Ebenezer, Lebanon County, PA.

4.4.4.8.1 MIRIAM IDA DEITER was born on 28 November 1908, Valley View, Schuylkill County, PA. She married WALTER VINCENT TOBIAS, son of GEORGE TOBIAS and MATILDA EISENHAUER, on 6 December 1931, St. Luke's Episcopal Church, Lebanon, Lebanon County, PA. She married JAMES J. SCHECK after 1945. She died on 19 February 2000, at age 91. She was buried at Covenant Greenwood Cemetery, Ebenezer, Lebanon County, PA.

4.4.4.8.1.1 ALTA MIRIAM TOBIAS was born on 29 November 1934. She was baptized on 28 February 1935, St. Luke's Episcopal Church, Lebanon, Lebanon County, PA.

4.4.4.8.2 WILFRED CHARLES DEITER was born on 14 September 1912. He married MILDRED L. FARNSLER on 18 November 1933, Lebanon, Lebanon County, PA. He died on 7 March 1992, at age 79. He was buried at Indiantown Gap National Cemetery, Annville, Lebanon County, PA.

4.4.4.8.3 EVELYN EMMA DEITER was born on 24 November 1915, Lebanon County, PA. She married (--?--) MANTHONE. She married ALLEN EARL RITTER. She died on 10 November 1992, at age 76. She was buried on 13 November 1992, at Highspire Cemetery, Highspire, Dauphin County, PA.

4.4.4.8.3.1 MARGO MANTHONE was born circa 1937.

4.4.4.8.4 EUGENE ELWOOD DEITER was born on 14 June 1921, Lebanon, Lebanon County, PA. He married ESTHER A. SATTAZAHN, daughter of WARREN I. SATTAZAHN and ESTHER A. LEHMAN. He died on 24 August 1983, at age 62. He was buried at Covenant Greenwood Cemetery, Ebenezer, Lebanon County, PA.

4.4.4.8.4.1 LINDA DEITER married THOMAS RHENN.

4.4.4.9 GERTRUDE MAE DEITER was born on 10 October 1887, Sacramento, Schuylkill County, PA. She married FRANKLIN ELLSWORTH SCHEIB on 27 February 1904. She died on 16 April 1929, Good Spring, Schuylkill County, PA, at age 41. She was buried on 20 April 1929, at Church of God Cemetery, Valley View, Schuylkill County, PA.

4.4.4.9.1 EVA VIOLA SCHEIB was born on 20 September 1904, Schuylkill County, PA. She married JOHN WILLIAM GARDNER. She married PAUL KEIM WALTERS after 1945. She died on 16 September 1987, Dauphin County, PA, at age 82. She was buried at Shoops Cemetery, Harrisburg, Dauphin County, PA.

4.4.4.9.1.1 JOHN WILLIAM GARDNER was born on 12 September 1930. He married SHIRLEY A. MUSSLEMAN. He died on 10 August 2002, Holy Spirit Hospital, Camp Hill, Cumberland County, PA, at age 71. He was buried at Rolling Green Memorial Park, Camp Hill, Cumberland County, PA.

4.4.4.9.2 ALBERT EARL SCHEIB was born on 9 October 1906, Hegins, Schuylkill County, PA. He married CARRIE VIOLA MOSER, daughter of ARCHIBALD A. MOSER and IDA CARRIE WIEST. He died in April 1969, at age 62. He was buried at Church of God Cemetery, Valley View,

Schuylkill County, PA. Some sources record that he died in 1968 Clearfield, Clearfield County, PA.

4.4.4.9.2.1 GERALD SCHEIB

4.4.4.9.3 ALVENA MARIE SCHEIB was born on 27 February 1910. She married **WALTON SNYDER DAVIS SR.**, son of **CHARLES LEMUEL DAVIS** and **MAUDE IRENE STOUFFER.** She died on 21 August 1999, Blue Ridge Haven Convalescent Center, Harrisburg, Dauphin County, PA, at age 89. She was buried at Rolling Green Memorial Park, Harrisburg, Dauphin County, PA.

4.4.4.9.3.1 KAY LOUISE DAVIS married **JAMES PAUL LURING**.

4.4.4.9.3.1.1 KEVIN JAMES LURING

4.4.4.9.3.2 WALTON SNYDER DAVIS JR. married **PATRICIA JANE STANDISH**.

4.4.4.9.3.2.1 JAMES KALLEN DAVIS married **STEPHANIE COLEMAN**, daughter of **ROBERT COLEMAN** and **PATRICIA SMITH**.

4.4.4.9.3.2.1.1 CAROLINE JANE DAVIS

4.4.4.9.3.2.1.2 GRIFFIN MYLES DAVIS

4.4.4.9.3.2.1.3 LYDIA FRANCES DAVIS

4.4.4.9.4 FLORENCE SCHEIB was born circa 1914. She married **ROY EZRA SCHWALM**, son of **EZRA NORMAN SCHWALM** and **LAURA JANE SCHRADER,** on 31 March 1934, Dauphin County, PA.

4.4.4.9.4.1 JOANN GERTRUDE SCHWALM was born on 5 February 1934, Pottstown, Montgomery County, PA. She married **LESLIE CLEVELAND LAFON**, son of **LESLIE C. LAFON** and **FERN KASH**, on 31 August 1957, Albemarle County, VA. She and **LESLIE CLEVELAND LAFON** were divorced on 21 December 1979 Albemarle County, VA.

4.4.4.9.4.1.1 LARRY LAFON

4.4.4.9.4.1.2 LESLIE LAFON

4.4.4.9.4.2 CAROLYN SCHWALM was born circa 1936. She married **DELBERT PAUL**.

4.4.4.9.4.2.1 DEBORAH PAUL

4.4.4.9.4.2.2 GRADY PAUL

4.4.5 ELIZABETH SCHWALM KLINGER is also referred to as **LIZZIE** in some sources. She was born on 12 March 1850. She married **SAMUEL K MAURER**. She died on 27 December 1930, Philadelphia, Philadelphia County, PA, at age 80. She was buried on 30 December 1930, at Hillside Cemetery, Roslyn, Montgomery County, PA. Cemetery is also known as Ardsley Burial Park.

4.4.5.1 AGNES M. MAURER was born on 12 January 1871, Ashland, Schuylkill County, PA. She died on 17 May 1951, Philadelphia, Philadelphia County, PA, at age 80. She was buried on 21 May 1951, at Hillside Cemetery, Roslyn, Montgomery County, PA.

4.4.5.2 HELEN VIOLA MAURER was born on 17 February 1880, Ashland, Schuylkill County, PA. She married **HARVEY H. COLBATH**, son of **JOHN COLBATH** and **MARY CAMPBELL,** circa 1910. She died on 28 May 1959, Philadelphia, Philadelphia County, PA, at age 79. She was buried on 2 June 1959, at West Laurel Hill Cemetery, Bala Cynwyd, Montgomery County, PA.

4.4.5.2.1 HELEN DOROTHY COLBATH was born on 7 March 1915, Philadelphia, Philadelphia County, PA. She married **CHARLES R. THOMPSON**. She died on 18 April 2005, at age 90. She was buried at Greenwood Cemetery, Tuckerton, Ocean County, NJ.

4.4.5.2.1.1 CHARLES RALPH THOMPSON was born on 15 August 1932, Philadelphia, Philadelphia County, PA. He was baptized on 15 October 1933, St. Matthew's Methodist Episcopal Church, Philadelphia, Philadelphia County, PA. He died on 15 March 1997, at age 64.

4.4.5.3 RALPH EMERSON MAURER was born on 29 March 1885. He died on 5 December 1916, Montgomery County, PA, at age 31. He was buried on 8 December 1916, at Ardsley Burial Park, Montgomery County, PA. Cemetery is also known as Hillside Cemetery.

4.4.5.4 GRACE GERTRUDE MAURER was born on 8 April 1887. She married **(--?--) MAKINSON**. She died on 18 July 1922, War Veterans Hospital, Mont Alto, Franklin County, PA, at age 35. She was buried at Hillside Cemetery, Roslyn, Montgomery County, PA.

4.4.5.5 ARTHUR S. MAURER was born on 10 April 1887, Ashland, Schuylkill County, PA. He married **ROSE MARY SMILEY** on 9 April 1956, San Francisco County, CA. He died on 28 April 1960, University Hospital, Philadelphia, Philadelphia County, PA, at age 73.

4.4.6 DANIEL S. KLINGER was born circa 1852. He married **MARY MAURER**, daughter of **JOHN W. MAURER** and **CATHARINE KUTZ**.

4.4.6.1 VICTORIA KLINGER was born on 17 June 1874. She married **(--?--) WILLIARD**. She married **PATRICK MEROLD** circa 1907. She died in 1950.

4.4.6.1.1 GURNEY EDWARD WILLIARD was born on 20 October 1892, Valley View, Schuylkill County, PA. He married **SUSAN (--?--)**.

4.4.6.1.1.1 JOHN WILLIARD was born circa 1910.

4.4.6.1.1.2 ANNA WILLIARD was born circa 1916.

4.4.6.1.2 EVA M. WILLIARD was born in January 1897.

4.4.6.1.3 MARY A. WILLIARD was born in March 1899.

4.4.6.1.4 LAWRENCE EUGENE MEROLD was born on 24 July 1907, Tower City, Schuylkill County, PA. He married **MINNIE JANE SINES** on 26 November 1936, Summit County, OH. He died on 8 April 1943, in military action when a truck he was driving struck a mine. Lawrence was a Warrant Officer JG in the 18th Regiment of the 1st Infantry Division. Tunisia at age 35. He was buried at Rose Hill Park, Akron, Summit County, OH.

4.4.6.1.5 HARRY MEROLD was born circa 1911.

4.4.6.1.6 RUFUS MARK MEROLD was born on 5 October 1915, Tower City, Schuylkill County, PA. He married **ESTELLA MAY KIMBLE**, daughter of **THOMAS G. KIMBLE** and **MARY M. MUNTZING**, on 20 January 1943, Summit County, OH. He died on 24 March 1998, Celina, Mercer County, OH, at age 82. He was buried at Swamp College Cemetery, Celina, Mercer County, OH.

4.4.6.2 CURTIN KLINGER also went by the name of **GURTY**. He was born on 17 October 1878. He died on 2 May 1888, at age 9. He was buried at Church of God Cemetery, Valley View, Schuylkill County, PA.

4.4.6.3 JOSEPH S. KLINGER was born on 21 January 1879, Schuylkill County, PA. He married **BLANCHE ELIZABETH HOFFMAN**, daughter of **CHARLES CORNELIUS HOFFMAN** and **ANGELINE MESSERSMITH**. He died on 23 June 1916, Tower City, Schuylkill County, PA, at age 37. He was buried on 27 June 1916, at Greenwood Cemetery, Tower City, Schuylkill County, PA.

4.4.6.3.1 FRED JOSEPH KLINGER was born on 25 May 1911. He married **VIVA GALE HELMICK** on 17 October 1942, Wellsburg, Brooke County, WV. He died on 28 May 1956, Seattle, King County, WA, at age 45. He was buried at Greenwood Cemetery, Tower City, Schuylkill County, PA.

4.4.6.4 HARRY H. KLINGER was born on 12 April 1881. He married **ELSIE BOWERS**. He died on 14 December 1943, Philadelphia, Philadelphia County, PA, at age 62. He was buried on 18 December 1943, at NJ.

4.4.6.5 RUFUS KLINGER was born on 7 April 1883, Valley View, Schuylkill County, PA. He married **M. MAUDE LEWIS**, daughter of **THOMAS MORGAN LEWIS** and **AGNES JANETHA SIMMONS**. He died on 6 August 1916, Williamstown, Dauphin County, PA, at age 33. He was buried on 9 August 1916, at Fairview Cemetery, Williamstown, Dauphin County, PA.

4.4.6.6 LLOYD EDWARD KLINGER was born on 8 February 1886, Frackville, Schuylkill County, PA. He married **CATHARINE LOUISE MEINHARDT**, daughter of **GUSTAV MEINHARDT** and **WILHELMINE LEOPOLD**, on 25 November 1911, Zion Evangelical Lutheran Church, Tamaqua, Schuylkill County, PA. He died in December 1972, at age 86.

4.4.6.6.1 GUSTAV FREDERICK KLINGER is also referred to as **AUGUSTUS KLINGER** in some sources. He was born on 20 June 1912, Tower City, Schuylkill County, PA. He died on 6 February 1999, at age 86.

4.4.6.6.2 WILHELMINA MARY KLINGER was born circa 1915. She was born on 29 March 1915, Schuylkill County, PA.

4.4.6.6.3 RUTH L. KLINGER was born circa 1916. Some sources record that she was born circa 1921.

4.4.6.6.4 DAVID DANIEL KLINGER was born on 16 February 1917, Schuylkill County, PA. Some sources record that he was born on 26 October 1916. He died on 24 January 2013, at age 95.

4.4.6.7 WALTER KLINGER was born on 6 April 1889, Frackville, Schuylkill County, PA. He married **CLARA MARY TROUTMAN.** He died on 22 April 1962, Rest Haven Home, North Manheim Township, Schuylkill County, PA, at age 73. He was buried on 25 April 1962, at Greenwood Cemetery, Tower City, Schuylkill County, PA.

4.4.6.7.1 BRUCE W. KLINGER was born on 26 September 1912. He married **RUTH NAOMI WARFEL,** daughter of **MILTON S. WARFEL** and **JANE R. ETZWEILER,** on 12 August 1940, Lucas County, OH. He died on 3 July 1974, at age 61. He was buried at Fairview Cemetery, Williamstown, Dauphin County, PA.

4.4.6.7.2 MARY E. KLINGER was born circa 1915. She married **LLOYD UNDERKOFFLER.**

4.4.6.7.3 DOROTHY KLINGER was born on 25 September 1916, Williamstown, Dauphin County, PA. She married **BEN L. BOHR.** She died on 28 November 2002, at age 86. She was buried at Barbours Cemetery, Barbours, Lycoming County, PA.

4.4.6.7.4 MARIAN BETTY KLINGER was born on 28 February 1924, Tower City, Schuylkill County, PA. She married **GEORGE A. WELSH.** She died on 27 February 1989, New Cumberland, Cumberland County, PA, at age 64. She was buried at Tri-County Memorial Gardens, Lewisberry, York County, PA.

4.4.6.7.5 HELEN ALICE KLINGER was born on 17 October 1926. She married **CLAIR EDWARD WHITCOMB,** son of **GEORGE WHITCOMB** and **ERTHA WILLIARD,** on 22 December 1945, Tower City, Schuylkill County, PA. She died in September 1986, Elizabethville, Dauphin County, PA, at age 59. She was buried at Fairview Cemetery, Williamstown, Dauphin County, PA.

4.4.6.7.6 LARRY DALE KLINGER was born on 3 January 1932, Tower City, Schuylkill County, PA. He died on 13 November 1992, at age 60. He was buried at Quantico National Cemetery, Quantico, Prince William County, VA.

4.4.6.8 JOHN KLINGER was born in February 1891. Some sources record that he was born on 10 February 1892, Valley View, Schuylkill County, PA. He married **SARAH ELLA HOFFMAN,** daughter of **CORNELIUS O. HOFFMAN** and **ANGELINA (--?--),** circa 1910. He died on 9 December 1947, at age 56.

4.4.6.8.1 MARK ROBERT KLINGER was born circa 1911.

4.4.6.8.2 NINA LORAINE KLINGER was born on 12 December 1915, Akron, Summit County, OH. She married **WILLIAM E. CAMPBELL** before 1940. She died on 9 February 2002, Akron, Summit County, OH, at age 86.

4.4.6.8.2.1 KYRA LYNN CAMPBELL was born circa 1943. She married **DOUGLAS WALTER HAYN,** son of **HENRY HAYN** and **ETHEL FORD,** on 16 November 1968, Summit County, OH.

4.4.6.8.3 ELDA DONNA KLINGER was born on 6 February 1918. She married **KENNETH WALTER FAIRCHILD,** son of **WALTER FAIRCHILD** and **FLORENCE SIVRILING,** on 18 September 1937, Summit County, OH.

4.4.6.8.3.1 JULIE LORAYNE FAIRCHILD was born in 1948. She married **RICHARD HERBERT MENDELSON** on 18 July 1976, Summit County, OH.

4.4.7 MARY KLINGER is also referred to as **POLLY** in some sources. She was born circa 1853. She married **JOHN H. BRESSLER.**

4.4.7.1 FRANCES BRESSLER was born circa 1874.

4.4.7.2 IRVIN BRESSLER was born on 17 October 1876. He died in December 1966, at age 90.

4.4.7.3 BERTHA BRESSLER is also referred to as **BURDIE** in some sources. She was born circa 1972.

4.4.7.3.1 ELDA (--?--)

4.4.8 FREDERICK S. KLINGER was born on 8 February 1856. He married **KATIE T. MILLER,** daughter of **ABRAHAM MILLER** and **MARGARET TROOP,** circa 1882. He died on 6 August 1927, at age 71. He was buried at Cedar Hill Cemetery, Ephrata, Lancaster County, PA.

4.4.8.1 LILLIAN C. KLINGER was born on 5 November 1883. She married **CHARLES GAUL MYERS,** son of **ALDUS J. MYERS** and **JENNIE GAUL.** She died on 11 April 1961, Parkersburg, Chester County, PA, at age 77.

4.4.8.1.1 A. RALPH MYERS was born on 9 March 1903, Lancaster County, PA. He married **ISABEL C. ARMSTRONG,** daughter of **SAMUEL H. ARMSTRONG** and **MASRY ELLEN WHITEMAN,**

on 22 June 1929, Coatesville, Chester County, PA. He died on 20 June 1942, Downingtown, Chester County, PA, at age 39.

4.4.8.1.2 ANNA KATHRYN MYERS was born on 7 February 1905, Strasburg, Lancaster County, PA. She married an unknown person circa 1926. She married **CARLTON J. ESHLEMAN** on 10 April 1926, Coatesville, Chester County, PA. According to a newspaper obituary, For most of her life, Anna lived in Coatesville, PA where for many years she was executive secretary to the president and CEO of Lukens Steel Co. in Coatesville. She died on 25 January 2006, Tel Hai Nursing Home, Honey Brook, Chester County, PA, at age 100.

4.4.8.1.3 CHARLES F. MYERS was born circa 1910. He married **HAZEL W. KRIXER**.

4.4.8.1.3.1 DORIS MYERS was born circa 1936. She married **WILLIAM A. ORTH**.

4.4.8.1.3.1.1 VICTORIA ORTH

4.4.8.1.3.1.2 SANDRA ORTH

4.4.8.1.4 EDWARD KLINGER MYERS was born on 11 April 1913, Ephrata, Lancaster County, PA. He married **CHARLOTTE SMITH**. He died on 18 April 1994, at age 81.

4.4.8.1.4.1 CAROLYN ANN MYERS married **RICHARD A. CUMMINS**.

4.4.8.1.4.1.1 BRYAN EDWARD CUMMINS

4.4.8.1.4.2 EDWARD S. MYERS

4.4.8.1.5 ROBERT MATTHEW MYERS was born on 19 November 1915, Ephrata, Lancaster County, PA. He married **VIRGINIA BURDAN**. He died on 15 July 1989, at age 73.

4.4.8.1.5.1 ROBERT B. MYERS

4.4.8.1.5.2 DOROTHEA C. MYERS married **TIMOTHY WIDDOWS**.

4.4.8.2 EDWARD MILLER KLINGER was born on 28 January 1886, Ephrata Township, Lancaster County, PA. He died on 17 September 1959, Philadelphia, Philadelphia County, PA, at age 73. He was buried on 25 September 1959, at Fairview Cemetery, Coatesville, Chester County, PA. Edward never married.

4.4.8.3 GERTRUDE E. KLINGER was born in January 1894. She married **MATTHEW ELER**, son of **LEONARD ELER** and **EMMA (--?--),** in 1914, Philadelphia, Philadelphia County, PA.

4.4.8.3.1 DORIS ROBERTA ELER was born on 2 June 1915, New Brunswick, Middlesex County, NJ. She married **LYNN H. LANSBERRY**. She died on 12 May 2004, New Haven, New Haven County, CT, at age 88.

4.4.8.3.1.1 SCOTT LANSBERRY married **DEBORAH CARLE**.

4.4.8.3.1.1.1 GEOFFREY LANSBERRY

4.4.8.3.1.1.2 HOLLY LANSBERRY

4.4.8.3.1.1.3 JASON LANSBERRY

4.4.8.3.1.2 BARBARA LANSBERRY was born on 28 July 1939. She married **CLINTON MARPLE**.

4.4.8.3.1.2.1 RUSSELL MARPLE

4.4.8.3.1.2.2 DOUGLAS MARPLE

4.4.8.3.1.2.3 BRUCE MARPLE

4.4.8.3.1.2.4 ERIC MARPLE

4.4.9 PETER KLINGER was born circa 1859.

4.4.10 BARBARA S. KLINGER was born on 12 September 1860. She married **MILTON D. UNDERKOFFLER**, son of **DAVID UNDERKOFFLER** and **MAGDALENA DOCKEY,** circa 1878. She died on 31 March 1946, South Lebanon Township, Lebanon County, PA, at age 85. She was buried on 3 April 1946, at Covenant Greenwood Cemetery, Ebenezer Township, Lebanon County, PA.

4.4.10.1 MINNIE P. UNDERKOFFLER was born on 28 March 1879, Valley View, Schuylkill County, PA. She married **CHARLES ELIAS FETTEROLF**, son of **ELIAS FETTEROLF** and **PHOEBE EMMA HUNTZINGER,** on 18 January 1902, Annville, Lebanon County, PA. She died on 27 April 1947, Hegins, Schuylkill County, PA, at age 68. She was buried on 30 April 1947, at Friedens Union Cemetery, Hegins, Schuylkill County, PA.

4.4.10.1.1 ARLAND ALBERT UNDERKOFFLER is also referred to as **ARLAND A. OCHS** in some sources. He was born on 25 January 1899. Some sources record that he was born circa 1898. He married **MARY REICH** circa 1918. He died on 20 March 1957, Lebanon, Lebanon County, PA, at age 58. He was buried on 25 March 1957, at Covenant Greenwood Cemetery, Ebenezer Township, Lebanon County, PA.

> **4.4.10.1.1.1 ARLAND A. UNDERKOFFLER JR.**

> **4.4.10.1.1.2 MARLIN UNDERKOFFLER** was born on 29 November 1919. He died on 18 June 1978, at age 58. He was buried at Covenant Greenwood Cemetery, Ebenezer Township, Lebanon County, PA.

> **4.4.10.1.1.3 HAROLD UNDERKOFFLER** was born on 21 December 1920. He married **MARGUERITE E. DEMMY**. He died on 25 August 1995, at age 74. He was buried at Covenant Greenwood Cemetery, Ebenezer Township, Lebanon County, PA.

>> **4.4.10.1.1.3.1 HAROLD UNDERKOFFLER JR.**

>> **4.4.10.1.1.3.2 EDWARD UNDERKOFFLER**

4.4.10.1.2 ALLEN C. FETTEROLF was born on 25 June 1902, Annville, Lebanon County, PA. He married **MARGARET F. KEELER**. He was baptized on 6 February 1938, Trinity Reformed Church, Philadelphia, Philadelphia County, PA. He died on 21 July 1951, Polyclinic Hospital, Harrisburg, Dauphin County, PA, at age 49. He was buried on 25 July 1951, at Rolling Green Memorial Park, Camp Hill, Cumberland County, PA.

> **4.4.10.1.2.1 JUDITH FETTEROLF** married (--?--) **WIEGAND**.

> **4.4.10.1.2.2 JOHN KEELER FETTEROLF** was born on 16 November 1937, Philadelphia, Philadelphia County, PA. He married **LINDA M. KERSTETTER**. He died on 30 September 1996, Shiloh, York County, PA, at age 58.

>> **4.4.10.1.2.2.1 ROBERT FETTEROLF**

>> **4.4.10.1.2.2.2 JANEEN FETTEROLF** married (--?--) **SNELL**.

4.4.10.1.3 MAUDE M. FETTEROLF was born on 30 October 1904, Hegins Township, Schuylkill County, PA. She married **ERNEST HUNTZINGER**, son of **ALVIN B. HUNTZINGER** and **C. A. SALTZER**, on 7 July 1922, Friedens Lutheran Church, Hegins, Schuylkill County, PA. She died on 17 October 1927, Pottsville, Schuylkill County, PA, at age 22, as the result of injuries received in an auto accident. She was buried on 20 October 1927, at Friedens Union Cemetery, Hegins, Schuylkill County, PA.

> **4.4.10.1.3.1 MARGARET MARDELLE HUNTZINGER** was born on 2 February 1923, Hegins, Schuylkill County, PA. She married **DELMER E. TREFSGER**, son of **WILLIAM MILLARD TREFSGER** and **ALMA M. HEPLER**. She died on 30 July 1990, at age 67. She was buried at Friedens Union Cemetery, Hegins, Schuylkill County, PA.

>> **4.4.10.1.3.1.1 DANIEL TREFSGER** married **ROMAINE** (--?--).

>> **4.4.10.1.3.1.2 DELMER TREFSGER JR.**

> **4.4.10.1.3.2 ELIZABETH L. HUNTZINGER** was born circa 1926. Elizabeth is listed in the 1940 Census as age 14, living in the household of her father and his second wife, Ruth. This suggests that Elizabeth was born before Maude's death in 1927. The 1930 Census lists her as "Bettyleu" and as the stepdaughter of Ernest Huntzinger, confirming that she was the daughter of Maude Fetterolf.

4.4.10.1.4 JOSEPH IRVIN FETTEROLF was born on 31 July 1905, Pitman, Schuylkill County, PA. He married **BESSIE MAE BENSINGER**, daughter of **FRANCIS W. BENSINGER** and **EMMA JANE CARL**. At the time of the 1930 census, Joseph and Bessie had been married 3 years and were living in Hegins Township, Schuylkill County, PA. He was a time keeper for a construction company. They had 2 children. He died in October 1974, at age 69. He was buried at Saint Peters United Methodist Church Cemetery, Fearnot, Schuylkill County, PA.

> **4.4.10.1.4.1 RICHARD JOSEPH FETTEROLF** was born on 11 December 1927, Hegins, Schuylkill County, PA. He died in October 1984, at age 56. He was buried at Calvary Cemetery, Mount Carbon, Schuylkill County, PA.

> **4.4.10.1.4.2 JACK DAVID FETTEROLF** was born on 4 January 1930, Hegins, Schuylkill County, PA. He married **MARIAN ELEANOR HERB**, daughter of **THOMAS E. HERB** and **MABEL M. STUTZMAN**. He died on 16 April 2007, Ashland State Hospital, Butler Township,

Schuylkill County, PA, at age 77. He was buried at Friedens Union Cemetery, Hegins, Schuylkill County, PA.

> **4.4.10.1.4.2.1 ROMAINE FETTEROLF** married **BARRY R. DAUB**, son of **RONALD DAUB** and **B. MARIE (--?--)**.
>> **4.4.10.1.4.2.1.1 HEIDI MARIE DAUB** married **SCOTT SOYSTER**.
>>> **4.4.10.1.4.2.1.1.1 JACK WALTER SOYSTER**
>>> **4.4.10.1.4.2.1.1.2 ANNA LYNN SOYSTER**
>> **4.4.10.1.4.2.1.2 CLINTON DANIEL DAUB**
>> **4.4.10.1.4.2.1.3 HAYLEY REBECCA DAUB**
>
> **4.4.10.1.4.2.2 TOMMY JOE FETTEROLF** was born on 31 March 1948, Ashland State Hospital, Ashland, Schuylkill County, PA. He died on 31 March 1948, Ashland State Hospital, Ashland, Schuylkill County, PA. He was buried on 1 April 1948, at Friedens Union Cemetery, Hegins, Schuylkill County, PA.

4.4.10.1.4.3 WILLIAM F. FETTEROLF was born on 25 May 1932, Pottsville, Schuylkill County, PA. He married **NORMA F. SCHULTZ** circa 1953. He died on 11 April 2012, Penn State Milton Hershey Medical Center, Hershey, Dauphin County, PA, at age 79. According to a newspaper obituary, William lived in Hegins, PA. He was a 1950 graduate of the former Hegins Township High School. He was an Army veteran of the Korean War. After his discharge from the Army, he began working for his father at Fetterolf's Meat Market, Hegins. In 1974, he became the owner of Fetterolf's Meat Market. After selling the meat market in 1996, he worked part time for Bixler's Meat Market. He was buried on 16 April 2012, at Friedens United Church of Christ Cemetery, Hegins, Schuylkill County, PA.

> **4.4.10.1.4.3.1 DAVID F. FETTEROLF** married **CHERYL (--?--)**. David lives in Hegins, PA.
>
> **4.4.10.1.4.3.2 SUSAN F. FETTEROLF.** Susan lives in Lancaster, PA.

4.4.10.1.4.4 ANN LOUISE FETTEROLF was born on 19 March 1936. She married **NED JOSEPH PEIFER** on 2 October 1957, Friedens UCC Church, Hegins, Schuylkill County, PA. She died on 23 November 2016, Millersburg, Dauphin County, PA, at age 80. She was buried on 30 November 2016, at Saint David's Reformed Church Cemetery, Killinger, Dauphin County, PA.

> **4.4.10.1.4.4.1 SHELLEY ANN PEIFER** was born on 18 September 1958, Pittsville, Schuylkill County, PA. She married **STEVE HEINBAUGH** on 1 June 1984, Saint David's Reformed Church, Killinger, Dauphin County, PA.
>> **4.4.10.1.4.4.1.1 BENJAMIN J. HEINBAUGH** was born on 26 July 1988.
>> **4.4.10.1.4.4.1.2 RACHEL E. HEINBAUGH** was born on 4 December 1991.
>
> **4.4.10.1.4.4.2 REBECCA I. PEIFER** was born on 2 December 1963, Harrisburg, Dauphin County, PA. She married **GREG ULSH** on 1 November 1985, Saint David's Reformed Church, Killinger, Dauphin County, PA.
>> **4.4.10.1.4.4.2.1 MATTHEW P. ULSH** was born on 10 November 1991.
>> **4.4.10.1.4.4.2.2 ADAM R. ULSH** was born on 13 August 1994.

4.4.10.1.5 IRENE E. FETTEROLF was born circa 1908.

4.4.10.1.6 CHARLES ELIAS FETTEROLF JR. was born on 20 March 1916, Pitman, Schuylkill County, PA. He was baptized on 1 April 1931, Friedens Reformed Church, Hegins, Schuylkill County, PA. He married **HELEN E. (--?--)**. He died on 6 January 1975, at age 58. He was buried on 10 January 1975, at Citizen's Cemetery, Lavelle, Schuylkill County, PA.

4.4.10.1.7 JAMES MILTON FETTEROLF was born on 20 February 1921. He was baptized on 1 April 1936, Friedens Reformed Church, Hegins, Schuylkill County, PA.

4.4.10.2 HELEN UNDERKOFFLER was born on 20 July 1884. Although Helen is listed among Barbara and Milton's children in the Journal of the Johannes Schwalm Association, according to the 1910 US Census, Barbara only gave birth to 8 children. Helen would be the ninth. There is nothing in either the 1920 or 1930 Census that identifies another daughter named Helen. She married **HARRY G. SMITH**, son of **JOHN B. SMITH** and **SUSAN MATTERNESS**, on 28 January 1905, Annville, Lebanon County,

PA. She died on 21 March 1940, Lebanon, Lebanon County, PA, at age 55. She was buried on 25 March 1940, at Covenant Greenwood Cemetery, Ebenezer, Lebanon County, PA.

 4.4.10.2.1 ESTHER S. SMITH was born on 13 December 1906. She married **LUKE I. MAYER**, son of **HARRY W. MAYER** and **EDITH F. STONG,** circa 1928. She married **DELMAR V. RITTLE**, son of **PAUL RITTLE** and **LAURA WAGAMAN,** on 25 September 1948, North Lebanon Township, Lebanon County, PA.

  4.4.10.2.1.1 EDWARD H. MAYER was born on 4 June 1930, Pittsburgh, Allegheny County, PA. He married **PATRICIA CARBAUGH.** He married **AUDREY GARMAN.** He died on 8 May 2013, at age 82.

   4.4.10.2.1.1.1 SUE MAYER

   4.4.10.2.1.1.2 BRADLEY MAYER

  4.4.10.2.1.2 THOMAS MAYER was born on 30 November 1931. He married **ELIZABETH BRIGHT.**

   4.4.10.2.1.2.1 JENNIFER MAYER

 4.4.10.2.2 ALMA I. SMITH was born circa 1920. She married **CHARLES F. KNESEL**, son of **CHARLES H. KNESEL** and **GERTRUDE KELLER,** on 6 June 1942, Lebanon County, PA.

  4.4.10.2.2.1 DAVID KNESEL married **NEAL ASHCROFT.**

   4.4.10.2.2.1.1 VERONICA KNESEL

   4.4.10.2.2.1.2 JENNIFER KNESEL

  4.4.10.2.2.2 PATRICIA KNESEL married **BILL BLIZZARD.**

   4.4.10.2.2.2.1 CHARLES BLIZZARD

   4.4.10.2.2.2.2 ZACK BLIZZARD

  4.4.10.2.2.3 THOMAS KNESEL

  4.4.10.2.2.4 CHARLES KNESEL JR.

4.4.10.3 HARRY J. UNDERKOFFLER was born on 14 November 1886, Hegins Township, Schuylkill County, PA. He married **MABEL MARY BOLTZ**, daughter of **ABRAHAM BOLTZ** and **LIZZIE (--?--)**, circa 1905. He married **MARY E. SNYDER** after 1910. He died on 5 September 1966, Lebanon, Lebanon County, PA, at age 79. He was buried at Mount Lebanon Cemetery, Lebanon, Lebanon County, PA.

 4.4.10.3.1 RALPH STEPHEN UNDERKOFFLER was born circa 1905. He married **MARIE C. MCCULLOUGH**, daughter of **JOSEPH R. MCCULLOUGH** and **MARY A. (--?--)**, circa 1925. There is a Ralph Steven Underkoffler, born 5 Apr 1905, died 11 Feb 1975, buried in the Los Angeles National Cemetery in Los Angeles, CA. It is unclear whether this is the same person.

  4.4.10.3.1.1 RALPH STEPHEN UNDERKOFFLER JR. was born on 13 May 1925, Philadelphia, Philadelphia County, PA. He died on 25 November 1986, at age 61.

  4.4.10.3.1.2 JOSEPH THOMAS UNDERKOFFLER was born on 26 September 1928, Philadelphia, Philadelphia County, PA. He died on 2 August 1991, at age 62.

  4.4.10.3.1.3 CATHERINE MARIE UNDERKOFFLER is also referred to as **MARIE CATHERINE UNDERKOFFLER** in some sources. She was born on 27 December 1929, Philadelphia, Philadelphia County, PA. She married **(--?--) LEBLANC.** She married **(--?--) BRON.** She died on 3 May 2004, Woodbury, Gloucester County, NJ, at age 74. She was buried at Eglington Cemetery, Clarksboro, Gloucester County, NJ.

  4.4.10.3.1.4 CATHERINE N. UNDERKOFFLER was born circa 1930.

  4.4.10.3.1.5 WILLIAM CHARLES UNDERKOFFLER was born on 16 December 1937, Philadelphia, Philadelphia County, PA. He married **JACQUELINE (--?--).** He died on 15 October 1984, at age 46. He was buried at Saint John Neumann Cemetery, Chalfont, Bucks County, PA.

 4.4.10.3.2 AARON MILTON UNDERKOFFLER was born on 28 December 1906, North Annville Township, Lebanon County, PA. He married **MIRIAM STEEL**, daughter of **JOHN STEEL** and **MADELINE WALTERS.** He married **GENVIEVE ANGEL** after 1930. He died on 22 September 1990, Alameda County, CA, at age 83.

  4.4.10.3.2.1 GREGORY UNDERKOFFLER married **JULIE COX.**

4.4.10.3.2.1.1 GREGORY UNDERKOFFLER JR.

4.4.10.3.3 WILLIAM HOWARD TAFT UNDERKOFFLER was born on 7 November 1908, Lebanon County, PA. He died in 1933. He was buried at Mount Lebanon Cemetery, Lebanon, Lebanon County, PA.

4.4.10.4 HERMAN W. UNDERKOFFLER is also referred to as **HERMAN A. UNDERKOFFLER** in some sources. He was born on 8 September 1890, Valley View, Schuylkill County, PA. He married **DERTHA WEHRY**, daughter of **JOSEPH WEHRY** and **HANNAH LONG,** on 25 March 1916, Lebanon, Lebanon County, PA. He died on 27 December 1938, Lebanon, Lebanon County, PA, at age 48. He was buried on 31 December 1938, at Covenant Greenwood Cemetery, Ebenezer Township, Lebanon County, PA. Some sources record that he died on 28 December 1939.

4.4.10.4.1 ALMA J. UNDERKOFFLER was born on 11 October 1916. She married **HENRY M. UHLER**, son of **HARRY CLARENCE UHLER** and **SADIE A. KLICK**. She died in October 1977. She was buried at Covenant Greenwood Cemetery, Ebenezer, Lebanon County, PA.

4.4.10.4.1.1 MARY UHLER

4.4.10.4.1.2 JAY HENRY UHLER was born on 14 December 1939.

4.4.10.5 ESTHER J. UNDERKOFFLER was born on 5 January 1893, Lebanon, Lebanon County, PA. She married **RAYMOND W. MCCONNELL**, son of **EDWARD MCCONNELL** and **MARGARET SNYDER**, on 14 April 1917, Lebanon, Lebanon County, PA. She died on 10 April 1953, Lebanon, Lebanon County, PA, at age 60. She was buried on 14 April 1953, at Covenant Greenwood Cemetery, Ebenezer, Lebanon County, PA.

4.4.10.5.1 ROBERT R. MCCONNELL is also referred to as **BUD** in some sources. He was born circa 1917. He married **MILDRED E. WILHELM**, daughter of **J. AMSON WILHELM** and **CLARE E. HOTTENSTEIN,** on 23 November 1939, Lebanon County, PA.

4.4.10.5.1.1 CAROL MCCONNELL married (--?--) **KLOPP**.

4.4.10.5.1.1.1 SCOTT KLOPP

4.4.10.5.1.2 CATHY MCCONNELL married (--?--) **DIEM**.

4.4.10.5.2 ELWOOD MCCONNELL was born circa 1920. He married **CAMELIA PELLERITE**.

4.4.10.5.2.1 COLLEEN MCCONNELL married (--?--) **BEISSWANGER**.

4.4.10.5.2.2 SHARON MCCONNELL married (--?--) **BONANNO**.

4.4.10.5.2.3 PATRICIA MCCONNELL

4.4.10.5.2.4 MARY ELLEN MCCONNELL

4.4.10.5.3 PEARL MCCONNELL was born circa 1923. She married **ARTHUR CAMPBELL**.

4.4.10.5.3.1 RUSTY CAMPBELL

4.4.10.5.3.2 JULIE CAMPBELL

4.4.10.5.3.3 TOMMY CAMPBELL

4.4.10.6 NELLIE MAY UNDERKOFFLER is also referred to as **MELLIE M.** in some sources. She was born on 2 October 1896, Valley View, Schuylkill County, PA. She died on 28 October 1962, South Lebanon Township, Lebanon County, PA, at age 66. She was buried on 31 October 1962, at Covenant Greenwood Cemetery, Ebenezer, Lebanon County, PA. Never married.

4.4.10.7 TOLBERT HENRY UNDERKOFFLER is also referred to as **TALBERT H. UNDERKOFFLER** in some sources. He was born on 4 September 1898. He married **ELLA HAAS**, daughter of **HENRY HAAS** and **FANNIE WHITE,** on 30 April 1918, Lebanon County, PA. He died in February 1981, at age 82. He was buried at Hopeland United Methodist Church Cemetery, Hopeland, Lancaster County, PA.

4.4.10.7.1 BARBARA UNDERKOFFLER married (--?--) **WHITCRAFT**.

4.4.10.7.2 BERTHA M. UNDERKOFFLER was born circa 1918.

4.4.10.7.3 HENRY MARK UNDERKOFFLER was born circa 1921. He died in 1939. He was buried at Hopeland Cemetery, Hopeland, Lancaster County, PA.

4.4.10.7.4 CHRISTINE J. UNDERKOFFLER married (--?--) **WALTZ**. She was born circa 1923.

4.4.10.7.5 CLAIR E. UNDERKOFFLER was born on 21 December 1923. He married **ERMA ELIZABETH URBAN**, daughter of **ARTHUR URBAN** and **ALICE EARHART**. He died on 27 August 1979, at age 55. He was buried at Millersville Mennonite Cemetery, Millersville, Lancaster County, PA.

4.4.10.7.5.1 LARRY UNDERKOFFLER married DEBBIE (--?--).

4.4.10.7.5.2 TERRY UNDERKOFFLER married WANDA (--?--).

4.4.10.7.5.3 CAROL ANN UNDERKOFFLER was born on 15 February 1949, Lancaster, Lancaster County, PA. She married EVERETT L. CAMPBELL. She died on 9 August 2010, Leola, Lancaster County, PA, at age 61. She was buried on 17 August 2010, at Millersville Mennonite Cemetery, Millersville, Lancaster County, PA.

4.4.10.7.5.3.1 JASON C. CAMPBELL married SANDY (--?--).

4.4.10.7.5.3.2 DANA P. CAMPBELL married MONICA (--?--).

4.4.10.7.5.3.3 MATTHEW P. CAMPBELL married BRANDY (--?--).

4.4.10.7.6 MILDRED J. UNDERKOFFLER was born circa 1925.

4.4.10.7.7 TOLBERT UNDERKOFFLER JR. married JANE (--?--). He was born on 19 August 1927.

4.4.10.7.8 KATHRYN JUNE UNDERKOFFLER also went by the name of KITTY. She was born on 4 June 1929. She married ELWOOD BOWMAN. She died on 18 September 2010, at age 81. She was buried at Hopeland United Methodist Church Cemetery, Hopeland, Lancaster County, PA.

4.4.10.7.8.1 GARY L. BOWMAN married BARBARA (--?--).

4.4.10.7.8.2 BRIAN E. BOWMAN married TRACY (--?--).

4.4.10.7.9 RONALD LEE UNDERKOFFLER was born on 9 February 1940, Lancaster County, PA. He died on 26 September 2005, at age 65. He was buried at Good/s Mennonite Cemetery, Elizabethtown, Lancaster County, PA.

4.4.10.8 VINCENT K. UNDERKOFFLER is also referred to as VINCENT M. UNDERKOFFLER in some sources. He was born on 23 November 1902. Some sources record that he was born circa 1893. He married DOROTHY LITTLE circa 1924. He died on 24 July 1962, at age 59. He was buried at Grand View Memorial Park, Annville, Lebanon County, PA.

4.4.10.8.1 DORIS UNDERKOFFLER was born circa 1924. She married JAMES ARNOLD.

4.4.10.8.1.1 GREGORY ARNOLD married MARY JO GRACI.

4.4.10.8.1.1.1 JAIME ARNOLD

4.4.10.8.1.2 EILEEN ARNOLD

4.4.10.8.2 VINCENT M. UNDERKOFFLER JR. was born circa 1925. He married CAMELIA PELLERITE. He married BLANCHE BUDY.

4.4.10.8.3 JAMES M.A. UNDERKOFFLER was born circa 1928. He married PHYLLIS KARLI.

4.4.10.8.3.1 JAMES UNDERKOFFLER JR.

4.4.10.8.3.2 PATRICIA UNDERKOFFLER

4.5 JUSTINA KLINGER was born on 6 July 1829. She married JACOB SCHWALM, son of FREDERICK SCHWALM and CATHARINA STEIN, circa 1845. She died on 3 March 1897, at home, Hubley Township, Schuylkill County, PA, at age 67. She was buried at St. Peter's United Methodist Church Cemetery, Fearnot, Hubley Township, Schuylkill County, PA.

4.5.1 FIETTA SCHWALM is also referred to as FYETTA SCHWALM in some sources. She was born on 7 October 1847, Pennsylvania. Some sources record that she was born in October 1845. She married HENRY HAUPT HEPLER, son of JACOB MAURER HEPLER and ELISABETHA HAUPT, in 1864. Some sources suggest that she and HENRY HAUPT HEPLER were married in 1866. She died on 21 January 1917, Ashland, Schuylkill County, PA, at age 69. She was buried on 25 January 1917, at Brock Cemetery, Ashland, Schuylkill County, PA.

4.5.1.1 ELIZABETH HEPLER was born on 5 July 1866, Schuylkill County, PA. She married THOMAS HUGHES circa 1890. She died on 14 November 1918, Ashland, Schuylkill County, PA, at age 52. She was buried on 18 November 1918, at Brock Cemetery, Ashland, Schuylkill County, PA.

4.5.1.2 MONROE S. HEPLER was born circa 1868. Some sources record that he was born in 1870. He died on 2 April 1900, Ashland, Schuylkill County, PA. He was buried at Brock Cemetery, Ashland, Schuylkill County, PA.

4.5.1.3 JACOB HENRY HEPLER was born on 2 September 1869, Schuylkill County, PA. He died on 23 September 1871, Schuylkill County, PA, at age 2. He was buried at Saint Paul's United Church of Christ Cemetery, Sacramento, Schuylkill County, PA.

4.5.1.4 OSCAR SAMUEL HEPLER was born on 18 December 1873, Hubley Township, Schuylkill County, PA. He married **IDA MAY LONG** circa 1898. He died on 5 September 1956, Ashland, Schuylkill County, PA, at age 82. He was buried on 10 September 1956, at Christ Church Cemetery, Fountain Springs, Schuylkill County, PA.

    4.5.1.4.1 IRENE E. HEPLER was born on 13 March 1898. She married **WILLARD D. GEIST**, son of **JOHN B. GEIST** and **LAUREL STITZER**. She died on 30 December 1963, Bristol, Bucks County, PA, at age 65.

        4.5.1.4.1.1 ROBERT WILLARD GEIST was born on 24 April 1930, Ashland, Schuylkill County, PA. He died on 7 March 1997, at age 66. He was buried at Indiantown Gap National Cemetery, Annville, Lebanon County, PA.

    4.5.1.4.2 LILLIAN B. HEPLER was born on 10 January 1903, Ashland, Schuylkill County, PA. She died on 7 December 1907, Ashland, Schuylkill County, PA, at age 4. She was buried on 8 December 1907, at Brock Cemetery, Ashland, Schuylkill County, PA.

4.5.1.5 CHARLES S. HEPLER was born circa 1875.

4.5.1.6 ALICE S. HEPLER was born circa 1877.

4.5.1.7 CATHARINE HEPLER is also referred to as **KATIE** in some sources. She was born on 8 June 1879, Schuylkill County, PA. She married **DAVID FRANKLIN GROVE**, son of **JOSEPH GROVE** and **REBECCA (--?--)**, on 23 August 1900, Ashland, Schuylkill County, PA. She died on 8 May 1959, Northampton, Northampton County, PA, at age 79. She was buried on 11 May 1959, at Fairview Cemetery, Northampton, Northampton County, PA.

    4.5.1.7.1 EARL H. GROVE was born on 18 June 1901. He married **ELEANORA TRANSUE**, daughter of **HARRY TRANSUE** and **CARRIE VAN DORN RANDELL,** on 30 October 1929, Allentown, Lehigh County, PA. He died in July 1973, at age 72.

        4.5.1.7.1.1 CARLYN GROVE is also referred to as **CARLEAN GROVE** in some sources. She was born circa 1928.

        4.5.1.7.1.2 ROBERTA GROVE was born circa 1935.

    4.5.1.7.2 GRACE DORIS GROVE was born on 20 January 1912, Northampton County, PA. She married **HAROLD Q. DOTTER**, son of **WILLIAM DOTTER** and **MINNIE RINGER,** on 26 August 1933, Allentown, Lehigh County, PA. She died on 19 August 1997, Belleville, Mifflin County, PA, at age 85. She was buried at Fairview Cemetery, Northampton, Northampton County, PA.

        4.5.1.7.2.1 DAVID W. DOTTER was born on 4 December 1933, Northampton, Northampton County, PA. He died on 1 February 1985, Fountain Hill, Lehigh County, PA, at age 51. He was buried at Fairview Cemetery, Northampton, Northampton County, PA.

        4.5.1.7.2.2 DIANE MARIE DOTTER was born on 14 June 1937, Northampton, Northampton County, PA. She married **(--?--) AMATO**. She died on 17 April 2005, at age 67.

4.5.2 SAMUEL EMANUEL SCHWALM was born on 9 June 1848. He married **SARAH ELIZABETH STRAUB**. He married **ELLEN VESTA GEIST**, daughter of **JACOB GEIST** and **CATHERINE SCHWARTZ**, on 9 June 1889, Schuylkill County, PA. He died on 29 June 1913, at age 65. He was buried at Saint Peters United Methodist Church Cemetery, Fearnot, Schuylkill County, PA.

    4.5.2.1 EZRA NORMAN SCHWALM was born in August 1872. He married **LAURA JANE SCHRADER**, daughter of **JACOB SCHRADER** and **SARAH (--?--)**, circa 1902. Ezra became a deaf mute in childhood, as a result of a viral fever; Ezra's wife Laura was also a deaf mute. He died in 1932. He was buried at Friedens Union Cemetery, Hegins, Schuylkill County, PA.

        4.5.2.1.1 RUTH SCHWALM was born on 19 July 1903. She married **HERBERT B. SCHECK**. She died on 30 May 1963, Monterey County, CA, at age 59.

        4.5.2.1.2 ROY EZRA SCHWALM was born on 15 July 1905. He was baptized on 16 October 1905, Frieden's Reformed Church, Hegins, Schuylkill County, PA. He married **FLORENCE SCHEIB**, daughter of **FRANKLIN ELLSWORTH SCHEIB** and **GERTRUDE MAE DEITER,** on 31 March 1934, Dauphin County, PA. He married **GRACE E. (--?--)** before 1940. He died on 1 June 1975, at age 69. He was buried at Saint Johns Cemetery, Tamaqua, Schuylkill County, PA.

            4.5.2.1.2.1 JOANN GERTRUDE SCHWALM (see above)

                4.5.2.1.2.1.1 LARRY LAFON (see above)

                4.5.2.1.2.1.2 LESLIE LAFON (see above)

4.5.2.1.2.2 CAROLYN SCHWALM (see above)

4.5.2.1.2.2.1 DEBORAH PAUL (see above)

4.5.2.1.2.2.2 GRADY PAUL (see above)

4.5.2.1.3 PAUL JACOB SCHWALM is also referred to as **PAUL J. SWALM** in some sources. He was born on 1 July 1908, Tremont, Schuylkill County, PA. He married **DOROTHY RIST**. He lived in Ripon, WI. He died on 23 April 2000, Ripon Medical Center, Ripon, WI, at age 91. He was buried on 26 April 2000, at Garden of the Cross Cemetery, Ripon, WI.

4.5.2.1.3.1 LOIS MARIE SCHWALM was born on 31 October 1928, York Farm, Pottsville, Schuylkill County, PA. She married **KERMIT WEISKE**, son of **CHARLES WEISKE** and **WINIFRED (--?--)**. She lived in WI.

4.5.2.1.3.1.1 JANE WEISKE

4.5.2.1.3.1.2 STEPHEN WEISKE married **LYNN HERRIOT**.

4.5.2.1.3.1.2.1 LAURA WEISKE

4.5.2.1.3.1.2.2 BRIAN HERRIOT WEISKE married **CLAIRE (--?--)**.

4.5.2.1.3.1.2.3 STEPHANIE WEISKE

4.5.2.1.3.1.3 MARY WEISKE

4.5.2.1.3.1.4 MICHAEL WEISKE

4.5.2.1.3.2 EDMUND P. SCHWALM was born on 18 December 1929, Pottsville, Schuylkill County, PA. He died on 24 July 1988, Good Samaritan Hospital, Pottsville, Schuylkill County, PA, at age 58. He was buried at Charles M. Barber Cemetery, Pottsville, Schuylkill County, PA.

4.5.2.1.4 NORMAN EDWARD SCHWALM was born on 14 August 1910. Some sources record that he was born on 14 August 1908, Tremont, Schuylkill County, PA. The birth date listed in the death certificate is inconsistent with Census records and the birth date of Norman's siblings. He married **ANNA LILECK**, daughter of **PETER LILECK**. He died on 12 January 1938, Schuylkill Township, Schuylkill County, PA, at age 27. He was buried on 15 January 1938, at Presbyterian Cemetery, Pottsville, Schuylkill County, PA.

4.5.2.1.4.1 NORMAN ELIAS SCHWALM was born in 1934. He married **SHIRLEY ANN RINKENBERG** on 15 February 1958, North Hollywood, Los Angeles County, CA.

4.5.2.1.4.1.1 KEITH EDWARD SCHWALM was born on 5 February 1960, Santa Clara County, CA. He married **CATHERINE MCCOMBE** on 10 January 1981, Santa Clara County, CA. He and **CATHERINE MCCOMBE** were divorced. He married **ELISE DUNGAN** in 1991.

4.5.2.1.4.1.1.1 MICHAEL KENNETH SCHWALM was born in 1980, Mountain View, Santa Clara County, CA. He married **DESIREE KALANDROS.**

4.5.2.1.4.1.1.2 KIMBERLY ELISE SCHWALM was born in 1992, Los Gatos, Santa Clara County, CA.

4.5.2.1.4.1.2 LINDA ANN SCHWALM was born in 1963, San Francisco, San Francisco County, CA. She married **TONY L. SCOTT** on 17 December 1983, Los Angeles County, CA. She married **RICK LEE MONTOYA** in 1986, Cupertino, Santa Clara County, CA.

4.5.2.1.4.1.2.1 SAMANTHA ANN MONTOYA was born in 1988, Mountain View, Santa Clara County, CA. She married **ERICK AMBRIS** in 2008, Roseville, Placer County, CA.

4.5.2.1.4.1.2.1.1 LANDON LEE AMBRIS was born in 2009, Roseville, Placer County, CA.

4.5.2.1.4.1.2.2 RYAN LEE MONTOYA was born in 1991, Mountain View, Santa Clara County, CA.

4.5.2.2 IRA CLAYTON SCHWALM was born on 28 June 1877, Pitman, Schuylkill County, PA. He married **TAMIE KESSLER**, daughter of **ELIAS KESSLER** and **ELIZABETH STUTZMAN,** circa 1896. He died on 24 September 1947, Valley View, Schuylkill County, PA, at age 70. He was buried on 29 September 1947, at St. Andrew's United Methodist Church Cemetery, Valley View, Schuylkill County, PA.

4.5.2.2.1 IVA IRENE SCHWALM was born on 22 January 1898. She married **STANLEY HARNER.** She married **HARRY O. DONLEAVY.** She died in 1971. She was buried at St. Andrew's United Methodist Church Cemetery, Valley View, Schuylkill County, PA.

> **4.5.2.2.1.1 KERMIT IVAN HARNER** was born on 28 September 1925, Valley View, Schuylkill County, PA. He married **BETTE (--?--).** He died on 16 September 2005, Hartford Hospital, Hartford, Hartford County, CT, at age 79. He was buried at Windsor Veterans Memorial Cemetery, Windsor, Hartford County, PA.
>
>> **4.5.2.2.1.1.1 KATHRYN HARNER** married **STEPHEN SMITH.**
>>
>> **4.5.2.2.1.1.2 DEBORAH HARNER** married **MARK GRIFFIN.**
>>
>> **4.5.2.2.1.1.3 JEFFREY HARNER** married **ELIZABETH (--?--).**
>>
>> **4.5.2.2.1.1.4 JODI HARNER** married **RICHARD HENDERSON.** She is also referred to as **JODI** in some sources.
>>
>> **4.5.2.2.1.1.5 RONALD HARNER**

4.5.2.2.2 FRED F. SCHWALM was born on 23 September 1899. He married **MARY BERGEY,** daughter of **W. ELLIS BERGEY** and **ELLA BOGENWREATH,** on 25 December 1924, St. Andrew's Church, Valley View, Schuylkill County, PA. Prior to his death, Fred was living in the vicinity of Valley View, Schuylkill County, PA. He died on 8 July 1981, Hershey Medical Center, Dauphin County, PA, at age 81. He was buried at St. Andrew's Church Cemetery, Valley View, Schuylkill County, PA.

> **4.5.2.2.2.1 LUCILLE ODENE SCHWALM** was born on 25 December 1925. She married **JOHN S. CURRY,** son of **JOHN K. CURRY** and **EDITH SHENK.** She married **JOHN G. BRUBAKER,** son of **PHARES BRUBAKER** and **LIZZIE GRAYBILL,** after 1984.
>
>> **4.5.2.2.2.1.1 LUANNE CURRY** was born on 14 August 1950, Polyclinic Hospital, Harrisburg, Dauphin County, PA. She married **JAMES F. REESE,** son of **FRANKLIN JOHN REESE** and **SHIRLEY BARTH,** in July 1976, Bernville, Berks County, PA.
>>
>>> **4.5.2.2.2.1.1.1 SARAH CURRY REESE** was born on 4 April 1980, Reading Hospital, Reading, Berks County, PA. She died on 5 April 1980, Harrisburg Hospital, Harrisburg, Dauphin County, PA. She was buried at Fishburn United Methodist Church Cemetery, Hershey, Dauphin County, PA.
>>>
>>> **4.5.2.2.2.1.1.2 LEAH IRENE REESE** was born on 15 May 1983, Reading Hospital, Reading, Berks County, PA. She married **DAVID MATHEW USFASZEWSKI** on 17 October 2009, Friedens Evangelical Lutheran Church, Bernville, Berks County, PA.
>>>
>>> **4.5.2.2.2.1.1.3 JOHN FRANKLIN REESE** was born on 21 June 1983, Lankenau Hospital, Philadelphia, Philadelphia County, PA. He married **BECKY DANNER** on 1 June 2013.
>>>
>>>> **4.5.2.2.2.1.1.3.1 KAILI SARAH REESE** was born on 11 June 2014.
>>>
>>> **4.5.2.2.2.1.1.4 SAMUEL IRA REESE** was born on 21 June 1983, Lankenau Hospital, Philadelphia, Philadelphia County, PA.
>>
>> **4.5.2.2.2.1.2 JOHN SHENK CURRY JR.** was born on 29 April 1952, Harrisburg, Dauphin County, PA. He married **VICKIE LOVE,** daughter of **JAMES LOVE** and **SHIRLEY (--?--),** on 28 July 1979, Hershey, Dauphin County, PA.
>>
>>> **4.5.2.2.2.1.2.1 APRIL LOVE CURRY** was born on 7 June 1986, Harrisburg, Dauphin County, PA.
>>>
>>> **4.5.2.2.2.1.2.2 VANESSA LYNN CURRY** was born on 15 March 1990.
>>
>> **4.5.2.2.2.1.3 SALLY JANE CURRY** was born on 21 January 1954, Hershey, Dauphin County, PA. She married **NATHAN PAUL BACON,** son of **JOHN BACON** and **LORETTA (--?--),** on 14 May 1978, Mont Alto, Franklin County, PA.
>>
>>> **4.5.2.2.2.1.3.1 KARL JOHANN BACON** was born on 22 November 1989.
>>
>> **4.5.2.2.2.1.4 PAMELA K. CURRY** was born on 29 July 1955. She died on 8 October 1977, in an automobile accident at Routes 22 and 743 East Hanover Township, Dauphin County, PA, at age 22. She was buried on 11 October 1977, at Fishburn United Methodist Church Cemetery, Hershey, Derry Township, Dauphin County, PA.

4.5.2.2.2.1.5 JENNIFER L. CURRY was born on 6 December 1961, Hershey, Dauphin County, PA. She died on 6 December 1961, Hershey, Dauphin County, PA. She was buried at Fishburn United Methodist Church Cemetery, Hershey, Dauphin County, PA.

4.5.2.2.2.2 RENO PALMER SCHWALM was born on 1 September 1929, Valley View, Schuylkill County, PA. He married **HELEN D. STUTZMAN**, daughter of **RAYMOND R. STUTZMAN** and **GERTRUDE STRAUB**, on 28 June 1952, Sacramento, Schuylkill County, PA. He died on 21 September 1995, Hubley Township, Schuylkill County, PA, at age 66. He was buried on 25 September 1995, at St. Andrew's United Church of Christ Cemetery, Valley View, Hegins Township, Schuylkill County, PA.

4.5.2.2.2.2.1 NAN ELIZABETH SCHWALM was born on 23 July 1954, Pottsville, Schuylkill County, PA. She married **BERNARD SADOSKI JR.** on 30 June 1979, Valley View, Schuylkill County, PA.

4.5.2.2.2.2.2 ANDREW EDWARD SCHWALM was born on 25 May 1957, Pottsville, Schuylkill County, PA. He married **EILEEN JONES.**

4.5.2.2.2.2.2.1 ROBERT JOSEPH SCHWALM was born on 4 February 1986.

4.5.2.2.2.2.2.2 AUBREY NOEL SCHWALM was born on 4 December 1990.

4.5.2.2.3 CLAYTON ALLEN SCHWALM was born on 26 August 1901. Prior to his death, Clayton was living in the vicinity of Valley View, Schuylkill County, PA. He died in September 1967, at age 66. He was buried at St. Andrew's United Methodist Church Cemetery, Valley View, Schuylkill County, PA.

4.5.2.2.4 CHARLES LEE SCHWALM was born on 24 November 1904. He died in 1906. He was buried at St. Andrew's United Methodist Church Cemetery, Valley View, Schuylkill County, PA.

4.5.2.2.5 H. ALLEN SCHWALM is also referred to as **HARRY A. SCHWALM** in some sources. He was born on 9 May 1906. He married **GRACE V. SPOTTS** on 13 December 1926, St. Andrew's United Methodist Church, Valley View, Schuylkill County, PA. Prior to his death, Harry was living in the vicinity of Valley View, Schuylkill County, PA. He died in July 1972, at age 66. He was buried at St. Andrew's United Methodist Church Cemetery, Valley View, Schuylkill County, PA.

4.5.2.2.5.1 MARION ELANORE SCHWALM was born on 15 December 1927. She married **AUSTIN S. FURMAN** on 26 June 1946, St. Andrew's United Methodist Church Cemetery, Valley View, Schuylkill County, PA.

4.5.2.2.5.2 BARBARA ANN ELIZABETH SCHWALM was born on 24 August 1930, Valley View, Schuylkill County, PA. She married **LEX I. BLACK** on 11 February 1950, St. Andrew's United Methodist Church Cemetery, Valley View, Schuylkill County, PA. She died on 30 October 2008, at age 78. According to a newspaper obituary, Barbara retired from the Harrisburg Police Department, but earlier she had been employed by the Polyclinic Hospital, Harrisburg School District, Uptown Senior Citizens Center, American Red Cross and Sam's Club. She also served as Secretary on the Senior Citizens Center's Board of Directors and was a member of the Board of Directors of the American Red Cross Safety Programs Clinic, as well as a volunteer for the American Red Cross for over fifteen years as a First Aid Instructor and as a First Aid Instructor trainer. She received the Hall of Fame Award for outstanding and unselfish service in the field of First Aid.

4.5.2.2.5.2.1 BONNIE BLACK married **SAMUEL O'KANE.**

4.5.2.2.5.2.1.1 KRISTIN O'KANE married (--?--) **HIGGINS.**

4.5.2.2.5.2.2 KEITH BLACK married **ANN MCDONALD.**

4.5.2.2.5.2.3 GAIL BLACK

4.5.2.2.6 HILDA M. SCHWALM was born on 28 August 1910. She married **JOHN W. BERGEY** on 26 December 1931, St. Andrew's Church, Valley View, Schuylkill County, PA. Prior to her death, Hilda was living in the vicinity of Valley View, Schuylkill County, PA. She died in May 1978, at age 67. She was buried at St. Andrew's United Methodist Church Cemetery, Valley View, Schuylkill County, PA.

4.5.2.2.6.1 WILLIAM CLYDE BERGEY was born on 22 August 1933, Valley View, Schuylkill County, PA. He married **DORTHA R. HAYES**, daughter of **HORACE HAYES** and **DESSIE** (--?--), circa 1956. He died on 21 September 2010, Dallas, Dallas County, TX, at age 77. He was buried on 24 September 2010, at Resthaven Memorial Park, Corsicana, Navarro County, TX.

- **4.5.2.2.6.1.1 ROBERT BERGEY**
  - **4.5.2.2.6.1.1.1 BRANDY BERGEY**
  - **4.5.2.2.6.1.1.2 BLAIR BERGEY**
  - **4.5.2.2.6.1.1.3 JONATHAN BERGEY**
- **4.5.2.2.6.1.2 BARBARA BERGEY** married (--?--) **STRMISKA**.
  - **4.5.2.2.6.1.2.1 JOSCELYN STRMISKA** married (--?--) **VANDEVENTER**.
    - **4.5.2.2.6.1.2.1.1 RHEA VANDEVENTER**
    - **4.5.2.2.6.1.2.1.2 KHYLEI VANDEVENTER**
    - **4.5.2.2.6.1.2.1.3 ABIGAYLE VANDEVENTER** married (--?--) **CASTENADA**.
  - **4.5.2.2.6.1.2.2 JOELYN MARIE STRMISKA** was born on 26 April 1998, Corsicana, TX.
  - **4.5.2.2.6.1.2.3 JAELYN MARIE STRMISKA** was born on 26 April 1998, Corsicana, Navarro County, TX.

4.5.2.2.6.2 ROBERT EUGENE BERGEY was born on 9 May 1935.

4.5.2.2.6.3 CONSTANCE LOU BERGEY was born on 1 December 1937. She married **DONALD E. SCHEIB**, son of **LESTER L. SCHEIB** and **MARGARET E. TROUTMAN**.

- **4.5.2.2.6.3.1 DONNA SCHEIB** married **JAMES REED**. She married **JAMES MARTIN**.
  - **4.5.2.2.6.3.1.1 AMY LYNNE REED** married **WILLIAM SONNEN**.
    - **4.5.2.2.6.3.1.1.1 CHEYENNE CAITLIN SONNEN** was born on 11 April 1998, Good Samaritan Hospital, Pottsville, Schuylkill County, PA.
- **4.5.2.2.6.3.2 JOY SCHEIB**
- **4.5.2.2.6.3.3 EDDIE SCHEIB**
- **4.5.2.2.6.3.4 JOHN SCHEIB** married **TAMMY** (--?--).
  - **4.5.2.2.6.3.4.1 JADE AIMEE-LOUISE SCHEIB** was born on 5 September 1996.
  - **4.5.2.2.6.3.4.2 MADDISON SUSAN-MARIE SCHEIB** was born on 22 March 1998, Good Samaritan Hospital, Pottsville, Schuylkill County, PA.

4.5.2.2.6.4 JOYCE MARIE BERGEY was born on 1 February 1941. She married **CARMEN D. SCICCHITANO**.

- **4.5.2.2.6.4.1 LISA SCICCHITANO**
- **4.5.2.2.6.4.2 MELISSA SCICCHITANO**
- **4.5.2.2.6.4.3 CARMEN D. SCICCHITANO JR.** was born circa 1972. He died on 4 September 1997, 635 17th Street, Prospect Park, PA. He was buried at St. Peter and St. Paul Greek Orthodox Church Cemetery, Mt. Carmel, PA.

4.5.2.2.6.5 JOANNE GAIL BERGEY was born on 29 October 1947. She married **JERRY L. STIELY**, son of **HARRY ALLEN STIELY** and **EVELYN ELSIE KLINGER**, circa 1965.

- **4.5.2.2.6.5.1 TERRI J. STIELY** married **DEAN HERB** on 12 September 1987, Frieden's United Church of Christ, Hegins, Schuylkill County, PA. Terri lives in Halifax, PA.
  - **4.5.2.2.6.5.1.1 NIKKI MARIE HERB** was born on 3 June 1989, Harrisburg Hospital, Harrisburg, Dauphin County, PA. She married **RYAN LEHR**, son of **JORDAN LEHR** and **SHARON** (--?--), on 4 June 2011.
  - **4.5.2.2.6.5.1.2 HEIDI ELIZABETH HERB** was born on 26 July 1992.
- **4.5.2.2.6.5.2 KRIS L. STIELY** married **VICKI WHITESEL**, daughter of **RON WHITESEL** and **DONNA MEETZ**. He lived in Sacramento, Hubley Township, Schuylkill County, PA. Kris lives in Fearnot, PA.
  - **4.5.2.2.6.5.2.1 JOHN MICHAEL STIELY** was born on 17 May 1999, Good Samaritan Regional Medical Center, Pottsville, Schuylkill County, PA.
  - **4.5.2.2.6.5.2.2 BEN WILLIAM STIELY** was born on 16 September 2001.

4.5.2.2.7 Ray Alvin Schwalm was born on 13 March 1918, Valley View, Schuylkill County, PA. He married **Enid Eunice Berry**, daughter of **Ernest Leslie Berry,** on 25 October 1941, Vancouver, British Columbia, CA. After being raised in Valley View, PA, Ray received his undergraduate degree from Millersville University and graduate degrees from Oregon State University. After serving in the Canadian Air Force in World War II, Ray was a technology professor at Western Washington State College in Bellingham, Washington. An article on his life appeared in the 2005 issue of The Hessians: Journal of the Johannes Schwalm Historical Association. Prior to his death, Ray was living in the Bellingham area, Whatcom County, WA. He died on 8 August 1987, at age 69. He was buried at Greenacres Memorial Park, Ferndale, Whatcom County, WA.

    4.5.2.2.7.1 Roger Sherwood Schwalm was born on 2 January 1943. He married **Annette Engel**. He married **Claudia Harris**. He married **Linda Bradley**.

        4.5.2.2.7.1.1 Roger Raymond Schwalm Sr. married **Cassandra Covington**.

            4.5.2.2.7.1.1.1 Roger Raymond Schwalm Jr. married **Diane Fulton**.

                4.5.2.2.7.1.1.1.1 Aziza Rashuan Annette Schwalm was born on 6 May 2007.

        4.5.2.2.7.1.2 Scott Berry Schwalm married **Paula Creech**.

            4.5.2.2.7.1.2.1 Amanda Jean Schwalm married **Clifford Dozier**.

                4.5.2.2.7.1.2.1.1 Summer Lee Dozier was born on 11 June 2005.

        4.5.2.2.7.1.3 Christopher Littlefield

    4.5.2.2.7.2 Patricia Diane Schwalm was born on 30 September 1944. She married (--?--) **Littlefield**. She married **Jerry Driscoll**.

        4.5.2.2.7.2.1 Melissa Littlefield married **Ray Amaro**.

            4.5.2.2.7.2.1.1 Drake Hero Amaro was born on 26 August 2002.

        4.5.2.2.7.2.2 Christopher Littlefield

        4.5.2.2.7.2.3 Donald Sean Driscoll married **Shelley Lynn Rubinger** on 26 April 2003.

            4.5.2.2.7.2.3.1 Zachary Rubinger was born before April 2003.

            4.5.2.2.7.2.3.2 Sean Harris Driscoll was born on 9 August 2003.

4.5.2.3 Eda May Schwalm is also referred to as **Edith Schwalm** in some sources. She was born on 25 April 1879. Eda was the housekeeper for Dr. and Mrs. William J. O'Brien in Philadelphia for many years. According to an article in the Philadelphia Inquirer, upon his death on March 4, 1940, Dr. O'Brien bequeathed Eda the sum of $50,000 for her "loyalty, kindness, and devotion." She died on 1 May 1955, Philadelphia General Hospital, Philadelphia, Philadelphia County, PA, at age 76. She was buried on 1 May 1955, at Friedens Union Cemetery, Hegins, Schuylkill County, PA.

4.5.2.4 Elvin Ray Schwalm was born on 9 April 1881. He married **Edna Williard**. Prior to his death, Elvin was living in the vicinity of Reading, Berks County, PA. He died on 17 August 1968, at age 87. He was buried at Frieden's Union Cemetery, Hegins, Schuylkill County, PA.

    4.5.2.4.1 Anna Irene Schwalm was born on 14 December 1903. She was baptized on 18 March 1904, St. Paul (Artz's) Lutheran and Reformed Church, Sacramento, Schuylkill County, PA. She married **William E. Ressler**, son of **Frank J. Ressler** and **Mary S. Otto**. She died on 28 May 1988, at home, 404 Douglas Street, Reading, Berks County, PA, at age 84. She was buried at Frieden's Cemetery, Hegins, Schuylkill County, PA.

        4.5.2.4.1.1 Vincent Roland Ressler was born on 22 October 1922, Hegins, Schuylkill County, PA. He died on 21 February 1972, Reading, Berks County, PA, at age 49. He was buried at Friedens Union Cemetery, Hegins, Schuylkill County, PA.

    4.5.2.4.2 William Arthur Schwalm was born on 3 September 1906, Schuylkill County, PA. He was baptized on 7 October 1906, Friedens Reformed Church, Hegins, Schuylkill County, PA. He married **Hilda R. Bowman**, daughter of **Ellsworth W. Bowman** and **Mary Smeltz,** on 1 January 1929, Friedens Reformed Church, Hegins, Schuylkill County, PA. Prior to his death, William was living in the vicinity of Frackville, Schuylkill County, PA. He died in March 1976, Frackville, Schuylkill County, PA, at age 69. He was buried at Frieden's Union Cemetery, Hegins, Schuylkill County, PA.

4.5.2.4.3 CHARLES ALBERT SCHWALM was born on 28 December 1909, Hegins, Schuylkill County, PA. He married **FLORENCE MYRTLE GLASS**, daughter of **WILLIAM SYLVESTER GLASS** and **AMANDA F. HARTZ,** on 15 February 1930, Elkton, Cecil County, MD. He died on 2 November 1993, at home, 3533 Pricetown Road, Fleetwood, Berks County, PA, at age 83. He was buried at Forest Hills Memorial Park, Reiffton, Berks County, PA.

> **4.5.2.4.3.1 SHIRLEY BELLE SCHWALM** was born circa 1932. She married **CARSON LEROY HART** on 27 November 1952, Holy Spirit Church, Reading, Berks County, PA. She married **EDWARD CROSBY HOWE** on 4 August 1957, Oklahoma.
>
>> **4.5.2.4.3.1.1 CHARLES WYNN HOWE** was born on 25 May 1958, Reading, Berks County, PA. He married **MARCELE L. ANDERSON** on 5 May 1980, Monticello, Piatt County, IL.
>>
>> **4.5.2.4.3.1.2 JERRIANNE HOWE** was born on 3 November 1960, Reading, Berks County, PA. She married **FRANK WOODS** on 13 February 1988, Houston, Harris County, TX. She and **FRANK WOODS** were divorced circa 1995.
>>
>>> **4.5.2.4.3.1.2.1 ELISA DONEE WOODS** was born on 11 February 1989, Houston, Harris County, TX.
>
> **4.5.2.4.3.2 GERALDINE A. SCHWALM** was born on 25 July 1939. She married **ERIC ALLMER.**

4.5.2.4.4 EDA MAY SCHWALM was born on 20 April 1915. She died on 3 April 1916. She was buried at Frieden's Union Cemetery, Hegins, Schuylkill County, PA.

4.5.2.4.5 MARK ALTON SCHWALM was born on 6 November 1918, Hegins, Schuylkill County, PA. He married **HELEN BERTHA FAGER**, daughter of **LEWIS L. FAGER** and **CAROLINE SCHUTT**, on 25 April 1943, St. Matthew's Lutheran Church, Reading, Berks County, PA. He died on 25 December 2013, Sun Prairie, WI, at age 95. According to a newspaper obituary, Mark went to McCann School of Business in Reading, PA, and was then hired by GE for whom he worked for 42 years. After retiring from GE in 1979, he focused on his passions -- history, genealogy, and travel. He helped to form the Johannes Schwalm Historical Association concentrating on Hessian soldiers of the Revolutionary War.

Mark lived in Greenville, SC for 23 years before moving to Wisconsin.

> **4.5.2.4.5.1 JOANNE SCHWALM** married **JOHN M. JONES.**
>
>> **4.5.2.4.5.1.1 LISA C. JONES** married **SCOTT PANHORST.**
>>
>> **4.5.2.4.5.1.2 HEATHER JONES**
>
> **4.5.2.4.5.2 ANN SCHWALM** was born on 7 February 1947, Baltimore, Baltimore County, MD. She married **ARLYNN SCHWANKE** on 20 September 1969, Cleveland Heights, Cuyahoga County, OH.
>
>> **4.5.2.4.5.2.1 TODD DANIEL SCHWANKE** was born on 3 September 1972, Madison, Dane County, WI. He married **MARSHA ALLEN** on 20 May 2006, Bristol Lutheran Church, Sun Prairie, WI. Todd is a technical specialist at the University of Wisconsin-Milwaukee.
>>
>> **4.5.2.4.5.2.2 AMY ANN SCHWANKE** was born on 3 February 1977, Madison, Dane County, WI. She died before 2014.
>>
>> **4.5.2.4.5.2.3 MARK WALTER SCHWANKE** was born on 22 May 1980, Madison, Dane County, WI.
>>
>> **4.5.2.4.5.2.4 ERICA ANN SCHWANKE** was born on 30 May 1984, Seoul, South Korea.
>
> **4.5.2.4.5.3 KARL E. SCHWALM** was born on 20 May 1948, Baltimore, Baltimore County, MD. He married **SHARON E. GANUS**. Karl is a practicing physician in Oakland, MD. Recently, he stopped delivering babies after delivering more than 2,500 in his career.
>
>> **4.5.2.4.5.3.1 MICHAEL JOHANNES SCHWALM** was born on 18 August 1982.

4.5.2.4.6 WALLACE A. SCHWALM was born on 28 June 1922. He died on 23 June 1923, Hegins Township, Schuylkill County, PA. He was buried on 25 June 1923, at Frieden's Union Cemetery, Hegins, Schuylkill County, PA.

4.5.2.5 JAMES A. SCHWALM was born in January 1884. He died in 1905. He was buried at Friedens Union Cemetery, Hegins, Schuylkill County, PA.

4.5.2.6 MARIETTA MAUDE SCHWALM was born in 1887. She died on 10 September 1906. She was buried at Friedens Union Cemetery, Hegins, Schuylkill County, PA. It is not clear whether Marietta is a daughter of Samuel or not. She is buried alongside two of Samuel's children, James and Eda, but she is not listed in the 1900 Census as living in Samuel and Ellen's household. Nor does she appear to be listed anywhere else in the 1900 Census in Schulkill County. There does not appear to be any death certificate for her in Pennsylvania, at least among the online lists at ancestry.com.

There is, however, a listing in Samuel's household for a "Maud Millholand" born September, 1887, identified as a "servant." Curiously, there is a "Roswell Millholand" born Dec. 1891 who is shown as a "Son" of Ellen Schwalm.

4.5.2.7 MABEL L. SCHWALM is also referred to as **MABELLE SCHWALM** in some sources. She was born in November 1886. Some sources record that she was born on 8 November 1888, Pennsylvania. She married **FREDERIC HAIGH** on 5 November 1938, Ontario, San Bernardino County, CA. The San Bernardino County Sun reported on November 3, 1938, that a marriage license was issued to "Frederic Haigh, 71, England, and Mabelle Schwalm, 51, both residents of Los Angeles." A few days later the same paper reported that "Dr. Frederic Haigh, 71-year old Hollywood physician, and Miss Mabelle Schwalm, 51, Los Angles, were married here [Ontario] today [November 5] by Judge J.F. Hamilton in his chambers at city hall. Passenger ship records indicate that a Mabelle Haigh, born c. 1887 in Valley View, PA, sailed from Los Angeles, CA, on December 22, 1950, bound for Honolulu, HI, aboard the SS Lurline, with the return trip leaving Honolulu on January 10, 1951. She died on 18 January 1958, Los Angeles County, CA, at age 71. She was buried at Forest Lawn Memorial Park (Glendale), Glendale, Los Angeles County, CA.

4.5.2.8 ROSWELL JACOB SCHWALM was born on 18 December 1891, Hegins, Schuylkill County, PA. He married **MARIE TERESE ROTHERMEL**, daughter of **DAVID L. ROTHERMEL** and **HARRIET FLORY**. He died on 20 January 1961, Lancaster General Hospital, Lancaster, Lancaster County, PA, at age 69. He was buried on 24 January 1961, at Woodward Hill Cemetery, Lancaster, Lancaster County, PA.

> **4.5.2.8.1 MARIE ELIZABETH SCHWALM** was born on 24 June 1921. She married **HERBERT M. DENLINGER**, son of **JOHN CLETUS DENLINGER** and **STELLA KEELEY MYERS,** on 30 August 1947. She died on 31 August 2005, at age 84. She was buried at Saint Pauls Evangelical Lutheran Cemetery, Silver Spring Township, Cumberland County, PA.
>
>> **4.5.2.8.1.1 JOHN R. DENLINGER**
>>
>> **4.5.2.8.1.2 CHRISTINE DENLINGER**
>>
>> **4.5.2.8.1.3 ROSWELL DENLINGER**

4.5.2.9 BERNICE AMELIA HANNAH SCHWALM was born on 13 September 1898. She was baptized on 7 January 1899, Frieden's Reformed Church, Hegins, Schuylkill County, PA. She died on 24 October 1899, at age 1. She was buried at Saint Peters United Methodist Church Cemetery, Fearnot, Schuylkill County, PA.

4.5.2.10 MARY ELLEN SCHWALM was born on 21 July 1900. She was baptized on 28 October 1900, Frieden's Reformed Church, Hegins, Schuylkill County, PA. She married **JOHN MERL SHULTZ**, son of **J. FRANK SHULTZ** and **SUSAN MILLER**. Prior to her death, Mary was living in the vicinity of Lancaster, Lancaster County, PA. She died in January 1972, at age 71. She was buried at Cedar Lawn Cemetery, Lancaster, Lancaster County, PA.

> **4.5.2.10.1 NANCY RUTH SHULTZ** was born on 30 July 1928, Lancaster County, PA. She married **JOHN CLAIRE DUFFY**, son of **J. WILLIAM DUFFY** and **ADA MILLER**. She died on 8 October 1961, Lancaster, Lancaster County, PA, at age 33. She was buried at Millersville Mennonite Cemetery, Millersville, Lancaster County, PA.
>
>> **4.5.2.10.1.1 DANIEL J. DUFFY**
>>
>> **4.5.2.10.1.2 KATHLEEN S. DUFFY** was born on 14 November 1949, Lancaster, Lancaster County, PA. She married **DON C. BIEMENSDERFER**. She married **WILLIAM E. HARLAN** circa 1986. She died on 29 January 2011, Branford, New Haven County, CT, at age 61. She was buried at Millersville Mennonite Cemetery, Millersville, Lancaster County, PA.
>>
>>> **4.5.2.10.1.2.1 STEPHANIE BIEMENSDERFER** married (--?--) **CARBONE**.
>>>
>>> **4.5.2.10.1.2.2 ELIZABETH HARLAN**
>>>
>>> **4.5.2.10.1.2.3 WILLIAM HARLAN JR.**

4.5.2.10.1.3 STEPHEN R. DUFFY was born on 3 August 1955, Lancaster County, PA. He died on 22 August 1955, Lancaster, Lancaster County, PA. He was buried on 24 August 1955, at Millersville Mennonite Cemetery, Millersville, Lancaster County, PA.

4.5.2.11 GRACE KATHARINE SCHWALM was born on 25 March 1902. She was baptized on 9 June 1902, Frieden's Reformed Church, Hegins, Schuylkill County, PA. She married LEONARD BARTH.

4.5.2.11.1 HAROLD LEONARD BARTH was born on 2 November 1920, Lancaster, Lancaster County, PA. He married MARGARET DICKOL. He died on 2 October 1991, Philadelphia, PA, at age 70. He was buried on 7 October 1991, at Oakland Cemetery, Philadelphia, PA.

4.5.2.11.1.1 SANDRA BARTH married GEORGE POWELL.

4.5.2.11.1.1.1 SUSAN POWELL

4.5.2.11.1.1.2 THERESA POWELL

4.5.2.11.1.1.3 KAREN MARIE POWELL was born on 29 November 1980, Philadelphia, PA.

4.5.2.11.1.2 WARREN BARTH married MARY HORSTMAN.

4.5.2.11.1.2.1 KEVIN BARTH

4.5.2.11.1.2.2 KIMBERLY BARTH

4.5.2.11.2 RAYMOND E. BARTH was born on 6 June 1922. He married MARY FRANCES HOLZAPFEL. He died on 5 January 1972, Norfolk, VA, at age 49. He was buried at Forest Lawn Cemetery, Norfolk, VA.

4.5.2.11.2.1 VIRGINIA BARTH married JOHN SRNKA.

4.5.2.11.2.1.1 CHRISTOPHER SRNKA

4.5.2.11.2.1.2 SCOTT SRNKA

4.5.2.11.2.2 DAVID A. BARTH was born on 25 March 1952. He died on 18 June 1972, at age 20. He was buried at Forest Lawn Cemetery, Norfolk, VA.

4.5.2.11.3 RICHARD CARL BARTH was born on 31 August 1926, St. Joseph's Hospital, Lancaster, Lancaster County, PA. He married SABINA RUDENAUER, daughter of CARL RUDENAUER and ANNA SCHMIDT, on 3 April 1948. He died on 22 July 2002, at age 75. He was buried at Lakeview Memorial Park, Cinnaminson, Burlington County, NJ.

4.5.2.11.3.1 RICHARD CARL BARTH JR. was born on 1 August 1949. He married CAROL A. RABBITT. Richard became the Assistant Secretary for Policy Development of the Department of Homeland Security.

4.5.2.11.3.1.1 AMELIA CHRISTINE BARTH was born on 24 November 1981.

4.5.2.11.3.1.2 ALEXANDER CARL BARTH was born on 22 February 1985, Washington, DC.

4.5.2.11.3.2 ROBERT GEORGE BARTH married CHARLENE VANDERGRIFT. He was born on 17 December 1950.

4.5.2.11.3.2.1 CYNTHIA GRACE BARTH married MICHAEL ANTHONY BOVINO on 25 September 2004, Haddonfield United Methodist Church, Haddonfield, NJ.

4.5.2.11.3.2.1.1 ANTHONY ROBERT BOVINO was born on 21 November 2007.

4.5.2.11.3.2.1.2 JOSEPH MICHAEL BOVINO was born on 21 November 2007.

4.5.2.11.3.2.2 GREGORY ROBERT BARTH was born on 3 March 1978. He married STEPHANIE ZURN.

4.5.2.11.3.2.2.1 ASHLEY PAIGE BARTH was born on 4 March 2008.

4.5.2.11.3.2.2.2 ZACHARY CARTER BARTH was born on 3 February 2010.

4.5.2.11.3.3 KARAN SABINA BARTH was born on 19 November 1952, Darby, Delaware County, PA. She died on 25 February 1954, University Hospital, Philadelphia, Philadelphia County, PA, at age 1. She was buried on 1 March 1954, at Old Cathedral Cemetery, Philadelphia, Philadelphia County, PA.

4.5.2.11.3.4 KARIN SABINA BARTH was born on 28 March 1955.

4.5.2.11.3.5 KENNETH CHARLES BARTH was born on 18 April 1959. He married EMILY PIERCE.

4.5.2.11.3.5.1 NICOLE LEE BARTH was born on 25 June 1979. She married THEODORE HINES on 15 February 2002.

4.5.2.11.3.5.1.1 KILEY RAE HINES was born on 12 October 2005.

4.5.2.11.3.5.1.2 JILLIAN LYNNAE HINES was born on 2 April 2009. She was baptized on 28 June 2009, First United Methodist Church, Moorestown, Burlington County, NJ.

4.5.2.11.3.5.1.3 REED THOMAS HINES was born on 13 June 2014.

4.5.2.11.3.5.2 RICHARD CARL BARTH II was born on 2 February 1981, Philadelphia, PA. He married CHRISTINE BOZARTH. He married JACKIE (--?--).

4.5.2.11.3.5.2.1 ANNA ELIZABETH BARTH was born on 25 November 2002.

4.5.2.12 THEODORE R. SCHWALM is also referred to as RAYMOND THEODORE SCHWALM in some sources. He was born on 12 May 1906, on the Shadle Farm in Deep Creek Valley, Valley View, Schuylkill County, PA. Some sources record that he was born on 21 July 1906. He was baptized on 21 August 1906, Frieden's Reformed Church, Hegins, Schuylkill County, PA. He married EDNA MOORE on 12 June 1926. He died on 29 September 1991, St. Joseph's Hospital, Lancaster, Lancaster County, PA, at age 85. He was buried at Riverview Burial Park, Lancaster, Lancaster County, PA.

4.5.2.12.1 MARY ELLEN SCHWALM is also referred to as MARYELLEN SCHWALM in some sources. She was born on 13 June 1928, Lancaster, Lancaster County, PA. She married JOHN RICHARD GOCKLEY on 10 June 1950. She died in April 1978, at age 49.

4.5.2.12.1.1 SUSAN GOCKLEY married STEVEN BROWN.

4.5.2.12.1.1.1 JASON BROWN was born on 20 November 1979.

4.5.2.12.1.1.2 JENIFER BROWN was born on 24 September 1981.

4.5.2.12.1.2 LISA GOCKLEY married WALTER PETERS on 5 November 1981, Lancaster, Lancaster County, PA.

4.5.2.12.1.2.1 STEPHANIE PETERS

4.5.2.12.1.2.2 MICHELLE PETERS

4.5.2.12.1.3 ROBERT THEODORE GOCKLEY was born on 7 April 1952, Lancaster County, PA. He died on 20 April 1952, Lancaster General Hospital, Lancaster, Lancaster County, PA. He was buried on 22 April 1952, at Riverview Burial Park, Lancaster, Lancaster County, PA.

4.5.3 CATHERINE SCHWALM was born on 5 October 1849. Some sources record that she was born on 5 April 1847, Schuylkill County, PA. She married ABRAHAM CARL. She died on 20 March 1873, at age 23. Some sources record that she died on 20 March 1871 Pottsville, Schuylkill County, PA. She was buried at Saint Pauls United Church of Christ Cemetery, Sacramento, Schuylkill County, PA.

4.5.3.1 FREDERICK MONROE CARL was born on 21 November 1870, Tower City, Schuylkill County, PA. He married ANNIE STAPLE on 29 August 1891, Camden, Camden County, NJ. He died on 16 February 1921, Reading, Berks County, PA, at age 50. He was buried on 19 February 1921, at Greenwood Cemetery, Tower City, Schuylkill County, PA.

4.5.3.1.1 WILLIAM C. CARL was born in March 1892. He married MARGARET YINGST on 15 August 1913, Wilmington, New Castle County, DE. He married LULU MALONE.

4.5.3.1.1.1 ELIZABETH CARL

4.5.3.1.1.2 FREDERICK W. CARL married MARY GALLAGHER. He married NANCY HOFFMAN.

4.5.3.1.1.2.1 DOROTHY CARL married JOSEPH MAZZO JR.

4.5.3.1.1.2.1.1 KATHLEEN MAZZO

4.5.3.1.1.2.1.2 JOSEPH MAZZO III

4.5.3.1.1.2.2 FREDERICK M. CARL

4.5.3.1.1.2.3 WILLIAM F. CARL

4.5.4 HANNAH SCHWALM was born on 17 September 1851, Schuylkill County, PA. She married JARED BOHN FAUST, son of REUBEN EIRICH FAUST and MARY ANN BOHN, in October 1870. She died on 24 March 1926, Reading, Berks County, PA, at age 74. She was buried on 29 March 1926, at Charles Evans Cemetery, Reading, Berks County, PA.

4.5.4.1 OSCAR M. FAUST was born on 8 April 1871, Valley View, Schuylkill County, PA. He died on 12 April 1873, Valley View, Schuylkill County, PA, at age 2. He was buried at Saint Pauls United Church of Christ Cemetery, Sacramento, Schuylkill County, PA.

4.5.4.2 WILLIAM H. FAUST was born on 7 April 1874, Reading, Berks County, PA. He married **MARY JANE BOUCHAT**, daughter of **WILLIAM BOUCHAT** and **MARY J. (--?--)**, on 18 June 1895, Reading, Berks County, PA. He died on 12 April 1921, Easton, Northampton County, PA, at age 47. He was buried at Charles Evans Cemetery, Reading, Berks County, PA.

4.5.4.2.1 WARREN JARED FAUST was born on 31 January 1896. He was baptized on 29 March 1896, St. Barnabas Episcopal Church, Reading, Berks County, PA. He married **MARY ELLEN FELTON**. He died in December 1978, Bridgeport, Fairfield County, CT, at age 82. He was buried at Lakeview Cemetery, Bridgeport, Fairfield County, CT.

4.5.4.2.2 HELEN BOUCHAT FAUST was born on 22 May 1897, Reading, Berks County, PA. She married **JOSEPH J. SCHMIDT**.

4.5.4.2.2.1 JOSEPH SCHMIDT was born circa 1928.

4.5.4.3 ANNA FRANCES FAUST was born on 10 February 1876, Reading, Berks County, PA. She married **WILSON HENRY EISENBROWN**, son of **PENROSE F. EISENBROWN** and **SARAH (--?--)**, on 15 January 1896, Reading, Berks County, PA. She died on 22 January 1957, West Reading, Berks County, PA, at age 80. She was buried on 25 January 1957, at Charles Evans Cemetery, Reading, Berks County, PA.

4.5.4.3.1 SARAH E. EISENBROWN was born on 4 January 1897. She married **HARRY FRANCIS RAHN** before 1920. She died on 6 January 1984, at age 87. She was buried at Charles Evans Cemetery, Reading, Berks County, PA.

4.5.4.3.1.1 INFANT DAUGHTER JANET ISOBEL RAHN was born on 31 July 1924, Reading, Berks County, PA. She died on 1 August 1924, Reading, Berks County, PA. She was buried at Charles Evans Cemetery, Reading, Berks County, PA.

4.5.4.3.1.2 FRANCES HAHN married **ELMER C. ALLWINE**. She was born circa 1927.

4.5.4.3.1.2.1 DANIEL ALLWINE

4.5.4.3.1.2.2 DAVID ALLWINE

4.5.4.3.1.3 WILSON HAHN was born circa 1931.

4.5.4.3.2 RUTH EISENBROWN was born in 1899, Reading, Berks County, PA. She died on 3 February 1965, Berks County, PA. She was buried at Charles Evans Cemetery, Reading, Berks County, PA.

4.5.4.3.3 ANNA MAY EISENBROWN was born on 14 May 1906, Reading, Berks County, PA. She married **(--?--) FREY**. She married **(--?--) SCHMIDT**. She died on 17 March 1994, at age 87. She was buried at Charles Evans Cemetery, Reading, Berks County, PA.

4.5.5 GEORGE WASHINGTON SCHWALM was born on 16 June 1853, Fearnot, Schuylkill County, PA. He died on 3 November 1856, Schuylkill County, PA, at age 3. He was buried at St. Paul (Artz's) Lutheran and Reformed Church, Sacramento, Schuylkill County, PA.

4.5.6 JUSTINA E. SCHWALM was born on 11 August 1855, Fearnot, Schuylkill County, PA. She married **CHARLES M. HOFFMAN** circa 1877. She died on 9 March 1926, Tremont, Schuylkill County, PA, at age 70. She was buried on 13 March 1926, at Saint Peters United Methodist Church Cemetery, Fearnot, Schuylkill County, PA.

4.5.6.1 ALICE J. HOFFMAN was born on 13 December 1876, Fearnot, Schuylkill County, PA. She married **JAMES SALTZER** before 1896. She married **HENRY GRANT HERB**, son of **HENRY HERB** and **MATILDA MAURER**, circa 1899. She died on 14 January 1946, Allentown, Lehigh County, PA, at age 69. She was buried on 17 January 1946, at Saint Peters United Methodist Church Cemetery, Fearnot, Schuylkill County, PA.

4.5.6.1.1 ETHEL SALTZER was born in March 1896. She married **WILSON SCHAEFFER**, son of **FRANK SCHAEFFER** and **ELIZABETH FEGLEY**. She married **ELMER GARDNER** after 1930. She married **LESTER KERSCHNER**.

4.5.6.1.1.1 GRACE ALICE SCHAEFFER was born in 1912. She married **EDWARD B. CHAPMAN**, son of **JOHN B. CHAPMAN** and **DORA J. KIEHL**, circa 1930. She married **ROBERT ELLSWORTH BONAWITZ**. She died in October 1971. She was buried at Saint John's Lutheran Church Cemetery, Pine Grove, Schuylkill County, PA.

4.5.6.1.1.1.1 SHIRLEY D. CHAPMAN was born on 29 February 1932. She married GLENN A. FURMAN, son of ASHER K. FURMAN and ELIZABETH D. YOUNG. She married CARL RICHARD BAUM, son of MORRIS BAUM and CLARA A. HOLSBERG, on 23 January 1988.

    4.5.6.1.1.1.1.1 CRAIG FURMAN

    4.5.6.1.1.1.1.2 CORIE FURMAN

4.5.6.1.1.1.2 MICHELLE BONAWITZ married RICHARD L. WETZEL.

    4.5.6.1.1.1.2.1 ANDREW WETZEL

4.5.6.1.1.2 ELMER K. GARDNER married JOAN BARRY.

4.5.6.1.2 RAY CHARLIE HOFFMAN HERB was born on 16 December 1902. He was baptized on 14 March 1903, St. Andrews United Methodist Church, Valley View, Schuylkill County, PA. He married BERNICE L. DEIBLER, daughter of ARTHUR DEIBLER and HANNA MATILDA SNYDER. He died on 28 October 1969, Fulton County, GA, at age 66. He was buried at First Presbyterian Church Cemetery, Metuchen, Middlesex County, NJ.

    4.5.6.1.2.1 JANICE LUCILLE HERB was born on 9 December 1940. She married THOR W. RINDEN.

    4.5.6.1.2.2 SALLY SNYDER HERB was born on 18 June 1942.

4.5.6.1.3 HENRY GUY HERB was born on 6 April 1909, Schuylkill County, PA. He died on 4 September 1909, Pottsville Hospital, Pottsville, Schuylkill County, PA. He was buried on 6 September 1909, at Saint Peters United Methodist Church Cemetery, Fearnot, Schuylkill County, PA.

4.5.6.1.4 EARLE ALBERT HERB was born on 5 April 1912. He married MATILDA S. REEDY, daughter of FRANKLIN M. REEDY and MARY M. YOUNG, before 1 April 1940. He died on 16 October 1992, Leon County, FL, at age 80. He was buried at Culley's MeadowWood Memorial Park, Tallahassee, Leon County, FL.

    4.5.6.1.4.1 JANET DOROTHY HERB was born on 12 December 1930. She died on 14 September 1938, at age 7. She was buried at Newfoundland Methodist Cemetery, Newfoundland, Passaic County, NJ.

    4.5.6.1.4.2 MARY ALICE HERB was born on 20 August 1940. She married R. CARSON DYAL.

4.5.7 JACOB NATHANIEL SCHWALM is also referred to as NATHANIEL J. SCHWALM in some sources. He was born on 12 November 1857, Schuylkill County, PA. He married HANNAH KLINE, daughter of GEORGE KLINE and CAROLINE ARTZ, circa 1879. He died on 23 July 1938, Williamstown, Dauphin County, PA, at age 80. He was buried on 25 July 1938, at Fairview Cemetery, Williamstown, Dauphin County, PA.

4.5.7.1 NORA C. SCHWALM was born on 28 September 1879. She married HARRY WILLIAM RANK, son of J.L. RANK and SUSANNA (--?--), on 31 December 1900, Williamstown, Dauphin County, PA. She died on 29 April 1961, West Reading, Berks County, PA, at age 81. She was buried on 3 May 1961, at Fairview Cemetery, Williamstown, Dauphin County, PA.

    4.5.7.1.1 ALLEN W. RANK was born on 14 May 1901. He married HELEN B. SHAFFER. He died on 2 June 1974, at age 73. He was buried at Charles Evans Cemetery, Reading, Berks County, PA.

        4.5.7.1.1.1 DARRELL SHAFFER RANK was born on 11 March 1926, Reading, Berks County, PA. He married GLORIA D'ERCOLE. He died on 26 March 2005, at age 79. He was buried at Indiantown Gap National Cemetery, Annville, Lebanon County, PA.

            4.5.7.1.1.1.1 KEVIN RANK

4.5.7.2 STANFORD W. SCHWALM was born on 10 May 1888, Valley View, Schuylkill County, PA. He married ANNA E. STEIN, daughter of ISAAC F. STEIN and ADALINE ROW, on 20 March 1914, Harrisburg, Dauphin County, PA. He died on 28 April 1943, at age 54.

    4.5.7.2.1 WARREN STANFORD SWALM was born on 23 August 1914, Williamstown, Dauphin County, PA. He married BERNICE AUMAN. He died on 17 July 2000, at age 85. He was buried at Aulenbach's Cemetery, Mount Penn, Berks County, PA.

        4.5.7.2.1.1 CAROL SCHWALM married RALPH MARINO.

            4.5.7.2.1.1.1 RALPH J. MARINO

4.5.7.2.1.1.2 VINCENT J. MARINO

4.5.7.2.1.1.3 CAROL L. MARINO

4.5.7.2.1.2 LISA ANN SCHWALM married (--?--) HEYDNER.

4.5.7.2.1.3 DARRELL WARREN SWALM was born on 17 October 1941, Reading, Berks County, PA. He married MARIE ANNE BEN on 28 May 1993, Miami-Dade County, FL. He died on 7 November 1998, at home, 125 Tumbleweed Drive, Blandon, PA, at age 57. He was buried at Berks County Memorial Gardens, Maidencreek Township, Berks County, PA.

4.5.7.2.2 RAY ALLEN SCHWALM was born on 12 January 1920. He was baptized on 29 February 1920, Immanuel Evangelical Lutheran Church, Williamstown, Dauphin County, PA.

4.5.8 MARY A. SCHWALM was born on 5 December 1859. She married SAMUEL C. HERB, son of HENRY HERB and CATHERINE COLEMAN, circa 1877. She died on 21 August 1920, at age 60. She was buried on 25 August 1920, at St. Peter's (Artz) United Methodist Church, Fearnot, Schuylkill County, PA.

4.5.8.1 CHARLES OSCAR MILTON HERB is also referred to as OSCAR HERB in some sources. He was born on 28 June 1877, Schuylkill County, PA. He married HANNAH ELIZABETH SHADE, daughter of REUBEN H. SHADE and AMELIA JANE TROUTMAN WIEST, on 25 March 1899. He died on 6 October 1938, Tower City, Schuylkill County, PA, at age 61. He was buried on 9 October 1938, at Greenwood Cemetery, Tower City, Schuylkill County, PA.

4.5.8.1.1 WARREN OSCAR HERB (see above)

4.5.8.1.1.1 BETTY IRENE HERB (see above)

4.5.8.1.1.1.1 WARREN THOMAS REIGHTLER (see above)

4.5.8.1.2 EVA MAE HERB (see above)

4.5.8.1.2.1 KARL LEO UNDERKOFFLER (see above)

4.5.8.2 CURTIN M. HERB was born on 15 December 1882, Schuylkill County, PA. He died on 9 November 1894, Schuylkill County, PA, at age 11. He was buried at Saint Peters United Methodist Church Cemetery, Fearnot, Schuylkill County, PA.

4.5.9 HENRY E. SCHWALM was born on 17 January 1862, Fearnot, Schuylkill County, PA. He married CATHERINE A. SALTZER, daughter of JOHN W. SALTZER and MARY CLARK, circa 1883. He died on 10 September 1933, Hubley Township, Schuylkill County, PA, at age 71. He was buried on 14 September 1933, at St. Peter's United Methodist Church Cemetery, Fearnot, Hubley Township, Schuylkill County, PA.

4.5.9.1 LEON LINSCOTT SCHWALM was born on 17 January 1884, Fearnot, Schuylkill County, PA. Some sources record that he was born on 14 January 1884, Fearnot, Schuylkill County, PA. He married SALLY EDNA DIETRICH on 29 July 1911, Frieden's Reformed Church, Hegins, Schuylkill County, PA. He died on 7 February 1945, Spring Glen, Schuylkill County, PA, at age 61. He was buried on 11 February 1945, at Saint Paul's United Church of Christ Cemetery, Sacramento, Schuylkill County, PA.

4.5.9.1.1 HOMER RAYMOND SCHWALM was born on 27 October 1911, Spring Glen, Schuylkill County, PA. He was baptized on 24 January 1912, St. Andrew's United Methodist Church, Valley View, Schuylkill County, PA. He married DOROTHY HANNAH ROTHERMEL, daughter of CHARLES A. ROTHERMEL and CARRIE A. KAHLER. He died on 8 January 1975, Spring Glen, Schuylkill County, PA, at age 63. He was buried at Saint Paul's United Church of Christ Cemetery, Sacramento, Schuylkill County, PA.

4.5.9.1.2 ELVA C. SCHWALM was born on 22 December 1913, Spring Glen, Schuylkill County, PA. She married CHARLES HERMAN KIEFER, son of AARON ALVIN KIEFER and EMMA SHAFFER, on 23 November 1940, Hegins, Schuylkill County, PA. She lived in Hegins, Schuylkill County, PA. She died on 7 April 1996, Good Samaritan Regional Medical Center, Pottsville, Schuylkill County, PA, at age 82. She was buried at United Methodist Cemetery, Hegins, Schuylkill County, PA.

4.5.9.1.2.1 LEE A. KIEFER was born in 1941. He married LINDA RUCH.

4.5.9.1.2.1.1 AARON KIEFER

4.5.9.1.2.1.1.1 JARED KIEFER

4.5.9.1.2.1.1.2 JOSHUA KIEFER

4.5.9.1.2.1.2 KATHY KIEFER married TROY MAURER, son of TERRANCE WILLIAM MAURER and BONNIE WIEST.

4.5.9.1.2.1.2.1 SETH WILLIAM MAURER was born on 20 February 1990, Good Samaritan Hospital, Pottsville, Schuylkill County, PA. On October 17, 2008, Seth graduated with honors at Lakeland Air Force Base. He married MEGAN ELIZABETH BETZ, daughter of HAROLD BETZ and BETH ANN (--?--), on 8 June 2013, Frieden's Lutheran Church, Hegins, Schuylkill County, PA.

4.5.9.1.2.1.2.1.1 BRIELLE ISABELLA MAURER was born on 10 June 2013, Minot, Ward County, ND.

4.5.9.1.2.1.2.2 EVAN GARRET MAURER was born on 24 January 1992, Good Samaritan Hospital, Pottsville, Schuylkill County, PA.

4.5.9.1.2.1.2.3 CHASE AVERY MAURER was born on 6 September 1996, Good Samaritan Regional Medical Center, Pottsville, Schuylkill County, PA.

4.5.9.1.2.1.2.4 (--?--) MAURER was born on 6 September 1996, Good Samaritan Regional Medical Center, Pottsville, Schuylkill County, PA.

4.5.9.1.2.1.2.5 CHELSEA MAE-LYNN MAURER was born on 15 June 2000.

4.5.9.1.3 ERMA A. SCHWALM was born in 1916. She married LESTER S. GUTSHALL, son of WILLMER J. GUTSHALL and MAUD I. (--?--), on 4 June 1938, Harrisburg, Dauphin County, PA. She died on 13 July 1989, Leader East Nursing and Rehabilitation Center, Harrisburg, Dauphin County, PA. She was buried at Woodland Memorial Gardens, Lower Paxton Township, Dauphin County, PA.

4.5.9.1.3.1 RONALD L. GUTSHALL was born on 11 October 1938. He married GLORIA JOHNSTON.

4.5.9.1.3.1.1 DON GUTSHALL was born on 23 May 1960. He married LORI (--?--). He married BARBARA SANTOS BLOOM on 8 August 2009.

4.5.9.1.3.1.1.1 JENNIFER GUTSHALL was born on 25 August 1986.

4.5.9.1.3.1.2 JEFFREY GUTSHALL was born on 24 May 1963.

4.5.9.1.3.1.3 BRIAN GUTSHALL was born on 2 August 1964.

4.5.9.1.3.1.3.1 BRIAN GUTSHALL was born on 17 April 1987.

4.5.9.1.3.1.3.2 JEREMY GUTSHALL was born on 24 February 1989.

4.5.9.1.3.2 DEAN GUTSHALL was born on 17 May 1947. He married ANNA LOUISE SCHAFFNER, daughter of RAY SCHAFFNER and BERNICE HAND.

4.5.9.1.3.2.1 TROY GUTSHALL

4.5.9.1.3.2.1.1 EMILY RAE GUTSHALL

4.5.9.1.3.2.2 CHAD GUTSHALL

4.5.9.1.3.2.3 COLBY GUTSHALL

4.5.9.1.4 EDNA I. SCHWALM was born on 18 January 1920, Spring Glen, Schuylkill County, PA. She married WILLIAM T. SCHRAWDER, son of ELMER SCHRAWDER and OLEDA SCHEIB, on 24 December 1948, St. Andrew's Church, Valley View, Schuylkill County, PA. She died on 16 September 2007, Holy Spirit Hospital, Camp Hill, Cumberland County, PA, at age 87. According to a newspaper obituary, Edna lived in Spring Glen, Schuylkill County, PA. She was a retired seamstress, but also worked on the family farm. She served as a pianist for the St. Mark's Sunday school. She was buried on 20 September 2007, at St. Mark's United Methodist Cemetery, Spring Glen, Schuylkill County, PA.

4.5.9.2 BEULAH ESTE SCHWALM was born on 6 August 1888, Fearnot, Schuylkill County, PA. She married WILLIAM ISAAC KLINGER, son of WILLIAM S. KLINGER and SUSANNAH SCHADEL, on 16 November 1907, Hegins, Schuylkill County, PA. At the time of her death, Beulah was living in Hegins, Schuylkill County, PA. She died on 6 November 1966, at age 78. She was buried at Spring Glen, Schuylkill County, PA.

4.5.9.2.1 KATHRYN SUSANNAH KLINGER was born on 21 August 1917, Spring Glen, Hubley Township, Schuylkill County, PA. She married CARL W. LUBOLD, son of CLINTON LUBOLD and MARY (--?--), on 24 June 1939, St. Andrew's Church, Valley View, Schuylkill County, PA. She lived in Annville, Lebanon County, PA. She died on 12 November 2001, Kindred Place, Annville, Lebanon County, PA, at age 84. She was buried at St. Mark's United Methodist Church Cemetery, Spring Glen, Hubley Township, Schuylkill County, PA.

4.5.9.2.1.1 CARL WILLIAM LUBOLD JR. was born on 20 April 1940. He married NATALIE SOMMERS.

4.5.9.2.1.1.1 WILLIAM KLINGER LUBOLD was born after 1970.

4.5.9.2.2 WILLIAM HENRY KLINGER was born on 10 February 1919, Spring Glen, Schuylkill County, PA. He married MARY AMELIA KESSLER, daughter of MOSES LEON KESSLER and MINNIE EULALIA DEIBERT, on 24 August 1940, Zion (Klinger's) Church, Erdman, Lykens Township, Dauphin County, PA. William's wife Mary was the author of a Klinger family history published in 1989, "Klingers from the Odenwald, Hesse, Germany." He died on 21 February 1978, at age 59. He was buried on 25 February 1978, at Zion (Klinger's) Church, Erdman, Lykens Township, Dauphin County, PA.

4.5.9.2.2.1 MARY ANN KLINGER was born on 19 May 1947. She married BARRY LYNN TSCHOPP, son of RUSSELL TSCHOPP and ANNA MOWERY, on 28 November 1965, Zion (Klinger's) Church, Erdman, Lykens Township, Dauphin County, PA. Mary lives in York County, PA.

4.5.9.2.2.1.1 ANN MARIE TSCHOPP was born on 28 May 1966, Harrisburg, Dauphin County, PA.

4.5.9.2.2.1.2 BARRY LYNN TSCHOPP JR. was born on 30 September 1969, Sunbury, Northumberland County, PA.

4.5.9.3 MASON R. SCHWALM was born on 10 August 1891, Fearnot, Schuylkill County, PA. He died on 17 November 1962, Fearnot, Schuylkill County, PA, at age 71.

4.5.9.4 TESSIE M. SCHWALM was born on 2 March 1894. She married CLINTON ARTHUR KOPPENHAVER, son of CALVIN OSCAR KOPPENHAVER and SARAH L. HEBERLING, on 30 November 1912, St. Andrew's Church, Valley View, Schuylkill County, PA. She died on 13 August 1968, at age 74.

4.5.9.4.1 IVAN P. KOPPENHAVER was born on 23 April 1913. He married THELMA E. MORGAN. He died in July 1967, at age 54. He was buried at Saint Mark's United Brethren Cemetery, Spring Glen, Schuylkill County, PA.

4.5.9.4.1.1 BARBARA J. KOPPENHAVER was born circa 1937, Valley View, Schuylkill County, PA. She married DONALD H. KISSINGER, son of HAROLD EARL KISSINGER and ERSAL AGNES ROSE, Valley View, Schuylkill County, PA.

4.5.9.4.1.1.1 RICKY KISSINGER was born on 29 May 1957, Spring Glen, Schuylkill County, PA. He married TERRI UPDEGROVE Muir, PA. He married DAWN (--?--).

4.5.9.4.1.1.1.1 JOEL RICHARD KISSINGER was born on 13 December 1983. He died on 20 May 2014, Texas at age 30.

4.5.9.4.1.1.2 LORI KISSINGER was born on 19 February 1963, Sacramento, Schuylkill County, PA.

4.5.9.4.1.1.3 CRAIG KISSINGER was born on 23 January 1967, Sacramento, Schuylkill County, PA.

4.5.9.4.1.2 LENWOOD KOPPENHAVER was born circa 1942. He married LINDA SCHADE.

4.5.9.4.1.2.1 TIMOTHY KOPPENHAVER

4.5.9.4.2 ELWOOD J. KOPPENHAVER was born on 11 December 1914. He married ROMIE ONEIDA KIMMEL, daughter of GEORGE KIMMEL and EMMA (--?--). He died on 25 December 1991, Polyclinic Medical Center, Harrisburg, Dauphin County, PA, at age 77. He was buried at St. Mark's Cemetery, Spring Glen, Hubley Township, Schuylkill County, PA. According to a newspaper obituary, Elwood was retired from Valley View Enterprises in Valley View, and lived in Spring Glen, Schuylkill County, PA.

4.5.9.4.2.1 RITA KOPPENHAVER

4.5.9.4.2.2 KEVIN KOPPENHAVER

4.5.9.4.2.3 NANCY K. KOPPENHAVER was born on 4 July 1939. She married LEON MARK SCHADLE, son of RAY WOODROW WILSON SHADLE and EVA MAY KLINGER, on 8 October 1955.

4.5.9.4.2.3.1 YVONNE LEE SHADLE was born on 27 January 1958, Schuylkill County, PA. She was baptized on 5 April 1959, Zion (Klinger's) Lutheran Church, Erdman, Dauphin County, PA. She married **LESTER ADAMS** circa 1975.

> **4.5.9.4.2.3.1.1 JASON ADAMS** was born on 11 October 1977. He married **HOLLI** (--?--).
>
> **4.5.9.4.2.3.1.2 BRETT ADAMS** was born on 12 May 1980.

4.5.9.4.2.3.2 LORI SHADLE was born on 2 February 1960, Schuylkill County, PA. She married **DENNIS BOYD** circa 1982.

> **4.5.9.4.2.3.2.1 JESSICA BOYD**
>
> **4.5.9.4.2.3.2.2 BRIAN BOYD**

4.5.9.4.2.3.3 L. MARK SHADLE was born on 27 December 1968, Schuylkill County, PA. He married **PENNI** (--?--).

> **4.5.9.4.2.3.3.1 ALYSSA SHADLE**
>
> **4.5.9.4.2.3.3.2 MEGAN SHADLE** is also referred to as **MEGAN SCHADLE** in some sources.

4.5.9.4.3 HENRY C. KOPPENHAVER was born on 1 May 1928, Spring Glen, Schuylkill County, PA. He married **DELORES PALMER**. He married **KAREN D. COMFORT** on 19 November 1974. He died on 5 July 1999, Evangelical Community Hospital, Lewisburg, PA, at age 71. He was buried at United Lutheran Church Cemetery, Sunbury, Northumberland County, PA.

> **4.5.9.4.3.1 ROXANN KOPPENHAVER** married **BILL ZERBE**.
>
> > **4.5.9.4.3.1.1 COREY ZERBE**
>
> **4.5.9.4.3.2 KEVIN KOPPENHAVER** married **CHRISTINE** (--?--).
>
> > **4.5.9.4.3.2.1 DEREK KOPPENHAVER**
> >
> > **4.5.9.4.3.2.2 TIANA KOPPENHAVER**

4.5.9.5 HATTIE PRUELLA SCHWALM was born on 6 November 1895. Some sources record that she was born on 6 November 1896, Hegins Township, Schuylkill County, PA. She married **WILLIAM H. MAUSER**, son of **WILLIAM MAUSER** and **ELLEN** (--?--), on 2 May 1925, Valley View, Schuylkill County, PA. She died on 17 July 1961, North Manheim Township, Schuylkill County, PA, at age 65. She was buried on 20 July 1961, at Saint Peters United Methodist Church Cemetery, Fearnot, Schuylkill County, PA.

4.5.10 MONROE ELLSWORTH PETER SCHWALM was born on 17 April 1864, Dauphin County, PA. Some sources record that he was born on 17 April 1864, Hubley Township, Schuylkill County, PA. Some sources record that he was born in April 1865. He married **ELIZABETH LAVINIA ALICE CARL**, daughter of **DANIEL CARL** and **CATHERINE SCHAFFER**, circa 1894. He died on 16 September 1937, Dauphin County, PA, at age 73. He was buried on 21 September 1937, at St. Peter's United Methodist Church Cemetery, Fearnot, Hubley Township, Schuylkill County, PA.

> **4.5.10.1 SADIE MABEL SCHWALM** was born in January 1895. She married **HARRY EDWIN SCHADE**, son of **VICTORIA SHADE**. She died in September 1977, at age 82. She was buried at Saint Peters United Methodist Church Cemetery, Fearnot, Schuylkill County, PA.
>
> > **4.5.10.1.1 INFANT SCHADE** was born circa 1914. She died on 5 October 1914. She was buried at Saint Peters United Methodist Church Cemetery, Fearnot, Schuylkill County, PA.
> >
> > **4.5.10.1.2 MAE A. SCHADE** was born on 9 January 1916. She married **LEO BIXLER**. She married (--?--) **LAHR**. She died on 30 January 1996, Gratz Park Terrace, Gratz, Dauphin County, PA, at age 80. She was buried at St. Peter's United Methodist Church Cemetery, Fearnot, Schuylkill County, PA.
> >
> > > **4.5.10.1.2.1 MERRILL L. BIXLER** married **BARBARA SALADA**.
> > >
> > > > **4.5.10.1.2.1.1 APRIL BIXLER**
> >
> > **4.5.10.1.3 LEROY J. SCHADE** was born on 4 April 1918, Fearnot, Schuylkill County, PA. He married **DOROTHY LEONA BRENNEMAN**. He died on 27 November 1987, at age 69. He was buried at Reisterstown Community Cemetery, Reisterstown, Baltimore County, MD.
> >
> > > **4.5.10.1.3.1 PHYLLIS SCHADE**
> > >
> > > **4.5.10.1.3.2 DAVID SCHADE** married **PAMELA ROBINSON**.

4.5.10.1.3.3 DONALD SCHADE

4.5.10.1.3.4 BETTY SCHADE married **RONALD DUTTERER**.

4.5.10.1.3.4.1 RONALD DUTTERER

4.5.10.1.3.4.2 MICHELLE DUTTERER

4.5.10.1.3.4.3 THERESA DUTTERER

4.5.10.1.4 WARREN MONROE SCHADE was born on 26 February 1922. He married **DOROTHY L. BOWMAN**, daughter of **GEORGE A. BOWMAN** and **KATIE WESNER**. He died on 24 August 1982, at age 60. He was buried at Woodlawn Memorial Gardens, Harrisburg, Dauphin County, PA.

4.5.10.1.4.1 MARY ELLEN SCHADE married **WILLIAM G. MARTZ SR.**

4.5.10.1.4.1.1 MELISSA ANN MARTZ married **MATTHEW CRAIG BOOKS** on 28 October 1989, Trinity Evangelical Church, Middletown, PA.

4.5.10.1.4.1.2 WILLIAM G. MARTZ JR.

4.5.10.1.4.2 NANCY SCHADE married **GARY DEIMLER**.

4.5.10.1.4.2.1 CRAIG DEIMLER

4.5.10.1.4.2.2 LORI DEIMLER

4.5.10.1.4.3 LEAH SCHADE married **EDWARD W. ZOHN**. She married **WILLIAM BIBB**.

4.5.10.1.5 INFANT SCHADE was born on 29 September 1925. He/she died on 29 September 1925. He/she was buried at Saint Peters United Methodist Church Cemetery, Fearnot, Schuylkill County, PA.

4.5.10.1.6 BETTY JOAN SCHADE was born on 8 April 1932, Schuylkill County, PA. She was baptized on 16 October 1932, St. Andrew's United Methodist Church, Valley View, Schuylkill County, PA. She married **ALFRED WOLFGANG**, son of **WILLIAM EARL WOLFGANG** and **VERNA L. SLOTTERBUCK**, on 4 April 1953, St. Andrew's United Methodist Church, Valley View, Schuylkill County, PA. She died on 7 March 1970, at age 37. She was buried at St. Peter's (Schwalm's) United Methodist Church Cemetery, Fearnot, Schuylkill County, PA.

4.5.10.1.6.1 DEBORAH K. WOLFGANG was born on 4 April 1953. She was baptized on 5 May 1955, Evangelical Congregational Church, Berrysburg, Dauphin County, PA. She married **ROGER JOHNS** on 19 May 1972, Evangelical Congregational Church, Berrysburg, Dauphin County, PA.

4.5.10.1.6.1.1 KEVIN JOHNS was born on 22 October 1973.

4.5.10.1.6.1.2 STACY JOHNS was born on 29 August 1977.

4.5.10.1.6.2 RANDY WOLFGANG was born on 20 August 1958, Dauphin County, PA. He married **DIANE MARIE SCHMELTZ**, daughter of **LESTER SCHMELTZ** and **RUTH GERTIE KISSINGER**, circa 1978.

4.5.10.1.6.2.1 ADAM L. WOLFGANG (see above)

4.5.10.1.6.2.2 REBEKAH SUE WOLFGANG (see above)

4.5.10.1.7 LUKE HARRY SCHADE was born on 25 February 1940, Fearnot, Schuylkill County, PA. He was baptized on 19 March 1940, St. Andrew's United Methodist Church, Valley View, Schuylkill County, PA. He married **SHIRLEY MAURER**. He died on 30 March 2012, ManorCare, Camp Hill, Cumberland County, PA, at age 72. According to a newspaper obituary, Luke lived in Harrisburg and retired from the United Parcel Service.

4.5.10.1.7.1 DEBORAH J. SCHADE married **JEFF STINE**. Deborah lives in Martinsburg, WV.

4.5.10.1.7.1.1 MATTHEW STINE

4.5.10.1.7.2 CATHY SCHADE married **BUTCH KING**. Cathy lives in Etters, PA.

4.5.10.1.7.2.1 MICHAEL KING married **RONI** (--?--).

4.5.10.1.7.2.1.1 DYLAN KING

4.5.10.1.7.3 JAMES A. SCHADE married **ROBIN** (--?--). James lives in Mechanicsburg, PA.

4.5.10.1.7.4 DAVID L. SCHADE married **JEN** (--?--). David lives in New Cumberland, PA.

4.5.10.2 EDNA KATIE SCHWALM was born on 16 November 1897, Fearnot, Schuylkill County, PA. She died on 15 August 1899, Fearnot, Schuylkill County, PA, at age 1. She was buried at Saint Peter's United Methodist Church Cemetery, Fearnot, Dauphin County, PA.

4.5.10.3 HARRY RAY SCHWALM is also referred to as **HENRY RAY SCHWALM** in some sources. He was born on 26 September 1899, Hubley Township, Schuylkill County, PA. He married **EMMA E. STRAUB** circa 1918. He died on 19 July 1964, Butler Township, Schuylkill County, PA, at age 64. He was buried on 22 July 1964, at Saint Peter's United Methodist Church Cemetery, Fearnot, Schuylkill County, PA.

4.5.10.3.1 MARY SCHWALM

4.5.10.3.2 MABEL E. SCHWALM was born on 31 March 1918. She married **GEORGE LEBO.** Prior to her death, Mabel lived in the vicinity of Parlin, Middlesex County, NJ. She died on 5 July 1989, at age 71.

4.5.10.3.2.1 LAMAR LEBO married **MARYANN MOLLITER.**

4.5.10.3.2.1.1 FRANK LEBO

4.5.10.3.2.1.2 MICHELLE LEBO

4.5.10.3.2.1.3 JENNIFER LEBO

4.5.10.3.2.2 DORIS LEBO

4.5.10.3.3 PETER MONROE SCHWALM was born on 20 October 1926, Schuylkill County, PA. He married **HAZEL MARIE MOWER**, daughter of **PETER MOWER** and **MINNIE (--?--)**, on 30 October 1948, St. Andrew's Church, Valley View, Schuylkill County, PA. He died on 11 March 1989, Zephyr Hills, Pasco County, FL, at age 62. He was buried at St. Peter's (Schwalm's) Cemetery, Fearnot, Schuylkill County, PA.

4.5.10.3.3.1 ELLEN MARIE SCHWALM was born on 14 August 1949. She married **(--?--) LONG.**

4.5.10.3.3.2 LINDA LOU SCHWALM was born on 16 May 1951. She married **(--?--) NEUNER.**

4.5.10.4 ROY S. SCHWALM was born on 12 June 1904, Schuylkill County, PA. He married **EVA M. WARFIELD** on 12 August 1922, St. Andrew's Church, Valley View, Schuylkill County, PA. At the time of his death, Roy was separated from his wife. He died on 20 December 1955, Harrisburg Hospital, Harrisburg, Dauphin County, PA, at age 51. He was buried on 24 December 1955, at United Methodist Church Cemetery, Idaville, Adams County, PA.

4.5.10.4.1 RUSSELL LEE SCHWALM was born on 9 November 1922. He married **MARGARET MELLI.** He died on 4 May 1985, Veterans Administration Hospital, Lebanon, Lebanon County, PA, at age 62. He was buried at Indiantown Gap National Cemetery, Annville, Lebanon County, PA.

4.5.10.4.1.1 SANDRA M. SCHWALM married **JAMES SLEIGHTER.**

4.5.10.4.1.1.1 JAMES SLEIGHTER JR.

4.5.10.4.1.2 RUSSELL J. SCHWALM

4.5.10.4.1.3 WAYNE SCHWALM

4.5.10.4.2 LEON LAMAR SCHWALM was born on 20 September 1926. Some sources record that he was born on 20 September 1927. He married **PHYLLIS R. WEAVER**, daughter of **GEORGE WEAVER** and **MARY TEETER**. He died on 15 June 1980, Dauphin, Lower Paxton Township, Dauphin County, PA, at age 52. He was buried at Woodlawn Memorial Gardens, Harrisburg, Dauphin County, PA.

4.5.10.4.2.1 BRADLEY SCHWALM died before 5 June 2002.

4.5.10.4.2.2 STEPHEN L. SCHWALM married **JOAN HAEDERER.**

4.5.10.4.2.2.1 MARTHA ANN SCHWALM

4.5.10.4.2.2.2 MICHAEL A. SCHWALM

4.5.10.4.2.2.3 CHAD R. SCHWALM was born on 5 June 1977, Harrisburg, Dauphin County, PA. He died on 3 January 2007, as a result of an auto accident at age 29. According to a newspaper obituary, Chad lived in Dauphin, PA, and worked for Excel in Hamden Township, Dauphin County. He was buried at Woodland Memorial Gardens, Lower Paxton Township, Dauphin County, PA.

4.5.10.4.2.3 ELIZABETH M. SCHWALM married **(--?--) WILSON.**

4.5.10.4.2.4 ROBERT SCHWALM

4.5.10.5 ALLEN M. SCHWALM was born on 23 June 1910. He married RUTH ALVERETA SNYDER, daughter of JOHN SNYDER and CARRIE KLINE, on 30 January 1932, St. Andrew's Church, Valley View, Schuylkill County, PA. Prior to his death, Allen lived in the vicinity of Valley View, Schuylkill County, PA. He died in September 1974, at age 64. He was buried at Saint Peter's United Methodist Church Cemetery, Fearnot, Schuylkill County, PA.

4.5.10.5.1 ERNEST L. SCHWALM married JOAN L. HEPNER on 2 July 1955, St. Andrew's Church, Valley View, Schuylkill County, PA.

4.5.10.5.2 (--?--) SCHWALM died circa 1915, in infancy.

4.5.10.5.3 ROGER LEE SCHWALM was born on 23 April 1943. He married MARGARET DORMAN.

4.5.10.5.3.1 KENNETH SCHWALM

4.5.10.5.3.2 JAMES ANDREW SCHWALM was born on 5 March 1979.

4.5.10.6 INFANT SCHWALM was born on 10 November 1915, Fearnot, Schuylkill County, PA. He/she died on 10 November 1915, Fearnot, Schuylkill County, PA.

4.5.11 MARY E. SCHWALM is also referred to as POLLY in some sources. She was born on 28 February 1866, Schuylkill County, PA. She died on 11 November 1880, Schuylkill County, PA, at age 14. She was buried at Saint Peters United Methodist Church Cemetery, Fearnot, Schuylkill County, PA.

4.5.12 ELLEN BARBARA JUSTINA SCHWALM was born on 28 January 1870, Fearnot, Schuylkill County, PA. She married CHARLES M. MILLER, son of JOHN MILLER, circa 1891. She married VICTOR BLYLER circa 1905. She died on 8 May 1958, South Heidelberg Township, Berks County, PA, at age 88. She was buried at Saint Peters United Methodist Church Cemetery, Fearnot, Schuylkill County, PA.

4.5.12.1 FRED WILLIAM MILLER was born on 28 March 1891, Spring Glen, Schuylkill County, PA. He married MINNIE KIMMEL. He died on 7 October 1948, Pottsville, Schuylkill County, PA, at age 57. He was buried at St. Mark's United Methodist Church, Spring Glen, Schuylkill County, PA.

4.5.12.1.1 LEROY C. MILLER married ROSE MCGREADY.

4.5.12.1.1.1 CHARLES R. MILLER married CAROL MADY.

4.5.12.1.1.1.1 JEFFREY MILLER

4.5.12.1.1.1.2 MICHAEL MILLER

4.5.12.1.1.1.3 CYNTHIA MILLER

4.5.12.1.1.2 JUDITH MILLER married DEL HERBERT.

4.5.12.1.1.2.1 DOUGLAS S. HERBERT

4.5.12.2 JAMES E. MILLER was born on 11 February 1894, Fearnot, Schuylkill County, PA. He married ELVA M. HARNER, daughter of REILLY ELLSWORTH HARNER and FRANCES SALOMA ELIZABETH SCHWALM. He died on 20 March 1986, Austin, TX, at age 92, at the home of his son, Ned. He was buried at Saint Andrews United Methodist Church Cemetery, Valley View, Schuylkill County, PA.

4.5.12.2.1 JAMES E. MILLER JR. was born in 1918.

4.5.12.2.2 MARY ELVA MILLER was born in 1919. She married LANSTON MENTZER, son of HARRY M. MENTZER and CARRIE W. MYERS.

4.5.12.2.3 NED E. MILLER was born on 10 April 1923. He married MILDRED HENRY. He died on 2 June 1999, at age 76.

4.5.12.2.3.1 DIANE L. MILLER married JOEL REED.

4.5.12.2.3.2 JUDITH L. MILLER married RANDY TROJAN.

4.5.12.2.3.3 NANCY K. MILLER married GUION HOBBS.

4.5.12.2.3.3.1 RYAN HOBBS

4.5.12.3 CURTIN RAY MILLER is also referred to as J. CURTIS AND CURTIS R. MILLER in some sources. He was born on 24 August 1895, Fearnot, Schuylkill County, PA. He married BERTHA UNGER. He died in 1974. He was buried at St. Mark's United Methodist Church, Spring Glen, Schuylkill County, PA.

4.5.12.3.1 CHARLES VICTOR MILLER was born on 28 November 1915, Gratz, Dauphin County, PA. He married HELEN MAE HOFFMAN, daughter of CLAYTON HOFFMAN and ESTELLA

ERDMAN. He died on 6 May 1991, Good Samaritan Hospital, Lebanon, Lebanon County, PA, at age 75. He was buried at Gravel Hill Cemetery, Lebanon County, PA.

> **4.5.12.3.1.1 SANDRA MILLER** married **ROBERT VAN AKEN**. She married **(--?--) RAUCHUT**.
>
>> **4.5.12.3.1.1.1 SHAWN M. RAUCHUT** married **LESLIE (--?--)**. He is also referred to as **SHAWN VAN AKEN** in some sources.
>>
>> **4.5.12.3.1.1.2 DOUGLAS C. RAUCHUT** married **JEAN (--?--)**.
>>
>> **4.5.12.3.1.1.3 GLENN A. RAUCHUT** married **CORRINE (--?--)**.
>
> **4.5.12.3.1.2 MARGARET MILLER** married **RONALD SPANGLER**. She also went by the name of **PEGGY**. She died before December 2006.
>
>> **4.5.12.3.1.2.1 MISHON SPANGLER** married **DOUGLAS EBERLY**.

4.5.12.3.2 LAURETTA E. MILLER was born circa 1919, Pennsylvania. She married **ANDREW OLINICK**.

> **4.5.12.3.2.1 MICHAEL OLINICK**
>
> **4.5.12.3.2.2 STEPHEN OLINICK**
>
> **4.5.12.3.2.3 PAUL OLINICK**
>
> **4.5.12.3.2.4 PATRICIA OLINICK**
>
>> **4.5.12.3.2.4.1 CASSANDRA OLINICK**
>>
>> **4.5.12.3.2.4.2 ARIANA OLINICK**

4.5.12.3.3 BETTY E. MILLER was born circa 1920. She married **PAUL GRUMBINE**. She married **JOHN KOPECKY**.

> **4.5.12.3.3.1 PAUL GRUMBINE**
>
> **4.5.12.3.3.2 KAREN KOPECKY**

4.5.12.4 ESTHER MILLER is also referred to as **ESTA J.** in some sources. She was born on 17 August 1897, Schuylkill County, PA. She married **DEWEY S. ARTZ**. She died on 30 December 1960, Hamburg, Berks County, PA, at age 63. She was buried on 3 January 1961, at Salem-Berne Methodist Church Cemetery, Tilden Township, Berks County, PA.

> **4.5.12.4.1 ANNA MAE ARTZ** was born on 20 May 1919, Spring Glen, Schuylkill County, PA. She died on 7 April 2005, Manor Care Health Services, Inc., West Reading, Berks County, PA, at age 85. She was buried at Salem-Berne Methodist Church Cemetery, Tilden Township, Berks County, PA.

4.5.12.5 BEULAH IRENE BLYLER was born on 4 November 1906, Hubley Township, Schuylkill County, PA. She married **WILLIAM F. DUNLEAVY**. She died in January 1972, Berks County, PA, at age 65. She was buried at Saint Peter's United Methodist Church Cemetery, Fearnot, Schuylkill County, PA.

> **4.5.12.5.1 CARL F. DUNLEAVY**
>
> **4.5.12.5.2 DANIEL W. DUNLEAVY** married **ROBERTA POTTEIGER**.
>
> **4.5.12.5.3 BARBARA DUNLEAVY** was born circa 1935. She married **JOHN F. KLEIN**.
>
>> **4.5.12.5.3.1 JACQUELINE KLEIN**
>>
>> **4.5.12.5.3.2 MICHAEL KLEIN**
>
> **4.5.12.5.4 ROSE ANN DUNLEAVY** was born circa 1937. She married **WILLIAM C. ENGLE**.
>
>> **4.5.12.5.4.1 DUANE ENGLE**
>>
>> **4.5.12.5.4.2 PAMELA ENGLE**
>>
>> **4.5.12.5.4.3 BRIAN ENGLE**

4.5.13 TORRIE SCHWALM was born on 1 April 1873. She died on 17 April 1873. She was buried at St. Paul (Artz's) Lutheran and Reformed Church, Sacramento, Schuylkill County, PA.

4.6 ELIZABETH KLINGER was born on 14 July 1831, Spring Glen, Schuylkill County, PA. She married **SAMUEL SCHWALM**, son of **FREDERICK SCHWALM** and **CATHARINA STEIN**, circa 1850. She died on 11 December 1921, at age 90. She was buried at St. Andrew's Church Cemetery, Valley View, Schuylkill County, PA.

4.6.1 AGATHA V. SCHWALM is also referred to as AGATHA BARBARA in some sources. She was born on 15 February 1851, Hegins Township, Schuylkill County, PA. She was baptized on 6 March 1851, St. Paul's (Artz's) Lutheran and Reformed Church, Sacramento, Schuylkill County, PA. She married PAUL WOLFGANG circa 1873. She died on 24 November 1929, Valley View, Schuylkill County, PA, at age 78. She was buried on 28 November 1929, at St. Andrew's United Methodist Church, Valley View, Schuylkill County, PA.

4.6.1.1 TORY ISABELLE WOLFGANG is also referred to as BELLA WOLFGANG in some sources. She was born in 1874. She married WILLIAM H. TROUTMAN. She died in 1950. She was buried at St. Andrew's United Methodist Church, Valley View, Hegins Township, Schuylkill County, PA.

4.6.1.1.1 RAY A. TROUTMAN was born on 2 February 1896, Valley View, Hegins Township, Schuylkill County, PA. He married FLORENCE D. HERB, daughter of ELVIN K. HERB and MINNIE KLOUSER. Ray served in World War I as a member of the 7th Field Artillery. He was awarded a silver star for his conduct during the Aisne-Marne offensive of July 18 to July 25, in France. Ray was a school teacher in Hegins Township. There is a short biography of Ray in the 1988 Journal of the Johannes Schwalm Historical Association, vol. 3, no. 4, p. 73. He lived in Valley View, Schuylkill County, PA. He died on 30 March 1984, Valley View, Hegins Township, Schuylkill County, PA, at age 88. He was buried on 3 April 1984, at Church of God Cemetery, Valley View, Hegins Township, Schuylkill County, PA.

4.6.1.1.1.1 HELEN TROUTMAN married GUY SCHLEGEL. She married JACK RICKELS.

4.6.1.1.1.2 FERNE ISABEL TROUTMAN married LOUIS MAHAR.

4.6.1.1.1.2.1 JERROLD MAHAR married BETH SWAVELY. He is also referred to as GERALD MOHAR in some sources.

4.6.1.1.1.2.2 STEPHEN MAHAR is also referred to as STEVEN MOHAR in some sources.

4.6.1.1.1.2.3 MICHAEL MAHAR is also referred to as MICHAEL MOHAR in some sources.

4.6.1.1.1.2.4 EDWARD MAHAR is also referred to as EDWARD MOHAR in some sources.

4.6.1.1.1.3 WILLIAM H. TROUTMAN married ELLEN WOLFE.

4.6.1.1.1.3.1 CAROL ANN TROUTMAN married MATTHEW RENNER.

4.6.1.1.1.3.1.1 KATHY RENNER

4.6.1.1.1.3.2 ROBERT A. TROUTMAN married KAREN SIGMUNDSEN.

4.6.1.1.1.3.2.1 KATHY TROUTMAN

4.6.1.1.1.3.3 JOHN TROUTMAN

4.6.1.1.1.3.4 RAY A. TROUTMAN

4.6.1.1.1.4 JAMES TROUTMAN married ELAINE BUETER.

4.6.1.1.1.4.1 WILLIAM HOWARD TROUTMAN

4.6.1.1.1.5 GENE TROUTMAN married BEVERLY HARTMAN.

4.6.1.1.1.5.1 MICHELLE TROUTMAN

4.6.1.1.1.5.2 CRAIG TROUTMAN

4.6.1.1.1.5.3 SCOTT TROUTMAN

4.6.1.1.1.5.4 TANYA TROUTMAN

4.6.1.1.1.5.5 JASON TROUTMAN

4.6.1.1.1.6 GLENN TROUTMAN married MARY FOLEY.

4.6.1.1.1.6.1 KEVIN TROUTMAN

4.6.1.1.1.6.2 MARK TROUTMAN

4.6.1.1.2 GERTRUDE MABEL TROUTMAN was born on 28 August 1897. She was baptized on 10 January 1898, St. Andrew's United Methodist Church, Valley View, Hegins Township, Schuylkill County, PA. She married GURNEY ALLEN KLINGER, son of ALFRED KLINGER and HANNA MATTERN, on 25 June 1921, St. Andrew's Church, Valley View, Schuylkill County, PA. She died in 1969. She was buried at St. Andrew's Church Cemetery, Valley View, Schuylkill County, PA.

4.6.1.1.2.1 ARTHUR ALLEN KLINGER was born on 21 January 1923, Tremont, Schuylkill County, PA. He married ALMA BRYANT circa 1945. He married VIOLET M. KLINGER, daughter of **Eston Raymond Klinger** and **Carrie Edna Henninger,** on 6 March 1955, Berrysburg, Dauphin County, PA. He died on 28 October 2003, Holy Spirit Hospital, East Pennsboro Township, Dauphin County, PA, at age 80. He was buried at Peace United Church of Christ Cemetery, Berrysburg, Dauphin County, PA.

4.6.1.1.2.1.1 Kenneth Allen Klinger was born on 5 October 1946.

4.6.1.1.2.2 Kenneth Kermit Klinger was born on 3 December 1924, Tremont, Schuylkill County, PA. He married **Betty E. Stiely**, daughter of **Fred Stiely** and **Verna E. Harner,** on 19 August 1951, St. Andrew's Church, Valley View, Schuylkill County, PA. Kenneth served in the US Army during the Korean War. He died on 23 March 1991, 1100 East Grand Ave., Tower City, Schuylkill County, PA, at age 66. He was buried at Fort Indiantown Gap National Cemetery, Annville, Lebanon County, PA.

4.6.1.1.2.2.1 Keith Kermit Klinger was born on 21 July 1952, Lykens, Dauphin County, PA. He was baptized on 7 September 1952, St. Andrew's Church, Valley View, Schuylkill County, PA. He married **Helen Michaels** on 31 July 1971, Schuylkill County, PA. He and **Helen Michaels** were divorced. He died on 27 October 2013, Tower City, Schuylkill County, PA, at age 61. He was buried on 31 October 2013, at Saint Andrews United Methodist Church Cemetery, Valley View, Schuylkill County, PA.

4.6.1.1.2.2.1.1 Tanya L. Klinger married **Ryan Sims.**

4.6.1.1.2.2.1.1.1 Sydney Sims

4.6.1.1.2.2.1.1.2 Erica Sims

4.6.1.1.2.2.1.2 Eric Klinger was born on 13 September 1978, Lebanon, Lebanon County, PA. He died on 13 September 1978, Lebanon, Lebanon County, PA.

4.6.1.1.2.2.2 Karl Kenneth Klinger was born on 21 July 1952, Lykens, Dauphin County, PA. He was baptized on 7 September 1954, St. Andrew's Church, Valley View, Schuylkill County, PA. He married **Yvonne M. (--?--).** He died on 16 September 2014, Schuylkill Medical Center-East, Pottsville, Schuylkill County, PA, at age 62. He was buried on 20 September 2014, at Saint Andrews United Methodist Church Cemetery, Valley View, Schuylkill County, PA.

4.6.1.1.2.2.2.1 Kussandra Klinger

4.6.1.1.2.2.2.2 Janelle Klinger married **Sean Limric.**

4.6.1.1.2.2.3 Roger Klinger was born circa 1956.

4.6.1.1.2.3 Ralph W. Klinger was born on 16 January 1927, Tremont, Schuylkill County, PA. He married **Ethel Mae Kopp**, daughter of **Frank Kopp** and **Helen Snyder,** circa 1952. He died on 1 March 2013, Dauphin County, PA, at age 86. He was buried on 7 March 2013, at Woodlawn Memorial Gardens, Harrisburg, Dauphin County, PA.

4.6.1.1.2.3.1 Thomas R. Klinger was born on 27 December 1953, Lykens, Dauphin County, PA. He married **Margaret M. Smith** circa 1975. He died on 21 February 2013, Dauphin County, PA, at age 59. He was buried on 27 February 2013, at Blue Ridge Memorial Gardens, Harrisburg, Dauphin County, PA.

4.6.1.1.2.3.1.1 Andrew T. Klinger was born circa 1976. He married **Brenna J. (--?--).**

4.6.1.1.2.3.1.1.1 Kaelynn Klinger

4.6.1.1.2.3.1.2 Sarah E. Klinger was born circa 1978. She married **Nelson R. Llewellen.**

4.6.1.1.2.3.2 Wendy Lee Klinger was born on 20 December 1955, Lykens, Dauphin County, PA. She married **Ralph Jones** circa 1977. She died on 11 April 2001, at age 45. She was buried at Pine Grove Cemetery, Corry, Erie County, PA.

4.6.1.1.2.3.2.1 Justin Jones was born circa 1978.

4.6.1.1.2.4 Ruth Klinger was born on 12 March 1935. She married **Alfred Kuehn**, son of **Walter Kuehn** and **Hedwig Dick.** The Journal of the Johannes Schwalm Historical Association, vol. 1., no. 1, p. 11, contains an unclear listing for the children of Ruth and Alfred. In the original edition of the book, two children were listed for Ruth and Alfred -- Karen and Sharon, along with several children who were adopted -- Paul, Elaine, Joan, and "child." The listing makes it appear as though these adopted children were children of Karen, although that point was not entirely clear. In the later Journal listing, the adopted children, apparently as children of Ruth and Alfred, are listed under the names Paul, Elayne, Janet, and Beverly, and after the listing for "Cheryl," as a child of both Ruth and Alfred, the listing contains a parenthetical notation: "(not Karen, Sharon)." Apparently, this suggests that Karen and Sharon were to be omitted altogether from the listings for Ruth and Alfred's children, although that is unclear. There is also a listing for a child named "Christopher," but it is unclear whether that listing was intended as a listing for Ruth and Alfred or for Ruth's cousin Kenneth Troutman. She died on 22 April 1985, Wayne, NJ, at age 50.

4.6.1.1.2.4.1 KAREN KUEHN. According to some sources, Karen is listed as a child of Ruth Klinger, but this is probably incorrect.

4.6.1.1.2.4.1.1 PAUL (--?--)

4.6.1.1.2.4.1.2 ELAINE (--?--)

4.6.1.1.2.4.1.3 JOAN (--?--)

4.6.1.1.2.4.2 SHARON KUEHN. According to some sources, Sharon is listed as a child of Ruth Klinger, but this is probably incorrect.

4.6.1.1.2.4.3 PAUL KUEHN married **BECKY (--?--)**.

4.6.1.1.2.4.4 ELAYNE KUEHN married **RONALD ENGEBRETSEN**.

4.6.1.1.2.4.5 JANET KUEHN married **MICHAEL SCHUTZ**.

4.6.1.1.2.4.6 BEVERLY KUEHN married **JONATHAN ULFENG**.

4.6.1.1.2.4.7 CHERYL KUEHN married **OTTO SANCHEZ**.

4.6.1.1.3 EVA AMILIA TROUTMAN was born on 8 May 1899. She was baptized on 17 September 1899, St. Andrew's United Methodist Church, Valley View, Hegins Township, Schuylkill County, PA. She married **GEORGE ALVIN KOPPENHAVER**, son of **TORPETUS KOPPENHAVER** and **MARGUERITE ELIZABETH METZ**, on 31 March 1923, St. Andrew's United Methodist Church, Valley View, Hegins Township, Schuylkill County, PA. She died on 15 January 1980, at home, Valley View, Hegins Township, Schuylkill County, PA, at age 80.

4.6.1.1.3.1 CHESTER LEE KOPPENHAVER was born on 6 January 1928, Hegins, Schuylkill County, PA. He married **ALICE KESSLER**. He died on 6 May 1994, at home, R.D. # 1, Leesport, Berks County, PA, at age 66. He was buried at Church of God Cemetery, Valley View, Hegins Township, Schuylkill County, PA.

4.6.1.1.3.1.1 CLAIR KOPPENHAVER

4.6.1.1.3.1.2 LEE KOPPENHAVER

4.6.1.1.3.1.3 AMY KOPPENHAVER

4.6.1.1.4 EDNA ELIZABETH TROUTMAN was born on 26 June 1901. She was baptized on 29 December 1901, St. Andrew's United Methodist Church, Valley View, Hegins Township, Schuylkill County, PA. She married **EARL BUTZ**. She died on 18 August 1989, Lehigh Westminster Village Nursing Home, Allentown, Lehigh County, PA, at age 88. She was buried at Church of God Cemetery, Valley View, Hegins Township, Schuylkill County, PA.

4.6.1.1.4.1 ROBERT BUTZ married **PHYLLIS WHITE**. He married **CHARLETTE GOLDEN**.

4.6.1.1.4.1.1 DIANA BUTZ

4.6.1.1.4.1.2 TOMMY BUTZ

4.6.1.1.5 FLORENCE EMMA TROUTMAN was born on 16 August 1903. She was baptized on 27 December 1903, St. Andrew's United Methodist Church, Valley View, Hegins Township, Schuylkill County, PA. She died on 8 December 1914, at age 11. She was buried at St. Andrew's United Methodist Church, Valley View, Hegins Township, Schuylkill County, PA.

4.6.1.1.6 LAURA MAE TROUTMAN was born on 19 January 1906. She married **HARRY DEITRICK** on 12 October 1935. She died on 22 January 1985, at home, Hegins, Schuylkill County, PA, at age 79.

4.6.1.1.6.1 DAVID D. DEITRICK was born on 5 June 1941. He married **HILDA SCHEIB**. In 1998, David was living on Idlywood Drive, Winchester, VA. He died on 30 April 1998, University Hospital, San Antonio, TX, at age 56.

4.6.1.1.6.1.1 DONALD DEITRICK

4.6.1.1.6.1.2 HOLLY DEITRICK

4.6.1.1.6.1.3 KELLY DEITRICK

4.6.1.1.6.2 LORRAINE G. DEITRICK is also referred to as LORRAINE D. DIETRICH in some sources. She was born on 3 May 1946. She married THOMAS EDISON OLDHAM, son of WYLIE A. OLDHAM and DORIS E. BALL, on 16 July 1994, St. Andrew's United Methodist Church, Valley View, Schuylkill County, PA.

4.6.1.1.7 HOWARD W. TROUTMAN was born in 1910. He married IRENE M. DEITRICH, daughter of CHARLES S. DEITRICH and MARY ANN BROSIUS, in 1935. Howard and his wife Irene founded and operated Troutman's Greenhouse in Valley View, PA, until his death. He died in 1954. He was buried at Church of God Cemetery, Valley View, Schuylkill County, PA.

4.6.1.1.7.1 KENNETH C. TROUTMAN was born circa 1937. He married LINDA HOLMES.

4.6.1.1.7.1.1 CHRISTOPHER R. TROUTMAN

4.6.1.1.7.1.1.1 KYRA ANN TROUTMAN was born on 10 January 2005.

4.6.1.1.7.2 CARL L. TROUTMAN married MARLA J. BRUZIK.

4.6.1.1.8 ELVIN K. TROUTMAN was born on 29 July 1912, Valley View, Hegins Township, Schuylkill County, PA. He married MILDRED SAVIDGE, daughter of JONAS SAVIDGE and LOTTIE HOFFMAN. Elvin was a teacher. There is a short biography of Elvin in the 1988 Journal of the Johannes Schwalm Historical Association, vol. 3, no. 4, p. 76. He died on 1 January 1991, Good Samaritan Hospital, Pottsville, Schuylkill County, PA, at age 78. Prior to his death, Elvin was living at 309 East Mountain Road, Hegins, Schuylkill County, PA.

4.6.1.1.8.1 DOUGLAS TROUTMAN

4.6.1.1.9 BRUCE HERMAN TROUTMAN was born on 12 July 1914. He was baptized on 20 September 1914, St. Andrew's United Methodist Church, Valley View, Hegins Township, Schuylkill County, PA. He married ORPHA M. SNYDER, daughter of VICTOR C. SNYDER and EDNA F. ROMBERGER. He lived in Pitman, Schuylkill County, PA. He died on 19 July 1998, Good Samaritan Regional Medical Center, Pottsville, Schuylkill County, PA, at age 84. He was buried at Zion Evangelical Congregational Church, Pitman, Schuylkill County, PA.

4.6.1.1.9.1 PHYLLIS TROUTMAN married RODGER MERWINE. She is also referred to as PHYLISS in some sources. Phyliss lives in Pitman, PA.

4.6.1.1.9.1.1 KRIS W. MERWINE married WENDY RUNKLE, daughter of CHARLES L. RUNKLE and IRENE LONG.

4.6.1.1.9.1.1.1 ELSIE MARIE MERWINE was born on 18 May 1994.

4.6.1.1.9.1.2 KELLY M. MERWINE married MICHAEL A. SCHEIB, son of DONALD SCHEIB and KAREN (--?--), on 26 December 2003, St. Paul's E.C. Church, Pitman, Schuylkill County, PA.

4.6.1.1.9.2 RONALD V. TROUTMAN was born on 16 November 1937, Ashland Hospital, Ashland, Schuylkill County, PA. He married JOSEPHINE ESCANEZ on 24 October 1956. He died on 21 June 2013, Geisinger Medical Center, Danville, Montour County, PA, at age 75. According to a newspaper obituary, Ronald lived in Atlas, PA, where he worked as an auto mechanic and service manager. He was last employed at B & L in Shamokin, PA. He was buried on 25 June 2013, at All Saints Cemetery, Bear Gap, Northumberland County, PA.

4.6.1.1.9.2.1 DEBORA TROUTMAN. Debora lives in Atlas. PA.

4.6.1.1.9.2.2 JAMES TROUTMAN married TONI (--?--). Jim lives in Atlas, PA.

4.6.1.1.9.2.3 RODNEY TROUTMAN married DAWN (--?--). Rod lives in Mowry, PA.

4.6.1.2 AMELIA ELIZABETH WOLFGANG was born on 18 June 1876. She married JOHN GEORGE ROMBERGER JR., son of JOHN GEORGE ROMBERGER and HANNAH CLARK, circa 1896. She died on 29 October 1943, Valley View, Schuylkill County, PA, at age 67. She was buried at St. Andrew's United Methodist Church, Valley View, Hegins Township, Schuylkill County, PA.

4.6.1.2.1 PAUL FRANKLIN ROMBERGER was born on 25 January 1897. He was baptized on 13 June 1897, St. Andrew's United Methodist Church, Valley View, Hegins Township, Schuylkill County, PA. Some sources record that he was born on 23 January 1897. He married ALMA GERTRUDE SNYDER, daughter of EDGAR L. SNYDER and ALFRETTA (--?--). He married EMMA

STROHECKER. Prior to his death, Paul was living in the vicinity of Valley View, Schuylkill County, PA. He died on 1 October 1975, at age 78.

4.6.1.2.1.1 BERNICE ALVERTA ROMBERGER was born on 6 January 1926. She married **JOE MCCARTHY**. She married **HERBERT GROSS SR.**

4.6.1.2.1.1.1 PAUL FRANKLIN MCCARTHY was born on 30 January 1947.

4.6.1.2.1.1.2 HERBERT GROSS JR. was born on 25 September 1949.

4.6.1.2.2 EDWARD VERNON ROMBERGER is also referred to as **VERNON EDWARD ROMBERGER** in some sources. He was born on 17 July 1898. He was baptized on 23 February 1899, St. Andrew's United Methodist Church, Valley View, Hegins Township, Schuylkill County, PA. Some sources record that he was born on 17 July 1894. He married **ANNIE M. HENRY**, daughter of **JACOB HENRY** and **MIRAH (--?--)**. Prior to his death, "Vernon" was living in the vicinity of Valley View, Schuylkill County, PA. He died on 11 March 1980, at age 81. He was buried at Saint Andrews United Methodist Church Cemetery, Valley View, Schuylkill County, PA.

4.6.1.2.2.1 ERMA ELMIRA ROMBERGER was born on 11 December 1920. She married **WILLIAM ALLEN ROBERTS**. She married **JOSEPH GABLE**.

4.6.1.2.2.1.1 WILLIAM KENNETH ROBERTS was born on 21 January 1947. He died on 10 October 1970, at age 23.

4.6.1.2.2.1.2 EDWARD ALLEN ROBERTS was born on 31 May 1950.

4.6.1.2.2.2 ROBERT ROLAND ROMBERGER was born on 13 April 1923. He married **MARY DOROTHY MAYNARD**. He died on 4 January 1974, at age 50. He was buried at Grand Rapids, Kent County, MI.

4.6.1.2.2.2.1 CAROL ROMBERGER was born on 5 May 1944.

4.6.1.2.2.2.2 ROBERT EDWARD ROMBERGER was born on 13 November 1946.

4.6.1.2.2.3 BETTY JEAN ROMBERGER was born on 19 July 1925. She married **THEODORE WILLIAM MAURER**, son of **CLARK SNYDER MAURER** and **EMMA KATHRYN HECKERT**, on 5 August 1944.

4.6.1.2.2.3.1 TERRANCE WILLIAM MAURER was born on 12 November 1947. He married **BONNIE WIEST**, daughter of **RAY C. WIEST** and **DOROTHY F. ERDMAN**.

4.6.1.2.2.3.1.1 TODD MAURER was born on 11 February 1964. He married **LORI HENNING**, daughter of **LARRY HENNING** and **SUSAN WILLIER**.

4.6.1.2.2.3.1.1.1 LOREN MAURER

4.6.1.2.2.3.1.1.2 COLLIN RAY MAURER was born on 17 February 1996.

4.6.1.2.2.3.1.2 TROY MAURER was born on 6 December 1967. He married **KATHY KIEFER**, daughter of **LEE A. KIEFER** and **LINDA RUCH**.

4.6.1.2.2.3.1.2.1 SETH WILLIAM MAURER (see above)

4.6.1.2.2.3.1.2.1.1 BRIELLE ISABELLA MAURER (see above)

4.6.1.2.2.3.1.2.2 EVAN GARRET MAURER (see above)

4.6.1.2.2.3.1.2.3 CHASE AVERY MAURER (see above)

4.6.1.2.2.3.1.2.4 (--?--) MAURER (see above)

4.6.1.2.2.3.1.2.5 CHELSEA MAE-LYNN MAURER (see above)

4.6.1.2.2.3.1.3 TAMMY MAURER was born on 3 April 1969. She married **MARK SNYDER**.

4.6.1.2.2.3.1.3.1 NICOLE SNYDER

4.6.1.2.2.3.1.3.2 HUNTER MARK SNYDER was born on 30 May 1996.

4.6.1.2.2.3.1.4 TRICIA MAURER was born on 26 May 1972. She married **BROOKE TRAUTWEIN**, son of **ROBERT TRAUTWEIN** and **GAIL (--?--)**. She married **(--?--) TAMBURELLI**.

4.6.1.2.2.3.1.4.1 TAYLOR LAKEN TRAUTWEIN was born on 14 February 1994.

4.6.1.2.2.3.2 THOMAS AMBROSE MAURER was born on 1 November 1950. He married **CHERYL STRAUB**.

4.6.1.2.2.3.3 VERNON CLARK MAURER was born on 22 July 1953.

4.6.1.2.3 ARLAND SETH ROMBERGER was born on 10 March 1900, Valley View, Schuylkill County, PA. He was baptized on 3 October 1900, St. Andrew's United Methodist Church, Valley View, Hegins Township, Schuylkill County, PA. He married ETHEL CHARLOTTE SILLIMAN, daughter of HARRY F. SILLIMAN and CORA L. JACKETT, on 24 October 1939, Elkhart, IN. He died on 1 May 1967, Woodstock, McHenry County, IL, at age 67. He was buried at Oakland Cemetery, Woodstock, McHenry County, IL.

4.6.1.2.3.1 JOHN SILLIMAN ROMBERGER was born on 30 November 1945. He married BONNIE JUANITA STARKEY.

4.6.1.2.3.1.1 JOHN SETH ROMBERGER was born on 9 May 1975.

4.6.1.2.3.2 ARLAND STEPHEN ROMBERGER was born on 9 April 1949.

4.6.1.2.4 ELLEN MARY ROMBERGER was born on 5 September 1902. She was baptized on 14 February 1903, St. Andrew's United Methodist Church, Valley View, Hegins Township, Schuylkill County, PA. She married GUY FREDERICK RADEL, son of FRANK RADEL and LUCY KLOCK. She married CHARLES BROWN on 11 February 1964. She died on 31 May 1976, at age 73. She was buried in 1977, at Stone Valley Cemetery, Hickory Corners, Northumberland County, PA.

4.6.1.2.4.1 ELIZABETH MAE RADEL was born on 5 April 1934. She married ROBERT HARTMAN Stroudsburg, Monroe County, PA. She married WAYNE E. MCSHEEHY on 21 December 1960, Butler, Butler County, PA.

4.6.1.2.4.1.1 ROBIN ELLEN HARTMAN was born on 25 September 1956.

4.6.1.2.4.1.2 ANDREA MCSHEEHY

4.6.1.2.4.1.3 KEVIN WAYNE MCSHEEHY was born on 5 September 1961.

4.6.1.2.4.1.4 SEAN DALE MCSHEEHY was born on 3 December 1962.

4.6.1.2.4.1.5 KELLY KATHLEEN MCSHEEHY was born on 5 March 1968.

4.6.1.2.4.2 THOMAS R. RADEL was born on 16 March 1937. He married DARLETTE MAUSSER. He married ANNETTE PAUL.

4.6.1.2.4.2.1 TAMMY RADEL married JIM KLOCK. She married LINN WENRICH.

4.6.1.2.4.2.1.1 ROBBIE KLOCK was born on 2 December 1983. He married KILEY SHADE.

4.6.1.2.4.2.1.1.1 BAILEY KLOCK was born before 2004.

4.6.1.2.4.2.1.1.2 TIEGAN J. KLOCK was born on 8 July 2004, Pottsville Hospital, Pottsville, Schuylkill County, PA.

4.6.1.2.4.2.1.2 NIKKI KLOCK was born on 31 May 1985.

4.6.1.2.4.2.1.3 MICHAEL WENRICH was born on 24 March 1989.

4.6.1.2.4.2.1.4 DERRON WENRICH was born on 24 July 1993.

4.6.1.2.4.2.2 KHRIS ELAINE RADEL was born in September 1958. She married STEPHEN B. YUSLUM, son of STEPHEN E. YUSLUM and MARGARET DOYLE.

4.6.1.2.4.2.2.1 STEVEN THOMAS YUSLUM was born in 1982. He married MELISSA JOLENE PAGE, daughter of GARY PAGE and YVONNE KOPPENHAVER, on 17 June 2006, Lykens Glen Park, Dauphin County, PA. He married RACHEL (--?--).

4.6.1.2.4.2.2.1.1 STEPHEN TYLER YUSLUM was born on 6 April 2001, Pottsville Hospital, Pottsville, Schuylkill County, PA.

4.6.1.2.4.2.2.1.2 MCKENZIE ADDISON YUSLUM was born on 6 November 2007, Pottsville Hospital, Pottsville, Schuylkill County, PA.

4.6.1.2.4.2.2.2 ASHLEY KHRISTEN YUSLUM was born on 4 April 1984. She married JERE SIEMANSKI.

4.6.1.2.4.2.3 JANA LEA RADEL was born on 30 July 1976. She married DALE L. STACKHOUSE JR., son of DALE STACKHOUSE and ROSE (--?--), Tannersville, PA. In 2000, Jana was living in Bloomsburg, PA.

4.6.1.2.4.2.3.1 MYAH ROSE STACKHOUSE was born on 25 October 2002.

4.6.1.2.4.2.3.2 MACI RADEL STACKHOUSE was born on 19 December 2005, Bloomsburg Hospital, Bloomsburg, PA.

4.6.1.2.5 CHARLES RAYMOND ROMBERGER was born on 11 November 1904, Hegins, Schuylkill County, PA. He was baptized on 4 May 1905, St. Andrew's United Methodist Church, Valley View, Hegins Township, Schuylkill County, PA. He married **EVA M. DEITRICH**. He married **ARLENE G. FETTEROLF**, daughter of **HARRY PETER LEROY FETTEROLF** and **JENNIE LEBO**. He died on 31 January 1987, Pottsville Hospital, Pottsville, Schuylkill County, PA, at age 82. He was buried at St. Andrew's United Methodist Church, Valley View, Hegins Township, Schuylkill County, PA. Prior to his death, Charles was living at 1324 East Grand Ave., Tower City, Schuylkill County, PA.

4.6.1.2.5.1 ROGER LAMAR ROMBERGER was born on 21 February 1931, Hegins, Schuylkill County, PA. Some sources record that he was born on 20 February 1930. He married **KATHRYN ELEANORE MACE**, daughter of **ALLEN WOODWORTH MACE** and **DELLA JENNIE WIEST**. He died on 18 February 2013, Schuylkill Medical Center - East Norwegian Street, Pottsville, Schuylkill County, PA, at age 81. According to a newspaper obituary, Roger lived in Hegins, PA. He was a 1948 graduate of the former Hegins Township High School, and served for 22 years in the Air Force. Later, he drove a school bus for many years for Tri-Valley school district. He was buried on 25 February 2013, at Indiantown Gap National Cemetery, Annville, Lebanon County, PA.

4.6.1.2.5.1.1 MICHAEL ROGER ROMBERGER was born on 31 August 1953. He married **SAMANTHA (--?--)**. Michael lives in York, PA.

4.6.1.2.5.1.2 RICHARD LEE ROMBERGER was born on 31 July 1958. He married **LINDA FOSS** on 7 November 1981. Richard lives in Lakeland, GA.

4.6.1.2.5.1.2.1 LAURIE ALICE ROMBERGER was born on 21 April 1982.

4.6.1.2.5.2 MARY JEAN ROMBERGER was born on 31 December 1934. She married **CHESTER MORGAN** on 15 September 1951, Frieden's Lutheran Church, Hegins, Schuylkill County, PA. Jean lives in Hegins, PA.

4.6.1.2.5.2.1 MATT MORGAN

4.6.1.2.5.2.2 DEBRA LOUISE MORGAN was born on 3 October 1952. She married **(--?--) HOAGLAND**. She married **(--?--) LUCAS**.

4.6.1.2.5.2.3 CRAIG EUGENE MORGAN was born on 8 November 1953.

4.6.1.2.5.2.4 DENISE MORGAN was born in January 1956.

4.6.1.2.5.2.5 DONNA JEAN MORGAN was born in December 1960. She married **(--?--) RICKERT**.

4.6.1.2.5.3 ALICE I. ROMBERGER was born on 21 February 1936. She died on 17 December 2002, Citrus Memorial Hospital, Inverness, FL, at age 66. She was buried on 28 December 2002, at Friedens Union Cemetery, Hegins, Schuylkill County, PA.

4.6.1.2.6 HANNAH AGATHA ROMBERGER was born on 18 November 1906, Valley View, Schuylkill County, PA. She married **JACK HENLEY**, son of **JOHN WILLIAMS** and **MABLE HENLEY**, on 20 July 1946, Methodist Church, Woodstock, McHenry County, IL. She died on 26 February 2001, San Antonio, Bexar County, TX, at age 94

4.6.1.2.6.1 GARY EARL HENLEY was born in 1948. He married **REBECCA FUTRELL**.

4.6.1.2.6.1.1 STEPHEN HENLEY

4.6.1.2.6.1.2 MATTHEW HENLEY

4.6.1.2.6.2 REBECCA ELIZABETH HENLEY was born in September 1951.

4.6.1.2.7 LEONA MAY ROMBERGER was born on 28 August 1914, Valley View, Schuylkill County, PA. She married **STANLEY MILLER**, son of **EMORY MILLER** and **KATIE STRAUB**, on 2 July 1938, Valley View, Schuylkill County, PA. She lived in Old Mill Road, Valley View, Schuylkill County, PA. She died on 17 September 2004, Friendly Nursing Home, Pitman, Schuylkill County, PA, at age 90. According to a newspaper obituary, Leona graduated from Hegins Township High School and the Pottsville Beauty Culture School. She was buried at St. Andrew's United Methodist Church Cemetery, Valley View, Schuylkill County, PA.

4.6.1.2.7.1 KATHRYN ANN MILLER was born on 22 February 1940. She married **CURTIS W. ATKINSON** on 17 September 1963, Basel, Switzerland.

4.6.1.2.7.1.1 DOUGLAS CRAIG ATKINSON was born on 4 April 1965, Wiesbaden, Germany. He married **WENDY ANN MURPHY**.

4.6.1.2.7.1.1.1 LAUREN ASHLEY BABCOCK was born on 26 September 1986.

4.6.1.2.7.1.1.2 EMILY GRACE ATKINSON was born on 27 May 1997.

4.6.1.2.7.1.2 DEBRA YVONNE ATKINSON was born on 14 February 1967, West Virginia. She married RUSSELL L. CUMMINS.

4.6.1.2.7.1.2.1 ISAAC LEE CUMMINS was born on 31 August 1991.

4.6.1.2.7.1.2.2 CHARITY C. CUMMINS was born on 9 July 1997.

4.6.1.2.7.2 MARY ELLEN MILLER was born on 15 October 1945. She married JERRY KRAMMES.

4.6.1.2.7.2.1 JOHN MICHAEL KRAMMES was born on 26 July 1978.

4.6.1.3 MARY E. WOLFGANG was born in May 1880. She married JOHN EMERSON RICKERT. She died in 1964. She was buried at St. Andrew's United Methodist Church, Valley View, Hegins Township, Schuylkill County, PA.

4.6.1.3.1 HARRY MELVIN RICKERT was born on 15 February 1899. He was baptized on 28 October 1899, St. Andrew's United Methodist Church, Valley View, Hegins Township, Schuylkill County, PA. He married WINIFRED SPANOTIUS. He married EVELYN C. REIF. He died in April 1987, Phoebe Home, Allentown, Lehigh County, PA, at age 88.

4.6.1.3.1.1 JOYCE W. RICKERT married RICHARD ZIMMERMAN.

4.6.1.3.1.1.1 CRAIG ZIMMERMAN

4.6.1.3.1.1.2 KENT ZIMMERMAN

4.6.1.3.1.1.3 JAN ZIMMERMAN

4.6.1.3.1.2 DOROTHEA RICKERT married ALFRED REDFIELD. She was born on 10 July 1923. She died on 13 February 2002, at age 78.

4.6.1.3.1.2.1 SCOTT REDFIELD

4.6.1.3.1.2.2 DEBRA REDFIELD

4.6.1.4 CLARA ESTELLA WOLFGANG is also referred to as CARRIE AND FLORA E. in some sources. She was born on 5 August 1886. Some sources record that she was born in August 1887. She married CHARLES MONROE UNDERKOFFLER, son of ELIAS UNDERKOFFLER and CATHERINE ANN SCHROPE, on 13 January 1906. She died on 15 January 1951, Valley View, Schuylkill County, PA, at age 63. She was buried at St. Andrew's United Methodist Church, Valley View, Hegins Township, Schuylkill County, PA.

4.6.1.4.1 RUSSELL VERNON UNDERKOFFLER was born on 15 August 1906. He married MARTHA AMELIA SNYDER, daughter of CHARLES E. SNYDER and MABEL (--?--), on 28 April 1928. He died in August 1972. He was buried at All Saints Cemetery, Elysburg, Northumberland County, PA.

4.6.1.4.1.1 RUTH JEANNETTE UNDERKOFFLER was born on 9 December 1928. She married FRANCIS JOSEPH WOODS JR. on 2 December 1950.

4.6.1.4.1.1.1 FRANCIS JOSEPH WOODS III was born on 29 April 1952.

4.6.1.4.1.1.2 RICHARD RUSSELL WOODS was born on 2 September 1954.

4.6.1.4.1.1.3 JOAN ELLEN WOODS was born on 23 August 1956.

4.6.1.4.1.2 GENE RUSSELL UNDERKOFFLER was born on 6 December 1930. He married LUCY MARCELENE COSTELLO on 28 August 1957.

4.6.1.4.1.2.1 RUSSELL GENE UNDERKOFFLER was born on 8 August 1958.

4.6.1.4.1.2.2 LISA MARIE UNDERKOFFLER was born on 8 July 1962.

4.6.1.4.1.3 ROBERT CHARLES UNDERKOFFLER was born on 17 July 1934, Mount Carmel, Northumberland County, PA. He married MARY ANN GAGLIARDI on 21 June 1958. He died on 5 April 2000, at age 65.

4.6.1.4.1.3.1 KRISTINE ANTINETTE UNDERKOFFLER was born on 21 May 1959.

4.6.1.4.1.3.2 GAYLE JEAN UNDERKOFFLER was born on 27 January 1962.

4.6.1.4.2 ALVIN WILSON UNDERKOFFLER was born on 24 March 1908. He married OLIVE ANGELINE SELL on 13 June 1933. He died on 4 February 1975, at age 66.

4.6.1.4.2.1 KITTY ANN UNDERKOFFLER was born on 20 November 1934. She married **HOWARD E. SAMUELS** on 11 June 1955.

4.6.1.4.2.1.1 JENNIFER SUSAN SAMUELS was born on 26 October 1956.

4.6.2 FRANKLIN HENRY SCHWALM was born on 22 June 1853, Valley View, Schuylkill County, PA. He was baptized on 21 August 1853, St. Paul's (Artz's) Lutheran and Reformed Church, Sacramento, Schuylkill County, PA. He married **CATHERINE A. WOLFGANG**, daughter of **JACOB WOLFGANG** and **ELIZABETH BLYLER**, on 17 March 1878. A newspaper article that appeared, when Frank was 81 years old, in the *Upper Dauphin (Millersburg) Sentinel*, 6 Jan. 1933 (reprinted in the 1982 Journal of Johannes Schwalm Historical Association) contains a colorful story about Frank's life. He died on 9 March 1935, Hegins Township, Schuylkill County, PA, at age 81. He was buried at Saint Andrews United Methodist Church Cemetery, Valley View, Schuylkill County, PA.

4.6.2.1 FRANCES SALOMA ELIZABETH SCHWALM was born on 21 June 1874. She married **REILLY ELLSWORTH HARNER**, son of **GEORGE B. HARNER** and **MARIA WOLFGANG**, on 17 June 1893. She died in November 1950, at age 76. She was buried at Saint Andrews United Methodist Church Cemetery, Valley View, Schuylkill County, PA.

4.6.2.1.1 JOHN FREMONT HARNER was born on 11 December 1893, Valley View, Schuylkill County, PA. He married **LILLIE ALBERTA SCHMELTZ**, daughter of **MONROE SCHMELTZ** and **EMMA SEVILLA HERB**, on 3 March 1917. He died on 2 June 1959, Schuylkill County, PA, at age 65. He died on 2 June 1959, Pottsville Hospital, Pottsville, Schuylkill County, PA, at age 65. He was buried on 6 June 1959, at Lutheran Church Cemetery, Tremont, Schuylkill County, PA.

4.6.2.1.1.1 DORA HARNER was born on 16 September 1917, Tremont, Schuylkill County, PA. She married **CLARENCE A. KOHR**. She married **CLARENCE SCHNECK**. She died on 1 October 2015, Schuylkill Medical Center-East Norwegian Street, Pottsville, Schuylkill County, PA, at age 98. She was buried on 5 October 2015, at St. John's Lutheran Church Cemetery, Tremont, Schuylkill County, PA.

4.6.2.1.1.1.1 JOHN E. KOHR married **CATHARINE KIMMEL**.

4.6.2.1.1.1.1.1 MICHAEL D. KOHR married **LYNE (--?--)**.

4.6.2.1.1.1.1.1.1 SAMUEL KOHR

4.6.2.1.1.1.1.1.2 BENJAMIN KOHR

4.6.2.1.2 ELVA M. HARNER was born on 25 June 1895. She married **JAMES E. MILLER**, son of **CHARLES M. MILLER** and **ELLEN BARBARA JUSTINA SCHWALM**. She died on 28 March 1984, Geisinger Medical Center, Danville, Montour County, PA, at age 88. She was buried on 1 April 1984, at Saint Andrews United Methodist Church Cemetery, Valley View, Schuylkill County, PA.

4.6.2.1.2.1 JAMES E. MILLER JR. (see above)

4.6.2.1.2.2 MARY ELVA MILLER (see above)

4.6.2.1.2.3 NED E. MILLER (see above)

4.6.2.1.2.3.1 DIANE L. MILLER (see above)

4.6.2.1.2.3.2 JUDITH L. MILLER (see above)

4.6.2.1.2.3.3 NANCY K. MILLER (see above)

4.6.2.1.2.3.3.1 RYAN HOBBS (see above)

4.6.2.1.3 GEORGE F. HARNER was born on 6 February 1897. He was baptized on 18 January 1898, Saint Andrews United Methodist Church, Valley View, Schuylkill County, PA. He married **DAISY TROUTMAN**. He died before 1984.

4.6.2.1.3.1 HELEN HARNER married **JOHN BOYER**.

4.6.2.1.3.2 DAISY N. HARNER was born on 20 October 1918, Hegins, Schuylkill County, PA. She married **HARRY MARTZ**. Prior to her death, Daisy was living at 89 Powells Valley Road, Dauphin County, PA. She died on 12 April 2001, PinnacleHealth, Harrisburg, Dauphin County, PA, at age 82. She was buried at Zion (Klinger's) Church Cemetery, Erdman, Lykens Township, Dauphin County, PA.

4.6.2.1.3.2.1 JAMES H. MARTZ married **JACQUALINE SHRAWDER**.

4.6.2.1.3.2.1.1 KIMBRA MARTZ

4.6.2.1.3.2.1.2 DOUGLAS MARTZ

4.6.2.1.3.2.2 CAROLE A. MARTZ married **JOHN W. LAUDENSLAGER**, son of **JAY W. LAUDENSLAGER** and **MARY CROWLEY**.

4.6.2.1.3.2.2.1 ROBERT LAUDENSLAGER. Robert lives in Millersburg, PA.

4.6.2.1.3.2.2.2 TODD LAUDENSLAGER. Todd lives in Elizabethville, PA.

4.6.2.1.3.2.2.3 KEVIN LAUDENSLAGER married **AMY (--?--)**. Kevin lives in Elizabethville, PA.

4.6.2.1.3.2.2.4 BRADLEY LAUDENSLAGER married **NANCY (--?--)**. Bradley lives near Lykens, PA.

4.6.2.1.4 VERNA E. HARNER was born on 27 July 1900, Valley View, Schuylkill County, PA. She married **FRED STIELY**. She died on 22 January 1992, Good Samaritan Medical Center, Pottsville, Schuylkill County, PA, at age 91. She was buried at St. Andrew's United Methodist Church Cemetery, Valley View, Hegins Township, Schuylkill County, PA.

4.6.2.1.4.1 WARREN FRED STIELY was born on 9 June 1920, Valley View, Hegins Township, Schuylkill County, PA. He married **JOYCE AMELIA BLOUCH**, daughter of **WILBERT T. BLOUCH** and **ANNA L. PEFFLEY**. He died on 30 November 1985, at home, Lebanon, Lebanon County, PA, at age 65. He was buried at Covenant Greenwood Cemetery, Ebenezer, Lebanon County, PA.

4.6.2.1.4.1.1 TINA E. STIELY was born circa 1956. She married **(--?--) DETWEILER**.

4.6.2.1.4.1.1.1 JENNIFER DETWEILER

4.6.2.1.4.1.2 ANNE LOUISE STIELY was born circa 1957. She married **STEPHEN TYLER**.

4.6.2.1.4.1.2.1 TOBAN TYLER

4.6.2.1.4.1.2.2 TABATHA TYLER

4.6.2.1.4.2 BETTY E. STIELY was born on 25 October 1924, Hegins, Schuylkill County, PA. She married **KENNETH KERMIT KLINGER**, son of **GURNEY ALLEN KLINGER** and **GERTRUDE MABEL TROUTMAN**, on 19 August 1951, St. Andrew's Church, Valley View, Schuylkill County, PA. She died on 22 December 2014, Carolyn Croxton Slane Residence, Harrisburg, Dauphin County, PA, at age 90. She was buried on 29 December 2015, at St. Andrew's Methodist Church Cemetery, Valley View, Schuylkill County, PA.

4.6.2.1.4.2.1 KEITH KERMIT KLINGER (see above)

4.6.2.1.4.2.1.1 TANYA L. KLINGER (see above)

4.6.2.1.4.2.1.1.1 SYDNEY SIMS (see above)

4.6.2.1.4.2.1.1.2 ERICA SIMS (see above)

4.6.2.1.4.2.1.2 ERIC KLINGER (see above)

4.6.2.1.4.2.2 KARL KENNETH KLINGER (see above)

4.6.2.1.4.2.2.1 KUSSANDRA KLINGER (see above)

4.6.2.1.4.2.2.2 JANELLE KLINGER (see above)

4.6.2.1.4.2.3 ROGER KLINGER (see above)

4.6.2.1.5 GRACE L. HARNER was born circa 1905, Valley View, Hegins Township, Schuylkill County, PA. She married **WILLIAM L. BOWER**. Prior to her death, Grace was living at 317 South 23rd Street, Allentown, Lehigh County, PA. She died on 2 November 2003, Phoebe Home, Allentown, Lehigh County, PA. She was buried at Fairview Cemetery, Allentown, Lehigh County, PA.

4.6.2.1.5.1 BARBARA F. BOWER was born in 1930. She married **CHARLES FISH**. She married **(--?--) DIAZ**.

4.6.2.1.5.1.1 KAREN A. FISH

4.6.2.1.5.1.2 GREGORY FISH

4.6.2.1.6 LESLIE ELLSWORTH HARNER was born on 25 November 1909. Some sources record that he was born on 25 November 1919. He married **HILDA MARGARET HENRY**, daughter of **CHARLES HENRY** and **LOTTIE (--?--)**, circa 1933. He was inducted into Pennsylvania Sports Hall of Fame, for his exploits as a baseball pitcher. His playing days ended in 1941 following a mine accident. He lived in Pine Grove, Schuylkill County, PA. He died on 4 November 2000, Reading Hospital and Medical Center, Reading, Berks County, PA, at age 80. He was buried at St.

Andrew's United Methodist Church Cemetery, Valley View, Hegins Township, Schuylkill County, PA.

 4.6.2.1.6.1 JANICE HARNER married **GEORGE WOLFE**. Janice lives in Wyomissing, PA.

  4.6.2.1.6.1.1 MICHAEL WOLFE married **JUDY (--?--)**. Michael and Judy live in Portland, ME.

  4.6.2.1.6.1.2 ALISON WOLFE married **(--?--) IZZO**. Alison and her husband live in Hummelstown, PA.

 4.6.2.1.6.2 JANE M. HARNER married **RONALD BARNES**. Jane and Ronald live in New Cumberland, PA.

  4.6.2.1.6.2.1 JEFFREY BARNES married **ANN (--?--)**. Jeff and his Ann live in Santa Maria, CA.

  4.6.2.1.6.2.2 ERIC BARNES married **MARIA (--?--)**. Eric and Maria live in Pottstown, PA.

4.6.2.2 KATIE ELLA NORA SCHWALM was born on 23 May 1879, Schuylkill County, PA. She married **HOWARD G. SCHACH**. In 1929, Katie and Howard were operating a bakery in Florence, CO, but later returned to Pennsylvania where they operated a bakery for many years at the corner of Tenth and Buttonwood Streets in Reading, PA. She died on 29 November 1945, Reading, Berks County, PA, at age 66. She was buried at Saint Andrews United Methodist Church Cemetery, Valley View, Schuylkill County, PA.

 4.6.2.2.1 MARY SCHACH was born on 16 April 1899. She married **VOLLIE POSEY**. Beginning in 1989, Mary resided at Cornwall Manor, Lebanon, Lebanon County, PA. Previously, she had lived at 350 North 10th Street, Reading, PA. She died on 24 May 1998, Cornwall Manor, Lebanon, Lebanon County, PA, at age 99. She was buried at St. Andrew's United Methodist Church Cemetery, Valley View, Hegins Township, Schuylkill County, PA.

  4.6.2.2.1.1 NAOMI POSEY died in childhood.

 4.6.2.2.2 VERNA SCHACH was born circa 1902. She married **CHARLES ELVIN SEITZ**. She died before 1989.

  4.6.2.2.2.1 HELEN E SEITZ was born on 5 September 1922. She married **WILLIAM A. FISHER**, son of **MORRIS R. FISHER** and **AMELIA WENTZEL**, circa 1944. She died on 8 April 2008, Reading Hospital, Reading, Berks County, PA, at age 85.

   4.6.2.2.2.1.1 DAVID W. FISHER married **JOANNE WENRICH**.

    4.6.2.2.2.1.1.1 SHANNON FISHER

    4.6.2.2.2.1.1.2 SHAWN FISHER

   4.6.2.2.2.1.2 SUSAN E. FISHER married **RONALD L. JAMES SR.**

    4.6.2.2.2.1.2.1 JENNIFER JAMES

    4.6.2.2.2.1.2.2 RONALD JAMES JR.

     4.6.2.2.2.1.2.2.1 BRENDEN JAMES

     4.6.2.2.2.1.2.2.2 KAYLA JAMES

     4.6.2.2.2.1.2.2.3 TAYLOR JAMES

   4.6.2.2.2.1.3 MARK D. FISHER

    4.6.2.2.2.1.3.1 TELLY FISHER

 4.6.2.2.3 MARTHA MAE SCHACH was born on 22 February 1904, Valley View, Schuylkill County, PA. She married **LUTHER AMOS WEIK**, son of **HARRY W. WEIK** and **MARY MAGDALENA PALM**. She died on 4 November 1985, Holy Family Manor Nursing Center, Bethlehem, PA, at age 81. She was buried at Fairview Cemetery, Shillington, Berks County, PA.

  4.6.2.2.3.1 ANN M. WEIK was born circa 1932. She married **RICHARD CASSAR**.

   4.6.2.2.3.1.1 THOMAS E. CASSAR married **JILL SANDERS**. In 1995, Thomas was living at 210 West 15th Street, New York, NY.

    4.6.2.2.3.1.1.1 RACHEL MOORE CASSAR was born on 10 February 1992.

    4.6.2.2.3.1.1.2 GRACE ANASTASIA CASSAR was born on 1 September 1995, New York, NY.

4.6.2.2.3.1.2 JAMES CASSAR

4.6.2.2.3.1.3 DAVID CASSAR was born in 1960. He died on 25 December 2014, Marcus Hook, Delaware County, PA. He was buried on 3 January 2015, at Brandywine Baptist Church Cemetery, Chadds Ford, Delaware County, PA.

4.6.2.2.3.2 JEAN L. WEIK was born circa 1936. She married MERLIN F. HERTZOG, son of CHARLES HERTZOG and ESTHER RITZMAN.

4.6.2.2.3.2.1 BETH ANN HERTZOG married (--?--) RUCH.

4.6.2.2.3.2.1.1 CHRISTOPHER RUCH

4.6.2.2.3.2.1.2 MATTHEW RUCH

4.6.2.2.3.2.2 JOANNE HERTZOG married ROBERT KERN.

4.6.2.2.3.2.2.1 STEPHANIE KERN

4.6.2.2.3.2.2.2 GREG KERN

4.6.2.2.3.2.3 CAROL ANN HERTZOG married (--?--) MILOT.

4.6.2.2.3.2.4 NANCY B. HERTZOG married RICHARD COVELL.

4.6.2.2.4 NAOMI KATHRYN SCHACH was born on 9 February 1911. She was baptized on 7 May 1911, Saint Andrews United Methodist Church, Valley View, Schuylkill County, PA. She died on 23 February 1913, at age 2 of diphtheria. She was buried at Valley View, Schuylkill County, PA.

4.6.2.2.5 PAUL SCHACH was born on 30 October 1915. He married RUTH YOHN. In 1998, Paul was emeritus professor of Germanic languages at the University of Nebraska. After earning his Ph. D. in Germanic languages and literature from the University of Pennsylvania in 1949, he taught at Albright College and, beginning in 1951, at the University of Nebraska. He died on 20 October 1998, at home, Lincoln, NE, at age 82. Some sources record that he died on 13 October 1998. He was buried at Lincoln Memorial Park Mausoleum, Lincoln, Lancaster County, NE.

4.6.2.2.5.1 JOAN M. SCHACH

4.6.2.2.5.2 KATHERINE SCHACH married WILLIAM COOK.

4.6.2.2.5.3 PAULA R. SCHACH

4.6.2.2.6 JOHN HOWARD SCHACH was born on 8 January 1922, Tremont, Schuylkill County, PA. He married ADELAIDE KATHERINE LEVAN, daughter of ABRAM LEVAN and CATHARINE (--?--), on 9 June 1943. He died on 2 September 2008, Lower Heidelberg Township, Berks County, PA, at age 86. He was buried on 26 November 2008, at Charles Evans Cemetery, Reading, Berks County, PA.

4.6.2.2.6.1 JOHN HOWARD SCHACH JR. married BEVERLY ERNST. He married JESSICA GAGLIARDI. According to a 2007 article in the Reading Eagle, John is a retired US Airways pilot and currently the Fire Commissioner of Spring Township, Berks County, PA.

4.6.2.2.6.1.1 NICOLE M. SCHACH married PAUL W. BLEILER. She married DAVID V. RIOS.

4.6.2.2.6.1.1.1 CAITLYN NICOLE BLEILER was born on 22 November 2000.

4.6.2.2.6.1.1.2 MADISYN JADE BLEILER was born on 22 August 2003.

4.6.2.2.6.1.2 JONATHAN A. SCHACH married SALLY CLEMENT.

4.6.2.3 SAMUEL ELLSWORTH SCHWALM was born on 23 June 1881. He married JENNIE NORA SNYDER, daughter of JOHN SNYDER and AMANDA (--?--), on 5 January 1901, St. Andrew's United Methodist Church, Valley View, Schuylkill County, PA. He died in 1967. He was buried at St. Andrew's United Methodist Church Cemetery, Valley View, Schuylkill County, PA.

4.6.2.3.1 CALVIN FRANKLIN SCHWALM was born on 4 May 1901, Valley View, Schuylkill County, PA. He married IDA SOPHIA STIELY, daughter of PERRY M. STIELY and HARRIETTE SNYDER, on 27 November 1920, St. Andrew's Church, Valley View, Schuylkill County, PA. He died on 3 January 1938, Fremont, Schuylkill County, PA, at age 36. He was buried on 7 January 1938, at St. Andrew's Church Cemetery, Valley View, Schuylkill County, PA.

4.6.2.3.1.1 KERMIT KENNETH SCHWALM was born on 20 October 1921. He was baptized on 25 December 1921, St. Andrew's United Methodist Church, Valley View, Schuylkill County, PA. He died in 1923. He was buried at St. Andrew's Church Cemetery, Valley View, Schuylkill County, PA.

4.6.2.3.1.2 JOYCE BETTY SCHWALM was born on 3 October 1922. She was baptized on 15 February 1923, St. Andrew's United Methodist Church, Valley View, Schuylkill County, PA. She married **CLAYTON LEROY KOPPENHAVER**, son of **ANDREW CLEVELAND KOPPENHAVER** and **KATIE A. STRAUB**, on 19 July 1941, St. Andrew's Church, Valley View, Schuylkill County, PA. She died on 11 November 2005, Milton S. Hershey Penn State Medical Center, Hershey, Derry Township, Dauphin County, PA, at age 83. According to a newspaper obituary, Joyce lived in Hegins and, before that, Tremont, Schuylkill County, PA. She was a primary volunteer for Volunteer Home Care, Pine Grove, for the two years prior to her death. She was buried on 16 November 2005, at Church of God Cemetery, Valley View, Schuylkill County, PA.

4.6.2.3.1.2.1 RONALD EUGENE KOPPENHAVER was born on 18 December 1941, Warren Hospital, Pottsville, Schuylkill County, PA. He married **DARLA LAYNE SREWAET** on 21 March 1964. He married **LAURA MAY DONMOYER** on 20 April 1980. He died on 20 August 2002, Integris Baptist Medical Center, Oklahoma City, OK, at age 60. According to a newspaper obituary, Ronald lived in Oklahoma City, OK, where he was a caregiver at Comprehensive Community Services, Oklahoma City. He was buried at Church of God Cemetery, Valley View, Hegins Township, Schuylkill County, PA.

4.6.2.3.1.2.1.1 KELLY L. KOPPENHAVER married (--?--) **MILLER**.

4.6.2.3.1.2.2 GARY CLAYTON KOPPENHAVER was born on 11 February 1946, Warren Hospital, Pottsville, Schuylkill County, PA. He died on 6 May 2015, Health and Rehabilitation Center, Tremont, Schuylkill County, PA, at age 69. He was buried at Church of God Cemetery, Valley View, Schuylkill County, PA.

4.6.2.3.1.2.3 RANDALL EARL KOPPENHAVER was born on 2 September 1946, Hegins, Schuylkill County, PA. Some sources record that he was born on 2 September 1948. He married **CHRISTINE DENISE BANGO** on 23 October 1976.

4.6.2.3.1.2.3.1 JEREMY JUSTIN KOPPENHAVER was born on 8 December 1981.

4.6.2.3.1.2.3.2 TIMOTHY JUSTIN KOPPENHAVER was born on 10 January 1984.

4.6.2.3.1.2.4 SAMUEL PERRY KOPPENHAVER was born on 24 December 1949, Hegins, Schuylkill County, PA. Prior to his death, Samuel lived at 511 South Center Street, Pottsville, Schuylkill County, PA. He died on 19 February 2001, Pottsville Hospital, Pottsville, Schuylkill County, PA, at age 51. He was buried at Church of God Cemetery, Valley View, Hegins Township, Schuylkill County, PA.

4.6.2.3.1.2.5 KEITH ALAN KOPPENHAVER was born on 5 January 1956, Tremont, Schuylkill County, PA. Prior to his death, Keith lived in Tremont, Schuylkill County, PA. He died on 3 September 1989, Hershey Medical Center, Dauphin County, PA, at age 33. He was buried at Church of God Cemetery, Valley View, Hegins Township, Schuylkill County, PA.

4.6.2.3.1.2.6 KATHY ANN KOPPENHAVER was born on 15 March 1957, Tremont, Schuylkill County, PA. She married **RICKY ALLEN WANAMAKER**, son of **DELANO WANAMAKER** and **ARLENE (--?--)**, on 6 August 1982.

4.6.2.3.1.2.6.1 JASON ALLEN WANAMAKER was born on 16 February 1982, Schuylkill County, PA. He died in 1999.

4.6.2.3.1.2.6.2 LACIE ALICE WANAMAKER is also referred to as **LACREANNE WANAMAKER** in some sources. She was born on 12 July 1991, Pottsville, Schuylkill County, PA.

4.6.2.3.1.2.7 WENDY KAY KOPPENHAVER was born on 28 June 1962, Pottsville, Schuylkill County, PA. She died on 28 June 1962, Pottsville, Schuylkill County, PA.

4.6.2.3.1.2.8 JAMES LEE KOPPENHAVER was born on 25 July 1964, Pottsville, Schuylkill County, PA. He married **BRENDA LOUISE BIXLER** on 28 June 1986.

4.6.2.3.1.2.8.1 STEPHANIE KAY KOPPENHAVER was born on 23 November 1990, Pottsville, Schuylkill County, PA. She married **LUKE DANIEL DRAKE**, son of **DAVID DRAKE** and **KATIE (--?--)**, in June 2014.

4.6.2.3.1.2.8.2 MATTHEW MILES KOPPENHAVER was born on 10 November 1991, Pottsville, Schuylkill County, PA.

4.6.2.3.1.3 LYLE REUBEN SCHWALM was born on 19 February 1924, Valley View, Schuylkill County, PA. He was baptized on 3 September 1924, St. Andrew's United Methodist Church, Valley View, Schuylkill County, PA. He married JANET R. MYERS. He and JANET R. MYERS were divorced. He married SANDRA MCKEE. He died on 11 January 2013, Langhorne Manor, Bucks County, PA, at age 88. He was buried at Ulster Catholic/Immaculate Conception, Ulster, Bradford County, PA.

4.6.2.3.1.4 JEAN IRIS SCHWALM was born on 19 May 1926, Tremont, Schuylkill County, PA. She was baptized on 9 February 1927, St. Andrew's United Methodist Church, Valley View, Schuylkill County, PA. She married CARL ETHAN HEINLY, son of ETHAN HEINLY and LILLIE FEGLEY. She died on 7 July 2011, Country Meadows, Wyomissing, Berks County, PA, at age 85. She was buried on 13 July 2011, at Forest Hills Memorial Park, Reiffton, Berks County, PA.

    4.6.2.3.1.4.1 CARLA J. HEINLY married THOMAS P. HECKMAN.

        4.6.2.3.1.4.1.1 HOLLY A. HECKMAN

    4.6.2.3.1.4.2 MARY JANE HEINLY married JOHN R. HOOKS.

        4.6.2.3.1.4.2.1 SUZANNE HOOKS

        4.6.2.3.1.4.2.2 MEGAN E. HOOKS

    4.6.2.3.1.4.3 SALLY A. HEINLY married DAVID E. GILES.

        4.6.2.3.1.4.3.1 JENNIFER GILES

        4.6.2.3.1.4.3.2 CHRISTINA GILES

        4.6.2.3.1.4.3.3 CAROLINE GILES

    4.6.2.3.1.4.4 KENNETH C. HEINLY married LYNNE LAURENCE.

    4.6.2.3.1.4.5 JEFFREY A. HEINLY married JENNIFER (--?--).

    4.6.2.3.1.4.6 AMY L. HEINLY married JOHN SOCKEL.

4.6.2.3.1.5 JERRED FRANKLIN SCHWALM was born on 27 January 1927. He was baptized on 9 February 1927, St. Andrew's United Methodist Church, Valley View, Schuylkill County, PA. He married RUTH M. BURGERT, daughter of DAVID R. BURGERT and MARY DUTT, on 30 July 1949.

    4.6.2.3.1.5.1 BRUCE J. SCHWALM married RITA K. ADAMS.

        4.6.2.3.1.5.1.1 ANDREA L. SCHWALM married BRIAN HILLIARD on 30 April 2005.

            4.6.2.3.1.5.1.1.1 TUCKER J. HILLIARD

    4.6.2.3.1.5.2 BETH JAN SCHWALM married TROY ALAN ADAM circa 1988, St. Paul's Church of Christ, Kutztown, PA.

        4.6.2.3.1.5.2.1 KATIE BETH ADAM was born on 14 November 1987.

        4.6.2.3.1.5.2.2 KEEGAN TROY ADAM was born on 15 September 1993.

    4.6.2.3.1.5.3 BRADLEY JACK SCHWALM married KAY A. FLICKER circa 1988, St. Paul's Lutheran Church, Metztown, PA.

        4.6.2.3.1.5.3.1 ARIELLE LYNN SCHWALM was born on 28 June 1989.

        4.6.2.3.1.5.3.2 JEREMIAH F. SCHWALM was born on 27 March 1992.

    4.6.2.3.1.5.4 BURT J. SCHWALM was born on 30 May 1955. He married MARGO A. HOFFMAN.

    4.6.2.3.1.5.5 KAREN RUTH SCHWALM was born on 25 February 1960, Kutztown, Berks County, PA. She died on 26 April 1961, Philadelphia, Philadelphia County, PA, at age 1. She was buried at Maidencreek Cemetery, Blandon, Berks County, PA.

4.6.2.3.1.6 MARY ELIZABETH SCHWALM was born on 27 February 1931. She was baptized on 8 April 1931, St. Andrew's United Methodist Church, Valley View, Schuylkill County, PA. She married ALEX J. STROVINSKY. She died on 16 October 2011, at age 80. She was buried on 19 October 2011, at Jefferson Barracks National Cemetery, Lemay, St. Louis County, MO.

    4.6.2.3.1.6.1 MICHAEL J. STROVINSKY married CINDY (--?--).

    4.6.2.3.1.6.2 MARY A. STROVINSKY married GARY KANE.

4.6.2.3.2 EDITH I. SCHWALM was born circa 1905. She married **DAVID ROSENBLUTH**, son of **MORRIS ROSENBLUTH** and **ESTHER (--?--)**, after 1930. She died on 28 October 1995.

4.6.2.3.2.1 WANDA M. ROSENBLUTH was born circa 1936. She married **WILLIAM J. KINKAID**.

4.6.2.3.2.1.1 GARY DOUGLAS KINKAID was born in May 1959.

4.6.2.3.2.1.1.1 BECKY KINKAID

4.6.2.3.2.1.1.2 KATY KINKAID

4.6.2.3.3 BERTHA ESTHER SCHWALM was born on 14 March 1907, Hegins, Schuylkill County, PA. She married **ROBERT EVANS GOUDY**, son of **JOHN GOUDY** and **MARY EVANS**. She died on 2 April 1997, Riverside Regional Medical Center, Peninsula, NC, at age 90. She was buried at Maplewood Cemetery, Wilson, Wilson County, NC.

4.6.2.3.3.1 ROBERT S. GOUDY married **JANICE G. MCKELVEY**.

4.6.2.3.3.1.1 SARAH E. GOUDY

4.6.2.3.3.1.2 AMANDA B. GOUDY

4.6.2.3.3.2 SUZANNE M. GOUDY married **THOMAS A. INSLEY JR.**

4.6.2.3.4 HENRY LESTER SCHWALM was born on 9 June 1910, Valley View, Schuylkill County, PA. He died on 29 June 1910, Hegins, Schuylkill County, PA. The cause of death was narcosis resulting from an overdose of medicine. He was buried on 2 July 1910, at St. Andrew's United Methodist Church Cemetery, Valley View, Schuylkill County, PA.

4.6.2.3.5 FLORENCE D. SCHWALM was born on 1 May 1916. She married **ROBERT W. MINNICH**, son of **GEORGE D. MINNICH** and **ADA DIANNA SALTZER**. She married **THOMAS LEROY MORGAN**, son of **EMERSON MORGAN** and **ANNIE SHADE**. She died on 24 October 2000, Good Samaritan Regional Medical Center, Pottsville, Schuylkill County, PA, at age 84. She was buried at St. Andrew's Church Cemetery, Valley View, Hegins Township, Schuylkill County, PA.

4.6.2.3.5.1 DONNA MAE MINNICH was born on 21 April 1934. She married **JOHN JOSEPH CONNOLLY JR.** She married **CLAYTON CHRISTIAN**. She died on 24 November 2013, at age 79. She was buried on 2 December 2013, at Washington Crossing National Cemetery, Newton, Bucks County, PA.

4.6.2.3.5.1.1 JEFFREY J. CONNOLLY

4.6.2.3.5.1.2 KENNETH M. CONNOLLY

4.6.2.3.5.1.3 JOHN JOSEPH CONNOLLY III was born on 21 November 1954. He married **GRETCHEN ALLEN**. He died on 24 November 2010, at age 56. He was buried on 1 December 2010, at Washington Crossing National Cemetery, Newton, Bucks County, PA.

4.6.2.3.5.1.3.1 CHRISTINE CONNOLLY

4.6.2.3.5.1.3.2 JAMIE CONNOLLY

4.6.2.3.5.1.3.3 KATHERINE CONNOLLY

4.6.2.3.5.1.3.4 MICHAEL CONNOLLY

4.6.2.3.5.1.4 JENNY ELIZABETH CONNOLLY was born on 10 November 1960.

4.6.2.3.5.1.5 LINDA CHRISTIAN married **BILL KRAUSE**.

4.6.2.3.5.1.6 DONNA CHRISTIAN married **MARTY MCCARTHY**.

4.6.2.3.5.2 CAROLYN MORGAN married **RUSSELL SCHREFFLER**.

4.6.2.3.5.3 THOMAS D. MORGAN married **SUSAN HERB**. He married **CHRISTINE LUCAS**.

4.6.2.3.5.3.1 KENNETH M. MORGAN married **TINA NICOLE STIELY**, daughter of **DONNIE STIELY** and **LINDA (--?--)**.

4.6.2.3.5.3.1.1 HEATHER GEIST MORGAN was born circa 1992.

4.6.2.3.5.3.1.2 TIFFANI GEIST MORGAN was born circa 1996.

4.6.2.3.5.3.1.3 KENNETH MICHAEL MORGAN JR. was born on 24 February 1998.

4.6.2.3.5.3.1.4 ASHLEY NICOLE MORGAN was born on 17 May 1999, Pottsville Hospital, Pottsville, Schuylkill County, PA.

4.6.2.3.5.3.2 BOBBIE JO MORGAN

4.6.2.3.5.3.3 JENNIFER MORGAN married MICHAEL WILLIAM HERB, son of DAVID J. HERB and CAROL ANN BENSINGER.

4.6.2.3.5.3.3.1 TESSA ANN HERB was born on 4 July 2006, Pottsville Hospital, Pottsville, Schuylkill County, PA.

4.6.2.3.5.3.3.2 TAYLOR LYNN HERB was born on 18 December 2009, Pottsville Hospital, Pottsville, Schuylkill County, PA.

4.6.2.3.5.3.4 AMANDA MORGAN

4.6.2.3.5.3.5 THOMAS D. MORGAN JR.

4.6.2.3.5.4 JOHN L. MORGAN married DONNA (--?--).

4.6.2.3.5.5 JANET A. MORGAN was born on 20 December 1951, Valley View, Schuylkill County, PA. She married RICHARD L. ERNFIELD. She married JAMES D. SMITH. She married JOHN NEVADOMSKY. She died on 14 October 1999, Good Samaritan Regional Medical Center, Pottsville, Schuylkill County, PA, at age 47.

4.6.2.3.5.5.1 JESSICA (--?--) married (--?--) ROSENBERGER.

4.6.2.3.5.5.2 ALYSON (--?--) married (--?--) CLAUSER.

4.6.2.3.5.5.3 BRITTANY (--?--) married (--?--) HELLER.

4.6.2.3.5.5.4 AMY L. ERNFIELD married (--?--) UPDEGRAVE.

4.6.2.3.6 MARIAN ISABEL SCHWALM was born on 17 September 1917, Valley View, Schuylkill County, PA. She married LAWRENCE JOHN ROMBERGER. Prior to her death, Marian lived at 1411 Valley Drive, Lykens, Dauphin County, PA. She died on 15 June 2004, Nottingham Village, Northumberland, Northumberland County, PA, at age 86. She was buried on 19 June 2004, at Simeon's Cemetery, Gratz, Dauphin County, PA.

4.6.2.3.6.1 MARIE A. ROMBERGER married CLARENCE LAMAR RUNKLE, son of LESTER A. RUNKLE and GERTIE CRISSINGER.

4.6.2.3.6.1.1 JOANNE MARIE RUNKLE married JEFFREY B. ALLEN on 6 May 1996, St. Paul's United Church of Christ, Sellersville, PA.

4.6.2.3.6.1.1.1 GRIFFIN MATTHEW ALLEN was born on 12 May 2000.

4.6.2.3.6.1.1.2 CAMERON MICHAEL ALLEN was born on 17 February 2005.

4.6.2.3.6.1.2 MICHAEL RUNKLE married DESIREE HARTMAN.

4.6.2.3.6.1.2.1 MOXLEY BENJAMIN RUNKLE was born on 29 December 2005.

4.6.2.3.6.1.2.2 LYMAN ELIAS RUNKLE was born on 16 January 2008.

4.6.2.3.7 WAYNE SAMUEL SCHWALM was born on 27 November 1918, Valley View, Schuylkill County, PA. He married ALEESE MCLAIN, daughter of JOHN WESLEY MCLAIN and RUTH HASTY, on 8 April 1944, Camden, SC. He died on 23 October 2009, at his home, Fort Worth, TX, at age 90. He was buried on 26 October 2009, at Memory Gardens Cemetery, Mineral Wells, TX. According to a newspaper obituary, Wayne moved from Bainbridge, Georgia to Mineral Wells in 1956 to work with Southern Airways Helicopter Pilot School. Later he served as Director of Aircraft Maintenance, Assistant General Manager, and General Manager. He was survived by granddaughters Jennifer Hoover and her husband and Kelly of Overland Park, Kansas, and Emily May, and her husband Aaron, of Fort Worth, along with four great-grandchildren: Sidney and Zoe Harwell, Kayla and Ashley Hoover.

4.6.2.3.7.1 JOSEPH S. SCHWALM

4.6.2.3.7.2 WAYNE SAMUEL SCHWALM JR. also went by the name of SAM. He was born on 24 September 1945. He married WYNETTE DALE on 5 December 1970, Dallas, TX. Sam lives in Fort Worth, TX.

4.6.2.3.7.2.1 JENNIFER DALE SCHWALM was born on 6 October 1974, Denton County, TX. She married KELLY HOOVER.

4.6.2.3.7.2.1.1 KAYLA JENNIFER HOOVER

4.6.2.3.7.2.2 EMILY DAWN SCHWALM was born on 25 November 1976, Tarrant County, TX. She married JARRAD HARWELL. She married AARON MAY.

4.6.2.3.7.2.2.1 SIDNEY HARWELL

4.6.2.3.7.2.2.2 ZOE HARWELL

4.6.2.3.7.3 SANDRA LEE SCHWALM was born on 9 October 1950. Sandra lives in Weatherford, TX.

4.6.2.3.8 FRED JUNIOR SCHWALM was born on 22 March 1921. Some sources record that he was born on 22 March 1922. He was baptized on 14 October 1923, St. Andrew's United Methodist Church, Valley View, Schuylkill County, PA. He married **BESSIE MAY ENDERS**, daughter of **PHILLIP ELLSWORTH ENDERS** and **CARRIE (--?--),** on 13 April 1952, St. Andrew's Church, Valley View, Schuylkill County, PA. Fred lives in Valley View, PA.

4.6.2.3.8.1 JOSEPH SAMUEL SCHWALM was born on 26 February 1953. He was baptized on 5 April 1953, St. Andrew's United Methodist Church, Valley View, Schuylkill County, PA. He married **LINDA (--?--).**

4.6.2.3.8.2 DANIEL CALVIN SCHWALM was born on 15 June 1954. He was baptized on 12 September 1954, St. Andrew's United Methodist Church, Valley View, Schuylkill County, PA. He married **KAREN L. FESIG**.

4.6.2.3.8.2.1 MATTHEW SCHWALM was born in 1978. He married **ASHLEY HINKEL** on 16 June 2007, Saint Andrews United Methodist Church, Valley View, Schuylkill County, PA.

4.6.2.3.8.2.2 ADAM SCHWALM was born on 21 January 1984, Good Samaritan Regional Medical Center, Pottsville, Schuylkill County, PA.

4.6.2.3.8.3 AARON FRANKLIN SCHWALM was born on 15 February 1958. He was baptized on 13 April 1958, St. Andrew's United Methodist Church, Valley View, Schuylkill County, PA. He married **DUANE KEHLER**. He married **BONNIE LUDWIG**, daughter of **ROBERT LUDWIG** and **MARJORIE (--?--)**.

4.6.2.3.8.3.1 MICHAEL B. SCHWALM was born on 12 April 1977.

4.6.2.3.8.3.2 JAMES SCHWALM was born on 22 October 1987.

4.6.2.3.8.4 SAMUEL E. SCHWALM was born on 10 September 1959. He married **ROBIN SEAHOLTZ**, daughter of **PAUL SEAHOLTZ** and **BARBARA HOFER**. He and **ROBIN SEAHOLTZ** were divorced.

4.6.2.3.8.4.1 STU SCHWALM was born in 1978.

4.6.2.3.8.4.2 NATHANIEL SCHWALM was born circa 1980. He married **ASHLEY BARGE** in 2008.

4.6.2.3.9 JUNE HELEN SCHWALM was born on 10 January 1924, Valley View, Schuylkill County, PA. She was baptized on 31 October 1924, St. Andrew's United Methodist Church, Valley View, Schuylkill County, PA. She married **EDWARD J. CURRAN SR.**, son of **JAMES F. CURRAN** and **FLORENCE CATHERINE BOWES**. She died on 14 September 2004, Lower Buck Hospital, Bristol Township, Bucks County, PA, at age 80. She was buried on 20 September 2004, at Whitemarsh Memorial Park, Ambler, Montgomery County, PA.

4.6.2.3.9.1 EDWARD J. CURRAN JR. married **MARIE J. DIGUILIO**.

4.6.2.3.9.1.1 EDWARD E. CURRAN

4.6.2.3.9.1.2 REGINA L. CURRAN

4.6.2.3.9.2 KIM CURRAN married **JEFF PELTZ**.

4.6.2.3.9.3 ROBIN A. CURRAN married **BILL MCMANUS**.

4.6.2.3.9.4 SUSAN J. CURRAN married **RON RICHARDSON**.

4.6.2.3.9.5 PATRICIA J. CURRAN was born on 28 October 1948, Philadelphia, Philadelphia County, PA. She married **JOHN PASCHLEY**. She married **CHARLES FRANCIS MERIANO SR.** circa 2005. She died on 29 April 2012, at age 63. She was buried at Washington Crossing National Cemetery, Newtown, Bucks County, PA.

4.6.2.3.9.5.1 CHRISTINE PASCHLEY married **JIM CREIGHTON**.

4.6.2.3.9.5.2 CATHLEEN J. PASCHLEY married **(--?--) HOROWITZ**.

4.6.2.3.9.5.3 JAN MARIE PASCHLEY married **(--?--) ZEMITIS**.

4.6.2.3.10 BRUCE ELVIN SCHWALM was born on 19 February 1925, Valley View, Schuylkill County, PA. He was baptized on 17 April 1927, St. Andrew's United Methodist Church, Valley View, Schuylkill County, PA. He married **HILDEGARD SABLOTNY**. Bruce lives in Petersburg, VA.

4.6.2.3.10.1 FRANK E. SCHWALM

4.6.2.3.10.2 TIMOTHY A. SCHWALM married JANET (--?--).

4.6.2.3.10.2.1 KRISTEN L. SCHWALM was born on 24 November 1994.

4.6.2.3.10.2.2 CAMERON A. SCHWALM was born on 18 March 1999.

4.6.2.3.10.3 HENRY A. SCHWALM was born circa 1949. He married CAROLYN (--?--). He died on 8 April 2014, Petersburg, VA.

4.6.2.3.10.3.1 JENNIE E. SCHWALM

4.6.2.3.10.3.2 REBECCA SCHWALM

4.6.2.4 CLARENCE WILLIAM SCHWALM was born on 2 August 1884, Hegins Township, Schuylkill County, PA. He married ANNA M. RYLAND circa 1915. He died on 2 November 1948, Shoemakersville, Berks County, PA, at age 64. He was buried on 6 November 1948, at Saint Andrews United Methodist Church, Valley View, Schuylkill County, PA.

4.6.2.5 LILLY AGNES SCHWALM was born on 18 December 1886. She died on 27 October 1893, at age 6. She was buried at St. Andrew's Church Cemetery, Valley View, Schuylkill County, PA.

4.6.2.6 MARY ALICE SCHWALM was born on 12 September 1891. She married JOHN HARRISON LAUDENSLAGER, son of CHARLES I. LAUDENSLAGER and CATHARINE AMANDA ROMBERGER, in 1913, Philadelphia, Philadelphia County, PA. She died in 1966. She was buried at St. Andrew's United Methodist Church Cemetery, Valley View, Schuylkill County, PA.

4.6.2.6.1 HERMAN SYLVESTER LAUDENSLAGER was born on 10 April 1913, Valley View, Schuylkill County, PA. He was baptized on 27 July 1913, St. Andrew's United Methodist Church, Valley View, Schuylkill County, PA. He died on 17 July 1915, Valley View, Schuylkill County, PA, at age 2. He was buried at St. Andrew's United Methodist Church Cemetery, Valley View, Schuylkill County, PA.

4.6.2.6.2 DORA KATHRYN LAUDENSLAGER was born on 2 July 1916, Valley View, Schuylkill County, PA. She was baptized on 1 June 1919, St. Andrew's United Methodist Church, Valley View, Schuylkill County, PA. She married ROBERT L. BLAIR on 17 January 1942, St. Andrew's United Methodist Church, Valley View, Schuylkill County, PA. She died on 20 September 2005, Good Samaritan Hospital, Lebanon, Lebanon County, PA, at age 89. She was buried at St. Andrews Cemetery, Valley View, Schuylkill County, PA.

4.6.2.6.2.1 MARY ALICE BLAIR was born on 3 December 1943. She was baptized on 5 March 1944, St. Andrew's United Methodist Church, Valley View, Schuylkill County, PA. She married DANIEL HERNER.

4.6.2.6.2.1.1 DANIELLE HERNER

4.6.2.6.2.1.2 HEIDI HERNER

4.6.2.6.2.2 JANET LEE BLAIR was born on 30 October 1951. She was baptized on 3 February 1952, St. Andrew's United Methodist Church, Valley View, Schuylkill County, PA. She married LARRY MILLER.

4.6.2.6.2.2.1 SHANE MILLER

4.6.2.6.2.2.2 TRAVIS MILLER

4.6.2.6.3 MARY JEAN LAUDENSLAGER was born on 20 December 1917, Valley View, Schuylkill County, PA. She was baptized on 1 June 1919, St. Andrew's United Methodist Church, Valley View, Schuylkill County, PA. She married GEORGE WILLIAM FRONK, son of GEORGE FRONK and OLIVE RICHARDS, on 25 December 1938, St. Andrew's United Methodist Church, Valley View, Schuylkill County, PA. She died on 18 June 2014, Schuylkill Medical Center-East Norwegian Street, Pottsville, Schuylkill County, PA, at age 96. She was buried on 21 June 2014, at St. Andrew's United Methodist Church Cemetery, Valley View, Schuylkill County, PA.

4.6.2.6.3.1 ANN LOUISE FRONK was born on 20 October 1939. She was baptized on 24 August 1940, St. Andrew's United Methodist Church, Valley View, Schuylkill County, PA. She married WARREN H. KLINGER on 15 June 1957, St. Andrew's Church, Valley View, Schuylkill County, PA. She married PETER SCHILIRO. Ann lives in Warrington, PA.

4.6.2.6.3.1.1 TIMOTHY KLINGER married WENDY (--?--).

4.6.2.6.3.1.1.1 BRITTANY KLINGER

4.6.2.6.3.1.2 JEFFREY KLINGER married SANDRA (--?--).

4.6.2.6.3.1.2.1 JUSTIN KLINGER

4.6.2.6.3.1.2.2 KATELYN KLINGER

4.6.2.6.3.1.3 JANICE KLINGER

4.6.2.6.3.1.4 JEAN KLINGER

4.6.2.6.3.1.5 JAMES KLINGER

4.6.2.6.3.2 JOHN LAMAR FRONK was born on 6 January 1943. He was baptized on 5 February 1944, St. Andrew's United Methodist Church, Valley View, Schuylkill County, PA. He married DIANE (--?--). He married ELIZABETH PICCOLO. John lives in Millersburg, PA.

4.6.2.6.3.2.1 JENNA FRONK was born in 1980.

4.6.2.6.3.3 JANICE MARIE FRONK was born on 13 December 1946. She was baptized on 27 September 1947, St. Andrew's United Methodist Church, Valley View, Schuylkill County, PA. She married GARY HODGE. Janice lives in Camarillo, CA.

4.6.2.6.3.3.1 AMBER HODGE

4.6.2.6.3.3.2 SEAN HODGE

4.6.2.6.3.4 JEAN MARY FRONK was born on 9 January 1948. She was baptized on 11 November 1950, St. Andrew's United Methodist Church, Valley View, Schuylkill County, PA. She married JACK L. HERB, son of JOHN L. HERB and MARTHA FRANCIS SHADE.

4.6.2.6.3.4.1 AMANDA HERB married MATHEW HOROSCHAK in December 2006, St. Andrew's United Methodist Church, Valley View, Schuylkill County, PA. Amanda is an elementary school teacher in the Blue Mountain School District, while her husband Matthew is a science and math teacher in the Schuylkill Haven Area School District.

4.6.2.6.3.4.2 NICHOLE HERB married MICHAEL POLETTI.

4.6.2.6.3.4.2.1 AVA GRACE POLETTI was born on 1 March 2007.

4.6.2.6.3.4.3 JULIE HERB

4.6.2.6.3.5 JAMES W. FRONK was born on 11 September 1954, Pottsville, Schuylkill County, PA. He married DIANE (--?--) circa 1996. He died on 11 June 2011, Orlando, FL, at age 56. According to a newspaper obituary, James, who lived in Orlando, FL, was a 1971 graduate of Tri-Valley High School and a 1975 graduate of Kutztown University. After teaching sixth grade science and math at Upper Dauphin Area Middle School, he then became a pilot and taught flying lessons at Reading Airport. He later was employed as a pilot for USAir, Delta Airlines, and was a captain for Jet Blue, until becoming ill. He was buried on 18 June 2011, at Woodlawn Memorial Park, Gotha, FL.

4.6.2.6.3.5.1 JAMES FRONK

4.6.2.6.3.5.2 JOSEPH FRONK

4.6.2.6.3.5.3 SAMANTHA FRONK married RAY KNOWLES. Samantha and her brothers all live in Florida.

4.6.2.6.3.5.3.1 ANDREW KNOWLES

4.6.2.6.3.5.3.2 JACK KNOWLES

4.6.2.6.4 HELEN MARIE LAUDENSLAGER is also referred to as MARIE H. LAUDENSLAGER in some sources. She was born on 6 January 1921, Valley View, Schuylkill County, PA. She was baptized on 5 January 1924, St. Andrew's United Methodist Church, Valley View, Schuylkill County, PA. "Marie" served in the US Navy from 1942 until 1946. She married LEWIS LIEBERT JR., son of LEWIS LIEBERT and EMMA (--?--), on 25 September 1949, St. Andrew's United Methodist Church, Valley View, Schuylkill County, PA. She died on 8 September 1994, Hershey, Dauphin County, PA, at age 73. She was buried at Grand View Memorial Park, Annville, Lebanon County, PA.

4.6.2.6.4.1 DIANE MARIE LEIBERT was born on 23 December 1950. She was baptized on 29 April 1951, St. Andrew's United Methodist Church, Valley View, Schuylkill County, PA. She married THOMAS BLOUCH.

4.6.2.6.4.1.1 CHRISTINE BLOUCH

4.6.2.6.4.1.2 JASON BLOUCH

4.6.2.6.4.2 PATRICIA ANN LEIBERT was born on 16 June 1952. She was baptized on 21 December 1952, St. Andrew's United Methodist Church, Valley View, Schuylkill County, PA. She married **JERRY BOWMAN**.

> **4.6.2.6.4.2.1 KIM BOWMAN**
>
> **4.6.2.6.4.2.2 STEVEN BOWMAN**

4.6.2.6.4.3 KATHRYN I. LEIBERT was born circa 1957. She married **BRUCE GALLI**.

> **4.6.2.6.4.3.1 ALYNA GALLI**
>
> **4.6.2.6.4.3.2 LEWIS GALLI**
>
> **4.6.2.6.4.3.3 ALEXANDER GALLI**

4.6.2.6.5 LENORE MAY LAUDENSLAGER was born on 20 April 1923, Valley View, Schuylkill County, PA. She was baptized on 5 January 1924, St. Andrew's United Methodist Church, Valley View, Schuylkill County, PA. She married **JAMES EARL LEBO JR.**, son of **JAMES EARL LEBO** and **IRENE F. HERROLD**. She died on 26 July 2004, Hyman Caplan Pavilion, Lebanon, Lebanon County, PA, at age 81. She was buried on 30 July 2004, at Gravel Hill Cemetery, Palmyra, Lebanon County, PA.

> **4.6.2.6.5.1 LINDA I. LEBO** married **EDWARD MOFFET**.
>
>> **4.6.2.6.5.1.1 DAVID AARON MOFFET**
>>
>> **4.6.2.6.5.1.2 ERIC ADAM MOFFET**
>>
>> **4.6.2.6.5.1.3 ALEX EDWARDE MOFFET**
>
> **4.6.2.6.5.2 KATHRYN L. LEBO** married **SAMUEL S. CHAMBERS JR.**
>
>> **4.6.2.6.5.2.1 SAMUEL JAMES CHAMBERS**
>
> **4.6.2.6.5.3 JAMES ROBERT LEBO** married **KATE V. HANNON**.
>
>> **4.6.2.6.5.3.1 THEISEN JAMES LEBO**

4.6.2.7 TILLIE I. SCHWALM was born on 22 November 1894. She married **JAMES STUTZMAN**, son of **JOEL STUTZMAN** and **AMANDA ZERBE**. She married **HARRISON UPDEGRAVE**, son of **EDWARD UPDEGRAVE** and **AMANDA BIXLER**, after 1930. She died in August 1970, at age 75. She was buried at Saint Andrews United Methodist Church Cemetery, Valley View, Schuylkill County, PA.

> **4.6.2.7.1 LEROY J. STUTZMAN** was born on 5 November 1914, Valley View, Schuylkill County, PA. He married **MABEL GRACE SCHWALM**, daughter of **HARVEY EDWARD SCHWALM** and **MARY ALICE KLINGER**, on 5 June 1938, St. Andrew's Church, Valley View, Schuylkill County, PA. Prior to his death, Leroy was living at 1244 West Main Street, Valley View, Schuylkill County, PA. He died on 3 August 1995, Good Samaritan Regional Medical Center, Pottsville, Schuylkill County, PA, at age 80. He was buried on 6 August 1995, at St. Andrew's Cemetery, Valley View, Hegins Township, Schuylkill County, PA.
>
>> **4.6.2.7.1.1 JAMES LEROY STUTZMAN** was born on 5 November 1938. He was baptized on 21 January 1939, Saint Andrews United Methodist Church, Valley View, Schuylkill County, PA. He married **HILLDEGARD WENDT**, daughter of **FRANZ WENDT** and **KATRINA (--?--)**.
>>
>>> **4.6.2.7.1.1.1 ELKE BRIGGITTA STUTZMAN** was born on 3 December 1960, Pottsville, Schuylkill County, PA. She married **SCOTT ISENBERG**.
>>>
>>>> **4.6.2.7.1.1.1.1 CHANDRA LYNNE ISENBERG** was born on 15 April 1984.
>>>>
>>>> **4.6.2.7.1.1.1.2 BRITT CHARLES ISENBERG** was born on 3 January 1986, Holy Spirit Hospital, Camp Hill, Cumberland County, PA.
>>>>
>>>> **4.6.2.7.1.1.1.3 DUSTIN JAMES ISENBERG** was born on 3 January 1986, Holy Spirit Hospital, Camp Hill, Cumberland County, PA.
>>>
>>> **4.6.2.7.1.1.2 STEFANIE SUE STUTZMAN** is also referred to as **STEFANIE** in some sources. She was born on 21 January 1974, Holy Spirit Hospital, Camp Hill, Cumberland County, PA. She married **RAMEY FEIDT**, son of **WILLIAM FEIDT** and **JEAN (--?--)**.
>>>
>>>> **4.6.2.7.1.1.2.1 STELLA ROSE FEIDT** was born on 18 May 2009, Harrisburg Hospital, Harrisburg, Dauphin County, PA.
>>
>> **4.6.2.7.1.2 JOEL FRED STUTZMAN** was born on 17 May 1941, Valley View, Schuylkill County, PA. He was baptized on 24 August 1941, St Andrew's United Methodist Church,

Valley View, Schuylkill County, PA. He married **CAROL ANN WILLIER**, daughter of **ALBERT F. WILLIER** and **TILLIE ROSE KAHLER**.

4.6.2.7.1.2.1 **STEVEN JOEL STUTZMAN** was born on 1 June 1960, Schuylkill County, PA. He married **KYRA J. VANDERGRIFT** on 27 March 1993, Trinity United Church of Christ, East Petersburg, PA. He died on 25 March 2016, Heart of Lancaster Regional Medical Center, Lititz, Lancaster County, PA, at age 55.

4.6.2.7.1.2.1.1 **ALYSSA LYNN STUTZMAN** was born on 21 August 2000.

4.6.2.7.1.2.2 **JAMES SCOTT STUTZMAN** was born on 27 July 1964. He married **MARGO DELLINGER**. He married **KERRY (--?--)**.

4.6.2.7.1.2.2.1 **DANIEL J. STUTZMAN** was born on 27 August 1988.

4.6.2.7.1.2.3 **JULIE ANN STUTZMAN** was born on 28 November 1970. She married **JEFFREY MILNE**, son of **GERALD MILNE** and **BONNIE (--?--)**. In 2001, Julie was living in Chester Springs, PA.

4.6.2.7.1.2.3.1 **KENZIE MARIE MILNE** was born on 5 June 2001, Paoli Memorial Hospital, Paoli, PA.

4.6.2.7.1.2.4 **JOEL ANDREW STUTZMAN** was born on 21 May 1975, Pottsville, Schuylkill County, PA. He married **SANTINA GATTO**, daughter of **TOM GATTO** and **YVONNE (--?--)**.

4.6.2.7.1.2.4.1 **JOEL ETHAN STUTZMAN** was born on 1 February 2008.

4.6.2.7.1.2.5 **EDWARD STUTZMAN** was born circa 1977.

4.6.2.7.1.3 **EDWARD KEITH STUTZMAN** was born on 25 April 1947, Valley View, Schuylkill County, PA. He married **CYNTHIA LOU HOFFMAN**, daughter of **WILLIAM RICHARD HOFFMAN** and **MARIAN RICE STUTZMAN**, circa 1958. He died on 5 September 2013, Arden Courts, Harrisburg, Dauphin County, PA, at age 66.

4.6.2.7.1.3.1 **MELISSA J. STUTZMAN** was born on 12 January 1969, Holy Spirit Hospital, Camp Hill, Cumberland County, PA.

4.6.2.7.1.3.2 **TIMOTHY EDWARD STUTZMAN** was born on 21 March 1974, Holy Spirit Hospital, Camp Hill, Cumberland County, PA.

4.6.2.7.2 **LILLIAN I. STUTZMAN** was born on 19 September 1915. She married **RUSSEL CONWELL REIDER**, son of **BENJAMIN F. REIDER** and **AMANDA E. (--?--)**. She died on 22 December 2007, at age 92. According to Social Security listings, Lillian's "last residence" was Daytona Beach, Volusia County, FL, while she received her last Social Security benefit in Spring City, Chester County, PA. She was buried at Highland Memorial Park, Pottstown, Montgomery County, PA.

4.6.2.7.2.1 **LILLIAN RIDER**

4.6.2.7.2.2 **RUSSELL C. RIDER** was born circa 1932.

4.6.2.7.2.2.1 **JUDITH RIDER**

4.6.2.7.2.2.2 **RUSSELL RIDER**

4.6.2.7.2.2.3 **MICHAEL RIDER**

4.6.2.7.2.3 **JAMES F. RIDER** was born circa 1933.

4.6.2.7.2.3.1 **PATRICIA RIDER**

4.6.2.7.2.3.2 **JAMIE RIDER**

4.6.2.7.2.3.3 **KIMBERLY RIDER**

4.6.2.7.2.3.4 **BRIGIT RIDER**

4.6.2.7.2.3.5 **HILLARY RIDER**

4.6.2.7.2.4 **WILLIAM L. RIDER** was born circa 1935.

4.6.2.7.2.4.1 **TYRUS RIDER**

4.6.2.7.2.4.2 **TRACEY RIDER**

4.6.2.7.2.4.3 **RANDALL RIDER**

4.6.2.7.2.5 **JOHN L. RIDER** was born circa 1937.

4.6.2.7.2.5.1 **SAMUEL RIDER**

4.6.2.7.2.5.2 JILL RIDER

4.6.2.7.3 LLOYD MONROE STUTZMAN was born on 13 November 1916. He married HILDA ALVERTA KNORR, daughter of CLARENCE RAYMOND KNORR and ALVERTA HILDA SNYDER, on 7 October 1940, Maryland. He died on 17 March 1998, Hershey Medical Center, Dauphin County, PA, at age 81. He was buried at Frieden's Church Cemetery, Hegins, Schuylkill County, PA.

4.6.2.7.3.1 LAMAR L. STUTZMAN married ELIZABETH A. SCHROPE, daughter of PAUL SIMON SCHROPE SR. and IRENE A. HUNTZINGER. Lamar lives in Lebanon, PA.

4.6.2.7.3.1.1 ERIC L. STUTZMAN

4.6.2.7.3.1.2 INGRID A. STUTZMAN

4.6.2.7.3.2 BARBARA A. STUTZMAN married ROGER WETZEL, son of NELSON O. WETZEL and KATHRYN HEIM. Barbara lives in Valley View, PA.

4.6.2.7.3.2.1 KRIS ALAN WETZEL married KRISTA L. CLARK, daughter of ROBERT CLARK and CYNTHIA (--?--), on 30 May 1998, St. Andrew's United Methodist Church, Valley View, Schuylkill County, PA.

4.6.2.7.3.2.1.1 KADEN ALAN WETZEL was born on 3 February 2003.

4.6.2.7.3.2.1.2 KAMERON ALAN WETZEL was born on 3 January 2005, Harrisburg Hospital, Harrisburg, Dauphin County, PA.

4.6.2.7.3.2.2 MISTI WETZEL married KENT CONWAY, son of CLARK CONWAY and JOAN (--?--), on 6 December 2003, Christ United Methodist Church, Lansdale, PA.

4.6.2.7.3.3 GARY STUTZMAN married AHE (--?--).

4.6.2.7.3.4 DEBRA K. STUTZMAN married ERNEST WERTZ, son of KAY WERTZ and ALICE (--?--). She married JOHN STIELY. Debra lives in Elizabethville, PA.

4.6.2.7.3.4.1 JEFFREY WERTZ married MICHELLE KRAMMES.

4.6.2.7.3.4.1.1 DEVIN RAY WERTZ was born on 3 November 2003.

4.6.2.7.3.4.2 MICHAEL WERTZ married JENNIFER HUNTZINGER, daughter of CRAIG HUNTZINGER and JEAN KLOCK, on 26 December 1998, St. Paul's Lutheran Church, Millersburg, Dauphin County, PA.

4.6.2.7.3.4.2.1 JILLIAN MIKAYLA WERTZ was born on 22 February 2005, Harrisburg Hospital, Harrisburg, Dauphin County, PA.

4.6.2.7.3.4.2.2 BRODY MICHAEL WERTZ was born on 12 August 2009, Harrisburg Hospital, Harrisburg, Dauphin County, PA.

4.6.2.7.3.4.2.3 AVERY JEAN WERTZ was born on 12 August 2009, Harrisburg Hospital, Harrisburg, Dauphin County, PA.

4.6.2.7.4 FRANK J. STUTZMAN was born on 22 March 1918, Valley View, Schuylkill County, PA. He married BETTY DEEMER. Prior to his death, Frank was living at 209 McKinley Ave., Reading, Berks County, PA. He died on 5 November 1993, Berks County Home-Berks Heim, Bern Township, Berks County, PA, at age 75. He was buried on 9 November 1993, at Gethsemane Cemetery, Hyde Park, Berks County, PA.

4.6.2.7.5 FRANCES ISABEL UPDEGRAVE was born on 19 January 1931, Valley View, Schuylkill County, PA. She married FORREST IRVIN HERB on 30 June 1951, Valley View, Schuylkill County, PA. She died on 29 November 2012, Holy Spirit Hospital, Camp Hill, Cumberland County, PA, at age 81. According to a newspaper obituary, Frances, who lived in Valley View, PA, was a seamstress in local garment factories prior to her retirement. She was buried on 4 December 2012, at St. Andrew's United Methodist Church Cemetery, Valley View, Schuylkill County, PA.

4.6.2.7.5.1 THOMAS R. HERB married LISA KOLVA, daughter of GALEN KOLVA and ARLENE (--?--). Thomas lives in Lewisberry, PA.

4.6.2.7.5.1.1 BRYSON THOMAS HERB was born on 2 April 1997.

4.6.2.7.5.2 JACK S. HERB married TINA CHARTIS. Jack lives in Harrisburg, PA.

4.6.2.7.5.2.1 NICHOLAS THOMAS HERB was born on 23 November 1987. He married KATHLEEN RUTH ELLIS, daughter of DAVID ELLIS, on 11 October 2014, Grace United Methodist Church, Millersburg, Dauphin County, PA.

4.6.2.7.5.3 DIANE LOUISE HERB was born on 10 August 1957, Pottsville, Schuylkill County, PA. She married **HAROLD PAUL ROMBERGER**, son of **HAROLD C. ROMBERGER** and **ORPAH NAOMI SCHWALM,** on 25 June 1983, Saint Andrews United Methodist Church, Valley View, Schuylkill County, PA. Diane lives in Valley View, PA.

4.6.2.7.5.3.1 DANIEL JAMES ROMBERGER was born on 28 October 1991.

4.6.2.7.5.3.2 ALEXA DIANNE ROMBERGER was born on 12 March 1999, Pottsville Hospital, Pottsville, Schuylkill County, PA.

4.6.2.7.5.4 BARBARA ANN HERB was born circa 1968. She married **JOHN GARRET WOLFGANG**, son of **JOHN R. WOLFGANG** and **EMMA (--?--),** on 27 June 1992.

4.6.2.7.5.4.1 JARED MICHAEL WOLFGANG was born on 4 March 1992.

4.6.2.7.6 LUCILLE MARIE UPDEGRAVE was born on 23 July 1934, Valley View, Schuylkill County, PA. She married **DONALD FRANKLIN GEIST**, son of **GUY GEIST** and **BEULAH WIEST,** circa 1955. She died on 17 November 2009, Tremont Health and Rehabilitation Center, Tremont, Schuylkill County, PA, at age 75. According to a newspaper obituary, After graduating from Hegins Township High School and McCann School of Business, Pottsville, Lucille and her husband owned and operated the former Valley Home Center. She had also been employed as a bookkeeper for the former Starr's Poultry and the former Starr's Hardware, both of Valley View. She was buried on 20 November 2009, at Saint Andrews United Methodist Church Cemetery, Valley View, Schuylkill County, PA.

4.6.2.7.6.1 LUANN M. GEIST married **GARY CARPENTER**.

4.6.2.7.6.1.1 DAVID G. CARPENTER

4.6.2.7.6.2 WILLIAM D. GEIST was born on 4 December 1958, Pottsville, Schuylkill County, PA. He married **ROBYN M. HOFFMAN**, daughter of **WILLIAM RICHARD HOFFMAN** and **MARIAN ALICE STUTZMAN,** circa 1978. He died on 2 August 2013, Reading, Berks County, PA, at age 54.

4.6.2.7.6.2.1 KRISTI L. GEIST married **THOMAS DUFFY.**

4.6.2.7.6.2.1.1 NOAH DUFFY

4.6.2.7.6.2.2 ANGELA M. GEIST

4.6.2.7.6.2.2.1 BRYCE GEIST

4.6.2.7.6.2.3 AMY L. GEIST married (--?--) **LISK**.

4.6.2.7.6.2.4 MANDY L. GEIST married (--?--) **BELL**.

4.6.2.8 JOHN JACOB SCHWALM was born on 29 April 1899, Valley View, Schuylkill County, PA. He married **ELSIE MAE NEY**, daughter of **WILLIAM NEY** and **ELIZABETH MILLER**. John owned and operated Schwalm's Bakery in Tremont, Schuylkill County, PA, for 30 years. John and Elsie had no children. He died on 21 October 1983, Tremont, Schuylkill County, PA, at age 84. He was buried on 24 October 1983, at Church of God Cemetery, Valley View, Schuylkill County, PA.

4.6.3 HARRISON MONROE SCHWALM was born in 1855. He married **MARGARET SPOHN**, daughter of **PETER SPOHN** and **CATHERINE (--?--)**. He died in 1922. He was buried at Olive Cemetery, Wakarusa, Elkhart County, IN.

4.6.3.1 CLARA ALICE SCHWALM was born on 25 May 1877. She married **ELMER BOWERS**, son of **JACOB BOWERS** and **MARTHA ANN (--?--),** on 10 January 1895, St. Joseph County, IN. She died on 4 June 1953, Goshen, Elkhart County, IN, at age 76. She was buried at Olive Cemetery, Wakarusa, Elkhart County, IN.

4.6.3.1.1 UNA M. BOWERS was born in 1895. She married **NOBLE SEARER**, son of **GEORGE W. SEARER** and **SUSAN WEBER,** in 1918. She died in 1974. She was buried at Olive Cemetery, Wakarusa, Elkhart County, IN.

4.6.3.1.1.1 NOBLE SEARER JR. married **MARTHA SCHNORR**.

4.6.3.1.1.1.1 EVALINE SEARER

4.6.3.1.1.1.2 FRANK SEARER

4.6.3.1.1.1.3 MICHELLE SEARER

4.6.3.1.1.2 NORMAN J. SEARER married **ABLGRIN (--?--).**

4.6.3.1.1.2.1 NORMAN J. SEARER JR.

4.6.3.1.1.2.2 GARY SEARER

4.6.3.1.1.2.3 KATHY SEARER

4.6.3.1.1.2.4 DAVID SEARER

4.6.3.1.1.2.5 LORI ANN SEARER

4.6.3.1.1.3 HERMAN SEARER died before 9 October 2005.

4.6.3.1.1.4 AUDREY BERNICE SEARER is also referred to as **AUDREY ELIZABETH SEARER** in some sources. She was born on 18 January 1921, Harrison Township, Elkhart County, IN. She married **LOWELL DEAN BERGER**, son of **HERMAN BERGER** and **GLADY YOCKEY,** on 9 August 1945, Newport, Newport County, RI. She died on 3 June 2013, Elkhart General Hospital, Elkhart, Elkhart County, IN, at age 92. She was buried on 8 June 2013, at Bremen Municipal Cemetery, Bremen, Marshall County, IN.

4.6.3.1.1.4.1 GEORGE BERGER married **DIANN WISNIEWSKI.**

4.6.3.1.1.4.2 MARK BERGER married **FRAN (--?--).**

4.6.3.1.1.4.3 THOMAS ALLEN BERGER was born on 15 March 1949, Elkhart, Elkhart County, IN. He married **JEAN ELLEN PARKS** on 26 April 1969, Elkhart, Elkhart County, IN. He died on 12 June 2002, at age 53.

4.6.3.1.1.4.3.1 MICHAEL BERGER

4.6.3.1.1.5 KEITH SEARER was born on 19 June 1923, Baugo Township, Elkhart County, IN. He died on 11 October 2005, Miller's Merry Manor, Columbia City, Whitley County, IN, at age 82. He was buried on 13 October 2005, at Olive Cemetery, Wakarusa, Elkhart County, IN.

4.6.3.1.1.6 RICHARD OWEN SEARER was born on 3 November 1925, Mishawaka, St. Joseph County, IN. He married **RUTH MAXINE LEONARD**, daughter of **WALTER C. LEONARD** and **CARRIE WHITAKER,** circa 1960, Mishawaka, St. Joseph County, IN. He died on 17 July 2014, Morning View Health Care Facility, South Bend, St. Joseph County, IN, at age 88.

4.6.3.1.1.6.1 RICHARD OWEN SEARER JR. married **AMY (--?--).**

4.6.3.1.1.6.2 CAROLINE K. SEARER married **DAVE ANGLEMYER.**

4.6.3.1.1.6.3 ROBERT E. SEARER married **GLENDA GOINS.**

4.6.3.1.1.7 MAX NEWELL SEARER was born on 30 March 1928. He married **LOUISE ALFONSINE VANDAMME**, daughter of **LOUIS VANDAMME** and **MARGARET DEBOE,** in July 1948, Mishawaka, St. Joseph County, IN.

4.6.3.1.1.7.1 KAREN SEARER

4.6.3.1.1.8 ROBERT CARLISLE SEARER was born on 10 November 1930, South Bend, St. Joseph County, IN. He married **MARLENE HOWELL**. He married **BETTY J. WELLS** on 6 July 1979, Hobart, Lake County, IN.

4.6.3.1.1.8.1 ROBERT SEARER

4.6.3.1.1.8.2 JAMES SEARER

4.6.3.1.1.8.3 JOHN SEARER

4.6.3.1.2 CLEM HERMAN BOWERS was born on 23 December 1897, St. Joseph County, IN. He married **PEARL SUMMERS** on 28 September 1919, Elkhart County, IN. He married **CECIL MARIE WHITEHEAD**, daughter of **SAMUEL E. WHITEHEAD** and **DOSHIA PETERS,** in June 1928. He died on 27 June 1984, Goshen, Elkhart County, IN, at age 86. He was buried at New Paris Cemetery, New Paris, Elkhart County, IN.

4.6.3.1.2.1 STILLBORN SON BOWERS was born on 20 October 1920, Baugo Township, Elkhart County, IN. He died on 20 October 1920, Baugo Township, Elkhart County, IN.

4.6.3.1.2.2 ELMER JUNIOR BOWERS was born on 28 March 1925, Jackson Township, Elkhart County, IN. He married **VIRGINIA RAE STRYKER**, daughter of **CLAYTON STRYKER** and **FAY ARNOLD**, on 17 October 1948. He died on 22 March 2014, St Joseph Regional Medical Center, Mishawaka, St. Joseph County, IN, at age 88. He was buried on 28 March 2014, at Violett Cemetery., Goshen, Elkhart County, IN.

4.6.3.1.2.2.1 STEPHEN EDWARD BOWERS married **JANE YODER.** He was born in 1951.

4.6.3.1.2.2.1.1 RYAN BOWERS

4.6.3.1.2.2.1.2 RACHEL BOWERS

4.6.3.1.2.2.2 PAUL EUGENE BOWERS was born in 1959. He married **LORI MOWAN.** He married **LUCINDA ANN SCHWALM**, daughter of **DEAN LAMAR SCHWALM** and **ANNA LUCINDA DOUMA,** on 22 December 1990, Goshen, Elkhart County, IN.

4.6.3.1.2.2.2.1 ERIN BOWERS

4.6.3.1.2.2.2.2 JENNIFER BOWERS

4.6.3.1.2.2.3 JOHN DAVID BOWERS was born in 1962.

4.6.3.1.2.3 PAUL EUGENE BOWERS was born on 10 August 1930. He married **BARBARA (--?--).** He died on 26 November 1958, at age 28. He was buried at New Paris Cemetery, New Paris, Elkhart County, IN.

4.6.3.1.2.3.1 MELODY BOWERS

4.6.3.1.2.3.2 TONI BOWERS

4.6.3.1.2.4 ANNA B. KENDALL was born circa 1922. Her father was Ralph S. Kendall. She married **(--?--) HINSHAW.** She died before 2 May 2015.

4.6.3.1.2.5 EILEEN ESTHER KENDALL was born on 31 December 1922, Elkhart County, IN. Her father was Ralph S. Kendall. She married **DEVON FORREST HIGGINS,** son of **ARTHUR HIGGINS** and **ROSA KITSON,** in June 1942.

4.6.3.1.2.6 PHILIP LAMAR BOWERS was born on 18 October 1932, Elkhart, Elkhart County, IN. He married **SHIRLEY J. HAHN** on 30 March 1952. He died on 2 May 2015, Miller's Merry Manor, Wakarusa, Elkhart County, IN, at age 82. He was buried on 6 May 2015, at Olive Cemetery, Wakarusa, Elkhart County, IN.

4.6.3.1.2.6.1 RICHIE BOWERS married **DEBORAH PRICE.**

4.6.3.1.2.6.1.1 SCOTT A. BOWERS

4.6.3.1.2.6.2 STEPHANIE BOWERS married **BOB MCGAUGHEY.**

4.6.3.1.2.6.3 RONSON S. BOWERS married **JULIE (--?--).**

4.6.3.1.2.7 CAROLINE ANN BOWERS was born on 25 August 1936, Goshen, Elkhart County, IN. She married **EVERETT MILLER.** She married **TONI BUNGER.**

4.6.3.1.2.7.1 PENNY MILLER

4.6.3.1.2.7.2 MICHAEL MILLER

4.6.3.1.2.7.3 MITCH MILLER

4.6.3.1.2.7.4 TODD MILLER

4.6.3.1.3 CLEO MAE BOWERS was born on 24 September 1899. She married **HUBERT VANCE,** son of **OWEN E. VANCE** and **LOVINA WEAVER,** in April 1924. She died on 29 April 1985, Goshen, Elkhart County, IN, at age 85.

4.6.3.1.3.1 ELISABETH VANCE married **ROBERT WEIDA.**

4.6.3.1.3.2 MARY LOUISE VANCE was born on 27 February 1925, Elkhart County, IN. She married **THOMAS ROBERT RIETHOF,** son of **HENRY RIETHOF** and **MARIE DEUTSCH,** in August 1949. She died on 4 October 2010, Harleysville, Montgomery County, PA, at age 85. She was buried at George Washington Memorial Park Cemetery, Plymouth Meeting, Montgomery County, PA.

4.6.3.1.4 HARRISON ELLSWORTH BOWERS was born on 12 March 1904. He married **FRIEDA LOUISE MILLER**, daughter of **AMOS S. MILLER** and **MAUDE M. RUPERT,** on 14 February 1926. He died on 22 May 1976, South Bend, St. Joseph County, IN, at age 72. He was buried at Union Center Cemetery, Nappanee, Elkhart County, IN.

4.6.3.1.4.1 DAVID LYLE BOWERS was born on 24 August 1934, Elkhart, Elkhart County, IN. He married **JOANNE M. TATE** on 21 July 1957, Shreve, Wayne County, OH. He died on 27 November 2015, Lebanon, Warren County, OH, at age 81. He was buried at Union Center Cemetery, Nappanee, Elkhart County, IN.

4.6.3.1.4.1.1 ROBIN JOAN BOWERS married **(--?--) BONNELL.**

4.6.3.1.4.1.2 SCOTT DAVID BOWERS married **SHERRIE (--?--).**

4.6.3.1.5 KATHRYN ELIZABETH BOWERS was born on 14 July 1909, Elkhart County, IN. She married **LEVI J. ARNOLD,** son of **CHARLES M. ARNOLD** and **SARAH J. BROWN,** on 8 June 1929,

Goshen, Elkhart County, IN. She died on 19 January 1988, Goshen, Elkhart County, IN, at age 78. She was buried at Violett Cemetery, Goshen, Elkhart County, IN.

> **4.6.3.1.5.1 GARY ARNOLD**
>
> **4.6.3.1.5.2 ELOINE KATHRYN ARNOLD** was born on 9 February 1909, Elkhart, Elkhart County, IN. She married **WAYNE THEOBALD**.
>
>> **4.6.3.1.5.2.1 MARK THEOBALD**
>>
>> **4.6.3.1.5.2.2 PETER THEOBALD**
>>
>> **4.6.3.1.5.2.3 AMY THEOBALD**
>
> **4.6.3.1.5.3 CAROL SUE ARNOLD** was born circa 1937. She married **ROBIN ROBERTS**.
>
>> **4.6.3.1.5.3.1 JULIA ROBERTS**
>>
>> **4.6.3.1.5.3.2 EILEEN C. ROBERTS**

4.6.3.1.6 RUTH NAOMI BOWERS was born on 28 June 1912, Olive Township, Elkhart County, IN. She married **WAYNE MONEYHEFFER**, son of **JACOB MONEYHEFFER** and **OMA NEWCOMER**, in October 1937. She died on 22 September 1971, New Paris, Elkhart County, IN, at age 59. She was buried at Whitehead Cemetery, New Paris, Elkhart County, IN.

> **4.6.3.1.6.1 MARGARET MONEYHEFFER** married **DALE LOVE**. She married **JOHN HUSTED**.
>
>> **4.6.3.1.6.1.1 GREGORY LOVE**
>>
>> **4.6.3.1.6.1.2 THOMAS LOVE**
>
> **4.6.3.1.6.2 DONALD MONEYHEFFER** married **BARBARA HAUSBERGER**.
>
>> **4.6.3.1.6.2.1 KIMBERLY MONEYHEFFER**
>>
>> **4.6.3.1.6.2.2 DEBORAH MONEYHEFFER**

4.6.3.2 SAMUEL FREMONT SCHWALM was born on 29 August 1879, St. Joseph County, IN. He married **EDNA HOOVER** on 21 December 1899. He died on 20 October 1940, Goshen, Elkhart County, IN, at age 61. He was buried at Olive Cemetery, Wakarusa, Elkhart County, IN.

> **4.6.3.2.1 GLETA BERNICE SCHWALM** was born on 11 April 1903. She married **JOHN GALEN WHITEHEAD**, son of **GEORGE A. WHITEHEAD** and **NETTIE NEFF,** in March 1924. She died on 15 November 1987, Goshen, Elkhart County, IN, at age 84. She was buried at Violett Cemetery, Goshen, Elkhart County, IN.
>
>> **4.6.3.2.1.1 WILLIAM DEAN WHITEHEAD** was born on 11 February 1925, New Paris, Elkhart County, IN. He married **MARCIA CRIPE**. He died on 16 May 2008, Indianapolis, Marion County, IN, at age 83. He was buried at Oaklawn Memorial Gardens, Fishers, Hamilton County, IN.
>>
>>> **4.6.3.2.1.1.1 CAMORA D. WHITEHEAD** married **PAUL AMOS**.
>>>
>>> **4.6.3.2.1.1.2 THOMAS M. WHITEHEAD** married **CINDY (--?--)**.
>>>
>>>> **4.6.3.2.1.1.2.1 TYLER WHITEHEAD**
>>>>
>>>> **4.6.3.2.1.1.2.2 SPENCER WHITEHEAD**
>>>>
>>>> **4.6.3.2.1.1.2.3 HILLARY WHITEHEAD**
>
>> **4.6.3.2.1.2 WAYNE SCHWALM WHITEHEAD** was born on 23 May 1926, New Paris, Elkhart County, IN. He married **GLORIA JUNE CART**, daughter of **CHESTER L. CART** and **MARIE BLANCHARD,** in November 1949.
>>
>>> **4.6.3.2.1.2.1 STEPHEN W. WHITEHEAD**
>>>
>>> **4.6.3.2.1.2.2 JANELL MARIE WHITEHEAD** married **(--?--) RINK**.
>
>> **4.6.3.2.1.3 DORIS EVELYN WHITEHEAD** was born on 31 December 1938, Goshen, Elkhart County, IN. She married **DEAN SPEICHER**.
>>
>>> **4.6.3.2.1.3.1 DONELLE SUE SPEICHER** was born circa 1967. She married **STEVEN LAWRENCE ZUNKER**, son of **LAWRENCE ZUNKER** and **MARY CHRISTINE (--?--),** on 31 December 2000, Osceola, Elkhart County, IN.

4.6.3.3 HARVEY W. SCHWALM was born on 22 January 1882, St. Joseph County, IN. He married **SUSIE MILLER**, daughter of **JOSIAH MILLER** and **MARY HOOVER**, on 20 January 1906. He died in 1922. He was buried at Yellow Creek Brick Cemetery, Southwest, Elkhart County, IN.

4.6.3.3.1 MERLE LAMAR SCHWALM was born on 16 February 1909, Wakarusa, Elkhart County, IN. He married **FLORENCE EDNA SHANK**, daughter of **JOHN SHANK** and **AGNES CHRISTOPHEL**, on 28 May 1927. He died on 23 January 2000, Goshen, Elkhart County, IN, at age 90. He was buried at Violett Cemetery, Goshen, Elkhart County, IN.

    4.6.3.3.1.1 DONNA JEAN SCHWALM was born on 19 September 1927, Goshen, Elkhart County, IN. She married **RICHARD ALAN KERCHER**, son of **OTIS KERCHER** and **GENEVIEVE WILLIAMS**, in August 1947. She married **HAROLD SCHROCK**.

        4.6.3.3.1.1.1 DAVID KERCHER married **MAXINE NOYES**.

        4.6.3.3.1.1.2 MARK KERCHER married **DENISE BURNS**.

            4.6.3.3.1.1.2.1 CHRISTOPHER KERCHER

        4.6.3.3.1.1.3 CRAIG KERCHER married **ANTOINETTA WEBB**.

    4.6.3.3.1.2 DEAN LAMAR SCHWALM was born on 23 July 1929, Goshen, Elkhart County, IN. He married **ANNA LUCINDA DOUMA** on 26 August 1953, Church of the Brethren, Goshen, Elkhart County, IN. He died on 27 November 2014, Goshen, Elkhart County, IN, at age 85.

        4.6.3.3.1.2.1 WYNN SCHWALM married **COLLEEN COY**. He married **JULIE (--?--)**.

            4.6.3.3.1.2.1.1 RYAN SCHWALM

        4.6.3.3.1.2.2 TIMOTHY SCHWALM married **BEVERLY FULWIDER**.

            4.6.3.3.1.2.2.1 WINSTON SCHWALM

        4.6.3.3.1.2.3 LUCINDA ANN SCHWALM married **PAUL EUGENE BOWERS**, son of **ELMER JUNIOR BOWERS** and **VIRGINIA RAE STRYKER**, on 22 December 1990, Goshen, Elkhart County, IN.

    4.6.3.3.1.3 JANE IRIS SCHWALM was born on 23 September 1932, Goshen, Elkhart County, IN. She married **ROBERT W. MILLER**.

        4.6.3.3.1.3.1 PAMELA MILLER married **KEVIN CRAIN**.

            4.6.3.3.1.3.1.1 ALLISON CRAIN

            4.6.3.3.1.3.1.2 JONATHAN ROBERT CRAIN is also referred to as **JACK** in some sources.

        4.6.3.3.1.3.2 TODD WESLEY MILLER

4.6.3.4 LIZZIE MAY SCHWALM was born on 15 September 1884, Olive Township, Elkhart County, IN. She married **ELMER EBY** on 13 December 1902. She died on 2 October 1966, Wakarusa, Elkhart County, IN, at age 82. She was buried at Olive Cemetery, Wakarusa, Elkhart County, IN.

    4.6.3.4.1 KERMIT RAY EBY was born on 21 September 1903, St. Joseph County, IN. He married **RETHA LEONE FISH**, daughter of **AMOS A. FISH** and **ANNA MAY KINDIG**, in June 1927. He died on 10 August 1962, at age 58. He was buried on 13 August 1962, at Olive Cemetery, Wakarusa, Elkhart County, IN.

        4.6.3.4.1.1 SYLVIA EBY married **BILL BAIRD**.

            4.6.3.4.1.1.1 BILLY BAIRD

            4.6.3.4.1.1.2 LYNN BAIRD

        4.6.3.4.1.2 DANIEL EBY married **GAIL (--?--)**.

            4.6.3.4.1.2.1 CURTIS EBY

        4.6.3.4.1.3 KERMIT RAY EBY JR. was born on 6 August 1931. He married **RUTH FESSELE** on 18 February 1954. He died on 18 October 2010, at age 79.

            4.6.3.4.1.3.1 KERMIT EBY III married **STEPHANIE (--?--)**.

            4.6.3.4.1.3.2 RETHELISA R. EBY married **FRANC ORTEGA**. She is also referred to as **LISA** in some sources.

            4.6.3.4.1.3.3 BETTINA L. EBY married **RICHARD COOL**.

    4.6.3.4.2 GRACE MARGARET EBY was born on 12 October 1905, St. Joseph County, IN. She married **RONALD FLOYD WORKMAN**, son of **COLUMBUS JAY WORKMAN** and **MAY ELIZABETH RICE**, in March 1930.

        4.6.3.4.2.1 DEAN WORKMAN married **RETTA ELKSINS**.

            4.6.3.4.2.1.1 DANNY WORKMAN

4.6.3.4.2.1.2 NANCY WORKMAN

4.6.3.4.2.1.3 NINA G. WORKMAN

4.6.3.4.2.2 DAVID WORKMAN married SHIRLEY (--?--).

4.6.3.4.2.2.1 MICHAEL WORKMAN

4.6.3.4.2.3 DONNA M. WORKMAN was born on 1 January 1932, Mount Vernon, Knox County, OH. She married NEIL STAATS on 23 August 1953. She died on 2 July 2013, Colonial Manor Health Care Center, Loudonville, Ashland County, OH, at age 81. She was buried on 8 July 2013, at Wesley Chapel Cemetery, Knox, Knox County, OH.

4.6.3.4.2.3.1 PAUL E. STAATS married MARY LOU (--?--).

4.6.3.4.2.3.1.1 DOUG STAATS married LINDSEY (--?--).

4.6.3.4.2.3.1.2 NATHAN STAATS married ANDREA (--?--).

4.6.3.4.2.3.2 DENISE STAATS married MARK O'DONELL.

4.6.3.4.2.3.2.1 GARRETT O'DONELL

4.6.3.4.2.4 RONALD WORKMAN was born circa 1935.

4.6.3.4.3 MIRIAM LUCILLE EBY was born on 22 September 1908. She died on 30 April 1984, Elkhart, Elkhart County, IN, at age 75. She was buried on 2 May 1984, at Olive Cemetery, Wakarusa, Elkhart County, IN. Miriam was a school teacher who never married.

4.6.3.4.4 MABEL HELEN EBY was born on 7 October 1913, St. Joseph County, IN. She married ARTHUR LAMAR PAULUS, son of RALPH LEROY PAULUS and TREVA VICTORIA PLETCHER, on 24 December 1934. She died on 22 September 1998, Elkhart, Elkhart County, IN, at age 84.

4.6.3.4.4.1 BYRON PAULUS married SUE WILDEN.

4.6.3.4.4.2 CAROLINE PAULUS married JACK JESSE.

4.6.3.4.4.2.1 JACLYN D. JESSE

4.6.3.4.4.2.2 JONATHAN E. JESSE

4.6.3.4.4.3 DONALD PAULUS married TANYA BAKER.

4.6.3.4.4.3.1 TRENA M. PAULUS

4.6.3.4.4.3.2 HEIDI E. PAULUS

4.6.3.4.4.4 DENNIS PAULUS married MARY (--?--).

4.6.3.4.4.5 CARL FREDERICK PAULUS was born on 16 July 1936, Elkhart, Elkhart County, IN. He married BARBARA MACK, daughter of CARL ALLEN MACK and BERNICE HYDE, on 7 October 1961.

4.6.3.4.4.5.1 TRACY L. PAULUS

4.6.3.4.4.5.2 TREVOR L. PAULUS married JENNIFER (--?--).

4.6.3.4.4.5.3 TARA L. PAULUS married JAMES MCGEHEE.

4.6.3.4.4.5.4 TAMRA PAULUS married ROBERT EICHELBERGER.

4.6.3.4.4.6 ROBERT DUANE PAULUS was born on 7 May 1944. He died on 29 June 1969, action by hostile fire, Quang Ting Province, Republic of Vietnam, at age 25. He was buried on 11 July 1969, at Olive Cemetery, Wakarusa, Elkhart County, IN.

4.6.3.4.4.7 MARILYN ELAINE PAULUS was born on 9 September 1946. She died on 9 September 1946. She was buried at Olive Cemetery, Wakarusa, Elkhart County, IN.

4.6.3.4.4.8 DAWN MARIE PAULUS was born on 1 January 1948. She died on 1 January 1948. She was buried at Olive Cemetery, Wakarusa, Elkhart County, IN.

4.6.3.4.5 ELMER LEONARD EBY was born on 30 September 1922, Wakarusa, Elkhart County, IN. He married ESTHER MARIE MILLER, daughter of CLETUS MILLER and CLARA FERRIEDA, in October 1943. He died on 10 April 1996, Wakarusa, Elkhart County, IN, at age 73. He was buried at Olive Cemetery, Wakarusa, Elkhart County, IN.

4.6.3.4.5.1 JUDY EBY married VICTOR DRAPEZA. She married LARRY LONG.

4.6.3.4.5.1.1 CHRISTINA DRAPEZA

4.6.3.4.5.1.2 DONA LONG

4.6.3.4.5.1.3 COREY LONG

4.6.3.4.5.2 DAVID EBY married **DENISE ERBAUGH**.

4.6.3.4.5.2.1 RYAN D. EBY

4.6.3.4.5.2.2 ALICIA R. EBY

4.6.3.4.5.3 JANICE EBY married **RICHARD SHIVLEY**.

4.6.3.5 VERNON FRANKLIN SCHWALM was born on 10 April 1887. He married **FLORENCE STUDEBAKER**. He died on 10 May 1972, North Manchester, Wabash County, IN, at age 85. He was buried on 13 May 1972, at Oaklawn Cemetery, North Manchester, Wabash County, IN.

4.6.3.5.1 BETTY SCHWALM married **ROBERT KIMMEL**. She was born circa 1920.

4.6.3.5.1.1 JUDY R. KIMMEL

4.6.3.5.1.2 PEGGY A. KIMMEL married **DAVID HOLLOWELL**.

4.6.3.5.1.3 JEAN L. KIMMEL married **GARY CONNALLY**.

4.6.3.6 GERTRUDE SCHWALM was born on 24 July 1893, St. Joseph County, IN. She married **GEORGE W. PHILIPS**, son of **LEWIS F. PHILIPS** and **ALICE MILLER**, in May 1917, North Manchester County, IN. She died on 18 June 1972, Goshen, Elkhart County, IN, at age 78. She was buried on 21 June 1972, at Rock Run Cemetery, Goshen, Elkhart County, IN.

4.6.3.6.1 DOROTHY MARIE PHILIPS was born on 28 June 1922, Walton, Cass County, IN. She married **PAUL W. HARRINGTON**, son of **HOVEY HARRINGTON** and **AUDREY CRUME**, on 20 November 1943, Elkhart, Elkhart County, IN. She and **PAUL W. HARRINGTON** were divorced in 1944 Dade County, FL. She married **DONALD LARSON**.

4.6.3.7 ARTHUR HARRISON SCHWALM was born on 14 January 1896. He married **MABEL SARAH HOMES**, daughter of **DAVID HOMES** and **ALMIRA LONG**, on 20 January 1915, Goshen, Elkhart County, IN. He married **HAZEL NAOMI HOREIN**, daughter of **GEORGE HOREIN** and **SARAH JANE WELDY**, before 1 April 1940. He died on 14 January 1980, Wakarusa, Elkhart County, IN, at age 84.

4.6.3.7.1 MARIE BERNICE SCHWALM was born on 1 April 1916, Elkhart County, IN. She married **WARREN DEVON HARTMAN**, son of **HARVEY HARTMAN** and **GEORGIA SEESE**, on 17 February 1940. She died on 20 February 2011, Miller's Merry Manor, Wakarusa, Elkhart County, IN, at age 94.

4.6.3.7.1.1 RUDY HARTMAN married **LAVONDA STAHLEY**.

4.6.3.7.1.1.1 MARK HARTMAN

4.6.3.7.1.1.2 TODD A. HARTMAN

4.6.3.7.1.2 MAX HARTMAN married **HELENE HOBART**. He married **BRENDA (--?--)**.

4.6.3.7.1.2.1 ANDREW HARTMAN

4.6.3.7.1.2.2 JOY HARTMAN

4.6.3.7.1.3 TOM HARTMAN married **JOYCE (--?--)**.

4.6.3.7.1.3.1 JENNIFER L. HARTMAN

4.6.3.7.1.3.2 RYAN HARTMAN

4.6.3.7.1.4 TERRY HARTMAN married **SUSAN HANNON**.

4.6.3.7.1.4.1 WESLEY HARTMAN

4.6.3.7.1.4.2 JAYSON HARTMAN

4.6.3.7.2 BEULAH LOUISE SCHWALM was born on 7 July 1922, Wakarusa, Elkhart County, IN. She married **C.J. HOWE**, son of **C. J. HOWE** and **WILMA IRENE GRANT**. She died on 10 April 1999, at age 76. She was buried at Oak Grove Cemetery, Hillsdale, Hillsdale County, MI.

4.6.3.7.2.1 CYNTHIA HOWE married **ROY MEYER**.

4.6.3.7.2.1.1 ASHLEY MEYER

4.6.3.7.2.2 CONRAD JEFFREY HOWE was born on 14 February 1951, Hillsdale County, MI. He married **SANDRA STANLEY** on 27 March 1993. He died on 13 December 2007, Angola, Steuben County, IN, at age 56.

4.6.3.7.3 DALE EUGENE SCHWALM was born on 20 July 1930, Olive, Elkhart County, IN. He married **ARLENE JANETTE SCHMUCKER**, daughter of **DANIEL M. SCHMUCKER** and **FLORENCE BASSINGER**, in June 1950. He married **LORNA JEAN TROXEL** on 29 December 1978, Wakarusa, Elkhart County, IN.

4.6.3.7.3.1 WANDA SCHWALM married KENNETH CLEM.

4.6.3.7.3.2 STEVEN E. SCHWALM was born on 10 February 1952, Elkhart, Elkhart County, IN. He married CONNIE SUE STICKEL, daughter of ELLA MAE (--?--). He died on 10 September 2005, Lake County, FL, at age 53. He was buried on 15 October 2005, at Shiloh Cemetery, Fruitland Park, Lake County, FL.

- **4.6.3.7.3.2.1** TAMMY LYNN SCHWALM
- **4.6.3.7.3.2.2** TRACY M. SCHWALM

4.6.3.7.4 LOIS SCHWALM was born on 4 August 1934, Olive, Elkhart County, IN. She married LEE HARTMAN.

- **4.6.3.7.4.1** SUSAN K. HARTMAN
- **4.6.3.7.4.2** DIANE L. HARTMAN
- **4.6.3.7.4.3** JANE A. HARTMAN

4.6.3.7.5 ESTHER ELNORA SCHWALM was born on 15 January 1918. She married EARL LAMAR HUSBAND, son of ELGIE HUSBAND and ETHEL MARY LONG, in October 1937. She died on 10 November 2015, Miller's Merry Manor, Wakarusa, Elkhart County, IN, at age 97. She was buried on 15 November 2015, at Olive Cemetery, Wakarusa, Elkhart County, IN.

- **4.6.3.7.5.1** ELLA L. HUSBAND married ROBERT STITES.
  - **4.6.3.7.5.1.1** ROBERT STITES
- **4.6.3.7.5.2** EVELYN MARIE HUSBAND married ROBERT BUSS. She was born on 8 June 1938, Elkhart County, IN.
  - **4.6.3.7.5.2.1** CYNTHIA BUSS
  - **4.6.3.7.5.2.2** PENNY BUSS
  - **4.6.3.7.5.2.3** ROBERT S. BUSS
  - **4.6.3.7.5.2.4** MICHAEL LEE BUSS was born circa 1960. He married ANNETTE RENEE STRYCKER, daughter of MAX STRYCKER and JULINE (--?--), on 18 August 1990, Goshen, Elkhart County, IN.
- **4.6.3.7.5.3** EDITH LOUISE HUSBAND was born on 21 April 1940, Elkhart County, IN. She married PAUL S. HOCKMAN on 15 October 1966, Wakarusa, Elkhart County, IN.
  - **4.6.3.7.5.3.1** PAUL R. HOCKMAN
  - **4.6.3.7.5.3.2** LINDA L. HOCKMAN
  - **4.6.3.7.5.3.3** CONNIE S. HOCKMAN

4.6.3.7.6 MARGARET A. SCHWALM was born on 26 September 1919, Wakarusa, Elkhart County, IN. She married RUSSELL NUSBAUM in 1938, Wakarusa, Elkhart County, IN. She died on 27 June 2014, Miller's Merry Manor, Wakarusa, Elkhart County, IN, at age 94. She was buried at Olive Cemetery, Wakarusa, Elkhart County, IN.

- **4.6.3.7.6.1** LAMAR NUSBAUM married CHARLENE CULP.
  - **4.6.3.7.6.1.1** RODNEY NUSBAUM
  - **4.6.3.7.6.1.2** SHIELA NUSBAUM
- **4.6.3.7.6.2** DEAN NUSBAUM married HELEN MILLER.
  - **4.6.3.7.6.2.1** KELLY NUSBAUM
  - **4.6.3.7.6.2.2** LISA NUSBAUM
- **4.6.3.7.6.3** WAYNE NUSBAUM married BETTY ELRID. He married DIANE (--?--).
  - **4.6.3.7.6.3.1** BILLY W. NUSBAUM

4.6.3.7.6.4 JANE ANN NUSBAUM was born on 7 April 1944, Elkhart General Hospital, Elkhart, Elkhart County, IN. She died on 9 April 1944, Elkhart General Hospital, Elkhart, Elkhart County, IN. She was buried on 9 April 1944, at Olive Cemetery, Wakarusa, Elkhart County, IN.

4.6.3.7.6.5 JEAN ELLEN NUSBAUM was born on 7 April 1944, Elkhart General Hospital, Elkhart, Elkhart County, IN. She died on 8 April 1944, Elkhart General Hospital, Elkhart, Elkhart County, IN. She was buried on 9 April 1944, at Olive Cemetery, Wakarusa, Elkhart County, IN.

4.6.3.7.7 FREMONT EDWARD SCHWALM was born on 24 October 1924. He married **NORMA JEAN COOK** on 17 February 1944. He died on 25 August 1985, at age 60. He was buried at Prairie Street Cemetery, Elkhart, Elkhart County, IN.

4.6.3.8 NORA MYRTLE SCHWALM was born on 11 October 1899, St. Joseph County, IN. She married **HARVEY E. PLETCHER**, son of **ABRAM PLETCHER** and **ELIZABETH WEAVER**, on 7 March 1909, Pleasant Hill, Elkhart County, IN. She married **M.C. AGLEY** after 1937. She died on 1 August 1978, Timbercrest Home, North Manchester, Wabash County, IN, at age 78. She was buried on 3 August 1978, at Rock Run Cemetery, Goshen, Elkhart County, IN.

4.6.3.8.1 HAROLD EDGAR PLETCHER married **MARIE (--?--)**. He was born on 3 April 1910, Goshen, Elkhart County, IN. He married **LENORE H. HAHN**, daughter of **VERN HAHN** and **MARTHA ABIGAIL GORE**, in September 1932. He died in 2000. He was buried at Olive Cemetery, Wakarusa, Elkhart County, IN.

4.6.3.8.1.1 LARRY PLETCHER married **CAROL (--?--)**.

4.6.3.8.1.2 HENRY EDGAR PLETCHER was born on 26 April 1939. He died on 6 December 1961, at age 22. He was buried at Olive Cemetery, Wakarusa, Elkhart County, IN.

4.6.3.8.2 DONALD EUGENE PLETCHER was born on 6 June 1915, Goshen, Elkhart County, IN. He married **ALETHA VONDURANT** on 10 September 1938. He died on 14 October 2006, Asheville, Buncombe County, NC, at age 91.

4.6.3.8.2.1 REBECCA PLETCHER married **WILLIAM DIXON**. She married **JAY LEINBECK**. She married **PAUL BATES**.

4.6.3.8.2.1.1 WILLIAM DIXON married **MILENA (--?--)**.

4.6.3.8.2.1.1.1 WILL DIXON

4.6.3.8.2.1.1.2 NATALIA DIXON

4.6.3.8.2.2 STEPHEN PLETCHER married **JANET (--?--)**.

4.6.3.8.2.2.1 BRIAN PLETCHER

4.6.3.8.2.3 KATHLEEN PLETCHER married **JAY COOGAN**.

4.6.3.8.2.3.1 ADAM COOGAN

4.6.3.8.2.3.2 ELIZA COOGAN

4.6.3.8.3 HOWARD W. PLETCHER was born on 14 June 1918, Goshen, Elkhart County, IN. He married **BETTY BUCHANAN** on 27 October 1940. He died on 1 November 1999, at age 81. He was buried on 4 November 1999, at Olive Cemetery, Wakarusa, Elkhart County, IN.

4.6.3.8.3.1 HOWARD R. PLETCHER married **MARGARET (--?--)**.

4.6.3.8.3.2 PHILIP PLETCHER married **PEGGY BOSSTICK**.

4.6.3.8.3.2.1 PAMELA PLETCHER

4.6.3.8.3.3 JEAN PLETCHER

4.6.3.8.3.4 STANLEY K. PLETCHER was born on 11 December 1947, Elkhart, Elkhart County, IN. He died on 18 April 2016, Goshen, Elkhart County, IN, at age 68. He was buried at Olive Cemetery, Wakarusa, Elkhart County, IN.

4.6.3.8.3.4.1 NORA PLETCHER

4.6.3.8.3.4.2 MOLLY PLETCHER

4.6.4 SAMUEL PETER SCHWALM was born on 10 October 1858. He was baptized on 13 February 1859, St. Paul's (Artz's) Lutheran and Reformed Church, Sacramento, Schuylkill County, PA. He married **AGNES MINERVA BENSINGER**, daughter of **GEORGE BENSINGER** and **LOUISA KLINGER**, circa 1878. He died in 1927. He was buried at St. Andrew's Church Cemetery, Valley View, Schuylkill County, PA. A photograph of Samuel and Agnes's family appears in the 2006 edition of the Journal of the Johannes Schwalm Historical Association.

4.6.4.1 INFANT DAUGHTER SCHWALM was born on 20 February 1879. She died on 23 February 1879. She was buried at Saint Andrews United Methodist Church Cemetery, Valley View, Schuylkill County, PA.

4.6.4.2 FREMONT HARRISON SCHWALM was born on 8 January 1882. He married **JENNIE M. KLINGER**, daughter of **SAMUEL KLINGER** and **MARY COLEMAN**, on 28 July 1900, St. Andrew's

Church, Valley View, Schuylkill County, PA. He died on 8 April 1948, at age 66. He was buried at St. Andrew's Church Cemetery, Valley View, Schuylkill County, PA.

4.6.4.2.1 SAMUEL KLINGER SCHWALM was born on 25 December 1904. He was baptized on 23 April 1905, St. Andrew's United Methodist Church, Valley View, Schuylkill County, PA. He married BEULAH MAE UNDERKOFFLER, daughter of ELVIN LAWRENCE UNDERKOFFLER and BESSIE FIETTA REEDY, on 5 July 1925. He died on 29 December 1949, at age 45. He was buried at St. Andrew's Church Cemetery, Valley View, Schuylkill County, PA.

4.6.4.2.1.1 AGNES VIRGINIA SCHWALM was born on 25 December 1925, Pennsylvania. She married JAMES LEROY RICKERT on 5 June 1948. She and JAMES LEROY RICKERT were divorced on 4 February 1964.

4.6.4.2.1.1.1 RAMONA MARIE RICKERT was born on 14 October 1948.

4.6.4.2.1.2 HUGH SAMUEL SCHWALM was born on 11 January 1928, Pennsylvania. He married EMILY JANET KLOUSER, daughter of DEWEY KLOUSER and LIZZIE E. (--?--), on 16 April 1949. He married NANCY JANE (--?--).

4.6.4.2.1.2.1 STEPHEN SCHWALM was born on 24 November 1949. He married MELISSA MESSIMER on 28 January 1969. He married (--?--) WAGNER on 16 October 1976.

4.6.4.2.1.2.2 CYNTHIA LOUISE SCHWALM was born on 17 September 1951.

4.6.4.2.2 VERNON FRANCES SCHWALM was born on 16 December 1910. He died on 23 May 1911. He was buried at St. Andrew's Church Cemetery, Valley View, Schuylkill County, PA.

4.6.4.3 FRANCES SCHWALM was born in 1916. She died in 1917.

4.6.5 REILLEY A. SCHWALM is also referred to as REILLY in some sources. He was born on 7 September 1861, Pennsylvania. He married EVA ELLEN KIMMEL, daughter of EVANS KIMMEL and ELIZABETH BARKER, circa 1878. He married POLLY JANE HOFFMAN, daughter of EMANUEL HOFFMAN and FIETTA SHADEL, after 1891. He died on 30 August 1925, Frailey, Schuylkill County, PA, at age 63. He was buried on 2 September 1925, at St. Andrew's United Methodist Church Cemetery, Valley View, Schuylkill County, PA.

4.6.5.1 MARY ELIZABETH SCHWALM was born on 26 September 1881, Donaldson, Schuylkill County, PA. She married LESLIE TREVOR JONES, son of WILLIAM F. JONES and ELIZABETH ANNE JENKINS, on 22 April 1903, Donaldson, Schuylkill County, PA. She died on 16 May 1955, Pottsville, Schuylkill County, PA, at age 73. She was buried at Greenwood Cemetery, Tower City, Schuylkill County, PA.

4.6.5.1.1 KENNETH S. JONES was born on 12 May 1906, Tower City, Schuylkill County, PA. He married ELIZABETH E. MCCRONE, daughter of AGIS A. MCCRONE and ELIZABETH M. (--?--). Between 1951 and 1989, Kenneth lived in Shrewsbury, MA. He died on 20 December 1989, Medical Center of Central Massachusetts - Hahnemann, Worcester, MA, at age 83. He was buried at Mountain View Cemetery, Shrewsbury, Worcester County, MA.

4.6.5.1.1.1 GERALD K. JONES married RACHEL L. WEST.

4.6.5.1.1.1.1 STEPHEN G. JONES

4.6.5.1.1.1.2 BRIAN L. JONES

4.6.5.1.1.1.3 DAREN K. JONES

4.6.5.1.2 IRENE JONES was born circa 1910.

4.6.5.1.3 GRACE ELIZABETH JONES was born on 20 January 1917, Donaldson, Schuylkill County, PA. She married HOWARD E. GAGE. She died on 2 April 1999, St. Joseph's Medical Center, Reading, Berks County, PA, at age 82. She was buried at Greenwood Cemetery, Tower City, Schuylkill County, PA, PA.

4.6.5.1.3.1 BARBARA GAGE married JEROME BERNSTEIN.

4.6.5.1.3.1.1 ADAM G. BERNSTEIN

4.6.5.1.3.1.2 JOSHUA E. BERNSTEIN

4.6.5.1.3.2 JOHN H. GAGE

4.6.5.2 CARRIE ESTELLA SCHWALM is also referred to as CAROLINE in some sources. She was born on 29 May 1883. She married JESSIE ALONZO HATTER, son of FRANKLIN M. HATTER and AMANDA LOUISE ERDMAN, on 28 December 1904, Tremont, Schuylkill County, PA. She died in 1943.

4.6.5.2.1 EVELYN HATTER married **PAUL LAWRENCE**. She died on 30 May 1988, Sun City, CA.

4.6.5.3 HARRY RAY SCHWALM was born on 12 July 1894, Donaldson, Schuylkill County, PA. He married **ADA E. WOODRIDGE**, daughter of **WILLIAM A. WOODRIDGE** and **ELIZABETH SHERMAN**. He died on 2 April 1963, Pottsville, Schuylkill County, PA, at age 68. He was buried on 4 May 1963, at Fort Lincoln Cemetery, Brentwood, Prince George's County, MD.

> **4.6.5.3.1 HARRY ALFRED SCHWALM** was born on 19 December 1916, Washington, DC. He married **FLORENCE ELIZABETH SMITH**, daughter of **JAMES VERNON SMITH** and **GERTRUDE LANGTRY,** on 15 April 1939, Arlington, VA. He died on 10 June 1991, at age 74.
>
>> **4.6.5.3.1.1 JOAN SCHWALM** married **LARRY SNEAD**.
>>
>>> **4.6.5.3.1.1.1 JOHN SNEAD**
>>>
>>> **4.6.5.3.1.1.2 KAREN SNEAD**
>>
>> **4.6.5.3.1.2 SHIRLEY A. SCHWALM** married **ROY LERMAN**.
>>
>>> **4.6.5.3.1.2.1 ETHAN LERMAN**
>>
>> **4.6.5.3.1.3 MARY E. SCHWALM** married **EDWARD T. HILL**.

4.6.5.4 BRUCE FRANKLIN SCHWALM was born on 20 July 1896, Donaldson, Schuylkill County, PA. He married **ENOLA MILLER**. He married **FREDA WHITE**.

> **4.6.5.4.1 ARLENE SCHWALM** married **WILLIAM MCCLOY**.
>
>> **4.6.5.4.1.1 SANDRA MCCLOY** married **JOHN E. DEWER**.
>>
>>> **4.6.5.4.1.1.1 NATHAN DEWER**
>>>
>>> **4.6.5.4.1.1.2 MARGARET DEWER**
>>>
>>> **4.6.5.4.1.1.3 KATE DEWER**
>>
>> **4.6.5.4.1.2 BRUCE M. MCCLOY**
>
> **4.6.5.4.2 BRUCE SCHWALM JR.**

4.6.5.5 LEE WAYNE SCHWALM was born on 16 November 1898. He was baptized on 20 August 1899, St. Andrew's United Methodist Church, Valley View, Schuylkill County, PA. He married **M. WIEDMAN**. He married **ANNA ELIZABETH BOWMAN**. He died on 11 July 1964, Columbia County, FL, at age 65. He was buried at Arlington National Cemetery, Arlington, VA.

> **4.6.5.5.1 LOU SCHWALM** was born circa 1928.

4.6.5.6 (--?--) SCHWALM was born on 10 September 1901. He died on 13 September 1901. He was buried at St. Andrew's United Methodist Church Cemetery, Valley View, Schuylkill County, PA.

4.6.5.7 LESLIE J. SCHWALM was born on 17 June 1905. He married **ELEANOR BETZ**, daughter of **HARRY BETZ** and **BESSIE MORGAN**. He died in January 1981, at age 75. He was buried at Charles Baber Cemetery, Pottsville, Schuylkill County, PA.

> **4.6.5.7.1 CAROL SCHWALM** married **ROBERT NAGLE**.
>
>> **4.6.5.7.1.1 DEBORAH NAGLE**
>>
>> **4.6.5.7.1.2 KIMBERLY NAGLE**
>
> **4.6.5.7.2 JANET E. SCHWALM** married **FRANKLIN PROPST**. She was born circa 1936.
>
>> **4.6.5.7.2.1 WILLIAM ANDREW PROPST**
>>
>> **4.6.5.7.2.2 CHRISTOPHER D. PROPST**
>>
>>> **4.6.5.7.2.2.1 KIRSTEN M. PROPST**
>>>
>>> **4.6.5.7.2.2.2 CHRISTOPHER L. PROPST**

4.6.6 MARY ELIZABETH SCHWALM is also referred to as **LIZZIE AND MARY ELIZABETH** in some sources. She was born on 27 November 1865. She married **ALFRED HAROLD REED**, son of **LEVI REED** and **ROSANNA CATHARINE HERING,** in 1887. She died on 23 March 1939, at age 73. She was buried on 26 March 1939, at St. Andrew's United Methodist Church, Valley View, Hegins Township, Schuylkill County, PA.

> **4.6.6.1 HARVEY ALFRED REED** was born on 14 September 1887, Valley View, Schuylkill County, PA. He married **ESTELLA YODER**, daughter of **FRANKLIN REED YODER** and **ELEANORE CAROLINE GABLE,** on 25 June 1910, Hegins, Schuylkill County, PA. He died on 11 April 1944, Hegins Township, Schuylkill County, PA, at age 56. He was buried on 14 April 1944, at Friedens Union Cemetery, Hegins, Schuylkill County, PA.

4.6.6.1.1 PALMER HAROLD REED was born on 2 February 1911, Hegins, Schuylkill County, PA. He married **MILDRED TORELL REED**, daughter of **RUFUS REED** and **AUGUSTA STUTZMAN**. Prior to his death, Palmer was living at 1135 West Main Street, Valley View, Schuylkill County, PA. He died on 21 March 1991, Hershey Medical Center, Hershey, Dauphin County, PA, at age 80. He was buried at Frieden's Cemetery, Hegins, Schuylkill County, PA.

4.6.6.1.1.1 PALMER HAROLD REED JR. was born on 30 April 1935, Valley View, Schuylkill County, PA. He married **LUCILLE YVONNE KISSINGER**, daughter of **HARRY KISSINGER** and **GRACE STEILY**, on 4 July 1958, Valley View, Schuylkill County, PA.

4.6.6.1.1.1.1 CAROL ANN REED was born on 30 December 1959, Valley View, Schuylkill County, PA. She married **WARREN RUSSELL CARL JR.**, son of **WARREN RUSSELL CARL** and **SHIRLEY STITZMAN**, on 8 September 1979.

4.6.6.1.1.1.1.1 AMANDA LOUISE CARL was born on 6 February 1980, Gratz, Dauphin County, PA.

4.6.6.1.1.1.1.1.1 TRAVIS LETTICH was born on 15 September 1999.

4.6.6.1.1.1.1.1.2 KYLA FETZER was born on 22 August 2003.

4.6.6.1.1.1.1.2 SHAWN MICHAEL CARL was born on 31 May 1982, Gratz, Dauphin County, PA. He married **MANDY MARGERUM**, daughter of **ANTHONY MARGERUM** and **VIRGINIA (--?--)**, on 12 June 2010, Harrisburg Country Club, Harrisburg, Dauphin County, PA.

4.6.6.1.1.1.1.2.1 MAGNOLIA SAGE CARL was born on 21 March 2012, Harrisburg Hospital, Harrisburg, Dauphin County, PA.

4.6.6.1.1.1.2 SHARON LOUISE REED was born on 26 January 1962, Valley View, Schuylkill County, PA.

4.6.6.1.1.1.2.1 TIFFANY NATASHA (--?--) was born on 19 August 1996.

4.6.6.1.1.1.3 SHARON LOUISE REED was born on 26 January 1962, Valley View, Schuylkill County, PA.

4.6.6.1.1.1.3.1 TIFFANY NATASHA REED was born on 19 August 1996, York, York County, PA.

4.6.6.1.1.2 FREDERIC DAVID REED was born on 18 March 1937, Valley View, Schuylkill County, PA. He married **BARBARA ANN YURICK**, daughter of **PETER YURICK** and **EVELYN GOETZ**, on 23 August 1958, Lansford, Carbon County, PA.

4.6.6.1.1.2.1 JANET ELAINE REED was born on 20 December 1961, Birmingham, Jefferson County, AL. She married **JONATHAN DRESSER BLAKE**, son of **DICK BLAKE** and **JEANNE (--?--)**, on 25 May 2002, First Congregational UCC Church, Williamstown, Berkshire County, MA.

4.6.6.1.1.2.1.1 EMMA MARIE BLAKE was born on 29 July 2003, Cheshire, New Haven County, CT.

4.6.6.1.1.2.2 DAVID ALAN REED was born on 14 May 1964, Louisville, Jefferson County, KY. He married **KIM FRAN PACE**, daughter of **JIM PACE** and **CONNIE (--?--)**, on 10 July 1993, Lake Oswego, OR. He and **KIM FRAN PACE** were divorced.

4.6.6.1.1.2.2.1 MAKENZIE FRAN REED was born on 30 June 1994, Portland, Multnomah County, OR.

4.6.6.1.1.3 BRUCE LAMAR REED was born on 24 December 1942, Valley View, Schuylkill County, PA. He married **MAUREEN MARIE MALINOWSKI**, daughter of **ALBERT MALINOWSKI** and **HELEN PESARCHICK**, on 30 July 1966, Mount Carmel, Northumberland County, PA. He and **MAUREEN MARIE MALINOWSKI** were divorced in 1996. He married **SUSAN GAY SWEENEY**, daughter of **PAUL EDWARD SWEENEY** and **MARGARET ANN GILES**, in 1999.

4.6.6.1.1.3.1 JEFFREY PETER REED was born on 13 April 1971, Lancaster, Lancaster County, PA.

4.6.6.1.1.3.2 COURTNEY LYN REED was born on 9 May 1978, Lancaster, Lancaster County, PA. She married **RICHARD CHARLES STORK**, son of **THOMAS WILLIAM STORK** and **JOSEPHINE ELIZABETH HAEFNER**, on 14 December 2001, Good Shepherd Lutheran Church, Lancaster, Lancaster County, PA.

4.6.6.1.1.3.2.1 (--?--) STORK was born in 2006.

4.6.6.1.1.3.2.2 HUNTER THOMAS STORK was born on 27 March 2009, Lancaster General Hospital, Lancaster, Lancaster County, PA.

4.6.6.1.2 CHESTER HARVEY REED was born on 2 November 1913, Hegins Township, Schuylkill County, PA. He married MARIAN ELIZABETH SCHROPE, daughter of IRVIN H. SCHROPE and ALICE CATHERINE MELLEFONT, on 9 February 1936, Lisburn Church of God, Mechanicsburg, Cumberland County, PA. He died on 30 January 2003, Schuylkill Center, Genesis Elder Care Network, Pottsville, Schuylkill County, PA, at age 89. He was buried on 3 February 2003, at Saint Andrews United Methodist Church Cemetery, Valley View, Schuylkill County, PA.

4.6.6.1.2.1 DONALD CHESTER REED was born on 8 June 1936, Valley View, Schuylkill County, PA. He married PATRICIA ANN WILSON, daughter of CLAUDE KELLOGG WILSON JR. and CHARLOTTE MARY WALKER, on 2 January 1958, Towson, Baltimore County, MD. Don has compiled extensive genealogies of the descendants of Johannes Schwalm, including the 3 children of Peter Klinger and Catharine Wiest who married children of Frederick Schwalm and Catharina Stein.

4.6.6.1.2.1.1 DONALD CHESTER REED JR. was born on 28 January 1960, St. Joseph Hospital, Syracuse, Onondaga County, NY. He was baptized in 1961, Saint Andrews United Methodist Church, Valley View, Schuylkill County, PA. He married PAMELA ANN THOMPSON, daughter of WILLIAM THOMPSON and AUDREY FORREY, on 22 February 1986, First Presbyterian Church, York, York County, PA.

4.6.6.1.2.1.1.1 SHANNON ELIZABETH REED was born on 4 July 1988, Lancaster General Hospital, Lancaster, Lancaster County, PA.

4.6.6.1.2.1.1.2 BRITTANY LEE REED was born on 20 April 1991, Lancaster General Hospital, Lancaster, Lancaster County, PA.

4.6.6.1.2.1.1.3 CHELSEA LYNN REED was born on 21 July 1992, Lancaster General Hospital, Lancaster, Lancaster County, PA.

4.6.6.1.2.1.2 PAMELA WILSON REED was born on 19 October 1961, Ellis Hospital, Schenectady, Schenectady County, NY. She was baptized on 7 January 1962, Calvary Methodist Church, Niskayunah, Schenectady County, NY. She married MICHAEL EDWARD YUNGINGER, son of RONALD EUGENE YUNGINGER and ANNA MAE BUTZ, on 11 April 1987, Grandview United Methodist Church, Lancaster, Lancaster County, PA.

4.6.6.1.2.1.2.1 ADAM MICHAEL YUNGINGER was born on 26 October 1992, Lancaster General Hospital, Lancaster, Lancaster County, PA. He was baptized on 21 February 1993, Grandview United Methodist Church, Lancaster, Lancaster County, PA.

4.6.6.1.2.1.2.2 ALEXANDER REED YUNGINGER was born on 10 March 1998, Hershey Medical Center, Hershey, Dauphin County, PA. He died on 10 March 1998, Hershey Medical Center, Hershey, Dauphin County, PA.

4.6.6.1.2.1.2.3 AMY PATRICIA YUNGINGER was born on 15 May 2000, Lancaster General Hospital, Lancaster, Lancaster County, PA.

4.6.6.1.2.2 ALICE MARIAN REED was born on 1 June 1947, Pottsville Hospital, Pottsville, Schuylkill County, PA. She was baptized on 9 May 1948, Saint Andrews United Methodist Church, Valley View, Schuylkill County, PA. She married DENNIS MARLIN MILLER, son of MARLIN MONROE MILLER and GRACE DELLA BIXLER, on 11 July 1964, Saint Andrews United Methodist Church, Valley View, Schuylkill County, PA.

4.6.6.1.2.2.1 ROBERT DENNIS MILLER was born on 18 November 1964, Pottsville Good Samaritan Hospital, Pottsville, Schuylkill County, PA. He married MELISSA DEETER, daughter of JUNIOR ROGER DEETER and DIANE LUCILLE BOWMAN, on 1 September 1990, Saint Andrews United Methodist Church, Valley View, Schuylkill County, PA.

4.6.6.1.2.2.1.1 COLTON ROBERT MILLER was born on 23 January 1993, Good Samaritan Regional Medical Center, Pottsville, Schuylkill County, PA.

4.6.6.1.2.2.1.2 DUSTIN DENNIS MILLER was born on 1 April 1995, Good Samaritan Regional Medical Center, Pottsville, Schuylkill County, PA.

4.6.6.1.2.2.2 RICHARD SCOTT MILLER was born on 28 February 1968, Good Samaritan Hospital, Pottsville, Schuylkill County, PA. He married **TRACEY ANN ARTZ**, daughter of **DONALD AARON ARTZ** and **BONNIE LOU LUCAS**, on 7 March 1992, Frieden's Lutheran Church, Hegins, Schuylkill County, PA.

4.6.6.1.2.2.2.1 OLIVIA GRACE MILLER was born on 28 August 1992, Good Samaritan Hospital, Pottsville, Schuylkill County, PA.

4.6.6.1.2.2.2.2 DALTON RICHARD MILLER was born on 11 August 1994, Good Samaritan Hospital, Pottsville, Schuylkill County, PA.

4.6.6.2 ESTELLA MAY REED was born on 19 July 1889. She died on 10 August 1890, at age 1. She was buried at Friedens Union Cemetery, Hegins, Schuylkill County, PA.

4.6.6.3 FREMONT H. REED was born on 8 September 1891. He died on 10 February 1893, at age 1. He was buried at Friedens Union Cemetery, Hegins, Schuylkill County, PA.

4.6.6.4 ALICE E. REED was born on 5 March 1894. She died on 15 May 1895, at age 1. Some sources record that she was born on 5 March 1897. Some sources record that she died in 1899. She was buried at Friedens Union Cemetery, Hegins, Schuylkill County, PA.

4.6.6.5 NELSON REED was born on 11 May 1896, Hegins, Schuylkill County, PA. He married **MINNIE REBER**, daughter of **DAVID REBER** and **ELLEN FESSLER**, on 5 August 1922, Saint Andrews United Methodist Church, Valley View, Schuylkill County, PA. He died in an auto accident, on 26 September 1932, Reading, Berks County, PA, at age 36. He was buried on 27 September 1932, at Trinity Lutheran Church Cemetery, Valley View, Schuylkill County, PA.

4.6.6.5.1 LAMAR NELSON REED was born circa 1930. He married **EDITH EFFRON**, daughter of **JACOB EFFRON** and **JENNIE (--?--)**, Fort Sam Houston, San Antonio, Bexar County, TX.

4.6.6.5.1.1 ERIC RAND REED was born on 5 December 1954, Pottsville, Schuylkill County, PA. He married **JOAN ELLEN HAMBURGER** in March 1984, Haddon Heights, Camden County, NJ.

4.6.6.5.1.1.1 DAVID ALEXANDER REED was born on 12 December 1985, Prince George's County Hospital, Prince George's County, MD.

4.6.6.5.1.1.2 ALIZA JACQUELINE REED was born on 17 April 1988, Silver Spring, Montgomery County, MD.

4.6.6.5.1.1.3 SUZANNE KAROLINE REED was born on 10 August 1989, Fairfax, VA.

4.6.6.5.1.2 DOUGLAS WARREN REED was born on 20 September 1957, Bellefonte, Centre County, PA.

4.6.6.6 ALVERTA EVA REED was born on 1 September 1900, Valley View, Schuylkill County, PA. She married **RAY H. HERB** on 15 March 1919, St. Andrew's United Methodist Church, Valley View, Hegins Township, Schuylkill County, PA. She died on 9 April 1936, Pottsville Hospital, Pottsville, Schuylkill County, PA, at age 35. She was buried at St. Andrew's United Methodist Church, Valley View, Hegins Township, Schuylkill County, PA.

4.6.6.6.1 VIVIAN ALVERTA HERB is also referred to as **VIVIAN REED** in some sources but the listing of Vivian's maiden name as "Reed" may be in error. Vivian is listed at three different places in the Johannes Schwalm Historical Association materials, twice as being the daughter of Alverta Reed and Ray H. Herb, and once as the daughter of Nelson Reed and Minnie Reber. It would appear that the "Herb" name is more likely correct. She was born on 11 October 1919, Valley View, Schuylkill County, PA. She married **WILLIAM HENRY LEININGER**, son of **HENRY A. LEININGER** and **SALLY A. STARR**, on 5 September 1941, Orwigsburg, Schuylkill County, PA. She died on 5 December 2003, Hummelstown, Dauphin County, PA, at age 84.

4.6.6.6.1.1 WILLIAM H. LEININGER JR. was born on 23 June 1942, Pottsville, Schuylkill County, PA. He married **LAURA C. MAULFAIR**. He married **CAROL A. FASNACHT**, daughter of **RUSSEL FASNACHT** and **MARY M. WEBB**.

4.6.6.6.1.1.1 MARK DOUGLAS FASNACHT was born on 9 November 1958, Hershey, Dauphin County, PA. He married **BOBBIE JO TENNANT**. He married **DEBORAH ANN PRICE**. He married **JULIE E. MAY**, daughter of **EARL EDWARD MAY** and **JOYCE IONE GROFF**. He died on 21 May 2014, Milton S. Hershey Medical Center, Hershey, Dauphin County, PA, at age 55. He was buried on 29 May 2014, at Middletown Cemetery, Middletown, Dauphin County, PA.

4.6.6.6.1.1.1.1 MEGAN A. FASNACHT

4.6.6.6.1.1.2 DOUGLAS WAYNE LEININGER was born on 7 October 1968, Hershey, Dauphin County, PA. He married KATHRYN MARIE HENRY, daughter of BENJAMIN HENRY and GLORIA (--?--), on 8 June 1991.

4.6.6.6.1.1.2.1 DOUGLAS JAMES LEININGER was born on 28 May 1993.

4.6.6.6.1.1.2.2 JOHNATHAN MICHAEL LEININGER was born on 24 February 1995.

4.6.6.6.1.1.3 ANDREW R. LEININGER was born on 22 July 1974, Harrisburg, Dauphin County, PA.

4.6.6.6.1.2 NORMAN RAY LEININGER was born on 15 November 1943, Pottsville, Schuylkill County, PA. He married BARBARA DETWEILER on 15 July 1966, Hummelstown, Dauphin County, PA. He and BARBARA DETWEILER were divorced in June 1977. He married BETTY JANE FOX.

4.6.6.6.1.2.1 NEVIN JERROLL LEININGER was born on 9 December 1966, Hershey, Dauphin County, PA. He married MICHELE L. BOONE, daughter of EARL BOONE and NORMA (--?--), on 28 June 1986.

4.6.6.6.1.2.1.1 AMBER MARILYN LEININGER was born on 23 February 1987, York, York County, PA.

4.6.6.6.1.2.1.2 KENNETH RANDALL LEININGER was born on 2 March 1992.

4.6.6.6.1.2.2 COREY JAY LEININGER was born on 6 March 1972, Hershey, Dauphin County, PA. He married ALICE LENGLE.

4.6.6.6.1.2.2.1 JADE LYNN LEININGER was born on 5 September 1990.

4.6.6.6.2 PHAON RAY HERB was born on 22 May 1921, Valley View, Schuylkill County, PA. He was baptized on 5 September 1921, St. Andrew's United Methodist Church, Valley View, Hegins Township, Schuylkill County, PA. He married VIRGINIA CHARLOTTE SHUGARS, daughter of GEORGE SHUGARS and CHARLOTTE DEARBORN, on 27 November 1946, Minersville, Schuylkill County, PA. He died on 25 December 2010, at age 89. He was buried at Schuylkill Memorial Park, Schuylkill Haven, Schuylkill County, PA.

4.6.6.6.2.1 RICHARD PHAON HERB was born on 31 July 1947, Pottsville, Schuylkill County, PA. He married LINDA C. GOURLEY. Richard lives in Strasburg, CO.

4.6.6.6.2.1.1 NATHANIEL RICHARD HERB was born on 23 January 1970. He married TRACI (--?--).

4.6.6.6.2.1.1.1 CARSON HERB

4.6.6.6.2.1.1.2 BRODY HERB

4.6.6.6.2.1.2 ETHAN WILLIAM HERB was born on 21 June 1975.

4.6.6.6.2.2 THOMAS GEORGE HERB was born on 25 March 1952. He married VIOLA JOAN FRANKLIN, daughter of GEORGE WILLIAM FRANKLIN and VIOLA CATHERINE PITCOCK, on 25 November 1994, Manassas, VA.

4.6.6.6.3 OTIS S. HERB was born on 12 May 1924, Valley View, Schuylkill County, PA. He married EDNA E. SCOTT, daughter of WALTER H. SCOTT and EDNA E. (--?--), on 21 June 1947, Philadelphia, Philadelphia County, PA. He died on 27 November 2012, at age 88. He was buried at Hillside Cemetery, Roslyn, Montgomery County, PA.

4.6.6.6.3.1 ROBERT SCOTT HERB was born on 6 January 1950, Philadelphia, Philadelphia County, PA. He married JUDITH A. STOWELL on 23 August 1975, Denver, Denver County, CO. He married PAMELA ANN LAUER on 16 December 1989, Australia.

4.6.6.6.3.2 KENNETH STANFORD HERB was born on 6 May 1951, Philadelphia, Philadelphia County, PA. He married PATRICIA ANN REPPE, daughter of NORMAN REPPE and JOAN (--?--), on 19 April 1975, Philadelphia, Philadelphia County, PA.

4.6.6.6.3.2.1 KENNETH SCOTT HERB was born on 17 June 1980, Fairless Hills, Bucks County, PA.

4.6.6.6.3.3 RONALD KEITH HERB was born on 21 January 1958, Levittown, Bucks County, PA. He married REBECCA BUCKLEY on 12 September 1981, Lake Ariel, Wayne County, PA. He and REBECCA BUCKLEY were divorced in 1997. He married ROBIN SMOYER KELLER after 1997.

4.6.6.6.3.3.1 LAUREN BUCKLEY HERB was born on 31 October 1988, Bryn Mawr, PA.

4.6.6.6.3.3.2 KEVIN SCOTT HERB was born on 1 April 1992, Reading, Berks County, PA.

4.6.6.6.3.3.3 DILLON MAXWELL HERB was born on 5 October 1994, Reading, Berks County, PA.

4.6.6.6.4 ELSIE ELIZABETH HERB was born on 3 November 1925, Valley View, Schuylkill County, PA. She was baptized on 22 November 1925, St. Andrew's United Methodist Church, Valley View, Hegins Township, Schuylkill County, PA. She married **FRANCIS JOSEPH ERK**, son of **FREDERICK JACOB ERK** and **MARY FRANCES (--?--),** on 15 March 1946, Elkton, Cecil County, MD. She died on 7 July 2013, Montrose, Montrose County, CO, at age 87. She was buried at Rosita Cemetery, Rosita, Custer County, CO.

4.6.6.6.4.1 FRANCIS JOSEPH ERK JR. was born on 16 December 1946, Bayonne, Hudson County, NJ. He married **JUNE ANN WALTON** on 21 June 1971, Oreland, Montgomery County, PA.

4.6.6.6.4.1.1 KENDRA ANN ERK was born on 9 October 1983, Mahopac, Putnam County, NJ.

4.6.6.6.4.2 FREDERICK RAY ERK was born on 16 December 1946, Bayonne, Hudson County, NJ. He married **MARY LOU KRATOVILE** on 21 July 1972, Gibraltar.

4.6.6.6.4.2.1 JASON MICHAEL ERK was born on 1 September 1976, Doylestown, Bucks County, PA.

4.6.6.6.4.2.2 TODD FRANCIS ERK was born on 15 April 1982, Doylestown, Bucks County, PA.

4.6.6.6.4.3 KAREN ELIZABETH ERK was born on 11 November 1948, Long Island, NY. She married **ROGER WESLEY CORNELL**, son of **DAVID LEROY CORNELL** and **GWENDOLYN IRENE SMITH,** on 18 February 1971, Oreland, Montgomery County, PA.

4.6.6.6.4.3.1 EMILE ELIZABETH CORNELL was born on 24 August 1982, Boulder, Boulder County, CO.

4.6.6.6.4.3.2 LAURIE ROSE CORNELL was born on 29 December 1984, Boulder, Boulder County, CO.

4.6.6.6.4.4 DONNA MARIE ERK was born on 20 January 1955, Abington, Montgomery County, PA. She married **HENRY MICHAEL WOLLUM**, son of **HENRY MARVIN WOLLUM** and **ODILE AMITA AMO,** on 15 July 1978, Eldorado Springs, Boulder County, CO.

4.6.6.6.4.4.1 CARLA JUSTINE WOLLUM was born on 27 September 1985, Boulder, Boulder County, CO.

4.6.6.6.4.4.2 HENRY MARSHALL WOLLUM was born on 16 September 1988, Boulder, Boulder County, CO.

4.6.6.6.5 JAY JOSEPH HERB was born on 5 February 1928, Orwigsburg, Schuylkill County, PA. He married **EMOGENE WHITMAN**, daughter of **JARVIS COOPER WHITMAN** and **IDA MAE (--?--),** on 16 February 1951, Chimacum, Jefferson County, WA. He died on 15 October 1986, Port Townsend, Jefferson County, WA, at age 58.

4.6.6.6.5.1 RANDY JAY HERB was born on 4 September 1951, Port Townsend, Jefferson County, WA. He married **SHIRLEY L. MORGAN** on 11 November 1989. He married **CINDY L. SMITH**. He married **APRIL D. HECK**. He married **MARIAN EATON.**

4.6.6.6.5.1.1 RYAN J. HERB

4.6.6.6.5.2 DARCI JEAN HERB was born on 13 December 1958, Port Townsend, Jefferson County, WA. She married **JOSEPH WILLIAM CLOUSE**, son of **ROBERT CLOUSE** and **SARAH (--?--),** on 28 May 1976, Port Townsend, Jefferson County, WA.

4.6.6.6.5.2.1 JUSTIN WILLIAM CLOUSE was born on 7 October 1080, Port Townsend, Jefferson County, WA.

4.6.6.6.5.2.2 KRISTOFER JOSEPH CLOUSE was born on 12 December 1976, Port Townsend, Jefferson County, WA.

4.6.6.6.5.3 TRACI ANN HERB was born on 18 January 1963, Port Townsend, Jefferson County, WA. She married **DALE G. SEWARD** Port Angeles, Clallam County, WA.

4.6.6.6.5.4 JOEL RAY HERB was born on 9 August 1969, Port Townsend, Jefferson County, WA.

4.6.6.6.6 JAMES HENSIL HERB was born on 11 June 1930, Orwigsburg, Schuylkill County, PA. He married BETTY MAE REBER, daughter of DEWEY I. REBER and FRANCES MCMICHAEL, on 7 July 1951, Cornwall, Lebanon County, PA. He died on 21 January 2012, VA Medical Center, Lebanon, Lebanon County, PA, at age 81. He was buried on 26 January 2012, at Indiantown Gap National Cemetery, Annville, Lebanon County, PA.

4.6.6.6.6.1 LINDA MAE HERB was born on 22 May 1952, Hershey, Dauphin County, PA. She married JAMES WILLIAM HORSTICK, son of JOHN F. HORSTICK and KATHERINE (--?--), on 10 August 1974, Palmyra, Lebanon County, PA. Linda lives in Lebanon, PA.

4.6.6.6.6.1.1 JAMES WILLIAM HORSTICK II was born on 28 September 1977, Hershey, Dauphin County, PA.

4.6.6.6.6.1.2 NICHOLAS ALLEN HORSTICK was born on 16 February 1986, Harrisburg, Dauphin County, PA.

4.6.6.6.6.1.3 JONATHAN WESLEY HORSTICK was born on 27 February 1988, Harrisburg, Dauphin County, PA.

4.6.6.6.6.2 BRENDA JEAN HERB was born on 22 January 1957, Hershey, Dauphin County, PA. She married MICHAEL DAVID MILLER, son of WILBUR MILLER and ELLA (--?--), on 22 May 1976, Hershey, Dauphin County, PA. Brenda lives in Lebanon, PA.

4.6.6.6.6.2.1 ALLISON KAY MILLER was born on 4 November 1977, Harrisburg, Dauphin County, PA.

4.6.6.6.6.2.2 TODD MICHAEL MILLER was born on 28 January 1980, Harrisburg, Dauphin County, PA.

4.6.6.6.6.2.3 MATTHEW DAVID MILLER was born on 24 October 1984.

4.6.6.6.7 JUNE M. HERB was born on 22 June 1932, Orwigsburg, Schuylkill County, PA. She married CLARENCE WILLIAM EBBERT, son of CLARENCE L. EBBERT and RHEA STOUT, on 22 June 1951, Drexel Hill, Delaware County, PA. She died on 29 April 2014, at age 81.

4.6.6.6.7.1 WILLIAM HERB EBBERT was born on 24 August 1952, Lehighton, Carbon County, PA.

4.6.6.6.7.2 ALYCE MARIE EBBERT was born on 13 November 1955, Pottstown, Montgomery County, PA. She married LOUIS EARL VOLBERDING JR., son of LOUIS EARL VOLBERDING SR. and FLORENCE PAYTON, on 6 June 1976, Pueblo, Pueblo County, CO.

4.6.6.6.7.2.1 LISEL ZANE VOLBERDING was born on 28 April 1979, Colby, Thomas County, KS.

4.6.6.6.7.2.2 TZEITEL A. VOLBERDING was born on 17 March 1983, Colby, Thomas County, KS.

4.6.6.6.7.2.3 TABOR BRIANNE VOLBERDING was born on 8 June 1986, Colby, Thomas County, KS.

4.6.6.6.7.2.4 TEGAN CORRINE VOLBERDING was born on 10 January 1991, Carson City, NV.

4.6.6.6.7.2.5 TOBEN LE VOLBERDING was born on 1 October 1992, Carson City, NV.

4.6.6.6.7.3 JAMES RICHARD EBBERT was born on 20 October 1967, Port Huron, St. Clair County, MI. He married JONNIE LEE BLACKWELDER on 22 June 1994, Port Orange, Volusia County, FL.

4.6.6.6.8 JOHN R. HERB was born on 13 July 1935, Orwigsburg, Schuylkill County, PA. He married SANDRA GAYLE RESSLER, daughter of OSCAR RESSLER and VERNA ELIZABETH MILLER, on 1 September 1956, Trinity Lutheran Church, Valley View, Schuylkill County, PA. He died on 16 February 2010, at his home on Mountain Road, Hegins, Schuylkill County, PA, at age 74. According to a newspaper obituary, John graduated from Hegins Township High School and attended the University of Maryland. He served in the Army 11th Airborne during the Korean War, stationed in France. He was employed by AT&T, Sears, Spread Eagle Farms, Witmer Motors and the Engle-Rissinger Auto Group. He was buried on 20 February 2010, at St, Andrews United Methodist Cemetery, Valley View, Schuylkill County, PA.

4.6.6.6.8.1 HOLLY HERB was born on 17 September 1963, Harrisburg, Dauphin County, PA. She married DANIEL JOSEPH ROBINSKI, son of JOSEPH ROBINSKI and EILEEN BUCZYNSKI, on 17 September 1988, Zion (Stone Valley) Church, Hickory Corners, Northumberland County, PA. She married TODD DRUMHEISER. In 2010, Holly was living in Selinsgrove, Northumberland County, PA.

4.6.6.6.8.1.1 JACOB REED ROBINSKI was born on 24 July 1992, Harrisburg Hospital, Harrisburg, Dauphin County, PA.

4.6.6.6.8.1.2 JACOB REED ROBINSKI was born on 24 July 1992, Harrisburg, Dauphin County, PA.

4.6.6.7 MARGARET REED is also referred to as MARGARETTA I. REED in some sources. She was born in 1904. She died in 1912. She was buried at St. Andrew's United Methodist Church, Valley View, Hegins Township, Schuylkill County, PA.

4.6.7 SYNARY ELLSWORTH SCHWALM was born on 12 April 1868, Valley View, Hegins Township, Schuylkill County, PA. He married EMMA SALERA ISABELLA SALTZER, daughter of WILLIAM SALTZER and LYDIA (--?--), on 30 May 1889. He died on 27 January 1923, Pottsville, Schuylkill County, PA, at age 54. He was buried at St. Andrew's Church Cemetery, Valley View, Schuylkill County, PA.

4.6.7.1 GURNEY HARRISON SCHWALM was born on 2 July 1890, Valley View, Schuylkill County, PA. He married MARY SEVILLA SHADLE, daughter of ROBERT WILSON SHADLE and SARAH PHILLIPS, circa 1912. He died on 28 April 1972, Schuylkill County, PA, at age 81. He was buried at Trinity Lutheran Church Cemetery, Valley View, Schuylkill County, PA.

4.6.7.1.1 WILSON ELLSWORTH SCHWALM is also referred to as WILSON F. SCHWALM in some sources. He was born on 20 October 1912, Schuylkill County, PA. He married ARLENE MORGAN, daughter of JOSEPH I. MORGAN and CHARLOTTE CATHERINE HOUSER. He married DOROTHY HANNAH ROTHERMEL, daughter of CHARLES A. ROTHERMEL and CARRIE A. KAHLER. Prior to his death, Wilson was living in Sacramento, Schuylkill County, PA. He died on 14 February 1993, Good Samaritan Regional Medical Center, Pottsville, Schuylkill County, PA, at age 80. He was buried at Salem United Methodist Cemetery, Weishample, Barry Township, Schuylkill County, PA.

4.6.7.1.1.1 DIANE SCHWALM married JAMES RESSLER, son of EUGENE RESSLER and PHYLLIS KESSLER.

4.6.7.1.1.1.1 KRISTIAN RESSLER is also referred to as KRISTIN AND KIRSTEN in some sources. He was born on 4 July 1968, Valley View, Schuylkill County, PA. He married CAM CHAU.

4.6.7.1.1.1.1.1 JAMES HENRY RESSLER is also referred to as JAMES HENRY CHAU in some sources.

4.6.7.1.1.1.1.2 SPENSER EUGENE RESSLER is also referred to as SPENCER EUGENE CHAU in some sources.

4.6.7.1.1.1.2 HEATH RESSLER was born on 15 October 1969, Valley View, Schuylkill County, PA. He married LISA SUBICK.

4.6.7.1.1.1.2.1 COURTNEY MARIE RESSLER

4.6.7.1.1.1.2.2 LARISSA ELIZABETH RESSLER

4.6.7.1.1.1.3 VALISSA CHANTEL RESSLER was born on 23 March 1972, Valley View, Schuylkill County, PA. She married LAMONT MARK MASSER, son of MARK MASSER and ARLENE MAE WILLIER, on 4 June 1994, St. Andrew's United Methodist Church, Valley View, Schuylkill County, PA. In 1998, Valissa was living in Leck Kill, Northumberland County, PA.

4.6.7.1.1.1.3.1 REBECCA CATHERINE MASSER was born on 3 May 1998.

4.6.7.1.1.1.3.2 JOSHUA LAMONT MASSER was born on 6 January 2001, Geisinger Medical Center, Danville, Montour County, PA.

4.6.7.1.1.1.3.3 CHLOE ELIZABETH MASSER was born on 29 November 2005.

4.6.7.1.1.2 WALTER WILSON SCHWALM was born on 24 October 1951, Schuylkill County, PA. He was baptized on 13 April 1952, Friedens Reformed Church, Hegins, Schuylkill County, PA. He married JOANNE PATRICIA SHADLE, daughter of MONROE JOEL SHADLE and **ANNIS M. HUNTZINGER,** on 25 April 1970. He married **CAROL A. WITMER** on 17 July 2015, Wellsboro, Tioga County, PA.

> **4.6.7.1.1.2.1 MICHAEL NEIL SCHWALM** was born on 10 September 1970.
>
> **4.6.7.1.1.2.2 JENNIFER SUE SCHWALM** was born on 11 July 1978. She married **COREY MATTHEW SHADLE,** son of **RICHARD SHADLE** and **WANDA (--?--),** on 20 October 2001.
>
>> **4.6.7.1.1.2.2.1 EMMA MARIE SHADLE** was born on 20 August 2006, Pottsville, Schuylkill County, PA.
>>
>> **4.6.7.1.1.2.2.2 CALEB RICHARD SHADLE** was born on 10 November 2015, Hegins, Schuylkill County, PA.

4.6.7.1.2 CATHERINE ISABELLE SCHWALM was born on 24 May 1915, Valley View, Schuylkill County, PA. She married **LEE JACOB WARFIELD,** son of **ERNIE WARFIELD** and **MABEL WILLIARD,** on 29 May 1937, Trinity Lutheran Church, Valley View, Schuylkill County, PA. She died on 26 September 2011, Hershey Medical Center, Derry Township, Dauphin County, PA, at age 96. According to a newspaper obituary, Catherine lived in Reinerton, PA. She was a 1933 graduate of Hegins Twp. High School where she was a homemaker and assisted her late husband Lee in operating the former Esso/Exxon gas station in Reinerton for 40 years. She was buried at Fairview Cemetery, Williamstown, Dauphin County, PA.

> **4.6.7.1.2.1 ELLEN WARFIELD** married **MICHAEL BARKOS.** Ellen lives in Williamstown, PA.
>
>> **4.6.7.1.2.1.1 MICHELLE BARKOS** married **SCOTT CARL.** She married **(--?--) FLYNN.**
>>
>>> **4.6.7.1.2.1.1.1 ELISE NICOLE CARL** was born on 19 January 1988, Harrisburg Hospital, Harrisburg, Dauphin County, PA.
>>
>> **4.6.7.1.2.1.2 NICOLE BARKOS**
>>
>> **4.6.7.1.2.1.3 CARLA BARKOS** was born on 25 August 1969. She married **SAMUEL DAVID WYNN JR.**
>>
>>> **4.6.7.1.2.1.3.1 SAMUEL JACOB WYNN**
>>>
>>> **4.6.7.1.2.1.3.2 LUKE THOMAS WYNN** was born on 12 July 1995.
>
> **4.6.7.1.2.2 KENNETH WARFIELD** died in infancy.
>
> **4.6.7.1.2.3 CAROL A. WARFIELD** married **GEORGE A. TALLMAN,** son of **GEORGE W. TALLMAN** and **CHRISTINA E. SWOYER.** Carol lives in Tower City, PA.
>
> **4.6.7.1.2.4 NANCY WARFIELD** was born circa 1937. She married **GARY J. THOMPSON,** son of **JOSEPH THOMPSON** and **KATHRYN RITZMAN,** circa 1957. Nancy lives in Reinerton, PA.
>
>> **4.6.7.1.2.4.1 DARRYL THOMPSON**
>>
>> **4.6.7.1.2.4.2 TERRI A. THOMPSON** married **JASON MICHAEL GROW** on 23 August 1997, Christ United Methodist Church, Tower City, Schuylkill County, PA. She married **(--?--) CATHERS.**
>>
>>> **4.6.7.1.2.4.2.1 MAX CATHERS**
>>>
>>> **4.6.7.1.2.4.2.2 ALEXA GROW**

4.6.7.1.3 MARK MILLIARD SCHWALM was born on 5 December 1917, Valley View, Hegins Township, Schuylkill County, PA. He married **BETTY SCHOLL.** He married **ADELE IVOLENE DREIBELBIS,** daughter of **CHARLES DREIBELBIS** and **BEULAH HART.** He died on 5 September 2003, at his home Lykens, Dauphin County, PA, at age 85. According to a newspaper obituary, Mark was an Army veteran of World War II. He later worked for Don's Food Rite, in Lykens, and the former Cooper's Bakery. He was buried at Indiantown Gap National Cemetery, Annville, Lebanon County, PA.

> **4.6.7.1.3.1 JUDITH A. SHAFFER**
>
> **4.6.7.1.3.2 ROBERT M. SHAFFER**

4.6.7.1.4 GEORGE HARRISON SCHWALM was born on 14 November 1919, Valley View, Schuylkill County, PA. He married **RUTH EVELYN KOPPENHAVER,** daughter of **ABNER RALPH KOPPENHAVER** and **HELEN MABEL OSSMAN,** circa 1952. He died on 1 December 2009, The Manor at Susquehanna Village, Millersburg, Dauphin County, PA, at age 90. According to a newspaper obituary, George lived in Valley View, PA. He retired as a clerk for Midway Supermarket, in Valley View. Earlier, he and his wife had owned and operated a grocery store in Valley View. George enjoyed providing mobile grocery service to many area residents. He had also worked for the former Bud Kimmel General Store, Valley View. George served as a director of the Johannes Schwalm Historical Association Inc., and enjoyed researching the Schwalm genealogy. He had traveled to the Schwalm homeland in Germany while doing his research. He was buried on 6 December 2009, at Trinity Lutheran Church Cemetery, Valley View, Schuylkill County, PA.

4.6.7.1.5 EMMA SARAH SCHWALM was born on 6 November 1921, Hegins, Schuylkill County, PA. She married **DONALD T. STOKES.** Prior to her death, Emma, who formerly lived in Hegins Township, Schuylkill County, PA, was living at the Thornwald Nursing Home, Carlisle, Cumberland County, PA. She died on 6 November 2002, Carlisle Hospital, Carlisle, PA, at age 81. She was buried at Woodlawn Memorial Gardens, Lower Paxton Township, Dauphin County, PA.

4.6.7.1.5.1 EUGENE STOKES married **WENDY MARTIN.**

4.6.7.1.6 FRANK HENRY SCHWALM was born on 28 January 1924, Valley View, Schuylkill County, PA. He married **MARGARET NEY**, daughter of **EARL NEY** and **MINNIE ATHEY.** He died on 29 March 2007, ManorCare Health Services, Pottsville, Schuylkill County, PA, at age 83. According to a newspaper obituary, Frank lived in Valley View, Schuylkill County, PA. He was an Army veteran of World War II and was retired from Bethlehem Steel. He was buried on 2 April 2007, at Indiantown Gap National Cemetery, Annville, Lebanon County, PA.

4.6.7.1.6.1 JEFFREY SCHWALM married **TINA MOYER.**

4.6.7.1.6.1.1 MARK DAVID SCHWALM was born on 30 October 1983, Osteopathic Hospital, Allentown, Lehigh County, PA.

4.6.7.1.7 MARY JANE SCHWALM was born on 11 August 1926, Valley View, Schuylkill County, PA. She married **JAMES L. RUNKLE**, son of **CHESTER RUNKLE** and **PAULINE NORA SCHWALM,** on 9 February 1945. She was buried on 5 July 1996, at St. Paul's United Church of Christ Cemetery, Sacramento, Hubley Township, Schuylkill County, PA. She died on 2 July 1997, at her home on School Street Spring Glen, Hubley Township, Schuylkill County, PA, at age 70.

4.6.7.1.7.1 GARY L. RUNKLE married **BARBARA KISSINGER.**

4.6.7.1.7.1.1 BYRON RUNKLE

4.6.7.1.7.1.2 KARYN S. RUNKLE

4.6.7.1.7.2 GAIL RUNKLE married **DALE OTTO SCHROPE**, son of **NED WALLACE SCHROPE** and **ANNETTA P. OTTO.** She married **TERRY DALLEN.**

4.6.7.1.7.2.1 KIRBY SCHROPE was born on 19 September 1966, Harrisburg, Dauphin County, PA.

4.6.7.1.7.2.2 ERIC BRAD SCHROPE was born on 13 January 1973, Williamsport, Lycoming County, PA.

4.6.7.1.7.3 LINDA C. RUNKLE married **JEFFREY BROSIUS.**

4.6.7.1.7.4 CYNTHIA A. RUNKLE married **KEN GROSS.**

4.6.7.1.7.5 ROBERT D. RUNKLE married an unknown person. He married **SUSAN P. ERDMAN**, daughter of **ELWOOD EMERY ERDMAN** and **IRENE MAE SCHWALM,** on 15 September 1979.

4.6.7.1.7.5.1 JORDAN JAMES RUNKLE was born on 14 April 1991, Good Samaritan Regional Medical Center, Pottsville, Schuylkill County, PA.

4.6.7.1.7.6 SHARON SUE RUNKLE was born in 1952. She died in 1964. She was buried at St. Paul's (Artz's) Cemetery, Sacramento, Schuylkill County, PA.

4.6.7.2 ALMA MAY SCHWALM was born on 29 September 1891, Valley View, Schuylkill County, PA. She married **DANIEL H. WILLIARD**, son of **HENRY OSCAR WILLIARD** and **BARBARA AMANDA MILLER,** on 19 November 1919, Dallas County, IA.

4.6.7.2.1 FLORA WILLIARD

4.6.7.3 HATTIE ESTELLA SCHWALM was born on 6 December 1893, Valley View, Schuylkill County, IA. She married **LEROY W. KIESLING**, son of **JOHN A. KIESLING** and **SARAH M. SHADLE,** after 1920. She died on 2 February 1974, at age 80.

4.6.7.4 HARVEY RUSSELL SCHWALM was born on 17 June 1898, Valley View, Schuylkill County, IA. He married **CLARA DILLON** in 1924, TX. He died on 11 September 1948, at age 50. He was buried at Bryan City Cemetery, Bryan, Brazos County, TX.

> **4.6.7.4.1 DOROTHY E. SCHWALM** was born in 1925, in TX. She married **(--?--) WILLIER**.
>
>> **4.6.7.4.1.1 BILL WILLIER**
>>
>> **4.6.7.4.1.2 RUSSELL WILLIER**
>>
>> **4.6.7.4.1.3 KAREN WILLIER**

4.6.7.5 MILLARD STANLEY SCHWALM was born on 6 September 1900. He married **IRENE MAE BIXLER**, daughter of **MONROE BIXLER** and **SARAH ANNIE BOWERS**, on 20 November 1920, St. Andrew's Church, Valley View, Schuylkill County, PA. He died in 1944. He was buried at St. Andrew's Church Cemetery, Valley View, Schuylkill County, PA.

> **4.6.7.5.1 VERA IRENE SCHWALM** was born on 27 May 1921. She married **MARK ALLEN KIMMEL** on 18 July 1942, Gettysburg, Adams County, PA. Vera is the owner of a farm that has been in the Schwalm family since 1851. The farm was awarded a designation as a Pennsylvania Century Farm. The farm was purchased in 1851 by Frederick and Sarah Schwalm, from whom it latter passed to Samuel Schwalm, his son Ellsworth Schwalm, Vera's grandfather, Guerney Schwalm (Vera's uncle), and Millard Schwalm (Vera's father), before it was acquired by Vera and her husband Mark Kimmel in 1960. Vera's family recollections are the subject of a detailed article in the 2004 Journal of the Johannes Schwalm Historical Association.
>
>> **4.6.7.5.1.1 DORIS JEAN KIMMEL** was born on 5 January 1943. She died on 18 January 1944, at age 1. She was buried at St. Andrew's Church Cemetery, Valley View, Schuylkill County, PA.
>>
>> **4.6.7.5.1.2 GLENN MILLARD KIMMEL** was born on 29 January 1952. He married **LINDA JANE SCHREFFLER**, daughter of **MERL SCHREFFLER** and **RHEA SWINEHART**, on 25 August 1973, St. Andrew's United Methodist Church, Valley View, Schuylkill County, PA.
>>
>>> **4.6.7.5.1.2.1 RYAN KIMMEL**
>>>
>>>> **4.6.7.5.1.2.1.1 QUINTON KIMMEL**
>>>>
>>>> **4.6.7.5.1.2.1.2 NEVIN KIMMEL**
>>>>
>>>> **4.6.7.5.1.2.1.3 SHAYANNE KIMMEL**
>>
>> **4.6.7.5.1.3 PEGGY JANE KIMMEL** was born on 28 July 1955, Pottsville, Schuylkill County, PA. She married **LARRY RICHARD MILLER**, son of **LEWIS FRANKLIN MILLER** and **JOAN ELIZABETH CONRAD**, on 23 August 1975. She died on 28 June 2014, Geisinger Medical Center, Danville, Montour County, PA, at age 58. She was buried on 2 July 2014, at Saint Andrews United Methodist Church Cemetery, Valley View, Schuylkill County, PA.
>>
>>> **4.6.7.5.1.3.1 JENNIFER J. MILLER** was born on 30 March 1982. She married **KYLE KERSTETTER**.
>>>
>>>> **4.6.7.5.1.3.1.1 HAILEY P. KERSTETTER**
>>>
>>> **4.6.7.5.1.3.2 KELLY M. MILLER** was born on 5 February 1987. She married **CHARLES J. CARTER JR.**
>>>
>>>> **4.6.7.5.1.3.2.1 ANGELA M. CARTER**
>>
>> **4.6.7.5.1.4 CAROL KIMMEL** was born on 22 September 1956. She married **LEROY SHUEY** on 31 May 1975, Methodist Church, Weishample, Schuylkill County, PA.
>>
>>> **4.6.7.5.1.4.1 SHARON SHUEY** was born on 21 March 1976, Ashland Hospital, Ashland, Schuylkill County, PA.
>>>
>>> **4.6.7.5.1.4.2 MARK SHUEY** was born on 21 September 1977, Ashland Hospital, Ashland, Schuylkill County, PA.
>>>
>>>> **4.6.7.5.1.4.2.1 ANNIE JANE WENRICH** was born on 6 August 2004, Pottsville, Schuylkill County, PA.
>>>
>>> **4.6.7.5.1.4.3 MICHAEL SHUEY** was born on 21 September 1977, Ashland Hospital, Ashland, Schuylkill County, PA.
>
> **4.6.7.5.2 CLAIR MILLARD SCHWALM** was born on 11 February 1926, Valley View, Schuylkill County, PA. He was baptized on 9 May 1926, St. Andrew's United Methodist Church, Valley View, Schuylkill County, PA. He married **RUTH A. COLEMAN**, daughter of **HOMER R. COLEMAN**

and **ANNETTA SALOME MAE UMHOLTZ,** on 28 July 1945, St. Andrew's Church, Valley View, Schuylkill County, PA. He married **WILMA R. TROUTMAN,** daughter of **ROY TROUTMAN** and **MARTHA BOBB,** after 1966. He married **JOAN MACE MCCURLEY** circa 1988. He died on 3 October 2011, Catawissa, Northumberland County, PA, at age 85, at his home on Levi Lane. According to a newspaper obituary, prior to his death, Clair lived in Catawissa, PA. In his earlier years, he attended the Valley View area schools and then served with the Navy during World War II. He was owner and operator of Schwalm's Cafe, Valley View, for more than ten years, and was also employed as a coal miner and a truck driver. He was a member of the Underground Rescue EMT. From 1988 to 1996, he spent his time traveling through the country in his RV. He was buried at New Rosemont Cemetery, Espy, Columbia County, PA.

 4.6.7.5.2.1 CAROL SCHWALM married **(--?--) PASIRBA.**

 4.6.7.5.2.2 CLAIRE LOUISE SCHWALM was born on 17 September 1946. She married **JAMES NICKSIC.** Claire lives in Lititz, PA.

  4.6.7.5.2.2.1 LISA NICKSIC married **(--?--) HANN.**

   4.6.7.5.2.2.1.1 LOGAN HANN

  4.6.7.5.2.2.2 STACY NICKSIC married **(--?--) MILLER.**

   4.6.7.5.2.2.2.1 HAILEY MILLER

   4.6.7.5.2.2.2.2 TREY MILLER

 4.6.7.5.2.3 DEBORAH SCHWALM married **WILLIAM E. SCHWARTZ,** son of **IRVIN E. SCHWARTZ** and **ANNA MARIA JOOSS,** on 20 July 1968. Deborah lives in Hegins, PA.

  4.6.7.5.2.3.1 BRIAN SCHWARTZ was born on 30 April 1969.

   4.6.7.5.2.3.1.1 JACOB SCHWARTZ

   4.6.7.5.2.3.1.2 WILLIAM SCHWARTZ

  4.6.7.5.2.3.2 JILL SCHWARTZ was born on 31 March 1971.

 4.6.7.5.2.4 KEVIN SCHWALM married **SHIRLEY (--?--).** Kevin lives in Pitman, PA.

 4.6.7.5.2.5 JODI SCHWALM married **JAMES SPOTTS.** Jodi lives in Pottsville, PA.

  4.6.7.5.2.5.1 SYDNEY SPOTTS

  4.6.7.5.2.5.2 CADEY SPOTTS

 4.6.7.5.2.6 STEVEN T. SCHWALM was born in 1957. Steven lives in Lavelle, PA.

  4.6.7.5.2.6.1 ASHTON SCHWALM

4.6.7.5.3 DORA MAE SCHWALM was born on 29 October 1936. She married **WILLIAM WAGNER.**

 4.6.7.5.3.1 DANIEL WAGNER married **LINDA HORNBERGER,** daughter of **CHARLES HORNBERGER** and **SARAH (--?--).**

  4.6.7.5.3.1.1 KYLE DANIEL WAGNER was born on 17 July 1988.

  4.6.7.5.3.1.2 RYAN ANDREW WAGNER was born on 3 April 1989.

  4.6.7.5.3.1.3 JULIE DANIELLE WAGNER was born on 25 March 1993, Pottsville Hospital, Pottsville, Schuylkill County, PA.

 4.6.7.5.3.2 REV. DAVID WAGNER married **PEGGY L. KLINGER,** daughter of **PAUL R. KLINGER** and **NANCY L. KLOUSER.**

  4.6.7.5.3.2.1 CHARISSA WAGNER was born circa 1985. She married **(--?--) ZON.**

   4.6.7.5.3.2.1.1 AUDRIANNA ZON

  4.6.7.5.3.2.2 BENJAMIN LUKE WAGNER was born on 19 December 1989, Columbia City, IN.

  4.6.7.5.3.2.3 ARIEL GRACE WAGNER was born on 25 June 1993, South Whitley, IN.

 4.6.7.5.3.3 DALE WAGNER married **KELLY SHIRO.**

  4.6.7.5.3.3.1 DANELLE CHARLENE WAGNER was born on 20 May 1986.

  4.6.7.5.3.3.2 STEPHANIE ANN WAGNER was born on 10 June 1988, Harrisburg, Dauphin County, PA. She married **LUKE KIEFFER,** son of **DAVID KIEFFER** and **TENA (--?--),** in June 2014.

4.6.7.6 BEATRICE ISABELLA SCHWALM was born on 10 February 1902, Valley View, Schuylkill County, PA. She married **ROBERT W. LUCE** circa 1926. She died on 28 August 1986, Wormleysburg, PA, at age 84. A collection of Beatrice's recollections, collected by her daughter, appears in the 1998 Journal of the Johannes Schwalm Historical Association.

- **4.6.7.6.1 NANCY J. LUCE** married **LARRY GLINES**.
    - **4.6.7.6.1.1 LARRY GLINES**
    - **4.6.7.6.1.2 SUZANNE GLINES**
    - **4.6.7.6.1.3 DAWN GLINES**
    - **4.6.7.6.1.4 ROGER GLINES**
- **4.6.7.6.2 ROBERT W. LUCE JR.** married **SYLVIA MEYERS**.
    - **4.6.7.6.2.1 STEVEN D. LUCE** died on 26 April 1984.
    - **4.6.7.6.2.2 MICHELLE LUCE**
    - **4.6.7.6.2.3 ERIC LUCE**

4.6.7.6.3 JEAN M. LUCE was born on 26 February 1927. She married **ROBERT J. MASTELLER**. Prior to her death, Jean, formerly of Paxtang, PA, was living at the Ecumenical Retirement Village, Susquehanna Township, Dauphin County, PA. She died on 14 August 1999, at age 72. She was buried at Paxton Churchyard, Dauphin County, PA.

- **4.6.7.6.3.1 JOHN R. MASTELLER** married **SUSAN YOUNG**.
    - **4.6.7.6.3.1.1 AMY MASTELLER** was born in 1978.
    - **4.6.7.6.3.1.2 MICHAEL JOHN MASTELLER** was born on 18 September 1979.
- **4.6.7.6.3.2 BARBARA L. MASTELLER** married **MARK L. DEVENEY** on 20 June 1981.

4.6.7.6.4 VIRGINIA L. LUCE was born circa 1929. She married **MELVIN DUNN**.

- **4.6.7.6.4.1 LESLIE A. DUNN** married **JOHN ESSEX**.
    - **4.6.7.6.4.1.1 SARAH ESSEX** was born in 1978.
    - **4.6.7.6.4.1.2 KATHLEEN MICHELLE ESSEX** was born on 17 March 1981.
    - **4.6.7.6.4.1.3 BETH ANN ESSEX** was born on 26 August 1993.
- **4.6.7.6.4.2 DIANNE DUNN** married **WILLIAM HOMAN**. She is also referred to as **DIANE LUCE HOMAN** in some sources.
    - **4.6.7.6.4.2.1 KRISTOFF THEODORE HOMAN** was born on 8 May 1980.
- **4.6.7.6.4.3 REBECCA DUNN** married **ALAN ZURAWSKI**.

4.6.7.6.5 BARBARA LUCE was born circa 1930. She died in infancy.

4.6.7.7 ALBERT ELLSWORTH SCHWALM was born on 30 June 1904, Valley View, Schuylkill County, PA. He married **MARTHA NEY**, daughter of **RUFUS NEY** and **NELLIE (--?--)**, on 23 February 1929, St. Andrew's Church, Valley View, Schuylkill County, PA. He married **DIVA (--?--)**. At the time of his death, Albert was living at 1674 Palm Ave., San Diego, CA. He died on 24 September 1985, San Diego, San Diego County, CA, at age 81. Some sources record that he died on 25 September 1985.

- **4.6.7.7.1 ALBERT F. SCHWALM**

4.6.7.8 LILLIAN IRENE SCHWALM was born on 18 October 1905, Valley View, Schuylkill County, PA. She married **ROBERT J. MARZOLF**, son of **JOHN MARZOLF** and **ALWINE (--?--)**. She lived in 326 Ninth Street, New Cumberland, PA. She died on 16 February 1991, Harrisburg Hospital, Harrisburg, Dauphin County, PA, at age 85. She was buried at Rolling Green Memorial Park, Lower Allen Township, Cumberland County, PA.

- **4.6.7.8.1 ALICE E. MARZOLF**
- **4.6.7.8.2 IRENE MARZOLF** married **RICHARD LEONARD**.
    - **4.6.7.8.2.1 ELAINE LEONARD**
    - **4.6.7.8.2.2 PETER LEONARD**
    - **4.6.7.8.2.3 BETH LEONARD**
    - **4.6.7.8.2.4 JOY LEONARD**
    - **4.6.7.8.2.5 ANDY LEONARD**
- **4.6.7.8.3 TOM MARZOLF** married **BONNIE STARK**.

4.6.7.8.4 MARY L. MARZOLF married **JOHN TWIGG**.

4.6.7.8.4.1 WENDY TWIGG

4.6.7.8.4.2 MICHAEL TWIGG

4.6.7.8.4.3 JENNIFER TWIGG

4.6.7.9 GLADYS NAOMI SCHWALM was born on 1 January 1908, Valley View, Schuylkill County, PA. She married **GEORGE SAVAGE**. Prior to her death, Gladys was living at 315 Eighth Street, New Cumberland, Cumberland County, PA. She died on 17 May 1991, Fairview Village Nursing Home, Fairview Township, Cumberland County, PA, at age 83. She was buried at Mt. Olivet Cemetery, Fairview Township, Cumberland County, PA.

4.6.7.9.1 DONALD SAVAGE

4.6.7.9.2 GEORGE E. SAVAGE was born circa 1939. He married **FAYE (--?--)**. He died on 2 June 1998, at home, New Cumberland, Cumberland County, PA. He was buried at Mt. Olivet Cemetery, Fairview Township, York County, PA.

4.6.8 INFANT SON SCHWALM was born on 15 February 1870. He died on 15 February 1870. He was buried at St. Paul's (Artz's) Church Cemetery, Sacramento, Schuylkill County, PA.

4.6.9 ALICE MARIE SCHWALM was born on 4 April 1871. She married **WILLIAM H. GESSNER** circa 1896. She died in 1953.

4.6.9.1 IVA MINERVA GESSNER is also referred to as **IVY** in some sources. She was born on 3 April 1897, Valley View, Schuylkill County, PA. She married **JOHN CLARK ROBINSON SR.** in 1924. She died on 4 July 1995, Nottingham Village, Northumberland, Northumberland County, PA, at age 98. She was buried at Evergreen Cemetery, Selinsgrove, Snyder County, PA.

4.6.9.1.1 ELIZABETH ROBINSON also went by the name of **BETTY**. She was born on 29 January 1925, Spring Mills, Centre County, PA. She married **EARLE F. MILLER** on 22 March 1942. According to a newspaper obituary, Elizabeth lived on Comly Road, Turbotville, PA. She was a graduate of Spring Mills High School and Geisinger Medical Center School of Nursing in 1946. Betty worked as a Navy Cadet Nurse and as a pediatric nurse at Geisinger, in Danville. She received a proclamation from the Pennsylvania Historical and Museum Commission for 33 years of service to the Warrior Run Fort Freeland Heritage Society. She was buried on 21 February 2007, at Turbotville Cemetery, Turbotville, Northumberland County, PA.

4.6.9.1.2 JOHN C. ROBINSON JR. was born on 27 December 1932. He married **PEGGI LIVINGSTON**. John lives in Wayne, PA.

4.6.9.1.2.1 REBECCA ROBINSON was born in 1974.

4.6.9.1.2.2 JOHN CLARK ROBINSON III was born in 1968.

4.6.9.1.2.3 THOMAS ROBINSON was born in 1971.

4.6.9.2 GEORGE SAMUEL GESSNER was born on 21 July 1898. He married **FLORENCE CORNELL**. At the time of his death, George was living in Kintnersville, Bucks County, PA. He died on 21 October 1979, Kintnersville, Bucks County, PA, at age 81.

4.6.9.2.1 WILLIAM ELWOOD GESSNER was born in 1925. He married **DOROTHY THYGESON**. He married **DORIS SIEGFRIED**.

4.6.9.2.1.1 WILLIAM GESSNER

4.6.9.2.1.2 VICTORIA ANN GESSNER was born in 1954.

4.6.9.2.1.3 VALERIE GESSNER was born in 1957.

4.6.9.2.2 RICHARD W. GESSNER married **SUSAN WILLIAMS**. He was born in 1928.

4.6.9.2.2.1 RICHARD W. GESSNER JR. was born in 1952.

4.6.9.2.2.2 ROBERT GESSNER was born in 1954.

4.6.9.2.2.3 ELIZABETH GESSNER was born in 1956.

4.6.9.2.3 JAMES S. GESSNER was born in 1933.

4.6.9.3 GRACE UNA GESSNER was born on 26 February 1907. She married **JAMES STUART BARR**. She died on 28 April 1997, at age 90. She was buried at West Laurel Hill Cemetery, Bala Cynwyd, Montgomery County, PA.

4.6.10 FRANCIS SCHWALM was born on 20 April 1875. He died on 21 October 1880, at age 5. He was buried at St. Paul's (Artz's) Church Cemetery, Sacramento, Schuylkill County, PA.

4.7 EDWARD KLINGER is also referred to as **HENRY EDWARD MORTON** in some sources. He was born circa 1832. He married **ANNA OTTO**, daughter of **JONATHAN OTTO** and **SUSANNAH BRESSLER,** on 24 August 1851. He and **ANNA OTTO** were divorced on 9 September 1858 Schuylkill County, PA, on grounds of desertion by Edward, beginning 16 Aug 1855. Edward served in the US Army, Company L, 3rd Regiment, Pennsylvania Calvary, during the Civil War but then deserted. Service records list an Edward Klinger, sometimes listed with the middle initial "W" and sometimes with the middle initial "E," as enlisting for service on August 22, 1861. Apparently, Edward Klinger deserted on February 22, 1863. Other evidence confirms that this was likely Edward. Testimony of Valentine Savage in connection with the Estate of Peter Klinger indicates that Edward "went West" in the mid 1850's, but occasionally visited his family in Pennsylvania. According to this testimony, Edward used the surname "Moreton" [Morton] because he had deserted from the army. He married **ALICE DEAR** on 22 January 1873. Alice was from Syracuse, NY. Edward not only moved around but also often went by other names, such as Edward Morton, Henry Morton, H.E. Morton, or Harry Morton. The testimony of his brother Israel in connection with their Father's Estate proceedings confirms the basic facts that he was married at least twice, the second time in St. Louis, MO, had 2 children, one by each spouse. Edward (under the name Henry Edward Morton) filed a petition for divorce from his second wife, Alice, in St. Louis County, Missouri in February, 1877. According to the divorce petition, they lived together until December 10, 1875, after which they lived separately. The divorce from Alice was granted in April, 1877. He married **ELIZABETH PATTERSON** on 16 February 1878, St. Louis, MO. He died on 11 July 1878, St. Louis, MO. He was buried at Potter's Field, St. Louis, MO.

> **4.7.1 TOBIAS KLINGER** is also referred to as **TOBIAS CLINGER** in some sources. He was born on 18 January 1855, Schuylkill County, PA. He married **MAUDE COOK**, daughter of **LAWSON COOK,** on 29 January 1902. He died on 22 February 1924, Julian, Nemaha County, NE, at age 69. He was buried at Camp Creek Cemetery, Otoe County, NE.
>
> > **4.7.1.1 ANNA MARGARET KLINGER** was born on 25 November 1902, in Nebraska. She married **CHARLES EDWARD FEILEN**, son of **JOHN FEILEN** and **LOUISE KOMMA**. She died in June 1982, Julian, Nemaha, NE, at age 79.
> >
> > > **4.7.1.1.1 KENNETH DARYL FEILEN** is also referred to as **DERYLE** in some sources. He was born on 3 June 1923, Julian, NE. He married **EMMA E. SPORHASE**, daughter of **JOHN SPORHASE** and **ANNA EHLERS,** on 16 January 1943. He died in August 1984, at age 61.
> > >
> > > > **4.7.1.1.1.1 GEORGE E. FEILEN** was born on 22 February 1943, Nebraska City, Otoe County, NE. He married **ROWENE (--?--)**. He died on 2 September 2014, Council Bluffs, Pottawattamie County, IA, at age 71. He was buried at Ridgewood Cemetery, Council Bluffs, Pottawattamie County, IA. George was a foreman for Wonder Bread and later worked in the Council Bluffs School System at Carter Lake Elementary.
> > > >
> > > > **4.7.1.1.1.2 KENNETH J. FEILEN** was born on 15 August 1946. He married **MARGE (--?--)**. He died on 6 March 2008, Council Bluffs, Pottawattamie County, IA, at age 61.
> > > >
> > > > **4.7.1.1.1.3 JERRY FEILEN** married **DEBBIE (--?--)**.
> > > >
> > > > **4.7.1.1.1.4 ROGER FEILEN** married **KAREN (--?--)**.
> > > >
> > > > **4.7.1.1.1.5 LARRY FEILEN** married **KAYE (--?--)**.
> > > >
> > > > **4.7.1.1.1.6 ROSEANN MARIE FEILEN** was born on 5 February 1963. She died before 2005.
> > >
> > > **4.7.1.1.2 MARGARET JEAN FEILEN** was born on 26 October 1930, Nebraska City, Otoe County, NE. She married **HOWARD CHRISTENSEN** circa 1953. She died on 21 January 2004, Council Bluffs, Pottawattamie County, IA, at age 73.
> > >
> > > > **4.7.1.1.2.1 CHRIS CHRISTENSEN**
> >
> > **4.7.1.2 LOTTIE BELL KLINGER** was born on 11 April 1904, in Nebraska. She married **FAY MILL JONES** after 1920. She died on 3 August 1991, at age 87. She was buried at Wyuka Cemetery, Nebraska City, Otoe County, NE.
> >
> > > **4.7.1.2.1 RUTH JONES** was born circa 1924.
> >
> > **4.7.1.3 WILLIAM C. KLINGER** was born circa 1907, in Nebraska.
> >
> > **4.7.1.4 MARY FLORENCE KLINGER** was born in 1908, in Nebraska. She married **LESTER G. LEIDIGH** after 1930. She died on 21 June 1986. She was buried at Wyuka Cemetery, Nebraska City, Otoe County, NE.

4.7.1.5 HILDA LOUISE KLINGER was born in 1910, in Nebraska. She married **ALVIN W. STEINHOFF**, son of **HENRY D. STEINHOFF** and **SOPHIA M. ALBERS**. She died in 1993. She was buried at Park Hill Cemetery, Syracuse, Otoe County, NE.

4.7.1.5.1 KENNETH D. STEINHOFF was born on 9 January 1935.

4.7.1.5.2 RICHARD A. STEINHOFF was born on 19 October 1939. He married **BRENDA NABER** in May 1960, Lincoln, NE.

4.7.2 IDA EMMA KLINGER is also referred to as **IDA MORTON** in some sources. She was born on 29 September 1874, in Missouri. In 1882, Thomas C. Martin was appointed by the Probate Court for the City of St. Louis as Curator (or guardian) of the estate Ida Klinger who was then 7 years and 11 months old. An affidavit by Clara J. Miller, the mother of Edward's third wife, Elizabeth, indicates that after Edward's divorce from Alice, Edward and Elizabeth took care of Ida, but Edward's death left Elizabeth in "destitute circumstances," whereupon Ida was given over to the care of Thomas Martin. The affidavit also states that Elizabeth had remarried and was then living in Leadville, CO. After Thomas Martin's wife died in the 1880's, Ida apparently was sent to live with a sister of Thomas Martin and then later to an aunt's home in Des Moines, IA. Sometime later, according to family history as related by Margaret Downing, Ida's mother Alice took Ida to Canada, where Ida was enrolled at the Convent of Sacred Heart, in Calgary, Alberta. She married **FREDERICK HERBERT GIBBS** on 12 April 1896, Winnipeg, Manitoba, Canada. She died on 9 April 1920, at age 45. She was buried at Memorial Park, Grand Forks, Grand Forks County, ND.

4.7.2.1 NELLIE GIBBS was born on 4 October 1894, Winnipeg, Manitoba, Canada. Some sources record that she was born around 1900, but Nellie was listed as 4 years old in June 1900, at the time of the 1900 Census. She married **EINER JENSEN** circa 1916. She married **JULIUS RUDAHL** after 1930. She died on 12 September 1982, San Mateo, CA, at age 87. At Nellie's request, her daughter Pauline gave Nellie's date of birth as 4 Oct 1901 for her tombstone and death certificate. Her Social Security records list the date of birth as 4 October 1900, but the correct date was 4 October 1894.

4.7.2.1.1 MARLENE JUNE RUDAHL was born circa 1933. She married **LOUIE PETERSON**. She and **LOUIE PETERSON** were divorced.

4.7.2.1.1.1 JAY PETERSON

4.7.2.1.1.2 STEVEN PETERSON

4.7.2.1.1.3 TENA PETERSON

4.7.2.1.2 PAULENE OLIVE RUDAHL was born circa 1937. She married **PHILIP NELSON**. She and **PHILIP NELSON** were divorced. She married **TOM MCCORMICK**. She and **TOM MCCORMICK** were divorced.

4.7.2.1.2.1 KELLY MCCORMICK married **CHRIS MCHENRY**.

4.7.2.1.2.1.1 ELLA MCHENRY

4.7.2.1.2.2 WES MCCORMICK married **SANDRA (--?--)**.

4.7.2.2 FREDERICK EUGENE GIBBS was born on 9 January 1898, Grand Forks, ND. He married **NELLIE HELEN MULVANEY**, daughter of **MATTHEW MULVANEY** and **ELIZA (--?--)**, circa 1926, by common law marriage. He died on 11 August 1972, Ramsey County, MN, at age 74.

4.7.2.3 OLIVE IDA GIBBS was born on 23 February 1900. She married **ALBERT RINDFLEISCH**. She died on 19 October 1974, Ramsey County, MN, at age 74.

4.7.2.3.1 ALBERT E. RINDFLEISCH was born on 8 April 1928.

4.7.2.3.1.1 MATTHEW RINDFLEISCH

4.7.2.3.1.2 AUDREY RINDFLEISCH

4.7.2.3.1.3 ROGER RINDFLEISCH

4.7.2.3.1.4 ALLEN RINDFLEISCH

4.7.2.3.2 CAROL ANN RINDFLEISCH was born on 29 December 1932. She married **DONALD R.C. SPIESS**. She died on 28 April 1987, at age 54.

4.7.2.3.3 DONNA F. RINDFLEISCH married **FLOYD PINOTTI**.

4.7.2.3.3.1 MICHAEL ALBERT PINOTTI

4.7.2.3.3.2 DANIEL PINOTTI

4.7.2.3.3.3 JOSEPH C. PINOTTI

4.7.2.3.4 RITA KAY RINDFLEISCH was born on 25 November 1935. She married **WILLIAM C. MACDONALD.** Rita, who lives in Minnesota, has compiled much information on the descendants of Ida Emma Klinger.

- **4.7.2.3.4.1 WILLIAM CHARLES MACDONALD** was born on 5 August 1963.
- **4.7.2.3.4.2 THOMAS EDWARD MACDONALD** was born on 20 January 1966.
- **4.7.2.3.4.3 CAROLE JEANNE MACDONALD** was born on 1 February 1968.

4.7.2.4 CHARLES EDWARD GIBBS was born in 1903, Grand Forks, ND. He married **OLGA KOWALSKI.** He died on 16 June 1972, Chicago, Cook County, IL. He was buried at Mt. Hope Cemetery.

- **4.7.2.4.1 MELVIN GIBBS** was born on 10 December 1930. He died in 1934.

4.8 ABRAHAM KLINGER was born circa 1836. Abraham, who may have died young, was listed in the 1850 Census, but it is not clear if he was Peter and Catharine's son.

4.9 AGATHA CATHERINE KLINGER was born on 12 January 1837. Some sources record that she was born on 16 June 1837, Schuylkill County, PA. She was confirmed on 9 April 1852 St. Paul's (Artz's) Church, Sacramento, Hubley Township, Schuylkill County, PA. She married **JACOB EMERICH FERTIG** on 18 June 1854, Schuylkill County, PA. She died on 17 December 1888, Philadelphia, Philadelphia County, PA, at age 51. She was buried at St. John's (Kimmel's) Lutheran and Reformed Church Cemetery, Philadelphia, Barry Township, Schuylkill County`, PA.

4.9.1 WALLACE KLINGER FERTIG was born on 25 October 1855, Schuylkill County, PA. He married **ELMIRA SEITZ**, daughter of **JACOB SEITZ** and **EMMA ARTZ,** on 3 June 1876. He married **CAROLINE EMMA KLINE**, daughter of **GEORGE KLINE** and **CAROLINE ARTZ,** on 6 September 1889, Atlantic City, NJ. He died on 28 January 1916, at age 60. He was buried at Mount Carmel Cemetery, Mount Carmel, Northumberland County, PA.

4.9.1.1 LULA FERTIG was born on 23 May 1878, Helfenstein, Schuylkill County, PA. She married **EDWIN S. WILLIAMS** on 23 June 1900, New Franklin, Franklin County, PA. She died on 1 June 1905, at age 27. She was buried at St. John's (Kimmel's) Lutheran and Reformed Church Cemetery, Barry Township, Schuylkill County`, PA.

4.9.1.1.1 WALTER STANLEY WILLIAMS was born on 20 April 1901, Mount Carmel, Northumberland County, PA. He died on 14 April 1926, Burkburnett, Wichita County, TX, at age 24. He was buried at Burkburnett Memorial Cemetery, Burkburnett, Wichita County, TX. Walter was an oilfield worker in Texas.

4.9.1.2 HARRY FREMONT FERTIG was born on 2 March 1885, Mount Carmel, Northumberland County, PA. He married **CAROLINE CATHERINE OWENS** on 13 December 1909, Mount Carmel, Northumberland County, PA. He died on 16 October 1918, at age 33 , during the Spanish Influenza Epidemic. Harry was a carpenter and worked for the Pennsylvania Railroad Coal and Iron Co. He was buried at Mount Carmel Cemetery, Mount Carmel, Northumberland County, PA.

4.9.1.2.1 FREMONT WALLACE FERTIG was born on 6 October 1912, Mount Carmel, Northumberland County, PA. Some sources record that he was born on 6 October 1912, Camden, NJ. He married **RUTH MIRIAM SHOMPER** on 4 August 1936, Corning, NY. He died on 21 December 1989, at age 77. He was buried at Halifax, Dauphin County, PA.

4.9.1.2.1.1 CORINDA RUTH FERTIG was born in 1938. She married **ROBERT KREIDLER.** Corinda is a registered nurse.

4.9.1.2.1.1.1 JOHN R. KREIDLER was born on 10 December 1960. He married **LAURIE WOODBURY.**

- **4.9.1.2.1.1.1.1 TIMOTHY KREIDLER**
- **4.9.1.2.1.1.1.2 TYLER KREIDLER**

4.9.1.2.1.1.2 JANET R. KREIDLER was born on 8 March 1963. She married **ROBERT METTLER.**

4.9.1.2.1.1.3 JAMES FERTIG KREIDLER was born on 3 June 1964. He married **LISA HAUP.**

- **4.9.1.2.1.1.3.1 CURTIS J. KREIDLER**
- **4.9.1.2.1.1.3.2 COREY A. KREIDLER**

4.9.1.2.1.2 CAROLINE HARRIET FERTIG was born in 1942. She married **REV. WILLIAM K. ADAMS**. Caroline is a registered nurse.

4.9.1.2.1.2.1 DEBORAH LYNN ADAMS was born on 9 August 1964. She married **MARK T. THOMPSON**.

4.9.1.2.1.2.1.1 WILLIAM A. THOMPSON

4.9.1.2.1.2.1.2 KATHERINE R. THOMPSON

4.9.1.2.1.2.1.3 LINDSEY M. THOMPSON

4.9.1.2.1.2.1.4 CARRIE N. THOMPSON

4.9.1.2.1.2.2 WILLIAM KELSEY ADAMS JR. was born on 7 October 1965. He married **P. JOY BALDWIN**.

4.9.1.2.1.2.2.1 KELSEY A. ADAMS

4.9.1.2.1.2.2.2 CASSIDY J. ADAMS

4.9.1.2.1.2.3 DAVID STUART ADAMS was born on 3 August 1970. He married **CONNIE M. SEALS**.

4.9.1.2.1.2.3.1 HOLLY D. ADAMS

4.9.1.2.1.3 RUTH ANN FERTIG was born in 1953. She married **THOMAS LOGAN**.

4.9.1.2.1.3.1 HEATHER LOGAN

4.9.1.2.2 PAULINE OWENS FERTIG was born on 24 November 1916, Shamokin, Northumberland County, PA. She married **DR. ARTHUR SERVER** on 28 November 1942, Rapidan Arsenal, Edison, NJ. She married **SIDNEY SMITH** after 1967. She died on 16 August 2002, in New Jersey, at age 85. She was buried at Hollywood Memorial Park, Union, NJ. Pauline was a registered nurse. During World War II, she was a 1st Lieutenant in the US Army serving as a nurse in Europe.

4.9.1.2.2.1 GARY SANFORD SERVER was born on 10 December 1950.

4.9.1.2.2.2 JON ALAN SERVER was born on 17 July 1956.

4.9.1.2.3 HARRIET OWENS FERTIG was born on 5 February 1919, Mount Carmel, Northumberland County, PA. She married **GLENN ARTHUR SMITH** on 10 October 1945. She died on 10 January 1995, Okeechobee, FL, at age 75. Harriet was a registered nurse.

4.9.1.2.3.1 BARRY ARTHUR SMITH was born on 30 June 1948. He married **SALLY R. PITMAN**.

4.9.1.2.3.2 PERRY OWENS SMITH was born on 23 October 1954. He married **BEVERLY L. BAIN**.

4.9.1.3 ANNIE VIOLA FERTIG is also referred to as **ANNA F. FERTIG** in some sources. She was born on 2 November 1890. She was baptized on 27 August 1891, Grace Evangelical Lutheran Church, Mount Carmel, Northumberland County, PA. She married **ROBERT W. ELTRINGHAM**, son of **THOMAS S. ELTRINGHAM** and **AGNES WEIR**, on 19 June 1911, Williamsport, Lycoming County, PA. She died on 12 February 1977, at age 86. She was buried at Mount Carmel Cemetery, Mount Carmel, Northumberland County, PA. Annie graduated from the Ashland State General Hospital School of Nursing in 1910 and lived in Frackville, PA.

4.9.1.3.1 ELIZABETH ELTRINGHAM also went by the name of **BETTY**. She was born on 8 December 1911. She married **JOHN FRANCIS CHRISTIE** on 10 April 1939. She died on 13 September 1991, at age 79. Betty graduated from the Bryn Mawr School of Nursing and lived in Bryn Mawr, PA.

4.9.1.3.1.1 JOHN F. CHRISTIE III was born on 22 July 1940. He married **PENELOPE (--?--)**.

4.9.1.3.1.1.1 DANIELLE CHRISTIE was born on 27 January 1971.

4.9.1.3.1.1.2 J. ALEXANDER CHRISTIE was born on 9 January 1974.

4.9.1.3.1.2 MICHAEL CHRISTIE was born on 22 October 1945. He died on 22 May 1960, at age 14 as a result of injuries received in a bicycle accident.

4.9.1.3.2 MARION ANNA ELTRINGHAM was born on 5 April 1913. She married **WILLIAM J. ROBERTS** on 17 June 1936. She died on 8 June 1984, at age 71. She was buried at Odd Fellows Cemetery, Frackville, Schuylkill County, PA.

4.9.1.3.2.1 ELIZABETH ANN ROBERTS was born on 2 April 1937. She married **JEROME YESALAVAGE**, son of **ALBERT A. YESALAVAGE** and **ADELE A. URBAN,** on 21 June 1958. She married **GERALD NESVOLD** on 31 August 1985. Elizabeth lives in Pitman, PA.

    4.9.1.3.2.1.1 KERRY JEROME YESALAVAGE was born on 12 May 1961.

        4.9.1.3.2.1.1.1 NICOLE MARIE YESALAVAGE was born on 15 September 1987.

            4.9.1.3.2.1.1.1.1 CORA MAE CUFF was born on 26 November 2013.

    4.9.1.3.2.1.2 LISA JANE YESALAVAGE was born on 10 April 1967. She married **TIMOTHY WRIGHT** on 17 May 1991.

        4.9.1.3.2.1.2.1 GRACE ELIZABETH WRIGHT was born on 24 June 1999.

    4.9.1.3.2.1.3 MAX ADAM YESALAVAGE was born on 31 August 1973.

4.9.1.3.2.2 SUSAN MARY ROBERTS was born on 16 June 1947. She married **JOHN J. CANTWELL** on 29 May 1970. Susan lives in Pottsville, PA.

    4.9.1.3.2.2.1 JOHN JAMES CANTWELL JR. was born on 20 January 1974.

        4.9.1.3.2.2.1.1 BRIDGHID ANYA CANTWELL was born on 16 March 2002.

        4.9.1.3.2.2.1.2 TIERNEY ELIZABETH CANTWELL was born on 16 March 2002.

        4.9.1.3.2.2.1.3 RORY KATHRYN CANTWELL was born on 14 October 2003.

    4.9.1.3.2.2.2 JEREMY ROBERTS CANTWELL was born on 19 May 1977.

4.9.1.3.2.3 REX ANTHONY ROBERTS was born on 23 November 1953. Rex lives in Brooklyn Heights, NY.

4.9.1.3.3 ROBERT WEIR ELTRINGHAM II was born on 2 October 1927. He married **EDITH CHARLOTTE PARKER**, daughter of **ISAIAH PARKER** and **CHARLOTTE GOLDSWORTHY,** on 25 February 1950. He died on 28 October 2012, Care Central Center at Homewood-Plumcreek, Hanover, PA, at age 85. He was buried at Meadow Branch Cemetery, Westminster, Carroll County, MD.

    4.9.1.3.3.1 CAROL JEAN ELTRINGHAM was born on 22 May 1957. She married **CHARLES R. WEYRAUCH III.** Carol lives in Salt Lake City, UT.

    4.9.1.3.3.2 LORI PARKER ELTRINGHAM was born on 31 March 1962. She died on 22 April 1983, at age 21. She was buried at Meadow Branch Cemetery, Westminster, Carroll County, MD. Lori, while a student at Indiana University of Pennsylvania, was killed in an auto accident by a drunk driver.

4.9.1.4 MINNIE ALBERTA MIRIAM FERTIG also went by the name of **MICK.** She was born on 11 April 1893. She was baptized on 24 June 1897, Grace Lutheran Church, Mount Carmel, Northumberland County, PA. She married **JEROME B. GRAY.** She died on 30 June 1958, at age 65. Minnie (Miriam) was a graduate of Chester County Hospital School of Nursing and served as a public health nurse in Philadelphia.

4.9.1.4.1 ALICE HOOPES GRAY was born on 16 April 1924, Cambridge, MA. She died on 25 July 2014, Barclay Friends, West Chester, PA, at age 90. According to a newspaper obituary, Alice grew up in The Dower House on North High Street in West Chester, purportedly the oldest home in town, restored by the noted novelist Joseph Hergesheimer. She lived at that address most of her life. Alice won many golfing honors, including the Dorothy Campbell Howe Cup at Merion in 1964. Her amateur career culminated with two Pennsylvania State Women's Amateur golf championships in 1961 and 1963. With little monetary gain possible for women golf professionals in the sixties, Alice become a ladies pro and instructor first at West Chester Golf & Country Club and later at Edgmont Country Club in Newtown Square. Her non-sport interests included gardening and watercolor painting. A recollection of her life accompanied by many photos is available at https://sites.google.com/site/alicegrayremembered/.

4.9.1.4.2 JANE BETHEL GRAY was born on 24 November 1925. She married **PHILIP JAMISON** on 11 October 1950. She died on 16 February 2008, at age 82. Jane was a watercolor artist who lived in West Chester, PA, with her husband, Philip, who is a well-known painter.

    4.9.1.4.2.1 PHILIP JAMISON III. Philip lives in West Chester, PA.

    4.9.1.4.2.2 LINDA B. JAMISON was born on 12 January 1955. Linda and her identical twin sister Terry achieved some notoriety as the "Psychic Twins" in connection with predictions they made concerning terrorist attacks in 2002. They live in Los Angeles, CA.

4.9.1.4.2.3 TERRY JANE JAMISON was born on 12 January 1955.

4.9.1.5 ALMA LEE FERTIG was born on 19 September 1894, Mount Carmel, Northumberland County, PA. She was baptized on 24 June 1897, Grace Lutheran Church, Mount Carmel, Northumberland County, PA. She married JOHN WALTER BERGSTRESSER, son of SAMUEL EDWARD BERGSTRESSER and CLARA KELLER. She died on 21 February 1962, Allentown, Lehigh County, PA, at age 67. She was buried on 24 February 1962, at Mount Carmel Cemetery, Mount Carmel, Northumberland County, PA. Alma was a school teacher. After earning a teaching certificate from Bloomsburg College, Alma taught in Helfenstein, Gordon, and Trevorton, PA. She was also an accomplished singer.

4.9.1.5.1 CAROLINE FERTIG BERGSTRESSER was born on 15 November 1923. She married GLENN BLAINE SMITH, son of J. WARREN SMITH and EDNA RUPP, on 22 December 1945, Grace Lutheran Church, Mount Carmel, Northumberland County, PA. She died on 27 August 2006, Allentown, Lehigh County, PA, at age 82. She was buried at Mount Carmel Cemetery, Mount Carmel, Northumberland County, PA. Carolyn attended Dickinson Seminary in Williamsport, PA, and later worked for the Allentown School District. Her husband Glenn was a wrestling coach in Bellefonte and later in Allentown.

4.9.1.5.1.1 KIMBER DAVID SMITH was born on 29 September 1948.

4.9.1.5.1.2 CARROLL LEE SMITH was born on 14 June 1952. She married ROBERT E. LEE JR. on 23 June 1973, United States Naval Academy, Annapolis, MD.

4.9.1.6 WALTER K. FERTIG was born on 18 December 1900, Mount Carmel, Northumberland County, PA. He married MARIE STRIDE EDWARDS on 6 October 1922, Sunbury, Northumberland County, PA. He died on 22 February 1983, Geisinger Hospital, Danville, Montour County, PA, at age 82. He was buried at Mount Carmel Cemetery, Mount Carmel, Northumberland County, PA. Walter lived in Mount Carmel, PA, and worked for Prudential Insurance for 42 years.

4.9.1.6.1 WALTER K. FERTIG was born on 31 December 1927, Mount Carmel, Northumberland County, PA. He began military service on 16 March 1946. He ended military service on 21 September 1947. He married PHYLLIS L. LERCH on 17 May 1952. He died on 10 March 1998, Waynesboro Hospital, Waynesboro, Franklin County, PA, at age 70. According to a newspaper obituary, Walter was known as "Kay." He was a 1945 graduate of Mount Carmel High School; and a 1951 graduate of Penn State College with a degree in forestry. He served in the U.S. Army and was employed by the Army Map Service from 1951 to 1957. He was later employed by the Central Intelligence Agency from 1957 until his retirement in 1980. He was buried at Mount Carmel Cemetery, Mount Carmel, Northumberland County, PA.

4.9.1.6.1.1 WYNN K. FERTIG was born on 27 January 1960, Washington, DC. Wynn lives in Frederick, MD.

4.9.1.6.2 MARGARET ANN FERTIG was born on 28 July 1936, Danville, Montour County, PA. She married EDWARD J. DOWNING on 16 May 1959, Grace Lutheran Church, Mount Carmel, Northumberland County, PA. Margaret provided much of the research and the development of the listings of the descendants of Agatha Catherine Klinger.

4.9.1.6.2.1 DIANE ELAINE DOWNING was born on 23 October 1960, Okinawa, Japan. She married H. SCOTT STADLER on 28 November 1987, Fort Meyer Chapel, Fort Meyer, VA. Diane is an assistant professor at Health Sciences University in Portland, OR.

4.9.1.6.2.1.1 CHRISTOPHER SCOTT STADLER was born on 4 September 1989, Iowa City, IA.

4.9.1.6.2.1.2 EMILY PAIGE STADLER was born on 27 July 1993, Iowa City, IA.

4.9.1.6.2.1.3 JONATHON MICHAEL STADLER was born on 1 April 1995, Iowa City, IA.

4.9.1.6.2.2 EDWARD ANDREW DOWNING was born on 21 January 1964, Bellefonte, Centre County, PA. "Drew" is currently living in Hawaii on assignment as a civilian employee of the US Army.

4.9.1.6.2.2.1 BRYCE EDWARD DOWNING was born on 12 May 1996, Alexandria, VA.

4.9.1.6.2.2.2 PEYTON ANDREW DOWNING was born on 4 February 2000, Troy, MI.

4.9.1.6.2.3 MEGAN MARY DOWNING was born on 11 August 1970, Tripler Army Medical Center, Honolulu, HI. She married DAVID CHRISTOPHER CHASE. Megan is a teacher at the Waldorf School in Richmond, VA.

4.9.1.6.2.3.1 SOPHIE MARIE CHASE was born on 1 July 1996, Charlottesville, Albemarle County, VA.

4.9.1.6.2.3.2 GEORGIA LOUISE CHASE was born on 15 October 2001, Richmond, VA.

4.9.1.6.2.3.3 DAVID ELIAS CHASE was born on 15 January 2004, Richmond, VA.

4.9.1.6.2.4 MARGARET PAULINE DOWNING was born on 11 December 1971, Tripler Army Medical Center, Honolulu, HI. She married **WILLIAM M. HECKER** on 22 June 2002. Margaret is an RN and lives in Lakewood, CO.

4.9.1.6.2.4.1 ISABEL ANN HECKER was born on 15 July 2003, Denver, CO.

4.9.2 ALICE FERTIG was born on 28 January 1858. She married **EMERSON WEBSTER FARROW**, son of **SILAS FARROW** and **CHARITY MILLER**. She died on 20 March 1876, Helfenstein, Schuylkill County, PA, at age 18, of postpartum hemorrhage. She was buried at St. John's (Kimmel's) Lutheran Church Cemetery, Barry Township, Schuylkill County, PA.

4.9.2.1 ALICE AGATHA FARROW was born on 20 March 1876, Helfenstein, Schuylkill County, PA. She married **CLEMENT SCHNEIDER** in September 1895, Church of Our Lady, Mount Carmel, Northumberland County, PA. She died on 16 June 1958, at age 82. She was buried at St. Mary's Cemetery, Mount Carmel, Northumberland County, PA.

4.9.2.1.1 MILDRED SCHNEIDER was born on 16 August 1901. She married **BURTON M. MILLARD**, son of **DR. BENJAMIN J. MILLARD** and **LOTTIE R. (--?--)**. She died on 26 December 1986, at age 85. She was buried at Mount Carmel Cemetery, Mount Carmel, Northumberland County, PA.

4.9.2.1.1.1 MARY ALICE MILLARD was born circa 1924.

4.9.2.1.1.2 ANNE S. MILLARD was born circa 1928.

4.9.2.1.2 RAMONA SCHNEIDER was born on 16 August 1901. Some sources record that she was born on 16 August 1902. She married **JOHN CECIL** circa 1929. She died in an auto accident on 13 July 1968, at age 66. She was buried at Saint Mary's Cemetery, Mount Carmel, Northumberland County, PA. Ramona was a high School teacher in Mount Carmel, PA.

4.9.2.1.2.1 JACQUELINE CECIL was born in 1931.

4.9.2.1.3 PAUL SCHNEIDER was born on 30 October 1903. Some sources record that he was born on 28 October 1904. He married **HANNAH G. BOSCHE**. He died on 23 June 1981, at age 77. He was buried at Saint Mary's Cemetery, Mount Carmel, Northumberland County, PA. Paul was a dentist in Mount Carmel, PA.

4.9.2.1.3.1 PAUL CHRISTIAN SCHNEIDER was born circa 1934. He married **MARY PALUMBIS**. He died on 23 June 1981.

4.9.2.1.3.2 PATRICIA ANN SCHNEIDER was born after 1940. She married **DAVID FOSTER**.

4.9.2.1.4 ANNA MARGARET SCHNEIDER is also referred to as **ANNE** in some sources. She was born on 14 May 1906. She married **ANTHONY C. ANDRULONIS**, son of **ANTHONY ANDRULONIS** and **ANNA (--?--)**, before 1940. She died on 27 November 1986, at age 80. She was buried at Saint Mary's Cemetery, Mount Carmel, Northumberland County, PA.

4.9.2.1.4.1 JEROME A. ANDRULONIS was born in 1943. He married **JOANNE (--?--)**.

4.9.2.1.4.1.1 JOANE ANDRULONIS

4.9.2.1.4.1.2 BUCKEY ANDRULONIS

4.9.2.1.4.1.3 ANNE MARIE ANDRULONIS

4.9.2.1.4.2 PAUL ANTHONY ANDRULONIS was born on 6 May 1946. He married **SYLVIA (--?--)**. He died on 27 September 1999, West Hartford, Hartford County, CT, at age 53. He was buried at Saint Mary's Cemetery, Mount Carmel, Northumberland County, PA. Paul was a child psychiatrist in Hartford, CT.

4.9.2.1.4.2.1 ANTHONY ANDRULONIS was born in 1971.

4.9.2.1.4.2.2 CHRISSIE ANDRULONIS was born in 1974.

4.9.2.1.4.2.3 DAVID ANDRULONIS was born in 1977.

4.9.2.1.5 CLEMENT JOHN SCHNEIDER was born on 2 January 1909. Some sources record that he was born on 1 January 1909. He married **VALERIA BETZ**, daughter of **JOSEPH P. BETZ** and **AMELIA M. (--?--)**, circa 1929. He died on 27 May 1991, San Diego, CA, at age 82.

4.9.2.1.5.1 CLEM JOSEPH SCHNEIDER JR. was born on 14 April 1934. He died on 28 May 1972, at age 38.

4.9.2.1.5.2 VALERIE ANNE SCHNEIDER was born after 1940. She married **DAVID M. BREAM**.

4.9.2.1.6 ALICE SCHNEIDER was born on 20 June 1920. Some sources record that she was born in 1915. She married **JOHN HIGGINS** on 12 August 1943. She died on 5 October 2005, at age 85.

4.9.2.1.6.1 BONNIE ALICE HIGGINS was born on 1 May 1944. She married **GERALD WASCAVAGE**.

4.9.2.1.6.1.1 BRIAN WASCAVAGE was born in 1966.

4.9.2.1.6.1.2 MICHAILYN WASCAVAGE was born in 1968.

4.9.2.1.6.1.3 KRISA WASCAVAGE was born in 1978.

4.9.2.1.6.1.4 KEVIN WASCAVAGE was born in 1979.

4.9.2.1.6.1.5 ALISON WASCAVAGE was born in 1981.

4.9.2.1.6.2 MARY MARGARET HIGGINS was born in September 1946. She married **FRANCIS VOTTERO**.

4.9.2.1.6.2.1 ALICIA VOTTERO was born in 1969.

4.9.2.1.6.2.2 SCOTT VOTTERO was born in 1971.

4.9.2.1.6.2.3 MARK VOTTERO was born in 1973.

4.9.2.1.6.2.4 JANELLE VOTTERO was born in 1976.

4.9.2.1.6.3 JOHN J. HIGGINS was born in August 1948. He married **DOLORES PALITYEA**.

4.9.2.1.6.3.1 MARIA HIGGINS was born in 1971.

4.9.2.1.6.3.2 SEAN HIGGINS was born in 1975.

4.9.2.1.6.3.3 ERIN HIGGINS was born in 1981.

4.9.2.1.6.4 MICHAEL HIGGINS was born in September 1951, Mount Carmel, Northumberland County, PA. He married **PATRICIA PITTELLO**.

4.9.2.1.6.4.1 MICHAEL HIGGINS was born circa 1976.

4.9.2.1.6.4.2 ERIC HIGGINS was born circa 1978.

4.9.2.1.6.4.3 TRICIA HIGGINS was born circa 1981.

4.9.2.1.6.5 GERARD HIGGINS was born in September 1951, Mount Carmel, Northumberland County, PA. He married **DOROTHY JEFFREY**.

4.9.2.1.6.5.1 GERARD HIGGINS was born circa 1975.

4.9.2.1.6.5.2 JEFFRY HIGGINS was born circa 1980.

4.9.2.1.6.6 LEE ANN HIGGINS was born on 17 April 1954. She married **JOSEPH MATTUCCI**.

4.9.2.1.6.6.1 JOSEPH MATTUCCI was born circa 1979.

4.9.2.1.6.6.2 DANIEL MATTUCCI was born circa 1981.

4.9.2.1.6.6.3 JANINE MATTUCCI was born circa 1984.

4.9.3 FREMONT F. FERTIG was born in 1864, Schuylkill County, PA. Some sources record that he was born on 12 September 1865, Taylorsville, Schuylkill County, PA. He married **MARY MAGDALINE KEIFFER**, daughter of **JONATHAN KEIFFER** and **SARAH KEHRES**. He died on 21 October 1901, Helfenstein, Schuylkill County, PA, as a result of a fall from a roof. He was buried at St. John's (Kimmel's) Lutheran and Reformed Church Cemetery, Barry Township, Schuylkill County`, PA.

4.9.3.1 FREDERICK WALLACE FERTIG was born on 10 June 1891, Helfenstein, Schuylkill County, PA. In 1917, when he registered for the draft in World War I, Fred was living in Philadelphia and working as a stenographer for Henry & West, on Chestnut Street. From November 1, 1917 through June 3, 1919, Fred served with the Headquarters Company, 310th Field Artillery Unit which saw action in France. He married **ROSEMARY SCHWAN**, daughter of **HERMAN SCHWAN** and **ADA (--?--)**, on 31 July 1922. Fred attended business school in Philadelphia and later worked as a field accountant for the Pennsylvania Unemployment Commission. He and Rosemary were the postmasters in Helfenstein for many years. He died on 27 July 1955, Ashland State Hospital, Butler Township, Schuylkill County, PA, at age 64. He was buried at Northumberland Memorial Park, Stonington, Northumberland County, PA, under the name "Alfred W. Fertig."

4.9.3.1.1 GRETCHEN SCHWAN FERTIG was born on 28 August 1923, Helfenstein, Schuylkill County, PA. She married **NICHOLAS REVOTSKIE**, son of **MARTIN REVOTSKIE** and **SOFIE (--?--)**, on 20 June 1942, Annapolis, MD. Nicholas was attending the US Naval Academy in Annapolis.

4.9.3.1.1.1 PETER REVOTSKIE was born on 8 November 1944. He married **VIRGINIA MARSHALL**. He married **DIANE RING**.

4.9.3.1.1.1.1 MISCHA REVOTSKIE was born on 19 August 1976.

4.9.3.1.1.1.2 SHANTI REVOTSKIE was born on 19 August 1976.

4.9.3.1.1.2 SUSAN REVOTSKIE was born on 25 January 1948. She married **ERNEST DOUGLAS BROWN JR.**, son of **ERNEST BROWN SR.** and **ALBERTA COLEMAN**.

4.9.3.1.1.2.1 RAFAEL JABULANI ZWANAI BROWN was born on 2 December 1972.

4.9.3.1.1.2.2 NICHOLAS KALAFYA BROWN was born on 4 May 1976.

4.9.3.1.1.2.3 MACEO NKRUMAH BROWN was born on 5 February 1983.

4.9.3.1.1.2.4 NAIMA CAMILLE BROWN was born on 22 August 1986.

4.9.3.1.1.3 MICHAEL REVOTSKIE was born on 8 August 1953. He married **KATHLEEN REILLY**.

4.9.3.1.1.3.1 ALISHA REVOTSKIE was born on 21 October 1984.

4.9.3.1.1.3.2 SHALEEN REVOTSKIE was born on 5 April 1986.

4.9.3.1.1.3.3 MELISSA REVOTSKIE was born on 10 August 1987.

4.9.3.1.1.4 JILL REVOTSKIE was born on 3 April 1956. She married **LAURENCE ELLIOT JUNDA**.

4.9.3.1.1.4.1 KALEN JUNDA was born on 27 September 1983.

4.9.3.1.1.4.2 SEAN JUNDA was born on 7 January 1987.

4.9.3.2 FLORENCE MAE FERTIG was born in August 1894. She married **HARRY CLAYTON WELKER**, son of **ADAM WELKER SR.** and **KATIE PAUL**, on 3 June 1916. She died in 1972. She was buried at Citizens Cemetery, Lavelle, Schuylkill County, PA.

4.9.3.2.1 VIRGINIA M. WELKER was born on 15 February 1918, Lavelle, Schuylkill County, PA. She married **CARLOS IRA WETZEL**, son of **HENRY IRVIN WETZEL** and **ALICE CLARA WIEST**. She died on 24 October 2013, Geisinger-Shamokin Community Hospital, Shamokin, Northumberland County, PA, at age 95. She was buried at Brock Cemetery, Ashland, Schuylkill County, PA.

4.9.3.2.1.1 RONALD E. WETZEL (see above)

4.9.3.2.1.2 GERALD C. WETZEL (see above)

4.9.3.2.1.2.1 GAIL WETZEL (see above)

4.9.3.2.1.2.2 CHERYL WETZEL (see above)

4.9.3.2.1.2.3 CINDY WETZEL (see above)

4.9.3.2.1.2.4 DAWN WETZEL (see above)

4.9.3.2.1.2.5 WENDY WETZEL (see above)

4.9.3.2.1.2.6 GERALD C. WETZEL JR. (see above)

4.9.3.2.1.2.6.1 GERALD C. WETZEL III (see above)

4.9.3.2.1.2.6.2 KRISTA WETZEL (see above)

4.9.3.2.1.3 DONALD G. WETZEL (see above)

4.9.3.2.1.3.1 BRENDA WETZEL (see above)

4.9.3.2.1.3.2 DEBBIE WETZEL (see above)

4.9.3.2.2 MARION CAROLINE WELKER was born on 22 April 1919, Lavelle, Schuylkill County, PA. She married **CHARLES J. MALARKEY**. She died on 19 July 2010, Manor Care, Pottsville, Schuylkill County, PA, at age 91. According to a newspaper obituary, Marion was a graduate of both Ashland High School and Ashland State General Hospital School of Nursing.

4.9.3.2.2.1 WILLIAM J. MALARKEY married **LATITIA HOSLER**.

4.9.3.2.2.1.1 DENNIS MALARKEY

4.9.3.2.2.1.2 AMELIA MALARKEY

4.9.3.2.2.2 DENNIS C. MALARKEY was born in 1940. He married CAROL DIXON.

    4.9.3.2.2.2.1 WILLIAM MALARKEY

    4.9.3.2.2.2.2 THOMAS MALARKEY

4.9.3.2.3 NETTIE E. WELKER was born on 17 September 1920, Lavelle, Schuylkill County, PA. She married ANDREW A. SAPUTO. She died on 29 December 1968, at age 48.

    4.9.3.2.3.1 JAMES SAPUTO

        4.9.3.2.3.1.1 SUSANNE C. SAPUTO

        4.9.3.2.3.1.2 CHRISTOPHER SAPUTO

    4.9.3.2.3.2 RANDY SAPUTO

4.9.3.2.4 HARRIET AGATHA WELKER was born on 26 July 1926, Lavelle, Schuylkill County, PA. She married WILLIAM POWELL THOMAS circa April 1949. She died on 14 December 2001, Elizabethtown, PA, at age 75. She was buried at Citizens Cemetery, Lavelle, Schuylkill County, PA.

    4.9.3.2.4.1 WILLIAM J. THOMAS

    4.9.3.2.4.2 BARBARA THOMAS

    4.9.3.2.4.3 JEFFREY THOMAS

4.9.3.3 FRANK WILLIAM FERTIG was born on 16 July 1897, Helfenstein, Schuylkill County, PA. He married HELEN E. WEIKEL, daughter of ELLSWORTH WEIKEL and CORA ELLEN DUNKELBERGER, on 24 March 1919, Gowan City, Northumberland County, PA. He died on 4 February 1972, Geisinger Hospital, Danville, Montour County, PA, at age 74. He was buried at Saint Paul's Reformed Church Cemetery, Gowan City, Northumberland County, PA. Frank retired from the Atlantic Refining Company.

4.9.3.3.1 EVELYN ARLENE FERTIG was born on 26 August 1920. She died on 3 March 1924, at age 3. She was buried at Saint Paul's Reformed Church Cemetery, Gowan City, Northumberland County, PA.

4.9.3.3.2 FRANKLIN ELLSWORTH FERTIG was born on 12 April 1922, Shamokin, Northumberland County, PA. He married GERTRUDE BERNICE BECKETT, daughter of HAROLD BECKETT and SUSAN MILLS, on 9 June 1944. He died on 12 January 2007, Taylor Hospice, Ridley Park, Delaware County, PA, at age 84. Franklin graduated from Susquehanna University and attended Penn State and Harvard. He served in the US Navy from 1943 to 1046 and later taught music at Northumberland High School, in Northumberland, PA.

    4.9.3.3.2.1 GLENN PAUL FERTIG was born on 29 June 1945, Chelsea, Suffolk County, MA. He died on 15 August 1948, at age 3. He was buried at Northumberland, Northumberland County, PA.

    4.9.3.3.2.2 GREGORY HAROLD FERTIG was born on 29 September 1950.

    4.9.3.3.2.3 MARK FRANKLIN FERTIG was born on 27 July 1954. He married DOROTHY VIOLIN on 1 November 1974.

        4.9.3.3.2.3.1 NICHOLAS GLENN FERTIG was born on 20 January 1982. He married JESSE SMITH.

            4.9.3.3.2.3.1.1 BRIAN NICHOLAS FERTIG was born in 1999.

    4.9.3.3.2.4 JEFFREY DAVID FERTIG was born on 22 May 1958. He married JEANNETTE WRIGHT on 29 July 1989.

        4.9.3.3.2.4.1 HARMONY JOY FERTIG was born on 12 June 1990.

        4.9.3.3.2.4.2 HANS JEFFREY FERTIG was born on 13 July 1993.

        4.9.3.3.2.4.3 HOLLYN FERTIG was born on 23 May 1995.

4.9.3.3.3 HELEN JUNE FERTIG was born on 23 June 1925, Shamokin, Northumberland County, PA. She married ROBERT J. SEEBOLD, son of NELSON SEEBOLD and MARY J. SCHREFFLER, on 3 October 1948.

    4.9.3.3.3.1 ROBERT NELSON SEEBOLD was born on 23 April 1952. He married RHONDA BEST on 6 October 1990.

        4.9.3.3.3.1.1 ROBERT JOSEPH SEEBOLD was born on 18 November 1994.

        4.9.3.3.3.1.2 DANIEL JACOB SEEBOLD was born on 25 May 1996.

4.9.3.3.3.2 ANN ELIZABETH SEEBOLD was born on 22 June 1955. She married **WILLIAM SCHMIDT**. She married **RONALD DILKS**.

    4.9.3.3.3.2.1 JOHN ANDERSON SCHMIDT was born on 18 May 1983.

    4.9.3.3.3.2.2 SARAH ELIZABETH SCHMIDT was born on 18 May 1985.

4.9.3.3.4 CORA NANCY FERTIG was born on 8 January 1927, Shamokin, Northumberland County, PA. She married **MARLIN SCHOVIN**. She married **WILLIAM GEORGE HAZELTINE**, son of **ESMOND EVERETT HAZELTINE** and **KATIE MAE MOYER**, on 29 December 1950. She married **HERMAN LAMPE BENNETT**, son of **HARRY RAYMOND BENNETT** and **GRACE ALICE LAMPE**.

    4.9.3.3.4.1 SHARON LEE SCHOVIN was born on 16 December 1946. She married **FRED GANGLOFF** on 24 April 1970. She married **VICTOR REID**.

        4.9.3.3.4.1.1 ASHLEY REID was born in 1989. She married **WEBSTER TOLBERT**.

            4.9.3.3.4.1.1.1 ARIANNA MARIAH TOLBERT

            4.9.3.3.4.1.1.2 AAMANI JADE TOLBERT was born in 2008.

4.9.3.3.5 SHIRLEY GRACE FERTIG was born on 24 November 1928. She married **JOSEPH EDGAR CALLENDER**, son of **HARRY LEROY CALLENDER** and **AMY E. NEWITT**, on 23 March 1947.

    4.9.3.3.5.1 KAREN JO CALLENDER was born in 1948. She married **STEVEN MULL** on 17 June 1965. She married **RICHARD KEEFER** on 3 July 1983.

        4.9.3.3.5.1.1 CRAIG ALAN MULL is also referred to as **CRAIG CALLENDER** in some sources. Alan was later adopted by Shirley and Joseph and used the surname "Callender."

    4.9.3.3.5.2 JANICE ANN CALLENDER was born on 31 January 1953. She married **DALE FRYMOYER** on 31 July 1971. She married **CLEMENT ROHRER**.

        4.9.3.3.5.2.1 AMY CHRISTINE FRYMOYER was born on 13 November 1973. She married **WESLEY BUCK** on 8 October 1994.

            4.9.3.3.5.2.1.1 GLENN WESLEY BUCK was born in 1997.

            4.9.3.3.5.2.1.2 GARRETT DILLON BUCK was born in 2000.

            4.9.3.3.5.2.1.3 MEGAN ELIZABETH BUCK was born in 2002.

            4.9.3.3.5.2.1.4 ISAAC ROLAND BUCK was born in 2005.

    4.9.3.3.5.3 LINDA KAY CALLENDER was born on 23 December 1959. She died on 15 February 1977, at age 17.

4.9.3.3.6 VERA LOUISE FERTIG was born on 20 August 1931, Shamokin, Northumberland County, PA. She married **JACK L. BENNER**, son of **WILMONT BENNER** and **MYRA (--?--)**, on 1 July 1951. She died on 22 June 2012, Ellicott City, MD, at age 80. According to a newspaper obituary, Vera graduated as valedictorian from Northumberland High School. She was employed by the Northumberland Water Co., the Atlantic Refining Co., and the Air Force. Her body was donated to Anatomy Gifts Registry.

    4.9.3.3.6.1 CYNTHIA LOU BENNER was born on 12 May 1957. She married **CARY CHANDLER** on 14 October 1989.

        4.9.3.3.6.1.1 CAROLYN ASHLEY CHANDLER was born in 1991.

        4.9.3.3.6.1.2 DANIELLE MARIE CHANDLER was born on 12 December 1995.

    4.9.3.3.6.2 LINDA LEE BENNER was born on 24 March 1960. She married **JAMES SMITH** on 17 October 1987.

        4.9.3.3.6.2.1 CLINTON JAMES SMITH was born on 11 June 1990.

        4.9.3.3.6.2.2 JUSTIN BENNER SMITH was born on 16 July 1994.

        4.9.3.3.6.2.3 JACK WOODROW SMITH was born in 1997.

    4.9.3.3.6.3 MYRA LYNN BENNER was born on 13 August 1962. She married **DAVID WIEMAN** on 15 October 1994.

        4.9.3.3.6.3.1 ALEXANDRA CLARA WIEMAN was born in 1998.

        4.9.3.3.6.3.2 BENNER MATTHEW WIEMAN was born in 2003.

4.9.3.3.7 CAROLYN MARIE FERTIG was born on 30 November 1940. She married **RICHARD MILLER** on 16 June 1962.

4.9.3.3.7.1 CRAIG ARTHUR MILLER was born on 6 May 1963. He married NANCY MORGAN on 9 June 1990.

    4.9.3.3.7.1.1 STUART MILLER was born on 10 February 1965.

    4.9.3.3.7.1.2 ELIJAH MILLER was born on 4 June 1996.

    4.9.3.3.7.1.3 CAROL ANN ELIZABETH MILLER was born in 1998.

4.9.3.3.7.2 MARCI LOUISE MILLER was born on 24 April 1965. She married WILLIAM MCDERMOTT III on 14 September 1991.

    4.9.3.3.7.2.1 WILLIAM MCDERMOTT IV was born on 2 February 1994.

    4.9.3.3.7.2.2 RICHARD ARTHUR MCDERMOTT was born in 1996.

4.9.3.3.7.3 BYRON RICHARD MILLER was born on 3 May 1968. He married ELISE ABRAMS on 1 July 1995.

4.9.3.4 CARRIE FERTIG was born on 11 January 1899. She married JOSEPH LEWIS PAUL, son of HENRY W. PAUL and AGNES LAVENA STROHECKER, before 1920. She died on 2 April 1980, Allentown, Lehigh County, PA, at age 81. She was buried at Citizens Cemetery, Lavelle, Schuylkill County, PA.

4.9.3.4.1 GLENN FERTIG PAUL SR. was born on 11 April 1922, Lavelle, Schuylkill County, PA. He married EVELYN PEOPLES GREGORY circa 1944. He died on 3 May 2014, Gwinnett Medical Center, Lawrenceville, Gwinnett County, GA, at age 92. According to a newspaper obituary, Glenn attended Gettysburg College (PA) for one year, and then transferred and graduated from Maryville College (TN). Immediately following graduation, he enlisted in the US Navy and attended Midshipman's School at Notre Dame University, serving as a Second Lieutenant in the Navy during WWII, in both the Atlantic (Battle of Normandy) and Pacific theaters. Following the war, the Pauls moved to Atlanta, GA where he was employed by the Grinnell Company, and later General Motor's Fisher Body Division in Atlanta.

4.9.3.4.1.1 SUSAN GREGORY PAUL was born on 29 April 1951. She married CHARLES ALMAN DUNCAN. She and CHARLES ALMAN DUNCAN were divorced. She married (--?--) TYLER.

    4.9.3.4.1.1.1 GREGORY ALMAN DUNCAN was born on 26 February 1978.

    4.9.3.4.1.1.2 LAUREN LEIGH DUNCAN was born on 29 October 1981. She married DARIN SCUDDER.

4.9.3.4.1.2 PAMELA RENEE PAUL was born on 5 November 1955. She married MICHAEL LYNN ROBERTS. She and MICHAEL LYNN ROBERTS were divorced. She married HAROLD BAMBERG.

    4.9.3.4.1.2.1 LINDSEY MICHELLE ROBERTS

    4.9.3.4.1.2.2 LESLIE NICHOLE ROBERTS married (--?--) MIYATA.

4.9.3.4.1.3 GLENN FERTIG PAUL JR. was born on 8 September 1962. He married PAMELA CASH. He married LEE TURNER.

    4.9.3.4.1.3.1 ABBIE PAUL married ROBERT MILLER.

        4.9.3.4.1.3.1.1 LANDON MILLER

    4.9.3.4.1.3.2 ALEX PAUL

4.9.3.4.2 BETTY RENEE PAUL was born on 27 May 1925, Lavelle, Schuylkill County, PA. She died on 8 January 2012, Brethren Village, Lancaster, Lancaster County, PA, at age 86. According to a newspaper obituary, Renee served as Associate Professor of Special Education at Kutztown University, Associate Professor of Special Education at Gwynedd-Mercy College, and Director of Education at the Melmark School in Berwyn, PA. She served as a missionary in Kenya for four years and for two years in Congo (Zaire), both assignments with the Africa Inland Mission. Prior to her work in the mission field, she was a psychologist and served in various teaching positions with the Allentown School District for over twenty years. She was buried at Citizens Cemetery, Lavelle, Schuylkill County, PA.

4.10 PETER KLINGER was born circa 1839. Peter, who may have died young, was listed in the 1850 Census, but it is not clear if he was Peter and Catharine's son.

4.11 EVA ELIZABETH KLINGER was born on 7 October 1840. Some sources record that she was born in August 1840. She married **VALENTINE SAVIDGE**, son of **VALENTINE SAVIDGE** and **MARY REED**, circa 1856. She died on 16 May 1917, at age 76. She was buried at Hegins, Schuylkill County, PA.

4.11.1 OLIVER K. SAVIDGE was born in 1859. He married **EMMA DUNKLEBERGER** circa 1890. He married **LINDA HOLLENBACH** after 1910. He died in 1944.

4.11.2 MORRISON SAVIDGE was born circa 1861.

4.11.3 MARY ELIZABETH SAVIDGE was born circa 16 March 1857. Some sources record that she was born in 1863. She died on 31 May 1863. She was buried at St, Andrew's Church Cemetery, Valley View, Schuylkill County, PA.

4.11.4 ELIAS SAVIDGE was born on 20 July 1864. He died on 23 June 1865. He was buried at St, Andrew's Church Cemetery, Valley View, Schuylkill County, PA.

4.11.5 SAMUEL K. SAVIDGE was born on 2 June 1866. He married **MARY MAGLADA BOYER** in June 1887. He died on 10 February 1942, at age 75. He was buried at Hegins, Schuylkill County, PA.

4.11.5.1 DANIEL SAVIDGE died Delaware.

4.11.5.2 MARY ALICE SAVIDGE was born on 19 April 1890, Hegins Township, Schuylkill County, PA. She married **IRWIN FRANCIS SCHLEGEL** in November 1909. Some sources suggest that she was married in 1911. She died in 1972.

4.11.5.2.1 CHARLES W. SCHLEGEL was born on 12 June 1910. He died in 1976.

4.11.5.2.2 HARLAN EDGAR SCHLEGEL was born on 14 March 1916, Hubley Township, Schuylkill County, PA. He married **ELIZABETH MAE KUKLA** on 18 June 1938, Sacramento, PA. He died on 25 December 1990, RD, Hegins, Schuylkill County, PA, at age 74.

4.11.5.2.2.1 LANIER HAROLD SCHLEGEL was born on 14 June 1939, Hubley Township, Schuylkill County, PA. He married **DENA JANE EBERT** on 19 August 1961. He married **DENISE KLINE** on 14 December 1991, Skippack, PA.

4.11.5.2.2.1.1 DEBRA SUSAN SCHLEGEL was born on 19 February 1962, Reading, Berks County, PA. She married **WILLIAM GRAY ROSS** on 20 September 1986, Royersford, PA.

4.11.5.2.2.1.1.1 MELISSA GRAY ROSS was born on 23 January 1989, Flemington, NJ.

4.11.5.2.2.1.1.2 ELIZABETH MARIE ROSS was born on 31 August 1991, Flemington, NJ.

4.11.5.2.3 IRVIN JOHN SCHLEGEL was born on 27 December 1920. He married **EDNA VIOLA SCHWARTZ** on 23 March 1940, Valley View, Schuylkill County, PA. He died on 4 October 1996, Harrisburg, Dauphin County, PA, at age 75.

4.11.5.2.3.1 VERA EDNA SCHLEGEL was born on 6 May 1941, Hegins, Schuylkill County, PA. She married **ROGER GENE MAURER**, son of **CLARENCE O. MAURER** and **PEARL ELNORA KLINGER,** on 15 April 1961, Valley View, Schuylkill County, PA. She died on 22 January 2004, at her home Lancaster, Lancaster County, PA, at age 62. She was buried on 27 January 2004, at Church of God Cemetery, Valley View, Schuylkill County, PA.

4.11.5.2.3.1.1 SHARON LOUISE MAURER was born on 9 February 1962, Pottsville, Schuylkill County, PA. She married **MICHAEL VINCENT SARCINELLO** on 26 August 1989, Lancaster, Lancaster County, PA.

4.11.5.2.3.1.1.1 ANDREW PATRICK SARCINELLO was born on 3 January 1992, Chester County, PA.

4.11.5.2.3.1.1.2 DANA MICHELLE SARCINELLO was born on 7 May 1995, Chester County, PA.

4.11.5.2.3.1.2 RANDALL ALLEN MAURER was born on 19 December 1963, Allentown, Lehigh County, PA.

4.11.5.2.3.1.3 JOHN RICHARD MAURER was born on 18 January 1965, Allentown, Lehigh County, PA. He married **CHRISTINE MARY EHLEITER** on 10 October 1987, Lancaster, Lancaster County, PA.

4.11.5.2.3.1.3.1 COLIN PERTHEMORE MAURER was born on 19 February 1993, Arlington, Virginia.

4.11.5.2.3.1.3.2 Rebecca Cate Maurer was born on 27 September 1995, Arlington, Virginia.

4.11.5.2.3.1.4 Bryan Roger Maurer is also referred to as **Brian Roger Maurer** in some sources. He was born on 17 February 1970, Lancaster, Lancaster County, PA.

4.11.5.2.3.2 Doris Elaine Schlegel was born on 4 June 1949, Spring Glen, PA. She married **Steve Williams** on 10 May 1969, Valley View, Schuylkill County, PA.

4.11.5.2.3.2.1 Michael John Williams was born on 5 July 1970, Harrisburg, Dauphin County, PA.

4.11.5.2.3.2.2 Ryan Todd Williams was born on 22 May 1975, Harrisburg, Dauphin County, PA.

4.11.5.2.3.2.3 Jarad Andrew Williams was born on 16 June 1982, Harrisburg, Dauphin County, PA.

4.11.5.2.3.3 Brenda Eileen Schlegel was born on 15 July 1955, Pottsville, Schuylkill County, PA. She married **John Williamson** on 29 December 1977, Salt Lake City, UT.

4.11.5.2.3.3.1 Melanie Brook Williamson was born on 16 December 1978, Salt Lake City, UT.

4.11.5.2.3.3.2 Jessica Williamson was born on 13 August 1981, Salt Lake City, UT.

4.11.5.2.3.3.3 Camille Williamson was born on 2 June 1983, Salt Lake City, UT.

4.11.5.2.3.4 Daniel Eugene Schlegel was born on 18 August 1958, Pottsville, Schuylkill County, PA. He married **Christine Mae Miller** on 5 November 1977, Weishample. He married **Roseanne Rooney** on 12 March 1983, Weishample. He died on 29 May 1990, Sacramento, PA, at age 31.

4.11.5.2.3.4.1 Chad Schlegel was born on 27 July 1979.

4.11.5.2.4 Miriam Schlegel was born on 10 July 1922, RD, Hegins, Schuylkill County, PA. She married **Kenneth O. Williams** on 10 January 1946.

4.11.5.2.5 Annie Cordella Schlegel was born on 16 April 1928, Sacramento, PA. She married **Robert Raymond Coleman** on 2 July 1947, Elkton, MD.

4.11.5.2.5.1 James L. Coleman was born on 21 December 1950, Harrisburg, Dauphin County, PA. He married **Shelly Humiston** on 6 February 1971, Stamford, NY. He married **Patricia Gustin** on 26 October 1985.

4.11.5.2.5.1.1 Charles Eric Coleman was born on 22 August 1971, Stamford, NY.

4.11.5.2.5.1.2 Christine Anne Coleman was born on 9 November 1974, Stamford, NY.

4.11.5.2.5.1.3 Sarah Marie Coleman was born on 23 January 1987, Albany, NY.

4.11.5.2.5.2 Thomas Wayne Coleman was born on 19 November 1952, Lykens, Dauphin County, PA. He married **Marla Jan Ginenthal** on 15 September 1971.

4.11.5.2.5.2.1 Michael David Coleman was born on 4 July 1977, Schenectady, NY.

4.11.5.2.5.2.2 Timothy Wayne Coleman was born on 9 June 1981, Schenectady, NY.

4.11.5.3 William V. Savidge was born on 3 March 1892, Hegins Township, Schuylkill County, PA. He married **Sadie Miller**. Prior to his death, William was living in the vicinity of Millersburg, Dauphin County, PA. He died in December 1978, at age 86.

4.11.5.4 Harry M. Savidge is also referred to as **Harrison** in some sources. He was born in March 1894, Hegins, Schuylkill County, PA. He married **Nora Alice Schwartz**. He married **Lillian Hepler** on 24 January 1930. He died in 1978.

4.11.5.4.1 Paul Lester Savidge was born on 11 June 1916, Hegins, Schuylkill County, PA. He died on 18 December 1993, Spring Glen, PA, at age 77.

4.11.5.4.2 Catherine Savidge was born circa 1918.

4.11.5.4.3 Clair M. Savidge was born circa 1925.

4.11.5.5 Susanna H. Savidge was born on 4 February 1896, Hegins Township, Schuylkill County, PA. She married **Ralph Gilbert**.

4.11.5.5.1 MABEL GILBERT was born on 15 October 1936. She married **GENE THOMAS ROMBERGER** on 14 June 1958, Sacramento, PA.

4.11.5.6 GEORGE WASHINGTON SAVIDGE was born in August 1897. He married **EFFIE H. (--?--)** circa 1917. He married **MAUDE H. STRAUB**. He married **MARTHA WIEST**. He died Delaware.

4.11.5.6.1 MARK E. SAVIDGE was born circa 1917.

4.11.5.6.2 HOWARD M. SAVIDGE was born circa 1920.

4.11.5.6.3 HELEN S. SAVIDGE was born circa 1921.

4.11.5.6.4 CARRIE E. SAVIDGE was born circa 1925.

4.11.5.6.5 MAE I. SAVIDGE was born circa 1927.

4.11.5.7 JENNIE A. SAVIDGE was born in January 1899, Hegins Township, Schuylkill County, PA. She married **DONALD MOYER**.

4.11.5.8 JOHN E. SAVIDGE was born in 1901. He died on 1 November 1905.

4.11.5.9 JAMES E. SAVIDGE was born on 26 March 1902. He married **JENNIE SHADEL** on 18 September 1937. Prior to his death, James was living in the vicinity of Spring Glen, Schuylkill County, PA. He died in November 1976, at age 74.

4.11.5.10 CATHERINE M. SAVIDGE is also referred to as **KATHERINE** in some sources. She was born on 20 September 1903, Hegins Township, Schuylkill County, PA. She married **GUERNEY EDWARD MILLER**, son of **FRANKLIN B. MILLER** and **TAMIE SEVILLA MORGAN**, circa 1937. She died on 27 July 1971, at age 67. She died on 27 July 1971, at age 67.

4.11.5.10.1 DOROTHY MARIA MILLER was born on 9 March 1939. She married **LEWIS ANUSZEWSKI**.

4.11.5.10.1.1 MICHELLE ANN ANUSZEWSKI married **HERBERT S. FOREMAN**. She was born on 4 March 1958.

4.11.5.10.1.1.1 CORRINE ELIZABETH FOREMAN was born on 7 July 1975.

4.11.5.10.1.2 SCOTT JOSEPH ANUSZEWSKI was born on 23 March 1962.

4.11.5.10.1.3 CARA LYNNE ANUSZEWSKI was born on 3 March 1965.

4.11.5.10.1.4 ANDREA EDEN ANUSZEWSKI was born on 4 December 1967.

4.11.5.10.2 CLARENCE MILLER was born on 23 October 1948. He married **PATRICIA ANN MARKS**.

4.11.5.10.2.1 CINDY ANN MILLER was born on 7 January 1970.

4.11.5.10.2.2 KIMBERLY ANN MILLER was born on 15 June 1971.

4.11.5.10.2.3 TIMOTHY DAVID MILLER was born on 3 January 1979.

4.11.5.11 FRANK F. SAVIDGE was born on 30 September 1905, Hegins Township, Schuylkill County, PA. He married **FLORENCE CARL**. Prior to his death, Frank was living in the vicinity of Tremont, Schuylkill County, PA. He died on 14 June 1988, at age 82.

4.11.5.12 LAURA E. SAVIDGE was born in 1907, Hegins Township, Schuylkill County, PA. She married **CHARLES HEIM**. She married **RUFUS MONROE KIMMEL**, son of **JOHN K. KIMMEL** and **LOVINA WOLFGANG**, on 31 December 1934, Hegins, Schuylkill County, PA. She died in June 1967, Danville, Montour County, PA. She was buried at Saint Johns United Church of Christ Cemetery, Ashland, Schuylkill County, PA.

4.11.5.12.1 GUY W. HEIM is also referred to as **GUY KIMMEL** in some sources. He was born on 5 September 1925.

4.11.5.12.2 DANIEL KIMMEL died before 8 November 2007.

4.11.5.12.3 JOHN KIMMEL was born circa 1931.

4.11.5.12.4 MARY KIMMEL was born on 31 January 1933, Barry Township, Schuylkill County, PA. She died on 26 July 1933, Barry Township, Schuylkill County, PA.

4.11.5.12.5 MELVIN L. KIMMEL was born on 8 June 1934, Hegins Township, Schuylkill County, PA. He died on 6 November 2007, Pottsville Hospital, Pottsville, Schuylkill County, PA, at age 73. According to a newspaper obituary, Melvin lived in Ashland, Schuylkill County, PA. During the Korean War, he served in the Army as a truck mechanic. Later, he was employed as a coal miner by the Hegins Mining Company and eventually retired from the Porter Tunnel Coal

Company, Tower City, Schuylkill County, PA. He was buried on 9 November 2007, at St. John Cemetery, Barry Township, Schuylkill County, PA.

4.11.5.12.6 MARIE KIMMEL was born circa 1936. She married **MICHAEL BANACH.**

4.11.5.12.7 MONROE KIMMEL was born on 27 April 1938, Hegins, Schuylkill County, PA. He died on 23 January 1959, in a coal mining accident Columbia County, PA, at age 20. He was buried at Saint Johns United Church of Christ Cemetery, Ashland, Schuylkill County, PA. Monroe was never married.

4.11.5.12.8 PALMER E. KIMMEL was born on 2 July 1941, Hegins Township, Schuylkill County, PA. He married **LILIAN BECKER** circa 1968. He died on 26 November 2016, Broad Mountain Nursing Center, Frackville, Schuylkill County, PA, at age 75. He was buried on 30 November 2016, at Citizens Cemetery, Lavelle, Schuylkill County, PA.

> **4.11.5.12.8.1 RUBY KIMMEL** married **JOSEPH M. COYLE SR.**
>
> > **4.11.5.12.8.1.1 AMANDA COYLE**
> >
> > **4.11.5.12.8.1.2 JOSEPH M. COYLE JR.**
>
> **4.11.5.12.8.2 PAUL E. KIMMEL SR.** married **BETH (--?--).**
>
> > **4.11.5.12.8.2.1 JOSHUA KIMMEL**
> >
> > **4.11.5.12.8.2.2 MATTHEW KIMMEL**
> >
> > **4.11.5.12.8.2.3 TROY KIMMEL**
> >
> > **4.11.5.12.8.2.4 PAUL E. KIMMEL JR.**

4.11.5.13 CHARLES D. SAVIDGE was born in 1910.

4.11.5.14 MAUDE SAVIDGE was born circa 1913. She married **JOHNSON F. SMITH** on 4 January 1936, Friedens Church.

4.11.6 FREMONT K. SAVIDGE was born on 21 May 1868. He died on 10 May 1908, at age 39. He was buried at Hegins, Schuylkill County, PA.

4.11.7 SEVILLA SAVIDGE is also referred to as **ALICE SEVILLA** in some sources. She was born in December 1871. Some sources record that she was born in 1870. She married **WILLIAM LAUNDERS** after 1910. She died in 1948, Hegins, Schuylkill County, PA.

4.11.8 DANIEL K. SAVIDGE was born in 1873. He died in 1873.

4.11.9 LIZZIE SAVIDGE was born on 3 November 1874. She married **DANIEL HARNER.** She died in 1956. She was buried at Hegins, Schuylkill County, PA.

4.11.10 INFANT SAVIDGE was born circa 22 December 1876. He/she died on 31 December 1876. He/she was buried at St, Andrew's Church Cemetery, Valley View, Schuylkill County, PA.

4.11.11 KATIE ANNIE SAVIDGE was born circa 21 February 1877, Hegins Township, Schuylkill County, PA. She married **RALPH MORGAN.** She died on 9 July 1934, Warne Hospital, Pottsville, Schuylkill County, PA. She was buried on 12 July 1934, at Friedens Union Cemetery, Hegins, Schuylkill County, PA.

4.11.12 WILLIAM K. SAVIDGE was born in April 1881. Some sources record that he was born in April 1888. He died in 1946.

4.12 SARAH KLINGER was born circa 1841. Sarah, who may have died young, was listed in the 1850 Census, but it is not clear if she was Peter and Catharine's child.

5 JOHANN GEORGE KLINGER is also referred to as **GEORGE P. KLINGER** in some sources. He was born on 7 January 1798, Lykens Township, Dauphin County, PA. He was baptized on 23 February 1798, Zion (Klinger's) Church, Erdman, Lykens Township, Dauphin County, PA. He married **ELIZABETH STEIN**, daughter of **PETER STEIN** and **HANNAH COLEMAN,** circa 1822, Lykens Township, Dauphin County, PA. He died on 16 September 1880, Erdman, Lykens Township, Dauphin County, PA, at age 82. He was buried at Zion (Klinger's) Church, Erdman, Lykens Township, Dauphin County, PA.

5.1 JACOB KLINGER was born on 12 May 1823, Lykens Township, Dauphin County, PA.

5.2 ANN JULIAN KLINGER is also referred to as **ANNA JULIANNA AND ANGELINA** in some sources. She was born on 1 September 1824, Klingerstown, Schuylkill County, PA. She was baptized on 17 October 1824, Zion (Klinger's) Church, Erdman, Lykens Township, Dauphin County, PA. She married **DANIEL MERKEL WIEST**, son of **JOHANNES WIEST** and **CATHARINE MERKEL,** circa 1842, Klingerstown, Schuylkill County, PA. She died on 5 May 1854, Klingerstown, Schuylkill County, PA, at age 29. She was buried at Zion (Klinger's) Church, Erdman, Lykens Township, Dauphin County, PA.

5.2.1 (--?--) WIEST was born on 23 September 1843, Klingerstown, Schuylkill County, PA. He died on 23 September 1843, Klingerstown, Schuylkill County, PA.

5.2.2 DANIEL MERKEL WIEST is also referred to as **DANIEL WIEST JR.** in some sources. He was born on 4 January 1846, Klingerstown, Schuylkill County, PA. He died on 21 August 1846, Klingerstown, Schuylkill County, PA.

5.2.3 FRANZ KLINGER WIEST is also referred to as **FRANTZ K. AND FRANCIS WIEST** in some sources. He was born on 18 June 1847, Schwaben Creek, Northumberland County, PA. Frantz Wiest served in Co. A, 50th Pennsylvania Infantry, during the Civil War. He and his brother Heiram were captured and interned in the infamous Libby Prison, where Heiram died. Frantz spent the greater part of his life in Alaska and the Pacific Northwest, engaged in silver mining. He visited Klingerstown in 1916.

    5.2.3.1 GEORGE FRANKLIN WEIST is also referred to as **FRANK WIEST** in some sources. He was born in 1866, Leck Kill, Northumberland County, PA. He married **MARY A. (--?--)** circa 1887. George Franklin Wiest was a resident of the Schwaben Creek area and a lumberman by occupation. He died on 2 January 1947, Leck Kill, Northumberland County, PA. He was buried at St. John's Lutheran and Reformed Church Cemetery, Leck Kill, Upper Mahanoy Township, Northumberland County, PA.

        5.2.3.1.1 (--?--) WEIST married **(--?--) PAUL**.

        5.2.3.1.2 EDWARD H. WEIST was born in October 1888, Leck Kill, Northumberland County, PA.

            5.2.3.1.2.1 ELIZABETH WEIST married **HENRY LAUDENSLAGER**, son of **JOSEPH DANIEL LAUDENSLAGER** and **LAURA ALVENA WIEST**. She is also referred to as **BETTY WEIST** in some sources.

                5.2.3.1.2.1.1 LAWRENCE LAUDENSLAGER

                5.2.3.1.2.1.2 ROCHELLE LAUDENSLAGER

                5.2.3.1.2.1.3 CAROL LAUDENSLAGER

                5.2.3.1.2.1.4 ROGER LAUDENSLAGER

            5.2.3.1.2.2 WALTER WEIST was born PA.

                5.2.3.1.2.2.1 LENA WEIST was born Pitman, Schuylkill County, PA.

                5.2.3.1.2.2.2 RALPH WEIST was born Pitman, Schuylkill County, PA.

                5.2.3.1.2.2.3 JEAN WEIST was born Pitman, Schuylkill County, PA.

        5.2.3.1.3 KATIE WIEST. Some sources list this Katie as a daughter of Frank and Mary Wiest, but that appears to be incorrect. In 1900, they had a daughter named Katie, who was then 11 years old, and Mary had given birth to only 2 children (Edward and Katie). Moreover, the date of birth listed for this Katie is roughly the same as the date of birth of Edward. For these reasons, this listing for a daughter Katie, born around October 1888 and died round the same time, appears to be incorrect. She was born circa 1 October 1888, Leck Kill, Northumberland County, PA. She died on 1 October 1888, Leck Kill, Northumberland County, PA. She was buried at St. John's Lutheran and Reformed Church Cemetery, Leck Kill, Upper Mahanoy Township, Northumberland County, PA.

        5.2.3.1.4 KATIE J. WEIST was born in May 1891.

5.2.4 JULIANNA WIEST was born on 24 October 1844, Klingerstown, Schuylkill County, PA. Some sources record that she was born on 6 August 1848. She married **WILLIAM DUBENDORF** circa 1862. She died on 19 July 1922, Urban, Northumberland County, PA, at age 73. She was buried at St. John's Lutheran and Reformed Church Cemetery, Urban, Jordan Township, Northumberland County, PA.

    5.2.4.1 JOHN DUBENDORF was born on 24 April 1862, Hebe, Jordan Township, Northumberland County, PA. He died on 13 March 1866, Urban, Northumberland County, PA, at age 3.

    5.2.4.2 MARY J. DUBENDORF was born on 26 December 1863, Hebe, Jordan Township, Northumberland County, PA. She died on 6 January 1866, Hebe, Jordan Township, Northumberland County, PA, at age 2.

    5.2.4.3 SARAH DUBENDORF was born in 1865, Hebe, Jordan Township, Northumberland County, PA. She died on 28 December 1865, Hebe, Jordan Township, Northumberland County, PA.

    5.2.4.4 EMMA S. DUBENDORF was born on 6 April 1867, Hebe, Jordan Township, Northumberland County, PA. She married **HENRY A. WOLFE**, son of **HENRY WOLFE** and **REBECCA ADAM**, circa 1885. She died on 18 March 1938, Hebe, Jordan Township, Northumberland County, PA, at age 70. She was buried at St. John's Lutheran and Reformed Church Cemetery, Urban, Northumberland County, PA.

5.2.4.4.1 MARY WOLFE was born in June 1886, Pennsylvania.

5.2.4.4.2 WILLIAM OSCAR WOLF is also referred to as OSCAR W. WOLF in some sources. He was born in January 1889. He married BEULAH M. BROSIUS, daughter of JAMES L. BROSIUS, circa 1910. He died in 1953. He was buried at St. John's Lutheran and Reformed Church Cemetery, Urban, Northumberland County, PA.

    5.2.4.4.2.1 MELVIN S. WOLF was born circa 1910.

5.2.4.4.3 HARVEY E. WOLF was born in 1891. He married MAY A. SCHLEGEL, daughter of EDWARD SCHLEGEL and EMMA J. SCHAFFER, circa 1911. He died in 1960. He was buried at St. John's Lutheran and Reformed Church Cemetery, Urban, Northumberland County, PA.

    5.2.4.4.3.1 NEVIN L. WOLF was born on 27 April 1911. He married DOROTHY J. BOHNER. He died on 8 December 1969, at age 58. He was buried at St. John's Lutheran and Reformed Church Cemetery, Urban, Northumberland County, PA.

    5.2.4.4.3.2 EDWARD R. WOLF was born in 1913. He married MARTHA M. (--?--). He died in 1956. He was buried at St. John's Lutheran and Reformed Church Cemetery, Urban, Northumberland County, PA.

    5.2.4.4.3.3 LAWRENCE D. WOLF was born in 1919. He married FLORENCE A. (--?--). He died in 1963. He was buried at St. John's Lutheran and Reformed Church Cemetery, Urban, Northumberland County, PA.

    5.2.4.4.3.4 GLADLIS WOLF was born circa 1925.

5.2.4.4.4 (--?--) WOLFE was born on 10 October 1894. He/she died on 10 October 1894. He/she was buried at St. John's Lutheran and Reformed Church Cemetery, Urban, Northumberland County, PA.

5.2.4.4.5 NORA S. WOLFE was born circa 1901.

5.2.4.5 SEVILA DUBENDORF was born circa 1871.

5.2.4.6 WILLIAM DUBENDORF JR. was born on 19 October 1872, Hebe, Jordan Township, Northumberland County, PA. He died on 25 August 1873, Hebe, Jordan Township, Northumberland County, PA.

5.2.4.7 ADAM DUBENDORF was born circa 1876.

5.2.4.8 ALBERT DUBENDORF was born in 1879.

5.2.4.9 CHARLES DUBENDORF was born in January 1881.

5.2.4.10 SAMUEL DUBENDORF was born in August 1883. Some sources record that he was born circa 1859.

5.2.4.11 DAVID DUBENDORF was born in May 1885.

5.2.4.12 DANIEL DUBENDORF was born in November 1889.

5.2.5 ALBERT KLINGER WIEST was born circa 1849, Klingerstown, Schuylkill County, PA. He married PRISCILLA ADAMS circa 1870. Other sources indicate that Albert Klinger Wiest was a miner and that he made his home in Tower City, Schuylkill County, PA. He died Tower City, Schuylkill County, PA.

    5.2.5.1 FRANCIS WIEST was born Klingerstown, Schuylkill County, PA. He married IDA WITMER. The list of children of Francis and Ida is uncertain. According to the 1910 Census, Ida was no longer married to Francis but rather to John F. Schreffler. Perhaps Francis had died by that time. In any event, Ida was listed as the mother of 6 children, four of whom -- Harry, Harper, Clarence, and Harvey -- were living with her then. Those four along with Edward would comprise 5 of Ida's 6 children, but the precise identity of the sixth child is not clear. A number of sources list a number of additional children for Ida and Francis. He died in 1917.

    5.2.5.1.1 HENRY WIEST

    5.2.5.1.2 TILLIE WIEST married (--?--) ROWE.

    5.2.5.1.3 ELIZABETH WIEST married (--?--) COX.

    5.2.5.1.4 EDWARD WITMER WIEST. Edward Wiest was a miner and made his home in Wiconisco, Dauphin Co.,PA. He was killed in a mining accident. He is also referred to as EDWARD WEIST in some sources. He was born on 19 April 1886, Tower City, Schuylkill County, PA. He married FLORENCE MACHAMER circa 1909, PA. He died on 2 July 1937, Harrisburg Hospital, Harrisburg, Dauphin County, PA, at age 51, as a result of injuries incurred in a mining accident in Lykens, PA. He was buried on 4 July 1937, at Calvary United Methodist Cemetery, Wiconisco, Dauphin County, PA.

5.2.5.1.4.1 VELMA BEATRICE WIEST was born on 4 February 1910, Wiconisco, Dauphin County, PA. She married **AMBROSE RICHARD BOPP**, son of **WILLIAM H. BOPP** and **AMELIA BERGER**, on 9 August 1938, Harrisburg, Dauphin County, PA. She died on 16 February 1984, at age 74. She was buried at Sacred Heart Cemetery, Williamstown, Dauphin County, PA.

5.2.5.1.4.1.1 RICHARD A. BOPP was born circa 1939.

5.2.5.1.4.2 EMMA D. WIEST was born on 21 April 1912, Wiconisco, Dauphin County, PA. She married **JOSEPH J. YOURGAL** PA. She died on 10 February 1951, Pottsville Hospital, Pottsville, Schuylkill County, PA, at age 38. She was buried on 14 February 1957, at Calvary United Methodist Cemetery, Wiconisco, Dauphin County, PA.

5.2.5.1.4.3 ERNEST J. WIEST is also referred to as **ERNEST J. WEIST** in some sources. He was born on 24 August 1917, Wiconisco, Dauphin County, PA. He married **ORPHA ERDMAN**, daughter of **CARLOS ERDMAN** and **CORA (--?--)**, on 17 February 1940. He died on 19 November 2013, Lykens, Dauphin County, PA, at age 96.

5.2.5.1.4.4 KENNETH CLYDE WIEST is also referred to as **KENNETH WEIST** in some sources. He was born on 11 March 1925, Wiconisco, Dauphin County, PA. He died in July 1976, at age 51. He was buried at Calvary United Methodist Cemetery, Wiconisco, Dauphin County, PA.

5.2.5.1.5 HARRY A. WIEST was born in May 1893. Harry made his home in Wiconisco.

5.2.5.1.6 HARPER H. WIEST was born circa 1894. Harper made his home in Harrisburg. In 1930, he was a salesman for a biscuit company.

5.2.5.1.7 CLARENCE F. WIEST was born circa 1897. He married **SADIE (--?--)** circa 1922. Clarence made his home in Williamstown.

5.2.5.1.8 HARVEY E. WIEST was born circa 1901.

5.2.6 HEIRAM KLINGER WIEST was born on 6 August 1848, Klingerstown, Schuylkill County, PA. Some sources record that he was born on 4 January 1846. He died in May 1862, Libby Prison as a POW in the Civil War, Richmond, VA, at age 16. Some sources record that he died in May 1864 Libby Prison (Civil War), VA. The Wiest Family History notes that Heiram Klinger Wiest served in Co. A, 50th Pennsylvania Infantry, during the Civil War. He and his brother Frantz were captured and interned in the infamous Libby Prison. Each morning, it was the practice to gather up the bodies of those who had died during the night and bury them -- a feeble attempt to control the diseases that ravaged so many of the prisoners. Frantz survived his internment and tells the following story: One morning when the "death wagon" was making its rounds, Heiram was very sick. The guards decided that he wouldn't survive day and threw him on the wagon with the others that were to be buried.

5.2.7 JOHANNES WIEST was born on 30 January 1851, Klingerstown, Schuylkill County, PA. He died on 20 July 1851, Klingerstown, Schuylkill County, PA.

5.2.8 RITSCHART WIEST was born on 8 March 1852, Klingerstown, Schuylkill County, PA. He died on 8 May 1852, Klingerstown, Schuylkill County, PA.

5.2.9 SCHARTEL KLINGER WIEST is also referred to as **SCHERTEL AND SHARDEL WIEST** in some sources. He was born in 1853, Klingerstown, Schuylkill County, PA. He married **JANE WAGNER**. He married **CAROLINE (--?--)**. He died circa 1905, Mount Carmel, Northumberland County, PA.

5.2.9.1 CORBIN WIEST was born Mount Carmel, Northumberland County, PA. He died Mount Carmel, Northumberland County, PA.

5.2.9.2 WILLIAM VICTOR WIEST was born on 7 February 1873, Mount Carmel, Northumberland County, PA. He married **ELIZA CARL** circa 1896. Some sources suggest that he was married to **POLLY MINERVA ERDMAN**, but church records at Salem Church, Rough and Ready, show that William's wife (between the years of at least 1903 and the time of his death in 1906) was "Eliza" or "Lizzie" Carl. He died on 31 March 1906, in a mining accident, Gordon, Schuylkill County, PA, at age 33. He was buried at Rough and Ready, Schuylkill County, PA.

5.2.9.2.1 ELIZABETH WIEST

5.2.9.2.2 WILLIAM V. WIEST JR.

5.2.9.2.3 LOTTIE WIEST was born in January 1899.

5.2.9.2.4 MAMIE G. WIEST was born circa 1901.

5.2.9.2.5 MATTIE ELIZABETH WIEST was born on 28 February 1903. She was baptized on 3 April 1906, Salem (Herb's) Church, Rough and Ready, Schuylkill County, PA.

5.2.9.2.6 DANIEL WILLIAM WIEST was born on 23 July 1906, Gordon, Schuylkill County, PA.

5.2.9.2.7 THOMAS E. WIEST was born circa 1907.

5.2.9.3 WALTER M. WIEST was born on 2 August 1880, Mount Carmel, Northumberland County, PA. He married MINNIE M. THOMAS circa 1900. He married ELVIRA MAE KLINE circa 1930. He died on 27 May 1937, Mount Carmel, Northumberland County, PA, at age 56.

5.2.9.4 RICHARD WIEST was born circa 1875.

5.2.10 FELIX KLINGER WIEST was born on 27 April 1854, Klingerstown, Schuylkill County, PA. He married SARA WILLIAMSON, daughter of SAMUEL WILLIAMSON and CATHARINE (--?--). He died on 26 December 1909, Shamokin, Northumberland County, PA, at age 55. He was buried at Shamokin Cemetery, Shamokin, Northumberland County, PA.

5.2.10.1 ISAAC TIMBER WIEST also went by the name of TIM OR TIMOTHY. He was born on 27 January 1875, Klingerstown, Schuylkill County, PA. He married NELLIE A. TASKER circa 1905, Shamokin, Northumberland County, PA. He died on 19 August 1946, Shamokin, Northumberland County, PA, at age 71. He was buried at IOOF Cemetery, Shamokin, Northumberland County, PA.

5.2.10.1.1 HARRY GEORGE WIEST was born circa 1906, Shamokin, Northumberland County, PA. He died in 1962, Paterson, NJ.

5.2.10.1.1.1 CHILD WIEST was born circa 1925.

5.2.10.1.2 VIOLET MAY WIEST was born in 1908, Shamokin, Northumberland County, PA. She married DAVID WYNN circa 1934. She died Shamokin, Northumberland County, PA. She was buried at IOOF Cemetery, Shamokin, Northumberland County, PA.

5.2.10.1.2.1 GAYLE J. WYNN was born circa 1935, Shamokin, Northumberland County, PA. She married (--?--) DEITRICK.

5.2.10.1.2.2 ELAINE L. WYNN was born circa 1936, Shamokin, Northumberland County, PA. She married (--?--) DONNELY. She married WILLIAM R. SHAFFER.

5.2.10.2 WILLIAM JAMES WIEST was born on 12 December 1876. He married ROSANNA CHRISTINA SIMMENDINGER, daughter of JOHN SIMMENDINGER JR. and SARA ALICE HOUSER, on 18 June 1902, Shamokin, Northumberland County, PA. He died on 13 January 1959, at age 82. He was buried at Shamokin Cemetery, Shamokin, Northumberland County, PA.

5.2.10.2.1 WILLIAM IRVINE WIEST was born on 25 July 1903, Shamokin, Northumberland County, PA. He married GRACE IONA SCHLEIF on 30 July 1930, Shamokin, Northumberland County, PA. He died on 11 October 1968, Shamokin, Northumberland County, PA, at age 65. He was buried at Northumberland Memorial Park, Stonington, Shamokin Township, Northumberland County, PA.

5.2.10.2.1.1 GRACE IONA WIEST was born on 3 May 1932, Shamokin, Northumberland County, PA. She married RICHARD ATWOOD TREA on 21 June 1952, Shamokin, Northumberland County, PA. She married WILLIAM LANXNER on 15 November 1984.

5.2.10.2.1.1.1 RICHARD EDWARD TREA also went by the name of RICKY. He was born on 10 November 1953.

5.2.10.2.1.2 BARBARA CAROLYN WIEST was born on 1 December 1937, Shamokin, Northumberland County, PA. She married JOHN THOMAS MCCARTHY JR. on 4 July 1962. She died on 8 October 1971, Washington, DC, at age 33.

5.2.10.2.1.2.1 JOHN THOMAS III MCCARTHY was born on 8 May 1964. He married DENISE ELIZABETH BUSARD on 24 August 1991.

5.2.10.2.1.2.2 ELIZABETH CAROLYN MCCARTHY was born on 11 October 1966.

5.2.10.2.2 SARA LEAH WIEST was born on 14 January 1905, Shamokin, Northumberland County, PA. She married JOSEPH CHAMPION HALL, son of JAMES GEORGE HALL and MARY ELIZABETH CHAMPION, on 26 June 1935, St. John's Reformed Church, Shamokin, Northumberland County, PA. She died on 31 May 1981, Shamokin, Northumberland County, PA, at age 76. She was buried at Odd Fellows Cemetery, Shamokin, Northumberland County, PA.

5.2.10.2.2.1 BRUCE TRAVIS HALL was born on 19 January 1937, Geisinger Hospital, Danville, Montour County, PA. He married WINNIE ELIZABETH SHAFFER, daughter of

KIMBER CLEAVER SHAFFER and ADAHA DOROTHY PALMER, on 1 September 1962, Grace Lutheran Church, Shamokin, Northumberland County, PA. He died on 8 October 2011, Annapolis, MD, at age 74. According to a newspaper obituary, Bruce was a 1954 graduate of Shamokin High School and received a bachelor of science in electrical engineering from Penn State University in 1962.

From 1962 to 1976, he worked for HRB-Singer Inc. in State College and was later employed with IIT Research Institute (now Alion Science and Technology) in Annapolis from 1976 until his retirement in 2006.

He served in the U.S. Navy as an FT2 from 1954 to 1957, at the United States Naval Training Center in Bainbridge, Md., on the USS Albany CA-123 and the USS Des Moines CA-134.

Bruce's hobbies included researching genealogy and family history, model railroading and bowling. Bruce attended the Shamokin public schools, graduating from Shamokin Area High School in May 1954. After graduation, he enlisted in the U.S. Navy, serving on active duty from June 1954 to November 1957, where he attained the rank of (gun) fire control technician 2nd class (FT2). Following his separation from active duty, he was retained in the inactive reserve from November 1957 to June 1962. After his separation from the Navy, he enrolled in the Pennsylvania State University where he earned a bachelor's degree in electrical engineering in June 1962. He completed his eight-year obligation and received his honorable discharge from the Navy on the same day he graduated from Penn State.

Bruce was employed by HRB-Singer, Inc., State College, PA, and IIT Research Institute, Annapolis, MD.

    5.2.10.2.2.1.1 VALERIE LEIGH HALL (see above)

        5.2.10.2.2.1.1.1 JEREMY ERIK ARKLEY (see above)

        5.2.10.2.2.1.1.2 JARON TRAVIS ARKLEY (see above)

    5.2.10.2.2.1.2 BONNIE JOY HALL (see above)

        5.2.10.2.2.1.2.1 ANDREW ZACHARY LINGELBACH (see above)

        5.2.10.2.2.1.2.2 JACOB RYAN LINGELBACH (see above)

    5.2.10.2.2.1.3 HOLLY LYNN HALL (see above)

        5.2.10.2.2.1.3.1 JOSEPH CARL HOUGHTON (see above)

        5.2.10.2.2.1.3.2 MELISSA LEE HOUGHTON (see above)

        5.2.10.2.2.1.3.3 JENNIFER ELIZABETH HOUGHTON (see above)

        5.2.10.2.2.1.3.4 LOUIS REUBEN HOUGHTON (see above)

        5.2.10.2.2.1.3.5 JAMES MADISON HOUGHTON (see above)

    5.2.10.2.2.1.4 SHARI JEANNE HALL (see above)

        5.2.10.2.2.1.4.1 SARAH ELIZABETH JONES (see above)

        5.2.10.2.2.1.4.2 LAURA GRACE JONES (see above)

5.2.10.2.2.2 WILLIAM GARTH HALL was born on 27 May 1938. He married **CONSTANCE DOROTHY KOONS** on 5 May 1962, CT. He married **JOANNE RANKIN** on 4 November 1977. He married **MARGARET REAGEN** on 14 February 1987. He married **MARTHA LAMARR FISHER** on 28 October 1992, Jacksonville, FL.

    5.2.10.2.2.2.1 GARTH CHAMPION HALL was born on 27 December 1962, CT.

    5.2.10.2.2.2.2 CHRYSTAL DAWNETTE HALL was born on 22 January 1964, CT.

5.2.10.2.3 HELEN MYRTLE WIEST was born on 20 February 1908, Shamokin, Northumberland County, PA. She died on 1 April 1914, Shamokin, Northumberland County, PA, at age 6.

5.2.10.2.4 ROSE ANNA WIEST was born on 9 April 1913, Shamokin, Northumberland County, PA. She married **JOSEPH PITTELLI** on 30 September 1951, Shamokin, Northumberland County, PA. She died on 8 March 1976, Philadelphia, PA, at age 62.

5.2.10.2.5 JOHN ROBERT WIEST was born on 9 April 1913, Shamokin, Northumberland County, PA. He married **KATHERINE HOKENSON** on 10 June 1937. He died on 23 June 1981, Quincy, Adams County, IL, at age 68.

5.2.10.2.5.1 JOHN HOKENSON WIEST was born on 1 November 1943. He married ELIZABETH (--?--) on 30 November 1986. He died on 24 December 1991, at age 48.

5.2.10.2.5.2 MADELYN ROSE WIEST was born on 17 March 1949. She married ROBERT WILLIAM HAGEMANN on 25 June 1971.

5.2.10.2.5.2.1 JENNIFER LYNN HAGEMANN was born on 19 December 1974.

5.2.10.2.5.2.2 JOHN WILLIAM HAGEMANN was born on 7 May 1978.

5.2.10.2.5.3 JACQUELINE KAY WIEST was born on 27 January 1956. She married KEITH RICHARD FORSYTH on 8 September 1979, Burlington, NC.

5.2.10.2.6 RUTH ETHEL WIEST was born on 1 October 1915, Shamokin, Northumberland County, PA. She died on 30 March 1974, Atlantic City, NJ, at age 58.

5.2.10.3 GEORGE DANIEL WIEST was born on 4 November 1878, Klingerstown, Schuylkill County, PA. He married POLLY ERDMAN circa 1900. He died on 31 December 1951, Philadelphia, PA, at age 73. He was buried at Shamokin Cemetery, Shamokin, Northumberland County, PA.

5.2.10.3.1 EMMA OTTILLA WIEST was born on 10 June 1901, Philadelphia, PA. She married LESLIE HARFORD. She died in 1960, PA.

5.2.10.3.1.1 LEE SHARTLE HARFORD was born on 2 December 1920.

5.2.10.3.2 BESSIE MILDRED WIEST was born on 26 February 1905, Philadelphia, PA. She died on 7 April 1921, Rough and Ready, Schuylkill County, PA, at age 16.

5.2.10.3.3 FLORENCE WINIFRED WIEST was born on 8 August 1907, PA. She married SAMUEL B. MARSHALL circa 1928. She married DAVID LYONS after 1930. She died on 18 February 1980, Lake Wales, Polk County, FL, at age 72.

5.2.10.3.3.1 LOUISE DIANE MARSHALL was born on 16 October 1929. She married FREDERICK JAMES BATSON JR. on 23 August 1950.

5.2.10.3.3.1.1 DIANE SHARTLE BATSON married JOHN BRISTOW CART. She was born on 30 October 1951.

5.2.10.3.3.1.1.1 JAMES KITTINGER CART was born on 11 May 1988.

5.2.10.3.3.1.1.2 ELIZABETH BATSON CART was born on 5 March 1990.

5.2.10.3.3.1.2 MARGARET KITTINGER BATSON was born on 22 March 1956. She married WILLIAM JOHN ZWIEBEL.

5.2.10.3.3.1.2.1 COLIN BATSON ZWIEBEL was born on 25 October 1989.

5.2.10.3.3.1.2.2 AARON BATSON ZWIEBEL was born on 23 June 1991.

5.2.10.4 PHILIP PENROSE WIEST was born on 22 November 1882. He married OTTILLIA DRUMHEISER circa 1904. He died on 2 July 1963, at age 80. He was buried at Odd Fellows Cemetery, Shamokin, Northumberland County, PA.

5.2.10.4.1 ALLAN A. WIEST is also referred to as ALLEN A. WIEST in some sources. He was born on 30 October 1907. He married ELIZABETH AMANDA YEAGER, daughter of EUGENE YEAGER and HELEN KERSTETTER. He died on 14 November 1980, at age 73. He was buried at Odd Fellows Cemetery, Shamokin, Northumberland County, PA.

5.2.10.4.1.1 REV. KENNETH WIEST married MARY SOCK.

5.2.10.4.1.2 HELEN LOUISE WIEST married RONALD LEHNER.

5.3 MOSES KLINGER was born on 1 December 1827, Lykens Township, Dauphin County, PA. He married ANGELINE SHOFFSTALL, daughter of SAMUEL SCHOFFSTALL and ELIZABETH SCHMELTZ, circa 1850, PA. He died on 1 August 1901, Lykens Township, Dauphin County, PA, at age 73. He was buried at Zion (Klinger's) Church, Erdman, Lykens Township, Dauphin County, PA.

5.3.1 ELMIRA MYAH KLINGER is also referred to as MYHIA AND ELMIRA ELIZABETH in some sources. She was born in 1851, Lykens Township, Dauphin County, PA. She married JONATHAN C. WILLIARD, son of JONATHAN WILLIARD and CATHARINE KLINGER, circa 1871, Lykens Township, Dauphin County, PA. She died on 27 May 1927, Erdman, Lykens Township, Dauphin County, PA. She was buried at Zion (Klinger's) Church Cemetery, Erdman, Lykens Township, Dauphin County, PA.

5.3.1.1 CATHERINE ELIZABETH WILLIARD was born on 30 April 1876, Gratz, Dauphin County, PA. She was baptized on 3 June 1876, Zion (Klinger's) Church, Erdman, Lykens Township, Dauphin

County, PA. She married **JOHN MINNICH**. She died on 26 June 1957, Gratz, Dauphin County, PA, at age 81. She was buried at Simeon United Lutheran Church, Gratz, Dauphin County, PA.

5.3.1.2 MARY MCCLATA WILLIARD was born on 19 September 1877, Lykens Township, Dauphin County, PA. She was baptized on 22 December 1877, Zion (Klinger's) Church, Erdman, Lykens Township, Dauphin County, PA. She married **THEODORE KLINGER**, son of **FRANCIS KLINGER** and **HARRIET TROUTMAN,** on 15 November 1893, Hegins, Schuylkill County, PA. She died on 24 April 1942, Harrisburg, Dauphin County, PA, at age 64. She was buried at St. John's Lutheran Church Cemetery, Berrysburg, Dauphin County, PA.

5.3.1.2.1 ESTON RAYMOND KLINGER was born on 15 May 1895, Lykens Township, Dauphin County, PA. He married **CARRIE EDNA HENNINGER**, daughter of **ISAAC HENNINGER** and **ETTA ROMBERGER,** on 2 June 1917, Berrysburg, Dauphin County, PA. Prior to his death, Eston was living in the vicinity of Elizabethville, Dauphin County, PA. He died on 27 June 1972, Harrisburg, Dauphin County, PA, at age 77. He was buried on 30 June 1972, at Peace United Church of Christ Cemetery, Berrysburg, Dauphin County, PA.

5.3.1.2.1.1 VIOLET M. KLINGER was born on 28 December 1917, RD, Elizabethville, Lykens Township, Dauphin County, PA. She married **ARTHUR ALLEN KLINGER**, son of **GURNEY ALLEN KLINGER** and **GERTRUDE MABEL TROUTMAN,** on 6 March 1955, Berrysburg, Dauphin County, PA. She died on 7 January 2011, The Manor at Susquehanna Village, Millersburg, Dauphin County, PA, at age 93. According to a newspaper obituary, Prior to entering Susquehanna Village, Violet lived in Elizabethville, PA. She retired from Swab Wagon Co., Elizabethville, as a secretary with over 20 years of service. She was buried on 12 January 2011, at U.C.C. Reformed Cemetery, Berrysburg, Dauphin County, PA.

5.3.1.2.1.2 ERNEST LEROY KLINGER is also referred to as **LEROY E.** in some sources. He was born on 14 February 1920, Mifflin Township, Dauphin County, PA. He married **RENEE I. HOLTZMAN**, daughter of **GEORGE HOLTZMAN** and **SELENA BEIBLER,** on 25 March 1946, Elizabethville, Dauphin County, PA. He died on 9 October 2008, Elizabethville, Dauphin County, PA, at age 88, at his home on Church Street. According to a newspaper obituary, Ernest lived in Elizabethville, Dauphin County, PA where he founded and operated Klinger Machinery, Inc. After graduating from what was then the Lykens Valley Vocational High School in Berrysburg and Central Penn Business School, in Harrisburg, he served in the U. S. Army during World War II in the 265th Engineer Combat Battalion. He was buried on 13 October 2008, at Sweitzers Memorial Cemetery, Berrysburg, Dauphin County, PA.

5.3.1.2.1.2.1 ERNEST LAMAR KLINGER is also referred to as **EUGENE LAMAR KLINGER** in some sources. He was born on 25 November 1946, Mifflin Township, Dauphin County, PA. He married **ADELE E. (--?--)** circa 1965. He and **ADELE E. (--?--)** were divorced. Lamar graduated from the University of Louisiana, Baton Rouge, LA, and is currently the president of Klinger Machinery in Elizabethville, PA. Lamar lives in Elizabethville, PA.

5.3.1.2.1.2.2 LINDA J. KLINGER was born on 1 March 1950. Linda lives in Harrisburg, PA.

5.3.1.2.1.2.3 LOIS E. KLINGER was born on 14 August 1953. She married **JEFFREY MILLER**. Lois lives in West Lafayette, IN.

5.3.1.2.1.2.3.1 ANDREW J. MILLER married **HAGIT (--?--)**. Andrew lives in Oakland, CA.

5.3.1.2.1.2.3.2 ADAM LAWSON MILLER married **LACEY (--?--)**. Adam lives in Indianapolis, IN.

5.3.1.2.1.3 EARL ESTON KLINGER is also referred to as **EARL L. KLINGER** in some sources. He was born on 14 January 1922, RD, Elizabethville, Dauphin County, PA. He married **MILDRED PHOEBE BURRELL**, daughter of **PETER G. BURRELL** and **MAUDE C. LAHR**. Prior to his death, Earl was living in the vicinity of Sun City West, Maricopa County, AZ. He died on 15 June 1995, at age 73. He was buried at Sunland Memorial Park, Phoenix, AZ.

5.3.1.2.1.3.1 RICHARD E. KLINGER was born on 19 June 1946. He married **RUTH ANN PFEIL**.

5.3.1.2.1.3.1.1 ADRIANE ALLYN KLINGER

5.3.1.2.1.3.2 SUSAN E. KLINGER was born on 28 September 1950. She married LARRY R. KOMERNICKY on 26 February 1971, Elizabethville, Dauphin County, PA.

    5.3.1.2.1.3.2.1 HEATHER KOMERNICKY

    5.3.1.2.1.3.2.2 JARED KOMERNICKY

5.3.1.2.1.3.3 ROBERT EUGENE KLINGER was born on 12 May 1957, Harrisburg, Dauphin County, PA. He married LORRIE LYNN MILLER, daughter of THOMAS MILLER, circa 1978.

    5.3.1.2.1.3.3.1 MORGAN ALAINA KLINGER was born on 29 October 1991, Harrisburg, Dauphin County, PA.

5.3.1.2.1.4 FERN LILLIAN KLINGER was born on 9 March 1925, RD, Elizabethville, Dauphin County, PA. She died on 10 November 1933, Harrisburg, Dauphin County, PA, at age 8. She was buried at Peace United Church of Christ Cemetery, Berrysburg, Dauphin County, PA.

5.3.1.2.1.5 LORRAINE MARCELLA KLINGER was born on 20 March 1933, RD, Elizabethville, Dauphin County, PA. She married CLYDE MARVIN WITMER, son of EDWIN WITMER and MAE SNYDER, on 30 June 1953.

    5.3.1.2.1.5.1 LARRY CLYDE WITMER was born on 29 December 1957.

    5.3.1.2.1.5.2 RANDY LEE WITMER was born on 23 February 1960.

    5.3.1.2.1.5.3 GARY TODD WITMER was born on 10 January 1962.

5.3.1.2.2 HARRY ALBERT KLINGER was born on 4 May 1897, RD, Elizabethville, Dauphin County, PA. He married MINNIE AGNES HAIN, daughter of JOHN HAIN and CECILIA BROWN, on 7 June 1919, Berrysburg, Dauphin County, PA. Harry and Minnie had no children. He died on 10 May 1964, Harrisburg, Dauphin County, PA, at age 67. He was buried at Evangelical United Brethren Church Cemetery, Berrysburg, Dauphin County, PA.

5.3.1.2.3 MINNIE M. KLINGER was born on 1 March 1898, Lykens Township, Dauphin County, PA. She married RAY W. MYERS on 6 February 1917, Elizabethville, Dauphin County, PA. She died on 5 December 1952, RD, Millersburg, Dauphin County, PA, at age 54. She was buried at Salem (Wert's) Lutheran Church Cemetery, Killinger, Dauphin County, PA.

    5.3.1.2.3.1 EVELYN MYERS was born on 18 October 1918, Killinger, Dauphin County, PA. She married JAMES BORDNER. She died on 28 August 1965, Millersburg, Dauphin County, PA, at age 46. She was buried at Salem (Wert's) Lutheran Church Cemetery, Killinger, Dauphin County, PA.

    5.3.1.2.3.2 MARLIN THEODORE MYERS was born on 3 March 1921, Killinger, Dauphin County, PA. He was baptized on 8 May 1921, St. John's Lutheran Church, Berrysburg, Dauphin County, PA. Some sources record that he was born Millersburg RD, Dauphin County, PA. He married SUSAN P. RAMBERGER, daughter of CHARLES RAMBERGER and EDNA KNORR. He died on 3 June 1968, Killinger, Dauphin County, PA, at age 47. He was buried at Salem (Wert's) Lutheran Church Cemetery, Killinger, Dauphin County, PA.

        5.3.1.2.3.2.1 JANE MYERS was born on 27 November 1946. Jane lives in Camp Hill, PA.

            5.3.1.2.3.2.1.1 BRIAN SMITH married MICHELLE (--?--).

            5.3.1.2.3.2.1.2 CHET SMITH married ANGIE (--?--).

        5.3.1.2.3.2.2 DENNIS MYERS was born on 1 May 1952. He married SUE (--?--). Dennis lives in Millersburg, PA.

            5.3.1.2.3.2.2.1 DAVID MYERS

            5.3.1.2.3.2.2.2 MIKE MYERS married BECKY (--?--).

5.3.1.2.4 HATTIE IRENE KLINGER was born on 13 September 1900, RD, Elizabethville, Dauphin County, PA. She married ISAAC LEROY HOWARD, son of WILLIAM HOWARD and SADIE ROMBERGER, circa 1918, Dauphin County, PA. She died on 6 April 1969, Elizabethville, Dauphin County, PA, at age 68. She was buried at St. John's (Hill) Lutheran Church, near Berrysburg, Dauphin County, PA.

    5.3.1.2.4.1 LAURETTA FAYE HOWARD was born on 31 August 1919, RD, Elizabethville, Dauphin County, PA. She married GEORGE W BOYER in April 1941, Elizabethville, Dauphin

County, PA. She died on 7 November 2000, at age 81. She was buried at Oakhill Cemetery, Millersburg, Dauphin County, PA.

    5.3.1.2.4.1.1 CAROLYN DARNETA BOYER was born on 24 December 1943, Killinger, Dauphin County, PA. She married **JAMES ZERBY**.

        5.3.1.2.4.1.1.1 ANGELA ZERBY was born on 19 August 1962.

        5.3.1.2.4.1.1.2 TRISHA ZERBY is also referred to as **CHRIS** in some sources. She was born on 9 December 1969.

    5.3.1.2.4.1.2 GERALD RONALD BOYER was born on 29 November 1946, Killinger, Dauphin County, PA. He married **ANNETTE THORNBUSH**. He married **CELESTE HOUGE**.

5.3.1.2.4.2 NORWOOD CLEON HOWARD was born on 22 October 1920, RD, Elizabethville, Dauphin County, PA. Norwood was unmarried. According to Mary Klinger's book (p. 278), he was "killed in a coal hole (bootlegging) on Hegins Mountain." He died on 19 February 1939, Good Springs, Schuylkill County, PA, at age 18. He was buried at St. John's (Hill) Lutheran Church, near Berrysburg, Dauphin County, PA.

5.3.1.2.4.3 MARY ELLEN HOWARD was born on 29 November 1921, RD, Lykens, Dauphin County, PA. She married **JOHN ELWOOD HOOVER**, son of **PAUL CLAYTON HOOVER** and **LIZZIE MAE KLINGER**, on 28 October 1942, Brownsville, TX. She died on 7 August 2006, at age 84. She was buried at Woodlawn Gardens, Harrisburg, Dauphin County, PA. Prior to her death, Mary was living in the vicinity of Lewistown, Mifflin County, PA.

    5.3.1.2.4.3.1 BONITA LOU HOOVER was born on 20 July 1943. She married **JERRY EDWIN BOYER**.

        5.3.1.2.4.3.1.1 JEREMY TODD BOYER

        5.3.1.2.4.3.1.2 JERREL HOWARD BOYER

        5.3.1.2.4.3.1.3 JESSICA MARYANN BOYER

    5.3.1.2.4.3.2 JOHN ELWOOD HOOVER was born on 10 March 1951, RD, Millersburg, Dauphin County, PA. He married **BARBARA LONG**.

5.3.1.2.4.4 ALBERTA MAE HOWARD was born on 3 November 1923, RD, Elizabethville, Dauphin County, PA. She married **HOMER ALLEN DEIBLER**, son of **JOHN DEIBLER** and **LAURA UMHOLTZ**, on 27 February 1943, Rife, Dauphin County, PA. She married **PAUL LEON BROWN**, son of **SYLVESTER C. BROWN** and **RUTH A. SNYDER**, on 30 June 1956. She died on 28 December 1992, Pillow, Dauphin County, PA, at age 69. She was buried on 31 December 1992, at Zion (Hoover's) Lutheran and Reformed Church Cemetery, Rife, Dauphin County, PA.

    5.3.1.2.4.4.1 KAYE JOANNE DEIBLER was born on 22 May 1945, Harrisburg, Dauphin County, PA. She married **WARREN E. THOMA** on 25 October 1969, Shamokin, Northumberland County, PA.

        5.3.1.2.4.4.1.1 SHERRI THOMA

    5.3.1.2.4.4.2 INFANT SON DEIBLER died in infancy. He was born in 1947.

    5.3.1.2.4.4.3 THOMAS ALLEN DEIBLER was born on 13 October 1949, RD, Millersburg, Dauphin County, PA.

    5.3.1.2.4.4.4 PATRICIA DIANNE BROWN was born on 31 August 1958, Harrisburg, Dauphin County, PA. She married **THOMAS EDWARD DEITRICH**. She died on 27 October 1982, at age 24.

        5.3.1.2.4.4.4.1 BRENT THOMAS DEITRICH

    5.3.1.2.4.4.5 TAMMY JOANNE BROWN was born on 10 September 1965, Danville, Montour County, PA.

5.3.1.2.4.5 ROBERT ALTON HOWARD was born on 4 February 1924, RD, Elizabethville, Dauphin County, PA. He married **MARIE HARTMAN**, daughter of **RALPH HARTMAN** and **ELAH (--?--)**, on 7 August 1943, St. John's Church. He died on 12 September 1969, Danville, Montour County, PA, at age 45. He was buried at Maple Grove Cemetery, Elizabethville, Dauphin County, PA.

5.3.1.2.4.5.1 NANCY LOU HOWARD was born on 29 January 1944, RD, Millersburg, Dauphin County, PA. She died on 30 January 1944, RD, Millersburg, Dauphin County, PA.

5.3.1.2.4.5.2 VICKE LEE HOWARD was born on 25 May 1950, Harrisburg, Dauphin County, PA. She died on 3 March 1968, Halifax, Dauphin County, PA, at age 17.

5.3.1.2.4.5.3 ROBERT ALTON HOWARD was born on 7 August 1963.

5.3.1.2.4.6 MARK ALBERT HOWARD was born on 10 October 1926, Elizabethville, Dauphin County, PA. He married JUNE WIEST. He married WILMA SHAMROCK on 20 September 1956. He died on 19 January 1977, Chambersburg, Franklin County, PA, at age 50. He was buried at Spring Hill Cemetery, Shippensburg, PA.

5.3.1.2.4.6.1 MARK E. HOWARD was born on 28 February 1959.

5.3.1.2.4.6.2 DEITRA HOWARD was born on 13 February 1960.

5.3.1.2.4.6.3 SHARON HOWARD was born on 9 January 1961.

5.3.1.2.4.6.4 BRYAN L. HOWARD was born on 24 February 1962.

5.3.1.2.4.6.5 SHAWNA HOWARD was born on 31 August 1963.

5.3.1.2.4.6.6 STACY HOWARD was born on 11 March 1965.

5.3.1.2.4.6.7 PATRICK HOWARD was born on 26 July 1966.

5.3.1.2.4.7 EUGENE ISAAC HOWARD was born on 7 November 1927, RD, Lykens, Dauphin County, PA. He married DOROTHY PEIFFER on 19 July 1948. He married JANE MUNDORF. He died on 23 February 1988, Harrisburg, Dauphin County, PA, at age 60. He was buried at Middletown, Dauphin County, PA.

5.3.1.2.4.7.1 BARBARA HOWARD was born on 15 March 1949. She married RANDY WIEST.

5.3.1.2.4.7.1.1 RANDY EUGENE WIEST

5.3.1.2.4.7.1.2 KERRY LYNN WIEST

5.3.1.2.4.7.2 RITA RENEE HOWARD was born on 13 July 1952. She married NORMAN L MAURER. She married CHARLES PINKERTON.

5.3.1.2.4.7.2.1 JEFFRY ALLEN MAURER

5.3.1.2.4.7.3 CAROL HOWARD was born on 13 October 1954. She married RALPH KLOCK.

5.3.1.2.4.7.3.1 PAMELA YVONNE KLOCK

5.3.1.2.4.7.3.2 ANGELA KLOCK

5.3.1.2.4.7.4 MARILYN R. HOWARD is also referred to as MARLIN in some sources. She was born on 1 September 1956. She married IRA RAY ANTES.

5.3.1.2.4.7.4.1 AMBER ALYSIA ANTES

5.3.1.2.4.7.4.2 MANDY ADELLE ANTES

5.3.1.2.4.7.5 DENISE HOWARD was born on 1 August 1959. She married JAMES GOTTSHELL.

5.3.1.2.4.7.5.1 JAMIE LYNN GOTTSHELL

5.3.1.2.4.7.5.2 AMY SUE GOTTSHELL

5.3.1.2.4.8 PEARL GERALDINE HOWARD was born on 9 September 1930. She married MARLIN LEROY BUFFINGTON, son of MILTON O. BUFFINGTON and MAUDE E. KLINGER. Pearl lives in Halifax, PA.

5.3.1.2.4.8.1 LEONARD BUFFINGTON (see above)

5.3.1.2.4.8.2 JEFFREY BUFFINGTON (see above)

5.3.1.2.4.8.2.1 JEFFREY LYNN BUFFINGTON (see above)

5.3.1.2.4.8.2.2 JENNIFER LYNN BUFFINGTON (see above)

5.3.1.2.4.8.3 CRAIG BUFFINGTON (see above)

5.3.1.2.4.8.4 KEITH ALAN BUFFINGTON (see above)

5.3.1.2.4.8.4.1 ELIJAH ALAN BUFFINGTON (see above)

5.3.1.2.4.8.5 TINA BUFFINGTON (see above)

5.3.1.2.4.8.5.1 CHAD AARON BUFFINGTON (see above)

5.3.1.2.4.9 FEARL KATHLEEN HOWARD was born on 9 September 1930, RD, Lykens, Dauphin County, PA. She married GERALD ROBERT LENKER, son of CLARENCE I. LENKER and STELLA WIEST. She died on 22 September 2006, Geisinger Medical Center, Danville, Montour County, PA, at age 76. She was buried on 26 September 2006, at St. John's Lutheran Church Cemetery, near Berrysburg, Dauphin County, PA. According to a newspaper obituary, Fearl lived in Pillow, PA.

5.3.1.2.4.9.1 SANDRA KATHLEEN LENKER (see above)

5.3.1.2.4.9.2 DEBRA ROBERTA LENKER (see above)

5.3.1.2.4.10 DONALD WILLIAM HOWARD also went by the name of CHAPPY. He was born on 4 December 1931, Mifflin Township, Dauphin County, PA. He married CATHERINE ARINE MOWERY, daughter of JOHN MOWERY and DOROTHY FREDERICK. He died on 21 May 2015, at his home Millersburg, Dauphin County, PA, at age 83. According to a newspaper obituary, Donald retired from Brubaker Tool Co. in Millersburg and before that was a milkman for 30 years with various companies.

5.3.1.2.4.10.1 DOUGLAS LEE HOWARD was born on 24 August 1955, Harrisburg, Dauphin County, PA. He married PATTY (--?--).

5.3.1.2.4.10.2 EDWARD JOHN HOWARD married CAROL (--?--). He was born on 2 November 1960, Harrisburg, Dauphin County, PA.

5.3.1.2.4.10.3 SCOTT LEROY HOWARD was born on 21 May 1967, Harrisburg, Dauphin County, PA. He married CONNIE ENDERS.

5.3.1.2.4.11 HAROLD THEODORE HOWARD was born on 4 December 1931, Elizabethville, Dauphin County, PA. He married ELIZABETH ROSE DICKINSON, daughter of GEORGE DICKINSON and BRIDGET MCCABE, on 5 March 1955, St. John's Church.

5.3.1.2.4.11.1 DENNIS GEORGE HOWARD married DONNA JO NOLTE. He was born on 6 January 1956, Elizabethville, Dauphin County, PA.

5.3.1.2.4.11.2 WENDY BRIDGET HOWARD was born on 19 December 1961, Harrisburg, Dauphin County, PA.

5.3.1.2.4.11.3 JOHN DAVID HOWARD was born on 26 February 1965, Harrisburg, Dauphin County, PA.

5.3.1.2.4.12 RICHARD LEROY HOWARD was born on 31 January 1934, RD, Lykens, Dauphin County, PA. He married DOROTHY MARY SHAFFER, daughter of JOSEPH SHAFFER and MARY ZEIDERS, on 29 June 1953, County Line, Northumberland County, PA. Some sources suggest that he and DOROTHY MARY SHAFFER were married on 29 June 1957 County Line United Methodist Church, County Line, Northumberland County, PA. He died on 10 January 2010, at his home, Millersburg, Dauphin County, PA, at age 75. According to a newspaper obituary, Rich, who lived in Millersburg, was a veteran of the US Air Force in the Korean War. In 1992, he retired as an automotive/truck mechanic after many years of working at Brenner Motors in Harrisburg. In 1996, at the Hospital of University of Pennsylvania in Philadelphia, he became a double lung transplant recipient. He was buried on 14 January 2010, at Evangelical Cemetery, County Line, Northumberland County, PA.

5.3.1.2.4.12.1 KATHLEEN MARIE HOWARD was born on 28 March 1958, Harrisburg, Dauphin County, PA. She married JOSEPH PETER BEGANI on 14 March 1981, Grace United Methodist Church, Millersburg, Dauphin County, PA. Kathleen and her family live in Millersburg, PA.

5.3.1.2.4.12.1.1 NATHAN JOSEPH BEGANI married SHARA (--?--). Nathan and his wife live in Nashville, TN.

5.3.1.2.4.12.2 WAYNE RICHARD HOWARD was born on 14 October 1959, Harrisburg, Dauphin County, PA. He married DIANE MARIE NICE on 26 January 1980, Grace United Methodist Church, Millersburg, Dauphin County, PA. He married ANGELA FRANCES GALBRAITH on 27 July 1985, Trinity United Methodist Church, Elizabethville, Dauphin County, PA. Wayne lives in Elizabethville, PA.

5.3.1.2.4.12.2.1 MATHEW WAYNE HOWARD married **SANDRA (--?--)**. Matthew and Sandra live in Fairbanks, AK.

    5.3.1.2.4.12.2.1.1 DONOVAN HOWARD

5.3.1.2.4.12.2.2 SHAWN ELIZAH HOWARD. Shawn lives in Millersburg, PA.

5.3.1.2.4.12.2.3 COLBY MICHAEL HOWARD. Colby lives in Sevierville, TN.

5.3.1.2.4.12.3 RANDALL EUGENE HOWARD was born on 19 November 1961, Harrisburg, Dauphin County, PA. He married **CRYSTALE MICHELLE SCHULTZ** on 7 April 1984, St. Paul's Lutheran Church, Millersburg, Dauphin County, PA. He married **CRYSTAL ANN YEAGER** on 13 November 1993, United Methodist Church, Halifax, Dauphin County, PA. Randall lives in Millersburg, PA.

    5.3.1.2.4.12.3.1 JEREMY RANDALL HOWARD. Jeremy lives in Millersburg, PA.

5.3.1.2.4.12.4 ALAN DALE HOWARD was born on 21 July 1963, Harrisburg, Dauphin County, PA. He married **HEATHER ANN LAWLEY** on 21 April 1990, Grace United Methodist Church, Millersburg, Dauphin County, PA. Alan and his family live in Millersburg, PA.

    5.3.1.2.4.12.4.1 TESSA MORGAN HOWARD

    5.3.1.2.4.12.4.2 JOSHUA ALAN HOWARD

5.3.1.2.4.12.5 BRENDA ELAINE HOWARD was born on 27 February 1965, Harrisburg, Dauphin County, PA. She married **STEPHEN JOHN CARUSO** on 12 June 1993, Grace United Methodist Church, Millersburg, Dauphin County, PA. Brenda and her family live in Harrisburg, PA.

    5.3.1.2.4.12.5.1 JORDAN ALEXIS CARUSO

    5.3.1.2.4.12.5.2 DOMINIC CARUSO

5.3.1.2.4.13 KENNETH LAMAR HOWARD was born on 19 June 1936, RD, Lykens, Dauphin County, PA. He died on 29 April 1937, Harrisburg, Dauphin County, PA.

5.3.1.2.5 MARK FRANKLIN KLINGER was born on 10 January 1902, RD, Elizabethville, Dauphin County, PA. He married **EVA ALVESTA TROUTMAN**, daughter of **JOHN HENRY TROUTMAN** and **CORA MAY ROTHERMOL,** on 3 May 1928, Elizabethville, Dauphin County, PA. He died on 25 November 1981, Harrisburg, Dauphin Co., PA, at age 79. He was buried on 28 November 1981, at Maple Grove Cemetery, Elizabethville, Dauphin Co., PA.

5.3.1.2.5.1 FRANCES MADELINE KLINGER was born on 23 August 1928, Washington Township, Dauphin County, PA. Some sources record that she was born on 24 August 1928, Loyalton, PA. She married **HENRY E. SHOMPER** on 24 December 1945, Baltimore, Baltimore (city), MD. Some sources suggest that she and **HENRY E. SHOMPER** were married Elizabethville, Dauphin County, PA.

    5.3.1.2.5.1.1 RICHARD LEROY SHOMPER was born on 18 October 1946, Elizabethville, Dauphin Co., PA. He married **GLORIA HOOVER** on 27 June 1974, PA.

        5.3.1.2.5.1.1.1 ROBIN SHOMPER was born on 19 June 1980, Harrisburg, Dauphin Co., PA.

    5.3.1.2.5.1.2 SHIRLEY JEAN SHOMPER was born on 15 October 1948, Elizabethville, Dauphin Co., PA. She married **JAMES LEE ROCK** on 2 March 1969.

        5.3.1.2.5.1.2.1 SCOTT LEE ROCK was born on 13 November 1968, Harrisburg, Dauphin Co., PA. He married **ROBIN MICHELLE HOFFMAN** on 27 October 1995, Lutheran Church, Pillow, Dauphin Co., PA.

        5.3.1.2.5.1.2.2 KIMBERLY ROCK was born on 30 April 1970, Harrisburg, Dauphin Co., PA. She married **MICHAEL MORRIS** on 2 September 1995.

    5.3.1.2.5.1.3 DAVID LESTER SHOMPER was born on 25 January 1952, Dauphin Co., PA. He married **MELANIE CHUBB** on 19 July 1975, PA. He married **KAREN L. ZERBY** on 8 February 1986, PA.

        5.3.1.2.5.1.3.1 DANECA M SHOMPER was born on 27 July 1978, Harrisburg, Dauphin Co., PA.

        5.3.1.2.5.1.3.2 LANDON DAVID SHOMPER was born on 19 November 1986, Harrisburg, Dauphin Co., PA.

5.3.1.2.5.1.4 JOHN EDWARD SHOMPER SR. was born on 25 March 1953, Dauphin Co., PA. He married an unknown person. He married **CINTHIA SEELER** on 25 October 1975, PA.

> **5.3.1.2.5.1.4.1 JOHN EDWARD SHOMPER JR.** was born on 16 December 1983, Harrisburg, Dauphin Co., PA.
>
> **5.3.1.2.5.1.4.2 JESSICA C. SHOMPER** was born on 16 December 1983, Harrisburg, Dauphin Co., PA.
>
> **5.3.1.2.5.1.4.3 FELICIA SHOMPER** was born on 8 February 1990, Harrisburg, Dauphin Co., PA.

5.3.1.2.5.2 EILEEN MARIE KLINGER is also referred to as **EILEEN GWENERVE KLINGER** in some sources. She was born on 21 January 1931, Loyalton, Dauphin County, PA. She was baptized on 21 August 1932, the home of Theodore Klinger, Dauphin Co., PA. She married **ERNEST NELSON DIETRICH**, son of **HARRIS EDGAR DIETRICH** and **AMELIA HOFFMAN,** on 1 October 1949, Evangelical United Brethren Church, Loyalton, Dauphin Co., PA. She married **BRIGHT MATTIS**, son of **BLAIR MATTIS** and **CLARA BYERLY,** Elizabethville, Dauphin County, PA. She married **BRIGHT BYRLEY MATTIS (WW-II)** after 1960, Elizabethville, Dauphin Co., PA. She died on 5 June 2004, Dauphin Co., PA, at age 73. She was buried on 21 June 2004, at Maple Grove Cemetery, Elizabethville, Dauphin Co., PA.

> **5.3.1.2.5.2.1 MARK CARL DIETRICH** was born on 15 February 1952. He was born on 15 February 1952, Zeldin Hospital, Lykens, Dauphin Co., PA. He married **RONI MARIE HUGHES** on 14 June 1973, PA. He married **RONI MARIE HUGHES.**
>
>> **5.3.1.2.5.2.1.1 JASON EARL DIETRICH** was born on 15 July 1983, Harrisburg, Dauphin Co., PA.
>>
>> **5.3.1.2.5.2.1.2 RYAN ALEXANDER DIETRICH** was born on 1 May 1986, Harrisburg, Dauphin Co., PA.
>>
>> **5.3.1.2.5.2.1.3 JASON PREL DIETRICH**
>>
>> **5.3.1.2.5.2.1.4 RYAN ALEXANDER DIETRICH**
>
> **5.3.1.2.5.2.2 MILLIE MAE DIETRICH** was born on 9 January 1958, Harrisburg, Dauphin Co., PA. She married **DAVID LARRY WEBSTER** on 18 December 1976, PA.
>
>> **5.3.1.2.5.2.2.1 JENNIFER MARIE WEBSTER** was born on 14 September 1977, Harrisburg, Dauphin Co., PA.
>>
>> **5.3.1.2.5.2.2.2 JOSHUA CALEB WEBSTER** was born on 14 March 1979, Harrisburg, Dauphin Co., PA.

5.3.1.2.5.3 CARL RICHARD KLINGER was born on 30 December 1932, Big Run, Dauphin Co., PA. He was baptized on 11 February 1934, Dauphin Co., PA. He married **PATRICIA ANN SHAFFER**, daughter of **ROBERT SHAFFER** and **ETHEL HERMAN,** circa 1958, PA.

> **5.3.1.2.5.3.1 DANE ANDREW KLINGER** was born on 23 August 1960, Montgomery Hospital, Norristown, Montgomery Co., PA. He married **LIZABETH FLETCHER** on 29 April 1985.
>
>> **5.3.1.2.5.3.1.1 MARK FRANKLIN KLINGER** is also referred to as **MARK BRANDON KLINGER** in some sources. He was born on 28 January 1990, Dauphin Co., PA.
>
> **5.3.1.2.5.3.2 LANCE NATHANAEL KLINGER** was born on 9 May 1966, Harrisburg, Dauphin Co., PA. He married **VICKI (--?--)** on 1 December 2002, PA.

5.3.1.2.6 HOMER WILBER KLINGER was born on 16 April 1903, Loyalton, Dauphin County, PA. He married **MADIE MAE DANIELS**, daughter of **JOEL ELMER DANIELS** and **MARY RISSINGER,** on 28 December 1923, Fredericksburg, Lebanon County, PA. Homer and Madie lived in the Reinerton-Tower City area of Schuylkill County, where Homer worked as a driller in the coal mines. He died on 10 March 1927, at home, Tower City, Schuylkill County, PA, at age 23. He was buried at St. John's (Hill) Lutheran Cemetery, Berrysburg, Dauphin County, PA.

> **5.3.1.2.6.1 ELSIE MAE KLINGER** was born on 23 May 1924, Millersburg, Dauphin County, PA. She married **JAMES MARVIN EAVES**, son of **PIERSON LEE EAVES** and **MARY OCTAVIA TOMLINSON,** on 18 April 1945, Childress County, TX. For a number of years, Elsie and her husband James, who live in Georgetown, TX, maintained an extensive family history website that included many family photos and reminiscences relating to the Klinger family.

5.3.1.2.6.1.1 JAMES BERNARD EAVES was born on 8 February 1947, Vaughan Memorial Hospital, Selma, Dallas County, AL. He married CLAUDIA ELAINE COOK on 18 March 1972, First Baptist Church, Anderson, Anderson County, SC. Jimmy graduated from the US Air Force Academy in 1969 and in 1986 received his MD degree from University of Arkansas Medical School.

5.3.1.2.6.1.1.1 CHRISTOPHER FRANKLIN EAVES was born on 28 March 1974, Desert Samaritan Hospital, Mesa, Maricopa County, AZ. He was named Chad Franklin Eaves at birth, but had his name legally changed to Christopher Franklin Eaves about 1986. He married DARLENA D. SAMPSON on 11 December 1999, Las Vegas, Clark Co., NV. He and DARLENA D. SAMPSON were divorced before 10 September 2003. Tyla had two children before her marriage to Chris F. Eaves. Her son, Kyler, lives with Tyla and Chris. Her daughter, Juliana, was adopted by Chris Eaves after he married her mother.

5.3.1.2.6.1.1.1.1 CHRISTOPHER JAMES (CJ) EAVES was born on 11 January 2004, AK.

5.3.1.2.6.1.1.1.2 HAILEY AUTUMN EAVES was born on 27 January 2007, AK.

5.3.1.2.6.1.1.2 AUTUMN HEATHER EAVES was born on 12 March 1981, Willford Hall AF Medical Center, San Antonio, Bexar County, TX. She married ASHLEY DYLAN CALL on 25 June 2005, Harmon Residence, Girdwood, Anchorage, AK. She and ASHLEY DYLAN CALL were divorced in 2017.

5.3.1.2.6.1.1.3 ERIN ELIZABETH EAVES was born on 5 February 1979, Little Rock, Pulaski County, AR. She married CHRISTOPHER PHILIP ULMER on 22 April 2004, AK. She and CHRISTOPHER PHILIP ULMER were divorced in 2012. She married SCOTT SMITH in 2014, Las Vegas, Clark County, NV. She and SCOTT SMITH were divorced before 2017.

5.3.1.2.6.1.2 MARVIN LEE EAVES is also referred to as MARTY in some sources. He was born on 14 February 1962, Tinker AF Base Hospital, Midwest City, Oklahoma Co., OK. He married VERONICA MARRITE RAHR, daughter of RICHARD RAHR and VIRGINIA STEHLING, on 31 March 1990, Dallas, Dallas County, TX.

5.3.1.2.6.1.2.1 RYAN LEE EAVES was born on 8 January 1992, Presbyterian Hospital, Margot Perot Women's Annex, Dallas, Dallas Co., TX.

5.3.1.2.6.1.2.2 ASHLEE ANN EAVES was born on 3 July 1995, Presbyterian Hospital, Margot Perot Women's Annex, Dallas, Dallas Co., TX.

5.3.1.2.6.2 JEAN MARY KLINGER was born on 11 November 1925, on Theodore Klinger's farm near Berrysburg, Mifflin Township, Dauphin County, PA. She married LEE WILLIAMS on 27 December 1947, Atlanta, Fulton County, GA. She died on 13 April 2000, DeKalb Medical Center, Decatur, DeKalb County, GA, at age 74. She was buried on 16 April 2000, at Melwood Cemetery, Stone Mountain, DeKalb County, GA.

5.3.1.2.6.2.1 SANDRA LEE WILLIAMS married JIMMIE RAY CHAVES on 12 June 1971, First Baptist Church, Clarkston, DeKalb County, GA.

5.3.1.2.6.2.1.1 GINA LEE CHAVES

5.3.1.2.6.2.1.2 MICHAEL RAY CHAVES

5.3.1.2.6.2.2 DONNA JEAN WILLIAMS married PAUL D. HOLLOWAY SR. in August 1968, Clarkston, DeKalb County, GA. She and PAUL D. HOLLOWAY SR. were divorced. She married LARRY JANOSKI in 1974, DeKalb County, GA. She and LARRY JANOSKI were divorced. She married LES STANLEY in 1982, Georgia. She and LES STANLEY were divorced.

5.3.1.2.6.2.2.1 PAUL D. HOLLOWAY JR. married JEANETTE WARNER on 19 June 1999, Georgia.

5.3.1.2.6.2.2.1.1 MADELYNN TAYLOR HOLLOWAY

5.3.1.2.6.2.2.1.2 RYAN DANIEL HOLLOWAY

5.3.1.2.6.2.2.2 TRACEY L. HOLLOWAY married JOSEPH GRABLE on 4 July 1999, Georgia.

5.3.1.2.6.2.2.2.1 FORD MARSHALL GRABLE

5.3.1.2.6.2.3 KENNETH WAYNE WILLIAMS married CECILE MCCLAIN. He married DEBORAH ANN LIVELY.

    5.3.1.2.6.2.3.1 JAMIE WAYNE WILLIAMS

    5.3.1.2.6.2.3.2 ZACHRY WILLIAMS

    5.3.1.2.6.2.3.3 MALLORY MICHELLE WILLIAMS

5.3.1.2.6.2.4 DONALD EUGENE WILLIAMS was born on 4 December 1950, Clarkston, DeKalb County, GA. He died on 13 December 1950, Clarkston, DeKalb County, GA.

5.3.1.2.6.3 RUTH ELIZABETH KLINGER was born on 7 March 1927, Reinerton, Schuylkill County, PA. She died on 10 March 1928, Millersburg, Dauphin County, PA, at age 1. Some sources record that she died on 13 March 1928. She was buried at St. John's Lutheran Church Cemetery, Berrysburg, Dauphin County, PA.

5.3.1.2.7 VERNA MAY KLINGER was born on 11 June 1905, Oakdale, Dauphin County, PA. Some sources record that she was born on 11 June 1905, in Elizabethville or Loyalton, Dauphin County, PA. She married HOMER ARTHUR LEBO, son of IRA M. LEBO and KATE POLM, on 19 April 1924, Elizabethville, Dauphin County, PA. She married ISAAC LEROY HOWARD, son of WILLIAM HOWARD and SADIE ROMBERGER, on 19 June 1971, St John's (Hill) Lutheran Church, Dauphin County, PA. She died on 27 January 1995, Polyclinic Hospital, Harrisburg, Dauphin County, PA, at age 89. She was buried at St. John's (Hill) Lutheran Church, near Berrysburg, Dauphin County, PA.

5.3.1.2.7.1 HOMER ARTHUR LEBO was born on 25 October 1924, Mifflin Township, Dauphin County, PA. He died on 5 November 1924, Mifflin Township, Dauphin County, PA. He was buried at St. John's (Hill) Lutheran Church, near Berrysburg, Dauphin County, PA.

5.3.1.2.7.2 THEODORE MILTON LEBO also went by the name of TED. He was born on 7 May 1926, Elizabethville, Dauphin County, PA. He married SHIRLEY SUE LEITZEL, daughter of FRED LEITZEL and HATTIE IRENE BORDNER. Theodore had 4 step-children, who were children of Theodore's wife Shirley Sue Leitzel and her first husband Whitey Schreffler. These were Douglas (b. 19 May 1951); Dolores (b. 17 April 1953), Daniel (b. 22 November 1955), and Donald (b. 28 February 1957). It is unknown whether Theodore formally adopted them or not. Prior to his death, Theodore was living in or near Elizabethville, Dauphin County, PA. He died on 30 April 1998, at age 71. He was buried at St. John's (Hill) Lutheran Church, near Berrysburg, Dauphin County, PA.

5.3.1.2.7.3 ROBERT ARTHUR LEBO was born on 9 January 1928, Elizabethville, Dauphin County, PA. He married MYRTLE VIOLA LONG, daughter of ROY LONG and NORA ADAMS, on 31 December 1949, Williamstown, PA. He died in 1995, Kissimmee, Osceola County, FL.

    5.3.1.2.7.3.1 ROBERT ARTHUR LEBO was born on 19 September 1950, San Francisco, CA. He married BARBARA ANN SPAETH on 18 September 1971.

        5.3.1.2.7.3.1.1 JASON MICHAEL LEBO

        5.3.1.2.7.3.1.2 KIMBERLY ANN LEBO

        5.3.1.2.7.3.1.3 KELLY LYNNE LEBO

        5.3.1.2.7.3.1.4 KARI MARIE LEBO

        5.3.1.2.7.3.1.5 KRISTEN MICHELLE LEBO was born on 12 May 1950.

5.3.1.2.7.4 ARNOLD KLINGER LEBO also went by the name of ARNIE. He was born on 17 August 1928. Some sources record that he was born on 17 August 1929, Elizabethville, Dauphin County, PA. He was baptized on 6 October 1929, St. John's (Hill) Lutheran Church, near Berrysburg, Dauphin County, PA. He married VIRGINIA MAE MURPHY, daughter of THOMAS MURPHY and GLENIS (--?--), on 14 June 1950, Panama Canal Zone, Panama. He and VIRGINIA MAE MURPHY were divorced. He married ESTHER HARGROVE. Prior to his death, Arnold was living in or near Riverview, Hillsborough County, FL. He died on 19 April 1979, Hudson, FL, at age 49. He was buried on 24 April 1979, at Greenwood Cemetery, Wayne, Wayne County, MI.

    5.3.1.2.7.4.1 PENELOPE ANN LEBO was born on 17 October 1953, Holloman Air Force Base, NM. She married DALE WEAVER on 10 June 1972, Hummelstown, PA.

        5.3.1.2.7.4.1.1 CHRISIANNA WEAVER died at birth.

        5.3.1.2.7.4.1.2 JENNIFER WEAVER was born on 28 April 1974.

5.3.1.2.7.4.2 **PAMELA GAIL LEBO** was born on 28 November 1954, Holloman Air Force Base, NM. She married **RICHARD LEADER** on 14 April 1974, Harrisburg, Dauphin County, PA. She married **RANDY SHUEY.**

5.3.1.2.7.4.3 **KIM LOUISE LEBO** was born on 26 September 1957, Allentown, Lehigh County, PA. She married **STANLEY WHEELER.**

5.3.1.2.7.4.3.1 JOHN WHEELER

5.3.1.2.7.5 **JAMES DONALD LEBO** was born on 2 January 1933, Elizabethville, Dauphin County, PA. He married **BETTY J. HARE**, daughter of **ROBERT HARE** and **AMELIA SMITH,** on 3 April 1955, London, UK. He and **BETTY J. HARE** were divorced on 19 September 1972 Harris County, TX. He married **PATRICIA A. STUPPY**, daughter of **WALTER STUPPY** and **AGNES KRAMER.** He died on 22 January 2014, Adamsville, AL, at age 81.

5.3.1.2.7.5.1 **FAUNE LEBO** was born on 31 January 1960, Harrisburg, Dauphin County, PA. She married **LAVAUN COLE.**

5.3.1.2.7.5.1.1 EMILIA REE COLE

5.3.1.2.7.5.2 **APRIL LOUISE LEBO** was born on 18 May 1962, Norfolk, VA.

5.3.1.2.7.5.3 **JAMES ROBERT LEBO** was born on 20 December 1965, London, England, UK.

5.3.1.2.7.6 **BURMA MAE LEBO** was born on 27 February 1936, Elizabethville, Dauphin County, PA. She died on 3 May 1940, Harrisburg, Dauphin County, PA, at age 4. She was buried at St. John's (Hill) Lutheran Church, near Berrysburg, Dauphin County, PA.

5.3.1.2.8 **LILLIE FAY KLINGER** was born on 20 November 1906, Washington Township, Dauphin County, PA. She married **HOMER NATHANIEL FEIDT**, son of **WILLIAM A. FEIDT** and **KATIE M. BOYER,** on 6 September 1924, Elizabethville, Dauphin County, PA. She died on 25 June 1990, Rife, Dauphin County, PA, at age 83.

5.3.1.2.8.1 **MARY MINERVA FEIDT** was born on 22 November 1924, Mifflin Township, Dauphin County, PA. She died on 1 October 1929, Elizabethville, Dauphin County, PA, at age 4.

5.3.1.2.8.2 **WILLIAM THEODORE FEIDT** was born on 22 February 1929, RD, Millersburg, Dauphin County, PA. He married **JEAN MAE NEITER**, daughter of **FRED NEITER** and **IDA SCHMELTZ.** He died on 18 December 1984, Millersburg RD, Dauphin County, PA, at age 55.

5.3.1.2.8.2.1 **RICKY WILLIAM FEIDT** was born on 6 August 1956. He married **KIMBRA YVONNE MARTZ.**

5.3.1.2.8.2.1.1 SHAUN WILLIAM FEIDT

5.3.1.2.8.2.1.2 TROY JAMES FEIDT

5.3.1.2.8.2.2 **RANDY LEE FEIDT** was born on 19 August 1958.

5.3.1.2.8.2.3 **RUSTY LYNN FEIDT** was born on 9 December 1959. He married **MICHELLE RENE KROMMES.**

5.3.1.2.8.2.4 **RAMEY LAMAR FEIDT** was born on 17 December 1968.

5.3.1.2.8.3 **DALE HOMER FEIDT** was born on 24 August 1930, RD, Millersburg, Dauphin County, PA. He married **ARLENE M. LENKER**, daughter of **ROY LENKER** and **DOROTHY DINGER,** on 29 January 1956, Elizabethville, Dauphin County, PA.

5.3.1.2.8.3.1 **RODNEY ALLEN FEIDT** was born on 10 August 1959, Harrisburg, Dauphin County, PA. He married **ANNETTE KATHERINE DEPPEN.**

5.3.1.2.8.3.2 **BRENDA SUE FEIDT** was born on 4 December 1961, Harrisburg, Dauphin County, PA. She married **RONALD LEE KERSTETTER.**

5.3.1.2.8.3.3 **BRIAN ALLEN FEIDT** was born on 8 July 1969, Harrisburg, Dauphin County, PA. He died on 19 May 1982, at age 12.

5.3.1.2.8.4 **LEE NATHANIEL FEIDT** was born on 2 March 1932, RD, Millersburg, Dauphin County, PA. He married **PATTY LOU RILAND**, daughter of **FRANK RILAND** and **SARAH ENDERS,** on 17 April 1954, Millersburg, Dauphin County, PA.

5.3.1.2.8.4.1 **JEFFREY LEE FEIDT** was born on 23 April 1963, Harrisburg, Dauphin County, PA.

5.3.1.2.8.5 GLENN EDGAR FEIDT was born on 4 December 1933, RD, Millersburg, Dauphin County, PA. He married JOAN D. SULTZBACH, daughter of EARL SULTZBACH and SALLIE YERGES, on 1 November 1952, Millersburg, Dauphin County, PA.

5.3.1.2.8.5.1 RUTHANNA COLEEN FEIDT was born on 27 November 1954, Harrisburg, Dauphin County, PA. She married JOEL MARK MALEHORN on 6 April 1974, Millersburg, Dauphin County, PA.

5.3.1.2.8.5.1.1 JANNA MICHELLE MALEHORN

5.3.1.2.8.5.1.2 JADE OLIVIA MALEHORN

5.3.1.2.8.6 RAHN HENRY FEIDT was born on 26 July 1940, RD, Millersburg, Dauphin County, PA. He married CAROL ANN BROSIUS on 29 July 1961.

5.3.1.2.8.6.1 BONNIE ELAINE FEIDT is also referred to as BONNIE L. in some sources. She was born on 9 January 1961, Harrisburg, Dauphin County, PA. She married KEVIN JEFFREY TROUTMAN.

5.3.1.2.8.6.1.1 KRISTOPHER DOUGLAS TROUTMAN

5.3.1.2.8.6.2 RAHN DOUGLAS FEIDT was born on 22 January 1966, Harrisburg, Dauphin County, PA. He married BARBARA BOWMAN YOUNG.

5.3.1.2.8.7 JOYCE MARIE FEIDT was born on 25 April 1949, Harrisburg, Dauphin County, PA. She married JOHN BRABITS, son of EDWARD BRABITS and DOROTHY FESSE, on 11 November 1972, RD, Millersburg, Dauphin County, PA.

5.3.1.2.9 BEATRICE D. KLINGER was born on 1 October 1911, RD, Elizabethville, Dauphin County, PA. She died on 1 April 1914, Dauphin, Dauphin County, PA, at age 2.

5.3.1.2.10 MARGARET ETHEL KLINGER was born on 2 April 1916, RD, Elizabethville, Dauphin County, PA. She married LEE SAMUEL SNYDER, son of WILLIAM SNYDER and (--?--) HINKLE. Prior to her death, Margaret was living in or near Millersburg, Dauphin County, PA. She died on 1 August 2003, at age 87. She was buried at St. John's (Hill) Lutheran Church, Berrysburg, Dauphin County, PA.

5.3.1.2.10.1 DALE EUGENE SNYDER was born on 21 September 1945, RD, Millersburg, Dauphin County, PA. He married JAN ARLA BOWMAN on 7 March 1965, Halifax, Dauphin County, PA.

5.3.1.2.10.1.1 CHADWICK BOWMAN SNYDER

5.3.1.2.10.1.2 JENNIFER REBECCA SNYDER was born on 11 June 1971. She married VINCENT WARDFORD.

5.3.1.2.10.1.2.1 ALEXIS VICTORIA SNYDER

5.3.1.3 ELI THEODORE WILLIARD is also referred to as ELIAS in some sources. He was born on 10 May 1879. He was baptized on 15 June 1879, Zion (Klinger's) Church, Erdman, Lykens Township, Dauphin County, PA. He died in 1882.

5.3.1.4 DORSEY ANGELINE WILLIARD is also referred to as DOROTHY EVANGELINE WILLIARD in some sources. She was born on 6 February 1881, Gratz, Dauphin County, PA. She was baptized on 26 March 1881, Zion (Klinger's) Church, Erdman, Lykens Township, Dauphin County, PA. She married EDWIN GUERNEY KLINGER, son of WILLIAM S. KLINGER and SUSANNAH SCHADEL.

5.3.1.4.1 EDWIN GURNEY KLINGER JR. was born in 1900, Branchdale, Schuylkill County, PA. Some sources record that he was born circa 1901. He married HELEN C. WILLIAMS circa 1921, PA. He died in 1966, Tremont, Schuylkill County, PA. He was buried in 1966, at Old Reformed Church Cemetery, Tremont, Schuylkill County, PA.

5.3.1.4.1.1 EDWIN KLINGER was born circa 1923, Tremont, Schuylkill County, PA.

5.3.1.4.1.2 CASANDRA KLINGER married an unknown person. She was born circa 1925, Tremont, Schuylkill County, PA.

5.3.1.4.2 IRVIN WILLIAM KLINGER was born in 1902, Tower City, Schuylkill County, PA. Some sources record that he was born in 1903. He married MARTHA GAUNTLETT circa 1921, PA. He died on 14 June 1975, Schuylkill County, PA. He was buried at St. John's Lutheran Church Cemetery, Tremont, Schuylkill County, PA.

5.3.1.4.2.1 FERNE A. KLINGER was born on 2 April 1926, Branchdale, Schuylkill County, PA. She married RAYMOND EDWARD DONMOYER circa 1946, PA. She died on 13 March

2003, Milton S. Hershey Medical Center, Hershey, Dauphin County, PA, at age 76. She was buried at St. John's Lutheran Church Cemetery, Tremont, Schuylkill County, PA.

5.3.1.4.2.1.1 BAMBI DONMOYER married (--?--) **SHAAK**.

5.3.1.4.2.1.2 FERNE DONMOYER was born circa 1947, Schuylkill County, PA. She died circa 1947, Schuylkill County, PA.

5.3.1.4.2.1.3 TERRY DONMOYER was born circa 1950, Schuylkill County, PA.

5.3.1.4.2.1.4 WENDY DONMOYER was born on 30 December 1959, Pottsville, Schuylkill County, PA. She married **KENNETH GRAEFF** circa 1977. She died on 1 September 2010, at her home on 125 Centre St., Donaldson, Schuylkill County, PA, at age 50.

5.3.1.4.2.1.4.1 KENNETH GRAEFF

5.3.1.4.2.1.4.2 AMY GRAEFF was born circa 1967, Schuylkill County, PA. She married **DAN SHADLE**.

5.3.1.4.2.1.4.2.1 CHLOE SHADLE was born circa 1987, Schuylkill County, PA.

5.3.1.4.2.1.4.2.2 DANIEL SHADLE was born circa 1990, Schuylkill County, PA.

5.3.1.4.2.1.4.2.3 EMMA SHADLE was born circa 1992, Schuylkill County, PA.

5.3.1.4.2.1.4.2.4 GABRIELLE SHADLE was born on 12 December 2005, Schuylkill County, PA.

5.3.1.4.2.2 WILLIAM IRVIN KLINGER is also referred to as **BILLY KLINGER** in some sources. He was born in 1927, Tremont, Schuylkill County, PA. He died in 1993, Tremont, Schuylkill County, PA. He was buried in 1993, at Odd Fellow Lodge Cemetery, Shamokin, Northumberland County, PA.

5.3.1.4.3 ELLEN VERTIE KLINGER was born on 23 February 1904, Branchdale, Schuylkill County, PA. She was baptized on 17 January 1905, St. Andrew's United Methodist Church, Valley View, Schuylkill County, PA. She married **WALTER DANIEL SCHINKEL** circa 1922, PA. She married **CHARLES HENRY DAVIDSON** in 1930, PA. She died on 24 March 1950, Shamokin, Northumberland Co., PA, at age 46. She was buried at Odd Fellow Lodge Cemetery, Shamokin, Northumberland Co., PA.

5.3.1.4.3.1 JUNE SCHINKEL was born on 24 January 1925, Branchdale, Schuylkill County, PA. She married **MARTIN VAN BUREN STEWART** on 17 July 1943, Bonham, Fannin Co., TX.

5.3.1.4.3.1.1 MARTIN VAN BUREN STEWART JR. married **BETTY MCNEELEY**. He was born on 7 July 1944, Shamokin Hospital, Shamokin, Northumberland Co., PA.

5.3.1.4.3.1.2 DENNIS MARSHALL STEWART was born on 9 October 1948, Geisinger Hospital, Danville, Montour Co., PA. He married **JULIE DICKEN** circa 1976. He married **GERI HOPPER SCOTT** in January 2000.

5.3.1.4.3.1.2.1 MARSHALL SHANE STEWART was born on 30 October 1978.

5.3.1.4.3.1.2.2 ASPEN DAWN STEWART was born on 23 May 1982.

5.3.1.4.3.1.3 MITCHELL WAYNE STEWART was born on 24 August 1955, Lackland A.F.B. Hospital, San Antonio, Bexar, TX.

5.3.1.4.3.1.4 CYNTHIA ELLEN STEWART was born on 11 March 1960, Turner AFB Hospital, Albany, Dougherty Co., GA. She married **WILLIAM EUGENE GRAHAM (GW)**.

5.3.1.4.3.1.4.1 SAMANTHA NICOLLE GRAHAM was born on 18 November 1989.

5.3.1.4.3.1.4.2 KTHAN ROBERT GRAHAM was born on 1 May 1995.

5.3.1.4.4 CLINTON J. KLINGER was born in 1905, Branchdale, Schuylkill County, PA. He married **MARGARET SYKES** circa 1927. He died in 1963, Northumberland Co., PA. He was buried at Northumberland Memorial Cemetery, Stonington, Northumberland County, PA.

5.3.1.4.4.1 DOROTHY KLINGER was born circa 1929, Shamokin, Northumberland County, PA. She married **ANDREW J. DREBITKO SR.** PA.

5.3.1.4.4.1.1 SHARON DREBITKO was born circa 1947, Schuylkill County, PA.

5.3.1.4.4.1.2 ANDREW J. DREBITKO JR. was born circa 1950, Schuylkill County, PA.

5.3.1.4.4.1.2.1 ANDREW J. DREBITKO III was born circa 1985, Schuylkill County, PA. He died on 1 May 2006, Union Co., PA.

5.3.1.4.5 RALPH MOSES KLINGER was born on 6 September 1908, Heckscherville, Schuylkill County, PA. He married **SARAH ROBERTA MCCLAIN** circa 1927, PA. He married **SARAH ROBERTA MCCLAIN**. He died in 1996, Shamokin, Northumberland Co., PA. He was buried in 1996, at Odd Fellow Lodge Cemetery, Shamokin, Northumberland Co., PA.

5.3.1.4.5.1 ROBERTA ELLEN KLINGER was born on 1 April 1931, Shamokin, Northumberland Co., PA. She married **RICHARD LLOYD SIREN** circa 1949, PA. She died on 22 July 2006, Mountain View Nursing and Rehabilitation Center in Coal Twp., Northumberland Co., PA, at age 75.

5.3.1.4.5.1.1 PAMELA SIREN was born circa 1951, PA. She married **WILLIAM KEMP** circa 1974.

5.3.1.4.5.1.1.1 SARAH KEMP was born circa 1975.

5.3.1.4.5.1.1.2 AL KEMP was born circa 1977.

5.3.1.4.5.1.2 DR. SUSAN MICHELE SIREN was born on 16 September 1955, PA.

5.3.1.4.5.2 RALPH KLINGER was born on 9 November 1933, Shamokin, Northumberland Co., PA. He died on 11 November 2015, Shamokin, Northumberland County, PA, at age 82. He was buried at Odd Fellows Cemetery, Shamokin, Northumberland County, PA.

5.3.1.4.6 ARTHUR G. KLINGER was born on 6 September 1909. He married **MARY F. BECK**. He died on 29 May 1954, Philadelphia, Philadelphia County, PA, at age 44. He was buried on 3 June 1954, at Shamokin Cemetery, Shamokin, Northumberland County, PA.

5.3.1.4.6.1 ARTHUR N. KLINGER was born on 16 October 1932. He died on 9 February 2006, at age 73.

5.3.1.4.6.2 NORMA J. KLINGER was born circa 1934.

5.3.1.4.6.3 WESLEY V. KLINGER was born circa 1936.

5.3.1.5 EMMA JANE WILLIARD was born on 3 May 1884, Gratz, Dauphin County, PA. She was baptized on 6 August 1884, Zion (Klinger's) Church, Erdman, Lykens Township, Dauphin County, PA. She married **ISRAEL DANIELS**, son of **JOEL DANIELS** and **ANNA MARIA CAROLINA KLINGER,** circa 1904, Lykens Township, Dauphin County, PA. She married **CLAUDE SAMUEL BUFFINGTON**, son of **JOHN JACOB BUFFINGTON** and **CLARA L. KISSINGER,** after 1920. Some sources suggest that she and **CLAUDE SAMUEL BUFFINGTON** were married circa 1916 Lykens Township, Dauphin County, PA, but this appears to be inconsistent with the Census records. Prior to her death, Emma was living in or near Gratz, Dauphin County, PA. She died in December 1973, at age 89. She was buried at Gratz, Dauphin County, PA.

5.3.1.5.1 ALVIN R. DANIEL was born in 1904. He married **MABEL BRETZIUS**. He died in 1976.

5.3.1.5.1.1 BUDDY DANIEL was born in 1926. He died in 1936, when hit by a car while he was sledding, Gratz, Dauphin County, PA.

5.3.1.6 MOSES ALVIN WILLIARD was born in 1889, Lykens Township, Dauphin County, PA. He married **CATHERINE IRENE SITLINGER**, daughter of **GEORGE EDWARD SITLINGER** and **SARAH LOUISE GOOD,** on 18 June 1910, Friedens Reformed Church, Hegins, Schuylkill County, PA. He died on 24 November 1953, Lykens Township, Dauphin Co., PA. He was buried on 29 November 1953, at Zion (Klinger's) Lutheran Church Cemetery, Erdman, Dauphin Co., PA.

5.3.1.6.1 ALVIN RAY WILLIARD was born circa 1912. He was born on 1 February 1912, Lykens Township, Dauphin Co., PA. He was baptized on 5 April 1912, Simeon Lutheran Church, Gratz, Dauphin Co., PA. He married **MAE A. DANIEL** circa 1928, PA. He married **SARAH ARLENE WILLIARD**, daughter of **HARVEY MCKINLEY WILLIARD** and **CARRIE MINERVA SNYDER**. He married **SARAH ARLENE WILLIARD**, daughter of **HARVEY MCKINLEY WILLIARD** and **CARRIE MINERVA SNYDER,** on 12 April 1941, Zion (Klinger's) Lutheran Church, Erdman, Dauphin Co., PA. He died on 25 February 1976, Dauphin Co., PA, at age 64. He was buried on 28 February 1976, at Zion (Klinger's) Lutheran Church Cemetery, Erdman, Dauphin Co., PA.

5.3.1.6.1.1 JUNE ANNABELLE WILLIARD was born on 5 November 1930, PA. She was baptized on 29 March 1939, Friedens Reformed Church, Hegins, Schuylkill County, PA.

5.3.1.6.1.2 DEBRA SUE WILLIARD was born on 9 June 1958, Schuylkill County, PA. She married **ROB SMYRE** circa 1982. She married **MARLIN E. WIEST JR.**, son of **MARLIN E. WIEST** and **MARCIA MILDRED MORRIS,** on 3 September 1987, Zion (Klinger's) Lutheran Church, Erdman, Dauphin Co., PA. She married **JEFFREY BENNETT** on 29 May 1995, Las

Vegas, Clark Co., NV. She married an unknown person on 29 May 1995, Las Vegas, Clark Co., NV.

5.3.1.6.1.2.1 MATTHEW GEORGE SMYRE was born circa 1984.

5.3.1.6.1.2.2 KYLE WIEST (see above)

5.3.1.6.1.3 PATRICIA DELORES WILLIARD is also referred to as **PATSY WILLIARD** in some sources. She was born on 5 February 1941, Schuylkill County, PA. She married **ALLEN ESTON SHIRO** on 31 October 1959, Zion (Klinger's) Lutheran Church, Erdman, Dauphin Co., PA.

5.3.1.6.1.3.1 RICKY ALLEN SHIRO was born on 29 March 1960, Pottsville, Schuylkill County, PA. He was baptized on 22 May 1960, Evangelical Congregational Church, Gratz, Dauphin Co., PA. He married **BARBARA JEAN STEEL** on 11 April 1981, Evangelical Congregational Church, Gratz, Dauphin Co., PA.

5.3.1.6.1.3.1.1 STEVEN MICHAEL SHIRO was born on 26 September 1983, Pottsville, Schuylkill County, PA. He was baptized on 27 November 1983, Evangelical Congregational Church, Berrysburg, Dauphin Co., PA.

5.3.1.6.1.3.1.2 VALERIE MARIE SHIRO was born on 1 September 1986, Harrisburg, Dauphin Co., PA. He was baptized on 16 November 1986, Evangelical Congregational Church, Berrysburg, Dauphin Co., PA.

5.3.1.6.1.3.1.3 BRYAN ALLEN SHIRO was born on 23 October 1989, Harrisburg, Dauphin Co., PA. He was baptized on 24 December 1989, Evangelical Congregational Church, Berrysburg, Dauphin Co., PA.

5.3.1.6.1.3.2 TINA ANN SHIRO was born on 31 March 1962, Pottsville, Schuylkill County, PA. She was baptized on 13 May 1962, Evangelical Congregational Church, Gratz, Dauphin Co., PA. She married **JAMES NOVINGER** on 26 March 1983, Evangelical Congregational Church, Gratz, Dauphin Co., PA.

5.3.1.6.1.3.2.1 TRICIA NOVINGER was born on 12 May 1984, PA.

5.3.1.6.1.3.2.2 NATALIE NICOLE NOVINGER was born on 16 December 1987, PA. She died on 17 December 1987, PA.

5.3.1.6.1.3.2.3 ROSE MARIE NOVINGER was born on 22 August 1989, PA.

5.3.1.6.1.3.2.4 LAURA NOVINGER was born on 28 March 1993, PA.

5.3.1.6.1.3.3 KELLY MARIE SHIRO was born on 12 August 1964, Pottsville, Schuylkill County, PA. She was baptized on 25 October 1964, Evangelical Congregational Church, Gratz, Dauphin Co., PA. She married **DALE MILLARD WAGNER** on 24 August 1985, St. Andrew's United Methodist Church, Valley View, Schuylkill County, PA.

5.3.1.6.1.3.3.1 DANELLE CHARLENE WAGNER was born on 20 May 1986, Harrisburg, Dauphin Co., PA. She was baptized on 3 August 1986, Evangelical Congregational Church, Berrysburg, Dauphin Co., PA.

5.3.1.6.1.3.3.2 STEPHANIE ANN WAGNER was born on 10 June 1988, Harrisburg, Dauphin Co., PA. She was baptized on 18 September 1988, Evangelical Congregational Church, Berrysburg, Dauphin Co., PA.

5.3.1.6.1.3.4 SHELLY KAY SHIRO was born on 18 April 1966, Good Samaritan Hospital, Pottsville, Schuylkill County, PA. She was baptized on 19 June 1966, Evangelical Congregational Church, Gratz, Dauphin Co., PA. She married **JEFFREY MAYNARD GEIST** on 18 October 1986, Friedens United Church of Christ, Hegins, Schuylkill County, PA.

5.3.1.6.1.3.4.1 ANDREW JEFF GEIST was born on 26 December 1988, PA.

5.3.1.6.1.3.4.2 ANDREA KAY GEIST was born on 4 April 1992, PA.

5.3.1.6.1.3.5 AUDREY CAROL SHIRO was born on 27 December 1967, Pottsville, Schuylkill County, PA. She was baptized on 25 February 1968, Evangelical Congregational Church, Gratz, Dauphin Co., PA. She married **KERRY JOSEPH KEMBEL** on 18 June 1988, Evangelical Congregational Church, Berrysburg, Dauphin Co., PA. She married **(--?--) (--?--)** on 21 June 1997.

5.3.1.6.1.3.5.1 JOSHUA JOSEPH KEMBEL was born on 4 August 1986, Pottsville, Schuylkill County, PA. He was baptized on 28 September 1986, Evangelical Congregational Church, Berrysburg, Dauphin Co., PA.

5.3.1.6.1.3.5.2 JORDAN ALLEN KEMBEL was born on 13 December 1989, Pottsville, Schuylkill County, PA. He was baptized on 25 March 1990, Evangelical Congregational Church, Berrysburg, Dauphin Co., PA.

5.3.1.6.1.3.5.3 (--?--) (--?--) was born on 9 December 1997.

5.3.1.6.1.3.5.4 CARISSA WALELA MARROCCO was born on 29 April 2001.

5.3.1.6.1.3.6 DOLORES ELAINE SHIRO was born on 13 February 1969, Pottsville, Schuylkill County, PA. She was baptized on 6 April 1969, Evangelical Congregational Church, Gratz, Dauphin Co., PA. She married **BRIAN E. LONG** on 9 March 1991, Evangelical Congregational Church, Berrysburg, Dauphin Co., PA.

5.3.1.6.1.3.6.1 KYLE ERNEST LONG was born on 7 July 1991, Pottsville, Schuylkill County, PA. He was baptized on 8 September 1991, Evangelical Congregational Church, Berrysburg, Dauphin Co., PA.

5.3.1.6.1.3.6.2 KASEY MARIE LONG was born on 9 April 1994, Pottsville, Schuylkill County, PA.

5.3.1.6.1.3.7 HEIDI ARLENE SHIRO was born on 5 June 1971, Pottsville, Schuylkill County, PA. She was baptized on 8 August 1971, Evangelical Congregational Church, Gratz, Dauphin Co., PA. She married **BRIAN KOPPENHAVER** on 8 May 1993, PA.

5.3.1.6.1.3.7.1 ASHLEY NICOLE KOPPENHAVER was born on 2 September 1993, Dauphin Co., PA.

5.3.1.6.1.3.7.2 AMBER CHRISTINE KOPPENHAVER was born on 17 March 1996, Harrisburg Hospital, Harrisburg, Dauphin Co., PA.

5.3.1.6.1.3.7.3 MASON ALEXANDER KOPPENHAVER was born on 20 July 2000, Harrisburg Hospital, Harrisburg, Dauphin Co., PA.

5.3.1.6.1.3.8 VICKI SUE SHIRO was born on 1 January 1974, Pottsville, Schuylkill County, PA. She was baptized in 1974, Evangelical Congregational Church, Gratz, Dauphin Co., PA. She married **KEITH ANDREW REYNOLDS** on 18 August 2001, Christ Church, Carlisle, Cumberland Co., PA.

5.3.1.6.1.4 RONALD ALVIN WILLIARD was born on 29 September 1944, Schuylkill County, PA. He married **BETTY LOU PHILLIPS** on 5 September 1964, Zion (Klinger's) Lutheran Church, Erdman, Dauphin Co., PA. He married **RUTH ELLA ROTHERMEL**, daughter of **ELWOOD LESTER ROTHERMEL** and **BERNICE N. SNYDER**, on 31 July 1976, PA.

5.3.1.6.1.4.1 WENDY LOU WILLIARD was born on 4 February 1965, Pottsville, Schuylkill County, PA. She was baptized on 25 April 1965, Zion (Klinger's) Lutheran Church, Erdman, Dauphin Co., PA. She married **JEFFREY ALLEN MARTZ** on 20 March 1982, Zion (Klinger's) Lutheran Church, Erdman, Dauphin Co., PA.

5.3.1.6.1.4.1.1 ALANA MARIE MARTZ was born on 30 August 1982, Polyclinic Medical Center, Harrisburg, Dauphin Co., PA. She was baptized on 12 December 1982, St. Luke's United Church of Christ, Malta, Northumberland Co., PA.

5.3.1.6.1.4.1.2 JANELLE ELIZABETH MARTZ was born on 27 October 1984, Polyclinic Medical Center, Harrisburg, Dauphin Co., PA. She was baptized on 12 May 1985, St. Luke's United Church of Christ, Malta, Northumberland Co., PA.

5.3.1.6.1.4.1.3 JASPAR ALLEN MARTZ was born on 8 January 1987, Polyclinic Medical Center, Harrisburg, Dauphin Co., PA.

5.3.1.6.1.4.1.4 ALLISON HEATHER MARTZ was born on 13 January 1990, Polyclinic Medical Center, Harrisburg, Dauphin Co., PA.

5.3.1.6.1.4.1.5 ALYSSA LUELLAN MARTZ was born on 25 July 1994, Polyclinic Medical Center, Harrisburg, Dauphin Co., PA.

5.3.1.6.1.4.2 SHERRI ANN WILLIARD was born on 1 June 1967, Good Samaritan Hospital, Pottsville, Schuylkill County, PA. She was baptized on 22 October 1967, Zion (Klinger's) Lutheran Church, Erdman, Dauphin Co., PA. She married **RODNEY LEE TAYLOR** on 28 June 1986, Himmel Church, Rebuck, Northumberland Co., PA. She married **GARY RAY MILLER** on 18 May 2002, PA. She married an unknown person on 18 May 2002, PA.

 5.3.1.6.1.4.2.1 CHASE LANDON MILLER was born circa 2004, Kazakhstan.

5.3.1.6.1.5 TRUDY DARLENE WILLIARD was born on 8 June 1947, Schuylkill County, PA. She was baptized on 29 July 1947, Zion (Klinger's) Lutheran Church, Erdman, Dauphin Co., PA. She married **LYNN EDWARD CONRAD** on 18 June 1966, Zion (Klinger's) Lutheran Church, Erdman, Dauphin Co., PA.

 5.3.1.6.1.5.1 EDWARD LYNN CONRAD was born on 21 September 1967, Nürnburg, Germany. He married **DEBRA ANN ADAMS** on 8 November 1986, St. Andrew's United Methodist Church, Valley View, Schuylkill County, PA.

  5.3.1.6.1.5.1.1 AMANDA LYNN CONRAD was born on 2 March 1987, Hazelton, Luzerne Co., PA.

  5.3.1.6.1.5.1.2 NATOSHA CONRAD was born on 18 February 1988, Pottsville, Schuylkill County, PA.

 5.3.1.6.1.5.2 MICHAEL LYNN CONRAD was born on 16 May 1972. He married **ROXANNE CATHERINE ORNER** on 24 June 2000, Friedens United Church of Christ, Hegins, Schuylkill County, PA.

5.3.1.6.1.6 TAMMY JANE WILLIARD was born on 29 May 1960, Schuylkill County, PA. She married **RICHARD LEE WENRICH**, son of **WHELAN ELLIS WENRICH** and **ANNA MAE KISSINGER,** on 24 June 1978, Zion (Klinger's) Lutheran Church, Erdman, Dauphin Co., PA.

 5.3.1.6.1.6.1 JENNIFER ROSE WENRICH (see above)

 5.3.1.6.1.6.2 JESSICA ANN WENRICH (see above)

5.3.1.6.2 MARTHA IRENE WILLIARD was born on 29 July 1914, Lykens Township, Dauphin Co., PA. She was baptized on 17 October 1914, Simeon Lutheran Church, Gratz, Dauphin Co., PA. She married **RAY CLAYTON TROUTMAN**, son of **VICTOR WILLIAM TROUTMAN** and **SALLIE BAUM WIEST**. She and **RAY CLAYTON TROUTMAN** were divorced. She married **LEON SAMUEL STRAUB**, son of **SAMUEL HOMER STRAUB** and **KATE ALVERTA DEIBERT,** circa 1961, PA. She died on 17 December 2004, Dauphin Co., PA, at age 90. She was buried on 21 December 2004, at Zion (Klinger's) Lutheran Church Cemetery, Erdman, Dauphin Co., PA.

 5.3.1.6.2.1 KEITH WAYNE STRAUB was born on 28 February 1963, Dauphin Co., PA. He was baptized on 27 February 1972, Zion (Klinger's) Lutheran Church, Erdman, Dauphin Co., PA. He married **TRACY ANN MILLER** on 16 July 1983, Zion (Klinger's) Lutheran Church, Erdman, Dauphin Co., PA.

  5.3.1.6.2.1.1 AMY LYNN STRAUB was born on 28 July 1984, PA. She was baptized on 13 October 1984, Zion (Klinger's) Lutheran Church, Erdman, Dauphin Co., PA.

  5.3.1.6.2.1.2 JESSICA K. STRAUB was born on 9 March 1990, PA.

5.3.1.7 ANNIE L. WILLIARD was born on 1 May 1891, Gratz, Dauphin County, PA. She married **SAMUEL HARRY STRAUB**, son of **TOBIAS ALBERT STRAUB** and **MARY E. LOW,** on 1 July 1916, Zion (Klinger's) Church, Erdman, Lykens Township, Dauphin County, PA. She died on 8 March 1959, at age 67.

 5.3.1.7.1 HARVEY T. STRAUB was born circa 1911.

5.3.2 CATHARINE KLINGER was born on 6 November 1852, Lykens Township, Dauphin County, PA. She died on 17 February 1854, PA at age 1.

5.3.3 ELIZABETH KLINGER was born on 30 October 1853. Some sources record that she was born in 1850. On page 396, Mary Klinger, Klingers from the Odenwald, Hesse, Germany, suggests that Elizabeth married Daniel S. Klinger, son of William and Rebecca Schofftsall Klinger, and cross-references her material on them (pp. 228-29), but on those pages there is no mention of Elizabeth Klinger. In fact, those pages list Daniel S. Klinger's wife as "Lizzie Erdman." She died on 13 March 1903, at age 49. She was buried at Gratz, Dauphin County, PA.

5.3.4 GEORGE M. KLINGER was born on 10 August 1854, Lykens Township, Dauphin County, PA. He was baptized on 17 September 1854, Zion (Klinger's) Church, Erdman, Lykens Township, Dauphin County, PA. Some sources record that he was born on 11 August 1853. He married **JULIANN KOPPENHAVER** circa 1887, Lykens Township, Dauphin County, PA. He died on 11 July 1911, PA at age 56. He was buried at Zion (Klinger's) Church, Erdman, Lykens Township, Dauphin County, PA.

5.3.4.1 MABEL PEARL KLINGER is also referred to as **PEARLIE MABEL** in some sources. She was born in October 1883. Some sources record that she was born in 1884. She married **WILLIAM OSCAR KLINGER**, son of **MARCUS KLINGER** and **ELIZABETH DELP,** circa 1899. She died on 26 February 1951. She was buried at St. Michael's Lutheran and Reformed Church Cemetery, Klingerstown, Schuylkill County, PA.

5.3.4.1.1 CARLOS EDWIN KLINGER is also referred to as **EDWIN C.** in some sources. He was born on 15 March 1900, near Klingerstown, Schuylkill County, PA. He was baptized on 22 April 1900, St. Michael's Church, Klingerstown, Schuylkill County, PA. Prior to his death, Carlos was living in or near Sunbury, Northumberland County, PA. He died on 15 January 1968, at age 67. Some sources record that he died on 22 January 1968 Sunbury Hospital, Sunbury, Northumberland County, PA. Other sources record that he died on 23 January 1968. He was buried on 26 January 1968, at St. Michael's Church, Klingerstown, Schuylkill County, PA.

5.3.4.1.2 KATIE ALMEDA KLINGER is also referred to as **EVA AND CATHERINE** in some sources. She was born on 25 March 1901, Lykens Township, Dauphin County, PA. She married **LESTER LEROY KLINGER**, son of **DANIEL M. KLINGER** and **EMALINE ARBOGAST,** on 22 June 1918, St. Michael's Church, Klingerstown, Schuylkill County, PA. Katie and her husband Lester were first cousins, once removed. She married **(--?--) BROWN.** She married **SCOTT SUNDAY.** Prior to her death, Katie was living in or near Gratz, Northumberland County, PA. She died in September 1986, Millersburg, Dauphin County, PA, at age 85. She was buried at St. Peter's United Methodist Church Cemetery, Fearnot, Schuylkill County, PA, where her tombstone lists her name as "Katie Sunday Klinger."

5.3.4.1.2.1 GALEN OSCAR KLINGER is also referred to as **GALEN C.** in some sources. He was born on 15 June 1919. He was baptized on 18 July 1919, St. Michael's Church, Klingerstown, Schuylkill County, PA. He married **IRENE MAE HARNER** on 5 September 1942. Galen was a milk truck driver in Hegins, PA. He was a sergeant in the US Army during World War II. He died on 22 July 1988, at age 69. He was buried on 26 July 2016, at Church of God Cemetery, Valley View, Schuylkill County, PA.

5.3.4.1.2.1.1 GARY OSCAR KLINGER is also referred to as **GARY GALEN KLINGER** in some sources. He was born on 17 January 1947.

5.3.4.1.2.2 IDA LORETTA KLINGER is also referred to as **IDA LAURETTA** in some sources. She was born on 12 January 1921, Lykens Township, Dauphin County, PA. She was baptized on 6 March 1921, Zion (Klinger's) Church, Erdman, Lykens Township, Dauphin County, PA. She married **GUY RUFUS HARNER**, son of **RUFUS HARNER** and **BERTHA BOATMAN,** on 21 September 1935. She married **MELVIN NEWTON KOPPENHAVER.** She died on 7 February 2013, The Kepler Home, Elizabethville, Dauphin County, PA, at age 92. She was buried on 11 February 2013, at Church of God Cemetery, Valley View, Schuylkill County, PA.

5.3.4.1.2.2.1 LESTER RUFUS HARNER was born on 2 June 1936, Valley View, Schuylkill County, PA. He married **RUTHANNA MAY NICE**, daughter of **ARTHUR NICE** and **MARY BOYER.** He died on 24 November 2002, Camp Hill, Cumberland County, PA, at age 66. He was buried at Maple Grove Cemetery, Elizabethville, Dauphin County, PA.

5.3.4.1.2.2.1.1 BRENDA LOU HARNER

5.3.4.1.2.2.1.2 BRYANT KIETH HARNER

5.3.4.1.2.2.2 CAROLYN DOLLY HARNER was born on 4 February 1938. She died on 17 October 1946, at age 8.

5.3.4.1.2.2.3 MARILYN IRENE HARNER was born on 12 January 1944. She married **MARK SHAFFER.**

5.3.4.1.2.2.3.1 THOMAS LEE SHAFFER

5.3.4.1.2.2.3.2 MINDY SHAFFER

5.3.4.1.2.2.3.3 TIMOTHY SHAFFER died before 2013.

5.3.4.1.2.2.4 RICHARD DEAN HARNER married **DORA (--?--).** He was born on 16 December 1945.

5.3.4.1.2.2.4.1 RICHARD HARNER

5.3.4.1.2.2.4.2 JAMES HARNER

5.3.4.1.2.3 MELBA K. KLINGER is also referred to as **MELBA CATHERINE KLINGER** in some sources. She was born on 15 August 1923, Sacramento, Schuylkill County, PA. She was baptized on 16 November 1923, St. Michael's Church, Klingerstown, Schuylkill County, PA. She married **RAYMOND CURTIS CROUTHARMEL**, son of **SAMUEL K. CROUTHARMEL** and **MARY E. ZIPF**. She died on 6 October 2014, at her home Halifax, Dauphin County, PA, at age 91. She was buried on 11 October 2014, at Stone Valley Cemetery, Hickory Corners, Northumberland County, PA.

    5.3.4.1.2.3.1 DENNIS RAY CROUTHARMEL was born on 20 March 1941.

    5.3.4.1.2.3.2 LARRY CURTIS CROUTHARMEL was born on 2 March 1942.

    5.3.4.1.2.3.3 TERRY GENE CROUTHARMEL was born on 12 November 1943.

    5.3.4.1.2.3.4 KAREN DIANE CROUTHARMEL was born on 4 January 1950. She married (--?--) **MACKENBEE**.

    5.3.4.1.2.3.5 CARL ALLEN CROUTHARMEL was born on 17 October 1953.

    5.3.4.1.2.3.6 DARRYL LEE CROUTHARMEL was born on 23 April 1955.

5.3.4.1.2.4 CHESTER LEROY KLINGER was born on 28 September 1925, Fearnot, Schuylkill County, PA. He was baptized on 1 November 1925, St. Michael's Church, Klingerstown, Schuylkill County, PA. Some sources record that he was born on 28 September 1928. Chester was a private first class in the US Army during World War II. He married **ALBERTA KAHLER** on 21 July 1945, St. Andrew's Church, Valley View, Schuylkill County, PA. He died on 4 December 2003, Coaldale, Wiconisco Township, Dauphin County, PA, at age 75. According to a newspaper obituary, Chester was an Army veteran of World War II who received a Purple Heart, Bronze Star, Good Conduct Medal, Expert Marksman's Medal, Valorous Service Medal and Silver Star. He was a retired coal miner. He was buried on 9 December 2003, at Calvary United Methodist Cemetery, Wiconisco, Wiconisco Township, Dauphin County, PA.

    5.3.4.1.2.4.1 JEAN PAUL KLINGER

    5.3.4.1.2.4.2 MICHAEL A. KLINGER

    5.3.4.1.2.4.3 BONITA KLINGER married (--?--) **PAUL**.

    5.3.4.1.2.4.4 SUSAN KLINGER died before 8 December 2003.

    5.3.4.1.2.4.5 TRUDY KLINGER

    5.3.4.1.2.4.6 DAVID DEAN KLINGER was born on 9 July 1941.

    5.3.4.1.2.4.7 STEVEN LEROY KLINGER was born on 30 March 1948.

5.3.4.1.2.5 VIOLET BETTY KLINGER was born on 18 September 1930, Hubley Township, Schuylkill County, PA. She married **MARLIN HARVEY REBUCK**, son of **HARRY E. REBUCK** and **MABEL A. KAHLER**. She died on 2 December 2016, Sunbury Community Hospital, Sunbury, Northumberland County, PA, at age 86. She was buried on 6 December 2016, at Himmel's Church Cemetery, Rebuck, Northumberland County, PA.

    5.3.4.1.2.5.1 TODD B. REBUCK was born on 8 July 1961, Harrisburg, Dauphin County, PA. He married **SHELLY HARNER**. He died on 26 June 2013, at his home Gratz, Dauphin County, PA, at age 51. He was buried on 29 June 2013, at Himmel Church Cemetery, Rebuck, Northumberland County, PA.

        5.3.4.1.2.5.1.1 SHAWN REBUCK was born on 22 February 1988.

    5.3.4.1.2.5.2 TONYA L. REBUCK was born on 22 December 1969. She married **THOMAS REINHARD**. She married **SCOTT LATSHA**.

        5.3.4.1.2.5.2.1 JAYNA KATIE REINHARD was born on 17 May 1993.

5.3.4.1.2.6 EILEEN MAY KLINGER is also referred to as **EILENE** in some sources. She was born on 2 May 1932, Fearnot, Schuylkill County, PA. She married **CLAIR ERNEST LEITZEL**, son of **LAWRENCE S. LEITZEL** and **ALMA MARY EDNA MOYER,** circa 1948. She died on 26 December 2015, The Manor, Susquehanna Village, Millersburg, Dauphin County, PA, at age 83. She was buried on 29 December 2015, at Union Cemetery, Gratz, Dauphin County, PA.

    5.3.4.1.2.6.1 CAROL LEITZEL was born on 9 June 1951, Lykens, Dauphin County, PA. She married an unknown person. She married **STUART ALLEN ROMBERGER**, son of

HAROLD C. ROMBERGER and ORPAH NAOMI SCHWALM, on 9 September 1972, Hegins, Schuylkill County, PA.

5.3.4.1.2.6.1.1 KELLY YVONNE ROMBERGER was born on 20 December 1975. She married BRIAN MUSOLINO, son of VINCE MUSOLINO and JAMIE (--?--).

5.3.4.1.2.6.1.1.1 MYKENNA ADELL MUSOLINO was born on 2 February 2002, Geisinger Medical Center, Danville, Montour County, PA.

5.3.4.1.2.6.1.2 KRISTIE ANN ROMBERGER was born on 15 February 1977. She married WAYNE KLINGER on 8 September 2001, Friedens Lutheran Church, Hegins, Schuylkill County, PA.

5.3.4.1.2.6.2 GLENN ELDON LEITZEL was born on 23 December 1953, Gratz, Dauphin County, PA. He married ALYCE HATTER, daughter of JACQUE HATTER and IRIS ROMAIN(E) DUNLEAVY, circa 1974, PA.

5.3.4.1.2.6.2.1 RAHN LEITZEL

5.3.4.1.2.6.2.2 AMANDA LEITZEL

5.3.4.1.2.6.3 ANNETTE ANGELA LEITZEL was born on 7 June 1960. She married (--?--) VERBISH. She married ROBERT FETTEROLF.

5.3.4.1.3 STELLA MAY KLINGER is also referred to as STELLA MAE in some sources. She was born on 13 February 1903. Some sources record that she was born on 13 March 1903. She was baptized on 19 April 1903, St. Michael's Church, Klingerstown, Schuylkill County, PA. She married DANIEL EMANUEL KLINGER, son of ELIAS WILLIAM KLINGER and KATHRYN GORDON, on 13 July 1918, St. Michael's Church, Klingerstown, Schuylkill County, PA. Prior to her death, Stella was living in or near Valley View, Schuylkill County, PA. She died on 21 May 1976, at age 73. She was buried on 24 May 1976, at Zion (Klinger's) Church Cemetery, Erdman, Lykens Township, Dauphin County, PA.

5.3.4.1.3.1 LEON OSCAR KLINGER was born on 4 January 1919. He married ELVA IRENE HARNER, daughter of JOHN HARNER and EVA SCHUCKER, on 9 July 1938, Valley View, Schuylkill County, PA. He lived in Sacramento, Schuylkill County, PA. He died on 20 May 2001, at age 82.

5.3.4.1.3.1.1 GENE KLINGER was born on 18 November 1938, Valley View, Schuylkill County, PA. He married JEAN LEFFLER, daughter of LINCOLN LEFFLER and ELLEN BOHNER, on 11 June 1960, Zion (Klinger's) Church, Erdman, Lykens Township, Dauphin County, PA.

5.3.4.1.3.1.1.1 TAMMY KLINGER was born on 1 December 1961. She married DAVID NEISWENDER on 10 October 1981.

5.3.4.1.3.1.1.1.1 MICHAEL NEISWENDER

5.3.4.1.3.1.1.2 MICHAEL KLINGER was born on 11 January 1968.

5.3.4.1.3.1.2 DOROTHY KLINGER was born on 16 June 1941, Valley View, Schuylkill County, PA. She married GUY LEFFLER, son of LINCOLN LEFFLER and ELLEN BOHNER, on 27 November 1958. She married RAY YEICH on 2 September 1967. She lived in Harrisburg, Dauphin County, PA.

5.3.4.1.3.1.3 DIANE M. KLINGER was born on 11 June 1942, Valley View, Schuylkill County, PA. She married HARRY M. MAUSSER on 8 June 1963, Zion (Klinger's) Church, Erdman, Lykens Township, Dauphin County, PA.

5.3.4.1.3.1.3.1 HARRY MAUSSER was born on 2 March 1964. He married RHODA KOHR on 11 June 1983.

5.3.4.1.3.1.3.1.1 ASHLEY MAUSSER was born on 6 April 1984.

5.3.4.1.3.1.3.1.2 ALISA MAUSSER was born on 2 December 1985, Dover Air Force Base, DE.

5.3.4.1.3.1.3.1.3 AMANDA MAUSSER was born on 31 May 1987, Beale Air Force Base, CA.

5.3.4.1.3.1.3.1.4 ALEXIS MAUSSER was born on 25 September 1992, Beale Air Force Base, CA.

5.3.4.1.3.1.3.2 DEBBIE MAUSSER was born on 21 November 1968.

5.3.4.1.3.1.4 JOY ANNE KLINGER was born on 3 November 1943, Hegins, Schuylkill County, PA. She was baptized on 28 October 1952, Zion (Klinger's) Church, Erdman, Lykens Township, Dauphin County, PA. She married **M. THANK NGUYEN.** She married **HAROLD SCHADEL** in 1965, Zion (Klinger's) Church, Erdman, Lykens Township, Dauphin County, PA. She died in 1969. She was buried at Zion (Klinger's) Church, Erdman, Lykens Township, Dauphin County, PA.

    5.3.4.1.3.1.4.1 BRENDA SCHADEL was born on 3 June 1965.

5.3.4.1.3.1.5 JAMES LEE KLINGER was born on 25 May 1945, near Sacramento, Schuylkill County, PA. He was baptized on 28 October 1952, Zion (Klinger's) Church, Erdman, Lykens Township, Dauphin County, PA. He married **PENNY LAUDENSLAGER**, daughter of **HAVEN LAUDENSLAGER** and **RUTH YODER,** on 22 February 1964, Simeon's Church, Gratz, Dauphin County, PA. He lived in Millersburg, Dauphin County, PA.

    5.3.4.1.3.1.5.1 SHERRI LEE KLINGER was born on 25 July 1964, Harrisburg, Dauphin County, PA. She married **RODNEY ALLEN MESSNER**, son of **ROBERT A. MESSNER** and **SANDRA WILLOW,** in March 1982. She married **JOHN F. HEBDA.**

        5.3.4.1.3.1.5.1.1 BRENT ALLEN MESSNER

            5.3.4.1.3.1.5.1.1.1 CAMERON A. MESSNER

        5.3.4.1.3.1.5.1.2 BRANDON JAMES MESSNER was born on 30 March 1985, Onslow Memorial Hospital, Jacksonville, Onslow County, NC. He died on 6 October 2014, Highspire, Dauphin County, PA, at age 29. He was buried at Riverview Memorial Gardens, Halifax, Dauphin County, PA.

5.3.4.1.3.1.6 LEON OSCAR KLINGER JR. was born on 1 November 1947, near Sacramento, Schuylkill County, PA. He was baptized on 28 October 1952, Zion (Klinger's) Church, Erdman, Lykens Township, Dauphin County, PA. He married **JANET L. SITLINGER**, daughter of **RUSSELL BENJAMIN SITLINGER** and **MARY A. SHADLE,** on 24 April 1971, Zion (Klinger's) Church, Erdman, Lykens Township, Dauphin County, PA. He lived in Gratz, Dauphin County, PA.

    5.3.4.1.3.1.6.1 PAMELA SUE KLINGER was born on 16 August 1971, Dauphin Co., PA. She was baptized on 17 October 1971, Zion (Klinger's) Lutheran Church, Erdman, Dauphin Co, PA. She married **TROY EUGENE MILLARD** on 18 October 1998, St. John's (Hill) Lutheran Church, near Berrysburg, Dauphin Co., PA. She married an unknown person on 18 October 1998, St. John's (Hill) Lutheran Church, near Berrysburg, Dauphin Co., PA.

        5.3.4.1.3.1.6.1.1 BROOKE AMANDA MILLARD was born on 2 June 1999, Holy Spirit Hospital, Camp Hill, Cumberland Co., PA.

    5.3.4.1.3.1.6.2 MICHELLE KLINGER was born on 22 February 1974, Dauphin Co., PA. She was baptized on 10 March 1974, Zion (Klinger's) Lutheran Church, Erdman, Dauphin Co., PA.

5.3.4.1.3.1.7 ROSE MARIE KLINGER was born on 11 November 1947. Some sources record that she was born on 11 November 1946, near Sacramento, Schuylkill County, PA. She was baptized on 28 October 1952, Zion (Klinger's) Church, Erdman, Lykens Township, Dauphin County, PA. She married **JOE FRANTZ** on 4 May 1968, Zion (Klinger's) Church, Erdman, Lykens Township, Dauphin County, PA. She lived in Erdman, Lykens Township, Dauphin County, PA.

    5.3.4.1.3.1.7.1 RADELL FRANTZ was born on 6 September 1968.

5.3.4.1.3.1.8 RODNEY RAY KLINGER was born on 18 March 1952, near Sacramento, Schuylkill County, PA. He was baptized on 28 October 1952, Zion (Klinger's) Church, Erdman, Lykens Township, Dauphin County, PA. He married **BRENDA WIEST** on 25 March 1972, Zion (Klinger's) Church, Erdman, Lykens Township, Dauphin County, PA.

    5.3.4.1.3.1.8.1 JENIFER KLINGER was born on 28 September 1972.

    5.3.4.1.3.1.8.2 JASON KLINGER was born on 15 February 1979.

5.3.4.1.3.2 ALVIN ELIAS KLINGER was born on 9 November 1920. He was baptized on 30 October 1921, St. Michael's Church, Klingerstown, Schuylkill County, PA. Some sources record that he was born on 30 October 1921. Some source record that he was baptized on 9

November 1921 Salem (Herb's) Church, Rough and Ready, Schuylkill County, PA. He married **VELMA KATHRYN ERDMAN**, daughter of **JOHN JASPER ERDMAN** and **ELURA GRACE STARR**, on 1 March 1941, St. Andrew's Church, Valley View, Schuylkill County, PA. Alvin served in the US Army during World War II. He lived in Valley View, Hegins Township, Schuylkill County, PA. He died on 13 January 1997, Schuylkill Manor, Pottsville, Schuylkill County, PA, at age 76. He was buried at Christ Church Cemetery, Fountain Springs, Schuylkill County, PA. According to some sources he was buried at St. Andrew's Cemetery, Valley View, Schuylkill County, PA.

5.3.4.1.3.2.1 CAROLYN KLINGER married (--?--) **BUFFINGTON**.

5.3.4.1.3.2.1.1 JULIE BUFFINGTON

5.3.4.1.3.2.1.2 ANN BUFFINGTON

5.3.4.1.3.2.2 KENNETH ALVIN KLINGER was born on 16 July 1941, Valley View, Schuylkill County, PA. He married **CAROLYN K. MERVINE**. He died on 31 January 1999, at his home West Grove, Chester County, PA, at age 57. According to a newspaper obituary, Kenneth was a research chemist for Montel Inc., in Elkton, MD. He was buried on 4 February 1999, at Laurel Hill Memorial Gardens, Columbia, Lancaster County, PA.

5.3.4.1.3.2.2.1 CATHY S. KLINGER

5.3.4.1.3.2.2.2 MICHAEL S. KLINGER

5.3.4.1.3.2.2.3 LORI ANN KLINGER was born on 28 May 1960, Pottsville, Schuylkill County, PA. She died on 23 July 1992, Tulsa, Tulsa County, PA, at age 32. She was buried at Friedens Union Cemetery, Hegins, Schuylkill County, PA.

5.3.4.1.3.2.3 SANDRA LEE KLINGER was born on 5 March 1943. She married **LARRY LAMAR WILLIARD**, son of **MELVIN HARVEY WILLIARD** and **ELSIE JENNIE BOYER**, on 26 January 1963, Zion (Klinger's) Lutheran Church, Erdman, Dauphin Co., PA.

5.3.4.1.3.2.3.1 KERRY LAMAR WILLIARD was born on 7 January 1963, Dauphin Co., PA.

5.3.4.1.3.2.3.2 DAVID ALLEN WILLIARD was born on 4 August 1964, Dauphin Co., PA.

5.3.4.1.3.2.3.3 MELISSA WILLIARD was born circa 1968, Dauphin Co., PA.

5.3.4.1.4 VENA ALPHA KLINGER is also referred to as **VERNA, VENIE, WINNIE, AND VINNIE** in some sources. She was born on 8 June 1905. She was baptized on 6 August 1905. She married **ALBERT TOBIAS STROHECKER**, son of **WILLIAM P. STROHECKER** and **SARAH E. BOHNER**, circa 1925. She died in 1938. She was buried at St. David's Lutheran and Reformed Church Cemetery, Hebe, Northumberland County, PA.

5.3.4.1.4.1 MARLIN LEE KLINGER is also referred to as **MARLIN LEO AND MARLIN O.** in some sources. Some sources record that he was born on 24 January 1921, Klingerstown, Schuylkill County, PA. He married **ARABEL C. STRAUB**, daughter of **HARRY AUSTIN STRAUB** and **HILDA E. WENRICH**, on 18 July 1942, St. Michael's Church, Klingerstown, Schuylkill County, PA. He died on 20 April 2011, Spring Glen, Schuylkill County, PA, at age 90. According to a newspaper obituary, Marlin worked in the coal industry for Legal Coal Company, Kocher Coal Company, and retired from Mercury Coal Company in 1987. He was buried on 26 April 2011, at Zion (Klinger's) Lutheran Church Cemetery, Erdman, Dauphin County, PA.

5.3.4.1.4.1.1 MARLIN LAMAR KLINGER JR. was born on 2 February 1943, Lykens, Dauphin County, PA. He was baptized on 11 March 1943, St. Michael's Church, Klingerstown, Upper Mahantango Township, Schuylkill County, PA. He married **BETTY SUE BOWLING**. He died on 2 September 2001, Oneonta, Blount County, AL, at age 58. He was buried at Oak Hill Cemetery, Oneonta, AL.

5.3.4.1.4.1.1.1 MATTHEW KLINGER. Matthew lives in Oneonta, AL.

5.3.4.1.4.1.2 DENNIS ERROL KLINGER was born on 14 April 1944. He was baptized on 7 June 1944, St. Michael's Church, Klingerstown, Schuylkill County, PA. He married **CHARLOTTE GEIST**, daughter of **LAWRENCE GEIST** and **ANNA (--?--)**, in 1964, Hegins, Schuylkill County, PA. In 1989, Dennis was living in Camp Hill, Cumberland County, PA.

5.3.4.1.4.1.2.1 DOUGLAS KLINGER was born on 26 March 1967. He married **CHERIE (--?--).** Douglas lives in Dallas, PA.

5.3.4.1.4.1.2.2 TRACY KLINGER was born on 5 February 1971. She married **PETE GERVASIO.** Tracy lives in Harrisburg, PA.

5.3.4.1.4.1.3 CAROL ANN KLINGER was born on 28 January 1947. She was baptized on 31 May 1947, St. Michael's Church, Klingerstown, Schuylkill County, PA. She married **DOUGLAS HEPLER.** Carole lives in Spring Glen, PA.

5.3.4.1.4.1.3.1 CHRIS HEPLER married **WANDA (--?--).** Chris lives in Kernersville, NC.

5.3.4.1.4.1.3.2 JAMES HEPLER. James lives in Durham, NC.

5.3.4.1.4.1.4 CYNTHIA LOUISE KLINGER also went by the name of **CINDY.** She was born on 25 March 1959. She married **GARY WEDDE.** Cindy lives in Elysburg, PA.

5.3.4.1.4.1.4.1 BRANDON WEDDE married **MELINDA (--?--).** Brandon lives in Pittsburgh, PA.

5.3.4.1.4.1.5 TIMOTHY SCOTT KLINGER was born on 28 March 1968. He was baptized on 2 June 1968, Zion (Klinger's) Church, Erdman, Lykens Township, Dauphin County, PA. He married **NADINE (--?--).**

5.3.4.1.4.2 ARLENE M. SEIGER was born on 25 April 1924, Klingerstown, Schuylkill County, PA. She married **HENRY S. BROWN.** She died on 4 December 2013, Manor Care, Sunbury, Northumberland County, PA, at age 89. According to a newspaper obituary, Arlene was raised by her grandparents, W.O. and Pearl Mable Klinger. She owned and operated Arlene Brown's Beauty Shop, Klingerstown, for 50 years and had previously been employed at Carl's Store, Spring Glen, Boyer's Butcher Shop, Klingerstown, and Dormar Manufacturing, Gratz. She was buried on 9 December 2013, at Salem Church Cemetery, Rough and Ready, Schuylkill County, PA.

5.3.4.1.4.2.1 ELAINE BROWN married **(--?--) REED.** Elaine lives in Wiconisco, PA.

5.3.4.1.4.2.1.1 MICHAEL REED. Michael is a minister in Trafford, PA.

5.3.4.1.4.2.2 LYNN BROWN. Lynn lives in East Pittsburgh, PA.

5.3.4.1.4.2.2.1 MATTHEW BROWN

5.3.4.1.4.2.2.2 SAMANTHA BROWN

5.3.4.1.4.2.3 MICHELLE BROWN married **JOHN RAUTZAHN.** Michelle lives in Williamstown, PA.

5.3.4.1.4.2.3.1 JOSEPH RAUTZAHN

5.3.4.1.4.3 MARGARET FAY STROHECKER was born on 25 October 1926, Upper Mahantango Township, Schuylkill County, PA. She was baptized on 25 November 1926, Salem (Herb's) Church, Rough and Ready, Northumberland County, PA.

5.3.4.1.4.4 MABEL SAVILLA STROHECKER was born on 12 November 1927, Klingerstown, Schuylkill County, PA. She was baptized on 2 January 1928, Salem (Herb's) Church, Rough and Ready, Schuylkill County, PA.

5.3.4.1.4.5 ROBERT NEAL STROHECKER was born on 16 October 1928, Klingerstown, Schuylkill County, PA. He was baptized on 11 November 1928, Salem (Herb's) Church, Rough and Ready, Schuylkill County, PA. He died before 2013.

5.3.4.1.4.6 LUCILLA MAE STROHECKER was born on 8 October 1929, Klingerstown, Schuylkill County, PA. She was baptized on 2 September 1930, Salem (Herb's) Church, Rough and Ready, Schuylkill County, PA.

5.3.4.1.5 HOMER ALVIN KLINGER was born on 22 April 1907. He was baptized on 7 July 1907, St. Michael's Church, Klingerstown, Schuylkill County, PA. He married **FERN M. HAAS,** daughter of **PALMER C. HAAS** and **MAMIE JEMIMAH DIETZ,** circa 1931. He died on 28 February 1991, at age 83. He was buried on 4 March 1991, at Salem Cemetery, Schuylkill County, PA.

5.3.4.1.5.1 JOAN EMILY KLINGER was born circa 1936. She married **WALLACE GLENN BARNES,** son of **WILLIAM BARNES** and **ELIZABETH GUESSNER,** circa 1960.

5.3.4.1.5.1.1 ROBIN S. BARNES was born in 1964.

5.3.4.1.5.1.2 JEFFREY S. BARNES was born in 1965.

5.3.4.1.5.1.3 ELIZABETH BARNES was born in 1967. She married **(--?--) COURTRIGHT**.

5.3.4.1.6 RALPH RAYMOND KLINGER is also referred to as **RALPH H. KLINGER** in some sources. He was born on 6 April 1909. He was baptized on 31 May 1909, St. Michael's Church, Klingerstown, Schuylkill County, PA. He married **HILDA S. MATTERN**, daughter of **SAMUEL H. MATTERN** and **LIZZIE S. REINER**, on 26 August 1933, St. Michael's Church, Klingerstown, Schuylkill County, PA. He died on 11 May 1985, Geisinger Medical Center, Danville, Montour County, PA, at age 76. He was buried on 15 May 1985, at St. John's Lutheran Church Cemetery, Leck Kill, Northumberland County, PA.

5.3.4.1.6.1 SUSIE E. KLINGER married **(--?--) REEDER**.

5.3.4.1.6.2 ERNEST L. KLINGER

5.3.4.1.6.3 RACHEL P. KLINGER married **(--?--) HEPLER**.

5.3.4.1.6.4 LAMAR R. KLINGER was born on 8 January 1934. He married **LARONA A. WIEST**, daughter of **CLARENCE EDWIN WIEST** and **IRENE KATHERINE REED**, on 27 August 1955, Salem (Herb's) Church, Rough and Ready, Schuylkill County, PA. He died on 17 February 1974, at age 40. He was buried at St. Michael's Lutheran Church Cemetery, Klingerstown, Schuylkill County, PA.

> **5.3.4.1.6.4.1 CHARLENE KAY KLINGER** (see above)
>> **5.3.4.1.6.4.1.1 SARAH ELIZABETH WOODRING** (see above)
>> **5.3.4.1.6.4.1.2 EMILY WOODRING** (see above)
> **5.3.4.1.6.4.2 BONITA EILEEN KLINGER** (see above)
>> **5.3.4.1.6.4.2.1 ASHLEY JAMES SNYDER** (see above)
>>> **5.3.4.1.6.4.2.1.1 ALEXANDRA GRACE SNYDER** (see above)
>> **5.3.4.1.6.4.2.2 ALEXIS LAMAR SNYDER** (see above)
> **5.3.4.1.6.4.3 BRIAN LAMAR KLINGER** (see above)
>> **5.3.4.1.6.4.3.1 TRISHIA NICOLE KLINGER** (see above)
>> **5.3.4.1.6.4.3.2 ALYSSA MARIE KLINGER** (see above)
> **5.3.4.1.6.4.4 TODD LAMAR KLINGER** (see above)
>> **5.3.4.1.6.4.4.1 DELANEY KATHERINE KLINGER** (see above)
>> **5.3.4.1.6.4.4.2 RHETT CHARLES KLINGER** (see above)

5.3.4.1.6.5 BRYANT R. KLINGER was born in 1939.

5.3.4.1.7 RAY MELVIN KLINGER was born on 31 October 1910. He was baptized on 12 February 1911, St. Michael's Church, Klingerstown, Schuylkill County, PA. He died in December 1991, at age 81. He was buried at St. Michael's Lutheran Church Cemetery, Klingerstown, Schuylkill County, PA.

5.3.4.1.8 HELEN IRENE KLINGER was born on 2 April 1913, RR1, Klingerstown, PA. She was baptized on 1 May 1913, St. Michael's Church, Klingerstown, Schuylkill County, PA. She married **STANLEY A. WOLFGANG** on 24 June 1933, St. Michael's Church, Klingerstown, Schuylkill County, PA. She died on 21 August 2001, Susquehanna Lutheran Village, Millersburg, Dauphin County, PA, at age 88. Some sources record that she died on 24 August 2001. She was buried at Salem Cemetery, Rough and Ready, Upper Mahantango Township, Schuylkill County, PA.

5.3.4.1.8.1 GLENN D. WOLFGANG married **DORIS (--?--)**.

5.3.4.1.8.2 MAE IRENE WOLFGANG was born on 5 January 1934. She was baptized on 13 March 1934, Salem (Herb's) Church, Rough and Ready, Schuylkill County, PA. She married **CHRISTIAN HAUSSLER**.

5.3.4.1.8.3 ALLEN STANLEY WOLFGANG was born on 11 December 1935. He was baptized on 18 March 1936, Salem (Herb's) Church, Rough and Ready, Schuylkill County, PA.

5.3.4.1.8.4 EARL ALFRED WOLFGANG married **BETTY (--?--)**. He was born on 18 August 1937. He was baptized on 15 November 1937, Salem (Herb's) Church, Rough and Ready, Schuylkill County, PA.

5.3.4.1.9 LUCY ALVENA KLINGER is also referred to as **LUCIE** in some sources. She was born on 7 November 1915. She was baptized on 5 January 1916, St. Michael's Church, Klingerstown, Schuylkill County, PA. Some sources record that she was born on 7 November 1916. She married

Fred J. Clark. She died on 2 January 2007, at the home of her daughter, Hegins, Schuylkill County, PA, at age 90. According to a newspaper obituary, Lucy lived in Hegins, Schuylkill County, PA, and provided child care for area families for 34 years. She was buried on 5 January 2007, at St. Andrew's Church Cemetery, Valley View, Schuylkill County, PA.

5.3.4.1.9.1 Jacky L. Clark died before 2 January 2007.

5.3.4.1.9.2 Anna G. Clark married **Clyde Miller.**

5.3.4.1.9.2.1 Steven C. Miller

5.3.4.1.9.3 Paul M. Clark was born on 3 August 1936, Mahantongo Township, Schuylkill County, PA. He died on 7 July 2010, at the home of his sister Anna G. Miller, Hegins, Schuylkill County, PA, at age 73. According to a newspaper obituary, Paul served in the U.S. Air Force. Later, he was employed as a groomsman at Penn National Race Track, Grantville. He was buried on 10 July 2010, at Indiantown Gap Military Cemetery, Annville, Lebanon County, PA.

5.3.4.1.9.3.1 Philip G. Clark

5.3.4.1.9.3.1.1 Dominique Clark

5.3.4.1.10 Eva Juliana Klinger was born on 20 August 1919. She married **(--?--) Brown.** She married **Luther Edwin Brown,** son of **A. Wilson Brown** and **Emma Howerter,** circa 1943.

5.3.4.1.10.1 Richard C. Brown

5.3.4.1.10.2 Sandra M. Brown married **(--?--) Angst.**

5.3.4.1.11 Paul William Klinger was born on 3 September 1923, Klingerstown, Schuylkill County, PA. He was baptized on 28 September 1923, St. Michael's Church, Klingerstown, Schuylkill County, PA. He married **Marian Geraldine Snyder,** daughter of **Charles Snyder** and **Mabel A. Hoch,** on 12 December 1945. He died on 7 November 2010, Hershey Medical Center, Hershey, Dauphin County, PA, at age 87. According to a newspaper obituary, Paul owned K-Hogs Farm at Klingerstown and worked as a butcher with the former Boyer Meats. He was buried on 11 November 2010, at St. Michael's Lutheran Church Cemetery, Klingerstown, Schuylkill County, PA.

5.3.4.1.11.1 Sharon Sandra Klinger was born on 10 January 1947. She married **Marlin Erdman,** son of **Marlin Erdman** and **Fern Shade,** on 14 August 1971.

5.3.4.1.11.1.1 Jeffrey William Erdman was born on 15 January 1972. He married **Kimberly Fazio.**

5.3.4.1.11.1.2 Chris Marie Erdman was born on 23 December 1976.

5.3.4.1.11.2 Donald Paul Klinger was born on 24 March 1951. He was baptized on 29 April 1951, St. Michael's Church, Klingerstown, Schuylkill County, PA. He married **Joan Mae Morgan** on 18 April 1970.

5.3.4.1.11.2.1 Eric Donald Klinger was born on 10 October 1970.

5.3.4.1.11.2.2 Loriann Klinger was born on 8 September 1972.

5.3.4.1.11.3 Donna Marie Klinger was born on 24 March 1951. She was baptized on 29 April 1951, St. Michael's Church, Klingerstown, Schuylkill County, PA. She married **Harold Dunston** on 7 April 1973. She married **Glenn Troutman.**

5.3.4.1.12 Guy Junior Klinger was born on 3 October 1928, RR 1, Klingerstown, Schuylkill County, PA. He was baptized on 23 December 1928, St. Michael's Church, Klingerstown, Schuylkill County, PA. He died on 17 May 2008, Friendly Nursing Home, Pitman, Schuylkill County, PA, at age 79. According to a newspaper obituary, Guy was known as "Junior." He had lived in Klingerstown, Elysburg, and Danville. After being educated in the Klingerstown area schools, he was a farm laborer, who enjoyed the outdoors and working on farms. He was buried on 21 May 2008, at St. Michael's Lutheran Church Cemetery, Klingerstown, Schuylkill County, PA.

5.3.4.2 Harry Allen Klinger is also referred to as **Henry Allen and Harry E. Klinger** in some sources. He was born on 4 December 1887. He was baptized on 29 April 1888, Zion (Klinger's) Church, Erdman, Lykens Township, Dauphin County, PA. He married **Virgie R. Wolf** on 28 September 1907, Zion (Klinger's) Church, Erdman, Lykens Township, Dauphin County, PA. He died in 1956. He was buried at Simeon Church Cemetery, Gratz, Dauphin County, PA.

5.3.4.2.1 LUTHER RAYMOND KLINGER was born on 28 January 1908. He married ERNESTINE A. (--?--) circa 1927. He died on 2 August 1960, at age 52.

5.3.4.2.2 CHARLES OSCAR KLINGER was born on 14 May 1909. He married HELEN IRENE STEELY, daughter of WILLIAM D. STEELY and JENNIE EDNA SALTZER, on 11 June 1928, Dauphin County, PA. He married CATHERINE R. (--?--). He died on 8 December 1989, at age 80. He was buried at Laureldale Cemetery, Tuckerton, Berks County, PA.

> **5.3.4.2.2.1** HAROLD STANLEY KLINGER was born on 18 March 1931, Gratz, Dauphin County, PA. He died on 11 March 2006, at age 74. He was buried at Florida National Cemetery, Bushnell, Sumter County, FL.
>
> **5.3.4.2.2.2** LARRY ALVIN KLINGER was born on 5 October 1932, Gratz, Dauphin County, PA. He died on 7 December 2015, Catawba Valley Medical Center, Hickory, NC, at age 83.
>
> **5.3.4.2.2.3** HARRY KLINGER was born circa 1933.
>
> **5.3.4.2.2.4** CARL E. KLINGER was born on 18 March 1936.
>
> **5.3.4.2.2.5** ALICE E. KLINGER was born on 3 June 1937, Gratz, Dauphin County, PA. She married LYNWOOD D. HENRY circa 1956. She was buried at Pleasant View Cemetery, Sinking Spring, Berks County, PA.
>
>> **5.3.4.2.2.5.1** KURT L. HENRY married CHRISTINE A. (--?--).
>>
>> **5.3.4.2.2.5.2** ROBIN L. HENRY married JAMES R. LASH.
>>
>> **5.3.4.2.2.5.3** ROGER L. HENRY married KATHLEEN L. (--?--).
>>
>> **5.3.4.2.2.5.4** LISA L. HENRY married JOHN E. KOWALCZYK.
>>
>>> **5.3.4.2.2.5.4.1** ALEX KOWALCZYK
>>>
>>> **5.3.4.2.2.5.4.2** ANNA KOWALCZYK
>
> **5.3.4.2.2.6** IRENE M. KLINGER was born on 11 September 1939. She married CRAIG D. LEFFLER. She and CRAIG D. LEFFLER were divorced on 6 September 1979 Hennepin County, MN. She married WALDO B. ASP on 31 December 1980, Hennepin County, MN.

5.3.4.2.3 LEROY ELIAS KLINGER was born on 30 July 1911, Spring Glen, Schuylkill County, PA. He married LILLIAN A. BAER. Prior to his death, Leroy was living in or near Wernersville, Berks County, PA. He died on 28 May 2000, Manor Care, West Reading, PA, at age 88. He was buried at Pleasant View Cemetery, Berks County, PA.

> **5.3.4.2.3.1** RICHARD M. KLINGER died in 1993.
>
> **5.3.4.2.3.2** FORREST G. KLINGER
>
> **5.3.4.2.3.3** ELWOOD L. KLINGER
>
> **5.3.4.2.3.4** GENE L. KLINGER
>
> **5.3.4.2.3.5** BRUCE H. KLINGER
>
> **5.3.4.2.3.6** DENNIS G. KLINGER
>
> **5.3.4.2.3.7** DORIS KLINGER married (?) SHADEL.
>
> **5.3.4.2.3.8** MARLIN D. KLINGER

5.3.4.2.4 GUY G. KLINGER was born on 23 February 1915, Gratz, Dauphin County, PA. He married DOROTHY E. TROUTMAN, daughter of JOHN E. TROUTMAN and ANNIE F. YEAKLEY. Guy served in US Army during World War II. He died on 13 February 2001, Reading Hospital, West Reading, PA, at age 85. He was buried at Pleasant View Cemetery, Berks County, PA.

> **5.3.4.2.4.1** WILLIAM G. KLINGER
>
> **5.3.4.2.4.2** GLEN D. KLINGER
>
> **5.3.4.2.4.3** JUNE A. KLINGER married (--?--) BOYER.
>
> **5.3.4.2.4.4** EILEEN R. KLINGER married (?) WHITE.

5.3.4.2.5 KATHRYN JULIAN KLINGER was born on 13 September 1924.

5.3.4.2.6 EVA NAOMI KLINGER was born on 26 January 1927, Gratz, Dauphin County, PA. She married EUSTACIO MARINO SR., son of ANTONIO MARINO and ANGELINA MODESTO, in 1942. She died on 7 January 2017, at age 89.

> **5.3.4.2.6.1** PAMELA MARINO married WILLIAM F. MUNROE. She married TERENCE DOWD.

5.3.4.2.6.2 EUSTACIO RICHARD MARINO JR. married HEIDI (--?--).

5.3.4.3 ESTON EMANUEL KLINGER is also referred to as EMANUEL E. AND ESTON EMIL in some sources. He was born circa 8 January 1890. He married VERNA MAE KLINGER, daughter of ELMER MICHAEL KLINGER and MARY CATHERINE ENGLE, on 30 May 1914, Frieden's Reformed Church, Hegins, Schuylkill County, PA. He died on 29 October 1940. He was buried at Zion (Klinger's) Church Cemetery, Erdman, Lykens Township, Dauphin County, PA.

- **5.3.4.3.1** JOHN ELWOOD KLINGER (see above)
    - **5.3.4.3.1.1** VIOLET KLINGER (see above)
    - **5.3.4.3.1.2** ALMA E. KLINGER (see above)
    - **5.3.4.3.1.3** KENNETH F. KLINGER (see above)
- **5.3.4.3.2** BLANCHE IRENE KLINGER (see above)
    - **5.3.4.3.2.1** MILDRED MARIE SCHEIB (see above)
    - **5.3.4.3.2.2** JOHNNY ALLEN OSCAR SCHEIB (see above)
- **5.3.4.3.3** WILLIAM GUY KLINGER (see above)
- **5.3.4.3.4** THOMAS LEROY KLINGER (see above)
    - **5.3.4.3.4.1** RICHARD KLINGER (see above)
    - **5.3.4.3.4.2** VIRGINIA KLINGER (see above)
    - **5.3.4.3.4.3** KATHRYN SUSAN MAE KLINGER (see above)
    - **5.3.4.3.4.4** JANET RENEE KLINGER (see above)
    - **5.3.4.3.4.5** BRENDA LEE KLINGER (see above)
    - **5.3.4.3.4.6** VICKIE JEAN KLINGER (see above)
        - **5.3.4.3.4.6.1** STACY M. CHUBB (see above)
        - **5.3.4.3.4.6.2** BRIAN K. CHUBB (see above)
            - **5.3.4.3.4.6.2.1** BROOKE CHUBB (see above)
            - **5.3.4.3.4.6.2.2** MOLLY CHUBB (see above)
            - **5.3.4.3.4.6.2.3** FELISHA CHUBB (see above)
            - **5.3.4.3.4.6.2.4** MAKAYLA CHUBB (see above)
            - **5.3.4.3.4.6.2.5** CODIE ALLEN CHUBB (see above)
        - **5.3.4.3.4.6.3** SONYA L. CHUBB (see above)
    - **5.3.4.3.4.7** JACQUELINE L. KLINGER (see above)
- **5.3.4.3.5** BETTY MAY KLINGER (see above)
- **5.3.4.3.6** SELIN HERMAN KLINGER (see above)
- **5.3.4.3.7** GEORGE ELMER KLINGER (see above)

5.3.4.4 CARRIE EDNA KLINGER was born on 25 March 1896. She was baptized on 14 June 1896, Zion (Klinger's) Church, Erdman, Lykens Township, Dauphin County, PA. She died on 7 April 1905, at age 9. She was buried at Zion (Klinger's) Church Cemetery, Erdman, Lykens Township, Dauphin County, PA.

5.3.5 DANIEL M. KLINGER was born on 3 February 1860, Lykens Township, Dauphin County, PA. Some sources record that he was born in 1852. He married EMALINE ARBOGAST, daughter of ISRAEL ARBOGAST and ANGELINA (--?--), circa 1878, Lykens Township, Dauphin County, PA. He died on 10 September 1919, Lykens Township, Dauphin County, PA, at age 59. He was buried at Zion (Klinger's) Church, Erdman, Lykens Township, Dauphin County, PA.

5.3.5.1 MARY LOUISE KLINGER was born on 17 May 1879, Lykens Township, Dauphin County, PA. She married MICHAEL EDWIN HERMAN circa 1896, Lykens Township, Dauphin County, PA. She died on 26 September 1942, Washington Township, Dauphin County, PA, at age 63.

5.3.5.1.1 HARRY ALLEN HERMAN was born on 17 April 1897, Washington Township, Dauphin Co., PA. He married SADIE ELEANOR ROWE on 15 September 1917. He died in 1960, Schuylkill County, PA. He was buried in 1960, at Maple Grove Cemetery, Elizabethville, Dauphin Co., PA.

5.3.5.1.1.1 DAVID ALLEN HERMAN was born on 23 December 1918, Tower City, Schuylkill County, PA. He married EMMA DELONG on 24 November 1945.

5.3.5.1.1.1.1 JOHN DAVID HERMAN was born on 1 November 1946.

5.3.5.1.1.2 HELEN IRENE HERMAN was born on 8 October 1921, Tower City, Schuylkill County, PA. She married **MARK WILLIAM UNDERKOFFLER** on 28 October 1939. She died in June 1995, at age 73. Prior to her death, Helen lived in Tower City, Schuylkill County, PA.

5.3.5.1.1.2.1 LORI UNDERKOFFLER married (--?--) **BOND**.

5.3.5.1.1.2.2 ROBERT UNDERKOFFLER

5.3.5.1.1.2.3 EILEEN UNDERKOFFLER married (--?--) **TROUTMAN**.

5.3.5.1.1.2.4 KENNETH W. UNDERKOFFLER was born on 30 January 1954. He died on 5 November 2005, at age 51.

5.3.5.1.1.2.5 MARK W. UNDERKOFFLER also went by the name of **MICK**. He was born on 16 May 1959, Pottsville, Schuylkill County, PA. He married **CHRISTINA BOYER** circa 1985. He died on 8 September 2010, Williams Township, Schuylkill County, PA, at age 51. According to a newspaper obituary, Mark lived in Tower City, Schuylkill County, PA. He was a graduate of Williams Valley High School and a machinist at Dauphin Precision Tool, Millersburg, for 20 years. He was also a skilled auto mechanic. He was buried on 11 September 2010, at St. Peter's Reformed Church Cemetery, Orwin, Schuylkill County, PA.

5.3.5.1.1.2.5.1 SHARYN D. UNDERKOFFLER

5.3.5.1.1.2.5.2 MARK W. UNDERKOFFLER III married **CASSANDRA** (--?--).

5.3.5.1.1.2.5.3 ANDREW J. UNDERKOFFLER

5.3.5.1.1.2.5.4 BRYAN K. UNDERKOFFLER

5.3.5.1.1.2.6 LAMAR L. UNDERKOFFLER also went by the name of **RED**. He was born on 5 February 1963, Pottsville, Schuylkill County, PA. He died on 24 January 2011, Schuylkill Medical Center-South, Pottsville, Schuylkill County, PA, at age 47. He was buried at Maple Grove Cemetery, Elizabethville, Dauphin County, PA. According to a newspaper obituary, Lamar was a graduate of Williams Valley High School and lived in Tower City, Schuylkill County, PA.

5.3.5.1.1.2.6.1 TIMOTHY WALSH

5.3.5.1.1.3 ETHEL MARIE HERMAN was born on 4 April 1925, Tower City, Schuylkill County, PA. She married **JOHN WILLIAMS HUMMEL** on 21 July 1945.

5.3.5.1.1.4 WILLIAM HARRY HERMAN was born on 3 May 1926, Tower City, Schuylkill County, PA. He married **LOIS MARIE BADDORF** on 10 December 1949.

5.3.5.1.1.5 PAUL EDWARD HERMAN was born on 25 December 1928, Tower City, Schuylkill County, PA. He married **DONNA MCNEAL** on 27 August 1955.

5.3.5.1.1.6 CLARENCE LEROY HERMAN was born on 9 July 1937, Tower City, Schuylkill County, PA. He married **MARIE ELAINE WEAVER** on 27 July 1957.

5.3.5.1.2 THOMAS E. HERMAN was born circa 1899. Some sources record that he was born circa 1900.

5.3.5.1.3 MARY E. J. HERMAN was born circa 1903.

5.3.5.1.4 MILDRED M. HERMAN was born circa 1905.

5.3.5.1.5 MABEL H. HERMAN was born circa 1907.

5.3.5.1.6 LEON L. HERMAN was born circa 1911.

5.3.5.1.7 FLOYD E. HERMAN was born circa 1914.

5.3.5.1.8 MYRTLE M. HERMAN was born circa 1917.

5.3.5.2 GEORGE ALLEN KLINGER is also referred to as **ALLEN G. KLINGER** in some sources. He was born on 23 January 1881, Lykens Township, Dauphin County, PA. He married **SIDNEY ANN MESSERSMITH** circa 1902, Elizabethville, Dauphin County, PA. He died in 1964, Allensville, PA.

5.3.5.2.1 ROSA E. KLINGER was born circa 1902.

5.3.5.2.2 GALEN H. KLINGER was born circa 28 February 1902. He died on 16 April 1902. He was buried at Salem Lutheran and Reformed Church, Elizabethville, Dauphin County, PA.

5.3.5.3 GUERNEY ISRAEL KLINGER was born on 7 November 1882, Lykens Township, Dauphin County, PA. He married **SALLIE AGNES REBUCK**, daughter of **EMANUEL REBUCK** and **JULIANA**

SHADE, circa 1904, Erdman, Lykens Township, Dauphin County, PA. He died on 23 October 1936, Erdman, Lykens Township, Dauphin County, PA, at age 53. He was buried on 27 October 1936, at Zion (Klinger's) Church Cemetery, Erdman, Dauphin County, PA.

    5.3.5.3.1 MABEL KLINGER was born on 28 March 1906. She married **JOSEPH SALADA** on 3 July 1924. Prior to her death, Mabel was living in or near Valley View, Schuylkill County, PA. She died on 11 January 1989, at age 82.

        5.3.5.3.1.1 ARLENE FLORENCE SALADA was born on 18 November 1924. She married **HAVEN EDWIN ERDMAN**, son of **FAIRES M. ERDMAN** and **BEULAH MINERVA TROUTMAN**, on 6 March 1943. Prior to her death, Arlene was living in or near Valley View, Schuylkill County, PA. She died in August 1974, at age 49.

            5.3.5.3.1.1.1 GERALD DEAN ERDMAN was born on 16 August 1948.

            5.3.5.3.1.1.2 TERRY LEE ERDMAN was born on 23 October 1949.

        5.3.5.3.1.2 LEROY IRWIN SALADA was born on 16 April 1926. Some sources record that he was born on 26 April 1926, Valley View, Schuylkill County, PA. He married **MARY ELEANOR SCHEIB**, daughter of **HOMER WILLIAM SCHEIB** and **MARY JUSTINA SHAFFER**, circa 1945, PA. He died on 9 May 1997, Valley View, Schuylkill County, PA, at age 71. He was buried on 12 May 1997, at Simeon United Lutheran Church Cemetery, Gratz, Dauphin Co., PA.

            5.3.5.3.1.2.1 SANDRA ELAINE SALADA was born on 21 October 1947, Schuylkill County, PA. She was baptized on 24 July 1948, St. Andrew's United Methodist Church, Valley View, Schuylkill County, PA.

        5.3.5.3.1.3 FAYNE LAMAS SALADA married **EVA LOWES**. He was born on 12 November 1927. He married **DORIS JOANNE BIXLER**, daughter of **ROBERT CALVIN BIXLER** and **SUSANNAH REBECCA KISSINGER**, on 17 July 1954, Valley View, Schuylkill County, PA.

            5.3.5.3.1.3.1 RONALD E. SALLADA

            5.3.5.3.1.3.2 FAYNE LAMA SALADA was born on 22 January 1957.

            5.3.5.3.1.3.3 ROBERT ALLEN SALADA was born on 17 August 1963.

        5.3.5.3.1.4 RENEE JOANNA SALADA was born on 15 December 1937. She married **HAROLD EDWARD DANIELS**.

        5.3.5.3.1.5 GARY JOSEPH SALADA was born on 22 August 1943. He married **SHIRLEY MAE SCHAFFLER**.

5.3.5.3.2 CLARENCE E. KLINGER was born on 29 July 1908, Erdman, Lykens Township, Dauphin County, PA. He married **ESTHER MAY MILLER**, daughter of **JACOB MILLER** and **MARY WOLFGANG**, on 29 July 1930. He died on 27 December 1968, Fearnot, Schuylkill County, PA, at age 60. He was buried at St. Peter's United Methodist Church Cemetery, Fearnot, Schuylkill County, PA.

        5.3.5.3.2.1 CLARENCE M. KLINGER was born on 7 October 1930. Clarence served as a corporal in the US Army during the Korean War. He married **MABEL LAMAE BOYER**, daughter of **RAMSEY BOYER** and **ARLENE DERK**, on 9 April 1954. He died in March 1998, at age 67. He was buried at St. Peter's United Methodist Church Cemetery, Fearnot, Schuylkill County, PA.

            5.3.5.3.2.1.1 LIZA KLINGER. Liza lives in Tower City, PA.

            5.3.5.3.2.1.2 STEPHANIE LYNN KLINGER was born on 10 October 1956. She married **KENNETH GOLDEN**. Stephanie lives in Tower City, PA.

                5.3.5.3.2.1.2.1 SHELLY GOLDEN married (--?--) **SLOUGH**.

                5.3.5.3.2.1.2.2 DAWN GOLDEN married (--?--) **SHUTT**.

                5.3.5.3.2.1.2.3 MICHAEL K. GOLDEN was born on 27 August 1978, Pottsville, Schuylkill County, PA. He married **CORY L. MESSICK**. He died on 12 October 2016, Good Samaritan Hospital, Lebanon, Lebanon County, PA, at age 38.

                    5.3.5.3.2.1.2.3.1 KRISTEN GOLDEN

                    5.3.5.3.2.1.2.3.2 ALAN GOLDEN

            5.3.5.3.2.1.3 CLARENCE M. KLINGER was born on 6 October 1958. Clarence lives in Tower City, PA.

5.3.5.3.3 ADA IRENE KLINGER was born on 28 June 1914, Erdman, Dauphin County, PA. She married **JOHN DAVID TROUTMAN**, son of **VICTOR WILLIAM TROUTMAN** and **SALLIE BAUM WIEST**, on 3 July 1930, Frieden's Reformed Church, Hegins, Schuylkill County, PA. She died on 16 November 2001, Klingerstown, Schuylkill County, PA, at age 87. She was buried on 20 November 2001, at Zion (Klinger's) Church, Erdman, Lykens Township, Dauphin County, PA.

> **5.3.5.3.3.1 GUY CLIFFORD TROUTMAN** also went by the name of **JOHNNY**. He was born on 3 September 1930. He married **JUNO A. ENDERS** on 15 December 1948.
>
> > **5.3.5.3.3.1.1 LINDA SUE TROUTMAN** was born on 26 October 1950. She married **HAROLD GEISE** on 25 September 1971.
> >
> > > **5.3.5.3.3.1.1.1 MELANIE GEISE** was born on 2 September 1980.
> > >
> > > **5.3.5.3.3.1.1.2 GABRIEL GEISE** was born on 2 January 1985.
> >
> > **5.3.5.3.3.1.2 DENNIS LAMAR TROUTMAN** was born on 23 July 1952.

5.3.5.3.4 GERTRUDE MAE KLINGER also went by the name of **GERTIE**. She was born on 9 November 1916. She married **LEE MARLIN DANIEL**, son of **GERMAN DANIELS** and **SALLIE E. WELKER**. She married **JOHN KIRBY STIELY**. Prior to her death, Gertie was living in or near Williamstown, Dauphin County, PA. She died on 7 March 2002, at age 85.

> **5.3.5.3.4.1 LARRY L. DANIEL** was born on 6 May 1938. He married **JEAN MC NAMORO**. Larry lives in Williamstown, Dauphin County, PA.
>
> > **5.3.5.3.4.1.1 DENISE DANIEL**
> >
> > **5.3.5.3.4.1.2 CHRIS DANIEL**
> >
> > **5.3.5.3.4.1.3 MIKE DANIEL**
> >
> > **5.3.5.3.4.1.4 JENNY DANIEL**
>
> **5.3.5.3.4.2 SALLY ANN DANIEL** was born on 20 June 1940. She married **THOMAS HEPLER**, son of **JAMES FRED HEPLER** and **MAE ENDERS**, on 14 June 1958. Sally lives in Gratz, Dauphin County, PA.
>
> > **5.3.5.3.4.2.1 JEFFREY T. HEPLER** was born on 13 October 1958. He married **BRENDA HEANEY**.
> >
> > > **5.3.5.3.4.2.1.1 ABIGAIL HEPLER**
> > >
> > > **5.3.5.3.4.2.1.2 VICTORIA HEPLER**
> >
> > **5.3.5.3.4.2.2 RHONDA HEPLER** was born in 1960. She married **JEFF SWAB**.
> >
> > > **5.3.5.3.4.2.2.1 ALEX SWAB**
> > >
> > > **5.3.5.3.4.2.2.2 LORA SWAB**
> >
> > **5.3.5.3.4.2.3 MARSHALL HEPLER** was born in 1962.
> >
> > **5.3.5.3.4.2.4 GOLDINE HEPLER** is also referred to as **GOLDEEN** in some sources. She was born in 1964.
>
> **5.3.5.3.4.3 PAUL IRWIN DANIEL** was born on 29 December 1942. He married **RUTH DELORES SCHAEFFLER**, daughter of **DAVID R. SCHAEFFLER** and **FLORENCE WITMER**, on 27 May 1967, Dalmatia, Northumberland County, PA. He died on 12 July 2008, at his home on Park Road, Herndon, Northumberland County, PA, at age 65. According to a newspaper obituary, Paul, who lived in Herndon, Northumberland County, PA, worked as a steelworker at Bethlehem Steel, Steelton, PA. He was buried on 17 July 2008, at Riverview Memorial Gardens, Halifax, Dauphin County, PA.
>
> > **5.3.5.3.4.3.1 TODD ERIC DANIEL** was born on 12 September 1968. He died on 2 August 1994, at age 25.
> >
> > **5.3.5.3.4.3.2 MICHELLE DAWN DANIEL** is also referred to as **SHELLY** in some sources. She was born on 31 March 1971. Michelle lives in Sunbury, PA.
>
> **5.3.5.3.4.4 JOHN ROGER STIELY** was born on 27 May 1950, Dauphin County, PA. He married **PEGGY DIANE STRAUB**, daughter of **LEO GEORGE STRAUB** and **NORMA J. KESSLER**, on 19 July 1969, Erdman, Lykens Township, Dauphin County, PA. He and **PEGGY STRAUB** were divorced before 1988. John lives in Elizabethville, Dauphin County, PA.
>
> > **5.3.5.3.4.4.1 ERIC CHRISTOPHER STIELY** was born on 5 November 1969.
> >
> > **5.3.5.3.4.4.2 ANGELA DIANE STIELY** was born on 15 April 1972, Dauphin County, PA.

5.3.5.3.4.5 CLAIR STIELY was born on 22 November 1953. Clair lives in Mechanicsburg, PA.

5.3.5.3.5 IRWIN RAY KLINGER was born on 17 June 1920, Erdman, Lykens Township, Dauphin County, PA. Some sources record that he was born on 17 June 1917, Erdman, Lykens Township, Dauphin County, PA. Although Irwin's obituary lists his date of birth as 17 June 1917, he is not listed among his parents' children in the 1920 Census, while he is listed as 9 years old at the time of the 1930 Census, suggesting that the correct year of birth should be 1920, which is consistent with other sources. He died on 17 July 2002, Veterans Administration Hospital, Lebanon, Lebanon County, PA, at age 82. According to a newspaper obituary, Irwin, who had earned a doctorate, retired as principal of the Upper Dauphin Elementary Schools. He was a veteran of World War II, serving in seven different campaigns in North Africa, Sicily, Normandy, Battle of the Bulge, Luxembourg, France and Germany, between 1941 and 1945. Beginning in 1978, he taught grades one through eight in Amish North Mountain View School and later in the South Mountain View School. He was also a Pennsylvania Dutch playwright, writing for the Dutch Forsumling, and he taught Pennsylvania German (Dutch) classes. As a local historian, he compiled the history of Zion (Klinger's) Church, Erdman and helped the Gratz Historical Society collect material for a book on Lykens Township. In later years, he lived in Elizabethville, Dauphin County, PA. He was buried on 20 July 2002, at Zion (Klinger's) Church Cemetery, Erdman, Lykens Township, Dauphin County, PA.

5.3.5.4 HARRY SAMUEL KLINGER was born on 19 March 1884, Lykens Township, Dauphin County, PA. He married **REGINA (--?--)** on 4 July 1920, St. Andrew's Church, Valley View, Schuylkill County, PA. He died on 14 April 1939, at age 55. Some sources record that he died in 1938 Fearnot, Schuylkill County, PA. He was buried at St. Peter's United Methodist Church Cemetery, Fearnot, Schuylkill County, PA.

5.3.5.4.1 IRENE S. KLINGER was born circa 1915.

5.3.5.4.2 JOHN M. KLINGER was born circa 1918.

5.3.5.4.3 CARRIE V. KLINGER was born circa 1918.

5.3.5.5 DANIEL ESTON KLINGER was born on 8 April 1886, Lykens Township, Dauphin County, PA. Some sources record that he was born in March 1886. He married **BESSIE ELIZABETH BUSH**, daughter of **FRANKLIN B. BUSH** and **FRANCES LORETTA TROUTMAN**, on 27 October 1906. He died on 31 December 1947, Taylorsville, Schuylkill County, PA, at age 61. He was buried at St. John's (Kimmel's) Evangelical Lutheran Church Cemetery, Deep Creek Valley, Barry Township, Schuylkill County, PA.

5.3.5.5.1 MELBA BLANCHE KLINGER is also referred to as **MELVA** in some sources. She was born on 4 December 1907. She married **GEORGE KEYSOCK**. Prior to her death, Melba was living in or near Ashland, Schuylkill County, PA. She died on 13 February 1997, at age 89.

5.3.5.5.2 HOMER MARLIN KLINGER was born on 14 May 1909, Barry Township, Schuylkill County, PA. He married **EDITH G. REED**. Prior to his death, Homer was living in the vicinity of Gordon, Schuylkill County, PA. He died on 22 October 1974, at age 65. He was buried at St. John's (Kimmel's) Evangelical Lutheran Church Cemetery, Deep Creek Valley, Barry Township, Schuylkill County, PA.

5.3.5.5.2.1 STEPHANIE KLINGER married **ANTHONY WILLIAMS**.

5.3.5.5.2.1.1 ANTHONY WILLIAMS

5.3.5.5.2.1.2 MORGAN REID WILLIAMS was born on 23 March 1993.

5.3.5.5.2.2 MARY ANN KLINGER was born on 27 October 1932, Barry Township, Schuylkill County, PA. She married **RUSSELL RICKARD** on 26 February 1955. She is also referred to as **MARY ANN RICKERT** in some sources. Mary Ann lives in Caryville, TN.

5.3.5.5.2.2.1 DAVID LEE RICKARD was born on 22 April 1956. He married **KATHLEEN ROBERTSON**. He married **FRANCES GRAHAM**.

5.3.5.5.2.2.1.1 MICHAEL RICKARD was born on 17 August 1987.

5.3.5.5.2.2.1.2 MATTHEW RICKARD was born on 29 April 1992.

5.3.5.5.2.2.2 MARK RICKARD was born on 10 August 1960.

5.3.5.5.2.3 JOYCE MARIE KLINGER was born on 17 May 1935. She married KARL KLINGER on 9 June 1956. She married CARMEL GARIPOLI circa 1969. Joyce lived in Reading, Berks County, PA. She died on 15 October 2002, at age 67.

5.3.5.5.2.3.1 DEBRA LOUISE KLINGER was born on 22 June 1955. She married GREG GAENZLE.

5.3.5.5.2.3.1.1 JAMIE LYNN GAENZLE was born on 30 August 1982.

5.3.5.5.2.3.1.2 NICOLE MARIE GAENZLE was born on 16 August 1984.

5.3.5.5.2.3.2 DANIEL LEWIS KLINGER was born on 5 January 1958. He married JOETTE GILLAE.

5.3.5.5.2.3.2.1 DANIELLE LYNN KLINGER was born on 26 April 1983.

5.3.5.5.2.3.2.2 LAUREN ASHLEY KLINGER was born on 29 August 1986.

5.3.5.5.2.3.3 DENNIS LEE KLINGER was born on 24 November 1959. He married TINA MARIE HILBERT.

5.3.5.5.2.3.4 TONI JO GARIPOLI was born on 5 September 1970. She married BRETT CONROY on 21 October 1989.

5.3.5.5.2.4 GENE REED KLINGER was born on 7 January 1938. He married IDA MARIE MCANDREW, daughter of JOSEPH L. MCANDREW and IDA MARIE RHOADES, on 20 December 1975. Gene lives in Ashland, PA.

5.3.5.5.2.4.1 THERESA KLINGER married (--?--) CONIPITSKI.

5.3.5.5.2.4.2 GENE REED KLINGER II was born on 20 June 1976.

5.3.5.5.2.4.3 JENNIFER ANNE KLINGER was born on 24 January 1979.

5.3.5.5.2.5 CONSTANCE MAE KLINGER also went by the name of CONNIE. She was born on 16 March 1941. She married CLAIR HASKER in 1961. Constance lived in Reading, Berks County, PA. She died on 30 May 1999, at age 58.

5.3.5.5.2.5.1 STEPHANIE JO HASKER was born on 9 October 1962.

5.3.5.5.2.5.2 ERIC R. HASKER was born on 16 October 1964. He married JUSTINE ANTOLONI. He died on 2 October 2005, at age 40.

5.3.5.5.2.5.2.1 TAYLOR MARIE HASKER was born on 24 August 1992.

5.3.5.5.2.6 YVONNE KLINGER also went by the name of VONNIE. She was born on 9 February 1949. She married THOMAS MANLEY. Yvonne lives in Ashland, PA.

5.3.5.5.2.6.1 ANGELA MARIE KLINGER was born on 2 September 1968. She married EUGENE ZDIERA on 24 August 1991.

5.3.5.5.2.6.1.1 MICHAEL THOMAS ZDIERA was born on 23 February 1992.

5.3.5.5.2.6.2 THOMAS MANLEY II was born on 22 February 1970.

5.3.5.5.2.6.3 STEPHEN MANLEY was born on 16 February 1972.

5.3.5.5.2.7 JAMES DANIEL KLINGER was born on 24 March 1953. He married BONNIE DENGLER, daughter of ROY W. DENGLER and JERALDINE MAURER, on 1 March 1975. He died on 5 December 1992, at age 39.

5.3.5.5.2.7.1 MICHAEL DAVID KLINGER was born on 10 January 1976, Pottsville, Schuylkill County, PA. He married ANGELA DIETZ, daughter of EARL DIETZ and JOANNE CONTI. He died on 11 August 2008, at his home on Centre Street, Ashland, Schuylkill County, PA, at age 32. According to a newspaper obituary, Michael was a 1994 graduate of North Schuylkill High School.

5.3.5.5.2.7.1.1 VICTOR J. KLINGER was born on 21 June 2002, Pottsville, Schuylkill County, PA. He died on 29 January 2008, in a fire at his home, 509 Center St., Ashland, Schuylkill County, PA, at age 5. He was buried on 2 February 2008, at St. John's Cemetery, Barry Township, Schuylkill County, PA.

5.3.5.5.2.7.1.2 AUDREY D. KLINGER was born on 28 January 2005, Pottsville, Schuylkill County, PA. She died on 29 January 2008, in a fire at her home, 509 Center St., Ashland, Schuylkill County, PA, at age 3. She was buried on 2 February 2008, at St. John's Cemetery, Barry Township, Schuylkill County, PA.

5.3.5.5.2.7.1.3 GUNNAR KLINGER was born circa June 2006.

5.3.5.5.2.7.2 JEREMY JACOB KLINGER was born on 18 October 1977. Jeremy lives in Mifflinburg, PA.

5.3.5.5.2.7.3 JAROD MATTHEW KLINGER is also referred to as **JARRED** in some sources. He was born on 14 July 1980. Jarred lives in Ashland, PA.

5.3.5.5.2.7.4 CHANTELLE ALICIA KLINGER was born on 12 February 1982. Chantelle lives in Ashland, PA.

5.3.5.5.2.8 ROBERT KEITH KLINGER also went by the name of **ROCKY**. He was born on 14 June 1956, Fountain Springs, Schuylkill County, PA. He married **PATRICIA RINGO** on 12 November 1977. He married **DEBBIE APONICK** on 14 February 1991. He died on 27 June 2008, at home, 510 McKnight Street, Gordon, Schuylkill County, PA, at age 52. According to a newspaper obituary, Robert graduated from North Schuylkill High School and was employed as a materials handler for Gould's Pump Company in Ashland, PA, until his retirement.

5.3.5.5.2.8.1 DARYL ROBERT KLINGER was born on 5 April 1978. He married **ANGELA JOY EAGLE** on 27 October 2007. Daryl is an information technology professional and lives in Sanford, FL.

5.3.5.5.2.8.1.1 ALEXANDER XAVIER KLINGER also goes by the name of **ALEX**. He was born on 29 July 1997.

5.3.5.5.2.8.1.2 ZAK ALLEN KLINGER was born on 29 July 1998.

5.3.5.5.2.8.2 SHEILA GRADWELL was adopted.

5.3.5.5.2.8.3 JENNA GRADWELL was adopted.

5.3.5.5.3 HOWARD ALBERT KLINGER was born on 7 January 1911. He married **MARY JANE (--?--)**. He died on 22 April 1955, at age 44. He was buried at St. John's (Kimmel's) Evangelical Lutheran Church Cemetery, Deep Creek Valley, Barry Township, Schuylkill County, PA.

5.3.5.5.3.1 JON LEIGH KLINGER died at age 20 months. He was buried at St. John's (Kimmel's) Evangelical Lutheran Church Cemetery, Deep Creek Valley, Barry Township, Schuylkill County, PA.

5.3.5.5.4 GLADYS ELIZABETH KLINGER was born on 8 September 1915, Taylorsville, Barry Township, Schuylkill County, PA. She was baptized on 24 September 1915, St. John's (Kimmel's) German Reformed Church, Barry Township, Schuylkill County, PA. She married **KARL KEHLER** on 2 June 1935. Prior to her death, Gladys was living in or near Easton, Northampton County, PA. She died on 9 January 1998, at age 82.

5.3.5.5.4.1 JANICE CORINNE KEHLER was born on 4 March 1936. She married **ALBERT KUEBLER** on 2 June 1956.

5.3.5.5.4.1.1 BETH ANN KUEBLER was born on 11 December 1958. She married **MART DEAN VARVEL** on 16 May 1992.

5.3.5.5.4.1.2 LAURIE JO KUEBLER was born on 26 July 1962. She married **RICHARD ALAN PALMER** on 20 October 1984.

5.3.5.5.4.1.2.1 ANDREW MICHAEL PALMER was born on 26 March 1992.

5.3.5.5.4.2 KARL ROBERT KEHLER was born on 29 March 1943. He married **SUSANNE METZGAR** on 22 December 1967.

5.3.5.5.4.2.1 CARL JOSHUA KEHLER was born on 2 January 1976.

5.3.5.5.4.2.2 JEREMY JOHN KEHLER was born on 30 August 1977.

5.3.5.5.4.2.3 JENNIFER KEHLER was born on 29 May 1979.

5.3.5.5.5 FAYE FRANCES KLINGER is also referred to as **FANNIE AND FAY** in some sources. She was born on 4 August 1917. She married **ALPHONONSO MATALONAS** on 22 December 1937, Frieden's Reformed Church, Hegins, Schuylkill County, PA. She died on 22 October 1992, at age 75. She died on 2 October 1992, at age 75. Prior to her death, Faye was living in the vicinity of Ashland, Schuylkill County, PA.

5.3.5.5.5.1 GERALD MATALONAS married **ROSEMARY RAPOLI** in 1962.

5.3.5.5.5.1.1 ROSEMARY MATALONAS

5.3.5.5.5.1.2 GERALD MATALONAS

5.3.5.5.5.2 DIANE MATALONAS married DAVID MINNICK.

5.3.5.5.6 HAROLD EDWIN KLINGER was born on 28 April 1919. He married MARY JANE SCHROPE. He married IRENE E. OSMAN, daughter of ELMER OSMAN and EMMA SCHUCKER. He died on 15 April 1984, Citrus County, FL, at age 64. He was buried at Fero Memorial Gardens Cemetery, Beverly Hills, Citrus County, FL.

5.3.5.5.6.1 BONNIE KLINGER

5.3.5.5.6.2 PATRICIA KLINGER was born circa 1937. She married WILLIAM ENNIS in October 1955.

5.3.5.5.6.2.1 STEPHEN ENNIS married ROBIN (--?--).

5.3.5.5.6.2.2 INFANT DAUGHTER ENNIS was born on 7 December 1955. She died on 8 December 1955, Ashland State Hospital, Ashland, Schuylkill County, PA. She was buried on 9 December 1955, at Kimmel's Church Cemetery, Barry Township, Schuylkill County, PA.

5.3.5.5.6.2.3 SUZANNE ENNIS was born on 20 March 1957, Ashland, Schuylkill County, PA. She married HOWARD SMITH circa 1975. She died on 27 September 2009, at her home Ashland, Schuylkill County, PA, at age 52. She was buried at Brock Cemetery, Ashland, Schuylkill County, PA.

5.3.5.5.6.2.3.1 DAWN SMITH married SHAWN REED.

5.3.5.5.6.2.3.2 COURTNEY SMITH

5.3.5.5.6.2.3.3 HOWARD SMITH married CHRISTINA (--?--).

5.3.5.5.6.2.4 WILLIAM ENNIS SR. was born on 31 October 1961, Fountain Springs, Schuylkill County, PA. He married BERDINE MANHART on 10 August 1989. He died on 22 September 2015, at his home Wilberton #2, Columbia County, PA, at age 53. He was buried on 26 September 2015, at St. Joseph's Cemetery, Fountain Springs, Schuylkill County, PA.

5.3.5.5.6.2.4.1 BROOKE ENNIS

5.3.5.5.6.2.4.2 WILLIAM ENNIS JR.

5.3.5.5.6.3 CAROL ANN KLINGER was born circa 1938. She married DAVID DAVILLA in 1959.

5.3.5.5.6.4 JOHN KLINGER was born on 10 November 1947, Ashland, Schuylkill County, PA. He died on 9 July 1949, Ashland State Hospital, Ashland, Schuylkill County, PA, at age 1. He was buried on 12 July 1949, at Kimmel's Church Cemetery, Barry Township, Schuylkill County, PA.

5.3.5.5.6.5 RICK E. KLINGER married CAROL (--?--). Rick lives in Crystal River, FL.

5.3.5.5.6.5.1 MISTI KLINGER

5.3.5.5.7 NELSON DANIEL KLINGER was born on 12 September 1922. He married MARY OMLOR. He died in December 1989, at age 67.

5.3.5.5.7.1 PAMELA KLINGER

5.3.5.5.8 MARGARET JANE KLINGER is also referred to as PEGGY in some sources. She was born on 17 May 1924. She married EARL KLEWS. She died before 31 October 2007.

5.3.5.5.8.1 PEGGY KLEWS

5.3.5.5.8.2 KAREN KLEWS

5.3.5.5.8.3 EARL KLEWS JR. was born circa 1957. He died on 14 September 1963.

5.3.5.5.8.4 DEBRA KLEWS

5.3.5.5.8.5 DANIEL KLEWS

5.3.5.5.8.6 BLANCHE KLEWS

5.3.5.5.8.7 (--?--) KLEWS was born on 29 March 1963.

5.3.5.5.9 JACQUELINE JANICE KLINGER was born on 16 September 1925, Barry Township, Schuylkill County, PA. She was baptized on 6 December 1925, Frieden's Reformed Church, Hegins, Schuylkill County, PA. She married LEROY E. TROUTMAN, son of EDWIN TROUTMAN and MAMIE MAURER, on 1 July 1944. She died on 31 October 2007, Friendly Nursing Home, Pitman, Schuylkill County, PA, at age 82. According to a newspaper obituary, Jacqueline lived at

1360 Taylorsville Road, Ashland, PA. After graduating from Hegins Township High School, in the class of 1943, she was a sewing machine operator for Ashland Shirt Factory until her retirement in 1987. She was buried on 3 November 2007, at St. John's Church Cemetery, Barry Township, Schuylkill County, PA.

 5.3.5.5.9.1 **JUDITH ANN TROUTMAN** also went by the name of **JUDY**. She was born on 9 October 1944, Barry Township, Schuylkill County, PA. She married **BERNARD KLUSMAN** on 20 January 1962. She married **RICHARD W. FRITZ**.

  5.3.5.5.9.1.1 **LORI ANN KLUSMAN** was born on 19 November 1963. She married **ROBIN SMITH** on 22 May 1982.

   5.3.5.5.9.1.1.1 **STEPHANIE SMITH** died before 14 July 2006.

   5.3.5.5.9.1.1.2 **JAMIE SMITH** was born on 18 September 1983.

   5.3.5.5.9.1.1.3 **LINDSAY SMITH** was born on 3 December 1985.

  5.3.5.5.9.1.2 **BERNARD KLUSMAN** was born on 27 August 1965. He married **MICHELLE MYERS** on 18 July 1992.

   5.3.5.5.9.1.2.1 **KENDRICK KLUSMAN** died before 14 July 2006.

   5.3.5.5.9.1.2.2 **TY KLUSMAN** was born on 12 May 1980.

 5.3.5.5.9.2 **DONNA RAE TROUTMAN** was born on 22 December 1945, Barry Township, Schuylkill County, PA. She was baptized on 27 January 1946, St. John's (Kimmel's) German Reformed Church, Barry Township, Schuylkill County, PA. She married **ELVIN KRISE** on 21 March 1964.

  5.3.5.5.9.2.1 **TAMMY LYNN KRISE** was born on 6 October 1968. She married **JULIUS LYNCH** on 15 August 1992.

  5.3.5.5.9.2.2 **KELLY ANN KRISE** was born on 31 May 1970.

  5.3.5.5.9.2.3 **VICKIE SUE KRISE** was born on 19 December 1971.

 5.3.5.5.9.3 **LINDA LOU TROUTMAN** was born on 7 January 1947, Barry Township, Schuylkill County, PA. She was baptized on 6 April 1947, St. John's (Kimmel's) German Reformed Church, Barry Township, Schuylkill County, PA. She married **LOWELL ALLEN NEWTON** on 22 May 1971.

  5.3.5.5.9.3.1 **AMY LYNN NEWTON** was born on 12 February 1972.

 5.3.5.5.9.4 **KAREN LEE TROUTMAN** was born on 9 June 1951, Barry Township, Schuylkill County, PA. She married **PAUL HEPLER** on 13 May 1974.

  5.3.5.5.9.4.1 **PAUL LEROY HEPLER** was born on 23 February 1975.

  5.3.5.5.9.4.2 **HEATHER ANN HEPLER** was born on 4 December 1978.

 5.3.5.5.9.5 **SUSAN TROUTMAN** was born on 8 November 1955. She married **CHARLES KLINGER** on 18 August 1984.

  5.3.5.5.9.5.1 **MARISSA KLINGER** was born on 9 April 1998.

5.3.5.6 **MOSES KLINGER** was born on 21 December 1888, Lykens Township, Dauphin County, PA. He died on 17 March 1889, Lykens Township, Dauphin County, PA.

5.3.5.7 **OSCAR PRESTON KLINGER** was born on 18 December 1889, Lykens Township, Dauphin County, PA. He was baptized on 23 February 1890, Simeon Lutheran Church, Gratz, Dauphin County, PA. He married **KATIE ALICE KEITER**. He died on 27 April 1916, Elizabethville, Dauphin County, PA, at age 26.

5.3.5.8 **(--?--) KLINGER** was born on 16 April 1894. He died circa 1894. He was buried at St. Jacob's (Miller's) Lutheran and Reformed Church, Powell's Valley, Dauphin County, PA.

5.3.5.9 **LESTER LEROY KLINGER** was born on 6 January 1897, Lykens Township, Dauphin County, PA. Some sources record that he was born on 6 January 1899. He married **KATIE ALMEDA KLINGER**, daughter of **WILLIAM OSCAR KLINGER** and **MABEL PEARL KLINGER**, on 22 June 1918, St. Michael's Church, Klingerstown, Schuylkill County, PA. Lester and Katie were first cousins, once removed. He died on 8 January 1947, at age 50. He was buried at St. Peter's United Methodist Church Cemetery, Fearnot, Schuylkill County, PA.

 5.3.5.9.1 **GALEN OSCAR KLINGER** (see above)

  5.3.5.9.1.1 **GARY OSCAR KLINGER** (see above)

5.3.5.9.2 IDA LORETTA KLINGER (see above)
 5.3.5.9.2.1 LESTER RUFUS HARNER (see above)
  5.3.5.9.2.1.1 BRENDA LOU HARNER (see above)
  5.3.5.9.2.1.2 BRYANT KIETH HARNER (see above)
 5.3.5.9.2.2 CAROLYN DOLLY HARNER (see above)
 5.3.5.9.2.3 MARILYN IRENE HARNER (see above)
  5.3.5.9.2.3.1 THOMAS LEE SHAFFER (see above)
  5.3.5.9.2.3.2 MINDY SHAFFER (see above)
  5.3.5.9.2.3.3 TIMOTHY SHAFFER (see above)
 5.3.5.9.2.4 RICHARD DEAN HARNER (see above)
  5.3.5.9.2.4.1 RICHARD HARNER (see above)
  5.3.5.9.2.4.2 JAMES HARNER (see above)
5.3.5.9.3 MELBA K. KLINGER (see above)
 5.3.5.9.3.1 DENNIS RAY CROUTHARMEL (see above)
 5.3.5.9.3.2 LARRY CURTIS CROUTHARMEL (see above)
 5.3.5.9.3.3 TERRY GENE CROUTHARMEL (see above)
 5.3.5.9.3.4 KAREN DIANE CROUTHARMEL (see above)
 5.3.5.9.3.5 CARL ALLEN CROUTHARMEL (see above)
 5.3.5.9.3.6 DARRYL LEE CROUTHARMEL (see above)
5.3.5.9.4 CHESTER LEROY KLINGER (see above)
 5.3.5.9.4.1 JEAN PAUL KLINGER (see above)
 5.3.5.9.4.2 MICHAEL A. KLINGER (see above)
 5.3.5.9.4.3 BONITA KLINGER (see above)
 5.3.5.9.4.4 SUSAN KLINGER (see above)
 5.3.5.9.4.5 TRUDY KLINGER (see above)
 5.3.5.9.4.6 DAVID DEAN KLINGER (see above)
 5.3.5.9.4.7 STEVEN LEROY KLINGER (see above)
5.3.5.9.5 VIOLET BETTY KLINGER (see above)
 5.3.5.9.5.1 TODD B. REBUCK (see above)
  5.3.5.9.5.1.1 SHAWN REBUCK (see above)
 5.3.5.9.5.2 TONYA L. REBUCK (see above)
  5.3.5.9.5.2.1 JAYNA KATIE REINHARD (see above)
5.3.5.9.6 EILEEN MAY KLINGER (see above)
 5.3.5.9.6.1 CAROL LEITZEL (see above)
  5.3.5.9.6.1.1 KELLY YVONNE ROMBERGER (see above)
   5.3.5.9.6.1.1.1 MYKENNA ADELL MUSOLINO (see above)
  5.3.5.9.6.1.2 KRISTIE ANN ROMBERGER (see above)
 5.3.5.9.6.2 GLENN ELDON LEITZEL (see above)
  5.3.5.9.6.2.1 RAHN LEITZEL (see above)
  5.3.5.9.6.2.2 AMANDA LEITZEL (see above)
 5.3.5.9.6.3 ANNETTE ANGELA LEITZEL (see above)

5.3.5.10 FORREST EDWARD KLINGER was born on 21 May 1901, Lykens Township, Dauphin County, PA. He married **ELLEN MABEL GROFF**. He died on 30 March 1983, Polyclinic Medical Center, Harrisburg, Dauphin County, PA, at age 81. He was buried on 4 April 1983, at Maple Grove Cemetery, Elizabethville, Dauphin County, PA.

5.3.6 MARY ELLEN KLINGER was born on 10 June 1862, Lykens Township, Dauphin County, PA. She was baptized on 13 July 1862, Zion (Klinger's) Church, Erdman, Lykens Township, Dauphin County, PA. She married **JOHN S. STRAUB** circa 1884.

5.3.6.1 SAMUEL FREDERICK STRAUB is also referred to as **FRED SAMUEL STRAUB** in some sources. He was born on 26 August 1885. He was baptized on 14 September 1885, Zion (Klinger's) Church, Erdman, Lykens Township, Dauphin County, PA. He married an unknown person circa 1906. He married **MINA ESTELLA ARTZ**, daughter of **HENRY K. ARTZ** and **CHRISTIANA C. MANN,** circa 1906. He died in January 1968, at age 82.

    5.3.6.1.1 BEATRICE MAY STRAUB was born on 17 September 1907. She died on 25 October 1907, Hubley Township, Schuylkill County, PA.

    5.3.6.1.2 GEORGE H. STRAUB was born circa September 1908.

    5.3.6.1.3 MINNIE MILDRED STRAUB was born on 15 June 1910. She was baptized on 2 October 1910, Saint Pauls Lutheran and Reformed Church, Sacramento, Schuylkill County, PA. She married **NORMA R. OTTO** circa 1927.

        5.3.6.1.3.1 JANICE D. OTTO was born circa 1928.

5.3.6.2 WILLIAM ALBERT STRAUB is also referred to as **ALBERT WILLIAM** in some sources. He was born on 10 December 1888. He was baptized on 17 February 1889, Zion (Klinger's) Church, Erdman, Lykens Township, Dauphin County, PA. He married **MABEL E. HERNER** on 2 December 1913, St. Andrew's United Methodist Church, Valley View, Schuylkill County, PA. He died on 18 November 1947, Valley View, Schuylkill County, PA, at age 58. He was buried at St. Andrew's United Methodist Church Cemetery, Valley View, Schuylkill County, PA.

    5.3.6.2.1 MARY P. STRAUB was born circa 1914. She was baptized on 28 September 1914, St. Andrew's United Methodist Church, Valley View, Schuylkill County, PA.

    5.3.6.2.2 RUBY ALVENA STRAUB was born on 3 May 1915. She was baptized on 1 July 1917, St. Andrew's United Methodist Church, Valley View, Schuylkill County, PA.

    5.3.6.2.3 MAHLON WILLIAM STRAUB was born on 18 November 1919. He was baptized on 11 April 1920, St. Andrew's United Methodist Church, Valley View, Schuylkill County, PA. Prior to his death, Mahlon was living in or near Sarasota, Sarasota County, FL. He died on 15 January 1999, at age 79.

5.3.6.3 KATIE A. STRAUB is also referred to as **KATIE ANGELINE STRAUB** in some sources. She was born in November 1892. Some sources record that she was born circa 1886. She married **ANDREW CLEVELAND KOPPENHAVER**, son of **SAMUEL SYLVESTER KOPPENHAVER** and **SARAH ELMIRA JEMIMA ARTZ,** on 10 October 1911, Lutheran Parsonage, Hegins, Schuylkill County, PA. She died in 1966. She was buried at St. Paul's (Artz) Church Cemetery, Sacramento, Hubley Township, Schuylkill County, PA.

    5.3.6.3.1 CHILD KOPPENHAVER was born circa 1912, Hegins RD 1, Schuylkill County, PA. He/she died circa 1912, Hegins RD 1, Schuylkill County, PA.

    5.3.6.3.2 HELEN NAOMI KOPPENHAVER was born on 28 April 1913, Hegins RD 1, Schuylkill County, PA. She married **PAUL KLINGER**, son of **JONATHAN GRANT KLINGER** and **CORA NEUMEISTER,** on 21 June 1932. She married **EDWARD MILLER** circa 1964. She died on 18 July 1968, Pottsville, Schuylkill County, PA, at age 55.

        5.3.6.3.2.1 ELEANORE CORA KLINGER was born on 5 September 1932, Hegins, Schuylkill County, PA. She married **LLOYD FRANCIS SCHWARTZ** on 28 September 1950.

            5.3.6.3.2.1.1 LLOYD FRANCIS SCHWARTZ JR. was born on 9 November 1951, Schuylkill County, PA. He married **STEPHANIE ANN RAUDABAUCH** on 9 June 1973.

                5.3.6.3.2.1.1.1 NATHAN SCOTT SCHWARTZ was born on 7 April 1974.

                5.3.6.3.2.1.1.2 ERIC ANDREW SCHWARTZ was born on 13 April 1977.

            5.3.6.3.2.1.2 BONITA LEE SCHWARTZ was born on 30 January 1954, Pottsville, Schuylkill County, PA. She married **ARGIMIRO SANCHEZ** circa January 1992, Panama.

                5.3.6.3.2.1.2.1 GINO ANTHONY SANCHEZ was born circa 15 December 1995, LaSalle, LaSalle County, IL.

            5.3.6.3.2.1.3 RENA MARIE SCHWARTZ was born on 31 December 1962, Schuylkill County, PA. She married **BRYAN WAYNE TETER** on 13 September 1980.

                5.3.6.3.2.1.3.1 BRYAN CURTIS TETER was born on 29 September 1984.

                5.3.6.3.2.1.3.2 ANDREW PHILIP TETER was born on 7 December 1986.

                5.3.6.3.2.1.3.3 RACHEL ELINA TETER was born on 21 January 1988.

5.3.6.3.2.2 EUGENE JACKSON KLINGER was born on 11 November 1934, Schuylkill County, PA. He died on 27 February 1948, Schuylkill County, PA, at age 13.

5.3.6.3.3 RUSSELL CLEVELAND KOPPENHAVER was born on 14 December 1914, Hegins RD 1, Schuylkill County, PA. He married **MARY AMANDA COLEMAN**, daughter of **HOMER RALPH COLEMAN** and **ANETTA SALOME MAE UMHOLTZ**, on 25 June 1938. Prior to his death, "Russel" was living in or near Sacramento, Schuylkill County, PA. He died in January 1996, at age 81.

5.3.6.3.3.1 BRENDA LEE KOPPENHAVER was born on 14 August 1947. She married **TERRY JOSEPH HOFFMAN** on 3 July 1965.

5.3.6.3.3.1.1 VICKI LYNN HOFFMAN was born on 15 January 1966. She married **WILLIAM WEBER** on 9 April 1988, St. Paul's Church, Sacramento, Schuylkill County, PA.

5.3.6.3.3.1.1.1 JULIANN WEBER

5.3.6.3.3.1.1.2 JENNILYN NICHOLE WEBER was born on 25 May 1991, Pottsville, Schuylkill County, PA.

5.3.6.3.3.1.2 MICHELLE LYNN HOFFMAN was born on 5 December 1977. She married **(--?--) SMITH**.

5.3.6.3.3.1.2.1 BRAYDEN SMITH

5.3.6.3.3.1.2.2 BRODY SMITH

5.3.6.3.3.1.2.3 BRIELLE SMITH

5.3.6.3.4 HOWARD MAYNARD KOPPENHAVER was born on 12 August 1916, Hegins RD 1, Schuylkill County, PA. He married **DORIS RUTH KIMMEL**, daughter of **LESTER KIMMEL** and **BERTHA ALSPACH**, on 8 August 1946. He died on 15 March 1990, Pottsville, Schuylkill County, PA, at age 73.

5.3.6.3.4.1 CAROL ANN KOPPENHAVER also went by the name of **KOPPY**. She was born on 24 February 1947, Pottsville, Schuylkill County, PA. She married **DAVID FRANK ZIMMERMAN** on 2 July 1966. She married **RICHARD FESSLER** on 16 June 1979. She died on 14 September 2009, Reading Hospital and Medical Center, West Reading, Berks County, PA, at age 62. According to a newspaper obituary, Carol lived on N. Pine St., Tremont, PA. She had been employed by the State Department of Highways and by the former Canoe Manufacturing, Pine Grove. She was buried on 19 September 2009, at German Reformed Church Cemetery, Tremont, Schuylkill County, PA.

5.3.6.3.4.1.1 JILL DENISE ZIMMERMAN is also referred to as **JOE D.** in some sources. She was born on 9 July 1969. She married **(--?--) BAIN**. She married **(--?--) MADENFORD**.

5.3.6.3.4.1.1.1 BROOKE ELYSE BAIN was born on 19 November 1987.

5.3.6.3.4.1.2 RICHARD D. FESSLER JR. Richard was Carol's stepson.

5.3.6.3.4.1.3 MELISSA M. FESSLER. Melissa was Carol's stepdaughter. She married **(--?--) CAMPBELL**.

5.3.6.3.4.1.4 PARRISH JORDAN FESSLER was born on 27 November 1979.

5.3.6.3.4.2 LINDA KAY KOPPENHAVER was born on 31 December 1950. She married **TERRY LEE LEVAN** on 6 January 1970. She married **ROY MOWERY**. Linda lives in Huntingdon, PA.

5.3.6.3.4.2.1 NIKI LEE LEVAN was born on 6 January 1970.

5.3.6.3.4.3 FAY MARIE KOPPENHAVER was born on 24 September 1960. She married **DANIEL STEFFIE** on 28 July 1979. Fay lives in Schuylkill Haven, PA.

5.3.6.3.4.3.1 DANIEL HOWARD STEFFIE was born on 9 November 1979.

5.3.6.3.4.4 JOY SUE KOPPENHAVER was born on 23 March 1962. She married **KERRY ARTHUR THOMPSON** on 25 August 1984. Joy lives in Donaldson, PA.

5.3.6.3.4.4.1 ADAM KERRY THOMPSON was born on 21 February 1985.

5.3.6.3.4.4.2 ERIC MALCOLM THOMPSON was born on 18 April 1987.

5.3.6.3.5 CLAYTON LEROY KOPPENHAVER was born on 9 February 1918. He was born on 9 February 1918, Hegins RD 1, Schuylkill County, PA. He married **JOYCE BETTY SCHWALM**, daughter of **CALVIN FRANKLIN SCHWALM** and **IDA SOPHIA STIELY**, on 19 July 1941, St.

Andrew's Church, Valley View, Schuylkill County, PA. He lived in 201 Vaux Avenue, Tremont, Schuylkill County, PA. He died on 20 June 2000, Pottsville Hospital, Pottsville, Schuylkill County, PA, at age 82. He was buried at Church of God Cemetery, Valley View, Hegins Township, Schuylkill County, PA.

> **5.3.6.3.5.1** RONALD EUGENE KOPPENHAVER (see above)
>> **5.3.6.3.5.1.1** KELLY L. KOPPENHAVER (see above)
>
> **5.3.6.3.5.2** GARY CLAYTON KOPPENHAVER (see above)
>
> **5.3.6.3.5.3** RANDALL EARL KOPPENHAVER (see above)
>> **5.3.6.3.5.3.1** JEREMY JUSTIN KOPPENHAVER (see above)
>>
>> **5.3.6.3.5.3.2** TIMOTHY JUSTIN KOPPENHAVER (see above)
>
> **5.3.6.3.5.4** SAMUEL PERRY KOPPENHAVER (see above)
>
> **5.3.6.3.5.5** KEITH ALAN KOPPENHAVER (see above)
>
> **5.3.6.3.5.6** KATHY ANN KOPPENHAVER (see above)
>> **5.3.6.3.5.6.1** JASON ALLEN WANAMAKER (see above)
>>
>> **5.3.6.3.5.6.2** LACIE ALICE WANAMAKER (see above)
>
> **5.3.6.3.5.7** WENDY KAY KOPPENHAVER (see above)
>
> **5.3.6.3.5.8** JAMES LEE KOPPENHAVER (see above)
>> **5.3.6.3.5.8.1** STEPHANIE KAY KOPPENHAVER (see above)
>>
>> **5.3.6.3.5.8.2** MATTHEW MILES KOPPENHAVER (see above)

5.3.6.3.6 WARREN SYLVESTER KOPPENHAVER was born on 10 February 1920, Hegins RD 1, Schuylkill County, PA. He married LOUISE RITA FUHRMAN on 16 August 1944. He died on 15 December 2010, Lancaster General Hospital, Lancaster, Lancaster County, PA, at age 90. He was buried on 18 December 2010, at Chelten Hills Abbey, Philadelphia, Philadelphia County, PA. According to a newspaper obituary, Warren was a 1941 graduate of West Chester State Teacher's College with a dual degree in Science Education and Music. Warren taught Chemistry and Physics at Ridley Township High School and then became an industrial engineer for Westinghouse, where he worked for several decades before retiring before 1990. In 2006, Warren authored a book called "The Rocking Chair - A Tool for Your Health."

> **5.3.6.3.6.1** DAWN SHERRY KOPPENHAVER was born on 20 January 1953. She married ALBERT JOSEPH PEPE on 25 March 1978. She married ALBERT ARRON MAZZONE on 1 January 1983.
>> **5.3.6.3.6.1.1** DAVID WHITNEY BURTON MAZZONE was born on 17 June 1983. He married SARAH (--?--).
>>
>> **5.3.6.3.6.1.2** DANIEL WESTLEY BRANDON MAZZONE was born on 3 April 1985.
>
> **5.3.6.3.6.2** APRIL MELODY KOPPENHAVER was born on 5 December 1955. She married BARRY LEE VANAULEN on 7 August 1982. She married DAVID E. GAUL II.
>> **5.3.6.3.6.2.1** JERED LEE BRODERICK VANAULEN is also referred to as JERED KOPPENHAVER in some sources. He was born on 24 July 1992.

5.3.6.3.7 CARLOS DANIEL KOPPENHAVER was born on 5 December 1923, Hegins RD 1, Schuylkill County, PA. He married HELEN MAE ROMBERGER, daughter of HARRY CLARK ROMBERGER and MYRTLE MAE KUNTZELMAN. Carlos and his wife Helen operated a general store in Klingerstown, Schuylkill County. The store, which was the original general store in Klingerstown, was established by H.C. Romberger, Helen's father, and was later known as "Koppy's Store." He died on 25 September 1997, at age 73. He was buried at St. Michael's Church, Klingerstown, Schuylkill County, PA. The tombstone contains a World War II marker with a US Marine Corps designation. Prior to his death, Carlos was living in the vicinity of Klingerstown, Schuylkill County, PA.

> **5.3.6.3.7.1** DAVID HARRY KOPPENHAVER (see above)
>> **5.3.6.3.7.1.1** KARA KAY KOPPENHAVER (see above)
>>
>> **5.3.6.3.7.1.2** KRISTEN KYLEE KOPPENHAVER (see above)
>
> **5.3.6.3.7.2** MARY ALICE KOPPENHAVER (see above)
>> **5.3.6.3.7.2.1** CASEY ALLISON FIELD (see above)

5.3.6.3.7.2.2 LINDSEY RAGAN FIELD (see above)

5.3.6.3.7.3 REBECCA KAY KOPPENHAVER (see above)

5.3.6.3.7.3.1 KURT ROBERT KLINE (see above)

5.3.6.3.7.3.2 DREW CARLOS KLINE (see above)

5.3.6.3.7.4 JANE MARIE KOPPENHAVER (see above)

5.3.6.3.7.4.1 DANIEL THOMAS WEIGEL (see above)

5.3.6.3.7.4.2 LEAH MARIE GENEVIEVE WEIGEL (see above)

5.3.6.3.8 CHILD KOPPENHAVER was born circa 1930, Hegins RD 1, Schuylkill County, PA. He/she died circa 1930, Hegins RD 1, Schuylkill County, PA.

5.3.6.3.9 ANDREW ALFRED KOPPENHAVER was born on 2 May 1932, Hegins RD 1, Schuylkill County, PA. He married JOAN MARIE HUNTZINGER on 27 July 1957, Frieden's Lutheran Church, Hegins, Schuylkill County, PA. He died on 17 May 2015, Winchester Medical Center, Winchester, VA, at age 83. According to a newspaper obituary, Andrew worked as a coal miner before attending Penn State University and earning a degree in Electrical Engineering. He then served in the Army Reserve and was called to active duty during the Berlin crises where he served as the executive officer of a signal corps radio relay company. After his military service he worked for General Dynamics in Rochester, NY working on Anti-Submarine Warfare equipment and Tactical Air Navigation systems. Later, he was employed by the ITT Electro-Physics labs in Maryland where he worked on over-the-horizon radars. From 1975 until his retirement in 1996 he worked for the Illinois Institute of Technology at the Electromagnetic Compatibility Analysis Center in Annapolis, MD as a Research Engineer working on military exercise compatibility, NASA launch compatibility, and the Next Generation Doppler Weather Radar (NEXRAD).

Andy was also an avid genealogist compiling the data which became the basis for the publication "The Life and American Ancestry of Andrew Alfred Koppenhaver." He was buried on 13 June 2015, at Lutheran Memorial Garden of Mount Hebron Cemetery, Winchester, VA.

5.3.6.3.9.1 ANDREW ALAN KOPPENHAVER was born on 16 May 1959, Rochester, Monroe County, NY. He married SUSANA ALATORRE PELAYO on 28 May 1983, Bowie, Prince George's County, MD.

5.3.6.3.9.1.1 BENJAMIN ANDREW KOPPENHAVER was born on 2 April 1991, Reston, Fairfax County, VA.

5.3.6.3.9.1.2 REBECCA ANNE KOPPENHAVER was born on 14 January 1994, Reston, Fairfax County, VA.

5.3.6.3.9.2 MARK DAVID KOPPENHAVER was born on 12 September 1961, Rochester, Monroe County, NY. He married BRENDA ANN WATSON on 23 August 1986, Mormon Church, Bowie, Prince George's County, MD.

5.3.6.3.9.2.1 KRISTY ANN KOPPENHAVER was born on 30 January 1987, Annapolis, Anne Arundel County, MD.

5.3.6.3.9.2.2 KYLE REED KOPPENHAVER was born on 18 January 1989, Annapolis, Anne Arundel County, MD.

5.3.6.3.9.2.3 HUNTER DAVID KOPPENHAVER was born on 1 November 1995, Leesburg, Loudoun County, VA.

5.3.6.3.9.3 TIMOTHY JAY KOPPENHAVER was born on 1 December 1964, Cheverly, Prince George's County, MD. He married ALLISON JAYE MITCHELL on 23 May 1987, Purcellville, Loudoun County, VA.

5.3.6.3.9.3.1 BROOKE KATHRYN KOPPENHAVER was born on 13 May 1990, Leesburg, Loudoun County, VA.

5.3.6.3.9.3.2 COLLEEN MORGAN KOPPENHAVER was born on 15 October 1992, Leesburg, Loudoun County, VA.

5.3.6.4 MOSES HOMER STRAUB was born in February 1895. Some sources identify Moses Homer Straub with a Samuel Homer Straub, who is buried at Klinger's Church. That Homer died 22 Sep. 1944. From the age given at his death in the Church Records, Samuel Homer would have been born on 6 Sep. 1895. The 1930 Census for Lykens Township lists a Homer S. Straub, born c. 1895, as married to Katie A., age 32. According to the Census listings, they were married around 1917. The Klinger's

Church records list a marriage for a Homer S. Straub and Katie A. Deibert on 4 Mar. 1916. According to the 1920 Census, however, M. Homer Straub was still single and living with his parents in Hubley Township, Schuylkill County. For this reason, it appears that the Samuel Homer Straub buried at Klinger's Church is a different person and was not the son of Mary Ellen Klinger and John S. Straub. The Social Security Death Index contains a listing for a "Moses Straub," born 8 Feb 1895, died Nov 1979 in Lebanon, Lebanon County, PA.

5.3.6.5 MAUDY HANNAH STRAUB was born on 25 January 1897. She was baptized on 15 May 1897, Zion (Klinger's) Church, Erdman, Lykens Township, Dauphin County, PA.

5.3.7 MINNIE KLINGER was born circa 1863.

5.3.8 SAM BRADY KLINGER is also referred to as **BRADY SAM** in some sources. He was born on 14 June 1866, Lykens Township, Dauphin County, PA. He was baptized on 4 November 1866, Zion (Klinger's) Church, Erdman, Lykens Township, Dauphin County, PA. He married **MARY ELIZABETH WILLIARD**, daughter of **GEORGE D. WILLIARD** and **AMANDA MILLER**, circa 1886. He died on 2 July 1949, Williamstown, Dauphin County, PA, at age 83. He was buried on 5 July 1949, at Fairview Cemetery, Williamstown, Dauphin County, PA.

5.3.8.1 ARTHUR E. KLINGER is also referred to as **ARTIE ALONZO KLINGER** in some sources. He also went by the name of **ARDIE**. He was born on 10 July 1889, Gratz, Dauphin County, PA. He was baptized on 18 October 1889, Simeon Lutheran Church, Gratz, Dauphin County, PA. Some sources record that he was born on 10 July 1888. He married **PEARL E. PAUL**, daughter of **MILTON J. PAUL** and **AGNES RUBENDALL**. He died on 28 October 1950, Williams Township, Dauphin County, PA, at age 62.

5.3.8.2 MILLY BUELLA KLINGER is also referred to as **MILDRED P.** in some sources. She was born on 28 May 1893. She was baptized on 16 July 1893, Zion (Klinger's) Church, Erdman, Lykens Township, Dauphin County, PA.

5.3.8.3 EMMA LOUISA KLINGER was born on 7 October 1898. She was baptized on 2 April 1899, Zion (Klinger's) Church, Erdman, Lykens Township, Dauphin County, PA. Some sources record that she was born in October 1899. She married **NORMAN C. HETRICK** circa 1924. She died in September 1978, at age 79. She was buried at Valhalla Memory Gardens, Bloomington, Monroe County, IN.

5.3.8.3.1 JANE HETRICK was born circa 1924.

5.3.8.3.2 CHARLES HETRICK was born circa 1931.

5.3.8.4 CHARLES HARVEY KLINGER was born on 16 September 1900. He was baptized on 4 March 1901, Zion (Klinger's) Church, Erdman, Lykens Township, Dauphin County, PA.

5.3.8.5 HARRY WALTER KLINGER was born on 11 October 1909, Williamstown, Dauphin County, PA. He was baptized on 17 July 1910, Immanuel Evangelical Lutheran Church, Williamstown, Dauphin County, PA. He married **MILDRED M. KLINGER**, daughter of **JAMES ARTHUR KLINGER** and **MABEL E. SNYDER**. He died in 1978. He was buried at Mellinger Mennonite Cemetery, Lancaster, Lancaster County, PA.

5.3.8.5.1 JAMES H. KLINGER (see above)

5.3.8.5.1.1 ROBERT KLINGER (see above)

5.3.8.5.1.2 NANCY ANN KLINGER (see above)

5.3.8.5.2 MARTHA JEAN KLINGER (see above)

5.3.9 ANNA CEBILLA KLINGER is also referred to as **EMMA CEBILLA AND EMMA S.** in some sources. She was born on 19 August 1875. She was baptized on 6 November 1878, Zion (Klinger's) Church, Erdman, Lykens Township, Dauphin County, PA. She married **NATHAN A. KLINGER**, son of **J. HENRY KLINGER** and **KATE SCHADEL**. She died on 15 August 1897, Erdman, Lykens Township, Dauphin County, PA, at age 21. Anna died soon after the birth of her second child.

5.3.9.1 EDWIN RAY KLINGER was born on 31 October 1894. He married **VERDIE MINNIE MAUSSER**, daughter of **JACOB MAUSSER** and **AMANDA PAUL**, on 15 December 1915, Zion (Klinger's) Church, Erdman, Lykens Township, Dauphin County, PA. He died on 11 November 1981, at age 87. He was buried on 13 November 1987, at Zion (Klinger's) Church, Erdman, Lykens Township, Dauphin County, PA.

5.3.9.1.1 MAE ELIZABETH KLINGER was born on 18 August 1925. She was baptized on 17 January 1926, Zion (Klinger's) Church, Erdman, Lykens Township, Dauphin County, PA. She married **LEROY C. SMELTZ**, son of **ROY SCHMELTZ** and **VERNA WAGNER**. She died on 28

March 1981, at age 55. She was buried on 31 March 1981, at Zion (Klinger's) Church, Erdman, Lykens Township, Dauphin County, PA.

    5.3.9.1.1.1 JOYCE SMELTZ married **LYNN DEITRICH**.

    5.3.9.1.1.2 NANCY SMELTZ married **JIM HALLOWELL**.

5.3.9.2 GEORGE FRANKLIN KLINGER is also referred to as **GEORGE B. KLINGER** in some sources. He was born on 2 August 1897, Lykens Township, Dauphin Co., PA. He was baptized on 17 August 1897, Zion (Klinger's) Lutheran Church, Erdman, Dauphin Co., PA. Some sources record that he was born on 1 August 1897. After his mother died in childbirth, George was raised by his mother's sister Mary (Mrs. Daniel Kissinger), while his brother Edwin stayed with his grandparents. He married **NETTIE E. SCHEIB**, daughter of **WILLIAM H. SCHIEB** and **ANNA ELISABETH KISSINGER**, on 16 November 1918, Simeon Lutheran Church, Gratz, Dauphin County, PA. He died in March 1984, at age 86. He was buried at Gratz, Dauphin County, PA.

    5.3.9.2.1 INFANT DAUGHTER KLINGER was born in 1920, Dauphin Co., PA. She died in 1920, Dauphin Co., PA.

    5.3.9.2.2 MARIE EMMA KLINGER was born on 8 February 1923, Gratz, Montour County, PA. She was baptized on 11 March 1923, Simeon Lutheran Church, Gratz, Dauphin County, PA. She married **GILBERT CHARLES KOPPENHAVER**, son of **BENJAMIN HARRISON KOPPENHAVER** and **VERNA CARL**, on 9 October 1943, Simeon Lutheran Church, Gratz, Dauphin County, PA.

        5.3.9.2.2.1 GARY GILBERT KOPPENHAVER was born on 8 April 1945. He was baptized on 18 April 1945, Simeon Lutheran Church, Gratz, Dauphin County, PA. He married **CAROL ANN KOCHER**, daughter of **KENNETH KERMIT KOCHER** and **MARIE ELEANOR REISH**.

            5.3.9.2.2.1.1 STACY KOPPENHAVER was born on 5 February 1970, Dauphin Co., PA.

        5.3.9.2.2.2 BRUCE CARL KOPPENHAVER was born on 24 September 1949, Montour County, PA. He was baptized on 30 October 1949, Simeon Lutheran Church, Gratz, Dauphin County, PA. He married **LINDA NEY** circa 1972.

            5.3.9.2.2.2.1 NICOLE KOPPENHAVER was born circa 1974, PA.

        5.3.9.2.2.3 JANE KOPPENHAVER was born on 30 March 1953, Dauphin County, PA. She married **RODNEY LEE SHADE**, son of **JACK EUGENE SHADE SR.** and **JANICE KISSINGER**, circa 1973.

            5.3.9.2.2.3.1 TARA JANE SHADE was born on 12 October 1976, Dauphin County, PA.

            5.3.9.2.2.3.2 MATTHEW RODNEY SHADE was born on 28 December 1977, Dauphin County, PA. He married **MEGAN (--?--)**.

    5.3.9.2.3 GLENN R. KLINGER married **GLORIA SPOTTS**, daughter of **CARL SPOTTS** and **ETHEL BOWER**. He married **GLORIA SPOTTS** PA. He was born circa 1925, Gratz, Dauphin Co., PA.

        5.3.9.2.3.1 SCOTT KLINGER

        5.3.9.2.3.2 STEVEN KLINGER

        5.3.9.2.3.3 KEITH KLINGER married **BARBARA FERSTER**.

        5.3.9.2.3.4 SCOTT KLINGER was born circa 1946, Dauphin Co., PA.

        5.3.9.2.3.5 STEVEN KLINGER was born circa 1948, Dauphin Co., PA.

        5.3.9.2.3.6 KEITH R KLINGER was born on 29 October 1967, PA. He married **BARBARA A. FERSTER** circa 1997, PA.

            5.3.9.2.3.6.1 (--?--) KLINGER was born on 5 October 1999, Polyclinic Hospital, Harrisburg, Dauphin Co., PA.

    5.3.9.2.4 RUSSELL WILLIAM KLINGER was born on 26 July 1927, Gratz, Dauphin Co., PA. He was baptized on 4 September 1927, Simeon Lutheran Church, Gratz, Dauphin County, PA. He died on 19 September 1938, Dauphin County, PA, at age 11. He was buried at Simeon United Lutheran Church Cemetery, Gratz, Dauphin Co., PA.

5.4 SAMUEL KLINGER was born on 27 April 1830, Lykens Township, Dauphin County, PA. He was baptized on 27 June 1830, Zion (Klinger's) Church, Erdman, Lykens Township, Dauphin County, PA. He married **CATHERINE WILLIARD**, daughter of **JOHN L. WILLIARD** and **MARY WIEST**, circa 1855, Dauphin, Dauphin County, PA. Samuel was also a grist mill operator in the Klingerstown area. He died before 1900.

    5.4.1 ENJALINE KLINGER is also referred to as **ANGELINE, ANJELINE, AND ANNA** in some sources. She was born on 26 July 1856, Lykens Township, Dauphin County, PA. She was baptized on 7 September

1856, Zion (Klinger's) Church, Erdman, Lykens Township, Dauphin County, PA. She married **LEO REEDINGER**, son of **FREDOLINE REEDINGER** and **EPHRACINA (--?--)**, in 1884. Some sources suggest that she and **LEO REEDINGER** were married in 1876. The Census records for the Wiconisco area of Dauphin County list a couple named Anna and Leo Readinger (variously spelled) from 1900 through 1930. According to the 1880 Census, Leo was born in Baden, Germany around 1864, to Fredoline (age 60) and Ephracina (age 62) Reatdinger, both of whom were born in Baden, Germany. Fredoline was a shoemaker. If this Leo Readinger was Angeline's husband, they were likely married after 1880, probably around 1884. The 1900 Census lists a household for Leo (age 36) and Annie Riedinger (age 44) that included 5 children: August, 15; James L., 13; Samuel M., 12; Julia K., 9; and Laura M., 2. Leo was listed as working at a coal mine. The 1910 Census lists Leo and Anna Reedinger as married 25 years. Anna had given birth to 8 children, 6 of whom were then living. Leo was working as a coal miner. Leo and Annie were living with 5 of their children: August M., 25; James L., 23; Samuel A., 22; Julia L., 20; and Laura M., 12. By 1920, Leo and Anna's household included just August and Laura. August was a laborer for a contractor, while Laura was a "looper" in a hosiery mill. The birth dates given for Anna in these Census listings are consistent with the birth date of Angeline Klinger, and it is likely she who is referred to in these listings.

    5.4.1.1 AUGUST M. REEDINGER was born circa 1884.

    5.4.1.2 JAMES L. REEDINGER was born circa 1886.

    5.4.1.3 SAMUEL M. REEDINGER was born circa 1887.

    5.4.1.4 JULIA K. REEDINGER was born circa 1890.

    5.4.1.5 LAURA M. REEDINGER was born circa 1897.

5.4.2 MARIA ANNA KLINGER is also referred to as **MARY** in some sources. She was born on 4 May 1859. She was baptized on 14 August 1859, Zion (Klinger's) Church Cemetery, Erdman, Lykens Township, Dauphin County, PA. She married **GABRIEL MILLER** circa 1879.

    5.4.2.1 BERTHA M. MILLER was born in December 1881.

    5.4.2.2 JAMES A. MILLER was born in December 1885.

    5.4.2.3 NEWTON WILLIAMS MILLER was born on 11 November 1888. He was baptized on 18 February 1889, Zion (Klinger's) Church, Erdman, Lykens Township, Dauphin County, PA. He married **LIZZIE ARTZ** on 19 February 1910, Zion (Klinger's) Church, Erdman, Lykens Township, Dauphin County, PA.

    5.4.2.4 NOLEN EDWARD MILLER was born circa 5 December 1891, Lykens Township, Dauphin County, PA. He died on 8 April 1938, Hubley Township, Schuylkill County, PA. Nolen was a miner.

    5.4.2.5 HARRY R. MILLER was born in July 1896.

5.4.3 EMMA EMELIA KLINGER is also referred to as **EMMA EMILIE** in some sources. She was born on 23 June 1861, Lykens Township, Dauphin County, PA. She was baptized on 29 September 1861, Zion (Klinger's) Church, Erdman, Lykens Township, Dauphin County, PA.

5.4.4 ELIZABETH ELLEN KLINGER is also referred to as **ELISABETH ALLENS** in some sources. She was born on 9 July 1864, Lykens Township, Dauphin County, PA. She was baptized on 11 September 1864, Zion (Klinger's) Church, Erdman, Lykens Township, Dauphin County, PA.

5.4.5 GEORGE BRADY KLINGER was born on 30 January 1867, Lykens Township, Dauphin County, PA. He was baptized on 19 May 1867, Zion (Klinger's) Church, Erdman, Lykens Township, Dauphin County, PA. He married **ELLEN JANE SNYDER** circa 1887, PA. He died on 22 December 1949, Dauphin County, PA, at age 82. He was buried at Calvary United Methodist Cemetery, Wiconisco, Dauphin County, PA.

    5.4.5.1 GEORGE MORRIS KLINGER was born on 3 October 1889, Wiconisco, Dauphin Co., PA. He was baptized on 24 October 1891, Lykens Circuit Evangelical Congregational Church, Dauphin Co., PA. He married **MARY CELESTA METZ**, daughter of **WILLIAM HENRY METZ** and **MAGDALENA AMELIA LENTZ**, in 1910. He married **MINNIE M. BERKEBILE**, daughter of **WILLIAM BERKEBILE**, before 1930. He died on 17 May 1934, Schuylkill County, PA, at age 44.

        5.4.5.1.1 GEORGE WILLIAM KLINGER was born circa April 1910. He was born on 11 April 1910, Wiconisco, Dauphin Co., PA. He was baptized on 29 May 1910, St. John's (Hill) Lutheran Church, near Berrysburg, Dauphin Co., PA. He married **THELMA CARDELLA KOCHER** on 6 July 1929, St. John's (Hill) Lutheran Church, near Berrysburg, Dauphin Co., PA. He married **DORA T. SHOMPER** on 12 April 1975, PA. He died on 17 December 2000, Susquehanna Lutheran Village, Millersburg, Dauphin Co., PA. He was buried after 27 December 2000.

5.4.5.1.1.1 CAROLYN LOIS KLINGER was born on 11 November 1939, Dauphin Co., PA. She was baptized on 10 December 1939, St. John's (Hill) Lutheran Church, near Berrysburg, Dauphin Co., PA. She married **DONALD ERENBERG** circa 1960.

5.4.5.1.1.1.1 RICHARD MARK ERENBERG was born on 17 April 1962.

5.4.5.1.1.1.2 JOAN ERENBERG was born on 22 February 1968.

5.4.5.1.1.2 NEALE E. KLINGER was born on 30 July 1943, Dauphin Co., PA. He married **JUDY TARBUTTON** circa 1968. He died on 17 October 1976, Dauphin Co., PA, at age 33. He was buried after 17 October 1976, at St Peter's (Hoffman's) Church Cemetery in Lykens Township, Dauphin Co., PA.

5.4.5.1.1.3 CHARLOTTE KLINGER was born on 20 June 1945, Dauphin Co., PA. She married **PAUL CHRIST** circa 1963. She married **(--?--) GOMEZ** after 1965.

5.4.5.1.1.3.1 NICHOLAS MARTIN CHRIST was born on 15 January 1965.

5.4.5.1.2 LUELLA KLINGER was born on 4 October 1911, Tower City, Schuylkill County, PA. She married **(--?--) UMBERGER** circa 1932.

5.4.5.1.3 VIOLET KLINGER was born on 28 March 1915, Schuylkill County, PA. She married **(--?--) SHUEY** circa 1935.

5.4.5.1.4 EARL ERNEST KLINGER was born on 17 May 1917, Kantner, Schuylkill County, PA. He married **JUNE M. CARL**, daughter of **WALTER LAWRENCE CARL** and **KATIE M. KAHLER**. He died on 2 June 1959, VA Hospital, Lebanon County, PA, at age 42. He was buried at Greenwood Cemetery, Tower City, Schuylkill County, PA.

5.4.5.1.4.1 KAY LORRAINE KLINGER was born in 1947. She married **BARRY PAUL KLINGER**, son of **PAUL CLINTON KLINGER** and **JENNIE MAE KEENE**.

5.4.5.1.4.1.1 PAMELA M. KLINGER was born in 1964. She married **PHILIP SCOTT FETTERHOFF** on 26 October 1985, Schuylkill County, PA.

5.4.5.1.5 VIVIAN D. KLINGER was born in 1918, Schuylkill County, PA. She married **MARK ADAMS** circa 1938.

5.4.5.1.5.1 ROBERT ADAMS. Robert lives in Tamaqua, PA.

5.4.5.1.5.2 LEONARD ROY ADAMS was born on 25 September 1944, Tower City, Schuylkill County, PA. He married **MARIAN (--?--)**. He died on 27 December 2011, Monticello, KY, at age 67. According to a newspaper obituary, Leonard was a Navy veteran who then worked for the USDA Soil Conservation Division until his retirement. He lived in Monticello, KY.

5.4.5.1.6 VERNON L. KLINGER. Some sources indicate that Vernon was the son of George Morris Klinger. Based on Census records, Vernon would likely have been born after 1930. He married **JEAN M. O'NEILL**, daughter of **JOSEPH O'NEILL** and **JULIA NICKLO**, circa 1956.

5.4.5.1.6.1 CAROLE A. KLINGER. Carole lives in Harrisburg, PA.

5.4.5.1.6.2 KAREN J. KLINGER. Karen lives in New Cumberland, PA.

5.4.5.1.6.3 KAY M. KLINGER married **(--?--) LIVELSBERGER**. Kay lives in Mt. Joy, PA.

5.4.5.1.6.4 CARL L. KLINGER. Carl lives in Tower City, PA.

5.4.5.1.6.5 CHRIS V. KLINGER. Chris lives in Tower City, PA.

5.4.5.2 MYRL E. KLINGER was born on 10 December 1890. She died on 30 August 1898, at age 7. She was buried at Calvary United Methodist Church Cemetery, Wiconisco, Dauphin County, PA.

5.4.5.3 WALTER ROHRMAN KLINGER was born on 31 March 1893, Wiconisco, Dauphin County, PA. He married **OLIVE ANN ELIZABETH WATERS**. He died on 16 February 1941, Wiconisco, Dauphin County, PA, at age 47, from miner's asthma. He was buried at Calvary United Methodist Church Cemetery, Wiconisco, Dauphin County, PA.

5.4.5.3.1 GEORGE KLINGER was born circa 1915.

5.4.5.3.2 EVELYN KLINGER was born circa 1917. She married **ALBERT PARSONS**. She died before 2015.

5.4.5.3.2.1 RONALD PARSONS was born circa 1933. He died before 2015.

5.4.5.3.2.2 EVELYN FAY PARSONS was born on 7 October 1937, Wiconisco, Dauphin County, PA. She married **(--?--) NEITER**. She died on 15 March 2015, Wiconisco, Dauphin

County, PA, at age 77. She was buried at Calvary United Methodist Church Cemetery, Wiconisco, Dauphin County, PA.

> **5.4.5.3.2.2.1 THOMAS H. NEITER**
>
> **5.4.5.3.2.2.2 TIMOTHY A. NEITER**
>
> **5.4.5.3.2.2.3 DEBRA F. NEITER** married (--?--) **HELMAN**.
>
> **5.4.5.3.2.2.4 KATHY L. NEITER** married (--?--) **CAWTHERN**.

5.4.5.3.2.3 DOROTHY PARSONS was born after 1939. She married (--?--) **GEPHART**.

5.4.5.3.3 ARLENE KLINGER was born circa 1919.

5.4.5.3.4 ROBERT KLINGER was born circa 1922.

5.4.5.3.5 WILLIAM KLINGER was born circa 1927.

5.4.5.3.6 EUGENE DAVID KLINGER was born on 27 August 1930, Dauphin County, PA. He died on 22 January 1955, Wiconisco, Dauphin County, PA, at age 24 in a house fire. He was buried at Calvary United Methodist Church Cemetery, Wiconisco, Dauphin County, PA.

5.4.5.3.7 JOYCE MARIE KLINGER was born on 3 August 1933, Wiconisco, Dauphin County, PA. She married **GEORGE THOMAS WHEATCROFT JR.** According to some sources, Joyce moved to Michigan in 1956. She died on 22 July 2002, Pontiac, Oakland County, MI, at age 68. She was buried at White Chapel Memorial Park Cemetery, Troy, Oakland County, MI.

> **5.4.5.3.7.1 GEORGE THOMAS WHEATCROFT III** was born on 14 March 1960, Pontiac, Oakland County, MI. He died on 26 September 2002, Lake Orion, Oakland County, MI, at age 42. He was buried at Christian Memorial Cultural Center Cemetery, Rochester Hills, Oakland County, MI.

5.4.5.4 SAMUEL TYRUS KLINGER was born on 23 December 1894.

5.4.5.5 HARRY L. KLINGER was born in October 1899. He died before 1910.

5.4.5.6 JOHN F. KLINGER was born on 26 August 1901. He died on 3 October 1907, at age 6. He was buried at Calvary United Methodist Church Cemetery, Wiconisco, Dauphin County, PA.

5.4.5.7 LEROY KLINGER was born on 29 March 1904. He died on 7 November 1904. He was buried at Calvary United Methodist Church Cemetery, Wiconisco, Dauphin County, PA.

5.4.5.8 EVA KLINGER was born circa 1905.

5.4.5.9 INFANT KLINGER was born in October 1910. He died on 8 October 1910. He was buried at Calvary United Methodist Church Cemetery, Wiconisco, Dauphin County, PA.

5.4.5.10 IRA G. KLINGER was born circa 1911.

5.4.6 JOHN FRANCIS KLINGER is also referred to as **FRANCIS** in some sources. He was born on 31 March 1870, Lykens Township, Dauphin County, PA. He married **LYDIA MC CLADE MILLER** circa 1893, PA.

5.4.6.1 VERNA V. KLINGER was born circa 1903.

5.4.6.2 STELLA I. KLINGER was born circa 1905.

5.4.7 JULIA KLINGER is also referred to as **JULIANN** in some sources. She was born on 5 January 1873, Lykens Township, Dauphin County, PA. She married **WILLIAM GRELL** circa 1893.

5.4.8 SAMUEL MORRIS KLINGER is also referred to as **SAMUEL B.** in some sources. He was born on 17 March 1874, Wiconisco, Dauphin County, PA. He was baptized on 14 May 1874, Zion (Klinger's) Church, Erdman, Lykens Township, Dauphin County, PA. He married **ELEANOR EDWARDS**, daughter of **THOMAS EDWARDS** and **MARY COLLIER**, on 19 September 1893, Wiconisco, Dauphin County, PA. He died on 15 December 1943, at age 69. He was buried at Wiconisco, PA.

5.4.8.1 RUTH DEVONA KLINGER was born on 20 May 1910, Wiconisco, Dauphin County, PA. Some sources record that she was born on 10 May 1910, Wiconisco, Dauphin County, PA. She married **VERNON CHARLES GOODLING**, son of **HENRY K. GOODLING** and **IDA SELENA MATTER**, on 9 November 1927. She died on 10 July 1960, Harrisburg Hospital, Harrisburg, Dauphin County, PA, at age 50. She was buried on 13 July 1960, at Oak Hill Cemetery, Millersburg, Dauphin County, PA.

> **5.4.8.1.1 VERNON HAROLD GOODLING** was born on 10 May 1927, Wiconisco, Dauphin County, PA. He married **BETTY JANE BACHTELL** circa 1950. He died on 18 February 2008, Quincy Village Nursing Home, Quincy, Franklin County, PA, at age 80. He was buried on 23 February 2008, at Oak Hill Cemetery Mausoleum, Millersburg, Dauphin County, PA.
>
> > **5.4.8.1.1.1 LONNIE ALLEN GOODLING** was born on 4 September 1952, Dauphin Co., PA.

5.4.8.1.1.2 DEBRA MARLENE GOODLING married (--?--) JONES.

5.4.8.1.1.3 JACK RICHARDSON GOODLING is also referred to as JACK R. BACHTELL SR. in some sources. He was born on 15 August 1946, Hagerstown, Washington County, MD. He married TERRY L. WALBORN circa 1966. He died on 5 February 2014, Harrisburg Hospital, Harrisburg, Dauphin County, PA, at age 67. He was buried on 8 February 2014, at Riverview Memorial Gardens, Halifax, Dauphin County, PA.

5.4.8.1.1.3.1 BRENDA BACHTELL married DON MASLIN.

5.4.8.1.1.3.2 JACK R. BACHTELL JR.

5.4.8.1.1.3.3 RONALD BACHTELL

5.4.8.1.1.3.4 LEVI BACHTELL

5.4.8.2 HAYDEN MORRIS KLINGER was born on 12 November 1894, Lykens, Dauphin County, PA. He married JULIA KATHARINE REEDINGER on 10 June 1920. He died on 2 February 1940, at age 45.

5.4.8.2.1 DOROTHY ANNA KLINGER was born on 23 April 1923. She married GEORGE DAVID ADAMS on 29 August 1943.

5.4.8.2.1.1 CONNIE LEE ADAMS was born on 1 May 1948. She married GERALD LEROY GILBERT on 9 July 1966.

5.4.8.2.1.1.1 JOHN DAVID GILBERT was born on 10 August 1967.

5.4.8.2.1.1.2 TERESA LOUISE GILBERT was born on 18 April 1969. She married DOUGLAS SCOTT UNDERKOFFLER on 28 June 1986.

5.4.8.2.1.1.2.1 REBECCA LYNN UNDERKOFFLER was born on 25 September 1986.

5.4.8.2.1.2 DAVID EARL ADAMS was born on 27 July 1953. He married LINDA MARIA RHODY on 23 March 1980.

5.4.8.2.1.2.1 LISA MARIE ADAMS was born on 6 October 1980.

5.4.8.2.1.2.2 LAMAR DAVID ADAMS was born on 4 December 1982.

5.4.8.2.1.2.3 KIMBERLY ANN ADAMS was born on 10 January 1985.

5.4.8.2.2 ARLENE JUNE KLINGER was born on 15 February 1927, Wiconisco, Dauphin County, PA. She married CARL EDWIN DEITRICH SR., son of HARRY CARL DIETRICH and DORA SHILEY, on 12 November 1944. She died on 29 November 2013, Tremont Health and Rehabilitation Center, Tremont, Schuylkill County, PA, at age 86.

5.4.8.2.2.1 CAROL DEITRICH married CLARK ENDERS. She was born on 15 June 1944.

5.4.8.2.2.1.1 KEN ENDERS

5.4.8.2.2.1.2 TAMMY ENDERS

5.4.8.2.2.1.3 KENNY (--?--) was born on 16 February 1966.

5.4.8.2.2.1.4 TAMMY (--?--) was born on 23 January 1969.

5.4.8.2.2.2 SHIRLEY DEITRICH was born on 1 June 1948.

5.4.8.2.2.3 BOBBY DEITRICH was born on 23 August 1952.

5.4.8.2.2.4 CARL E. DEITRICH JR. was born on 16 December 1953. He married CHRYSTAL CREDITROLE. He married FEYE MESSNER, daughter of JERRY MESSNER.

5.4.8.2.2.4.1 HEATH DEITRICH

5.4.8.2.2.5 MILDRED DEITRICH was born on 1 February 1957. She married CARL BETTINGER JR.

5.4.8.2.3 ROBERT HAYDEN KLINGER was born circa 1920. Some sources record that he was born on 28 May 1927. He married MILDRED VAN BEHAN.

5.4.8.3 LESTER SAMUEL KLINGER was born on 27 May 1899, Lykens, Dauphin County, PA. He was unmarried. He died on 26 May 1958, Wiconisco, Dauphin County, PA, at age 58. He was buried at Calvary United Methodist Church Cemetery, Wiconisco, Dauphin County, PA.

5.4.8.4 HOMER LEE KLINGER was born in November 1896. Some sources record that he was born on 17 November 1889, Wiconisco, PA. He married KATHERINE ADELAIDE GOEHRINGER, daughter of HENRY GOTTLIEB GOEHRINGER and SARAH ADELAIDE KEYS, circa 1919, Elkton, MD. He died on 1 April 1956, at age 66. He was buried at Bethel Cemetery, Camden, NJ.

5.4.8.4.1 MARIAN ADELAIDE KLINGER was born on 24 September 1920, Philadelphia, Philadelphia County, PA. Some sources record that she was born on 4 September 1921, Philadelphia, PA. She was unmarried. She died on 19 October 1995, in New Jersey, at age 75. She was buried at Bethel Memorial Park, Pennsauken, Camden County, NJ.

5.4.8.4.2 DORIS ETHEL KLINGER was born on 8 January 1923, Philadelphia, PA. She married **HENRY FRANKLIN SHARP** on 4 October 1941.

5.4.8.4.3 WILLIAM HOMER KLINGER was born on 16 February 1925, Philadelphia, PA. He married **ELEANORE POWELL** on 6 December 1947.

5.4.8.4.4 ESTHER JULIA KLINGER was born circa 1928. Some sources record that she was born on 23 October 1923, Philadelphia, PA. She married **FRANK DAVIS MEDD** on 4 August 1956.

5.4.8.5 MYRON FREDERICK KLINGER was born on 24 June 1901, Wiconisco, Dauphin County, PA. He married **MARY FORNEY** circa 1923. He and **MARY FORNEY** were divorced before 1930. He died on 27 November 1932, State Hospital, Harrisburg, Dauphin County, PA, at age 31.

5.4.8.6 CARL COLLIER KLINGER was born on 15 August 1903. He married **VERNA ADELINE EVITTS**, daughter of **WILLIAM EVITTS** and **ADELINE DAVIDS**, circa 1924. He married **EDNA C. MORRIS** after 1938. He died in July 1978, at age 74. He was buried at Woodlawn Memorial Gardens, Harrisburg, Dauphin County, PA.

5.4.8.6.1 EVELYN KLINGER was born circa 1924.

5.4.8.6.2 PHYLLIS KLINGER was born circa 1925.

5.4.8.7 MARY KATHERINE KLINGER was born on 8 June 1907, Wiconisco, Dauphin County, PA. She married **ROY AMBROSE MACHAMER**, son of **JOHN A. MACHAMER** and **SARA E. (--?--)**, circa 1921. Some sources suggest that she and **ROY AMBROSE MACHAMER** were married in 1922. She died on 7 June 1990, Community General Osteopathic Hospital, Harrisburg, Dauphin County, PA, at age 82. She was buried at Blue Ridge Memorial Gardens, Harrisburg, Dauphin County, PA.

5.4.8.8 FLORIS KLINGER was born on 17 July 1908, Wiconisco, Dauphin County, PA. She died on 18 March 1910, Wiconisco, Dauphin County, PA, at age 1. She was buried at Calvary United Methodist Church Cemetery, Wiconisco, Dauphin County, PA.

5.4.8.9 ETHEL ARLINE KLINGER was born on 10 April 1914, Wiconisco, Dauphin County, PA. She married **DONALD KATERMAN HUNTER**. She died on 27 June 1991, Nashville, Davidson County, TN, at age 77. She was buried on 30 June 1991, at Greenwood Cemetery, Tower City, Schuylkill County, PA.

5.4.8.9.1 RUTH HUNTER married **(--?--) CHYKE**.

5.4.8.10 SAMUEL RAY KLINGER was born on 6 December 1917, Wiconisco, Dauphin Co., PA. Some sources record that he was born on 6 December 1912. He married **FLORA ADELINE BEVANS** circa 1944, Washington, D.C. He died on 18 January 1971, Veterans Hospital, Lebanon, Lebanon County, PA, at age 53. He was buried at Ft. Indiantown Gap National Cemetery, Annville, Lebanon Co., PA.

5.4.8.10.1 MADELINE C. KLINGER is also referred to as in some sources. She was born on 28 June 1946, Dauphin Co., PA. She married **DONALD LAMAR LAING JR.** circa 1972, PA.

5.4.8.10.2 LINDA ELAINE KLINGER was born on 23 July 1948, Dauphin Co., PA. She married **CHARLES MERVIN WERTZ** on 18 September 1967, PA. She married **(--?--) FELTMATE**.

5.4.8.10.2.1 CHARLES SAMUEL WERTZ was born on 26 January 1969, Dauphin Co., PA. He married **MARILYN RENEE FUHRMAN** on 14 October 1989, Zion (Stone Valley) Church, Halifax, Dauphin Co., PA.

5.4.8.10.2.1.1 JACQUELINE MARIE WERTZ was born on 26 May 1990, Dauphin Co., PA.

5.4.8.10.2.1.2 ALLISON NIKOL WERTZ was born on 13 February 1993, Dauphin Co., PA.

5.4.8.10.2.1.3 CHARLES JOSEPH WERTZ was born on 12 December 2000, Dauphin Co., PA.

5.4.8.10.3 SAMUEL RUSSELL KLINGER was born on 16 July 1954, Dauphin Co., PA. He married **JO ANN JONES** in 1975. He married **MALINDA HOY**, daughter of **EUGENE A. HOY** and **DOROTHY E. BROWN**, in 1997.

5.4.8.10.3.1 SAMUEL KLINGER was born in 1979, Dauphin Co., PA.

5.4.8.10.3.2 Laura Klinger was born on 18 January 1981, Dauphin Co., PA.

5.4.8.10.3.3 Lisa Klinger was born on 18 January 1981, Dauphin Co., PA.

5.4.8.10.3.4 Russell Eugene Klinger was born circa 1999, Dauphin Co., PA.

5.4.8.10.4 Douglas Howard Klinger was born on 7 November 1957, Harrisburg, Dauphin County, PA. He married **Brenda Shoffler** in 1983, Porter Township, Muir, Schuylkill County, PA. He died on 17 July 2015, at age 57. He was buried on 23 July 2015, at Calvary United Methodist Church Cemetery, Wiconisco, Dauphin County, PA.

5.4.8.10.4.1 Jenna M. Klinger was born in 1983, PA.

5.5 Elizabeth Klinger was born on 23 May 1835, Lykens Township, Dauphin County, PA. She was baptized on 16 August 1835, Zion (Klinger's) Church, Erdman, Lykens Township, Dauphin County, PA.

5.6 Hannah Klinger was born on 1 June 1842, Lykens Township, Dauphin County, PA. She was baptized on 14 August 1842, Zion (Klinger's) Church, Erdman, Lykens Township, Dauphin County, PA. She married **Samuel Straub**. She died on 25 November 1886, Lykens Township, Dauphin County, PA, at age 44. She was buried at Zion (Klinger's) Church, Erdman, Lykens Township, Dauphin County, PA.

5.6.1 Tobias Albert Straub is also referred to as **Tobias O.** in some sources. He was born on 14 June 1857. Some sources record that he was born in January 1858. He was baptized on 1 March 1858, Zion (Klinger's) Church, Erdman, Lykens Township, Dauphin County, PA. He married **Mary E. Low** circa 1885. He died in 1934. He was buried at Zion (Klinger's) Church Cemetery, Erdman, Lykens Township, Dauphin County, PA.

5.6.1.1 Samuel Harry Straub is also referred to as **Harry S.** in some sources. He was born on 11 September 1881. He married **Annie L. Williard**, daughter of **Jonathan C. Williard** and **Elmira Myah Klinger**, on 1 July 1916, Zion (Klinger's) Church, Erdman, Lykens Township, Dauphin County, PA. He died in 1963.

5.6.1.1.1 Harvey T. Straub (see above)

5.6.1.2 Geirmon Andrew Straub is also referred to as **Garman A., Geirman A., and German A.** in some sources. He was born on 22 June 1886, Dauphin County, PA. He was confirmed on 5 November 1904 Zion (Klinger's) Church, Erdman, Lykens Township, Dauphin County, PA. He married **Alice Frances Goodman**, daughter of **Nathan Goodman** and **Sarah (--?--)**, on 22 March 1913, St. David's Lutheran and Reformed Church, Hebe, Northumberland County, PA. When he registered for the World War II draft (1942), Geirmon was living in Herndon, PA, and working at the Tressler Lumber Co. in Trevorton, PA. He died in July 1970, at age 84. He was buried at St. David's Lutheran and Reformed Church Cemetery, Hebe, Northumberland County, PA. He was buried on 12 June 2013, at Calvary United Methodist Cemetery, Wiconisco, Dauphin County, PA.

5.6.1.2.1 Iva Straub married **(--?--) Hoffman**. Iva lives in Millersburg, PA.

5.6.1.2.2 Charles Alvin Straub was born on 7 August 1914. He was baptized on 5 September 1914, St. David's Lutheran and Reformed Church, Hebe, Northumberland County, PA. He died before 2013.

5.6.1.2.3 Stanley L. Straub was born on 4 February 1917, Northumberland County, PA. He married **Winifred C. Byerly**. He died on 16 March 2003, Kinkora Pythian Home, Duncannon, Perry County, PA, at age 86. He was buried on 19 March 2003, at Rolling Green Memorial Park, Camp Hill, Cumberland County, PA.

5.6.1.2.3.1 Phyllis J. Straub married **(--?--) Brooks**.

5.6.1.2.3.2 Janet L. Straub

5.6.1.2.3.3 Ronald L. Straub

5.6.1.2.3.4 Terry E. Straub

5.6.1.2.4 Mary S. Straub was born on 5 February 1919, Lykens, Dauphin County, PA. She married **Elvin Philip Romberger**, son of **Charles Isaac Romberger** and **Minerva A. Latsha**. She died in July 1987, at age 68.

5.6.1.2.5 Meda E. Straub was born on 19 July 1921, Hebe, Northumberland County, PA. She married **Charles F. Miller**, son of **Daniel Miller** and **Carrie Williams**. She died on 6 September 2013, The Manor at Susquehanna Village, Millersburg, Dauphin County, PA, at age 92.

5.6.1.2.5.1 Judy A. Miller married **Jake Klinger**. Judy lives in Tower City, PA.

5.6.1.2.5.2 Ruth Miller married **Bill Hoffman.** Ruth lives in Berrysburg, PA.

5.6.1.2.6 Nelson T. Straub was born in 1925, Northumberland County, PA. He married **Mary Leitzel.** He died on 11 February 2012, Spring Creek Health and Rehab Center, Harrisburg, Dauphin County, PA. According to a newspaper obituary, Nelson retired from Harrisburg Dairies; and worked at Kocher's Store and Don's Food Rite. He lived in Elizabethville, PA. He was buried on 15 February 2012, at Riverview Memorial Gardens, Halifax, Dauphin County, PA.

5.6.1.2.6.1 Ernest Straub died before 2012.

5.6.1.2.6.2 Barbara Straub married **(--?--) Novinger.** Barbara lives in Falling Waters, WV.

5.6.1.2.7 Marian A. Straub is also referred to as **Marion** in some sources. She was born on 15 February 1926, Jordan Township, Northumberland County, PA. She married **Walter Strohecker** on 19 August 1944. She died on 16 March 2012, The Manor at Susquehanna Village, Millersburg, Dauphin County, PA, at age 86. According to a newspaper obituary, Marian lived in Herndon, PA. She worked as a Machine Operator at Calvin Kline factory in Millersburg. She was buried on 20 March 2012, at St. David's Lutheran and Reformed Church Cemetery, Hebe, Northumberland County, PA.

5.6.1.2.7.1 Doris Strohecker married **Chester Wise.** Doris lives in Halifax, PA.

5.6.1.2.7.1.1 Randy Wise

5.6.1.2.7.1.2 Shelly Wise

5.6.1.2.7.2 Delroy Strohecker married **Sandra (--?--).**

5.6.1.2.8 Lee Straub was born circa 1928. Lee lives in Hebe, PA.

5.6.1.3 Esten Homer Straub is also referred to as **Eston** in some sources. He was born in March 1889. He was confirmed on 4 November 1908 Zion (Klinger's) Church, Erdman, Lykens Township, Dauphin County, PA. He died on 15 May 1939, Fearnot, Schuylkill County, PA, at age 50. He was buried on 18 May 1939, at U.B. Cemetery, Fearnot, Schuylkill County, PA.

5.6.1.4 Charles W. Straub is also referred to as **Walter C.** in some sources. He was born on 21 August 1890. He was baptized on 26 October 1890, Zion (Klinger's) Church, Erdman, Lykens Township, Dauphin County, PA.

5.6.1.5 Katie Hannah Straub was born on 24 February 1892. She was baptized on 24 April 1892, Zion (Klinger's) Church, Erdman, Lykens Township, Dauphin County, PA. She was confirmed on 14 November 1909 Zion (Klinger's) Church, Erdman, Lykens Township, Dauphin County, PA.

5.6.1.6 Carrie R. Straub was born in July 1893.

5.6.1.7 Emina Ellen Straub is also referred to as **Annie** in some sources. She was born on 29 June 1899. She was baptized on 12 November 1899, Zion (Klinger's) Church, Erdman, Lykens Township, Dauphin County, PA.

5.6.2 John Straub was born circa 1861. He married **Mary Klinger.**

5.6.3 George Brady Straub is also referred to as **Brady G.** in some sources. He was born on 12 April 1863, PA. He was baptized on 19 August 1863, Zion (Klinger's) Church, Erdman, Lykens Township, Dauphin County, PA. He married **Catherine Senora Klinger,** daughter of **Francis Klinger** and **Harriet Troutman,** circa 1889, PA. He died on 19 October 1949, at age 86. He was buried at Zion (Klinger's) Church, Erdman, Lykens Township, Dauphin County, PA.

5.6.3.1 Edgar W. Straub was born in May 1888. He married **Estella L. Strohecker** on 6 June 1908, Zion (Klinger's) Church, Erdman, Lykens Township, Dauphin County, PA.

5.6.3.1.1 Alvena Mae Straub is also referred to as **Elvina May Straub** in some sources. She is also referred to as **Mary A. Romberger** in some sources. She was born on 4 September 1908. She was baptized on 18 October 1908, Zion (Klinger's) Church, Erdman, Lykens Township, Dauphin County, PA. She married **Allen Clark Romberger,** son of **Isaiah Klinger Romberger** and **Elmira Clark,** on 20 November 1926, St. Michael's Lutheran Church, Klingerstown, Schuylkill County, PA. She died in August 1981, at age 72. She was buried at St. Michael's Church, Klingerstown, Schuylkill County, PA.

5.6.3.1.1.1 Allen Isaiah Romberger (see above)

5.6.3.1.1.1.1 Kristene Lea Romberger (see above)

5.6.3.1.1.1.2 Michael Allen Romberger (see above)

5.6.3.1.1.1.3 CLARK ALLEN ROMBERGER (see above)

5.6.3.1.1.2 ALICE LORRAINE ROMBERGER (see above)

5.6.3.1.1.2.1 ANN MARIE WILLIARD (see above)

5.6.3.1.1.2.2 JACK RUSSELL WILLIARD JR. (see above)

5.6.3.1.1.2.2.1 LUKE WILLIARD (see above)

5.6.3.1.1.2.2.2 ZACH HERSHEL WILLIARD (see above)

5.6.3.1.1.2.3 JEFFREY ALLEN WILLIARD (see above)

5.6.3.1.2 MARY ARLENA STRAUB was born on 23 October 1909. She was baptized on 10 December 1909, Zion (Klinger's) Church, Erdman, Lykens Township, Dauphin County, PA.

5.6.3.1.3 MINNIE VIOLA STRAUB was born on 7 March 1911. She was baptized on 14 May 1911, Zion (Klinger's) Church, Erdman, Lykens Township, Dauphin County, PA.

5.6.3.1.4 HOWARD EDWARD STRAUB was born on 21 October 1913. He was baptized on 15 March 1914, Zion (Klinger's) Church, Erdman, Lykens Township, Dauphin County, PA.

5.6.3.1.5 MINERVA C. STRAUB was born circa 1915.

5.6.3.1.6 RUSSELL E. STRAUB was born circa 1917.

5.6.3.1.7 DORA E. STRAUB was born circa 1919.

5.6.3.1.8 ROBERT B. STRAUB was born circa 1927.

5.6.3.2 BEULAH M. STRAUB was born on 15 November 1890, Lykens Township, Dauphin County, PA. She married LLOYD ERVIN TROUTMAN, son of BENNEVILLE R. TROUTMAN and LOUISA SEVILLA KLINGER, circa 1908, Zion (Klinger's) Church, Erdman, Lykens Township, Dauphin County, PA. She died in August 1959, Gratz, Dauphin County, PA, at age 68.

5.6.3.2.1 ALLEN RAY TROUTMAN was born on 15 December 1908, Lykens Township, Dauphin County, PA. He married ANNA FETTER, daughter of CHARLES H. FETTER and ELIZABETH BEISEL, circa 1926, Pennsylvania.

5.6.3.2.1.1 NOBLE TROUTMAN was born on 26 January 1931, Gratz, Dauphin County, PA. He married LORRAINE ZHABLOCKI. He married LORRAINE ZHABLOCKI circa 1949, Pennsylvania.

5.6.3.2.1.2 ELSIE TROUTMAN was born on 4 September 1935, Dauphin County, PA. Some sources record that she was born on 4 September 1931. She married JOHN KEHLY.

5.6.3.2.2 CHARLES LLOYD TROUTMAN was born on 25 April 1911.

5.6.3.2.3 MARGARET VIOLA TROUTMAN was born on 18 October 1912, Klingerstown, Schuylkill County, PA. She married LEON MATTERN. She died on 19 June 2006, The Manor at Susquehanna Village, Millersburg, Dauphin County, PA, at age 93. According to a newspaper obituary, Margaret lived at 622 Union Street, Millersburg, Dauphin County, PA. Margaret and her husband Leon were frequent participants in the Klinger's Church annual Dutch play and picnic held at Klinger's Church in Erdman. She was buried on 23 June 2006, at Zion (Klinger's) Church Cemetery, Erdman, Lykens Township, Dauphin County, PA.

5.6.3.2.3.1 ROMAINE E. MATTERN married (--?--) ERDMAN.

5.6.3.2.3.1.1 GARY ERDMAN

5.6.3.2.3.1.2 RANDY ERDMAN

5.6.3.2.3.2 DORENE M. MATTERN married DAVID HAWLEY.

5.6.3.2.3.3 DALE MATTERN died before 2006.

5.6.3.2.4 ALMA TROUTMAN was born circa 1915. She married RAYMOND BECHTEL.

5.6.3.2.5 THOMAS E. TROUTMAN was born in 1920. He married PAULINE REINER. He died in 1953, drowned in Shamokin Dam. He was buried at Zion (Klinger's) Church, Erdman, Lykens Township, Dauphin County, PA.

5.6.3.3 ALMA STRAUB was born circa 1891, Lykens Township, Dauphin County, PA. She married LESTER GEIST circa 1925, PA.

5.6.3.3.1 TOM GEIST married JOYCE LAUDENSLAYER, daughter of JAY LAUDENSLAYER and MARY CRAWLEY.

5.6.3.4 ARTHUR HARRISON STRAUB was born on 23 June 1892, Lykens Township, Dauphin County, PA. He married **EDNA ELIZABETH MAUSSER,** daughter of **JACOB MAUSSER** and **AMANDA PAUL,** circa 1910, PA. He died on 13 December 1960, Spring Glen, Schuylkill County, PA, at age 68. Arthur was a miner.

5.6.3.4.1 GERTRUDE STRAUB was born on 18 April 1912, Lykens Township, Dauphin County, PA. She married **RAYMOND R. STUTZMAN,** son of **ALBERT STUTZMAN** and **FRANCES ARTZ,** in April 1928, Valley View, Schuylkill County, PA.

5.6.3.4.1.1 FRANCES E. STUTZMAN was born on 6 January 1928, Sacramento, Schuylkill County, PA. Some sources record that she was born on 1 July 1928, Spring Glen, Schuylkill County, PA. She married **LAMAR MINNICH,** son of **WILLIAM MINNICH** and **RUTH BECHTEL,** on 24 December 1960, Hegins, Schuylkill County, PA. She died on 26 June 2006, at home, 546 Greenwood Road, Tower City, Schuylkill County, PA, at age 77. According to a newspaper obituary, Frances lived at 546 Greenwood Road, Tower City, Schuylkill County, PA. She was a seamstress in the garment industry.

5.6.3.4.1.1.1 HOLLY MINNICH was born Pottsville, Schuylkill County, PA. She married **STEVEN ALEXANDER.**

5.6.3.4.1.1.2 JUSTINE L. MINNICH is also referred to as **TINA** in some sources. She was born on 2 December 1962, Pottsville, Schuylkill County, PA. She married **RONN MARSHALL.**

5.6.3.4.1.1.3 ROXANNE R. MINNICH was born on 18 January 1966. She married **(--?--) NYE.**

5.6.3.4.1.2 HELEN D. STUTZMAN was born on 1 March 1933, Sacramento, Schuylkill County, PA. She married **RENO PALMER SCHWALM,** son of **FRED F. SCHWALM** and **MARY BERGEY,** on 28 June 1952, Sacramento, Schuylkill County, PA.

5.6.3.4.1.2.1 NAN ELIZABETH SCHWALM (see above)

5.6.3.4.1.2.2 ANDREW EDWARD SCHWALM (see above)

5.6.3.4.1.2.2.1 ROBERT JOSEPH SCHWALM (see above)

5.6.3.4.1.2.2.2 AUBREY NOEL SCHWALM (see above)

5.6.3.4.1.3 WILLIAM L. STUTZMAN was born on 6 October 1942, Sacramento, Schuylkill County, PA. He married **DORIS R. PRICE,** daughter of **ROBERT PRICE** and **RUTH ESBIN,** on 7 December 1963, Goshen, Chester County, PA.

5.6.3.4.1.3.1 SUSAN ELIZABETH STUTZMAN was born on 14 December 1966.

5.6.3.4.1.3.2 ARTHUR W. STUTZMAN was born on 21 June 1968.

5.6.3.4.1.3.3 RUTH ANNA STUTZMAN was born on 7 June 1970.

5.6.3.4.2 NAOMI ELIZABETH STRAUB was born on 10 December 1916, Spring Glen, Schuylkill County, PA. She was baptized on 28 January 1917, Zion (Klinger's) Church, Erdman, Lykens Township, Dauphin County, PA. She married **RAY HEPLER,** son of **HARRY HEPLER** and **DATIE STRAUB.** She died in 1951. She was buried at Sacramento, Schuylkill County, PA.

5.6.3.4.3 PAUL ARTHUR STRAUB was born on 31 December 1918, Spring Glen, Schuylkill County, PA. He was baptized on 4 March 1919, Zion (Klinger's) Church, Erdman, Lykens Township, Dauphin County, PA. He married **GROVENE WIEST.**

5.6.3.4.4 DOROTHY K. STRAUB was born on 31 December 1922, Spring Glen, Schuylkill County, PA. She married **(--?--) RESSLER,** son of **MORRIS RESSLER** and **EDNA MAUSSER.** Dorothy was a registered nurse. Prior to her death, Dorothy was living in the vicinity of Baltimore, MD. She died in September 1989, at age 66.

5.6.3.4.5 ALMA WINIFRED STRAUB was born on 1 September 1926, Spring Glen, Schuylkill County, PA. She was baptized on 6 December 1926, Zion (Klinger's) Church, Erdman, Lykens Township, Dauphin County, PA. She married **MARLIN E. KOPPENHAVER,** son of **JONATHON D. KOPPENHAVER** and **VERNA ROMBERGER,** on 16 February 1946, Valley View, Schuylkill County, PA.

5.6.3.4.5.1 RICHARD E. KOPPENHAVER was born on 26 April 1947.

5.6.3.4.6 VIOLET MAY STRAUB was born on 20 July 1930, Spring Glen, Schuylkill County, PA. She was baptized on 20 September 1930, Zion (Klinger's) Church, Erdman, Lykens Township,

Dauphin County, PA. She married **LARRY DEEL**. She married **DAVID BECHTEL**. She married **WILLIAM MCELROY**. Violet was a registered nurse.

5.6.3.5 AMELIA VIOLA STRAUB was born on 5 February 1894, Lykens Township, Dauphin County, PA. She died on 5 February 1894. She was buried at Zion (Klinger's) Church Cemetery, Erdman, Lykens Township, Dauphin County, PA. According to a number of sources, Amelia Viola Straub married Ira Schlegel around 1912, but according to the Klinger's Church History, Amelia, the daughter of George Brady and Catharina Straub, died Feb. 5, 1894, apparently in infancy. According to those sources, Amelia and Ira had a daughter named Dora, born 24 Oct. 1919. Census records suggest, however, that Ira Schlegel's wife, "Hannah" was not born until about 1903, making it unlikely that she was George Brady Straub's daughter Amelia. It is more likely that Ira Schlegel married Amelia's sister Bertha Hannah Straub.

5.6.3.6 SAMUEL HOMER STRAUB is also referred to as **HOMER SAMUEL** in some sources. He was born on 6 July 1895. He was baptized on 6 October 1895, Zion (Klinger's) Church, Erdman, Lykens Township, Dauphin County, PA. He married **KATE ALVERTA DEIBERT**, daughter of **SAMUEL D. DEIBERT** and **SARAH ELDA FETTEROLF**, on 4 March 1916, Zion (Klinger's) Church, Erdman, Lykens Township, Dauphin County, PA. He died on 22 September 1944, at age 49. He was buried at Zion (Klinger's) Church Cemetery, Erdman, Lykens Township, Dauphin County, PA.

> **5.6.3.6.1 MASON STRAUB** died before 2012.
>
> **5.6.3.6.2 ELVIN WILSON STRAUB** was born on 1 November 1915. He was baptized on 17 May 1916, Zion (Klinger's) Church, Erdman, Lykens Township, Dauphin County, PA. He married **FLORENCE E. (--?--)**. He married **LAURETTA E. WILLIARD** on 1 August 1942. He died in 1988. He was buried at Zion (Klinger's) Lutheran Church Cemetery, Erdman, Dauphin County, PA.
>
> **5.6.3.6.3 MINNIE HELEN STRAUB** was born on 4 February 1917. She was baptized on 21 April 1917, Zion (Klinger's) Church, Erdman, Lykens Township, Dauphin County, PA. She married **RAY WILLIAM LARK** on 23 January 1943, Zion (Klinger's) Church, Erdman, Lykens Township, Dauphin County, PA. She married **CLARENCE W. BROSIOUS**. She died in 1995. She was buried at Zion (Klinger's) Lutheran Church Cemetery, Erdman, Dauphin County, PA.
>
> **5.6.3.6.4 ANNIE TEMA STRAUB** is also referred to as **TAMMIE STRAUB** in some sources. She was born on 26 March 1918. She was baptized on 30 May 1918, Zion (Klinger's) Church, Erdman, Lykens Township, Dauphin County, PA. She married **CHARLES ELWOOD LAUDENSLAGER**, son of **HARRY VICTOR LAUDENSLAGER** and **EDNA FIETTA CARL**, on 30 August 1941, Zion (Klinger's) Church, Erdman, Lykens Township, Dauphin County, PA. She died on 9 July 2010, at her home Gratz, Dauphin County, PA, at age 92. She was buried at Zion (Klinger's) Lutheran Church Cemetery, Erdman, Dauphin County, PA.
>
>> **5.6.3.6.4.1 JUDY L. LAUDENSLAGER** married **D. RANDALL REED** on 23 April 1966, Zion (Klinger's) Lutheran Church, Erdman, Dauphin County, PA.
>>
>> **5.6.3.6.4.2 TERRY GEORGE LAUDENSLAGER** was born on 29 December 1941. He was baptized on 27 March 1942, Zion (Klinger's) Lutheran Church, Erdman, Dauphin County, PA. He married **DRINDA YVONNE STRAUB**, daughter of **CHARLES AUSTIN STRAUB** and **MIANA ELIZABETH KEEN**, on 26 February 1974, Zion (Klinger's) Lutheran Church, Erdman, Dauphin County, PA.
>>
>>> **5.6.3.6.4.2.1 TIFFANY ANN LAUDENSLAGER** was born on 2 July 1974. She was baptized on 8 September 1974, Zion (Klinger's) Lutheran Church, Erdman, Dauphin County, PA. She married **ERIC WILLIAM FEIDT** on 1 November 1997.
>>
>> **5.6.3.6.4.3 ROBERT LEON LAUDENSLAGER** was born on 30 August 1943. He was baptized on 26 January 1944, Zion (Klinger's) Lutheran Church, Erdman, Dauphin County, PA. He married **CAROL (--?--)**.
>
> **5.6.3.6.5 VIVIAN ELDA STRAUB** was born on 18 November 1919, Erdman, Dauphin County, PA. She was baptized on 22 February 1920, Zion (Klinger's) Church, Erdman, Lykens Township, Dauphin County, PA. She married **KELVIN LINCOLN BOWMAN** on 18 June 1938, Zion (Klinger's) Church, Erdman, Lykens Township, Dauphin County, PA. She died on 6 June 2012, Friendly Nursing Home, Pitman, Schuylkill County, PA, at age 92. She was buried on 9 June 2012, at Zion (Klinger's) Lutheran Church Cemetery, Erdman, Dauphin County, PA.
>
>> **5.6.3.6.5.1 TERRY HOMER BOWMAN** was born on 12 September 1938. He died on 15 September 1938, Lykens Township, Dauphin County, PA.

5.6.3.6.5.2 RANDY LEE BOWMAN was born on 30 August 1944, Dauphin County, PA. He was baptized on 2 October 1944, Zion (Klinger's) Lutheran Church, Erdman, Dauphin County, PA. He married **BARBARA E. WIEST** on 8 February 1964, Zion (Klinger's) Lutheran Church, Erdman, Dauphin County, PA.

5.6.3.6.5.2.1 TERRI LEE BOWMAN was born on 9 April 1964. She was baptized on 29 April 1964, Zion (Klinger's) Lutheran Church, Erdman, Dauphin County, PA. She married **ROBBY ALLEN BINGAMAN**, son of **REV. ROBERT ALLEN BINGAMAN** and **ALANE VIRGINIA MOYER**, circa 1991.

5.6.3.6.5.2.2 TONI LEE BOWMAN was born on 1 July 1965. She was baptized on 14 November 1965, Zion (Klinger's) Lutheran Church, Erdman, Dauphin County, PA.

5.6.3.6.6 LEON SAMUEL STRAUB was born on 12 January 1921, Dauphin Co., PA. He was baptized on 5 May 1921, Berrysburg Evangelical Congregational Circuit, Dauphin Co., PA. He married **MARTHA IRENE WILLIARD**, daughter of **MOSES ALVIN WILLIARD** and **CATHERINE IRENE SITLINGER**, circa 1961, PA. He died in March 2002, Dauphin Co., PA, at age 81. He was buried at Zion (Klinger's) Lutheran Church, Erdman, Dauphin County, PA.

5.6.3.6.6.1 KEITH WAYNE STRAUB (see above)

5.6.3.6.6.1.1 AMY LYNN STRAUB (see above)

5.6.3.6.6.1.2 JESSICA K. STRAUB (see above)

5.6.3.7 RAYMOND STRAUB was born on 16 December 1896, Lykens, Dauphin County, PA. He was baptized on 18 April 1897, Zion (Klinger's) Church, Erdman, Lykens Township, Dauphin County, PA. He married **FLORENCE KLOCK** circa 1916. He died before 2007.

5.6.3.7.1 LESTER STRAUB died before 14 August 2007.

5.6.3.7.2 DEAN STRAUB

5.6.3.7.3 DELBERT STRAUB

5.6.3.7.4 ESTHER STRAUB married **(--?--) CULBERT**.

5.6.3.7.5 HELEN M. STRAUB was born circa 1917. She married **(--?--) KLINGER**. She died before 14 August 2007.

5.6.3.7.6 AILENE M. STRAUB was born in 1919. She married **(--?--) FEGLEY**. She was born before 14 August 2007.

5.6.3.7.7 MARK R. STRAUB was born on 16 June 1921, Tremont, Schuylkill County, PA. He married **PAULINE MEYERS** circa 1947. He died on 14 August 2007, Good Samaritan Regional Medical Center, Schuylkill County, PA, at age 86. According to a newspaper obituary, Mark lived in Donaldson, Schuylkill County, PA. During World War II, he served as a tech sergeant in the Army Air Corps and received the European-African-Middle Eastern Medal, the Good Conduct Medal and the World War II Victory Medal. He was buried on 17 August 2007, at St. John's Lutheran Church Cemetery, Pine Grove, Schuylkill County, PA.

5.6.3.7.7.1 RONALD M. STRAUB SR. died before 14 August 2007.

5.6.3.7.7.2 JUDY STRAUB married **(--?--) GANLY**. She died before 14 August 2007.

5.6.3.7.7.3 CAROLYN STRAUB married **(--?--) WAGNER**.

5.6.3.7.8 LAWRENCE STRAUB was born circa 1923. He died before 14 August 2007.

5.6.3.7.9 DAVID STRAUB was born in 1925. He died before 14 August 2007.

5.6.3.8 MAMIE ALICE STRAUB was born on 19 January 1898. She was baptized on 23 May 1898, Zion (Klinger's) Church, Erdman, Lykens Township, Dauphin County, PA.

5.6.3.9 HARRY AUSTIN STRAUB was born on 10 May 1899, Lykens Township, Dauphin County, PA. He was baptized on 23 July 1899, Zion (Klinger's) Church, Erdman, Lykens Township, Dauphin County, PA. He married **HILDA E. WENRICH**, daughter of **CHARLES WENRICH** and **KATIE HOFFMAN**, on 8 September 1923, Valley View, Schuylkill County, PA. He died on 25 May 1996, at age 97. He was buried at Zion (Klinger's) Lutheran Church Cemetery, Erdman, Dauphin County, PA.

5.6.3.9.1 MILES VENUS STRAUB was born on 21 October 1923, Spring Glen, Schuylkill County, PA. He was baptized on 8 December 1923, Zion (Klinger's) Church, Erdman, Lykens Township, Dauphin County, PA. He died on 18 December 1944, in World War II, Germany, at age 21. He was buried circa 1948, at Zion (Klinger's) Church, Erdman, Lykens Township, Dauphin County, PA.

5.6.3.9.2 ARABEL C. STRAUB was born on 7 March 1925, Sacramento, Schuylkill County, PA. She married **MARLIN LEE KLINGER**, son of **DANIEL EMANUEL KLINGER** and **VENA ALPHA KLINGER**, on 18 July 1942, St. Michael's Church, Klingerstown, Schuylkill County, PA.

    5.6.3.9.2.1 MARLIN LAMAR KLINGER JR. (see above)

        5.6.3.9.2.1.1 MATTHEW KLINGER (see above)

    5.6.3.9.2.2 DENNIS ERROL KLINGER (see above)

        5.6.3.9.2.2.1 DOUGLAS KLINGER (see above)

        5.6.3.9.2.2.2 TRACY KLINGER (see above)

    5.6.3.9.2.3 CAROL ANN KLINGER (see above)

        5.6.3.9.2.3.1 CHRIS HEPLER (see above)

        5.6.3.9.2.3.2 JAMES HEPLER (see above)

    5.6.3.9.2.4 CYNTHIA LOUISE KLINGER (see above)

        5.6.3.9.2.4.1 BRANDON WEDDE (see above)

    5.6.3.9.2.5 TIMOTHY SCOTT KLINGER (see above)

5.6.3.9.3 LEO GEORGE STRAUB was born on 20 January 1928, Lykens Township, Dauphin County, PA. He was baptized on 25 November 1928, Zion (Klinger's) Church, Erdman, Lykens Township, Dauphin County, PA. Some sources record that he was born on 21 January 1928, Valley View, Schuylkill County, PA. He married **NORMA J. KESSLER**, daughter of **AARON EZRA KESSLER** and **DAISY ARDELLA TROUTMAN**, on 26 August 1950, Erdman, Lykens Township, Dauphin County, PA. He died on 11 September 1974, Lykens Township, Dauphin County, PA, at age 46. He was buried on 13 September 1974, at Zion (Klinger's) Church Cemetery, Erdman, Lykens Township, Dauphin County, PA.

    5.6.3.9.3.1 PEGGY DIANE STRAUB was born on 10 April 1951, Danville, Montour County, PA. She married **JOHN ROGER STIELY**, son of **JOHN KIRBY STIELY** and **GERTRUDE MAE KLINGER**, on 19 July 1969, Erdman, Lykens Township, Dauphin County, PA. She married **LAMAR MALONE** after 1973.

        5.6.3.9.3.1.1 ERIC CHRISTOPHER STIELY (see above)

        5.6.3.9.3.1.2 ANGELA DIANE STIELY (see above)

    5.6.3.9.3.2 DEBRA SUE STRAUB was born on 12 March 1953, Danville, Montour County, PA. She married **STEVEN DANIEL KNORR**.

        5.6.3.9.3.2.1 STEPHANIE DIANE KNORR was born on 11 May 1973, Lykens Township, Dauphin County, PA.

        5.6.3.9.3.2.2 RACHEL ANN KNORR was born on 25 July 1980.

    5.6.3.9.3.3 LYNN LEO STRAUB was born on 26 August 1957. He married **VALEN TINIA MARTIN**.

        5.6.3.9.3.3.1 JEREMY MARTIN STRAUB was born on 2 November 1985, Lykens Township, Dauphin County, PA.

    5.6.3.9.3.4 PENNY L. STRAUB was born on 11 November 1968, Harrisburg, Dauphin County, PA.

5.6.3.9.4 HARRY DEAN STRAUB was born on 30 May 1929, Valley View, Schuylkill County, PA. He was baptized on 20 September 1930, Zion (Klinger's) Church, Erdman, Lykens Township, Dauphin County, PA. He died on 21 December 2013, the Manor at Susquehanna Village, Millersburg, Dauphin County, PA, at age 84. According to a newspaper obituary, Harry lived in Lykens Township, Dauphin County, PA, and worked for Penn DOT for many years until his retirement. He was buried on 28 December 2013, at Zion (Klinger's) Lutheran Church Cemetery, Erdman, Dauphin County, PA.

5.6.3.9.5 CHARLES AUSTIN STRAUB was born on 16 November 1926. He was baptized on 26 December 1926, Zion (Klinger's) Church, Erdman, Lykens Township, Dauphin County, PA. Some sources record that he was born on 6 November 1926, Valley View, Schuylkill County, PA. He married **MIANA ELIZABETH KEEN**, daughter of **CHARLES H. KEEN** and **DAISY P. KEMP**.

5.6.3.9.5.1 DUANE CHARLES STRAUB was born on 25 November 1948, Sunbury Hospital, Sunbury, Northumberland County, PA. He married **LINDA HENNINGER**, daughter of **WILLIAM PENROSE HENNINGER** and **HELEN MAE REISCH**, on 23 October 1962.

5.6.3.9.5.1.1 SEAN ARTHUR STRAUB was born on 23 September 1985.

5.6.3.9.5.2 DRINDA YVONNE STRAUB was born on 5 April 1951, Lykens, Dauphin County, PA. She married **JEFFREY WITMER** circa 1968. She married **TERRY GEORGE LAUDENSLAGER**, son of **CHARLES ELWOOD LAUDENSLAGER** and **ANNIE TEMA STRAUB,** on 26 February 1974, Zion (Klinger's) Lutheran Church, Erdman, Dauphin County, PA.

5.6.3.9.5.2.1 TONYA A. WITMER was born on 13 January 1970.

5.6.3.9.5.2.2 TIFFANY ANN LAUDENSLAGER (see above)

5.6.3.9.5.3 DIANN ELIZABETH STRAUB was born on 2 July 1954, Lykens, Dauphin County, PA.

5.6.3.9.6 RONALD EUGENE STRAUB was born on 23 March 1934, Erdman, Dauphin County, PA. He was baptized on 16 September 1934, Zion (Klinger's) Church, Erdman, Lykens Township, Dauphin County, PA. He married **MARY D. ANDREWS**, daughter of **EDITH COOPER,** on 30 September 1961, Salem (Herb's) Lutheran Church, Rough and Ready, Schuylkill County, PA. He died on 9 July 2005, Klingerstown, Schuylkill County, PA, at age 71, at his residence on Hoffman Road. He was buried on 13 July 2005, at Salem (Herb's) UCC Cemetery, Rough and Ready, Schuylkill County, PA.

5.6.3.9.6.1 LORI ANN STRAUB was born on 18 August 1961.

5.6.3.9.6.2 MICHAEL DAVID STRAUB was born on 10 April 1965, Camp Hill, Cumberland County, PA. He was baptized on 11 July 1965, Zion (Klinger's) Church, Erdman, Lykens Township, Dauphin County, PA. He married **AUDREY SNYDER** on 10 March 2007. He died on 1 December 2010, SUN Community Care Hospice, Community Hospital, Sunbury, Northumberland County, PA, at age 45. He was buried on 6 December 2010, at Salem (Herb's) UCC Cemetery, Rough and Ready, Schuylkill County, PA.

5.6.3.9.6.2.1 DAVID MICHAEL STRAUB

5.6.3.9.6.2.2 STEPHEN MICHAEL STRAUB

5.6.3.9.7 DELROY FAYNE STRAUB SR. was born on 8 October 1940, RD, Lykens, Dauphin County, PA. He married **ALICE R. WILLIARD**, daughter of **DONALD R. WILLIARD** and **HELEN G. SEITZ**, on 16 December 1961, Zion (Klinger's) Church, Erdman, Lykens Township, Dauphin County, PA. He died on 26 October 2001, at age 61. He was buried at Zion Lutheran Church Cemetery, Lykens, Dauphin County, PA.

5.6.3.9.7.1 DELROY F. STRAUB was born on 19 May 1962, Harrisburg Hospital, Harrisburg, Dauphin County, PA.

5.6.3.9.7.2 BRADLEY J. STRAUB was born on 10 September 1964, Harrisburg Hospital, Harrisburg, Dauphin County, PA.

5.6.3.9.8 LARRY LAMAR STRAUB was born on 18 March 1942, Lykens Township, Dauphin County, PA. He was baptized on 15 November 1942, Zion (Klinger's) Church, Erdman, Lykens Township, Dauphin County, PA. He married **SHIRLEY HOFFMAN**, daughter of **REBA HOFFMAN,** on 27 February 1965, Valley View, Schuylkill County, PA.

5.6.3.9.9 MARY ELLEN STRAUB was born on 2 November 1945. She was baptized on 9 March 1946, Zion (Klinger's) Church, Erdman, Lykens Township, Dauphin County, PA. She married **MICHAEL SPYA**, son of **JOHN SPYA** and **JULIA LEVONICK,** on 8 June 1969, Osceola Mills, PA. Mary is a registered nurse.

5.6.3.9.9.1 MICHAEL SPYA was born on 20 May 1970, Tyrone, PA.

5.6.3.9.9.2 STEPHEN JAMES SPYA was born on 24 March 1972, Tyrone, PA.

5.6.3.9.10 GLENN ALLEN STRAUB was born on 14 December 1947. He was baptized on 2 April 1948, Zion (Klinger's) Church, Erdman, Lykens Township, Dauphin County, PA. Some sources record that he was born on 28 December 1948, Lykens Township, Dauphin County, PA. He married **LINDA HOKE** after 1970.

5.6.3.10 RALPH EDWIN STRAUB was born on 28 August 1901, Lykens Township, Dauphin County, PA. He was baptized on 22 December 1901, Zion (Klinger's) Church, Erdman, Lykens Township, Dauphin County, PA. He married **HILDA B. BOYER**, daughter of **CHARLES BOYER** and **CARRIE**

(--?--), on 3 March 1928, Zion (Klinger's) Church, Erdman, Lykens Township, Dauphin County, PA. He died on 29 June 1941, at age 39. He was buried at Zion (Klinger's) Church Cemetery, Erdman, Lykens Township, Dauphin County, PA.

    5.6.3.10.1 JEAN STRAUB was born circa 1928. She married **(--?--) HENNINGER**.

    5.6.3.10.2 CLAIR S. STRAUB was born circa 1930.

5.6.3.11 BERTHA HANNAH STRAUB is also referred to as **HANNAH BERTHA STRAUB** in some sources. She was born on 4 January 1903. She was baptized on 10 May 1903, Zion (Klinger's) Church, Erdman, Lykens Township, Dauphin County, PA. She married **IRA DANIEL SCHLEGEL**, son of **CHARLES DANIEL SCHLEGEL** and **MARY SMITH,** circa 1920. She died in May 1973, at age 70.

    5.6.3.11.1 DORA I. SCHLEGEL was born on 24 October 1919, Schuylkill County, PA. She married **HENRY O. SCHOTT**. She died on 25 November 1958, Montgomery County, PA, at age 39. She was buried at Lutheran Cemetery, Valley View, Schuylkill County, PA.

    5.6.3.11.2 RICHARD D. SCHLEGEL was Lutheran Minister. He was born on 12 May 1934, Valley View, Schuylkill County, PA. He married **MARY ALICE STUTZMAN** circa 1960. He died on 13 September 2014, St. Clair County, MI, at age 80.

        5.6.3.11.2.1 MATTHEW SCHLEGEL married **KRISTIN (--?--)**.

            5.6.3.11.2.1.1 MICHAEL SCHLEGEL

            5.6.3.11.2.1.2 DEVON SCHLEGEL

        5.6.3.11.2.2 KRISTA SCHLEGEL married **(--?--) RICKEL**.

            5.6.3.11.2.2.1 ANTHONY RICKEL

            5.6.3.11.2.2.2 ALEC RICKEL

5.6.3.12 LUMA FAY STRAUB was born on 21 November 1906, Lykens Township, Dauphin County, PA. She was baptized on 21 April 1907, Zion (Klinger's) Church, Erdman, Lykens Township, Dauphin County, PA. She married **WILLIAM WALLACE SCHLEGEL** circa 1926.

    5.6.3.12.1 WILLARD SCHLEGEL was born in 1927.

    5.6.3.12.2 JEAN E. SCHLEGEL was born in 1932. She died in 1954. She was buried at Zion (Klinger's) Church, Erdman, Lykens Township, Dauphin County, PA.

5.6.3.13 ROY IRVIN STRAUB was born on 9 August 1908. He was baptized on 1 November 1908, Zion (Klinger's) Church, Erdman, Lykens Township, Dauphin County, PA.

5.6.3.14 LOTTIE ALMA STRAUB was born on 3 May 1913. She was baptized on 21 June 1913, Zion (Klinger's) Church, Erdman, Lykens Township, Dauphin County, PA.

5.6.3.15 HELEN MARIE STRAUB was born on 17 July 1910. Some sources record that she was born on 17 July 1920. She married **LEON MILLER**.

5.6.4 MARY ELIZABETH STRAUB was born on 22 September 1864. She was baptized on 17 June 1865, Zion (Klinger's) Church, Erdman, Lykens Township, Dauphin County, PA.

5.6.5 OSCAR W. STRAUB is also referred to as **WILLIAM OSCAR STRAUB** in some sources. He was born circa 7 December 1869. He married **EMMA JANE HOKE**. He died on 2 August 1930. He was buried at Zion (Klinger's) Church Cemetery, Erdman, Lykens Township, Dauphin County, PA.

    5.6.5.1 (--?--) STRAUB died on 22 April 1910, in infancy.

    5.6.5.2 (--?--) STRAUB was born on 2 October 1893. He died on 5 October 1893.

    5.6.5.3 RAYMOND TOBIAS STRAUB was born on 4 October 1897. He was baptized on 6 March 1898, Zion (Klinger's) Church, Erdman, Lykens Township, Dauphin County, PA. He married **GRACE A. RADELL** on 21 June 1919, Zion (Klinger's) Church, Erdman, Lykens Township, Dauphin County, PA. He died on 13 July 1971, at age 73. He was buried on 17 July 1971, at Zion (Klinger's) Church Cemetery, Erdman, Lykens Township, Dauphin County, PA.

    5.6.5.4 CLARENCE GUY STRAUB was born on 2 May 1903. He was baptized on 5 July 1903, Zion (Klinger's) Church, Erdman, Lykens Township, Dauphin County, PA. He married **CORA ANNETTE JACOBS** on 30 January 1926, Zion (Klinger's) Church, Erdman, Lykens Township, Dauphin County, PA. He died on 26 May 1971, at age 68. He was buried on 29 May 1971, at Zion (Klinger's) Church Cemetery, Erdman, Lykens Township, Dauphin County, PA.

        5.6.5.4.1 DOROTHY JEAN STRAUB was born on 6 July 1926, Gratz, Dauphin County, PA. Some sources record that she was born on 16 July 1926. She was baptized on 7 August 1926, Zion

(Klinger's) Church, Erdman, Lykens Township, Dauphin County, PA. She married **KERMIT WILSON KISSINGER**, son of **DANIEL FRANKLIN KISSINGER** and **MARY AMANDA HOFFMAN,** on 15 December 1945, Zion (Klinger's) Church, Erdman, Lykens Township, Dauphin County, PA.

5.6.5.4.1.1 DOLORES ELAINE KISSINGER was born on 10 August 1946, PA. She was baptized on 10 November 1946, Zion (Klinger's) Lutheran Church, Erdman, Dauphin Co., PA. She married **ROY LAMAR CLARK** circa 1965, PA.

5.6.5.4.1.1.1 (--?--) **CLARK** was born circa 1967, PA.

5.6.5.4.1.1.2 ANGELA CLARK was born on 20 January 1967, PA. She married **BRADY NEUGARD** circa 1990, PA.

5.6.5.4.1.1.2.1 BRITTNEY LYNNE NEUGARD was born on 26 December 1992, PA.

5.6.5.4.1.1.2.2 BROCKTON PAUL NEUGARD was born on 9 March 1998, PA.

5.6.5.4.1.2 RICHARD MICHAEL KISSINGER was born on 29 July 1947, PA. He married **DEBORAH** (--?--) circa 1970.

5.6.5.4.1.3 DENNIS KEITH KISSINGER SR. was born on 10 July 1948, PA. He was baptized on 27 March 1949, Zion (Klinger's) Lutheran Church, Erdman, Dauphin Co., PA. He married **MARY LOUISE RUMBERGER** on 8 May 1971, PA.

5.6.5.4.1.3.1 DENNIS KEITH KISSINGER JR. was born on 28 October 1971, PA.

5.6.5.4.1.4 BONITA LOUISE KISSINGER was born on 11 November 1949, PA. She was baptized on 23 June 1950, Zion (Klinger's) Lutheran Church, Erdman, Dauphin Co., PA. She married **JEROME KISSINGER** circa 1970, PA.

5.6.5.4.1.4.1 GREGORY KISSINGER was born circa 1972, PA.

5.6.5.4.1.4.2 MICHELLE KISSINGER was born circa 1974, PA.

5.6.5.4.1.5 GREGORY KISSINGER was born circa 1951, PA. He married **PATRICIA** (--?--).

5.6.5.4.1.6 MICHELLE A. KISSINGER was born circa 1953, PA. She married **WILLIAM CORSNITZ JR.**

5.6.5.4.2 CAROLYN MARY STRAUB was born on 15 January 1940. She was baptized on 3 March 1940, Zion (Klinger's) Church, Erdman, Lykens Township, Dauphin County, PA. She married **CARL ROMBERGER**.

5.6.5.5 ROY EDWIN STRAUB was born on 13 January 1906. He died on 21 March 1907, at age 1. He was buried at Zion (Klinger's) Church Cemetery, Erdman, Lykens Township, Dauphin County, PA.

6 JOHANNES P. KLINGER is also referred to as **JOHN P. KLINGER** in some sources. He was born on 18 March 1802. He married **MARGARETHA SHADE**, daughter of **JOHN SHADE** and **HANNAH HOFFA.** He married **SARAH** (--?--). He died on 11 October 1873, at age 71. He was buried at St. Paul's (Artz) Church Cemetery, Sacramento, Hubley Township, Schuylkill County, PA.

6.1 JULIANNA KLINGER is also referred to as **JULIA ANN KLINGER** in some sources. She was born on 24 February 1823. She was baptized on 6 April 1823, Zion (Klinger's) Lutheran Church, Erdman, Dauphin County, PA. She married **JOHN J. CARL**, son of **JOHANN JACOB CARL** and **MARIA SARAH SCHAFFER**. She married **JACOB FRYMOYER** circa 1856. She died on 19 March 1904, at age 81. She was buried at Sharon Cemetery, Wilton, Muscatine County, IA.

6.1.1 JOHN CARL was born on 10 July 1845, Northumberland County, PA. He married **SARAH A. WOLFE**. He died on 28 January 1912, Herndon, Northumberland County, PA, at age 66. He was buried on 1 February 1912, at Herndon Cemetery, Herndon, Northumberland County, PA.

6.1.1.1 MARY JANE CARL is also referred to as **JENNIE MARY CARL** in some sources. She was born on 29 January 1883. She was baptized on 13 March 1883, St. John's Evangelical Lutheran Church, Jackson Township, Northumberland County, PA. She married **WILLIAM S. DRUMHELLER**, son of **HENRY Z. DRUMHELLER** and **ABBIE SHIPE,** on 21 May 1902, Northumberland County, PA. She died on 10 July 1970, at age 87. She was buried at Herndon Cemetery, Herndon, Northumberland County, PA.

6.1.1.1.1 MARION NAOMI DRUMHELLER was born on 27 August 1908, Herndon, Northumberland County, PA. She died on 13 January 2006, at age 97.

6.1.1.2 MINNIE CARL was born on 22 April 1887. She died on 30 December 1888, at age 1. She was buried at Herndon Cemetery, Herndon, Northumberland County, PA.

6.1.1.3 JOHN RAYMOND CARL was born on 17 March 1892. He died on 10 July 1972, at age 80. He was buried at Herndon Cemetery, Herndon, Northumberland County, PA.

6.1.2 HENRY A. CARL was born on 23 March 1850, Jackson Township, Northumberland County, PA. He married **REBECCA KOBEL**, daughter of **GEORGE KOBEL** and **CATHERINE SNYDER**, circa 1870. He died on 14 May 1930, Jackson Township, Northumberland County, PA, at age 80. He was buried at Herndon Cemetery, Herndon, Northumberland County, PA.

6.1.2.1 JOHN WASHINGTON CARL was born on 22 February 1882. He married **GRACE DORTHA MATOTT**, daughter of **HENRY MATOTT** and **JOSEPHINE MUNSON**, on 29 April 1917, Clinton County, NY. He died on 23 May 1947, at age 65. He was buried at Riverview Cemetery, Chazy, Clinton County, NY.

6.1.2.2 CLARENCE ELRO CARL was born on 22 October 1883. He married **MARY H. BURNS**, daughter of **ANNA M. (--?--)**. He died on 26 June 1922, Sunbury, Northumberland County, PA, at age 38.

6.1.2.3 QUINCY JAY CARL was born on 9 October 1888, Jackson Township, Northumberland County, PA. He died on 30 April 1963, Community Hospital, Sunbury, Northumberland County, PA, at age 74. He was buried on 4 May 1963, at Herndon Cemetery, Herndon, Northumberland County, PA.

6.1.2.4 CLYDE A. CARL was born on 22 February 1890. He married **CARRIE MYRL ROTHERMEL**, daughter of **JAMES ROTHERMEL** and **EMMA J. BOHNER**. He died in October 1971, at age 81. He was buried at Saint Paul's United Church of Christ Cemetery, Urban, Northumberland County, PA.

6.1.2.4.1 CHARLES CARL died before 25 December 2009.

6.1.2.4.2 HENRY CARL

6.1.2.4.3 JEAN CARL

6.1.2.4.4 ROBERT CARL died before 25 December 2009.

6.1.2.4.5 DANIEL P. CARL was born on 7 August 1931, Herndon, Northumberland County, PA. He married **BETTY (--?--)**. He died on 25 December 2009, Geisinger Medical Center, Danville, Montour County, PA, at age 78. He was buried on 29 December 2009, at Northumberland Memorial Park,, Stonington, Northumberland County, PA.

6.1.2.4.5.1 JULIE CARL married **ERNIE SCHREFFLER**.

6.1.2.4.5.1.1 JEREMIAH SCHREFFLER

6.1.2.4.5.1.1.1 NOLAN SCHREFFLER

6.1.2.4.5.2 TERRY CARL married **BARBARA (--?--)**.

6.1.2.4.5.2.1 TERRI LEE CARL died before 25 December 2009.

6.1.2.5 JAMES FRANKLIN CARL was born on 10 August 1891. He married **BERTHA VIOLA ZEIDERS**. He died on 6 December 1979, at age 88.

6.1.2.5.1 HENRY W. CARL was born on 31 July 1917. He died on 10 May 1918. He was buried at Herndon Cemetery, Herndon, Northumberland County, PA.

6.1.2.5.2 JAMES QUINCY ALLEN CARL was born on 4 July 1919. He married **MARTHA RUTH LASEK**. He died on 18 June 2009, at age 89. He was buried at Herndon Cemetery, Herndon, Northumberland County, PA.

6.1.2.5.3 RALPH ROLAND CARL was born on 20 June 1925, Herndon, Northumberland County, PA. He married **BETTY R. FEGLEY**, daughter of **SAMUEL FEGLEY** and **RUTH BAHNER**. He died on 2 April 1999, Millersburg, Dauphin County, PA, at age 73. He was buried at Saint Davids Reformed Church Cemetery, Killinger, Dauphin County, PA.

6.1.2.5.3.1 GARY CARL died before 29 June 2014.

6.1.2.5.4 FREDERICK E. CARL was born in 1938. He died on 16 April 1958. He was buried at Herndon Cemetery, Herndon, Northumberland County, PA.

6.1.2.6 MARY F. R. CARL was born in May 1894.

6.1.2.7 HELEN V. CARL was born on 22 May 1897. She died on 18 July 1897. She was buried at Herndon Cemetery, Herndon, Northumberland County, PA.

6.1.3 EMMA JANE FRYMOYER was born on 22 January 1857. She married **ADAM FRANK BEARD** circa 1881. She died on 27 May 1933, at age 76.

6.1.3.1 BLANCHE MAY BEARD was born on 23 June 1889, Cedar County, IA. She married **OLIVER E. KELLEY**, son of **ABSOLOM KELLEY** and **HELEN BOYNTON**, on 25 December 1908, Wilton, Muscatine County, IA. She died on 19 February 1991, Wilton Nursing Home, Wilton, Muscatine County, IA, at age 101. She was buried at Oakdale Cemetery, Wilton, Muscatine County, IA.

6.1.3.1.1 NEVIN ELLSWORTH KELLEY was born on 18 April 1919, Cedar County, IA. He married **DOROTHY M. JENKINS**, daughter of **EVAN JENKINS** and **ELIZABETH ANGEL**, on 4 January 1941, Blue Grass, IA. He died on 16 January 2008, Iowa City, Johnson County, IA, at age 88. He was buried at Oakdale Cemetery, Wilton, Muscatine County, IA.

6.1.3.1.2 HILBERT FRANK KELLEY was born on 11 April 1921, Cedar County, IA. He married **MARY JANE ATKINSON**, daughter of **EARL EDWARD ATKINSON** and **IRENE KELLY**, on 30 November 1941, Presbyterian Church, Wilton, Muscatine County, IA. He died on 7 February 1991, Wilton, Muscatine County, IA, at age 69. He was buried on 11 February 1991, at Oakdale Cemetery, Wilton, Muscatine County, IA.

6.1.3.2 CORA ANN BEARD was born on 11 August 1892, Wilton, Muscatine County, IA. She died on 24 January 1966, Wilton, Muscatine County, IA, at age 73. She was buried on 26 January 1966, at Oakdale Cemetery, Wilton, Muscatine County, IA.

6.1.4 JAMES K. FRYMOYER was born on 12 August 1859. He married **AMANDA BURRIS ARMENTROUT** on 14 April 1897, Muscatine County, IA. He died on 2 January 1941, Cedar County, IA, at age 81. He was buried at Oakdale Cemetery, Wilton, Muscatine County, IA.

6.1.4.1 GEORGIA RAE FRYMOYER was born on 18 October 1901. She married **ERWIN WRIGHT ALVERSON**. She died on 9 March 1992, at age 90. She was buried at Green Hills Memorial Park, Rancho Palos Verdes, Los Angeles County, CA.

6.1.4.1.1 LINDA LUCILLE ALVERSON was born on 22 August 1929, Hammond, Lake County, IN. She married **ANTHONY AYUSO** on 2 July 1977, Orange County, CA.

6.1.5 ALICE FRYMOYER was born circa 1865. She married **FRANKLIN SMITH**, son of **ASA SMITH** and **JULIA TRULINGER**, on 17 August 1886, Cedar County, IA.

6.2 SAMUEL KLINGER was born on 16 September 1824. Some sources record that he was born on 16 September 1825. He married **MAGDALENA KLINGER**, daughter of **JOHANN GEORGE KLINGER** and **CATHERINE SCHMELTZ**, circa 1849, PA. He married **MARY KAUFFMAN**. He died on 4 February 1903, at age 78. He was buried on 8 February 1903, at Wolf's Crossroads Cemetery, Rockefeller Township, Northumberland County, PA.

6.2.1 ELIAS KLINGER was born on 17 March 1850, near Sacramento, Schuylkill County, PA. He married **FLORA METZ**. He died on 16 March 1927, at age 76. He was buried at Odd Fellows Cemetery, Shamokin, Northumberland County, PA.

6.2.1.1 CATHERINE M. KLINGER also went by the name of **KATIE**. She was born on 5 September 1875. She married **HARRY E. SHERIFF**. She died on 27 November 1952, at age 77. She was buried at IOOF Cemetery, Shamokin, Northumberland County, PA.

6.2.1.1.1 CLARENCE E. SHERIFF was born circa 1899, Pennsylvania.

6.2.1.1.2 MARGARET E. SHERIFF was born circa 1907, Pennsylvania.

6.2.1.1.3 RALPH SHERIFF was born in 1909, Pennsylvania.

6.2.1.2 HOWARD KLINGER was born in 1876. He married **MARY KEAR**.

6.2.1.2.1 DOROTHY KLINGER

6.2.1.3 ANNE E. KLINGER was born on 3 July 1879. She married **FRED SHULTZ**. She married **AUGUST PARSONS**. She died on 12 May 1956, at age 76. She was buried at IOOF Cemetery, Shamokin, Northumberland County, PA.

6.2.1.4 MAUDE KLINGER is also referred to as **EMMA M.** in some sources. She was born on 10 May 1880. She married **WILLIAM L. DUNMOYER**, son of **HENRY DUNMOYER** and **ELLEN THOMAS**, circa 1898. She died on 11 January 1956, at age 75. She was buried at IOOF Cemetery, Shamokin, Northumberland County, PA.

6.2.1.5 ALVARETTA KLINGER is also referred to as **ALVA E. AND AMELIA** in some sources. She was born on 12 February 1882. She married **HARRY E. MUTCHLER** circa 1899. She died on 29 November 1963, at age 81. She was buried at IOOF Cemetery, Shamokin, Northumberland County, PA.

6.2.1.5.1 BEATRICE E. MUTCHLER was born on 21 December 1899. She married **PALMER G. KRAMER** after 1920. She died on 20 November 1968, at age 68.

6.2.1.5.2 HOWARD J. MUTCHLER was born on 3 August 1901. He married **MARY B. NEIBAUER** after 1920. He died on 6 March 1945, at age 43.

6.2.1.5.3 ROLAND E. MUTCHLER is also referred to as **ROLLAND** in some sources. He was born on 9 March 1903. He married **SARAH C. FISHER**, daughter of **CHARLES FISHER** and **MARY HOFFMAN,** circa 1927. He died on 18 May 1959, at age 56.

6.2.1.5.3.1 JEAN MUTCHLER was born circa 1930.

6.2.1.5.4 HELEN C. MUTCHLER was born circa 1906.

6.2.1.5.5 EILEEN A. MUTCHLER is also referred to as **IRENE** in some sources. She was born on 24 March 1908. She married **LEWIS T. NUSS** circa 1928. Prior to her death, Eileen was living in Lancaster, Lancaster County, PA. She died on 1 March 1977, at age 68.

6.2.1.5.6 HARRY E. MUTCHLER JR. was born circa 1913.

6.2.1.6 JENNIE KLINGER was born on 12 December 1883. Some sources record that she was born in 1884. She married **WILLIAM MITCHELE**. She died on 7 June 1949.

6.2.1.7 FRANK KLINGER is also referred to as **WILLIAM FRANKLIN KLINGER** in some sources. He was born on 29 April 1885. Some sources record that he was born in 1886. He married **ELIZABETH PHILIPS** circa 1905. He died on 17 May 1957, Cleveland, Cuyahoga County, OH.

6.2.1.7.1 NORMAN E. KLINGER was born on 30 November 1905, Pennsylvania. He married **GENNIE (--?--)** circa 1926. Prior to his death, Norman was living in Lehigh Acres, Lee County, FL. He died on 3 December 1992, at age 87.

6.2.1.7.1.1 JUNE KLINGER was born circa 1928, Ohio.

6.2.1.7.2 MARGARET KLINGER was born circa 1913, Pennsylvania.

6.2.1.8 MINNIE KLINGER was born in October 1887. Some sources record that she was born in 1888. She married **WILLIAM J. FISHER** circa 1910.

6.2.1.8.1 LEO C. FISHER was born on 16 February 1909. He died on 13 July 1995, at age 86. Prior to his death, Leo was living in Shamokin, Northumberland County, PA.

6.2.1.8.2 RAYMOND FISHER was born on 3 June 1911. He died in December 1976, at age 65. Prior to his death, Raymond was living in Shamokin, Northumberland County, PA.

6.2.1.8.3 PEARL E. FISHER was born on 13 August 1915, Shamokin, Northumberland County, PA. She married **LEWIS S. KLINGER**, son of **JOHN IRVIN KLINGER** and **LIZZIE E. MORT**. She died on 29 April 2008, Shamokin Area Community Hospital, Shamokin, Northumberland County, PA, at age 92. According to a newspaper obituary, Pearl lived at 810 Franklin Ave., Trevorton, Northumberland County, PA. She was a retired seamstress who worked in local garment factories. She was buried on 3 May 2008, at Northumberland Memorial Park, Stonington, Northumberland County, PA.

6.2.1.8.3.1 MARGIE J. KLINGER was born on 20 August 1933. She married **JOHN M. FOIERI**. She died on 1 June 2000, at age 66.

6.2.1.8.3.1.1 JOHN L. FOIERI married **LAVONNE (--?--)**.

6.2.1.8.3.1.1.1 JENNIFER FOIERI married **LARRY KEIM**.

6.2.1.8.3.1.1.1.1 CAITLIN KEIM

6.2.1.8.3.1.1.1.2 CORTNEY KEIM

6.2.1.8.3.1.1.2 TIA FOIERI married **JOHN REIDINGER**.

6.2.1.8.3.1.1.2.1 JOHN COLBY

6.2.1.8.3.1.1.2.2 CHLOE REIDINGER

6.2.1.8.4 PAULINE FISHER was born on 13 August 1915, Shamokin, Northumberland County, PA. She married **(--?--) PERSING**. She died on 22 January 2000, at age 84. Prior to her death, Pauline was living in Coal Township, Northumberland County, PA.

6.2.1.8.5 MAUDE E. FISHER was born on 7 August 1917, Shamokin, Northumberland County, PA. She married **EDWARD NEIBAUER**. She died on 26 December 2006, at age 89. According to a newspaper obituary, Maude was garment worker in Coal Township. Prior to her death, she lived on Owl Street, and later at the Mountain View Manor Nursing and Rehabilitation Center. She was an avid bowler and fisherwoman. She was buried on 29 December 2006, at St. Edward Cemetery, Coal Township, Northumberland County, PA.

6.2.1.9 RAYMOND E. KLINGER was born on 15 September 1889. He married ETHEL HENRY. He died on 15 August 1926, Memorial Hospital, Philadelphia, Philadelphia County, PA, at age 36. He was buried on 19 August 1926, at Westminster Cemetery, Bala Cynwyd, Montgomery County, PA.

6.2.1.9.1 CHARLES KLINGER was born in 1915, Pennsylvania.

6.2.1.9.2 RAYMOND MONROE KLINGER was born on 11 June 1918, Philadelphia, Philadelphia County, PA. He married CHARLOTTE B. (--?--). He died on 28 April 1992, at age 73. He was buried at Henlopen Memorial Park, Milton, Sussex County, DE.

6.2.1.9.3 JOHN KLINGER was born circa 1924.

6.2.1.9.4 SARAH KLINGER was born circa 1925.

6.2.1.10 HAROLD J. KLINGER was born on 22 April 1894, Shamokin, Northumberland County, PA. Some sources record that he was born in 1892. He married JENNIE E. QUARTZ, daughter of WILBERT QUARTZ and JENNIE (--?--), circa 1915. He died on 30 November 1964, Shamokin State Hospital, Coal Township, Northumberland County, PA, at age 70. He was buried on 3 December 1964, at IOOF Cemetery, Shamokin, Northumberland County, PA.

6.2.1.10.1 JENNIE E. KLINGER is also referred to as JAN in some sources. She was born on 9 December 1917, Pennsylvania. She married WILFRED ROTH. She died on 30 December 2008, at age 91.

6.2.1.10.2 WILBERT ELIAS KLINGER was born on 15 December 1919, Pennsylvania. He died on 28 August 1997, at age 77.

6.2.1.10.3 WILLIAM FRANKLIN KLINGER was born on 27 August 1924, Shamokin, Northumberland County, PA. He married MARTHA THOMPSON. He died on 31 July 1997, at age 72. He was buried at Saint Marks Church Cemetery, Pennsburg, Montgomery County, PA.

6.2.1.10.3.1 WILLIAM G. KLINGER SR. married CHRISTINE (--?--).

6.2.1.10.3.2 DONNA M. KLINGER was born on 10 May 1947, Shamokin, Northumberland County, PA. She married (--?--) HENRICK. She died on 7 November 2016, Red Hill, Montgomery County, PA, at age 69. She was buried on 18 November 2016, at Saint Marks Church Cemetery, Pennsburg, Montgomery County, PA.

6.2.1.10.3.2.1 SCOTT HENRICK married ANGELA (--?--).

6.2.1.10.3.2.1.1 RYAN HENRICK

6.2.1.10.4 JOHN LEWIS KLINGER was born on 19 July 1926, Shamokin, Northumberland County, PA. He died on 17 October 2000, at age 74. He was buried at Indiantown Gap National Cemetery, Annville, Lebanon County, PA.

6.2.1.10.5 ANNA E. KLINGER also went by the name of ANNIE. She was born on 5 February 1929, Shamokin, Northumberland County, PA. She married GERALD M. LINDEMUTH. She died on 6 June 2012, Ashland, Schuylkill County, PA, at age 83 at her residence on Dutchtown Road. According to a newspaper obituary, Anna was a graduate of the former Shamokin High School, and was employed as a nurse's aide at the former Ashland State General Hospital, Fountain Springs, until its closing. She and her late husband also operated a family farm. She was buried on 9 June 2012.

6.2.1.10.5.1 CONNIE LINDEMUTH married WILLIAM WYDRA SR.

6.2.1.10.5.1.1 PRISETHANE WYDRA died before 2012.

6.2.1.10.5.1.2 WILLIAM WYDRA JR.

6.2.1.10.5.1.3 ADRIENNE WYDRA

6.2.1.10.5.2 ROBERT LINDEMUTH

6.2.1.10.5.3 DONNA LINDEMUTH

6.2.1.10.6 HAROLD KLINGER was born circa 1935. He died before 2012.

6.2.1.11 ELWOOD ELIAS KLINGER was born on 5 June 1896. He married SAVADA LENTZ, daughter of ELMER LENTZ and MINNIE (--?--). He married CATHARINE SCHAFFER. He died on 8 July 1955, Shamokin, Northumberland County, PA, at age 59. He was buried at IOOF Cemetery, Shamokin, Northumberland County, PA.

6.2.1.11.1 ELWOOD ELSWORTH KLINGER was born in 1914.

6.2.1.11.1.1 DENNIS KLINGER was born in 1945.

6.2.1.11.1.1.1 Dennis Klinger was born in 1968.

6.2.1.11.2 Harold Klinger was born circa 1916, Pennsylvania.

6.2.1.11.3 Calvin Klinger

6.2.2 Samuel Emanuel Klinger was born on 28 November 1851, near Sacramento, Schuylkill County, PA. Some sources record that he was born in November 1850, Pennsylvania. He married **Harriet I. Dunkleberger**, daughter of **George Dunkleberger** and **Catherine Rebuck,** in 1875. He died on 2 July 1923, at age 71. He was buried at Pomfret Manor Cemetery, Sunbury, Northumberland County, PA.

6.2.2.1 Stella M. Klinger was born in October 1879, Pennsylvania. She married **Henry C. Worrell** circa 1895.

6.2.2.1.1 Hazel C. Worrell was born in July 1896.

6.2.2.1.2 Mary G. Worrell was born in January 1898. She married **Rhodes James Mock**. She died before 1930.

6.2.2.1.2.1 Mildred Mock was born circa 1919.

6.2.2.1.2.2 James Mock was born circa 1922.

6.2.2.1.3 Jennie M. Worrell was born in October 1899.

6.2.2.1.4 Helen Worrell was born circa 1903.

6.2.2.1.5 Harriet Worrell was born circa 1904.

6.2.2.2 Claude Klinger was born on 29 November 1882, Pennsylvania. He married **Anna Eliza Fisher** circa 1912. Prior to his death, Claude was living in Sunbury, Northumberland County, PA. He died in April 1969, at age 86.

6.2.2.2.1 Ruth Isabell Klinger was born on 1 January 1916, Sunbury, Northumberland County, PA. She married **Albert E. Heath** on 25 March 1937. She died on 19 June 2008, The Villages Regional Hospital, The Villages, FL, at age 92. According to a newspaper obituary, Ruth, who lived in Woodward, PA, attended Sunbury High School and graduated from York School of Nursing, after which she was employed at York Hospital. Later she worked at the Geisinger Medical Center, Danville, where she retired as a nurse anesthetist. Ruth was survived by five grandchildren, Joanne Martin of New Holland, Dawn Heath of Yardly, Brian Heath of New Holland, Elizabeth Gohn of Dillsburg and Wade Heath Jr. of Dover; six great-grandchildren; two great-great-grandchildren; and a longtime friend, Auther Bobb of Woodward. She was buried on 22 June 2008, at Woodward Cemetery, Woodward, Centre County, PA.

6.2.2.2.1.1 Wade Heath married **Linda Lee** (--?--).

6.2.2.2.1.1.1 Wade Heath Jr.

6.2.2.2.1.2 Gary Heath is also referred to as **A.G. Heath** in some sources. He was born on 12 December 1940. He died on 19 August 2004, at age 63.

6.2.2.2.2 Paul Ellsworth Klinger was born on 31 October 1919. He was baptized on 28 May 1928, Eden Evangelical Lutheran Church, Plum Creek, Northumberland County, PA. He married **Annabelle M. Heintzelman**, daughter of **John Heintzelman** and **Leva** (--?--), on 7 March 1953. He died on 21 February 2000, at age 80. According to an obituary for his wife, Paul had the following grandchildren: Kathy Mott, Tony Klinger, Jeff Lesher, Jenny Macklin, Josh Karli and Alicia Karli, and 10 great-grandchildren.

6.2.2.2.2.1 Jeanette Klinger married **Terry Lesher**. Jeanette lives in Sunbury, PA.

6.2.2.2.2.1.1 Jeff Lesher

6.2.2.2.2.2 Donna Klinger married **Rich Esposito**. She is also referred to as **Donna Burns** in some sources. Donna lives in Elizabethtown, PA.

6.2.2.2.2.3 Roger Klinger married **Mary** (--?--). Roger lives in Delaware.

6.2.2.2.2.4 Barry Klinger married **Roberta** (--?--). Barry lives in California.

6.2.2.2.3 Harriet Faye Klinger was born on 3 July 1926. She was baptized on 28 May 1928, Eden Evangelical Lutheran Church, Plum Creek, Northumberland County, PA. She married **(--?--) Kitchen.**

6.2.2.3 Palmer Eugene Klinger was born on 20 February 1882, Sunbury, Northumberland County, PA. Some sources record that he was born on 20 February 1880. Some sources record that he was born in February 1881, Pennsylvania. He married **Jennie Anna Brosius**, daughter of **Charles**

BROSIUS and SUSAN DEPPEN, circa 1901. According to some sources, Palmer was living in Detroit, Michigan around 1940, but in 1942, according to World War II draft registration cards, Palmer was living in Northumberland County, PA. He died on 12 August 1949, at age 68. He was buried at Pomfret Manor Cemetery, Sunbury, Northumberland County, PA.

    6.2.2.3.1 ARTHUR B. KLINGER was born circa 1902.

    6.2.2.3.2 ETHEL M. KLINGER was born circa 1904. She married **EARL BRIGAND**.

        6.2.2.3.2.1 SHIRLEY BRIGAND

        6.2.2.3.2.2 ROBERT BRIGAND

    6.2.2.3.3 RALPH C. KLINGER was born circa 1906.

    6.2.2.3.4 GLADYS V. KLINGER was born in 1909.

6.2.2.4 EMORY R. KLINGER was born on 2 July 1885, Pennsylvania. He married **MYRTLE A. CONRAD**, daughter of **SAMUEL CONRAD**. Prior to his death, Emory was living in Sunbury, Northumberland County, PA. He died on 10 December 1967, at age 82. He was buried at Pomfret Manor Cemetery, Sunbury, Northumberland County, PA.

6.2.2.5 FAY KLINGER is also referred to as **BESSIE FAYE KLINGER** in some sources. She was born on 6 January 1888, Pennsylvania. She married **WALTER S. SANDERS**. She died on 23 August 1943, at age 55. She was buried at Pomfret Manor Cemetery, Sunbury, Northumberland County, PA.

6.2.2.6 EARL CLYDE KLINGER was born on 10 October 1889, Pennsylvania. He died on 25 November 1948, at age 59. He was buried at Pomfret Manor Cemetery, Sunbury, Northumberland County, PA.

6.2.2.7 EMMA L. KLINGER was born in December 1891, Pennsylvania. Some sources record that she was born on 8 December 1892. She died on 5 December 1976. She was buried at Pomfret Manor Cemetery, Sunbury, Northumberland County, PA.

6.2.2.8 MARY C. KLINGER was born in April 1893, Pennsylvania.

6.2.2.9 MABEL R. KLINGER was born on 19 July 1896. Some sources record that she was born in July 1894, Pennsylvania. She married **FREDERICK T. LEPLEY** circa 1920. She died in December 1978, at age 84. She was buried at West Side Cemetery, Monroe Township, Snyder County, PA.

    6.2.2.9.1 FREDERICK E. LEPLEY was born on 9 May 1921. He died on 12 September 1987, at age 66.

        6.2.2.9.1.1 THOMAS LEPLEY

    6.2.2.9.2 EMMA LEPLEY was born on 2 August 1925, Sunbury, Northumberland County, PA. She married **ERNEST KORTEN JR.** on 27 June 1948, Zion Lutheran Church, Sunbury, Northumberland County, PA. She died on 21 May 2010, Sunbury, Northumberland County, PA, at age 84, at her home on RR 2. According to a newspaper obituary, Emma Jane worked as a licensed x-ray technician at the Sunbury Community Hospital and the Selinsgrove Center until her retirement. She and her husband also operated a Tastee Freeze in Danville for four years.

6.2.2.10 DONALD KLINGER is also referred to as **GEORGE D. KLINGER** in some sources. He was born in December 1898, Pennsylvania.

6.2.3 AMELIA E. KLINGER was born on 5 January 1854. She married **CHARLES H. WETZEL**, son of **CHARLES WETZEL** and **HANNAH HEIM**, circa 1875. She died on 13 July 1914, Rockefeller Township, Northumberland County, PA, at age 60. She was buried at Fairview Cemetery, Wiconisco, Dauphin County, PA.

    6.2.3.1 TAMIE A. WETZEL was born circa 1875. She died in 1915. She was buried at Fairview Cemetery, Wiconisco, Dauphin County, PA.

    6.2.3.2 DELLA B. WETZEL was born circa 1877.

    6.2.3.3 LILLIE M. WETZEL married **JOHN CAMERON**. She was born circa 1878.

        6.2.3.3.1 VERNA AMELIA CAMERON was born on 14 October 1897. She was baptized on 6 January 1898, Emmanuel Evangelical Lutheran Church, Wolf's Crossroads, Rockefeller Township, Northumberland County, PA.

    6.2.3.4 EMMA J. WETZEL was born on 17 July 1879. She died on 4 January 1894, at age 14. She was buried on 4 April 1894, at Emmanuel Evangelical Lutheran Church Cemetery, Wolf's Crossroads, Rockefeller Township, Northumberland County, PA.

    6.2.3.5 SIDNEY S. WETZEL was born circa 1882, Pennsylvania. She married **(--?--) NEIDIG**.

6.2.3.5.1 DAVID A. NEIDIG was born circa 1907, Pennsylvania.

6.2.3.5.2 HELEN M. NEIDIG was born circa 1908, Pennsylvania.

6.2.3.6 MAZIE M. WETZEL was born in May 1884, Pennsylvania.

6.2.3.7 SADIE ISABELLA WETZEL was born on 14 March 1894, Seven Points, Northumberland County, PA. She was baptized on 27 May 1894, Emmanuel Evangelical Lutheran Church, Wolf's Crossroads, Rockefeller Township, Northumberland County, PA. She married **EAMIL FROMME** on 6 June 1912, Williamstown, Dauphin County, PA. She died on 14 September 1979, Middletown, Dauphin County, PA, at age 85. She was buried at Fairview Cemetery, Wiconisco, Dauphin County, PA.

6.2.3.7.1 ROBERT FROMME was born circa 1921.

6.2.3.7.2 LILLIAN MARIE FROMME was born on 7 July 1924, Williamstown Junction, Dauphin County, PA. She died on 29 January 1998, at age 73.

6.2.4 GABRIEL KLINGER was born on 16 October 1855. He married **CLARA MILISSA WOLF**, daughter of **HENRY H. WOLF** and **HANNAH E. YORDY**, on 28 August 1881, Eden Evangelical Lutheran Church, Rockefeller Township, Northumberland County, PA. He died on 9 January 1941, at age 85. He was buried at Emmanuel Evangelical Lutheran Church, Wolf's Crossroads, Rockefeller Township, Northumberland County, PA.

6.2.4.1 HATTIE MILISSA KLINGER was born on 5 July 1882, Northumberland County, PA. She married **CLAYTON C. BARTHOLOMEW**, son of **VALENTINE BARTHOLOMEW** and **AMELIA HAUCK**, circa 1901. She died on 3 September 1960, Jacob's Nursing Home, Penn Township, Snyder County, PA, at age 78. She was buried on 6 September 1960, at Wolf's Cross Roads Lutheran Cemetery, Rockefeller Township, Northumberland County, PA.

6.2.4.1.1 HELEN AMELIA BARTHOLOMEW was born on 5 May 1902. She married **HOWARD E. DAGLE**, son of **JOHN DAGLE** and **MARGARET HOUSEL**.

6.2.4.1.1.1 CLAYTON DAGLE was born on 7 October 1922. He died on 18 October 1924, at age 2.

6.2.4.1.2 HERBERT ELWOOD BARTHOLOMEW was born on 20 December 1903. He married **GRACE THOMAS**. He died in September 1985, at age 81.

6.2.4.1.2.1 PAUL BARTHOLOMEW. Paul lives in Northumberland, PA.

6.2.4.1.2.2 FRANKLIN BARTHOLOMEW died before 2011.

6.2.4.1.2.3 SHIRLEY BARTHOLOMEW married **(--?--) MULL**. Shirley lives in Selinsgrove, PA.

6.2.4.1.2.4 JOYCE BARTHOLOMEW married **(--?--) HEIMBACH**. Joyce lives in Snydertown, PA.

6.2.4.1.2.5 ROBERT BARTHOLOMEW. Robert lives in Snydertown, PA.

6.2.4.1.2.6 HERBERT BARTHOLOMEW JR. died before 2011.

6.2.4.1.2.7 MILDRED BARTHOLOMEW was born circa 1929. She married **(--?--) KNOEBEL**. Mildred lives in Sunbury, PA.

6.2.4.1.2.8 CLAYTON E. BARTHOLOMEW was born on 10 August 1931, Rockefeller Township, Northumberland County, PA. He married **JANICE M. KLINGER** on 27 September 1985. He died on 28 June 2011, Geisinger Medical Center, Danville, Montour County, PA, at age 79. According to a newspaper obituary, Clayton lived in Trevorton, PA. He served in the Army during the Korean War from Jan. 7, 1949, to Sept. 2, 1952. He retired from Wilhold Co., Sunbury, as a mechanic. He was buried at Northumberland Memorial Park, Stonington, Northumberland County, PA.

6.2.4.1.2.8.1 CLAYTON R. BARTHOLOMEW. Clayton lives in Trevorton, PA.

6.2.4.1.2.8.2 PAUL BARTHOLOMEW married **TINA (--?--)**. Paul lives in Marion Heights, PA.

6.2.4.1.3 HOWARD VALENTINE BARTHOLOMEW was born on 30 December 1906. He died on 3 March 1919, at age 12. He was buried at Wolf's Cross Roads Cemetery, Rockefeller Township, Northumberland County, PA.

6.2.4.1.4 WARD EMERSON BARTHOLOMEW was born on 19 October 1908. He died on 28 February 1919, at age 10. He was buried at Wolf's Cross Roads Cemetery, Rockefeller Township, Northumberland County, PA.

6.2.4.1.5 RUTH IRENE BARTHOLOMEW was born on 15 January 1910. She married **DAVID MCCORRISTON**.

6.2.4.1.6 CLARE ELIZABETH BARTHOLOMEW was born on 2 April 1911. She married **JOHN ATKINSON**.

6.2.4.1.7 EFFENGER G. BARTHOLOMEW was born on 7 September 1912. He married **GLADYS WATERS**.

6.2.4.1.8 JOHN KELLAR BARTHOLOMEW was born on 17 December 1913. He married **MILDRED HOFFMAN**.

6.2.4.1.9 BRUCE BARTHOLOMEW was born circa 1915. Some sources record that he was born circa 1918. He married **RUTH HUMMEL**.

6.2.4.2 SAMUEL LLOYD KLINGER was born on 3 November 1883. He married **CHARLOTTE FANNIE WETZLER**, daughter of **JOHYN NICHOLAS WETZLER** and **CLARA NATHALIA WALZ,** circa 1905. He died on 4 July 1952, Glenolden, Delaware County, PA, at age 68. He was buried on 7 July 1952, at Arlington Cemetery, Drexel Hill, Delaware County, PA.

6.2.4.2.1 JOHN LUKE KLINGER was born on 17 September 1905. He married **HAZEL EMERICK**.

6.2.4.2.2 GRACE ELIZABETH KLINGER was born on 12 February 1908. She married **HARVEY C. KNAPP**.

6.2.4.2.3 MIRIAM VIRGINIA KLINGER was born on 14 December 1912. She married **WILLIAM ALBERT MCFANN**, son of **WILLIAM ALBERT MCFANN**.

6.2.4.3 HENRY ROLAND KLINGER was born on 30 November 1883, Dornsife, Northumberland County, PA. He married **ALICE MAY ZARTMAN** circa 1904. He died in August 1969, at age 85.

6.2.4.3.1 MARTHA NAOMI KLINGER was born on 24 August 1906, Sunbury, Northumberland County, PA. She married **RAYMOND C. STOUDT**, son of **ALFRED H. STOUDT** and **SALLIE E. CROUTHAMEL**. She died in 1977. She was buried at Greenwood Cemetery, Allentown, Lehigh County, PA.

6.2.4.3.1.1 ROBERT R. STOUDT was born on 12 October 1927. He died on 11 September 1937, Allentown, Lehigh County, PA, at age 9. He was buried at Greenwood Cemetery, Allentown, Lehigh County, PA.

6.2.4.3.1.2 DONALD H. STOUDT was born circa 1929.

6.2.4.3.1.3 RAYMOND C. STOUDT JR. was born circa 1938.

6.2.4.3.2 CLYDE GABRIEL JOSEPH KLINGER was born on 5 April 1908, Rockefeller Township, Northumberland County, PA. He married **RUTH ERSILLA PRY**, daughter of **HARRY THOMAS PRY** and **ADDIE REBECCA WOODBRIDGE**. He died in October 1979, at age 71. Prior to his death, Clyde was living in Allentown, Lehigh County, PA.

6.2.4.3.2.1 PATRICIA KLINGER was born circa 1937.

6.2.4.3.2.2 GRANT CLYDE KLINGER was born on 29 August 1938, Allentown, Lehigh County, PA. He married **DAWN DIDRA**, daughter of **CHARLES DIDRA** and **FLORENCE REICHARD,** circa 1957. He died on 21 May 1995, Allentown, Lehigh County, PA, at age 56. He was buried at Saint Mark's Cemetery, Allentown, Lehigh County, PA.

6.2.4.3.3 PAUL D. KLINGER was born on 24 October 1909. He married **LILLIAN (--?--)**. He died on 10 July 1991, at age 81.

6.2.4.3.4 BERNICE KLINGER was born on 30 April 1912. She died on 13 February 1913, Sunbury, Northumberland County, PA. She was buried at Saint Luke's Cemetery, Sunbury, Northumberland County, PA.

6.2.4.3.5 GEORGE W. KLINGER was born on 30 July 1918. He died on 30 July 1918, Allentown, Lehigh County, PA.

6.2.4.3.6 RUTH M. KLINGER was born in 1919, Pennsylvania.

6.2.4.3.7 CLARA E. KLINGER was born circa 1923, Pennsylvania.

6.2.4.4 ROY EUGENE KLINGER was born on 14 December 1884. He was baptized on 31 August 1885, Emmanuel Evangelical Lutheran Church, Wolf's Crossroads, Northumberland County, PA. He died on

5 December 1902, at age 17. He was buried at Emmanuel Evangelical Lutheran Church Cemetery, Wolf's Crossroads, Northumberland County, PA.

6.2.4.5 EDNA VIOLA KLINGER was born on 14 December 1884. She died on 29 August 1885. She was buried on 31 August 1885, at Emmanuel Evangelical Lutheran Church Cemetery, Wolf's Crossroads, Northumberland County, PA.

6.2.4.6 IRVIN ALBERT KLINGER was born on 30 March 1886, Trevorton, Schuylkill County, PA. He married **LYDIA DAVIS**, daughter of **WILLIAM B. DAVIS** and **MARGARET (--?--)**, circa 1906. He died on 27 February 1958, Williamsport Hospital, Williamsport, Lycoming County, PA, at age 71. He was buried on 2 March 1958, at Wolf's Cross Roads Cemetery, Rockefeller Township, Northumberland County, PA.

> **6.2.4.6.1 IRVIN ALBERT KLINGER JR.** was born on 12 March 1916, Wilkes Barre, Luzerne County, PA. He married **VIRGINIA LOUISE RAWLS**, daughter of **ALBERT DUPREE RAWLS** and **ANNIE LOREEN FLYNN**, on 28 March 1943, Phoebus, Elizabeth City County, VA. He died on 5 August 1989, Petersburg, VA, at age 73. He was buried at Sunset Memorial Park, Chester, Chesterfield County, VA.

>> **6.2.4.6.1.1 KENNETH RAYMOND KLINGER** married **SHIRLEY (--?--)**. He married **PAMELA RAY COCHRAN** circa 1973. He and **PAMELA RAY COCHRAN** were divorced.

>>> **6.2.4.6.1.1.1 JENNIFER COCHRAN KLINGER** was born on 5 June 1975. She married **SERGIO MICHAEL LEON** on 30 May 1998.

>>>> **6.2.4.6.1.1.1.1 MICHAEL IRVIN LEON** was born on 6 March 2005.

>>>> **6.2.4.6.1.1.1.2 SOPHIA MAE LEON** was born on 25 July 2007.

> **6.2.4.6.2 ALFRED RAYMOND KLINGER** was born on 22 June 1918, Wilkes Barre, Luzerne County, PA. He married **LUCILLE MADALINE HARRIS**, daughter of **CLARENCE HARRIS** and **PEARL JENNINGS**, circa 1939. He died on 20 February 2007, at age 88.

>> **6.2.4.6.2.1 ALFRED RAYMOND KLINGER JR.** was born on 18 October 1942, Williamsport, Lycoming County, PA. He married **GABRIELLA ANGELA CAPRANI** circa 1968. He died on 3 April 2001, Bedford, Middlesex County, MA, at age 58.

>>> **6.2.4.6.2.1.1 SILVIA MARIE KLINGER** is also referred to as **SIVIA CLINGER** in some sources. She was born circa 1970.

>>> **6.2.4.6.2.1.2 CINZIA KLINGER** was born in 1971. She married **(--?--) BIBB**.

>>> **6.2.4.6.2.1.3 CHRISTINE ANGELA KLINGER** is also referred to as **KRISTINE CLINGER** in some sources. She was born circa 1984.

6.2.4.7 BESSIE AURELIA KLINGER was born on 2 August 1887. She married **CLAUD EMANUEL BROSIOUS**, son of **ELIAS BROSIOUS** and **MAHALA (--?--)**. She died in December 1918, at age 31. She was buried at Wolf's Cross Roads Cemetery, Wolf's Cross Roads, Northumberland County, PA.

> **6.2.4.7.1 ARTHUR REUBEN BROSIUS** was born on 20 November 1913. He married **ELENORE BRAMLEY**. He died before 2015.

> **6.2.4.7.2 CLARA ELIZABETH BROSIUS** is also referred to as **CLARA ELIZABETH BROSCIOUS** in some sources. She was born on 2 August 1915, Augustaville, Northumberland County, PA. She married **RUSSELL FREDERICK NAHODIL SR.**, son of **FRANZ NAHODIL** and **BLANCHE LULU LYTLE**, on 6 August 1936. She died on 29 March 2015, at age 99. According to a newspaper obituary, Clara, who lived in Shamokin, PA, worked in food service her entire life. She worked as a cafeteria manager for the Arrow Shirt Company as well as for Weller Vending. She was buried at Northumberland Memorial Park, Stonington, Northumberland County, PA.

>> **6.2.4.7.2.1 ROSLYN NAHODIL** married **WAYNE KOMARA**.

>> **6.2.4.7.2.2 JANE NAHODIL** married **(--?--) LONG**.

>> **6.2.4.7.2.3 RUSSELL NAHODIL JR.** married **KIM (--?--)**.

>> **6.2.4.7.2.4 REV. RICHARD NAHODIL** married **BETH (--?--)**.

>> **6.2.4.7.2.5 DIANE NAHODIL** died before 2015.

6.2.4.8 ARCHIE CLYDE KLINGER was born on 18 June 1889. He married **LYDIA O'NIELL**. He died on 11 October 1964, at age 75. He was buried at Roselawn Cemetery, Berwick, Columbia County, PA.

> **6.2.4.8.1 THELMA IRIS KLINGER** was born on 20 August 1911. She married **JAY RUSSELL PETERS**, son of **WILLIAM DANIEL PETERS** and **MARY JANE RIEGEL**, on 26 December 1953. She

died on 7 January 1977, at age 65. She was buried at Roselawn Cemetery, Berwick, Columbia County, PA.

6.2.4.8.2 MINA EVELYN KLINGER was born on 20 October 1912.

6.2.4.9 OLIVE MAY KLINGER was born on 30 September 1890. She married GROVER C. WYNN. She died on 28 June 1978, Los Angeles, CA, at age 87. She was buried at Rose Hills Memorial Park, Whittier, Los Angeles County, CA.

6.2.4.9.1 GROVER IRVIN WYNN was born on 25 March 1914. He married DOLA MARIE IRVIN, daughter of JAMES ARTHUR IRVIN and PEARL SUTTON, on 2 June 1935, Bartlett, IA. He married MARGARET PATRICIA CALDERWOOD, daughter of WILLARD S. CALDERWOOD and MARGARET ELLIOTT, on 24 February 1962, Los Angeles, Los Angeles County, CA. He died in December 1974, at age 60.

6.2.4.9.1.1 KATHERINE MARIE WYNN was born on 29 June 1937, Los Angeles County, CA.

6.2.4.9.2 DOROTHY ARLINE WYNN was born on 14 November 1916, Danville, Montour County, PA. She married LEIGHTON B. REED. She died on 17 August 2007, at age 90. She was buried at Sidney Cemetery, Sidney, Fremont County, IA.

6.2.4.9.3 ROBERT CHARLES WYNN was born on 10 September 1919. He married MAE (--?--) before 1940. He died on 25 April 1945, Luzon, Philippines, at age 25. Robert was a private first class in Company G, 27th Infantry Regiment, 25th Division of the US Army. He was originally buried in the Philippines but was disinterred and reburied in the US. He was buried on 25 February 1949, at Fort Rosencrans National Cemetery, San Diego, San Diego County, CA.

6.2.4.10 ANNIE JANNETTE KLINGER was born on 1 January 1892. She died in August 1893, at age 1.

6.2.4.11 REMUS ELMER KLINGER was born on 16 February 1893. He died in August 1893.

6.2.4.12 EMMA ELIZABETH KLINGER was born on 2 May 1894. She married J. FRANKLIN DAGLE circa 1916. She died in 1940.

6.2.4.12.1 JOHN CLAIR DAGLE married JACQUALIN HENDERSON. He was born on 30 October 1920.

6.2.4.13 ALICE ELISE KLINGER was born on 26 September 1895. She married CRAYTON HOMER SPECHT on 25 December 1917, Shamokin, Northumberland County, PA. She died on 30 March 1989, Selinsgrove, Snyder County, PA, at age 93.

6.2.4.13.1 CLIFTON REARICK SPECHT was born on 15 January 1919. He married HELEN RACHAEL STEFFEN. He died in June 1982, at age 63.

6.2.4.13.2 ELLEN ENDORA SPECHT was born on 28 March 1920. She married BANKS BILGER. She died before 2010.

6.2.4.13.3 WILDA PAULINE SPECHT is also referred to as HILDA T. in some sources. She was born on 8 February 1922, Tharptown, Northumberland County, PA. She married MARLYN S. HACKENBURG on 21 December 1938. She died on 29 August 2010, Winfield, Union County, PA, at age 88, at her home. According to a newspaper obituary, Wilda was a homemaker most of her life, but was employed at J.G. Ott Manufacturing, Selinsgrove, and Bob Rader chicken dressing plant, Lithia Springs. She enjoyed bird watching, crossword puzzles, flowers and making craft items with plastic canvas to give to her friends. She was also active in the Senior Citizen Center, Penns Creek. She was buried on 2 September 2010, at Globe Mills Cemetery, Middleburg, Snyder County, PA.

6.2.4.13.3.1 NANCY L. HACKENBURG was born on 10 November 1940. She married RANDALL BONNIE. She died on 1 October 2008, at age 67.

6.2.4.13.4 CHARLES THEODORE SPECHT was born on 25 September 1923. He married ESTHER MILLER. He died on 23 October 1993, at age 70. At the time of his death, Charles was living in the vicinity of Rochester, NY.

6.2.4.13.5 CRAYTON HOMER SPECHT was born on 19 October 1925. He died in 1928. He died before 2010.

6.2.4.13.6 HATTIE MARIE SPECHT was born on 1 January 1927. She died in 1927.

6.2.4.13.7 WANDA MAY SPECHT was born on 28 December 1927. She married JERALD LONG.

6.2.4.13.8 RUTH IRIS SPECHT was born on 10 July 1929. She married JOHN KELLY. She married WILLIAM FLOWERS. She married (--?--) COOK. She married LEROY BAKER.

6.2.4.13.9 EDWIN CLAIR SPECHT was born on 27 September 1933. He married **JANNETTE NAUGLE.** He died on 25 August 1995, at age 61.

6.2.4.13.10 MIRIAM ELIZABETH SPECHT was born on 20 December 1933.

6.2.4.14 JOHN FRAZIER KLINGER was born on 5 September 1898. He married **SARAH ELIZABETH ROSS,** daughter of **CHARLES E. ROSS** and **EVA A. EISTER,** circa 1921. He died on 22 September 1968, at age 70. He was buried at Wolf's Cross Roads Cemetery, Rockefeller Township, Northumberland County, PA.

6.2.4.14.1 CHARLES FRAZIER KLINGER was born on 22 May 1922. He married **MARTHA MARTIN.** He died before 18 November 2008.

6.2.4.14.2 BETTY ELNORA KLINGER was born on 18 August 1923. She married **LEON BADMAN.** She married **(--?--) HOCH.** Betty lives in Quakertown, PA.

6.2.4.14.3 RICHARD GABRIEL KLINGER was born on 21 February 1925, Plum Creek, Northumberland County, PA. He married **DOROTHY L. MANGUS,** daughter of **ORVILLE MANGUS** and **ROSE MCGOUGH,** circa 1944. He died on 18 November 2008, Geisinger Medical Center, Danville, Montour County, PA, at age 83. According to a newspaper obituary, Richard who was known as "Dick" lived on Scenic Drive, Danville, PA. He served in the Air Force and was later employed for 27 years at Merck, Riverside, PA, as a first line supervisor. He was buried on 21 November 2008, at Odd Fellows Cemetery, Danville, Montour County, PA.

6.2.4.14.3.1 LINDA KLINGER married **RICHARD BYERLY.** Linda and her husband live in Rebuck, PA.

6.2.4.14.3.2 RICK KLINGER married **SHARON (--?--).** Rick and his wife live in Riverside, PA.

6.2.4.14.4 JUNE ELIZABETH KLINGER was born on 15 June 1926. She married **EMERSON REITZ.** June lives in Sunbury, PA.

6.2.4.14.5 SHIRLEY LOIS KLINGER was born on 18 November 1928, Sunbury, Northumberland County, PA. Some sources record that she was born on 18 November 1929. She married **LEROY SNYDER** on 3 December 1951, PA. She married **FRED KLINGER** on 27 December 1974. She died on 23 November 2010, Osceola Regional Hospital, Kissimmee, FL, at age 81. According to a newspaper obituary, Shirley attended the Sunbury schools and then worked for David Knit, Northumberland, Pa., and Scottys Lumber in Florida. She also lived in Roy, UT.

6.2.4.14.5.1 SAMUEL SNYDER married **CINDY (--?--).** Samuel lives in Kratzerville, PA.

6.2.4.14.5.2 JUDY SNYDER married **(--?--) BELL.** Patricia lives in Jacksonville, FL.

6.2.4.14.5.3 LOIS ANN SNYDER was born on 12 July 1953, Dauphin Co., PA. She married **TRACY UMSTEAD.** Lois lives in Selinsgrove, PA.

6.2.4.14.5.4 CARL LEROY SNYDER was born on 20 August 1954, Dauphin Co., PA. Carl lives in Roy, UT.

6.2.4.14.5.5 PATRICIA JEAN SNYDER was born on 23 March 1957, Dauphin Co., PA. Patricia lives in Clover, SC.

6.2.4.14.6 JOSEPHINE EVA KLINGER was born on 27 January 1931. She married **LARRY MILLER.** Josephine lives in Maryland.

6.2.4.14.7 JOHN JUNIOR KLINGER was born on 20 September 1932. He married **SALLY HARRY.** He died before 18 November 2008.

6.2.4.14.8 JEANNETTE MAY KLINGER is also referred to as **JEANETTE AND JANET** in some sources. She was born on 16 October 1934. She married **ROBERT HEDDINGS.** She married **(--?--) BLAIR.** Jeanette lives in Idaho.

6.2.4.15 ELLEN MAY KLINGER was born on 29 September 1901. She married **GEORGE WARDEN WYNN,** son of **GEORGE W. WYNN** and **FLORA RENN,** circa 1921. Ellen lived in Sunbury, PA. She died on 3 January 1967, at age 65. She was buried at Wolf's Crossroads Cemetery, Rockefeller Township, Northumberland County, PA.

6.2.4.15.1 GEORGE WARDEN WYNN JR. was born on 23 November 1922. Some sources record that he was born on 22 November 1922. George lived in Poplar, Douglas County, WI. He died on 9 February 1988, at age 65.

6.2.4.15.2 CLIFFORD CALVIN WYNN was born on 11 July 1924. Clifford lives in White Haven, FL.

6.2.4.15.3 KEITH LARUE WYNN was born on 22 June 1929. Keith lives in Standardsville, VA.

6.2.4.15.4 GERALDINE FLORA WYNN was born on 1 July 1931, Sunbury, Northumberland County, PA. She died on 16 July 2008, Golden Living Center Mansion, Sunbury, Northumberland County, PA, at age 77. According to a newspaper obituary, Geraldine, who lived at 130 S. Front St., Sunbury, PA, was employed in Kmart stores in Buffalo, N.Y., Bloomsburg, PA, and Shamokin Dam, PA, as office manager, until her retirement in 1981. She was buried on 19 July 2008, at United Lutheran Cemetery, Seven Points Road, Sunbury, Northumberland County, PA.

6.2.4.15.5 KARL DAVID WYNN is also referred to as **CARL** in some sources. He was born on 11 January 1933. Karl lives in Blaisdel, NY.

6.2.4.16 LAURA BELLE KLINGER was born on 5 December 1902. She died on 7 December 1907, at age 5. Some sources record that she died in 1908. She was buried at Wolf's Cross Roads Cemetery, Rockefeller Township, Northumberland County, PA.

6.2.4.17 JAMES ROBERT KLINGER was born on 8 June 1906. He married **HELEN M. MARKS** circa 1922. He died on 10 November 1972, at age 66.

6.2.4.17.1 GLADYS EMMA KLINGER was born on 27 March 1924. She married **CHARLES HOLLENBACH**.

6.2.4.17.2 JAMES ROBERT KLINGER was born on 24 August 1926. He married **JUNE HEIMBACH**.

6.2.4.17.3 DOROTHY HELEN KLINGER was born on 27 December 1927. She married **CLAUDE WENRICH**.

6.2.4.17.4 GRANT ELWOOD KLINGER was born on 24 January 1929, Sunbury, Northumberland County, PA. He married **BERNICE ROWE**, daughter of **PAUL ROWE** and **KATIE WALTER**, on 28 January 1950, Zion Lutheran Church, Kratzerville, Northumberland County, PA.

6.2.4.17.4.1 SHERRY KLINGER was born on 22 July 1950, Lewisburg Hospital, Lewisburg, PA. She married **GEORGE E. ISENBERG**, son of **SAMUEL PAUL ISENBERG** and **MARTHA SNYDER**, on 28 March 1970, Laurelton, PA. She married **(--?--) BEAVER**. She died before 2015.

6.2.4.17.4.1.1 TRACEY ANN ISENBERG was born on 3 October 1970, Sunbury, Northumberland County, PA.

6.2.4.17.4.1.2 JOSEPH ROBERT ISENBERG was born on 22 July 1972.

6.2.4.17.4.2 KEITH A. KLINGER was born on 23 September 1952, Lewisburg Hospital, Lewisburg, PA.

6.2.4.17.4.3 DENNIS KLINGER was born on 11 September 1954, Lewisburg Hospital, Lewisburg, PA. He married **KATHRYN WILLIAMS** on 25 November 1972, Sunbury, Northumberland County, PA.

6.2.4.17.4.4 CAROL KLINGER was born on 5 April 1956, Lewisburg Hospital, Lewisburg, PA. She married **(--?--) MCCREARY**.

6.2.4.17.4.5 TERRY KLINGER was born on 28 November 1959, Lewisburg Hospital, Lewisburg, PA.

6.2.4.17.4.6 TINA KLINGER was born on 10 August 1961, Lewisburg Hospital, Lewisburg, PA. She married **(--?--) MULL**.

6.2.4.17.4.7 PAUL JAMES KLINGER was born on 12 November 1963, Lewisburg Hospital, Lewisburg, PA.

6.2.4.17.5 MARIAN KAY KLINGER was born on 17 December 1931. She married **MARSHALL QUICK**. She married **WAYNE GIBBONS**. She married **HENRY MENGLE**.

6.2.4.17.6 FREDERICK CLAIR KLINGER was born on 25 April 1934. He married **JEAN DUNKLE**.

6.2.4.17.7 NETTIE JANE KLINGER was born on 25 April 1934. She married **MARLIN BELL**.

6.2.4.17.8 CLAIR MARDEN KLINGER was born on 15 September 1935. He married **DARLENE NEWBERRY**, daughter of **STEPHEN NEWBERRY** and **MARGARET GINGRICH**, on 11 October 1958.

6.2.4.17.8.1 CLAIR KLINGER married **LELIA (--?--)**.

6.2.4.17.8.2 TROY KLINGER married HOPE (--?--).

6.2.4.17.8.3 ANNETTE KLINGER married ALAN SUTTON.

6.2.4.17.9 EVELYN MAY KLINGER was born on 30 October 1936. She married GEORGE LETTERMAN.

6.2.4.17.10 ELSIE LOUISE KLINGER was born on 17 February 1938. She married CLAIR SPANGLER.

6.2.4.17.11 KENNETH LEE KLINGER was born on 5 February 1943. He married BARBARA UMHOLTZ.

6.2.4.17.12 JANET MARIE KLINGER was born on 30 July 1944. She married LAMAR ALLEN CAMPBELL.

6.2.5 CATHARINE JANE KLINGER was born on 22 October 1857. She died in 1925. She was buried at Emmanuel Evangelical Lutheran Church, Wolf's Crossroads, Rockefeller Township, Northumberland County, PA.

6.2.6 JULIA ANN KLINGER was born on 8 January 1860. She died on 11 January 1863, at age 3. She was buried at Emanuel's (Old Lantz) Church, Rockefeller Township, Northumberland County, PA.

6.2.7 MARIA MAGDALENA KLINGER is also referred to as MARY in some sources. She was born on 8 January 1862. She was baptized on 13 January 1863, Emmanuel Evangelical Lutheran Church, Wolf's Crossroads, Northumberland County, PA. She died on 28 April 1876, at age 14. She was buried at Emanuel's (Old Lantz) Church, Rockefeller Township, Northumberland County, PA.

6.2.8 ISABELLA JANE KLINGER was born on 14 July 1864, Northumberland County, PA. She was baptized on 1 October 1865, Emmanuel Evangelical Lutheran Church, Wolf's Crossroads, Northumberland County, PA. She married EZRA PERCIVAL SCHIVE. She died on 15 October 1916, at age 52. She was buried at Odd Fellows Cemetery, Shamokin, Northumberland County, PA.

6.2.9 JOHN GEORGE KLINGER was born on 17 November 1866, Seven Points, Northumberland County, PA. Some sources record that he was born in November 1867. He married ELIZABETH DEWITT, daughter of WILLIAM W. DEWITT and MARY LATSHA, on 16 January 1890. He died on 18 April 1939, at age 72. He was buried at Pomfret Manor Cemetery, Sunbury, Northumberland County, PA.

6.2.9.1 HARRY WILLIAM KLINGER was born on 11 September 1893. He died on 11 November 1969, at age 76. He was buried at Pomfret Manor Cemetery, Sunbury, Northumberland County, PA.

6.2.9.2 EDGAR DEWITT KLINGER was born in 1897. He married MARY SHIELD.

6.2.10 WILLIAM EGGERS KLINGER was born on 7 October 1868. He was baptized on 21 June 1869, Emmanuel Evangelical Lutheran Church, Wolf's Crossroads, Northumberland County, PA. He died on 9 November 1873, at age 5. He was buried at Emanuel's (Old Lantz) Church, Rockefeller Township, Northumberland County, PA.

6.2.11 PETER LLOYD KLINGER was born on 7 September 1870. He was baptized on 7 May 1871, Emmanuel Evangelical Lutheran Church, Wolf's Crossroads, Northumberland County, PA. Some sources record that he was born in 1869. Peter and his brother Daniel were twins. He married CARRIE E. FAUSOLD, daughter of ELIAS FAUSOLD and LYDIA HEPNER, on 28 September 1890, Eden Evangelical Lutheran Church, Rockefeller Township, Northumberland County, PA. In 1985, the Sunbury Daily Item reprinted a picture taken soon after 1900 that showed Peter L. Klinger, "who lived on a farm along Plum Creek, near Sunbury," posing on the front of a Pennsylvania Railroad steam freight engine with the train's crew. He died on 6 January 1961, at age 90. He was buried at Wolf's Cross Roads Cemetery, Rockefeller Township, Northumberland County, PA.

6.2.11.1 LEONA GRACE KLINGER was born in 1891. She married CLAYTON M. GEARHART, son of FRANK GEARHART and ANNA M. YEAGER, on 22 June 1908. She died on 2 December 1937, from brain tumor. Some sources record that she died on 19 December 1937. She was buried at Eden Evangelical Lutheran Church, Plum Creek, Rockefeller Township, Northumberland County, PA.

6.2.11.1.1 ERNEST EUGENE GEARHART was born on 1 November 1908. He was baptized on 10 January 1909, Eden Evangelical Lutheran Church, Rockefeller Township, Northumberland County, PA. He was confirmed on 19 July 1925 Eden Evangelical Lutheran Church, Rockefeller Township, Northumberland County, PA. He married ANNA MAE MILLER on 4 August 1929, Eden Evangelical Lutheran Church, Rockefeller Township, Northumberland County, PA. Prior to his death, Ernest was living in Sunbury, Northumberland County, PA. He died on 12 February 1997, at age 88.

6.2.11.1.1.1 DOLORES MAE GEARHART was born on 29 January 1931. She was baptized on 28 October 1934, Eden Evangelical Lutheran Church, Rockefeller Township, Northumberland County, PA.

6.2.11.1.1.2 NORMAN CLARENCE GEARHART was born on 18 December 1932. He was baptized on 28 October 1934, Eden Evangelical Lutheran Church, Rockefeller Township, Northumberland County, PA.

6.2.11.1.1.3 GARY LEE GEARHART was born on 17 April 1935. He was baptized on 28 March 1937, Eden Evangelical Lutheran Church, Rockefeller Township, Northumberland County, PA.

6.2.11.1.2 LLOYD RAYMOND GEARHART was born on 28 February 1910. He was baptized on 17 February 1924, Eden Evangelical Lutheran Church, Rockefeller Township, Northumberland County, PA. He was unmarried. He died before 2007.

6.2.11.1.3 THELMA LEAH GEARHART was born on 22 May 1911. She was baptized on 17 February 1924, Eden Evangelical Lutheran Church, Rockefeller Township, Northumberland County, PA. She married **GERALD REMLEY**. She died in March 1975, at age 63.

6.2.11.1.4 GRACE IRENE GEARHART was born on 3 May 1913. She was baptized on 17 February 1924, Eden Evangelical Lutheran Church, Rockefeller Township, Northumberland County, PA. She married **STANLEY WEBB**. Prior to her death, Grace was living in Radcliff, Hardin County, KY. She died on 12 May 2005, at age 92.

6.2.11.1.5 FLORENCE GERTRUDE GEARHART was born on 1 May 1915, Sunbury, Northumberland County, PA. She was baptized on 17 February 1924, Eden Evangelical Lutheran Church, Rockefeller Township, Northumberland County, PA. She married **ROBERT STEPHENS**. She died on 12 October 2007, Wayne, MI, at age 92. According to a newspaper obituary, Florence was employed as a private secretary for the Detroit Diesel Co. and was living in Wayne, MI, at the time of her death. She was buried on 23 October 2007, at Northumberland Memorial Garden, Stonington, Northumberland County, PA.

6.2.11.1.6 HAROLD LEROY GEARHART was born on 1 November 1916. He was baptized on 17 February 1924, Eden Evangelical Lutheran Church, Rockefeller Township, Northumberland County, PA. He married **ANNA BELL**. Prior to his death, Harold was living in Danville, Montour County, PA. He died on 18 August 1995, at age 78.

6.2.11.1.7 CLAIR CLAYTON GEARHART was born on 26 June 1926. He was baptized on 14 July 1929, Eden Evangelical Lutheran Church, Rockefeller Township, Northumberland County, PA. He was unmarried. Prior to his death, Clair was living in Flourtown, Montgomery County, PA. He died on 22 February 1997, at age 70.

6.2.11.1.8 ARTHUR MONROE GEARHART was born on 15 March 1929. He was baptized on 14 July 1929, Eden Evangelical Lutheran Church, Rockefeller Township, Northumberland County, PA. He married **HARRIET GIRTON**. Prior to his death, Arthur was living in Grahamsville, Sullivan County, NY. He died on 12 June 1996, at age 67.

6.2.11.2 AMMON LAWRENCE KLINGER was born on 19 February 1892. Some sources record that he was born in 1893. He married **MARY LONG** in 1912. He married **MARY ALICE BEATTY**, daughter of **JAMES W. BEATTY** and **DOROTHY (--?--)**. He married **ELEANOR M. HARTMAN**, daughter of **CHARLES B. HARTMAN** and **M. GRACE WAGAMAN**, on 5 September 1925. According to Carlos Klinger, who knew Ammon, during the 1950's, Ammon owned a fuel oil distributorship and a gas station in Waynesboro. Prior to his death, Ammon was living in the vicinity of Waynesboro, Franklin County, PA. He died on 25 April 1986. He was buried at Green Hill Cemetery, Waynesboro, Franklin County, PA.

6.2.11.2.1 ANNA OLIVE KLINGER was born in May 1913. She married **(--?--) HEATH**.

6.2.11.2.2 DOROTHY KLINGER was born on 12 March 1917. She married **WILLIAM BYERS PRICE**. She died in August 1974, at age 57. She was buried at Green Hill Cemetery, Waynesboro, Franklin County, PA.

6.2.11.2.2.1 WILLIAM KLINGER PRICE was born on 2 October 1951, Winchester, Frederick County, VA. He died on 5 October 1951. He was buried at Green Hill Cemetery, Waynesboro, Franklin County, PA.

6.2.11.3 OSCAR W. KLINGER was born on 23 September 1897. He married **MABEL M. BOYER**, daughter of **CLOYD BOYER** and **BERTHA NACE**, after 1920. He died on 17 March 1963, at age 65. He was buried at Northumberland Memorial Cemetery, Stonington, Northumberland County, PA.

- **6.2.11.3.1 RUSSELL KLINGER**
- **6.2.11.3.2 EVELYN KLINGER**
- **6.2.11.3.3 ELEANOR JANE KLINGER** was born circa 1943.

6.2.11.4 FLORENCE J. KLINGER was born on 6 July 1899. She married **ROBERT M. LAUVER**, son of **ADAM B. LAUVER** and **JOANNA I. CONRAD**. She died on 13 October 1939, Snydertown, Northumberland County, PA, at age 40. She was buried at Stonington Baptist Church Cemetery, Stonington, Northumberland County, PA.

- **6.2.11.4.1 CHARLES E. LAUVER** was born on 12 September 1918, Northumberland County, PA. He married **JUNE S. LUPOLD**. He died in November 1972, at age 54.
  - **6.2.11.4.1.1 JEAN LOUISE LAUVER** married (--?--) **GEISWITE**. She was born on 21 June 1938, Sunbury, Northumberland County, PA. She died on 26 April 1998, at age 59.
  - **6.2.11.4.1.2 CHARLES RONALD LAUVER** was born on 30 April 1939, Sunbury, Northumberland County, PA. He married **ROSALIE MABLE** (--?--). He died on 7 May 1961, Community Hospital, Sunbury, Northumberland County, PA, at age 22. He was buried on 9 May 1961, at Fairview Cemetery, Verdilla, Snyder County, PA.
- **6.2.11.4.2 ROBERT O. LAUVER SR.** was born on 14 September 1922, Shamokin, Northumberland County, PA. He married **ESTHER MAE REICHENBACH**. He died on 11 June 2013, Providence Place Retirement Center, Chambersburg, Franklin County, PA, at age 90. He was buried on 14 June 2013, at Parklawn Memorial Gardens, Chambersburg, Franklin County, PA.
  - **6.2.11.4.2.1 ROBERT O. LAUVER JR.** married **BOBBIE** (--?--).
    - **6.2.11.4.2.1.1 TAMMY LAUVER** married **GREG SCHUCHMAN**.
      - **6.2.11.4.2.1.1.1 KENDYL SCHUCHMAN**
    - **6.2.11.4.2.1.2 CHRYSTAL LAUVER** married (--?--) **SATTAZAHN**.
      - **6.2.11.4.2.1.2.1 DARYA SATTAZAHN**
    - **6.2.11.4.2.1.3 DR. ROBERT LAUVER III** married **JESSICA** (--?--).
      - **6.2.11.4.2.1.3.1 AUSTIN LAUVER**
      - **6.2.11.4.2.1.3.2 JULLIAN LAUVER**
- **6.2.11.4.3 FREDEREICK L. LAUVER** was born on 18 May 1924. He died on 27 June 1977, at age 53. He was buried at Norland Cemetery, Greene Township, Franklin County, PA.
- **6.2.11.4.4 CLYDE LAUVER** was born circa 1931. He married **NANCY** (--?--).

6.2.11.5 HOMER C. KLINGER was born on 8 July 1901. He married **MARION E. DAGLE** circa 1925. Prior to his death, Homer was living in the vicinity of Elizabethtown, Lancaster County, PA. He died on 1 October 1988, at age 87.

- **6.2.11.5.1 MARLIN KLINGER**
- **6.2.11.5.2 LOIS KLINGER**
- **6.2.11.5.3 LLOYD E. KLINGER** was born circa 1918.

6.2.11.6 WARREN STANLEY KLINGER was born on 13 July 1903. He was unmarried. Prior to his death, Warren was living in the vicinity of Sunbury, Northumberland County, PA. He died in January 1978, at age 74.

6.2.11.7 PAUL W. KLINGER was born on 2 January 1910. He married **EVELYN M. BURNS**, daughter of **ERMY BURNS** and **EMILY CORKINS**. He died on 7 January 1975, at age 65. He was buried at Northumberland Memorial Park, Stonington, Northumberland County, PA.

- **6.2.11.7.1 CHERYL KLINGER** married **JOHN MEREDITH**.
- **6.2.11.7.2 KAREN KLINGER** was born in 1947. She married **KIMBER HOFFMAN**.

6.2.12 DANIEL LEWIS KLINGER was born on 7 September 1870. He was baptized on 7 May 1871, Emmanuel Evangelical Lutheran Church, Wolf's Crossroads, Northumberland County, PA. Some sources record that he was born in 1869. He died on 9 October 1873, at age 3. Some sources record that he died in 1872.

6.3 CAROLINA KLINGER is also referred to as **CAROLINE** in some sources. She was born on 18 February 1826. She was baptized on 30 April 1826, Zion (Klinger's) Church, Erdman, Lykens Township, Dauphin County, PA. She married **SIMON BLYLER**, son of **MICHAEL BLYLER** and **MARIA BURKET**, on 28 August 1844. In 1873, Carolina and Simon purchased Lot # 17 in Gratz, Dauphin County, PA, from Jacob and Hannah Buffington. The Gratz History says that Simon, after serving in the Civil War, was employed for 16 years as a stonemason for the Pennsylvania Railroad. Later, he and Carolina moved to Gratz. She died on 3 September 1895, at age 69. She was buried at Gratz, Dauphin County, PA.

6.3.1 ALICE BLYLER died in childhood.

6.3.2 WILLIAM H. BLYLER was born circa 1845. He married **ELIZABETH (--?--)**.

6.3.2.1 WILLIAM BLYLER was born circa 1869.

6.3.3 SAMUEL EMAMUEL BLYLER was born on 4 April 1847. Some sources record that he was born circa 1843. He married **MARY F. (--?--)** circa 1873. According to some sources, Samuel was also a hotel proprietor in Lebanon, PA.

6.3.3.1 GERTRUDE J. BLYLER was born in March 1879.

6.3.3.2 WILLIAM E. BLYLER was born in April 1880.

6.3.3.3 PEARL BLYLER was born in October 1881.

6.3.3.4 OTTIE BLYLER was born in March 1886.

6.3.4 JOHN PRESTON BLYLER was born on 21 January 1849. Some sources record that he was born circa 1847. He married **EMMA BARTHO** circa 1870. He died on 27 May 1933, Williamstown, Dauphin County, PA.

6.3.4.1 HARVEY BLYLER was born in 1871. He married **ANNIE CATHERINE HESS**, daughter of **EDWARD A. HESS** and **MARY JANE SNYDER**. He died in 1953. He was buried at Fairview Cemetery, Williamstown, Dauphin County, PA.

6.3.4.1.1 NORMAN G. BLYLER was born in 1896. He died in 1913. He was buried at Seyberts Cemetery, Williamstown, Dauphin County, PA.

6.3.4.1.2 RALPH E. BLYLER was born in 1905. He died in 1908. He was buried at Seyberts Cemetery, Williamstown, Dauphin County, PA.

6.3.4.1.3 CHARLES M. BLYLER was born in 1907. He died in 1909. He was buried at Seyberts Cemetery, Williamstown, Dauphin County, PA.

6.3.4.2 ALBERT BLYLER was born in December 1874.

6.3.4.3 FRANCIS BLYLER was born circa 1875.

6.3.4.4 DANIEL BLYLER was born on 20 July 1878. He died on 25 October 1897, at age 19. He was buried at Seyberts Cemetery, Williamstown, Dauphin County, PA.

6.3.4.5 GURNEY G. BLYLER was born in October 1880. He married **MARY A. MOFFETT** on 25 February 1902, Williamstown, Dauphin County, PA. He died in 1927. He was buried at Fairview Cemetery, Williamstown, Dauphin County, PA.

6.3.4.5.1 ROBERT PRESTON BLYLER was born on 19 September 1902, Williamstown, Dauphin County, PA. He died in April 1981, at age 78.

6.3.4.6 HERMAN E. BLYLER married **NORA LEONA (--?--)**. He was born on 7 September 1881. Some sources record that he was born in September 1882. He died on 14 December 1909, Blair County, PA, at age 28. He was buried at Rose Hill Cemetery, Altoona, Blair County, PA.

6.3.4.7 PEARL BLYLER was born in May 1886.

6.3.4.8 BERTIE BLYLER was born in October 1888.

6.3.4.9 WALTER BLYLER was born in November 1890.

6.3.4.10 MARTHA FLORENCE BLYLER also went by the name of **MATTIE**. She was born on 21 December 1894, Williamstown, Dauphin County, PA. Some sources record that she was born in December 1892. She married **DAVID BENDER**. She married **HARRY EDWARD MYERS** after 1919. She died on 11 July 1952, Tower City, Schuylkill County, PA, at age 57. She was buried at Greenwood Cemetery, Tower City, Schuylkill County, PA.

6.3.4.10.1 DAVID LEE BENDER was born on 23 February 1919, Williamstown, Dauphin County, PA. He married **JANE E. (--?--)**. He died on 3 April 1979, Camp Hill, Cumberland County, PA, at age 60. He was buried at Greenwood Cemetery, Tower City, Schuylkill County, PA.

6.3.4.10.2 JOYCE MARIE MYERS was born on 12 June 1924, Tower City, Schuylkill County, PA. She married **DONALD H. BEHNEY** circa 1945. She died on 19 October 1999, Camp Hill, Cumberland County, PA, at age 75. She was buried at Saint Peters Reformed Cemetery, Orwin, Schuylkill County, PA.

    6.3.4.10.2.1 LORI BEHNEY

    6.3.4.10.2.2 MICHAEL BEHNEY

6.3.5 DANIEL C. BLYLER was born on 17 October 1851, Schuylkill County, PA. He married **ADELINE SUSAN DANIEL**, daughter of **GEORGE DANIEL** and **ELIZABETH HOFFMAN,** on 14 July 1877. From about 1883 until 1901, Daniel operated the hotel called Union House in Gratz, Dauphin County. After selling the property in 1901, Daniel and his family moved to Reading, Berks County, PA. He died in 1934.

    6.3.5.1 ANNA M. BLYLER is also referred to as **ANNIE** in some sources. She was born in November 1877.

    6.3.5.2 EDNA M BLYLER was born in January 1882, Pennsylvania.

    6.3.5.3 HOMER C. BLYLER was born in January 1884, Pennsylvania. Homer was a baseball player who returned to Gratz to open a men's hat store.

    6.3.5.4 ARTHUR GARFIELD BLYLER was born in June 1885. He married **MAUD MABEL MILLER** in 1910. Arthur owned a men's hat shop in Harrisburg, PA, called "Plymouth Hat Store."

    6.3.5.5 MARGARET F. BLYLER also went by the name of **MAGGIE**. She was born in February 1889. Margaret was nurse in Reading before serving in World War I at Camp Meade. Later she moved to Buffalo, NY.

    6.3.5.6 ALBERT E. BLYLER was born in October 1892.

    6.3.5.7 VERNA O. BLYLER was born in July 1895.

6.3.6 FRANK P. BLYLER is also referred to as **FRANKLIN** in some sources. He was born on 13 March 1855. He married **VICTORIA ANN MILLER**, daughter of **HENRY MILLER** and **HANNAH KLINGER,** circa 1874.

    6.3.6.1 RAPHAEL BLYLER died in childhood.

    6.3.6.2 HARPER W. BLYLER was born in 1877. He married **JENNIE M. EDINGER** circa 1901. He married **GERTRUDE M. (--?--)** circa 1922.

        6.3.6.2.1 ELIZABETH E. BLYLER was born circa 1902.

        6.3.6.2.2 DONALD W. BLYLER was born circa 1923.

    6.3.6.3 EARL M. BLYLER was born in 1882.

    6.3.6.4 MAE M. BLYLER is also referred to as **MABEL AND MAY** in some sources. She was born in 1890.

    6.3.6.5 RUTH ESTHER BLYLER is also referred to as **ESTHER R.** in some sources. She was born in July 1892. She married **ARTHUR M. EBY** before 1920.

        6.3.6.5.1 JANE V. EBY was born in 1918.

    6.3.6.6 HARRY BLYLER was born in 1895.

6.3.7 EMMA L. BLYLER is also referred to as **EMELINE** in some sources. She was born in August 1856. Emma was not listed among Simon and Caroline's household at the time of the 1860 Census, but there was a 4-year old child listed named "Caroline" who would have been about Emma's age (about 3 years 10 months) at the time. She married **AARON A. UMHOLTZ**. In 1900, Emma, a widow, was living in Gratz with 2 of her sons, Harper, a huckster, and George, who later became a barber. She died in 1936.

    6.3.7.1 VERGIE UMHOLTZ married **(--?--) STAHL**.

        6.3.7.1.1 FRANCES STAHL

    6.3.7.2 CAROLINE CORINDA UMHOLTZ also went by the name of **CARRIE**. She was born on 2 June 1874. She married **(--?--) SHERIDAN**. She died on 31 December 1945, at age 71.

        6.3.7.2.1 JAMES SHERIDAN

    6.3.7.3 HERMAN HARPER UMHOLTZ was born on 12 January 1876. He died in 1929.

    6.3.7.4 GEORGE F. UMHOLTZ was born on 28 February 1885. He married **FRONIE OSSMAN**, daughter of **JOHN H. OSSMAN** and **ELLEN S. (--?--)**. He died on 5 November 1947, at age 62.

    6.3.7.5 E. RAY UMHOLTZ was born in 1890. He died in 1894.

6.3.8 URIAH BLYLER was born circa 1858. Uriah was not listed among Simon and Caroline's household at the time of the 1860 Census, although he was listed in the 1870 Census.

6.3.9 JOSEPH BLYLER was born circa 1859.

6.3.10 CHARLES MONROE BLYLER was born on 7 February 1864. He married **ELIZABETH HESS,** daughter of **HARRY HESS** and **ELIZABETH UMHOLTZ,** on 11 October 1883, Lutheran Church, Elizabethville, Dauphin County, PA. He died on 29 December 1913, at age 49.

    6.3.10.1 MARLA MAY BLYLER was born on 17 May 1884. She died before 1900.

    6.3.10.2 HARRY EDWIN BLYLER was born on 3 June 1886. He married **NINA RETTINGER** on 17 November 1906, E.U.B. Church, Lykens, Dauphin County, PA.

        6.3.10.2.1 PAUL BLYLER was born circa 1907. He married **ELINOR BORG**.

            6.3.10.2.1.1 BRENDA NINA BLYLER married (--?--) **HOWE**.

        6.3.10.2.2 MARIE BLYLER was born circa 1913.

        6.3.10.2.3 RAY BLYLER was born circa 1915.

        6.3.10.2.4 ROSS BLYLER is also referred to as **ROSCOE** in some sources. He was born circa 1918.

        6.3.10.2.5 MARGARIE BLYLER was born in 1925.

    6.3.10.3 JENNIE IRENE BLYLER was born on 8 April 1888. Some source record that she was baptized on 6 April 1888. She married **DR. PERLEY E. DOWNING**, son of **BENTON E. DOWNING** and **LIZZIE E. (--?--),** circa 1919. Prior to her death, Jennie was living in the vicinity of West Palm Beach, Palm Beach County, FL. She died in December 1985, at age 97.

        6.3.10.3.1 JEANNETTE E. DOWNING was born in 1925.

    6.3.10.4 EARL ROSCOE BLYLER was born on 11 January 1892. He married **GRAYCE I. RITZMAN** before 1920. He died in 1948.

        6.3.10.4.1 ROBERT BLYLER died before 2012.

        6.3.10.4.2 NEALE R. BLYLER was born circa 1922. He died before 2012.

        6.3.10.4.3 PATRICIA G. BLYLER was born on 28 February 1929. She married **CARL KNOUSE**. She married **GUY A. MILLER**. She died on 9 March 2012, Pleasant Acres Nursing & Rehabilitation Center, York, York County, PA, at age 83. According to a newspaper obituary, Patricia was a highly skilled and successful seamstress. She created special occasion and custom wedding gowns. Patricia also raised and showed champion Pomeranians. She also loved gardening, travel. As a certified bowling instructor and member of the USBC Hall of Fame, she taught the elderly and children the sport of bowling.

            6.3.10.4.3.1 GUY MILLER

                6.3.10.4.3.1.1 GUY MILLER II

                6.3.10.4.3.1.2 RYAN MILLER

            6.3.10.4.3.2 PENNY MILLER married (--?--) **SPENCER**.

                6.3.10.4.3.2.1 CARL SPENCER

                6.3.10.4.3.2.2 SAMUEL SPENCER

            6.3.10.4.3.3 SUSAN MILLER married (--?--) **SEPAVICH**.

                6.3.10.4.3.3.1 VICTORIA SEPAVICH

    6.3.10.5 ELDA BLYLER was born in March 1894. She married **PHAON REHRER**.

    6.3.10.6 EVA CAROLINE BLYLER was born on 31 December 1896. She married **CLARENCE E. MILLER**. She died in 1957.

        6.3.10.6.1 ROBERT MILLER was born in December 1919.

        6.3.10.6.2 JAMES MILLER was born circa 1920. James may be a duplicate listing for Robert Miller.

        6.3.10.6.3 MARY MILLER was born circa 1922. She married **WALTER DANIEL**.

    6.3.10.7 HEISTER P. BLYLER was born on 1 January 1900. He married **BERTHA LEBO**, daughter of **DR. WILLIAM LEBO** and **PRUELLA HUNTZINGER**, circa 1925. Prior to his death, Heister was living in the vicinity of Millersburg, Dauphin County, PA. He died in June 1984, at age 84.

        6.3.10.7.1 BARBARA BLYLER

6.3.10.7.2 ELLERSLIE BLYLER

6.3.10.7.3 CLARETA BLYLER is also referred to as **CLARITA** in some sources. She was born circa 1928.

6.3.10.8 ROY ALFRED BLYLER was born on 1 July 1903. He married **HILDA SNYDER**, daughter of **CHARLES SNYDER**, circa 1926. He died in 1973. He was buried at Simeon Church Cemetery, Gratz, Dauphin County, PA.

6.3.10.8.1 CHARLES BLYLER was born circa January 1928.

6.4 WILLIAM H. KLINGER is also referred to as **WILHELM** in some sources. He was born on 23 February 1829. He was baptized on 9 May 1829, Zion (Klinger's) Church, Erdman, Lykens Township, Dauphin County, PA. He married **MARIA M. KAUFFMAN**, daughter of **JACOB KAUFFMAN** and **LYDIA DREHER**, in September 1854. He died on 28 September 1916, at age 87. According to Mary Klinger's book, William was buried at either St. John's (Kimmel's) Lutheran and Reformed Church Cemetery in Barry Township, Schuylkill County, or "at Weishample," but published cemetery listings for Kimmel's Church, for the Church of God Cemetery in Weishample, and for the Salem EUB United Methodist Church in Weishample do not appear to include William.

6.4.1 EMMA CLARA KLINGER was born on 3 August 1855, Schuylkill County, PA. She married **JOHN WILLIAM FRITZ JR.** She died on 21 January 1946, Shamokin State Hospital, Zerbe Township, Northumberland County, PA, at age 90. She was buried on 24 January 1946, at Zion Lutheran Cemetery, Trevorton, Northumberland County, PA.

6.4.1.1 EDNA MARIA FRITZ was born on 16 August 1886, Trevorton, Northumberland County, PA. She married **JOSIAH BLAYDON**. She died on 14 September 1980, Gardena, Los Angeles County, CA, at age 94. She was buried at Greenwood Cemetery, Trevorton, Northumberland County, PA.

6.4.1.1.1 ROBERT WILLIAM BLAYDON was born on 27 August 1917, Shamokin, Northumberland County, PA. He married **HARRIETT (--?--)**. He died on 4 April 2005, at age 87. He was buried at Greenwood Cemetery, Trevorton, Northumberland County, PA.

6.4.1.1.1.1 RONALD BLAYDON was born circa 1939.

6.4.1.1.2 FLORENCE NAOMI BLAYDON was born on 3 October 1919, Shamokin, Northumberland County, PA. She married **SEYMOUR S. BERNSTEIN** on 28 July 1946, Philadelphia, Philadelphia County, PA. She died on 26 June 2003, Middletown, Dauphin County, PA, at age 83. She was buried at Greenwood Cemetery, Trevorton, Northumberland County, PA.

6.4.1.1.2.1 JOSEPH BERNSTEIN

6.4.1.1.2.2 THOMAS BERNSTEIN

6.4.1.2 ELLEN C. FRITZ was born on 26 October 1891. She married **RAYMOND C. BUFFINGTON**, son of **HARRY G. BUFFINGTON** and **IDA CLARA SHAFFER**. She died in 1972. She was buried at Greenwood Cemetery, Trevorton, Northumberland County, PA.

6.4.1.2.1 EMMA MARIE BUFFINGTON was born on 30 May 1913. She married **ROY STEVEN GARMAN**, son of **BERT E. GARMAN** and **VERSA E. DUNKELBERGER**. She died on 7 November 1991, at age 78. She was buried at Greenwood Cemetery, Trevorton, Northumberland County, PA.

6.4.1.2.1.1 BARRY E. GARMAN was born in 1938. He died in 1938. He was buried at Greenwood Cemetery, Trevorton, Northumberland County, PA.

6.4.1.2.1.2 SANDRA L. GARMAN was born in 1941. She died in 1960. She was buried at Greenwood Cemetery, Trevorton, Northumberland County, PA.

6.4.1.2.2 DONALD W. BUFFINGTON was born on 14 January 1915. He married **CARRIE A. WILLIARD**, daughter of **DANIEL FRANKLIN WILLIARD** and **SARAH JANE BROWER**. He died on 20 July 2003, at age 88. He was buried at Maple Grove Cemetery, Elizabethville, Dauphin County, PA.

6.4.1.3 MILTON CALVIN FRITZ was born on 19 October 1895. He died on 30 January 1901, Northumberland County, PA, at age 5. He was buried at Greenwood Cemetery, Trevorton, Northumberland County, PA.

6.4.1.4 WILLIAM PHILIP FRITZ was born on 20 December 1898. He died on 25 January 1901, Northumberland County, PA, at age 2. He was buried at Greenwood Cemetery, Trevorton, Northumberland County, PA.

6.4.2 CHARLES F. KLINGER was born in February 1857. He married **SARAH (--?--)**. He died in 1917. He was buried at Greenwood Cemetery, Tower City, Schuylkill County, PA.

6.4.3 LYDIA A. KLINGER was born on 7 March 1858. She married GEORGE M. KANTNER, son of FRANKLIN KANTNER and CAROLINE KERSCHNER. She died on 22 March 1916, at age 58. She was buried at Greenwood Cemetery, Tower City, Schuylkill County, PA.

6.4.3.1 MINNIE KANTNER was born circa 1877, Pennsylvania.

6.4.3.2 HATTIE ESTELLE KANTNER was born on 22 March 1879, Porter Township, Schuylkill County, PA. She married WILLIAM FRANCIS HOFFMAN in 1897. She died on 15 July 1967, Los Angeles, Los Angeles County, CA, at age 88. She was buried at Forest Lawn Memorial Park (Hollywood Hills), Los Angeles, Los Angeles County, CA.

6.4.3.2.1 LEROY KANTNER HOFFMAN SR. was born on 9 December 1897, Reading, Berks County, PA. He married EMMA CHRISTINE HATCH, daughter of HENRY HARRY HATCH and ELIZABETH MARIE GLIDEHAUS. He died on 18 February 1985, Los Angeles, Los Angeles County, CA, at age 87. He was buried at Rose Hills Memorial Park, Whittier, Los Angeles County, CA.

6.4.3.2.1.1 EMMA RAMONA HOFFMAN was born on 9 March 1919, Ramona, Washington County, OK. She married MARION ARTHUR COLEGROVE, son of ARTHUR JAMES COLEGROVE and MARTHA GERTRUDE ANDERSON. She died on 28 June 2004, Provo, Utah County, UT, at age 85. She was buried at Rose Hills Memorial Park, Whittier, Los Angeles County, CA.

6.4.3.2.1.2 LEROY KANTNER HOFFMAN JR. was born on 8 January 1922, Ramona, Washington County, OK. He married MARILYN GATES. He and MARILYN GATES were divorced in May 1977 Los Angeles County, CA. He died on 19 December 1989, at age 67. He was buried at Rose Hills Memorial Park, Whittier, Los Angeles County, CA.

6.4.3.2.1.3 NORMAN LEE HOFFMAN was born on 4 July 1928. He married ALICE EDNA HOGSETT. He died on 13 November 2011, at age 83.

6.4.3.2.1.3.1 ALICE EDNA HOFFMAN was born on 12 November 1956. She died on 5 September 1979, at age 22. She was buried at Valhalla Memorial Park, North Hollywood, Los Angeles County, CA.

6.4.3.2.2 HILBERT GRIFFITHS HOFFMAN was born on 20 June 1903, Tower City, Schuylkill County, PA. He married BLANCHE JOSEPHINE SHINDLER, daughter of JOHN WILLIAM SHINDLER and MARY UNDERKOFFLER, circa 1924. He died in 1942. He was buried at Greenwood Cemetery, Tower City, Schuylkill County, PA.

6.4.3.2.2.1 BETH ESTELLA HOFFMAN was born on 10 August 1924, Tower City, Schuylkill County, PA. She married HARRY EDWARD HOLDEN, son of HARRY EDWARD HOLDEN SR. and KATHERINE M. SCHREINER. She died on 2 February 2015, Health and Rehabilitation Center, Tremont, Schuylkill County, PA, at age 90. She was buried at Greenwood Cemetery, Tower City, Schuylkill County, PA.

6.4.3.2.2.1.1 BETH ANN HOLDEN married KERRY RICHARDS.

6.4.3.2.2.1.1.1 CRYSTAL RICHARDS

6.4.3.2.2.1.1.2 CHAD RICHARDS married JODY (--?--).

6.4.3.2.2.1.2 SUSAN JANE HOLDEN was born on 6 April 1953, Lykens, Dauphin County, PA. She died on 29 May 1958, Lykens, Dauphin County, PA, at age 5. She was buried on 2 June 1958, at Greenwood Cemetery, Tower City, Schuylkill County, PA.

6.4.3.2.2.2 BEN DAVID HOFFMAN was born on 15 September 1926, Tower City, Schuylkill County, PA. He died on 11 December 1999, at age 73.

6.4.3.3 EDWARD F. KANTNER is also referred to as EDWIN in some sources. He was born in October 1880, Pennsylvania. He married EMMA R. (--?--) circa 1907.

6.4.3.3.1 LOLA M. KANTNER was born circa 1908, Pennsylvania.

6.4.3.3.2 THELMA W. KANTNER was born circa 1918, Pennsylvania.

6.4.3.4 HARRY W. KANTNER was born in December 1882, Pennsylvania.

6.4.3.5 MAY KANTNER was born in April 1885.

6.4.3.6 ALICE GRACE KANTNER was born in September 1887, Pennsylvania.

6.4.3.7 CLARK A. KANTNER was born in October 1889, Pennsylvania.

6.4.3.8 FREDA H. KANTNER was born in May 1894, Pennsylvania. She married ROBERT LUDWIG circa 1917.

    6.4.3.8.1 JANE G. LUDWIG was born circa 1924, Pennsylvania.

    6.4.3.8.2 LaVERNE K. LUDWIG was born circa 1925, Pennsylvania.

6.4.4 ALFRED KLINGER was born on 20 March 1859. He married MARY A. WERTZ, daughter of RILEY WERTZ and KATHERINE JURY, circa 1891. He died on 29 November 1947, Polyclinic Hospital, Harrisburg, Dauphin County, PA, at age 88. He was buried on 3 December 1947, at Halifax United Methodist Church Cemetery, Halifax, Dauphin County, PA.

    6.4.4.1 HARRY WILBUR KLINGER was born on 19 April 1892, Tower City, Schuylkill County, PA. He married MARY ESTHER BORDNER, daughter of JOHN C. BORDNER and MARY BOWER. He married ESTHER N. (--?--). He died on 8 April 1987, at age 94.

        6.4.4.1.1 DONALD ALFRED KLINGER was born on 30 May 1918, Sunbury, Northumberland County, PA. He was baptized on 4 June 1918, Zion Lutheran Church, Sunbury, Northumberland County, PA. He died on 3 April 1995, at age 76. He was buried at Resurrection Cemetery, Harrisburg, Dauphin County, PA.

    6.4.4.2 LOTTIE ALICE KLINGER was born in April 1893. She married HARRY BENDER PUTT, son of CHARLES B. PUTT and SAREPTA V. BENDER, on 7 April 1913, Dauphin County, PA. She married GEORGE WILLIAM COWLES. She died on 23 July 1981, at age 88. She was buried at Halifax United Methodist Church Cemetery, Halifax, Dauphin County, PA.

6.4.5 HARRY T. KLINGER was born in May 1863. He married ELIZABETH C. FETTER circa 1896. He died in 1927.

    6.4.5.1 MARY R. KLINGER was born in September 1897, Pennsylvania.

6.4.6 LILLIAN LOUISE KLINGER also went by the name of LILLIE. She was born on 28 July 1863. She married JAMES LEWIS, son of JAMES LEWIS and HARRIET DANIELS. She died on 18 September 1953, Tower City, Schuylkill County, PA, at age 90. She was buried on 22 September 1953, at Greenwood Cemetery, Tower City, Schuylkill County, PA.

    6.4.6.1 WILLIAM HENRY LEWIS was born on 6 April 1881, Tower City, Schuylkill County, PA. He died on 15 February 1966, at age 84. He was buried at Greenwood Cemetery, Tower City, Schuylkill County, PA.

    6.4.6.2 CHARLES ALFRED LEWIS was born on 28 June 1883, Tower City, Schuylkill County, PA. He married ELIZABETH ELLEN ADAMS, daughter of WILLIAM ADAMS (--?--) and ELLEN DYER, circa 1907. He died in 1968. He was buried at Greenwood Cemetery, Tower City, Schuylkill County, PA.

        6.4.6.2.1 MAY E. LEWIS is also referred to as ELSIE in some sources. She was born circa 1907.

        6.4.6.2.2 ELVA R. LEWIS was born in 1910.

        6.4.6.2.3 IVAN C. LEWIS was born circa 1922.

    6.4.6.3 ARTHUR DAVID LEWIS was born on 6 October 1886, Williamstown, Dauphin County, PA. He married MAUDE A. PHILLIPS, daughter of EDWIN PHILLIPS and EMMA ACKER.

        6.4.6.3.1 JEAN LEWIS was born on 7 September 1912, Tower City, Schuylkill County, PA. She married (--?--) LEHMAN. She died on 4 March 2003, at age 90.

    6.4.6.4 GARFIELD J. LEWIS is also referred to as JAMES GARFIELD LEWIS in some sources. He was born on 17 June 1889, Tower City, Schuylkill County, PA. He married ELIZABETH EVE ADAMS, daughter of JAMES HENRY ADAMS and MARY ELIZABETH FETTERHOFF, in 1916. He died in May 1973, at age 83.

        6.4.6.4.1 JAMES G. LEWIS was born on 19 June 1915, Tower City, Schuylkill County, PA. He married MARY E. HOWE. He married GLADYS E. PENTZ. He died on 31 July 2011, Palm Coast, Flagler County, FL, at age 96. He was buried on 5 August 2011, at Woodlawn Memorial Gardens, Harrisburg, Dauphin County, PA.

            6.4.6.4.1.1 AUDREY LEWIS married JOEL ROSEN.

                6.4.6.4.1.1.1 ANISSA ROSEN

                6.4.6.4.1.1.2 JAN L. ROSEN

            6.4.6.4.1.2 JAMIE LEWIS was born on 30 May 1958. She died on 21 April 2000, Harrisburg, Dauphin County, PA, at age 41. She was buried at Woodlawn Memorial Gardens, Dauphin County, PA.

6.4.6.4.2 AUDREY LEWIS married **(--?--) KNOWLES**. She was born circa 1918.

6.4.6.4.3 ELIZABETH LOUISE LEWIS was born on 20 December 1921, Tower City, Schuylkill County, PA. She married **MARLIN RAYMOND EHRHART**, son of **JAMES R. EHRHART** and **LILLIAN J. UNDERKOFFLER,** on 7 July 1946, Lebanon County, PA. She died on 26 September 2006, at age 84.

6.4.6.4.4 RHODA HARRIET LEWIS was born on 24 January 1924, Tower City, Schuylkill County, PA. She married **(--?--) MYERS**. She died on 29 November 2000, at age 76.

6.4.6.4.5 JOHN LLEWELLYN LEWIS was born on 31 December 1925, Tower City, Schuylkill County, PA. He died on 26 April 1998, at age 72.

6.4.6.4.6 RUTH DELPHINE LEWIS was born on 21 March 1928. She married **ALEXANDER GLADFELTER**. She died on 1 May 2011, Port Charlotte, Charlotte County, FL, at age 83.

6.4.6.4.7 EMMA JANE LEWIS was born on 28 January 1931, Tower City, Schuylkill County, PA. She married **EDGAR NEAL KOPP**, son of **EDGAR A. KOPP** and **PAULINE M. SNYDER**. She died on 8 January 2007, at age 75. She was buried at Indiantown Gap National Cemetery, Annville, Lebanon County, PA.

    6.4.6.4.7.1 STEVEN KOPP

    6.4.6.4.7.2 KATHY KOPP married **JOHN MISIAK**.

6.4.6.5 MARY JANES LEWIS was born on 31 October 1891. She died on 29 November 1897, at age 6. She was buried at Greenwood Cemetery, Tower City, Schuylkill County, PA.

6.4.6.6 FLORENCE L. LEWIS was born on 25 February 1894. She married **IVAN CLYDE WATKINS**. She died in 1979. She was buried at Greenwood Cemetery, Tower City, Schuylkill County, PA.

6.4.6.7 ELLA G. LEWIS was born on 25 July 1897. She died on 2 July 1993, Dallas County, TX, at age 95. She was buried at Restland Memorial Park, Dallas, Dallas County, TX.

6.4.6.8 EMMA M. LEWIS was born on 25 July 1899. She married **TIMOTHY BENNEVILLE KEHLER**, son of **JOSEPH KEHLER** and **LOUISA KIEFFER**. She died on 21 October 1995, Dallas County, TX, at age 96. She was buried at Restland Memorial Park, Dallas, Dallas County, TX.

    6.4.6.8.1 EMMA LOU KEHLER was born circa 1921.

    6.4.6.8.2 JOYCE KEHLER was born circa 1923.

    6.4.6.8.3 CONSTANCE J. KEHLER was born circa 1927.

6.4.7 AMANDA E. KLINGER was born circa 1865. She married **ROBERT ROBINSON** circa 1891. She died in 1916.

6.4.8 SARAH ALICE KLINGER was born on 28 March 1868, Fearnot, Schuylkill County, PA. She married **WILLIAM LEWIS FREDERICK KNECHT**, son of **CHARLES FREDERICK KNECHT** and **PAULINE EISENSTECK,** circa 1888. She died on 23 May 1961, Tower City, Schuylkill County, PA, at age 93. She was buried on 26 May 1961, at Greenwood Cemetery, Tower City, Schuylkill County, PA.

6.4.8.1 ROY LEO KNECHT was born on 10 June 1888, Tower City, Schuylkill County, PA. He married **JOSIE BONNING** on 27 March 1920, Russellville, Pope County, AR. He died on 5 April 1962, at age 73. He was buried at Memorial Park Cemetery, Heavener, Le Fore County, OK.

    6.4.8.1.1 GILBERT WILLIAM KNECHT was born on 2 July 1920, Monroe, Le Fore County, OK. He died on 21 September 2013, Tulsa, Tulsa County, OK, at age 93. He was buried at Memorial Park Cemetery, Tulsa, Tulsa County, OK.

6.4.8.2 CHARLES ALBERT KNECHT was born on 17 September 1890. He died on 20 March 1895, at age 4. He was buried at Greenwood Cemetery, Tower City, Schuylkill County, PA.

6.4.8.3 WILLIAM KENNETH KNECHT was born on 3 May 1892. He married **AGNES C. NORBETH**, daughter of **DOMINIKAS NORBUNTAS** and **AGNES VINGIS BROWN,** on 8 January 1915, Sebastian County, AR. He died in August 1970, at age 78. He was buried at Greenwood Cemetery, Tower City, Schuylkill County, PA.

    6.4.8.3.1 FREDERICK VERNON KNECHT was born on 6 November 1915, Calhoun, Le Flore County.

6.4.8.4 JESSE GILBERT KNECHT was born on 15 June 1894, Tower City, Schuylkill County, PA. He married **MARY ANN POWELL** after 1910. He died on 4 October 1918, Winchester, England, at age 24, while serving with the 509th Motor Truck Company of the US Army. He was buried at Greenwood Cemetery, Tower City, Schuylkill County, PA.

6.4.8.5 MYRA ANNETTA KNECHT was born on 20 September 1899. She died on 9 May 1900. She was buried at Greenwood Cemetery, Tower City, Schuylkill County, PA.

6.4.8.6 MILDRED ALICE KNECHT was born on 1 March 1901. She married **ALBERT FAUST ERB**, son of **GEORGE B. ERB** and **ALICE (--?--),** before 1930. She died on 5 December 1997, at age 96. She was buried at Highland Memorial Park, Pottstown, Montgomery County, PA.

    6.4.8.6.1 ALBERT ERB was born circa 1932.

    6.4.8.6.2 ALICE LOUISE ERB was born circa 1934.

6.4.8.7 MERLE ARLINE KNECHT was born on 10 July 1904. She died on 31 October 1998, at age 94. She was buried at Greenwood Cemetery, Tower City, Schuylkill County, PA.

6.4.8.8 LOUISE BEATRICE KNECHT was born on 20 March 1908, Tower City, Schuylkill County, PA. She married **PHILIP SAMUEL BORKE**, son of **GEORGE BORKE** and **ANNA KATHERINE HAMELELHE**. She died on 10 June 1994, Hershey, Dauphin County, PA, at age 86. She was buried at Greenwood Cemetery, Tower City, Schuylkill County, PA.

6.4.8.9 KARL E. KNECHT was born on 2 May 1911. He was baptized on 25 December 1911, St. Paul's Lutheran Church, Tower City, Schuylkill County, PA. He married **SARA ELLEN MATTERN**, daughter of **JOHN FRANKLIN MATTERN** and **LIZZIE M. FISS**. He died in April 1974, at age 62. He was buried at Blair Memorial Park, Bellwood, Blair County, PA.

6.4.9 WILLIAM PERCIVAL KLINGER was born on 28 May 1870, Tower City, Schuylkill County, PA. He married **CATHERINE E. BAILEY**, daughter of **WILLIAM BAILEY** and **ISABEL LEBO**, circa 1894. He died on 19 July 1954, Tower City, Schuylkill County, PA, at age 84. He was buried on 22 July 1954, at Greenwood Cemetery, Tower City, Schuylkill County, PA.

    6.4.9.1 CHARLES WILLIAM KLINGER was born on 11 August 1895, Tower City, Schuylkill County, PA. He married **EDNA MAY FOREMAN**. He died on 18 January 1970, Harrisburg, Dauphin County, PA, at age 74. He was buried at Greenwood Cemetery, Tower City, Schuylkill County, PA.

        6.4.9.1.1 MAE IRENE KLINGER was born on 6 August 1916, Tower City, Schuylkill County, PA. She married **PETER WILLIAM SHEEHAN**. She died on 5 November 1968, Lebanon, Lebanon County, PA, at age 52. She was buried at Mount Lebanon Cemetery, Lebanon, Lebanon County, PA.

        6.4.9.1.2 DONALD WILLIAM KLINGER was born on 18 August 1919, Tower City, Schuylkill County, PA. He died on 6 October 2004, Hampton, VA, at age 85.

        6.4.9.1.3 JEANNE V. KLINGER was born on 3 March 1921, Tower City, Schuylkill County, PA. She married **JOHN T. BROSNAN**. She died on 19 October 1973, Hershey Medical Center, Hershey, Dauphin County, PA, at age 52. She was buried at Grand View Memorial Park, Annville, Lebanon County, PA.

            6.4.9.1.3.1 KAREN A. BROSNAN

            6.4.9.1.3.2 MARY E. BROSNAN

            6.4.9.1.3.3 (--?--) BROSNAN married **THOMAS C. HOOVEN**.

        6.4.9.1.4 IVAN C. KLINGER was born in 1924. He died in 1924. He was buried at Greenwood Cemetery, Tower City, Schuylkill County, PA.

        6.4.9.1.5 DEAN R. KLINGER was born on 22 January 1927, Tower City, Schuylkill County, PA. He married **FAY B. RHOADS**, daughter of **ELWOOD RHOADS** and **HANNAH BRETZ**, on 17 March 1951. He died on 9 November 2011, Manor Care, Lebanon, Lebanon County, PA, at age 84. He was buried at Mount Lebanon Cemetery, Lebanon, Lebanon County, PA.

            6.4.9.1.5.1 AMY JO KLINGER married **CHUCK HANSELL**.

                6.4.9.1.5.1.1 JASON M. HANSELL

                6.4.9.1.5.1.2 CHRISTOPHER D. HANSELL

                6.4.9.1.5.1.3 CHARLES B. HANSELL

                6.4.9.1.5.1.4 ADAM B. HANSELL

                6.4.9.1.5.1.5 NATHAN C. HANSELL

            6.4.9.1.5.2 RICHARD C. KLINGER married **MICHELLE (--?--)**.

                6.4.9.1.5.2.1 JONATHON KLINGER

                6.4.9.1.5.2.2 DEAN M. KLINGER

6.4.9.1.5.2.3 **DAVID S. KLINGER**

6.4.9.1.5.3 **DEAN E. KLINGER** was born on 4 September 1953. He died on 16 July 2006, at age 52. He was buried at Mount Lebanon Cemetery, Lebanon, Lebanon County, PA.

6.4.9.1.6 **KENNETH KARL KLINGER** was born on 4 September 1928, Tower City, Schuylkill County, PA. He died on 27 March 1955, VA Hospital, South Lebanon Township, Lebanon County, PA, at age 26. He was buried on 31 March 1955, at Greenwood Cemetery, Tower City, Schuylkill County, PA. Kenneth never married.

6.4.9.1.7 **CAROL K. KLINGER** married **HENRY BRANDT**. She was born circa 1934.

6.4.9.1.8 **RONALD N. KLINGER** was born on 9 January 1936, Tower City, Schuylkill County, PA. He died on 16 January 1973, Harrisburg, Dauphin County, PA, at age 37.

6.4.9.2 **GUY FRANKLIN KLINGER** was born on 10 March 1897. He died circa 1903. He was buried at Greenwood Cemetery, Tower City, Schuylkill County, PA.

6.4.9.3 **LEROY H. KLINGER** was born on 5 January 1899, Tower City, Schuylkill County, PA. He died on 21 October 1918, Tower City, Schuylkill County, PA, at age 19. He was buried on 24 October 1918, at Greenwood Cemetery, Tower City, Schuylkill County, PA.

6.4.9.4 **PAULINE KLINGER** was born in March 1900. She died circa 1905. She was buried at Greenwood Cemetery, Tower City, Schuylkill County, PA.

6.4.9.5 **IRENE F. KLINGER** was born on 17 January 1901. She married **HERBERT W. GROVE**, son of **HARRY C. GROVE** and **EMMA R. (--?--),** circa 1927. She died in April 1986, at age 85.

6.4.9.5.1 **JO ANNE GROVE** was born circa 1935.

6.4.9.6 **KATHERINE B. KLINGER** was born on 25 November 1905. She married **JOSEPH BEBO**. She died on 2 March 1987, at age 81. She was buried at Greenwood Cemetery, Tower City, Schuylkill County, PA.

6.4.9.7 **MERLE E. KLINGER** was born in 1906. She died on 14 January 1917, Tower City, Schuylkill County, PA. She was buried at Greenwood Cemetery, Tower City, Schuylkill County, PA.

6.4.9.8 **HELEN ARLEAN KLINGER** was born on 10 September 1909, Tower City, Schuylkill County, PA. She died on 22 January 1916, Tower City, Schuylkill County, PA, at age 6. She was buried on 24 January 1916, at Greenwood Cemetery, Tower City, Schuylkill County, PA.

6.4.9.9 **ISABELLE B. KLINGER** was born on 2 November 1910, Tower City, Schuylkill County, PA. She married **FREDERICK GOTTSHALL ROMBERGER**, son of **ALVIN NATHAN ROMBERGER** and **MARY ALICE GOTTSHALL,** on 24 February 1940, Winchester, VA. She died on 28 August 2000, New Cumberland, Cumberland County, PA, at age 89. She was buried at Calvary United Methodist Cemetery, Wiconisco, Dauphin County, PA.

6.4.9.10 **HARRY BENNETT KLINGER** was born on 4 March 1912, Tower City, Schuylkill County, PA. He married **MARGARET M. (--?--)**. He died on 5 March 1997, at age 85. He was buried at Zion United Methodist Church Cemetery, Red Lion, York County, PA.

6.4.9.11 **GRACE MARIA KLINGER** was born on 2 September 1914, Tower City, Schuylkill County, PA. She married **ROBERT D. KOLVA**. She died on 13 July 1990, New Cumberland, Cumberland County, PA, at age 75. She was buried at Greenwood Cemetery, Tower City, Schuylkill County, PA.

6.4.10 **PRISCILLA JANE KLINGER** was born on 13 January 1873, Schuylkill County, PA. She married **NELSON RISCHE**, son of **HENRY RISCHE** and **MARYAN KINES**, circa 1891. She died on 28 December 1940, Palmyra, Lebanon County, PA, at age 67. She was buried at Greenwood Cemetery, Tower City, Schuylkill County, PA.

6.4.10.1 **MAUDE I. RISCHE** was born on 10 November 1891, Schuylkill County, PA. She married **CHARLES A. BAIER**, son of **CHARLES BAIER** and **MARY ELIZABETH (--?--)**. She died on 4 April 1960, Philadelphia, Philadelphia County, PA, at age 68.

6.4.10.1.1 **KARL CLIFFORD BAIER** was born on 11 June 1911, Tower City, Schuylkill County, PA. He married **BLANCHE E. HORLEY**. He died on 20 February 1989, at age 77. He was buried at Tennessee State Veterans Cemetery, Knoxville, Knox County, TN.

6.4.10.1.2 **BROOKE RISCHE BAIER** was born on 30 December 1916, Tower City, Schuylkill County, PA. He married **SHIRLEY E. JONES**. He married **ELBERTA M. STELLWAGEN** on 17 August 1996. He died on 9 May 2013, Skagit County, WA, at age 96.

6.4.10.1.2.1 **JANE BAIER** married **TIM NELSON**.

6.4.10.1.2.2 DOUGLAS BAIER

6.4.10.1.2.3 KATHI BAIER married **DENNIS MELVILLE**.

6.4.10.1.2.3.1 BROOKE MELVILLE

6.4.10.1.3 HOWARD NELSON BAIER was born on 9 April 1918, Tower City, Schuylkill County, PA. He married **MARY PATRICIA ALTWATER**, daughter of **FRANK ROSS ALTWATER** and **ANNABELLE STEWART,** on 14 June 1942, Lebanon County, PA. He died on 3 August 2006, at age 88.

6.4.10.2 CORRINE H. RISCHE was born on 5 June 1893. She died on 15 November 1893. She was buried at Greenwood Cemetery, Tower City, Schuylkill County, PA.

6.4.10.3 DOROTHY M. RISCHE was born on 6 February 1902, Tower City, Schuylkill County, PA. She married **ERNEST J. HAND.** She died in childbirth on 21 March 1929, Tower City, Schuylkill County, PA, at age 27. She was buried on 24 March 1929, at Greenwood Cemetery, Tower City, Schuylkill County, PA.

6.4.10.3.1 STILLBORN SON HAND was born on 21 March 1929, Tower City, Schuylkill County, PA. He died on 21 March 1929, Tower City, Schuylkill County, PA. He was buried on 24 March 1929, at Greenwood Cemetery, Tower City, Schuylkill County, PA.

6.4.10.4 MARK NELSON RISCHE was born on 14 April 1904, Tower City, Schuylkill County, PA. He married **MINERVA E. MILLAR**, daughter of **ALBERT MILLAR** and **MARY ADA REED,** on 1 October 1927, Dauphin County, PA. He married **MARTHA E. HEATH** on 21 June 1947, Mecklenburg County, NC. He died on 18 August 1985, Pinellas County, FL, at age 81. He was buried at Arlington National Cemetery, Arlington, Arlington County, VA.

6.4.11 BESSIE MAY KLINGER was born on 26 December 1879, Pennsylvania. She married **EDWARD LUTHER RAMER**. She died on 21 June 1920, Quakertown, Bucks County, PA, at age 40. She was buried on 25 June 1920, at Greenwood Cemetery, Tower City, Schuylkill County, PA.

6.4.11.1 CORRINE DORCAS RAMER was born on 16 February 1910. She married **WALTER SCHMIDT KOSTENBADER**, son of **THOMAS DANIEL KOSTENBADER** and **NELLIE E. SCHMIDT**. She died on 13 November 1982, at age 72. She was buried at Greenwood Cemetery, Nazareth, Northampton County, PA.

6.4.11.2 RHODA LUCILLE RAMER was born on 31 August 1913, Wiconisco, Dauphin County, PA. She married **(--?--) JOHNSON**. She died in April 1977, at age 63. She was buried at Greenwood Cemetery, Nazareth, Northampton County, PA.

6.4.11.3 JEAN ELEANOR RAMER was born on 6 March 1917, Slatington, Lehigh County, PA. Jean served in the US Army from January 1944 through 2 March 1946. She married **GEORGE B. HODAC**. She and **GEORGE B. HODAC** were divorced on 24 January 1975 Washoe County, NV. She died on 20 November 1978, at age 61. She was buried at Calverton National Cemetery, Calverton, Suffolk County, NY.

6.5 ELISABETH KLINGER was born on 29 December 1834. She was baptized on 16 April 1835, Zion (Klinger's) Church, Erdman, Lykens Township, Dauphin County, PA. She died on 1 May 1873, at age 38. She was buried at St. Paul's (Artz) Church Cemetery, Sacramento, Hubley Township, Schuylkill County, PA.

6.6 ANNA MARIA KLINGER was born on 1 January 1838. She was baptized on 29 April 1838, Zion (Klinger's) Church, Erdman, Lykens Township, Dauphin County, PA.

6.7 MARAGETHA KLINGER was born on 23 November 1840. She was baptized on 1 March 1841, Zion (Klinger's) Church, Erdman, Lykens Township, Dauphin County, PA.

6.8 ELIZABETH CHRISTINA KLINGER was born on 2 February 1845. She was baptized on 26 March 1845, Zion (Klinger's) Church, Erdman, Lykens Township, Dauphin County, PA.

6.9 ALFRED KLINGER was born on 9 May 1847. Some sources record that he was born on 2 May 1847. He was baptized on 10 June 1847, Zion (Klinger's) Church, Erdman, Lykens Township, Dauphin County, PA. He married **MARY E. FUNK** before 1870. He died on 24 March 1882, Perry County, PA, at age 34. He was buried at Liverpool Union Cemetery, Liverpool, Perry County, PA. According to information at Findagrave.com:

A Civil War veteran, he enlisted in Harrisburg February 9, 1865, mustered into federal service there February 14 as a private with Co. L, 13th Pennsylvania Cavalry (117th Pa), and honorably discharged July 13, 1865, by general order.

After the war, he married Mary [Funk] and fathered Harry W. (b. 02/19/73, d. 06/28/74). By 1870, he was living in Liverpool, Perry County, where he was a member of Post 409, G.A.R.

6.9.1 HARRY W. KLINGER was born on 19 February 1873. He died on 28 June 1874, at age 1. He was buried at Liverpool Union Cemetery, Liverpool, Perry County, PA.

6.10 CERENUS KLINGER is also referred to as **SERENES EMORY KLINGER** in some sources. He was born on 7 April 1850. Some sources record that he was born on 10 April 1850. He was baptized on 5 May 1850, Zion (Klinger's) Church, Erdman, Lykens Township, Dauphin County, PA. He married **AGNES A. FRANK**, daughter of **PHILIP FRANK**. He died on 29 January 1921, Liverpool, Perry County, PA, at age 70. He was buried on 1 February 1921, at Liverpool Union Cemetery, Liverpool, Perry County, PA.

6.10.1 JOHN HENRY KLINGER was born on 29 July 1877. He died on 22 February 1886, at age 8. He was buried at Liverpool Union Cemetery, Liverpool, Perry County, PA.

6.10.2 CHESTER ARTHUR KLINGER is also referred to as **CHARLES ARTHUR KLINGER** in some sources. He was born on 6 December 1881, Liverpool, Perry County, PA. He married **PEARL M. ISENBERG**. He died on 17 January 1939, Altoona, Blair County, PA, at age 57. He was buried on 20 January 1939, at Rose Hill Cemetery, Altoona, Blair County, PA.

6.10.2.1 CLAUDINE A. KLINGER was born on 12 October 1910, Altoona, Blair County, PA. She married **H. EUGENE OAKES**, son of **DELBERT OAKES** and **SUSAN MILLS**, on 18 August 1931, Cumberland, Allegany County, MD. She died on 14 April 1987, Altoona, Blair County, PA, at age 76. She was buried on 16 April 1987, at Alto Reste Burial Park, Altoona, Blair County, PA.

6.10.2.2 RAY MELVIN KLINGER was born on 8 January 1921, Altoona, Blair County, PA. He married **ELLEN E. (--?--)**. He died on 14 September 2005, at age 84. He was buried at Alto Reste Burial Park, Altoona, Blair County, PA.

6.10.3 JENNIE E. KLINGER was born in October 1883, Liverpool, Perry County, PA. She married **J. WARREN STAILY**, son of **HORACE B. STAILY** and **MARY EMMA (--?--)**, in 1907, Philadelphia County, PA. She died on 13 August 1947, Liverpool, Perry County, PA, at age 63. She was buried on 17 August 1947, at Liverpool Union Cemetery, Liverpool, Perry County, PA.

6.10.4 MYRTIE ARDELLA KLINGER was born on 14 April 1885. She married **WILLIAM T. ALBRIGHT**, son of **SAMUEL ALBRIGHT** and **SUSAN (--?--)**, on 15 October 1903, Liverpool, Perry County, PA. She died on 19 January 1925, Liverpool, Perry County, PA, at age 39. She was buried on 1 February 1925, at Liverpool Union Cemetery, Liverpool, Perry County, PA.

6.10.4.1 JULIA A. ALBRIGHT was born circa 1904.

6.10.5 EMERY S. KLINGER was born on 1 September 1889. He died on 24 December 1901, at age 12.

7 ALEXANDER KLINGER was born on 28 May 1805, Lykens Township, Dauphin County, PA. He was baptized in 1805, Zion (Klinger's) Church, Erdman, Lykens Township, Dauphin County, PA. He married **MAGDALENA SCHMELTZ**, daughter of **ANDREAS SCHMELTZ** and **ANNA MARIA WALLER**. He died on 2 May 1876, Washington Township, Dauphin County, PA, at age 70. He was buried at Oakdale E. U. B. Cemetery, Oakdale, Washington Township, Dauphin County, PA.

7.1 SIMON KLINGER was born on 27 December 1827. He married **MARY ANN SWAB** after 1 June 1850. He died on 20 March 1901, at age 73. Some sources record that he died on 20 March 1902. He was buried at Maple Grove Cemetery, Elizabethville, Dauphin County, PA.

7.1.1 ALFRED KLINGER was born on 10 December 1851, Dauphin County, PA. He married **MARIA ELIZABETH TROUTMAN**, daughter of **DANIEL TROUTMAN** and **ELIZABETH BUSH**, on 19 November 1876. He died on 9 June 1923, Elizabethville, Dauphin County, PA, at age 71. He was buried at Maple Grove Cemetery, Elizabethville, Dauphin County, PA.

7.1.1.1 NORA AGNES KLINGER is also referred to as **AGNESS** in some sources. She was born on 16 October 1878, Dauphin County, PA. Some sources record that she was born in December 1879. She married **WILLIAM A. KEEFER**. She died on 4 February 1956, Elizabethville, Dauphin County, PA, at age 77. She was buried at Maple Grove Cemetery, Elizabethville, Dauphin County, PA.

7.1.1.2 ANNIE B. KLINGER was born on 27 November 1879, Dauphin County, PA. She married **MARLIN FERREE**. She died on 18 January 1975, at age 95. She was buried at Maple Grove Cemetery, Elizabethville, Dauphin County, PA.

7.1.1.3 MARTHA MAE KLINGER was born on 21 April 1881. Some sources record that she was born in 1885. She married **FREDERICK ERNEST HALLER**. She died on 9 April 1955, Washington, DC, at age 73. She was buried at Arlington National Cemetery, Arlington, VA.

7.1.1.4 HOMER RAMER KLINGER was born on 6 March 1883, near Berrysburg, Dauphin County, PA. He was baptized on 6 April 1883, Oakdale Church, Oakdale, Washington Township, Dauphin County,

PA. He died on 3 November 1884, at age 1. Some sources record that he died on 7 April 1883, but this date may not be correct. He was buried at Oakdale Church Cemetery, Dauphin County, PA.

7.1.1.5 MOODY N. KLINGER was born on 27 February 1885, Dauphin County, PA. He died on 3 September 1910, Dauphin County, PA, at age 25. He was buried at Maple Grove Cemetery, Elizabethville, Dauphin County, PA.

7.1.1.6 MINNIE BULAH KLINGER was born on 11 September 1887. She married **CLAYTON ALLEN WETZEL**. She died on 19 May 1960, at age 72. She was buried at Maple Grove Cemetery, Elizabethville, Dauphin County, PA.

7.1.1.7 WILLIAM DELROY KLINGER is also referred to as **WILLIAM L. KLINGER** in some sources. He was born on 23 February 1890, Upper Paxton Township, Dauphin County, PA. He married **CARRIE MANERVA MILLER**, daughter of **IRA OLIVER MILLER** and **JULIA A. GLACE,** circa 1916. He died on 21 February 1967, Millersburg, Dauphin County, PA, at age 76. Some sources record that he died on 21 February 1967 Middleburg, Snyder County, PA. He was buried at Maple Grove Cemetery, Elizabethville, Dauphin County, PA.

> **7.1.1.7.1 CHESTER R. KLINGER** was born on 19 January 1917, Elizabethville, Dauphin County, PA. He married **ERNESTINE E. DANIELS** on 9 April 1939, Wiconisco, PA. He died on 19 June 1981, Harrisburg, Dauphin County, PA, at age 64.
>
>> **7.1.1.7.1.1 DONALD EUGENE KLINGER** was born on 18 June 1940, Camden, NJ. He married **ESTER JANE ENGLISH** on 22 November 1961, Tower City, Schuylkill County, PA.
>>
>>> **7.1.1.7.1.1.1 STEVEN KLINGER** married **DEBORAH (--?--)**.
>>>
>>>> **7.1.1.7.1.1.1.1 STEVEN SCOTT KLINGER** was born on 10 May 1990.
>>>
>>> **7.1.1.7.1.1.2 DONALD EUGENE KLINGER JR.** was born on 31 October 1963. He married **SHARON (--?--)**.
>>>
>>>> **7.1.1.7.1.1.2.1 COLIN JOSEPH KLINGER**
>>>>
>>>> **7.1.1.7.1.1.2.2 SARAH LYNN KLINGER** was born on 1 May 1989.
>>>>
>>>> **7.1.1.7.1.1.2.3 MICHAEL KLINGER** was born on 13 December 1990.
>>>
>>> **7.1.1.7.1.1.3 KRISTA MARIE KLINGER** was born on 28 June 1971. She married **BRANDEN WAYNE ALEXANDER**.
>>>
>>>> **7.1.1.7.1.1.3.1 BRITTANY MARIE ALEXANDER** was born on 25 March 1994.
>>
>> **7.1.1.7.1.2 BARBARA KLINGER** was born on 8 January 1942, Wiconisco, PA. She married **HARVEY DENNIS FROMME** in November 1965, Wiconisco, PA.
>>
>>> **7.1.1.7.1.2.1 SHERRI ANN FROMME** was born on 7 December 1966, Harrisburg, Dauphin County, PA. She married **ANTHONY JAMES URVAN** on 24 December 1992.
>>>
>>>> **7.1.1.7.1.2.1.1 ALYSSA RENA URVAN** was born on 5 June 1993, Perry, GA.
>>>>
>>>> **7.1.1.7.1.2.1.2 ROBERT M. URVAN** was born on 16 May 1994, Perry, GA. He died on 16 May 1994, Perry, GA.
>>>>
>>>> **7.1.1.7.1.2.1.3 CARL M. URVAN** was born on 16 May 1994, Perry, GA. He died on 16 May 1994, Perry, GA.
>>>>
>>>> **7.1.1.7.1.2.1.4 MARC A. URVAN** was born on 16 May 1994, Perry, GA. He died on 16 May 1994, Perry, GA.
>>>
>>> **7.1.1.7.1.2.2 TAMMI LYNN FROMME** was born on 12 April 1969, Harrisburg, Dauphin County, PA. She married **THOMAS EDWARD SEIDERS**.
>>>
>>>> **7.1.1.7.1.2.2.1 ERIC THOMAS SEIDERS** was born on 21 January 1989.
>
> **7.1.1.7.2 HAROLD E. KLINGER** was born on 23 May 1921, Dauphin County, PA. He married **MARGARET MARIA KEITER**, daughter of **HOMER KEITER** and **LILLIAN M. ARNOLD,** on 18 April 1941, Hagerstown, Washington County, MD. He died on 11 August 1968, Harrisburg, Dauphin County, PA, at age 47. He was buried at Maple Grove Cemetery, Elizabethville, Dauphin County, PA.
>
>> **7.1.1.7.2.1 DAWN LANETTE KLINGER** was born on 6 December 1942. She married **DAVID UNDERKOFFLER**. She married **RONALD ROMBERGER** Rife, Dauphin County, PA. She married **JAMES RISSINGER**.

7.1.1.7.2.1.1 Douglas Underkoffler was born on 12 March 1968. He married **Terri (--?--)**.

    7.1.1.7.2.1.1.1 Rebecka Lynn Underkoffler

7.1.1.7.2.1.2 Angela Renae Romberger was born on 12 January 1976. She married **(--?--) Schadel**.

7.1.1.7.2.2 Rickey Eugene Klinger was born on 22 January 1954. He married **Linda (--?--)**.

7.1.1.7.3 Leona Irene Klinger was born on 28 March 1924. She married **Albert Salvator Sgrignoli**, son of **Mauro Sgrignoli** and **Feliciana Magaro**, circa 1942. She married **Thomas Charles Glorius** on 19 June 1959. She died on 8 June 1974, at age 50.

    7.1.1.7.3.1 Gayle Ann Sgrignoli was born on 13 May 1943. She married **George Ernest Herold** on 20 May 1966. She died on 14 August 2015, Harrisburg Hospital, Harrisburg, Dauphin County, PA, at age 72.

        7.1.1.7.3.1.1 Sherri Herold married **John Laughlin**.

        7.1.1.7.3.1.2 Sherri Lynn Herold was born on 20 July 1967.

    7.1.1.7.3.2 Keith Eugene Sgrignoli was born on 7 December 1948. He married **Dolores Jones** on 30 August 1969.

        7.1.1.7.3.2.1 Jeffrey William Sgrignoli was born on 7 January 1975.

    7.1.1.7.3.3 Deborah Kay Glorius was born on 3 August 1960.

7.1.1.8 Sallie E. Klinger was born on 26 February 1893. She died on 10 March 1893. She was buried at Oakdale Church Cemetery, Washington Township, Dauphin County, PA.

7.1.1.9 Mellie E. Klinger was born on 29 August 1894. She died on 28 January 1897, at age 2. She was buried at Oakdale Church Cemetery, Washington Township, Dauphin County, PA.

7.1.1.10 Bernice Pauline Klinger was born on 31 December 1895, Rife, Dauphin County, PA. She was baptized on 30 August 1896, Elizabethville, Dauphin County, PA. She married **Thomas Milton Hartman** circa 1917. Prior to her death, Bernice was living in Elizabethville, Dauphin County, PA. She died in May 1975, Harrisburg, Dauphin County, PA, at age 79.

    7.1.1.10.1 Henry H. Hartman was born in 1917, Washington Township, Dauphin County, PA. He married **Garnet Dixon** in 1950, Harrisburg, Dauphin County, PA. He died in 1980, San Diego, CA.

        7.1.1.10.1.1 Douglas Hartman was born on 9 October 1950. He married **Terry Lynn Bowers**.

            7.1.1.10.1.1.1 Lisa Hartman

            7.1.1.10.1.1.2 James Hartman

        7.1.1.10.1.2 Christine Hartman was born on 21 November 1953. She married **David Llewellyn**.

            7.1.1.10.1.2.1 David Llewellyn

            7.1.1.10.1.2.2 Katherine Llewellyn

        7.1.1.10.1.3 Carol Hartman was born on 1 May 1956. She married **Robert Jensen**. She married **(--?--) Kahler**.

            7.1.1.10.1.3.1 Jennifer Jensen

            7.1.1.10.1.3.2 Christian Jensen

    7.1.1.10.2 Eleanor Marie Hartman was born on 30 September 1918, Washington Township, Dauphin County, PA. She married **Eugene Hoffman** on 19 August 1944, Lykens, Dauphin County, PA. Prior to her death, Eleanor was living in the vicinity of Lykens, Dauphin County, PA. She died on 6 June 1997, at age 78.

    7.1.1.10.3 Thomas J. Hartman was born on 3 March 1921, Washington Township, Dauphin County, PA. Some sources record that he was born on 4 March 1921. He married **Eva Reitinger** in December 1941. Prior to his death, Thomas was living in the vicinity of Camp Hill, Cumberland County, PA. He died on 7 February 2001, at age 79.

        7.1.1.10.3.1 Maxine Hartman was born on 9 February 1943. She married **John Botts**.

            7.1.1.10.3.1.1 Michelle Botts

7.1.1.10.3.1.2 SUSANNE BOTTS

7.1.1.10.3.1.3 JILL BOTTS

7.1.1.10.4 PAUL FRANKLIN HARTMAN was born in 1922, Washington Township, Dauphin County, PA. He married ELEANOR MARIE (--?--) in 1948, Mifflin Twp., Dauphin County, PA. He died in 1970, Elizabethville, Dauphin County, PA.

- **7.1.1.10.4.1** PERCILLA HARTMAN was born circa 1951. She married EDWARD KOHLER.

  - **7.1.1.10.4.1.1** VERONICA KOHLER was born circa 1976.
  - **7.1.1.10.4.1.2** PATRICK KOHLER was born circa 1978.
  - **7.1.1.10.4.1.3** JOSEPH KOHLER was born circa 1980.
  - **7.1.1.10.4.1.4** CHARLES KOHLER was born circa 1982.

- **7.1.1.10.4.2** TIMOTHY HARTMAN was born circa 1955. He married LORIE MILLER.

  - **7.1.1.10.4.2.1** JENINE HARTMAN was born circa 1976.
  - **7.1.1.10.4.2.2** LONI HARTMAN was born circa 1981.
  - **7.1.1.10.4.2.3** LACI HARTMAN was born circa 1985.
  - **7.1.1.10.4.2.4** JILLIAN HARTMAN was born circa 1988.
  - **7.1.1.10.4.2.5** TONI HARTMAN was born circa 1992.

7.1.1.10.5 HILDA HARTMAN was born on 1 February 1923, Elizabethville, Dauphin County, PA. She married TONY FORLIZZI in 1948, MD.

- **7.1.1.10.5.1** LORIE FORLIZZI was born circa 1960. She married RICHARD CARLSON circa 1990.
- **7.1.1.10.5.2** JODIE FORLIZZI was born circa 1962.

7.1.1.11 CHARLES A. KLINGER was born on 16 February 1897. He died on 16 February 1897.

7.1.1.12 OLIVE MARIA KLINGER was born on 26 September 1901, Rife, Dauphin County, PA. She was baptized on 30 March 1902, Elizabethville, Dauphin County, PA. Some sources record that she was born on 26 September 1902, Rife, Dauphin County, PA. She married PAUL DEIBLER NOVINGER circa 1925. Prior to her death, Olive was living in the vicinity of Camp Hill, Cumberland County, PA. She was buried at Maple Grove Cemetery, Elizabethville, Dauphin County, PA. She died on 23 July 1997, Millersburg, Dauphin County, PA, at age 94.

7.1.2 HENRY JOHN KLINGER is also referred to as JOHN HENRY KLINGER in some sources. He was born in March 1852. Some sources record that he was born on 22 March 1853. He married CATHERINE ANNIE KOPPENHAVER circa 1883. He died on 6 June 1901, at age 48. He was buried at Oakdale Church Cemetery, Washington Township, Dauphin County, PA.

7.1.2.1 CARRIE E. KLINGER died before 1 June 1900, at age 1 year 8 months. She was buried at Oakdale Church Cemetery, Washington Township, Dauphin County, PA.

7.1.2.2 DANIEL EDWARD KLINGER was born on 9 April 1885. He married GACE A. (--?--). He died in February 1968, at age 82.

- **7.1.2.2.1** MARTHA A. KLINGER

7.1.2.3 AARON H. KLINGER was born in July 1887. He married SUSAN AMELIA SCHAFFER. He died on 12 November 1911, at age 24. He was buried at St. John's Lutheran Church Cemetery, Berrysburg, Dauphin County, PA.

- **7.1.2.3.1** JOSEPH KLINGER was born in 1908. He died in 1941.

7.1.2.4 CHARLES A. KLINGER was born on 9 October 1888. He married ALICE B. MARKEL after 1910. He died on 11 June 1964, at age 75. Some sources record that he died on 4 June 1964. He was buried at St. John's Lutheran Church Cemetery, Berrysburg, Dauphin County, PA.

- **7.1.2.4.1** ROY K. KLINGER was born circa April 1915, Pennsylvania. He died before 1964.

- **7.1.2.4.2** ARLENE R. KLINGER is also referred to as ERLINE in some sources. She was born on 23 August 1917, Pennsylvania. She married (--?--) PUNCH. She married FLOYD HARMAN. She died on 16 August 1990, at age 72.

  - **7.1.2.4.2.1** LARRY D. PUNCH
  - **7.1.2.4.2.2** NANCY PUNCH married (--?--) ZAPCIC.

7.1.2.4.3 VIOLET E. KLINGER was born circa October 1919, Pennsylvania. Violet was not listed with her family in the 1930 Census.

7.1.2.4.4 MARK I. KLINGER was born on 29 July 1922, Elizabethville, Dauphin County, PA. Although Mark's obituary published in the Harrisburg Patriot-News states that his parents were "John" and Alice Klinger, the 1930 Census records for Washington Township, Dauphin County (which includes Elizabethville) list a Mark I. Klinger, born circa 1922, as the son of "Charles A." and Alice B. Klinger. He married **ELSIE I. HEBERLING.** He died on 27 July 2008, Harrisburg Hospital, Harrisburg, Dauphin County, PA, at age 85. According to a newspaper obituary, Mark lived in Millersburg, PA. He was a veteran of the US Army, serving in the Pacific during World War II, and was awarded the Purple Heart. Later, he worked as at the Middletown Military Base. He was buried on 30 July 2008, at Maple Grove Cemetery, Elizabethville, Dauphin County, PA.

    7.1.2.4.4.1 RONALD LEE KLINGER was born on 3 June 1947. He died on 10 September 2006, at home, Elizabethville, Dauphin County, PA, at age 59. According to a newspaper obituary, Ronald lived in Elizabethville, Dauphin County, PA. He was a bus driver at CAT Share-a-ride and previously for Dauphin County Transportation. He had also worked for Swab Wagon Company, all of Elizabethville.

7.1.2.4.5 BETTY JANE KLINGER is also referred to as **BETTY L. KLINGER** in some sources. She was born on 30 May 1935, Elizabethville, Dauphin County, PA. She died on 9 May 2012, ManorCare Health Services, Lebanon, Dauphin County, PA, at age 76. She was buried on 16 May 2012, at Maple Grove Cemetery, Elizabethville, Dauphin County, PA.

7.1.2.5 JOHN B. KLINGER was born in December 1894, Pennsylvania. John served in the Headquarters Company of the 316th Infantry Division during World War I. He died circa 2 May 1933. Some sources record that he died in 1946. He was buried at St. John's Lutheran Church Cemetery, Berrysburg, Dauphin County, PA.

7.1.2.6 MARY E. KLINGER was born in June 1900. She married **MARK EDGAR STINE.** She died on 27 February 1978, at age 77.

7.1.3 JAMES KLINGER was born on 12 March 1855, Dauphin County, PA. He married **MARY E. KERSTETTER** before 1880. He married **SEVILLA J. BOYER** on 26 November 1891, Dauphin County, PA. He died on 4 October 1916, Dauphin County, PA, at age 61. He was buried at Oak Hill Cemetery, Millersburg, Dauphin County, PA.

7.1.3.1 NORMAN HOWARD KLINGER was born on 6 November 1881. He died on 27 October 1954, at age 72. He was buried at Oak Hill Cemetery, Millersburg, Dauphin County, PA.

7.1.3.2 HOMER EDWIN KLINGER was born on 10 July 1883. He married **KATIE ELLEN MATTER**, daughter of **IRA A. MATTER** and **MARY ELLEN JURY.** He died on 18 February 1952, at age 68. He was buried at Oak Hill Cemetery, Millersburg, Dauphin County, PA.

    7.1.3.2.1 IRENE A. KLINGER was born on 3 January 1913. She died on 5 November 1990, at age 77. Irene never married.

    7.1.3.2.2 JAMES E. KLINGER was born on 19 June 1914. He died on 1 August 1996, at age 82. He was buried at Oak Hill Cemetery, Millersburg, Dauphin County, PA.

    7.1.3.2.3 PAULINE ANNA KLINGER was born on 13 July 1915. She married **PAUL S. MURRAY.** She died on 14 December 1990, at age 75. She was buried at Woodlawn Memorial Gardens, Lower Paxton Township, Dauphin County, PA.

    7.1.3.2.4 LAURA S. KLINGER was born on 17 February 1920. She died on 12 December 1995, at age 75. She was buried at Oak Hill Cemetery, Millersburg, Dauphin County, PA. Laura never married.

    7.1.3.2.5 RUTH MARIE KLINGER was born on 18 March 1922. She married **NEVIN SCHREFFLER.** She married **HERMAN EUGENE HOKE.** She died on 9 November 2011, Community General Osteopathic Hospital, Harrisburg, Dauphin County, PA, at age 89. According to a newspaper obituary, Ruth lived in Dalmatia, PA. She retired from the former Creative Playthings in Herndon. She was buried on 12 November 2011, at Oak Hill Cemetery, Millersburg, Dauphin County, PA.

        7.1.3.2.5.1 JOAN MARIE SCHREFFLER was born on 17 April 1942. She married **ARDEN ADAMS.** Joan lives in Meyerstown, PA.

            7.1.3.2.5.1.1 TROY K. ADAMS died before 2011.

7.1.3.2.5.2 CAROL ANN HOKE was born on 19 December 1946. She married JERRY GRAFF. Carol lives in Millersburg, PA.

7.1.3.2.5.3 PATRICIA ELLEN HOKE was born on 20 December 1950. She married DONALD HOCH. Patricia lives in Dalmatia, PA.

7.1.3.2.6 CLARA A. KLINGER was born on 15 April 1923. She married RUSSEL J. HOOVER. She and RUSSEL J. HOOVER were divorced. She married JOHN R. KEIM. She died on 1 October 1996, at age 73.

7.1.3.2.6.1 RONALD HOOVER died in infancy.

7.1.3.2.6.2 KENNETH L. HOOVER

7.1.3.2.6.3 RUSSEL J. HOOVER JR.

7.1.3.2.7 HOMER ALBERT KLINGER was born on 10 June 1924. He died on 19 July 1993, at age 69. Homer never married.

7.1.3.2.8 SARA JANE KLINGER is also referred to as SAL in some sources. She was born on 13 February 1926, Millersburg, Dauphin County, PA. She married ALLEN FRANKLIN LENKER, son of CHARLES ALLEN LENKER SR. and GERTRUDE ISABELLA KLINGER. She married ROBERT HARNER. She died on 7 October 2012, the Manor at Susquehanna Village, Millersburg, Dauphin County, PA, at age 86. According to a newspaper obituary, Sal was retired from Dauphin County transportation services and had worked at the former Koppy's store in Lenkerville. She was buried on 11 October 2012, at Riverview Memorial Gardens, Halifax, Dauphin County, PA.

7.1.3.2.8.1 DAVID ALLEN LENKER (see above)

7.1.3.2.8.1.1 LINETTE LENKER (see above)

7.1.3.2.8.1.2 NATHANIEL LENKER (see above)

7.1.3.2.8.1.3 SARAH LENKER (see above)

7.1.3.2.8.2 JOAN MARIE LENKER (see above)

7.1.3.2.8.2.1 MATTHEW ALLEN CHUBB (see above)

7.1.3.3 FRANKLIN ANTHONY KLINGER was born on 17 January 1888, Upper Paxton Township, Dauphin County, PA. He married SADIE EDNA ROTHERMEL, daughter of SOLOMON ROTHERMEL and ELIZABETH (--?--), circa 1904. He died on 2 October 1939, Lower Allen Township, Cumberland County, PA, at age 51. He was buried at Rolling Green Memorial Park, Camp Hill, Cumberland County, PA.

7.1.3.3.1 NORMAN ELMER KLINGER is also referred to as HARRY ELMER KLINGER in some sources. He was born on 22 March 1906, Millersburg, Dauphin County, PA. He married RUTH ELLEN SHILEY, daughter of OSCAR SHILEY and KATIE SHOOP. He died in December 1980, at age 74. He was buried at Greenwood Cemetery, Tower City, Schuylkill County, PA.

7.1.3.3.1.1 JOYCE M. KLINGER was born circa 1938. She married THOMAS JOSEPH CROFT, son of THOMAS CROFT and SOPHIA B. ROBEBACKER, on 10 July 1965, Los Angeles County, CA.

7.1.3.3.1.1.1 ANN MARIE CROFT married KEITH CUBA.

7.1.3.3.1.1.2 SUSAN CROFT

7.1.3.3.2 MYRL IRENE KLINGER was born on 26 February 1908, Berrysburg, Dauphin County, PA. She married ALBERT CALVIN HECKERT on 28 February 1925. She died on 3 May 2012, Manor Care, Camp Hill, Cumberland County, PA, at age 104. According to a newspaper obituary, Myrl lived in Camp Hill and formerly of Harrisburg, PA. She lived independently and in her own home until the age of 97.

Myrl raised her niece, Myrl V. (Rittner) Busler, as her daughter from the age of two. She was buried at Rolling Green Memorial Park, Camp Hill, Cumberland County, PA.

7.1.3.3.3 MARTHA VIOLA KLINGER was born on 29 March 1915. She married ARTHUR P. SHADE SR. She died on 24 September 2005, at age 90.

7.1.3.3.3.1 ELLEN S. SHADE

7.1.3.3.3.2 ERNEST E. SHADE

7.1.3.3.3.3 ARTHUR P. SHADE JR.

7.1.3.3.3.4 WILLIAM FRANKLIN SHADE

7.1.3.3.4 **FAY M. KLINGER** was born on 12 September 1917. She married **DAVID E. RITTNER**. She died on 28 August 2004, at age 86.

    7.1.3.3.4.1 **JAN H. RITTNER**

    7.1.3.3.4.2 **PATRICIA D. RITTNER**

    7.1.3.3.4.3 **MYRL V. RITTNER**

7.1.3.3.5 **ESTHER R. KLINGER** was born on 8 May 1919. She married **ROBERT WARD**. She died on 28 December 2005, at age 86.

    7.1.3.3.5.1 **LARRY WARD** died before 2008.

    7.1.3.3.5.2 **SHIRLEY WARD**

7.1.3.3.6 **ROBERT FRANKLIN KLINGER** was born on 15 March 1921. He died on 1 January 1995, at age 73.

7.1.3.3.7 **PAUL EUGENE KLINGER** was born on 31 December 1928. He married **HAZEL BILLOW**. He married **HELEN G. VOGELSONG**.

    7.1.3.3.7.1 **CYNTHIA ANN KLINGER** married **JAMES TIBBINS**. She married **THOMAS WILLIAMS**.

    7.1.3.3.7.2 **RONALD PAUL KLINGER** married **SHERRY (--?--)**.

    7.1.3.3.7.3 **DEBORAH K. KLINGER**

7.1.3.4 **MARY E. KLINGER** was born on 13 July 1894. She married **JOHN HENRY HENNINGER** circa 1915. She died on 15 September 1973, at age 79.

    7.1.3.4.1 **EVELYN M. HENNINGER** was born on 22 April 1916. She married **ROBERT E. BROWN**. She died on 3 October 2007, at age 91.

    7.1.3.4.2 **WINIFRED A. HENNINGER** was born on 13 March 1920. She married **JOSEPH HEIM**. She died on 29 June 2001, at age 81.

    7.1.3.4.3 **ETHEL L. HENNINGER** was born circa 1922. She married **JOHN KNAUB**.

7.1.4 **WELLINGTON E. KLINGER** was born on 18 March 1858, Matterstown, PA. He married **AMANDA E. WILBERT**, daughter of **PHILIP WILBERT** and **CATHARINE MATTER**, on 8 July 1880, Oakdale Church, Dauphin County, PA. Wellington and Amanda lived east of the Spread Eagle Plant in Elizabethville, Dauphin County, PA. He died on 4 February 1936, Elizabethville, Dauphin County, PA, at age 77.

7.1.4.1 **EDITH CATHERINE KLINGER** is also referred to as **ESTHER** in some sources. She was born on 12 October 1882, Oakdale, Washington Township, Dauphin County, PA. She was baptized on 7 February 1883, in parents' home, Washington Township, Dauphin County, PA. She married **FRANK W. PAUL**, son of **JOHN PAUL** and **SUSANNA MILLER**, on 23 October 1904, St. James Lutheran Church. She died on 18 December 1947, Elizabethville, Dauphin County, PA, at age 65.

    7.1.4.1.1 **DOROTHY ELLEN PAUL** was born on 28 September 1906. She died in 1907.

    7.1.4.1.2 **MARTIN LUTHER PAUL** was born on 15 February 1908.

7.1.4.2 **ROSCOE MILTON KLINGER** was born on 25 April 1885, Berrysburg, Dauphin County, PA. He was baptized on 24 June 1888, Berrysburg, Dauphin County, PA. He married **ELLEN REBECCA SCHAEFFER**, daughter of **LEVI SCHAEFFER** and **ELIZABETH YEAGER**. Prior to his death, Roscoe was living in the vicinity of Harrisburg, Dauphin County, PA. He died in October 1978, at age 93. He was buried at Maple Grove Cemetery, Elizabethville, Dauphin County, PA.

    7.1.4.2.1 **MILDRED NETTIE KLINGER** was born on 20 June 1910. She married **RUSSELL HOY** on 20 April 1933. Mildred and Russell lived near Millersburg, Dauphin County, PA. She died on 27 December 1989, Dauphin County, PA, at age 79. She was buried on 30 December 1989, at Maple Grove Cemetery, Elizabethville, Dauphin County, PA.

        7.1.4.2.1.1 **JANET M. HOY** married **KENNETH R. ADAMS**, son of **EDWARD ADAMS** and **IVA REBUCK**.

            7.1.4.2.1.1.1 **RICKY ADAMS** married **LISA (--?--)**.

            7.1.4.2.1.1.2 **PAMELA ADAMS** is also referred to as **TAMMIE ADAMS** in some sources.

        7.1.4.2.1.2 **WINIFRED LORRAINE HOY** was born on 13 February 1937, Dauphin County, PA. She died on 13 February 1937, Dauphin County, PA. She was buried at Maple Grove Cemetery, Elizabethville, Dauphin County, PA.

7.1.4.2.2 ERMA L. KLINGER is also referred to as **IRMA** in some sources. She was born on 24 November 1923. She married **MELVIN ROBERT LEBO**, son of **HARVEY W. LEBO** and **AMANDA ETZWEILER**. She married **RUSSELL WALTER** after 1959. She died on 23 October 1994, Millersburg, Dauphin County, PA, at age 70. She was buried at Maple Grove Cemetery, Elizabethville, Dauphin County, PA.

    7.1.4.2.2.1 MELVIN LEBO married **MARY KLINGER**, daughter of **ERNEST KLINGER** and **ALMA ROTHERMOL**.

    7.1.4.2.2.2 MICHAEL LEBO

    7.1.4.2.2.3 CHAD WALTERS

7.1.4.2.3 MARCELLA SADIE KLINGER is also referred to as **MARSELLA SADIE KLINGER** in some sources. She was born on 1 June 1924, Washington Township, Dauphin County, PA. She married **CLAYTON MALCOM SNYDER**, son of **CLAYTON SNYDER**, circa 1942. Marcella and Clayton lived in Elizabethtown, PA. She died on 2 January 2010, The Manor at Susquehanna Village, Millersburg, Dauphin County, PA, at age 85.

    7.1.4.2.3.1 DIANE SNYDER married **FRANK CASWELL**. She married **(--?--) CASCIO**.

    7.1.4.2.3.2 JOANINE SNYDER is also referred to as **JO ANN** in some sources. She married **MICHAEL KREINER**. She married **(--?--) RICHIE**.

    7.1.4.2.3.3 JEFFREY SNYDER married **BARBARA FRY**.

    7.1.4.2.3.4 PAUL SNYDER

    7.1.4.2.3.5 WINIFRED SNYDER. Some sources do not list Winifred as a child of Marcella and Clayton. She was not mentioned in Marcella (Klinger) Snyder's obituary.

7.1.4.2.4 KATHRYN H. KLINGER was born on 20 August 1925, Elizabethville, Dauphin County, PA. She married **TIMOTHY H. SCHREFFLER**, son of **SAMUEL SCHREFFLER** and **KATIE JEMIMA DONMOYER**, on 24 December 1947. Kathryn and Timothy lived in Pillow, Dauphin County, PA. She died on 6 October 2001, Millersburg, Dauphin County, PA, at age 76. She was buried at Maple Grove Cemetery, Elizabethville, Dauphin County, PA.

    7.1.4.2.4.1 ANTHONY L. SCHREFFLER

    7.1.4.2.4.2 TIMOTHY T. SCHREFFLER

    7.1.4.2.4.3 JO ELLEN SCHREFFLER was born on 12 November 1949.

    7.1.4.2.4.4 INFANT SCHREFFLER was born on 17 January 1956.

7.1.4.3 STILLBORN INFANT KLINGER was born on 5 August 1891. He/she died on 5 August 1891.

7.1.4.4 STILLBORN INFANT KLINGER was born on 8 August 1893. He/she died on 8 August 1893.

7.1.4.5 CHARLOTTE KLINGER was born in 1896. There is a tombstone, in the same plot as Wellington and Amanda Klinger, listing Charlotte (1898-1935) with a son "Bobby Jr." (1926-1928). Based on this, Mary Klinger, Klingers from the Odenwald, Hesse, Germany, p. 405, concludes that she was the daughter of Wellington and Amanda. This may be in error. According to the 1900 and 1910 Census listings, Wellington and Amanda had 5 children born before 1910, only 3 of whom, "Esther," Roscoc, and Ralph, were living in 1900. This would suggest that Charlotte was not the daughter of Wellington and Amanda. She died in 1935.

7.1.4.6 RALPH WILBERT KLINGER was born on 11 July 1898, Elizabethville, Dauphin County, PA. He was baptized on 19 February 1900, Elizabethville, Dauphin County, PA. He married **LOTTIE (--?--)** circa 1921. He married **KATHRYN S. ROTHERMEL**, daughter of **JAMES ROTHERMEL** and **EMMA C. BOHNER**. He married **EDNA ALBERTA HAND** on 2 January 1937. He died on 1 August 1970, at age 72. Prior to his death, Ralph was living in Lykens, Dauphin County, PA.

    7.1.4.6.1 ELLA J. KLINGER was born on 13 July 1929. She married **(--?--) GRAEFF**. Prior to her death, Ella was living in the vicinity of Gratz, Dauphin County, PA. She died on 29 January 1993, at age 63.

        7.1.4.6.1.1 SCOTT GRAEFF married **MELISSA (--?--)**.

            7.1.4.6.1.1.1 BRIAN GRAEFF

            7.1.4.6.1.1.2 ASHLEY GRAEFF

            7.1.4.6.1.1.3 JENNIFER GRAEFF

            7.1.4.6.1.1.4 KIMBERLY GRAEFF

7.1.5 FRANCES KLINGER is also referred to as **FRANCIS AND FANNIE** in some sources. She was born in October 1860, Pennsylvania. Some sources record that she was born in 1861. She married **SIMON A. HOLTZMAN** circa 1887.

7.1.5.1 MARK G. HOLTZMAN was born circa 1887, Pennsylvania. He married **ETHEL W. (--?--)** circa 1912.

7.1.5.1.1 FRANCIS L. HOLTZMAN was born in 1913.

7.1.5.1.2 GEORGE T. HOLTZMAN was born in 1915.

7.1.5.1.3 THOMAS W. HOLTZMAN was born in 1918.

7.1.6 JEREMIAH KLINGER is also referred to as **JERRY** in some sources. He was born on 29 December 1861. He married **AGNES S. SMELTZER**, daughter of **JONAS SMELTZER** and **SARAH (--?--)**, circa 1892. Some sources suggest that he and **AGNES S. SMELTZER** were married circa 1894. He died on 20 November 1939, at age 77. He was buried at Zion Lutheran and Reformed Church Cemetery, Rife, Dauphin County, PA.

7.1.6.1 RALPH HARRISON LANDIS was born on 28 March 1890. The 1900 Census lists Ralph as a "son" of Jeremiah. The 1910 Census, however, lists Jeremiah's wife Agnes as the mother of 4 children. This suggests either that Ralph was not Agnes's son or that the listing of Ralph as Jeremiah's son is not correct. An obituary for Jay W. Klinger lists Ralph as a half-brother, suggesting that he was a son of Agnes Smeltzer and another man. He married **LYDIA (--?--)**.

7.1.6.2 HARRY A. KLINGER was born on 12 November 1894. He married **MARY ESTHER BORDNER**, daughter of **JOHN W. BORDNER** and **MARY C. BOWERS**. He married **ALICE HOFFMAN**. He died on 23 April 1944, at age 49.

7.1.6.2.1 DONALD A. KLINGER was born on 30 May 1918. He died on 3 April 1995, at age 76.

7.1.6.2.2 ROSANNA KLINGER was born on 27 October 1921. She married **MELVIN D. SCHNOOR**. She died on 1 December 2003, at age 82.

7.1.6.2.2.1 JACQUELYN SCHNOOR

7.1.6.2.2.2 CRAIG SCHNOOR

7.1.6.2.3 ROBERT KLINGER was born on 13 October 1923. He died on 21 July 1993, at age 69.

7.1.6.3 FRANK EDWARD KLINGER was born on 29 March 1896. He married **FLORA MAY CLEMSON**. He died circa 1963. He was buried at United Methodist Church Cemetery, Halifax, Dauphin County, PA.

7.1.6.4 JAY W. KLINGER was born on 2 April 1905, Upper Paxton Township, Dauphin County, PA. He married **ROZELLA M. HOY**, daughter of **HARRY ULYSSES HOY** and **SADIE L. WEAVER**, circa 1926. He died on 1 November 1955, at age 50. He was buried at Zion Lutheran and Reformed Church Cemetery, Rife, Dauphin County, PA.

7.1.6.4.1 SARAH ANNETTA KLINGER was born on 25 July 1929. She married **CHARLES D. LENKER**. She died on 7 January 1999, Millersburg, Dauphin County, PA, at age 69. She was buried at Salem Lutheran Church Cemetery, Millersburg, Dauphin County, PA.

7.1.6.4.2 ROY W. KLINGER was born on 12 May 1932. He married **MARGARET (--?--)**. He died on 1 June 1983, at age 51. He was buried at Riverview Memorial Gardens, Halifax, Dauphin County, PA.

7.1.6.4.3 GUY E. KLINGER

7.1.6.5 SARAH E. KLINGER was born on 31 January 1908, Upper Paxton Township, Dauphin County, PA. She married **ELMER D. KEITER** on 24 August 1940, Rev. Stanley C. Baker, officiating. She died on 21 February 1963, at age 55. She was buried at Oak Hill Cemetery, Millersburg, Dauphin County, PA.

7.1.7 ANNA S. KLINGER. Other sources record that she was also known as **ANNIE W. KLINGER**. She was born circa October 1862. Some sources record that she was born in October 1865. Other sources record that she was born circa 1864. She married **WILLIS O'NEILL** on 22 August 1885, Oakdale Church, Dauphin County, PA. She died on 5 May 1944, Chambersburg, Franklin County, PA, at age 78.

7.1.7.1 BERTHA BULAH O'NEILL was born on 12 October 1886. She was baptized on 25 February 1889, Curtin, Dauphin County, PA.

7.1.7.2 LAURA ETTA O'NEILL was born on 14 December 1887, Curtin, Dauphin County, PA. She was baptized on 22 April 1888, Curtin, Dauphin County, PA. She married **SILAS RAY COLDREN**. She died on 30 April 1956, at age 68.

- **7.1.7.2.1 MARTHA A. COLDREN**
- **7.1.7.2.2 ELWOOD O. COLDREN**
- **7.1.7.2.3 GERALDINE COLDREN**
- **7.1.7.2.4 ELNORA L. COLDREN**

7.1.7.3 WILLIAM OSCAR O'NEILL was born on 14 September 1890, Killinger, Dauphin County, PA. He was baptized on 1 February 1891, Killinger, Dauphin County, PA. He died in 1891.

7.1.7.4 MONA HELEN O'NEILL was born on 12 June 1892. She died on 5 January 1904, at age 11.

7.1.7.5 ETHEL IRENE O'NEILL was born on 15 December 1900. She died on 31 December 1903, at age 3.

7.1.7.6 ANNA M. O'NEILL was born circa 1905. Some sources record that she was born circa 1906. She married **(--?--) POTEIGER** circa 1927.

7.1.8 MARY KLINGER was born in 1867. Some sources record that she was born in 1870.

7.2 BENNEVILLE KLINGER was born on 19 December 1829. He died on 14 June 1849, at age 19. He was buried at Oakdale Cemetery, Oakdale, Dauphin County, PA.

7.3 CATHARINE KLINGER was born on 24 August 1831. She was baptized on 13 November 1831, Zion (Klinger's) Church, Erdman, Lykens Township, Dauphin County, PA. She married **JACOB BOWMAN**, son of **ABRAHAM BOWMAN** and **ANNA ELIZABETH FROST**.

7.4 DANIEL A. KLINGER was born on 12 January 1834, Dauphin County, PA. He married **EMMALINE LEBO**, daughter of **JONATHAN LEBO** and **ELIZABETH BECHTEL**, circa 1860. He began military service on 18 June 1863. He ended military service on 30 July 1863. Daniel served as a private in Company K of the 26th Regiment of the Pennsylvania Infantry Volunteers during the Civil War. According to some sources, he was also a watchmaker. He died on 13 January 1908, Dauphin County, PA, at age 74. He was buried at Oakdale Cemetery, Oakdale, Dauphin County, PA.

7.4.1 ALMEDA MAGDALENA KLINGER is also referred to as **ALMEDIA AND ALMATA** in some sources. She was born on 13 September 1863, Dauphin County, PA. She married **GEORGE H. BURRELL**, son of **JOHN BURRELL** and **POLLY TROUTMAN,** circa 1883. She died on 2 March 1947, Loyalton, Dauphin County, PA, at age 83. She was buried on 6 March 1947, at Maple Grove Cemetery, Elizabethville, Dauphin County, PA.

7.4.1.1 LAURA E. BURRELL was born on 17 November 1883, Berrysburg, Dauphin County, PA. She married **SALEM C. MOYER**, son of **MANDAN MOYER** and **ELMIRA (--?--)**. She died on 10 September 1953, Washington Township, Dauphin County, PA, at age 69. She was buried on 14 September 1953, at Oak Hill Cemetery, Millersburg, Dauphin County, PA.

7.4.1.1.1 MARK S. MOYER was born circa 1904.

7.4.1.1.2 MARTHA E. MOYER was born circa 1907.

7.4.1.1.3 ETHEL LAURA MOYER was born on 24 November 1909, Schuylkill County, PA. She died on 12 February 1911, New Ringgold, Schuylkill County, PA, at age 1. She was buried at Drehersville, Drehersville, Schuylkill County, PA.

7.4.1.1.4 PAUL C. MOYER was born in 1911. He died in 1921. He was buried at Oak Hill Cemetery, Millersburg, Dauphin County, PA.

7.4.1.1.5 LUKE MANDAN MOYER was born on 19 October 1912. He died on 19 October 1912. He was buried at Drehersville, Drehersville, Schuylkill County, PA.

7.4.1.1.6 SALEM CLAIR MOYER was born on 4 September 1918, Millersburg, Dauphin County, PA. He died on 17 May 1966, at age 47. He was buried at Montandon Cemetery, Montandon, Northumberland County, PA.

7.4.1.1.7 GRACE EMMALINE MOYER was born on 25 February 1921, Millersburg, Dauphin County, PA. She died on 15 June 1995, at age 74.

7.4.1.2 WALTER DANIEL BURRELL is also referred to as **DANIEL WALTER BURRELL** in some sources. He was born on 30 October 1886, New Ringgold, Schuylkill County, PA. He married **MINERVA REBECCA RAUENZAHN**, daughter of **JOEL LLEWELLYN RAUENZAHN** and **ELLEN FIELDS**.

He died on 16 March 1962, Laureldale, Berks County, PA, at age 75. He was buried on 20 March 1962, at Gernants Cemetery, Leesport, Berks County, PA.

7.4.1.2.1 FRANCES ALMEDA BURRELL was born on 16 February 1924, Reading, Berks County, PA. She married **DOMINIC J. DEAMGELO**, son of **DONATO DEAMGELO** and **MARIA CAVALUCCI**. She died on 19 September 1994, at age 70. She was buried at Forest Hills Memorial Park, Reiffton, Berks County, PA.

7.4.1.2.2 ELSIE BURRELL was born circa 1929.

7.4.1.3 LLOYD EDWARD BURRELL was born in 1888, Dauphin County, PA. He died in 1890, Dauphin County, PA.

7.4.1.4 LYDIA E. BURRELL was born on 21 April 1889. She died on 2 May 1890, at age 1.

7.4.1.5 WILLIAM E. BURRELL is also referred to as **WILLIAM ROY BURRELL** in some sources. He was born on 21 January 1890. He died on 8 July 1890.

7.4.1.6 JOHN DAVID BURRELL was born on 16 May 1891. He died on 16 February 1892.

7.4.1.7 HATTIE EVA BURRELL was born on 30 January 1893, Berrysburg, Dauphin County, PA. She married **WILLIAM EDWARD MATTER**, son of **REBECCA BATDORF**. She died on 12 March 1986, at age 93. She was buried at Maple Grove Cemetery, Elizabethville, Dauphin County, PA.

7.4.1.7.1 GLENN EDWARD MATTER was born on 28 May 1914. He married **MARGARET L. JOHNS**. He died on 24 April 2005, at age 90. He was buried at Maple Grove Cemetery, Elizabethville, Dauphin County, PA.

7.4.1.7.1.1 JON WILLIAM MATTER was born on 31 May 1937.

7.4.1.7.1.2 PAUL EUGENE MATTER was born on 6 July 1942.

7.4.1.7.2 HAROLD E. MATTER was born circa 1925.

7.4.1.8 LILLIE MAY BURRELL was born on 11 November 1895, Elizabethville, Dauphin County, PA. She married **ARTHUR A. BURRELL**. She died on 11 March 1961, Susquehanna Township, Dauphin County, PA, at age 65. She was buried on 14 March 1961, at Prospect Hill Cemetery, Harrisburg, Dauphin County, PA.

7.4.1.9 ALVIN GEORGE BURRELL died in 1895. He was born on 7 July 1896, Lock Haven, Clinton County, PA. Some sources record that he was born on 7 July 1899. He married **EFFIE M. LUPOLD**, daughter of **HARVEY E. LUPOLD** and **CLARA J. MILLER**. He was buried at Jacobs United Methodist Church Cemetery, Waynesville, Dauphin County, PA.

7.4.1.9.1 RICHARD A. BURRELL was born on 10 December 1923, Harrisburg, Dauphin County, PA. He married **PAULINE LOUISE EARLY** on 8 April 1945.

7.4.1.9.1.1 BARBARA ANN BURRELL was born on 16 October 1946, Polyclinic Hospital, Harrisburg, Dauphin County, PA. She married **JOHN FASICK** on 26 January 1963.

7.4.1.9.1.1.1 TERRI FASICK was born on 23 September 1963. She married **MICHAEL O'KEEFE** on 31 August 1985.

7.4.1.9.1.1.1.1 KATIE O'KEEFE was born on 23 April 1986.

7.4.1.9.1.2 DEBRA CYNTHIA BURRELL was born on 31 August 1951.

7.4.1.9.1.3 CHERYL EARLY BURRELL was born on 13 August 1953, Dauphin County, PA. She married **CHARLES ALBRIGHT** on 26 April 1975.

7.4.1.9.1.3.1 RYAN CHARLES ALBRIGHT was born on 27 January 1979, Harrisburg, Dauphin County, PA.

7.4.1.9.1.3.2 BRANDON RICHARD ALBRIGHT was born on 23 March 1981, Harrisburg, Dauphin County, PA.

7.4.1.9.1.3.3 ASHLEY BURRELL ALBRIGHT was born on 14 June 1983, Harrisburg, Dauphin County, PA.

7.4.1.9.2 JOANNE WINIFRED BURRELL was born on 23 July 1929, Dauphin County, PA. She married **RUSSELL ROSE SCHAFFNER JR.**, son of **RUSSELL R. SCHAFFNER** and **ESTHER M. KLINEYOUNG**, in 1947, Dauphin County, PA. She died on 27 January 2003, at age 73.

7.4.1.9.2.1 COLLEEN SCHAFFNER was born circa 1948. She married **QUENT KERSTEN** in 1971.

7.4.1.9.2.1.1 TODD KERSTEN

7.4.1.9.2.2 BROCK SCHAFFNER was born circa 1950. He married JUDITH HINES.

    7.4.1.9.2.2.1 JILL SCHAFFNER

    7.4.1.9.2.2.2 JASON SCHAFFNER

7.4.1.9.2.3 LESLIE SCHAFFNER was born circa 1952. She married MARVIN NEWMAN in 1970. She married MICHAEL ADAMS circa 1976.

    7.4.1.9.2.3.1 JULIE NEWMAN

    7.4.1.9.2.3.2 JENNIFER NEWMAN

    7.4.1.9.2.3.3 LUKE ADAMS

    7.4.1.9.2.3.4 JESSE ADAMS

    7.4.1.9.2.3.5 AARON ADAMS

7.4.1.9.2.4 ROCK CHRISTIAN SCHAFFNER was born on 4 July 1954, Dauphin County, PA. He died on 18 November 1971, Dauphin County, PA, at age 17.

7.4.1.9.2.5 MARK LEE SCHAFFNER was born circa 1965.

7.4.1.10 RALPH CLAIR BURRELL SR. was born on 14 September 1897, Washington Township, Berrysburg, Dauphin County, PA. He married PRUDENCE SARAH ELLEN HARNER, daughter of FREDERICK CHARLES HARNER and HATTIE PERSTELLA SHADLE, on 1 June 1918, Dauphin Co., PA. He died on 4 August 1989, Dauphin County, PA, at age 91. He was buried at Maple Grove Cemetery, Elizabethville, Dauphin County, PA.

7.4.1.10.1 CARL R. BURRELL was born on 8 April 1919, Harrisburg, Dauphin County, PA. He married ADDA VERDILLA LATSHA on 14 January 1945, St. John's (Hill) Lutheran Church, near Berrysburg, Dauphin Co., PA. He married BEVERLY J. CAREY on 17 April 1954, PA. He married SHIRLEY MARIE BOHNER, daughter of ALBERT R. BOHNER and GEORGIANNA CAMPBELL, circa 1956, PA. He died on 17 August 2006, Mechanicsburg, Cumberland County, PA, at age 87. He was buried at Blue Ridge Memorial Gardens, Harrisburg, Dauphin County, PA.

7.4.1.10.1.1 BENJAMIN CARL BURRELL was born on 5 October 1957, Harrisburg, Dauphin County, PA. He died on 15 January 2013, Harrisburg, Dauphin County, PA, at age 55. He was buried on 21 June 2013, at Blue Ridge Memorial Gardens, Harrisburg, Dauphin County, PA.

7.4.1.10.2 GILBERT EUGENE BURRELL was born on 7 September 1921, Dauphin County, PA. He married MARGARET ELLEN HOOVER on 3 January 1942, St. John's Lutheran Church, Lykens, Dauphin Co., PA. He died on 5 March 1991, Dauphin Co., PA, at age 69. He was buried after 5 March 1991, at Riverview Memorial Gardens, Halifax, Dauphin Co., PA.

7.4.1.10.2.1 LINDA DARLENE BURRELL was born on 16 March 1947, Dauphin Co., PA. She married JOHN KENT HASSINGER JR. PA. She married DAVID R. HERB circa 1965. She married JOHN WILLIAM LENKER JR. on 2 October 1999, Zion (Stone Valley) Church, Hickory Corners, Northumberland Co., PA.

7.4.1.10.2.1.1 KAREN A. HERB was born circa 1967, Dauphin Co., PA. She married TAB A. BLASSER circa 1997, PA.

7.4.1.10.2.1.1.1 CHASE BENJAMIN BLASSER was born on 13 July 1999, Polyclinic Hospital, Harrisburg, Dauphin Co., PA.

7.4.1.10.2.2 GAIL EILEEN BURRELL was born on 14 July 1951, Dauphin Co., PA. She was baptized on 20 April 1952, Evangelical United Brethren Church, Loyalton, Dauphin Co., PA. She married GARY LEE BIXLER circa 1968, PA.

7.4.1.10.2.2.1 BRIAN LEE BIXLER was born on 28 October 1970, Dauphin Co., PA. He was baptized on 28 February 1971, Immanuel United Methodist Church, Loyalton, Dauphin Co., PA. He married MARY DIETRICH circa 1995, PA.

7.4.1.10.2.2.1.1 EMILEE ALYSSA BIXLER was born on 6 November 1997, Harrisburg Hospital, Harrisburg, Dauphin Co., PA. She was baptized on 14 February 1998, Calvary United Methodist Church, Wiconisco, Dauphin Co., PA.

7.4.1.10.2.2.1.2 LAUREN ELIZABETH BIXLER was born on 17 April 2001, Harrisburg Hospital, Harrisburg, Dauphin Co., PA.

7.4.1.10.2.2.2 BRAD LEE BIXLER was born on 8 June 1976, Dauphin Co., PA. He was baptized on 20 June 1976, Immanuel United Methodist Church, Loyalton, Dauphin Co.,

PA. He married **ANGELIA LYNN SNYDER** on 9 September 2000, Glenn Park, Lykens, Dauphin Co., PA.

7.4.1.10.2.3 CAROLANN BURRELL was born on 17 October 1953, Dauphin Co., PA. She married **LYNN H. BOPP** on 6 December 1980.

7.4.1.10.2.3.1 ALEXANDRIA LYNN BOPP was born on 18 May 1981, PA.

7.4.1.10.3 IRENE ELIZABETH BURRELL was born on 31 October 1923, Dauphin County, PA. She married **PAUL D. KING** circa 1945. She married **BURNETT LAFEAM KOCHER** before 1958, PA.

7.4.1.10.4 RALPH C. BURRELL JR. was born on 9 May 1928, Dauphin Co., PA. He married **LORETTA MAE LAHR** circa October 1949, PA. He died on 12 January 1976, Dauphin Co., PA, at age 47. He was buried at Maple Grove Cemetery, Elizabethville, Dauphin Co., PA.

7.4.1.10.4.1 DENNIS CLAIR BURRELL was born on 12 December 1950, Dauphin Co., PA. He was baptized on 25 March 1951, Evangelical United Brethren Church, Loyalton, Dauphin Co., PA. He married **KAREN (--?--)** circa 1972.

7.4.1.10.4.1.1 GABRIEL BURRELL was born circa 1974.

7.4.1.10.4.1.2 NATHANIEL BURRELL was born circa 1976.

7.4.1.10.4.1.3 (--?--) BURRELL was born circa 1978.

7.4.1.10.4.1.4 (--?--) BURRELL was born circa 1980.

7.4.1.10.4.2 KAREN ELIZABETH BURRELL was born on 17 December 1952, Dauphin Co., PA. She was baptized on 5 April 1953, Zion Evangelical (Oakdale) Church, Dauphin Co., PA.

7.4.1.10.4.3 SANDRA BURRELL was born on 4 October 1954, Dauphin Co., PA. She married **DALE E. SCHWARTZ** circa 1974, PA.

7.4.1.10.4.3.1 TOBI SCHWARTZ was born in 1976, Dauphin Co., PA.

7.4.1.10.4.4 PAUL C. BURRELL was born on 6 July 1961, Dauphin Co., PA. He married **ALINDA A. KULP** circa 1980, PA.

7.4.1.10.4.4.1 JEREMY P. BURRELL was born on 24 June 1981, Dauphin Co., PA.

7.4.1.11 LEON E. BURRELL was born on 29 March 1902. He married **MARY REIGLE**. He died on 10 April 2001, Elizabethtown, Lancaster County, PA, at age 99. He was buried at Hummelstown Cemetery, Hummelstown, Dauphin County, PA.

7.4.1.12 CLARENCE J. BURRELL was born on 1 August 1904. He married **EDNA A. HUGGINS**. He died in April 1984, at age 79. He was buried at Shoop's Garden of Rest, Harrisburg, Dauphin County, PA.

7.4.1.12.1 RICHARD EUGENE BURRELL was born on 3 August 1926, Harrisburg, Dauphin County. He died on 27 June 1999, at age 72.

7.4.1.12.2 LARRY G. BURRELL was born on 20 June 1936. He died on 12 October 2010, at age 74.

7.4.2 KIRBY JONATHAN KLINGER was born on 16 February 1865, Washington Township, Dauphin County, PA. He married **MAGGIE MCCLATA SCHADEL** circa 1885. He died on 23 January 1926, Washington Township, Dauphin County, PA, at age 60. Some sources record that he died on 24 January 1926. He was buried at Oakdale Church Cemetery, Washington Township, Dauphin County, PA.

7.4.2.1 HOMER AUBURN KLINGER was born on 21 February 1886, Wiconisco, Dauphin County, PA. He was baptized on 26 June 1887, Loyalton, Dauphin County, PA. He married **GERTRUDE ELMA DUBENDORF** on 12 January 1915. He married **LAURA SPECHT** on 27 October 1934. He died on 7 February 1946, Millersburg, Dauphin County, PA, at age 59.

7.4.2.2 DOSIE DARLENE KLINGER is also referred to as **JOSIE** in some sources. She was born on 31 January 1888, Wiconisco, Dauphin County, PA. She was baptized on 1 January 1896, Berrysburg, Dauphin County, PA. She married **FRANKLIN H. HENNINGER**, son of **HENRY W. HENNINGER** and **MARY J. (--?--)**, on 29 October 1910, Berrysburg, Dauphin County, PA. She died on 30 August 1952, Berrysburg, Dauphin County, PA, at age 64.

7.4.2.2.1 ALMA PAULINE HENNINGER was born on 27 January 1911, Oakdale, Dauphin County, PA. She was baptized on 16 April 1912, Elizabethville, Dauphin County, PA. She married **(--?--) SCHAFFER**. She died on 10 February 1997, at age 86.

7.4.2.2.2 HILDA D. HENNINGER was born on 13 August 1912. She married **(--?--) STRAUB**. She died on 13 March 2002, at age 89.

7.4.2.2.3 FERLE GLADYS HENNINGER also went by the name of **GLADYS**. She was born on 8 November 1916, Elizabethville, Dauphin County, PA. She was baptized on 15 March 1917, Elizabethville, Dauphin County, PA. She married **ALLEN (--?--) SHETTERLY**. She died on 13 October 2012, the Manor at Susquehanna Village, Millersburg, Dauphin County, PA, at age 95. According to a newspaper obituary, Gladys lived in Berrysburg and was a retired seamstress who worked at various sewing factories in the area. She was buried on 17 October 2012, at Sweitzers Memorial Cemetery, Berrysburg, Dauphin County, PA.

7.4.2.2.3.1 FRED SHETTERLY married **REBECCA (--?--)**.

7.4.2.2.3.1.1 FREDERICK JASON SHETTERLY

7.4.2.2.3.1.2 SHAWNA SHETTERLY married **(--?--) LUCAS**.

7.4.2.2.3.1.2.1 BRYCE LUCAS

7.4.2.2.3.1.3 NICOLE SHETTERLY

7.4.2.2.3.2 SHARON SHETTERLY married **MARK SPRAUER**.

7.4.2.2.3.2.1 SHARI SPRAUER married **(--?--) KOLVA**.

7.4.2.2.4 RUTH NAOMI HENNINGER was born on 16 February 1919, Oakdale, Mifflin Township, Dauphin County, PA. Some sources record that she was born on 14 February 1919, Mifflin Township, Dauphin County, PA. She married **HERMAN E. SHAFFER**. She died on 18 May 2011, the Manor at Susquehanna Village, Millersburg, Dauphin County, PA, at age 92. According to a newspaper obituary, Ruth lived in Elizabethville and had been employed by Ames Shower Curtain, Millersburg, and Kochers IGA, Elizabethville. She was buried on 25 May 2011, at Emmanuel Wesleyan Church, Gratz, Dauphin County, PA.

7.4.2.2.4.1 PHILIP E. SHAFFER married **JANE LAUDENBACH**. Philip lives in Gratz, PA.

7.4.2.2.4.1.1 TODD SHAFFER married **DARLENE FAUST**. Todd lives in Lykens, PA.

7.4.2.2.4.1.1.1 BROOKE SHAFFER

7.4.2.2.4.1.1.2 BRITTNEY SHAFFER

7.4.2.2.4.1.1.3 DAKOTA SHAFFER

7.4.2.3 HERMIE PHRODA KLINGER was born on 16 February 1890. She was baptized on 1 January 1896, Berrysburg, Dauphin County, PA. She married **CHARLES N. NEIMAN** on 25 May 1907. She died on 1 August 1958, Berrysburg, Dauphin County, PA, at age 68.

7.4.2.3.1 DELTON WILBUR NEIMAN was born on 7 November 1907, Mifflin Township, Dauphin County, PA. He was baptized on 30 October 1908, Mifflin Township, Dauphin County, PA. He died in November 1966. Prior to his death, Delton was living in the vicinity of, Wiconisco, Dauphin County, PA.

7.4.2.3.2 MARY HILDA NEIMAN was born on 13 June 1909, Mifflin Township, Dauphin County, PA. She was baptized on 17 December 1910, Elizabethville, Dauphin County, PA.

7.4.2.3.3 MELVIN ARLINGTON NEIMAN was born on 15 September 1911, Oakdale, Dauphin County, PA. He was baptized on 11 February 1912, Oakdale, Dauphin County, PA. He married **MARY L. MILLER** on 27 October 1934, Washington Township, Dauphin County, PA. Prior to his death, Melvin was living in the vicinity of Millersburg, Dauphin County, PA. He died on 16 December 1993, at age 82.

7.4.2.3.3.1 EVELYN MAE NEIMAN was born on 20 December 1934, Elizabethville RD, Dauphin County, PA. She was baptized on 3 January 1938, Berrysburg, Dauphin County, PA.

7.4.2.4 RONNIE DRUELLA KLINGER is also referred to as **RONIE** in some sources. She was born on 3 December 1892, Berrysburg, Dauphin County, PA. She was baptized on 1 January 1896, Berrysburg, Dauphin County, PA. She married **HARVEY JEREMIAH MATTER**, son of **PETER ADAM MATTER** and **REBECCA BATDORF**, on 11 October 1913, Elizabethville, Dauphin County, PA. She died on 1 December 1979, Harrisburg Hospital, Harrisburg, Dauphin County, PA, at age 86. She was buried at Oak Hill Cemetery, Millersburg, Dauphin County, PA.

7.4.2.4.1 MARK KLINGER MATTER was born on 8 April 1914. He married **ARLENE AMANDA HARTMAN** on 26 June 1938, Allentown, Lehigh County, PA. He died on 22 April 1985, at age 71. He was buried at Reed City, Osceola County, MI.

7.4.2.4.1.1 KIRBY DOUGLAS MATTER was born on 20 July 1943. He married **NGUYEN THI BACH LOAN** on 18 April 1967, Saigon, Vietnam.

7.4.2.4.1.1.1 KALLY N. MATTER was born on 4 December 1970. She married **FRANK S. RUSSELL** on 20 March 1997, Dana Point, Monterey County, CA.

7.4.2.4.1.2 MARILYN ARLENE MATTER was born on 4 September 1948. She married **RONALD HERBERT MULLER** on 30 May 1968, Howell, Livingston County, MI.

7.4.2.4.1.3 MARK KEVIN MATTER was born on 15 October 1952. He married **MARCIA ANN MASON** on 22 May 1976, Birmingham, Oakland County, MI.

7.4.2.4.1.3.1 LAUREN E. MATTER was born on 24 October 1983.

7.4.2.4.1.3.2 KRISTEN A. MATTER was born on 9 January 1992.

7.4.2.4.2 HARVEY LEROY MATTER also went by the name of **HICKORY**. He was born on 15 May 1915. He married **GLADYS HAMMAKER** on 3 November 1946, Millersville, Lancaster County, PA. He died on 25 September 1983, at age 68. He was buried at Oak Hill Cemetery, Millersburg, Dauphin County, PA.

7.4.2.4.2.1 LORETTA LOUISE MATTER was born on 6 June 1947. She married **RAY LEROY KOHR**, son of **RAY N. KOHR** and **EVA J. KREINER**, on 26 February 1966, Millersburg, Dauphin County, PA.

7.4.2.4.2.1.1 TRISHA L. KOHR married **NOEL W. FALK**.

7.4.2.4.2.1.2 SHELBY B. KOHR married **JEFF A. SHADE**.

7.4.2.4.2.1.3 ERIN R. KOHR married **JOEL M. HILTON**.

7.4.2.4.2.2 DAVID LEROY MATTER was born on 2 September 1950. He married **CYNTHIA ANN CHUBB** on 23 July 1983, Millersburg, Dauphin County, PA.

7.4.2.4.2.2.1 DANIEL ALEXANDER MATTER was born on 13 September 1985.

7.4.2.4.2.2.2 GRANT DREW MATTER was born on 26 June 1992.

7.4.2.4.3 MARLIN EUGENE MATTER also went by the name of **RED**. He was born on 21 June 1920. He married **MILDRED P. HOFFMAN** on 15 November 1940, MD. He died on 1 December 1983, at age 63. He was buried at Riverview Memorial Gardens, Halifax, Dauphin County, PA.

7.4.2.4.3.1 RICHARD EUGENE MATTER was born on 19 July 1940. He married **LOUISE GROVER** on 5 February 1965, Halifax, Dauphin County, PA. He died on 28 November 1980, at age 40. He was buried at El Camino Memorial Park, San Diego, San Diego County, CA.

7.4.2.4.3.1.1 NANCY MATTER

7.4.2.4.3.2 EARL LEROY MATTER was born on 20 August 1942. He married **CAROL CLAYBAUGH** on 6 February 1965, Watts Township, Perry County, PA.

7.4.2.4.3.2.1 FREDERICK MATTER was born on 15 June 1967.

7.4.2.4.3.2.2 TERESA MATTER was born on 19 June 1969. She married **DEAN MCNAUGHTON**.

7.4.2.4.3.3 KIM LAMARR MATTER was born on 20 May 1955. He married **ROSE NONECKERE** on 15 March 1975, Killinger, Dauphin County, PA. He married **DEBORAH MILLER** on 14 March 1998, Halifax, Dauphin County, PA.

7.4.2.4.3.4 JAMES LEE MATTER was born on 30 December 1956. He married **HELEN ANN DEIHL** on 12 July 1997, Duncannon, Perry County, PA.

7.4.2.4.3.5 JANET LOUISE MATTER was born on 30 December 1956. She married **DENNIS RING** on 29 September 1990, Harrisburg, Dauphin County, PA.

7.4.2.4.4 RUTH N. MATTER was born on 12 February 1926. She married **CHARLES BURTON COOK**.

7.4.2.4.5 MARY ELIZABETH MATTER was born on 9 February 1928. She married **MARK RAY BLASSER**, son of **RAY M. BLASSER** and **IVY E. KRABER**, on 6 October 1957, Grace EUB Church, Millersburg, Dauphin County, PA. She died on 20 December 1999, at age 71. She was buried at Oak Hill Cemetery, Millersburg, Dauphin County, PA.

7.4.2.4.5.1 ANN BLASSER married **PETER AUSKELIS**. She is also referred to as **ANYA** in some sources. Ann lives in Portland, OR.

7.4.2.4.5.2 ANDREW BLASSER married **DENISE (--?--)**. Andrew lives in Harrisburg, PA.

7.4.2.4.5.3 BETH BLASSER married **DANIEL DIETRICK**. Beth lives in Baltimore, MD.

7.4.2.4.5.3.1 EHREN DIETRICK

7.4.2.4.5.3.2 D**UNCAN** D**IETRICK**

7.4.2.4.5.3.3 C**HARLES** D**IETRICK**

7.4.2.4.6 W**INIFRED** M. M**ATTER** was born on 12 December 1934. She married J**AMES** W. G**OULD** on 2 October 1954, Millersburg, Dauphin County, PA.

7.4.2.5 K**ATIE** E**MMELINE** K**LINGER** was born on 14 May 1895, Berrysburg, Dauphin County, PA. She was baptized on 1 January 1896, Oakdale Evangelical Congregational Church, Dauphin Co., PA. She married J**OSEPH** E**LMER** K**OPPENHAVER**, son of T**HEOPHILUS** M K**OPPENHAVER** and S**USAN** A**DALINE** G**OOD,** on 6 April 1912, St. John's (Hill) Lutheran Church, Berrysburg, Dauphin County, PA. She died on 1 September 1967, Polyclinic Hospital, Harrisburg, Craven County, PA, at age 72. She was buried at Oak Hill Cemetery, Millersburg, Dauphin County, PA.

7.4.2.5.1 H**AROLD** F**LOYD** K**OPPENHAVER** was born on 3 September 1912, Washington Township, Dauphin Co., PA. He was baptized on 18 April 1913, St. John's (Hill) Lutheran Church, near Berrysburg, Dauphin Co., PA. He married C**HRISTINE** E**THEL** H**ARPER**, daughter of E**DWARD** A**UGUSTS** H**ARPER** and C**ORA** L**OUISE** N**ACE,** circa 1946. He died on 25 December 1971, Millersburg, Dauphin Co., PA, at age 59. He was buried at Riverview Memorial Gardens, Halifax, Dauphin Co., PA.

7.4.2.5.1.1 A**NNA** M**AY** K**OPPENHAVER** was born circa 1948, Dauphin Co., PA. She married J**EROME** K**OPEC** circa 1970.

7.4.2.5.1.1.1 K**AREN** K**OPEC** was born circa 1972.

7.4.2.5.1.1.2 K**ATHY** K**OPEC** was born circa 1974.

7.4.2.5.1.1.3 K**EVIN** K**OPEC** was born circa 1976.

7.4.2.5.1.1.4 K**ARLA** K**OPEC** was born circa 1978.

7.4.2.5.1.1.5 K**RISTINE** K**OPEC** was born circa 1980.

7.4.2.5.1.1.6 K**IMBERLY** K**OPEC** was born circa 1982.

7.4.2.5.1.2 F**LOYD** H**AROLD** K**OPPENHAVER** was born on 2 March 1950, Dauphin Co., PA. He married J**OYCE** W**RIGHT** on 28 June 1968.

7.4.2.5.1.2.1 B**ETH** A**NN** K**OPPENHAVER** was born on 16 September 1970, Dauphin Co., PA.

7.4.2.5.1.2.1.1 A**NDREW** M**ICHAEL** W**ELKER** was born on 13 May 1987, Dauphin Co., PA.

7.4.2.5.1.2.1.2 M**IKKI** R**OCHELLE** D**AVIS** was born on 22 December 1989, Dauphin Co., PA.

7.4.2.5.2 H**OMER** H. K**OPPENHAVER** was born on 6 May 1916, Dauphin County, NC. He was baptized on 14 May 1916, Oakdale Evangelical Congregational Circuit, Dauphin Co., PA. He married M**ARGUERITE** E. B**ONAWITZ** circa 1936, PA. He married J**EAN** B**ECKER**. He died on 20 April 1957, Polyclinic Hospital, Harrisburg, Dauphin Co., PA, at age 40. He was buried on 24 April 1957, at Schuylkill Haven, Schuylkill County, PA.

7.4.2.5.2.1 D**ONALD** K**OPPENHAVER** was born circa 1938, PA.

7.4.2.5.3 M**IRIAM** A. K**OPPENHAVER** was born on 19 July 1920, Lenkerville, Dauphin County, PA. She married J**OSEPH** R**ALPH** H**ARPER**, son of C**ORA** L**OUISE** N**ACE**, on 29 January 1939, Dauphin Co., PA. She died on 17 November 2007, Harrisburg Hospital, Harrisburg, Dauphin County, PA, at age 87. According to a newspaper obituary, Miriam lived in Millersburg, Dauphin County, PA, and retired from the Puritan Fashions, Millersburg. She was buried on 20 November 2007, at Riverview Memorial Gardens, Halifax, Dauphin County, PA.

7.4.2.5.3.1 B**RUCE** E**DWARD** H**ARPER** was born on 26 September 1939, Dauphin Co., PA. He married C**AROL** A**NN** E**TZWEILER** on 1 December 1962, Wesleyan Church, Millersburg, Dauphin Co., PA.

7.4.2.5.3.1.1 S**COTT** M. H**ARPER** was born on 30 January 1964, Dauphin Co., PA. He married A**MY** L**OGAN** on 16 December 1989.

7.4.2.5.3.1.2 S**ONDRA** L. H**ARPER** was born on 18 September 1965, Dauphin Co., PA.

7.4.2.5.3.1.3 S**HERRY** A. H**ARPER** was born on 1 June 1968, Dauphin Co., PA. She married B**RIAN** M**ATTIS** on 29 November 1986, Dauphin Co., PA.

7.4.2.5.3.1.3.1 H**EATHER** M**ATTIS** was born on 20 January 1987, Dauphin Co., PA.

7.4.2.5.3.1.3.2 KARA MATTIS was born circa 1991, Dauphin Co., PA.

7.4.2.5.3.1.3.3 BAILEY ELISABETH MATTIS was born on 22 April 1997, Dauphin Co., PA.

7.4.2.5.3.1.3.4 LACEY MATTIS was born on 15 August 1998, Vandenberg AFB, CA.

7.4.2.5.3.2 JAMES LAMAR HARPER was born on 13 November 1941, Dauphin County, PA. He married GERALDINE MARIE HINKLE on 25 November 1961.

7.4.2.5.3.2.1 WALTER J. HARPER was born on 15 December 1962.

7.4.2.5.3.2.2 AUDREY M. HARPER was born in February 1964.

7.4.2.5.3.3 HAROLD J. HARPER was born on 17 December 1947, Dauphin Co., PA.

7.4.2.5.4 MYRTLE EMELINE KOPPENHAVER was born on 19 September 1927, Upper Paxton Township, Millersburg, Dauphin Co., PA. She was born circa October 1927. She married ROBERT C. GEORGE circa 1944.

7.4.2.5.4.1 MARCI LOU GEORGE was born on 6 March 1946. She married KENNETH BOYER circa 1967.

7.4.2.5.4.1.1 ASHLEY BOYER was born on 22 June 1969.

7.4.2.5.5 EARL LAMAR KOPPENHAVER was born on 6 December 1929, Upper Paxton Township, Dauphin Co., PA. He died on 9 July 1934, Millersburg, Dauphin County, PA, at age 4. He was buried on 12 July 1934, at Oak Hill Cemetery, Millersburg, Dauphin County, PA.

7.4.2.6 MYRTLE LARADA KLINGER was born on 18 April 1898. She died on 28 September 1900, at age 2. She was buried at Oakdale Church Cemetery, Washington Township, Dauphin County, PA.

7.4.2.7 MORROW GODBEY KLINGER was born on 1 June 1900. He married NORMA AGNES NELSON, daughter of WILLIAM J. NELSON and MARGARET M. BOWMAN, circa 1922. He married SUSAN ALVERTA WELKER after 1933. Some sources list Jackie Klinger as a child of Morrow Klinger and his second wife Susan Welker born c. 1936, but the 1940 Census listing for their household does not include such a child. He died on 15 March 1963, Middletown Township, Delaware County, PA, at age 62. He was buried on 19 March 1963, at Edgewood Memorial Park, Glen Mills, Delaware County, PA.

7.4.2.7.1 STILLBORN SON KLINGER was born on 21 November 1926, Millersburg, Dauphin County, PA. He died on 21 November 1926, Millersburg, Dauphin County, PA.

7.4.2.7.2 HAROLD LAMAR KLINGER was born on 13 March 1931, Millersburg, Dauphin County, PA. He married JANE C. STILES on 2 May 1952, Philadelphia, PA.

7.4.2.7.2.1 CYNTHIA KLINGER was born on 23 August 1954, Philadelphia, PA. She married THOMAS SAMUEL WOLFE, son of THOMAS FRANKLIN WOLFE and EMMA RUTH WITMER, on 26 October 1974, Philadelphia, PA.

7.4.2.7.2.1.1 AMY JEAN WOLFE was born on 17 October 1979, Philadelphia, PA.

7.4.2.7.2.1.2 NATHAN THOMAS WOLFE was born on 9 July 1981, Philadelphia, PA.

7.4.2.7.2.1.3 LAURIE ELLEN WOLFE was born on 4 July 1983, Philadelphia, PA.

7.4.2.7.2.1.4 EMILY CHRISTINE WOLFE was born on 13 May 1986, Philadelphia, PA.

7.4.2.7.2.2 GARY LAMAR KLINGER was born on 28 November 1956, Philadelphia, PA. He married JENNIFER VESTAL in April 1978, Philadelphia, PA. He married CAROL (--?--) on 10 November 1996.

7.4.2.7.2.2.1 JAMIE LEIGH KLINGER was born on 12 January 1979, Philadelphia, PA.

7.4.2.7.2.2.2 JASON LAMAR KLINGER was born on 7 January 1981, Philadelphia, PA.

7.4.2.7.2.3 SANDRA JEAN KLINGER was born on 14 September 1958, Philadelphia, PA. She married MIKE BONNEY.

7.4.2.7.2.4 PAMELA LEE KLINGER was born on 14 September 1958, Media, PA. She died on 18 November 2015, Lee County, FL, at age 57.

7.4.2.8 BESSIE HILDA KLINGER was born on 10 June 1902, Mifflin Township, Dauphin County, PA. She married JAY CHRISTIAN on 27 November 1924, Hegins, Schuylkill County, PA. She died on 26 May 1998, Millersburg, Dauphin County, PA, at age 95.

7.4.2.9 MARY ALMEDA KLINGER was born on 24 June 1904, Berrysburg, Dauphin County, PA. She married CLARION A. HECKERT, son of JOHN W. HECKERT and AMELIA (--?--), on 20 June 1931,

Millersburg, Dauphin County, PA. She died on 18 June 1971, Millersburg, Dauphin County, PA, at age 66.

7.4.2.10 FERLE MACHALA KLINGER was born on 8 November 1905, Berrysburg, Dauphin County, PA. She married **MARION EDWARD LENKER**, son of **MORRIS E. LENKER** and **DORA L. (--?--)**, on 16 August 1928. She died on 5 May 1988, Millersburg, Dauphin County, PA, at age 82.

7.4.3 PRESTON A. KLINGER was born in 1867. He married **ANNIE M. HOFFMAN.** He died in 1895. He was buried at Maple Grove Cemetery, Elizabethville, Dauphin County, PA.

7.4.3.1 LAURA AGNES KLINGER was born on 2 April 1890, Loyalton, Dauphin County, PA. She was baptized on 23 June 1895, Loyalton, Dauphin County, PA.

7.4.3.2 EDNA IRENE KLINGER was born on 24 February 1892, Loyalton, Dauphin County, PA. She was baptized on 23 June 1895, Loyalton, Dauphin County, PA. She married **HARVEY DANIEL HELT**, son of **DAVID DANIEL HELT** and **CATHERINE A. SNYDER.** She died on 15 August 1985, at age 93. She was buried at Maple Grove Cemetery, Elizabethville, Dauphin County, PA.

7.4.3.2.1 DANIEL P. HELT was born on 4 November 1919, Lykens, Dauphin County, PA. He died on 21 January 1920, Dauphin County, PA. He was buried at Maple Grove Cemetery, Elizabethville, Dauphin County, PA.

7.4.3.3 PRESTON ELIAS KLINGER was born on 28 January 1895, Loyalton, Dauphin County, PA. He was baptized on 23 June 1895, Loyalton, Dauphin County, PA. He married **CORA SHIPPY**, daughter of **PERRY SHIPPY** and **CLARA L. RUNKLE**, before 5 June 1917. On June 5, 1927, according to a World War I draft registration card, Preston was married and living in Green County, WI, where he was a self-employed tanner. At the time of his draft registration for World War II, in 1942, Preston was living at RR 1, Lena, West Point Township, Stephenson County, IL. He was listed as self-employed, 5' 3 1/2" tall, weight 140 lbs, with hazel eyes and brown hair. He died on 27 January 1952, at age 56. He was buried at Silent Hill Cemetery, McConnell, Stephenson County, IL.

7.4.3.3.1 LAURA V. KLINGER was born on 28 June 1917, Monroe, Green County, WI. She married **WILLIAM A. RICE** on 28 June 1938, Lanark, Carroll County, IL. She died on 26 October 2016, Rockford, Winnebago County, IL, at age 99. She was buried at Chapel Hill Memorial Gardens, Freeport, Stephenson County, IL.

7.4.3.3.1.1 WILLIAM ARTHUR RICE was born circa 1937. He married **KAY (--?--)**.

7.4.3.3.1.1.1 JUCINDA RICE

7.4.3.3.1.1.2 EDWIN RICE married **SUE (--?--)**.

7.4.3.3.1.1.3 KIRK RICE

7.4.3.3.1.1.4 MICHELLE RICE

7.4.3.3.1.1.5 DRINDA RICE

7.4.3.3.1.2 LINDA RICE married **JOE GREENHAW.**

7.4.3.3.2 GOLDIE INEZ KLINGER was born on 26 September 1918, Lena, IL. She married **EDWARD CRABB** before 1945. She was baptized on 2 January 1945, Loyalton Revival Meeting, Loyalton, PA. She married **RAY MAURER** circa 1948. She died on 4 May 2007, Elizabethville, Dauphin County, PA, at age 88. According to a newspaper obituary, Goldie, who was a long-time self-employed lifetime farmer and as well as working at the Nedrich Shirt factory, lived in Elizabethville, PA. She enjoyed working outdoor in the fields, her garden and with her animals. She was buried at Riverview Memorial Gardens, Halifax, Dauphin County, PA.

7.4.3.3.2.1 BENJAMIN CRABB married **MOLLY (--?--)**.

7.4.3.3.2.2 DANIEL CRABB married **SANDY (--?--)**.

7.4.3.3.3 ROY RAYMOND KLINGER was born on 18 October 1919, in Illinois. He died on 4 August 1925, Stephenson County, IL, at age 5. He was buried at Silent Hill Cemetery, McConnell, Stephenson County, IL.

7.4.3.3.4 DOROTHY MAE KLINGER was born on 9 October 1922, Lena RD, Stephenson County, IL. She married **(--?--) SMECK**. She died on 1 January 2015, Elizabethville, Dauphin County, PA, at age 92.

7.4.3.3.4.1 JOE SMECK

7.4.3.3.4.1.1 JOSEPH SMECK married **JASMINE (--?--)**.

7.4.3.3.4.1.2 JULIE SMECK married **JOHN CARLUCCI.**

7.4.3.3.4.1.2.1 JOHN JOSEPH CARLUCCI

7.4.3.3.4.1.2.2 MICHAEL CARLUCCI

7.4.3.3.4.1.2.3 NICHOLAS CARLUCCI

7.4.3.3.4.1.2.4 MIA CARLUCCI

7.4.3.3.5 JONATHAN D. KLINGER was born on 18 September 1927, Lena, IL. He married HILDA MILLER circa 1948. He died on 18 August 2012, Harrisburg Hospital, Harrisburg, Dauphin County, PA, at age 84. According to a newspaper obituary, Jonathan, who lived in Loyalton, PA, was co-owner of the R & K Diner, Route 209, Elizabethville, PA. He was survived by three grandsons: Mike Klinger, Elizabethville, Kyle Klinger, New Jersey and Kory Klinger, Halifax; and a granddaughter: Ann Morgan, North Carolina.

7.4.3.3.5.1 ROY KLINGER. Roy lives in Loyalton, PA.

7.4.3.3.5.2 RANDY KLINGER. Randy lives in Elizabethville, PA.

7.4.4 EDWIN M. KLINGER was born in August 1869. He married KATIE L. HOFFMAN on 25 August 1890, Washington Township, PA. He died in 1948. He was buried at Maple Grove Cemetery, Elizabethville, Dauphin County, PA.

7.4.4.1 WALTER EDWIN KLINGER was born on 12 October 1897, Loyalton, Dauphin County, PA. He was baptized on 6 February 1898, Loyalton, Dauphin County, PA. He died on 27 January 1975, Lebanon, Lebanon County, PA, at age 77. He was buried at Maple Grove Cemetery, Elizabethville, Dauphin County, PA.

7.4.4.2 EFFIE EMELINE KLINGER was born on 6 June 1907, Loyalton, Dauphin County, PA. She was baptized on 12 November 1907, Loyalton, Dauphin County, PA. She married CLYDE JACOB MILLER, son of HARRISON MILLER and EMMA JANE HUNTZINGER, circa 1917. She married DANIEL ADAM ROW. She died on 27 June 2006, Loyalton, Dauphin County, PA, at age 98. She was buried at Maple Grove Cemetery, Elizabethville, Dauphin County, PA.

7.4.4.2.1 BETTY R. MILLER married RALPH EDWIN LEBO JR., son of RALPH EDWIN LEBO and LOTTIE IRENE LEITZEL, on 24 December 1948, Salem Lutheran Church, Elizabethville, Dauphin County, PA.

7.4.4.2.1.1 BARBARA ANN LEBO married GARY LEE SCHEIB, son of NEVIN O. SCHEIB and MYRTLE BORDNER, circa 1968. She married JOHN F. DIAKOW JR., son of JOHN F. DIAKOW and MARTHA PRISCILLA KLINGER, circa 1976. She and JOHN F. DIAKOW JR. were divorced. She married (--?--) NOVINGER.

7.4.4.2.1.1.1 RACHEL A. DIAKOW (see above)

7.4.4.2.1.1.2 NATHAN J. DIAKOW (see above)

7.4.5 AGNES E. KLINGER was born on 11 January 1873, Dauphin County, PA. She married SOLOMON SHERMAN GOOD, son of DANIEL A. GOOD and SARAH D. HESS, on 28 February 1892. According to the Comprehensive History of Gratz, Solomon Good served as an apprentice miller to Jonas Swab and later left the area and "lived in many places along the East Coast." She died on 10 December 1952, Loyalton, Dauphin County, PA, at age 79. She was buried at Maple Grove Cemetery, Elizabethville, Dauphin County, PA.

7.4.5.1 ROY DANIEL GOOD was born on 14 January 1895, Loyalton, Dauphin County, PA. He was baptized on 23 June 1895, Loyalton, Dauphin County, PA.

7.4.5.2 WARREN L. GOOD was born circa 1896.

7.5 JACOB KLINGER was born on 19 April 1838. Jacob served in the Civil War. He married MARIA MARIAH HERNER in 1872. He died on 23 August 1903, at age 65. He was buried at Maple Grove Cemetery, Elizabethville, Dauphin County, PA.

7.5.1 MAGGIE R. KLINGER is also referred to as MAGGIE WISE in some sources. She was born in July 1872. She married BENJAMIN FRANKLIN WEISS, son of DANIEL WISE and REBECCA (--?--), on 7 May 1893, Oakdale Church, Dauphin County, PA. She died on 12 November 1948, at age 76. She was buried at Maple Grove Cemetery, Elizabethville, Dauphin County, PA.

7.5.1.1 HATTIE NAOMI WISE was born on 27 August 1897. She married LESTER ALVIN ENDERS, son of IRA AUSTIN ENDERS and AMANDA ALICE WARFEL. She died on 10 September 1985, at age 88. She was buried at Fairview Cemetery, Enders, Dauphin County, PA.

7.5.1.1.1 ROBERT A. ENDERS

7.5.1.1.2 MYRA ENDERS married (--?--) HOFFMAN.

7.5.1.1.3 PAUL W. ENDERS

7.5.1.1.4 EILEEN NAOMI ENDERS was born on 2 November 1920, Dauphin County, PA. She married **GEORGE W. ADOLPH**, son of **JOSEPH S. ADOLPH** and **DAISY C. NYE**, on 15 September 1944. She died on 19 September 2016, Corydon, Harrison County, IN, at age 95. She was buried on 23 September 2016, at Bethlehem Cemetery, Crandall, Harrison County, IN.

7.5.1.1.5 EVELYN RENEE ENDERS was born on 6 September 1924, Dauphin County, PA. She married **JOHN EDWARD URICH**. She died on 3 February 1993, Halifax, Dauphin County, PA, at age 68. She was buried at Halifax United Methodist Church, Halifax, Dauphin County, PA.

> **7.5.1.1.5.1 JOHN E. URICH JR.**
>
> **7.5.1.1.5.2 DAVE J. URICH**
>
> **7.5.1.1.5.3 DANIEL B. URICH**
>
> **7.5.1.1.5.4 RENEE E. URICH** married (--?--) RUSSELL.
>
> **7.5.1.1.5.5 KANDACE L. URICH** married (--?--) SZILAGE.

7.5.1.2 DANIEL K. WEISS is also referred to as **DANIEL K. WISE** in some sources. He was born in August 1899. He married **MAYME M. (--?--)**.

7.5.1.2.1 SHIRLEY E. WISE was born circa 1923.

7.5.1.2.2 JUNE E. WISE was born circa 1925.

7.5.1.2.3 FAYE P. WISE was born circa 1926.

7.5.1.2.4 D. RICHARD WISE was born in 1929.

7.5.1.3 CHARLES MARLIN WISE is also referred to as **CHARLES M. WISE** in some sources. He was born on 10 November 1903, Elizabethville, Dauphin County, PA. He married **KATIE JULIAN LENKER**, daughter of **ISAAC NEWTON LENKER** and **BEULAH ELIZABETH PAUL**, circa 1925. He died on 1 March 1971, Dauphin County, PA, at age 67. He was buried at Maple Grove Cemetery, Elizabethville, Dauphin County, PA.

7.5.1.3.1 ROMAIN N. WISE was born on 16 May 1926, Dauphin County, PA. He married **ARLENE MAY KOPPENHAVER**, daughter of **IRA CALMON KOPPENHAVER** and **IDA ESTA SCHWALM**. He died on 13 March 1993, Harrisburg, Dauphin County, PA, at age 66. He was buried at Maple Grove Cemetery, Elizabethville, Dauphin County, PA.

7.5.1.3.2 NEAL FRANKLIN WISE was born on 22 April 1928, Dauphin County, PA. He married **MARIE A. WIEST**, daughter of **FRANKLIN WIEST** and **MOLLY SALTZER**. He died on 23 December 1963, Dauphin County, PA, at age 35. He was buried at Maple Grove Cemetery, Elizabethville, Dauphin County, PA.

7.5.1.3.2.1 CINDY MAE WISE was born on 16 August 1949, Dauphin County, PA. She died on 16 September 2005, Dauphin County, PA, at age 56. She was buried at Maple Grove Cemetery, Elizabethville, Dauphin County, PA.

7.5.1.4 MARK FRANKLIN WISE was born on 25 October 1905, Dauphin County, PA. He married **EVELYN FAY DOCKEY**, daughter of **DANIEL DOCKEY** and **CORA KEBOCH**. He died on 2 March 2002, Dauphin County, PA, at age 96. He was buried at Maple Grove Cemetery, Elizabethville, Dauphin County, PA.

7.5.1.5 TRUMAN WILLIAM WISE is also referred to as **WILLIAM T. WISE** in some sources. He was born on 18 November 1908, Dauphin County, PA. Some sources record that he was born circa March 1909. He married **MILDRED IRENE GOTTSHALL**, daughter of **WILLIAM R. GOTTSHALL** and **SALLIE REBECCA KEBAUGH**. He died on 7 January 1992, Millersburg, Dauphin County, PA, at age 83. He was buried at Maple Grove Cemetery, Elizabethville, Dauphin County, PA.

7.5.1.5.1 INFANT SON WISE was born on 8 April 1938. He died on 8 April 1938. He was buried at Maple Grove Cemetery, Elizabethville, Dauphin County, PA.

7.5.2 FREDERICK E. KLINGER was born in 1874. He married **SUSAN ADALINE HETRICK**, daughter of **PETER HETRICK** and **MARGARET JANE BAKER**, on 2 October 1897. He died on 4 December 1942. He was buried at Maple Grove Cemetery, Elizabethville, Dauphin County, PA.

7.5.2.1 MARY EDNA KLINGER was born circa 1898, Dauphin County, PA. She died on 11 March 1969, Harrisburg, Dauphin County, PA. She was buried at Maple Grove Cemetery, Elizabethville, Dauphin County, PA.

7.5.3 WILLIAM A. KLINGER was born on 26 April 1876, Dauphin County, PA. He died on 31 July 1959, Dauphin County, PA, at age 83. He was buried at Maple Grove Cemetery, Elizabethville, Dauphin County, PA.

7.5.4 SALLIE E. KLINGER is also referred to as **SARAH** in some sources. She was born in March 1878.

7.5.5 ADA CLEDA KLINGER is also referred to as **ADIE** in some sources. She was born on 30 June 1885, Dauphin County, PA. She died on 24 September 1961, Dauphin County, PA, at age 76. She was buried at Maple Grove Cemetery, Elizabethville, Dauphin County, PA.

7.5.6 CATHERINE EDITH KLINGER was born on 30 June 1886, Oakdale, Dauphin County, PA. She was baptized, Oakdale, Dauphin County, PA.

7.6 JONATHAN KLINGER was born on 26 March 1840. Some sources record that he was born in 1838. He married **HETTIE UHLER**, daughter of **MICHAEL UHLER** and **HETTIE WETZEL**, on 19 April 1869. He died in 1922. He was buried at Maple Grove Cemetery, Elizabethville, Dauphin County, PA.

7.7 SARAH KLINGER was born in 1842. She married **EDWARD ROMBERGER**, son of **DANIEL ROMBERGER** and **HANNAH BERGSTRESSER**, on 10 January 1866, Oakdale Church, Rev. Jacob Adams officiating, Oakdale, Dauphin County, PA. She died on 26 January 1897. She was buried at Maple Grove Cemetery, Elizabethville, Dauphin County, PA. Some sources record that she died on 10 January 1867.

7.7.1 ALICE ROMBERGER was born circa 1869.

7.7.2 ELMER W. ROMBERGER was born in 1872. Some sources record that he was born in September 1873. He married **FRANCES E. BOYER**, daughter of **JOHN W. BOYER** and **LIDIA (--?--)**, circa 1899. He died on 31 October 1942.

7.7.2.1 PAUL W. ROMBERGER was born circa 1900.

7.8 ELIAS KLINGER was born in November 1844. Some sources record that he was born on 26 November 1843. He married **MARY ELLEN UMHOLTZ**, daughter of **SAMUEL UMHOLTZ** and **ELIZABETH HARNER**, on 2 August 1868. He died on 11 January 1908, at age 63. He was buried at Simeon's Cemetery, Gratz, Dauphin County, PA.

7.8.1 LOTTA KLINGER was born circa 1868.

7.8.2 LAVIA M. KLINGER is also referred to as **LORA M. AND LAIRA** in some sources. She was born circa 1869.

7.9 MARIETTA KLINGER is also referred to as **MARETTA AND MARY E. KLINGER** in some sources. She was born in 1847. She married **THOMAS B. MOYER** circa 1865. She died on 5 July 1908. She was buried at Oakdale E.U.B. Church Cemetery, Dauphin County, PA.

7.9.1 MAGGIE MOYER was born circa 1872.

7.9.2 ANNIE R. MOYER was born circa 1875.

7.9.3 JOHN EDGAR MOYER was born on 1 February 1878, Loyalton, Dauphin County, PA. He married **MARY EDNA ROMBERGER**. He died on 17 December 1956, Dauphin County, PA, at age 78. He was buried at Simeon United Lutheran Church Cemetery, Gratz, Dauphin County, PA.

7.9.3.1 ALMA MARY EDNA MOYER was born on 18 September 1902. She married **LAWRENCE S. LEITZEL**, son of **GEORGE ADAM TROUTMAN LEITZEL** and **CATHERINE ALICE SNYDER**, circa 1919. She married **WALTER H. DAVIS** after 1945. She died on 4 January 1992, Elizabethville, Dauphin County, PA, at age 89. She was buried at Simeon United Lutheran Church Cemetery, Gratz, Dauphin County, PA.

7.9.3.1.1 MARK EDGAR LEITZEL was born on 28 June 1920. He married **ARLENE SNOKE** circa 1940. He died in 1992.

7.9.3.1.1.1 BARBARA ANN LEITZEL married **JAMES BOYCE CONLEY**. She was born on 3 January 1941.

7.9.3.1.1.1.1 MICHAEL JAMES CONLEY was born on 7 June 1968.

7.9.3.1.1.2 BETTY MARIE LEITZEL was born on 3 January 1941. She married **ROBERT W. LEHMAN** circa 1957.

7.9.3.1.1.2.1 KATHLEEN CHRISTINA LEHMAN was born on 8 March 1958.

7.9.3.1.1.2.2 ROBIN MARY LEHMAN was born on 25 April 1962.

7.9.3.1.1.2.3 DEBRA JEAN LEHMAN was born on 2 July 1966.

7.9.3.1.1.3 ROBERT MARK LEITZEL was born on 9 April 1947. He married **PEGGY YOUNG** circa 1966. He married **JANET KLYTZ** after 1970.

7.9.3.1.1.3.1 ROBERT LEE LEITZEL was born on 17 December 1966.

7.9.3.1.1.3.2 AMY SUE LEITZEL was born on 2 August 1969.

7.9.3.1.1.4 BRENDA KAY LEITZEL was born on 13 April 1953. She married **MARTIN REIS** circa 1969.

7.9.3.1.1.4.1 TAMMY SUE REIS was born on 20 April 1970.

7.9.3.1.1.4.2 JAMES MARTIN REIS was born on 3 April 1972.

7.9.3.1.1.5 TERRY ALLEN LEITZEL married **DEBBIE MOORE**. He was born on 7 January 1958.

7.9.3.1.1.5.1 MARK ALLEN LEITZEL

7.9.3.1.2 CLAIR ERNEST LEITZEL was born on 29 September 1921, Lykens RD, Dauphin County, PA. He married **EILEEN MAY KLINGER**, daughter of **LESTER LEROY KLINGER** and **KATIE ALMEDA KLINGER,** circa 1948. He died on 20 August 2007, The Manor at Susquehanna Village, Millersburg, Dauphin County, PA, at age 85. According to a newspaper obituary, Clair lived in Gratz, Dauphin County, PA, after serving in the U.S. Army in World War II. He was buried on 24 August 2007, at Gratz Union Cemetery, Gratz, Dauphin County, PA.

7.9.3.1.2.1 CAROL LEITZEL (see above)

7.9.3.1.2.1.1 KELLY YVONNE ROMBERGER (see above)

7.9.3.1.2.1.1.1 MYKENNA ADELL MUSOLINO (see above)

7.9.3.1.2.1.2 KRISTIE ANN ROMBERGER (see above)

7.9.3.1.2.2 GLENN ELDON LEITZEL (see above)

7.9.3.1.2.2.1 RAHN LEITZEL (see above)

7.9.3.1.2.2.2 AMANDA LEITZEL (see above)

7.9.3.1.2.3 ANNETTE ANGELA LEITZEL (see above)

7.9.3.1.3 WAYNE ALTON LEITZEL was born on 26 December 1923, Gratz, Dauphin County, PA. He married **MARIAN M. COLEMAN**, daughter of **ALFRED RAY COLEMAN** and **SADIE I. WEIDMAN**. He died on 5 February 1998, York, York County, PA, at age 74. He was buried at Saint Peters Reformed Church Cemetery, Orwin, Schuylkill County, PA.

7.9.3.1.3.1 WAYNE ROBERT LEITZEL was born on 6 March 1949. He married **CHERYL ANN PICOLA**.

7.9.3.1.3.1.1 WAYNE ROBERT LEITZEL JR was born on 26 December 1969.

7.9.3.1.3.1.2 JASON LEITZEL was born in April 1975.

7.9.3.1.4 JOHN ADAM LEITZEL was born on 18 December 1924, Dauphin County, PA. He married **RUBY FETTEROLF**. He died on 4 February 1995, Pottsville, Schuylkill County, PA, at age 70. He was buried at Simeon United Lutheran Church Cemetery, Gratz, Dauphin County, PA.

7.9.3.1.4.1 ROBERT LEITZEL was born on 14 January 1958.

7.9.3.1.4.1.1 NIKKI ANN LEITZEL was born in December 1992.

7.9.3.1.5 MARY J. LEITZEL was born on 18 July 1926. She married **NELSON T. STRAUB**, son of **GEIRMON STRAUB** and **ALICE GOODMAN**.

7.9.3.1.5.1 ERNEST E. STRAUB is also referred to as **ERNEST R. STRAUB** in some sources. He was born on 28 February 1947. He married **BRENDA WEAVER**. Ernest served in the US Army in Vietnam. He died on 9 March 1996, at age 49. He was buried on 13 March 1996, at Indiantown Gap National Cemetery, Annville, Lebanon County, PA.

7.9.3.1.5.1.1 ERIC EUGENE STRAUB married **CATHY SNYDER**. He was born on 11 May 1970.

7.9.3.1.5.2 BARBARA STRAUB was born on 7 March 1948. She married **GEORGE COLEMAN** circa 1968. She married **KENNETH L. NOVINGER** circa 1973. Barbara lives in Fallingwaters, WV.

7.9.3.1.6 ANNA MAE LEITZEL was born on 20 July 1928. She married **RAY C. PEIFER**.

7.9.3.1.6.1 TRUMAN PEIFER was born on 2 May 1947. He married **DOLORES HUMMEL**.

7.9.3.1.6.1.1 DWAYNE PEIFER was born after 1967.

7.9.3.1.6.2 ARTHUR PEIFER was born on 31 March 1950.

7.9.3.1.6.3 CATHERINE PEIFER was born on 4 April 1953. She married **MICHAEL HOOVER**.

7.9.3.1.6.3.1 MATTHEW WALTER HOOVER

7.9.3.1.7 LAWRENCE KENNETH LEITZEL was born on 12 April 1930. He married **HANNELOR FRIEDA HERMINE KITZING** circa 1955. He died on 15 May 1979, at age 49. He was buried at Simeon United Lutheran Church Cemetery, Gratz, Dauphin County, PA.

7.9.3.1.7.1 ALLEN LaRUE LEITZEL was born on 30 August 1956.

7.9.3.1.7.2 SHARON LOU LEITZEL was born on 19 March 1958. She married (--?--) **HOOVER**.

7.9.3.1.7.3 AARON LYNN LEITZEL was born on 31 March 1963.

7.9.3.1.7.4 SHAUNTELL LOUISE LEITZEL was born on 12 September 1966.

7.9.3.1.7.5 SHAPPELL LEONA LEITZEL was born on 18 March 1969.

7.9.3.1.8 CHARLES NALDY LEITZEL was born on 10 June 1932. He married **JANET BOLIN**.

7.9.3.1.8.1 SUSAN R. LEITZEL was born on 15 March 1955. She married **ROBERT** (--?--).

7.9.3.1.8.2 DENNIS C. LEITZEL was born on 19 June 1956.

7.9.3.1.8.3 JAMES E. LEITZEL was born on 7 August 1957.

7.9.3.1.8.4 CHRISTINE E. LEITZEL was born on 8 February 1959.

7.9.3.1.8.5 MICHAEL W. LEITZEL was born on 9 August 1965.

7.9.3.1.9 JAMES M. LEITZEL married **MARY ANN KERWIN**. He was born on 9 April 1943.

7.9.3.1.9.1 JENNIFER ANN LEITZEL was born on 10 October 1969.

7.9.3.1.9.2 SHANNON LEITZEL was born after 1970.

8 HANNA KLINGER was born on 21 October 1807, Lykens Township, Dauphin County, PA. She was baptized on 21 March 1808, Zion (Klinger's) Church, Erdman, Lykens Township, Dauphin County, PA. She married **MICHAEL DIETZ**, son of **JOHANN CONRAD DIETZ** and **MARGARED MAGDALENA SCHORNMAN**. She died on 27 April 1885, Rough and Ready, Schuylkill County, PA, at age 77. She was buried at Salem Church, Rough and Ready, Schuylkill County, PA.

8.1 JONATHAN DIETZ is also referred to as **ADAM, JONAS, JUNIUS, AND "JUNE" (PRONOUNCED "YOU-EN")** in some sources. He was born on 9 February 1828, Gratz, Dauphin County, PA. He was baptized on 11 May 1828, Zion (Klinger's) Church, Erdman, Lykens Township, Dauphin County, PA. Some sources record that he was born on 8 February 1828, Gratz, Dauphin County, PA. He married **ENGILINA KNORR**, daughter of **DAVID KNORR** and **ANNA MARIA KISSINGER**. He died on 24 June 1906, Rough and Ready, Schuylkill County, PA, at age 78. Some sources record that he died on 21 June 1906 Rough and Ready, Schuylkill County, PA. He was buried at Salem Church, Rough and Ready, Schuylkill County, PA.

8.1.1 ELLAMINA DIETZ was born on 8 February 1852. She married **JOHANNES F. BRAUN**. Ellamina's husband's surname is variously given as either "Baum" or "Braun." She died on 24 September 1874, at age 22. She was buried at Salem Church, Rough and Ready, Schuylkill County, PA.

8.1.2 AARON DIETZ was born circa 1856.

8.1.3 SARAH DIETZ was born circa 1860.

8.1.4 EMMA DIETZ was born circa 1861.

8.1.5 LAVINA DIETZ was born circa 1868.

8.2 KITTY DIETZ was born on 8 October 1829.

8.3 DANIEL DIETZ was born in 1833. Some sources record that he was born circa 1835. He married **SUSANNAH KNORR**, daughter of **DAVID KNORR** and **ANNA MARIA KISSINGER**.

8.3.1 JOEL DIETZ was born circa 1856.

8.3.2 KATE DIETZ was born circa 1862.

8.3.3 AGNES DIETZ was born circa 1872.

8.3.4 LILLY MAY DIETZ was born circa 1878.

8.4 FIETTA DIETZ was born on 28 January 1838, Upper Mahantango Township, Schuylkill County, PA. Some sources record that she was born on 8 October 1829. She married **HENRY KNORR**, son of **DAVID KNORR** and

ANNA MARIA KISSINGER, circa 1857. She died on 5 June 1917, Harrisburg, Dauphin County, PA, at age 79. She was buried on 9 June 1917, at Paxtang, Paxtang, Dauphin County, PA.

8.4.1 CAROLINE KNORR is also referred to as **CAROLINA** in some sources. She was born on 16 October 1854, Schuylkill County, PA. She married **HENRY RETTINGER** circa 1876. Some sources record that she died in 1914, Harrisburg, Dauphin County, PA, but that appears to be inconsistent with the US Census listings. She died on 18 September 1943, Harrisburg, Dauphin County, PA, at age 88. She was buried on 21 September 1943, at Harrisburg Cemetery, Harrisburg, Dauphin County, PA.

8.4.1.1 EDGAR SOLOMON RETTINGER was born on 21 August 1876, Lykens, Dauphin County, PA. He married **JENNIE MAY PALMER**, daughter of **ADAM PALMER** and **REBECCA ROW**, on 12 March 1897, Zion Evangelical Lutheran Church, Lykens, Dauphin County, PA. He married **ROSA MARY ELLEN FISSEL**, daughter of **ELIAS FISSEL** and **ELLEN DIEHL**, after 1 April 1910. He died on 29 January 1956, Harrisburg, Dauphin County, PA, at age 79. He was buried on 1 February 1956, at Shoops Cemetery, Harrisburg, Dauphin County, PA.

8.4.1.1.1 MARY ELIZABETH RETTINGER was born on 10 December 1904, Lykens, Dauphin County, PA. She was baptized on 8 January 1905, Zion Evangelical Lutheran Church, Lykens, Dauphin County, PA. She married **RALPH EUGENE WOLFE**, son of **GEORGE W. WOLFE** and **AMANDA FUNKHOUSER**, on 1 September 1923, Dauphin County, PA. She died on 21 August 1956, Juniata, Blair County, PA, at age 51. She was buried on 24 August 1956, at Grandview Cemetery, Altoona, Blair County, PA.

8.4.1.1.1.1 RALPH EUGENE WOLFE was born on 29 June 1924, Harrisburg, Dauphin County, PA. He died on 23 January 1971, at age 46. He was buried at Grandview Cemetery, Johnstown, Cambria County, PA.

8.4.1.1.1.2 DONALD EDGAR WOLFE was born on 13 December 1925, Harrisburg, Dauphin County, PA. He married **RUBY M. ALLISON**, daughter of **ANGUS ALLISON** and **ANNIE MACKAY**, on 25 August 1947, Winchester, VA. He died on 14 April 2003, at age 77.

8.4.1.1.1.2.1 DENISE S. WOLFE married **LEMAN PADELFORD**.

8.4.1.1.1.2.2 DONALD T. WOLFE died before 23 October 2009.

8.4.1.1.1.3 GEORGE STANLEY WOLFE was born on 26 February 1928, Harrisburg, Dauphin County, PA. He married **CHERRY ANN FLECK**, daughter of **THOMAS MAXWELL FLECK** and **LOIS CHERRY**. He died on 3 July 1992, at age 64. He was buried at Grandview Cemetery, Johnstown, Cambria County, PA.

8.4.1.1.1.3.1 TOM WOLFE

8.4.1.1.1.3.2 GEORGE WOLFE married **MARCELLA (--?--)**.

8.4.1.1.1.4 FREDERICK WAYNE WOLFE was born on 7 October 1937, Harrisburg, Dauphin County, PA. He married **NANCY HELEN ROBERTSON** in February 1959, Orange County, FL. He died on 19 October 1995, Polk County, FL, at age 58. He was buried at Rolling Hills Cemetery, Winter Haven, Polk County, FL.

8.4.1.1.2 ELLEN CAROLYN RETTINGER was born on 30 September 1911, Harrisburg, Dauphin County, PA. She married **WILBUR GROSS BRYAN**, son of **CHARLES C. BRYAN** and **MYRTLE O. GROSS**, on 15 February 1928, Dauphin County, PA. She died on 26 November 2001, Dauphin County, PA, at age 90. She was buried on 29 November 2001, at Chestnut Hill Cemetery, Mechanicsburg, Cumberland County, PA.

8.4.1.1.2.1 DOROTHY L. BRYAN was born on 12 December 1928, Harrisburg, Dauphin County, PA. She married **EARL LEROY WOODALL**. She died in July 1985, at age 56. She was buried at Blue Ridge Memorial Gardens, Harrisburg, Dauphin County, PA.

8.4.1.1.2.1.1 ELLEN L. WOODALL married **(--?--) SIMPSON**.

8.4.1.1.2.1.2 BRYAN K. WOODALL

8.4.1.1.3 MYRTLE RETTINGER was born on 2 April 1915, Harrisburg, Dauphin County, PA. She married **GEORGE A. HOERNER JR.**, son of **GEORGE A. HOERNER SR.** and **MAY BLACK**, on 30 October 1933, Dauphin County, PA. She died in 1978, Dauphin County, PA. She was buried at Shoops Cemetery, Harrisburg, Dauphin County, PA.

8.4.1.1.3.1 GLENN A. HOERNER was born in 1936.

8.4.1.2 REBECCA RETTINGER was born in January 1880.

8.4.1.3 SUSAN MAY RETTINGER also went by the name of SUSIE. She was born on 5 August 1882. She was baptized on 25 December 1882, Zion Evangelical Lutheran Church, Lykens, Dauphin County, PA. She married GEORGE RAYMOND MORGANS, son of WILLIAM MORGANS and MARY ANN (--?--), on 6 December 1902, Lykens, Dauphin County, PA.

    8.4.1.3.1 ALICE MORGANS was born circa 1903.

    8.4.1.3.2 MABEL MORGANS was born on 27 July 1906, Mauch Chunk, Carbon County, PA.

    8.4.1.3.3 WILLIAM MORGANS was born circa 1908.

8.4.1.4 JENNIE EDNA RETTINGER was born on 26 February 1884, Lykens, Dauphin County, PA. She married CHARLES MONROE SHOMPER on 22 August 1903, Lykens, Dauphin County, PA. She died on 2 April 1962, Lykens, Dauphin County, PA, at age 78. She was buried on 6 April 1962, at Patriotic Order Sons of America Cemetery, Lykens, Dauphin County, PA.

    8.4.1.4.1 ELSIE ARLENE SHOMPER was born on 8 April 1904, Dauphin County, PA. She was baptized on 10 July 1904, Zion Evangelical Lutheran Church, Lykens, Dauphin County, PA. She married EDWARD HAROLD BODDORFF, son of FRED BODDORFF and JENNIE RASBATCH, on 15 August 1924, Dauphin County, PA. She died on 8 January 1969, at age 64. She was buried at Calvary United Methodist Church Cemetery, Wiconisco, Dauphin County, PA.

    8.4.1.4.2 HAROLD EUGENE SHOMPER was born on 4 October 1905. He was baptized on 10 March 1906, Zion Evangelical Lutheran Church, Lykens, Dauphin County, PA. He married DOROTHY ELLE PARTRIDGE, daughter of JOHN W. PARTRIDGE and SARAH MORGAN. He married DOROTHY L. WILLIAMS, daughter of THOMAS L. WILLIAMS and BLANCHE I. (--?--). He died in 1993. He was buried at Shamokin Cemetery, Shamokin, Northumberland County, PA.

        8.4.1.4.2.1 DOROTHY SHOMPER was born on 17 December 1940, Shamokin, Northumberland County, PA. She married BRUCE L. MCMANUS circa 1968. She died on 12 July 2006, Middletown, Delaware County, PA, at age 65. She was buried at Saints Peter and Paul Cemetery, Springfield, Delaware County, PA.

            8.4.1.4.2.1.1 DOROTHY MCMANUS married ADRIAN HALL.

            8.4.1.4.2.1.2 JOHN H. MCMANUS

            8.4.1.4.2.1.3 ANDREW W. MCMANUS

    8.4.1.4.3 RALPH EDWARD SHOMPER was born on 20 December 1907, Dauphin County, PA. He died on 10 September 1929, Harrisburg, Dauphin County, PA, at age 21. He was buried on 13 September 1929, at Patriotic Order Sons of America Cemetery, Lykens, Dauphin County, PA.

    8.4.1.4.4 CLYDE ALBERT SHOMPER was born on 9 December 1913, Lykens, Dauphin County, PA. He died on 1 October 1980, Wayne, Delaware County, PA, at age 66. He was buried at Patriotic Order Sons of America Cemetery, Lykens, Dauphin County, PA.

8.4.1.5 MABEL I. RETTINGER was born on 10 July 1887, Lykens, Dauphin County, PA. She married DORIE A. MOORE circa 1908. She died on 16 January 1962, Polyclinic Hospital, Harrisburg, Dauphin County, PA, at age 74. She was buried on 19 January 1962, at Rolling Green Memorial Park, Camp Hill, Cumberland County, PA.

    8.4.1.5.1 ELIZABETH CAROLINE MOORE was born on 18 November 1910, Harrisburg, Dauphin County, PA. She married WALTER RAY FEGAN, son of JAMES E. FEGAN and ANNIE F. SMITH, on 1 April 1939, Dauphin County, PA. She died on 28 July 2004, Mechanicsburg, Cumberland County, PA, at age 93. She was buried at Rolling Green Memorial Park, Camp Hill, Cumberland County, PA.

    8.4.1.5.2 MELVIN H. MOORE was born in 1912. He married MARY B. RIGHTER, daughter of JOHN M. RIGHTER and ANNA M. (--?--). He died in 1989. He was buried at East Harrisburg Cemetery, Harrisburg, Dauphin County, PA.

        8.4.1.5.2.1 MELVIN H. MOORE JR. was born circa 1937.

        8.4.1.5.2.2 STEPHANIE R. MOORE was born on 27 June 1939, Harrisburg, Dauphin County, PA. She died on 12 March 1950, Harrisburg Hospital, Harrisburg, Dauphin County, PA, at age 10. She was buried on 15 March 1950, at East Harrisburg Cemetery, Harrisburg, Dauphin County, PA.

    8.4.1.5.3 RUTH NAOMI MOORE was born on 29 April 1919, Harrisburg, Dauphin County, PA. She married JACK L. GOSNELL, son of HOBART GOSNELL and FLORENCE MACE, circa 1944.

She died on 13 August 1998, at age 79. She was buried at Blue Ridge Memorial Gardens, Harrisburg, Dauphin County, PA.

    8.4.1.5.3.1 **DORIS J. GOSNELL** married **JOSEPH GRAHAM.**

   8.4.1.5.4 **JAMES A. MOORE** was born circa December 1928.

  8.4.1.6 **RAYMOND CLARENCE RETTINGER** was born on 1 March 1888, Lykens, Dauphin County, PA. He died on 30 December 1947, Polyclinic Hospital, Harrisburg, Dauphin County, PA, at age 59. He was buried on 3 January 1948, at Harrisburg Cemetery, Harrisburg, Dauphin County, PA.

  8.4.1.7 **CLAUDE HENRY MATTHIAS RETTINGER** was born on 8 May 1897. He died on 13 December 1920, Harrisburg, Dauphin County, PA, at age 23. He was buried on 17 December 1920, at Harrisburg Cemetery, Harrisburg, Dauphin County, PA.

8.4.2 **AARON D. KNORR** was born in February 1857, Pennsylvania. Some sources record that he was born in 1858, PA. He married **MARY R. GIPPLE**, daughter of **CHRISTIAN GIPPLE** and **CATHERINE (--?--)**, circa 1876. Judging from the places of the births of their children, sometime between 1879 and about 1880 or 1881, Aaron and Mary moved from Pennsylvania to Kansas. Then, sometime between 1884 and 1891, they moved to the state of Washington. He died before 1920.

  8.4.2.1 **HATTIE L. KNORR** was born in December 1878, Pennsylvania.

  8.4.2.2 **SUSAN ALICE KNORR** was born in September 1881, Kansas. Some sources record that she was born circa 1880, Kansas. She married **CHRISTOPHER JOHN OLSEN ALMLEE** circa 1907.

    8.4.2.2.1 **ELSIE M. ALMLEE** was born circa January 1909, Oregon.

    8.4.2.2.2 **BERNICE MILDRED ALMLEE** was born in 1910, Washington.

      8.4.2.2.2.1 **NANCY JANE FOY**

        8.4.2.2.2.1.1 **JENELLE BENSON**

  8.4.2.3 **CLARA F. KNORR** was born in October 1884, Kansas.

  8.4.2.4 **BESSIE M. KNORR** was born in July 1891, Washington. Some sources record that she was born in 1892, Washington.

8.4.3 **HANNA KNORR** was born on 25 March 1860. Some sources record that she was born in March 1865, Pennsylvania. She married **JAMES SHANNON** circa 1883. She died on 4 November 1930, Hamilton, WA, at age 70.

  8.4.3.1 **HARVEY E. SHANNON** is also referred to as **HERVEY E. SHANNON** in some sources. He was born in December 1883, Kansas.

  8.4.3.2 **FREDERICK J. SHANNON** was born in April 1885, Kansas. He married **BLANSH (--?--)** between 1910 and 1920.

    8.4.3.2.1 **MERLE SHANNON** was born in 1911, Washington.

    8.4.3.2.2 **MAXINE SHANNON** was born in 1913, Washington.

    8.4.3.2.3 **NEIL SHANNON** was born in 1914, Washington.

  8.4.3.3 **CARRIE SHANNON** was born in June 1886, Kansas.

  8.4.3.4 **BESSIE SHANNON** was born in May 1888, Kansas.

  8.4.3.5 **ANNA M. SHANNON** also went by the name of **ANNIE**. She was born in October 1891, Washington.

  8.4.3.6 **ROBIN A. SHANNON** is also referred to as **ROBERT A. SHANNON** in some sources. He was born in October 1893, Washington.

  8.4.3.7 **SELMA B. SHANNON** is also referred to as **THELMA B. SHANNON** in some sources. She was born in February 1895, Washington.

8.4.4 **JULIANN KNORR** is also referred to as **JULIA KNORR** in some sources. She was born on 18 March 1862, PA. She married **CHRISTIAN J. GIPPLE**, son of **CHRISTIAN GIPPLE** and **MARY RITZMAN**. She and **CHRISTIAN J. GIPPLE** were divorced before 1910. She owned and operated the "Gipple House Hotel" in La Conner, WA. She died on 3 April 1911, Minor Hospital, Seattle, WA, at age 49. She was buried at Pleasant Ridge Cemetery, Mt. Vernon, WA.

  8.4.4.1 **AARON OTTO GIPPLE** also went by the name of **OTTO**. He was born on 28 December 1881, Kansas. He married **EDITH LEVINA MILLER**, daughter of **EDDIE L. MILLER** and **ANNA MARY DECHOW,** on 22 August 1906, Mt. Vernon, WA. He died on 16 January 1949, Tacoma, Pierce County, WA, at age 67. He was buried at Mountain View Cemetery, Tacoma, WA.

8.4.4.1.1 DONALD AARON GIPPLE was born on 16 September 1907, La Conner, WA. He married **MARY MICHIJALIA** circa 1928, Tacoma, WA. He died on 26 January 1974, at age 66. He was buried at Calvary Cemetery, Tacoma, Pierce County, WA.

8.4.4.1.1.1 MARLENE JOAN GIPPLE was born on 8 December 1930. She died on 21 February 1958, at age 27. She was buried at Calvary Cemetery, Tacoma, Pierce County, WA.

8.4.4.1.2 GERALD OWEN GIPPLE was born on 27 December 1915, Everett, Snohomish County, WA. He married **ALICE DOROTHY HANSON**, daughter of **HANS MARTIN HANSON** and **CHRISTINE HAUG,** on 11 March 1938, Portland, Multnomah County, OR. He was a tile contractor for Oregon Art Tile Co. He died on 9 March 1954, Portland, Multnomah County, OR, at age 38. He was buried at Mountain View Memorial Park, Lakewood, Pierce County, WA.

8.4.4.1.2.1 CAROL DIANNE GIPPLE was born on 8 April 1940, Tacoma, WA. She married **LYNNE ERROL MOYER** on 24 November 1958, Stevenson, WA.

8.4.4.1.2.2 MARION ADELLE GIPPLE was born on 24 March 1944, Portland, Multnomah County, OR. She married **WILLIAM C. CROSBY**. She married **JOHN FITZPATRICK**.

8.4.4.1.2.3 GERALD DONALD GIPPLE was born on 23 January 1947, Portland, Multnomah County, OR. He married **NANCY DARLENE WHARTON** Portland, Multnomah County, OR.

8.4.4.1.3 PATRICIA MARTHA GIPPLE was born on 18 January 1920, Tacoma, Pierce County, WA. She married **HAROLD OLAF OSTLING**, son of **AXEL H. OSTLING** and **WILMA K. (--?--)**. She died on 20 December 2005, Antioch, Contra Costa County, CA, at age 85.

8.4.4.1.3.1 NANCY OSTLING married **(--?--) STARKMAN**.

8.4.4.2 HARRY GIPPLE was born on 30 September 1883, Kansas City, KS. He married **EVA (--?--)** circa 1917. He died on 14 February 1948, Tacoma, WA, at age 64.

8.4.4.2.1 EVELYN GIPPLE was born circa 1917.

8.4.4.2.2 DOLORES GIPPLE was born circa 1919.

8.4.4.3 MARTHA MABEL GIPPLE was born on 13 June 1886, Miltonvale County, KS. She married **WILLIAM W. CONNER** in 1905, LaConner, WA. She died on 5 January 1951, Seattle, WA, at age 64.

8.4.4.4 VERNA MARY GIPPLE was born on 3 September 1890, Eagle Harbor, Bainbridge Island, WA. She married **RAYMOND L. VAUGHN** circa 1905, Vancouver, British Columbia, Canada. She married **JAMES A. HURLEY**. She died on 27 February 1983, Vancouver, British Columbia, Canada, at age 92.

8.4.4.4.1 NAOMI VAUGHN was born circa 1906, Washington.

8.4.5 MICHAEL KNORR was born in February 1864, Pennsylvania. He married **MARY FREY** circa 1885. He died in 1923, Williamstown, Dauphin County, PA.

8.4.5.1 MAZIE M. KNORR was born in August 1888. Some sources record that she was born circa 1884. She married **WELLINGTON MATTERN** on 9 January 1909, Upper Mahanoy Township, Northumberland County, PA.

8.4.5.2 HERMAN G. KNORR was born in March 1890, Pennsylvania.

8.4.5.3 MERRY F. KNORR is also referred to as **FLORENCE** in some sources. She was born in September 1891, Pennsylvania.

8.4.5.4 JAMES I. KNORR was born circa 1887, Pennsylvania. Some sources record that he was born in August 1895, Pennsylvania.

8.4.5.5 WILLIAM M. KNORR was born in September 1897.

8.4.5.6 MARY KNORR was born circa 1901.

8.4.5.7 MARTHA KNORR was born circa 1901.

8.4.6 CLARA REBECCA KNORR was born on 18 November 1866, PA. She was baptized on 11 May 1867, Union Salem Church, Berrysburg, Dauphin County, PA. She died on 26 September 1877, Tower City, Schuylkill County, PA, at age 10.

8.4.7 ALACE CLARA KNORR is also referred to as **ALICE** in some sources. She was born on 18 November 1868, PA. She died on 9 September 1877, Tower City, Schuylkill County, PA, at age 8.

8.5 HEINRICH DIETZ was born in 1843. He died in 1844. He was buried at Salem Church, Rough and Ready, Schuylkill County, PA.

8.6 NATHAN DIETZ was born on 28 April 1846, Schuylkill County, PA. He married **MARIA KNORR**, daughter of **DAVID KNORR** and **ANNA MARIA KISSINGER,** circa 1868. He died on 19 September 1924, Klingerstown,

Schuylkill County, PA, at age 78. He was buried on 23 September 1924, at Salem Church, Rough and Ready, Schuylkill County, PA.

8.6.1 **IRIE ELMER DIETZ** is also referred to as **ERIE ELMER, ELMER I., AND IRA DIETZ** in some sources. He was born on 2 July 1869. He married **LILLIE ALVERTTA STARR** circa 1890. He died on 29 May 1941, PA at age 71. He was buried at Salem Church Cemetery, Rough and Ready, Schuylkill County, PA.

8.6.1.1 **KATIE T. DIETZ** was born in January 1890. She died before 2000.

8.6.1.2 **MAMIE JEMIMAH DIETZ** is also referred to as **MAYME JEMIMA DIETZ** in some sources. She was born on 18 August 1891, Upper Mahantango Township, Schuylkill County, PA. She married **PALMER C. HAAS**. She died before 2000.

8.6.1.2.1 **FERN M. HAAS** was born circa 1911. She married **HOMER ALVIN KLINGER**, son of **WILLIAM OSCAR KLINGER** and **MABEL PEARL KLINGER**, circa 1931. She died in 2002. She was buried at Salem United Church of Christ Cemetery, Rough and Ready, Schuylkill County, PA.

8.6.1.2.1.1 **JOAN EMILY KLINGER** (see above)

8.6.1.2.1.1.1 **ROBIN S. BARNES** (see above)

8.6.1.2.1.1.2 **JEFFREY S. BARNES** (see above)

8.6.1.2.1.1.3 **ELIZABETH BARNES** (see above)

8.6.1.2.2 **ROMA M. HAAS** was born circa 1915.

8.6.1.2.3 **KERMIT PALMER HAAS** was born on 22 August 1922. He married **GAIL (--?--)**. He died on 23 December 1997, Lucas, OH, at age 75. He was buried at Salem United Church of Christ Cemetery, Rough and Ready, Schuylkill County, PA.

8.6.1.3 **EDNA S. DIETZ** was born in June 1893, Pennsylvania. She married **(--?--) MAURER**. She died before 2000.

8.6.1.4 **SADIE GERTRUDE DIETZ** was born on 1 March 1895, Upper Mahantango Township, Schuylkill County, PA. She married **(--?--) MAURER**. She died before 2000.

8.6.1.5 **LILY ESTHER DIETZ** was born on 16 March 1896, RR 1, Klingerstown, Schuylkill County, PA. She married **EARL HEPLER** circa 1922. She lived in RR 1, Pitman, Schuylkill County, PA. She died on 4 April 1999, Christiana Hospital, Newark, DE, at age 103. She was buried at Salem United Church of Christ Cemetery, Rough and Ready, Schuylkill County, PA.

8.6.1.6 **LUELLA FIETTA DIETZ** is also referred to as **LOUELLA** in some sources. She was born on 17 June 1897. She married **(--?--) MAURER**. She died before 2000.

8.6.1.7 **VERNA MARY REBECCA DIETZ** was born on 29 January 1899, Rough and Ready, PA. She married **(--?--) SEMEROD**. She died before 2000.

8.6.1.8 **EMMA FLORENCE HILDA DIETZ** was born on 10 October 1900, Rough and Ready, Schuylkill County, PA. She married **(--?--) GEIST** before 1920. She died before 2000.

8.6.1.9 **PEARL MAY DIETZ** was born on 8 May 1903, Rough and Ready, Schuylkill County, PA. She married **(--?--) KIEFFER**. She died before 2000.

8.6.1.10 **MILEN HERLEN DIETZ** is also referred to as **HERLAN DIETZ** in some sources. He was born on 10 June 1905. He died before 2000.

8.6.1.11 **RAY E. DIETZ** was born on 6 November 1909. He died on 9 March 1998, Good Samaritan Regional Medical Center, Pottsville, Schuylkill County, PA, at age 88.

8.6.1.11.1 **JAMES A. DIETZ**

8.6.1.11.2 **KAY V. DIETZ** married **(--?--) WILLIARD**.

8.6.1.11.3 **JEAN L. DIETZ** married **(--?--) SAVIDGE**.

8.6.1.12 **MARLYN DIETZ** is also referred to as **MARLIN S. DIETZ** in some sources. He was born in 1911, Pennsylvania. He died before 2000.

8.6.1.13 **WILLIARD K. DIETZ** was born in 1914, Pennsylvania. He died before 2000.

8.6.2 **DAVID M. DIETZ** is also referred to as **MONROE D.** in some sources. He was born on 17 April 1878.

8.7 **JOEL DIETZ** was born on 6 June 1848, Schuylkill County, PA. He married **LYDIA W. DUNKLEBERGER**, daughter of **DANIEL DUNKLEBERGER** and **CATHARINE WAGNER**. He died on 12 September 1907, Oceana County, MI, at age 59. He was buried at Elbridge Township Cemetery, Hart, Oceana County, MI.

8.7.1 **DONALD ELSWORTH DIETZ** was born on 7 July 1870.

8.7.2 WILLIAM O. DIETZ was born in 1872. He married **IDA A. HERSHBERGER**. He died in 1935. He was buried at Elbridge Township Cemetery, Hart, Oceana County, MI.

8.7.3 ELMIRA J. DIETZ was born on 3 March 1878. She married **(--?--) BUSHAW**. She married **HORACE J. LESSARD**, son of **ISADORE LESSARD** and **ADELAIDE LEBLANC**, on 2 June 1913, Ludington, Mason County, MI. She died on 17 October 1927, Mason County, MI, at age 49. She was buried at Pere Marquette Cemetery, Ludington, Mason County, MI.

8.7.4 LENA C. DIETZ was born on 19 February 1879. She married **FRANK L. NUTTALL**. She died on 1 June 1945, at age 66. She was buried at Elbridge Township Cemetery, Hart, Oceana County, MI.

>**8.7.4.1 HAZEL M. NUTTALL** was born in 1901. She married **ART STAPLES**. She died in 1980. She was buried at Mount Hope Cemetery, Shelby, Oceana County, MI.

>>**8.7.4.1.1 HERBERT G. STAPLES** was born in 1930. He died in 1931. He was buried at Mount Hope Cemetery, Shelby, Oceana County, MI.

>**8.7.4.2 GOLDIE MARIE NUTTALL** was born on 22 January 1912, Walkerville, Oceana County, MI. She married **JOHN LAWRENCE OVERHISER**, son of **KARL J. OVERHISER** and **NANCY ETHEL RISSER**, on 21 January 1937, Van Buren County, MI. She died on 10 September 1982, South Haven, Van Buren County, MI, at age 70. She was buried at McDowell Cemetery, South Haven Highlands, Allegan County, MI.

>>**8.7.4.2.1 JANET LOUISE OVERHISER** was born on 26 January 1938, South Haven, Van Buren County, MI. She married **HAROLD ROE** on 4 March 1955, First English Lutheran Church, South Haven, MI. She and **HAROLD ROE** were divorced in 1972. She married **EDMUND KASARDA** on 18 December 1974, Norfolk, NE. She and **EDMUND KASARDA** were divorced circa 1995. She died on 28 October 2000, Middlebury, Elkhart County, IN, at age 62. She was buried at Grace Lawn Cemetery, Middlebury, Elkhart County, IN.

>>>**8.7.4.2.1.1 STEPHEN ROE** died before 1972.

>>>**8.7.4.2.1.2 KIM ROE** was born in 1957, Van Buren County, MI. She married **DANA A. KESTER** in 1978, Trinity Lutheran Church, Paw Paw, Van Buren County, MI.

>>>>**8.7.4.2.1.2.1 T.J. KESTER** was born in July 1978, South Haven, Van Buren County, MI.

>>>>**8.7.4.2.1.2.2 TERRY KESTER** was born in May 1982, Plymouth, Sheboygan County, WI.

>>**8.7.4.2.2 MARJORIE ANN OVERHISER** was born on 14 June 1939, South Haven, Van Buren County, MI. She married **IVAN G. MARR**. She died on 4 March 1999, South Haven, Van Buren County, MI, at age 59. She was buried at McDowell Cemetery, South Haven Highlands, Allegan County, MI.

>>>**8.7.4.2.2.1 LARRY MARR** married **RUTH (--?--)**.

>>>**8.7.4.2.2.2 TERRY MARR**

>>>**8.7.4.2.2.3 DOUG MARR** married **NANCY (--?--)**.

>>>**8.7.4.2.2.4 GREG MARR** married **KAREN (--?--)**.

8.7.5 LYDIA DIETZ was born on 18 October 1887. She died on 11 July 1888. She was buried at Elbridge Township Cemetery, Hart, Oceana County, MI.

9 JOHANN ADAM KLINGER is also referred to as **JOHN ADAM KLINGER** in some sources. He was born on 18 February 1810, Lykens Township, Dauphin County, PA. He was baptized on 23 April 1810, Zion (Klinger's) Church, Erdman, Lykens Township, Dauphin County, PA. He married **LYDIA DORNHEIM**, daughter of **HENRY DORNHEIM** and **ANNA (--?--)**, circa 1834. According to some sources, John Adam and Lydia lived near the Hill (St. John's Lutheran) Church, Berrysburg, Dauphin County, PA. He died on 15 April 1885, Mifflin Township, Dauphin County, PA, at age 75. He was buried at St. John's Lutheran Church Cemetery, Berrysburg, Dauphin County, PA.

>**9.1 LYDIA KLINGER** was born on 24 January 1835. She died on 8 December 1872, at age 37. She was buried at St. John's Lutheran Church Cemetery, Berrysburg, Dauphin County, PA.

>**9.2 SAMUEL D. KLINGER** was born on 9 June 1838. He married **MARY (--?--)** circa 1859.

>**9.3 WILLIAM H. KLINGER** was born on 7 March 1840. He married **HANNAH ELIZA KEMMEREN** in 1869. He died on 28 April 1914, at age 74. He was buried at St. John's Lutheran Church Cemetery, Berrysburg, Dauphin County, PA.

>>**9.3.1 FANNIE ETTA KLINGER** was born on 15 February 1871. She was baptized on 2 March 1871, St. John's Lutheran Church, Berrysburg, Dauphin County, PA.

9.3.2 JOHN ADAM KLINGER was born on 20 January 1872. He was baptized on 5 May 1872, St. John's Lutheran Church, Berrysburg, Dauphin County, PA. He died on 5 January 1936, at age 63.

9.4 CAROLINE KLINGER was born on 21 January 1844. She was baptized on 25 April 1844, St. John's Lutheran Church, Berrysburg, Mifflin Township, Dauphin County, PA. She married **JEREMIAH R. CARL**, son of **JEREMIAH CARL** and **JULIANA RADEL**, on 5 February 1865, by Rev. C.S. Haman, Berrysburg Circuit, East Pennsylvania Conference Evangelical Association, Oakdale, Dauphin County, PA.

9.4.1 LINCOLN CALVIN CARL was born on 11 April 1866, Wiconisco Township, Dauphin County, PA. He married **ANNIE LAURIE CURTIS**, daughter of **CHARLES CURTIS** and **AMANDA MAIDENFORD**, circa 1887. He died in 1950.

9.4.1.1 CLARENCE CARL died in infancy. He was buried at Fairview Cemetery, Williamstown, Dauphin County, PA.

9.4.1.2 HERMAN LEROY CARL also went by the name of **BUD.** He was born on 30 April 1889. He married **EDITH (--?--).** He married **KATHERINE (--?--).** "Bud" served in World War I as a regimental supply sergeant in the 316th Infantry Division. Later he taught engineering and mathematics at the University of Pittsburgh, worked as RCA as a cost analyst, and also worked on the Manhattan Project, during World War II, on the development of the atomic bomb. He died on 13 July 1960, at age 71. He was buried at Fairview Cemetery, Williamstown, Dauphin County, PA.

9.4.1.3 GRACE CAROLINE CARL was born on 23 January 1893. Some sources record that she was born in January 1892. She married **CLAYTON C. RADEL** on 28 June 1917. She and **CLAYTON C. RADEL** were divorced. She died on 28 July 1980, Deptford, NJ, at age 88. She was buried at Fairview Cemetery, Williamstown, Dauphin County, PA.

9.4.1.3.1 PAUL HERMAN RADEL was born circa October 1918, Collingswood, Camden County, NJ. He died in 1941. He was buried at Fairview Cemetery, Williamstown, Dauphin County, PA.

9.4.1.3.2 LINCOLN CARL RADEL also went by the name of **CARL.** He was born on 24 October 1921, 401 West Comley Ave., West Collingswood, Camden County, NJ. He married **MOLLY LEE KIRBY.** He married **ANNAMAE MARIE NEVIL**, daughter of **JOSEPH MONTGOMERY NEVIL** and **ANNA MAE FORVOUR,** on 2 May 1947.

9.4.1.3.2.1 JOY ANN RADEL was born on 2 March 1948, West Jersey Hospital, Camden, Camden County, NJ. She married **BRUCE FRANCIS KLINE**, son of **JOSEPH HARRIS KLINE** and **MADALYN GLORIA KEMP,** on 20 June 1970, St. John's Catholic Church, Collingswood, NJ.

9.4.1.3.2.1.1 KEVIN DANIEL KLINE was born on 31 May 1978, West Jersey Hospital, Camden County, NJ. He married **KIMBERLY DEMPSY.** He and **KIMBERLY DEMPSY** were divorced.

9.4.1.3.2.1.1.1 CARL VINCENT KLINE also goes by the name of **C.K.** He was born on 2 April 2003, New Jersey.

9.4.1.3.2.1.2 JESSE CURTIS KLINE was born on 26 May 1979, West Jersey Hospital, Camden County, NJ. He married **ALISHA HAGLEIN** in June 2003. He and **ALISHA HAGLEIN** were divorced.

9.4.1.3.2.1.3 LAURA ASHLEY KLINE was born on 30 April 1982, West Jersey Hospital, Camden County, NJ.

9.4.1.3.2.2 CARLYNNE RADEL was born on 7 March 1951, West Jersey Hospital, Camden, Camden County, NJ. She married **BRUCE WILLIAM EDWARDS**, son of **LIONEL PATRICK EDWARDS** and **ELINORE WILSON,** on 27 October 1978, Collingswood, Camden County, NJ.

9.4.1.3.2.2.1 NICOLE RENE EDWARDS also goes by the name of **NIKKI.** She was born on 9 April 1982, Garden State Community Hospital, Marlton, NJ. Nikki supplied much information about the descendants of Johann Adam Klinger.

9.4.1.3.2.3 PAUL HERMAN RADEL was born on 9 February 1954, Camden, Camden County, NJ.

9.4.1.4 PAUL REVERE CARL was born on 12 April 1897. Paul graduated from the United States Military Academy, Class of 1917. He married **LYLLIAN OSSMAN** in 1919. He died on 10 September 1951, at age 54. He was buried at United States Military Academy Cemetery, West Point, Orange County, NY.

9.4.1.4.1 PAUL REVERE CARL JR. was born on 26 January 1922, Pennsylvania. He married **BETTY LEE DAUBENSPECK.**

9.4.1.4.1.1 ROBERT DOUGLAS CARL was born on 16 March 1951, New Jersey.

9.4.1.4.1.2 JOHN PRESTON CARL was born on 16 May 1955, New Jersey.

9.4.1.4.2 CAROLYN L. CARL was born in 1923, New Jersey. She married **JOHN SMITH BRADLEY.**

9.4.1.4.2.1 CARLA LYNN BRADLEY was born on 20 October 1950. She married **BRUCE EVANS** in 1972.

9.4.1.4.2.1.1 JARED SAXTON EVANS was born on 9 April 1981. He married **JULIANE (--?--)** in May 2007.

9.4.1.4.2.1.2 LINDSAY PAIGE EVANS married **JASON (--?--)**. She was born on 23 December 1983.

9.4.1.4.3 JEAN ROSELYN CARL was born in 1925.

9.4.2 CALVIN CARL was born circa 1869, Dauphin County, PA. Calvin's date of birth is uncertain. His name does not appear in a number of listings of the children of Caroline Klinger and Jeremiah Carl. One explanation for this might be that he died as a child. According to the 1900 Census, Caroline had 4 children, one of whom died before 1900. Calvin's name does not appear in any of the available Census listings between 1870 and 1900. He died before 1900.

9.4.3 HATTIE CARDELLA CARL was born circa 1879, Dauphin County, PA. Some sources record that she was born circa 1871. She married **TOM WAGNER.**

9.4.3.1 CARL WAGNER

9.4.3.2 NELLIE WAGNER

9.4.4 JAMES ABRAM GARFIELD CARL is also referred to as **JAMES G. CARL** in some sources. He was born on 30 July 1882, Dauphin County, PA. Some sources record that he was born circa 1874. He married **GERTRUDE EVANS HAINES**, daughter of **HESTER C. HAINES**, in 1907. He died in December 1963.

9.4.4.1 GERTRUDE CAROLINE CARL was born on 13 June 1908. Some sources record that she was born in July 1908, Pennsylvania. She married **CHARLES L. FORTUNE** in 1947. She died on 26 October 1986, at age 78.

9.5 MARY ANN KLINGER is also referred to as **MARIA ANNA** in some sources. She was born on 30 June 1845. She was baptized on 31 August 1845, St. John's Lutheran Church, Berrysburg, Mifflin Township, Dauphin County, PA. She married **EDWARD LENKER**, son of **PHILIP LENKER**, on 24 December 1865, Salem's Union Church, Berrysburg, Dauphin County, PA. She died on 3 April 1898, Dauphin County, PA, at age 52.

9.5.1 ROBERT LENKER was born circa 1864, Pennsylvania.

9.5.2 DAVID LUTHER LENKER was born in 1868, Pennsylvania. He married **FANNIE JANE HOOVER** circa 1893. He died on 16 January 1924. He was buried on 19 June 1924, at Salem Evangelical Lutheran Church Cemetery, Killinger, Upper Paxton Township, Dauphin County, PA.

9.5.2.1 HATTIE R. LENKER was born in 1894. Some sources record that she was born circa 1896, Pennsylvania. She married **HARVEY F. CROSSON** circa 1913. She died on 9 October 1958. She was buried on 13 October 1958, at Salem Evangelical Lutheran Church Cemetery, Killinger, Upper Paxton Township, Dauphin County, PA.

9.5.2.1.1 GEORGE E. CROSSON was born on 1 February 1915, Fisherville, Dauphin County, PA. He married **ANNA SAVILLA LETTICH** on 30 July 1960, Salem Lutheran Church, Elizabethville, Dauphin County, PA. He died on 9 December 1997, Harrisburg Hospital, Harrisburg, Dauphin County, PA, at age 82. He was buried at Simeon Church Cemetery, Gratz, Dauphin County, PA.

9.5.2.1.2 THELMA REBECCA CROSSON was born on 6 November 1923, Dauphin County, PA. She married **WILBUR WITMER LAUDENSLAGER**, son of **JOHN ADAM LAUDENSLAGER** and **LILLY ADELINE WITMER**, on 3 November 1939. She died on 9 October 1992, Holy Spirit Hospital, Camp Hill, Cumberland County, PA, at age 68. She was buried on 12 October 1992, at Emmanuel Wesleyan Cemetery, Gratz, Dauphin County, PA.

9.5.2.1.2.1 EVELYN LOUISE LAUDENSLAGER married **JOHN LAWRENCE YODER** on 27 August 1992.

9.5.2.1.2.2 DALLAS EUGENE LAUDENSLAGER married **YVONNE M. SNYDER** on 1 June 1968, Dauphin County, PA. He married **DIANE LEITZEL BIXLER** on 17 May 1975.

9.5.2.1.2.3 GARY LEE LAUDENSLAGER married **BARBARA HARNER**.

9.5.2.1.3 BERTHA E. CROSSON was born on 26 April 1926. She married **PAUL J. LONTZ** circa 1948. She died on 6 November 1996, Hershey Medical Center, Dauphin County, PA, at age 70.

9.5.2.1.3.1 CATHY A. LONTZ married **ROBERT WAYNE KAUFFMAN** circa 1971.

9.5.2.2 ANNIE M. LENKER was born circa 1897.

9.5.2.3 PAUL LUTHER LENKER was born on 3 January 1900, Dauphin County, Pennsylvania. He married **LOTTIE A. ENDERS**, daughter of **CHARLES A. ENDERS** and **LILLIE JANE HASSINGER,** on 24 November 1927, Elizabethville, Dauphin County, PA. He died in October 1962, Dauphin County, PA, at age 62. He was buried at Salem Evangelical Lutheran Church Cemetery, Killinger, Dauphin County, PA.

9.5.2.3.1 DOROTHEA LENKER

9.5.2.3.2 ROBERT J. LENKER

9.5.2.3.3 FLORENCE STONEROAD was born circa 1920. Florence was adopted.

9.5.2.3.4 CHARLES DAVID LENKER was born on 28 March 1928, Berrysburg, Dauphin County, PA. He married **SARAH ANNETTE KLINGER** on 11 February 1950, St. John's Lutheran Church, Berrysburg, Dauphin County, PA. He died on 20 November 2000, Millersburg, Dauphin County, PA, at age 72. He was buried at Salem Evangelical Lutheran Church Cemetery, Killinger, Upper Paxton Township, Dauphin County, PA.

9.5.2.3.5 FLOYD LUTHER LENKER was born on 25 August 1930.

9.5.2.3.5.1 LUANN MARIE LENKER

9.5.2.3.5.2 FLOYD LUTHER LENKER JR.

9.5.2.3.6 DONALD EUGENE LENKER was born on 29 July 1934. He was baptized on 21 April 1935, St. Paul's Evangelical Lutheran Church, Millersburg, Dauphin County, PA. He died on 24 February 2012, Hershey, Dauphin County, PA, at age 77.

9.5.2.3.7 LLOYD WILLIAM LENKER was born on 24 August 1936, Millersburg, Dauphin County, PA. He married **MARIE GESSNER** circa 1956. He died on 20 February 2014, Harrisburg Hospital, Harrisburg, Dauphin County, PA, at age 77. He was buried on 25 February 2014, at Oak Hill Cemetery, Millersburg, Dauphin County, PA.

9.5.2.3.7.1 STEVE LENKER married **LEANN (--?--)**.

9.5.2.3.7.2 MARLENE LENKER married **JOSEPH LEBO**.

9.5.2.3.7.3 MICHAEL LENKER married **GINA (--?--)**.

9.5.2.3.7.4 LLOYD W. LENKER JR. was born on 26 March 1958. Lloyd served in the military from 1976 until 1995. He married **KIEW CHAISONGKARM**, daughter of **RHIEN CHAISONGKARM** and **BAW KI PANG**, on 21 August 1987, Newport News, VA. He died on 24 February 2010, at age 51. He was buried at Oak Hill Cemetery, Millersburg, Dauphin County, PA.

9.5.2.3.7.4.1 CHRISTOPHER LENKER

9.5.2.3.8 PAUL EDWARD LENKER was born on 22 June 1939, Dauphin County, PA. He married **JOAN IRENE BURRELL**, daughter of **WILLIAM CHARLES BURRELL** and **EDNA IRENE WEAVER,** on 27 June 1959, Millersburg, Dauphin County, PA. He died on 10 January 1991, Millersburg, Dauphin County, PA, at age 51. He was buried at Riverview Memorial Gardens, Halifax, Dauphin County, PA.

9.5.2.3.8.1 EDWARD DEAN LENKER married **SHELLEY ROXANNE WILLIARD**, daughter of **ROBERT LEROY WILLIARD** and **MARGARET ARLENE ENDERS,** on 21 July 1984, Salem Lutheran Church, Elizabethville, Dauphin County, PA.

9.5.2.3.8.1.1 JASON EDWARD LENKER

9.5.2.3.8.1.2 NICHOLAS D. LENKER

9.5.2.3.8.2 ANGELA DAWN LENKER married **KENNETH D. HORCHLER** on 7 June 1986, Millersburg, Dauphin County, PA.

9.5.2.3.8.2.1 SUMMER NICOLE HORCHLER

9.5.2.3.8.2.2 CLARK BAUM

9.5.2.3.9 CLARENCE ANDREW LENKER was born on 16 October 1940.

9.5.2.4 BOYD L. LENKER was born circa 1903, Pennsylvania. He married **FLORENCE C. HOY** circa 1922.

9.5.2.4.1 RICHARD E. LENKER was born circa 1923, Millersburg, Dauphin County, PA. He married **EVA KURTZ**. He died on 23 August 2008, Manor Care Nursing Home, Camp Hill, Cumberland County, PA. According to a newspaper obituary, Richard served in the U. S. Navy during World War II as a Gunner's Mate in the European, African and Philippine Liberation campaigns. After the war, he was a truck driver for more than 40 years, driving 3.5 million accident-free miles.

9.5.2.4.1.1 TEDDY LENKER. Teddy lives in Lykens, PA.

9.5.2.4.2 FRANKLIN L. LENKER was born circa 1928. Frank lives in Millersburg, PA.

9.5.2.4.3 EVELYN LENKER died before 23 August 2008.

9.5.2.4.4 DOROTHY LENKER died before 23 August 2008.

9.5.2.4.5 SHIRLEY J. LENKER was born on 30 June 1935, Millersburg, Dauphin County, PA. She died on 24 February 2013, Holy Spirit Hospital, Camp Hill, Cumberland County, PA, at age 77. According to a newspaper obituary, Shirley lived in Millersburg, PA, and worked for Johnson Bailey and Muskin Shoe Co. both formerly of Millersburg, PA. She was buried on 1 March 2013, at Oak Hill Cemetery, Millersburg, Dauphin County, PA.

9.5.2.4.6 DOLORES LENKER married **RON LEISER**. Dolores lives in Millersburg, PA.

9.5.2.4.7 ROBERT LENKER. Robert lives in Millersburg, PA.

9.5.2.5 SALLIE M. LENKER was born in 1909, Pennsylvania.

9.5.3 ANNIE M. LENKER is also referred to as **MARY A.** in some sources. She was born circa 1872, Pennsylvania. She married **FRANKLIN B. NOVINGER** circa 1894.

9.5.3.1 RUTH PAULINE NOVINGER was born circa 1895.

9.5.3.2 EARL M. NOVINGER was born on 17 May 1901. Some sources record that he was born circa 1902, Pennsylvania. He married **FLORENCE D. (--?--)** circa 1925. He died in November 1970. Prior to his death, Earl was living in Harrisburg, Dauphin County.

9.6 JOHN H. KLINGER is also referred to as **HENRY KLINGER** in some sources. He was born circa 1847. Some sources record that he was born circa 1849. He married **ISABELLA J. HAAK** circa 1870.

9.6.1 CHARLES OLIVER KLINGER was born on 19 March 1873, Pennsylvania. He was baptized on 11 May 1873, Union Salem (Peace UCC) Church, Berrysburg, Dauphin County, PA.

9.6.2 ALICE JANE KLINGER is also referred to as **AMANDA** in some sources. She was born on 28 August 1875, Pennsylvania. She was baptized on 14 November 1875, St. John's Lutheran Church, Berrysburg, Dauphin County, PA. Some sources record that she was born circa 1874, Pennsylvania.

9.6.3 DANIEL MONROE KLINGER was born on 27 March 1877, Pennsylvania. He was baptized on 2 May 1877, St. John's Lutheran Church, Berrysburg, Dauphin County, PA. Some sources record that he was born circa 1876, Pennsylvania.

9.6.4 MARGARET S. KLINGER is also referred to as **MAGGIE, SALOMA AND LIDDIE** in some sources. She was born circa May 1880, Pennsylvania.

9.6.5 KATIE C. KLINGER was born on 3 December 1884. She died on 5 January 1885. She was buried at St. John's Lutheran Church Cemetery, Berrysburg, Dauphin County, PA.

9.6.6 ANNIE M. KLINGER was born in May 1886, Pennsylvania. Some sources record that she was born circa 1883, but the 1900 Census, which lists Annie's age as 17, lists her month of birth as what appears to be May of 1886.

9.6.7 EDMUND E. KLINGER is also referred to as **EDWARD** in some sources. He was born in February 1887, Pennsylvania.

9.6.8 CAROLINE ELLEN KLINGER also went by the name of **ELLEN**. She was born in September 1890, Pennsylvania.

9.7 MOSES KLINGER was born circa 1851.

9.8 DANIEL DAVID KLINGER was born on 22 August 1857. He was baptized on 8 December 1857, St. John's Lutheran Church, Berrysburg, Mifflin Township, Dauphin County, PA. He died on 23 February 1858. He was buried at St. John's Lutheran Church Cemetery, Berrysburg, Dauphin County, PA.

9.9 CHARLES MILTON KLINGER was born on 16 September 1860, Dauphin County, PA. He was baptized on 16 February 1861, St. John's Lutheran Church, Berrysburg, Mifflin Township, Dauphin County, PA. He died on 22 November 1861, at age 1 in a fire. He was buried at St. John's Lutheran Church Cemetery, Berrysburg, Dauphin County, PA.

10 JACOB S. KLINGER is also referred to as **JACOB P. KLINGER** in some sources. He was born on 29 January 1813, Lykens Township, Dauphin County, PA. He married **LOUISA ALSPACH**, daughter of **JOHN ALSPACH** and **MARY MAGDALENA HEITER**, before 29 May 1836. By deed dated 24 August 1844, Jacob's father Peter Klinger, transferred to Jacob 6 tracts of land comprising about 174 acres. These tracts included portions of 2 of Philip Klinger's 4 original holdings (parts of "Salem," "Mt. Holly," and "Klingerwell") as well as several tracts that were parts of land that Peter Klinger had patented himself. This transfer covered land in both Lykens Township Dauphin County and Upper Mahantango Township, Schuylkill County. He died on 23 January 1883, Erdman, Lykens Township, Dauphin County, PA, at age 69. He was buried at Zion (Klinger's) Church, Erdman, Lykens Township, Dauphin County, PA.

10.1 JOHN A. KLINGER was born circa 1837. He married **AMANDA MILLER**.

10.2 MARCUS KLINGER is also referred to as **MICHAEL** in some sources. He was born on 24 May 1838. He was baptized on 24 May 1839, Zion (Klinger's) Church, Erdman, Lykens Township, Dauphin County, PA. Some sources record that he was born on 24 May 1839, but this may be an erroneous reference to his baptismal date. Other sources record that he was born in April 1839. He married **ELIZABETH DELP**, daughter of **GEORGE DELP** and **CATHARINE BUSH**, circa 1861. He died on 6 February 1901, at age 62. He was buried at St. Michael's Church Cemetery, Klingerstown, Schuylkill County, PA.

10.2.1 ELSWORTH KLINGER was born on 28 October 1862. He married **IDA C. KNORR**, daughter of **ISAAC C. KNORR** and **ELIZABETH FETTEROLF**, circa 1885. He died on 9 January 1933, at age 70. He was buried at St. Michael's Church Cemetery, Klingerstown, Schuylkill County, PA.

10.2.1.1 CARRIE VESTA KLINGER is also referred to as **CARRIE A. AND CAROLINE VESTA KLINGER** in some sources. She was born on 2 May 1885. She married **CHARLES H. BOYER** on 25 November 1905, Zion (Klinger's) Church, Erdman, Lykens Township, Dauphin County, PA. She died on 23 November 1971, at age 86. She was buried at St. Michael's Church Cemetery, Klingerstown, Schuylkill County, PA.

10.2.1.1.1 MABEL IRENE BOYER was born on 14 October 1906. She died on 22 January 1907. She was buried at St. Michael's Church Cemetery, Klingerstown, Schuylkill County, PA.

10.2.1.1.2 HELEN MAE BOYER married (--?--) **ROTHERMEL**. She was born on 31 January 1908. She died before 2009.

10.2.1.1.3 MELVIN HENRY BOYER was born on 21 February 1910. He died on 19 November 1995, at age 85. Prior to his death, Melvin was living in Dornsife, Northumberland County, PA.

10.2.1.1.4 HARLIN L. BOYER is also referred to as **HARLEN** in some sources. He was born on 14 April 1912, Pennsylvania. He died on 8 March 1995, at age 82.

10.2.1.1.5 IVAN ELWOOD BOYER was born on 23 November 1919. Some sources record that he was born circa October 1919. He married **SOPHIA BELLE LAND**. He died on 13 May 1983. He was buried at St. Michael's Church Cemetery, Klingerstown, Schuylkill County, PA.

10.2.1.1.5.1 ELEANOR RACHEL BOYER was born on 8 June 1941. She was baptized on 12 September 1941, Salem (Herb's) Church, Rough and Ready, Schuylkill County, PA.

10.2.1.1.5.2 BETTY ROMAINE BOYER was born on 23 March 1943. She was baptized on 4 September 1943, Salem (Herb's) Church, Rough and Ready, Schuylkill County, PA. She married **EUGENE ALLEN WIEST**.

10.2.1.1.5.2.1 DENISE RENEE WIEST was born on 20 January 1965, Shamokin, Northumberland County, PA. She was baptized on 31 May 1965, Salem (Herb's) Church, Rough and Ready, Schuylkill County, PA.

10.2.1.1.5.3 EUGENE IVAN BOYER was born on 14 May 1945. He was baptized on 10 November 1945, St. Michael's Church, Klingerstown, Schuylkill County, PA. He married **IRENE MARY BEURY** on 27 February 1965, St. Michael's Church, Klingerstown, Schuylkill County, PA.

10.2.1.1.5.4 LEON BOYER was born on 22 January 1948.

10.2.1.1.5.5 EDWARD LOEB BOYER is also referred to as **EDWIN** in some sources. He was born on 22 January 1948. He was baptized on 3 April 1948, St. Michael's Church, Klingerstown, Schuylkill County, PA.

10.2.1.1.5.6 RUBY MAE BOYER was born on 28 March 1951. She was baptized on 10 August 1951, St. Michael's Church, Klingerstown, Schuylkill County, PA.

10.2.1.1.5.7 LINDA SUE BOYER was born on 6 November 1954, Dornsife, Northumberland County, PA. She was baptized on 2 April 1955, St. Michael's Church, Klingerstown, Schuylkill County, PA.

10.2.1.1.6 STERLIN ROY BOYER was born on 23 February 1922. He was baptized on 22 April 1922, St. Michael's Church, Klingerstown, Schuylkill County, PA. He married **ANNA VIRGINIA WERT**, daughter of **JEREMIAH FRANKLIN WERT** and **ANNIE REBECCA RIEGLE**. He died on 5 July 2010, Geisinger Medical Center, Danville, Montour County, PA, at age 88. He was buried on 9 July 2010, at Herndon Cemetery, Herndon, Northumberland County, PA. According to a newspaper obituary, Sterlin was a mechanic at the former Klingerstown Motors and at Boyer's Used Cars.

10.2.1.1.6.1 ROY STERLIN BOYER was born on 12 February 1943, Dornsife, Northumberland County, PA. He married **FAY HOWELL**. He died on 11 September 2015, Green Valley Skilled Nursing and Rehab Center, Pitman, Schuylkill County, PA, at age 72. He was buried on 15 September 2015, at Union Cemetery, Pillow, PA.

10.2.1.1.6.2 HENRY FRANKLIN BOYER was born on 30 April 1945. He married **INEZ (--?--)**.

10.2.1.1.6.2.1 TODD BOYER married **TINA (--?--)**.

10.2.1.1.7 BRYANT WOODROW BOYER is also referred to as **BRYAN** in some sources. He was born on 5 April 1924, Klingerstown, Schuylkill County, PA. Some sources record that he was born on 5 April 1923. He was baptized on 1 June 1924, St. Michael's Church, Klingerstown, Schuylkill County, PA. He died on 16 May 2009, Friendly Nursing Home, Pitman, Schuylkill County, PA, at age 86. According to a newspaper obituary, Bryant was a farmer in the Klingerstown area. He was buried on 20 May 2009, at St. Michael's Church Cemetery, Klingerstown, Schuylkill County, PA.

10.2.1.2 MABEL GERTRUDE KLINGER was born on 17 September 1891. She married **HENRY H. LESHER**, son of **HENRY LESHER**, circa 1908. She died on 21 September 1969, at age 78.

10.2.1.2.1 MINNIE LESHER was born circa October 1908, Pennsylvania.

10.2.1.2.2 MARLIN L. LESHER was born in 1910, Pennsylvania.

10.2.1.2.3 MARGARET I. LESHER was born in 1914, Pennsylvania.

10.2.1.2.4 GLENNON E. LESHER was born circa June 1916, Pennsylvania.

10.2.1.2.5 PAULINE E. LESHER was born circa July 1918, Pennsylvania.

10.2.1.2.6 VERNON LESHER was born circa 1924, Pennsylvania.

10.2.1.2.7 JEAN LESHER was born circa October 1925.

10.2.1.2.8 RUTH LESHER was born circa 1927, Pennsylvania.

10.2.1.2.9 JUNIOR LESHER was born circa September 1929, Pennsylvania.

10.2.1.3 ALLEN TIMOTHY KLINGER is also referred to as **ALLEN P. KLINGER** in some sources. He was born on 17 January 1894, Klingerstown, Schuylkill County, PA. He married **ALPHA F. STARR**, daughter of **OSCAR ADAM STARR** and **ELIZABETH SOPHRONIA KNORR**. He died on 15 February 1960, Shellsville, Dauphin County, PA, at age 66. According to a newspaper obituary, Allen T. Klinger, of Shellsville, PA, formerly a resident of Klingerstown, died very suddenly following a heart attack at Shellsville. He was a lumberman by trade. He was buried at Salem (Herb's) Church Cemetery, Rough and Ready, Schuylkill County, PA.

10.2.1.3.1 EVELYN ELSIE KLINGER was born on 29 May 1914. She was baptized on 19 July 1914, St. Michael's Church, Klingerstown, Schuylkill County, PA. She married **HARRY ALLEN STIELY**, son of **PERRY M. STIELY** and **HARRIETTE SNYDER**, on 17 September 1930, Salem (Herb's) Reformed Church, Rough and Ready, Schuylkill County, PA. She died on 21 November 1952, at age 38.

10.2.1.3.1.1 JIMMY STIELY is also referred to as **JIMMY SHEETZ** in some sources.

10.2.1.3.1.2 BOBBY STIELY

10.2.1.3.1.3 ALPHA STIELY married TERRY G. STROHECKER, son of FRED RAYMOND STROHECKER and EDNA M. PAUL.

10.2.1.3.1.3.1 RANDY STROHECKER was born on 4 October 1967.

10.2.1.3.1.4 DONALD STIELY

10.2.1.3.1.5 HARRY STIELY

10.2.1.3.1.6 PERRY ALVIN STIELY is also referred to as PERRY ALBERT STIELY in some sources. He was born on 28 January 1931. He was baptized on 22 February 1931, Salem (Herb's) Church, Rough and Ready, Schuylkill County, PA. He was buried at Salem (Herb's) Church Cemetery, Rough and Ready, Schuylkill County, PA. He died on 18 August 1941, at age 10.

10.2.1.3.1.7 EVELYN ESTHER STIELY was born on 14 May 1932. She was baptized on 27 June 1932, Salem (Herb's) Church, Rough and Ready, Schuylkill County, PA. She married (--?--) JONES.

10.2.1.3.1.8 GUY LEROY STIELY was born on 8 August 1933. He was baptized on 4 December 1933, Salem (Herb's) Church, Rough and Ready, Schuylkill County, PA. He died in 1936. He was buried at Salem (Herb's) Church Cemetery, Rough and Ready, Schuylkill County, PA.

10.2.1.3.1.9 GEORGE EARL STIELY was born on 22 November 1934. He was baptized on 21 March 1935, Salem (Herb's) Church, Rough and Ready, Schuylkill County, PA. There is a second baptism listed in the Salem Church records for George Earl Stiely. These records list the date of birth as 27 November 1934 and the date of the baptism as 21 March 1936.

10.2.1.3.1.10 NANCY JEANNETTE STIELY was born on 19 December 1935, Klingerstown, Schuylkill County, PA. She was baptized on 22 June 1936, Salem (Herb's) Church, Rough and Ready, Schuylkill County, PA. She married LAMAR FOULDS on 9 June 1953, in Maryland. She died on 21 January 2012, Rebuck, Northumberland County, PA, at age 76, at her daughter's home. According to a newspaper obituary, Nancy lived in Hunter Station, PA. She worked at the former Riverside and Muskins Shoe Factory in Millersburg and Wilson Manufacturing in Sunbury, and later worked as an independent mail truck carrier for the U.S. Postal Service. She was buried on 25 January 2012, at Northumberland Memorial Park, Stonington, Northumberland County, PA.

10.2.1.3.1.10.1 ROBYN FOULDS married GREGORY SNYDER. Robyn lives in Rebuck, PA.

10.2.1.3.1.10.2 RODNEY FOULDS married LINDA (--?--). Rodney lives in Herndon, PA.

10.2.1.3.1.10.3 RINDY FOULDS married MARLA (--?--). Rindy lives in Dornsife, PA.

10.2.1.3.1.11 DONA MARY STIELY is also referred to as DONNA in some sources. She was born on 9 May 1937. She was baptized on 2 January 1938, Salem (Herb's) Church, Rough and Ready, Schuylkill County, PA. She married (--?--) SARFINE. She died in November 1980, at age 43.

10.2.1.3.1.12 BEVERLY GRACE STIELY was born on 7 June 1938, Rough and Ready, Schuylkill County, PA. She was baptized on 8 July 1938, Salem (Herb's) Church, Rough and Ready, Schuylkill County, PA. She married WILLIAM H. WILLIARD, son of HOWARD W. WILLIARD and BESSIE (--?--). She died on 23 April 2014, Sun Home Hospice Care Center, Sunbury, Northumberland County, PA, at age 75. She was buried at Salem United Church of Christ Cemetery, Rough and Ready, Schuylkill County, PA.

10.2.1.3.1.12.1 GLENN LINCOLN WILLIARD was born on 12 February 1955, Ashland, Schuylkill County, PA. He died on 25 July 1965, at age 10. He was buried at Salem United Church of Christ Cemetery, Rough and Ready, Schuylkill County, PA.

10.2.1.3.1.12.2 DOUGLAS ERIC WILLIARD was born on 24 June 1969. He was baptized on 12 October 1969, Salem United Church of Christ, Rough and Ready, Schuylkill County, PA.

10.2.1.3.1.13 MARVIN STIELY was born on 20 July 1939. He died on 20 July 1939. He was buried at Salem United Church of Christ Cemetery, Rough and Ready, Schuylkill County, PA.

10.2.1.3.1.14 JESSE L. STIELY was born on 24 September 1940, Rough and Ready, Schuylkill County, PA. He died on 17 January 2015, Tremont Health and Rehabilitation Center, Tremont, Schuylkill County, PA, at age 74. He was buried on 24 January 2015, at Salem Cemetery, Rough and Ready, Schuylkill County, PA.

10.2.1.3.1.15 JERRY L. STIELY was born on 24 June 1944, Klingerstown, Schuylkill County, PA. He married **JOANNE GAIL BERGEY**, daughter of **JOHN W. BERGEY** and **HILDA M. SCHWALM**, circa 1965. He died on 23 October 2009, 327 N. Goodspring Road, Hegins, Schuylkill County, PA, at age 65, at his home. According to a newspaper obituary, Jerry was a 1963 graduate of Tri-Valley High School and a 1965 graduate of Williamsport Tech. He was employed as a heavy equipment operator by Frank Krammes Excavating, Sacramento, PA, and Pine Creek Coal Co., Spring Glen, PA.

    10.2.1.3.1.15.1 TERRI J. STIELY (see above)

        10.2.1.3.1.15.1.1 NIKKI MARIE HERB (see above)

        10.2.1.3.1.15.1.2 HEIDI ELIZABETH HERB (see above)

    10.2.1.3.1.15.2 KRIS L. STIELY (see above)

        10.2.1.3.1.15.2.1 JOHN MICHAEL STIELY (see above)

        10.2.1.3.1.15.2.2 BEN WILLIAM STIELY (see above)

10.2.1.3.1.16 PAUL ISAAC STIELY was born on 28 November 1949. He was baptized on 26 January 1950, Salem (Herb's) Church, Rough and Ready, Schuylkill County, PA.

10.2.1.3.1.17 IVAN ROGER STIELY is also referred to as **IVAN WYNN** in some sources. He was born on 16 May 1951. He was baptized on 7 June 1951, Salem (Herb's) Church, Rough and Ready, Schuylkill County, PA.

10.2.1.3.1.18 GLENN DAVID STIELY was born on 10 October 1952. He was baptized on 21 October 1952, Salem (Herb's) Church, Rough and Ready, Schuylkill County, PA. He died in 1954. He was buried at Salem (Herb's) Church Cemetery, Rough and Ready, Schuylkill County, PA.

10.2.1.3.2 GINNY KLINGER was born circa 1918. Some sources list Ginny as Allen Klinger's daughter, but she is not listed among his children in either the 1920 or 1930 Census.

10.2.1.3.3 GUY A. KLINGER was born in 1919, Pennsylvania. He married **STELLA V. KREITZER** in 1939, Salem Evangelical Lutheran and Reformed Church, Rough and Ready, Schuylkill County, PA. He died on 21 August 1971. He was buried at Salem Church Cemetery, Rough and Ready, Schuylkill County, PA.

    10.2.1.3.3.1 BARBARA KLINGER married **PAUL WILLIAM RAMBERGER**, son of **WILLIAM CLARENCE RAMBERGER** and **ANNA IRENE WOLFGANG**.

        10.2.1.3.3.1.1 KEITH RAMBERGER was born on 14 December 1964, Sunbury, Northumberland County, PA. He died on 25 July 2011, Dalmatia, Northumberland County, PA, at age 46, at his residence.

10.2.1.3.4 ESTHER DAISY KLINGER was born on 4 May 1929, Northumberland County, PA. She married **RAYMOND H. BOWMAN**. She died on 19 July 1971, Good Samaritan Hospital, PA, at age 42. She was buried on 22 July 1971, at Frieden's Cemetery, Hegins, Schuylkill County, PA. Esther was a sewing machine operator and lived in Valley View, PA.

10.2.1.4 VERNA MAE KLINGER was born on 30 March 1901. She married **STANLEY CLARK ROMBERGER**, son of **ISAIAH KLINGER ROMBERGER** and **ELMIRA CLARK**, on 4 October 1919. She died in July 1979, at age 78. She was buried at St. Michael's Church, Klingerstown, Schuylkill County, PA.

    10.2.1.4.1 QUENTIN STANLEY ROMBERGER (see above)

        10.2.1.4.1.1 DIANNE LEA ROMBERGER (see above)

            10.2.1.4.1.1.1 SHARON GALLAGHER (see above)

            10.2.1.4.1.1.2 SCOTTIE GALLAGHER (see above)

            10.2.1.4.1.1.3 STEPHANIE GALLAGHER (see above)

        10.2.1.4.1.2 DONNA LEE ROMBERGER (see above)

            10.2.1.4.1.2.1 BRIAN ROMBERGER (see above)

10.2.1.4.2 ROLAND RUSSEL ROMBERGER (see above)
 10.2.1.4.2.1 ROLAND JAMES ROMBERGER (see above)
 10.2.1.4.2.2 JOYCE ELIZABETH ROMBERGER (see above)
  10.2.1.4.2.2.1 GILLIAN LOVE (see above)
 10.2.1.4.2.3 BEVERLY VERNA ROMBERGER (see above)
  10.2.1.4.2.3.1 JESSE HARNER (see above)
  10.2.1.4.2.3.2 JAKE ROMBERGER HARNER (see above)
 10.2.1.4.2.4 GAIL ANN ROMBERGER (see above)
  10.2.1.4.2.4.1 ERIC NONNECKE (see above)
 10.2.1.4.2.5 RENEE MARY ROMBERGER (see above)
  10.2.1.4.2.5.1 PETER BREEN (see above)
  10.2.1.4.2.5.2 SCOTT BREEN (see above)
10.2.1.4.3 MARION ANNA ROMBERGER (see above)
 10.2.1.4.3.1 STEVEN EARL TROUTMAN (see above)
  10.2.1.4.3.1.1 MICHAEL TROUTMAN (see above)
  10.2.1.4.3.1.2 VALERIE TROUTMAN (see above)
 10.2.1.4.3.2 GLENN LAMAR TROUTMAN (see above)
  10.2.1.4.3.2.1 HEATHER LYNNE TROUTMAN (see above)
  10.2.1.4.3.2.2 MATTHEW JAMES TROUTMAN (see above)
  10.2.1.4.3.2.3 HILLARY APRIL TROUTMAN (see above)
 10.2.1.4.3.3 RUBY MARY TROUTMAN (see above)
  10.2.1.4.3.3.1 ANTONIO DAVID MICHETTI (see above)
  10.2.1.4.3.3.2 ROSALYNDA MARY MICHETTI (see above)
  10.2.1.4.3.3.3 ANGELINA MAE MICHETTI (see above)
  10.2.1.4.3.3.4 MARIA MELINDA MICHETTI (see above)
  10.2.1.4.3.3.5 YOLANDA MARION MICHETTI (see above)
10.2.1.4.4 LEE LAMAR ROMBERGER (see above)
 10.2.1.4.4.1 DALE LEE ROMBERGER (see above)
 10.2.1.4.4.2 JANE MARIE ROMBERGER (see above)
10.2.1.4.5 ROY ALBERT ROMBERGER (see above)
 10.2.1.4.5.1 ROBIN LEE ROMBERGER (see above)
10.2.1.4.6 MARK MARTIN ROMBERGER (see above)
 10.2.1.4.6.1 MICHAEL IRVIN ROMBERGER (see above)
10.2.1.4.7 BARBARA MARIE ROMBERGER (see above)
 10.2.1.4.7.1 VICKI LEE KOPPENHAVER (see above)
  10.2.1.4.7.1.1 ZANE DAVID ROMBERGER (see above)
 10.2.1.4.7.2 KELLY SUE KOPPENHAVER (see above)

10.2.2 CHARLES MILTON KLINGER was born on 27 June 1864, Upper Mahanoy Township, Northumberland County, PA. He married ELIZABETH SCHEIB, daughter of FRANKLIN SCHEIB and ELISABETH MOYER, on 28 March 1891, Pillow, Dauphin County, PA. He died on 19 February 1940, Erdman, Lykens Township, Dauphin County, PA, at age 75. He was buried on 24 February 1940, at Simeon Union Cemetery, Gratz, Dauphin County, PA.

 10.2.2.1 WALTER PRESTON KLINGER is also referred to as PRESTON W. in some sources. He was born on 4 July 1893, Klingerstown, Schuylkill County, PA. In 1917, when he registered for the draft in World War I, Walter was single and living in Reading, PA, where he was working as a blacksmith for the Reading Railroad. He married LYDIA H. MAURER circa 1919. He married CARRIE STUTZMAN after 1942. He died in October 1975, at age 82. Prior to his death, Walter was living in the vicinity of Wernersville, Berks County, PA.

10.2.2.1.1 FRANKLIN C. KLINGER was born on 31 March 1925, Hegins, Schuylkill County, PA. He married **FERNE M. IRVING.** He died on 10 July 2012, Messiah Village, Mechanicsburg, Cumberland County, PA, at age 87. According to a newspaper obituary, Franklin, who lived in Robesonia, served in the Navy on a submarine during World War II. Later he worked for ARCO Pipeline, Spring Township, for 36 years, retiring in 1984. He was buried at Schuylkill Memorial Park, Schuylkill Haven, Schuylkill County, PA.

> **10.2.2.1.1.1 KATHY M. KLINGER** married **GIFFORD BRINER.** Kathy lives in Mechanicsburg, PA.
>
> **10.2.2.1.1.2 LESLIE A. KLINGER.** Leslie lives in Hummelstown, PA.

10.2.2.1.2 ELEANOR KLINGER was born circa 1931.

10.2.2.1.3 MARIE KLINGER was born on 15 June 1932. She married **DONALD EUGENE ARTZ SR.**, son of **GUY ROSCOE ARTZ** and **ETHEL M. HUNTZINGER,** circa 1950, PA. She died on 11 November 1982, at age 50. She was buried at Friedens Union Cemetery, Hegins, Schuylkill County, PA. Prior to her death, Marie was living in Oswego, NY.

10.2.2.1.4 JEANNE KLINGER was born after 1940. She married **(--?--) NICHOLS.** Jeanne lives in Wylie, TX.

10.2.2.2 BEULAH ANNORA KLINGER was born on 27 July 1891. Some sources record that she was born in July 1892. Other sources record that she was born on 27 July 1887. She married **AUSTIN WALLACE COLEMAN**, son of **JOHN JACOB COLEMAN** and **SALLY LENKER,** on 16 March 1912, Simeon Lutheran Church, Gratz, Dauphin County, PA. She died on 18 October 1972, at age 85. Some sources record that she died on 14 October 1972.

> **10.2.2.2.1 MARK AUSTIN COLEMAN** was born on 13 October 1912. He was baptized on 17 November 1912, Simeon Lutheran Church, Gratz, Dauphin County, PA. He married **EVELYN MEADOWS.** He died before 2006.
>
>> **10.2.2.2.1.1 LINDA COLEMAN** was born in 1948. She married **EUGENE ATWELL.**
>>
>> **10.2.2.2.1.2 MARK COLEMAN** was born in 1951. He married **ANNA RODICHOK.**
>
> **10.2.2.2.2 ARTHUR EARL COLEMAN** was born on 17 August 1914. He was baptized on 4 October 1914, Simeon Lutheran Church, Gratz, Dauphin County, PA.
>
> **10.2.2.2.3 HILDA LUCILE COLEMAN** was born on 22 September 1915. She was baptized on 30 October 1915, Simeon Lutheran Church, Gratz, Dauphin County, PA. She married **LEO W. FLEGAL.** She died before 2006.
>
>> **10.2.2.2.3.1 TIMOTHY FLEGAL**
>>
>> **10.2.2.2.3.2 TERRY FLEGAL**
>>
>> **10.2.2.2.3.3 THEODORE FLEGAL**
>>
>> **10.2.2.2.3.4 WENDY FLEGAL**
>
> **10.2.2.2.4 SARAH E. COLEMAN** was born on 12 June 1917, Gratz, Dauphin County, PA. She married **RUSSELL L. LENKER.** She married **WILLIAM E. BECK.** She died on 14 October 2009, Carlisle Regional Medical Center, Carlisle, Cumberland County, PA, at age 92. According to a newspaper obituary, Sarah, who was also known as "Sally," lived in Carlisle and, previously, Colonial Park, PA, retired from the Commonwealth of PA Department of Community Affairs and from Nationwide Insurance Co., in Harrisburg.
>
>> **10.2.2.2.4.1 DONALD R. LENKER** was born in 1938. He married **PATRICIA S. ROBERTS.** Donald lives in Woodstock, VA.
>>
>>> **10.2.2.2.4.1.1 JEFFREY LENKER**
>>>
>>> **10.2.2.2.4.1.2 MICHAEL LENKER**
>>>
>>> **10.2.2.2.4.1.3 MEREDITH LENKER**
>
> **10.2.2.2.5 ETHEL IRENE COLEMAN** was born on 16 September 1918. She was baptized on 8 December 1918, Simeon Lutheran Church, Gratz, Dauphin County, PA. She married **GAYLORD GURTZ.** She died before 2006.
>
>> **10.2.2.2.5.1 DENNIS GURTZ** married **CAROLYN SPRING.**
>>
>> **10.2.2.2.5.2 MARTIN GURTZ** married **SHARON PATERSON.**

10.2.2.2.6 RUTH BUELLA COLEMAN was born on 1 August 1920. She was baptized on 29 August 1920, Simeon Lutheran Church, Gratz, Dauphin County, PA. She married **HOWARD LEBO.** She died before 2006.

 10.2.2.2.6.1 DEBORAH ANN LEBO was born in 1940. She married **RICHARD POHNER.**

 10.2.2.2.6.2 RICHARD LEBO was born in 1947.

 10.2.2.2.6.3 ROBERT LEBO was born in 1954. He married **CORINNE MARTIN.**

10.2.2.2.7 CHARLES JACOB COLEMAN was born on 3 October 1921. He was baptized on 20 November 1921, Simeon Lutheran Church, Gratz, Dauphin County, PA. Some sources record that he was born in 1922. He died in 1984.

10.2.2.2.8 ROBERT RAYMOND COLEMAN was born on 27 April 1924, Lykens Township, Dauphin County, PA. He was baptized on 1 June 1924, Simeon Lutheran Church, Gratz, Dauphin County, PA. He married **ANNA C. SCHLEGEL** in 1947. He died on 14 January 2006, Fox Hospital, Oneonta, NY, at age 81. According to a newspaper obituary, Robert enlisted in the Army Air Force in 1942 and served as Flight Engineer on a B-17 Flying Fortress in the Asiatic Pacific Theatre of operations, where he received a number of decorations. Later he worked for the Piasecki Helicopter Corporation and the Baldwin Locomotive Works as a Diesel Test Engineer. In 1947, he purchased a farm in Lykens Township, Dauphin County, PA. After selling the farm, he worked for the New York Farm Bureau and moved to the Catskill Mountains of New York. Later he worked in Chicago for the National American Farm Bureau Federation, eventually retiring as the Director of Special Marketing Services. He then moved back to the Catskill Mountains of New York.

 10.2.2.2.8.1 JAMES COLEMAN was born in 1950. He married **SHELLEY HUMISTON.** He married **PATRICIA GUSTIN.**

 10.2.2.2.8.2 THOMAS COLEMAN was born in 1952. He married **MARLA GINENTHAL.**

10.2.2.3 GEORGE ELMER KLINGER was born on 28 January 1896, Klingerstown, Schuylkill County, PA. At the time of his registration for the draft on June 5, 1917 for World War I, George was living in Reading, PA, where he worked as a blacksmith for the Philadelphia and Reading Railroad. He was not married. He married **LAURA MAY MINNICH,** daughter of **WILLIAM HENRY MINNICH** and **CORA ALICE HUNTZINGER,** on 2 March 1918, Friedens Evangelical Lutheran Church, Hegins, Schuylkill County, PA. He died in 1918. He was buried at Friedens Union Cemetery, Hegins, Schuylkill County, PA. His tombstone indicates "WW I."

 10.2.2.3.1 MIRIAM KLINGER is also referred to as **MERIAM ALICE KLINGER** in some sources. She was born on 28 June 1918. She married **AMBROSE J. MCDONALD,** son of **WILLIAM P. MCDONALD** and **HELEN (--?--),** after 1940. She died in July 1985, at age 67.

  10.2.2.3.1.1 WILLIAM P. MCDONALD was born on 5 January 1950, Pottsville, Schuylkill County, PA. He married **VERA (--?--).** He died on 12 January 2013, Stockton-on-Tees, England, at age 63. According to a newspaper obituary, William who was known as Bill" "lived in Stockton-on-Tees, England, where he worked more than 30 years as a groundsman for the council of Stockton. He was a 1968 graduate of Pine Grove Area High School and a veteran of the Air Force.

  Services in England took place at the Chapel of St. Bede, Teeside as well as in Schuylkill County, PA.

10.2.2.4 DANIEL CYRUS KLINGER was born on 13 November 1897. He was baptized on 8 April 1898, St. Michael's Church, Klingerstown, Schuylkill County, PA. He married **SADIE ALVERTA SNYDER,** daughter of **WILLIAM HENRY SNYDER** and **LILLIE FRANCES BROSIUS,** on 2 June 1923. He died on 2 April 1985, RD 1, Herndon, Northumberland County, PA, at age 87. He was buried on 6 April 1985, at Himmels Church, Rebuck, Washington Township, Northumberland County, PA.

 10.2.2.4.1 RAYMOND DANIEL KLINGER was born on 17 November 1923. He died in 1932.

 10.2.2.4.2 ROMAINE ELIZABETH KLINGER was born on 6 April 1935, Jordan Township, Northumberland County, PA. She married **WILLIAM H. PEIFER,** son of **EMERY E. PEIFER** and **GRACE O. (--?--),** on 27 February 1954, Urban, Northumberland County, PA. She died on 13 February 2015, Schuylkill Medical Center-South Jackson Street, Pottsville, Schuylkill County, PA, at age 79. According to a newspaper obituary, Romaine retired as a seamstress from Haven Line Industries, Schuylkill Haven, in 2001, and previously had been employed at the former

Summit Station Manufacturing Co., Pine Grove, Schuylkill County, PA. She was buried at Hetzel's Church Cemetery, Pine Grove, Schuylkill County, PA.

10.2.2.4.2.1 LEONARD D. PEIFER was born on 3 September 1954.

10.2.2.4.2.2 KAREN ANN PEIFER was born on 2 June 1965. She married **(--?--)** HOY.

10.2.2.4.2.2.1 JADZIA HOY

10.2.2.4.3 ARLENE DANETTA KLINGER was born on 2 January 1938, Northumberland County, PA. She married JAMES WILBERT, son of GEORGE E. WILBERT and CARRIE M. **(--?--)**, on 31 December 1955, Lutheran Parsonage, Millersburg, Dauphin County, PA. Arlene and James lived in Millersburg, PA. Arlene worked for Muskin Shoe Co., while James was a mechanic for Coca-Cola in Millersburg.

10.2.2.4.3.1 JAMES E. WILBERT was born on 1 August 1956, Harrisburg, Dauphin County, PA.

10.2.2.4.3.2 RODNEY C. WILBERT was born on 4 September 1960, Harrisburg, Dauphin County, PA.

10.2.2.4.3.3 MONICA LOU WILBERT was born on 12 January 1963, Harrisburg, Dauphin County, PA.

10.2.2.4.4 MELVIN WILLIAM KLINGER was born on 24 April 1942, Northumberland County, PA. He married JACKIE CONRAD on 18 January 1964, St. Matthew Lutheran Church, Shamokin Dam, Snyder County, PA. Melvin was a machine operator at Muskin Shoe Co., Millersburg, PA. He lived near Dalmatia, Northumberland County, PA.

10.2.2.4.4.1 MELVIN WILLIAM KLINGER JR. was born on 13 January 1965, Sunbury, Northumberland County, PA.

10.2.2.5 KATHERINE ESTELLA KLINGER also went by the name of KATIE. She was born on 10 January 1900. She was baptized on 22 April 1900, St. Michael's Church, Klingerstown, Schuylkill County, PA. She married WILLIAM M. RENNINGER circa 1923. Some sources suggest that she and WILLIAM M. RENNINGER were married circa 1920. She is also referred to as KATHERINE REININGER in some sources. She died in February 1983, Berks County, PA, at age 83.

10.2.2.5.1 LEROY RENNINGER

10.2.2.5.2 EARL W. RENNINGER was born on 4 May 1924, Branch Dale, Schuylkill County, PA. He married ESTHER MARIE SCHNECK on 11 December 1943. He died on 17 May 2009, Schuylkill Medical Center-East Norwegian Street, Pottsville, Schuylkill County, PA, at age 85. According to a newspaper obituary, Earl was a decorated veteran of World War II. He served in the Army 1943-1946 as a technical sergeant with Battery C, 669th Field Artillery Battalion. He received the Good Conduct Medal, the European, African, Middle Eastern Campaign Medal with one Bronze Star as well as the World War II Victory Medal. Later, Earl was the owner of Renninger's Garage, Newtown, where he worked all his life, providing mechanical and towing services as well as being a service provider for AAA. In 1953, Earl acquired ownership of Earl Renninger Inc., a school bus company, which has provided transportation for the Minersville Area School District for 56 years. He was buried on 21 May 2009, at Schuylkill Memorial Park, Schuylkill Haven, Schuylkill County, PA.

10.2.2.5.2.1 KAY RENNINGER married **(--?--)** KOCH. Kay lives in Newtown, PA.

10.2.2.5.2.2 DALE RENNINGER married DOLLY **(--?--)**.

10.2.2.5.2.3 WILLIAM RENNINGER married DEBORAH **(--?--)**. William lives in Newtown, PA.

10.2.2.5.3 ELSIE E. RENNINGER was born circa 1927, Pennsylvania. She married **(--?--)** MOYER. Elsie lives in Newtown, PA.

10.2.2.5.4 SARAH E. RENNINGER married **(--?--)** WETZEL. She was born circa August 1928, Pennsylvania.

10.2.2.6 MARTHA EDNA KLINGER was born on 4 March 1902. She was baptized on 25 April 1902, St. Michael's Church, Klingerstown, Schuylkill County, PA. She died on 28 April 1902. She was buried at St. Michael's Church Cemetery, Klingerstown, Schuylkill County, PA.

10.2.2.7 FLORENCE VIOLA KLINGER was born in July 1903, Dauphin County, PA. She died on 13 November 1920, at age 17. She was buried at Simeon Union Cemetery, Gratz, Dauphin County, PA.

10.2.2.8 CLAUDE ALBERT KLINGER is also referred to as **CLOYD** in some sources. He was born on 9 October 1903. He married **SADIE M. DUNKELBERGER** on 16 October 1924, Salem (Herb's) Church, Rough and Ready, Schuylkill County, PA. He married **HELEN SNYDER** after 1959. He died in 1983. He was buried at Frieden's Union Cemetery, Hegins, Schuylkill County, PA.

    10.2.2.8.1 BETTY MAE KLINGER was born on 4 May 1925. She married **WAYNE LESTER WOLFGANG**, son of **DAVID WOLFGANG** and **CARRIE SCHLEGEL**. She died on 22 September 2001, at age 76.

    10.2.2.8.2 CLAUDE SYLVESTER KLINGER JR. was born on 20 July 1927, Hegins, Schuylkill County, PA. He was baptized on 26 November 1927, Frieden's Reformed Church, Hegins, Schuylkill County, PA. He married **PHYLLIS SCHEIB** circa 1946. He died on 12 July 2001, South Lebanon Township, Lebanon County, PA, at age 73. He was buried at Indiantown Gap National Cemetery, Annville, Lebanon County, PA.

        10.2.2.8.2.1 DENNIS KLINGER

        10.2.2.8.2.2 DAVID KLINGER

        10.2.2.8.2.3 BRENDA KLINGER

        10.2.2.8.2.4 REBECCA KLINGER married **LOREN SNYDER**.

    10.2.2.8.3 DOLORES CATHERINE KLINGER was born on 4 June 1931, Hegins, Schuylkill County, PA. She died on 14 June 2007, at age 76.

    10.2.2.8.4 ROBERT HAROLD KLINGER was born on 29 July 1933, Hegins Township, Schuylkill County, PA. He died on 24 March 2005, Hershey Medical Center, Dauphin County, PA, at age 71. According to a newspaper obituary, Robert was a salesman for Mack Trucks, Inc., in Harrisburg. He served in the U.S. Army in Korea. He was buried on 29 March 2005, at Indiantown Gap National Cemetery, Annville, Lebanon County, PA.

        10.2.2.8.4.1 AUDREY M. KLINGER married **ROBERT SHENK**. She lived in Annville, Lebanon County, PA.

            10.2.2.8.4.1.1 ROSE SHENK

        10.2.2.8.4.2 BRIDGET C. KLINGER married **SHAWN WHEELER**. She lived in York Haven, PA.

            10.2.2.8.4.2.1 SHELBY WHEELER

            10.2.2.8.4.2.2 TAYLOR WHEELER

10.2.2.9 CHARLES EDGAR KLINGER was born on 6 October 1905. He married **HANNAH DANIEL** circa 1932. He died circa 1981, Harrisburg, Dauphin County, PA. He was buried at Simeon Union Cemetery, Gratz, Dauphin County, PA.

10.2.2.10 THOMAS MARCUS KLINGER was born on 7 September 1909. He was baptized on 9 October 1909, St. Michael's Church, Klingerstown, Schuylkill County, PA. He married **HANNAH DANIELS**, daughter of **GERMAN DANIELS** and **SALLIE E. WELKER**. He married **EVA M. HOFFMAN**, daughter of **HARVEY CLAIR HOFFMAN** and **MARY J. STARR**, on 26 August 1940, Zion (Klinger's) Church, Erdman, Lykens Township, Dauphin County, PA. He died on 16 October 1968, at age 59. He was buried at Zion (Klinger's) Church Cemetery, Erdman, Lykens Township, Dauphin County, PA.

    10.2.2.10.1 THOMAS CLAIR KLINGER was born on 31 May 1941, Erdman, Dauphin County, PA. He was baptized on 18 October 1941, Zion (Klinger's) Church, Erdman, Lykens Township, Dauphin County, PA. He married **MARIAN E. LAUDENSLAGER** on 2 July 1962. He died on 17 March 2014, Harrisburg Hospital, Harrisburg, Dauphin County, PA, at age 72.

        10.2.2.10.1.1 KATHRYN ANN KLINGER married **KERRY L. KOPPENHEFFER**.

            10.2.2.10.1.1.1 MINDY LYNN KOPPENHEFFER

            10.2.2.10.1.1.2 JENNIFER LEE KOPPENHEFFER married (--?--) **MOCK**.

                10.2.2.10.1.1.2.1 JESSICA MOCK

        10.2.2.10.1.2 LYNN EUGENE KLINGER was born on 17 October 1958. He died in October 1982.

        10.2.2.10.1.3 RANDY LEE KLINGER was born on 5 February 1960, Harrisburg, Dauphin County, PA. He died on 24 April 2014, Halifax, Dauphin County, PA, at age 54.

10.2.2.10.2 ROY ALLEN KLINGER was born on 28 January 1945. He was baptized on 2 March 1946, Zion (Klinger's) Church, Erdman, Lykens Township, Dauphin County, PA. He married **PEGGY (--?--).** In 2008, Roy was living in Erdman, Dauphin County, PA.

10.2.2.10.3 MARY LOU KLINGER was born on 30 May 1948, Pottsville, Schuylkill County, PA. She was baptized on 6 November 1948, Zion (Klinger's) Church, Erdman, Lykens Township, Dauphin County, PA. She married **KARL DEIBLER.** She died on 17 May 2008, York Hospital, York, York County, PA, at age 59, as a result of an auto accident. According to a newspaper obituary, Mary Lou was a 1966 graduate of Upper Dauphin High School, Elizabethville, and was employed as a beautician at Double Take Hair Salon in Manchester. She lived in Lewisberry. She was buried on 22 May 2008, at Zion (Klinger's) Church Cemetery, Erdman, Dauphin County, PA.

    10.2.2.10.3.1 LESLIE KLINGER

    10.2.2.10.3.2 ANN DEIBLER married **DAVID WOLF.**

10.2.2.10.4 LARRY LEE KLINGER was born on 6 December 1960. He was baptized on 5 November 1961, Zion (Klinger's) Church, Erdman, Lykens Township, Dauphin County, PA. He married **LORI (--?--).** In 2008, Larry was living in Spring Glen, Schuylkill County, PA.

10.2.2.11 RAY AUSTIN KLINGER is also referred to as **AUSTIN RAY KLINGER** in some sources. He was born on 14 August 1911. He was baptized on 26 September 1911, Simeon Lutheran Church, Gratz, Dauphin County, PA. He was confirmed on 27 November 1926 Zion (Klinger's) Church, Erdman, Lykens Township, Dauphin County, PA. He married **ELVA M. TSCHOPP** on 19 September 1932, Zion (Klinger's) Church, Erdman, Lykens Township, Dauphin County, PA. He died on 8 December 1979, at age 68. He was buried at Riverview Memorial Gardens, Halifax, Dauphin County, PA.

10.2.2.11.1 ROBERT EUGENE KLINGER was born on 6 February 1933. He was baptized on 25 December 1934, Zion (Klinger's) Church, Erdman, Lykens Township, Dauphin County, PA.

10.2.2.11.2 RUTH ESTHER KLINGER was born on 21 November 1934. She was baptized on 25 December 1934, Zion (Klinger's) Church, Erdman, Lykens Township, Dauphin County, PA.

10.2.2.11.3 KENNETH LAMAR KLINGER was born on 19 July 1936. He was baptized on 9 November 1936, Zion (Klinger's) Church, Erdman, Lykens Township, Dauphin County, PA.

10.2.2.11.4 SHIRLEY ANN KLINGER was born on 10 August 1941. She was baptized on 7 November 1941, Zion (Klinger's) Church, Erdman, Lykens Township, Dauphin County, PA.

10.2.2.11.5 RONALD AUSTIN KLINGER was born on 16 June 1943. He was baptized on 4 September 1948, Zion (Klinger's) Church, Erdman, Lykens Township, Dauphin County, PA.

10.2.2.11.6 JACKY LEE KLINGER was born on 23 November 1945. She was baptized on 4 September 1948, Zion (Klinger's) Church, Erdman, Lykens Township, Dauphin County, PA.

10.2.2.12 EVA MAY KLINGER was born on 6 May 1915. She was baptized on 24 July 1915, St. Michael's Church, Klingerstown, Schuylkill County, PA. She married **RAY WOODROW WILSON SHADLE,** son of **JAMES PHILLIPS SHADLE** and **EMMA BERTHA ROTHERMEL,** on 13 January 1932, Zion (Klinger's) Church, Erdman, Lykens Township, Dauphin County, PA. She married **FRANCIS I. PAUL** on 19 April 1958, Simeon Lutheran Church, Gratz, Dauphin County, PA. She died circa 1973, Dauphin County, PA. She was buried at Simeon Union Cemetery, Gratz, Dauphin County, PA.

10.2.2.12.1 RUSSELL RUE SCHADLE was born on 30 October 1934, Klingerstown, Schuylkill County, PA. He married **BETTY LORRAINE BINGAMAN,** daughter of **JOHN HENRY BINGAMAN** and **ALICE E. PHILLIPS,** on 29 August 1959, Simeon Union Church, Gratz, Dauphin County, PA. He died on 12 February 2010, Harrisburg Hospice Center, Harrisburg, Dauphin County, PA, at age 75. He was buried on 16 February 2010, at Simeon United Lutheran Church Cemetery, Gratz, Dauphin County, PA.

    10.2.2.12.1.1 ALICE MAE SHADLE (see above)

    10.2.2.12.1.2 JOHN RUSSELL SHADLE (see above)

10.2.2.12.2 VIOLET JANE SCHADLE was born on 19 May 1932, RR1, Dornsife, Northumberland County, PA. She married **RAYMOND GEORGE WILLIAMS** on 11 February 1950. She died on 28 October 2006, Sacramento, Dauphin County, PA, at age 74. According to a newspaper obituary, Violet lived on the Honeymoon Trail, Sacramento. She was a homemaker. When she was younger, she sold produce in the Tremont and Pottsville areas.

    10.2.2.12.2.1 GLENN P. WILLIAMS SR. married **LOIS COTNER** circa 1977. He died in 2005.

10.2.2.12.2.1.1 GLENN P. WILLIAMS JR.

10.2.2.12.2.2 BRIAN GRIFFITH WILLIAMS married SHARON WILLIARD circa 1983.

10.2.2.12.2.2.1 JAMES WILLIAMS

10.2.2.12.2.3 SHEILA J. WILLIAMS married STEVEN P. REED, son of PAUL DANIEL REED and EVA KATHRYN RABUCK, circa 1971.

10.2.2.12.2.3.1 SCOTT REED

10.2.2.12.2.4 HOLLY M. WILLIAMS married (--?--) ADAIR circa 1980.

10.2.2.12.2.4.1 JENNIFER ADAIR

10.2.2.12.2.5 GARY RAMON WILLIAMS was born on 5 September 1950. He died on 17 August 1969, at age 18. He was buried on 20 August 1969, at St. Paul's (Artz's) Church, Sacramento, Schuylkill County, PA.

10.2.2.12.3 LEON MARK SCHADLE was born on 13 March 1936, Sacramento, Schuylkill County, PA. He married NANCY K. KOPPENHAVER, daughter of ELWOOD J. KOPPENHAVER and ROMIE ONEIDA KIMMEL, on 8 October 1955. He died on 2 March 2006, Tower City, Schuylkill County, PA, at age 69. He was buried on 6 March 2006, at Greenwood Cemetery, Tower City, Schuylkill County, PA. According to a newspaper obituary, Leon lived at 101 E. Grand Ave, Tower City. He was the owner of Schadles Barber Shop for 49 years, he also owned and operated Schadles Garage for 32 years.

10.2.2.12.3.1 YVONNE LEE SHADLE (see above)

10.2.2.12.3.1.1 JASON ADAMS (see above)

10.2.2.12.3.1.2 BRETT ADAMS (see above)

10.2.2.12.3.2 LORI SHADLE (see above)

10.2.2.12.3.2.1 JESSICA BOYD (see above)

10.2.2.12.3.2.2 BRIAN BOYD (see above)

10.2.2.12.3.3 L. MARK SHADLE (see above)

10.2.2.12.3.3.1 ALYSSA SHADLE (see above)

10.2.2.12.3.3.2 MEGAN SHADLE (see above)

10.2.2.12.4 JAMES CHARLES SCHADLE was born on 4 July 1940, Sacramento, Schuylkill County, PA. He was baptized on 3 December 1940, Zion (Klinger's) Church, Erdman, Lykens Township, Dauphin County, PA. He married LORRAINE ESTHER KOPPENHAVER, daughter of HENRY FRANKLIN KOPPENHAVER and LULU ELLEN MILLER, on 15 April 1961, Erdman, Dauphin County, PA. He and LORRAINE ESTHER KOPPENHAVER were divorced in 1974. He died on 16 February 2005, at age 64. He was buried at Simeon United Lutheran Church Cemetery, Gratz, Dauphin County, PA.

10.2.2.12.4.1 LYNN CHARLES SHADLE (see above)

10.2.2.12.4.2 STEVEN JAMES SHADLE (see above)

10.2.2.12.4.2.1 STEVEN REID SHADLE (see above)

10.2.2.12.4.3 REBECCA SUE SHADLE (see above)

10.2.2.12.4.3.1 ALEXIS NICOLE MENTZER (see above)

10.2.2.12.5 RAY DALE SCHADLE is also referred to as ROY DALE SCHADLE in some sources. He was born on 26 March 1942. He was baptized on 25 April 1942, Zion (Klinger's) Church, Erdman, Lykens Township, Dauphin County, PA. He married JENNIE ARLENE HEDDINGS on 18 April 1964, Zion (Klinger's) Church, Erdman, Lykens Township, Dauphin County, PA.

10.2.2.12.5.1 GINA L SHADLE married JAMES ROACH circa 1984.

10.2.2.12.5.1.1 BRANDON TYLER ROACH

10.2.2.12.5.1.2 TRENT GARRICK ROACH was born on 2 December 1992.

10.2.2.12.5.2 LYNNETTE SHADLE

10.2.2.12.6 ELLEN PAUL married (--?--) JOHNSTON. An obituary for Ellen's brother Leon lists Ellen as his sister, but it is unclear whether her father was Ray Shadle or Francis Paul.

10.2.2.12.7 KAY ANN PAUL was born on 11 January 1946. She married EUGENE P. MATTER on 29 January 1966, Zion (Klinger's) Lutheran Church, Erdman, Dauphin County, PA. She died on 9

November 2009, at age 63. She was buried at St. Peter's (Hoffman's) United Church of Christ Cemetery, Lykens, Dauphin County, PA.

10.2.2.12.7.1 TINA MATTER

10.2.2.12.7.2 EUGENE MATTER JR.

10.2.2.12.7.3 DEWAYNE L. MATTER was born on 17 May 1968. He died on 19 May 1968.

10.2.2.12.8 INFANT PAUL was born in February 1950. He/she died on 14 February 1950.

10.2.3 AGNES KLINGER was born in 1865. Some sources record that she was born circa 1868. She married DANIEL SCHADEL WIEST, son of MOSES MERKEL WIEST and MARIA SCHADEL. She married CHARLES K. HERB on 21 May 1904, St. Michael's Lutheran Church, Klingerstown, Schuylkill County, PA. She died in 1937. She was buried at St. Michael's Lutheran Church Cemetery, Klingerstown, Schuylkill County, PA.

10.2.3.1 MARIE HELEN HERB was born on 31 March 1906. She married REV. RAYMOND A. KLINE, son of NOAH KLINE and MARIA E NACE, circa 1923. She died on 8 April 1981, at age 75. She was buried at Mount Hope Cemetery, Myerstown, Lebanon County, PA.

10.2.3.1.1 HELEN KLINE was born circa January 1926.

10.2.3.1.2 RAYMOND A. KLINE JR. was born circa 1927.

10.2.3.1.3 MARGUERITE KLINE was born circa 1928.

10.2.4 ALBERT HYRAM KLINGER was born in 1872. He married MABEL M. REBUCK circa 1913. Some sources suggest that he and MABEL M. REBUCK were married after 1920 because, in the 1920 Census, Mabel was listed in Albert's household as single and a servant. Albert was also listed as single. He died on 25 March 1960. He was buried at St. Michael's Church Cemetery, Klingerstown, Schuylkill County, PA.

10.2.4.1 KATIE M. KLINGER was born on 14 February 1917, Klingerstown, Schuylkill County, PA. She married JAY SMELTZ. She died on 16 April 2009, Sunbury Community Hospital Skilled Care Unit, Sunbury, Northumberland County, PA, at age 92. According to a newspaper obituary, Katie lived in Herndon, PA, and was a homemaker and cleaned the offices at Meckley's Limestone Inc. and also area homes. She was buried on 20 April 2009, at Himmel's Church Cemetery, Rebuck, Northumberland County, PA.

10.2.4.1.1 CARL SMELTZ married LINDA (--?--).

10.2.4.1.1.1 HEATHER SMELTZ married SCOTT FEESE.

10.2.4.1.1.1.1 JACOB FEESE

10.2.4.1.2 BRAD SMELTZ married JEN (--?--).

10.2.4.1.3 MATTHEW SMELTZ married NATALIE (--?--).

10.2.4.1.4 NANCY SMELTZ died in 1950, in infancy.

10.2.4.2 VINNIE A. KLINGER is also referred to as VIENNA KLINGER in some sources. She was born circa 1919, Pennsylvania. She married WALTER L. KLOCK, son of DANIEL N. KLOCK and MARTHA M. ERDMAN, on 2 June 1940, at the Lutheran parsonage, Herndon, Jackson Township, Northumberland County, PA, the Rev. Charles Snyder officiating.

10.2.4.2.1 DORIS KLOCK married CARL D. KAHLER circa 1961, St. Peter's Lutheran Church, Red Cross, Northumberland County, PA.

10.2.4.2.1.1 DANIEL LEROY KAHLER

10.2.4.2.1.2 TIMOTHY KAHLER married MISTY (--?--).

10.2.4.2.1.2.1 COURTNEY M. KAHLER was born on 27 May 1987.

10.2.4.2.1.3 ANDREW KAHLER

10.2.4.2.1.4 CATHERINE KAHLER married BRYAN J. ERB, son of RICKIE ERB and JANET GEMBERLING, on 12 December 1998, Himmel's Church, Rebuck, Washington Township, Northumberland County, PA.

10.2.4.2.2 SANDRA KLOCK married LEE E. REED, son of JOHN W. REED SR. and EDNA MICHAELS.

10.2.4.2.2.1 TODD REED married STACY DUNSWORTH, daughter of MIKE DUNSWORTH and KRIS (--?--).

10.2.4.2.2.1.1 CLAY MICHAEL REED

10.2.4.2.2.1.2 CONNOR LEE REED was born on 8 December 1993.

10.2.4.2.2.2 TY REED married **TRACY SCHEIB**. He lived in Gratz, Dauphin County, PA.

10.2.4.2.2.2.1 (--?--) REED was born on 27 August 1996, Polyclinic Medical Center, Harrisburg, Dauphin County, PA.

10.2.4.2.2.2.2 (--?--) REED was born circa 1999, Polyclinic Hospital, Harrisburg, Dauphin County, PA.

10.2.4.2.2.3 TARYN REED

10.2.4.3 WALTER A. KLINGER was born circa 1920, Pennsylvania. He died before 2009.

10.2.4.4 HOMER KLINGER was born on 8 April 1921. He died on 29 July 1921.

10.2.4.5 GEORGE R. KLINGER was born on 20 October 1924, Pennsylvania. He died on 6 February 1997, at age 72. Prior to his death, George was living in the Klingerstown, PA, area.

10.2.4.6 CHARLES M. KLINGER was born circa 1927, Pennsylvania. He died before 2009.

10.2.4.7 MYRTLE ELIZA KLINGER was born on 3 November 1928. She died on 7 March 1944, at age 15. She was buried at St. Michael's Church Cemetery, Klingerstown, Schuylkill County, PA.

10.2.4.8 BETTY A. KLINGER was born on 7 May 1930. She married **(--?--) WEHRY**. She died on 15 March 2004, at age 73.

10.2.4.9 PAULINE GRACE KLINGER was born on 30 October 1934. She was baptized on 10 June 1935, St. Michael's Church, Klingerstown, Schuylkill County, PA. She married **(--?--) KLOUSER**. She died on 14 May 2002, at age 67.

10.2.4.10 KENNETH RAYMOND KLINGER was born on 12 July 1937. He was baptized on 26 December 1937, St. Michael's Church, Klingerstown, Schuylkill County, PA. He died in March 1993, at age 55.

10.2.5 WILLIAM OSCAR KLINGER was born on 11 June 1874. He was baptized on 13 September 1874, Salem (Herb's) Church, Rough and Ready, Schuylkill County, PA. He married **MABEL PEARL KLINGER**, daughter of **GEORGE M. KLINGER** and **JULIANN KOPPENHAVER**, circa 1899. He died on 16 December 1965, at age 91. He was buried at St. Michael's Lutheran and Reformed Church Cemetery, Klingerstown, Schuylkill County, PA.

10.2.5.1 CARLOS EDWIN KLINGER (see above)

10.2.5.2 KATIE ALMEDA KLINGER (see above)

10.2.5.2.1 GALEN OSCAR KLINGER (see above)

10.2.5.2.1.1 GARY OSCAR KLINGER (see above)

10.2.5.2.2 IDA LORETTA KLINGER (see above)

10.2.5.2.2.1 LESTER RUFUS HARNER (see above)

10.2.5.2.2.1.1 BRENDA LOU HARNER (see above)

10.2.5.2.2.1.2 BRYANT KIETH HARNER (see above)

10.2.5.2.2.2 CAROLYN DOLLY HARNER (see above)

10.2.5.2.2.3 MARILYN IRENE HARNER (see above)

10.2.5.2.2.3.1 THOMAS LEE SHAFFER (see above)

10.2.5.2.2.3.2 MINDY SHAFFER (see above)

10.2.5.2.2.3.3 TIMOTHY SHAFFER (see above)

10.2.5.2.2.4 RICHARD DEAN HARNER (see above)

10.2.5.2.2.4.1 RICHARD HARNER (see above)

10.2.5.2.2.4.2 JAMES HARNER (see above)

10.2.5.2.3 MELBA K. KLINGER (see above)

10.2.5.2.3.1 DENNIS RAY CROUTHARMEL (see above)

10.2.5.2.3.2 LARRY CURTIS CROUTHARMEL (see above)

10.2.5.2.3.3 TERRY GENE CROUTHARMEL (see above)

10.2.5.2.3.4 KAREN DIANE CROUTHARMEL (see above)

10.2.5.2.3.5 CARL ALLEN CROUTHARMEL (see above)

10.2.5.2.3.6 DARRYL LEE CROUTHARMEL (see above)

  10.2.5.2.4 CHESTER LEROY KLINGER (see above)
   10.2.5.2.4.1 JEAN PAUL KLINGER (see above)
   10.2.5.2.4.2 MICHAEL A. KLINGER (see above)
   10.2.5.2.4.3 BONITA KLINGER (see above)
   10.2.5.2.4.4 SUSAN KLINGER (see above)
   10.2.5.2.4.5 TRUDY KLINGER (see above)
   10.2.5.2.4.6 DAVID DEAN KLINGER (see above)
   10.2.5.2.4.7 STEVEN LEROY KLINGER (see above)
  10.2.5.2.5 VIOLET BETTY KLINGER (see above)
   10.2.5.2.5.1 TODD B. REBUCK (see above)
    10.2.5.2.5.1.1 SHAWN REBUCK (see above)
   10.2.5.2.5.2 TONYA L. REBUCK (see above)
    10.2.5.2.5.2.1 JAYNA KATIE REINHARD (see above)
  10.2.5.2.6 EILEEN MAY KLINGER (see above)
   10.2.5.2.6.1 CAROL LEITZEL (see above)
    10.2.5.2.6.1.1 KELLY YVONNE ROMBERGER (see above)
     10.2.5.2.6.1.1.1 MYKENNA ADELL MUSOLINO (see above)
    10.2.5.2.6.1.2 KRISTIE ANN ROMBERGER (see above)
   10.2.5.2.6.2 GLENN ELDON LEITZEL (see above)
    10.2.5.2.6.2.1 RAHN LEITZEL (see above)
    10.2.5.2.6.2.2 AMANDA LEITZEL (see above)
   10.2.5.2.6.3 ANNETTE ANGELA LEITZEL (see above)
10.2.5.3 STELLA MAY KLINGER (see above)
 10.2.5.3.1 LEON OSCAR KLINGER (see above)
  10.2.5.3.1.1 GENE KLINGER (see above)
   10.2.5.3.1.1.1 TAMMY KLINGER (see above)
    10.2.5.3.1.1.1.1 MICHAEL NEISWENDER (see above)
   10.2.5.3.1.1.2 MICHAEL KLINGER (see above)
  10.2.5.3.1.2 DOROTHY KLINGER (see above)
  10.2.5.3.1.3 DIANE M. KLINGER (see above)
   10.2.5.3.1.3.1 HARRY MAUSSER (see above)
    10.2.5.3.1.3.1.1 ASHLEY MAUSSER (see above)
    10.2.5.3.1.3.1.2 ALISA MAUSSER (see above)
    10.2.5.3.1.3.1.3 AMANDA MAUSSER (see above)
    10.2.5.3.1.3.1.4 ALEXIS MAUSSER (see above)
   10.2.5.3.1.3.2 DEBBIE MAUSSER (see above)
  10.2.5.3.1.4 JOY ANNE KLINGER (see above)
   10.2.5.3.1.4.1 BRENDA SCHADEL (see above)
  10.2.5.3.1.5 JAMES LEE KLINGER (see above)
   10.2.5.3.1.5.1 SHERRI LEE KLINGER (see above)
    10.2.5.3.1.5.1.1 BRENT ALLEN MESSNER (see above)
     10.2.5.3.1.5.1.1.1 CAMERON A. MESSNER (see above)
    10.2.5.3.1.5.1.2 BRANDON JAMES MESSNER (see above)
  10.2.5.3.1.6 LEON OSCAR KLINGER JR. (see above)
   10.2.5.3.1.6.1 PAMELA SUE KLINGER (see above)
    10.2.5.3.1.6.1.1 BROOKE AMANDA MILLARD (see above)
   10.2.5.3.1.6.2 MICHELLE KLINGER (see above)

10.2.5.3.1.7 ROSE MARIE KLINGER (see above)
    10.2.5.3.1.7.1 RADELL FRANTZ (see above)
10.2.5.3.1.8 RODNEY RAY KLINGER (see above)
    10.2.5.3.1.8.1 JENIFER KLINGER (see above)
    10.2.5.3.1.8.2 JASON KLINGER (see above)
10.2.5.3.2 ALVIN ELIAS KLINGER (see above)
    10.2.5.3.2.1 CAROLYN KLINGER (see above)
        10.2.5.3.2.1.1 JULIE BUFFINGTON (see above)
        10.2.5.3.2.1.2 ANN BUFFINGTON (see above)
    10.2.5.3.2.2 KENNETH ALVIN KLINGER (see above)
        10.2.5.3.2.2.1 CATHY S. KLINGER (see above)
        10.2.5.3.2.2.2 MICHAEL S. KLINGER (see above)
        10.2.5.3.2.2.3 LORI ANN KLINGER (see above)
    10.2.5.3.2.3 SANDRA LEE KLINGER (see above)
        10.2.5.3.2.3.1 KERRY LAMAR WILLIARD (see above)
        10.2.5.3.2.3.2 DAVID ALLEN WILLIARD (see above)
        10.2.5.3.2.3.3 MELISSA WILLIARD (see above)
10.2.5.4 VENA ALPHA KLINGER (see above)
    10.2.5.4.1 MARLIN LEE KLINGER (see above)
        10.2.5.4.1.1 MARLIN LAMAR KLINGER JR. (see above)
            10.2.5.4.1.1.1 MATTHEW KLINGER (see above)
        10.2.5.4.1.2 DENNIS ERROL KLINGER (see above)
            10.2.5.4.1.2.1 DOUGLAS KLINGER (see above)
            10.2.5.4.1.2.2 TRACY KLINGER (see above)
        10.2.5.4.1.3 CAROL ANN KLINGER (see above)
            10.2.5.4.1.3.1 CHRIS HEPLER (see above)
            10.2.5.4.1.3.2 JAMES HEPLER (see above)
        10.2.5.4.1.4 CYNTHIA LOUISE KLINGER (see above)
            10.2.5.4.1.4.1 BRANDON WEDDE (see above)
        10.2.5.4.1.5 TIMOTHY SCOTT KLINGER (see above)
    10.2.5.4.2 ARLENE M. SEIGER (see above)
        10.2.5.4.2.1 ELAINE BROWN (see above)
            10.2.5.4.2.1.1 MICHAEL REED (see above)
        10.2.5.4.2.2 LYNN BROWN (see above)
            10.2.5.4.2.2.1 MATTHEW BROWN (see above)
            10.2.5.4.2.2.2 SAMANTHA BROWN (see above)
        10.2.5.4.2.3 MICHELLE BROWN (see above)
            10.2.5.4.2.3.1 JOSEPH RAUTZAHN (see above)
    10.2.5.4.3 MARGARET FAY STROHECKER (see above)
    10.2.5.4.4 MABEL SAVILLA STROHECKER (see above)
    10.2.5.4.5 ROBERT NEAL STROHECKER (see above)
    10.2.5.4.6 LUCILLA MAE STROHECKER (see above)
10.2.5.5 HOMER ALVIN KLINGER (see above)
    10.2.5.5.1 JOAN EMILY KLINGER (see above)
        10.2.5.5.1.1 ROBIN S. BARNES (see above)
        10.2.5.5.1.2 JEFFREY S. BARNES (see above)
        10.2.5.5.1.3 ELIZABETH BARNES (see above)

10.2.5.6 RALPH RAYMOND KLINGER (see above)
    10.2.5.6.1 SUSIE E. KLINGER (see above)
    10.2.5.6.2 ERNEST L. KLINGER (see above)
    10.2.5.6.3 RACHEL P. KLINGER (see above)
    10.2.5.6.4 LAMAR R. KLINGER (see above)
        10.2.5.6.4.1 CHARLENE KAY KLINGER (see above)
            10.2.5.6.4.1.1 SARAH ELIZABETH WOODRING (see above)
            10.2.5.6.4.1.2 EMILY WOODRING (see above)
        10.2.5.6.4.2 BONITA EILEEN KLINGER (see above)
            10.2.5.6.4.2.1 ASHLEY JAMES SNYDER (see above)
                10.2.5.6.4.2.1.1 ALEXANDRA GRACE SNYDER (see above)
            10.2.5.6.4.2.2 ALEXIS LAMAR SNYDER (see above)
        10.2.5.6.4.3 BRIAN LAMAR KLINGER (see above)
            10.2.5.6.4.3.1 TRISHIA NICOLE KLINGER (see above)
            10.2.5.6.4.3.2 ALYSSA MARIE KLINGER (see above)
        10.2.5.6.4.4 TODD LAMAR KLINGER (see above)
            10.2.5.6.4.4.1 DELANEY KATHERINE KLINGER (see above)
            10.2.5.6.4.4.2 RHETT CHARLES KLINGER (see above)
    10.2.5.6.5 BRYANT R. KLINGER (see above)
10.2.5.7 RAY MELVIN KLINGER (see above)
10.2.5.8 HELEN IRENE KLINGER (see above)
    10.2.5.8.1 GLENN D. WOLFGANG (see above)
    10.2.5.8.2 MAE IRENE WOLFGANG (see above)
    10.2.5.8.3 ALLEN STANLEY WOLFGANG (see above)
    10.2.5.8.4 EARL ALFRED WOLFGANG (see above)
10.2.5.9 LUCY ALVENA KLINGER (see above)
    10.2.5.9.1 JACKY L. CLARK (see above)
    10.2.5.9.2 ANNA G. CLARK (see above)
        10.2.5.9.2.1 STEVEN C. MILLER (see above)
    10.2.5.9.3 PAUL M. CLARK (see above)
        10.2.5.9.3.1 PHILIP G. CLARK (see above)
            10.2.5.9.3.1.1 DOMINIQUE CLARK (see above)
10.2.5.10 EVA JULIANA KLINGER (see above)
    10.2.5.10.1 RICHARD C. BROWN (see above)
    10.2.5.10.2 SANDRA M. BROWN (see above)
10.2.5.11 PAUL WILLIAM KLINGER (see above)
    10.2.5.11.1 SHARON SANDRA KLINGER (see above)
        10.2.5.11.1.1 JEFFREY WILLIAM ERDMAN (see above)
        10.2.5.11.1.2 CHRIS MARIE ERDMAN (see above)
    10.2.5.11.2 DONALD PAUL KLINGER (see above)
        10.2.5.11.2.1 ERIC DONALD KLINGER (see above)
        10.2.5.11.2.2 LORIANN KLINGER (see above)
    10.2.5.11.3 DONNA MARIE KLINGER (see above)
10.2.5.12 GUY JUNIOR KLINGER (see above)

10.2.6 HEYRAM A. KLINGER was born in February 1878, Pennsylvania. The 1900 Census lists "Heyram" as a son of Marcus and Elizabeth Klinger, but it is likely that this listing is a reference to their son Albert Hyram," although the birthdate appears to be inaccurate. The 1900 Census indicates that Elizabeth was the mother of only 5 children, all of whom were living in 1900. Her fifth child was born in 1874, 4 years before "Heyram," suggesting that this listing duplicates an earlier child. Also, there is no listing for a Heyram in the 1880 Census.

10.3 **MARIA ELISABETH KLINGER** is also referred to as **ELISABETH** in some sources. She was born on 16 April 1845. She was baptized on 15 June 1845, Zion (Klinger's) Church, Erdman, Lykens Township, Dauphin County, PA. She married **AMOS W. ROTHERMEL**, son of **ISAAC MONROE ROTHERMEL** and **HANNAH WIEST**, Klingerstown, Schuylkill County, PA.

    10.3.1 **ELWIN ROTHERMOL** (see above)

    10.3.2 **THEODORE ROTHERMOL** (see above)

    10.3.3 **MACLADA ROTHERMEL** (see above)

        10.3.3.1 **AMOS MORRIS** (see above)

        10.3.3.2 **BEATRICE MORRIS** (see above)

        10.3.3.3 **LOUIS MORRIS** (see above)

    10.3.4 **MILTON ROTHERMEL** (see above)

        10.3.4.1 **NORMAN LESTER ROTHERMEL** (see above)

        10.3.4.2 **DOROTHY PEARL ROTHERMEL** (see above)

        10.3.4.3 **HERBERT MILTON ROTHERMEL** (see above)

        10.3.4.4 **RUSSELL H. ROTHERMEL** (see above)

    10.3.5 **EDWIN ROTHERMEL** (see above)

        10.3.5.1 **EDWIN FRANCIS ROTHERMEL** (see above)

        10.3.5.2 **GLADYS MARGARET ROTHERMEL** (see above)

    10.3.6 **JOHN ROTHERMOL** (see above)

    10.3.7 **CHARLES K. ROTHERMEL** (see above)

        10.3.7.1 **CHARLES ROTHERMEL** (see above)

        10.3.7.2 **HARRY BURTON ROTHERMEL** (see above)

        10.3.7.3 **GLORIA ROTHERMEL** (see above)

    10.3.8 **JAMES ROTHERMEL** (see above)

    10.3.9 **INFANT ROTHERMOL** (see above)

    10.3.10 **LUCY ROTHERMEL** (see above)

    10.3.11 **CLAUDE L. ROTHERMEL** (see above)

        10.3.11.1 **MARY ROTHERMEL** (see above)

        10.3.11.2 **MARTHA ROTHERMEL** (see above)

        10.3.11.3 **HELEN ROTHERMEL** (see above)

10.4 **VIOLETTE KLINGER** is also referred to as **VIAH AND VIOLET** in some sources. She was born on 9 March 1847. She was baptized on 25 May 1847, Zion (Klinger's) Church, Erdman, Lykens Township, Dauphin County, PA. She married **JOSIAH D. SALTZER**. She died on 13 June 1907, near Klingerstown, Upper Mahantango Township, Schuylkill County, PA, at age 60. She was buried at Zion (Klinger's) Church Cemetery, Erdman, Lykens Township, Dauphin County, PA. The listings for Violette's children, which is drawn from several different sources, is not certain.

    10.4.1 **ANNIE SALTZER** was born near Klingerstown, Upper Mahantango Township, Schuylkill County, PA. She died near Klingerstown, Upper Mahantango Township, Schuylkill County, PA.

    10.4.2 **BUELL SALTZER** was born near Klingerstown, Upper Mahantango Township, Schuylkill County, PA. He died near Klingerstown, Upper Mahantango Township, Schuylkill County, PA.

    10.4.3 **CLARA SALTZER** was born near Klingerstown, Upper Mahantango Township, Schuylkill County, PA. She died near Klingerstown, Upper Mahantango Township, Schuylkill County, PA.

    10.4.4 **JEROMA SALTZER** was born near Klingerstown, Upper Mahantango Township, Schuylkill County, PA. She died near Klingerstown, Upper Mahantango Township, Schuylkill County, PA.

    10.4.5 **LINCOLN SALTZER** was born near Klingerstown, Upper Mahantango Township, Schuylkill County, PA. He died near Klingerstown, Upper Mahantango Township, Schuylkill County, PA.

10.4.6 ELLEN SALTZER was born near Klingerstown, Upper Mahantango Township, Schuylkill County, PA. She died near Klingerstown, Upper Mahantango Township, Schuylkill County, PA.

10.4.7 GABRIEL SALTZER was born near Klingerstown, Upper Mahantango Township, Schuylkill County, PA. He died near Klingerstown, Upper Mahantango Township, Schuylkill County, PA.

10.4.8 FREMONT SALTZER was born circa 1868, Pennsylvania.

10.4.9 MAGGIE SALTZER was born circa July 1869, near Klingerstown, Upper Mahantango Township, Schuylkill County, PA. She died circa 1873, near Klingerstown, Upper Mahantango Township, Schuylkill County, PA. She was buried at Zion (Klinger's) Church Cemetery, Erdman, Lykens Township, Dauphin County, PA.

10.4.10 FRANCES SALTZER was born circa 1874, Pennsylvania.

10.4.11 WILLIAM SALTZER was born circa 1876, Pennsylvania.

10.4.12 COLONEL SALTZER was born circa 1877, Pennsylvania.

10.4.13 HARRY HERBERT SALTZER was born on 14 March 1877, near Klingerstown, Upper Mahantango Township, Schuylkill County, PA.

10.4.14 ORSON SALTZER was born circa 1878, Pennsylvania.

10.4.15 MELVINA SALTZER was born in November 1879, Pennsylvania.

10.4.16 ELIAS WARRER SALTZER was born on 8 October 1886, near Klingerstown, Upper Mahantango Township, Schuylkill County, PA.

10.4.17 KATIE EVA SALTZER was born on 28 December 1890, near Klingerstown, Upper Mahantango Township, Schuylkill County, PA.

10.4.18 EDWIN BLAINE SALTZER was born on 22 October 1892, near Klingerstown, Upper Mahantango Township, Schuylkill County, PA.

10.5 TOBIAS KLINGER was born circa 1854. He married **(--?--) BATHOLD**.

10.5.1 WILLIAM KLINGER

10.5.2 CARRIE KLINGER

11 DANIEL KLINGER was born on 28 January 1816, near Erdman, Dauphin County, PA. He married **MARY ANN SCHOFFSTALL**, daughter of **JOHN SCHOFFSTALL** and **MARY MAGDALENA HOOVER,** before 1840. A hand drawn map, circa 1862, that is included as an exhibit in Irwin Klinger's, Klinger's Church History, shows a "D. Klinger" living southeast of the area in which Lubold's School was built (probably between 1862 and 1875). Daniel's father Peter died in 1858. A similar map, showing the taxable values of properties in Lykens Township in 1875 does show the Lubold's School. On the same map, however, "Dan'l Klinger" is listed as living on or near the Peter Klinger homestead, just south of Klinger's Church. This is consistent with information provided in 2001 by Carl Klinger, of Sacramento, PA, who indicated that the younger Daniel Klinger was born on a property now owned by Knorrs, that is located just south and east of what was formerly Lubold's School. This property is located along (and on the east side) of the Lubold's School Road. This also bears out the recollection of Carlos G. Klinger who remembers that his father (the younger Daniel's grandson, Guy) told him that Daniel Klinger had to buy the Peter Klinger homestead. The younger Daniel Klinger later lived there as well. Daniel and Mary Ann owned several lots in Gratz, PA. They acquired the adjacent lots 37 and 39 (just east of the Square on the north side of Market Street) on March 30, 1870. They sold both lots on March 17, 1882. On March 13, 1870, Daniel acquired a portion of a lot across the street (Lot 40), and used a building on the property for "a cabinet making shop." An 1876 tax assessment listed Daniel as owning a half lot with a cabinet making shop. This property was a sold on March 1, 1881. On October 19, 1879, Daniel was a communicant at Klinger's Church, Erdman, Lykens Township, Dauphin County. He died on 2 March 1899, Lykens Township, Dauphin County, PA, at age 83. According to the Affidavit of Death and Request for Letters of Administration filed in the Dauphin County Courthouse, March 8, 1899, Daniel died at 9:30 pm on 2 Mar 1899. He was survived by sons John, Daniel Jr., and Emanuel, all of Lykens Township, and daughters Mary Glantz or Nanticoke and Louise Knerr of Lykens Township. He was buried at Zion (Klinger's) Church Cemetery, Erdman, Lykens Township, Dauphin County, PA.

11.1 SUSANNAH KLINGER was born on 12 October 1840. She married **WILLIAM ROMBERGER**, son of **JOHANN CHRISTIAN ROMBERGER** and **SUSANNAH MATTER**. She died on 18 July 1877, at age 36. She was buried at Zion (Klinger's) Church, Erdman, Lykens Township, Dauphin County, PA.

11.1.1 ISAIAH KLINGER ROMBERGER was born on 23 May 1864. He married **ELMIRA CLARK**, daughter of **SAMUEL W. CLARK** and **JOHANNA WIEST**, circa 1884. Isaiah Romberger and his wife Elmira Clark owned the general store in Klingerstown, Schuylkill County, PA. He died on 21 April 1919, at age 54. He was buried at St. Michael's Church, Klingerstown, Schuylkill County, PA.

- **11.1.1.1** BERTHA VIOLA ROMBERGER (see above)
    - **11.1.1.1.1** (--?--) HAVICE (see above)
    - **11.1.1.1.2** ELMIRA F. HAVICE (see above)
        - **11.1.1.1.2.1** LUTHER C. WILLIAMS (see above)
        - **11.1.1.1.2.2** BERTHA C. WILLIAMS (see above)
- **11.1.1.2** SAMUEL WALTER ROMBERGER (see above)
- **11.1.1.3** THOMAS CLARK ROMBERGER (see above)
    - **11.1.1.3.1** JOHN ISAIAH ROMBERGER (see above)
        - **11.1.1.3.1.1** GENE THOMAS ROMBERGER (see above)
            - **11.1.1.3.1.1.1** GARY GENE ROMBERGER (see above)
                - **11.1.1.3.1.1.1.1** AMY MARIE ROMBERGER (see above)
                - **11.1.1.3.1.1.1.2** BRIAN ADAM ROMBERGER (see above)
            - **11.1.1.3.1.1.2** JOHN RALPH ROMBERGER (see above)
            - **11.1.1.3.1.1.3** LORI ANN ROMBERGER (see above)
                - **11.1.1.3.1.1.3.1** VALERIE GREEN (see above)
        - **11.1.1.3.1.2** CARL FRANCIS ROMBERGER (see above)
            - **11.1.1.3.1.2.1** COLLEEN ANN ROMBERGER (see above)
                - **11.1.1.3.1.2.1.1** HEATHER ANN SEIBEL (see above)
                - **11.1.1.3.1.2.1.2** CARLEE LYNN SEIBEL (see above)
            - **11.1.1.3.1.2.2** RANDY LEE ROMBERGER (see above)
        - **11.1.1.3.1.3** ROBERT LAMAR ROMBERGER (see above)
            - **11.1.1.3.1.3.1** JODY ANN ROMBERGER (see above)
            - **11.1.1.3.1.3.2** TINA ROMBERGER (see above)
    - **11.1.1.3.2** MAE ELMIRA ROMBERGER (see above)
    - **11.1.1.3.3** ROY ELWOOD ROMBERGER (see above)
        - **11.1.1.3.3.1** RONALD T. ROMBERGER (see above)
        - **11.1.1.3.3.2** LARRY E. ROMBERGER (see above)
        - **11.1.1.3.3.3** TERRY LEE ROMBERGER (see above)
            - **11.1.1.3.3.3.1** KAREN A. ROMBERGER (see above)
                - **11.1.1.3.3.3.1.1** KATELYNN PENDAL (see above)
            - **11.1.1.3.3.3.2** DIANE M. ROMBERGER (see above)
                - **11.1.1.3.3.3.2.1** BOBBY ANCHEFF (see above)
                - **11.1.1.3.3.3.2.2** BEN ANCHEFF (see above)
                - **11.1.1.3.3.3.2.3** OLIVIA ANCHEFF (see above)
            - **11.1.1.3.3.3.3** LEEANN ROMBERGER (see above)
                - **11.1.1.3.3.3.3.1** CAROLINE KLINGER (see above)
                - **11.1.1.3.3.3.3.2** OWEN KLINGER (see above)
        - **11.1.1.3.3.4** ROBERT W. ROMBERGER (see above)
    - **11.1.1.3.4** CURTIS RAY ROMBERGER (see above)
    - **11.1.1.3.5** EARL THOMAS ROMBERGER (see above)
        - **11.1.1.3.5.1** THOMAS STACE ROMBERGER (see above)
        - **11.1.1.3.5.2** GARY MICHAEL ROMBERGER (see above)
    - **11.1.1.3.6** RUSSELL ROLAND ROMBERGER (see above)
    - **11.1.1.3.7** ALMA JEAN ROMBERGER (see above)
    - **11.1.1.3.8** MARY LOU ROMBERGER (see above)
    - **11.1.1.3.9** MARION MARIE ROMBERGER (see above)
- **11.1.1.4** CHARLES ROMBERGER (see above)

11.1.1.5 HARRY CLARK ROMBERGER (see above)
    11.1.1.5.1 HELEN MAE ROMBERGER (see above)
        11.1.1.5.1.1 DAVID HARRY KOPPENHAVER (see above)
            11.1.1.5.1.1.1 KARA KAY KOPPENHAVER (see above)
            11.1.1.5.1.1.2 KRISTEN KYLEE KOPPENHAVER (see above)
        11.1.1.5.1.2 MARY ALICE KOPPENHAVER (see above)
            11.1.1.5.1.2.1 CASEY ALLISON FIELD (see above)
            11.1.1.5.1.2.2 LINDSEY RAGAN FIELD (see above)
        11.1.1.5.1.3 REBECCA KAY KOPPENHAVER (see above)
            11.1.1.5.1.3.1 KURT ROBERT KLINE (see above)
            11.1.1.5.1.3.2 DREW CARLOS KLINE (see above)
        11.1.1.5.1.4 JANE MARIE KOPPENHAVER (see above)
            11.1.1.5.1.4.1 DANIEL THOMAS WEIGEL (see above)
            11.1.1.5.1.4.2 LEAH MARIE GENEVIEVE WEIGEL (see above)
11.1.1.6 STANLEY CLARK ROMBERGER (see above)
    11.1.1.6.1 QUENTIN STANLEY ROMBERGER (see above)
        11.1.1.6.1.1 DIANNE LEA ROMBERGER (see above)
            11.1.1.6.1.1.1 SHARON GALLAGHER (see above)
            11.1.1.6.1.1.2 SCOTTIE GALLAGHER (see above)
            11.1.1.6.1.1.3 STEPHANIE GALLAGHER (see above)
        11.1.1.6.1.2 DONNA LEE ROMBERGER (see above)
            11.1.1.6.1.2.1 BRIAN ROMBERGER (see above)
    11.1.1.6.2 ROLAND RUSSEL ROMBERGER (see above)
        11.1.1.6.2.1 ROLAND JAMES ROMBERGER (see above)
        11.1.1.6.2.2 JOYCE ELIZABETH ROMBERGER (see above)
            11.1.1.6.2.2.1 GILLIAN LOVE (see above)
        11.1.1.6.2.3 BEVERLY VERNA ROMBERGER (see above)
            11.1.1.6.2.3.1 JESSE HARNER (see above)
            11.1.1.6.2.3.2 JAKE ROMBERGER HARNER (see above)
        11.1.1.6.2.4 GAIL ANN ROMBERGER (see above)
            11.1.1.6.2.4.1 ERIC NONNECKE (see above)
        11.1.1.6.2.5 RENEE MARY ROMBERGER (see above)
            11.1.1.6.2.5.1 PETER BREEN (see above)
            11.1.1.6.2.5.2 SCOTT BREEN (see above)
    11.1.1.6.3 MARION ANNA ROMBERGER (see above)
        11.1.1.6.3.1 STEVEN EARL TROUTMAN (see above)
            11.1.1.6.3.1.1 MICHAEL TROUTMAN (see above)
            11.1.1.6.3.1.2 VALERIE TROUTMAN (see above)
        11.1.1.6.3.2 GLENN LAMAR TROUTMAN (see above)
            11.1.1.6.3.2.1 HEATHER LYNNE TROUTMAN (see above)
            11.1.1.6.3.2.2 MATTHEW JAMES TROUTMAN (see above)
            11.1.1.6.3.2.3 HILLARY APRIL TROUTMAN (see above)
        11.1.1.6.3.3 RUBY MARY TROUTMAN (see above)
            11.1.1.6.3.3.1 ANTONIO DAVID MICHETTI (see above)
            11.1.1.6.3.3.2 ROSALYNDA MARY MICHETTI (see above)
            11.1.1.6.3.3.3 ANGELINA MAE MICHETTI (see above)
            11.1.1.6.3.3.4 MARIA MELINDA MICHETTI (see above)

      11.1.1.6.3.3.5 YOLANDA MARION MICHETTI (see above)
    11.1.1.6.4 LEE LAMAR ROMBERGER (see above)
     11.1.1.6.4.1 DALE LEE ROMBERGER (see above)
     11.1.1.6.4.2 JANE MARIE ROMBERGER (see above)
    11.1.1.6.5 ROY ALBERT ROMBERGER (see above)
     11.1.1.6.5.1 ROBIN LEE ROMBERGER (see above)
    11.1.1.6.6 MARK MARTIN ROMBERGER (see above)
     11.1.1.6.6.1 MICHAEL IRVIN ROMBERGER (see above)
    11.1.1.6.7 BARBARA MARIE ROMBERGER (see above)
     11.1.1.6.7.1 VICKI LEE KOPPENHAVER (see above)
      11.1.1.6.7.1.1 ZANE DAVID ROMBERGER (see above)
     11.1.1.6.7.2 KELLY SUE KOPPENHAVER (see above)
  11.1.1.7 STELLA JOANNA ROMBERGER (see above)
  11.1.1.8 ALLEN CLARK ROMBERGER (see above)
   11.1.1.8.1 ALLEN ISAIAH ROMBERGER (see above)
    11.1.1.8.1.1 KRISTENE LEA ROMBERGER (see above)
    11.1.1.8.1.2 MICHAEL ALLEN ROMBERGER (see above)
    11.1.1.8.1.3 CLARK ALLEN ROMBERGER (see above)
   11.1.1.8.2 ALICE LORRAINE ROMBERGER (see above)
    11.1.1.8.2.1 ANN MARIE WILLIARD (see above)
    11.1.1.8.2.2 JACK RUSSELL WILLIARD JR. (see above)
     11.1.1.8.2.2.1 LUKE WILLIARD (see above)
     11.1.1.8.2.2.2 ZACH HERSHEL WILLIARD (see above)
    11.1.1.8.2.3 JEFFREY ALLEN WILLIARD (see above)
  11.1.1.9 HELEN SUSANNAH ROMBERGER (see above)
   11.1.1.9.1 LaRUE HELEN ERDMAN (see above)
    11.1.1.9.1.1 ROBERT MACHAMER JR. (see above)
   11.1.1.9.2 STELLA HELEN ERDMAN (see above)
   11.1.1.9.3 SANDRA HELEN ERDMAN (see above)
   11.1.1.9.4 RUE OTIS ERDMAN JR. (see above)

11.1.2 CHARLES DANIEL ROMBERGER was born on 14 July 1866. He married **ELLA WOLF**, daughter of **JOHN C. WOLF** and **AMELIA KLINGER.** He died on 20 January 1895, at age 28.

 11.1.2.1 LULU ROMBERGER (see above)

 11.1.2.2 GERTRUDE ROMBERGER (see above)

11.1.3 MARY ANN ROMBERGER was born on 17 September 1868.

11.1.4 WILLIAM AUSTIN ROMBERGER was born on 11 December 1870. He married **EMMA CATHERINE WIEST**, daughter of **VICTOR BAUM WIEST** and **AMELIA TROUTMAN,** circa 1891. He died on 30 November 1928, at age 57. He was buried at St. Michael's Church, Klingerstown, Schuylkill County, PA.

 11.1.4.1 LILLIAN ALICE ROMBERGER was born on 30 September 1891. She married **MOSES RICHARD LEITZEL**, son of **WILLIAM OSCAR LEITZEL** and **EMMA SCHADEL WIEST,** after 1910. She died on 6 September 1974, Myerstown, Lebanon County, PA, at age 82.

  11.1.4.1.1 PAUL LEITZEL

  11.1.4.1.2 ROY RICHARD LEITZEL was born on 2 September 1916, Klingerstown, Schuylkill County, PA. He married **ELEANOR MESSERSMITH.** He married **PEARL REBER.** He died on 15 June 1999, Lebanon, Lebanon County, PA, at age 82.

   11.1.4.1.2.1 ELAINE LEITZEL married **LARRY WIEST.**

   11.1.4.1.2.2 VIRGINIA LEITZEL married **PAUL ENGLE.**

11.1.4.1.2.3 CAROL RUTH LEITZEL was born on 15 August 1945, Dauphin County, PA. She married ROBERT PETER STINE, son of PETER I. STINE and MARY MARIE UMHOLTZ, in 1966, PA.

> **11.1.4.1.2.3.1** JEFFREY ROBERT STINE married SHELLEY CAROL BROWN.
>> **11.1.4.1.2.3.1.1** ASHLEY CAROL STINE
>
> **11.1.4.1.2.3.2** AMY MARIE STINE

11.1.4.1.3 WILLIAM FORD LEITZEL was born on 21 April 1918. He married HILDA FAE KESSLER, daughter of CHARLES EDWIN KESSLER and MEDA MABEL PAUL, on 13 April 1940. He died on 22 March 1996, Klingerstown, Schuylkill County, PA, at age 77. He was buried at St. Michael's Lutheran Church Cemetery, Klingerstown, Schuylkill County, PA.

> **11.1.4.1.3.1** BONNIE LEITZEL married FRANK J. MILLER JR., son of FRANK MILLER and HELEN (--?--).
>
>> **11.1.4.1.3.1.1** VALERIE MILLER married NORMAN KOHLS. She lived in San Diego, CA.
>>> **11.1.4.1.3.1.1.1** KELLY KOHLS
>>> **11.1.4.1.3.1.1.2** SCOTT KOHLS
>>
>> **11.1.4.1.3.1.2** KIM MILLER married (--?--) LEVY.
>
> **11.1.4.1.3.2** THOMAS C. LEITZEL
>
> **11.1.4.1.3.3** PAUL LEITZEL married PEGGY (--?--).

11.1.4.2 FLORA EVA ROMBERGER was born on 8 January 1895. She died on 5 February 1895.

11.1.4.3 GERTRUDE CATHERINE ROMBERGER was born on 28 July 1896. She married CHARLES DANIEL SCHAFFER circa 1918. She died on 6 July 1989, at age 92.

11.1.4.4 MARY HAZEL ROMBERGER was born on 21 January 1899, Klingerstown, Schuylkill County, PA. She was baptized on 30 April 1899, St. Michael's Church, Klingerstown, Upper Mahantango Township, Schuylkill County, PA. She married IRWIN WILSON DEIBERT, son of EMANUEL W. DEIBERT and AMELIA JANE SHADE, circa 1916. She died on 23 July 1977, at age 78. She was buried at Zion (Klinger's) Church, Erdman, Lykens Township, Dauphin County, PA.

> **11.1.4.4.1** HELEN AMELIA DEIBERT was born on 7 April 1916, Fearnot, Schuylkill County, PA. She married LAWRENCE WOODROW BYERLY, son of ISAAC THEODORE BYERLY and TAMIE UBELLA ERDMAN, after 1930. She lived in Gratz, Dauphin County, PA. She died on 11 October 1995, Susquehanna Lutheran Village, Millersburg, Dauphin County, PA, at age 79. She was buried at Zion (Klinger's) Church Cemetery, Erdman, Lykens Township, Dauphin County, PA.
>
>> **11.1.4.4.1.1** DENNIS CHARLES BYERLY was born on 1 April 1936. He married MARY LOUISE MATLOCK.
>>> **11.1.4.4.1.1.1** DAVID BYERLY
>>> **11.1.4.4.1.1.2** DEBRA JEAN BYERLY was born on 13 June 1960.
>>> **11.1.4.4.1.1.3** DAWN MARIE BYERLY was born on 23 June 1961.
>>> **11.1.4.4.1.1.4** DIANNE LOUISE BYERLY was born on 15 December 1962.
>>
>> **11.1.4.4.1.2** ELAINE MARTHA BYERLY was born on 17 November 1939. She married DONALD LEWIS COLE.
>>> **11.1.4.4.1.2.1** AMITY COLE
>>> **11.1.4.4.1.2.2** GREGORY COLE
>>> **11.1.4.4.1.2.3** JEFFREY LEE COLE was born on 22 September 1959.
>>> **11.1.4.4.1.2.4** RACHEL LYNN COLE was born on 29 March 1962.
>
> **11.1.4.4.2** FAYE MARY DEIBERT was born on 25 January 1918. She married DARWIN FEGER. She married DUD WILLIER after 1952. She died on 18 June 1993, at age 75.
>
>> **11.1.4.4.2.1** LILA ELANORE DEIBERT was born on 18 February 1933. She married FRANKLIN CHARLES LAPRIOLA.
>>> **11.1.4.4.2.1.1** FRANKLIN CHARLES LAPRIOLA was born on 5 December 1952.
>>> **11.1.4.4.2.1.2** RANDY IRWIN LAPRIOLA was born on 19 January 1957.
>>
>> **11.1.4.4.2.2** LINDA MAE FEGER was born on 6 January 1951.

11.1.4.4.3 MABEL CATHARINE DEIBERT is also referred to as MAEBELLA DEIBERT in some sources. She was born on 20 August 1919. She married HARRIS EDWIN BUCHER. She and HARRIS EDWIN BUCHER were divorced. She married MARLIN R. SHADE, son of SAMUEL G. SHADE and BEULAH ELMIRA KISSINGER, after 1955. She died before 2001.

11.1.4.4.4 IRVIN LEROY DEIBERT was born on 15 March 1921. He died on 24 April 1937, Fountain Springs, Schuylkill County, PA, at age 16.

11.1.4.4.5 LILLIAN MAY DEIBERT was born on 24 May 1926, Klingerstown, Schuylkill County, PA. She married CLAIR ERNEST ERDMAN, son of FARUS RILEY ERDMAN and MACIE M. ENGLE, on 12 September 1942. She died on 3 June 2007, at home, Mechanicsburg, Cumberland County, PA, at age 81. According to a newspaper obituary, Lillian worked at the Dormar Shirt Factory in Gratz, Dauphin County, and at the Sears at the Capital City Mall, Camp Hill, Cumberland County, where she retired in 1992. She enjoyed quilting, reading, and doing crossword puzzles. She was buried on 7 June 2007, at Salem Cemetery, Rough and Ready, Schuylkill County, PA.

    11.1.4.4.5.1 CLAIR ERDMAN JR. married MICHELLE (--?--). In 2007, Clair was living in New Cumberland, Cumberland County, PA.

    11.1.4.4.5.2 GENE IRWIN ERDMAN was born on 16 April 1943. He married CAROLE WESSNER. In 2007, Gene was living in Livermore, CO.

        11.1.4.4.5.2.1 CHERYL ANN ERDMAN was born on 4 November 1961.

    11.1.4.4.5.3 SANDRA LILLIAN ERDMAN was born on 21 June 1945. She married DEAN SCHRECK. In 2007, Sandra was living in Sunbury, Northumberland County, PA.

11.1.4.5 MABEL AMELIA ROMBERGER was born on 20 March 1903. She died on 1 April 1903.

11.1.4.6 ANNA IRENE ROMBERGER was born on 14 August 1905, Klingerstown, Schuylkill County, PA. She was baptized on 5 November 1905, St. Michael's Church, Klingerstown, Schuylkill County, PA. She married LLOYD HOMER KESSLER, son of CHARLES HENRY KESSLER and MARY ELIZABETH ERDMAN, on 8 September 1925, Klingerstown, Schuylkill County, PA. She married FRANCIS XAVIER TREAS after 1930. She died in 1984.

    11.1.4.6.1 CATHERINE MARY KESSLER is also referred to as KATHRYN in some sources. She was born circa 1925. She married JOHN HECKERT.

        11.1.4.6.1.1 ELAINE HECKERT

        11.1.4.6.1.2 KAREN HECKERT

        11.1.4.6.1.3 JOHN HECKERT JR.

11.1.4.7 WILLIAM RAY WIEST ROMBERGER was born on 12 September 1907, Klingerstown, Schuylkill County, PA. He married MARY ELIZABETH STINE, daughter of JOHN W. STINE and MATILDA BEAVER, circa 1929. He died in April 1973, at age 65.

    11.1.4.7.1 ANNA IRENE ROMBERGER was born on 11 November 1930. Some sources record that she was born on 30 November 1930. She was baptized on 16 April 1931, St. Michael's Church, Klingerstown, Schuylkill County, PA. She married ROBERT RAY TROUTMAN, son of CHARLES TROUTMAN and CARRIE BEAVER, on 6 November 1949.

        11.1.4.7.1.1 ROBERT TROUTMAN JR. married ANN (--?--). Robert lives in Carlisle, PA.

        11.1.4.7.1.2 RICHARD TROUTMAN married KAREN (--?--). Richard lives in Millmont, PA.

        11.1.4.7.1.3 DONALD TROUTMAN married BRENDA (--?--). Donald lives in New Oxford, PA.

        11.1.4.7.1.4 TERRY TROUTMAN married JENNIFER (--?--). Terry lives in Klingerstown, PA.

11.1.5 HARRY KLINGER ROMBERGER was born on 11 June 1873. He married EMMA JANE SNYDER circa 1894. He died on 13 February 1939, at age 65.

    11.1.5.1 JENNIE IRENE ROMBERGER was born on 18 March 1894. She married JOHN LEITZEL before 1920. She died in 1960.

11.1.6 JOHN KLINGER ROMBERGER was born on 17 June 1876, Dauphin County, PA. He married ALICE AMELIA TROUTMAN, daughter of GEORGE L. TROUTMAN and MARY LOUISE WERT, on 13 January 1900, Oakdale Church, Oakdale, Dauphin County, PA. He married BLANCHE ELIZABETH HOFFMAN, daughter of CHARLES CORNELIUS HOFFMAN and ANGELINE MESSERSMITH, on 28 August 1920, Dauphin County, PA. He died on 16 January 1954, at age 77. He was buried at Maple Grove Cemetery, Elizabethville, Dauphin County, PA.

11.1.6.1 RALPH TROUTMAN ROMBERGER was born on 29 December 1900, Dauphin County, PA. He married **CARRIE ELISE BAHNER**, daughter of **ADAM FRANKLIN BOHNER** and **SARAH E. HAIN**, on 16 November 1918, Berrysburg, Dauphin County, PA. He died on 20 June 1974, Halifax, Dauphin County, PA, at age 73. He was buried at Maple Grove Cemetery, Elizabethville, Dauphin County, PA.

> **11.1.6.1.1 MARIE LEONA ROMBERGER** is also referred to as **MARIE LOUISE** in some sources. She was born on 22 October 1922. She married **CLARENCE WILLIAM BROSIUS**. She married **CLARENCE ENDERS**, son of **CHARLES A. ENDERS** and **LILLIE JANE HASSINGER**, on 9 July 1964.
>
>> **11.1.6.1.1.1 CAROL ANN BROSIUS** was born on 7 May 1944, Klingerstown, Schuylkill County, PA. She was born on 7 May 1944, Geisinger Medical Center, Danville, Montour County, PA. She married **RAHN HENRY FEIDT**, son of **HOMER NATHANIEL FEIDT** and **LILLIE FAY KLINGER**, on 29 July 1961.
>>
>>> **11.1.6.1.1.1.1 BONNIE ELAINE FEIDT** (see above)
>>>
>>>> **11.1.6.1.1.1.1.1 KRISTOPHER DOUGLAS TROUTMAN** (see above)
>>>
>>> **11.1.6.1.1.1.2 RAHN DOUGLAS FEIDT** (see above)
>
> **11.1.6.1.2 JOHN ALBERT ROMBERGER** was born on 25 December 1925, Klingerstown RD, Schuylkill County, PA. He married **MARGERY JANET DAVIS** circa 1950. After retiring as a biological research scientist from the Department of Agriculture in Maryland, John moved to Elizabethville, Dauphin County, PA. He was an active researcher in local and family history, with a particular interest in restoring old mills. He was buried on 9 January 2014, at Maple Grove Cemetery, Elizabethville, Dauphin County, PA.
>
>> **11.1.6.1.2.1 ANN IRENE ROMBERGER** was born on 25 February 1955. She married **(--?--) FONTAINE**. Ann lives in Richland, MI.
>>
>> **11.1.6.1.2.2 DANIEL DAVIS ROMBERGER** was born on 10 September 1956. Daniel lives in Silver Spring, MD.

11.1.6.2 JEAN ELIZABETH ROMBERGER was born on 5 April 1924, Tower City, Schuylkill County, PA. She married **RICHARD MALNICK**, son of **JOSEPH P. MALNICK** and **VERNA (--?--)**, in 1946, Hancock County, WV. She died on 22 July 2011, Tremont Health and Rehabilitation Center, Tremont, Schuylkill County, PA, at age 87. She was buried on 27 July 2011, at Greenwood Cemetery, Tower City, Schuylkill County, PA.

> **11.1.6.2.1 RICHARD S. MALNICK** married **KATHE (--?--)**.
>
>> **11.1.6.2.1.1 JONATHAN MALNICK**
>
> **11.1.6.2.2 SHARON A. MALNICK**
>
> **11.1.6.2.3 SHERI A. MALNICK** married **IRV MOYER**.
>
>> **11.1.6.2.3.1 LINDSEY MOYER**
>>
>> **11.1.6.2.3.2 ABBEY MOYER**

11.1.6.3 BETTY JANE ROMBERGER was born on 2 March 1932, Loyalton, Dauphin County, PA. She married **EARL FRANKLIN KOHR**, son of **HARVEY KOHR** and **AMELIA ESTELLA MILLER**. She married **CHARLES WILLIAM FETTERHOFF**, son of **WILLIAM HENRY FETTERHOFF** and **IDA REBECCA YOUNG**, after 1964. She died on 20 January 2006, Harrisburg Hospital, Harrisburg, Dauphin County, PA, at age 73. She was buried at Hershey Cemetery, Hershey, Dauphin County, PA.

11.2 JOHANNES KLINGER also went by the name of **JOHN**. He was born on 8 February 1843, Dauphin County, PA. For a time John, lived on the Peter Klinger homestead south of Klinger's Church and then later sold the farm to his brother Daniel and wife Sevilla Shaffer. He married **CHRISTIANA DEIBERT**, daughter of **WILLIAM DEIBERT** and **HANNAH B. WIEST**. He died on 26 May 1918, Lykens Township, Dauphin County, PA, at age 75. He was buried on 30 May 1918, at Zion (Klinger's) Lutheran Church Cemetery, Erdman, Dauphin County, PA.

> **11.2.1 HANNAH E. KLINGER** was born on 12 December 1865. She married **CHARLES MONROE SCHEIB**, son of **JOSHUA SCHEIB** and **ELIZABETH RAUDENBACH**, in 1883. She died on 20 May 1945, at age 79.
>
>> **11.2.1.1 EMMA JANE SCHEIB** is also referred to as **ANNIE J.** in some sources. She was born on 28 December 1884. She married **OSCAR CLARK**, son of **DAVID T. CLARK** and **ELEMIRA KLINGER**, circa 1908. She died in 1974.
>>
>>> **11.2.1.1.1 HARRY A. CLARK** was born in 1909. He died in 1911.
>>>
>>> **11.2.1.1.2 HANNAH CLARK** was born in 1912. She married **JAMES SEEGER**.

11.2.1.2 IRA G. SCHEIB was born in July 1888. He married LILLIAN BEACH.

11.2.1.3 BERTHA VESTA SCHEIB was born on 12 September 1891. She married HARRY G. RIEGEL. She died in 1959.

11.2.1.3.1 AVIS RIEGEL was born in 1916, Pennsylvania. She married IRA GOTSCHALL. She died before 2010.

11.2.1.3.2 PAUL RIEGEL was born in 1917. He married SALLY DRIVER. He died before 2010.

11.2.1.3.3 LEE A. RIEGEL also went by the name of PAP. He was born on 6 August 1923, Gratz, Dauphin County, PA. He married MIRIAM SHADE. He died on 14 November 2010, at age 87. According to a newspaper obituary, Lee, who lived on Fearnot Road, Sacramento, PA, was a World War II Army Air Corps veteran, serving in Bismarck Archipelago, New Guinea and the Philippines liberation. He was a retired carpenter with Mark Saultzbaugh Carpentry, Millersburg, and was a machinist with Brubakers, Millersburg. He was buried on 17 November 2010, at St. Peter's United Methodist Church Cemetery, Sacramento, Schuylkill County, PA.

11.2.1.3.3.1 BRENDA RIEGEL married JEFFREY GRIFFITHS (--?--). She married JAMES ZECHMAN.

11.2.1.3.3.1.1 MICHAEL GRIFFITHS married WENDI (--?--).

11.2.1.3.3.1.1.1 JEFFREY GRIFFITHS

11.2.1.3.3.1.1.2 GRACIE GRIFFITHS

11.2.1.3.3.1.1.3 ELLA GRIFFITHS

11.2.1.3.4 HANNAH RIEGEL was born circa July 1925. She married GLENN BRADLEY.

11.2.1.3.5 MARY RIEGEL was born circa December 1927. She married RICHARD SNYDER. She died before 2010.

11.2.1.4 AMELIA C. SCHEIB is also referred to as AMELIA G. AND MILLIE C. SCHEIB in some sources. She was born on 31 July 1895, Pennsylvania. She married RALPH F. DOCKEY, son of JONATHON DOCKEY and JOANNA GESNER, after 1920. Prior to her death, Amelia was living in the vicinity of Gratz, Dauphin County, PA. She died on 7 May 1990, at age 94.

11.2.1.4.1 HILDA A. DOCKEY was born on 28 February 1922, Lykens Township, Dauphin County, PA. She married LEE KNORR on 29 June 1940. Hilda lived on Knorr Lane, Elizabethville, PA. She died on 22 April 2009, The Manor at Susquehanna Village, Millersburg, Dauphin County, PA, at age 87. She was buried at Maple Grove Cemetery, Elizabethville, Dauphin County, PA.

11.2.1.4.1.1 RONALD KNORR married RUTH (--?--).

11.2.1.4.1.2 DENNIS KNORR married DEBORAH (--?--).

11.2.1.4.1.3 MARIE KNORR married GEORGE RESSLER.

11.2.1.4.1.4 KAREN KNORR married LARRY CONLEY.

11.2.1.4.2 HANNAH C. DOCKEY married (--?--) MAURER. She was born circa 1926, Pennsylvania.

11.2.1.4.3 GEORGE R. DOCKEY was born on 21 March 1929, Lykens Township, Dauphin County, PA. He married MINNIE A. STONEROAD. He died on 3 June 2009, at his home at 101 S. Market Street, Elizabethville, Dauphin County, PA, at age 80.

11.2.1.4.3.1 SHIRLEY DOCKEY married RICHARD HENNINGER.

11.2.1.4.3.2 GLENN E. COOK died before 2009.

11.2.1.5 MARY MAY SCHEIB was born on 21 March 1902, Pennsylvania. She married ALFRED STANLEY KLINGER, son of MONROE ELMER KLINGER and ELIZABETH K. ARTZ, on 27 September 1919, Simeon Lutheran Church, Gratz, Dauphin County, PA.

11.2.1.5.1 MARK MONROE KLINGER was born on 15 December 1919. He was baptized on 28 March 1920, Simeon Lutheran Church, Gratz, Dauphin County, PA. He married MAY A. ZERBE, daughter of CHARLES R. ZERBE and CARDIE A. WITMER. He died on 23 February 1997, Harrisburg, Dauphin County, PA, at age 77.

11.2.1.5.2 ALPHUS STANLEY KLINGER was born on 16 January 1921. He was baptized on 10 April 1921, Simeon Lutheran Church, Gratz, Dauphin County, PA. He began military service on 4 November 1942 when Alphus enlisted as a private in the Army Air Corps. He married HELEN R.

WATTS, daughter of GUY M. WATTS and MARTHA E. STROUP. He lived at 609 Light St, Millersburg, Dauphin County, PA. He died on 6 July 1990, at age 69.

11.2.1.5.2.1 LINDA M. KLINGER married (--?--) WELLS.

11.2.1.5.2.2 CHRISANN KLINGER married (--?--) FULKROAD.

11.2.1.5.2.3 ALPHUS S. KLINGER II married LINDA TRUNZO, daughter of THEODORE TRUNZO and NORMA HOFFMAN.

11.2.1.5.2.3.1 KARA KLINGER married (--?--) HALE.

11.2.1.5.2.4 GARY KLINGER

11.2.1.5.2.5 BRODRICK KLINGER

11.2.1.5.2.6 ANDY KLINGER

11.2.1.5.2.7 MATTHEW KLINGER

11.2.1.5.3 ANNA A. KLINGER was born circa 1922.

11.2.1.5.4 BLAIR ALTON KLINGER was born on 21 May 1924. He was baptized on 8 September 1924, Simeon Lutheran Church, Gratz, Dauphin County, PA. He died on 27 February 1942, at age 17. He was buried at Simeon Union Cemetery, Gratz, Dauphin County, PA.

11.2.1.5.5 BETTY JANE MAE KLINGER was born on 8 September 1926. She was baptized on 17 October 1926, Simeon Lutheran Church, Gratz, Dauphin County, PA.

11.2.1.5.6 CAROLYN MARIE KLINGER was born on 1 September 1929, Herndon, Northumberland County, PA. She married CHARLES J. LENHART, son of PAUL L. LENHART and EVELYN RIEGEL, circa 1951. She died on 8 April 2011, Carolyn Croxton Slane Hospice Residence, Susquehanna Township, Dauphin County, PA, at age 81. According to a newspaper obituary, Carolyn lived in Camp Hill, PA, and retired as a purchasing agent for the former New Cumberland Army Depot. She was buried at Indiantown Gap National Cemetery, Annville, Lebanon County, PA.

11.2.1.5.6.1 CHARLES J. LENHART JR. married GAIL P. (--?--).

11.2.1.5.6.1.1 EVELYN M. LENHART

11.2.1.5.6.1.2 ERIC M. LENHART

11.2.1.5.7 DONALD CLARENCE KLINGER also went by the name of JACK. He was born on 18 July 1934, Millersburg, Dauphin Co., PA. He married PAULINE ELIZABETH FULKROAD, daughter of LEROY NORMAN FULKROAD and MILDRED PAULINE HARRIS, on 28 November 1953. He died on 15 January 2012, Winter Haven, Polk County, FL, at age 77.

11.2.1.6 HARRY H. SCHEIB was born on 24 October 1905. He married ESTHER J. MAURER before 1930. He died in August 1984, at age 78. He was buried at Millersburg, Dauphin County, PA.

11.2.1.6.1 BONITA SCHEIB married HOMER CAMPBELL (--?--). Bonita lives in Berrysburg, PA.

11.2.1.6.1.1 BRYAN CAMPBELL

11.2.1.6.1.2 MICHAEL CAMPBELL

11.2.1.6.1.3 JON CAMPBELL

11.2.1.6.2 CAROL SCHEIB married LEONARD CONNOR. Carol lives in Salford, PA.

11.2.1.6.3 ROGER G. SCHEIB was born on 20 December 1928, Lykens Township, Dauphin County, PA. He married JUNE V. TROUTMAN. He died on 10 January 2010, at his home on Crissinger Road, Dornsife, Northumberland County, PA, at age 81. According to a newspaper obituary, Roger was educated in the Lykens Township schools and later was a farmer and was employed at Bethlehem Steel, Steelton, retiring in 1994. He lived in Dornsife. He was buried on 13 January 2010, at St. Peter's Lutheran Church Cemetery, Red Cross, Northumberland County, PA.

11.2.1.6.3.1 LINDA SCHEIB married ED BOYER.

11.2.1.6.3.1.1 MICHAEL BOYER

11.2.1.6.3.1.2 JASON BOYER

11.2.1.6.3.2 JEANNETTE SCHEIB married DAVID MATTER.

11.2.1.6.3.2.1 JARED MATTER

11.2.1.6.3.2.2 MORGAN MATTER

11.2.1.6.3.3 RICHARD G. SCHEIB married DENISE (--?--).

11.2.1.6.3.3.1 LAUREN SCHEIB

11.2.1.6.3.3.2 NATALIE SCHEIB

11.2.1.6.4 HARRY H. SCHEIB was born on 5 August 1931, Lykens Township, Dauphin County, PA. He married DIANA (--?--). He died on 9 July 2012, at age 80. He was buried on 14 July 2012, at Union Cemetery, Gratz, Dauphin County, PA. According to a newspaper obituary, Harry lived in South Carolina. He was a U.S. veteran of the Korean War.

11.2.1.6.4.1 MARK SCHEIB

11.2.1.6.5 GLORIA SCHEIB was born on 21 August 1934, Lykens Township, Dauphin County, PA. She married LAMAR CRABB circa 1960. She died on 3 March 2010, at home, Mechanicsburg, Cumberland County, PA, at age 75. According to a newspaper obituary, Gloria lived in Mechanicsburg, PA. After graduating from Hubley Township High School, she worked for the Pennsylvania Department of Labor and Industry as a data analyst supervisor for more than 41 years. She was buried on 6 March 2010, at Union Cemetery, Gratz, Dauphin County, PA.

11.2.2 AMELIA LORETTA KLINGER was born on 6 April 1872. She married DAVID CALVIN KLINGER, son of DAVID S. KLINGER and BARBARA MERKEL WIEST, on 6 November 1891. She died in 1954. She was buried at Fairview Cemetery, near Williamstown, Dauphin County, PA.

11.2.2.1 FRANCIS OLIVER KLINGER was born on 16 March 1892. He married MYRL R. SHULTZ, daughter of JOHN W. SHULTZ and ELLEN M. (--?--), between 1910 and 1920. Prior to his death, Francis was living in the vicinity of Lykens, Dauphin County, PA. He died in February 1972, at age 79.

11.2.2.1.1 DOROTHY M. KLINGER was born circa April 1919.

11.2.2.1.2 JOHN D. KLINGER was born on 21 January 1929. He married JOAN C. MCCREADY circa 1950. He died on 14 May 2009, Milton S. Hershey Medical Center, Derry Township, Dauphin County, PA, at age 80. According to a newspaper obituary, John, who was a veteran of the US Army in the Korean Conflict, retired as a machinist from Alfa Laval company. He was buried on 19 May 2009, at Cavalry United Methodist Church Cemetery, Wiconisco, Dauphin County, PA.

11.2.2.1.2.1 RANEE KLINGER died in infancy.

11.2.2.1.2.2 RUSTY KLINGER died in infancy.

11.2.2.2 KATIE REGINA KLINGER was born circa 1894.

11.2.2.3 HARRY A. KLINGER was born circa 1896. He married TESSIE (--?--) circa 1921.

11.2.2.3.1 MARK KLINGER was born circa 1922, Pennsylvania.

11.2.2.3.2 DORIS KLINGER married (--?--) HAIN. She was born circa 1924, Pennsylvania.

11.2.2.3.3 RAY WILLIAM KLINGER is also referred to as WILLIAM OR BILL in some sources. He was born on 27 June 1925. Ray was likely the son of Harry A. and Tessie M. Klinger. A "Ray William Klinger," born 27 Jun 1925, was baptized at Frieden's Reformed Church, Hegins, PA, on 22 November 1925. He married BEATRICE E. WERT, daughter of EARL WERT and MARGARET ORR. He died on 30 April 2005, Lykens, Dauphin County, PA, at age 79. According to a newspaper obituary, Ray was a retired self-employed auto repairman, an Army Veteran of World War II and the recipient of two purple hearts. He was buried on 4 May 2005, at Indiantown Gap National Cemetery, Lebanon County, PA.

11.2.2.3.3.1 WILLIAM KLINGER

11.2.2.3.3.2 KIRK KLINGER

11.2.2.3.3.3 DARLA KLINGER married (--?--) HEBER.

11.2.2.4 JOHN E. KLINGER was born circa 1899. He married SARAH (--?--) circa 1927.

11.2.2.5 CARLOS A. KLINGER was born circa 1902. He married MAE (--?--) circa 1925.

11.2.2.5.1 MARY KLINGER was born in June 1925.

11.2.2.6 FLORA M. KLINGER was born on 15 May 1905. She married PRESTON DUNLAP before 1940. She died on 30 November 1990, at age 85. She was buried on 5 December 1990, at Green Tree Church of the Brethren Cemetery, Oaks, Montgomery County, PA.

11.2.2.7 RICHARD ROOSEVELT KLINGER was born on 27 January 1908. He married **HELEN IRENE REED**, daughter of **WILLIAM HENRY REED** and **ELIZABETH KISSINGER,** on 29 August 1925, Simeon Lutheran Church, Gratz, Dauphin County, PA. According to a newspaper obituary, at the time of his death, Richard was the retired owner of Klinger's Repair Service in Lykens and was the founder of a tradition known as the "Lykens Santa Claus Truck." An article describing this tradition appears on the web site of the Lykens, PA, Liberty Hose Company No. 2 (http://www.lykenspa.com/santa.htm). Apparently, in 1934, Richard first used a four-cylinder truck decorated with evergreens to travel the streets of Lykens Borough with Santa Claus offering treats to children. Richard portrayed Santa, while his brother Carlos was an instrumental part in the operation. Initially, Richard had been employed in the coal mines, but in 1925 he opened a radio repair business. After the mines closed in 1930, he built his business into a hardware and appliance store. Prior to his death, Richard was living at Susquehanna Lutheran Village, Millersburg, Dauphin County, PA. He died on 25 January 1995, Community General Osteopathic Hospital, Lower Paxton Township, Dauphin County, PA, at age 86. He was buried at Calvary United Methodist Church Cemetery, Wiconisco, Dauphin County, PA.

11.2.2.7.1 MARIE LORANNA KLINGER is also referred to as **MARIE LORAINE KLINGER** in some sources. She was born on 2 November 1925, Pennsylvania. She was baptized on 24 January 1926, Simeon Lutheran Church, Gratz, Dauphin County, PA. She married **ROBERT ANDREWS.**

11.2.2.7.2 ROBERT JAMES KLINGER was born on 3 September 1928, Dauphin County, PA. He married **JEANNE ALICE WERTZ**, daughter of **ALBERT CLARENCE WERTZ** and **MILDRED IRENE SULTZBAUGH.** He died on 29 August 1984, Dauphin County, PA, at age 55. He was buried at Maple Grove Cemetery, Elizabethville, Dauphin County, PA.

11.2.2.7.3 RICHARD EARL KLINGER was born on 27 June 1930, Lykens, Dauphin County, PA. He married **AUDREY I. EILER**, daughter of **JAMES EILER** and **IRENE SEIP.** He died on 1 October 2011, Harrisburg Hospital, Harrisburg, Dauphin County, PA, at age 81. According to a newspaper obituary, Richard was a 1948 graduate of the former Lykens High School and also Elizabethtown College where he received his teaching degree. Richard was a past President of the Lykens Borough Council and past Board Member of the former Miners Bank of Lykens. Richard was also the owner of the former Lykens Valley Motors, the Lykens Bowling Alley and co-owner of Klinger's Repair. He was the second generation of Klinger's to sponsor and run the Santa Floats on Christmas Eve in Lykens. Richard was a Navy Veteran of the Korean War where he proudly served on the U.S.S. Wisconsin. He was buried on 6 October 2011, at Maple Grove Cemetery, Elizabethville, Dauphin County, PA.

11.2.2.7.3.1 RICHARD E. KLINGER married **JEANMARIE (--?--).** Richard lives in Lykens, PA.

11.2.2.7.3.2 BECKY I. KLINGER married **JOEL DAVIES.** Becky lives iin Lebanon, PA.

11.2.2.7.3.2.1 CHRIS MILLER married **BROOKE BEARD.**

11.2.2.7.3.2.1.1 ADDISON NOELLE MILLER was born on 7 December 2010.

11.2.2.7.4 DAVID CALVIN KLINGER was born circa 1939. He married **MARILYN NUTT.**

11.2.2.7.5 DONALD MARTIN KLINGER was born after 1939.

11.2.2.8 GRACE C. KLINGER was born in 1911, Pennsylvania.

11.2.2.9 VERA M. KLINGER was born in February 1916.

11.3 SAMUEL KLINGER was born on 8 April 1846. He married **MARY COLEMAN**, daughter of **SOLOMON COLEMAN** and **SUSANNAH (--?--).** He died on 23 July 1897, at age 51. He was buried at St. Peter's United Methodist Church Cemetery, Fearnot, Schuylkill County, PA.

11.3.1 JENNIE M. KLINGER was born on 20 July 1884. She married **FREMONT HARRISON SCHWALM**, son of **SAMUEL PETER SCHWALM** and **AGNES MINERVA BENSINGER,** on 28 July 1900, St. Andrew's Church, Valley View, Schuylkill County, PA. She died on 25 September 1947, at age 63. She was buried at St. Andrew's Church Cemetery, Valley View, Schuylkill County, PA.

11.3.1.1 SAMUEL KLINGER SCHWALM (see above)

11.3.1.1.1 AGNES VIRGINIA SCHWALM (see above)

11.3.1.1.1.1 RAMONA MARIE RICKERT (see above)

11.3.1.1.2 HUGH SAMUEL SCHWALM (see above)

11.3.1.1.2.1 STEPHEN SCHWALM (see above)

11.3.1.1.2.2 CYNTHIA LOUISE SCHWALM (see above)

11.3.1.2 VERNON FRANCES SCHWALM (see above)

11.3.2 EDWIN S. KLINGER is also referred to as **EDWARD KLINGER** in some sources. He was born in March 1886. He married **MINNIE M. SCHWALM,** daughter of **CHARLES HENRY SCHWALM** and **EMMA JANE DEPPEN,** circa 1906. He was buried at Elizabethville, Dauphin County, PA.

11.3.2.1 VERNA KLINGER (see above)

11.3.2.2 ALLEN E. KLINGER (see above)

11.3.2.3 MABEL V. KLINGER (see above)

11.3.2.3.1 MAY WAGNER (see above)

11.4 CATHARINE KLINGER was born on 15 July 1849. She was baptized on 23 September 1849, Zion (Klinger's) Church, Erdman, Lykens Township, Dauphin County, PA. She married **PHILIP MCKINNEY,** son of **PHILIP MCKINNEY** and **ESTHER ERDMAN,** on 26 January 1868, Rev. Isaac Stiely officiating, Lykens Township, Dauphin County, PA. She died on 7 February 1892, at age 42. She was buried at Zion (Klinger's) Church Cemetery, Erdman, Lykens Township, Dauphin County, PA.

11.4.1 LOUISA MCKINNEY was born on 4 December 1868.

11.4.2 THEODORE HENRY MCKINNEY was born on 27 December 1869. He married **ELIZABETH A. TROUTMAN,** daughter of **ISAAC L. TROUTMAN** and **MARY ANN KLINGER,** circa 1890.

11.4.2.1 DANIEL R. MCKINNEY was born circa 1893, Pennsylvania.

11.4.2.2 PEARL L. MCKINNEY was born circa 1900, Pennsylvania.

11.4.2.3 KATTIE M. MCKINNEY was born circa 1905, Pennsylvania.

11.4.2.4 HARRIE G. MCKINNEY was born circa 1907, Pennsylvania.

11.4.3 ANNORA MCKINNEY is also referred to as **ANORA AND NORA** in some sources. She was born on 17 March 1872. She was baptized on 9 May 1872, Zion (Klinger's) Church, Erdman, Lykens Township, Dauphin County, PA. She married **CHARLES REBUCK.**

11.4.4 SALLIE MCKINNEY was born on 1 September 1874. Some sources, including the Klinger's Church baptismal records, list Sallie's date of birth as September 1, 1872, but that date is less than 6 months after the date of birth of her sister Anora. For this reason, it is perhaps more likely that she was born in 1874, as is shown in the Klinger's Church Cemetery listings. She was baptized on 7 November 1874, Zion (Klinger's) Church, Erdman, Lykens Township, Dauphin County, PA. She died on 1 December 1876, at age 2. She was buried at Zion (Klinger's) Church Cemetery, Erdman, Lykens Township, Dauphin County, PA.

11.4.5 CORDELIA MCKINNEY was born on 21 June 1877, PA. She was baptized on 20 July 1877, Zion (Klinger's) Church, Erdman, Lykens Township, Dauphin County, PA. She married **FRANKLIN ADAM KLINGER,** son of **FRANCIS KLINGER** and **HARRIET TROUTMAN,** on 20 June 1895, Simeon Lutheran Church, Gratz, Dauphin County, PA. She died on 5 March 1897, at age 19. She was buried at Zion (Klinger's) Church, Erdman, Lykens Township, Dauphin County, PA.

11.4.5.1 KATIE A. KLINGER was born on 4 February 1896. She died on 26 March 1896. She was buried at Zion (Klinger's) Church, Erdman, Lykens Township, Dauphin County, PA.

11.4.6 DANIEL ARTHUR MCKINNEY was born on 2 February 1881. He died in 1940.

11.4.7 MARY ELIZABETH MCKINNEY was born on 21 February 1883.

11.4.8 CHARLES OLIVER MCKINNEY was born in August 1886. He married **JENNIE (--?--)** circa 1907. He died in 1913.

11.4.8.1 CATHERINE MCKINNEY was born circa 1908, Pennsylvania.

11.4.8.2 GUY MCKINNEY was born circa June 1909, Pennsylvania.

11.4.8.3 CHARLES A. MCKINNEY was born circa 1912, Pennsylvania.

11.5 DANIEL KLINGER JR. was born on 23 May 1852. He married **SEVILLA SHAFFER,** daughter of **DANIEL W. SHAFFER** and **ANNA MARIA BOHNER,** circa 1877. According to John Daniels, Daniel and Sevilla purchased the Peter Klinger homestead from Daniel's brother John. This was stated to Carlos Klinger on July 14, 1968. He died on 27 June 1919, Lykens Township, Dauphin County, PA, at age 67. He was buried on 30 June 1919, at Zion (Klinger's) Church, Erdman, Lykens Township, Dauphin County, PA.

11.5.1 MILTON C. KLINGER is also referred to as **CHARLES MILTON AND CARLOS MILTON KLINGER** in some sources. He was born on 27 February 1877, Northumberland County, PA, probably somewhere near Hebe, as he was baptized at St. David's Church in Hebe, although his death certificate lists his birthplace as Dauphin County. He was baptized on 3 June 1877, St. David's Lutheran and Reformed Church, Hebe,

Jordan Township, Northumberland County, PA. He married **SARAH ELLEN SCHWALM**, daughter of **FREDERICK STEIN SCHWALM** and **SARAH ANN RUBENDALL**, in August 1894. He died on 4 February 1918, Trevorton, Northumberland County, PA, at age 40 of a self-inflicted gun shot wound. At the time, Milton and Ellen were living in Trevorton, PA, just off Tenth Street, near the railroad. Sometime after Milton's death, Ellen moved her family to Shamokin and lived in half of a double house owned by her daughter and son-in-law Carrie and Grant Zimmerman. This is where Ellen was living at the time of the 1920 Census. He was buried on 8 February 1918, at Zion (Klinger's) Church, Erdman, Lykens Township, Dauphin County, PA.

11.5.1.1 GUY EDWIN KLINGER was born on 14 January 1895, Fearnot, Schuylkill County, PA. He was baptized on 28 April 1895, by the Rev. Oliver Schaeffer, pastor of the Reformed Church at Hegins, PA. Guy's parents were listed on the baptismal certificate as as "Milton" and "Ellen" Klinger. It is likely that the baptism was not performed in the Church itself. He was confirmed on 5 April 1912 Zion Evangelical Lutheran Church, Trevorton, Northumberland County, PA. Guy served in World War I as a Wagoner in Supply Company, 314th Infantry, 79th Division, which was organized as part of the American Expeditionary Force - World War I. The men of the 314th were trained at Camp Meade (later renamed Fort George G. Meade in 1929), Maryland. Guy was inducted at Sunbury, PA, on September 18, 1917, and was initially assigned to Company L, 314th Infantry. Beginning October 19, 1917, he was assigned to Supply Company as a wagoner. He served overseas from July 8, 1918, until May 26, 1919, just before his discharge on May 31, 1919.

The 314th arrived at Fort Meade in September, 1917 and completed training and sailed to France aboard the USS Leviathan in July, 1918. Upon arrival at Brest, France, they continued training until September 1918, then took part in the Meuse Argonne Offensive. Capturing the town of Malancourt on 26 September 1918, they assisted the 313th Infantry on the following day in the capture of the town of Montfaucon-d'Argonne. Montfaucon was a heavily defended area and observation post of the German army. Of the four Infantry regiments of the 79th Division involved in the offensive, the 314th was hardest-hit. It took several days to account for all the missing personnel and bring the regiment up 50 percent manning.

The 79th Division was relieved on 30 September and transferred to the Troyon sector. While there, they assumed a variety of duties, including holding the front. They shared the trenches with the 313th, 315th, and 316th Infantry Regiments. During this time, they were harassed with mustard gas, shelling, and enemy trench and air raids but held the line.

At the end of October, the 79th Division was again ordered to move to participate in the third phase of the Meuse Argonne Offensive. On 1 November 1918, the 314th advanced. By 9 November, they captured the towns of Crepion, Waville, and Moirey. The following day the unit captured Buisson Chaumont, Hill 328. On 11 November, the 314th advanced against Cote de Romagne and stopped firing at 11 a.m., at the time of the Armistice. By the end day, the 314th had made the greatest advance into German lines east of the Meuse River.

The regiment continued training, passed a review by General Pershing, and shipped home on 15 May 1919, aboard the USS Princess Matoika. Arriving at Hoboken, New Jersey on 26 May 1919, they were discharged from service at Camp Dix, New Jersey.

One Internet site offers the following chronology which closely matches Guy's service:

August 25, 1917 General Joseph H. Kuhn assigned to Camp Meade to organize and command the new 79th Division.

Sept. 19, 1917 First contingent of selected men arrived at Camp Meade.

April 6, 1918 Division paraded in Baltimore before President Wilson.

July 8, 1918 Sailed for France on the U.S.S. Leviathan.

July 15, 1918 Arrived in Brest, France.

July 25 - Sept. 8, 1918 Regimental training begun in the vicinity of Prauthoy, France.

Sept. 26, 1918 Commenced Meuse Argonne Offensive: Captured Malancourt, France.

Sept. 27, 1918 Montfaucon captured by the 313th Regiment, assisted by 314th Regiment on the right.

Sept. 28. 1918 Nantillois captured by 315th Regiment.

Sept. 30, 1918 Relieved by 3rd Division and moved to Troyon Sector.

Oct. 26-28, 1918 Relieved from Troyon Sector by 33rd Division.

Nov. 1, 1918 Participated in third phase of Meuse Argonne Offensive. Assigned to Belleu Bois and Bois de Chenes.

Nov. 6, 1918 The Borne du Cornouillier (Hill 378) captured by the 316th Regiment.

Nov. 9, 1918 Captured Crepion, Wavrille, Gibercy, and Moirey.

Nov. 10, 1918 Captured Hill 328.

Nov. 11, 1918 Moved against Cote de Romagne. Armistice ended operations.

April 12, 1919 Division reviewed by General Pershing at Orquevaux.

May 15, 1919 Sailed home on the U.S.S. Princess Matoika from St. Nazaire, France.

May 26, 1919 Arrived at Hoboken, New Jersey.

May 27-31, 1919 Discharged at Camp Dix, New Jersey. Guy was discharged from the Army. He married **HELEN LORENE LEMON**, daughter of **SIMON GRANT LEMON** and **MAGGIE VERDILLA SNYDER,** on 9 October 1920, Urban, Northumberland County, PA. The ceremony was performed by the Rev. William H. Kline, pastor of the Urban parish. When Guy and Helen were first married, they lived in Shamokin. In 1928 they moved to the Herndon area, where their sons Kenneth and Merle were born. In 1923, Guy and Helen were living at 1404 West Lynn Street, Shamokin, PA, at the southwest corner of Lynn and Ash streets. From about 1932 until about 1941, Guy and Helen operated a gas station in Herndon. They lived not far from the gas station. He died on 20 January 1961, Herndon, Northumberland County, PA, at age 66. According to a newspaper obituary, at the time of his death, Guy was living in Herndon, Northumberland County, PA, where he had lived for many years. Guy had been a street car operator and had operated a gas station in Herndon. Later he was employed as a machinist at the Alvord Tool Works at Millersburg, before his retirement. He was buried on 23 January 1961, at Herndon Cemetery, Herndon, Northumberland County, PA.

11.5.1.1.1 MARY ELLEN KLINGER was born on 25 June 1921, Shamokin, Northumberland County, PA. At the time Mary was born, Guy and Helen were living at 1117 Walnut Street in one-half of a double house. Grant and Carrie (Klinger) Zimmerman lived in the other half. She was baptized on 1 September 1921, Shamokin, Northumberland County, PA, by E. H. Gerhart. On 20 May 1930, Mary received a reading certificate. On 8 May 1935, Mary received her grammar school diploma in Herndon, PA. She died of pulmonary haemorrhage due to tuberculosis on 18 March 1942, Herndon, Northumberland County, PA, at age 20. She was buried on 22 May 1942, at Herndon Cemetery, Herndon, Northumberland County, PA.

11.5.1.1.2 CARLOS GRANT KLINGER was born on 15 March 1923, 5:30 pm, at 1404 Lynn Street, Shamokin, Northumberland County, PA. He was baptized on 3 May 1923, Shamokin, Northumberland County, PA. According to a newpaper article about students at Herndon High School (c. 1941), Carlos, nicknamed "Dewberry," lived in Shamokin for about 4 years, until his family purchased the gas station in Herndon and moved to Herndon, PA. Following graduation from Herndon High School, Class of 1941, Carlos enlisted in the US Navy 12 Dec 1942. At the time of enlistment, he was working as a machine operator at Glenn L. Martin CO., Baltimore MD, where he had been employed since April, 1942. Carlos completed boot camp at Bainbridge, MD, and then received additional Naval training at Norfolk, MD.

Most of his active duty time was spent aboard the USS Burke (DE 215/APD 65), where he was a water tender/boiler tender, second class. Carlos (Service # 245 33 21) reported for duty on the ship in Philadelphia, PA, the day it was commissioned, 20 August 1943, with Lt. Comdr. Edwin K. Winn in command.

According to the Dictionary of American Naval Fighting Ships:

"Following shakedown off Bermuda, the [Burke] participated in general type training in late September and October. On 29 October, she joined a convoy bound for Ireland and arrived safely at Londonderry on 11 November. Burke soon returned to New York and made eight more uneventful round-trip transatlantic voyages to escort convoys to Europe or North Africa and back. On 25 January 1945, the warship entered Sullivan's Dry Dock and Repair Corp. in Brooklyn, N.Y., for conversion to a high speed transport.

"Redesignated APD-65, Burke left the shipyard on 8 April and was slated for service in the war against Japan. Burke transited the Panama Canal and joined the Pacific Fleet on 1 May at Balboa. There, she also embarked officers and sailors for transportation to San Diego and, after reaching southern California, took on board more passengers for passage to Pearl Harbor. The high-speed transport's mission was to carry underwater demolition teams (UDT's) to assault areas for prelanding beach clearance. Burke trained with UDT's on Maui in preparation for service in the conquest of Okinawa.

"The fast transport arrived off Okinawa on 27 June after the major part of the struggle to take that island was over. She briefly served on picket duty off Ie Shima, but Burke's duty was cut short on 30 June, and she sailed for the Philippines. The high-speed transport trained near Legaspi on southeastern Luzon with other amphibious ships in preparation for the expected invasion of the Japanese home islands. However, the explosion of atomic bombs at Hiroshima and Nagasaki early in August demonstrated to Japan the futility of continuing the war, so Burke never had an opportunity to participate in an assault. She returned to Leyte and was there when the Japanese capitulated on 15 August.

"Burke escorted occupation forces to Japan and, as the formal surrender ceremony took place on board the battleship Missouri (BB-63) in Tokyo Bay on 2 September, the transport steamed up the channel and into the bay. Burke escorted convoys of occupation troops until 26 October then proceeded to Manila. After transporting men and equipment among the islands of the Philippine archipelago, Burke embarked returning veterans and headed for home. Upon arrival at San Diego, the fast transport disembarked her passengers and got underway for the east coast of the United States.

"In January 1946, Burke became the flagship for Transport Division (TransDiv) 121 and commenced operations with the Atlantic Fleet. She participated in fleet antisubmarine and amphibious exercises along the east coast and in the West Indies. She also trained UDT's and naval reservists."

Carlos disembarked in February, 1946, when the ship arrived at Norfolk, VA, just prior to his discharge from the Navy on 3 Mar 1946 in Bainbridge, MD.

May 15, 1950, Carlos went to work as a stationary fireman at Letterkenny Army Depot near Chambersburg, PA.

On October 30, 1951, Carlos was recalled from reserve duty to active duty, and was assigned to the Great Lakes Naval Training Center, Great Lakes IL. He served until 20 Dec 1952, when he was again discharged.

From the early 1950's until his retirement, Carlos worked at Letterkenney Army Depot, Franklin County, PA. Carlos and Marion lived in Chambersburg, PA for more than 50 years before relocating to Laramie, WY in 2007. He married **MARION THURSTON LONG**, daughter of **MAX ADAM LONG** and **RHODA ALAURA THURSTON,** on 2 January 1947, North Avenue Methodist Church, Baltimore, MD. A newspaper article reported that a dinner was held at he home of Mr. and Mrs. Max A. Long in Hickory Corners, Northumberland County, PA, to celebrate the wedding of their daughter, Marion to Carlos, of Herndon, Northumberland County, who was a navy veteran of World War II, of Herndon. The article reported that at the wedding, the bride wore a white wool dress with black accessories and had a corsage of tortoise shell roses. It also noted that Marion was formerly a cashier at the J. C. Penney Company store in Sunbury. At the time of the marriage, Carlos was employed at the Glenn L. Martin Company in Baltimore, where they planned to live. He died on 25 May 2014, Ivinison Memorial Hospital, Laramie, Albany County, WY, at age 91. He's cremated remains were interred on 25 April 2017, at Lincoln Cemetery, Chambersburg, Franklin County, PA.

11.5.1.1.2.1 MAX EDWIN KLINGER was born on 16 April 1952, Community Hospital, Sunbury, Northumberland County, PA. He was baptized, Zion Lutheran Church, Sunbury, Northumberland County, PA, by Rev. Robert W. Koons.

11.5.1.1.2.2 SUZANNE ALAURA KLINGER was born on 6 June 1957, Chambersburg Hospital, Chambersburg, Franklin County, PA. She was baptized, First Lutheran Church, Chambersburg, Franklin County, PA, by Rev. Roland W. Renkel. Suzanne is an academic reference librarian for the University of Washington, Tacoma. She lives in Gig Harbor, WA.

11.5.1.1.2.3 DAVID GRANT KLINGER was born on 14 August 1961, Chambersburg Hospital, Chambersburg, Franklin County, PA. He was baptized, First Lutheran Church, Chambersburg, Franklin County, PA. He married **DEBRA MAY STOFFER**, daughter of **NEAL STOFFER** and **JANICE STENDER,** on 5 October 1996, Peaceful Valley, CO. He and **DEBRA MAY STOFFER** were divorced in 2001 Longmont, Boulder County, CO. David retired from an environmental compliance firm and lives in Laramie, WY.

11.5.1.1.3 MERLE GUY KLINGER also went by the name of **GUY**. He was born on 20 November 1931, near Herndon, Jackson Township, Northumberland County, PA. He was baptized on 1 April 1932, at his parents' home, by Rev. G.E. Klick, Herndon RD, Jackson Township, Northumberland County, PA. He died on 9 March 2015, New York, NY, at age 83. He was buried on 17 March 2015, at Herndon Cemetery, Herndon, Northumberland County, PA. According to a newspaper obituary, After graduating from high school in Herndon, "Guy" went to New York City and attended the New York School of Interior Decoration, where he became an interior decorator. He was employed by several prestigious firms, including Hattie Carnegie in New York City.

11.5.1.1.4 KENNETH EDWARD KLINGER was born on 20 November 1931, near Herndon, Jackson Township, Northumberland County, PA. He was baptized on 1 April 1932, at his parents' home, by Rev. G.E. Klick, Herndon RD, Jackson Township, Northumberland County, PA. He married **EMMA JANE KLOCK**, daughter of **HERLIN HARLIN KLOCK** and **FLORENCE BEULAH TROUTMAN,** on 27 August 1955, Himmel's Church, Rebuck, Washington Township, Northumberland County, PA. The wedding was performed by Rev. Derl Troutman, Emma's cousin. After serving in the US Navy during the Korean War as an electrician aboard patrol craft USS PCE 882, Kenneth later became an apartment complex manager in New York City, before retiring to Hackettstown, NJ.

> **11.5.1.1.4.1 DEBORAH ANN KLINGER** was born on 11 August 1959, Brooklyn Hospital, Brooklyn, NY. She married **PAUL HOWARD TREXLER**, son of **BLAINE JOSEPH TREXLER** and **JEAN SCHUREMAN,** on 12 August 1978, Lutheran Church, Long Valley, NJ. She and **PAUL HOWARD TREXLER** were divorced in 1989. She married **CHADWICK DEAN** on 31 December 1994, Las Vegas, NV. She and **CHADWICK DEAN** were divorced on 24 December 2010 Roselle Park, NJ.
>
>> **11.5.1.1.4.1.1 ROBERT KENNETH DEAN** was born on 9 July 1995, Easton Hospital, Easton, PA. He was baptized, Nazareth, PA.
>
> **11.5.1.1.4.2 KEITH EDWARD KLINGER** was born on 18 August 1966, St. Vincent's Hospital, New York City, NY. He married **SUSAN SILVEIRA** on 21 October 1995, Our Lady of the Mountain Church, Schooleys Mountain, Long Valley, Morris County, NJ.
>
>> **11.5.1.1.4.2.1 KRISTINA MARIE KLINGER** was born in October 2003, Hackettstown, NJ. She was baptized, Our Lady of the Mountain Church, Schooleys Mountain, NJ.

11.5.1.2 CARRIE ELLEN KLINGER is also referred to as **CARRIE ETNA** in some sources. She was born on 8 February 1897, Trevorton, Northumberland County, PA. She was baptized on 18 April 1897, Zion (Klinger's) Church, Erdman, Lykens Township, Dauphin County, PA. Some sources record that she was born on 8 February 1896. She married **WILLIAM GRANT ZIMMERMAN**, son of **WILLIAM D. ZIMMERMAN** and **EMMA S. CARSTETTER,** on 12 June 1916. She died of pulmonary tuberculosis on 16 August 1924, at her residence 1422 Walnut Street, Shamokin, Northumberland County, PA, at age 27. She was buried on 20 August 1924, at IOOF Cemetery, Shamokin, Northumberland County, PA.

> **11.5.1.2.1 WILLIAM DANIEL ZIMMERMAN** was born on 29 April 1917, 1100 Block, West Walnut St., Shamokin, Northumberland County, PA. He married **LOLA SARAH KNORR**, daughter of **CLARENCE ALLEN KNORR** and **JENNIE KAHLER,** on 19 September 1943, St. John's Reformed Church, Shamokin, Northumberland County, PA. William was a bus driver and lived in Williamsport, Lycoming County, PA. He died on 10 June 1989, Williamsport, Lycoming County, PA, at age 72. He was buried on 14 June 1989, at IOOF Cemetery, Shamokin, Northumberland County, PA.
>
>> **11.5.1.2.1.1 ROBERT GRANT ZIMMERMAN** was born on 19 July 1947, Geisinger Hospital, Danville, Northumberland County, PA. He married **CHRISTINA LIPPHARDT** on 9 June 1973, Lutheran Church, Oberaula, Germany. He and **CHRISTINA LIPPHARDT** were divorced in August 1979 Jacksonville, FL. He married **JOAN LAWRENCE** on 28 July 1980, Naval Air Station, Jacksonville, FL.
>
> **11.5.1.2.2 ROBERT GRANT ZIMMERMAN** was born on 9 December 1919, 1100 Block, West Walnut St., Shamokin, Northumberland County, PA. He was baptized circa 1920, Grace Lutheran Church, Shamokin, Northumberland County, PA. Robert was a private in the 30th Infantry Division, 120th Regiment, Company D in World War II. As an MOS Heavy Machine Gunner, he served in France in World War II. His first encounter with the enemy was in July, 1944, in Normandy, near St. Lo. On August 11, 1944 he was taken prisoner at Montain, France, and was sent to Stalag 7A, Moosberg, Germany, August 30, 1944. A 1944 newspaper article listed Robert

as "missing in action." He was released from prison camp on May 8, 1945. He was then sent to First Ordinance Training Regiment, Aberdeen, MD, in August 1945, and was discharged December 13, 1945. He re-enlisted in the Air Force, October 16, 1946 and was sent to 81st Fighter Group, 91st Fighter Squadron, Wheeler Field, Hawaii. In September, 1947, he was an MOS Propeller Specialist S/Sgt and was reassigned to Kirtland AFB, NM, July, 1949. He was discharged from Fitzsimmons General Army Hospital, September, 1950. He married **MARGARET GAYDOS**, daughter of **JOHN GAYDOS** and **SUSANNA HALLIS,** on 7 January 1950, St. John's Church, Shamokin, Northumberland County, PA. He died on 23 February 1981, Holy Spirit Hospital, Camp Hill, Cumberland County, PA, at age 61. He was buried at IOOF Cemetery, Shamokin, Northumberland County, PA. According to some sources he was buried at Northumberland Memorial Park, Stonington, Northumberland County, PA.

11.5.1.2.2.1 DIANNE JAYNE ZIMMERMAN was born on 18 July 1951, Shamokin, Northumberland County, PA. She married **JOHN AARON BOOSE** on 16 November 1974.

11.5.1.2.2.1.1 JENNIFER ANN BOOSE was born on 9 March 1977, Camp Hill, Cumberland County, PA.

11.5.1.2.2.2 CYNTHIA ANN ZIMMERMAN was born on 13 September 1952, Shamokin, Northumberland County, PA. She married **MICHAEL AUSTIN CRIST** on 22 May 1971.

11.5.1.2.2.2.1 STACEY LYNN CRIST was born on 9 June 1972, Camp Hill, Cumberland County, PA.

11.5.1.2.2.2.2 SCOTT MICHAEL CRIST was born on 20 October 1974, Camp Hill, Cumberland County, PA.

11.5.1.2.2.2.3 THOMAS ROBERT CRIST was born on 21 June 1977, Harrisburg, Dauphin County, PA.

11.5.1.2.3 (--?--) **ZIMMERMAN** was born on 1 October 1921, 1300 Block, Independence St., Shamokin, Northumberland County, PA. Some sources list this child as a boy, while others list it as a girl. He died on 4 October 1921, Independence St., Shamokin, Northumberland County, PA. He was buried at IOOF Cemetery, Shamokin, Northumberland County, PA.

11.5.1.2.4 SARAH SEVILLA ZIMMERMAN was born on 16 December 1922, 1300 Block, Independence St., Shamokin, Northumberland County, PA. She married **MERLE EDWARD HOY**, son of **JOHN HOY** and **VERA (--?--),** on 22 November 1941, Elkton, MD. She died on 9 October 1972, Sunbury Community Hospital, Sunbury, Northumberland County, PA, at age 49. She was buried on 11 October 1972, at Jacob's UCC Church Cemetery, Reed's Station, Ralpho Township, Northumberland County, PA.

11.5.1.2.4.1 JOHN HOY

11.5.1.2.4.2 GEORGE HOY was born on 9 September 1942.

11.5.1.2.4.3 WILLIAM HOY was born on 24 April 1945.

11.5.1.2.4.4 BETTY LOU HOY was born on 14 January 1947. She married **RICHARD LEE WOODRUFF**, son of **LEE WOODRUFF** and **ALICE CAMPBELL,** on 27 April 1968. Betty lives in Mayberry Township, Montour County, PA, near Danville.

11.5.1.2.4.4.1 DEAN WOODRUFF married **DEBRA (--?--).** Dean lives in Danville, PA.

11.5.1.2.4.4.2 DEBRA WOODRUFF married **RICHARD SHUMAN.** Debra lives in Mainville, PA.

11.5.1.2.4.4.2.1 STEVEN SHUMAN

11.5.1.2.4.4.2.2 COURTNEY SHUMAN

11.5.1.2.4.4.3 MICHAEL WOODRUFF married **KAREN (--?--).** Michael lives in Danville, PA.

11.5.1.2.4.5 LINDA HOY was born on 22 March 1950. She married **(--?--) SNYDER.**

11.5.1.2.4.6 THOMAS M. HOY was born on 17 March 1953. He died on 28 June 1968, in automobile accident, Franklin Township, Columbia County, PA, at age 15.

11.5.1.3 CARLOS ALBERT KLINGER was born on 11 March 1899, Gratz, Dauphin County, PA. Carlos was a private in Company I, 119th Infantry, 28th Division and served in France, 1918-1919. Carlos died as a result of a mine accident on Feb. 21, 1920, at the North Franklin Colliery, in Trevorton, PA. He was buried the same day as his brother Fred. Apparently because of deep snow, his body was taken as far as Trevorton by trolley. A short newspaper account of the accident under the headline "Brothers Injured in Same Way at Same Hour" states:

"Two brothers, Carlos and Fred Klinger, of Shamokin, employed at widely separated collieries, were similarly injured at the same hour Saturday, the former dying at the state hospital a short time after his admittance, while the other is lying at the point of death, unapprised of the death of his brother. Both young men were squeezed between a trip of wagons and the rip of a gangway."

It is questionable whether this newspaper account is correct. According to other family members, Frederick was injured on Friday February 20 and, apparently, was first taken home. According to Roy M. Klinger, his brother, Fred's brother Carlos persuaded Fred to go to the hospital, where he died fourteen days later. Carlos was injured the next day, Saturday the 21st, in much the same way. Carlos was taken to Shamokin Hospital with head injuries and died in the operating room, the same day. He died on 21 February 1920, Coal Township, Northumberland County, PA, at age 20. He was buried on 26 February 1920, at Zion (Klinger's) Church, Erdman, Lykens Township, Dauphin County, PA.

11.5.1.4 FREDERICK DANIEL KLINGER also went by the name of **FRED.** He was born on 28 February 1901. Frederick died as result of mine accident on Friday, February 20, 1920, at the Cameron Colliery, Shamokin, PA. The accident occurred a day before his brother Carlos was killed in a similar accident in Trevorton, PA. Fred was apparently first taken home but then persuaded to go to the hospital where he remained until his death fourteen days later.

According to his brother, Roy M. Klinger, Fred, who was driving mules at the time, was squeezed between a group of mine cars and the side of a tunnel. A newspaper account of the accident suggests that both brothers were injured within one hour of each other. He died on 6 March 1920, State Hospital, Shamokin, Coal Township, Northumberland County, PA, at age 19. He was buried on 11 March 1920, at Zion (Klinger's) Church, Erdman, Lykens Township, Dauphin County, PA.

11.5.1.5 ROY MILTON KLINGER also went by the name of **SHORTY.** He was born on 19 September 1906, Halifax Township, Dauphin County, PA. He married **DORIS HELEN PRESHER**, daughter of **HERBERT LEROY PRESHER** and **DOLLIE MABEL LUNN,** on 3 August 1929, Cattaraugus County, NY. Roy served in the Navy during World War II, and was self-employed for 54 years, owning a shoe repair shop, dry cleaning business, a Western Auto store, and "Shorty's Sporting Goods." He was later employed by AVX Corp. in Olean, NY. He died on 10 September 1990, General Hospital, Olean, Cattaraugus County, NY, at age 83. He was buried at East Sharon Cemetery, Honeoye, Potter County, PA.

11.5.1.5.1 JOANNE ELLEN KLINGER was born on 26 March 1930, Shinglehouse, Potter County, PA. She married **ROBERT APPLEBY**, son of **GLENN APPLEBY** and **MINA HUBBARD,** on 10 September 1950, First Baptist Church, Shinglehouse, Potter County, PA. She died on 14 June 2012, Sweden Valley Manor, Coudersport, PA, at age 82. According to a funeral home obituary, Joanne was a graduate of Shinglehouse High School, class of 1948 and a graduate of Bryant and Stratton Business College in Buffalo, NY. She was employed by Montgomery Ward in Olean and then by First National Bank in Shinglehouse. She retired from the Oswayo Valley School District in Shinglehouse where she was employed as business manager. She was later employed as a sales clerk at Southwestern Fountain Company in Mesa, AZ. She was buried at Maple Grove Cemetery, Shinglehouse, Potter County, PA.

11.5.1.5.1.1 CYNTHIA ANN APPLEBY was born on 29 May 1953, Olean, NY. She married **DON V. GUSTON** on 1 April 1974. She married **JUDE DALE AUMAN** on 24 April 1979, Shinglehouse, Potter County, PA.

11.5.1.5.1.1.1 JOSHUA CHRISTOPHER GUSTON was born on 25 December 1974.

11.5.1.5.1.1.2 BRANDY JO AUMAN was born on 13 December 1979.

11.5.1.5.1.1.3 JUDE MATTHEW AUMAN was born on 21 March 1981.

11.5.1.5.1.1.4 MATTHEW LUKE AUMAN was born on 26 September 1983.

11.5.1.5.1.1.5 BETTY ANN AUMAN was born on 17 December 1985.

11.5.1.5.1.2 ROBIN JOLENE APPLEBY was born on 13 April 1957. She married **MICHAEL GOODE** on 30 June 1979, Shinglehouse, Potter County, PA.

11.5.1.5.1.2.1 ROBBY JOE GOODE was born on 24 March 1981.

11.5.1.5.2 JANETTE MABEL KLINGER was born on 18 May 1936, Shinglehouse, Potter County, PA. She married **RICHARD SHERWOOD** on 9 January 1956. She and **RICHARD SHERWOOD** were divorced. She married **DONALD MINGUS**, son of **HOWARD MINGUS** and **WINIFRED DAY**, Andover, NY.

> **11.5.1.5.2.1 MARK RICHARD SHERWOOD** was born on 24 February 1959, Olean, NY. He married **DIANA LEE SHORT** on 19 November 1982, Corning, NY.

> **11.5.1.5.2.2 JEFFREY SCOTT SHERWOOD** was born on 9 February 1962. He married **BRENDA BATES** on 14 February 1984, Dayton, OH.

>> **11.5.1.5.2.2.1 MILENA BRIEANNE SHERWOOD** was born on 2 October 1983, Dayton, OH.

11.5.1.6 SARAH SEVILLA KLINGER also went by the name of **SEVILLA.** She was born on 21 October 1909, near Fearnot, Hubley Township, Schuylkill County, PA. She was baptized on 12 December 1909, Zion (Klinger's) Church, Erdman, Lykens Township, Dauphin County, PA. She married **FRANK GIDEON SCHMELTZ**, son of **REUBEN SCHMELTZ** and **SARAH EMMA UNGER,** on 3 October 1928, Shamokin, Northumberland County, PA. She died on 31 October 1997, Community Hospital, Sunbury, Northumberland County, PA, at age 88. She was buried at Christ (White) Church Cemetery, Barnesville, Schuylkill County, PA. Sevilla was living at the Mansion Nursing Home in Sunbury, Northumberland County, PA, prior to her death. Previously she had lived in Grier City and West Hazelton, PA.

> **11.5.1.6.1 LEE DARWIN SCHMELTZ** was born on 26 December 1929, 1504 West Lynn Street, Shamokin, Northumberland County, PA. He married **MARY MARGRET GRIBBIN**, daughter of **WILLIAM F. GRIBBIN** and **MARGARET ANN CLARK,** on 14 February 1953, St. Edwards Church, Shamokin, Northumberland County, PA. He and **MARY MARGRET GRIBBIN** were divorced. Lee served in the US Army infantry in the Far East, including 2 tours of duty in Korea. During one tour, he suffered from frostbite and was hospitalized for 6 months in Japan. Subsequently, Lee was a coal miner for Peca Coal Company in Mahanoy City, Schuylkill County, PA, and worked as a miner-driller for various construction companies. Later he was a zoo keeper, mostly in the reptile division, at the National Zoological Park, Washington, DC. After he retired in 1974, Lee lived in Las Cruces, NM. He married **LAVINA WALKER**, daughter of **WILLIAM CLARK WALKER** and **MARY FLORENCE MARSHALL,** on 18 November 1995. He died on 24 July 2016, Hanover Hospital, Hanover, York County, PA, at age 86. He was buried at Cheltenham Veterans Cemetery, Cheltenham, Prince George's County, MD.

>> **11.5.1.6.1.1 WILLIAM FRANCIS SCHMELTZ** was born on 8 December 1953, Shamokin, Northumberland County, PA. In 2006, William was living in Las Cruces, NM. He died on 3 January 2012, at age 58.

>> **11.5.1.6.1.2 DONNA MARIE SCHMELTZ** was born on 22 August 1955, Shamokin, Northumberland County, PA. She died on 4 October 2008, at age 53.

>>> **11.5.1.6.1.2.1 DAWN SCHMELTZ**

>> **11.5.1.6.1.3 ALEXANDER JAMES SCHMELTZ** was born on 11 August 1964, Providence Hospital, Washington, DC. In 2006, Alexander was living in Stuart, FL.

>> **11.5.1.6.1.4 PATRICIA ANN SCHMELTZ** was born on 27 July 1968, Providence Hospital, Washington, DC. She married **DONALD THOMASON**. She married **(--?--) KAUFFMAN**. In 2016, Patricia was living in Thomasville, PA.

>>> **11.5.1.6.1.4.1 DONALD THOMASON JR.**

>>> **11.5.1.6.1.4.2 KAYLA KAUFFMAN**

>> **11.5.1.6.1.5 ANN MARGARET SCHMELTZ** was born on 30 September 1970, Providence Hospital, Washington, DC. She married **SCOTT WALKER**. In 2006, Ann was living in Laurel, MD.

>>> **11.5.1.6.1.5.1 JOSHUA WALKER**

> **11.5.1.6.2 MAE KATHRYN SCHMELTZ** was born on 6 May 1932, Frackville, Schuylkill County, PA. She was baptized in July 1932, by Rev. Gerhardt, Shamokin, Northumberland County, PA. She married **HERBERT KILBY**, son of **JAMES FRANKLIN KILBY** and **OSCEOLLA ARNOLD,** on 31 December 1952, Washington, DC. She died on 6 March 2000, District Heights, Prince Gorge's County, MD, at age 67.

11.5.1.6.2.1 ELLEN MARIE KILBY was born on 28 December 1953, Washington, DC. She married **ROBERT DALE BLIZARD** on 10 August 1974, Calvary Memorial Church, Hyattsville, MD.

11.5.1.6.2.1.1 CHRISTAL MICHELL BLIZARD was born on 3 September 1978.

11.5.1.6.2.1.2 ROBERT BLIZARD was born circa 1983.

11.5.1.6.2.2 HERBERT RUSSELL KILBY was born on 4 December 1956, Washington, DC. He married **JENNIFER LYNN THOMAS** on 22 November 1976, Baptist Temple, San Diego, CA.

11.5.1.6.2.2.1 HERBERT RUSSELL KILBY JR. is also referred to as **RUSTY** in some sources. He was born on 27 April 1979, Jacksonville, FL.

11.5.1.6.2.2.2 SEAN PATRICK KILBY was born on 10 August 1981, Yokohama, Japan.

11.5.1.6.2.3 FRANK WALTER KILBY was born on 23 July 1958, Washington, DC. He married **DEBORAH (--?--).**

11.5.1.6.3 GLENN IRA SCHMELTZ was born on 29 May 1943, Grier City, Schuylkill County, PA. He was baptized on 29 July 1943, Christ Evangelical Lutheran Church, Quakake, Schuylkill County, PA. He married **CARRIE JEAN DALTON**, daughter of **KENNETH EARL DALTON** and **VIRGIE MAE RICE,** on 6 April 1968, Hyattsville, MD. He died on 4 October 2003, Bowie, MD, at age 60.

11.5.1.6.3.1 DAVID LEE SCHMELTZ was born on 17 July 1971, Chicago, Cook County, IL. He married **SHARLEEN COCHRELL** on 29 May 1993.

11.5.1.6.3.1.1 REBECCA SCHMELTZ was born circa 1988.

11.5.1.6.3.1.2 TIFFANY RAE SCHMELTZ was born on 16 December 1992, Cheverly, MD. She married **GARRET LINDO.** She and **GARRET LINDO** were divorced on 21 October 2011 Alexandria, VA.

11.5.1.6.3.1.3 NICOLE LEIGH SCHMELTZ was born on 18 November 2005, Winchester, VA.

11.5.1.6.4 LOIS GRACE SCHMELTZ was born on 19 December 1946, Grier City, Schuylkill County, PA. She was baptized on 25 February 1947, Grier City, Schuylkill County, PA. She married **MAURICE JOSEPH CURCIO** on 24 April 1965, Redeemer Lutheran Church, Hyattsville, MD.

11.5.1.6.4.1 MARK JOHN CURCIO was born on 5 July 1966, Providence Hospital, Washington, DC. He was baptized on 31 July 1966.

11.5.1.6.4.2 KAREN SARAH CURCIO was born on 1 May 1971, Providence Hospital, Washington, DC. She was baptized on 13 June 1971. She married **ROBERT EUGENE BOLEY** on 28 June 1992.

11.5.1.7 IRA CHARLES KLINGER was born on 10 January 1915, Trevorton, Northumberland County, PA. He married **MARY ABIGAIL LANDAU**, daughter of **CHARLES B. LAUNDAU** and **SUSAN GIBBONS,** on 20 September 1947, Zion Lutheran Church, Sunbury, PA. Ira served in the US Army in the Philippines during World War II, and later was an auditor with the Internal Revenue Service and eventually a self-employed accountant in Sunbury, Northumberland County, PA. He and Mary lived on Market Street in Sunbury had no children. He died on 7 May 1993, Community Hospital, Sunbury, Northumberland County, PA, at age 78. He was buried on 10 May 1993, at Orchard Hills (West Side) Cemetery, Shamokin Dam, Snyder County, PA.

11.5.2 CARRIE ANERVA KLINGER was born on 17 November 1878. She was baptized on 3 March 1879, Zion (Klinger's) Church, Erdman, Lykens Township, Dauphin County, PA. She is also referred to as **CARRIE ENERVA AND CARRIE MINERVA** in some sources. She married **JONATHAN DANIELS**, son of **ISRAEL DANIELS,** on 13 March 1897, Zion (Klinger's) Church, Erdman, Lykens Township, Dauphin County, PA. She died on 12 February 1938, Philadelphia, Philadelphia County, PA, at age 59. She was buried on 16 February 1938, at Zion (Klinger's) Lutheran Church, Erdman, Lykens Township, Dauphin County, PA.

11.5.2.1 MAUDE MARIE DANIELS was born on 9 September 1897. She was baptized on 17 October 1897, Zion (Klinger's) Church, Erdman, Lykens Township, Dauphin County, PA. She died in 1900. She was buried at Zion (Klinger's) Lutheran Church Cemetery, Erdman, Dauphin County, PA.

11.5.2.2 WINNIE ALMA DANIELS was born on 10 August 1899, Lykens Township, Dauphin County, PA. She married **WILLIAM BOERNER** circa 1928. She died on 13 October 1981, Philadelphia, PA, at age 82. She was buried at Zion (Klinger's) Church, Erdman, Lykens Township, Dauphin County, PA.

11.5.2.3 HARRY W. DANIELS was born on 5 February 1902. He married **MADELENE (--?--)** after 1930. He died on 1 June 1990, Fitzgerald Mercy Medical Center, Darby, Delaware County, PA, at age 88. He was buried on 5 June 1990, at Saint Denis Cemetery, Havertown, Delaware County, PA.

    11.5.2.3.1 JAMES J. DANIELS

    11.5.2.3.2 JOSEPH J. DANIELS

11.5.2.4 DARWIN ROOSEVELT DANIELS is also referred to as **DAVID N. DANIELS** in some sources. He was born on 10 July 1903, Gratz, Dauphin County, PA. He married **VERA SHEETS**, daughter of **CLINTON SKELLY SHEETS** and **MARY L. GOLDSBOROUGH**, circa 1927. He and **VERA SHEETS** were divorced before 1953. He died on 25 July 1953, Philadelphia General Hospital, Philadelphia, Philadelphia County, PA, at age 50. He was buried on 29 July 1953, at Zion (Klinger's) Church, Erdman, Lykens Township, Dauphin County, PA.

11.5.3 EMMA LOUISE KLINGER was born on 28 February 1881, Lykens Township, Dauphin County, PA. She married **WILLIAM ELIAS KLINGER**, son of **FRANCIS KLINGER** and **HARRIET TROUTMAN**, circa 1899, Lykens Township, Dauphin County, PA. She died in 1947, Lykens Township, Dauphin County, PA. She was buried at Zion (Klinger's) Church, Erdman, Lykens Township, Dauphin County, PA.

11.5.3.1 CLARENCE RAYMOND KLINGER was born on 11 June 1899. He was baptized on 23 July 1899, Zion (Klinger's) Church, Erdman, Lykens Township, Dauphin County, PA. He married **MAE REBECCA KLINGER**, daughter of **DANIEL S. KLINGER** and **LIZZIE ERDMAN**, on 5 January 1921, Simeon Lutheran Church, Gratz, Dauphin County, PA. He died on 3 December 1960, at home, near Spring Glen, Schuylkill County, PA, at age 61. He was buried on 7 December 1960, at Union Cemetery, Gratz, Dauphin County, PA.

11.5.3.2 DAISY ALVENA KLINGER was born on 21 March 1902. She married **JEREMIAH I. KOPPENHAVER**, son of **MORRIS L. KOPPENHAVER** and **MARY A. BUFFINGTON**, circa 1925. She died on 2 January 1967, Good Samaritan Hospital, Pottsville, PA, at age 64. She was buried on 6 January 1967, at St. Mathew's Cemetery (Coleman's Church).

    11.5.3.2.1 MIRIAM EMMA KOPPENHAVER was born on 7 March 1922. She died on 6 August 1971, at the home of her sister Dorothy at age 49. She was buried on 10 August 1971, at St. Mathew's Cemetery (Coleman's Church).

    11.5.3.2.2 DOROTHY MARY KOPPENHAVER was born on 9 April 1924, Spring Glen, Schuylkill County, PA. She was confirmed on 20 November 1938 Saint Mathew's (Coleman's) Church, Lykens Township, Dauphin County, PA. She married **GEORGE CHARLES REINOEHL**, son of **ROY HENRY REINOEHL** and **HILDA RHEA MINERVA DEITER**, on 24 September 1943, Dauphin County, PA. She was buried on 1 June 2013, at St. Matthew's (Coleman's) Church Cemetery, Spring Glen, Schuylkill County, PA.

        11.5.3.2.2.1 TED JOHN REINOEHL (see above)

        11.5.3.2.2.2 LYNN GEORGE REINOEHL (see above)

11.5.4 HARRY DANIEL KLINGER was born on 24 February 1883, near Klingerstown, Schuylkill County, PA. He married **SALLIE A. ENGLE** circa 1904. He died on 8 February 1940, at age 56. He was buried at Zion (Klinger's) Church, Erdman, Lykens Township, Dauphin County, PA.

11.5.4.1 MARY SEVILLA KLINGER was born on 21 January 1908. She was baptized on 23 February 1908, Zion (Klinger's) Church, Erdman, Lykens Township, Dauphin County, PA. She married **HARLAN AUSTIN KLINGER**, son of **OLIVER CECIL KLINGER** and **FLOSSIE MAY STROHECKER**, on 14 April 1927, Zion (Klinger's) Church, Erdman, Lykens Township, Dauphin County, PA. Eventually Harlan inherited ownership of a general store in Klingerstown where Mary and Harlan operated a store in a building that, as of 2006, housed Boyer's Hardware Store. Mary and Harlan lived in an apartment above the store. Later Harlan and his 2 sons took over from his uncle Austin the Chevrolet dealership in Sacramento, Schuylkill County, PA. Mary and Harlan later sold the store and moved into an apartment in the Klingerstown Bank Building. She died on 17 April 1975, Klingerstown, Schuylkill County, PA, at age 67. She was buried on 21 April 1975, at Zion (Klinger's) Church, Erdman, Lykens Township, Dauphin County, PA.

    11.5.4.1.1 PAUL IVAN KLINGER was born on 23 August 1927, Erdman, Lykens Township, Dauphin County, PA. He married **ANNA KATHRYN ROTHERMOL**, daughter of **(--?--)**

Rothermol and **Minnie Schwalm**, on 8 November 1952, Zion (Klinger's) Church, Erdman, Lykens Township, Dauphin County, PA. He married **Marian Marie Mausser**, daughter of **Raymond Mausser** and **Grace Mildred Wagner**, on 8 January 1960. After April, 2003, Paul lived in Millersburg, Dauphin County, PA. He died on 29 October 2005, Millersburg, Dauphin County, PA, at age 78, at his home. According to a newspaper obituary, Paul served in the U.S. Army as a Specialist 3rd Class. Before moving to Millersburg in April 2003, Paul was an EMT for Hegins Area Ambulance and a member of the Hegins-Hubley Water Authority. He was also a school bus driver for Bowman Brothers in Valley View. Until the time of retirement, he was also a co-owner of Klinger Chevrolet in Sacramento, PA, with his brother, Carl. He was buried at Zion (Klinger's) Church, Erdman, Lykens Township, Dauphin County, PA.

> **11.5.4.1.1.1 Karen Marie Klinger** was born on 17 June 1954. She was baptized on 26 December 1954, Zion (Klinger's) Church, Erdman, Lykens Township, Dauphin County, PA.
>
> **11.5.4.1.1.2 Beverly Sue Klinger** was born on 23 October 1962, Pottsville, Schuylkill County, PA. She was baptized on 13 January 1963, Zion (Klinger's) Church, Erdman, Lykens Township, Dauphin County, PA. She married **David J. Hand**, son of **Gene Hand**, on 6 October 1984, Valley View, Schuylkill County, PA. She lived in Hegins, Schuylkill County, PA.

11.5.4.1.2 Carl Harlan Klinger was born on 15 February 1932, Lykens, Dauphin County, PA. He was baptized on 22 April 1932, Frieden's Reformed Church, Hegins, Schuylkill County, PA. He married **Carol Schminky**, daughter of **Joseph Nevin Schminky** and **Dorothy Smith**, on 14 August 1954, Gratz, Dauphin County, PA. Carl was co-owner with his brother Paul of Klinger Chevrolet in Sacramento, Schuylkill County, PA. He lives in Sacramento.

> **11.5.4.1.2.1 Sally Ann Klinger** was born on 16 September 1955, Danville, Montour County, PA. She married **Lewis Samuel Zimmerman**, son of **Lewis B. Zimmerman** and **Mildred Hoover**, on 28 April 1979, Sacramento, Schuylkill County, PA.
>
>> **11.5.4.1.2.1.1 Joseph Philip Zimmerman** was born on 3 March 1985, Pottsville, Schuylkill County, PA.
>>
>> **11.5.4.1.2.1.2 Kate Rebecca Zimmerman** was born on 24 September 1986, Pottsville, Schuylkill County, PA.
>
> **11.5.4.1.2.2 Timothy Carl Klinger** was born on 30 January 1960, Pottsville, Schuylkill County, PA. He married **Wendy Kay Wiest**, daughter of **Claus Maynarc Wiest** and **Joanna Joyce Troutman**, on 11 May 1985, Sacramento, Schuylkill County, PA. In 1995, Tim took over the family's Chevrolet dealership in Sacramento, PA. A history of the family's involvement with the dealership can be read at http://klingerchevrolet.com/aboutus.aspx.
>
>> **11.5.4.1.2.2.1 Brittney Kay Klinger** was born on 12 March 1986, Harrisburg, Dauphin County, PA. In 2008, Brittany graduated from Simmons College in Boston, MA, and subsequently took a job as catering and convention coordinator with the Westin Boston Hotel.
>>
>> **11.5.4.1.2.2.2 Turner Timothy Klinger** was born on 15 May 1991, Harrisburg, Dauphin County, PA.
>
> **11.5.4.1.2.3 Amy Louise Klinger** was born on 7 September 1962, Pottsville, Schuylkill County, PA. She died on 12 November 1983, at age 21. She was buried on 15 November 1983, at St. Paul's United Church of Christ, Sacramento, Schuylkill County, PA.
>
> **11.5.4.1.2.4 Jane Elizabeth Klinger** was born on 11 November 1965, Pottsville, Schuylkill County, PA. She married **Peter G. Savas**, son of **Constantine Savas** and **Catherine Francis**, on 6 April 1991, Salisbury, CT.
>
>> **11.5.4.1.2.4.1 Elizabeth Savas** was born on 29 September 1991, Denville, NJ.
>>
>> **11.5.4.1.2.4.2 Perry Savas** was born on 15 November 1992, Santa Ana, CA.
>>
>> **11.5.4.1.2.4.3 Hannah Savas** was born on 19 April 1994, Santa Ana, CA.
>>
>> **11.5.4.1.2.4.4 Tess Savas** was born on 30 October 1995, Framingham, MA.
>>
>> **11.5.4.1.2.4.5 Madison Savas** was born on 1 July 1997, Wellesley, MA.
>>
>> **11.5.4.1.2.4.6 Halley Savas** was born on 18 May 1999, Wellesley, MA.

11.5.4.2 Eva May Klinger was born on 15 February 1909. She was baptized on 16 February 1909, Zion (Klinger's) Church, Erdman, Lykens Township, Dauphin County, PA. She died on 16 February

1909. She was buried at Zion (Klinger's) Church Cemetery, Erdman, Lykens Township, Dauphin County, PA.

11.5.4.3 ALMA MARIE KLINGER was born on 27 October 1910. She was baptized on 15 November 1910, Zion (Klinger's) Church, Erdman, Lykens Township, Dauphin County, PA. Some sources record that she was born on 12 March 1907. She married **EARL MONROE OXENRIDER**, son of **HENRY ARCHIE OXENRIDER** and **HANNAH ELIZABETH STIELY**, on 21 March 1927, Leck Kill, Northumberland County, PA. She died on 19 April 1974, at home, near Klingerstown, Schuylkill County, PA, at age 63. She was buried on 22 April 1974, at Salem Cemetery, Rough and Ready, Schuylkill County, PA.

11.5.4.3.1 BERNICE ARLENE OXENRIDER also went by the name of **ARLENE**. She was born on 21 August 1927, near Lykens, Dauphin County, PA. She married **HAROLD W. HOFFMAN** on 22 June 1956, Elkton, MD. Arlene lives in Warminster, PA.

11.5.4.3.1.1 RITA MARIE HOFFMAN was born on 20 December 1966.

11.5.4.3.2 WILLARD EARL OXENRIDER was born on 14 July 1929, Rough and Ready, Schuylkill County, PA. Some sources record that he was born on 17 July 1929, Klingerstown, Schuylkill County, PA. He was baptized on 17 August 1929, Salem (Herb's) Church, Rough and Ready, Schuylkill County, PA. He married **ISABEL GLADYS KLINGER**, daughter of **CHARLES R. KLINGER** and **BEULAH M. HAIN**, on 24 December 1949. Willard lives in Herndon, PA.

11.5.4.3.2.1 DEBRA ANN OXENRIDER (see above)

11.5.4.3.2.1.1 CHRISTIE MARIE ERDMAN (see above)

11.5.4.3.2.1.2 STACEY LYNN ERDMAN (see above)

11.5.4.3.2.2 BILLIE EARL OXENRIDER (see above)

11.5.4.3.2.2.1 LYNNETTE ANN OXENRIDER (see above)

11.5.4.3.2.2.2 JASON EARL OXENRIDER (see above)

11.5.4.3.3 MARIE IRENE OXENRIDER is also referred to as **MARY IRENE** in some sources. She was born on 10 August 1931, Hepler, Schuylkill County, PA. She was baptized on 17 October 1931, Salem (Herb's) Church, Rough and Ready, Schuylkill County, PA. She married **BLAINE MCPHERSON**, son of **BLAINE MCPHERSON**, on 27 November 1952, Leck Kill, Northumberland County, PA. She died before 2012.

11.5.4.3.3.1 BLAINE MCPHERSON was born on 18 November 1953. He married **CAROL HELEN HALE** on 2 June 1979.

11.5.4.3.3.1.1 DAVID EARL MCPHERSON was born in 1980.

11.5.4.3.3.1.2 JENNIFER LEIGH MCPHERSON was born on 23 June 1981.

11.5.4.3.3.2 SHARON MARIE MCPHERSON was born on 27 November 1954. She married **LESTER GROSSMICH**.

11.5.4.3.3.2.1 JESSIE JAMES GROSSMICH was born on 30 January 1976.

11.5.4.3.3.2.2 SHERRIE ANN GROSSMICH was born on 12 August 1979.

11.5.4.3.3.3 CYNTHIA COLLEEN MCPHERSON was born on 29 January 1957. She married **GARY KUNI** on 16 November 1976.

11.5.4.3.3.3.1 GARY MICHAEL KUNI was born on 22 October 1977.

11.5.4.3.3.3.2 COLLEEN MARIE KUNI was born on 7 October 1980.

11.5.4.3.3.4 SUSAN CAROL MCPHERSON was born on 11 July 1959, Camden, NJ.

11.5.4.3.3.5 KAREN ANN MCPHERSON was born on 2 January 1966.

11.5.4.3.3.5.1 JOSEPH PAUL MCPHERSON was born on 28 February 1981.

11.5.4.3.4 RAY H. OXENRIDER was born on 10 December 1933, Klingerstown, Schuylkill County, PA. He was baptized on 22 April 1934, Salem (Herb's) Church, Rough and Ready, Schuylkill County, PA. Some sources record that he was born on 10 December 1933, Hepler, Schuylkill County, PA. He married **MARIE COSTELLO** on 19 September 1964. He married **DOROTHY WAGNER** on 27 June 1981. He died on 15 June 2012, SUN Community Care Hospice at Sunbury Community Hospital, Sunbury, Northumberland County, PA, at age 78. He was buried on 20 June 2012, at Salem UCC Church Cemetery, Rough and Ready, Schuylkill County, PA. According to a newspaper obituary, Ray was a graduate of Hegins High School and served in the

Korean War. He was employed by the United States Postal Service as a carrier serving Merchantville, NJ.

11.5.4.3.4.1 RALPH JONES. Ralph was Ray's step-son.

11.5.4.3.5 DEAN HAROLD OXENRIDER is also referred to as **DEAN HERALD OXENRIDER** in some sources. He was born on 19 June 1938, Mahantango Township, Schuylkill County, PA. He was baptized on 23 July 1938, Salem (Herb's) Church, Rough and Ready, Schuylkill County, PA. He married **MARVINE LEBO** on 28 December 1957, Red Cross, Northumberland County, PA. Dean lives in Herndon, PA.

11.5.4.3.5.1 TERESA ANN OXENRIDER was born on 30 July 1960. She married **TIMOTHY EMERSON MORGAN** on 5 April 1980.

11.5.4.3.5.1.1 MELISSA ANN MORGAN was born on 28 June 1981.

11.5.4.3.6 RITA MAE OXENRIDER was born on 11 September 1940, Geisinger Hospital, Danville, Montour County, PA. She was baptized on 20 October 1940, Salem (Herb's) Church, Rough and Ready, Schuylkill County, PA. She married **JOHN P. RYAN** on 12 April 1962. She and **JOHN P. RYAN** were divorced in 1968. She married **FRANK S. IDZIG** on 13 July 1974. Rita lives in Warminster, PA.

11.5.4.3.6.1 JOHN PATRICK RYAN was born on 22 October 1963.

11.5.4.3.6.2 PATRICIA MARIE RYAN was born on 27 December 1964.

11.5.4.3.7 LINDA LOU OXENRIDER was born on 13 March 1947, Pottsville General Hospital, Pottsville, Schuylkill County, PA. She was baptized on 3 May 1947, Salem (Herb's) Church, Rough and Ready, Schuylkill County, PA. She married **MICHAEL HERSHEY** on 15 April 1978, St. Paul's Church, Philadelphia, PA. Linda lives in Warminster, PA.

11.5.4.3.7.1 GAIL MARIE HERSHEY was born on 1 May 1969.

11.5.5 WILLIAM OSCAR KLINGER was born on 14 June 1885. He was baptized on 28 June 1885, Zion (Klinger's) Church, Erdman, Lykens Township, Dauphin County, PA. He married **IDA SEVILLA TOBIAS**, daughter of **WILLIAM TOBIAS** and **CAROLINE BERKHOUSE**, circa 1906. He died in 1962. He was buried at Zion (Klinger's) Church, Erdman, Lykens Township, Dauphin County, PA.

11.5.5.1 VERA MAE KLINGER was born on 25 January 1906. She was baptized on 11 March 1906, Zion (Klinger's) Church, Erdman, Lykens Township, Dauphin County, PA. She married **GURNEY GEORGE MARTZ**, son of **SAMUEL OSCAR MARTZ** and **MARY E. WILLIARD**, on 17 November 1925, Salem (Herb's) Church, Rough and Ready, Schuylkill County, PA. She married **SAMUEL BROWN**. She died on 1 August 1997, at age 91. She was buried at Zion (Klinger's) Church, Erdman, Lykens Township, Dauphin County, PA.

11.5.5.1.1 HARLAN OSCAR MARTZ was born on 24 February 1926, Dornsife, Northumberland County, PA. He was baptized on 2 April 1926, Salem (Herb's) Church, Rough and Ready, Schuylkill County, PA. He married **MABEL VIRGINIA LENIG**, daughter of **RALPH CLAIR LENIG** and **LENA ALICE LONG**, on 3 July 1949. He died on 17 August 1985, Geisinger Medical Center, Danville, Montour County, PA, at age 59. He was buried on 20 August 1985, at St. Peter's (Hoffman's) Church Cemetery, Lykens Township, Dauphin County, PA

11.5.5.1.1.1 DONNA VIRGINIA MARTZ was born on 20 December 1949, Danville, Montour County, PA. She married **LEONARD LEE SILKS**, son of **GEORGE O. SILKS JR.**, on 16 September 1967.

11.5.5.1.1.2 CAROLYN JEAN MARTZ was born on 22 August 1952, Lykens, Dauphin County, PA. She married **ERVIN JOHN WILLIAMS** on 7 November 1970.

11.5.5.1.1.2.1 JAMES WILLIAMS

11.5.5.1.1.3 LARRY HARLAN MARTZ was born on 27 April 1954, Lykens, Dauphin County, PA. He married **BONNIE DENISE ARTZ**, daughter of **EUGENE HOWARD ARTZ** and **GLORIA P. MILLER**, on 2 February 1980.

11.5.5.1.1.4 GARY LEE MARTZ was born on 23 October 1960, Danville, Montour County, PA.

11.5.5.1.2 MAE ARLENE MARTZ was born on 5 May 1927. She married **WILLIAM HERMAN MATTERN**, son of **LLOYD EDWARD MATTERN** and **MINNIE ELLEN RUNKLE**, on 8 August 1949.

11.5.5.1.2.1 DENNIS LEE MATTERN was born on 2 August 1950, stillborn.

11.5.5.1.2.2 LINDA CHARMAINE MATTERN was born on 16 July 1952. She married DALE EUGENE KLINGER, son of GURNEY ELWOOD KLINGER SR. and EDNA DEETER, on 14 April 1973.

>**11.5.5.1.2.2.1** SHELLY RENEE KLINGER was born on 14 September 1973. She married KARL WILLIARD, son of ELLWOOD WILLIARD SR. and BARBARA (--?--). In 2005, Shelly was living in Carbondale, IL.

>>**11.5.5.1.2.2.1.1** BROOKE WILLIARD was born circa 1989.

>>**11.5.5.1.2.2.1.2** KARLY WILLIARD was born on 6 May 1998.

>>**11.5.5.1.2.2.1.3** MADISON WILLIARD was born on 26 February 2000.

>>**11.5.5.1.2.2.1.4** ZACHARY WILLIARD was born on 26 February 2000.

>**11.5.5.1.2.2.2** KRISTY ELAINE KLINGER was born on 1 July 1976.

>**11.5.5.1.2.2.3** RYAN DALE KLINGER was born on 16 May 1978. He married ASHLEY WEINREICH, daughter of PAUL WEINREICH and JUDY (--?--), on 19 August 2006, St. Andrew's United Methodist Church, Valley View, Schuylkill County, PA.

11.5.5.1.3 BLANCHE JEAN MARTZ was born on 3 March 1931. She was baptized on 11 April 1931, Salem (Herb's) Church, Rough and Ready, Schuylkill County, PA. She married LESTER R. HARNER, son of GURNEY LEO HARNER and EDNA JANE CLARK, in December 1951. Blanche lives in Sacramento, PA.

>**11.5.5.1.3.1** DEBRA JEAN HARNER was born on 15 June 1954. She married ARTHUR SNYDER on 16 July 1976.

>>**11.5.5.1.3.1.1** NATHAN D. SNYDER

>>**11.5.5.1.3.1.2** CODY SNYDER

>**11.5.5.1.3.2** LONNIE EUGENE HARNER was born on 5 March 1957. He married GAIL WOLFGANG on 4 June 1983.

>>**11.5.5.1.3.2.1** ETHAN D. HARNER

>>>**11.5.5.1.3.2.1.1** TANYA J. HARNER married (--?--) KEITER.

11.5.5.1.4 CARL GURNEY MARTZ was born on 10 October 1933, Klingerstown, Schuylkill County, PA. He married MARY JANE HOKE, daughter of ALBERT W. HOKE and MARGARET A. BECHTEL, circa 1954. Carl was an equipment operator. He died on 8 January 2012, Harrisburg Hospital, Harrisburg, Dauphin County, PA, at age 78. According to a newspaper obituary, Carl's passion was baseball and he was instrumental in founding the little league and teener league of Elizabethville, and the American Legion League of UDA. He was buried on 13 January 2012, at St. Peters United Church of Christ Cemetery, Lykens, Dauphin County, PA.

>**11.5.5.1.4.1** STEVEN ALBERT MARTZ was born on 3 July 1955. He married SAVANNAH (--?--).

>**11.5.5.1.4.2** RANDY CARL MARTZ was born on 28 May 1956. He married LAURA BRADFORD on 22 November 1977, Columbia, SC. He married PAULA SHEFFLET on 29 October 1983, St. Louis, MO. Randy spent four seasons (1980-1983) as a pitcher with the Chicago Cubs and the Chicago White Sox. Randy lives in East Alton, IL.

>>**11.5.5.1.4.2.1** BRADFORD C. MARTZ was born on 3 February 1979.

>**11.5.5.1.4.3** TINA E. MARTZ was born on 5 December 1958. She married NORMAN BASSO. Tina lives in York, PA.

>**11.5.5.1.4.4** DAVID WILLIAM MARTZ was born on 26 October 1960. He married SUSAN PATRICK on 15 May 1982. David lives in Millersburg, PA.

>>**11.5.5.1.4.4.1** ANDREW D. MARTZ was born on 28 October 1983.

>**11.5.5.1.4.5** DENNIS SAMUEL MARTZ was born on 2 July 1963. He married TAMMY SKELTON on 27 November 1982. Dennis lives in Halifax, PA.

>>**11.5.5.1.4.5.1** NATASHA L. MARTZ was born on 7 August 1982.

11.5.5.2 FLOYD ALBERT KLINGER was born on 23 April 1912, Dornsife, Northumberland County, PA. He was baptized on 2 June 1912, Salem (Herb's) Church, Rough and Ready, Schuylkill County, PA. He married LAURA ALVERTA RAMBERGER, daughter of DANIEL EDGAR RAMBERGER and MARY EVA SNYDER, on 12 August 1933, Salem (Herb's) Church, Rough and Ready, Schuylkill

County, PA. He died on 16 June 1986, Geisinger Hospital, Danville, Northumberland County, PA, at age 74. According to a newspaper obituary, Floyd retired from farming in 1985. He was buried on 19 June 1986, at Salem Cemetery, Rough and Ready, Schuylkill County, PA.

11.5.5.2.1 (--?--) **KLINGER** was born circa 1934. He died in 1934.

11.5.5.2.2 **MARVIN EARL KLINGER** was born on 24 July 1935, Upper Mahanoy Township, Northumberland County, PA. He married **LENA MELINDA SNYDER**, daughter of **GUY JEFFERSON SNYDER** and **MARGARET IRENE HOCH**, on 18 December 1954, Himmel's Church, Rebuck, Washington Township, Northumberland County, PA.

11.5.5.2.2.1 **JEANNE IRENE KLINGER** was born on 1 September 1956, Lykens, Dauphin County, PA. She married **RICHARD CLYDE ADAMS**, son of **CLYDE C. ADAMS** and **ARABEL E. (--?--)**, on 21 June 1975, Himmel's Church, Rebuck, Washington Township, Northumberland County, PA.

11.5.5.2.2.2 **DENNIS LEE KLINGER** was born on 12 February 1959, Williamsport, Lycoming County, PA. He married **DENISE ANN KLACIK**, daughter of **THOMAS KLACIK** and **ESTHER FLESSATTI**, on 13 September 1980, Transfiguration Ukrainian Catholic Church, Shamokin, Northumberland County, PA.

11.5.5.2.2.2.1 **MERISSA KLINGER** was born on 1 January 1984, Evangelical Hospital, Lewisburg, PA.

11.5.5.2.2.3 **MICHAEL FLOYD KLINGER** was born on 19 August 1963, Sunbury, Northumberland County, PA. He married **KELLY EILEEN HAIN**, daughter of **KENNETH HAIN** and **JOYCE (--?--)**, on 2 May 1987, Himmel's Church, Rebuck, Northumberland County, PA.

11.5.5.2.2.3.1 **RYAN KLINGER** was born circa 1992.

11.5.5.2.2.3.2 **AMANDA KLINGER** was born circa 1997.

11.5.5.2.2.3.3 **COLLIN CHAD KLINGER** was born circa 1 January 2000.

11.5.5.2.3 **WILLARD LEE KLINGER** was born on 9 March 1942, Northumberland County, PA. He was baptized on 14 June 1942, Zion (Klinger's) Church, Erdman, Lykens Township, Dauphin County, PA. He married **CONNIE MAE NEIDIG**, daughter of **GEORGE FREEMAN NEIDIG** and **MAE BEATRICE MARTIN**, on 7 May 1960, Salem Church, Rough and Ready, Schuylkill County, PA. Williard is an electrician.

11.5.5.2.3.1 **DAWN LYNETTE KLINGER** was born on 16 March 1961, Community Hospital, Sunbury, Northumberland County, PA. She married **JAMES KRAMER**, son of **MELVIN G. KRAMER**, on 29 September 1985, Himmel's Church, Rebuck, Washington Township, Northumberland County, PA. Some sources suggest that she and **JAMES KRAMER** were married on 29 September 1984 Himmel's Church, Rebuck, Northumberland County, PA. She lived in West Cameron, Northumberland County, PA.

11.5.5.2.3.1.1 **ADAM JAMES KRAMER** was born on 18 January 1987.

11.5.5.2.3.1.2 **GRACE ELIZABETH KRAMER** was born on 30 June 1989.

11.5.5.2.3.2 **WILLARD LEE KLINGER JR.** was born on 9 November 1964, Community Hospital, Sunbury, Northumberland County, PA. He married **LORI KEIFFER** on 9 May 1987, Missionary Alliance Church, Watsontown, Northumberland County, PA. He lived in Northumberland, Northumberland County, PA.

11.5.5.2.3.2.1 **KEVIN FLOYD KLINGER** was born on 21 July 1986.

11.5.5.2.3.3 **GRACE ELAINE KLINGER** was born on 20 September 1966, Community Hospital, Sunbury, Northumberland County, PA. She married **DONALD BRUBAKER**, son of **WARREN BRUBAKER**, on 15 September 1991, Christ Wesleyan Church, Milton, Northumberland County, PA. She lived in R.D. 3, Sunbury, Northumberland County, PA.

11.5.5.2.3.3.1 **OLIVIA GRACE BRUBAKER** was born on 30 August 2001.

11.5.5.2.3.4 **DALE GEORGE KLINGER** was born on 4 September 1969, Community Hospital, Sunbury, Northumberland County, PA. He married **JENNIFER BRUBAKER**, daughter of **WARREN BRUBAKER**, on 4 May 1991, Augustaville Wesleyan Church, Augustaville, Northumberland County, PA. He lived in Paxinos, Northumberland County, PA.

11.5.5.2.3.4.1 **NATHAN DALE KLINGER** was born on 15 June 2001.

11.5.5.2.3.4.2 **EMILY KATHRYN KLINGER** was born on 7 April 2003.

11.5.6 CHARLES EDWIN KLINGER was born on 20 July 1887. He was baptized on 18 September 1887. He died on 18 September 1888, at age 1.

11.6 EMANUEL KLINGER is also referred to as **IMMANUEL** in some sources. He was born on 28 September 1856. He was baptized on 28 December 1856, Zion (Klinger's) Church, Erdman, Lykens Township, Dauphin County, PA. He married **CHRISTIANA SCHADEL**, daughter of **GEORGE H. SCHADEL** and **REBECCA TROUTMAN**, on 17 May 1874, Hegins, Schuylkill County, PA. Emanuel was the head carpenter for the building of the "new" Klinger's Church in 1894 and 1895. He died on 16 March 1928, at age 71. He was buried at Zion (Klinger's) Church, Erdman, Lykens Township, Dauphin County, PA.

11.6.1 MARY ALICE KLINGER was born on 21 September 1874. She married **HARVEY EDWARD SCHWALM**, son of **EDWARD SCHWALM** and **MATILDA LUCAS**, circa 1893. She died on 6 February 1961, Valley View, Schuylkill County, PA, at age 86. She was buried on 9 February 1961, at St. Andrew's Church Cemetery, Valley View, Schuylkill County, PA.

11.6.1.1 JENNY REBECCA SCHWALM was baptized on 20 March 1894, Zion (Klinger's) Lutheran Church, Erdman, Dauphin County, PA. She was born on 6 February 1894. She died on 2 January 1900, at age 5. She was buried at Zion (Klinger's) Church, Erdman, Lykens Township, Dauphin County, PA.

11.6.1.2 MINNIE ELDA SCHWALM is also referred to as **MINNIE A. SCHWALM** in some sources. She was born on 7 July 1896. She was baptized on 16 August 1896, Simeon Lutheran Church, Gratz, Dauphin County, PA. She married **THOMAS RADEL** circa 1913. She died in 1962.

11.6.1.2.1 RUTH O. RADEL was born in 1912, Pennsylvania. She married **HERMAN D. REED**.

11.6.1.2.1.1 CLAIR E. REED married **MAE GRABEY**.

11.6.1.2.1.1.1 ROBERT REED

11.6.1.2.1.1.2 REBECCA REED

11.6.1.2.1.2 MEREDITH E. REED married **GARY E. TRIPLETT**.

11.6.1.2.1.2.1 CHRISTOPHER TRIPLETT

11.6.1.2.2 MARY S. RADEL was born in 1914, Pennsylvania. She married **HENRY L. MENENDEZ**.

11.6.1.2.2.1 LOUIS R. MENENDEZ

11.6.1.2.3 ELEANOR RADEL was born in 1916, Pennsylvania. She married **GEORGE P. GARMAN**.

11.6.1.2.3.1 JANET M. GARMAN married **(--?--) BREACH**.

11.6.1.2.3.1.1 DONALD BREACH

11.6.1.2.3.2 KISLYNN G. GARMAN married **(--?--) WHITENIGHT**.

11.6.1.2.3.2.1 SUSAN WHITENIGHT

11.6.1.2.4 ROBERT R. RADEL was born circa 1920, Pennsylvania.

11.6.1.3 BESSIE EVA SCHWALM was born on 22 September 1899, Muir, PA. She married **GEORGE JAMES LUBOLD**, son of **CHARLES LUBOLD** and **KATIE ANN MILLER**, on 26 May 1917. She died on 15 February 1991, Pottsville, Schuylkill County, PA, at age 91. She was buried at Saint Andrews United Methodist Church Cemetery, Valley View, Schuylkill County, PA.

11.6.1.3.1 HELEN IRENE LUBOLD was born on 29 December 1917, Bear Valley, Hegins Township, Schuylkill County, PA. She married **PALMER D. SMELTZ**, son of **RILEY OSCAR SCHMELTZ** and **KATE ALICE DANIELS**, on 23 July 1937, St. Andrew's United Methodist Church, Valley View, Schuylkill County, PA. She died on 31 July 1965, at age 47. She was buried at Saint Andrew's United Methodist Church Cemetery, Valley View, Schuylkill County, PA.

11.6.1.3.1.1 PALMER DANIEL SMELTZ was born on 5 March 1938. He was baptized on 23 April 1938, St. Andrew's United Methodist Church, Valley View, Schuylkill County, PA.

11.6.1.3.1.2 BETTY JEAN SMELTZ was born on 7 March 1941. She was baptized on 2 May 1941, St. Andrew's United Methodist Church, Valley View, Schuylkill County, PA.

11.6.1.3.1.3 JAMES RILEY SMELTZ was born on 5 January 1944. He was baptized on 22 April 1944, St. Andrew's United Methodist Church, Valley View, Schuylkill County, PA.

11.6.1.3.2 EVA M. LUBOLD was born on 29 June 1919, Bear Valley, Hegins Township, Schuylkill County, PA. She married **HOMER JONATHAN KLINGER**, son of **JONATHAN GRANT KLINGER** and **CORA NEUMEISTER**, on 25 December 1937, St. Andrew's Church, Valley View, Schuylkill County, PA. She died on 3 September 1997, Valley View, Schuylkill County, PA, at age 78. She was buried at Saint Andrew's United Methodist Church Cemetery, Valley View, Schuylkill County, PA.

11.6.1.3.2.1 MARILYN MILDRED KLINGER was born on 27 August 1938.

11.6.1.3.2.2 BRUCE JAMES KLINGER was born on 5 June 1941.

11.6.1.3.2.3 RONALD GENE KLINGER was born on 24 November 1942.

11.6.1.3.2.4 ROBERT JAMAR KLINGER was born on 24 February 1945.

11.6.1.3.2.5 MARK DAVID KLINGER was born on 26 November 1953.

11.6.1.3.2.6 JOAN MARIE KLINGER was born on 7 January 1955.

11.6.1.3.3 HARVEY LUBOLD was born on 4 January 1921, Bear Valley, Hegins Township, Schuylkill County, PA. He married HILDA MARGARET MOYER, daughter of SAMUEL STANFORD MOYER and MABEL ESTELLA BIXLER.

11.6.1.3.3.1 HARVEY CHARLES LUBOLD JR. was born on 2 September 1942, Valley View, Schuylkill County, PA. He married FAYE RENEE SCHREFFLER, daughter of MARTIN SCHREFFLER and BETTY J. MORGAN, on 30 June 1962, Valley View, Schuylkill County, PA. He died on 8 March 2009, at his home, RR 3, Towanda, Towanda Township, Bradford County, PA, at age 66. According to a newspaper obituary, Harvey graduated from Tri-Valley High School Class of 1960 in Hegins, and Penn State University, where he received his degree in mechanical engineering. He was employed by GTE Sylvania in Towanda for 35 years, retiring as manager of the CAD-CAM Division in Engineering in 1998. During his years with Sylvania, Harvey designed many furnaces and secured several patents.

11.6.1.3.3.1.1 VICKI LUBOLD married (--?--) SCHMIDT.

11.6.1.3.3.1.2 STEPHANIE LUBOLD married (--?--) BOYLE.

11.6.1.3.3.2 LINDA MARIE LUBOLD was born on 17 January 1948. She married KIETH DONALD SCHEIB, son of DONALD SCHEIB and JANICE OTTO, on 17 June 1967. She and KIETH DONALD SCHEIB were divorced in 1971. She married JAMES SAPIANO on 19 June 1971, Valley View, Schuylkill County, PA.

11.6.1.3.3.3 AUDREY LOUISE LUBOLD was born on 7 November 1951. She married DALE GONGLOFF on 12 August 1972.

11.6.1.3.4 MELVIN JAMES LUBOLD was born on 9 March 1923, Bear Valley, Hegins Township, Schuylkill County, PA. He married GENEVIEVE HAINES Valley View, Schuylkill County, PA.

11.6.1.3.5 MARIE ANNIS LUBOLD was born on 26 April 1925. She died on 15 March 1926. She was buried at Zion (Klinger's) Church, Erdman, Lykens Township, Dauphin County, PA.

11.6.1.3.6 LUCILLE MARY LUBOLD was born on 30 March 1928, Valley View, Schuylkill County, PA. She married LESTER HERBERT LUDWIG, son of HERBERT WILLIAM LUDWIG and IRENE MAY KLINGER, on 6 October 1945, St. Andrew's United Methodist Church, Valley View, Schuylkill County, PA.

11.6.1.3.6.1 STEVEN LESTER LUDWIG was born on 27 June 1946, Schuylkill County, PA. He married PATRICIA HORNBERGER circa 1965.

11.6.1.3.6.1.1 TIMOTHY STEVEN LUDWIG was born on 22 July 1967. He married JUNE STALLER circa 1990.

11.6.1.3.6.1.1.1 BRYON LUDWIG was born circa 1992.

11.6.1.3.6.1.2 JEFFREY WILLIAM LUDWIG was born on 10 June 1970.

11.6.1.3.6.1.3 SUSAN DIANA LUDWIG was born on 28 December 1975.

11.6.1.3.6.2 MARIE ANN LUDWIG was born on 3 April 1951. She married ELVIN DARYL MORGAN circa 1968. She married TED JOHN REINOEHL, son of GEORGE CHARLES REINOEHL and DOROTHY MARY KOPPENHAVER, on 15 April 1978.

11.6.1.3.6.2.1 BRYAN KEITH MORGAN is also referred to as BRYAN MORGAN in some sources. He was born on 29 October 1969. He married STEPHANIE BLOCH circa 1992.

11.6.1.3.6.2.1.1 LISA ANN MORGAN was born circa 1994.

11.6.1.3.6.2.1.2 ANNA MAE MORGAN was born circa 1996.

11.6.1.3.6.2.1.3 JACHARY MORGAN was born circa 1995.

11.6.1.3.6.2.1.4 JOSHUA RYAN MORGAN was born on 10 March 1997.

11.6.1.3.6.2.1.5 NICHOLAS BRYCE MORGAN was born on 11 September 1998.

11.6.1.3.6.2.2 CHRISTOPHER CHARLES MORGAN was born on 28 March 1970. He married **PAULA KODACK** circa 1988.

11.6.1.3.6.2.2.1 JUSTIN MORGAN was born on 10 October 1990.

11.6.1.3.6.2.2.2 JARED MICHAEL MORGAN was born on 17 October 1993.

11.6.1.3.6.2.2.3 KATELYN C. MORGAN was born on 10 March 1997.

11.6.1.3.6.3 THOMAS HERBERT LUDWIG was born on 19 February 1954, Schuylkill County, PA. He married **DONNA RAE SMITH** circa 1978.

11.6.1.3.6.3.1 CHRYSTAL DAWN LUDWIG was born on 5 May 1980.

11.6.1.3.6.3.2 AMANDA KAY LUDWIG was born on 27 April 1983.

11.6.1.3.6.3.3 BETHANY NICOLE LUDWIG was born on 16 November 1987.

11.6.1.3.6.4 DONALD JAMES LUDWIG was born on 23 December 1955, Schuylkill County, PA. He died on 16 June 1971, Schuylkill County, PA, at age 15. He was buried at Salem E.U.B. United Methodist Church Cemetery, Weishample, Schuylkill County, PA.

11.6.1.3.6.5 CATHY MARILYN LUDWIG was born on 17 August 1960, Schuylkill County, PA.

11.6.1.3.6.6 KENNETH GLEN LUDWIG was born on 23 October 1964, Schuylkill County, PA.

11.6.1.3.6.6.1 JUDITH ANN LUDWIG was born on 28 March 1993.

11.6.1.3.6.7 ALICE KAY LUDWIG was born on 15 July 1966, Schuylkill County, PA. She married **KEVIN RONALD SCHEIB**, son of **ROBERT BENJAMIN SCHEIB** and **PHYLLIS EVA MAE PAUL**, on 27 May 1989, PA.

11.6.1.3.6.7.1 ZACHARY ROBERT SCHEIB was born on 8 October 1991, Schuylkill County, PA.

11.6.1.3.6.7.2 NATHAN TYLER SCHEIB was born on 13 July 1994, Schuylkill County, PA.

11.6.1.3.6.7.3 SAMUEL JAMES SCHEIB was born on 13 July 1994, Schuylkill County, PA.

11.6.1.3.6.7.4 DANIEL RONALD SCHEIB was born on 19 July 2000, Schuylkill County, PA.

11.6.1.3.7 WILLIAM ROGER LUBOLD was born on 10 January 1940, Valley View, Schuylkill County, PA. He married **RUTHANNE NATALIE TIETSWORTH** on 31 March 1956, Lavalle, PA.

11.6.1.4 ALMA MEDA SCHWALM was born on 19 January 1900, Pennsylvania. She married **HARVEY J. SCHADEL**. She died on 21 January 1926, Jordan Township, Northumberland County, PA, at age 26. She was buried on 25 January 1926, at Union Cemetery, Pillow, Northumberland County, PA.

11.6.1.4.1 EVA SCHADEL

11.6.1.4.2 MIRIANA SCHADEL

11.6.1.4.3 HARVEY SCHADEL

11.6.1.5 WILLIAM HARVEY SCHWALM is also referred to as **WILLIAM D. SCHWALM** in some sources. He was born in 1902, Pennsylvania. He married **MEDA MAE SCHWALM**, daughter of **ALBERT PETER SCHWALM** and **BARBARA A. CLARK**, circa 1919. He died in 1980. He was buried at Zion (Klinger's) Lutheran Church Cemetery, Erdman, Dauphin County, PA.

11.6.1.5.1 LORRAINE SCHWALM died before December 2003.

11.6.1.5.2 BRUCE D. SCHWALM married **BETTY HELLER**. He married **SYLVIA SNYDER**.

11.6.1.5.2.1 VINCENT SCHWALM

11.6.1.5.2.2 STEVEN SCHWALM

11.6.1.5.2.3 MICHAEL SNYDER

11.6.1.5.2.4 DOUGLAS SNYDER

11.6.1.5.2.5 SANDRA SCHWALM

11.6.1.5.3 LEON H. SCHWALM was born on 19 September 1918. He married **LILLIAN MACE**, daughter of **JAMES MACE** and **ERMA WEISS**, on 30 August 1941, St. Andrew's Church, Valley

View, Schuylkill County, PA. Prior to his death, Leon was living in the vicinity of Valley View, Schuylkill County, PA. He died on 7 January 1986, Reading Hospital and Medical Center, Reading, Berks County, PA, at age 67. He was buried at Saint Andrews United Methodist Church Cemetery, Valley View, Schuylkill County, PA.

11.6.1.5.3.1 LYNN EDWARD SCHWALM was born on 6 September 1942, Schuylkill County, PA. He was baptized on 7 December 1942, St. Andrew's United Methodist Church, Valley View, Schuylkill County, PA. He married an unknown person. He married **CONNIE ANN LETTICH**, daughter of **EARL HENRY LETTICH** and **BETTY L. SCHEIB**, circa 1963, PA. He died in 1965, Schuylkill County, PA. He was buried at St Andrew's United Methodist Church Cemetery, Valley View, Schuylkill County, PA.

11.6.1.5.3.2 DAVID HENRY SCHWALM was born on 28 July 1945. He married **AUDREY CONPROPST**.

11.6.1.5.3.2.1 SCOTT SCHWALM

11.6.1.5.3.2.2 DEBRA SCHWALM

11.6.1.5.3.2.3 HEATHER SCHWALM

11.6.1.5.3.3 RONALD WAYNE SCHWALM was born on 9 September 1960, Butler Township, Schuylkill County, PA. He died on 4 October 1960, A.C. Milliken Hospital, Pottsville, Schuylkill County, PA. He was buried on 6 October 1960, at Saint Andrews United Methodist Church Cemetery, Valley View, Schuylkill County, PA.

11.6.1.5.3.4 DONALD DUANE SCHWALM was born on 6 October 1960, Butler Township, Schuylkill County, PA. He married **BERNADETTE WEIDENSAUL** on 19 July 1986, St. Mauritius Catholic Church, Ashland, PA.

11.6.1.5.4 HELEN M. SCHWALM was born on 8 July 1920, Schuylkill County, PA. She married **HARLEY ALVIN HAUCK**, son of **ROBERT HAUCK** and **KATIE COLEMAN**. She died on 10 May 1980, Schuylkill County, PA, at age 59. She was buried at Church of Christ Cemetery, Fountain Springs, Schuylkill County, PA.

11.6.1.5.4.1 BARBARA HAUCK married **CHARLES STROHECKER**.

11.6.1.5.4.1.1 SUSAN STROHECKER

11.6.1.5.4.1.2 DEBRA STROHECKER

11.6.1.5.4.2 CAROL HAUCK married **DALE THOMPSON**.

11.6.1.5.4.2.1 RANDALL THOMPSON

11.6.1.5.4.2.2 LYNDON THOMPSON

11.6.1.5.4.3 HARLEY HAUCK JR. married **ELLEN CORDY**.

11.6.1.5.4.3.1 DEREK J. HAUCK married **KELLY STORM**. He married **TARA HARVEY**.

11.6.1.5.4.3.1.1 CAETLYN HAUCK

11.6.1.5.4.3.1.2 DAVID HAUCK

11.6.1.5.4.3.1.3 ANDREW HAUCK

11.6.1.5.5 ELEANOR MAY SCHWALM was born on 28 September 1922. She died on 4 April 1926, at age 3. She was buried at Zion (Klinger's) Lutheran Church Cemetery, Erdman, Dauphin County, PA.

11.6.1.5.6 ANNICE SCHWALM was born in 1927, Schuylkill County, PA. She married **ROBERT H. KLOUSER**, son of **CHARLES KLOUSER** and **KATIE KOPPENHAVER**. She lived in Hegins, Schuylkill County, PA. She died on 3 June 1979, Milton Hershey Medical Center, Dauphin County, PA. She was buried in 1980, at Church of God Cemetery, Valley View, Schuylkill County, PA.

11.6.1.5.6.1 YVONNE KLOUSER married **JACK SPECHT**.

11.6.1.5.6.1.1 SHANNON LEE SPECHT married **THOMAS MELIDEO**.

11.6.1.5.6.1.1.1 SOPHIA ROSE MELIDEO was born on 18 July 1999, Loudoun Hospital, Leesburg, VA.

11.6.1.5.6.1.2 SHANE SPECHT

11.6.1.5.6.1.3 SOMER ANNE SPECHT married **PRYCE PARKER**. She lived in Hershey, Dauphin County, PA.

11.6.1.5.6.1.3.1 MYAH ELIZA PARKER was born on 15 August 1996.

11.6.1.5.6.1.3.2 CLAUDIA MAE PARKER was born on 6 September 2002.

11.6.1.5.7 WILLIAM R. SCHWALM was born circa 1929, Valley View, Hegins Township, Schuylkill County, PA. He married ELLA MAE STROHECKER, daughter of GEORGE EMORY STROHECKER and A. VALERIA BEURY, circa 1950. He lived in Hatboro, PA. He died on 1 December 2003. He was buried on 19 November 2016, at Pine Grove Memorial Park, Warminster, Bucks County, PA.

11.6.1.5.7.1 DEBRA SCHWALM married CHRISTIAN NICKELS JR.

11.6.1.5.7.1.1 CHRISTIAN NICKELS III married ELIZABETH BOCH.

11.6.1.5.7.1.2 JONATHAN MICHAEL NICKELS married AMBER (--?--).

11.6.1.5.7.1.3 JILL KRISTIN NICKELS married DAN SCHAEFER.

11.6.1.5.7.2 WENDY SCHWALM married JAMES C. MORGAN.

11.6.1.5.7.2.1 AMANDA MORGAN

11.6.1.5.7.2.2 ALLISON MORGAN

11.6.1.5.7.2.3 JAYME MORGAN

11.6.1.5.7.2.4 JAMES C. MORGAN JR.

11.6.1.5.7.3 WILLIAM R. SCHWALM JR. married PAULA FREY. He married SUZANNE CREPS.

11.6.1.5.7.3.1 KIMBERLY FREY

11.6.1.5.7.3.2 JOHN SCHWALM

11.6.1.5.7.3.3 SUZANNE CREPS

11.6.1.5.7.4 RICHARD G. SCHWALM married JOANNE GORG.

11.6.1.5.7.4.1 RICHARD G. SCHWALM JR. married MEGHAN (--?--).

11.6.1.5.7.4.2 RANDALL WESLEY WILLIAM SCHWALM was born on 22 April 1985.

11.6.1.6 VERNA CHRISTIANA SCHWALM was born on 4 April 1909, Millersburg, Dauphin County, PA. She married CLIFFORD KENNETH SCHWALM, son of DANIEL A. SCHWALM and NORA MARGARET SNYDER, on 3 June 1926, St. Andrew's Church, Valley View, Schuylkill County, PA. She died on 18 August 1992, Susuehanna Lutheran Village, Millersburg, Dauphin County, PA, at age 83. She was buried at Saint Andrews United Methodist Church Cemetery, Valley View, Schuylkill County, PA.

11.6.1.6.1 CAROLYN ROJEAN SCHWALM was born on 23 June 1928. She married LYLE C. MILLER, son of WILLIAM D. MILLER and IVA KLOUSER, circa 1947.

11.6.1.6.1.1 DANIEL D. MILLER married BARBARA (--?--).

11.6.1.6.1.1.1 JOSH MILLER

11.6.1.6.1.1.2 KAYLA MILLER married (--?--) MASSER.

11.6.1.6.1.2 LUCINDA MILLER married WILLIAM R. REED.

11.6.1.6.1.2.1 BRETT REED

11.6.1.6.1.2.2 BRAD REED

11.6.1.7 ELDA MATILDA SCHWALM was born circa 1911, Pennsylvania. She married ROBERT GREEN after 1930. She died before 1976.

11.6.1.7.1 ROBERT GREEN

11.6.1.7.2 JAMES GREEN

11.6.1.7.3 MARGURITE GREEN

11.6.1.8 MABEL GRACE SCHWALM was born on 22 September 1914, Valley View Hegins Township, Schuylkill County, PA. She married LEROY J. STUTZMAN, son of JAMES STUTZMAN and TILLIE I. SCHWALM, on 5 June 1938, St. Andrew's Church, Valley View, Schuylkill County, PA. She died on 12 September 2001, Good Samaritan Regional Medical Center, Pottsville, Schuylkill County, PA, at age 86.

11.6.1.8.1 JAMES LEROY STUTZMAN (see above)

11.6.1.8.1.1 ELKE BRIGGITTA STUTZMAN (see above)

11.6.1.8.1.1.1 CHANDRA LYNNE ISENBERG (see above)

11.6.1.8.1.1.2 BRITT CHARLES ISENBERG (see above)

11.6.1.8.1.1.3 DUSTIN JAMES ISENBERG (see above)

11.6.1.8.1.2 STEFANIE SUE STUTZMAN (see above)

11.6.1.8.1.2.1 STELLA ROSE FEIDT (see above)

11.6.1.8.2 JOEL FRED STUTZMAN (see above)

11.6.1.8.2.1 STEVEN JOEL STUTZMAN (see above)

11.6.1.8.2.1.1 ALYSSA LYNN STUTZMAN (see above)

11.6.1.8.2.2 JAMES SCOTT STUTZMAN (see above)

11.6.1.8.2.2.1 DANIEL J. STUTZMAN (see above)

11.6.1.8.2.3 JULIE ANN STUTZMAN (see above)

11.6.1.8.2.3.1 KENZIE MARIE MILNE (see above)

11.6.1.8.2.4 JOEL ANDREW STUTZMAN (see above)

11.6.1.8.2.4.1 JOEL ETHAN STUTZMAN (see above)

11.6.1.8.2.5 EDWARD STUTZMAN (see above)

11.6.1.8.3 EDWARD KEITH STUTZMAN (see above)

11.6.1.8.3.1 MELISSA J. STUTZMAN (see above)

11.6.1.8.3.2 TIMOTHY EDWARD STUTZMAN (see above)

11.6.1.9 EDWARD SCHWALM was born on 15 October 1915, Schuylkill County, PA. He married CELECIA BAIMBRIDGE on 2 April 1936, St. Andrew's Church, Valley View, Schuylkill County, PA. He died on 12 September 1969, Harrisburg, Dauphin County, PA, at age 53. He was buried at Methodist Episcopal Cemetery, Williamstown, Dauphin County, PA.

11.6.1.9.1 DONALD EDWARD SCHWALM was born on 8 September 1936.

11.6.1.9.2 LARRY GORDON SCHWALM was born on 15 September 1938.

11.6.1.10 HILDA M. SCHWALM was born circa October 1917, Pennsylvania. She married LLOYD H. DONTON.

11.6.1.10.1 CAROLE JEAN DONTON married RICHARD B. ARTZ, son of EUGENE HOWARD ARTZ and GLORIA P. MILLER.

11.6.1.10.1.1 BRUCE L. ARTZ was born on 16 April 1960. He married JEANNIE FRY on 16 June 1984.

11.6.1.10.1.2 PAMELA ARTZ was born on 30 June 1961. She married ROBERT ELVIN KOPPENHAVER, son of ELVIN LEROY KOPPENHAVER and RUTH ELAINE DEITRICH, on 17 January 1987.

11.6.2 CHARLES DANIEL KLINGER was born on 21 February 1877, Gratz, Dauphin County, PA. He was baptized on 8 April 1877, Lutheran Theological Seminary, Gettysburg, Adams County, PA. He married EMMA JANE BOWMAN, daughter of DAVID BOWMAN and MARY CLARK, before 1918. In 1918 when he registered for the draft in World War I, Charles was married and living at 255 E. Market Street in Williamstown, Dauphin County, PA, where he was a carpenter foreman at the Susquehanna Colliery in Williamstown. He died on 17 November 1956, Williamstown, Dauphin County, PA, at age 79. He was buried at Fairview Cemetery, Williamstown, Dauphin County, PA.

11.6.3 CATHARINE KLINGER is also referred to as KATIE REBECCA in some sources. She was born on 28 May 1879. She was baptized on 27 October 1879, Zion (Klinger's) Church, Erdman, Lykens Township, Dauphin County, PA. She married THEODORE E. REBUCK, son of EMANUEL REBUCK and JULIANA SHADE, circa 1896. She died in 1946. She was buried at St. Paul's (Artz's) Church Cemetery, Sacramento, Schuylkill County, PA.

11.6.3.1 WALTER REBUCK was born in January 1897, Pennsylvania.

11.6.3.2 GURNEY E. RABUCK is also referred to as GURNEY REBUCK in some sources. He was born in April 1899, Pennsylvania. He married BEATRICE H. FETTERHOFF, daughter of PHILIP FETTERHOFF and MARGARET DERR, circa 1925. He died before 2008.

11.6.3.2.1 JOYCE REBUCK married CLIFFORD SHAFFER. Joyce lives in Nottingham, PA.

11.6.3.2.2 DONALD REBUCK married MARIE NOLAN.

11.6.3.2.3 EDITH REBUCK. Edith lives in Tower City, Schuylkill County, PA.

11.6.3.2.4 DORIS REBUCK married **CARL WETZEL.** Doris lives in Ashland, Schuylkill County, PA.

11.6.3.2.5 GURNEY REBUCK married **MARIE HOUSE.**

11.6.3.2.6 JACKIE RABUCK died before 20 December 2008.

11.6.3.2.7 LLOYD G. REBUCK was born on 5 June 1926, Pennsylvania. He married **BESSIE LONG**, daughter of **ROY LONG** and **NORA ADAMS**. He died on 13 December 1992, at age 66.

11.6.3.2.8 WILLIAM H. RABUCK was born on 9 November 1928, Tower City, Schuylkill County, PA. He married **MAE OSSMAN** circa 1961. He died on 21 October 2008, Geisinger Medical Center, Danville, Montour County, PA, at age 79. According to a newspaper obituary, William, who lived in Ashland, PA, was Navy veteran serving in World War II and Korea and was a retired supervisor for the City of Harrisburg Water Department.

11.6.3.2.8.1 JASON T. RABUCK

11.6.3.2.9 BERTHA M. RABUCK was born on 2 April 1930, Tower City, Schuylkill County, PA. She married **RUDOLF WEAVER**, son of **GEORGE WEAVER** and **MARGARET (--?--)**. She died on 20 December 2008, at her home, on Church Street, Muir, Schuylkill County, PA, at age 78. According to a newspaper obituary, Bertha retired from the Kinney Shoe Factory, in Millersburg, PA. She was buried on 27 December 2008, at Fairview Cemetery, Muir, Schuylkill County, PA.

11.6.3.2.9.1 BRENDA J. WEAVER married **ANTHONY HOST.** Brenda lives in Lykens, Dauphin County, PA.

11.6.3.2.9.2 SHELVA J. WEAVER married **MICHAEL KLINGER.** Shelva lives in Tremont, Schuylkill County, PA.

11.6.3.2.9.3 DEIRDRA J. WEAVER married **(--?--) DUNLEAVY.** Dierdra lives in Tremont, Schuylkill County, PA.

11.6.3.2.9.4 TARA J. WEAVER married **RICHARD STRAUB.** Tara lives in Muir, Schuylkill County, PA.

11.6.3.2.9.4.1 ERIC STRAUB

11.6.3.2.10 JAMES E. RABUCK was born on 21 September 1935, Sheridan, Schuylkill County, PA. He married **ETHEL E. ADAMS**, daughter of **WILLIAM M. ADAMS** and **VERNA SHILEY**, circa 1957. He died on 9 June 2009, at his home on Colliery Avenue, Tower City, Schuylkill County, PA, at age 73. According to a newspaper obituary, James was a Marine Corps veteran of the Korean War. He retired in 2000 from Richmond Screw and Anchor, Tremont. James was also an avid outdoorsman.

11.6.3.2.10.1 ROSE M. RABUCK

11.6.3.2.10.2 MARK L. RABUCK

11.6.3.2.10.3 RODNEY L. RABUCK

11.6.3.2.10.4 MELINDA J. RABUCK married **(--?--) HENDRICKS.**

11.6.3.2.10.4.1 CASSIDY HENDRICKS

11.6.3.2.10.4.2 WILLIAM HENDRICKS

11.6.3.2.10.4.3 JEFFREY HENDRICKS

11.6.3.2.10.4.4 ROSE HENDRICKS

11.6.3.2.10.4.5 ELIJAH HENDRICKS

11.6.3.2.10.4.6 JOSEPH HENDRICKS

11.6.3.3 ARTHUR REBUCK was born circa 1901, Pennsylvania.

11.6.3.4 ANNIE REBUCK was born circa 1904, Pennsylvania.

11.6.3.5 ALLEN A. REBUCK was born circa 1906, Pennsylvania.

11.6.3.6 HENRY REBUCK was born in 1909, Pennsylvania.

11.6.3.7 THEODORE REBUCK was born circa 1910, Pennsylvania.

11.6.3.8 ERNEST F. REBUCK was born circa 1912, Pennsylvania.

11.6.3.9 MARK L. REBUCK was born circa 1916, Pennsylvania.

11.6.3.10 ERMA M. REBUCK was born circa 1918, Pennsylvania.

11.6.3.11 CHARLES E. REBUCK was born circa November 1919, Pennsylvania.

11.6.4 CLARA EMMA MCCLAIDA KLINGER is also referred to as **CLAIRE AND CLARA M.** in some sources. She was born on 8 January 1882, Lykens Township, Dauphin County, PA. She married **JAMES ISAAC SCHEIB**, son of **FRANKLIN SCHEIB** and **ELISABETH MOYER**, circa 1899. She died on 22 October 1962, Friendly Home, Pitman, Schuylkill County, PA, at age 80. She was buried on 26 October 1962, at Spring Glen United Methodist Church Cemetery, Spring Glen, Hubley Township, Schuylkill County, PA. Some sources record that she died in 1957.

11.6.4.1 ALBERT OSCAR SCHEIB was born on 26 June 1899, Gratz, Dauphin County, PA. He married **CATHERINE ELIZABETH LUBOLD** on 8 November 1919, Zion (Klinger's) Lutheran Church, Erdman, Dauphin County, PA. He died on 28 April 1937, Williamstown, Dauphin County, PA. He was buried on 1 May 1937, at St. Mark's United Methodist Church Cemetery, Spring Glen, Schuylkill County, PA.

11.6.4.1.1 BESSIE EDNA SCHEIB was born on 13 October 1921, Valley View, Schuylkill County, PA. She was baptized on 13 November 1921, Zion (Klinger's) Lutheran Church, Erdman, Dauphin Co, PA. She married **ROY PERSHING HOLDEMAN**, son of **CLAYTON E. HOLDEMAN** and **ESTELLA LAURA SAUSSER,** on 19 October 1940, St Andrew's United Methodist Church, Valley View, Schuylkill County, PA.

11.6.4.1.1.1 GLORIA JEAN HOLDEMAN was born on 30 April 1941, Dauphin Co, PA. She married **LAMAR GENE KISSINGER**, son of **LESTER EMANUEL KISSINGER** and **RUBY STRAUB**, on 15 June 1959.

11.6.4.1.1.1.1 KELI KISSINGER is also referred to as **KELLY KISSINGER** in some sources. She was born on 14 July 1960. She married **STEVEN SHANNON** circa 1983.

11.6.4.1.1.1.2 RANDALL EUGENE KISSINGER was born on 26 May 1963, Reading, Berks County, PA. He married **MERITA MARIE HILL** on 5 June 1993.

11.6.4.1.1.1.3 CURTIS ALAN KISSINGER was born on 1 February 1967.

11.6.4.1.1.2 KENNETH HOLDEMAN was born circa 1943, Dauphin Co, PA. He married **VIRGINIA MAIDEN**. He married **DEBORAH (--?--)**.

11.6.4.1.1.2.1 CHRIS HOLDEMAN was born circa 1968, Dauphin Co., PA.

11.6.4.1.2 JUNE ROSE SCHEIB was born on 7 June 1926, Williamstown, Dauphin County, PA. She was baptized on 11 July 1926, St. Andrew's United Methodist Church, Valley View, Schuylkill County, PA. She married **WILLIARD A. DEIBERT** on 22 July 1944, St. Andrew's United Methodist Church, Valley View, Schuylkill County, PA. She married **WILLIARD ALLEN DEIBERT**, son of **GEORGE WILLIAM DEIBERT** and **GERTIE E. ERDMAN**, on 22 July 1944, St. Andrew's United Methodist Church, Valley View, Schuylkill County, PA. She married **GEORGE R. HOFFMAN**, son of **LEVI HOFFMAN** and **CORA SEAMON**, on 31 January 1948, Dauphin County, PA. She married **HAROLD GOUDY**. She died on 2 October 2010, The Manor at Susquehanna Village, Millersburg, Dauphin County, PA, at age 84. According to a newspaper obituary, June had worked at the former Muskin Shoe factory in Millersburg. She was buried at St. Mark's United Methodist Church Cemetery, Srping Glen, Schuylkill County, PA.

11.6.4.1.2.1 ANN MARIE (--?--) married **(--?--) BONAWITZ**.

11.6.4.1.2.1.1 CHARLES BONAWITZ IV

11.6.4.1.2.1.2 NICHOLAS BONAWITZ

11.6.4.1.2.1.3 ERIN BONAWITZ married **(--?--) GRIFFIN**.

11.6.4.1.2.2 DAVID A. HOFFMAN

11.6.4.1.2.3 BRENT N. HOFFMAN

11.6.4.2 VERNON ARTHUR SCHEIB was born on 17 October 1901. He married **EVA MABEL KISSINGER**. He died on 31 December 1971, at age 70.

11.6.4.2.1 RUBY SCHEIB married **JOHN SHERRY**.

11.6.4.2.2 ELWOOD SCHEIB

11.6.4.2.3 ANNIE M. SCHEIB was born in 1918. She married **AMOS SUNDAY**. She married **H.D. ABRAMSON**.

11.6.4.2.4 ETHEL SCHEIB was born on 28 December 1920. She married **CLAUDE L. KNORR**, son of **FREDERICK DANIEL KNORR** and **URSULA H. WOLFGANG**.

11.6.4.2.4.1 DENNIS KNORR was born circa 1942. Dennis lives in the vicinity of Gratz, Dauphin County, PA.

11.6.4.2.4.2 CLAUDE L KNORR was born on 20 September 1942. He married **ELLEN BLYLER**. Claude lives in Hegins, Schuylkill County, PA.

11.6.4.2.4.2.1 YVONNE KNORR was born on 1 April 1964. She married **RODNEY HEIM**.

11.6.4.2.4.2.1.1 RAHN HEIM was born on 28 May 1981.

11.6.4.2.4.2.2 HEATHER KNORR was born on 19 October 1976.

11.6.4.2.4.2.3 KENT KNORR was born on 29 June 1962.

11.6.4.2.4.3 CAROL KNORR was born circa 1944.

11.6.4.2.5 MARGARET SCHEIB was born circa June 1927, Pennsylvania. She married **CHARLES HERB**.

11.6.4.2.6 STANLEY SCHEIB was born circa September 1928, Pennsylvania. He married **MARIAN DITTON**. He married **LORRAINE HERB**.

11.6.4.3 CARLOS RUFUS SCHEIB was born on 14 December 1903, Gratz, Dauphin County, PA. He married **SADIE ALVERTA KLINGER**, daughter of **FRANKLIN ADAM KLINGER** and **ELLEN SEVILLA LETTICH**, on 18 February 1922, St. Andrew's United Methodist Church, Valley View, Schuylkill County, PA. He died on 2 April 1934, at age 30. He was buried at Spring Glen, Schuylkill County, PA.

11.6.4.3.1 HARRY FRANKLIN SCHEIB was born on 28 May 1922. He married **HELEN WILLIARD**, daughter of **PERRY WILLIARD**. He died on 5 March 1987, at age 64. He was buried on 8 March 1987, at St, Mark's Church Cemetery, Spring Glen, Schuylkill County, PA.

11.6.4.3.1.1 GARY SCHEIB was born on 23 May 1950.

11.6.4.3.1.1.1 KELLY SCHEIB

11.6.4.3.1.1.2 MEGAN SCHEIB

11.6.4.3.2 DALE LAMAR SCHEIB was born on 23 August 1933. He died in 1936. He was buried at Spring Glen United Methodist Cemetery, Spring Glen, Schuylkill County, PA.

11.6.4.4 AMMON ELLERSLIE SCHEIB was born on 8 June 1906, Lykens Township, Dauphin County, PA. He married **MAE SARAH MATTERN** on 17 September 1925. He died on 10 January 1961, Hubley Township, Schuylkill County, PA, at age 54. He was buried on 15 January 1961, at United Brethren Cemetery, Sacramento, Schuylkill County, PA. Ammon worked as a reamer in a machine shop.

11.6.4.4.1 MABEL IRENE SCHEIB was born on 17 February 1926. She was baptized on 25 April 1926, St. Andrew's United Methodist Church, Valley View, Schuylkill County, PA. She married **ROBERT ALLEN KANTZ** on 14 July 1945, St. Andrew's United Methodist Church, Valley View, Schuylkill County, PA.

11.6.4.4.1.1 SUSAN CAROL KANTZ was born on 4 July 1946, Dauphin Co., PA. She married **THOMAS DONAHUE** in September 1967.

11.6.4.4.1.1.1 CLAIRE ELIZABETH DONAHUE was born on 18 July 1970.

11.6.4.4.1.1.2 CATHARINE CAROL DONAHUE was born on 20 June 1972.

11.6.4.4.1.1.3 MEGHAN JEAN DONAHUE was born on 11 August 1975.

11.6.4.4.1.1.4 WILLIAM THOMAS DONAHUE was born on 11 August 1975.

11.6.4.4.1.2 MAUREEN LOUISE KANTZ was born on 27 March 1948, Dauphin Co., PA.

11.6.4.4.1.3 SALLY ANN KANTZ was born on 4 June 1949, Dauphin Co., PA. She married **THOMAS SUTCLIFFE JR.** circa 1971.

11.6.4.4.1.3.1 ANNIE ELIZABETH SUTCLIFFE was born on 6 June 1979.

11.6.4.4.1.3.2 JOHN ALLEN SUTCLIFFE was born on 15 July 1982.

11.6.4.4.1.3.3 MARK ANDREW SUTCLIFFE was born on 22 November 1983.

11.6.4.4.1.4 JANET EILEEN KANTZ was born on 6 December 1952, Dauphin Co., PA. She married **CHARLES W. HEAGY** circa 1972.

11.6.4.4.1.4.1 ROBERT CHARLES HEAGY was born on 27 June 1974.

11.6.4.4.1.4.2 DANIEL DAVID HEAGY was born on 24 March 1976.

11.6.4.4.1.4.3 RACHAEL ELIZABETH HEAGY was born on 20 June 1983.

11.6.4.4.2 ELVA ARLENE SCHIEB was born on 15 June 1927, Valley View, Schuylkill County, PA. She married **ROBERT BRYAN SCHMELTZ**, son of **WILLIAM HENRY SCHMELTZ** and **NORA MAY KLINGER**, on 15 September 1945, St. Adrew's United Methodist Church, Valley View, Schuylkill County, PA. She died on 5 August 2010, Ephrata Manor, Ephrata, Lancaster County, PA, at age 83. She was buried on 9 August 2010, at Zeltenreich Cemetery, New Holland, Lancaster County, PA.

11.6.4.4.2.1 MARILYN MAE SCHMELTZ was born on 24 October 1946, Ashland, Schuylkill County, PA. She married **HAL ROY BEASLEY** on 26 August 1972.

11.6.4.4.2.1.1 CHERYL LYNN BEASLEY was born on 15 May 1981.

11.6.4.4.2.1.2 JEFFREY ALAN BEASLEY was born on 6 September 1986.

11.6.4.4.2.2 SHARON EILEEN SCHMELTZ was born on 10 January 1950, Schuylkill County, PA. She married **GLENN JAMES LONGENECKER** on 3 May 1969.

11.6.4.4.2.2.1 JAMES GLENN LONGENECKER was born on 23 March 1970.

11.6.4.4.2.2.2 DOLLY MICHELLE LONGENECKER was born on 19 August 1973.

11.6.4.4.2.3 SHEILA MARIE SCHMELTZ was born on 14 November 1951.

11.6.4.4.2.4 BYRON ROBERT SCHMELTZ was born on 25 September 1953. He died on 20 June 1976, at age 22.

11.6.4.4.2.5 HENRY AMMON SCHMELTZ was born on 25 November 1955, Schuylkill County, PA. He married **SHARON LYNN NACE** on 1 June 1974.

11.6.4.4.2.5.1 STEPHEN MICHAEL SCHMELTZ was born on 4 February 1976.

11.6.4.4.2.5.2 CHRISTOPHER JOHN SCHMELTZ was born on 27 March 1980.

11.6.4.4.2.6 DAVID MONROE SCHMELTZ was born on 25 November 1955. He married **PAULA MARIE WERTZ** on 3 April 1982.

11.6.4.4.2.6.1 SABRINA MARIA SCHMELTZ was born on 22 June 1984.

11.6.4.4.2.6.2 RYAN MATTHEW SCHMELTZ was born on 13 August 1986.

11.6.4.4.2.6.3 AARON MICHAEL SCHMELTZ was born on 27 January 1989.

11.6.4.4.3 EDNA PAULINE SCHEIB was born on 6 December 1929, Valley View, Schuylkill County, PA. She married **ALLEN DANIEL ADAM REED**, son of **WILLIAM GARFIELD REED** and **STELLA CATHERINE SCHMELTZ**, on 17 September 1949, St. Andrew's United Methodist Church, Valley View, Schuylkill County, PA.

11.6.4.4.3.1 BRUCE ALLEN REED was born on 1 July 1951, Valley View, Schuylkill County, PA. He married **FAYE ANN FERREE** on 19 June 1971, Sacramento, Schuylkill County, PA.

11.6.4.4.3.1.1 STEVEN DALE REED was born on 10 May 1972, Pottsville, Schuylkill County, PA. He married **TORI LEIGH BARRY** in September 1994.

11.6.4.4.3.1.2 DAVID MICHAEL REED was born on 30 August 1979, Pottsville, Schuylkill County, PA.

11.6.4.4.3.2 DENNIS DALE REED was born on 22 October 1958, Lancaster, Lancaster County, PA. He married **WANDA LOU PORTZLINE** on 2 May 1987, Christ United Church of Christ, Fountain, Schuylkill County, PA. He married **KATHRYN EILEEN MACHAMER** after 1990.

11.6.4.4.3.3 TINA ELLEN REED was born on 13 April 1962, Lancaster, Lancaster County, PA.

11.6.4.4.3.4 ROSE ANN REED was born on 9 June 1964, Lancaster, Lancaster County, PA. She married **DENNIS ALLEN BERKLEY** on 19 February 1983. She married **KENNETH STEICH** on 6 September 1989.

11.6.4.4.3.4.1 MICHAEL ALLEN BERKLEY was born on 10 September 1983, Pottsville, Schuylkill County, PA.

11.6.4.4.3.4.2 KAYLA ANN WENHOLD STEICH was born on 29 November 1989, Pottsville, Schuylkill County, PA.

11.6.4.4.4 MARK ROY SCHEIB was born on 2 August 1933, Schuylkill County, PA. He was baptized on 15 October 1933, St. Andrew's United Methodist Church, Valley View, Schuylkill County, PA. He married **SHEILA HOWARD** on 3 September 1960.

11.6.4.4.5 MARY ELIZABETH SCHEIB was born on 28 January 1943, Schuylkill County, PA. She married **LAMAR EUGENE SHOMPER** on 3 September 1960.

>**11.6.4.4.5.1 DONNA LOUISE SHOMPER** was born on 7 October 1962. She married **DONALD BRUCE BRANDT** on 7 June 1980.
>
>>**11.6.4.4.5.1.1 DARREN CHRISTOPHER BRANDT** was born on 28 February 1981.
>>
>>**11.6.4.4.5.1.2 DEBORAH ANGELA BRANDT** was born on 29 October 1982.
>>
>>**11.6.4.4.5.1.3 DIANA REBEKAH BRANDT** was born on 9 May 1987.
>>
>>**11.6.4.4.5.1.4 DOROTHY KATHERINE BRANDT** was born on 9 May 1987.
>
>**11.6.4.4.5.2 JAMES LAMAR SHOMPER** was born on 29 March 1964. He married **WENDY BRUNELLE BROWN** on 12 May 1984.
>
>**11.6.4.4.5.3 THOMAS EDWARD SHOMPER** was born on 27 April 1972.

11.6.4.4.6 HILDA MARIE SCHEIB was born on 28 April 1945, Schuylkill County, PA. She was baptized on 29 July 1945, St. Andrew's United Methodist Church, Valley View, Schuylkill County, PA. She married **DAVID DONALD DIETRICH**, son of **HARRY F. DIETRICH** and **LAURA MAY TROUTMAN,** on 23 February 1963.

>**11.6.4.4.6.1 DONALD DAVID DIETRICH** was born on 21 July 1963, PA.
>
>**11.6.4.4.6.2 HOLLY ANN DIETRICH** was born on 13 January 1965, Schuylkill County, PA. She married **CHARLES MATTHEW NEWMAN** on 17 July 1987.
>
>**11.6.4.4.6.3 KELLY LYNN DIETRICH** was born on 10 February 1969, Schuylkill County, PA.

11.6.4.4.7 VERNA MAE SCHEIB was born on 14 November 1946, Schuylkill County, PA. She married **RONALD LANSTON HARNER** on 17 July 1965.

>**11.6.4.4.7.1 SCOTT ALBERT HARNER** was born on 24 November 1966, Schuylkill County, PA. He married **DEBRA ANN KILLE** on 6 May 1989.
>
>**11.6.4.4.7.2 TODD RONALD HARNER** was born on 24 November 1966, Schuylkill County, PA.
>
>**11.6.4.4.7.3 ANDREW AMMON HARNER** was born on 17 June 1970, Schuylkill County, PA.

11.6.4.5 IRVIN MONROE SCHEIB is also referred to as **IRVAN MONROE SCHEIB** in some sources. He was born on 10 September 1908, Gratz, Dauphin County, PA. He married **ANNA VIOLA WETZEL.** He died in June 1984, at age 75. He was buried at Saint Mark's United Brethren Cemetery, Spring Glen, Schuylkill County, PA.

>**11.6.4.5.1 LUKE ALFRED SCHEIB** was born on 4 November 1930, PA. He married **ARLEAH C. KAHLER** on 26 March 1948. He married **SHIRLEY A. MCCRACKIN**, daughter of **ROBERT MCCRACKIN** and **MARY (--?--),** after 1955.
>
>**11.6.4.5.2 DEAN IRVIN SCHEIB** was born on 4 November 1942. He married **RUBY JEAN DITTY**, daughter of **ROY EDWARD DITTY** and **MELVA PAULINE SCHAFFNER**, in 1960. He died on 11 October 1999, Harrisburg, Dauphin County, PA, at age 56. He was buried at Saint David's Reformed Church Cemetery, Killinger, Dauphin County, PA.
>
>>**11.6.4.5.2.1 ANGELA JEAN SCHEIB** was born in 1960.
>>
>>**11.6.4.5.2.2 CRYSTAL ANN SCHEIB** was born in 1963.

11.6.4.6 CATHRYN EDNA SCHEIB is also referred to as **CATHERINE** in some sources. She was born on 15 December 1911, Gratz, Dauphin County, PA. Some sources record that she was born on 16 December 1910, Gratz, Dauphin County, PA. She married **ALBERT F. KLOUSER**. She died in June 1975, at age 63. She was buried at Saint Paul's United Church of Christ Cemetery, Sacramento, Schuylkill County, PA.

>**11.6.4.6.1 ELSIE IRENE KLOUSER** was born on 25 February 1927, Valley View, Schuylkill County, PA. She married **GEORGE LOHR**, son of **JOHN LOHR** and **KATIE MILLER,** on 24 June 1944. She died on 5 February 2008, Pottsville Hospital, Pottsville, Schuylkill County, PA, at age 80. According to a newspaper obituary, Elsie lived at 244 Mahantongo St., Hegins, Schuylkill County, PA before she moved to the Friendly Nursing Home in Pitman. She retired as a

seamstress, after working at several garment factories in the area. She was buried on 9 February 2008, at St. Paul's Church Cemetery, Sacramento, Schuylkill County, PA.

11.6.4.6.1.1 GEORGETTA D. LOHR married **LANNY LUPOLD**. She is also referred to as **GEORGETTE** in some sources.

11.6.4.6.1.1.1 DR. CHRIS P. LUPOLD

11.6.4.6.1.1.2 AMY LUPOLD married **(--?--) BAIR**.

11.6.4.6.1.1.2.1 EMMA BAIR

11.6.4.6.1.1.2.2 NOAH BAIR

11.6.4.6.1.2 STEVEN S. LOHR married **PATTI (--?--)**.

11.6.4.6.1.2.1 BRITTANY M. LOHR

11.6.4.6.2 ELWOOD E. KLOUSER was born on 28 July 1929, Hegins Township, Schuylkill County, PA. He married **ARLEDA M. WEINREICH**. He died on 7 December 2008, Mount Carmel Nursing Center, Mount Carmel, Northumberland County, PA, at age 79. He was buried at Saint Andrew's United Methodist Church Cemetery, Valley View, Schuylkill County, PA.

11.6.4.6.3 FERN E. KLOUSER was born circa 1932. She married **DANIEL DIETRICH**.

11.6.4.6.3.1 LYNN DIETRICH married **JOYCE SCHMELTZ**, daughter of **LEROY SCHMELTZ** and **MAE KLINGER**.

11.6.4.6.3.2 (--?--) DIETRICH. Some sources suggest that she and **GEORGE LOHR** were married.

11.6.4.6.4 JAMES JACKSON KLOUSER was born on 20 December 1934, Schuylkill County, PA. He died on 12 August 1943, Schuylkill County, PA, at age 8. He was buried at Saint Paul's United Church of Christ Cemetery, Sacramento, Schuylkill County, PA.

11.6.4.6.5 JEANNETTE RUTH KLOUSER was born on 16 September 1936, Valley View, Schuylkill County, PA. She married **IRVIN MORGAN**. She died on 18 January 2001, Valley View, Schuylkill County, PA, at age 64. She was buried at Saint Andrew's United Methodist Church Cemetery, Valley View, Schuylkill County, PA.

11.6.4.7 RALPH ALVIN SCHEIB was born on 4 August 1914, Gratz, Dauphin County, PA. He married **HELEN JENNIE NEUGARD** on 25 December 1936. He died on 25 July 1992, at age 77.

11.6.4.7.1 MAE SCHEIB was born circa 1938, Dauphin Co., PA. She married **(--?--) JONES** circa 1959.

11.6.4.7.2 JANET HELEN SCHEIB was born on 20 July 1952, Dauphin County, PA. She married **(--?--) COSTA** circa 1974.

11.6.4.7.3 ALVIN RALPH SCHEIB was born on 3 March 1943, Dauphin Co., PA. He married **MARY SULLIVAN** circa 1965.

11.6.5 ALICE CHRISTIANNA KLINGER is also referred to as **ALTA KLINGER** in some sources. She was born on 2 June 1884, Klingerstown, Schuylkill County, PA. She was baptized on 5 October 1884, Zion (Klinger's) Church, Erdman, Lykens Township, Dauphin County, PA. She lived in Lykens, Dauphin County, PA. She married **HARVEY FRANKLIN SEILER**, son of **RICHARD TROUTMAN SEILER** and **AMELIA MAURER**, on 8 September 1904, Trinity Lutheran Church, Pottsville, Schuylkill County, PA. She married **HARVEY E. BENSINGER**, son of **ADAM BENNSINGER**, on 14 October 1909, St. Paul's (Artz's) United Church of Christ, Sacramento, Schuylkill County, PA. She married **FRANKLIN MARKEL SCHEIB**, son of **FRANKLIN SCHEIB** and **ELISABETH MOYER**, after 1930. She died on 18 January 1968, Pottsville, Schuylkill County, PA, at age 83. She was buried at St. Pauls (Artz's) United Church of Christ Cemetery, Sacramento, Schuylkill County, PA.

11.6.5.1 ERNEST SEILER is also referred to as **EARNEST W. SILER** in some sources. He was born circa 1905, in Pennsylvania. He married **BEULAH CAROLINE HECKLER**. He died circa 1946, in Pennsylvania.

11.6.5.1.1 CLYDE SEILER was born circa 1929, in Pennsylvania. He lived in Tower City, Schuylkill, Pennsylvania, United States. He married **ERIKA (--?--)** in December 1958, Munich, Bavaria, Germany.

11.6.5.1.1.1 LILLIAN SEILER was born on 27 April 1949, Munich, Bavaria, Germany. She married **DONALD WADDELL**.

11.6.5.1.1.1.1 ANGELA WADDELL was born on 27 March 1966, Huntsville, Madison County, AL. She married **SCOTT WADDELL**. She lived in Huntsville, AL.

11.6.5.1.1.1.1.1 CHRISTINA LEIGH WADDELL lived in Owens Cross Roads, AL. She was born on 29 June 1989. She died on 13 January 2013, at age 23. She was buried at Talucah, Morgan County, AL.

11.6.5.1.1.1.2 ANNETTE WADDELL was born on 17 September 1968, Huntsville, Madison County, AL. She married (--?--) **HUGHES**.

11.6.5.1.1.1.2.1 TAYLOR RAYE HUGHES was born on 27 June 2000.

11.6.5.1.1.2 CHRISTINA SEILER was born Brooklyn, NY. She married (--?--) **WHITAKER**.

11.6.5.1.1.2.1 BRIAN WHITAKER

11.6.5.1.1.2.2 STEPHANIE WHITAKER

11.6.5.1.1.3 DIANE SEILER was born on 26 October 1954. She married (--?--) **SMITH**.

11.6.5.1.1.3.1 SON 1 SMITH

11.6.5.1.1.3.2 SON 2 SMITH

11.6.5.1.1.3.3 SON 3 SMITH

11.6.5.1.1.4 GEORGE SEILER was born on 28 January 1963, Huntsville, Madison County, AL.

11.6.5.1.1.4.1 STEVEN SEILER was born on 27 June 1989, Huntsville, Madison County, AL.

11.6.5.1.2 FRANKLIN SEILER was born circa 1935, in Pennsylvania. He lived in Minersville, Schuylkill County, PA. He lived in Minersville, Schuylkill County, PA. He married **GLORIA LYONS**.

11.6.5.1.2.1 BARRY SEILER was born in 1960.

11.6.5.1.2.2 MARY SEILER was born in 1962. She married **JAMES HARRIS**. She married (--?--) **COLE**.

11.6.5.1.2.2.1 JAMES HARRIS

11.6.5.1.2.2.2 MARY COLE

11.6.5.1.3 MARY SEILER was born circa 1937, in Pennsylvania. She lived in Minersville, Schuylkill, Pennsylvania, United States. She married **DON MARPLE**.

11.6.5.1.3.1 DOUGLAS GENE MARPLE was born on 12 April 1962. He married **KIM** (--?--). He and **KIM** (--?--) were divorced. He married **CAROL HARRIS**. He married **KEELY LYNN HARRIS**.

11.6.5.1.3.2 DAVID SCOTT MARPLE was born on 20 February 1965. He died in December 1979, at age 14.

11.6.5.1.3.3 DANIEL KIRK MARPLE was born on 3 October 1970. He married **JANE ANDREWS** on 5 November 2011.

11.6.5.2 GEORGE HARVEY SEILER was born on 21 November 1906, Schuylkill County, PA. He died on 30 May 1908, Schuylkill County, PA, at age 1. He was buried at St. Paul's (Artz's) United Church of Christ Cemetery, Sacramento, Schuylkill County, PA.

11.6.5.3 SARAH RUTH FERN SEILER lived in Lorain, Ohio, United States. She was born on 8 October 1908, Sacramento, Schuylkill Schuylkill County, PA. She lived in Hubley, Schuylkill, Pennsylvania. She lived in Hubley, Schuylkill, Pennsylvania. She married **JOSEPH W ABROMITIS** on 17 July 1924, Elkton, MD. She lived in Minersville, Schuylkill, Pennsylvania. She married **ADAM GEORGE YURKONIS**. She died on 18 October 1999, Avon, Lorain County, OH, at age 91.

11.6.5.3.1 JOSEPH P. ABROMITIS is also referred to as **JOSEPH ABROMAITIS** in some sources. He was born on 23 June 1925, Minersville, Schuylkill County, PA. He lived in Minersville, Schuylkill, Pennsylvania. He married **LAURA LUISI**. He died on 17 November 1990, Bethlehem, PA, at age 65. He was buried at Allentown, Lehigh County, PA.

11.6.5.3.1.1 EUGENE ABROMITIS was born on 13 April 1947. Eugene served with the 25th Infantry as a rifleman near the Cambodian border during the Vietnam War. He married **MARIE E. SHERMAN**. He lived in Elkton, MD. He married **SAYURI** (--?--).

11.6.5.3.1.1.1 PETER JAMES ABROMITIS married **ANGELA CARLSON**.

11.6.5.3.1.1.1.1 ZOIE EMA ABROMITIS was born on 26 February 2007.

11.6.5.3.1.1.1.2 JACOB EVAN ABROMITIS was born on 6 February 2011.

11.6.5.3.1.1.2 SARAH ABROMITIS married **RICHARD BOWERS.**

11.6.5.3.1.1.2.1 RICHARD CHRISTOPHER BOWERS was born on 28 June 2008.

11.6.5.3.1.1.2.2 CHASE CHRISTIAN BOWERS was born in 2013.

11.6.5.3.1.1.3 REBECCA ANN ABROMITIS was born on 9 June 1975, Syracuse, Onondaga County, NY. She married **LAWRENCE WEBSTER WALDRIDGE JR.** She lived in Elkton, MD.

11.6.5.3.1.1.3.1 EMILY RENAY WALDRIDGE was born on 2 April 1999, Elkton, Cecil County, MD.

11.6.5.3.1.1.4 KEVIN ABROMITIS was born on 3 January 1994.

11.6.5.3.1.2 LAURA ABROMITIS was born circa 1952.

11.6.5.3.1.3 JOSEPH W. ABROMITIS was born on 15 January 1957. He lived in Allentown, PA.

11.6.5.3.1.4 DOUGLAS P. ABROMITIS was born circa 1961. He lived in Allentown, PA.

11.6.5.3.1.5 PHILLIP ABROMITIS was born on 21 March 1962. He lived in Perkasie, PA.

11.6.5.3.2 JOHN HARVEY ABROMITIS was born on 8 January 1929, Minersville, Schuylkill County, PA. He lived in Minersville, Schuylkill, Pennsylvania. He married **ANGELA M ROBERTI** on 19 June 1948, Brooklyn, King County, NY. He died on 31 March 2012, Hackettstown NJ at age 83. He was buried at Union Cemetery, Hackettstown, Warren County, NJ.

11.6.5.3.2.1 JOHN J. ABROMITIS SR. was born on 24 October 1948, Brooklyn, Kings County, NY. He married **JANE ANDERSON** in 1967. He and **JANE ANDERSON** were divorced in 1976. He married **LINDA ABBAZZIA** on 25 June 1981, Hackettstown, Warren County, NJ.

11.6.5.3.2.1.1 JOHN JOSEPH ABROMITIS JR was born on 18 September 1967, Newton, Sussex County, NJ. He married **EILEEN COHEN.**

11.6.5.3.2.1.1.1 MIA RENEE ABROMITIS was born on 5 February 2001, Hackettstown, Warren County, NJ.

11.6.5.3.2.1.2 KRISTIN ROSE ABROMITIS was born on 20 October 1981, Hackettstown, Warren County, NJ. She married **DAMIEN JACOBS.**

11.6.5.3.2.1.2.1 BRANDON BERTRAND JACOBS was born on 5 January 2010, in Virginia.

11.6.5.3.2.1.2.2 BRADLEY JOSEPH JACOBS was born on 30 April 2013.

11.6.5.3.2.1.3 THERESA ANN ABROMITIS was born on 17 December 1983, Hackettstown, Warren County, NJ.

11.6.5.3.2.2 MICHAEL WILLIAM ABROMITIS was born on 18 March 1953, Brooklyn, Kings County, NY. He married **SUSAN MILLER.**

11.6.5.3.2.2.1 MATTHEW MICHAEL ABROMITIS was born on 10 February 1996.

11.6.5.3.2.3 MARYANN ABROMITIS was born on 3 March 1954, Brooklyn, Kings County, NY. She married **PATRICK G. MCFADDEN SR** on 19 July 1975. She lived in Phillipsburg, NJ. She and **PATRICK G. MCFADDEN SR** were divorced in March 2011.

11.6.5.3.2.3.1 PATRICK G. MCFADDEN JR was born on 10 February 1976, Hackettstown, Warren County, NJ. He married **KAREN RICHMOND** on 9 September 2005.

11.6.5.3.2.3.2 MARISA A MCFADDEN was born on 31 January 1978, Phillipsburg, Warren County, NJ. She married **MICHAEL TAMBURELLO** on 30 August 2003, Crossed Keys Inn, Andover, NJ.

11.6.5.3.2.3.2.1 ALICE MAE TAMBURELLO was born on 25 September 2005, Hackettstown, Warren County, NJ.

11.6.5.3.2.3.2.2 LILY GRACE TAMBURELLO was born on 31 August 2007, Hackettstown, Warren County, NJ.

11.6.5.3.2.3.2.3 JULIA ROSE TAMBURELLO was born on 23 November 2009.

11.6.5.3.2.3.2.4 PHOEBE ELIZABETH TAMBURELLO was born on 24 March 2011.

11.6.5.3.2.3.2.5 JACKSON CHARLES TAMBURELLO was born on 30 April 2013, Hackettstown, Warren County, NJ.

11.6.5.3.2.4 JACQUELYN GERETTE ABROMITIS was born on 17 February 1963, Queens County, NY. Jacky, who lives in Great Meadows, NJ, was the source for much of the information on the descendants of Alice Christianna Klinger.

11.6.5.3.3 ARLENE ABROMITIS was born on 16 February 1931, in Pennsylvania. She married ORLANDO J. MOLLICA on 22 May 1948.

11.6.5.3.3.1 RONALD R MOLLICA lived in Houston, TX. He was born on 7 November 1951. He married DIANE M (--?--) on 8 May 1971. He lived in Houston, TX. He and DIANE M (--?--) were divorced on 20 October 1986 Harris County, TX. He married FREDA L ANDERSON on 25 August 1990, Harris County, TX.

11.6.5.3.3.1.1 JANINE MARIE MOLLICA was born on 16 September 1975.

11.6.5.3.3.1.2 MICHAEL ANTHONY MOLLICA was born on 4 November 1981. He married ASHLEY INEZ TULLGREN.

11.6.5.3.3.1.2.1 FALON INEZ MOLLICA was born on 28 June 2011.

11.6.5.3.3.2 CHRISTINE A. MOLLICA was born on 19 July 1957, Ridgewood, NJ. She married REX ARNOLD MCCLURE.

11.6.5.3.3.2.1 AMY LYNN MCCLURE was born on 3 May 1982, Wayne, NJ.

11.6.5.3.3.2.2 RYAN MATTHEW MCCLURE was born on 1 July 1985, Wayne, NJ.

11.6.5.3.4 WILLIAM P. ABROMITIS was born on 4 February 1932, Minersville, Schuylkill County, PA. He married THERESA AGNES MICKELBART, daughter of FRANCIS MICKELBART and PETRONELLA OVERLINGAS. He died on 20 December 1993, Euclid General Hospital, Mentor, Lake County, OH, at age 61. He was buried at All Souls Cemetery, Chardon, Geauga County, OH.

11.6.5.3.4.1 WILLIAM J ABROMITIS was born on 6 August 1955, Cleveland, OH. He married RHONDA THOMAS.

11.6.5.3.4.1.1 GARRETT ABROMITIS was born on 8 August 1988.

11.6.5.3.4.2 MARY ANN ABROMITIS was born on 21 October 1968, Cleveland, OH. She married VIDAS TATARUNAS. She lived in Cleveland, OH.

11.6.5.3.4.2.1 TADAS ANDRIUS TATARUNAS was born on 5 June 1999, Cleveland, Cuyahoga County, OH.

11.6.5.3.4.2.2 ALEKSA ROMA TATARUNAS was born on 5 July 2001, Cleveland, Cuyahoga County, OH.

11.6.5.3.4.2.3 OLIVIJA THERESA TATARUNAS was born on 5 July 2001, Cleveland, Cuyahoga County, OH.

11.6.5.3.5 PATRICIA ALICE ABROMITIS was born on 14 June 1936, Pottsville, PA. She married THOMAS BOHATCH. She died on 8 August 1998, Mentor, Lake County, OH, at age 62. She was buried at Mentor Municpal Cemetery, Mentor, Lake County, OH.

11.6.5.3.5.1 JEFFREY BOHATCH lived in Willowick, OH. He was born on 25 September 1954, Cleveland, OH.

11.6.5.3.5.2 KAREN D BOHATCH lived in Lake, Ohio, United States. She was born on 18 October 1958, Cleveland, OH. She married RICHARD T HUTCHINS on 18 October 1975.

11.6.5.3.5.3 PAMELA JEAN BOHATCH lived in Lake, Ohio, United States. She is also referred to as PAMELA JEAN KATONA in some sources. She was born on 11 October 1960, Cleveland, Cuyahoga County, OH. She married THOMAS J. LEKUTIS on 23 June 1979, Lake County, OH. She married CHRISTO KATONA on 18 November 1995, Lake County, OH. She died on 7 August 2002, Lake County, OH, at age 41. She was buried at Mentor Municipal Cemetery, Mentor, Lake County, OH.

11.6.5.3.6 ROBERT YURKONIS was born circa 1944. He married BETTY (--?--).

11.6.5.3.6.1 JULIE YURKONIS married (--?--) STILES.

11.6.5.3.6.1.1 BETHANY STILES

11.6.5.3.6.1.2 BRANDON STILES

11.6.5.3.6.2 ROBERT YURKONIS JR.

11.6.5.3.6.3 SCOTT LOUIS YURKONIS

11.6.5.4 FREDERICK HERMAN BENSINGER was born on 6 January 1911, Hegins, Hegins, Schuylkill, Pennsylvania, U.S.A. He was baptized on 22 April 1911, Valley View, Schuylkill, Pennsylvania. He lived in Hubley, Schuylkill, Pennsylvania. He lived in Minersville, Schuylkill, Pennsylvania. He married **MARY AUGUSTA SHUEY**, daughter of **DANIEL MILTON SHUEY** and **RUBY IRENE CLAUSER,** on 18 November 1933, Pottsville, Schuylkill County, PA. He died on 1 March 1971, Ann Arbor, Washtenaw, Michigan, U.S.A., at age 60. He was buried at Greenwood Cemetery, Tower City, Schuylkill County, PA.

11.6.5.4.1 JOAN ELLEN BENSINGER was born on 17 March 1934, Tower City, Schuylkill, Pennsylvania, United States. She died on 16 July 1969, White Plains, NY, at age 35.

11.6.5.4.2 RICHARD PAUL BENSINGER was born on 2 November 1935, Porter, Jefferson, Pennsylvania, United States. He married **CAROLE A. (--?--).** He died in November 1984, Ypsilanti, MI. He was buried at Union-Udell Cemetery, Ypsilanti, Washtenaw County, MI.

11.6.5.5 ROBERT IRA BENSINGER lived in Hubley Township, Schuylkill County, PA. He was born on 1 January 1920, Hegins Township, Schuylkill County, PA. He lived in Minersville, Schuylkill, Pennsylvania. He lived in Hegins, Schuylkill, Pennsylvania, United States. He married **TILLIE ARLENE SCHEIB**, daughter of **ELMER F. SCHEIB** and **BESSIE SUSAN MORGAN,** on 25 January 1941. He died on 5 February 1970, Williamstown, Dauphin County, PA, at age 50. He was buried at Fairview Cemetery, Williamstown, Dauphin County, PA.

11.6.5.5.1 LANCE BENSINGER

11.6.5.5.2 ROBERT BENSINGER JR.

11.6.6 GEORGE E. KLINGER was born on 16 September 1886. He died on 19 December 1895, at age 9. He was buried at Zion (Klinger's) Church, Erdman, Lykens Township, Dauphin County, PA.

11.6.7 HENRY WILSON KLINGER was born on 3 December 1888. He was baptized on 9 March 1889, Zion (Klinger's) Church, Erdman, Lykens Township, Dauphin County, PA. He married **CARRIE M. BOWMAN** on 1 March 1913, Frieden's Reformed Church, Hegins, Schuylkill County, PA. Prior to his death, Henry was living in the vicinity of Gratz, Dauphin County, PA. He died in September 1972, at age 83.

11.6.7.1 KERMIT WILSON KLINGER was born on 5 May 1914. He married **GLADYS B. ROMBERGER**, daughter of **CHARLES ROMBERGER** and **ALICE HARRIS.** He died on 29 February 1968, at age 53. He was buried at Simeon Cemetery, Gratz, Dauphin County, PA.

11.6.7.1.1 SHIRLEY BETTY KLINGER was born on 29 September 1935. She married **PAUL BYLE.** Shirley lives in Gratz, PA.

11.6.7.1.1.1 WILLIAM BYLE

11.6.7.1.1.2 LEONARD BYLE

11.6.7.1.2 EUGENE KERMIT KLINGER was born on 27 February 1949. He married **SHIRLEY SUE (--?--).** Eugene lives in Mechanicsburg, PA.

11.6.7.2 MAY C. KLINGER was born circa 1917, Pennsylvania. She married **MUSH TROUTMAN.** In 1989, May was living in Pillow, PA.

11.6.8 JAMES DAVID KLINGER was born on 23 February 1891, Lykens Township, Dauphin County, PA. He was baptized on 5 July 1891, Zion (Klinger's) Church, Erdman, Lykens Township, Dauphin County, PA. He married **JEMIMA REGINA KLINGER**, daughter of **HENRY S. KLINGER** and **EMMA MARY WIEST.** He died on 16 November 1964, Wernersville State Hospital, Wernersville, Berks County, PA, at age 73. According to a newspaper obituary, James was a retired carpenter who lived in Valley View, Schuylkill County, PA. He was buried at Zion (Klinger's) Church, Erdman, Lykens Township, Dauphin County, PA.

11.6.8.1 RAYMOND F. KLINGER was born circa 1911, Pennsylvania. He died before 1 November 2011.

11.6.8.2 GLENN A. KLINGER was born circa 1912, Pennsylvania. He married **MARGARET SCHADEL.** He died before 1 November 2011.

11.6.8.3 EMMA CHRISTIANA KLINGER was born on 14 December 1913. She married **(--?--) STARR.** She died before 2013.

11.6.8.4 ISABELLA J. KLINGER is also referred to as **ISABELLE** in some sources. She was born circa 1915, Pennsylvania. She died before 1 November 2011.

11.6.8.5 LENA MAE KLINGER was born on 26 May 1920, Spring Glen, Schuylkill County, PA. She married **RAYMOND MOSES KESSLER**, son of **MOSES LEON KESSLER** and **MINNIE EULALIA DEIBERT**. She died on 19 February 2013, The Manor at Susquehanna Village, Millersburg, Dauphin County, PA, at age 92. She was buried on 23 February 2013, at Zion (Klinger's) Lutheran Church Cemetery, Erdman, Dauphin County, PA. According to a newspaper obituary, Lena worked for the former Muskin Shoe Co., Millersburg, and as a field agent for the Pennsylvania Department of Agriculture, Harrisburg.

11.6.8.5.1 RICHARD RAYMOND KESSLER was born on 23 May 1941, Spring Glen, Schuylkill County, PA. He married **BETTE LOU WIDER** El Paso, TX.

11.6.8.5.1.1 AMY JULIA KESSLER

11.6.8.5.1.2 MICHAEL KESSLER

11.6.8.5.2 JAMES MICHAEL KESSLER was born on 18 August 1946, RD, Millersburg, Dauphin County, PA. He married **PRISCILLA ANN CHUBB**, daughter of **EARL E. CHUBB** and **EDNA LAHR,** circa 1968, Millersburg, Dauphin County, PA. He married **JANICE SUE COUCH**, daughter of **SIDNEY ADRIAN COUCH** and **BETTY JOAN (--?--),** on 8 June 1974, United Methodist Church, Waverly, Lackawanna County, PA.

11.6.8.5.2.1 JACQUILINE J. KESSLER was born on 30 September 1969, Seoul, South Korea.

11.6.8.5.2.2 KATHERINE DIANE KESSLER was born on 27 January 1977, Tunkhannock, Wyoming County, PA.

11.6.8.5.2.3 MATTHEW JAMES KESSLER was born on 24 December 1979, Binghamton, Broome County, NY.

11.6.8.5.3 MARY ELIZABETH KESSLER was born on 4 June 1951. She died on 3 March 1953, at age 1. She was buried at Zion (Klinger's) Lutheran Church Cemetery, Erdman, Dauphin County, PA.

11.6.8.5.4 ROBERT ANDREW KESSLER was born on 7 March 1954, RD, Millersburg, Dauphin County, PA. He married **JUDY BOYER**, daughter of **BOBBY BOYER.**

11.6.8.5.5 DAVID L. KESSLER was born on 10 December 1955, RD, Millersburg, Dauphin County, PA. He married **JEAN M. BOYER**, daughter of **DARWIN BOYER** and **MARGARET (--?--),** on 23 October 1976, Pillow, Dauphin County, PA.

11.6.8.5.5.1 TIONNE RAE KESSLER was born on 26 May 1978, Harrisburg, Dauphin County, PA.

11.6.8.6 RACHEL A. KLINGER was born circa 1922, Pennsylvania. She died before 1 November 2011.

11.6.8.7 BETTE C. KLINGER was born on 27 May 1924, Spring Glen, Schuylkill County, PA. She married **MELVIN L. BIXLER**. Mary Klinger refers to Betty as "Betty Bixler of blueberry fame," who lived on a farm north of Sacramento, Schuylkill County. She died on 1 November 2011, 1715 W. Maple Street, Valley View, Schuylkill County, PA, at age 87. According to a newspaper obituary, Bette was a 1941 graduate of the former Hubley Township High School. She was a seamstress in area garment factories and had also worked at the former Mitchell's Bakery, Valley View.

Bette volunteered for Good Samaritan Hospital, Pottsville, Diakon Volunteer Home Care and the Hillside SPCA. She was buried on 4 November 2011, at St. Andrew's United Methodist Church Cemetery, Valley View, Schuylkill County, PA.

11.6.9 JOHN ALEXANDER ALVIN KLINGER also went by the name of **ALVIN**. He was born on 23 February 1893. He was baptized on 26 March 1893, Zion (Klinger's) Church, Erdman, Lykens Township, Dauphin County, PA. He married **LILLIAN ONEDA TROUTMAN**, daughter of **HENRY LESHER TROUTMAN** and **ANGELINE TOBIAS,** circa 1912. Prior to his death, Alvin was living in the vicinity of Elizabethville, Dauphin County, PA. He died on 5 July 1978, at age 85. He was buried on 8 July 1978, at Zion (Klinger's) Church, Erdman, Lykens Township, Dauphin County, PA.

11.6.9.1 EVA CHRISTIANA KLINGER is also referred to as **EVA CHRISTINE KLINGER** in some sources. She was born on 6 July 1912, Pennsylvania. She was baptized on 13 October 1912, David's Lutheran & Reformed Church, Hebe, Northumberland County, PA. She married **EMORY WOODROW SNYDER**, son of **WILLIAM HENRY SNYDER** and **LILLIE FRANCES BROSIUS,** on 25 June 1931, Zion (Klinger's) Church, Erdman, Lykens Township, Dauphin County, PA. Eva lived in Elizabethville, PA.

She died on 28 April 1993, at age 80. She was buried at Zion (Klinger's) Church Cemetery, Erdman, Dauphin County, PA.

11.6.9.1.1 GUY ALVIN SNYDER was born on 3 August 1931, Gratz, Dauphin County, PA. He was baptized on 20 December 1931, Zion (Klinger's) Church, Erdman, Dauphin County, PA. He married **MIRIAM RUTH SHOOP**, daughter of **JAMES W. SHOOP** and **ESTHER MAE ENDERS,** on 5 October 1952, Salem Lutheran Church, Elizabethville, Dauphin County, PA. He died on 10 January 2015, at age 83, at his home in Dauphin County, PA. He was buried on 16 January 2015, at David's Church Cemetery, Killinger, Dauphin County, PA. According to a newspaper obituary, Guy was the owner of Snyder's Welding in Elizabethville.

11.6.9.1.1.1 STEPHEN JAMES SNYDER was born on 7 February 1953. He was baptized on 5 April 1953, Salem Lutheran Church, Elizabethville, Dauphin County, PA. He married **JODY M. (--?--)**. Stephen lives in Millersburg, PA.

11.6.9.1.1.2 WANDA MAE SNYDER was born on 1 June 1956. She was baptized on 23 December 1956, Salem Lutheran Church, Elizabethville, Dauphin County, PA. She married **(--?--) BECK**. Wanda lives in Carlisle, PA.

11.6.9.1.1.3 DAVID GUY SNYDER was born on 28 October 1957. He was baptized on 7 September 1958, Salem Lutheran Church, Elizabethville, Dauphin County, PA. David lives in Gratz, PA.

11.6.9.1.1.4 SONYA MARIE SNYDER was born on 28 August 1961. She was baptized on 9 September 1962, Salem Lutheran Church, Elizabethville, Dauphin County, PA. She married **(--?--) HOFFMAN**. Sonya lives in Halifax, PA.

11.6.9.1.1.5 JULIE CHRISTIANNA SNYDER was born on 31 October 1965. She was baptized on 10 April 1966, Salem Lutheran Church, Elizabethville, Dauphin County, PA. She married **(--?--) MIHAILOFF**. Julie lives in Millersburg, PA.

11.6.9.1.1.6 LISA MAE SNYDER was born on 8 August 1968. She was baptized on 7 October 1968, Salem Lutheran Church, Elizabethville, Dauphin County, PA. Lisa lives in Elizabethville, PA.

11.6.9.1.1.7 JENNIFER MAE SNYDER was born on 14 November 1970. She was baptized on 28 February 1971, Salem Lutheran Church, Elizabethville, Dauphin County, PA. She married **(--?--) GROSSER**. Jennifer lives in Halifax, PA.

11.6.9.1.1.8 AMY BETH SNYDER was born on 26 June 1973. She was baptized on 26 August 1973, Salem Lutheran Church, Elizabethville, Dauphin County, PA. Amy lives in Elizabethville, PA.

11.6.9.1.2 FLOYD EMORY SNYDER was born on 7 August 1934, Pillow, Dauphin County, PA. He married **SHARI RAY KEPPLEY**. A 1976 newspaper article reported that Floyd, a member of the Wyoming Air National Guard, had taken command of the 153rd Tactical Airlift Group in Cheyenne, Wyoming. A flight instructor for United Airlines, he was the first non-full-time commander of the 153rd. Floyd attended Williamsport Technical Institute and received a B.A. degree in mineral engineering from the Colorado School of Mines and a master's degree in business administration from the University of Colorado. He married **MARI AWATA**. He died on 24 January 2011, Brighton, CO, at age 76. He was buried on 27 February 2011, at Zion (Klinger's) Church Cemetery, Erdman, Dauphin County, PA.

11.6.9.1.3 GLENN WILLIAM SNYDER was born on 27 November 1937, Elizabethville, Dauphin County, PA. He was baptized on 27 March 1938, Zion (Klinger's) Church, Erdman, Dauphin County, PA. He married **HEIDI MULLER**.

11.6.9.1.4 DERLE MARLIN SNYDER was born on 20 June 1943, Elizabethville, Dauphin County, PA. He was baptized on 31 October 1943, Zion (Klinger's) Church, Erdman, Dauphin County, PA. He married **BETSY ANN RUTH**, daughter of **FRANKLIN WILLIAM RUTH JR**. and **PEARLE SHOWERS,** on 30 October 1965, United Methodist Church, Elizabethville, Dauphin County, PA.

11.6.9.1.4.1 KAREN RUTH SNYDER was born on 19 January 1977, Manchester, CT. Karen lives in Manchester, Hartford County, CT.

11.6.9.1.5 DARLENE LILLIAN SNYDER was born on 17 April 1945, Elizabethville, Dauphin County, PA. She married **MARK EUGENE STROHECKER**, son of **JOEL RAY STROHECKER** and **LILLIE CARVIE,** on 12 October 1963, United Methodist Church, Elizabethville, Dauphin County, PA. Darlene lives in Elizabethville, PA.

11.6.9.1.5.1 MARK EUGENE STROHECKER JR. married BETHANY A. ALEXANDER on 28 October 2000, First United Methodist Church, Millersburg, Dauphin County, PA.

11.6.9.1.5.2 CHRYSTAL ANN STROHECKER is also referred to as CRYSTAL in some sources. She was born on 19 September 1964, Pottsville, Schuylkill County, PA.

11.6.9.1.5.3 ANNETTE RENEE STROHECKER was born on 31 January 1967, Pottsville, Schuylkill County, PA.

11.6.9.1.5.4 GERALD MARK STROHECKER was born on 19 September 1969, Pottsville, Schuylkill County, PA.

11.6.9.1.6 JOYCE CHRISTIANA SNYDER is also referred to as JOYCE CHRISTIA in some sources. She was born on 7 July 1947, Elizabethville, Dauphin County, PA. She was baptized on 7 August 1947, Zion (Klinger's) Church, Erdman, Dauphin County, PA. She married DARRYL LEE REINFELD, son of GRANT MARCUS FREDERICK REINFELD and LILLIAN L. (--?--), on 11 February 1967, St. Paul's Lutheran Church, Millersburg, Dauphin County, PA.

11.6.9.1.6.1 MYCHELLE CHRISTINE REINFELD was born on 31 January 1967, Harrisburg, Dauphin County, PA.

11.6.9.1.6.2 KYMBERLY LEE REINFELD was born on 24 January 1968, Harrisburg, Dauphin County, PA.

11.6.9.1.6.3 DARRELL EMORY REINFELD was born on 4 March 1969, Camp Hill, Cumberland County, PA.

11.6.9.2 IVAH ANGELINA KLINGER was born on 1 May 1914, Dauphin County, PA. She died on 5 May 1917, Lykens, Dauphin County, PA, at age 3. She was buried at Zion (Klinger's) Lutheran Church Cemetery, Erdman, Dauphin County, PA.

11.6.9.3 MARLIN EMANUEL KLINGER was born on 3 January 1917, Gratz, Dauphin County, PA. He was baptized on 3 June 1917, Zion (Klinger's) Lutheran Church, Erdman, Dauphin County, PA. He married ANNA MARGARET GEBHART. Prior to his death, Marlin was living in the vicinity of Gratz, Dauphin County, PA. He died on 14 November 1993, at age 76. He was buried at Zion (Klinger's) Lutheran Church Cemetery, Erdman, Dauphin County, PA.

11.6.9.3.1 KENNETH WAYNE KLINGER was born on 25 April 1947. He was baptized on 25 December 1947, Zion (Klinger's) Lutheran Church, Erdman, Dauphin County, PA.

11.6.9.4 HERMAN HENRY KLINGER was born on 27 December 1920, Gratz, Dauphin County, PA. Some sources record that he was born on 27 December 1922. He married EDITH HANNAH KISSINGER, daughter of ERNEST MILTON KISSINGER and GERTRUDE SOPHIA WIEST. He died on 9 January 1987, Good Samaritan Hospital, Pottsville, Schuylkill County, PA, at age 64. According to a newspaper obituary, Herman lived in Spring Glen, PA, and worked at the Brubaker Tool Corp., Millersburg, PA, until his retirement. He was an Air Force veteran of World War II. He was buried at St. Paul's Church Cemetery, Sacramento, Schuylkill County, PA.

11.6.9.4.1 DOROTHY EDITH KLINGER (see above)

11.6.9.4.1.1 DANIEL E. BLYLER (see above)

11.6.9.4.1.1.1 SARA BLYLER (see above)

11.6.9.4.1.2 ANN MARIE BLYLER (see above)

11.6.9.4.1.3 CAROLE A. BLYLER (see above)

11.6.9.4.1.4 KAY M. BLYLER (see above)

11.6.9.4.2 LINDA MARIE KLINGER (see above)

11.6.9.5 ELSIE ONEDA KLINGER was born on 7 November 1923. She died on 14 May 1924. She was buried at Zion (Klinger's) Church, Erdman, Lykens Township, Dauphin County, PA.

11.6.9.6 ESTHER KATHRYN KLINGER was born on 20 February 1925, Gratz, Dauphin County, PA. She married RILAND GEORGE SCHEIDLER, son of GEORGE FRANKLIN SCHEIDLER and KATIE ROSELLEN AUCKER. She died on 31 March 2008, Selbyville, DE, at age 83. According to a newspaper obituary, Esther lived on Pine St. in Millersburg, PA, before moving in with her daughter in Selbyville, DE. She had previously worked at Nelson's Restaurant in Millersburg. She was buried at Zion Lutheran Cemetery, Rife, Dauphin County, PA.

11.6.9.6.1 DEBRA L. SCHEIDLER married (--?--) DUDLEY. Debra lives in Selbyville, DE.

11.6.9.6.2 Dean Marlin Scheidler was born on 14 June 1946. He died on 18 April 2000, Dauphin County, PA, at age 53.

11.6.9.6.3 Sheila Marie Scheidler was born on 27 June 1949. She married **(--?--) Reese**. Prior to her death, Sheila was living in the vicinity of Halifax, Dauphin County, PA. She died on 11 February 1999, Dauphin County, PA, at age 49.

11.6.9.7 Orpha Lillian Klinger is also referred to as **Oprha** in some sources. She was born on 20 January 1931. She married **(--?--) White**. In 1987, Orpha was living in York, PA. She died on 2 February 2002, at age 71.

11.6.10 Frederick Monroe Klinger also went by the name of **Fred**. He was born on 8 April 1895, Lykens Township, Dauphin County, PA. He was baptized on 16 June 1895, Zion (Klinger's) Church, Erdman, Lykens Township, Dauphin County, PA. He married **Jennie May Paul**, daughter of **Daniel S. Paul** and **Amelia Jane Schwalm**, on 5 October 1912, Erdman, Lykens Township, Dauphin County, PA. He died in 1978, Lykens Township, Dauphin County, PA. He was buried at Zion (Klinger's) Church, Erdman, Lykens Township, Dauphin County, PA.

11.6.10.1 Roy Marlin Klinger was born on 26 March 1914, Lykens Township, Dauphin County, PA. He was baptized on 5 July 1914, Zion (Klinger's) Church, Erdman, Lykens Township, Dauphin County, PA. He married **Helen Straub**. He died on 8 July 1989, at home, Millsboro, DE, at age 75. He was buried at Lutheran Cemetery, Tremont, Schuylkill County, PA.

11.6.10.1.1 Frederick Klinger married **Diana Sneck**.

11.6.10.1.1.1 Kim Klinger

11.6.10.1.1.2 Todd Klinger

11.6.10.1.1.3 Brady Klinger

11.6.10.1.2 Linda Klinger married **Phil Amos**.

11.6.10.1.3 Dennis Klinger

11.6.10.2 Earl Stanford Klinger was born on 23 February 1916, Lykens Township, Dauphin County, PA. He married **Margaret E. Hummel**. He lived in Tremont, Schuylkill County, PA. He died on 22 February 1998, Pottsville Hospital and Warner Clinic, Pottsville, Schuylkill County, PA, at age 81. He was buried at St' John's Lutheran Church Cemetery, Tremont, Schuylkill County, PA.

11.6.10.2.1 John W. Klinger was born on 21 June 1943, Pottsville, Schuylkill County, PA. He married **Lucile Natale**, daughter of **Carmen Natale** and **Alice (--?--)**, circa 1965. He died on 14 July 2005, at home, Tremont, Schuylkill County, PA, at age 62. According to a newspaper obituary, John was living at 10 N. Crescent St., Tremont, when he died. After graduating Tremont High School and Williamsport Technical Institute, John was employed by the former Garden State Tannery in Fleetwood, PA. He was buried at St. John's Lutheran Cemetery, Tremont, Schuylkill County, PA.

11.6.10.2.1.1 Barbara Klinger

11.6.10.2.1.2 John W. Klinger Jr.

11.6.10.3 Guy Irvin Klinger was born on 24 October 1917, Lykens Township, Dauphin County, PA. He died on 29 October 1917.

11.6.10.4 Stanley Emanuel Klinger was born on 12 August 1922, Spring Glen, Schuylkill County, PA. He married **Camille Hart**. Stanley was a First Lieutenant in the US Army during World War II. He died on 21 April 2007, at home, 126 Vaux Ave., Tremont, Schuylkill County, PA, at age 84. According to a newspaper obituary, Stanley served in the Army in World War II. He retired from the Richmond Screw Co., Tremont, and had previously worked at Scranton Electric. He was buried at Indiantown Gap National Cemetery, Annville, Lebanon County, PA.

11.6.10.4.1 Patricia Klinger married **Robert Diagastino**. She married **Steve Horner**. She died before 21 April 2007.

11.6.10.4.1.1 Robert Diagastino Jr.

11.6.10.4.1.2 John Diagastino died before 21 April 2007.

11.6.10.4.1.3 Michael Diagastino

11.6.10.4.1.4 Christine Diagastino

11.6.10.4.1.5 Thomas Diagastino

11.6.10.4.1.6 John Horner

11.6.10.4.2 CAROL KLINGER married ROGER BAUR. She married RICHARD BECKER.

    11.6.10.4.2.1 SHAWN BAUR

    11.6.10.4.2.2 TANYA BAUR

    11.6.10.4.2.3 RICHARD BECKER

    11.6.10.4.2.4 SHANNON BECKER

11.6.10.4.3 MICHAEL KLINGER married SHELVA WEAVER.

    11.6.10.4.3.1 MICHAEL KLINGER

11.6.10.4.4 JEFFREY KLINGER

11.6.11 IRA JACOB KLINGER was born on 19 May 1897, Lykens Township, Dauphin County, PA. He was baptized on 25 July 1897, Zion (Klinger's) Church, Erdman, Lykens Township, Dauphin County, PA. He married EVA M. ROTHERMEL, daughter of LAZARUS W. ROTHERMEL and EMMA L. BUSH, on 8 April 1916, Zion (Klinger's) Church, Erdman, Lykens Township, Dauphin County, PA. Prior to his death, Ira was living in Valley View, Schuylkill County, PA. He died in March 1969, at age 71. He was buried at Valley View, Schuylkill County, PA.

    11.6.11.1 MARY EMMA KLINGER (see above)

        11.6.11.1.1 TERRY L. STEHR (see above)

        11.6.11.1.2 CRAIG R. STEHR (see above)

        11.6.11.1.3 SUSAN K. STEHR (see above)

11.6.12 ESTON ISAIAH KLINGER was born on 12 March 1899. He was baptized on 30 April 1899, Zion (Klinger's) Church, Erdman, Lykens Township, Dauphin County, PA. He married ESTHER MIRALDA MAE RADEL on 26 October 1918, Zion (Klinger's) Church, Erdman, Lykens Township, Dauphin County, PA. At the time of his death, Eston was living in Klingerstown, Schuylkill County, PA. He died on 17 June 1966, at age 67. He was buried at Zion (Klinger's) Church, Erdman, Lykens Township, Dauphin County, PA.

    11.6.12.1 ERMA CATHERINE KLINGER was born on 7 February 1919. She was baptized on 1 May 1919, Zion (Klinger's) Church, Erdman, Lykens Township, Dauphin County, PA. She married PERRY HARRISON WILLIARD on 25 July 1936, Zion (Klinger's) Church, Erdman, Lykens Township, Dauphin County, PA. She died before 9 November 2010.

        11.6.12.1.1 IVAN WILLIARD

    11.6.12.2 IVAN JOHNNY KLINGER was born on 30 May 1921, Spring Glen, Schuylkill County, PA. He married DORIS EDITH MARTZ on 5 April 1947, Zion (Klinger's) Church, Erdman, Lykens Township, Dauphin County, PA. He died on 9 November 2010, Schuylkill Medical Center, East Norwegian Street, Pottsville, Schuylkill County, PA, at age 89. According to a newspaper obituary, Ivan served with the Army in the Philippines during World War II and was a recipient of the Purple Heart. After the war, he was a tire capper for Klinger and Stehr Inc., enjoyed working on his farm, and also worked as a mechanic and a blacksmith. Ivan enjoyed riding bicycle and delivered The Daily Item on his bike for many years. He also enjoyed flying kites and going to the beach. In his younger years, he enjoyed bowling, roller skating and going to drive-in movies, and he looked forward to sled riding with his children and grandchildren. He enjoyed listening to shortwave radio and was known to improvise antennas for better reception. He was buried on 13 November 2010, at Zion (Klinger's) Church Cemetery, Erdman, Dauphin County, PA.

        11.6.12.2.1 MARY JANE KLINGER married (--?--) EBRIGHT.

        11.6.12.2.2 BARBARA KLINGER married JAMES HOFER.

        11.6.12.2.3 RUTH KLINGER married GARY KEMBEL.

        11.6.12.2.4 ROXIE KLINGER married TIM SHEESLEY.

        11.6.12.2.5 RUTH ELLEN KLINGER was born on 27 July 1948. She was baptized on 20 August 1948, Zion (Klinger's) Church, Erdman, Lykens Township, Dauphin County, PA. She married GARY LEE KEMBEL on 31 August 1968, Zion (Klinger's) Church, Erdman, Lykens Township, Dauphin County, PA.

            11.6.12.2.5.1 GREGORY ALLEN KEMBEL was born on 8 May 1969. He was baptized on 27 July 1969, Zion (Klinger's) Church, Erdman, Lykens Township, Dauphin County, PA.

            11.6.12.2.5.2 DONALD LEE KEMBEL was born on 11 December 1970. He was baptized on 30 May 1971, Zion (Klinger's) Church, Erdman, Lykens Township, Dauphin County, PA.

11.6.12.2.5.3 MARY JANE KEMBEL was born on 14 May 1973. She was baptized on 9 September 1973, Zion (Klinger's) Church, Erdman, Lykens Township, Dauphin County, PA.

11.6.12.2.5.4 IVAN JAY KEMBEL was born on 12 February 1975. He was baptized on 14 March 1976, Zion (Klinger's) Church, Erdman, Lykens Township, Dauphin County, PA.

11.6.13 MEDA MAMIE KLINGER was born on 21 December 1902. Some sources record that she was born on 23 December 1902. She was baptized on 12 March 1903, Zion (Klinger's) Church, Erdman, Lykens Township, Dauphin County, PA. She married EDWIN WALLACE KNORR, son of WILLIAM EMMON KNORR and JANE ERDMAN, on 25 June 1929. She died on 12 February 1977, at age 74.

11.6.13.1 BRYANT EDWIN KLINGER is also referred to as BRYANT E. KNORR in some sources. He was born on 10 February 1923, Klingerstown, Schuylkill County, PA. He married HILDA G. HERB, daughter of EDWIN LEE HERB and IDA MINERVA REBUCK. He died on 5 September 1988, at age 65. He was buried at Riverview Memorial Gardens, Halifx, Dauphin County, PA.

11.6.13.1.1 PATSY KLINGER

11.6.13.1.2 RONALD KLINGER

11.6.13.2 ELSIE JENNIE BOYER is also referred to as ELSIE J. KNORR in some sources. She was born on 10 March 1927, Schuylkill County, PA. She was baptized on 9 May 1927, Zion (Klinger's) Lutheran Church Cemetery, Erdman, Dauphin Co., PA. She married MELVIN HARVEY WILLIARD, son of HARVEY MCKINLEY WILLIARD and CARRIE MINERVA SNYDER, on 12 June 1943, Zion (Klinger's) Lutheran Church, Erdman, Dauphin Co., PA. She died on 10 April 1957, Dauphin Co., PA, at age 30. She was buried on 14 April 1957, at St. Michael's Church Cemetery, Klingerstown, Schuylkill County, PA.

11.6.13.2.1 LARRY LAMAR WILLIARD was born on 24 September 1943, Dauphin Co., PA. He was baptized on 26 October 1943, Zion (Klinger's) Lutheran Church, Erdman, Dauphin Co., PA. He married SANDRA LEE KLINGER, daughter of ALVIN ELIAS KLINGER and VELMA KATHRYN ERDMAN, on 26 January 1963, Zion (Klinger's) Lutheran Church, Erdman, Dauphin Co., PA.

11.6.13.2.1.1 KERRY LAMAR WILLIARD (see above)

11.6.13.2.1.2 DAVID ALLEN WILLIARD (see above)

11.6.13.2.1.3 MELISSA WILLIARD (see above)

11.6.13.2.2 GERALDINE MAE WILLIARD was born on 11 June 1945, Dauphin Co., PA. She was baptized on 3 August 1945, Zion (Klinger's) Lutheran Church, Erdman, Dauphin Co., PA.

11.6.13.2.3 CHERYL DARLENE WILLIARD was born on 26 December 1948, Dauphin Co., PA. She was baptized on 12 February 1949, Zion (Klinger's) Lutheran Church, Erdman, Dauphin Co., PA. She married MARVIN IRA TOBIAS on 17 May 1969, Zion (Klinger's) Lutheran Church, Erdman, Dauphin Co., PA. She died on 3 January 1985, Northumberland Co., PA, at age 36. She was buried after 3 January 1985, at St. John's Lutheran & Reformed Church, Leck Hill, Northumberland Co., PA.

11.6.13.2.3.1 MICHAEL TOBIAS was born circa 1972, Northumberland Co., PA.

11.6.13.2.4 DALE MELVIN WILLIARD was born on 19 September 1951, PA. He married NOPHOT KITKLANG circa 1975. He died on 18 April 2004, Hegins, Schuylkill County, PA, at age 52.

11.6.13.2.4.1 RICHARD M. WILLIARD was born circa 1977, Schuylkill County, PA.

11.6.13.3 RAY ELWOOD KNORR was born on 7 April 1930, Klingerstown, Schuylkill County, PA. He married SALLIE CAROL on 1 October 1949. He died on 6 February 1987, at age 56.

11.6.13.3.1 RAY ELWOOD KNORR was born on 28 December 1949, Lykens, Dauphin County, PA. He married RENAE ROWLAND, daughter of JAMES T. ROWLAND ROWLAND SR. and THERESA SWOYER, on 1 May 1971.

11.6.13.3.1.1 DUANE KNORR was born circa 1972.

11.6.13.3.2 CHRISTINE DEBRA KNORR was born on 9 June 1953, Fearnot, Hubley Township, Schuylkill County, PA. She married JAY MCCARTHY on 9 June 1985.

11.6.13.3.3 SHEREE LEE SUSAN KNORR was born on 24 October 1956, Fearnot, Hubley Township, Schuylkill County, PA.

11.6.13.3.4 MICHELLE INEZ KNORR was born on 2 January 1972, Pottsville, Schuylkill County, PA.

11.6.13.4 WALLACE EDWARD KNORR was born on 9 July 1932, Lykens Township, Dauphin County, PA. He married **LAURA E. HERB** on 30 September 1950. He died on 16 December 2012, Geisinger Medical Center, Danville, Columbia County, PA, at age 80. According to a newspaper obituary, Wallace lived in Valley View, PA. He was a coal miner and a farmer, having worked in numerous area coal mines prior to his retirement. He was buried on 20 December 2012, at Zion (Klinger's) Lutheran Church, Erdman, Dauphin County, PA.

11.6.13.4.1 LEONARD EUGENE KNORR was born on 18 April 1950, Lykens, Dauphin County, PA. He married **KAREN WILLIARD** on 21 July 1973. Leonard lives in Dillsburg, PA.

11.6.13.4.1.1 MATTHEW KNORR was born circa 1975.

11.6.13.4.2 VIRGINIA ELAINE KNORR was born on 19 May 1955, Lykens, Dauphin County, PA. She married **JAMES OXENRIDER** on 15 October 1977. She and **JAMES OXENRIDER** were divorced. In 2012, Virginia and her partner Joan Krick were living in Northumberland, PA.

11.6.13.4.2.1 JENNIFER OXENRIDER was born circa 1979.

11.6.13.4.2.2 LUCY OXENRIDER was born circa 1981.

11.6.13.4.3 JULIE DIANE KNORR was born on 1 October 1957, Rebuck, Northumberland County, PA. She married **RAY DERCK** on 27 November 1973. Julie lives in Shamokin, PA.

11.6.13.4.3.1 MICHAEL DERCK was born circa 1975.

11.6.13.4.3.2 APRIL DERCK was born circa 1977.

11.6.13.5 DEAN LAMAR KNORR was born on 25 June 1941, Lykens Township, Dauphin County, PA. He married **DIANE ELIZABETH GOODERHAM** on 15 July 1972. He died on 26 March 2010, at his home on Lubbolds School Road, Lykens, Dauphin County, PA, at age 68. According to a newspaper obituary, Dean, who lived in Lykens, PA, was a 1959 graduate of Upper Dauphin High School and a 1964 graduate of Penn State University, with a bachelor of science degree in agricultural education. Dean retired in 1999, after 35 years of teaching agriculture in the Line Mountain School District. He was also a life-long farmer. He was buried on 29 March 2010, at Zion (Klinger's) Church Cemetery, Erdman, Dauphin County, PA.

11.6.13.5.1 KATE ELIZABETH KNORR was born on 9 April 1986, Danville, PA. At the time of her father's death, Kate was living in Springfield, VA, and was engaged to Michael Neely.

11.7 MARY ANNA KLINGER is also referred to as **MARIA ANNA KLINGER** in some sources. She was born on 15 July 1859, Dauphin County, PA. She was baptized on 22 April 1860, Zion (Klinger's) Church, Erdman, Lykens Township, Dauphin County, PA. She married **SAMUEL BAUM WIEST**, son of **SAMUEL MERKEL WIEST** and **ESTHER BAUM**. She married **REV. JOHN G. GLANTZ** after 1877, PA. She died on 22 October 1911, Nanticoke, Luzerne County, PA, at age 52. She was buried on 26 October 1911, at Hanover Cemetery, Nanticoke, Luzerne County, PA.

11.7.1 SALLIE ANN MINERVA WIEST was born on 16 November 1876, Klingerstown, Schuylkill County, PA. She was baptized on 10 February 1877, Zion (Klinger's) Church, Erdman, Lykens Township, Dauphin County, PA. She married **WILLIAM GINTER**, son of **GUSTAV GINTER** and **ANNA (--?--)**, circa 1897.

11.7.1.1 LAWRENCE ROY GINTER was born on 8 January 1899, Nanticoke, Luzerne County, PA. He married **LILLIAN URMSTON**. He died on 2 July 1955, West Goshen Township, Chester County, PA, at age 56. He was buried on 7 July 1955, at Fairview Cemetery, Coatesville, Chester County, PA.

11.7.1.1.1 LAWRENCE URMSTON GINTER was born on 30 June 1934, Coatesville, Chester County, PA. He married **ELEANOR LEWIS**. He and **ELEANOR LEWIS** were divorced before 2015. He died on 12 November 2015, Elizabethtown, Lancaster County, PA, at age 81. He was buried at Birmingham-Lafayette Cemetery, West Chester, Chester County, PA.

11.7.1.1.1.1 LAUREN GINTER married **(--?--) JACKSON**.

11.7.1.1.1.1.1 EMILY JACKSON

11.7.1.1.1.1.2 BEN JACKSON

11.7.1.1.1.1.3 PARKER JACKSON died before 12 November 2015.

11.7.1.1.1.2 LYNN GINTER married **(--?--) MAY**.

11.7.1.1.1.2.1 MADELEINE MAY

11.7.1.1.1.2.2 SAM MAY

11.7.1.1.1.3 LEIGH GINTER married **(--?--) CLARK BROOKS**.

11.7.1.1.1.3.1 HANNAH-LEIGH CLARK BROOKS

11.7.1.1.1.3.2 HALEY CLARK BROOKS

11.7.1.1.1.4 LIZABETH GINTER married (--?--) CONNORS.

11.7.1.1.1.4.1 NATALIE CONNORS

11.7.1.2 FLOYD SAMUEL GINTER was born on 6 March 1900. He married ROSE WYSHNER, daughter of PETER WYSHNER and ANTONIA KAULCHITUE, on 18 August 1929, Luzerne County, PA. He died in November 1970, at age 70.

11.7.1.2.1 ARLENE DELORES GINTER was born on 17 November 1930, Nanticoke, Luzerne County, PA. She married (--?--) IMBROLGLIA. She died in December 1981, at age 51.

11.7.1.2.2 EUGENE GINTER was born on 26 April 1931, Nanticoke, Luzerne County, PA. He died on 21 February 1940, Lehman Township, Luzerne County, PA, at age 8. He was buried on 26 February 1940, at Hanover Green Cemetery, Hanover Township, Luzerne County, PA.

11.7.1.2.3 MARILYN S. GINTER was born circa 1938.

11.7.1.3 DR. LEWIS GINTER was born circa 1902.

11.7.1.4 EARLE GINTER was born circa 1903.

11.7.1.5 CHARLES DANIEL GINTER was born on 6 April 1907, Nanticoke, Luzerne County, PA. He married LUCY BOYER, daughter of STEPHEN BOYER and SARAH EMANUEL, on 21 January 1935, Luzerne County, PA. He died on 6 September 1998, at age 91. He was buried at Fairview Cemetery, South Coatesville, Chester County, PA.

11.7.1.6 WILLARD GINTER was born on 27 November 1910, Nanticoke, Luzerne County, PA. He died on 27 November 1982, Plains, Luzerne County, PA, at age 72. He was buried at Hanover Green Cemetery, Hanover Green, Luzerne County, PA.

11.8 SARAH LOUISA KLINGER also went by the name of LOUISA. She was born on 9 November 1862, PA. Some sources record that she was born in December 1862. She was baptized on 24 May 1863, Zion (Klinger's) Church, Erdman, Lykens Township, Dauphin County, PA. She married JONATHAN KNOHR, son of HENRY KNOHR and HANNAH BUFFINGTON, circa 1882. She died on 19 March 1924, at age 61. She was buried on 23 March 1924, at Simeon Union Cemetery, Gratz, Dauphin County, PA.

11.8.1 DANIEL MILTON KNOHR was born on 3 December 1882. He was baptized on 8 February 1883, Zion (Klinger's) Church, Erdman, Lykens Township, Dauphin County, PA. Some sources record that he was born on 3 December 1883. He married JENNIE M. LEHR, daughter of DANIEL L. LEHR and MARY MAURER, circa 1910. He died on 17 February 1943, at age 59.

11.8.1.1 DANIEL LEWIS KNOHR also went by the name of LEWIS. He was born on 11 January 1911. He married ELSIE SCHLEGEL. He died in 1996.

11.8.1.2 ALLEN EDWARD KNOHR was born on 1 January 1913. He died on 10 September 1988, at age 75.

11.8.1.3 MARY LOUISE KNOHR was born on 1 December 1915. She died before 2012.

11.8.1.4 EARL LEHR KNOHR was born on 19 October 1918. He died in May 1986, at age 67.

11.8.1.5 RUTH IRENE KNOHR married (--?--) HUNTSINGER. She was born on 22 April 1924. She died in 1992.

11.8.1.6 RALPH JOSEPH KNOHR also went by the name of LEFTY. He was born on 18 December 1925, Gratz, Dauphin County, PA. He died on 20 January 2012, The Manor at Susquehanna Village, Millersburg, Dauphin County, PA, at age 86. According to a newspaper obituary, Ralph was a graduate of the former Hegins Township High School and Shippensburg University. After serving in the US Navy during World War II on the USS Apollo, he taught biology and physics at Upper Dauphin School District for many years. He was buried on 27 January 2012, at Union Cemetery, Gratz, Dauphin County, PA.

11.8.1.7 ALICE JEAN KNOHR married (--?--) HERB. She was born on 17 November 1928. She died before 2012.

11.8.1.8 JANET LUCILLE KNOHR was born on 11 November 1931. She married (--?--) EVANS. Janet lives in Germantown, TN.

11.8.2 HARRY IRVIN KNOHR was born on 2 November 1885. He died on 18 August 1961, Polyclinic Hospital, Harrisburg, Dauphin County, PA, at age 75. He was buried on 21 August 1961, at Simeon Union Cemetery, Gratz, Dauphin County, PA. Never married.

11.8.3 Mary L. Knohr was born on 15 May 1888. She married **William E. Philips** circa 1910. She died on 26 May 1940, at age 52. She was buried at Simeon Cemetery, Gratz, Dauphin County, PA.

    11.8.3.1 Vannie Philips was born on 2 June 1912. She married **Bill Swartz.**

    11.8.3.2 Effie Philips was born on 4 May 1914. She died in 1985.

11.8.4 Edmond K. Knohr is also referred to as **Edward** in some sources. He was born on 25 July 1894. He died in April 1968, at age 73. He was buried at Simeon Union Cemetery, Gratz, Dauphin County, PA.

Index to the Genealogical Listings

(--?--)
- (--?--) (1948-) 330
- (--?--) (1997-) 331
- Ablgrin 271
- Ada 302
- Adele 60
- Adele E. (1942-) 317
- Ahe 270
- Alfretta 252
- Alice 270, 395, 493
- Alice Baylor 93
- Allen Shetterly 411
- Alma (-2010) 194
- Alma M. (1933-) 74
- Alwine 293
- Alyson 264
- Amanda 127, 260
- Amanda Carolina (1867-1956) 72
- Amanda E. 269
- Amanda L. 197
- Amber 124, 478
- Amelia (1874-) 414
- Amelia M. (1892-1954) 301
- Amy 61, 258, 272
- Andrea 276
- Angela 128, 376
- Angelina 342
- Angelina (1862-) 222
- Angie 318
- Anita 96
- Anita M. 58
- Ann 259, 453
- Ann M. 121
- Ann Marie 481
- Anna 166, 167, 337, 426, 496
- Anna (1881-) 301
- Anna A. (1876-) 93
- Anna C. (1900-1984) 125
- Anna M. 373, 422
- Annie M. (1883-) 176
- Annie R. (1886-1952) 64
- Anny A. (1891-) 176
- Arabel E. (-2003) 473
- Arlene 261, 270
- Ashley 107, 164
- B. Marie 225
- Barbara 84, 131, 228, 273, 373, 472, 478
- Barbara A. (1939-2004) 76
- Barbara J. 218
- Becky 138, 251, 318
- Bessie (1914-) 433
- Beth 310, 381
- Beth Ann 242
- Betsey 113
- Bette 231
- Betty 82, 339, 373, 488
- Betty (1924-) 157
- Betty Joan 490
- Betty L. 131
- Blanche I. 422
- Blansh (1883-) 423
- Bobbie 387
- Bonnie 115, 171, 269
- Brandy 228
- Brenda 96, 277, 453
- Brenna J. 250
- Brigette 74
- Brittany 264
- Carol 180, 279, 321, 349, 367
- Carol (1960-) 414
- Carole A. (1937-) 489
- Caroline (1859-) 313
- Carolyn 266
- Carrie 371
- Carrie (1910-1977) 265
- Carrie M. 438
- Carrie M. (1878-1968) 127
- Carrie M. (1879-) 175
- Cassandra 343
- Catharina (1794-1854) 49
- Catharine 260, 314
- Catharine (1858-1947) 149
- Catherine 271
- Catherine (1821-) 423
- Catherine (1856-1883) 156
- Catherine R. (1914-1994) 341
- Charlotte B. (1920-) 376
- Cherie 338
- Cheryl 114, 225
- Christina 62, 349
- Christine 244, 376
- Christine A. 341
- Cindy 64, 180, 262, 274, 383
- Claire 230
- Connie 124, 179, 282
- Cora 313
- Cora Mae (1886-) 59
- Cordelia 131
- Corrine 248
- Cynthia 270
- Dawn 53, 113, 243, 252
- Deanna 131
- Debbie 228, 295
- Debbie S. 118
- Debby 92
- Deborah 205, 399, 438, 455, 467, 481
- Deborah (1949-) 372
- Deborah A. 79
- Debra 79, 464
- Dee 157
- Delores 98
- Denise 412, 457
- Dessie 233
- Diana 457
- Diane 200, 267, 278
- Diane M (1952-) 488
- Diva 293
- Dolly 438
- Dolores 74
- Donna 68, 182, 208, 264
- Donna J. 80
- Donna M. 125
- Dora 333
- Dora L. (1870-) 415
- Doris 339
- Dorothy (1860-) 386

Name	Page
Edith	427
Edith E.	179
Edith Mae (1887-1959)	207
Edna E.	285
Effie H. (1900-)	309
Elah	319
Elaine	251
Elda	222
Eleanor	62, 131, 147
Eleanor Marie	401
Eliza (1862-)	296
Elizabeth	50, 72, 204, 231, 388, 403
Elizabeth (1858-)	87
Elizabeth (1947-)	316
Elizabeth L. (1878-1946)	78
Elizabeth M.	280
Ella	287
Ella Mae	278
Ellen	52, 244
Ellen E. (1930-1995)	398
Ellen M. (1867-)	457
Ellen S. (1854-1936)	389
Elmira	407
Emma	74, 223, 243, 267, 271
Emma (1876-)	152
Emma R.	396
Emma R. (1884-)	392
Ephracina (1818-)	358
Erika (-2002)	485
Ernestine A. (1907-)	341
Esther	87, 263
Esther N. (1900-1987)	393
Ethel W. (1891-)	406
Eva	424
Eva C. (1907-1974)	55
Eva M.	50, 55, 72
Evelyn	199
Evie	92
Faye	294
Florence	94, 176
Florence A. (1918-)	312
Florence D. (1901-)	430
Florence E. (1920-1979)	367
Fran	272
Frances A.	165
Frances L. (1926-)	74
Francis	56
Frieda	95
Gace A. (1894-1985)	401
Gail	253, 275, 425
Gail P.	456
Gennie (1905-)	375
George F. Eash (1909-1980)	56
Gertrude	116
Gertrude (1908-2000)	209
Gertrude M. (1893-)	389
Gina	429
Gladys	193
Gladys L.	123
Glenis	325
Gloria	204, 285
Grace E. (1912-1995)	229
Grace O.	437
Gussie M. (1899-)	72
Gwendolyn Leone (1930-2006)	112
Hagit	317
Hanna E. (1890-)	158
Hannah	98
Hannah P.	54
Harriett (1922-)	391
Hattie P.	124
Heather	147
Heidi	342
Helen	114, 452
Helen (1892-)	437
Helen E. (1908-)	100
Helen E. (1917-1983)	225
Helena	61
Holli	244
Homer Campbell	456
Hope	385
Ida	52
Ida Mae	286
Inez	432
Irene	93
Irene L. (1904-)	83
Isobel	67
Jackie	84, 238
Jacqueline	226
Jacqueline M.	213
James	164
Jamie	335
Jan	157
Jane	129, 228
Jane (1851-)	204
Jane (1857-)	99
Jane E.	388
Janell	192
Janet	60, 68, 179, 266, 279
Jasmine	415
Jason	428
Jean	248, 268
Jean Andrea	132
Jean I. (1924-)	208
Jeanmarie	458
Jeanne	61, 282
Jeffrey Griffiths (-2010)	455
Jen	245, 442
Jennie	284, 376
Jennie (1883-1965)	459
Jennifer	262, 276, 453
Jennifer B.	72
Jenny	99
Jerilynn	79
Jessica	61, 264, 387
Jewel	198
Jo	54
Joan	56, 251, 270, 285
Joann	104, 187
Joanne	208, 301
Jodee	117
Jody	392
Jody M. (1958-)	491
Josephine	136
Josephine (1850-)	97
Joy	108
Joyce	191, 277, 473
Judy	180, 183, 259, 472
Juliane	428
Julie	273, 275

Juline	278
June	84, 194
Kandi	180
Karen	129, 156, 252, 295, 426, 453, 464
Karen (1952-)	410
Karen G.	204
Kate C.	70
Kathe	454
Katherine	123, 287, 427
Kathleen L.	341
Kathryn	87, 212
Kathy	94
Katie	261
Katie R. (1850-)	207
Katie R. (1868-)	175
Katrina	268
Kay	147, 415
Kaye	295
Kelly	191
Kenny (1966-)	361
Kerry	269
Kiley	147
Kim	216, 381, 486
Kris	442
Kristin	371
Lacey	317
Lavonne	375
LeAnn	429
Leighanne	198
Lelia	384
Leslie	248
Leva (-2010)	377
Lidia (1851-)	418
Lillian (1909-2005)	380
Lillian L.	492
Lily	168
Linda	179, 180, 191, 208, 263, 265, 400, 433, 442
Linda Lee	377
Lindsey	276
Lisa	124, 404
Lizzie	191
Lizzie (1865-)	226
Lizzie E.	280
Lizzie E. (1856-)	390
Lois	213
Loretta	231
Lori	242, 440
Lorraine (1927-)	139
Lorraine E. (1925-)	126
Lottie	258
Lottie (1897-)	405
Lottie R. (1874-1957)	301
Louella	123
Louisa (1856-1936)	80
Lucille	179
Lydia	50, 194, 288
Lydia (1887-)	406
Lyne	257
Mabel	67, 256
Madelene (1912-1984)	468
Mae	382
Mae (1907-)	457
Magdalina	56
Mahala	381
Mamie M. (1892-1968)	80
Marcella	421
Margaret	138, 209, 279, 406, 480, 490
Margaret (1852-)	381
Margaret E. (1941-2002)	63
Margaret M. (1912-1994)	396
Marge	295
Maria	259
Marian	215, 359
Marian L.	215
Marianne	136
Marie	279
Marie K. (1886-)	87
Marjorie	265
Marla	147, 433
Martha (1881-)	166
Martha Ann	271
Martha Drudge	92
Martha M. (1918-)	312
Mary	150, 175, 242, 276, 377, 426, 484
Mary (1914-)	198
Mary A.	226
Mary A. (1862-1938)	311
Mary Ann	155, 422
Mary C. (1865-)	96
Mary Christine	274
Mary E. (1863-)	83
Mary E. (1903-)	205
Mary Elizabeth	396
Mary Emma	398
Mary F. (1857-)	388
Mary Frances	286
Mary J.	239
Mary J. (1852-)	410
Mary J. (1864-1930)	89
Mary Jane	348
Mary L.	213
Mary Lou	276
Maud I.	242
Mauree	217
Mayme M. (1903-)	417
Megan	357
Meghan	478
Melinda	51, 338
Melissa	405
Michelle	318, 395, 453
Mildred A. (1908-)	205
Mildred S.	138
Milena	279
Minnie	211, 246
Minnie (1877-)	376
Minnie J. (1881-)	180
Mirah	253
Misty	442
Molly	415
Monica	228
Myra (1909-)	305
Myra (1945-)	102
Nadine	338
Nancy	258, 387, 426
Nancy Jane	280
Natalie	442
Nellie	293
Nickie (1982-)	102
Nora Leona	388
Norma	285

Ophelia F. (1932-) 79
Patricia 61, 78, 146, 191, 196, 372
Patti 130, 485
Patty 321
Paul 251
Pearson 214
Peggy 440, 452
Penelope 298
Penni 244
Penny 198
Phyllis 136
Rachel 254
Rebecca 194, 207, 229, 411
Rebecca (1832-) 416
Regina (1884-1944) 346
Rhonda 50
Rickann 115
Robert 420
Roberta 91, 377
Robin 245, 349
Romaine 224
Roni 245
Rosalie Mable 387
Rose 254
Rose E. (1888-) 65
Rowene 295
Ruth 426, 455
Ruth Ann 87
S. Alice 192
Sadie (1903-) 313
Sallie E. 158
Sally (1962-) 196
Samantha 255
Sandra 266, 296, 322, 364
Sandy 228, 415
Sara A. (1863-) 126
Sara E. (1860-) 362
Sarah 70, 72, 84, 229, 239, 286, 292, 354, 372
Sarah (1832-) 406
Sarah (1852-1931) 363
Sarah (1860-1930) 391
Sarah (1901-) 457
Sarah J. (1846-) 61
Sarah M. (1857-) 69
Savannah 472
Sayuri 486
Shan 99
Shane 147
Shara 321
Sharon 233, 383
Sharon (1963-) 399
Shelby 129
Sherrie 273
Sherry 191, 404
Shirley 114, 144, 231, 276, 292, 381
Shirley Sue 489
Sofie (1890-) 303
Sophia 99
Stephanie 275
Sue 130, 318, 415
Susan 128, 162, 213, 221, 398
Susanna 88, 240
Susannah (1811-) 458
Sylvia (1948-) 301
Tammy 233
Tammy (1969-) 361
Tena 292
Terri 400
Tessie (1897-) 457
Theresa 70
Tiffany Natasha (1996-) 282
Tina 128, 379, 432
Toni 252
Tracey 191
Traci 285
Tracy 96, 128, 228
Trish 131
Trisha 147
Ursula 187
Vera 437, 464
Verna (1895-1978) 454
Vicki (1968-) 323
Victoria 190
Virginia 282
Wanda 228, 289, 338
Wendi 455
Wendy 266
William Adams 393
Wilma K. (1897-) 424
Winifred 230
Wrela V 127
Yvonne 269
Yvonne (1950-) 102
Yvonne M. 250

Abbazzia
  Linda (1952-) 487
Abrams
  Elise 306
Abramson
  H.D. 481
Abromaitis
  Joseph (1925-1990) 486
Abromitis
  Arlene (1931-) 488
  Douglas P. (1961-) 487
  Eugene (1947-) 486
  Garrett (1988-) 488
  Jacob Evan (2011-) 487
  Jacquelyn Gerette (1963-) 488
  John Harvey (1929-2012) 487
  John J. Sr. (1948-) 487
  John Joseph Jr (1967-) 487
  Joseph P. (1925-1990) 486
  Joseph W (1896-1955) 486
  Joseph W. (1957-) 487
  Kevin (1994-) 487
  Kristin Rose (1981-) 487
  Laura (1952-) 487
  Mary Ann (1968-) 488
  Maryann (1954-) 487
  Matthew Michael (1996-) 487
  Mia Renee (2001-) 487
  Michael William (1953-) 487
  Patricia Alice (1936-1998) 488
  Peter James 486
  Phillip (1962-) 487
  Rebecca Ann (1975-) 487
  Sarah 487
  Theresa Ann (1983-) 487
  William J (1955-) 488

William P. (1932-1993) 488
Zoie Ema (2007-) 487

Acker
Emma 393

Adair
(--?--) 441
Jennifer 441

Adam
(--?--) 78
Katie Beth (1987-) 262
Keegan Troy (1993-) 262
Rebecca (1826-1907) 311
Troy Alan 262

Adams
Aaron 409
Alan (1913-) 176
Albert (1911-) 176
Anna Elizabeth (1873-1922) 175
Anne E. (1903-) 176
Arden 402
Barbara A. (1943-2000) 115
Beulah M. (1903-) 176
Brett (1980-) 244, 441
Cassidy J. 298
Charles B. (1884-1903) 143, 156
Charles Milton (1875-) 175
Charles N. (1888-) 175
Clarence Marlin (1908-1998) 175
Clayton Franklin (1890-) 176
Clyde C. (1918-2006) 473
Connie Lee (1948-) 361
David Earl (1953-) 361
David Stuart (1970-) 298
Deborah Lynn (1964-) 298
Debra Ann (1967-) 332
Edward (-2010) 404
Edward N. (1880-) 176
Elizabeth Ellen (1884-1947) 393
Elizabeth Eve (1887-1981) 393
Elizabeth M. (1925-) 176
Elmer J. (1896-) 175
Emanuel (1857-1925) 143
Emma (1873-1922) 175
Esther J. (1922-) 176
Ethel E. 480
Flora (1880-1932) 120
Florence A. (1902-) 175
Floyd M. (1910-) 176
Francis G. (1914-) 176
Frank E. (1916-) 176
George David (1921-) 361
George W. (1906-) 176
Guy 176
Hannah Sivilla (1866-1910) 174
Harold 176
Harold (1917-) 175
Harry F. (1890-) 175
Harry L. (1902-1977) 143, 156
Helen (1918-) 175
Helen (1922-) 147
Holly D. 298
Howard (1911-) 176
Isaac Monroe (1870-1915) 175
James (-1964) 143, 156
James Henry 393
Jason (1977-) 244, 441
Jeanne 176
Jeremiah K. P. (1902-) 176
Jesse 409
John Q. (1906-) 176
John Quincy (1882-) 176
Jon Paul Henry 198
Jonene 198
Kelsey A. 298
Kenneth 106, 176
Kenneth R. (1941-2010) 404
Kenneth W. (1921-) 176
Kent Allen 106
Kimberly Ann (1985-) 361
Lamar David (1982-) 361
Lee L. (1924-) 176
Leona (1934-) 133
Leonard Roy (1944-2011) 359
Lester 244
Lillian 176
Lindsay Jo 106
Lisa Marie (1980-) 361
Loranza (1868-1955) 175
Lucy (1916-) 176
Lucy A. (1892-) 175
Lucy May (1885-1921) 176
Luke 409
Margaret (1915-) 176
Mark (1916-) 359
Mark L. (1916-) 176
Mary M. 61
Michael 409
Mildred E. (1907-1956) 176
Milton S. (1895-1964) 143, 156
Miriam (1912-) 176
Monroe I. (1908-1957) 176
Nathan (1910-) 133
Nicholas 174
Nicholas Edwin (1880-) 176
Nicholas S. (1904-) 176
Nora 325, 480
Pamela 404
Paul (1902-) 176
Paul John Henry 198
Priscilla 312
Raymond C. (1905-1982) 175
Richard Clyde 473
Ricky 404
Rita K. 262
Robert 359
Robert (1923-) 176
Rolandus (1868-1955) 175
Roy 176
Roy H. (1897-1973) 175
Russell N. (1900-) 175
Ruth F. (1921-1967) 143, 156
Sadie O. (1900-1902) 143, 156
Sarah Ellen (1878-) 176
Shirley (1935-) 133
Tammie 404
Troy K. (-2011) 402
Verna M. (1894-) 175
W. Kay (1919-) 176
Warren (1917-1920) 143, 156
William K. (Rev.) (-2013) 298

William K. Rev. (-2013) 298
William Kelsey Jr. (1965-) 298
William M. 480
William Victor (1876-) 176

Addison
Paul (1907-) 175
Samuel 175

Adolph
George W. (1920-2004) 417
Joseph S. 417

Agley
M.C. 279

Airgood
Peggy Drudge 95

Akelaitis
Ron 198

Albers
Sophia M. (1885-1980) 296

Albert
Glen E. 58

Albright
Ashley Burrell (1983-) 408
Brandon Richard (1981-) 408
Charles (1954-) 408
Julia A. (1904-) 398
Ryan Charles (1979-) 408
Samuel 398
William T. 398

Alexander
Bethany A. 492
Branden Wayne (1971-) 399
Brittany Marie (1994-) 399
Jan 107
Steven 366

Allen
Alexis Nicole (1994-) 96
Bradan Roller (1998-) 96
Bradley Rollar 96
Cameron Michael (2005-) 264
Denise Marie 121
Donald Wayne (1943-) 184
Elizabeth Christine (1994-) 184
Gretchen 263
Griffin Matthew (2000-) 264
Jeffrey B. 264
Lisa Ann (1972-) 184
Marsha 235
Mary Joan (1933-) 123
Terry Michael (1969-) 184

Allex
Tammy (1961-) 164

Allison
Angus 421
Ruby M. (1927-2009) 421

Allmer
Eric 235

Allwine
Daniel 239
David 239
Elmer C. 239

Almlee
Bernice Mildred (1910-) 423
Christopher John Olsen (1870-) 423

Elsie M. (1909-) 423

Alspach
Bertha (-2007) 353
John (1780-1864) 431
Louisa (1810-1876) 176, 431

Altwater
Frank Ross 397
Mary Patricia (1919-) 397

Alvarez
Patricia 198

Alverson
Erwin Wright (1901-1990) 374
Linda Lucille (1929-) 374

Alvord
(--?--) 140

Amaro
Drake Hero (2002-) 234
Ray 234

Amato
(--?--) 229

Ambler
James H. (1922-) 76
James Herbert (1898-1950) 76
Jane Florence (1924-) 76

Ambris
Erick (1987-) 230
Landon Lee (2009-) 230

Ammerman
Margaret C. 59

Amo
Odile Amita 286

Amos
Paul 274
Phil 493

Ancheff
Ben 151, 449
Bobby 151, 449
George 151
Olivia 151, 449

Anders
Lee Edward (1923-1986) 73

Anderson
Ethel Ross (1904-1959) 84
Freda L (1960-) 488
Helen Marian Ardel (1922-) 91
Jane (1948-) 487
Marcele L. (1959-) 235
Martha Gertrude 392
Matthew M. (1880-) 84

Andrews
Audrey M. (1933-) 190
Jane 486
Mary D. 370
Robert 458

Andrulonis
Anne Marie 301
Anthony (1871-1937) 301
Anthony (1971-) 301
Anthony C. (1905-1982) 301
Buckey 301
Chrissie (1974-) 301
David (1977-) 301
Jerome A. (1943-) 301

Joane..301
Paul Anthony (1946-1999)...............................301
Angel
Elizabeth..374
Genvieve..226
Angeles
Alex Estrada (1975-).....................................71
Anglemyer
Dave..272
Anglin
Annetta Elton (1870-1961)..............................92
Angst
(--?--)..340
Anskis
Francis (1937-)...190
Antes
Amber Alysia..320
Ira Ray...320
Mandy Adelle..320
Antoloni
Justine..347
Anuszewski
Andrea Eden (1967-)..................................309
Cara Lynne (1965-).....................................309
Lewis...309
Michelle Ann (1958-)..................................309
Scott Joseph (1962-)....................................309
Aponick
Debbie..348
Appleby
Cynthia Ann (1953-)...................................465
Glenn...465
Robert (1929-1998).......................................465
Robin Jolene (1957-)...................................465
Aquino
Marilyn Ada..71
Arbogast
(--?--) (1918-)..144
Courtney Lynn (1986-)...............................144
Emaline (1862-1919)............................333, 342
Israel..342
Kathanne (1988-).......................................144
Kathleen Jo (1957-)....................................144
Robert Mark (1961-)..................................144
Seth William (1983-)..................................144
Shea Kimberly (1986-)...............................144
William Charles (1928-1984).......................144
William Charles Jr. (1953-)........................144
Archer
Nettie Bea..60
Archibald
Cynthia Lea...58
Arkley
Jaron Travis (1984-1984).......................145, 315
Jeremy Erik (1983-)............................145, 315
John K..144
Larry Erik (1958-)......................................144
Armentrout
Amanda Burris..374
Armstrong
Isabel C. (1904-1942)....................................222
Jerry..58
Jerry Jr. (1963-)..58

Samuel H...222
Arnold
Carol Sue (1937-).......................................274
Charles M..273
Eileen...228
Eloine Kathryn (1909-)...............................274
Fay...272
Gary...274
Gregory..228
Hattie Amelia (1883-1950).............................62
Jacob...64
Jaime..228
James...228
Levi J. (1901-1993).......................................273
Lillian M. (1907-2003).................................399
Osceolla...466
Randy L. (1964-)...197
William J. (1905-1958)...................................64
Artz
Anna Mae (1919-2005).................................248
Beverlyann (1938-)....................................102
Bonnie Denise (1957-)...............................471
Bruce L. (1960-)..479
Caroline..240, 297
Clarence...136
Cynthia S...136
Daniel...136
Daniel Webster (1901-1960).........................102
Dewey S. (1898-1953)..................................248
Donald Aaron (1949-).................................284
Donald Eugene Sr. (1928-1986)....................436
Edwin...136
Elias...135
Elizabeth K. (1877-1948)..............................455
Elmer E. (1874-1954)...................................219
Elwood Eugene (1934-1996)........................205
Emma (1830-1919).......................................297
Ernest R...135
Eston C. (1910-1970)....................................136
Eugene Howard (1932-1968)................471, 479
Faith E..205
Fayne Henry (1926-1931).............................103
Florence Alma (1901-1914)..........................219
Frances..366
Guy Roscoe (1899-1966)..............................436
Helen (1920-)..102
Henry K. (1858-1935)...........................102, 352
Howard Monroe (1895-1971).......................102
Irvin (1879-1937)..204
Irvin Rathmus (1939-2000)...........................205
Ivan Wayne (1909-1989)..............................204
James Monroe...102
James W..205
Jeffrey M...136
Jonathan...136
Katie..136
Lamar...136
Laura..136
Lawrence...135
Lawrence A...136
Lester...136
Linda..135
Lizzie...358
Mahlon R. (1930-2007).................................135
Marie M. (1922-)...103

Mark L. 136
Marvin G. (1928-1997) 138
Matthew 136
Mina Estella (1886-) 352
Pamela (1961-) 479
Pamela B. 205
Phyllis (1928-) 102
Ralph Arthur (1899-1945) 138
Raymond 136
Raymond Jr. 136
Richard B. (1940-) 479
Sarah Elmira Jemima (1858-1929) 352
Shawn J. 205
Stephanie K. 136
Stets (1930-2007) 135
Tracey Ann (1969-) 284
Tyler (1990-) 102
Vera Violet (1928-2016) 204
Walter 136
Warren E. 136
Wayne I. (1930-2017) 204

Aseman
Elsie B. (1905-) 97

Ashcroft
Neal 226

Asp
Waldo B. (1934-) 341

Athey
Clifford 214
Irene G. (1928-2013) 214
Lizzie 177
Minnie 290

Atkinson
Curtis W. 255
Debra Yvonne (1967-) 256
Douglas Craig (1965-) 255
Earl Edward 374
Emily Grace (1997-) 256
John 380
Mary Jane 374

Atwell
Eugene 436

Aucker
Katie Rosellen (1889-1939) 492

Auman
Bernice (-1999) 240
Betty Ann (1985-) 465
Brandy Jo (1979-) 465
Jude Dale 465
Jude Matthew (1981-) 465
Matthew Luke (1983-) 465

Aungst
Claude E. (1895-1979) 81
Lyman E. (1888-1928) 81
William R. (1913-1981) 216

Auskelis
Peter 412

Austria
Karen 62

Avery
Cornelia Paulina (1925-2005) 60

Awata
Mari 491

Ayuso
Anthony 374

Azinger
Richard 191
Vincent (1973-) 191

Babcock
Lauren Ashley (1986-) 256

Bachtell
Betty Jane (1924-2008) 360
Brenda 361
Jack R. Jr. 361
Jack R. Sr. (1946-2014) 361
Levi 361
Ronald 361

Backfisch
James 204

Bacon
John 231
Karl Johann (1989-) 231
Nathan Paul 231

Baddorf
Lois Marie (1930-) 343

Badman
Leon 383

Baer
Lillian A. (-1974) 341

Bahner
Carrie Elise (1897-1983) 454
Ruth 373

Bahney
Emma 218

Baier
Brooke Rische (1916-2013) 396
Charles 396
Charles A. (1887-1967) 396
Douglas 397
Howard Nelson (1918-2006) 397
Jane 396
Karl Clifford (1911-1989) 396
Kathi 397

Bailey
Catherine E. (1870-1942) 395
William 395
William F. 132

Baimbridge
Celecia 479

Bain
(--?--) 353
Beverly L. 298
Brooke Elyse (1987-) 353

Bainbridge
William 100

Bair
(--?--) 485
Bessie 50
Emma 485
Frances Grace 184
Noah 485

Baird
Bill 275
Billy 275
Lynn 275

Baker
   (--?--) 120, 217
   Leroy 382
   Margaret Jane 417
   Tanya 276

Baldwin
   P. Joy 298

Ball
   Doris E. 252

Bamberg
   Harold 306

Banach
   Michael 310

Bango
   Christine Denise 261

Barge
   Ashley 265

Barker
   Elizabeth (1837-1900) 280

Barkos
   Carla (1969-) 289
   Michael 289
   Michelle 289
   Nicole 289

Barnes
   Elizabeth (1967-) 339, 425, 445
   Eric 259
   Jeffrey 259
   Jeffrey S. (1965-) 338, 425, 445
   Raymond Martin 174
   Robin S. (1964-) 338, 425, 445
   Ronald 259
   Wallace Glenn (1923-2000) 338
   William (1885-1929) 338

Barnett
   Glenn Richard (1942-) 175

Barnhardt
   (--?--) 207

Barnhart
   Elizabeth 210

Barnum
   Thelma (1904-) 92

Barr
   Harriet 78
   James Stuart 294
   Ruth Etta (1908-1994) 62

Barry
   (--?--) 141, 187
   Allen Charles (1943-2015) 214
   Allen William (1922-2002) 214
   Anna Mae (1938-2015) 109
   Arthur Levi (1924-1999) 214
   Betty 109
   Carl Eugene (1940-) 109
   Carl R. (1932-) 214
   Catherine Lorraine (1926-1970) 215
   Charles Samuel (1918-1972) 214
   Clyde R. (1940-1941) 214
   Clyde Sidney (1916-1979) 214
   Dale 215
   Daniel Abraham (1916-1986) 109
   Daniel Edward (1970-) 110
   Darlene Lee (1951-) 110
   Diane Lynn (1968-) 109
   Donna 109
   Dorothy J. (1930-) 215
   Edwin Roy (1958-) 188
   Elmer Charles (1910-1940) 214
   Elsie Marie (1946-) 110
   Faith Elizabeth (1989-) 188
   Frosty (1935-2009) 109
   Guy Raymond (1920-1993) 214
   Helen Florence (1928-1929) 215
   Henry George (1885-1939) 213
   Irene E. (1908-1961) 213
   Jean 109
   Joan 240
   John 109
   John Earl (1897-1962) 187
   John Henry (1914-1992) 214
   Judy 109
   Karen 215
   Kathryn (1926-1970) 215
   Mae (1992-) 109
   Margaret Mae (1911-1975) 214
   Marian A. (1936-) 214
   Marianne C. (1971-) 109
   Marlin Eugene (1945-) 109
   Maryann (1971-) 109
   Meagan Holly (1986-) 188
   Michael K. (1956-1975) 214
   Rachel Louise (1989-) 188
   Ray Richard Jr. (1967-) 109
   Ray Richard Sr. (1943-2013) 109
   Robert 215
   Robert E. (1934-2012) 215
   Robert Jr. 215
   Roy Edward (1935-2009) 109
   Roy Edwin (1940-) 187
   Samantha Lee (1966-) 109
   Sandra Lee (1961-) 109
   Scott Earl (1961-) 188
   Stacy Lynn (1972-) 108, 109
   Tammy 110, 111
   Tori Leigh (1974-) 483

Barth
   Alexander Carl (1985-) 237
   Amelia Christine (1981-) 237
   Anna Elizabeth (2002-) 238
   Ashley Paige (2008-) 237
   Cynthia Grace 237
   David A. (1952-1972) 237
   Gregory Robert (1978-) 237
   Harold Leonard (1920-1991) 237
   Karan Sabina (1952-1954) 237
   Karin Sabina (1955-) 237
   Kenneth Charles (1959-) 237
   Kevin 237
   Kimberly 237
   Leonard 237
   Nicole Lee (1979-) 238
   Raymond E. (1922-1972) 237
   Richard Carl (1926-2002) 237
   Richard Carl II (1981-) 238
   Richard Carl Jr. (1949-) 237
   Robert George (1950-) 237
   Sandra 237
   Shirley 231

Virginia 237
Warren 237
Zachary Carter (2010-) 237

Bartho
Emma (1850-1918) 388

Bartholomew
Bruce (1915-) 380
Clare Elizabeth (1911-) 380
Clayton C. (1878-1958) 379
Clayton E. (1931-2011) 379
Clayton R. 379
Effenger G. (1912-) 380
Franklin 191
Franklin (-2011) 379
Helen Amelia (1902-) 379
Herbert Elwood (1903-1985) 379
Herbert Jr. (-2011) 379
Howard Valentine (1906-1919) 379
John Kellar (1913-) 380
Joyce 379
Mildred (1929-) 379
Paul 379
Richard (1965-) 191
Robert 379
Ruth Irene (1910-) 380
Shirley 379
Valentine (1836-1904) 379
Ward Emerson (1908-1919) 380

Bartlett
Alanna Leslie (2005-) 112
Jayden Aaron (2009-) 112
Jordan Austin (2009-) 112
Robert 112
Trythena Maxine (2005-) 112

Barto
Agnes 70
Anna B. (1908-) 70
Anna Pauline (1889-1958) 72
Brian Keith 70
Concepcion Q. (1950-) 71
Connie (1950-) 71
Cori Patricia (1976-) 71
Dana Elizabeth (1980-) 71
Dominic 70
Edward (1858-1943) 70
Edwin K. (1858-1943) 70
Effie L. (1882-1884) 71
Evelyn Elizabeth (1954-) 71
Florence (1899-) 70
Ginny (1949-) 71
Harry George (1957-) 71
Harry W. (1885-1939) 72
Hazel E. (1892-) 70
Henry Wilson 70
Henry Wilson (1908-1973) 70
Henry Wilson (1932-1996) 70
Hilda S. (1894-1977) 72
Isaac Jacob (1807-1874) 69
Joe 70
John 70
John Willis (1896-1972) 72
John Wilson (1860-1928) 70
Joseph (1962-) 71
Joseph Warren (1931-2016) 70
Julia (1947-) 70
Julianna Davis (1993-) 71
Julie 70
Kathleen 70
Lillian (1902-) 70
Lona Amon (1942-) 71
Marie 70
Marion R. (1903-) 72
Michael (1964-) 71
Michael Arthur 70
Mike 70
Nick (1989-) 70
Norman (1887-1888) 72
Reuben (1840-1912) 69
Robert E. (1890-1960) 72
Robert Joseph 70
Robert M. (1919-) 72
Robert William (1915-1982) 71
Ross F. (1911-) 70
Ruth Ellena (1947-) 70
Sarah 72
Susan Elizabeth (1863-) 72
Teresa 70
Van Adrian (1944-) 71
Virginia (1949-) 71
Warren 70
Warren Moyer (1909-1982) 70
Warren R. (1881-1929) 70
William F. (1913-) 70

Bashore
Audrey A. 80
Charlene M. 80
Edward H. (1928-2008) 80
Edward L. 80
Herbert 80
Wenda M. 80

Basseligia
Mark 77

Bassinger
Florence 277

Basso
Norman 472

Batdorf
Miriam L. (1899-1970) 143
Rebecca 408, 411

Bates
Brenda 466
Paul 279

Bathold
(--?--) 448

Batson
Diane Shartle (1951-) 316
Frederick James Jr. 316
Margaret Kittinger (1956-) 316

Battorf
Catherine (1807-1883) 201

Bauer
Christine Sophie (1927-1997) 51
Jacob 51

Baum
Carl Richard (1925-2011) 240
Clark 429
Esther (1820-1910) 166, 496
Mary Ann (1848-1931) 166
Morris 240

Sallie 181
Bauman
  Anna Maria (1788-1846) 150
Baumgartner
  Joseph 94
Baur
  Roger 494
  Shawn 494
  Tanya 494
Bax
  Charles J. Jr. (1942-   ) 127
Beach
  Lillian 455
Beacher
  Ruth Ann 199
Bean
  Mary Lillie (1864-1900) 118
Beard
  Adam Frank (1857-1934) 373
  Blanche May (1889-1991) 374
  Brooke 458
  Cora Ann (1892-1966) 374
Beasley
  Cheryl Lynn (1981-   ) 483
  Hal Roy 483
  Jeffrey Alan (1986-   ) 483
Beato
  (--?--) 198
  Julian 198
Beatty
  James W. (1857-   ) 386
  Mary Alice (1894-1950) 386
Beaudoin
  Jerome R. 60
  Marie G. (1931-2006) 60
Beaver
  (--?--) 157, 384
  Carrie (-2008) 453
  Matilda 453
Bebo
  Joseph 396
Bechtel
  David 367
  Donald R. 68, 122
  Elizabeth 407
  Harold H. (-1984) 68
  Harold K. (1941-2003) 68, 122
  Larry E. 68, 122
  Margaret A. 472
  Michael T. 68, 122
  Raymond 365
  Ruth 366
Beck
  (--?--) 491
  Hanna (1822-1846) 205
  James Philip (1907-1972) 55
  Jason 118
  John 55
  Mary F. (1911-1993) 329
  Randy 118
  William E. 436
Becker
  Harry C. (1912-1987) 78

Jean (1920-   ) 413
Lilian 310
Richard 494
Roxanne M. 197
Shannon 494
Beckett
  Gertrude Bernice (1924-2008) 304
  Harold (1896-   ) 304
Begani
  Joseph Peter 321
  Nathan Joseph 321
Behan
  Mildred Van (-1980) 361
Behney
  Donald H. (1922-2011) 389
  Lori 389
  Michael 389
Beibler
  Selena 317
Beilharz
  Amy 147
  Missy 147
  Rich 147
Beisel
  Elizabeth 365
  Lucetta (1824-1904) 161
Beisswanger
  (--?--) 227
Belack
  (--?--) 197
Beland
  Jeanette 215
Bell
  (--?--) 271, 383
  Anna 386
  Marlin 384
Bemiller
  Joyce 62
Ben
  Marie Anne 241
Bender
  Caleb 107
  David (-1919) 388
  David Lee (1919-1979) 388
  Eric 107
  Harold 117
  Sarepta V. 393
Benjamin
  Elizabeth (1831-1863) 51
Benner
  Cynthia Lou (1957-   ) 305
  Jack L. (1931-2005) 305
  Linda Lee (1960-   ) 305
  Myra Lynn (1962-   ) 305
  Wilmont (1905-   ) 305
Bennett
  Bernice Woofter (1920-   ) 92
  Harry Raymond (1883-1948) 305
  Herman Lampe (1913-2012) 305
  Jeffrey (1957-   ) 329
  Martha E. (1857-1922) 98
Bennsinger
  Adam (1856-   ) 485

Page 509

Bensinger
- Agnes Minerva (1861-1940) 279, 458
- Bessie Mae (1910-1965) 224
- Carol Ann (1958-) 264
- Francis W. 224
- Frederick Herman (1911-1971) 489
- George 279
- Harvey E. (1876-1928) 485
- Jennie 214
- Joan Ellen (1934-1969) 489
- Lance 489
- Richard Paul (1935-1984) 489
- Robert Ira (1920-1970) 489
- Robert Jr. 489
- Sarah (1853-1923) 149

Benson
- Jenelle 423

Berg
- Bert 91
- Bert David (1919-1979) 91
- Bonnie D. (1952-) 91
- Bonnie Dianne (1952-) 91
- James William (1922-2002) 91
- James William Jr. (1950-1950) 91
- Sharon A. (1950-) 91
- Sharon Ann (1950-) 91
- William Lystad (1897-1970) 91

Berger
- Amelia 313
- George 272
- Herman 272
- Lowell Dean (1922-2009) 272
- Mark 272
- Mary 77
- Michael 272
- Thomas Allen (1949-2002) 272

Bergey
- Barbara 233
- Blair 233
- Brandy 233
- Constance Lou (1937-) 233
- Joanne Gail (1947-) 233, 434
- John W. (1907-1988) 232, 434
- Jonathan 233
- Joyce Marie (1941-) 233
- Mary (1904-1992) 231, 366
- Robert 233
- Robert Eugene (1935-) 233
- W. Ellis 231
- William Clyde (1933-2010) 232

Bergstresser
- Caroline Fertig (1923-2006) 300
- Hannah (1818-1889) 418
- John Walter (1892-1964) 300
- Samuel Edward (1854-1928) 300

Berkebile
- Minnie M. (1885-1973) 358
- William (1867-) 358

Berkhouse
- Caroline 471

Berkley
- Dennis Allen (1962-) 483
- Michael Allen (1983-) 483

Bernstein
- Adam G. 280
- Jerome 280
- Joseph 391
- Joshua E. 280
- Seymour S. 391
- Thomas 391

Berry
- Enid Eunice (1920-2006) 234
- Ernest Leslie 234

Best
- Rhonda (1960-) 304

Bettinger
- Carl Jr. 361
- Sueann 117

Betz
- Eleanor (1904-1998) 281
- Harold 242
- Harry 281
- Joseph P. (1886-1950) 301
- Megan Elizabeth 242
- Valeria (1912-1950) 301

Beury
- A. Valeria 478
- Irene Mary 431

Bevans
- Flora Adeline (1921-1999) 362

Bibb
- (--?--) 381
- William 245

Bickel
- Mildred A. (1908-1977) 92

Bickhart
- Laura Mae (1925-) 87
- William S. 87

Biden
- Julie 135

Biegsler
- Anna Margaretha (1822-1854) 69

Biemensderfer
- Don C. 236
- Stephanie 236

Biggers
- Jeffrey Steven 103

Bigos
- Josephine C. 57

Bilger
- Banks 382

Billow
- Hazel 404

Bindley
- Artice (1936-) 133
- Catherine (1917-) 133
- Charles (1912-) 133
- Delbert (1920-) 133
- Frank 133
- Franklin (1902-) 133
- Leroy (1906-) 133
- Virginia (1932-) 133

Bingaman
- Alan Franklin (1968-) 89
- BellAnn (1964-) 89
- Betty Lorraine (1929-2013) 89, 440

Beverly 88
Byron Henry (1921-1987) 88
Catherine (1915-1985) 88
Celia Irene (1923-1999) 88, 170
Charles (-2007) 156
Charles C. (1863-1915) 168
Clarence Franklin (1926-) 88
Clarence H. (1884-1888) 168
Clinton Cleaver (1885-) 168
Dennis K. (1941-2007) 156
Donald Eugene (1927-) 89
Fred Robert (1919-1989) 88
Gail (1957-) 89
Gloria 88
James Monroe (1936-) 89
Jane Louise (1951-) 89
John 88
John Henry (1889-1961) 88, 440
John Jacob (1925-1991) 88
John W. (1825-1904) 88
Kathryn Minerva (1915-1985) 88
Keith (1955-) 89
Kenneth (1967-) 89
Larry (1958-) 89
Mary Ann (1957-) 89
Owen E. (1918-1986) 88
Richard Arlen (1931-) 89
Robby Allen 368
Robert Allen (1949-) 88
Robert Allen (Rev.) 368
Robert Allen Rev. 368
Ronald 88
Valerie (1951-) 89

Bingamin
Bellann (1964-) 114
Kermit (-1965) 111
Sandra Dee (1960-) 111

Binkley
Arlene 75

Bittikofer
Elisabeth (1849-1927) 92

Bivin
Winifred (1878-) 93

Bixler
Amanda 268
April 244
Brad Lee (1976-) 409
Brenda Louise 261
Brian Lee (1970-) 409
Darlene (1943-) 193
Diane Leitzel 428
Doris JoAnne (1935-) 344
Emilee Alyssa (1997-) 409
Franklin Daniel (1928-1957) 89
Franklin Daniel Jr. (1950-) 89
Garvin Sylvester 53
Gary Lee (1947-) 409
George 180
Grace Della 283
Guy L. (1908-1983) 193
Irene Mae (1903-2006) 291
Jean 182
Jean L. 126
Jean Marie (1935-2009) 53
Jennifer (1974-) 193
John 181
John W. (1912-1993) 53
Lauren Elizabeth (2001-) 409
Leo 244
Mabel Estella 475
Margaret Edith (1926-2001) 148
Matthew (1977-) 193
Melvin L. (1916-1989) 490
Merrill L. 244
Monroe 291
Robert Calvin (1901-1941) 344
Ronald (1940-) 193
Susan Jane (1875-1953) 120, 146, 181
Timothy James (1950-) 89
Virginia Dianne (1946-) 89

Black
Alan 62
Bonnie 232
Gail 232
Ike P. 64
Keith 232
Lex I. (1924-1994) 232
Lois M. (1929-2008) 64
Luther L. (1900-1942) 64
May 421
Robert 64

Blackwelder
Jonnie Lee 287

Blair
(--?--) 383
Janet Lee (1951-) 266
Mary Alice (1943-) 266
Robert L. (-1994) 266

Blake
Dick 282
Emma Marie (2003-) 282
Jonathan Dresser 282

Blanchard
Marie 274

Blascovick
Andrew 107

Blasser
Andrew 412
Ann 412
Anya 412
Beth 412
Chase Benjamin (1999-) 409
Mark Ray (1926-) 412
Ray M. 412
Tab A. (1965-) 409

Blaydon
Florence Naomi (1919-2003) 391
Josiah (1871-1946) 391
Robert William (1917-2005) 391
Ronald (1939-) 391

Bleiler
Caitlyn Nicole (2000-) 260
Madisyn Jade (2003-) 260
Paul W. 260

Blizard
Christal Michell (1978-) 467
Robert (1983-) 467
Robert Dale 467

Blizzard
    Bill 226
    Charles 226
    Zack 226
Bloch
    Kenneth A. (1927-1989) 152
    Rachael E. (1950-) 152
    Stephanie 475
Blood
    Ruth Irene 85
Bloom
    Barbara Santos 242
Blouch
    Christine 267
    Jason 267
    Joyce Amelia (1927-2005) 258
    Thomas 267
    Wilbert T. 258
Blyler
    Albert (1874-) 388
    Albert E. (1892-) 389
    Alice 388
    Ann Marie (1967-) 196, 492
    Anna M. (1877-) 389
    Annie (1877-) 389
    Arlene Ellen (1933-2015) 192
    Arthur Garfield (1885-) 389
    Barbara 390
    Bertie (1888-) 388
    Beulah Irene (1906-1972) 248
    Brenda Nina 390
    Carole A. (1969-) 196, 492
    Charles (1928-) 391
    Charles M. (1907-1909) 388
    Charles Monroe (1864-1913) 390
    Clareta (1928-) 391
    Clarita (1928-) 391
    Daniel 192
    Daniel (1878-1897) 388
    Daniel C. (1851-1934) 389
    Daniel E. (1962-) 195, 492
    Donald W. (1923-) 389
    Earl M. (1882-) 389
    Earl Roscoe (1892-1948) 390
    Edna M (1882-) 389
    Elda (1894-) 390
    Eleanor M. (1938-) 170
    Elizabeth (1836-1912) 257
    Elizabeth E. (1902-) 389
    Ellen 482
    Ellerslie 391
    Elmer 170
    Elmer C. (1915-1987) 195
    Elvin C. (1942-) 195
    Emeline (1856-1936) 389
    Emma L. (1856-1936) 389
    Esther R. (1892-) 389
    Eva Caroline (1896-1957) 390
    Francis (1875-) 388
    Frank P. (1855-) 389
    Franklin (1855-) 389
    Gertrude J. (1879-) 388
    Gurney G. (1880-1927) 388
    Harper W. (1877-) 389

    Harry (1895-) 389
    Harry Edwin (1886-) 390
    Harvey (1871-1953) 388
    Heister P. (1900-1984) 390
    Herman E. (1881-1909) 388
    Homer C. (1884-) 389
    Jennie Irene (1888-1985) 390
    John Preston (1847-1933) 388
    Joseph (1859-) 390
    Kay M. (1971-) 196, 492
    Mabel and May (1890-) 389
    Mae M. (1890-) 389
    Maggie (1889-) 389
    Margaret F. (1889-) 389
    Margarie (1925-) 390
    Marie (1913-) 390
    Marla May (1884-1900) 390
    Martha Florence (1894-1952) 388
    Mattie (1894-1952) 388
    Michael 388
    Neale R. (1922-2012) 390
    Norman G. (1896-1913) 388
    Ottie (1886-) 388
    Patricia G. (1929-2012) 390
    Paul (1907-) 390
    Pearl (1881-) 388
    Pearl (1886-) 388
    Ralph E. (1905-1908) 388
    Raphael 389
    Ray (1915-) 390
    Robert (-2012) 390
    Robert Preston (1902-1981) 388
    Roscoe (1918-) 390
    Ross (1918-) 390
    Roy Alfred (1903-1973) 391
    Ruth Esther (1892-) 389
    Samuel Emamuel (1843-) 388
    Sara (1997-) 196, 492
    Simon (1822-1897) 388
    Uriah (1858-) 390
    Verna O. (1895-) 389
    Victor 247
    Walter (1890-) 388
    William (1869-) 388
    William E. (1880-) 388
    William H. (1845-) 388
Boatman
    Bertha 333
Bobb
    Karl K. 157
    Kenneth E. 157, 203
    Martha 292
    Steven C. 157, 203
Boch
    Elizabeth 478
Boddeiger
    Elizabeth (1788-1865) 186
Boddorff
    Edward Harold (1903-1938) 422
    Fred 422
Boehringer
    Martin Luther 77
    Mildred Erb (1909-1939) 77

Boerner
William..468
Bogenwreath
Ella..231
Boggs
Bryan Toliver (1988-)..95
Casey Alan (1988-)...95
David Dean (1969-)...95
Donald Dean (1940-)...95
Jeffrey Jay (1966-)...95
John Hamilton (1936-2001)...95
Kenneth (1942-)...95
Kurt Thomas (1992-)...95
Mary Ellen (1934-)...95
Ralph F. (1913-1974)..95
Roger Allan (1960-)...95
Stephanie Michelle (1986-   ).......................................95
Tony Lee (1962-)...95
Bohatch
Jeffrey (1954-)..488
Karen D (1958-)..488
Pamela Jean (1960-2002)...488
Thomas...488
Bohn
Mary Ann..238
Bohner
(--?--)..160
Adam Franklin (1871-1944).......................................454
Albert R...409
Anna Maria (1831-1867).....................................169, 459
Arabella V. (1924-)...133
Arlene R. (1921-2011)...179
Boyd (1903-)...133
Charles A. (1889-1951)...141
Charles Robert (1926-)..141
Daniel W. (1856-1941)..51
David..51
Dean A. (1929-)...133
Donald K. (1957-   )..141
Dorah..120
Dorothy J. (1912-)...312
Elijah (1884-1969)...179
Ellen..171, 335
Emma C. (-2009)...405
Emma J. (1881-1920)..373
Flora L. (1925-)..141
Guy David (1954-)..141
Guy Emerson (1916-1993)..141
Harry Howard (1881-1952)...51
Irene C. (1910-)..141
Jean K. (1949-   )...141
John H. (1882-)..133
Laura R. (1894-   )...120
Leah E. (1919-   )...141
Lee W. (1920-   )..141
Lizzie...120
Lydia Jane (1892-1984)...134
Mamie C. (1898-   )..120
Marian (1912-)...141
Marion M. (1912-   )..141
Michael..119
Michael D. (1833-1913)...119
Owen E. (1923-   )...141
Robert..120
Robert T. (1952-   )..141
Sarah E. (1868-1958)...337
Sarah E. (1943-   )..141
Shirley Marie (1921-1995)..409
William C. (1937-   )...141
William L. (1926-   )..133
William T. (1852-1916)..134, 141
Yvonne Leah (1941-   )..141
Bohr
Ben L. (1916-1998)...222
Colby James..115
Eliza Maria (1875-1967)...75
Peter..115
Boley
Robert Eugene...467
Bolin
Janet (1937-   )...420
Boltz
Abraham (1868-   )...226
Gertrude..74
Mabel Mary (1887-1910)..226
Bomgardner
Cletus..172
Bonanno
(--?--)..227
Bonawitz
(--?--)..481
Charles IV...481
Erin..481
Marguerite E. (1919-1961)...413
Maria Catherine (1811-1892).......................................83
Michelle..240
Nicholas..481
Robert Ellsworth (1911-1987)....................................239
Ruth Ann...59
Bond
(--?--)..343
Bonnell
(--?--)..273
Bonney
Mike..414
Bonnie
Randall..382
Bonning
Josie...394
Books
Matthew Craig..245
Boone
Earl..285
Michele L. (1968-   )...285
Boose
Jennifer Ann (1977-   )..464
John Aaron..464
Bopp
Alexandria Lynn (1981-   )..410
Ambrose Richard (1906-1976)...................................313
Lynn H. (1949-   )..410
Richard A. (1939-   )...313
Tina M...214
William H..313
Bordner
Emma..119
Hattie Irene (1904-2000)...325

James ... 318
John C. ... 393
John W. ... 406
Mary Esther ... 393
Mary Esther (1892-1962) ... 406
Myrtle (1920-) ... 416

Borg
Elinor ... 390

Borke
George ... 395
Philip Samuel (1908-1984) ... 395

Bosche
Hannah G. (1908-2001) ... 301

Bosstick
Peggy ... 279

Bottiggi
Robert ... 82

Botts
Jill ... 401
John ... 400
Michelle ... 400
Susanne ... 401

Bouchat
Mary Jane (1875-) ... 239
William ... 239

Bovino
Anthony Robert (2007-) ... 237
Joseph Michael (2007-) ... 237
Michael Anthony ... 237

Bowen
Henry Edward (1926-1981) ... 123
James R. (1869-1907) ... 57
Margaret Elizabeth (1923-1998) ... 58
Myrtle Ellen (1918-1984) ... 57
Theodore Shelly (1893-1929) ... 57

Bower
Barbara F. (1930-) ... 258
Ethel ... 357
Leah (1926-) ... 142
Mary ... 393
Oscar ... 142
William L. (1890-2003) ... 258

Bowerman
David (1831-1910) ... 150
Judy Mae (1944-) ... 111

Bowers
(--?--) ... 200
Caroline Ann (1936-) ... 273
Chase Christian (2013-) ... 487
Clem Herman (1897-1984) ... 272
Cleo Mae (1899-1985) ... 273
David Lyle (1934-2015) ... 273
Elmer (1868-1946) ... 271
Elmer Junior (1925-2014) ... 272, 275
Elsie ... 221
Erin ... 273
Harrison Ellsworth (1904-1976) ... 273
Harry ... 98
Jacob ... 271
Jennifer ... 273
John David (1962-) ... 273
Kathryn Elizabeth (1909-1988) ... 273
Louise B. (1918-2014) ... 98
Mary C. ... 406
Melody ... 273
Paul Eugene (1930-1958) ... 273
Paul Eugene (1959-) ... 273, 275
Philip Lamar (1932-2015) ... 273
Rachel ... 273
Richard ... 487
Richard Christopher (2008-) ... 487
Richie ... 273
Robin Joan ... 273
Ronson S. ... 273
Ruth Naomi (1912-1971) ... 274
Ryan ... 272
Sarah Annie ... 291
Scott A. ... 273
Scott David ... 273
Stephanie ... 273
Stephen Edward (1951-) ... 272
Stillborn Son (1920-1920) ... 272
Terry Lynn ... 400
Toni ... 273
Una M. (1895-1974) ... 271

Bowersox
David ... 64

Bowes
Florence Catherine ... 265

Bowles
Nancy L. ... 104

Bowling
Betty Sue ... 337

Bowman
(--?--) ... 88
Abraham ... 407
Amanda Michelle ... 182
Anna Elizabeth (1892-1972) ... 281
Brian E. ... 228
Carrie M. (1896-) ... 489
Dan ... 182
David ... 156, 479
Debra (1958-) ... 192
Diane Lucille ... 283
Dorothy L. (-2014) ... 245
Edith Teresa (1879-1947) ... 217
Edna ... 156
Effie ... 98
Ellsworth W. ... 234
Elwood ... 228
Emma Jane (1873-1941) ... 479
Gary L. ... 228
George A. ... 245
Hilda R. (1910-2006) ... 234
Jacob ... 407
Jan Arla ... 327
Jerry ... 268
John A. ... 217
Kelvin Lincoln (1915-2006) ... 367
Kim ... 268
Linda (1963-) ... 192
Margaret M. ... 414
Mary Martha (1909-1957) ... 197
Randy Lee (1944-) ... 368
Raymond H. ... 434
Richard (1930-) ... 192
Richard II (1960-) ... 192
Steven ... 268
Terri Lee (1964-) ... 368

Terry Homer (1938-1938) 367
Toni Lee (1965-) 368
Boyd
   (--?--) 59
   Brian 244, 441
   Dennis 244
   Elizabeth (1958-) 197
   Jessica 244, 441
Boyer
   (--?--) 341
   Ashley (1969-) 414
   Betty Romaine (1943-) 431
   Blanche M. (1905-1953) 160
   Bobby 490
   Bryan (1923-2009) 432
   Bryant Woodrow (1923-2009) 432
   Carolyn Darneta (1943-) 319
   Carrie (1876-1959) 209
   Charles 370
   Charles H. (1885-1963) 431
   Chauncy E. (1889-1970) 203
   Christina 343
   Cloyd 387
   Darwin 490
   Ed 456
   Edward Loeb (1948-) 432
   Edwin (1948-) 432
   Eleanor E. 138
   Eleanor Rachel (1941-) 431
   Elizabeth 55
   Elsie Jennie (1927-1957) 337, 495
   Elura (1883-1935) 209
   Eugene Ivan (1945-) 431
   Frances E. (1878-) 418
   George W (1918-1976) 318
   Gerald Ronald (1946-) 319
   Grandee (1915-1916) 203
   Harlen (1912-1995) 431
   Harlin L. (1912-1995) 431
   Harry 166
   Helen Mae (1908-2009) 431
   Henry Franklin (1945-) 432
   Hilda B. (1909-1948) 370
   Ivan Elwood (1919-1983) 431
   Jacob A. (1871-1945) 160
   Jason 456
   Jean M. (1942-) 490
   Jeremy Todd 319
   Jerrel Howard 319
   Jerry Edwin 319
   Jessica MaryAnn 319
   John 257
   John T. 209
   John W. (1856-) 418
   Judy 490
   June M. 157
   Katie M. (1875-) 326
   Kenneth (1944-) 414
   Leon (1948-) 431
   Linda Sue (1954-) 432
   Lucy (1909-1985) 497
   Mabel Irene (1906-1907) 431
   Mabel Lamae (1937-2009) 344
   Mabel M. (1905-1969) 387
   Mark P. (1911-1913) 203
   Mary 333
   Mary Maglada (1869-1952) 307
   Melvin Henry (1910-1995) 431
   Michael 456
   Michelle Lynn (1969-) 184
   Michelle Lynn (1973-) 184
   Patrick Stephen (1999-) 188
   Ramsey 344
   Roy Sterlin (1943-2015) 432
   Ruby Mae (1951-) 432
   Sevilla J. (1860-1939) 402
   Stephen 497
   Stephen P. (1977-) 188
   Sterlin Roy (1922-2010) 432
   Thomas Leininger Jr. (1969-) 184
   Thomas Leininger Sr. (1948-) 184
   Todd 432
   Viola 139
   William 209
Boyle
   (--?--) 475
Boynton
   Helen 374
Bozarth
   Christine 238
Brabits
   Edward 327
   John (1945-) 327
Brackin
   Joseph 200
Bradbury
   Barbara Louise (1967-) 95
Bradford
   Laura 472
Bradley
   Carla Lynn (1950-) 428
   Glenn 455
   John Smith 428
   Linda 234
Braget
   Susan M. 179
Bramley
   Elenore 381
Brandt
   Alfred Adolph (1916-1988) 162
   Alfred Arlie (1943-) 162
   Arlee 162
   Darren Christopher (1981-) 484
   Deborah Angela (1982-) 484
   Diana Rebekah (1987-) 484
   Donald Bruce (1960-) 484
   Dorothy Katherine (1987-) 484
   Harold 138
   Henry 396
   Neil 162
Brannon
   (--?--) 190
Bransted
   Patricia Ann (1975-) 144
Braun
   Johannes F. 420
Bray
   Melissa Jo 194

        Thomas 194
Brazel
        Martha (1877-1940) 167
Breach
        (--?--) 474
        Donald 474
Bream
        David M. (1940-   ) 302
Bredekamp
        (--?--) 83
Breen
        Kevin 154
        Peter 154, 435, 450
        Scott 154, 435, 450
Brehmer
        Elizabeth Bertha (1884-1914) 122
Brennan
        Julia Maria 73
Brenneman
        Dorothy Leona (1914-2002) 244
Brensinger
        Catherine (1862-1940) 81
Breskius
        Cecelia 66
Bressler
        Bertha (1972-   ) 222
        Burdie (1972-   ) 222
        Clair L. (1935-   ) 53
        Frances (1874-   ) 222
        Irvin (1876-1966) 222
        John H. (1851-   ) 222
        Susannah (1805-1891) 295
        Thomas L. 53
        Timothy S. 53
Bretz
        Hannah 395
Bretzius
        Mabel (1906-   ) 329
Brigand
        Earl 378
        Robert 378
        Shirley 378
Bright
        Elizabeth 226
Briner
        Gifford 436
Brinkerhuff
        Frank 60
        Ida (1906-   ) 60
Brock
        Belle 167
Brodhecker
        Marilyn 90
Brommer
        John 84
        Michael 84
Bron
        (--?--) 226
Brooks
        (--?--) 363
Broscious
        Clara Elizabeth (1915-2015) 381

Brosious
        Clarence W. 367
        Claud Emanuel 381
        Edgar 67
        Elias 381
        Pauline M. (1919-2015) 67
        Sarah Frances (1872-   ) 133
Brosius
        Anna Dreibelbis 207
        Arthur Reuben (1913-2015) 381
        Balir E. (1930-2016) 157, 203
        Beulah M. (1890-1948) 312
        Carlos Ray (1895-1975) 157, 203
        Carol Ann (1944-   ) 327, 454
        Charles (1849-1904) 378
        Charles A. (1893-   ) 67
        Clara Elizabeth (1915-2015) 381
        Clarence William (1921-   ) 454
        David 157, 203
        Eleanor (1916-2016) 157, 203
        Fern M. (1923-2011) 157, 203
        Frances 176
        Fred 202
        Harold 202
        Harry W. (1896-1900) 67
        James L. (1882-   ) 312
        Jay Adam (1895-   ) 67
        Jeffrey 290
        Jennie Anna (1881-   ) 377
        John 202
        John Pershing (1926-2004) 157, 203
        Kirby 157, 203
        Lillie Frances (1877-1945) 437, 490
        Mabel 203
        Mary Ann (-2009) 252
        Mary C. (1915-2011) 157, 203
        Maurice E. (1874-1960) 157, 202
        Melvin R. (1920-1961) 157, 203
        Michael (1842-1925) 202
        William E. (1870-1955) 67
Brosnan
        (--?--) 395
        John T. (1915-1961) 395
        Karen A. 395
        Mary E. 395
Brower
        Sarah Jane 391
Brown
        (--?--) 80, 204, 333, 340
        A. Wilson (-2004) 340
        Agnes Vingis 394
        Cecilia 318
        Charles 170, 254
        Charles H. 110
        Dorothy E. 362
        Elaine 338, 445
        Elsie 130
        Emma 51
        Ernest Douglas Jr. (1947-2012) 303
        Ernest Sr. 303
        Ernest V. (1888-1971) 94
        Frances Fay (1912-1997) 94
        Harriet (1854-   ) 165
        Henry S. (1920-1994) 338
        Jason (1979-   ) 238

Jean F. (1927-2002) 200
Jenifer (1981-) 238
Joseph 194
Lillie 132
Luther Edwin (1921-2004) 340
Lynn 338, 445
Maceo Nkrumah (1983-) 303
Marian (1926-2008) 81
Matthew 338, 445
Michelle 338, 445
Naima Camille (1986-) 303
Nicholas Kalafya (1976-) 303
Patricia Dianne (1958-1982) 319
Paul Leon (1918-1988) 319
Rafael Jabulani Zwanai (1972-) 303
Richard C. 340, 446
Richard F. (-2008) 81
Robert (1948-) 145
Robert E. (1911-1997) 404
Samantha 338, 445
Samuel 471
Sandra M. 340, 446
Sarah J. 273
Shelley Carol 452
Steven 238
Sylvester C. 319
Tammy JoAnne (1965-) 319
Verna 136
Wendy Brunelle (1966-) 484
Wilmer J. (1890-1971) 194

Brubaker
Donald 473
Jennifer 473
John G. (1923-2009) 231
Olivia Grace (2001-) 473
Phares 231
Warren 473

Bruce
Janette L. 69

Brunk
Naomi E. 217

Bruzik
Marla J. 252

Bryan
Charles C. 421
Dorothy L. (1928-1985) 421
Wilbur Gross (1906-1951) 421

Bryant
Alma (1922-1954) 249
Kurt W. (1962-) 57

Bubb
Annie (1898-1904) 83
Benneville M. (1832-1914) 83
Esther G. (1924-) 83
Henry S. (1870-1968) 83
Mark H. (1902-) 83
Myrtle M. (1893-) 83
Richard S. (1930-) 83

Bubernack
(--?--) 125

Buchanan
Betty 279

Buchanon
Ashton Berkley (2000-) 148
Jaden Avery Malick (1998-) 148
Jason Avery (1975-) 148

Bucher
Harris Edwin (1924-) 453

Buck
Garrett Dillon (2000-) 305
Glenn Wesley (1997-) 305
Isaac Roland (2005-) 305
Megan Elizabeth (2002-) 305
Wesley 305

Buckley
Rebecca 285

Bucks
Hugh Ralph (1912-1991) 215

Buczynski
Eileen 288

Budy
Blanche 228

Bueck
Edith Cardella (1876-) 177

Buehler
John 70

Bueter
Elaine 249

Buffington
(--?--) 337
Abigail 121
Ann 337, 445
Blair LaMar (1932-2008) 121
Braden James (2006-) 135
Brent Russell 135
Brock William (2004-) 135
Bryce Russell (2008-) 135
Catherine E. (1846-1904) 69
Chad Aaron 121, 321
Cheryl 122
Claude Samuel (1890-1969) 329
Craig (1955-) 121, 320
Daniel Harold (1994-) 173
David B. (1940-2007) 121
Delores 109
Dennis Elvin (1944-) 121
Donald W. (1915-2003) 391
Douglas Harold (1960-) 173
Edwin B. (1912-1998) 120
Edwin E. (1912-1998) 120
Elijah Alan 121, 320
Elma Elaine (1940-) 120
Emma Marie (1913-1991) 391
Faye M. (1924-2006) 121
Gary Russell 135
Gilbert J. (1914-) 121
Grant (1889-1973) 173
Hannah 497
Hannah S. (1916-) 121
Harry G. 391
Helen M. (1912-) 120
Janice 120
Jean (1939-) 120
Jeffrey (1948-) 121, 320
Jeffrey Lynn 121, 320
Jennifer Lynn 121, 320
Johannes (1817-1899) 51
John Jacob (1861-1925) 329

    John Robert (1907-1959) 120
    Julie 337, 445
    Keith Alan (1957-) 121, 320
    Kelly A. 121
    Kevin Roy (1990-) 173
    Kristin 121
    Laura Irene (1906-1989) 120, 181
    Leonard (1946-1968) 121, 320
    Lorelea 121
    Lynette 122
    Marlin Leroy (1920-1993) 121, 320
    Mary A. (1868-1941) 468
    Melanie 121
    Milton O. (1883-1955) 120, 181, 320
    Randy D. 121
    Raymond C. (1892-1918) 391
    Ronald 121
    Ronald Edwin (1943-) 120
    Roxanne 121
    Roy (1932-) 173
    Roy E. (1909-) 103
    Royce E. (1909-) 103
    Sarah A. (1841-1924) 51
    Stephanie Jan (1963-) 173
    Taylor 121
    Tiger 122
    Tina (1959-) 121, 321
Buggy
    Ann E. 141
    James C. 140
    James C. (1936-1999) 140
    Jerome P. 141
    Kenneth J. 141
    Lisa M. 141
    William M. 141
Bunger
    Toni 273
Burdan
    Virginia 223
Burgert
    David R. 262
    Ruth M. (1928-2009) 262
Burgess
    Betty J. (1928-) 123
    Harry 123
Burket
    Maria 388
Burns
    Denise 275
    Donna 377
    Ermy 387
    Evelyn M. (1914-2006) 387
    Mary H. (1886-) 373
    Sarah Etta 92
    Tina (1974-) 184
    Una E. 137
Burrell
    (--?--) 101
    (--?--) (1978-) 410
    (--?--) (1980-) 410
    Alvin George (1896-1895) 408
    Arthur A. (1894-1976) 408
    Barbara Ann (1946-) 408
    Benjamin Carl (1957-2013) 409

    Carl R. (1919-2006) 409
    CarolAnn (1953-) 410
    Cheryl Early (1953-) 408
    Clarence J. (1904-1984) 410
    Daniel Walter (1886-1962) 407
    Debra Cynthia (1951-) 408
    Dennis Clair (1950-) 410
    Elsie (1929-) 408
    Frances Almeda (1924-1994) 408
    Gabriel (1974-) 410
    Gail Eileen (1951-) 409
    George H. (1858-1923) 407
    Gilbert Eugene (1921-1991) 409
    Hattie Eva (1893-1986) 408
    Irene Elizabeth (1923-) 410
    Jeremy P. (1981-) 410
    Joan Irene 429
    John 407
    John David (1891-1892) 408
    Karen Elizabeth (1952-) 410
    Larry G. (1936-2010) 410
    Laura E. (1883-1953) 407
    Leon E. (1902-2001) 410
    Lillie May (1895-1961) 408
    Linda Darlene (1947-) 409
    Lloyd Edward (1888-1890) 408
    Lydia E. (1889-1890) 408
    Mildred Phoebe (1917-1998) 317
    Nathaniel (1976-) 410
    Paul C. (1961-) 410
    Peter G. 317
    Ralph C. Jr. (1928-1976) 410
    Ralph Clair Sr. (1897-1989) 409
    Richard A. (1923-) 408
    Richard Eugene (1926-1999) 410
    Sandra (1954-) 410
    Walter Daniel (1886-1962) 407
    William Charles 429
    William E. (1890-1890) 408
    William Roy (1890-1890) 408
Busard
    Denise Elizabeth (1960-) 314
Bush
    Bessie Elizabeth (1886-1954) 346
    Catharine 431
    Catharine (1839-1893) 202
    Elizabeth (1822-1915) 398
    Elizabeth (1837-1889) 83
    Elsie 142
    Emma L. (1861-1929) 178, 494
    Franklin B. (1858-1936) 346
    Ida 219
    William J. 178
Bushaw
    (--?--) 426
Buss
    Cynthia 278
    Michael Lee (1960-) 278
    Penny 278
    Robert 278
    Robert S. 278
Butchinski
    Josephine 142

Butler
    (--?--) 167
    Delores (1909-) 167
    Maxine Edna (1914-) 167

Butz
    Anna Mae 283
    Diana 251
    Earl 251
    Robert 251
    Tommy 251

Byerly
    Clara 323
    David 452
    Dawn Marie (1961-) 452
    Debra Jean (1960-) 452
    Dennis Charles (1936-) 452
    Dianne Louise (1962-) 452
    Elaine Martha (1939-) 452
    Erique Adrienne (1973-) 108
    Isaac Theodore (1892-1983) 452
    Lawrence Woodrow (1913-1988) 452
    Leah 206
    Randolph Ira (1951-) 108
    Richard 383
    Winifred C. (1923-2003) 363

Byle
    Leonard 489
    Paul 489
    William 489

Cable
    Feeney E. 87

Cain
    Emerson 56

Calderwood
    Margaret Patricia (1925-) 382
    Willard S. 382

Calhoun
    Michael 138

Call
    Ashley Dylan (1980-) 324
    George Jackson (1925-2000) 55

Callahan
    (--?--) 209

Callender
    Craig 305
    Harry Leroy 305
    Janice Ann (1953-) 305
    Joseph Edgar (1928-2009) 305
    Karen Jo (1948-) 305
    Linda Kay (1959-1977) 305

Calloway
    Lola 109

Camaish
    Velma 166

Camden
    Bernadene Kay (1963-) 95

Cameron
    John 378
    Verna Amelia (1897-) 378

Campbell
    (--?--) 353
    Alice 464
    Arthur 227
    Bryan 456
    Dana P. 228
    Everett L. 228
    Georgianna 409
    Jason C. 228
    Jon 456
    Julie 227
    Kyra Lynn (1943-) 222
    Lamar Allen 385
    Margaret 98
    Mary 220
    Matthew P. 228
    Michael 456
    Rusty 227
    Theda Mae 141
    Tommy 227
    William E. (1915-) 222

Canford
    Mary 215

Cantwell
    Bridghid Anya (2002-) 299
    Jeremy Roberts (1977-) 299
    John J. 299
    John James Jr. (1974-) 299
    Rory Kathryn (2003-) 299
    Tierney Elizabeth (2002-) 299

Caprani
    Gabriella Angela (1944-) 381

Caral
    Anna 121

Carbaugh
    Patricia 226

Carbone
    (--?--) 236

Carder
    (--?--) 64

Carey
    Beverly J. 409

Carl
    (--?--) 56, 105, 122, 216
    Abraham (1850-1898) 238
    Amanda Louise (1980-) 282
    Ann 129
    Bud (1889-1960) 427
    Calvin (1869-1900) 428
    Carolyn L. (1923-) 428
    Charles (-2009) 373
    Clarence 427
    Clarence Elro (1883-1922) 373
    Clyde A. (1890-1971) 373
    Daniel 244
    Daniel P. (1931-2009) 373
    Dorothy 192, 238
    Edna Fietta 367
    Elise Nicole (1988-) 289
    Eliza (1874-) 313
    Elizabeth 238
    Elizabeth Lavinia Alice (1877-1936) 244
    Emma Jane 224
    Florence 309
    Frederick E. (1938-1958) 373
    Frederick M. 238
    Frederick Monroe (1870-1921) 238
    Frederick W. 238

Gary (-2014) 373
Gertrude Caroline (1908-1986) 428
Grace Caroline (1892-1980) 427
Hattie Cardella (1879-) 428
Helen V. (1897-1897) 373
Henry 373
Henry A. (1850-1930) 373
Henry W. (1917-1918) 373
Herman LeRoy (1889-1960) 427
James Abram Garfield (1874-1963) 428
James Franklin (1891-1979) 373
James G. (1874-1963) 428
James Quincy Allen (1919-2009) 373
Jean 373
Jean Roselyn (1925-) 428
Jennie Mary (1883-1970) 372
Jeremiah 427
Jeremiah R. (1841-) 427
Johann Jacob (1796-1862) 372
John 125
John (1845-1912) 372
John J. (1818-1854) 372
John Preston (1955-) 428
John Raymond (1892-1972) 373
John Washington (1882-1947) 373
Julie 373
June M. (1920-2007) 359
Lincoln Calvin (1866-1950) 427
Magnolia Sage (2012-) 282
Mary (1875-1919) 125
Mary F. R. (1894-) 373
Mary Jane (1883-1970) 372
Mattie (-2011) 180
Minnie (1887-1888) 372
Paul Revere (1897-1951) 427
Paul Revere Jr. (1922-) 428
Quincy Jay (1888-1963) 373
Ralph Roland (1925-1999) 373
Robert (-2009) 373
Robert Douglas (1951-) 428
Scott 289
Sebilla 146
Shawn Michael (1982-) 282
Terri Lee (-2009) 373
Terry 373
Verna 357
Walter Lawrence (1900-1962) 359
Warren Russell 282
Warren Russell Jr. (1955-) 282
William C. (1892-) 238
William F. 238

Carle
Deborah 223

Carlson
Angela 486
Hazel Margreta (1900-1976) 168
Randall 61
Richard 401

Carlucci
John 415
John Joseph 416
Mia 416
Michael 416
Nicholas 416

Carol
Sallie 495

Carpenter
David G. 271
Gary 271

Carr
(--?--) 108
Carole Elizabeth 175
Charles 208
Edmund George (1911-2001) 175
Emma Barbara 175
Gary Robert 175
George Edmund (1892-1966) 175
Joan 175
Linda Mary 175
Margaret Catherine 175
Patricia 175
Patricia A. 105, 106
Richard Edmund 175
Roger George 175
Sharon Estelle 175
Shirley Ann 175
Winston Paul (1913-1978) 175

Carstetter
Emma S. (1873-1947) 463

Cart
Chester L. 274
Elizabeth Batson (1990-) 316
Gloria June (1927-) 274
James Kittinger (1988-) 316
John Bristow 316

Carter
Angela M. 291
Charles J. Jr. 291

Cartwright
Estella 98

Caruso
Dominic 322
Jordan Alexis 322
Stephen John 322

Carvie
Lillie 491

Cascio
(--?--) 405

Cash
Pamela 306

Cassar
David (1960-2014) 260
Grace Anastasia (1995-) 259
James 260
Rachel Moore (1992-) 259
Richard 259
Thomas E. 259

Cassatt
Carrie Mae (1887-1951) 125
William 125

Cassler
Clara L (1883-) 98
Louis 98

Castenada
(--?--) 233

Caswell
Frank 405

Catalano
- Janice (1953-) 71

Cathers
- (--?--) 289
- Max 289

Cauffman
- Albert M. (1867-) 96
- Louise (1922-) 96
- Mary Evelyn (1925-) 97
- Russell (1899-1964) 96
- Wilma L. (1922-) 96

Cavalucci
- Maria 408

Cavanaugh
- Diane (1937-) 163

Cawthern
- (--?--) 360

Cecil
- Jacqueline (1931-) 301
- John (1907-) 301

Centrella
- James 58

Chaisongkarm
- Kiew (1952-) 429
- Rhien 429

Chambers
- Samuel James 268
- Samuel S. Jr. 268

Champion
- Mary Elizabeth (1876-1958) 314

Chandler
- Carolyn Ashley (1991-) 305
- Cary 305
- Danielle Marie (1995-) 305

Chapman
- Edward B. (1908-1945) 239
- John B 239
- Shirley D. (1932-) 240

Chartis
- Tina 270

Chase
- David Christopher 300
- David Elias (2004-) 301
- Georgia Louise (2001-) 301
- Sophie Marie (1996-) 301

Chau
- Cam 288
- James Henry 288
- Spencer Eugene 288

Chaves
- Gina Lee 324
- Jimmie Ray 324
- Michael Ray 324

Cheaney
- Sara Elaine (1974-) 145

Cherry
- Lois 421

Chilton
- (--?--) 90

Chisato
- Eric Vincent (1996-) 71
- Joylie Ibai (1993-) 70

Chris
- Trisha (1969-) 319
- Zerby (1969-) 319

Christ
- Mildred E. (1914-2013) 80
- Nicholas Martin (1965-) 359
- Paul (1939-) 359

Christensen
- Chris 295
- Howard 295

Christian
- Clayton 263
- Donna 263
- Jay 414
- Linda 263

Christie
- Danielle (1971-) 298
- J. Alexander (1974-) 298
- John F. III (1940-) 298
- John Francis (1912-1992) 298
- Michael (1945-1960) 298

Christophel
- Agnes 275

Chubb
- Brian K. (1970-2010) 128, 342
- Brooke 128, 342
- Codie Allen (1991-2011) 128, 342
- Cynthia Ann (1956-) 412
- Earl E. 490
- Emma Caroline (-1988) 196
- Felisha 128, 342
- James Edgar (1941-1997) 115
- Larry A 106
- Makayla 128, 342
- Matthew Allen (1978-) 106, 403
- Melanie (1956-) 322
- Molly 128, 342
- Priscilla Ann 490
- Robert Eugene (1952-2000) 128
- Rose A. (1925-) 104
- Sonya L. (1973-) 128, 342
- Stacy M. 128, 342

Chyke
- (--?--) 362

Cialini
- Catherine (1927-2007) 215
- Guerno 215

Cinninger
- Barbara Lou (1929-) 93
- Betty Ann (1930-) 93
- Bun (1906-) 93
- Charles P. (1906-) 93
- Donald J. (1900-) 93
- Edward A. (1913-) 93
- Hal Eugene (1933-) 93
- James D. (1929-) 93
- Joan E. (1925-) 93
- Joe Ann (1925-) 93
- John (1870-1953) 93
- John E. (1925-) 93
- Lee H. (1909-1910) 93
- LeRoy O. (1901-1973) 93
- Mary Ellen (1923-) 93
- Mary R. (1908-1908) 93

  Robert E. (1901-1986) 93
  Ruth M. (1897-1898) 93
  Verna Dean (1924-   ) 93
Cinqmars
  (--?--) 115
Cisco
  Timothy 62
Cissna
  Kevin James (1980-   ) 91
  Timothy P. (1950-   ) 91
  Timothy Paul (1950-   ) 91
Clancy
  David 116
Clark
  (--?--) (1967-   ) 372
  Angela (1967-   ) 372
  Anna G. 340, 446
  Anna Mary (1837-1908) 150
  Barbara A. (1874-1940) 182, 476
  Barbara Alice (1862-1907) 143, 156
  Calvin A. (-1960) 189
  Cassy Elizabeth (1864-1943) 143
  Catherine Elizabeth (1864-1943) 143, 156
  David T. (1849-1909) 454
  Dominique 340, 446
  Donald R. 112
  Edna Jane (1912-2000) 472
  Edward (1845-1864) 143, 156
  Elizabeth (1835-1861) 150
  Elmira (1866-1926) 150, 364, 434, 448
  Emma 201
  Esther (1856-   ) 156
  Franklin W. (1854-   ) 156
  Fred J. (-1969) 340
  Hannah 252
  Hannah (1912-   ) 454
  Harry A. (1909-1911) 454
  Hiram (1846-1864) 156
  Jacky L. (-2007) 340, 446
  James W. 189
  Johannes R. (1791-1855) 150
  John (1853-   ) 156
  John S. 194
  Jonathan 201
  Krista L. 270
  Kylee Cheyenne (1995-   ) 112
  Lisa K. (1965-2004) 189
  Margaret Ann 466
  Mary 241, 479
  Mary Amelia (1869-1944) 194
  Milessa Michele (1973-   ) 112
  Oscar (1878-1943) 454
  Paul M. (1936-2010) 340, 446
  Philip G. 340, 446
  Polly (1837-1908) 150
  Robert 270
  Robert (1946-   ) 112
  Roy Lamar (1939-   ) 372
  Samuel B. (1813-1858) 143, 150
  Samuel W. (1844-1905) 150, 448
  Tamara Leslie (1971-   ) 112
  Thomas (1852-1868) 156
Clark Brooks
  (--?--) 496
  Haley 497
  Hannah-Leigh 496
Clauser
  (--?--) 264
  Carrie Edna (1885-1952) 122
  Charles Austin Jr. (1911-1977) 122
  Charles Austin Sr. (1883-1955) 122
  John Killian (1863-1927) 122
  Mary (1890-1890) 122
  Ruby Irene 489
  Sadie Mae (1887-1983) 122
Clay
  Sandra L. 117
Claybaugh
  Carol (1945-   ) 412
Clem
  Kenneth 278
Clement
  Sally 260
Clemson
  Flora May (1890-1971) 406
Cline
  Carol Ann (1943-   ) 58
  Cecil Woodrow (1912-2006) 217
  David C. (1941-2005) 217
  Goldie 217
  Rodney J. 217
  William E. (1939-1994) 217
Clinehens
  (--?--) 98
Clinger
  Albert E. (1888-1957) 94
  Kristine (1984-   ) 381
  Sivia (1970-   ) 381
  Tobias (1855-1924) 295
Clough
  (--?--) 160
  Allen 141
Clouse
  Joseph William 286
  Justin William (1080-   ) 286
  Kristofer Joseph (1976-   ) 286
  Robert 286
Clouser
  Shirley 67
Coccia
  Maria 215
Cochran
  Albert B. (1929-2004) 64
  Albert Broyles Jr. (1949-1976) 64
  Linda S. 64
  Marianne 64
  Pamela Ray 381
Cochrell
  Sharleen (1971-   ) 467
Coe
  Amber 195
  Charles 195
  Heather 195
  Jennifer 195
Cohen
  Eileen (1960-   ) 487

Colbath
- Harvey H. (1878-1940) 220
- Helen Dorothy (1915-2005) 220
- John 220

Colby
- John 375

Coldren
- Elnora L. 407
- Elwood O. 407
- Geraldine 407
- Martha A. 407
- Silas Ray (1890-1936) 407

Cole
- (--?--) 486
- Amity 452
- Donald Lewis (1936-) 452
- Emilia Ree 326
- Gregory 452
- Jeffrey Lee (1959-) 452
- Lavaun 326
- Mary 486
- Rachel Lynn (1962-) 452

Colegrove
- Arthur James 392
- Marion Arthur (1921-1985) 392

Colella
- Albert 58
- Geraldine (1944-) 58

Coleman
- Albanus 169
- Alberta 303
- Alfred Ray (1907-1968) 419
- Arthur Earl (1914-) 436
- Austin Wallace (1883-1959) 436
- Catherine 241
- Charles Eric (1971-) 308
- Charles Jacob (1922-1984) 437
- Charles R. 63
- Christine Anne (1974-) 308
- Ethel Irene (1918-2006) 436
- Gail 204
- George 419
- Hannah (1770-1845) 310
- Hilda Lucile (1915-2006) 436
- Homer R. 291
- Homer Ralph (1895-1941) 353
- Ivan R. (1923-1997) 204
- James (1950-) 437
- James D. 63
- James G. (1937-2010) 63
- James L. (1950-) 308
- Jenny Cylvesta (1880-1945) 204
- John Jacob (1858-1920) 436
- Joseph D. (1906-1986) 63
- Joseph G. 63
- Katie (-1998) 477
- Linda (1948-) 436
- Marian M. (1930-1992) 419
- Mark (1951-) 436
- Mark Austin (1912-2006) 436
- Mary (1847-1908) 136, 279, 458
- Mary Amanda (1917-2015) 353
- Mary E. 63
- Michael David (1977-) 308
- Robert 220
- Robert Raymond (1924-) 308
- Robert Raymond (1924-2006) 437
- Ruth A. (1926-1966) 291
- Ruth Buella (1920-2006) 437
- Sarah E. (1917-2009) 436
- Sarah Marie (1987-) 308
- Solomon (1811-) 458
- Stephanie 220
- Stephen 204
- Thomas (1952-) 437
- Thomas Wayne (1952-) 308
- Timothy Wayne (1981-) 308
- Tyson 180

Coles
- George Thomas 218
- Gloria Romaine (1931-2004) 218

Collier
- Carolyn 95
- Mary 360

Comfort
- Karen D. 244

Conant
- Carol Lynn 116
- Denise Margaret 116
- Joyce Diane 116
- Richard Gordon (1938-) 116

Conipitski
- (--?--) 347

Conley
- James Boyce (1944-) 418
- Larry 455
- Michael James (1968-) 418

Conn
- Laura Wade (1969-) 96

Connally
- Gary 277

Conner
- William W. (1882-) 424

Connolly
- Christine 263
- Jamie 263
- Jeffrey J. 263
- Jenny Elizabeth (1960-) 263
- John Joseph III (1954-2010) 263
- John Joseph Jr. 263
- Katherine 263
- Kenneth M. 263
- Michael 263

Connor
- Leonard 456

Connors
- (--?--) 497
- Natalie 497

Conpropst
- Audrey 477

Conrad
- Alston (1996-) 188
- Amanda Lynn (1987-) 332
- Arlene F. (1930-) 87
- Catherine 136
- Charles (1909-) 50
- Edward Lynn (1967-) 332
- Harry F. (1878-) 50

    Howard O. (1883-) 87
    Jackie 438
    Joan Elizabeth 291
    Joanna I. (1863-1942) 387
    Joseph (1970-) 188
    Lynn Edward (1946-) 332
    Maxine J. (1928-) 87
    Michael Lynn (1972-) 332
    Myrtle A. (1886-1973) 378
    Natosha (1988-) 332
    Reily (1998-) 188
    Samuel (1858-) 378
    Steven Wilbert Jr. 130
    Steven Wilbert Sr. 130
    Theodore R. (1903-1976) 87
    Theodore Roosevelt Jr. (1926-2001) 87

Conroy
    Brett 347

Contento
    Omar 118

Conti
    Joanne 347

Conway
    Clark 270
    Kent 270

Coogan
    Adam 279
    Eliza 279
    Jay 279

Cook
    (--?--) 382
    Avonelle Lucille (1944-) 96
    Charles Burton (1924-) 412
    Claudia Elaine 324
    Cleason 64
    Glenn E. (-2009) 455
    John W. 62
    Lawson 295
    Mary Catherine (1905-1950) 64
    Maude (1896-1984) 295
    Norma Jean 279
    Randy (1972-2000) 164
    William 164, 260

Cool
    Richard 275

Cooper
    Edith 370

Copenhaver
    Henrietta 56

Cordy
    Ellen 477

Corkins
    Emily 387

Cornell
    David Leroy 286
    Emile Elizabeth (1982-) 286
    Florence 294
    Laurie Rose (1984-) 286
    Roger Wesley (1948-) 286

Corsnitz
    Evelyn Jueno (1932-1995) 109
    William Jr. 372

Costa
    (--?--) (1950-) 485

Costello
    Lucy Marcelene (1932-) 256
    Marie (-1979) 470

Cotner
    Lois 440

Couch
    Janice Sue (1946-) 490
    Sidney Adrian 490

Coulson
    Ella 59

Courtright
    (--?--) 339

Covell
    Richard 260

Covington
    Cassandra 234

Coward
    Dawna Kay (1973-) 71
    Julia A. (1982-) 71
    Kenneth W. (1939-) 71
    Kenneth W. Jr. (1980-) 71

Cowles
    George William (1889-1955) 393

Cox
    (--?--) 312
    Julie 226
    Melba 205

Coy
    Colleen 275

Coyle
    Amanda 310
    Joseph M. Jr. 310
    Joseph M. Sr. 310

Crabb
    Benjamin 415
    Daniel 415
    Edward 415
    Lamar 457

Crain
    Allison 275
    Jack 275
    Jonathan Robert 275
    Kevin 275

Crane
    Maxine 112

Crawley
    Mary 365

Creditrole
    Chrystal 361

Creech
    Paula 234

Creighton
    Jim 265

Creps
    Suzanne 478

Cresswell
    Mack Nelson 106

Creswell
    Wilma Leoda (1930-2003) 106

Criley
    Anthony 180
    Calvin 180
    Carl 180

Cripe
- Marcia 274

Crissinger
- Gertie 264

Crissman
- Ray 88

Crist
- Michael Austin 464
- Scott Michael (1974-) 464
- Stacey Lynn (1972-) 464
- Thomas Robert (1977-) 464

Croft
- Ann Marie 403
- Susan 403
- Thomas 403
- Thomas Joseph (1932-2007) 403

Crone
- Bessie Athey Vera (1886-) 177
- Flora 212
- John 177

Croop
- Collin 123
- Jenson 123
- William 123

Crosby
- William C. 424

Crosson
- Bertha E. (1926-1996) 429
- Ethel Jane (1928-) 103
- George E. (1915-1997) 428
- Harvey F. (1893-1968) 428
- Thelma Rebecca (1923-1992) 428

Crouthamel
- Sallie E. (1861-1934) 380

Croutharmel
- Carl Allen (1953-) 334, 351, 443
- Darryl Lee (1955-) 334, 351, 443
- Dennis Ray (1941-) 334, 351, 443
- Karen Diane (1950-) 334, 351, 443
- Larry Curtis (1942-) 334, 351, 443
- Raymond Curtis (1918-1986) 334
- Samuel K. 334
- Terry Gene (1943-) 334, 351, 443

Crowley
- Mary 258

Crume
- Audrey 277

Crumlich
- Donald 62
- Edward L. 62
- Lorri K. 62
- Scott L. 62
- Todd A. (1963-2014) 63

Crumroy
- Brenda Ross (1959-) 85
- Jenifer Ruth (1959-) 85
- Kimberly Ann (1964-) 85
- Otto Frederick Jr. (1934-) 85
- Otto Frederick Sr. 85

Cuba
- Keith 403

Cuff
- Cora Mae (2013-) 299

Culbert
- (--?--) 368

Cullather
- Dorothy Frances (1906-1979) 73
- Peter James 73

Cullision
- Lelah A. 98

Culp
- Charlene 278
- Margaret 123

Cummins
- Bryan Edward 223
- Charity C. (1997-) 256
- Isaac Lee (1991-) 256
- Richard A. 223
- Russell L. 256

Curcio
- Karen Sarah (1971-) 467
- Mark John (1966-) 467
- Maurice Joseph (1942-) 467

Curran
- Edward E. 265
- Edward J. Jr. 265
- Edward J. Sr. (1917-1981) 265
- James F. 265
- Kim 265
- Patricia J. (1948-2012) 265
- Regina L. 265
- Robin A. 265
- Susan J. 265

Curry
- April Love (1986-) 231
- Jennifer L. (1961-1961) 232
- John K. 231
- John S. (1922-1984) 231
- John Shenk Jr. (1952-) 231
- Luanne (1950-) 231
- Pamela K. (1955-1977) 231
- Sally Jane (1954-) 231
- Vanessa Lynn (1990-) 231

Curtis
- Annie Laurie (1870-) 427
- Charles 427

Dagata
- Catherine F. 73

Dagle
- Clayton (1922-1924) 379
- Howard E. (1902-1973) 379
- J. Franklin (1896-) 382
- John 379
- John Clair (1920-) 382
- Marion E. (1905-) 387

Dale
- Wynette 264

Daley
- Jerry 109

Dallen
- Terry 290

Dalton
- Carrie Jean (1938-1984) 467
- Kenneth Earl 467

Daniel
- Adeline Susan (1857-1926) 389

Alvin R. (1904-1976) 329
Buddy (1926-1936) 329
Chris 345
Denise 345
George 389
Hannah 439
Jenny 345
Larry L. (1938-) 345
Lee Marlin (1907-1945) 345
Mae A. (1914-) 329
Michelle Dawn (1971-) 345
Mike 345
Paul Irwin (1942-2008) 345
Sally Ann (1940-) 345
Shelly (1971-) 345
Todd Eric (1968-1994) 345
Walter 390

Daniels
Bennevell F. 61
Darwin Roosevelt (1903-1953) 468
David N. (1903-1953) 468
Ernestine E. (1914-1994) 399
German (1886-1947) 345, 439
Hannah 439
Harold Edward (1934-) 344
Harriet 393
Harry W. (1902-1990) 468
Israel 467
Israel (1859-1917) 329
James J. 468
Jeffrey 211
Joel (1830-1902) 329
Joel Elmer (1878-1918) 323
Jonathan (1875-1969) 467
Joseph J. 468
Kate Alice (1881-1957) 474
Madie Mae (1903-1974) 323
Malinda Jane (1851-1941) 61
Maude Marie (1897-1900) 467
Melvin S. (1916-2008) 210
Robert Melvin (1936-2003) 211
Stanford N. (1891-1966) 210
Winnie Alma (1899-1981) 468

Danielson
Duella (1905-) 93

Danner
Becky 231
Delores K. 61

Dashem
Elmer 124
Margaret Mae (1921-1994) 124

Dasher
Mabel E. (1879-1980) 94

Daub
Barry R. (1957-2015) 225
Clinton Daniel 225
Hayley Rebecca 225
Heidi Marie 225
Ronald 225

Daubenspeck
Betty Lee 428

Daubert
Celia I. (1895-1976) 82

Davids
Adeline 362

Davidson
Charles Henry (1901-1953) 328

Davies
Joel 458

Davilla
David 349

Davis
Albert W. (1881-1967) 100
Alma Jean (1927-) 102
Austin (1897-1989) 101
Belton Raymond (1895-1987) 101
Bettye (1962-) 71
Bryant Austin (1920-1921) 101
Carlos (1902-1986) 102
Caroline Jane 220
Catherine Annora (1888-1895) 101
Charles Clinton (1879-1944) 100
Charles Lemuel 220
Cora May (1886-1895) 101
Darwin D. (1920-1921) 100
Delphin D. (1907-) 100
Donald D. 54
Dwight 100
Edris Betty (1928-1996) 54
Elise Elura (1930-) 101
Emma Jane (1883-) 101
Eva A. (1901-1980) 102
Eva Grace (1918-2006) 101
Evelyn Mae (1922-1997) 54
Griffin Myles 220
Harry Austin (1897-1989) 101
Howard E. (1905-) 100
Ike or Charles Edmond (1902-1986) 102
James Kallen 220
John C. 53
Kay Louise 220
Lawrence Elwood (1933-) 101
Leon Jay (1916-) 101
Leroy Elwell (1912-1976) 100
Lola Marie (1905-1995) 102
Lydia (1888-1958) 381
Lydia Frances 220
Margery Janet (1929-) 454
Mel M. 54
Melvin H. (1922-1942) 101
Melvin Morrison (1924-2007) 54
Mikki Rochelle (1989-) 413
Moses William (1901-) 100
Philip Walter (1890-1965) 101
Reginald (1906-) 100
Russell (1913-) 100
Sallie Phebe Precilla (1892-1895) 101
Sarah Jean (1919-1986) 54
Shirley Carine (1929-1934) 102
Theresa 51
Wade Morrison (1885-1951) 53
Walter H. 418
Walter H. (1890-1965) 101
Walton Snyder Jr. 220
Walton Snyder Sr. (1907-1990) 220
Wellie C. (1915-1916) 101
Willard Stanly (1924-) 101
William Albert (1881-1967) 100

William B. (1849-) 381
William D. (1856-1930) 100

Dawes
(--?--) 190

Dawson
Alfred 123
Frank S. (1920-2008) 123

Day
Dennis 61
Winifred 466

DeAmgelo
Dominic J. (1915-1999) 408
Donato 408

Dean
Chadwick (1962-) 463
Robert Kenneth (1995-) 463

Dear
Alice 295

Dearborn
Charlotte 285

Dearment
Anna May Maria (1907-1941) 125

Dearmitt
Julia R. (1904-1971) 124

Deaven
Catharina Elizabeth 76

DeBoe
Margaret 272

Dechow
Anna Mary 423

Deel
Larry 367

Deemer
Betty 270

Deeter
Edna 472
Junior Roger 283
Mabel (1916-1989) 67
Melissa 283

DeFacis
(--?--) 187

Deibert
Christiana (1847-1934) 454
Chrystal 126
Clarence R. (1913-1997) 126
Emanuel W. (1850-1925) 452
Faye Mary (1918-1993) 452
Francis Samuel (1887-1952) 126
George E. (1861-) 126
George Edward Wiest 192
George Nathaniel (1929-2002) 192
George William 481
Guy T. (1956-2014) 126
Hannah Mary Ette (1880-1960) 195
Helen Amelia (1916-1995) 452
Helen I. (1915-1983) 126
Irvin Leroy (1921-1937) 453
Irwin Wilson (1897-1982) 452
Jay C. 126
Jessica Alexis (1994-) 192
Joseph 126, 127
Joseph C. (1923-2014) 126
Kate Alverta (1897-1968) 332, 367

Kori Nicole (1997-) 192
Lauran Ashley (1994-) 192
Leroy (1917-1967) 126
Lila Elanore (1933-) 452
Lillian May (1926-2007) 453
Mabel Catharine (1919-2001) 453
Maebella (1919-2001) 453
Michael George (1958-) 192
Minnie Eulalia (1895-1977) 243, 490
Samuel D. (1870-) 367
Tiffany 126
William 454
William Allen (1901-1975) 192
Williard A. 481
Williard Allen (1926-2001) 481

Deibler
Ann 440
Arthur 240
Bernice L. (1903-1995) 240
Elizabeth (1810-1889) 171
Homer Allen (1916-1951) 319
Infant Son (1947-) 319
John 319
Karl 440
Karl E. (1937-2009) 157, 203
Kaye JoAnne (1945-) 319
Leroy D. (1906-1964) 157
Rebecca (1831-1907) 119
Sandra E. 157, 203
Scott 157, 203
Shari 157, 203
Thomas Allen (1949-) 319

Deichert
Alverta M. (1907-1978) 79
Fred (1896-1968) 74
Howard Irvin (1923-2007) 74
Ivy Anna (1929-2007) 74
Lloyd Clair (1925-) 74
Ralph N. (1886-1956) 79

Deihl
Helen Ann (1956-) 412

Deimler
Craig 245
Gary 245
Lori 245

Deisher
Sandra L. 78

Deiter
Allen William (1903-1966) 217
Bessie M. (1891-1947) 215
Brenda 216
Catherine Estella (1880-1938) 219
Charles K. (1877-1935) 217
Christine Marie (1988-) 141
Dale W. (1934-2010) 216
Dennis 216
Diane 216
Elizabeth K. (1873-1932) 217
Ellen Jane (1868-1935) 213
Eugene Elwood (1921-1983) 219
Evelyn Emma (1915-1992) 219
Florence Agnes (1913-1971) 216
Fred (1872-1940) 217
Freda Mae (1917-1965) 216

Frederic (1872-1940) 217
Gertrude Mae (1887-1929) 219, 229
Harry K. (1885-1956) 219
Hilda Rhea Minerva (1904-1973) 218, 468
Ida (1864-1907) 213
James Albert 141
James Albert III (1980-) 141
James Ronald (1995-) 141
John D. 216
John H. (1842-1913) 213
John H. (1928-2013) 216
John Henry (1893-1955) 216
Linda 219
Lizzie (1873-1932) 217
Lottie C. (1895-1983) 216
Mabel Toledo (1890-1946) 213
Marguerite Cordella (1916-2008) 218
Merle Corrine (1915-1959) 216
Miriam Ida (1908-2000) 219
Myrle (1915-1959) 216
Myrtle Eleanor (1919-2016) 216
Myrtle I. (1896-1979) 217
Pearl Irene (1915-2007) 216
Robert D. (1932-2003) 216
Samuel K. (1870-1937) 213
Stephen 216
Todd 216
Wilfred Charles (1912-1992) 219
Willa Merle (1902-2008) 218

Deitrich
Bobby (1952-) 361
Brent Thomas 319
Carl E. Jr. (1953-) 361
Carl Edwin Sr. (1920-2011) 361
Carol (1944-) 361
Charles S. (-2009) 252
Eva M. 255
Heath 361
Irene M. (1915-2009) 252
Lynn 357
Mildred (1957-) 361
Ruth Elaine 479
Shirley (1948-) 361
Thomas Edward 319

Deitrick
(--?--) 314
David D. (1941-1998) 251
Donald 251
Harry (-1978) 251
Holly 252
Kelly 252
Lorraine G. (1946-) 252

Delano
Jennifer Lynn (1979-) 172
Salvatore (1949-) 172
Stephanie Ann (1980-) 172

Dell
Carolyn 139
Charles R. (1895-) 139
Donald L. (1929-) 139
Doris 139
May E. (1921-) 139
Robert W. (1926-) 139
William S. (1927-) 139

Dellinger
Margo 269

DeLong
Emma (1922-) 342

Delp
Elizabeth (1847-1932) 333, 431
George 431

Demmy
Marguerite E. (1922-1992) 224

Dempsy
Kimberly 427

Dengler
Bonnie (1955-1994) 347
Roy W. (1932-2008) 347

Denlinger
Christine 236
Herbert M. (1921-2000) 236
John Cletus 236
John R. 236
Roswell 236

Dennis
Howard 208

Deppen
Albert (1912-) 142
Alexander 202
Allen Simon (1889-1932) 134
Amanda Sinora (1874-) 140
Andrew Lee (1975-) 135
Anna (1922-) 139
Anna Helen (1904-) 139
Annette Katherine 326
Annie B. (1922-) 139
Anthony Michael (1974-) 135
Arthur (1899-) 142
Arvel 138
Arvel Grant (1893-) 139
Arvel Jr. (1933-) 139
Beatrice 138
Beatrice (1921-) 142
Betty (1927-) 139
Blanche (1908-) 139
C. Arthur (1882-1891) 142
Charles 139
Charles G. (1921-) 139
Charles J. (1876-1937) 141
Charles Ralph (1899-) 139
Charles W. (1881-) 133
Clarence Ray (1891-1918) 138
Daniel A. (1879-) 142
David Michael (1949-) 134
Delores LaMae (1938-) 134
Elizabeth (1858-1905) 132
Elmer (1910-) 142
Elwood 138
Emma Jane (1867-1931) 135, 459
Emma L. (1873-1937) 202
Emory Alvin (1898-1898) 133
Ernest G. (1923-1986) 139
Eva (1903-) 142
Eva Jane (1909-) 139
Fanny (1882-) 133
Florence Edna (1901-1940) 142
Floyd Edgar (1910-) 139
Forrest 139

H. Johnson (1865-1939) 134
Harlan F. (1902-) 133
Harold (1919-1939) 139
Harvey (1884-1884) 142
Harvey (1891-) 138
Hattie (1894-1899) 139
Heidi Marie (1971-) 135
Helen R. (1927-) 139
Henry W. (1833-1902) 132
James 139
John H. and Henry J. (1865-1939) 134
Katie (1888-) 133
Kenneth L. 128
Lynn Alan (1957-) 134
Mae C. E. (1924-2012) 68, 135
Mary (1897-) 141
Mary (1918-) 142
Mary Elizabeth (1959-1974) 134
Mary Fay (1916-) 139
Mary Lizabeth (1959-1974) 134
May 138
Melvin Oscar (1914-1915) 139
Mildred (-2012) 134
Millard 139
Minnie (1884-) 133
Miriam 138
Pearl (1905-) 142
Pearl (1922-) 139
Pearl Rebecca (1923-) 142
Ray Jonathan (1912-1997) 134
Ray Jonathan Jr. (1934-) 134
Ray Jonathon Jr. (1934-) 134
Richard (1925-) 139
Robert (1927-) 133
Roy Edwin (1913-1913) 139
Salarah and Selarah (1874-) 140
Samuel Grant (1870-) 138
Samuel Harry (1897-) 139
Sarah (1863-1924) 133
Scott 129
Stella (1897-1940) 142
Sula M. (1893-1932) 141
Susan (1856-1892) 378
Thomas Linkoln (1861-1861) 133
Thomas Ray (1966-) 134
Willard (1928-) 139
William 139
William (1859-1931) 133
William Henry (1901-) 139
William K. (1924-) 139
William Lloyd (1918-2000) 134
Zula and Sula T. (1893-1932) 141
Derck
April (1977-) 496
Michael (1975-) 496
Ray 496
D'Ercole
Gloria (1932-2012) 240
Derk
Arlene 344
Derr
Margaret 479
Detweiler
(--?--) 258
Barbara (1944-) 285

Jennifer 258
Deutsch
Marie 273
Deveney
Mark L. 293
Dewald
William 218
Dewalt
Anna 142
Helen (-2012) 131
Dewer
John E. 281
Kate 281
Margaret 281
Nathan 281
DeWitt
Elizabeth (1867-1941) 385
William W. 385
Diagastino
Christine 493
John (-2007) 493
Michael 493
Robert 493
Robert Jr. 493
Thomas 493
Diakow
Elizabeth L. 117
Gabrielle E. 117
John F. (1915-1992) 117, 416
John F. Jr. (1950-) 117, 416
Marsha E. (1947-) 117
Nathan J. (1977-1995) 117, 416
Rachel A. 117, 416
Diaz
(--?--) 258
Dick
Hedwig (1907-1990) 250
Dicken
Julie (1950-) 328
Dickinson
Elizabeth Rose (1931-) 321
George 321
Dickol
Margaret 237
Didra
Charles 380
Dawn (1938-2013) 380
Diebler
(--?--) 176
Diehl
Ellen 421
Diem
(--?--) 227
Dieter
(--?--) 82
Charles K. (1877-1935) 217
Solomon 213
Dietrich
(--?--) 128, 485
Alvin Howard (1932-2000) 104
Alvin Howard Jr. (1955-) 104
Bryan Keith 219
Daniel 485

David Donald (1941-1998) 484
Debby Kaye (1957-) 104
Donald David (1963-) 484
Ellen Marie (1911-2004) 103
Ernest Nelson (1916-1960) 323
Harris Edgar 323
Harry Carl (1886-1969) 361
Harry F. (1904-1978) 484
Holly Ann (1965-) 484
James Lamar (1941-1997) 219
Jason Earl (1983-) 323
Jason Prel 323
Judy Ann (1964-) 104
Kelly Lynn (1969-) 484
Lorraine D. (1946-) 252
Lynn 485
Mark Carl (1952-) 323
Marlene Jeanette (1938-) 219
Mary (1972-) 409
Mary Carol 218
Millie Mae (1958-) 323
Nancy Darlene (1961-) 104
Paul J. (1931-2004) 218
Phyllis Karen 218
Robert Willy 219
Ryan Alexander 323
Ryan Alexander (1986-) 323
Sally Edna 241
Tillie (1911-2004) 103
Trudy Ann (1964-) 104
William Charles (1936-) 219
William Walter (1915-1967) 218

Dietrick
Charles 413
Daniel 412
Duncan 413
Ehren 412

Dietz
Aaron (1856-) 420
Adam, Jonas, Junius, and 420
Agnes (1872-) 420
Angela 347
Daniel (1833-) 420
David M. (1878-) 425
Donald Elsworth (1870-) 425
Earl 347
Edna S. (1893-2000) 425
Ellamina (1852-1874) 420
Elmira J. (1878-1927) 426
Emma (1861-) 420
Emma Florence Hilda (1900-2000) 425
Erie Elmer, Elmer I., and Ira (1869-1941) 425
Fietta (1838-1917) 420
Heinrich (1843-1844) 424
Herlan (1905-2000) 425
Irie Elmer (1869-1941) 425
James A. 425
Jean L. 425
Joel (1848-1907) 425
Joel (1856-) 420
Johann Conrad (1752-1819) 420
Jonathan (1828-1906) 420
Kate (1862-) 420
Katie T. (1890-2000) 425
Kay V. 425

Kitty (1829-) 420
Lavina (1868-) 420
Lena C. (1879-1945) 426
Lilly May (1878-) 420
Lily Esther (1896-1999) 425
Louella (1897-2000) 425
Luella Fietta (1897-2000) 425
Lydia (1887-1888) 426
Mamie Jemimah (1891-2000) 338, 425
Marlin S. (1911-2000) 425
Marlyn (1911-2000) 425
Mayme Jemima (1891-2000) 425
Michael (1806-1882) 420
Milen Herlen (1905-2000) 425
Monroe D. (1878-) 425
Nathan (1846-1924) 424
Pearl May (1903-2000) 425
Ray E. (1909-1998) 425
Sadie Gertrude (1895-2000) 425
Sarah (1859-1920) 150
Sarah (1860-) 420
Verna Mary Rebecca (1899-2000) 425
William O. (1872-1935) 426
Williard K. (1914-2000) 425

DiGuilio
Marie J. 265

Dilks
Ronald 305

Dillon
Clara 291

Dinatale
(--?--) 80
Mario 80
Nino 80

Dinger
Annie 214
Dorothy 326

Disney
Josephine 113

Ditton
Marian 482

Ditty
Roy Edward (1917-2007) 484
Ruby Jean (1943-) 484

Ditzler
Anna Louisa (1880-1966) 73
Charles Allen (1903-1972) 74
Irvin Wilson 74
James Morris (1933-1981) 74

Divet
Darla 90

Dix
Beatrice S. (1942-) 190

Dixon
Carol 304
Garnet 400
Natalia 279
Will 279
William 279

Dobson
Anita (1946-) 145

Dockey
(--?--) 131
Benjamin F. (1848-1927) 119

    Daniel (1887-1968) 119, 417
    Evelyn Fay (1908-1995) 119, 417
    George R. (1929-2009) 455
    Hannah C. (1926-) 455
    Hilda A. (1922-2009) 455
    Jonathon (1874-1956) 455
    Lee Dale (1938-) 187
    Magdalena (1827-) 223
    Paul G. (1906-1982) 187
    Ralph F. (1899-1983) 455
    Shirley 455
    Vernon 117
    Viola C. 131
    Yvonne I. (1959-) 187

Doherty
    Diane Lee Allen (1946-) 174

Dolan
    (--?--) 212

Dolby
    (--?--) 125

Donahue
    Catharine Carol (1972-) 482
    Claire Elizabeth (1970-) 482
    Meghan Jean (1975-) 482
    Thomas (1944-) 482
    William Thomas (1975-) 482

Donleavy
    Harry O. 231

Donmoyer
    Bambi 328
    Ferne (1947-1947) 328
    Katie Jemima (1888-1961) 130, 405
    Laura May 261
    Monroe Edward 211
    Raymond Edward (1926-2003) 327
    Shirley Betty (1936-1937) 211
    Terry (1950-) 328
    Theodore (1915-1968) 211
    Wendy (1959-2010) 328

Donnely
    (--?--) 314

Donton
    Carole Jean 479
    Lloyd H. 479

Dorer
    Elmer E. (1917-1988) 63
    James E. (1940-) 63
    Ralph 63
    Richard E. (1940-) 63

Dorman
    Margaret 247

Dornheim
    Henry 426
    Lydia (1817-1894) 426

Dotter
    David W. (1933-1985) 229
    Diane Marie (1937-2005) 229
    Harold Q. (1910-1963) 229
    William 229

Dotterer
    Florence M. (1898-1960) 52
    Levi 52

Douma
    Anna Lucinda 273, 275

Dowd
    Terence 341

Downey
    (--?--) (1967-) 188
    Sarah C. (1868-) 84
    Shawn LeRoy 86

Downhour
    Alice J. (1921-) 97
    Claud (1897-) 97
    Frank F. (1918-1918) 97
    Jean F. (1930-) 97
    Ronald R. (1923-) 97

Downing
    Benton E. (1852-) 390
    Bryce Edward (1996-) 300
    Diane Elaine (1960-) 300
    Edward Andrew (1964-) 300
    Edward J. 300
    Jeannette E. (1925-) 390
    Margaret Pauline (1971-) 301
    Megan Mary (1970-) 300
    Perley E. (Dr.) (1881-) 390
    Perley E. Dr. (1881-) 390
    Peyton Andrew (2000-) 300

Doyle
    Jaime 106
    Jan 106
    Joseph 106
    Margaret 254

Dozier
    Clifford 234
    Summer Lee (2005-) 234

Drake
    David 261
    Luke Daniel 261

Drapeza
    Christina 276
    Victor 276

Drebitko
    Andrew J. III (1985-2006) 328
    Andrew J. Jr. (1950-) 328
    Andrew J. Sr. (1927-) 328
    Sharon (1947-) 328

Dreher
    Lydia (1812-1891) 391

Dreibelbis
    Adele Ivolene (1926-2004) 289
    Charles 289

Dreisbach
    (--?--) 171

Driscoll
    Donald Sean 234
    Jerry 234
    Sean Harris (2003-) 234

Driver
    Sally 455

Druckmiller
    Dane Scott (2000-) 183
    Scott David (1970-) 183
    Ty Scott (1997-) 183

Drum
    Sadie 214

Drumheiser
- Ottillia (1883-1946) 316
- Todd 288

Drumheller
- Henry Z. 372
- Marion Naomi (1908-2006) 372
- William S. (1880-1942) 372

Dubbs
- Albert G. (1881-1959) 51
- Jefferson 51
- Mary Emma (1920-1991) 52

Dubendorf
- Adam (1876-) 312
- Albert (1879-) 312
- Charles (1881-) 312
- Daniel (1889-) 312
- David (1885-) 312
- Emma S. (1867-1938) 311
- Gertrude Elma 410
- John (1862-1866) 311
- Mary J. (1863-1866) 311
- Samuel (1859-) 312
- Sarah (1865-1865) 311
- Sevila (1871-) 312
- William (1833-1902) 311
- William Jr. (1872-1873) 312

Duby
- Helen (1893-1974) 65

DuClos
- Jennifer Elaine (1972-) 58
- Richard Eugene 58

Dudley
- (--?--) 492

Duel
- June 91

Duffy
- Daniel J. 236
- J. William 236
- John Claire (1927-2006) 236
- Kathleen S. (1949-2011) 236
- Noah 271
- Stephen R. (1955-1955) 237
- Thomas 271

Duncan
- Charles Alman 306
- Gregory Alman (1978-) 306
- Lauren Leigh (1981-) 306

Dungan
- Elise (1960-) 230

Dunkelberger
- Betty 171
- Cora Ellen (1876-1957) 304
- Gary 148
- Gary Maynard (1957-) 148
- Helen T. (1910-1978) 77
- Sadie M. (1908-1959) 439
- Versa E. 391

Dunkle
- (--?--) 126
- Jean 384
- Roy S. (1904-1986) 126
- Solon R. (1872-1958) 126

Dunkleberger
- Daniel 425

- Emma (1853-1914) 307
- George (1810-) 377
- Harriet I. (1856-1938) 377
- Lydia W. (1849-1935) 425

Dunlap
- Preston (1902-1988) 457

Dunleavy
- (--?--) 480
- Barbara (1935-) 248
- Carl F. 248
- Daniel W. 248
- Iris Romain(e) (1936-) 335
- Rose Ann (1937-) 248
- William F. 248

Dunlevy
- Mae E. (1909-2008) 136
- Roseann 147
- William (-2008) 136

Dunmoyer
- Henry 374
- William L. (1879-1945) 374

Dunn
- Dianne 293
- Leslie A 293
- Melvin 293
- Rebecca 293

Dunston
- Harold 340

Dunsworth
- Mike 442
- Stacy 442

Durham
- Pauline 99

Durr
- Ann 66

Dussell
- Florence 60

Dutt
- Mary 262

Dutterer
- Michelle 245
- Ronald 245
- Theresa 245

Duttry
- Elias (1851-) 69
- Emma Jane 69

Dwyer
- (--?--) 192

Dyal
- R. Carson 240

Dyer
- Ellen 393

Eagle
- Angela Joy (1978-) 348

Earhart
- Alice 227

Early
- Pauline Louise 408

Eash
- James F. (1882-1920) 56

Easterling
- Emma 60

Eaton
- Marian 286

Eaves
- Ashlee Ann (1995-) 324
- Autumn Heather (1981-) 324
- Christopher Franklin (1974-) 324
- Christopher James (CJ) (2004-) 324
- Erin Elizabeth (1979-) 324
- Hailey Autumn (2007-) 324
- James Bernard (1947-) 324
- James Marvin 323
- Marvin Lee (1962-) 324
- Pierson Lee 323
- Ryan Lee (1992-) 324

Ebbert
- Alyce Marie (1955-) 287
- Clarence L. 287
- Clarence William (1926-) 287
- James Richard (1967-) 287
- William Herb (1952-) 287

Eberhart
- Bessie May (1905-1938) 51
- Melvin 51

Eberly
- Douglas 248

Ebersole
- June Elizabeth (1926-2012) 113
- Ralph 113

Ebert
- Betty J. (1926-) 88, 170
- Dena Jane (1939-) 307
- Sarah Elizabeth (1923-2007) 109

Ebey
- Charles Garfield (1878-1952) 78
- Norman W. (1915-1981) 78

Ebright
- (--?--) 494

Eby
- Alicia R. 277
- Arthur M. (1906-) 389
- Bettina L. 275
- Curtis 275
- Daniel 275
- David 277
- Elmer 275
- Elmer Leonard (1922-1996) 276
- Grace Margaret (1905-) 275
- Jane V. (1918-) 389
- Janice 277
- Judy 276
- Kermit III 275
- Kermit Ray (1903-1962) 275
- Kermit Ray Jr. (1931-2010) 275
- Lisa 275
- Mabel Helen (1913-1998) 276
- Miriam Lucille (1908-1984) 276
- Rethelisa R. 275
- Ryan D. 277
- Sylvia 275

Eckler
- Guy Tobias (1919-1994) 52
- Harry R. 52
- Mary 216

Edinger
- Jennie M. (1876-1920) 389

Edmonds
- Caroline 60

Edmondson
- Jewel A. 199

Edwards
- Bruce William 427
- Eleanor (1874-1955) 360
- Eliza (1860-) 111
- Lionel Patrick 427
- Marie Stride (1897-1972) 300
- Nicole Rene (1982-) 427
- Nikki (1982-) 427
- Thomas 360

Effron
- Edith 284
- Jacob 284

Eggleston
- Heather 107
- Joshua 107
- Michael A. 107

Egstad
- Raymond Henry (1919-1975) 164
- Ruth Ann (1947-) 164

Ehleiter
- Christine Mary (1964-) 307

Ehlers
- Anna 295

Ehrhart
- James R. 394
- Marlin Raymond (1921-) 394

Ehringer
- Andrew (1910-1969) 88
- Patricia (1939-) 88
- Shirley Lorraine (1936-) 88

Eichelberger
- Robert 276

Eichholtz
- Jacob Ely 50
- William F. (1872-1947) 50

Eiler
- Audrey I. (1931-2011) 458
- James 458

Eisenbrown
- Anna May (1906-1994) 239
- Penrose F. 239
- Ruth (1899-1965) 239
- Sarah E. (1897-1984) 239
- Wilson Henry (1872-1955) 239

Eisenhauer
- Matilda 219

Eisensteck
- Pauline 394

Eister
- Eva A. 383

Elder
- William Merle (1902-1980) 123

Eler
- Doris Roberta (1915-2004) 223
- Leonard 223
- Matthew (1886-1915) 223

Elfers
- Molly (1986-) 163
- Peter (1990-) 163

Elksins
- Retta 275

Ellenberger
- Donald Lee (1953-2002) 115

Eller
- Duncan 187
- Ernie 187
- Kyrsten 187

Elliott
- Florence (1870-1905) 74
- Margaret 382

Ellis
- David 270
- Kathleen Ruth 270

Elrid
- Betty 278

Eltringham
- Betty (1911-1991) 298
- Carol Jean (1957-) 299
- Elizabeth (1911-1991) 298
- Harry Alexander (1884-1919) 213
- Lori Parker (1962-1983) 299
- Marion Anna (1913-1984) 298
- Robert W. (1885-1942) 298
- Robert Weir II (1927-2012) 299
- Thomas S. (1858-1923) 298

Emanuel
- Sarah 497

Emberg
- (--?--) 216

Embury
- Mikayla Marie (1993-) 112
- Sean 112

Emerich
- Susanna (1839-1916) 72

Emerick
- Hazel 380

Enck
- Guy 73

Enders
- Bessie May (1930-2014) 265
- Charles A. 429, 454
- Clarence (1920-) 454
- Clark 361
- Connie 321
- Douglas 208
- Eileen Naomi (1920-2016) 417
- Esther Mae 491
- Evelyn Renee (1924-1993) 417
- Gail L. 111
- Ira Austin 416
- Juno A. (1930-) 345
- Ken 361
- Lester Alvin (1894-1972) 416
- Lottie A. (1910-1977) 429
- Mae 345
- Mae (1918-) 180
- Margaret Arlene 429
- Mark 208
- Myra 417
- Paul W. 208, 417
- Phillip Ellsworth (1898-1947) 265
- Raymond 208
- Robert A. 416
- Sarah 326
- Tammy 361

Endy
- Florence (1892-1930) 132

Engebretsen
- Ronald 251

Engel
- Annette 234

Engle
- Alice Estelle (1869-1946) 51
- Brian 248
- Calvin L. 119
- Daniel 119
- Duane 248
- Earl E. (1910-) 119
- Geraldine E. (1929-) 119
- Helen A. (1908-1987) 129, 184
- Henry W. 101
- Isaac 126
- Laurence C. (1922-) 119
- Macie M. (1904-) 128, 453
- Marlin D. (1915-) 119
- Mary Catherine (1873-1953) 126, 342
- Mildred P. (1908-) 119
- Pamela 248
- Paul 451
- Robert Lewis (1931-) 119
- Sallie A. (1885-1939) 468
- Sarah J. (1917-) 119
- William C. 248

English
- Abigaile 75
- Charles R. 114
- Ester Jane (1943-1995) 399
- Mason 75
- Matthew 75

Ennis
- (--?--) 199
- Brooke 349
- Infant daughter (1955-1955) 349
- Jared 199
- Stephen 349
- Suzanne (1957-2009) 349
- William 349
- William Jr. 349
- William Sr. (1961-2015) 349

Enterline
- (--?--) 148

Epler
- Artimissia (1873-1965) 91
- William 91

Epley
- Alexander 75
- Brad 75
- Zachary 75

Eppler
- Ethel E. (1916-) 98
- John Oliver 98
- Thelma M. (1912-) 98

Erb
- Albert (1932-) 395
- Albert Faust (1893-1969) 395
- Alice Louise (1934-) 395
- Bryan J. 442
- George B. 395
- Mamie 77
- Rickie 442

Erbaugh
- Denise 277

Erdman
- (--?--) 365
- Alvin S. (1867-1947) 198
- Amanda 213
- Amanda Louise (1862-1931) 280
- Ashlee Elizabeth (1986-) 103
- Barbara Elura (1894-1946) 101
- Carlos 313
- Cheryl Ann (1961-) 453
- Chris Marie (1976-) 340, 446
- Christie Marie (1975-) 129, 470
- Clair Ernest (1924-2011) 453
- Clair Jr. 453
- David Lynn 170
- Dorothy F. (1923-2006) 253
- Elwood Emery (1912-2009) 290
- Emery E. (1921-1983) 128
- Emma (1860-1941) 56
- Ernest C. (1927-1991) 129
- Estella 248
- Esther (1812-1892) 459
- Faires M. (1882-) 344
- Farus Riley (1888-1968) 128, 453
- Gary 365
- Gene Irwin (1943-) 453
- Gerald Dean (1948-) 344
- Gertie E. 481
- Harry Lee 170
- Haven Edwin (1919-) 344
- Herman W. (1896-2008) 129
- Jacob Joseph (1859-1899) 101
- Jacob W. (1819-1873) 198
- Jane 495
- Jeffrey William (1972-) 340, 446
- Jennie M. (1890-1962) 201
- John Jasper (1892-1937) 337
- Lamar E. 129
- LaRue Helen (1938-) 156, 451
- Lizzie (-1905) 468
- Margaret Irene (1919-2008) 149
- Marlin 340
- Martha M. (1896-1978) 442
- Mary Elizabeth (1867-1938) 453
- Orpha (1921-2010) 313
- Otis Oliver (1880-1931) 156
- Polly (1882-1957) 316
- Polly Minerva (1880-1957) 313
- Randy 365
- Randy L. 129
- Richard 129
- Ricky A. 170
- Ruby 147
- Rue Otis (1914-1994) 156
- Rue Otis Jr. (1951-) 156, 451
- Sandra Helen (1948-) 156, 451
- Sandra Lillian (1945-) 453
- Sharon 129
- Stacey Lynn (1979-) 129, 470
- Stella Helen (1942-) 156, 451
- Susan P. (1955-) 290
- Tamie Ubella (1894-1979) 452
- Terry Lee (1949-) 344
- Thomas 103
- Velma Kathryn (1923-1992) 337, 495
- Violet Arlene 170
- William Lamar 170
- William Ralph (1891-1957) 198

Erenberg
- Donald (1937-) 359
- Joan (1968-) 359
- Richard Mark (1962-) 359

Erickson
- Richard William (1947-) 57
- Shauna Marie (1982-) 57

Erk
- Donna Marie (1955-) 286
- Francis Joseph (1923-1998) 286
- Francis Joseph Jr. (1946-) 286
- Frederick Jacob 286
- Frederick Ray (1946-) 286
- Jason Michael (1976-) 286
- Karen Elizabeth (1948-) 286
- Kendra Ann (1983-) 286
- Todd Francis (1982-) 286

Ernfield
- Amy L. 264
- Richard L. 264

Ernst
- Beverly 260

Esbin
- Ruth (-1969) 366

Escanez
- Josephine 252

Eshbach
- Becky Lou (1962-) 86
- Cheryl Ann (1956-) 86
- James Douglas (1964-) 86
- James Robert (1933-) 86
- Kyle James (1991-) 87
- Tayler Marie (1995-) 87

Eshelman
- Elizabeth (1811-1880) 69

Eshleman
- Carlton J. (1898-1985) 223

Esposito
- Rich 377

Essex
- Beth Ann (1993-) 293
- John 293
- Kathleen Michelle (1981-) 293
- Sarah (1978-) 293

Essler
- Viola (1905-1964) 200

Etzweiler
- Amanda 405
- Carol Ann (1943-) 413
- Darwin P. (1914-1972) 53
- David H. 53
- Infant Son (1939-1939) 53

    Jane R. 222
    Kermit Leon (1920-1996) 53
    Marian (-2011) 56
    Philip John (1888-1959) 53
    William (1935-   ) 53

Evans
    (--?--) 64, 497
    Bruce 428
    Jared Saxton (1981-   ) 428
    Lindsay Paige (1983-   ) 428
    Mark M. 217
    Mary 263
    Miriam Arminta (1905-1994) 217
    Nancy Kay (1940-   ) 115

Evitts
    Verna Adeline (1899-1937) 362
    William 362

Ewing
    Blair Robert (2000-   ) 164
    Thomas McKinley (1998-   ) 164
    Thomas Scott 164

Fager
    Helen Bertha (1918-2013) 235
    Lewis L. 235

Fairchild
    Julie Lorayne (1948-   ) 222
    Kenneth Walter (1913-1975) 222
    Walter 222

Fake
    Amos 76
    Amos Ira (1908-1992) 77
    Ann L. 76
    Barry Hoffman (1940-   ) 76
    Clarence A. (1901-1986) 76
    Dale C. (1938-1996) 77
    Earl Elias (1899-1970) 76
    Earl Elias Jr. (1932-1996) 76
    Elaine G. (1931-   ) 73
    Elmer Norman (1878-1923) 73
    Ethel (1914-2016) 77
    Ethel (1935-   ) 73
    Harvey (1875-1953) 76
    Helen R. 76
    Irene Mildred (1911-1999) 77
    Jacqueline (1934-   ) 77
    Joan (1935-   ) 77
    Joan E. (1936-   ) 73
    Kenneth Harvey (1931-   ) 76
    Linda G. 76
    Lois E. 77
    Margaret A. (1928-   ) 73
    Marie E. 76
    Mary (1935-   ) 77
    Mary Louise (1928-   ) 77
    Nancy E. 77
    Nancy Jane (1932-1932) 77
    Paul Albert (1906-1977) 77
    Richard (1938-   ) 77
    Robert C. (1925-2010) 76
    Sharon G. 76
    Stella M. (1897-1987) 76
    Warren Henry (1898-1972) 73

Falck
    Sarah (1889-1917) 186

Falk
    Noel W. 412

Fandrich
    Dawn Babette (1956-   ) 162

Farnsler
    Mildred L. (1912-1996) 219

Farrell
    Leon Charles (1913-1991) 75

Farrow
    Alice Agatha (1876-1958) 301
    Emerson Webster (1846-1914) 301
    Silas 301

Fasick
    John 408
    Terri (1963-   ) 408

Fasnacht
    Carol A. (1939-2012) 284
    Mark Douglas (1958-2014) 284
    Megan A. 285
    Russel 284

Fauber
    Mary Magdalene 59

Fausold
    Carrie E. (1873-1940) 385
    Elias (1846-1914) 385

Faust
    Anna Frances (1876-1957) 239
    Darlene 411
    Helen Bouchat (1897-   ) 239
    Jared Bohn (1846-1911) 238
    Oscar M. (1871-1873) 239
    Reuben Eirich 238
    Warren Jared (1896-1978) 239
    William H. (1874-1921) 239

Fay
    James P. (1955-   ) 163
    Taylor Hamilton (1982-   ) 163

Fazio
    Kimberly 340

Fee
    Barbara 145

Feeley
    Chris 151

Feese
    Jacob 442
    Scott 442

Fegan
    James E. 422
    Walter Ray (1906-1986) 422

Feger
    Brenda Kay (1953-   ) 196
    Darwin (1916-   ) 452
    Dennis Leroy (1957-   ) 196
    Kirk A. 196
    Linda Mae (1951-   ) 452
    Marlin 196
    Shaun A. 196

Fegley
    (--?--) 368
    Betty R. (1928-2014) 373
    Effie 168
    Elizabeth 239
    Jeff 109

    Jeremiah Albert (1863-1949)..................................100
    Lillie 262
    Samuel 373

Feick
    Barbara (1774-1853) 132, 209

Feidt
    Bonnie Elaine 158
    Bonnie Elaine (1961-) 327, 454
    Bonnie L. (1961-) 327
    Brenda Sue (1961-) 326
    Brian Allen (1969-1982) 326
    Dale Homer (1930-) 326
    Eric William 367
    Glenn Edgar (1933-) 327
    Homer Nathaniel (1904-1992) 326, 454
    Jeffrey Lee (1963-) 326
    Joyce Marie (1949-) 327
    Lee Nathaniel (1932-) 326
    Mary Minerva (1924-1929) 326
    Rahn Douglas (1966-) 327, 454
    Rahn Henry (1940-) 327, 454
    Ramey 268
    Ramey LaMar (1968-) 326
    Randy Lee (1958-) 326
    Ricky William (1956-) 326
    Rodney Allen (1959-) 326
    Rusty Lynn (1959-) 326
    Ruthanna Coleen (1954-) 327
    Shaun William 326
    Stella Rose (2009-) 268, 479
    Troy James 326
    William 268
    William A. (1873-) 326
    William Theodore (1929-1984) 326

Feilen
    Charles Edward (1896-1984) 295
    Deryle (1923-1984) 295
    George E. (1943-2014) 295
    Jerry 295
    John (1872-) 295
    Kenneth Daryl (1923-1984) 295
    Kenneth J. (1946-2008) 295
    Larry 295
    Margaret Jean (1930-2004) 295
    Roger 295
    Roseann Marie (1963-2005) 295

Feltmate
    (--?--) 362

Felton
    (--?--) 194
    Mary Ellen (1895-1985) 239

Felty
    (--?--) (-1930) 80
    Levi Henry (1872-1952) 75
    Mary Ann (1940-) 75
    Ronald (1941-1991) 82
    Russell A. (1912-1992) 75

Fenstermacher
    Gilbert 131
    Rodney C. 131
    Sarah Elizabeth 169

Fenter
    Drew Michael (2000-) 163
    Lynsey Kanoelani (1997-) 163
    Philip Drew (1964-) 163

Fenzel
    Debra Kay (1954-) 103
    Frederick Alvin (1923-2005) 103
    Frederick Sr. (1892-1959) 103
    Karen Diane (1952-) 103

Ferguson
    Ellen Josephine (1937-) 98

Ferree
    Faye Ann (1951-) 483
    Marlin 398

Ferrieda
    Clara 276

Ferster
    Barbara 357
    Barbara A. (1970-) 357

Fertig
    Alice (1858-1876) 301
    Alma Lee (1894-1962) 300
    Anna F. (1890-1977) 298
    Annie Viola (1890-1977) 298
    Brian Nicholas (1999-) 304
    Caroline Harriet (1942-) 298
    Carolyn Marie (1940-) 305
    Carrie (1899-1980) 306
    Charles F. 201
    Cora Nancy (1927-) 305
    Corinda Ruth (1938-) 297
    Evelyn Arlene (1920-1924) 304
    Florence M. (1913-) 201
    Florence Mae (1894-1972) 199, 303
    Frank William (1897-1972) 304
    Franklin Ellsworth (1922-2007) 304
    Frederick Wallace (1891-1955) 302
    Fremont F. (1864-1901) 302
    Fremont Wallace (1912-1989) 297
    Glenn Paul (1945-1948) 304
    Gregory Harold (1950-) 304
    Gretchen Schwan (1923-) 303
    Guerney W. (1905-1918) 201
    Hans Jeffrey (1993-) 304
    Harmony Joy (1990-) 304
    Harriet Owens (1919-1995) 298
    Harry Fremont (1885-1918) 297
    Helen June (1925-) 304
    Hollyn (1995-) 304
    Jacob Emerich (1834-1882) 297
    Jeffrey David (1958-) 304
    John 201
    Lula (1878-1905) 297
    Margaret Ann (1936-) 300
    Mark Franklin (1954-) 304
    Mick (1893-1958) 299
    Minnie Alberta Miriam (1893-1958) 299
    Nicholas Glenn (1982-) 304
    Norman (1908-1908) 201
    Pauline Owens (1916-2002) 298
    Ruth Ann (1953-) 298
    Shirley Grace (1928-) 305
    Vera Louise (1931-2012) 305
    Wallace Klinger (1855-1916) 297
    Walter K. (1900-1983) 300
    Walter K. (1927-1998) 300
    Wynn K. (1960-) 300

Fesig
- Betty A. (1939-2009) 127
- George (-2009) 127
- Karen L. 265

Fesse
- Dorothy 327

Fessele
- Ruth 275

Fessler
- Ellen 284
- Harlan 211
- Jeremiah 213
- Melissa M. 353
- Naomi M. (1924-1964) 200
- Parrish Jordan (1979-) 353
- Richard 353
- Richard D. Jr. 353
- Thomas F. (1881-1962) 211
- Thomas Ward (1873-1955) 213

Feterolf
- Mary 52

Fetter
- Anna (1909-) 365
- Carol Ann (1937-) 169
- Charles H. (1867-1938) 365
- Elizabeth C. (1875-) 393
- Evelyn Elaine (1933-) 169
- Harry Nathan (1912-) 169
- Jean Blanche (1928-) 169
- Joan Blanche (1928-) 169
- Katie L. (1901-1964) 101
- Lamar Curtis (1927-) 169

Fetterhoff
- Beatrice H. (1908-1994) 479
- Charles William (1926-2001) 454
- Charlotte Ann (1924-1998) 215
- Christine 116
- Clifford David (1928-1975) 215
- Daniel M. (1889-1959) 215
- Donne E. 215
- Harold William (1921-1997) 215
- James M. (1944-2004) 116
- James M. Jr. 116
- Lawrence D. (1912-1963) 215
- Lorie Ann 116
- Mary Elizabeth 393
- Mildred Mae (1914-2000) 215
- Paul Milton (1917-1965) 215
- Philip 479
- Philip Scott (1963-) 359
- Sherry 116
- William Henry (1900-1968) 454

Fetterolf
- Allen C. (1902-1951) 224
- Ann Louise (1936-2016) 225
- Arlene G. (1921-1990) 255
- Charles Elias (1877-1978) 223
- Charles Elias Jr. (1916-1975) 225
- David F. 225
- Elias 223
- Elizabeth (1836-1913) 140, 431
- Emma Jane 194
- Harry Peter Leroy (1895-1950) 255
- Irene E. (1908-) 225
- Jack David (1930-2007) 224
- James Milton (1921-) 225
- Janeen 224
- John Keeler (1937-1996) 224
- Joseph Irvin (1905-1974) 224
- Judith 224
- Katie 120
- Maude M. (1904-1927) 224
- Mazie S. (1896-1921) 101
- Richard Joseph (1927-1984) 224
- Robert 224, 335
- Romaine 225
- Ruby (1930-) 419
- Sarah Elda (1867-1935) 367
- Susan F. 225
- Tommy Joe (1948-1948) 225
- William F. (1932-2012) 225

Fetzer
- Kyla (2003-) 282

Fick
- Maria Margaretha (1772-1847) 66

Fidler
- Carol 82
- Elvin William (1921-2000) 82
- Gary 82
- William 82

Field
- Casey Allison (1981-) 152, 354, 450
- Lindsey Ragan (1985-) 152, 355, 450
- Melvin Norman Jr. 152

Fields
- Ellen 407

Filer
- George 125
- Mary Tabitha (1906-1980) 125

Filippeli
- Marina (1976-) 58

Finsterbush
- Patricia A. (1944-) 111

Firestone
- (--?--) 69
- Amanda 69

Fish
- Amos A. 275
- Charles 258
- Gregory 258
- Karen A. 258
- Retha Leone (1905-1982) 275

Fisher
- Anna Eliza (1887-) 377
- Charles (1880-) 375
- David W. 259
- Leo C. (1909-1995) 375
- Mark D. 259
- Martha Lamarr 315
- Maude E. (1917-2006) 375
- Morris R. (-2006) 259
- Pauline (1915-2000) 375
- Pearl E. (1915-2008) 375
- Raymond (1911-1976) 375
- Sarah C. (1905-1974) 375
- Shannon 259
- Shawn 259
- Susan E. 259

Fiss
    Telly 259
    William A. (1921-2006) 259
    William J. (1886-) 375

Fiss
    Lizzie M. 395

Fissel
    Elias 421
    Rosa Mary Ellen (1881-1940) 421

Fite
    Ashley 116

Fitzpatrick
    John 424

FitzPatrick
    (--?--) 177

Fleck
    Cherry Ann (1832-2015) 421
    Thomas Maxwell 421

Flegal
    Leo W. (1903-1985) 436
    Terry 436
    Theodore 436
    Timothy 436
    Wendy 436

Fleming
    Andrea Lynn (1973-) 160
    Kristina Rene (1984-) 160
    Robert William (1948-) 160
    Verda (1918-) 144

Flessatti
    Esther 473

Fletcher
    Lizabeth (1958-) 323

Flicker
    Kay A. 262

Flook
    DeLinda Lee 183

Florick
    Sophie A. (1924-1994) 112

Flory
    Harriet 236

Flowers
    William 382

Flynn
    (--?--) 289
    Annie Loreen 381
    Kathryn B. 55

Focht
    Ann 216

Foieri
    Jennifer 375
    John L. 375
    John M. 375
    Tia 375

Foley
    Mary 249

Fontaine
    (--?--) 454

Ford
    Ethel 222

Foreman
    Corrine Elizabeth (1975-) 309
    Edna May (1895-1942) 395
    Herbert S. (1956-) 309

Forlizzi
    Jodie (1962-) 401
    Lorie (1960-) 401
    Tony (-1975) 401

Forney
    Carrie M. (1885-1930) 143
    Harry W. (1912-1967) 104
    John Henry (1884-1960) 104
    Mary 362

Forrester
    Lawrence 118

Forrey
    Audrey 283

Forse
    Robert 135
    William 135

Forsyth
    Keith Richard (1954-) 316

Fortenbaugh
    John 55
    John F. (1905-1974) 55

Fortune
    Charles L. 428

Forvour
    Anna Mae 427

Foss
    Linda (1958-) 255

Foster
    David 301

Foulds
    Lamar (-2010) 433
    Rindy 433
    Robyn 433
    Rodney 433

Fox
    (--?--) 105
    Betty Jane 285

Foy
    Nancy Jane 423

France
    Christiana (1817-1858) 51

Francis
    Catherine 469

Frank
    Agnes A. (1858-1919) 398
    Dorothy A. 176
    Edna (1910-) 119
    Gary A. 176
    Harvey J. (1889-) 119
    Philip 398
    Phillip K. 176

Franklin
    George William 285
    Pamala Ann (1965-) 165
    Viola Joan 285

Frantz
    Joe 336
    Nancy Lou 82
    Radell (1968-) 336, 445

Frederick
    Dorothy 321
    Llars 116
    Richard 116

Freeman
    Lloyal Ann 158
Frey
    (--?--) 239
    Kimberly 478
    Mary 424
    Paula 478
Frinkley
    Kaye 123
Fritz
    Edna Maria (1886-1980) 391
    Ellen C. (1891-1972) 391
    John William Jr. (1864-1935) 391
    Milton Calvin (1895-1901) 391
    Richard W. 350
    William Philip (1898-1901) 391
Fromme
    Eamil (1891-1963) 379
    Harvey Dennis (1944-   ) 399
    Lillian Marie (1924-1998) 379
    Robert (1921-   ) 379
    Sherri Ann (1966-   ) 399
    Tammi Lynn (1969-   ) 399
Fronk
    Ann Louise (1939-   ) 266
    George 266
    George William (1913-2010) 266
    James 267
    James W. (1954-2011) 267
    Janice Marie (1946-   ) 267
    Jean Mary (1948-   ) 267
    Jenna (1980-   ) 267
    John Lamar (1943-   ) 267
    Joseph 267
    Samantha 267
Frost
    Anna Elizabeth 407
Fry
    Barbara 405
    Jeannie 479
Frymoyer
    Alice (1865-   ) 374
    Amy Christine (1973-   ) 305
    Dale 305
    Emma Jane (1857-1933) 373
    Georgia Rae (1901-1992) 374
    Jacob (1828-1902) 372
    James K. (1859-1941) 374
Fuhrman
    Louise Rita 354
    Marilyn Renee (1970-   ) 362
Fulkroad
    (--?--) 456
    Gerald C. Sr. (1941-1998) 111
    Gerald Conrad Jr. 111
    Henry Adam 111
    Leroy Norman (1908-1988) 456
    Pauline Elizabeth (1934-   ) 456
    Tina Louise 111
Fulkrod
    Jay 158
Fulton
    Diane 234

Fultz
    Mabel Grace 87
Fulwider
    Beverly 275
Funk
    Mary E. 397
Funkhouser
    Amanda 421
Furhman
    Phillip III 88
Furman
    Asher K. 240
    Austin S. 232
    Corie 240
    Craig 240
    Glenn A. (1930-1984) 240
    Lot 211
    Mazie (1920-2008) 211
Futrell
    Rebecca 255
Gable
    Eleanore Caroline 281
    Joseph 253
Gabriel
    (--?--) 189
Gadel
    Caitlin 51
    David 52
    Paul 51
Gaenzle
    Greg 347
    Jamie Lynn (1982-   ) 347
    Nicole Marie (1984-   ) 347
Gage
    Barbara 280
    Howard E. 280
    John H. 280
Gagliardi
    Jessica 260
    Mary Ann 256
Galbraith
    Angela Frances 321
Gallagher
    George 153
    Mary 238
    Scottie (1973-   ) 153, 434, 450
    Sharon (1968-   ) 153, 434, 450
    Stephanie (1975-   ) 153, 434, 450
Galli
    Alexander 268
    Alyna 268
    Bruce 268
    Lewis 268
Gamber
    Louisa (1856-1921) 49
Gameral
    Margianne (1930-2000) 155
Gangloff
    Fred 305
Ganly
    (--?--) 368
Ganus
    Sharon E. (1951-   ) 235

Garbutt
- Jeff 178

Gardner
- Elmer 239
- Elmer K. 240
- John William (1898-1945) 219
- John William (1930-2002) 219

Garipoli
- Carmel (1930-) 347
- Toni Jo (1970-) 347

Garman
- Audrey 226
- Barry E. (1938-1938) 391
- Bert E. 391
- George P. 474
- Janet M. 474
- KisLynn G. 474
- Rosa 52
- Roy Steven (1912-1995) 391
- Sandra L. (1941-1960) 391

Gassert
- David 79

Gates
- Marilyn 392

Gatto
- Santina 269
- Tom 269

Gaul
- David E. II 354
- Jennie 222

Gauntlett
- Martha (1904-1975) 327

Gaydos
- John 464
- Margaret (1925-) 464

Gaynor
- Leona Sarah (1912-1994) 113

Gearhart
- Arthur Monroe (1929-1996) 386
- Clair Clayton (1926-1997) 386
- Clayton M. (1888-1968) 385
- Dolores Mae (1931-) 386
- Ernest Eugene (1908-1997) 385
- Florence Gertrude (1915-2007) 386
- Frank (1862-1951) 385
- Gary Lee (1935-) 386
- Grace Irene (1913-2005) 386
- Harold LeRoy (1916-1995) 386
- Kelly Ann (1960-) 95
- Lloyd Raymond (1910-2007) 386
- Norman Clarence (1932-) 386
- Thelma Leah (1911-1975) 386

Gebhart
- Anna Margaret (1911-1997) 492

Geise
- Gabriel (1985-) 345
- Harold (1946-) 345
- Melanie (1980-) 345
- Rachel Ellen (1873-) 141

Geist
- (--?--) 425
- Amy L. 271
- Andrea Kay (1992-) 330
- Andrew Jeff (1988-) 330
- Angela M. 271
- Bryce 271
- Charlotte (1944-) 337
- Donald Franklin (1930-) 271
- Ellen Vesta (1866-1928) 229
- Flossie E. (1890-1925) 194
- Guy (1902-1981) 271
- Jacob 229
- James Marvin (1953-2011) 171
- Jeffrey Maynard (1966-) 330
- John B. 229
- Kristi L. 271
- Lawrence 337
- Lester (1890-) 365
- LuAnn M. 271
- Mandy L. 271
- Marvin E. 171
- Robert Willard (1930-1997) 229
- Tom 365
- Vertie J. 192
- Willard D. (1898-1963) 229
- William D. (1958-2013) 271

Geistwite
- David Gordon (1966-) 171
- Eugene 171
- Heidi May (1970-) 171
- Linda Lou (1951-1951) 171
- Louella 171
- Randolph Alan (1955-) 171

Geiswite
- (--?--) 387

Gemberling
- Janet 442

General
- Frank Albert 62
- Ruth Elaine (1926-2004) 62

Gensemer
- Alexandra 72
- Catherine 72
- Ella Margaret (1917-) 72
- George John (1923-1983) 72
- George W. (1861-) 72
- Harry 72
- Harry J. 72
- Harry Z. (1894-) 72
- Harry Z. (1925-) 72
- Jack 72
- Jack (1923-1983) 72
- Red (1925-) 72

George
- Marci Lou (1946-) 414
- Robert C. (1924-) 414

Gephart
- (--?--) 360

Gerhart
- George John (1908-1967) 151

Gervasio
- Pete 338

Gesner
- Joanna (1876-1968) 455

Gessner
- (--?--) 186
- Elizabeth (1956-) 294

George Samuel (1898-1979) 294
Grace Una (1907-1997) 294
Henry (1840-1909) 157
Iva Minerva (1897-1995) 294
Ivy (1897-1995) 294
James S. (1933-   ) 294
Katie 179
Marie 429
Mary (1878-1934) 157, 203
Paul A. (1924-2004) 179
Renee J. 180
Richard W. (1928-   ) 294
Richard W. Jr. (1952-   ) 294
Robert (1954-   ) 294
Valerie (1957-   ) 294
Victoria Ann (1954-   ) 294
William 179, 294
William Elwood (1925-   ) 294
William H. (1862-   ) 294

Giannone
Catherine 58

Gibbons
Susan 467
Wayne 384

Gibbs
Charles Edward (1903-1972) 297
Frederick Eugene (1898-1972) 296
Frederick Herbert (1859-1920) 296
Melvin (1930-1934) 297
Nellie (1894-1982) 296
Olive Ida (1900-1974) 296

Giglio
Julie Anne (1965-   ) 85

Gilbert
Gerald LeRoy (1946-   ) 361
John David (1967-   ) 361
Mabel (1936-   ) 150, 309
Ralph 308
Teresa Louise (1969-   ) 361

Giles
Caroline 262
Christina 262
David E. 262
Jennifer 262
Margaret Ann 282

Gill
Eugene Robert (1925-2005) 54
Joseph A. 54

Gillae
Joette 347

Gillette
Jack 166

Gilmore
Jill 108

Gimbel
Josephine 65

Ginenthal
Marla 437
Marla Jan (1952-   ) 308

Gingrich
Aldus E. 217
Calvin B. 217
Clayton C. 217
Harold F. (1915-1973) 217

Margaret 384

Ginter
Arlene Delores (1930-1981) 497
Charles Daniel (1907-1998) 497
Earle (1903-   ) 497
Eugene (1931-1940) 497
Floyd Samuel (1900-1970) 497
Gustav 496
John 90
Lauren 496
Lawrence Roy (1899-1955) 496
Lawrence Urmston (1934-2015) 496
Leigh 496
Lewis (Dr.) (1902-   ) 497
Lewis Dr. (1902-   ) 497
Lizabeth 497
Lynn 496
Marilyn S. (1938-   ) 497
Sarah (1844-1919) 90
Willard (1910-1982) 497
William (1875-1939) 496

Gipple
Aaron Otto (1881-1949) 423
Carol Dianne (1940-   ) 424
Christian (1819-1877) 423
Christian J. (1856-1914) 423
Dolores (1919-   ) 424
Donald Aaron (1907-1974) 424
Evelyn (1917-   ) 424
Gerald Donald (1947-   ) 424
Gerald Owen (1915-1954) 424
Harry (1883-1948) 424
Marion Adelle (1944-   ) 424
Marlene Joan (1930-1958) 424
Martha Mabel (1886-1951) 424
Mary R. (1857-   ) 423
Otto (1881-1949) 423
Patricia Martha (1920-2005) 424
Verna Mary (1890-1983) 424

Girton
Harriet 386

Gise
Alfred I. (1886-   ) 52
George M. 52
Richard William (1907-   ) 53

Gish
Paul 90

Glace
Julia A. 399

Gladfelter
Alexander 394

Glantz
Jack 52
John G. (Rev.) (1830-1893) 496
John G. Rev. (1830-1893) 496

Glass
Florence Myrtle (1911-2013) 235
William Sylvester 235

Glem
Marie Clara (1928-   ) 152

Glidehaus
Elizabeth Marie 392

Glines
Dawn 293

Glinski
    Larry 293
    Roger 293
    Suzanne 293

Glinski
    Norman R. (1928-1986) 54

Glorius
    Deborah Kay (1960-) 400
    Thomas Charles (1919-) 400

Gockley
    John Richard 238
    Lisa 238
    Robert Theodore (1952-1952) 238
    Susan 238

Godfried
    Jean (1931-) 92

Goehringer
    Henry Gottlieb 361
    Katherine Adelaide (1902-) 361

Goetz
    Evelyn 282

Goins
    Glenda 272

Golden
    Alan 344
    Charlette 251
    Dawn 344
    Kenneth 344
    Kristen 344
    Michael K. (1978-2016) 344
    Shelly 344

Goldsborough
    Mary L. 468

Goldsmith
    Cheryl Lynn (1973-) 163
    Elizabeth Karen (1968-) 163
    James (1944-) 163

Goldsworthy
    Charlotte 299

Gomez
    (--?--) (1939-) 359

Gonder
    Charles Omar (1881-1958) 107
    Martha Gertrude (1903-2001) 107

Gongloff
    Dale 475

Good
    Daniel A. (1840-1922) 416
    Roy Daniel (1895-) 416
    Sarah Louise (1866-1889) 329
    Solomon Sherman (1865-1954) 416
    Susan Adaline (1868-1935) 413
    Warren L. (1896-) 416

Goode
    Michael 465
    Robby Joe (1981-) 465

Gooderham
    Diane Elizabeth 496

Goodling
    Debra Marlene 361
    Henry K. (1859-1907) 360
    Jack Richardson (1946-2014) 361
    Lonnie Allen (1952-) 360
    Vernon Charles (1907-1965) 360
    Vernon Harold (1927-2008) 360

Goodman
    Alice (-2012) 419
    Alice Frances (1895-1975) 363
    Nathan (1842-1910) 363

Goodrich
    Emma Florence (1886-1958) 94

Gordon
    Kathryn (1882-1966) 335

Gore
    Martha Abigail 279

Gorg
    Joanne 478

Gosnell
    Doris J. 423
    Hobart 422
    Jack L. (1924-2010) 422

Gotschall
    Ira455

Gotshall
    Clara 198

Gottschall
    William 119

Gottshall
    Carl (1909-1963) 205
    Earl W. (1902-1963) 205
    Ida M. (-2002) 195
    James M. (1875-1938) 205
    Mary Alice 396
    Michael 64
    Mildred Irene (1911-2001) 417
    William R. 417

Gottshell
    Amy Sue 320
    James 320
    Jamie Lynn 320

Goudy
    Amanda B. 263
    Harold (-2010) 481
    John 263
    Robert Evans (1900-1975) 263
    Robert S. 263
    Sarah E. 263
    Suzanne M. 263

Gould
    James W. (1930-) 413

Gourley
    Linda C. 285

Grabey
    Mae 474

Grable
    Ford Marshall 324
    Joseph 324

Graci
    Mary Jo 228

Gradwell
    Jenna 348
    Sheila 348

Graeff
    (--?--) 405
    Amy (1967-) 328
    Ashley 405
    Brian 405

Jennifer ... 405
Kenneth ... 328
Kenneth (1947-) ... 328
Kimberly ... 405
Phoebe ... 54
Scott ... 405

Graeger
Lucy ... 211

Graff
Jerry ... 403

Graham
Amy M. (1918-) ... 99
Calvin Stoey (1905-1983) ... 62
Deborah Louise ... 62
Emma N. (1913-) ... 99
Frances ... 346
James T. (1886-) ... 99
Joan Aileen ... 62
Joseph ... 423
Kthan Robert (1995-) ... 328
Robert Calvin ... 62
Robert Harvey (1928-2004) ... 62
Rosemary Ann ... 62
Samantha Nicolle (1989-) ... 328
William Eugene (GW) (1958-) ... 328

Grainey
(--?--) ... 190

Grant
Jennifer Nicole (1972-) ... 96
Wilma Irene ... 277

Grasset
Marie ... 178

Gray
Alice Hoopes (1924-2014) ... 299
Jane Bethel (1925-2008) ... 299
Jean ... 168
Jerome B. (1899-1986) ... 299
Paul ... 168
Robert ... 72
Robert G. ... 72
Teed ... 168

Graybill
Lizzie ... 231

Green
James ... 478
Margurite ... 478
Robert ... 478
Sherry Ann (1960-) ... 150
Steven ... 151
Valerie (1981-) ... 151, 449

Greenhaw
Joe ... 415

Gregory
Evelyn Peoples ... 306

Grell
William (1873-) ... 360

Gribbin
Mary Margret (1932-1994) ... 466
William F. ... 466

Griffin
(--?--) ... 481
Mark ... 231
Michael ... 118

Griffiths
Ella ... 455
Gracie ... 455
Jeffrey ... 455
Michael ... 455

Grim
Mae Christine ... 113

Grimm
Denise ... 112

Groff
Ellen Mabel ... 351
Joyce Ione ... 284

Gromley
Michael ... 104

Gronborg
Ole ... 85

Gross
Herbert Jr. (1949-) ... 253
Herbert Sr. ... 253
John ... 214
Ken ... 290
Mildred K. (1920-2015) ... 214
Myrtle O. ... 421

Grosser
(--?--) ... 491

Grossmich
Jessie James (1976-) ... 470
Lester ... 470
Sherrie Ann (1979-) ... 470

Grove
Carlean (1928-) ... 229
Carlyn (1928-) ... 229
David Franklin (1877-1949) ... 229
Earl H. (1901-1973) ... 229
Grace Doris (1912-1997) ... 229
Harry C. ... 396
Herbert W. ... 396
Jo Anne (1935-) ... 396
Joseph ... 229
Roberta (1935-) ... 229

Grover
Louise ... 412

Grow
Alexa ... 289
Jason Michael ... 289

Grube
Louise (1872-) ... 132

Grumbine
Paul ... 248

Guerrieri
Cole ... 124
Robert A. Jr. ... 124
Stacey L. ... 124
Tony ... 124
Zak ... 124

Guessner
Elizabeth (1905-1988) ... 338

Guest
Wilmer ... 89

Guise
Emory ... 62
Lola J. ... 62

Gunderman
    Shirley (1933-) 193
Gurtz
    Dennis 436
    Gaylord (1905-1963) 436
    Martin 436
Gusler
    Traci (1964-) 144
Gustin
    Patricia 437
    Patricia (1953-) 308
Guston
    Don V. 465
    Joshua Christopher (1974-) 465
Guthie
    Josephine 132
Gutshall
    Brian (1964-) 242
    Brian (1987-) 242
    Chad 242
    Colby 242
    Dean (1947-) 242
    Don (1960-) 242
    Emily Rae 242
    Jeffrey (1963-) 242
    Jennifer (1986-) 242
    Jeremy (1989-) 242
    Lester S. (1914-1987) 242
    Ronald L. (1938-) 242
    Troy 242
    Willmer J. 242
Guyer
    Mary J. (1879-) 57
    Minnie 54
Haak
    Emma 211
    Isabella J. (1852-) 430
Haas
    (--?--) 191
    Ella (1900-1972) 227
    Faith 147
    Fern M. (1911-2002) 338, 425
    Henry 227
    Kermit Palmer (1922-1997) 425
    Palmer C. (1892-) 338, 425
    Roma M. (1915-) 425
Hackenburg
    Marlyn S. (1917-2003) 382
    Nancy L. (1940-2008) 382
Haederer
    Joan 246
Haefner
    Josephine Elizabeth 282
Hagemann
    Jennifer Lynn (1974-) 316
    John William (1978-) 316
    Robert William (1949-) 316
Haglein
    Alisha 427
Hahn
    Frances (1927-) 239
    Lenore H. (1914-1969) 279
    Shirley J. (1931-) 273
    Vern 279
    Wilson (1931-) 239
Haigh
    Frederic (1867-1943) 236
Hain
    (--?--) 457
    Beulah M. (1904-1989) 128, 470
    Bryant Charles (1980-) 188
    Charles B. (1950-) 188
    Charles Edgar 188
    Charles Walter (1892-1969) 157
    John 318
    John W. (1871-1970) 157
    Kelly Eileen 473
    Kenneth 473
    Kylie Annie (1979-) 188
    Mabel (-2008) 81
    Martha Jane 158
    Minnie Agnes (1896-1981) 318
    Norman Jay (1923-2004) 157
    Sarah E. (1876-1940) 454
    Stacey Marie (1969-) 188
    Thomas N. 158
Haines
    (--?--) 123
    Genevieve 475
    Gertrude Evans (1904-) 428
    Hester C. (1850-) 428
Haldeman
    John 82
Hale
    (--?--) 456
    Carol Helen 470
Hall
    (--?--) (-2014) 79
    Adrian 422
    Bonnie Joy (1966-) 145, 315
    Bruce Travis (1937-2011) 144, 314
    Chrystal Dawnette (1964-) 315
    Garth Champion (1962-) 315
    Holly Lynn (1969-) 145, 315
    James George (1873-1943) 314
    Joseph Champion (1911-1992) 144, 314
    Shari Jeanne (1973-) 145, 315
    Valerie Leigh (1963-) 144, 315
    William Garth (1938-) 315
Haller
    Frederick Ernest (1888-1955) 398
Hallis
    Susanna 464
Hallowell
    Jim 357
Hamburger
    Joan Ellen (1955-) 284
    Mary 51
Hamelelhe
    Anna Katherine 395
Hamill
    (--?--) 190
Hamlin
    Sheri Sue (1956-) 95
Hammaker
    Gladys (1919-) 412

Hand
- Bernice 242
- David J. 469
- Edna Alberta 405
- Ernest J. (1898-1973) 397
- Gene 469
- Melba 216
- Rita Josephine 175
- Stillborn Son (1929-1929) 397

Hanez
- Helen Ann 99

Hanken
- Daniel (1953-) 189
- Julia (1961-) 189
- Laurie (1967-) 190
- Melissa (1957-) 189
- Robert (1924-) 189

Hann
- (--?--) 292
- Lillie Catherine 61
- Logan 292

Hannon
- Charles W. (1935-) 97
- Kate V. 268
- Susan 277
- William (1905-) 97

Hansell
- Adam B. 395
- Charles B. 395
- Christopher D. 395
- Chuck 395
- Jason M. 395
- Nathan C. 395

Hansen
- (--?--) 105

Hanson
- Alice Dorothy (1916-1977) 424
- Hans Martin 424

Hare
- Betty J. (1935-) 326
- Robert 326

Harford
- Lee Shartle (1920-) 316
- Leslie 316

Hargrove
- Esther (1930-) 325

Harkey
- Stephen 116

Harlan
- Elizabeth 236
- William E. 236
- William Jr. 236

Harman
- (--?--) 109, 180
- Floyd 401
- James 77

Harner
- Alissa 192
- Andrew Ammon (1970-) 484
- Barbara 429
- Brenda Lou 333, 351, 443
- Bryant Kieth 333, 351, 443
- Carolyn Dolly (1938-1946) 333, 351, 443
- Cornelius E. 49
- Corrnine M. (1929-) 49
- Daisy N. (1918-2001) 257
- Daniel (1868-1917) 310
- Deborah 231
- Debra Jean (1954-) 472
- Dora (1917-2015) 257
- Edward T. (1918-1918) 50
- Edwin Theodore (1880-1953) 49
- Elizabeth (1820-1855) 418
- Elva Irene (1921-) 335
- Elva M. (1895-1984) 247, 257
- Ethan D. 472
- Evelyn L. (1913-1966) 50
- Frank 153
- Frederick Charles (1876-1932) 409
- Gary (1947-) 188
- George B. 257
- George F. (1897-1984) 257
- Grace L. (1905-2003) 258
- Gurney Leo (1910-1994) 472
- Guy Rufus (1912-1958) 333
- Helen 257
- Irene Mae (1914-) 333
- Jake Romberger (1986-) 153, 435, 450
- James 333, 351, 443
- Jane M. 259
- Janice 259
- Jeffrey 231
- Jesse 153, 435, 450
- Jessica 153
- Jodi 231
- John (1896-) 335
- John Fremont (1893-1959) 257
- Judith R. (1937-) 49
- Kathryn 231
- Kermit Ivan (1925-2005) 231
- Leslie Ellsworth (1919-2000) 258
- Lester R. (1930-2011) 472
- Lester Rufus (1936-2002) 333, 351, 443
- Lonnie Eugene (1957-) 472
- Marilyn Irene (1944-) 333, 351, 443
- Mary Liza 170
- Nancy Marion (1932-1982) 182
- Prudence Sarah Ellen (1901-) 409
- Raymond Edward Charles (1906-1978) ... 49
- Raymond Edwin Charles (1936-1936) 49
- Reilly Ellsworth (1868-1933) 247, 257
- Richard 333, 351, 443
- Richard Dean (1945-) 333, 351, 443
- Robert 403
- Ronald 231
- Ronald Lanston (1942-) 484
- Rufus 333
- Scott Albert (1966-) 484
- Shelly 334
- Stanley 231
- Tanya J. 472
- Todd Ronald (1966-) 484
- Verna E. (1900-1992) 250, 258

Harper
- Audrey M. (1964-) 414
- Bruce Edward (1939-) 413
- Christine Ethel (1911-1999) 413
- Edward Augusts (1889-1973) 413

Harold J. (1947-) 414
James Lamar (1941-) 414
Joseph Ralph (1916-2008) 413
Scott M. (1964-) 413
Sherry A. (1968-) 413
Sondra L. (1965-) 413
Walter J. (1962-) 414

Harrier
Stewart 208

Harrington
Hovey 277
John 98
Mary Jacobs (1891-1920) 98
Paul W. 277

Harris
Alice 489
Beulah 206
Carol (-2003) 486
Carrie Irene 198
Clarence 381
Claudia 234
James 486
Keely Lynn 486
Lucille Madaline (1920-) 381
Lucretia 93
Maud Ethel (1884-1956) 122
Mildred Pauline (1911-) 456
Walter 206

Harrison
Ruth 53

Harry
Sally 383

Harsham
Vicki (1950-) 162

Hart
Beulah 289
Camille (1921-1987) 493
Carson Leroy 235

Hartley
Albert J. (1883-1951) 122

Hartman
Andrew 277
Ann 148
Ann Marie (1960-) 148
Arlene Amanda (1916-) 411
Benjamin Franklin (1935-1936) 149
Beverly 249
Carol (1956-) 400
Charles B. 386
Christine (1953-) 400
Desiree 264
Diane L. 278
Diane Marie (1975-) 149
Douglas (1950-) 400
Eddie (1959-) 149
Eddie Alexander (1926-) 148
Edwin (1881-1945) 148
Eleanor M. (1913-2000) 386
Eleanor Marie (1918-1997) 400
Greg Alan (1981-) 149
Greg Alan (1981-1993) 149
Harvey 277
Henry H. (1917-1980) 400
Hilda (1923-) 401
James 400
Jan 148
Jan Louise (1959-) 148
Jane A. 278
Jayson 277
Jenine (1976-) 401
Jennifer L. 277
Jennifer Sue (1970-) 149
Jillian (1988-) 401
Jonas 69
Joy 277
Katie Lovina (1897-1949) 183
Laci (1985-) 401
Lee 278
Lisa 400
Loni (1981-) 401
Lori A. (1961-) 149
Marie (1927-) 319
Mark 277
Max 277
Maxine (1943-) 400
Michael C. (1956-) 149
Michelle Lynn (1979-) 149
Paul Franklin (1922-1970) 401
Percilla (1951-) 401
Ralph 319
Raymond Edward (1906-1996) 148
Raymond Paul Jr. (1937-) 149
Richard Raymond (1928-) 148
Richard Raymond Jr. (1955-) 148
Robert 254
Robin Ellen (1956-) 254
Rodney C. (1958-) 149
Rudy 277
Ryan 277
Shelley Lynn (1956-2008) 148
Shirley Ruth (1930-1989) 149
Susan K. 278
Suzette Carol (1954-) 148
Terry 277
Thomas J. (1921-2001) 400
Thomas Milton (1887-1943) 400
Timothy (1955-) 401
Todd A. 277
Tom 277
Toni (1992-) 401
Vicki 148
Vicki Rae (1952-) 148
Warren Devon (1917-) 277
Wesley 277

Hartwell
Dorothy L. (1908-1964) 65

Hartwig
Sharon (1956-) 149

Hartz
Amanda F. 235
Lillie E. 213

Hartzell
Catherine E. (1908-1983) 146

Harvey
Tara 477

Harwell
Jarrad 264
Sidney 264

Zoe 264
Hasker
Clair (1937-) 347
Eric R. (1964-2005) 347
Stephanie Jo (1962-) 347
Taylor Marie (1992-) 347
Hassinger
John Allen 87
John Kent Jr. (1942-) 409
Lillie Jane 429, 454
Mable E. (1922-2016) 87
Hasson
(--?--) 76
Hasty
Ruth 264
Hatch
Emma Christine (1899-1990) 392
Henry Harry 392
Hatter
Alyce (1957-) 335
Betty J. (1920-1975) 214
Evelyn (-1988) 281
Franklin M. (1859-1915) 280
Jacque (1934-2004) 335
Jessie Alonzo (1883-1966) 280
Hauck
Amelia (1839-1921) 379
Andrew 477
Barbara 477
Caetlyn 477
Carol 477
David 477
Derek J. 477
Harley Alvin (1918-1997) 477
Harley Jr. 477
Robert (-1998) 477
Hauer
Christopher 74
George D. 74
Jason 74
Lester E. (1922-2013) 74
Lester E. Jr. 74
Susan L. 74
Haug
Christine 424
Haup
Lisa 297
Haupt
Elisabetha 228
Haurdel
Marie 210
Hausberger
Barbara 274
Haussler
Christian 339
Havice
(--?--) (-1906) 150, 449
Elamira or Elamina (1911-1984) 150
Elmira F. (1911-1984) 150, 449
Luther Calvin (1870-) 150
Hawk
Cynthia Ann (1953-) 144

Hawley
David 365
Hayes
Dortha R. 232
Horace 232
Hayn
Douglas Walter (1936-) 222
Henry 222
Hazeltine
Esmond Everett (1892-1949) 305
William George (1915-1974) 305
Head
Carson Elizabeth (2000-) 164
Daniel Robert (1938-2001) 164
David Daniel (1960-) 164
David Filer (1908-1992) 163
Kaitlan Marie (1996-) 164
Lisa Lynn (1961-) 164
Michael Scott (1956-) 163
Sharon June (1942-) 164
Tammi Sue (1957-) 163
Thomas Wilkie (1936-) 163
Thomas William (1970-) 164
Timothy Patrick (1961-) 164
Tori Lynn (1990-) 164
Trevor Nelson (1989-) 164
Headdress
Dale M. 178
Heagy
Charles W. (1950-) 482
Daniel David (1976-) 482
Rachael Elizabeth (1983-) 483
Robert Charles (1974-) 482
Heaney
Brenda 345
Heath
(--?--) 386
A.G. (1940-2004) 377
Albert E. (1914-2002) 377
Brenda (1965-) 191
Gary (1940-2004) 377
Jeffrey (1969-) 191
Martha E. (1907-1995) 397
Raymond R. (1944-) 191
Wade 377
Wade Jr. 377
Hebda
John F. 336
Heber
(--?--) 457
Heberling
Elsie I. (1916-2005) 402
Sarah L. (1855-1931) 137, 243
Heck
April D. 286
Hecker
Isabel Ann (2003-) 301
William M. 301
Heckert
Albert Calvin (1906-1989) 403
Clarion A. (1904-) 414
Daniel 87
Elaine 453

Page 548

    Emma Kathryn (1901-1979)..................253
    John...453
    John Jr...453
    John W. (1846-   )...........................414
    Karen...453
    Mary Ella (1854-   ).............................56

Heckler
    Beulah Caroline (1900-1942)..............485

Heckman
    Holly A..262
    Thomas P..262

Heddings
    Jennie Arlene...................................441
    Robert...383

Heffelfinger
    Grace I...76

Heider
    Harry..61
    Harry Calvin (1899-   ).........................61

Heilman
    Cheryl...51
    Cynthia A. (1950-2014)........................51
    Herman (1921-1995)............................51
    Lonnie..51
    Ruth Elizabeth (1904-2000)..................76
    Samuel W..76
    Todd...51

Heim
    Catherine (1848-1908).......................201
    Charles..309
    Guy W. (1925-   )...............................309
    Hannah..378
    Joan Arlene (1949-   ).........................183
    Joseph (1916-1985)............................404
    Kathryn...270
    Kenneth John (1968-   )......................183
    Rahn (1981-   )..................................482
    Rodney...482
    Samuel..201

Heimbach
    (--?--)...379
    Earl...213
    June..384
    William F...213

Heimbaugh
    Eunice..89

Hein
    Christine..82
    Jane..82
    Linda Diane (1952-2014).....................82
    Merritt Emory (1920-1981)..................82
    Thomas..82

Heinbach
    Katie..75

Heinbaugh
    Benjamin J. (1988-   ).........................225
    Rachel E. (1991-   )............................225
    Steve (1954-   )..................................225

Heinly
    Amy L...262
    Carl Ethan (1925-1996)......................262
    Carla J...262
    Ethan...262
    Jeffrey A..262

    Kenneth C..262
    Mary Jane...262
    Sally A..262

Heintzelman
    Annabelle M. (1923-2010)..................377
    John (-2010)...................................377

Heiser
    Flora...189

Heiter
    Mary Magdalena (1783-1859)............431

Heitzman
    Ida May....................................146, 182

Heller
    (--?--)...264
    Betty...476

Helman
    (--?--)...360

Helmick
    Viva Gale..221

Helt
    Daniel P. (1919-1920).........................415
    David Daniel.....................................415
    Harvey Daniel (1891-1943)................415

Hemm
    Doreen Lisa......................................144

Henderson
    Donna Leigh (1958-   ).......................144
    Jacqualin..382
    Richard...231

Hendricks
    (--?--)...480
    Cassidy...480
    Elijah..480
    Jeffrey..480
    Joseph..480
    Rose..480
    William...480

Henley
    Gary Earl (1948-   ).............................255
    Jack (1916-1990)................................255
    Mable...255
    Matthew..255
    Rebecca Elizabeth (1951-   )..............255
    Stephen...255

Henly
    Barton...67
    Sara..67
    Susan..67

Hennessy
    (--?--)...113

Henning
    Larry...253
    Lori...253

Henninger
    (--?--)...371
    Alma Pauline (1911-1997)..................410
    Carrie Edna (1895-1975)............250, 317
    Ethel L. (1922-   )...............................404
    Evelyn M. (1916-2007).......................404
    Ferle Gladys (1916-2012)...................411
    Franklin H. (1888-1968).....................410
    Gladys (1916-2012)............................411
    Henry W. (1845-   )............................410

Hilda D. (1912-2002) ... 410
Isaac ... 317
John Henry (1888-1932) ... 404
Linda ... 370
Richard ... 455
Ruth Naomi (1919-2011) ... 411
William Penrose ... 370
Winifred A. (1920-2001) ... 404

Henrick
(--?--) ... 376
Ryan ... 376
Scott ... 376

Henry
Annie M. (1899-1971) ... 253
Benjamin ... 285
Charles (-2008) ... 258
Ethel (1905-) ... 376
Hilda Margaret (1912-2008) ... 258
Jacob ... 253
Kathryn Marie ... 285
Kurt L. ... 341
Lisa L. ... 341
Lynwood D. ... 341
Mildred ... 247
Robin L. ... 341
Roger L. ... 341

Hentz
Debra (1955-) ... 197

Hepler
(--?--) ... 339
Abigail ... 345
Alice S. (1877-) ... 229
Alma M. ... 224
Austin (1913-) ... 137
Beulah Savilla (1899-1978) ... 219
Catharine (1879-1959) ... 229
Charles ... 219
Charles S. (1875-) ... 229
Chris ... 338, 369, 445
Donna ... 67
Doris Sidney (1922-2016) ... 214
Douglas ... 338
Earl (-1969) ... 425
Elizabeth (1866-1918) ... 228
Gertrude (1904-1972) ... 182
Goldeen (1964-) ... 345
Goldine (1964-) ... 345
Harry ... 366
Harry A. (1888-) ... 137
Heather Ann (1978-) ... 350
Henry Haupt (1838-1917) ... 228
Ida S. (1910-) ... 137
Irene E. (1898-1963) ... 229
Jacob Henry (1869-1871) ... 228
Jacob Maurer ... 228
James ... 338, 369, 445
James Fred (1908-1943) ... 345
Jeffrey T. (1958-) ... 345
Katie (1879-1959) ... 229
Lillian ... 308
Lillian B. (1903-1907) ... 229
Marshall (1962-) ... 345
Mary Grace ... 137
Mathilda (-1937) ... 132
Monroe S. (1868-1900) ... 228
Nancy ... 137
Oscar ... 214
Oscar Samuel (1873-1956) ... 229
Paul (1951-) ... 350
Paul Leroy (1975-) ... 350
Ray (1922-) ... 366
Rebecca (1833-1899) ... 217
Rhonda (1960-) ... 345
Thomas (1939-) ... 345
Victoria ... 345

Hepner
(--?--) ... 186
(--?--) (2000-) ... 196
Andrew (1972-) ... 196
Blanche ... 138
Cody Charles (1997-) ... 196
Ellen (1859-1943) ... 206
Joan L. ... 247
Lydia (1843-1905) ... 385
Samuel S. (1828-1894) ... 206

Herald
Lulu (1874-1962) ... 68

Herb
(--?--) ... 180, 497
Amanda ... 267
Anthony ... 193
Barbara Ann (1968-) ... 271
Betty Irene (1923-2002) ... 204, 241
Brenda Jean (1957-) ... 287
Brody ... 285
Bryson Thomas (1997-) ... 270
Carson ... 285
Charles ... 482
Charles Elsworth (1919-1969) ... 130
Charles K. (1855-1930) ... 442
Charles Oscar Milton (1877-1938) ... 204, 241
Curtin M. (1882-1894) ... 241
Daniel ... 100
Darci Jean (1958-) ... 286
David ... 55
David J. ... 264
David R. (1944-) ... 409
Dean ... 233
Diane Louise (1957-) ... 271
Dillon Maxwell (1994-) ... 286
Earle Albert (1912-1992) ... 240
Edwin L. ... 130
Edwin Lee (1895-1957) ... 130, 495
Elsie Elizabeth (1925-2013) ... 286
Elsie M. (1915-) ... 55
Elvin K. ... 249
Emma Sevilla (1878-1930) ... 257
Ethan William (1975-) ... 285
Eva Mae (1911-1986) ... 204, 241
Florence D. (1905-1999) ... 249
Forrest Irvin ... 270
Heidi Elizabeth (1992-) ... 233, 434
Henry ... 239, 241
Henry Grant (1875-1953) ... 239
Henry Guy (1909-1909) ... 240
Hilda G. (1924-2013) ... 495
Holly (1963-) ... 288
Jack L. ... 267
Jack S. ... 270
James Hensil (1930-2012) ... 287

Janet Dorothy (1930-1938) 240
Janice Lucille (1940-   ) 240
Jay Joseph (1928-1986) 286
Jeremy 104
Joel Ray (1969-   ) 287
John L. (1926-   ) 267
John R. (1935-2010) 287
Julie 267
June M. (1932-2014) 287
Karen A. (1967-   ) 409
Kenneth Scott (1980-   ) 285
Kenneth Stanford (1951-   ) 285
Kevin Scott (1992-   ) 286
Laura E. 496
Lauren Buckley (1988-   ) 286
Linda Mae (1952-   ) 287
Lorraine 482
Marian Eleanor (1929-1998) 224
Marie Helen (1906-1981) 442
Mary Alice (1940-   ) 240
Michael William (1976-   ) 264
Nathaniel Richard (1970-   ) 285
Nicholas Thomas (1987-   ) 270
Nichole 267
Nikki Marie (1989-   ) 233, 434
Oscar (1877-1938) 241
Otis S. (1924-2012) 285
Phaon Ray (1921-2010) 285
Randy Jay (1951-   ) 286
Ray Charlie Hoffman (1902-1969) 240
Ray H. (1900-1965) 284
Richard Phaon (1947-   ) 285
Robert Scott (1950-   ) 285
Ronald Keith (1958-   ) 285
Roy Paul (1961-   ) 130
Ryan J. 286
Sally Snyder (1942-   ) 240
Samuel C. (1859-1926) 204, 241
Sheila 193
Susan 263
Taylor Lynn (2009-   ) 264
Tessa Ann (2006-   ) 264
Thomas E. 224
Thomas George (1952-   ) 285
Thomas R. 270
Traci Ann (1963-   ) 286
Vivian Alverta (1919-2003) 284
Warren Oscar (1901-   ) 204, 241
Wayne 104

Herbert
Del 247
Douglas S. 247

Hering
Rosanna Catharine 281

Herman
Clarence Leroy (1937-   ) 343
David Allen (1918-   ) 342
Ethel 323
Ethel Marie (1925-   ) 343
Floyd E. (1914-   ) 343
Harry Allen (1897-1960) 342
Helen Irene (1921-1995) 343
John David (1946-   ) 343
Leon L. (1911-   ) 343
Mabel H. (1907-   ) 343

Mary E. J. (1903-   ) 343
Michael Edwin (1876-1927) 342
Mildred M. (1905-   ) 343
Myrtle M. (1917-   ) 343
Paul Edward (1928-   ) 343
Thomas E. (1899-   ) 343
William Harry (1926-   ) 343

Hern
Judy A. 178

Herner
(--?--) 100
Daniel 266
Danielle 266
Heidi 266
Mabel E. (1891-   ) 352
Maria Mariah (1844-1922) 416

Herold
George Ernest (1942-   ) 400
Sherri 400
Sherri Lynn (1967-   ) 400

Herr
David 201

Herring
Ruth Delma (1906-1933) 59
Sandra Joan (1943-   ) 183
Sarah N. (1852-1902) 166

Herriot
Lynn 230

Herrold
Irene F. 268

Hershberger
Ida A. (1879-1946) 426

Hershey
Gail Marie (1969-   ) 471
Kenneth C. 125
Michael 471
Virginia Mary (1896-1975) 60

Hertzel
Vera Mae (1931-1989) 112

Hertzog
Beth Ann 260
Carol Ann 260
Charles 260
JoAnne 260
Merlin F. (1932-2004) 260
Nancy B. 260

Hess
Annie Catherine (1875-1951) 388
Edward A. 388
Elizabeth (1865-1935) 390
Harry 390
Jacqueline (1931-   ) 139
Sarah D. (-1909) 416
Stewart 139
Susan Adaline 216

Hetrick
Charles (1931-   ) 356
Jane (1924-   ) 356
Norman C. (1900-1985) 356
Peter 417
Susan Adaline (1875-1950) 417

Heydner
(--?--) 241

Hiepler
- Arthur 217

Hiester
- Lillie 74

Higgins
- (--?--) 232
- Arthur 273
- Bonnie Alice (1944-) 302
- Devon Forrest (1923-) 273
- Eric (1978-) 302
- Erin (1981-) 302
- Gerard (1951-) 302
- Gerard (1975-) 302
- Jeffry (1980-) 302
- John (1921-2005) 302
- John J. (1948-) 302
- Lee Ann (1954-) 302
- Maria (1971-) 302
- Mary Margaret (1946-) 302
- Michael (1951-) 302
- Michael (1976-) 302
- Sean (1975-) 302
- Tricia (1981-) 302

Hilbert
- Tina Marie 347

Hill
- Ann (1913-) 97
- Craig 158
- Edward T. 281
- Maude 165
- Merita Marie (1965-) 481

Hilliard
- Brian 262
- Tucker J. 262

Hilton
- Joel M. 412

Hine
- Abigail Isorah (1883-1959) 50

Hines
- Jillian Lynnae (2009-) 238
- Judith 409
- Kiley Rae (2005-) 238
- Reed Thomas (2014-) 238
- Theodore 238

Hinkel
- Ashley 265

Hinkle
- (--?--) (-1930) 327
- Geraldine Marie (1933-) 414

Hinshaw
- (--?--) 273

Hinton
- Kristy Nicole (1993-) 85
- Lloyd Keith (1958-) 85

Hirte
- Rosina Esther 166

Hissey
- Frederick J. (1892-) 167
- Frederick T. (1859-) 167
- Infant Daughter (1918-1918) 167

Hoagland
- (--?--) 255

Hoast
- Sarah Elizabeth (1862-1910) 182

Hobart
- Helene 277

Hobbs
- Guion 247
- Ryan 247, 257

Hoch
- (--?--) 383
- Donald 403
- Mabel A. (1901-1985) 340
- Margaret Irene (1912-2007) 473

Hockman
- Connie S. 278
- Linda L. 278
- Paul R. 278
- Paul S. (1944-) 278

Hodac
- George B. 397

Hodge
- Amber 267
- Gary 267
- Sean 267

Hodgkins
- Sarah 182

Hoehnen
- Kathleen Savage (1958-) 71

Hoerner
- George A. Jr. (1906-1967) 421
- George A. Sr. 421
- Glenn A. (1936-) 421

Hofer
- Barbara 265
- James 494

Hoffa
- Hannah (1810-1894) 203, 372

Hoffman
- (--?--) 166, 363, 417, 491
- Alice (1902-) 406
- Alice Edna (1956-1979) 392
- Alice J. (1876-1946) 239
- Amelia 323
- Anna 201
- Anna Margaretha (1753-) 49
- Anna Priscilla 101
- Annie M. (1871-1927) 415
- April Gail 89
- Ben David (1926-1999) 392
- Beth Estella (1924-2015) 392
- Betty Florence (1923-) 169
- Bill 364
- Blanche Elizabeth (1890-1973) 221, 453
- Bobby (1928-) 169
- Bobby Albert (1929-1972) 173
- Brent N. 481
- Catherine E. (1888-) 119
- Charles Cornelius (1861-1915) 221, 453
- Charles M. (1856-1928) 239
- Clarence 140
- Clayton 247
- Cleo B. (1926-1926) 169
- Cornelius O. (1862-) 222
- Cynthia Lou (1946-) 269
- Dale John 114

Daniel (1836-) 66
David 66
David A. 481
Dawn Aelyn 114
Debra L 117
Dottie Katie (1921-) 169
Edward C. (1891-1927) 119
Elizabeth 389
Elizabeth (1777-) 49
Elizabeth Ellen (1867-1962) 185
Emanuel 66
Emanuel (1846-1917) 280
Emma Ramona (1919-2004) 392
Eugene (1919-1991) 400
Eva M. (1920-2006) 439
Fay 119
Frank 166
Galen Paul III (1970-) 188
Galen Paul Jr. (1956-) 188
George (1813-1854) 66
George R. (1908-1981) 481
Greta Jane (1972-) 188
Hannah (1807-1858) 210
Harold W. 470
Harvey Clair 439
Helen Mae (1921-2006) 247
Hilbert Griffiths (1903-1942) 392
Ira (1911-) 169
Jacob 166
Jacob Leroy (1930-) 170
John (1836-) 66
John C. (1888-1957) 64
John George (1771-1828) 66
Katie 368
Katie (1888-) 119
Katie L. (1873-1963) 416
Keith Bradley (1976-) 188
Kimber 387
Kyle Paul (1993-) 188
Leroy Kantner Jr. (1922-1989) 392
Leroy Kantner Sr. (1897-1985) 392
Levi 481
Lewis C. (1865-) 119
Lottie (-1991) 252
Lula Marie (1898-1971) 134
Margo A. (1956-2007) 262
Marilyn K. (1955-) 154
Mark Luther (1951-) 68
Mary (1879-) 375
Mary Amanda (1904-1988) 372
Michelle Lynn (1977-) 353
Mildred 380
Mildred P. (1920-1996) 412
Myrtle (-2007) 156
Nancy 180, 238
Nicholas Ryan (1979-) 68
Norma 456
Norman Lee (1928-2011) 392
Paul Donald 114
Polly Jane (1873-1957) 280
Reba 370
Renee Coleen 114
Rhoda Marilyn (1929-) 170
Richard D. 113
Rita Marie (1966-) 470
Robin Michelle (1970-) 322
Robyn M. 271
Rodney I. (1941-1941) 170
Roy (1914-) 119
Ruth (1902-2001) 76
Sarah Elizabeth (1910-1999) 64
Sarah Ella (1888-1972) 222
Scott Brian (1974-) 68
Sherry Ann 114
Shirley 370
Terry Joseph (-2015) 353
Thomas Alvin (1892-1943) 119
Tina Ellen (1960-) 173
Vicki Lynn (1966-) 353
Wesley 166
Willard 117
William Francis 392
William Richard 269, 271

Hoffner
Anzonetta Jane (1934-2012) 131
Elva 134
Russell (-2012) 131

Hogsett
Alice Edna (1928-2014) 392

Hoke
Albert W. 472
Alice Cora (1878-1945) 172
Carol Ann (1946-) 403
Corrine Olive Senora (1925-2005) 208
Daniel Belton (1902-1975) 208
Emma Jane (1871-1924) 371
Erma J. (1929-2014) 208
Herman Eugene (1923-1988) 402
Linda 370
Lynn L. (1952-1970) 208
Mary Jane (1936-) 472
Norwood Quentin (1921-1975) 208
Patricia Ellen (1950-) 403
Samantha (1969-) 111
Velva Ruby 81

Hokenson
Katherine 315

Holdeman
Chris (1968-) 481
Clayton E. (1897-1966) 481
Gloria Jean (1941-) 481
Kenneth (1943-) 481
Roy Pershing (1918-1982) 481

Holden
Beth Ann 392
Harry Edward (1919-2000) 392
Harry Edward Sr. 392
Susan Jane (1953-1958) 392

Holderman
Anna (1819-1900) 209
Harley E. (1888-1961) 98

Holdiman
Anna 213

Holena
Joan 110

Holl
Daniel A. (1984-) 178
James P. 178

Hollenbach
  Charles 384
  Linda (1882-) 307
  Mabel 133

Holloway
  Madelynn Taylor 324
  Paul D. Jr. 324
  Paul D. Sr. 324
  Ryan Daniel 324
  Sharon Lee 121
  Tracey L. 324

Hollowell
  David 277

Holmes
  Linda 252

Holsberg
  Clara A. 240

Holtzer
  Bill 158

Holtzman
  Francis L. (1913-) 406
  George 317
  George T. (1915-) 406
  Mark G. (1887-) 406
  Renee I. (1921-2014) 317
  Simon A. (1857-) 406
  Thomas W. (1918-) 406

Holwig
  Harry F. (1891-1949) 55
  Henry 55
  Levi D. (1846-1894) 56
  Margaret E. (1897-1925) 57
  Monroe Harvey (1871-1960) 56
  Myrtle E. (1895-1929) 56

Holzapfel
  Mary Frances 237

Homan
  Diane Luce 293
  Kristoff Theodore (1980-) 293
  William 293

Homes
  David 277
  Mabel Sarah (1893-1939) 277

Hooks
  John R. 262
  Megan E. 262
  Suzanne 262

Hoos
  Festus G. (1885-1966) 94

Hooven
  John Joseph II (1930-1991) 62
  John Joseph III (1953-) 62
  Linda Jo (1955-) 62
  Thomas C. 395
  Valerie A. (1984-) 62

Hoover
  (--?--) 196, 420
  Augustus G. 217
  Bonita Lou (1943-) 319
  Bruce 78
  Dale Edward 59
  Edna (1879-1955) 274
  Fannie Jane (1867-1936) 428
  Gloria (1950-) 322
  Harold 134
  Jean Marie (1938-) 134
  John Elwood (1919-2001) 319
  John Elwood (1951-) 319
  Junior 114
  Kayla Jennifer 264
  Kelly 264
  Kenneth L. 403
  Landon 119
  Margaret (1963-) 59
  Margaret Ellen (1924-2002) 409
  Mary 274
  Mary Magdalena (1779-1826) 67, 448
  Matthew Walter 420
  Merredith Doreen 114
  Michael 420
  Mildred 469
  Myrtle M. 217
  Paul Clayton (1894-1951) 319
  Ronald 403
  Russel J. (1920-2001) 403
  Russel J. Jr. 403
  Sandra Lee 114

Hopkins
  (--?--) 78

Hoppes
  Nedra Maxine 217

Hoppis
  Amanda 91

Hopple
  Margaret (1918-2007) 69

Horbach
  Canal (1928-) 199
  Robert C. (1918-1930) 199

Horchler
  Kenneth D. 429
  Summer Nicole 429

Horein
  George 277
  Hazel Naomi (1908-2007) 277

Horley
  Blanche E. (1911-2000) 396

Hornberger
  Charles 292
  Clarence E. (1904-) 155
  Linda 292
  Patricia 475

Horner
  John 493
  Maude 124
  Steve 493

Horoschak
  Mathew 267

Horowitz
  (--?--) 265

Horstick
  James William (1952-) 287
  James William II (1977-) 287
  John F. 287
  Jonathan Wesley (1988-) 287
  Nicholas Allen (1986-) 287

Horstman
  Mary 237

Horwath
Nadja (1941-) 199
Hoshauer
D.J. 138
Donald E. 138
Heather 138
Heidi 138
Hosler
Latitia 303
Host
Anthony 480
Hottenstein
Clare E. 227
Houck
Ammon I. (1864-1936) 185
Annie Della (1893-1937) 185
Infant (1887-1887) 185
Jennie Mabel (1893-1972) 185
Mazie E. (1895-1912) 185
Houge
Celeste 319
Houghton
Eric Daniel (1969-) 145
James Madison (2002-) 145, 315
Jennifer Elizabeth (1998-) 145, 315
Joseph Carl (1993-) 145, 315
Louis 145
Louis Reuben (1999-) 145, 315
Melissa Lee (1996-) 145, 315
House
John Robert (1856-1899) 63
Marie 480
Serilda Pearl (1889-1911) 63
Housel
Margaret 379
Houser
Charlotte Catherine 288
Sara Alice (1864-1923) 314
Houtz
Lynore K. 121
Howard
Alan Dale (1963-) 322
Alberta Mae (1923-1992) 319
Barbara (1949-) 320
Brenda Elaine (1965-) 322
Bryan L. (1962-) 320
Carol (1954-) 320
Chappy (1931-2015) 321
Colby Michael 322
Deitra (1960-) 320
Denise (1959-) 320
Dennis George (1956-) 321
Donald William (1931-2015) 321
Donovan 322
Douglas Lee (1955-) 321
Edward John (1960-) 321
Eugene Isaac (1927-1988) 320
Fearl Kathleen (1930-2006) 207, 321
Harold Theodore (1931-) 321
Isaac Leroy (1898-1988) 121, 207, 318, 325
Jeremy Randall 322
John David (1965-) 321
Joshua Alan 322
Kathleen Marie (1958-) 321
Kenneth LaMar (1936-1937) 322
Lauretta Faye (1919-2000) 318
Marilyn R. (1956-) 320
Mark Albert (1926-1977) 320
Mark E. (1959-) 320
Marlin (1956-) 320
Mary Ellen (1921-2006) 319
Mathew Wayne 322
Nancy Lou (1944-1944) 320
Norwood Cleon (1920-1939) 319
Patrick (1966-) 320
Pearl Geraldine (1930-) 121, 320
Randall Eugene (1961-) 322
Richard Leroy (1934-2010) 321
Rita Renee (1952-) 320
Robert Alton (1924-1969) 319
Robert Alton (1963-) 320
Scott Leroy (1967-) 321
Sharon (1961-) 320
Shawn Elizah 322
Shawna (1963-) 320
Sheila 484
Stacy (1965-) 320
Tessa Morgan 322
Vicke Lee (1950-1968) 320
Wayne Richard (1959-) 321
Wendy Bridget (1961-) 321
William 318, 325
Howe
(--?--) 390
C. J. 277
C.J. (1926-) 277
Charles Wynn (1958-) 235
Conrad Jeffrey (1951-2007) 277
Cynthia 277
Edward Crosby 235
Jerrianne (1960-) 235
Mary E. (-1984) 393
Howell
Fay 432
Mark 136
Marlene 272
Howerter
Emma (-2004) 340
Hoy
(--?--) 438
Anna Celeste (1872-1943) 160
Betty Lou (1947-) 464
Eugene A. (1937-2010) 362
Florence C. (1904-) 430
George (1942-) 464
Harry Ulysses 406
Jadzia 438
Janet M. 404
John 464
Linda (1950-) 464
Malinda (1962-) 362
Merle Edward 464
Rozella M. (1902-1979) 406
Russell 404
Thomas M. (1953-1968) 464
William (1945-) 464
Winifred Lorraine (1937-1937) 404
Hubbard
Mina 465

Huber
    Nicholas Bryan Christopher (1990-) 58
Hubler
    Donna 199
Hubley
    Alma Rebecca (1862-1946) 70
    Jonathan 70
Hudson
    Aela Murphy (2009-) 59
    Cora Roan (2002-) 59
    Jeffrey Allan (1972-) 59
    John A. 59
    Moira Elizabeth (2000-) 59
    Robert (1930-1980) 59
Huff
    Grace Jieyun 191
    Stephen 191
Huffmon
    Marie 124
Huggins
    Edna A. (1907-1973) 410
Hughes
    (--?--) 486
    Roni Marie 323
    Roni Marie (1954-) 323
    Rosine Elizabeth (1915-1996) 65
    Taylor Raye (2000-) 486
    Thomas 228
Humiston
    Shelley 437
    Shelly (1953-) 308
Hummel
    Aaron Robert (1977-) 58
    Alyssa Kate (2005-) 57
    Anthony Wallace (1970-) 57
    Barbara (1944-) 57
    Dolores 419
    Elsie 156
    Elsie Anna (1927-2016) 73
    Frederick 73
    Hollie Lynn (1968-) 57
    Joaquin Filippeli (2011-) 58
    John Williams (1917-) 343
    Karen Ruth (1947-) 112
    Kathryn Ann (1960-) 57
    Kevin Ian (1982-) 58
    Kingston Scott (2009-) 58
    LaMar Edward (1938-) 57
    Lawrence Edgar Jr. (1933-) 57
    Lawrence Edgar Sr. (1913-1976) 57
    Linda Elaine (1948-) 58
    Mandy Yates (1978-) 58
    Margaret E. (-1982) 493
    Raymond Albert (1910-1997) 112
    Richard 109
    Robert Eugene (1949-) 58
    Ruth (1919-) 380
    Teresa Marie (1956-) 57
    Valerie Elaine (1955-) 57
    William Henry (1874-1953) 57, 112
Hunter
    Donald Katerman (1908-1974) 362
    Edmund T. 118
    Keith E. (1968-1969) 118

    Ruth 362
Huntley
    Helen 166
    Jack J. 166
    Louella 166
Huntsinger
    (--?--) 497
    Sandra (1947-) 155
Huntzinger
    Alvin B. 224
    Annis M. (1929-) 289
    Carl 78
    Cora Alice (1869-1943) 437
    Cora Tamey (1872-1937) 213
    Craig 270
    Elizabeth L. (1926-) 224
    Emma Jane 416
    Ernest (1902-1980) 224
    Ethel M. (1904-1974) 436
    Henry 213
    Irene A. 270
    Jennifer 270
    Joan Marie 355
    Margaret Mardelle (1923-1990) 224
    Phoebe Emma 223
    Pruella 390
    Ruth M. 204
Huratiak
    Paul John (1931-2004) 218
Hurlburt
    (--?--) 125
Hurley
    James A. (1886-1956) 424
Hurst
    Carol Ann 163
Husband
    Earl LaMar 278
    Edith Louise (1940-) 278
    Elgie 278
    Ella L. 278
    Evelyn Marie (1938-) 278
Huss
    Elizabeth (-1881) 61, 65
Husted
    Antoinette 175
    Edyth 175
    George 174
    John 274
Hutchins
    Richard T (1956-) 488
Hyde
    Bernice 276
Ickes
    David Chase (1893-1957) 50
    Ridgely Helen (1928-2010) 50
    Turie S. 50
Idzig
    Frank S. 471
Illig
    Harry P. (1883-) 79
    Kathleen (1925-2006) 79
Imbrolglia
    (--?--) 497

Ingram
Clara W. (1897-1972) 211
Insley
Thomas A. Jr. 263
Irick
Robert 200
Irvin
Dola Marie (1915-) 382
James Arthur 382
Irving
Ferne M. 436
Isenberg
Britt Charles (1986-) 268, 479
Chandra Lynne (1984-) 268, 479
Dustin James (1986-) 268, 479
George E. (1948-) 384
Joseph Robert (1972-) 384
Pearl M. 398
Samuel Paul 384
Scott 268
Tracey Ann (1970-) 384
Iwamoto
Ray (1920-2000) 165
Raymond 165
Robert 165
Izzo
(--?--) 259
Jackett
Cora L. 254
Jackson
(--?--) 496
Ben 496
Emily 496
Parker (-2015) 496
Jacobs
Bradley Joseph (2013-) 487
Brandon Bertrand (2010-) 487
Cora Annette (1908-2002) 371
Damien (1980-) 487
Rae (1901-) 98
James
Brenden 259
Jennifer 259
Kayla 259
Ronald Jr. 259
Ronald L. Sr. 259
Taylor 259
Jamison
April M. (1982-) 179
David A. (1963-) 179
Donald R. 179
Linda B. (1955-) 299
Philip 299
Philip III 299
Shawna M. (1986-) 179
Steven T. (1965-) 179
Terry Jane (1955-) 300
Tina M. (1968-) 179
Jandle
Alvera C. (1955-) 110
Barbara Jane (1952-) 110
Calvin C. (1961-) 110
Coleman (1912-1996) 110
Coleman Nandor Jr. (1947-) 110
Richard R. (1959-1993) 110
Robert J. (1950-) 110
Janoski
Larry 324
Jeffrey
Dorothy 302
Jenkins
Dorothy M. 374
Elizabeth Anne 280
Evan 374
Jennings
Pearl 381
Jensen
Christian 400
Einer (-1927) 296
Jennifer 400
Robert 400
Jesse
Jack 276
Jaclyn D. 276
Jonathan E. 276
Johanides
Joseph Louis (1910-1994) 53
Johnom
Sonja Margaret (1930-) 113
Johns
(--?--) 168
Bess 168
Diane Louise (1957-) 160
Kevin (1973-) 245
Lester Arthur (1931-) 160
Lester Arthur Jr. (1959-) 160
Margaret L. (1910-2009) 408
Roger 245
Stacy (1977-) 245
Sula May 129
Vivian 168
Johnson
(--?--) 397
Celestia (1910-) 93
Joanna (1864-1906) 91
John 91
Richard Bolinger 81
Roy C. (1909-1986) 77
Vennetta 94
Johnston
(--?--) 441
Gloria (1938-) 242
Mary Lou 163
Jones
(--?--) 361, 433
(--?--) (1936-) 485
Anna Bell 64
Archie (1903-) 80
Bill 121
Brian L. 280
Daniel 122
Daren K. 280
Dolores (1948-) 400
Edward L. (1905-) 80
Eileen 232
Fay Mill (1897-1989) 295
Gerald K. 280
Grace Elizabeth (1917-1999) 280

Heather 235
Helen 177
Helen (1885-) 177
Howard S. (-1910) 80
Irene (1910-) 280
Jennie 55
Jo Ann (1956-) 362
John 212
John M. (1932-2014) 235
Joseph Christopher (1974-) 145
Justin (1978-) 250
Kenneth S. (1906-1989) 280
Laura Grace 145, 315
Leslie Trevor (1878-1957) 280
Linda 199
Lisa C. 235
Matilda M. (1883-1960) 212
Ralph 118, 250, 471
Ruth (1924-) 295
Sarah Elizabeth (2002-) 145, 315
Shirley E. 396
Stephen G. 280
William F. (1847-1943) 280

Jooss
Anna Maria 292

Josephson
Fred 137
John (1909-) 137
Marvin 137
Mary 137
Ruth 137
Wayne 137

Joss
Ellen H. 54

Junda
Kalen (1983-) 303
Laurence Elliot 303
Sean (1987-) 303

Jury
Earl 69
Katherine 393
Mary Ellen 402

Kahler
(--?--) 400
Alberta 334
Andrew 442
Arleah C. (1932-) 484
Carl D. 442
Carrie A. (1891-1949) 241, 288
Catherine 442
Courtney M. (1987-) 442
Daniel LeRoy 442
Elaine 130
Gary 130
Jennie 463
Katie M. (1899-1947) 359
Lisa 130
Mabel A. 334
Mildred Sophia (1911-2000) 130
Norman 130
Roy Marvin (1937-2014) 130
Tillie Rose 269
Timothy 442
Violet M. 117

Kalandros
Desiree 230

Kanaval
John Joseph (1930-) 152

Kandybowski
James Vincent 141

Kane
Gary 262

Kantner
Alice Grace (1887-) 392
Caroline 213
Clark A. (1889-) 392
Edward F. (1880-) 392
Edwin (1880-) 392
Franklin 392
Freda H. (1894-) 393
George M. (1851-1894) 392
Harry W. (1882-) 392
Hattie Estelle (1879-1967) 392
Lola M. (1908-) 392
May (1885-) 392
Minnie (1877-) 392
Thelma W. (1918-) 392

Kantz
Janet Eileen (1952-) 482
Maureen Louise (1948-) 482
Robert Allen (1929-1996) 482
Sally Ann (1949-) 482
Susan Carol (1946-) 482

Kapp
Allen Levi (1921-2004) 217
Arthur Harry (1922-1996) 217
Doris J. (1925-) 217
Grace R. (1930-2005) 217
Harry 217
Jean Romaine (1930-2005) 217
Levi R. 217
Lucille I. (1927-) 217

Karli
Phyllis 228

Kasarda
Edmund 426

Kash
Fern 220

Katona
Christo (1963-) 488
Pamela Jean (1960-2002) 488

Kauffman
(--?--) 466
Ada F. (1906-1983) 63
Alice M. (1909-1977) 63
Esther M. (1901-) 63
Hannah Rose (2007-) 86
Harry Edward (1902-) 63
Harry W. (1875-) 63
Howard (1898-) 63
Jacob (1808-1878) 391
Jeffrey Michael (2004-) 86
Kayla 466
Maria M. (1834-1907) 391
Mary (1835-1877) 374
Michael Scott (1973-) 86
Robert Wayne 429

Kaufman
    David Michael (1969-)..................................159
    Kaity (1994-)..159
    Kirby Alan (1964-)..159
    Larry Alfred (1930-)......................................159
    Lear Anthony (1971-).....................................159
    Michael J. (1967-)...159
    Michaela Marie (1997-)..................................159
    Scott Douglas (1961-)....................................159

Kaulchitue
    Antonia..497

Kear
    Mary...374

Kebaugh
    Cora Edna..119
    Sallie Rebecca...417

Keboch
    Cora..119, 417
    Daniel (1864-1945)..119
    Henry (1836-)..119
    Sallie (1890-)...119

Keckler
    Elva..139

Keefer
    Danielle...103
    Emmett Earl (1908-1978).................................94
    Owen Edward (1882-1950).............................94
    Richard..305
    William A. (1870-1940)..................................398

Keeler
    Margaret F. (1905-1993).................................224

Keeley
    Lynn A..159

Keen
    Charles H. (1892-1967)..................................369
    Elwood B..56
    James B..56
    Janice M. (1938-)..56
    Miana Elizabeth (1926-)........................367, 369

Keene
    Jennie Mae (1899-1994).................................359

Keener
    Dennis P..215
    John...215
    Pamela A...215
    Paul Henry (1922-2010).................................215

Keeney
    Myrle...128

Kehler
    Alissa...193
    Carl Joshua (1976-).......................................348
    Constance J. (1927-)......................................394
    Dorice A..193
    Duane..265
    Emma Lou (1921-)...394
    Janice Corinne (1936-)..................................348
    Jennifer (1979-)..348
    Jeremy John (1977-).......................................348
    Joseph..394
    Joyce (1923-)..394
    Karl (1913-1973)...348
    Karl Robert (1943-).......................................348
    Timothy Benneville (1899-1981)....................394

Kehly
    John (1933-)...365

Kehres
    Rosa...184
    Sarah...302

Keiffer
    Jonathan..302
    Lori..473
    Mary Magdaline (1868-1946)........................302

Keim
    Caitlin...375
    Cortney...375
    John R. (1919-1991).......................................403
    Larry...375

Keiser
    Arlene..140
    Cora V. (1894-1943).......................................185
    Elaine..140
    Emma..207
    Forrest Herb (-1940)......................................140
    Forrest Jr...140
    Wilbert..140

Keister
    Dave..87
    Hal...115
    Howie Eric..115

Keiter
    (--?--)...472
    Bessie..138
    Elmer D. (1900-1993).....................................406
    Homer (1896-1972)..399
    Jennie (1932-)..154
    Katie Alice..350
    Margaret Maria (1923-2015)..........................399

Keith
    Archibald (1924-)..98
    Emma B. (1916-)...97
    Ernest F. (1918-)..97
    Floyd E. (1918-)...97
    Floyd Ernest (1885-1934).................................97
    George S. (1914-)..97
    Lula May (1926-)..98
    Lulu M..98
    Marjorie L. (1919-)..97

Keller
    (--?--)...79
    Clara (1856-1906)..300
    Gertrude..226
    Robin Smoyer (1962-)...................................285

Kelley
    Absolom..374
    Hilbert Frank (1921-1991).............................374
    Nevin Ellsworth (1919-2008).........................374
    Oliver E. (1887-1958).....................................374

Kelly
    Christina..136
    Irene..374
    James...136
    John...382
    Margaret..98
    Stephen...136

Kembel
    Donald Lee (1970-)..494
    Gary..494

    Gary Lee 494
    Gregory Allen (1969-) 494
    Ivan Jay (1975-) 495
    Jordan Allen (1989-) 331
    Joshua Joseph (1986-) 331
    Kerry Joseph (1965-) 330
    Mary Jane (1973-) 495

Kemmeren
    Hannah Eliza (1846-1907) 426

Kemmerling
    Mary Ellen 79

Kemp
    Al (1977-) 329
    Daisy P. (1898-1986) 369
    Madalyn Gloria 427
    Sarah (1975-) 329
    William (1949-) 329

Kendall
    Anna B. (1922-2015) 273
    Eileen Esther (1922-) 273

Kennedy
    Lillian M. 60

Kent
    Irene (1900-) 139

Keough
    (--?--) 208

Keppler
    Angeline (1829-1897) 206

Keppley
    Shari Ray 491

Kercher
    Christopher 275
    Craig 275
    David 275
    Mark 275
    Otis 275
    Richard Alan (1925-1992) 275

Kern
    Greg 260
    Robert 260
    Stephanie 260

Kerr
    Alex 71
    Nicole (1977-) 71
    Robert (1951-) 71

Kerrs
    Martha 115

Kerschner
    Caroline 392
    Lester 239

Kershner
    Ronald 50

Kersten
    Quent 408
    Todd 408

Kerstetter
    Eva (1904-) 139
    Hailey P. 291
    Helen (-2011) 316
    Jennette (1877-1938) 84
    John (-1920) 84
    Kyle 291
    Linda M. 224

    Mary E. (1861-1890) 402
    Ronald Lee 326

Kerwin
    Mary Ann (1947-) 420

Kessler
    Aaron Ezra (1911-1969) 369
    Alice 251
    Amy Julia 490
    Catherine Mary (1925-) 453
    Charles Edwin (1892-1977) 452
    Charles Henry (1866-1940) 453
    Craig S. 104
    David L. (1955-) 490
    Elias 230
    Hilda Fae (1920-1999) 452
    Jacquiline J. (1969-) 490
    James Michael (1946-) 490
    Jean E. (1941-2012) 198
    John Earl (1920-2001) 198
    Katherine Diane (1977-) 490
    Kathryn (1925-) 453
    Larae Lynn (1938-) 103
    Lloyd Homer (1907-1941) 453
    Lorraine M. 182
    Mae Eleanor (1915-2007) 134
    Mark 138
    Mark William (1917-2008) 149
    Mary Amelia (1918-1992) 243
    Mary Elizabeth (1951-1953) 490
    Matthew James (1979-) 490
    Maude Irene (1887-1944) 58
    Michael 490
    Moses Leon (1894-1978) 243, 490
    Norma J. (1932-) 345, 369
    Phyllis 288
    Raymond Moses (1916-1989) 490
    Richard Raymond (1941-) 490
    Robert Andrew (1954-) 490
    Sinary Raymond (1896-1963) 134
    Tamie (1878-1959) 230
    Tionne Rae (1978-) 490
    Violet (1939-) 149

Kester
    Dana A. 426
    T.J. (1978-) 426
    Terry (1982-) 426

Kettering
    Elizabeth Fannie 76

Keys
    Sarah Adelaide 361

Keysock
    George (1911-1964) 346

Kidwell
    Earl 82
    Marguerite L. (1930-2014) 82

Kiefer
    Aaron 241
    Aaron Alvin 241
    Charles Herman (1910-1990) 241
    Jared 241
    Joshua 241
    Kathy 241, 253
    Lee A. (1941-) 241, 253

Kieffer
    (--?--) 193, 425
    David 292
    Louisa 394
    Luke 292

Kiehl
    Dora J. 239
    Helen A. (1919-2006) 116

Kiesling
    John A. 290
    Leroy W. 290

Kilby
    Ellen Marie (1953-) 467
    Frank Walter (1958-) 467
    Herbert (1924-2004) 466
    Herbert Russell (1956-) 467
    Herbert Russell Jr. (1979-) 467
    James Franklin 466
    Sean Patrick (1981-) 467

Kille
    Debra Ann (1968-) 484

Killheffer
    Mayme J. (1880-1962) 160

Kimble
    Estella May (1904-2002) 221
    Thomas G. 221

Kimmel
    Barbara 216
    Carol (1956-) 291
    Catharine 257
    Daniel (-2007) 309
    Doris Jean (1943-1944) 291
    Doris Ruth (1925-2007) 353
    Edward 211
    Eleanor Jean 216
    Eliza 49
    Erin Nicole (1983-) 185
    Eva Ellen (1861-1891) 280
    Evans (1833-1909) 280
    George 243
    Glenn Millard (1952-) 291
    Gregory Scott (1984-) 185
    Guy (1925-) 309
    Hannah 135
    Henry 216
    Jacqueline L 192
    Jean L. 277
    John (1931-) 309
    John K. (1861-1927) 309
    Joshua 310
    Judy R. 277
    Katherine 216
    Lester (-2007) 353
    Marie (1936-) 310
    Mark Allen (1917-1977) 291
    Mary (1933-1933) 309
    Mary A. (1879-1939) 211
    Matthew 310
    Melvin L. (1934-2007) 309
    Minnie 247
    Monroe (1938-1959) 310
    Nevin 291
    Palmer E. (1941-2016) 310
    Paul E. Jr. 310
    Paul E. Sr. 310
    Peggy A. 277
    Peggy Jane (1955-2014) 291
    Quinton 291
    Raymond L. (1917-2008) 216
    Robert 192, 277
    Romie Oneida (1915-2014) 243, 441
    Ronald George (1948-) 185
    Ruby 310
    Rufus Monroe (1894-1964) 309
    Ryan 291
    Shayanne 291
    Troy 310

Kincade
    Kristen (1968-) 165

Kinderman
    Anna L. (1894-) 53
    Charles 53

Kindig
    Anna May 275

Kindoom
    O.K. 178

Kines
    Maryan 396

King
    Butch 245
    Dylan 245
    Michael 245
    Orville 139
    Paul D. (1921-1986) 410
    Steven Wilbur (1945-) 57

Kingery
    Karen 120

Kinkaid
    Becky 263
    Gary Douglas (1959-) 263
    Katy 263
    William J. 263

Kinter
    Andrew G. (1840-1915) 61, 65
    Emma Long (1874-1971) 61
    Kathryn Matilda (1881-1948) 65

Kirby
    Molly Lee 427

Kissinger
    (--?--) 127
    Andrew 101
    Anna Elisabeth (1874-1929) 357
    Anna Mae (1934-) 197, 332
    Anna Maria (1808-1848) 420, 421, 424
    Arlene Mary (1930-2007) 196
    Barbara 290
    Beulah Elmira (1888-) 453
    Bonita Louise (1949-) 372
    Charles E. (-1988) 101
    Clara L. (1862-1938) 329
    Craig (1967-) 243
    Curtis Alan (1967-) 481
    Daniel (1838-1924) 169
    Daniel Franklin (1898-1986) 372
    Daniel Milton (1879-1945) 195
    Dennis Keith Jr. (1971-) 372
    Dennis Keith Sr. (1948-) 372
    Dolores Elaine (1946-) 372

Donald H. (1935-) 243
Donald Lee 128
Edith 196
Edith Hannah (1926-2009) 195, 492
Elizabeth (1877-1938) 458
Elwood Ernest (1938-2001) 198
Ernest Lamar (1958-) 196
Ernest Milton (1906-1947) 195, 492
Eva Mabel 481
Gabrielle 198
Gregory (1951-) 372
Gregory (1972-) 372
Harold Earl (1911-1972) 243
Harold Grant 128
Harry (1910-1964) 282
Janice (1934-) 357
Jerome (1947-) 372
Joel Richard (1983-2014) 243
Kate A. (1871-1954) 169
Kathryn 101
Keli (1960-) 481
Kelly (1960-) 481
Kermit Wilson (1923-) 372
Kimberly Sue (1963-) 198
Lamar Gene (1935-) 481
Larry E. (1968-) 198
LeRoy Charles (1932-2011) 196
Leroy Charles Jr. (1956-) 197
Lester Emanuel (1913-1969) 481
Lori (1963-) 243
Lucille Yvonne (1939-2007) 282
Marilyn D. (1952-2011) 128
Martha Marie (1932-) 195
Mary Lou (1948-2012) 196
Michelle (1974-) 372
Michelle A. (1953-) 372
Mike 198
Pamela Ann (1962-) 197
Randall Eugene (1963-) 481
Richard Michael (1947-) 372
Ricky (1957-) 243
Ronald 128
Roy 101
Ruth Gertie (1935-2014) 197, 245
Scott Paul (1961-) 196
Susannah Rebecca (1907-1983) 344
Todd Albert (1965-) 197
Trisha (1980-) 196
Tristan 198
Wanda Ann (1957-) 196
Willard Milton (1928-1974) 196

Kitchen
(--?--) 377

Kitklang
Nophot (1953-) 495

Kitson
James 103
Rosa 273

Kitzing
Hannelor Frieda Hermine (1933-) 420

Klacik
Denise Ann 473
Thomas 473

Klahr
Emma 80

Klein
(--?--) 110
Jacqueline 248
John F. 248
Michael 248

Klews
(--?--) (1963-) 349
Blanche 349
Daniel 349
Debra 349
Earl 349
Earl Jr. (1957-1963) 349
Karen 349
Peggy 349

Klick
George 211
John Wilson (1900-1958) 211
Sadie A. 227

Kline
Bruce Francis 427
C.K. (2003-) 427
Carl Vincent (2003-) 427
Caroline Emma (1870-1950) 297
Carrie 247
Denise (1954-) 307
Drew Carlos (1990-) 152, 355, 450
Elvira Mae (1894-1941) 314
George 240, 297
Hannah (1861-1950) 240
Helen (1926-) 442
Jesse Curtis (1979-) 427
Joseph Harris 427
Kevin Daniel (1978-) 427
Kurt Robert (1985-) 152, 355, 450
Laura Ashley (1982-) 427
Marguerite (1928-) 442
Noah (1860-1940) 442
Ray 194
Raymond A. (Rev.) (1897-1937) 442
Raymond A. Jr. (1927-) 442
Raymond A. Rev. (1897-1937) 442
Robert Warren 152
Wanda Joan (1941-1983) 194

Klineyoung
Esther M. 408

Klinger
(--?--) 100, 117, 122, 166, 368
(--?--) (1894-1894) 350
(--?--) (1934-1934) 473
(--?--) (1999-) 357
Aaron A. (1860-1914) 81
Aaron H. (1887-1911) 401
Abraham (1836-) 297
Abraham (1867-1950) 122
Ada Cleda (1885-1961) 418
Ada Irene (1914-2001) 345
Ada May (1906-2003) 170
Adam 114, 131
Adam (1860-1914) 81
Adam Monroe (1877-1925) 65
Adelia (1868-1926) 73
Adie (1885-1961) 418

Name	Page
Adriane Allyn	317
Agatha Catherine (1837-1888)	297
Agnes (1862-1926)	100
Agnes (1865-1937)	442
Agnes (1890-1961)	81
Agnes E. (1873-1952)	416
Agness (1878-1956)	398
Albert (1914-1914)	65
Albert Earl (1888-1957)	94
Albert Garfield (1884-)	59
Albert Hyram (1872-1960)	442
Albert Jefferson (1883-1970)	64
Alex (1997-)	348
Alexander (1805-1876)	398
Alexander W. (1875-1945)	146
Alexander Xavier (1997-)	348
Alfred (1847-1882)	397
Alfred (1851-1923)	398
Alfred (1851-1937)	249
Alfred (1859-1947)	393
Alfred Raymond (1918-2007)	381
Alfred Raymond Jr. (1942-2001)	381
Alfred Stanley (1902-1968)	455
Alice Christianna (1884-1968)	485
Alice E. (1937-)	341
Alice Elise (1895-1989)	382
Alice Jane (1874-)	430
Alice Regina (1903-1968)	147
Alice Sara (1904-1995)	83
Allen E. (1910-)	136, 459
Allen G. (1881-1964)	343
Allen Henry (1905-1947)	125
Allen P. (1894-1960)	432
Allen Timothy (1894-1960)	432
Allison	113
Alma E.	127, 342
Alma Marie (1910-1974)	129, 470
Alma R. (1908-1994)	62
Almeda Magdalena (1863-1947)	407
Almedia and Almata (1863-1947)	407
Aloma (1858-1928)	99
Alphus S. II	456
Alphus Stanley (1921-1990)	455
Alta (1884-1968)	485
Alva E. and Amelia (1882-1963)	374
Alvaretta (1882-1963)	374
Alvin (1893-1978)	490
Alvin Elias (1920-1997)	336, 445, 495
Alyssa Marie (1990-)	193, 339, 446
Amanda (1845-)	88
Amanda (1874-)	430
Amanda (1997-)	473
Amanda E. (1865-1916)	394
Amber Tye Cetess (1982-)	59
Amelia (1846-1920)	93, 451
Amelia Anne (2003-)	86
Amelia E. (1854-1914)	378
Amelia Loretta (1872-1954)	457
Ammon Lawrence (1893-1986)	386
Amy (1911-)	93
Amy Jo	395
Amy Louise (1962-1983)	469
Andrew	131
Andrew T. (1976-)	250
Andy	147, 456
Angela Marie (1968-)	347
Angeline, Anjeline, and Anna (1856-)	357
Angie	88
Ann Julian (1824-1854)	310
Anna A. (1922-)	456
Anna Catherine (1841-1901)	69
Anna Cebilla (1875-1897)	356
Anna E.	78
Anna E. (1929-2012)	376
Anna Julianna and Angelina (1824-1854)	310
Anna L. (1905-1983)	84
Anna Mae (1931-)	82
Anna Margaret (1902-1982)	295
Anna Maria (1838-)	397
Anna Maria Carolina (1841-1913)	329
Anna Olive (1913-)	386
Anna R. (1911-1958)	64
Anna S. (1865-1944)	406
Anna Zimmerman (1911-1958)	64
Anne E. (1879-1956)	374
Annette	385
Annie (1929-2012)	376
Annie B. (1879-1975)	398
Annie E. (1873-1931)	56
Annie Jannette (1892-1893)	382
Annie M. (1886-)	430
Annie Sevilla (1865-1925)	119
Annie W. (1865-1944)	406
Anthony	89
Anthony Phillip (1964-)	114
Anthony Robert	116
April	75
Archie (1903-)	80
Archie Clyde (1889-1964)	381
Ardie (1888-1950)	356
Arlene (1919-)	360
Arlene Danetta (1938-)	438
Arlene E. (1928-2014)	82
Arlene June (1927-2013)	361
Arlene R. (1917-1990)	401
Arthur (1878-)	98
Arthur Allen (1923-2003)	249, 317
Arthur B. (1902-)	378
Arthur E. (1888-1950)	356
Arthur G. (1909-1954)	329
Arthur J. (1880-)	90
Arthur Monroe (1947-)	99
Arthur N. (1932-2006)	329
Artie Alonzo (1888-1950)	356
Ashley	131
Audrey D. (2005-2008)	347
Audrey M.	439
Augustus (1912-1999)	221
Austin Ray (1911-1979)	440
B. Hope	124
Barbara	434, 493, 494
Barbara (1942-)	399
Barbara Jean (1936-)	85
Barbara S. (1860-1946)	223
Barry	377
Barry Paul (1946-)	359
Beatrice D. (1911-1914)	327
Beatrice Irene (1919-2006)	65
Beatrice M. (1911-)	80
Becky I.	458

Belton Eugene (1921-2001) 107
Belton Garfield (1899-1970) 107
Belva E. (1896-1989) 91
Benjamin F. (1860-1942) 99
Benneville (1829-1849) 407
Bernice (1912-1913) 380
Bernice Pauline (1895-1975) 400
Bertha E. (1884-) 87
Bertram L. (1931-2013) 201
Bessie Alice (1910-1986) 77
Bessie Aurelia (1887-1918) 381
Bessie Faye (1888-1943) 378
Bessie Hilda (1902-1998) 414
Bessie May (1879-1920) 397
Bette C. (1924-2011) 490
Betty (1833-1886) 49
Betty A. (1930-2004) 443
Betty Elnora (1923-) 383
Betty Ethel (1932-) 62
Betty F. (1927-) 79
Betty I. (1925-2017) 82
Betty Jane (1935-2012) 402
Betty Jane Mae (1926-) 456
Betty June (1927-2014) 129
Betty L. (1935-2012) 402
Betty Mae (1925-2001) 439
Betty May (1927-1996) 128, 342
Beulah Annora (1887-1972) 436
Beverly Sue (1962-) 469
Billie Jo 108
Billy (1927-1993) 328
Birtha (1884-) 87
Blair Alton (1924-1942) 456
Blanche Irene (1918-2007) 127, 342
Blanche O. (1894-1933) 90
Bonita 334, 351, 444
Bonita Eileen (1958-) 193, 339, 446
Bonnie 349
Bonnie (1958-) 193
Bonnie Marie (1961-) 118
Braden 124
Brady 493
Brady Sam (1866-1949) 356
Brenda 124, 439
Brenda Lee (1950-) 127, 342
Brenna A. 79
Brenton Anthony (1985-) 114
Brian 78
Brian Lamar (1962-) 193, 339, 446
Brian R. 92
Bridget C. 439
Brittany 266
Brittney Kay (1986-) 469
Brodrick 456
Bruce 78
Bruce H. 341
Bruce James (1941-) 475
Bruce W. (1912-1974) 222
Bryan (1962-) 193
Bryant Edwin (1923-1988) 495
Bryant R. (1939-) 339, 446
Calvin 377
Calvin Charles (1889-1970) 201
Calvin Gifford (1923-1993) 58
Calvin Gifford Jr. (1943-) 58

Carl Allen (1929-1989) 124
Carl Collier (1903-1978) 362
Carl E. (1936-) 341
Carl Harlan (1932-) 469
Carl L. 359
Carl Raymond (1920-2002) 87
Carl Richard (1932-) 323
Carlos A. (1902-) 457
Carlos Albert (1899-1920) 464
Carlos Edwin (1900-1968) 333, 443
Carlos Grant (1923-2014) 461
Carol 494
Carol (1956-) 384
Carol Ann (1938-) 349
Carol Ann (1947-) 338, 369, 445
Carol J. 87
Carol Jean (1941-) 131
Carol K. (1934-) 396
Carole A. 359
Carole L. 200
Carolina (1826-1895) 388
Caroline 151, 449
Caroline (1826-1895) 388
Caroline (1844-) 427
Caroline Ellen (1890-) 430
Carolyn 337, 445
Carolyn Lois (1939-) 359
Carolyn Marie (1929-2011) 456
Carrie 448
Carrie (1922-) 78
Carrie A. and Caroline Vesta (1885-1971) 431
Carrie Anerva (1878-1938) 467
Carrie E. (-1900) 401
Carrie Edna (1896-1905) 342
Carrie Elizabeth (1866-) 72
Carrie Ellen (1897-1924) 463
Carrie Enerva and Carrie Minerva (1878-1938) 467
Carrie Etna (1897-1924) 463
Carrie Rebecca (1879-1979) 81
Carrie V. (1918-) 346
Carrie Vesta (1885-1971) 431
Casandra (1925-) 327
Catharine 316
Catharine (-1848) 210
Catharine (1815-1847) 66
Catharine (1831-) 407
Catharine (1849-1892) 459
Catharine (1852-1854) 332
Catharine (1871-) 119
Catharine (1879-1946) 479
Catharine Jane (1857-1925) 385
Catherine (-1858) 49
Catherine Anna (1850-1935) 88
Catherine Edith (1886-) 418
Catherine Emma (1924-1997) 128
Catherine M. (1875-1952) 374
Catherine Senora (1871-1937) 364
Cathy S. 337, 445
Cerenus (1850-1921) 398
Ceylon (1929-2011) 128
Chantelle Alicia (1982-) 348
Charlene Kay (1956-) 192, 339, 446
Charles (1824-1887) 90
Charles (1888-1959) 66
Charles (1915-) 376

Charles (1961-) ... 350
Charles A. (1888-1964) ... 401
Charles A. (1897-1897) ... 401
Charles Arthur (1881-1939) ... 398
Charles Daniel (1877-1956) ... 479
Charles David (1929-) ... 129
Charles E. (1885-) ... 118
Charles E. (1885-1934) ... 98
Charles E. (1918-) ... 68, 122
Charles E. (1926-1989) ... 82
Charles Edgar (1905-1981) ... 439
Charles Edwin (1853-1916) ... 61
Charles Edwin (1887-1888) ... 474
Charles Edwin Jr. (1874-1927) ... 61
Charles F. (1857-1917) ... 391
Charles Franklin (1891-1949) ... 122
Charles Franklin Jr. (1923-1988) ... 123
Charles Frazier (1922-2008) ... 383
Charles Frederick (1867-1937) ... 92
Charles Harvey (1900-) ... 356
Charles Henry (1881-1971) ... 81
Charles M. (1927-2009) ... 443
Charles Milton (1860-1861) ... 431
Charles Milton (1864-1940) ... 435
Charles Milton and Carlos Milton (1877-1918) ... 459
Charles Monroe (1855-1905) ... 98
Charles Monroe (1878-1956) ... 68, 122
Charles Monroe (1917-1962) ... 98
Charles Oliver (1873-) ... 430
Charles Oscar (1909-1989) ... 341
Charles R. (1900-1956) ... 128, 470
Charles Ray (1883-) ... 94
Charles Richard (1930-1979) ... 62
Charles Ronald (1944-) ... 99
Charles W. (1910-) ... 80
Charles W. (1927-) ... 92
Charles William (1895-1970) ... 395
Charlotte (-2005) ... 125
Charlotte (1896-1935) ... 405
Charlotte (1945-) ... 359
Charlotte Betty (1923-2013) ... 66
Chauncey L. (1904-1979) ... 87
Cherie ... 108
Cheryl ... 387
Chester Arthur (1881-1939) ... 398
Chester Leroy (1928-2003) ... 334, 351, 444
Chester R. (1917-1981) ... 399
Chip or Gene (1940-1987) ... 85
Chris E. (1962-2014) ... 79
Chris V. ... 359
Chrisann ... 456
Christian Phillip (1993-) ... 114
Christiana (1861-1932) ... 101
Christine Angela (1984-) ... 381
Christine E. (1963-) ... 58
Christopher Norman (1974-) ... 116
Cindy (1959-) ... 338
Cindy Lou ... 82
Cinzia (1971-) ... 381
Clair ... 384
Clair Marden (1935-) ... 384
Claire and Clara M. (1882-1957) ... 481
Clara A. (1878-1900) ... 132
Clara A. (1923-1996) ... 403
Clara E. (1923-) ... 380
Clara Emma McClaida (1882-1957) ... 481
Clara Mala (1878-1900) ... 132
Clarence (1888-) ... 56
Clarence E. (1908-1968) ... 344
Clarence Franklin (1896-1954) ... 76
Clarence G. (1925-2017) ... 78
Clarence M. (1930-1998) ... 344
Clarence M. (1958-) ... 344
Clarence Mark (1889-1959) ... 58
Clarence Raymond (1899-1960) ... 468
Clarence W. (1914-1970) ... 63
Clark L. (1917-1939) ... 82
Claude (1882-1969) ... 377
Claude Albert (1903-1983) ... 439
Claude Sylvester Jr. (1927-2001) ... 439
Claudine A. (1910-1987) ... 398
Clayton Daniel (1886-1965) ... 66
Clifford H. ... 75
Clinton Charles (1868-1961) ... 91
Clinton J. (1905-1963) ... 328
Cloyd (1903-1983) ... 439
Clyde Gabriel Joseph (1908-1979) ... 380
Colin Joseph ... 399
Collin Chad (2000-) ... 473
Connie (1941-1999) ... 347
Constance Mae (1941-1999) ... 347
Cora (1875-) ... 119
Craig R. ... 87
Curtin (1878-1888) ... 221
Cynthia ... 92, 201
Cynthia (1954-) ... 414
Cynthia Ann ... 404
Cynthia Louise (1959-) ... 338, 369, 445
Daisy Alvena (1902-1967) ... 218, 468
Dale (1955-) ... 131
Dale Eugene (1953-) ... 108, 472
Dale George (1969-) ... 473
Dan ... 151
Dane Andrew (1960-) ... 323
Daniel ... 131
Daniel (1816-1899) ... 448
Daniel (1823-1837) ... 210
Daniel (1842-1863) ... 61
Daniel A. (1834-1908) ... 407
Daniel Cyrus (1897-1985) ... 437
Daniel David (1857-1858) ... 430
Daniel Edward (1885-1968) ... 401
Daniel Emanuel (1899-1956) ... 335, 369
Daniel Eston (1886-1947) ... 346
Daniel Jr. (1852-1919) ... 459
Daniel Lewis (1870-1873) ... 387
Daniel Lewis (1958-) ... 347
Daniel M. (1860-1919) ... 333, 342
Daniel Monroe (1876-) ... 430
Daniel S. (1851-1909) ... 468
Daniel S. (1852-) ... 221
Danielle Lynn (1983-) ... 347
Darla ... 457
Daryl Robert (1978-) ... 348
David ... 63, 439
David B. (1860-) ... 89
David Calvin (1870-1931) ... 457
David Calvin (1939-) ... 458
David Daniel (1917-2013) ... 222
David Dean (1941-) ... 334, 351, 444

David Grant (1961-)	462
David L.	87
David S.	396
David S. (1827-1916)	146, 457
David Stanley (1958-)	131
Dawn Lanette (1942-)	399
Dawn Lynette (1961-)	473
Dean	75
Dean E. (1953-2006)	396
Dean Ellwood (1936-1991)	131
Dean H.	81
Dean Jr.	131
Dean M.	395
Dean R. (1927-2011)	395
Debie Jo (1956-)	108
Deborah Ann (1959-)	463
Deborah K.	404
Debra A.	87
Debra Louise (1955-)	347
Delaney Katherine (2001-)	193, 339, 446
Delphine M. (1928-)	72
Denn A. (1936-)	125
Dennis	439, 493
Dennis (1945-)	376
Dennis (1954-)	384
Dennis (1968-)	377
Dennis Errol (1944-)	337, 369, 445
Dennis Eugene (1929-)	130
Dennis G.	341
Dennis Lee (1959-)	347, 473
DeWayne (1936-)	92
Diane	131
Diane M. (1942-)	335, 444
Dolores Catherine (1931-2007)	439
Donald (1898-)	378
Donald A.	130
Donald A. (1918-1995)	406
Donald Alfred (1918-1995)	393
Donald Clarence (1934-2012)	456
Donald Eugene (1940-)	399
Donald Eugene Jr. (1963-)	399
Donald H.	75
Donald Martin (1939-)	458
Donald Paul (1951-)	340, 446
Donald William (1919-2004)	395
Donna	377
Donna J.	62
Donna Lee (1946-)	114
Donna M.	154
Donna M. (1947-2016)	376
Donna Marie (1951-)	340, 446
Doris	341
Doris (1924-)	457
Doris Ethel (1923-)	362
Dorothy	374
Dorothy (1913-2000)	94
Dorothy (1916-2002)	222
Dorothy (1917-1974)	386
Dorothy (1929-)	328
Dorothy (1941-)	335, 444
Dorothy Alice (1928-)	124
Dorothy Anna (1923-)	361
Dorothy Edith (1945-)	195, 492
Dorothy Helen (1927-)	384
Dorothy Irene (1928-2001)	62
Dorothy M. (1919-)	457
Dorothy Mae (1922-2003)	125
Dorothy Mae (1922-2015)	415
Dosie Darlene (1888-1952)	410
Douglas	92, 147
Douglas (1967-)	338, 369, 445
Douglas Howard (1957-2015)	363
Douglas Robert	63
Earl Clyde (1889-1948)	378
Earl Ernest (1917-1959)	359
Earl Eston (1922-1995)	317
Earl L. (1922-1995)	317
Earl Lloyd (1898-1995)	92
Earl Stanford (1916-1998)	493
Earla Emma (1907-1963)	77
Earle D. (1903-)	84
Ed (1885-)	118
Edgar DeWitt (1897-)	385
Edith C. (1894-1982)	92
Edith Catherine (1882-1947)	404
Edith Jane (1937-)	114
Edith Julian (1883-1952)	66
Edith May (1883-1952)	66
Edmund E. (1887-)	430
Edna Irene (1892-1985)	415
Edna Viola (1884-1885)	381
Edward	124
Edward (1832-1878)	295
Edward (1886-)	459
Edward (1887-)	430
Edward (1887-1968)	81
Edward Ellsworth (1877-)	93
Edward Miller (1886-1959)	223
Edwin (1876-)	65
Edwin (1923-)	327
Edwin C. (1900-1968)	333
Edwin Charles (1902-1985)	62
Edwin Guerney (1879-1950)	327
Edwin Gurney Jr. (1900-1966)	327
Edwin M. (1869-1948)	416
Edwin Ray (1894-1981)	356
Edwin S. (1886-)	136, 459
Effie Emeline (1907-2006)	416
Eileen Gwenerve (1931-2004)	323
Eileen Marie (1931-2004)	323
Eileen May (1932-2015)	334, 351, 419, 444
Eileen R.	341
Eilene (1932-2015)	334
Elda Donna (1918-)	222
Eleanor (1903-1903)	84
Eleanor (1931-)	436
Eleanor Jane (1943-)	387
Eleanor Phyllis (1933-2014)	113
Eleanore Cora (1932-)	352
Elemira (1851-1934)	454
Eli (1844-1932)	72
Elias (1822-1889)	83
Elias (1835-1917)	217
Elias (1844-1908)	418
Elias (1844-1932)	72
Elias (1849-1926)	93
Elias (1850-1927)	374
Elias William (1872-1929)	335
Elisabeth (1834-1873)	397
Elisabeth (1845-)	447

Elisabeth Allens (1864-)	358
Elise (1885-1891)	81
Eliza (1879-)	65
Elizabeth	177
Elizabeth (-2009)	122
Elizabeth (1825-1858)	99
Elizabeth (1831-1921)	248
Elizabeth (1833-1886)	49
Elizabeth (1835-)	363
Elizabeth (1853-1903)	332
Elizabeth Christina (1845-)	397
Elizabeth Ellen (1864-)	358
Elizabeth May (1908-1971)	64
Elizabeth Sarah (1913-2009)	114
Elizabeth Schwalm (1850-1930)	220
Elizabeth Thelma (1925-2008)	125
Ella J. (1929-1993)	405
Ella Katie (1878-1970)	78
Ella Rebecca (1876-1950)	80
Ellen (1890-)	430
Ellen (1909-2000)	86
Ellen Ann (1957-)	59
Ellen Ethel (1909-2000)	86
Ellen May (1901-1967)	383
Ellen Vertie (1904-1950)	328
Elma Marie (1908-1913)	171
Elmer (1897-1939)	82
Elmer Elsworth (1865-1947)	91
Elmer F. (1888-)	118
Elmer Michael (1877-1954)	126, 342
Elmira Myah (1851-1927)	316, 363
Eloma (1858-1928)	99
Elsie Louise (1938-)	385
Elsie Mae (1924-)	323
Elsie Oneda (1923-1924)	492
Elsworth (1862-1933)	152, 431
Elvin Elias (1923-2007)	82
Elwood Elias (1896-1955)	376
Elwood Elsworth (1914-)	376
Elwood L.	341
Elwood Michael (1890-1966)	65
Emaline (1851-1911)	97
Emanual (1843-1917)	83
Emanuel (1843-1908)	90
Emanuel (1856-1928)	180, 474
Emanuel E. and Eston Emil (1890-1940)	342
Emanuel T. (1843-1917)	83
Emerson (2013-)	131
Emery S. (1889-1901)	398
Emily Kathryn (2003-)	473
Emma (1851-1911)	97
Emma (1868-)	61
Emma Cebilla and Emma S. (1875-1897)	356
Emma Christiana (1913-2013)	489
Emma Clara (1855-1946)	391
Emma Elizabeth (1894-1940)	382
Emma Emelia (1861-)	358
Emma Emilie (1861-)	358
Emma J. (1854-1929)	99
Emma Jane (1859-1933)	51
Emma L. (1891-1976)	378
Emma L. (1892-)	99
Emma Louisa (1898-1978)	356
Emma Louise (1881-1947)	468
Emma M. (1880-1956)	374
Emmanuel (1860-)	81
Emory R. (1885-1967)	378
Enjaline (1856-)	357
Eric (1978-1978)	250, 258
Eric Donald (1970-)	340, 446
Erline (1917-1990)	401
Erma Catherine (1919-2010)	494
Erma L. (1923-1994)	405
Ernest	405
Ernest L.	339, 446
Ernest Lamar (1946-)	317
Ernest Leroy (1920-2008)	317
Ernest Luther (1925-2011)	129, 184
Esther (1882-1947)	404
Esther Daisy (1929-1971)	434
Esther Julia (1923-)	362
Esther Kathryn (1925-2008)	492
Esther R. (1919-2005)	404
Eston Emanuel (1890-1940)	127, 342
Eston Isaiah (1899-1966)	494
Eston Raymond (1895-1972)	250, 317
Ethel Arline (1914-1991)	362
Ethel Ellen (1909-2000)	86
Ethel Laura (1900-1972)	61
Ethel M. (1904-)	378
Eugene David (1930-1955)	360
Eugene George (1932-2010)	79
Eugene Jackson (1934-1948)	353
Eugene Kermit (1949-)	489
Eugene Lamar (1946-)	317
Eugene or Gene (1905-1997)	84
Eugene R. (1935-2005)	82
Eva (1794-1870)	132
Eva (1883-)	98
Eva (1905-)	360
Eva and Catherine (1901-1986)	333
Eva Catharina (1820-1887)	209
Eva Christiana (1912-1993)	490
Eva Christine (1912-1993)	490
Eva Elizabeth (1840-1917)	307
Eva Juliana (1919-)	340, 446
Eva L. (1904-)	98
Eva May (1907-)	65
Eva May (1909-1909)	469
Eva May (1915-1973)	89, 174, 243, 440
Eva N. (1900-)	56
Eva Naomi (1927 2017)	341
Eva O. (1895-)	99
Eva Rena (1906-2005)	81
Eve Elizabeth (1794-1870)	132
Eve Elizabeth (1834-)	100
Evelyn	387
Evelyn (1917-2015)	359
Evelyn (1924-)	362
Evelyn Alberta (1931-2007)	80
Evelyn Elsie (1914-1952)	233, 432
Evelyn Kathleen (1927-2011)	118
Evelyn May (1936-)	385
Fannie and Fay (1917-1992)	348
Fannie Etta (1871-)	426
Fay (1888-1943)	378
Fay M. (1917-2004)	404
Faye Frances (1917-1992)	348
Felix H. (1872-1926)	217
Ferle Machala (1905-1988)	415

Fern Lillian (1925-1933) 318
Ferne A. (1926-2003) 327
Fietta 100
Fietta E. (1863-1932) 118
Flora A. (1874-) 126
Flora M. (1905-1990) 457
Florence J. (1899-1939) 387
Florence Viola (1903-1920) 438
Floris (1908-1910) 362
Floyd Albert (1912-1986) 472
Floyd Elmer (1925-2010) 129
Forest Eugene Jr. (1940-1987) 85
Forrest Edward (1901-1983) 351
Forrest Eugene Sr. (1905-1997) 84
Forrest G. 341
Forrest Gerald (2009-) 86
Frances (1861-) 406
Frances Madeline (1928-) 322
Francis (1851-1910) 170, 317, 364, 459, 468
Francis (1870-) 360
Francis and Fannie (1861-) 406
Francis Oliver (1892-1972) 457
Francis V. (1862-) 118
Francis W. (1862-) 118
Frank (1886-1957) 375
Frank Edward (1896-1963) 406
Frank Eugene (1973-) 108
Frank G. 64
Frank M. (1904-1904) 125
Franklin Adam (1875-1928) 459, 482
Franklin Anthony (1888-1939) 403
Franklin C. (1925-2012) 436
Fred 383
Fred (1895-1978) 493
Fred (1901-1920) 465
Fred Joseph (1911-1956) 221
Frederick 493
Frederick (1844-1907) 92
Frederick (1881-) 98
Frederick Clair (1934-) 384
Frederick Daniel (1901-1920) 465
Frederick E. (1874-1942) 417
Frederick Monroe (1895-1978) 493
Frederick S. (1856-1927) 222
Gabriel (1855-1941) 379
Galen C. (1919-1988) 333
Galen Chester (1914-1991) 65
Galen H. (1902-1902) 343
Galen Oscar (1919-1988) 333, 350, 443
Gary 60, 75, 456
Gary Galen (1947-) 333
Gary Lamar (1956-) 414
Gary Lee (1954-1974) 78
Gary Oscar (1947-) 333, 350, 443
Gayle Yvonne (1949-) 107
Gene (1938-) 335, 444
Gene L. 341
Gene Ray (1959-) 59
Gene Reed (1938-) 347
Gene Reed II (1976-) 347
George 81
George (1880-1966) 78
George (1915-) 359
George Allen (1881-1964) 343
George B. (1897-1984) 357

George Brady (1867-1949) 358
George D. (1898-) 378
George Dale (1942-) 114
George E. (1886-1895) 489
George E. (1938-2013) 92
George Elmer (1896-1918) 437
George Elmer (1936-2003) 128, 342
George Eugene (1923-1998) 117
George Franklin (1876-) 120
George Franklin (1897-1984) 357
George M. (1854-1911) 127, 332, 443
George Morris (1889-1934) 358
George P. (1798-1880) 310
George R. (1924-1997) 443
George W. (1876-) 120
George W. (1918-1918) 380
George William (1910-2000) 358
Georgina Delphine (1942-2009) 114
Gertie (1916-2002) 345
Gertrude E. (1894-) 223
Gertrude Isabella (1894-1977) 103, 403
Gertrude Isabelle (1894-1977) 103
Gertrude Mae (1916-2002) 345, 369
Getrude Alice (1898-1983) 124
Gilbert A. (1912-1962) 65
Ginny (1918-) 434
Gladys 64
Gladys Elizabeth (1915-1998) 348
Gladys Emma (1924-) 384
Gladys V. (1909-) 378
Glen D. 341
Glenn 113
Glenn A. (1912-2011) 489
Glenn Lamar (1944-1991) 132
Glenn R. (1925-) 357
Glenn Robert (1905-1970) 64
Goldie Inez (1918-2007) 415
Gordon E. M. (1873-1970) 83
Gordon Edwin (1885-1943) 170
Grace C. (1911-) 458
Grace Elaine (1966-) 473
Grace Elizabeth (1908-) 380
Grace Maria (1914-1990) 396
Grace Marie (1890-1964) 94
Grace Rebecca (1998-) 108
Grant Andrew (2000-) 108
Grant Clyde (1938-1995) 380
Grant Elwood (1929-) 384
Guerney (1881-) 126
Guerney Edward (1892-1957) 125
Guerney Israel (1882-1936) 343
Gunnar (2006-) 347
Gurney Allen (1892-1965) 249, 258, 317
Gurney Elwood Sr. (1928-1988) 472
Gurty (1878-1888) 221
Gustav Frederick (1912-1999) 221
Guy (1931-2015) 463
Guy A. (1919-1971) 434
Guy E. 406
Guy Edwin (1895-1961) 460
Guy Franklin (1897-1903) 396
Guy G. (1915-2001) 341
Guy G. (1927-2012) 79
Guy Irvin (1917-1917) 493
Guy Junior (1928-2008) 340, 446

Guy W. (1890-1922) 87
Guy W. (1919-2010) 87
Hanna (1807-1885) 420
Hannah (1835-) 100
Hannah (1838-1923) 389
Hannah (1842-1886) 363
Hannah E. (1865-1945) 454
Hannah M. (1909-1975) 81
Harlan Austin (1902-1966) 468
Harold (1916-) 377
Harold (1935-2012) 376
Harold E. (1921-1968) 399
Harold Edwin (1919-1984) 349
Harold J. (1894-1964) 376
Harold Lamar (1931-) 414
Harold Stanley (1931-2006) 341
Harriet Faye (1926-) 377
Harry 92
Harry (1933-) 341
Harry A. (1894-1944) 406
Harry A. (1896-) 457
Harry Albert (1897-1964) 318
Harry Allen (1887-1956) 340
Harry Bennett (1912-1997) 396
Harry Calvin (1881-1902) 94
Harry Clarence (1880-1947) 84
Harry Daniel (1883-1940) 468
Harry Elmer (1906-1980) 403
Harry Franklin (1880-1919) 59
Harry H. (1881-1943) 221
Harry Harvey (1876-1953) 77
Harry Jack (1930-) 92
Harry L. (1899-1910) 360
Harry Samuel (1884-1938) 346
Harry T. (1863-1927) 393
Harry Victor (1886-1958) 65
Harry W. (1873-1874) 398
Harry Walter (1909-1978) 90, 356
Harry Wilbur (1892-1987) 393
Harry William (1893-1969) 385
Harry Wilson (1875-1946) 91
Harvena (1919-2012) 75
Harvenia (1919-2012) 75
Harvey (1906-1978) 79
Harvey Edward (1869-1930) 125
Harvey Wilson (1918-2002) 75
Hattie Catherine (1903-1965) 111
Hattie Irene (1900-1969) 121, 207, 318
Hattie Milissa (1882-1960) 379
Hayden Morris (1894-1940) 361
Heath Allen 115
Heather 122
Helen Alice (1926-1986) 222
Helen Arlean (1909-1916) 396
Helen Irene (1913-2001) 339, 446
Helen M. (1905-1927) 62
Henry (1847-) 430
Henry (1904-) 92
Henry Allen and Harry E. (1887-1956) 340
Henry John (1853-1901) 401
Henry Robert (1944-) 116
Henry Roland (1883-1969) 380
Henry S. (1862-1942) 489
Henry Wadsworth (1917-2003) 116
Henry Wilson (1888-1972) 489

Herman Henry (1922-1987) 195, 492
Herman Paul (1913-1959) 77
Hermie Phroda (1890-1958) 411
Heyram A. (1878-) 446
Hilda Louise (1910-1993) 296
Homer (1921-1921) 443
Homer Albert (1924-1993) 403
Homer Alvin (1907-1991) 338, 425, 445
Homer Auburn (1886-1946) 410
Homer C. (1901-1988) 387
Homer Edwin (1883-1952) 106, 402
Homer Jonathan (1917-1971) 474
Homer Lee (1889-1956) 361
Homer Marlin (1909-1974) 346
Homer Ramer (1883-1884) 398
Homer Wilber (1903-1927) 323
Howard (1876-) 374
Howard Albert (1911-1955) 348
Howard J. (1924-) 81
Howard R. (1901-1987) 92
Hy. F. (1879-) 126
Iain (2011-) 131
Ida (1888-1943) 99
Ida (1910-) 64
Ida Emma (1874-1920) 296
Ida Lauretta (1921-2013) 333
Ida Loretta (1921-2013) 333, 351, 443
Ida Pearl (1876-1937) 63
Immanuel (1856-1928) 474
Inez Mae (1907-1994) 93
Infant (1896-1896) 124
Infant (1898-1898) 125
Infant (1910-1910) 360
Infant Daughter (1920-1920) 357
Infant Son (1901-1901) 146
Ira Charles (1915-1993) 467
Ira G. (1911-) 360
Ira G. (1912-1983) 80
Ira Jacob (1897-1969) 180, 494
Irene A. (1913-1990) 402
Irene F. (1901-1986) 396
Irene M. (1916-1982) 78
Irene M. (1939-) 341
Irene May (1906-1983) 475
Irene S. (1915-) 346
Irene S. and Lillie Irene (1900-1987) 108
Irma (1923-1994) 405
Irvin (1876-1937) 126
Irvin Albert (1886-1958) 381
Irvin Albert Jr. (1916-1989) 381
Irvin William (1902-1975) 327
Irwin Ray (1920-2002) 346
Isaac (1851-1935) 80
Isaac Jay (1876-1920) 83
Isabel Gladys (1931-1996) 129, 470
Isabella J. (1915-2011) 490
Isabella Jane (1864-1916) 385
Isabelle (1915-2011) 490
Isabelle B. (1910-2000) 396
Israel (1826-1900) 210
Israel (1878-1879) 84
Ivah Angelina (1914-1917) 492
Ivan C. (1924-1924) 395
Ivan Johnny (1921-2010) 494
Ivan R. (1902-1978) 92

Name	Page
Ivie R. (1917-)	80
J. Henry (1825-1905)	356
Jack (1934-2012)	456
Jacky Lee (1945-)	440
Jacob (1823-)	310
Jacob (1838-1903)	416
Jacob E. (1843-1899)	122
Jacob P. Klinger (1813-1883)	431
Jacob S. (1813-1883)	176, 431
Jacqueline	88, 92
Jacqueline Janice (1925-2007)	349
Jacqueline L. (1959-)	128, 342
Jadee	108
Jake	363
James	92, 267
James (1855-1916)	402
James (1856-1889)	65
James Arthur (1880-)	90, 356
James Daniel (1953-1992)	347
James David (1891-1964)	489
James E. (1914-1996)	402
James E. (1929-1968)	79
James Eugene (1938-)	115
James Eugene Jr.	115
James Franklin (1889-1965)	65
James H. (1935-2015)	90, 356
James Lee (1945-)	336, 444
James Robert (1906-1972)	384
James Robert (1915-1992)	115
James Robert (1926-)	384
Jamie Leigh (1979-)	414
Jan (1917-2008)	376
Jane Elizabeth (1965-)	469
Janelle	250, 258
Janet Marie (1938-1969)	82
Janet Marie (1944-)	385
Janet Renee (1950-)	127, 342
Janette Mabel (1936-)	465
Janice	75, 113, 267
Janice M. (1946-)	379
Janice Mary (1956-)	99
Jarod Matthew (1980-)	348
Jarred (1980-)	348
Jason (1979-)	336, 445
Jason Lamar (1981-)	414
Jasper Anthony (1886-1957)	87
Jay (1876-1920)	83
Jay W.	62
Jay W. (1905-1955)	406
Jean	75, 267
Jean Alberta (1914-)	94
Jean Charlotte (1919-2003)	123
Jean Elizabeth (1950-2009)	118
Jean Mary (1925-2000)	324
Jean Paul	334, 351, 444
Jeanette	377
Jeanette and Janet (1934-)	383
Jeanne (1940-)	436
Jeanne Irene (1956-)	473
Jeanne V. (1921-1973)	395
Jeannette May (1934-)	383
Jeffrey	82, 266, 494
Jemima Regina (1885-1952)	489
Jenifer (1972-)	336, 445
Jenna M. (1983-)	363
Jennie	205
Jennie (1859-1933)	51
Jennie (1884-1949)	375
Jennie (1909-1989)	79
Jennie E. (1883-1947)	398
Jennie E. (1917-2008)	376
Jennie I. (1896-1970)	126
Jennie M. (1884-1947)	279, 458
Jennifer Anne (1979-)	347
Jennifer Cochran (1975-)	381
Jennifer E.	117
Jeremiah (1861-1939)	406
Jeremy Jacob (1977-)	348
Jerry (1861-1939)	406
Jestina (1830-1859)	100
Jimmy I. (1929-)	81
Joan	79
Joan Emily (1936-)	338, 425, 445
Joan M.	77
Joan Marie (1955-)	475
Joan Ross (1931-)	85
Joanne Ellen (1930-2012)	465
Johann Adam (1810-1885)	426
Johann George (1787-1838)	374
Johann George (1798-1880)	310
Johann Peter (1773-1858)	49
Johann Peter (1796-1879)	209
Johann Philip (1792-1857)	49
Johannes (1811-1872)	49
Johannes (1843-1918)	454
Johannes (1847-1922)	80
Johannes P. (1802-1873)	372
John	60
John (1838-1913)	51
John (1843-1918)	454
John (1847-1922)	80
John (1891-1947)	222
John (1924-)	376
John (1947-1949)	349
John A. (1811-1872)	49
John A. (1837-)	431
John A. (1860-1884)	99
John A. (1866-1939)	60
John Adam (1810-1885)	426
John Adam (1849-)	88
John Adam (1872-1936)	427
John Alexander Alvin (1893-1978)	195, 490
John B. (1894-1946)	402
John D. (1929-2009)	457
John E. (1899-)	457
John Earle (1893-1964)	60
John Earle Jr. (1923-1986)	60
John Elwood (1916-1957)	127, 342
John F. (1893-1944)	92
John F. (1901-1907)	360
John Francis (1870-)	360
John Frazier (1898-1968)	383
John George (1866-1939)	385
John H. (1847-)	430
John Henry (1853-1901)	401
John Henry (1877-1886)	398
John Irvin (1885-1947)	375
John Junior (1932-2008)	383
John Lewis (1926-2000)	376
John Luke (1905-)	380

John M. (1918-)	346
John P. (1802-1873)	372
John Preston (1904-1979)	94
John R.	87
John Robert (1935-1935)	64
John S. (1861-1932)	150
John W. (1943-2005)	493
John W. Jr.	493
John Wesley (1876-1925)	59
Jon Leigh	348
Jonas (1845-1911)	126
Jonas (1856-1889)	65
Jonathan (1838-1922)	418
Jonathan D. (1927-2012)	416
Jonathan Grant (1886-1956)	352, 474
Jonathon	395
Joseph	131
Joseph (1844-1897)	61
Joseph (1908-1941)	401
Joseph Francis (1920-1989)	98
Joseph S. (1879-1916)	221
Josephine Eva (1931-)	383
Josie (1888-1952)	410
Jostia (1830-1859)	100
Joy Anne (1943-1969)	336, 444
Joyce (1932-)	125
Joyce M. (1938-)	403
Joyce Marie (1933-2002)	360
Joyce Marie (1935-2002)	347
Judith Ann (1947-)	116
Judy Pearl (1948-2006)	78
Julia (1873-)	360
Julia Ann (1823-1904)	372
Julia Ann (1860-1863)	385
Juliann (1873-)	360
Julianna (1823-1904)	372
June (1928-)	375
June A.	341
June E.	77
June Elizabeth (1926-)	383
Justin	267
Justin Robert (1981-)	59
Justina (1829-1897)	228
Justina (1847-1909)	210
Kaelynn	250
Kandy	130
Kara	456
Karen	201
Karen (1947-)	387
Karen J.	78, 359
Karen Lynne (1973-)	86
Karen Marie (1954-)	469
Karl	347
Karl Kenneth (1952-2014)	250, 258
Karl Ross (1970-)	86
Kate (1850-1935)	88
Kate (1861-1916)	51
Kate and Emma (1841-1901)	69
Kate E. (1878-1970)	78
Katelyn	267
Katherine	92
Katherine B. (1905-1987)	396
Katherine Estella (1900-1983)	438
Kathryn Ann	439
Kathryn H. (1925-2001)	405
Kathryn Julian (1924-)	341
Kathryn Susan Mae (1949-)	127, 342
Kathryn Susannah (1917-2001)	242
Kathy	201
Kathy Kay (1959-)	108
Kathy M.	436
Katie (1871-)	119
Katie (1875-1952)	374
Katie (1900-1983)	438
Katie A. (1896-1896)	459
Katie Almeda (1901-1986)	333, 350, 419, 443
Katie Beulah (1901-1987)	68, 122
Katie C. (1884-1885)	430
Katie Emmeline (1895-1967)	413
Katie M. (1917-2009)	442
Katie Rebecca (1879-1946)	479
Katie Regina (1894-)	457
Katina S.	87
Kay Lorraine (1947-)	359
Kay M.	359
Keith	82, 357
Keith A. (1952-)	384
Keith Edward (1966-)	463
Keith Kermit (1952-2013)	250, 258
Keith R (1967-)	357
Kelvin	130
Kenneth	130
Kenneth Allen (1946-)	250
Kenneth Alvin (1941-1999)	337, 445
Kenneth Edward (1931-)	463
Kenneth F. (1941-2011)	127, 342
Kenneth Karl (1928-1955)	396
Kenneth Kermit (1924-1991)	250, 258
Kenneth Lamar (1936-)	440
Kenneth Lee (1943-)	385
Kenneth Raymond	381
Kenneth Raymond (1937-1993)	443
Kenneth Ronald (1936-)	65
Kenneth Wayne (1947-)	492
Kermit Wilson (1914-1968)	489
Kevin	75
Kevin Ernest	88
Kevin Floyd (1986-)	473
Kim	493
Kirby Jonathan (1865-1926)	410
Kirk	457
Krista	130
Krista Marie (1971-)	399
Kristi	60
Kristina Marie (2003-)	463
Kristy Elaine (1976-)	472
Kurt Eugene (1979-)	86
Kussandra	250, 258
Lamar R. (1934-1974)	192, 339, 446
Lance Nathanael (1966-)	323
Landon Scott (2006-)	108
Larry Alvin (1932-2015)	341
Larry Dale (1932-1992)	222
Larry Joseph (1944-1993)	114
Larry Lee (1960-)	440
Larry P.	78
Laura (1981-)	363
Laura Agnes (1890-)	415
Laura Belle (1902-1907)	384
Laura S. (1920-1995)	402

Laura V. (1917-2016)	415
Lauren Ashley (1986-)	347
Laurie	201
Laurie Jean	82
Lavia M. (1869-)	418
Lavina (1849-)	80
Leah (1832-1859)	100
Leann	108
Lena (1929-)	201
Lena Mae (1920-2013)	490
Leon Oscar (1919-2001)	335, 444
Leon Oscar Jr. (1947-)	336, 444
Leon Ray (1909-1932)	201
Leona Grace (1891-1937)	385
Leona Irene (1924-1974)	400
Leroy (1904-1904)	360
Leroy E. (1920-2008)	317
Leroy Elias (1911-2000)	341
Leroy H. (1899-1918)	396
Leslie	440
Leslie A.	436
Lester Leroy (1897-1947)	333, 350, 419
Lester Samuel (1899-1958)	361
Lester Walter (1916-2000)	66
Lewis S. (1908-1976)	375
Lidia A. (1869-1931)	90
Lillian C. (1883-1961)	222
Lillian Louise (1863-1953)	393
Lillie (1863-1953)	393
Lillie (1874-)	61
Lillie Errena (1900-1987)	108
Lillie Fay (1906-1990)	326, 454
Lillie M. (1926-)	81
Lillie R. (1878-1960)	80
Lilly (1914-)	66
Linda	383, 493
Linda Elaine (1948-)	362
Linda J. (1950-)	317
Linda M.	456
Linda Marie (1954-)	196, 492
Lisa	81, 92
Lisa (1981-)	363
Liza	344
Lizzie (1850-1930)	220
Lizzie (1866-)	72
Lizzie Mae (1898-1968)	319
Lloyd E. (1918-)	387
Lloyd Edward (1886-1972)	221
Lois	64, 387
Lois E. (1953-)	317
Lonnie E.	79
Lora M. and Laira (1869-)	418
Loretta Frances (1912-2005)	123
Lori Ann (1960-1992)	337, 445
Loriann (1972-)	340, 446
Lorraine Marcella (1933-)	318
Lotta (1868-)	418
Lottie Alice (1893-1981)	393
Lottie Bell (1904-1991)	295
Louis Donald (1925-2002)	124
Louisa (1840-1924)	279
Louisa (1862-1924)	497
Louisa Sevilla (1860-1929)	365
Lousian (1857-)	89
Lucia (1859-1929)	89
Lucie (1916-2007)	339
Lucille M. (1924-)	123
Lucy (1857-)	89
Lucy (1859-1929)	89
Lucy A. (1881-1976)	80
Lucy Alvena (1916-2007)	339, 446
Luella (1911-)	359
Luther E. (1904-1989)	129, 184
Luther G. (1890-1922)	87
Luther L.	75
Luther Ralph (1924-1999)	75
Luther Raymond (1908-1960)	341
Lydia (1813-1858)	66
Lydia (1835-1872)	426
Lydia A. (1858-1916)	392
Lydia A. (1908-1997)	77
Lydia Ann (1858-)	66
Lynn Eugene (1958-1982)	439
Lynsay Michele (1986-)	59
Mabel (1906-1989)	344
Mabel Gertrude (1891-1969)	432
Mabel Pearl (1884-1951)	333, 350, 425, 443
Mabel R. (1894-1978)	378
Mabel R. (1897-)	118
Mabel V. (1911-)	136, 459
Madeline C. (1946-)	362
Mae	129, 485
Mae Elizabeth (1925-1981)	356
Mae Irene (1916-1968)	395
Mae Rebecca (1899-1953)	468
Magdalena (1830-1874)	374
Maggie R. (1872-1948)	119, 416
Maggie, Saloma and Liddie (1880-)	430
Maragetha (1840-)	397
Marcella Sadie (1924-2010)	405
Marcus (1838-1901)	333, 431
Maretta and Mary E. (1847-1908)	418
Margaret (1907-)	59
Margaret (1913-)	375
Margaret Alice (1909-2005)	189
Margaret Elizabeth (1942-)	58
Margaret Ethel (1916-2003)	327
Margaret Jane (1924-2007)	349
Margaret M. (1917-2009)	123
Margaret Marie (1939-)	111, 115
Margaret S. (1880-)	430
Margaret Savilla (1922-2005)	117
Margarette (1897-)	76
Margie J. (1933-2000)	375
Maria (1818-)	209
Maria Anna (1845-1898)	428
Maria Anna (1859-)	358
Maria Anna (1859-1911)	496
Maria Catharine (1847-1922)	213
Maria Elisabeth (1845-)	176, 447
Maria Magdalena (1862-1876)	385
Marian Adelaide (1920-1995)	362
Marian Betty (1924-1989)	222
Marian Kay (1931-)	384
Marian Romaine (1928-2011)	130
Marianne (1962-)	124
Marie (1932-1982)	436
Marie Emma (1923-)	357
Marie Loraine (1925-)	458
Marie Loranna (1925-)	458

Marietta (1847-1908) 418
Marilyn Mildred (1938-) 475
Marissa (1998-) 350
Mark 113
Mark (1922-) 457
Mark Brandon (1990-) 323
Mark David (1953-) 475
Mark Franklin (1902-1981) 322
Mark Franklin (1990-) 323
Mark I. (1922-2008) 402
Mark Monroe (1919-1997) 455
Mark Robert (1911-) 222
Marlin 387
Marlin D. 341
Marlin Emanuel (1917-1993) 492
Marlin Lamar Jr. (1943-2001) 337, 369, 445
Marlin Lee (1921-2011) 337, 369, 445
Marlin Leo and Marlin O. (1921-2011) 337
Marsella Sadie (1924-2010) 405
Martha A. 401
Martha A. (1922-2000) 66
Martha E. (1865-1873) 90
Martha E. (1899-1972) 76
Martha Edna (1902-1902) 438
Martha Eva (1934-2004) 65
Martha Jean (1938-) 90, 356
Martha Mae (1881-1955) 398
Martha Naomi (1906-1977) 380
Martha Priscilla (1922-1997) 117, 416
Martha Viola (1915-2005) 403
Marvin (1940-) 92
Marvin Earl (1935-) 473
Mary 64, 364, 405
Mary (1847-1922) 213
Mary (1853-) 222
Mary (1853-1937) 169
Mary (1859-) 358
Mary (1862-1876) 385
Mary (1867-) 407
Mary (1925-) 457
Mary Alice (1874-1961) 268, 474
Mary Almeda (1904-1971) 414
Mary Ann (1845-1898) 428
Mary Ann (1851-1919) 459
Mary Ann (1874-1948) 76
Mary Ann (1932-) 346
Mary Ann (1947) 243
Mary Ann (1959-) 98
Mary Anna (1859-1911) 496
Mary C. 130, 184
Mary C. (1893-) 378
Mary Catherine (1861-1916) 51
Mary Catherine (1938-) 114
Mary E. (1892-) 118
Mary E. (1894-1973) 404
Mary E. (1900-1978) 402
Mary E. (1915-) 222
Mary Edna (1898-1969) 417
Mary Eleanor (1910-1989) 65
Mary Elizabeth (1911-2002) 83
Mary Ellen (1862-) 351
Mary Ellen (1921-1942) 461
Mary Emma (1893-1973) 74
Mary Emma (1927-2009) 180, 494
Mary Florence (1908-1986) 295
Mary Jane 494
Mary Katherine (1907-1990) 362
Mary Kathlene (1921-2005) 125
Mary Laura (1867-1928) 83
Mary Lou (1948-2008) 440
Mary Louise (1879-1942) 342
Mary Louise (1943-) 115
Mary M. (1853-1854) 89
Mary R. (1897-) 393
Mary Ruby (1899-1996) 96
Mary Savilla 210
Mary Sevilla (1908-1975) 468
Matthew 337, 369, 445, 456
Maud Elnora (1892-1975) 103
Maude (1880-1956) 374
Maude A. (1885-1953) 90
Maude E. (1877-1952) 120, 181, 320
Maude Elizabeth (1892-1975) 103
Maude Mae (1898-1960) 147
Max Edwin (1952-) 462
May C. (1917-) 489
May Cristina (1916-) 159
Meda Mamie (1902-1977) 495
Melba Blanche (1907-1997) 346
Melba Catherine (1923-2014) 334
Melba K. (1923-2014) 334, 351, 443
Mellie E. (1894-1897) 400
Melva (1907-1997) 346
Melvin C. (1912-1935) 66
Melvin William (1942-) 438
Melvin William Jr. (1965-) 438
Meriam Alice (1918-1985) 437
Merissa (1984-) 473
Merle E. (1906-1917) 396
Merle Guy (1931-2015) 463
Micah 108
Michael 92, 480, 494
Michael (1838-1901) 431
Michael (1865-1910) 65
Michael (1968-) 335, 444
Michael (1990-) 399
Michael A. 334, 351, 444
Michael David (1976-2008) 347
Michael E. (1877-1954) 126
Michael Eugene (1953-2002) 115
Michael Floyd (1963-) 473
Michael S. 337, 445
Michelle (1974-) 336, 444
Mildred Jane (1925-) 118
Mildred M. (1911-1981) 90, 356
Mildred Nettie (1910-1989) 404
Mildred P. (1893-) 356
Milly Buella (1893-) 356
Milton C. (1877-1918) 459
Milton Harvey (1905-) 59
Mina Evelyn (1912-) 382
Minnie (1863-) 356
Minnie (1888-) 375
Minnie Bulah (1887-1960) 399
Minnie M. (1898-1952) 318
Minnie May (1895-1960) 150
Miriam (1918-1985) 437
Miriam Virginia (1912-) 380
Misti 349
Mitchell R. (1905-1964) 113

Monroe Elmer (1879-1938)..............................455
Moody N. (1885-1910)....................................399
Morgan Alaina (1991-)..................................318
Morris H. (1890-)..118
Morrow Godbey (1900-1963)..........................414
Moses (1827-1901)...316
Moses (1851-)...430
Moses (1888-1889)...350
Murrel Raymond (1895-1982)........................125
Myhia and Elmira Elizabeth (1851-1927).......316
Myrl E. (1890-1898).......................................359
Myrl Irene (1908-2012)...................................403
Myron Frederick (1901-1932)........................362
Myrtie Ardella (1885-1925)............................398
Myrtle (1907-)..59
Myrtle Eliza (1928-1944)................................443
Myrtle Larada (1898-1900).............................414
Myrtle Marie (1919-1997)..............................116
Nancy Ann..90, 356
Nancy L. (1935-1936).....................................79
Naomi Irene (1922-)......................................171
Nathan A. (1871-1964)...................................356
Nathan Dale (2001-).....................................473
Neale E. (1943-1976).....................................359
Nelson Daniel (1922-1989)............................349
Nettie Jane (1934-).......................................384
Nettie May (1875-1957)...................................93
Nicole..108, 114
Nina Loraine (1915-2002)..............................222
Noelle Catherine (2007-)................................86
Nora Agnes (1878-1956)................................398
Nora May (1900-1966)...................................483
Norma J. (1934-)...329
Norman E. (1905-1992).................................375
Norman Elmer (1906-1980)...........................403
Norman Howard (1881-1954)........................402
Olive Maria (1902-1997)................................401
Olive May (1890-1978)..................................382
Oliver Cecil (1884-1954)................................468
Oprha (1931-2002)...493
Orpha Lillian (1931-2002)..............................493
Oscar Preston (1889-1916).............................350
Oscar W. (1897-1963)....................................387
Owen..151, 449
Owen Michael (2004-)..................................108
Palmer Eugene (1881-1949)...........................377
Pamela..349
Pamela Lee (1958-2015)................................414
Pamela M. (1964-)..359
Pamela Sue (1971-)..............................336, 444
Pansey I. (1912-2004)......................................63
Patricia (-2007)..493
Patricia (1937-)......................................349, 380
Patsy...495
Pattilynn Louise (1951-).................................59
Paul (1909-2006)..352
Paul Clinton (1898-1968)...............................359
Paul D. (1909-1991).......................................380
Paul E. (1903-1998)...78
Paul Ellsworth (1919-2000)...........................377
Paul Eugene (1928-).....................................404
Paul Ivan (1927-2005)...................................468
Paul James (1963-).......................................384
Paul R. (1933-2009).......................................292
Paul W. (1910-1975)......................................387

Paul William (1923-2010) 340, 446
Paula 88
Pauline (1900-1905) 396
Pauline (1901-) 94
Pauline Anna (1915-1990) 402
Pauline Grace (1934-2002) 443
Pauline M. (1921-1923) 124
Pauline Marie (1927-1964) 130
Pearl Elnora (1915-2004) 307
Pearlie Mabel (1884-1951) 333
Peggy (1924-2007) 349
Peggy (1939-) 115
Peggy L. 292
Penro (1864-1936) 72
Penrose (1864-1936) 72
Percival (1842-1899) 72
Peter (1773-1858) 49
Peter (1838-1915) 68, 118
Peter (1839-) 306
Peter (1859-) 223
Peter F. (1895-) 118
Peter Lloyd (1870-1961) 385
Philip 60
Philip (1836-) 100
Philip (1840-1918) 59
Philip Carl (1824-1887) 90
Philip W. (1935-) 92
Phillip 114
Phillip (1868-1950) 103
Phillip William (1941-) 114
Phillip William Absalom (1908-1983)........... 113
Phoebe (1839-) 122
Phyllis (1925-) 362
Polly (1853-) 222
Pork (1942-) 114
Prescilla (1862-1929) 100
Preston A. (1867-1895) 415
Preston Elias (1895-1952) 415
Preston W. (1893-1975) 435
Prisciilla Jane (1873-1940) 396
Priscilla (1913-) 59
Priscilla Mae (1935-) 113
Rachel A. (1922-2011) 490
Rachel P. 339, 446
Ralph (1933-2015) 329
Ralph C. (1906-) 378
Ralph Elias (1894-1960) 75
Ralph H. (1909-1985) 339
Ralph H. (1918-1994) 65
Ralph Lester Jr. (1958-) 108
Ralph Lester Sr. (1935-1996) 108
Ralph Moses (1908-1996) 329
Ralph Raymond (1909-1985) 192, 339, 446
Ralph W. (1927-2013) 250
Ralph Wilbert (1898-1970) 405
Randall (1931-1961) 131
Randy 416
Randy Eugene (1960-) 108
Randy Eugene Jr. 108
Randy Lee (1960-2014) 439
Ranee 457
Ray Austin (1911-1979) 440
Ray Melvin (1910-1991) 339, 446
Ray Melvin (1921-2005) 398
Ray William (1925-2005) 457

Raymond Daniel (1923-1932) 437
Raymond E. (1889-1926) 376
Raymond F. (1911-2011) 489
Raymond Monroe (1918-1992) 376
Raymond Murrel (1923-1983) 126
Rebecca 439
Remus Elmer (1893-1893) 382
Rhett Charles (2003-) 193, 339, 446
Richard 127, 342
Richard C. 395
Richard C. (1928-) 124
Richard E. 458
Richard E. (1946-) 317
Richard Earl (1930-2011) 458
Richard Gabriel (1925-2008) 383
Richard M. (-1993) 341
Richard Roosevelt (1908-1995) 458
Rick 383
Rick E. 349
Rickey Eugene (1954-) 400
Robert 90, 356
Robert (1922-) 360
Robert (1923-1993) 406
Robert Anthony (1969-) 116
Robert Eugene (1933-) 440
Robert Eugene (1957-) 318
Robert Franklin (1921-1995) 404
Robert Harold (1933-2005) 439
Robert Hayden (1927-) 361
Robert Jamar (1945-) 475
Robert James (1928-1984) 458
Robert Joseph (1915-1997) 65
Robert Keith (1956-2008) 348
Robert Leroy Jr. 115
Robert Leroy Sr. (1941-2008) 115
Robert Mitchel (1925-2003) 113
Robert Raymond (1931-2004) 130
Robert Walter (1884-1915) 66
Robert Wayne (1936-2015) 63
Roberta Ellen (1931-2006) 329
Robyn 116
Rocky (1956-2008) 348
Rodney Ray (1952-) 336, 445
Roger 377
Roger (1956-) 250, 258
Roger P. (1929-) 94
Romaine Elizabeth (1935-2015) 437
Ronald 63, 495
Ronald Austin (1943-) 440
Ronald Eugene (1934-2015) 113
Ronald Gene (1942-) 475
Ronald L. 130
Ronald Lee (1947-2006) 402
Ronald N. (1936-1973) 396
Ronald Paul 404
Ronie (1892-1979) 411
Ronnie Druella (1892-1979) 411
Rosa E. (1902-) 343
Rosa Karoline (1894-) 65
Rosa Minerva (1866-1942) 54
Rosanna (1921-2003) 406
Roscoe Milton (1885-1978) 404
Rose Marie (1946-) 336, 445
Roxie 494
Roy 192, 416
Roy Allen (1945-) 440
Roy Edgar (1932-2013) 131
Roy Edward (1924-1992) 124
Roy Eugene (1884-1902) 380
Roy K. (1915-1964) 401
Roy Marlin (1914-1989) 493
Roy Milton (1906-1990) 465
Roy P. (1900-) 72
Roy Raymond (1919-1925) 415
Roy S. (1910-1973) 132
Roy W. (1890-1974) 80
Roy W. (1932-1983) 406
Ruby (1899-1996) 96
Rufus (1883-1916) 221
Russel Charles (1921-2012) 75
Russell 387
Russell Edwin (1926-2007) 62
Russell Eugene (1999-) 363
Russell William (1927-1938) 357
Rusty 457
Ruth 494
Ruth (1935-1985) 250
Ruth Ann (1933-) 92
Ruth Ann (1939-) 131
Ruth Devona (1910-1960) 360
Ruth Elizabeth (1927-1928) 325
Ruth Ellen (1948-) 494
Ruth Esther (1934-) 440
Ruth Isabell (1916-2008) 377
Ruth L. (1916-) 221
Ruth M. (1919-) 380
Ruth Marie (1922-2011) 402
Ryan (1992-) 473
Ryan Dale (1978-) 472
Sadie Alverta (1904-1983) 482
Sal (1926-2012) 403
Sallie (1868-) 119
Sallie (1870-1942) 73
Sallie E. (1878-) 418
Sallie E. (1893-1893) 400
Sallie Mae (1888-1903) 122
Sally Ann (1955-) 469
Salome (1819-) 69
Salomon (1820-1893) 69
Sam Brady (1866-1949) 90, 356
Samuel (1824-1903) 374
Samuel (1826-1897) 99
Samuel (1830-1900) 357
Samuel (1846-1897) 136, 279, 458
Samuel (1849-1860) 80
Samuel (1979-) 362
Samuel B. (1874-1943) 360
Samuel D. (1838-) 426
Samuel Elias (1894-1958) 82
Samuel Emanuel (1851-1923) 377
Samuel Lloyd (1883-1952) 380
Samuel Morris (1874-1943) 360
Samuel Ray (1917-1971) 362
Samuel Russell (1954-) 362
Samuel Tyrus (1894-) 360
Sandra Jean (1958-) 414
Sandra Joyce (1942-) 116
Sandra Lee (1943-) 337, 445, 495
Sara Jane (1926-2012) 106, 403
Sarah 100

Name	Page
Sarah (1841-)	310
Sarah (1842-1867)	418
Sarah (1878-)	418
Sarah (1925-)	376
Sarah A. (1868-)	119
Sarah Adella (1869-1939)	83
Sarah Alice (1868-1961)	394
Sarah and Salmi (1819-)	69
Sarah Annetta (1929-1999)	406
Sarah Annette (1929-1999)	429
Sarah C. (1918-2002)	78
Sarah Catherine (1870-1942)	73
Sarah E. (1908-1963)	406
Sarah E. (1978-)	250
Sarah Estella (1893-1952)	91
Sarah Glennette (1933-2010)	64
Sarah Louisa (1862-1924)	497
Sarah Lynn (1989-)	399
Sarah Sevilla (1909-1997)	466
Scott	124, 357
Scott (1946-)	357
Selin Herman (1929-2011)	128, 342
Serenes Emory (1850-1921)	398
Sevilla (1909-1997)	466
Sevilla Agnes (1865-1922)	122
Shanell Dawn Lynn (1973-)	59
Shanna C.	79
Sharon	82
Sharon Sandra (1947-)	340, 446
Shelly Renee (1973-)	472
Sherri Lee (1964-)	336, 444
Sherry (1950-2015)	384
Shirley (1936-)	130
Shirley Ann (1941-)	440
Shirley Betty (1935-)	489
Shirley Lois (1929-2010)	383
Shorty (1906-1990)	465
Silvia Marie (1970-)	381
Simon (1827-1901)	398
Solomon (1820-1893)	69
Sonya	108
Stanley Emanuel (1922-2007)	493
Stanley Howard (1930-2009)	131
Stanley Louis (1910-1983)	114
Stanley Roosevelt (1908-1995)	130
Stella (1887-)	80
Stella I. (1905-)	360
Stella M. (1879-)	377
Stella Mae (1903-1976)	335
Stella May (1903-1976)	335, 444
Stephanie	346
Stephanie Lynn (1956-)	344
Stephen	82
Stephen E.	130, 184
Steven	357, 399
Steven (1948-)	357
Steven E.	79
Steven Leroy (1948-)	334, 351, 444
Steven Scott (1990-)	399
Stillborn Infant (1891-1891)	405
Stillborn Infant (1893-1893)	405
Stillborn Son (1926-1926)	414
Sue (1942-2009)	114
Susan	92
Susan (-2003)	334, 351, 444
Susan (1879-)	66
Susan E. (1950-)	318
Susanna (1872-)	80
Susannah (1817-1885)	67
Susannah (1840-1877)	93, 150, 448
Susie E.	339, 446
Suzanne Alaura (1957-)	462
Suzanne Marie (-2015)	63
Suzette	113
Tammy	131
Tammy (1961-)	335, 444
Tanya L.	250, 258
Terry	131
Terry (1959-)	384
Thelma Iris (1911-1977)	381
Theodore (1876-1956)	317
Theodore Mark (1946-)	59
Theresa	347
Thomas	63
Thomas Clair (1941-2014)	439
Thomas Leroy (1926-1997)	127, 342
Thomas Marcus (1909-1968)	439
Thomas R. (1953-2013)	250
Tillie Sedora (1905-1994)	148
Timothy	124, 266
Timothy A.	87
Timothy Carl (1960-)	469
Timothy Scott (1968-)	338, 369, 445
Tina (1961-)	384
Tobias (1854-)	448
Tobias (1855-1924)	295
Toby	108
Todd	493
Todd Lamar (1969-)	193, 339, 446
Tracy (1971-)	338, 369, 445
Tracy Marie (1954-)	108
Trishia Nicole (1987-)	193, 339, 446
Troy	385
Trudy	334, 351, 444
Turner Timothy (1991-)	469
Ulyas Grand (1872-1873)	126
Valeria (1883-1900)	81
Vena Alpha (1905-1938)	337, 369, 445
Venus Crystin Tara (1967-)	59
Vera M. (1916-)	458
Vera Mae (1906-1997)	471
Verdie S. (1891-1968)	210
Verna (1908-1909)	136, 459
Verna Mae (1898-1977)	127, 342
Verna Mae (1901-1979)	152, 434
Verna May (1905-1995)	325
Verna V. (1903-)	360
Verna, Venie, Winnie, and Vinnie (1905-1938)	337
Vernon L.	359
Viah and Violet (1847-1907)	447
Vicki L.	92
Vickie Jean (1952-)	128, 342
Victor J. (2002-2008)	347
Victoria (1874-1950)	221
Victoria Diane (1973-)	116
Vienna (1919-)	442
Vinnie A. (1919-)	442
Viola Myrtle (1884-1953)	94
Violet (-2012)	127, 342
Violet (1915-)	359

Violet Betty (1930-2016) 334, 351, 444
Violet E. (1919-   ) 402
Violet M. (1917-2011) 249, 317
Violette (1847-1907) 447
Virginia 127, 342
Vivian D. (1918-   ) 359
Vonnie (1949-   ) 347
Walter (1889-1962) 222
Walter (1891-1891) 99
Walter A. (1920-2009) 443
Walter Edwin (1897-1975) 416
Walter Preston (1893-1975) 435
Walter Rohrman (1893-1941) 359
Wanda Mae (1939-1992) 65
Warren H. 266
Warren Stanley (1903-1978) 387
Wayne 335
Wayne Arthur (1929-2002) 76
Wellington E. (1858-1936) 404
Wendy Lee (1955-2001) 250
Wesley V. (1936-   ) 329
Wilbert Elias (1919-1997) 376
Wilhelm (1829-1916) 391
Wilhelmina Mary (1915-   ) 221
Willard Lee (1942-   ) 473
Willard Lee Jr. (1964-   ) 473
William 115, 448, 457
William (1874-   ) 61
William (1927-   ) 360
William (1940-   ) 92
William A. (1876-1959) 418
William C. (1907-   ) 295
William Delroy (1890-1967) 399
William Edward (1893-1929) 124
William Eggers (1868-1873) 385
William Elias (1881-1959) 468
William Elmer (1879-1944) 63
William Elmer (1933-   ) 131
William Franklin (1886-1957) 375
William Franklin (1924-1997) 376
William G. 341
William G. Sr. 376
William Guy (1923-1970) 127, 342
William H. (1829-1916) 391
William H. (1840-1914) 126
William H. (1854-1937) 89
William H. (1868-1909) 56
William H. (1920-   ) 65
William Henry (1842-   ) 122
William Henry (1859-   ) 100
William Henry (1919-1978) 243
William Homer (1925-   ) 362
William Irvin (1927-1993) 328
William Isaac (1887-1949) 242
William L. (1890-1967) 399
William or Bill (1925-2005) 457
William Oscar (1874-1965) 333, 350, 425, 443
William Oscar (1885-1962) 471
William Percival (1870-1954) 395
William R. (1868-1909) 56
William R. (1943-2016) 87
William S. (1854-1925) 242, 327
Willie (1874-   ) 61
Wilma E. (1907-   ) 98
Wilmer F. (1916-1980) 65

Wilson (1872-1962) 74
Yvonne (1949-   ) 347
Zak Allen (1998-   ) 348
Zoann 114

Klock
Angela 320
Bailey (2004-   ) 254
Bruce (1959-   ) 191
Daniel N . (1892-1986) 442
Darla (1958-   ) 191
Doris 442
Emma Jane (1937-   ) 463
Florence (1898-2007) 368
Herlin Harlin (1901-1947) 463
J. Robert (1934-   ) 191
Jean 270
Jean (1924-   ) 172
Jim 254
Lucy 254
Nikki (1985-   ) 254
Pamela Yvonne 320
Ralph 320
Robbie (1983-   ) 254
Robert Jr. (1964-   ) 191
Sandra 442
Tiegan J. (2004-   ) 254
Walter L. (1920-2000) 442

Klohr
Daniel 76

Klopp
(--?--) 227
Scott 227

Klouser
(--?--) 443
Albert F. (1906-1956) 484
Alvin 185
Charles 477
Dewey 280
Elsie Irene (1927-2008) 484
Elwood E. (1929-2008) 485
Emily Janet (1929-   ) 280
Fern E. (1932-   ) 485
Iva 478
James Jackson (1934-1943) 485
Jeannette Ruth (1936-2001) 485
Minnie 249
Nancy L. 292
Robert H. (1923-2005) 477
Yvonne 477

Klusman
Bernard (1941-2006) 350
Bernard (1965-   ) 350
Kendrick (-2006) 350
Lori Ann (1963-   ) 350
Ty (1980-   ) 350

Klytz
Janet 419

Knapp
Harvey C. 380

Knaub
John 404

Knecht
Charles Albert (1890-1895) 394
Charles Frederick 394

Frederick Vernon (1915-)..394
Gilbert William (1920-2013)......................................394
Jesse Gilbert (1894-1918) 394
Karl E. (1911-1974) 395
Louise Beatrice (1908-1994)......................................395
Merle Arline (1904-1998) 395
Mildred Alice (1901-1997) 395
Myra Annetta (1899-1900)...395
Roy Leo (1888-1962) 394
William Kenneth (1892-1970) 394
William Lewis Frederick (1865-1949) 394

Knell
George..56
Margaret E. (1916-1989)..56

Knerr
Mary..192

Knesel
Charles F. (1919-1992)..226
Charles H...226
Charles Jr...226
David...226
Jennifer..226
Patricia..226
Thomas..226
Veronica..226

Knight
Kenneth...97
Samuel..97

Knoebel
(--?--)..379

Knohr
Alice Jean (1928-2012)...497
Allen Edward (1913-1988)..497
Daniel Lewis (1911-1996)...497
Daniel Milton (1883-1943) 497
Earl Lehr (1918-1986)...497
Edmond K. (1894-1968)..498
Edward (1894-1968)...498
Harry Irvin (1885-1961)..497
Henry...497
Janet Lucille (1931-)..497
Jonathan (1863-1932)..497
Lefty (1925-2012)...497
Lewis (1911-1996)..497
Mary L. (1888-1940)...498
Mary Louise (1915-2012)...497
Ralph Joseph (1925-2012)...497
Ruth Irene (1924-1992)...497

Knorr
Aaron D. (1858-1920)...423
Alace Clara (1868-1877)...424
Alice (1868-1877)...424
Allen (1910-)...141
Amanda S. (1896-1896)..140
Bessie M. (1892-)..423
Boyd (1906-)..140
Bryant E. (1923-1988)...495
Carol (1944-)..482
Carolina (1854-1914)..421
Caroline (1854-1914)..421
Christine Debra (1953-)...495
Clara F. (1884-) 423
Clara Rebecca (1866-1877).......................................424
Clarence Allen (1886-1961)......................................463
Clarence Raymond (1895-1945)................................270
Claude L (1942-)...482
Claude L. (1917-2008)..482
David (1809-)...420, 424
Dean Lamar (1941-2010)..496
Dennis..455
Dennis (1942-)...482
Dolly (1930-)..140
Duane (1972-)..495
Edna...318
Edwin Wallace (1902-)..495
Elizabeth Sophronia (1872-1941) 186, 432
Elsie J. (1927-1957)..495
Engilina (1833-1879)..420
Florence (1891-) 424
Frederick Daniel (1894-1978)...................................482
Guerney E. (1894-1964) 140
Gurnie (1894-1964) 140
Hanna (1860-1930)...423
Hattie L. (1878-) 423
Heather (1976-)..482
Henry (1835-1901)..420
Herman G. (1890-)...424
Hilda Alverta (1920-2014)..270
Ida C. (1867-1949)..152, 431
Ina Lou (1934-) 140
Irene (1916-) 140
Isaac C. (1840-1890)..140, 431
James B. (1921-)..140
James H. (1921-)..140
James I. (1895-) 424
Julia (1862-1911)..423
Juliann (1862-1911)..423
Julie Diane (1957-)..496
Karen 455
Kate Elizabeth (1986-)...496
Kent (1962-)..482
Kermit (1914-)...141
Lee...455
Leonard Eugene (1950-) 496
Lizzie M. (1891-1918)..161
Lola Sarah (1919-2005)..463
Luther R. (1906-1908)..140
Mabel (1912-1963)...140
Margaret (-1940)..140
Maria (1838-1923)..424
Marie..455
Martha (1901-)...424
Mary (1901-)..424
Matthew (1975-)..496
Mazie M. (1884-)...424
Merry F. (1891-)...424
Michael (1864-1923)...424
Michelle Inez (1972-)..495
Rachel Ann (1980-)...369
Ray Elwood (1930-1987)..495
Ray Elwood (1949-) 495
Raymond G. (1927-)..140
Ronald..455
Rose Regina (1904-) 140
Rosie (1904-)..140
Sheree Lee Susan (1956-) 495
Stella (1898-)..140
Stephanie Diane (1973-) 369
Steven Daniel...369

Sula C. (1896-1896) 140
Sula G. (1896-1896) 140
Susan Alice (1880-) 423
Susannah (1836-) 420
Virginia Elaine (1955-) 496
Wallace Edward (1932-2012) 496
Walter LeRoy (1925-) 140
William Emmon 495
William M. (1897-) 424
Wilson Ellsworth (1866-1920) 140
Yvonne (1964-) 482

Knouse
Carl (-2012) 390
Daniel 157

Knowles
(--?--) 394
Andrew 267
Jack 267
Ray 267

Kobel
George 373
Rebecca (1854-1923) 373

Koble
Sally 211

Koch
(--?--) 438
Phoeby Ann (1829-1875) 100

Kocher
Burnett LaFeam (1922-1958) 410
Carol Ann (1947-) 357
Kenneth Kermit 357
Thelma Cardella (1913-1972) 358

Kock
Howard 189
Loretta Mae (1908-1993) 189

Kodack
Paula 476

Koesel
David Douglas (1946-) 123

Kohler
Amelia 214
Charles (1982-) 401
Edward 401
Joseph (1980-) 401
Lena 53
Patrick (1978-) 401
Veronica (1976-) 401

Kohlman
Elizabeth (1828-1898) 167

Kohls
Kelly 452
Norman 452
Scott 452

Kohr
(--?--) 127
Benjamin 257
Clarence A. (-1965) 257
Earl Franklin (1907-1964) 454
Erin R. 412
Harvey (1877-1965) 454
John 216
John E. 257
Michael D. 257
Ray Leroy (1944-2010) 412
Ray N. (-2010) 412
Rhoda (1964-) 335
Samuel 257
Shelby B. 412
Trisha L. 412

Kolva
(--?--) 411
Galen 270
Josephine (1896-) 140
Lisa 270
Robert D. (1912-1974) 396

Komara
Wayne 381

Komernicky
Heather 318
Jared 318
Larry R. 318

Komma
Louise (1874-) 295

Konyar
James 121
James Jr. 121

Koons
Charles Monroe (1864-1918) 66
Constance Dorothy (1941-) 315
Dwayne Lee (1969-) 107
Evelyn 115
Harry G. 128
Joelle Rene (1976-) 108
Matthew Edward (1994-) 108
Michael 66
Roger 107

Kopec
Jerome (1946-) 413
Karen (1972-) 413
Karla (1978-) 413
Kathy (1974-) 413
Kevin (1976-) 413
Kimberly (1982-) 413
Kristine (1980-) 413

Kopecky
John 248
Karen 248

Kopenhaver
Charles 133
Charles (-1940) 132
Elizabeth (1919-) 132
Emily E. (-1940) 132
Ethel (1917-) 132
Grace 132
Harry W. 132
Harvey (1879-1940) 133
Harvey Jr. 133
Helen 132
Howard (-1940) 136
Ivan (1916-) 132
Jared (1914-) 132
Margaret 132
Marian 132
Minnie (1884-1937) 133
Olven (1919-) 132
Rufus (1877-) 132
Sarah 132
Selin (1931-2016) 138

    Walter 132
    Warren 132
    William (-1940) 132
    William (1848-1925) 132

Kopp
    Edgar A. 394
    Edgar Neal (1933-2008) 394
    Ethel Mae (1927-2005) 250
    Frank 250
    Kathy 394
    Randall Warren 51
    Randi N. 52
    Sandra R. 52
    Steven 394
    Tonya M. 51

Koppenhaver
    Abner Ralph (-2007) 289
    Amber Christine (1996-) 331
    Amy 251
    Andrew Alan (1959-) 355
    Andrew Alfred (1932-2015) 355
    Andrew Cleveland (1884-1946) 152, 261, 352
    Anna Lucille (1929-2008) 138
    Anna May (1948-) 413
    April Melody (1955-) 354
    Arlene May (1927-1988) 138, 417
    Ashley Nicole (1993-) 331
    Barbara J. (1937-) 243
    Ben 136
    Benjamin Andrew (1991-) 355
    Benjamin Harrison 357
    Beth Ann (1970-) 413
    Betty Lucille (1924-2014) 184
    Brenda Lee (1947-) 353
    Brian (1969-) 331
    Brooke Kathryn (1990-) 355
    Bruce Carl (1949-) 357
    Calvin Charles (1924-2006) 138
    Calvin Oscar (1860-1933) 137, 243
    Carlos Daniel (1923-1997) 152, 354
    Carol Ann (1947-2009) 353
    Carol Ann (1972-) 174
    Catherine Annie (1861-1937) 401
    Ceylon Lamar (1931-2016) 138
    Chester Lee (1928-1994) 251
    Child (1912-1912) 352
    Child (1930-1930) 355
    Clair 251
    Clarence Robert (1902-1977) 184
    Clayton Leroy (1918-2000) 261, 353
    Clinton Arthur (1888-1954) 243
    Colleen Morgan (1992-) 355
    Daniel Martin (1927-2008) 138
    David C. 138
    David Harry (1948-) 152, 354, 450
    Dawn Sherry (1953-) 354
    Derek 244
    Donald (1938-) 413
    Donna L. 138
    Dorothy Mary (1924-) 218, 468, 475
    Earl Lamar (1929-1934) 414
    Elvin Leroy 479
    Elwood J. (1914-1991) 243, 441
    Ernest Henry (1925-1980) 138
    Fay Marie (1960-) 353

    Floyd Harold (1950-) 413
    Fred J. 138
    Gary Clayton (1946-2015) 261, 354
    Gary Gilbert (1945-) 357
    George Alvin (1895-1975) 251
    Gilbert Charles (1920-2005) 357
    Harold Floyd (1912-1971) 413
    Helen Naomi (1913-1968) 352
    Henry C. (1928-1999) 244
    Henry Franklin (1908-1962) 173, 441
    Homer H. (1916-1957) 413
    Howard Maynard (1916-1990) 353
    Hunter David (1995-) 355
    Ira Calmon (1894-1966) 137, 417
    Ira Elvin (1921-2008) 137
    Ivan P. (1913-1967) 243
    James Lee (1964-) 261, 354
    Jane (1953-) 357
    Jane Marie (1964-) 152, 355, 450
    Jered (1992-) 354
    Jeremiah I. (1897-1936) 218, 468
    Jeremy Justin (1981-) 261, 354
    Jonathon D. 366
    Joseph Elmer (1892-1965) 413
    Joy Sue (1962-) 353
    Juliann (1864-1906) 127, 332, 443
    Kara Kay (1979-) 152, 354, 450
    Kathy Ann (1957-) 261, 354
    Katie 477
    Keith Alan (1956-1989) 261, 354
    Kelly L. 261, 354
    Kelly Sue (1969-) 155, 435, 451
    Kevin 243, 244
    Koppy (1947-2009) 353
    Kristen Kylee (1985-) 152, 354, 450
    Kristy Ann (1987-) 355
    Kyle Reed (1989-) 355
    Larry Paul (1941-) 155
    Lee 251
    Lenwood (1942-) 243
    Linda Kay (1950-) 353
    Lorraine Esther (1944-) 174, 441
    Mae 214
    Mark David (1961-) 355
    Marlin E. 366
    Mary Alice (1952-) 152, 354, 450
    Mary Louise (1913-1999) 53
    Mary Naomi (1932-1996) 138
    Mason Alexander (2000-) 331
    Matthew Miles (1991-) 261, 354
    Melvin Newton (1915-1997) 333
    Michael Patrick (1965-) 174
    Miriam A. (1920-2007) 413
    Miriam Emma (1922-1971) 468
    Morris L. (1866-1915) 468
    Myrtle Emeline (1927-) 414
    Nancy K. (1939-) 243, 441
    Nicole (1974-) 357
    Patrick Ryan (1990-) 174
    Paul Albert (1917-) 155
    Philip Michael (1993-) 174
    Randall Earl (1946-) 261, 354
    Rebecca Anne (1994-) 355
    Rebecca Kay (1958-) 152, 355, 450
    Richard E. (1947-) 366

Rita 243
Robert Elvin (1955-) 479
Ronald Eugene (1941-2002) 261, 354
Roxann 244
Ruby Cathleen (1919-2008) 137
Russell Cleveland (1914-1996) 353
Ruth Evelyn (1916-2007) 289
Samuel Perry (1949-2001) 261, 354
Samuel Sylvester (1852-1927) 352
Samuel W. 53
Sarah 216
Stacy (1970-) 357
Stephanie Kay (1990-) 261, 354
Theophilus M (1867-1940) 413
Tiana 244
Timothy 243
Timothy Jay (1964-) 355
Timothy Justin (1984-) 261, 354
Torpetus (1860-1904) 251
Vicki Lee (1963-) 155, 435, 451
Warren Loraine (1922-2008) 137
Warren Sylvester (1920-2010) 354
Wendy Kay (1962-1962) 261, 354
William Harry (1941-) 173
Xandra 88
Yvonne 254

Koppenheffer
Ebbie Jane (1866-1942) 104
Jennifer Lee 439
Kerry L. (1958-) 439
Mindy Lynn 439

Korten
Ernest Jr. (-2000) 378

Kostenbader
Thomas Daniel 397
Walter Schmidt (1911-1969) 397

Kowalczyk
Alex 341
Anna 341
John E. 341

Kowalski
Olga (1906-1972) 297

Kraber
Ivy E. 412

Krahling
Emma Katherine (1939-2015) 62
Henry 62
Jacob (1911-1994) 62
Jacob Henry (1935-1985) 62

Krakoske
Gregory Michael (1962-) 98

Krall
Mabel 211
Mary 211

Kramer
(--?--) 91
Adam James (1987-) 473
Agnes 326
Anne M. 151
Delores 121
Grace Elizabeth (1989-) 473
James 473
Melvin G. 473
Palmer G. (1900-1949) 374

Krammes
Jerry 256
John Michael (1978-) 256
Michelle 270

Kratovile
Mary Lou 286

Kratzer
Albert Roosevelt (1906-1992) 137
Blanche Margaret (1907-) 137
Carrie Violet 131
Cathy 135
Chris 137
Clarence U. (1869-) 137
Guy Livingston (1911-1994) 137
Guy M. 137
Lana 135
Megan 68, 122, 135
Miriam Irene (1918-2003) 134
Paul Russell (1896-1949) 134
Ralph Henry (1921-1964) 137
Randy 68, 135
Verna S. (1904-1924) 137
William M. (1920-1966) 68, 135

Krause
Bill 263
Pearl Grace (1919-1990) 77

Kreidler
Corey A. 297
Curtis J. 297
James Fertig (1964-) 297
Janet R. (1963-) 297
John R. (1960-) 297
Robert 297
Timothy 297
Tyler 297

Kreiner
Eva J. 412
Michael 405

Kreiser
Charles Paul (1916-1997) 54
Delenore W. (1938-) 54
Robert 215
Samuel 54
Shelly 215

Kreisher
John 142

Kreitzer
Elsie M. 79
Stella V. (1922-1971) 434

Krise
Elvin (1943-) 350
Kelly Ann (1970-) 350
Tammy Lynn (1968-) 350
Vickie Sue (1971-) 350

Krissinger
Bertha E. 179

Krixer
Hazel W. (1909-) 223

Krohn
Karen 194

Krommes
Michelle Rene 326

Kroster
- Brandon ... 64
- Cody ... 64
- Kathy ... 64
- Kyle ... 64
- Linda ... 64
- Robert Jr. ... 64
- Robert P. (1920-2006) ... 64
- Sally ... 64

Kuebler
- Albert (1931-) ... 348
- Beth Ann (1958-) ... 348
- Laurie Jo (1962-) ... 348

Kuehn
- Alfred (1931-2015) ... 250
- Beverly ... 251
- Cheryl ... 251
- Elayne ... 251
- Janet ... 251
- Karen ... 251
- Paul ... 251
- Sharon ... 251
- Walter (1902-1992) ... 250

Kuentzler
- Dorothy B. ... 135

Kufta
- Robert ... 201

Kuharic
- (--?--) ... 64

Kukla
- Elizabeth Mae (1918-) ... 307

Kulp
- Alinda A. (1963-) ... 410
- Karen ... 89
- Linda ... 117

Kuni
- Colleen Marie (1980-) ... 470
- Gary ... 470
- Gary Michael (1977-) ... 470

Kunsman
- Rebecca (1773-1837) ... 66

Kuntzelman
- Myrtle Mae (1895-1957) ... 152, 354
- Wilson E. (1872-) ... 152

Kurtz
- Eva (-2008) ... 430
- Jennie E. (1885-1950) ... 79

Kutz
- Catharine ... 221

Lachman
- Jean Irene (1922-1998) ... 84

Lafon
- Larry ... 220, 229
- Leslie ... 220, 229
- Leslie C. ... 220
- Leslie Cleveland (1929-) ... 220

Lagerman
- Daniel ... 190
- David ... 190
- Sarah ... 190
- Timothy ... 190
- Timothy II ... 190

Lahr
- (--?--) ... 244
- Amelia C. (1884-1956) ... 179
- Carol L. (1967-) ... 195
- Daniel F. (1876-1883) ... 160
- Edna ... 490
- Elizabeth (1856-1901) ... 207
- Emma S. (1883-1906) ... 161
- Francis G. (1888-1910) ... 161
- Hannah R. (1880-1882) ... 161
- Henry ... 207
- Hilda Irene (1927-2011) ... 84
- Isaac (1820-1883) ... 83
- Isaac (1856-1938) ... 83
- Jacob (1862-) ... 84
- Joe ... 84
- John J. (1878-1881) ... 160
- Josiah (1845-1900) ... 158
- Kermit R. (1926-1992) ... 84
- Loretta Mae (1933-) ... 410
- Margaret F. (1903-) ... 83
- Maud (1892-1894) ... 161
- Maude C. ... 317
- Monroe I. (1878-1954) ... 160
- Peter (1872-1877) ... 160
- Ralph M. (1904-1969) ... 84
- Raymond W. ... 195
- Susan McClata (1871-1958) ... 158
- Terry Lee ... 89
- Victor W. (1885-1891) ... 161

Laing
- Bonita (1945-) ... 115
- Donald Lamar Jr. (1950-) ... 362

Lamb
- (--?--) ... 213
- Robert ... 107

Lamberson
- Violet (1864-) ... 65

Lamenza
- (--?--) ... 207

Lammers
- Josephine Margaret (1918-2009) ... 60

Lampe
- Grace Alice (1888-1931) ... 305

Land
- Sophia Belle ... 431

Landau
- Mary Abigail (1909-1998) ... 467

Landis
- Bradley ... 57
- Brian S. ... 213
- Henry B. (1937-1998) ... 213
- Irene E. (1930-1930) ... 213
- Jason Aaron (1993-) ... 57
- Jeramy Noah (2000-) ... 57
- John Kreider (1900-1969) ... 213
- John Kreider Jr. (1929-2004) ... 213
- John M. ... 213
- Jonah Elijah (1995-) ... 57
- Judy ... 213
- Julia Alexandra (1998-) ... 57
- Karl H. ... 214
- Linda I. ... 214
- Mark E. ... 214

Ralph Harrison (1890-) 406
Robert C. 213

Lang
Adam (1823-) 73

Langtry
Gertrude 281

Lansberry
Barbara (1939-) 223
Geoffrey 223
Holly 223
Jason 223
Lynn H. 223
Scott 223

Lantz
Pearl E. (1896-) 107

Lanxner
William (1926-1986) 314

Lapriola
Franklin Charles 452
Franklin Charles (1952-) 452
Randy Irwin (1957-) 452

Lark
Ray William 367

Larson
Donald 277
Eloise 91
Philip G. (1895-1982) 91
Phillip G. Jr. 91
Robert 91

Lasek
Martha Ruth 373

Lash
James R. 341

Laszlo
Sandow 74
Zoey 74

Latsha
Adda Verdilla (1921-1953) 409
Dawn (1959-) 196
Marqueen (1931-) 173
Mary 385
Minerva A. (1879-1921) 363
Scott 334

Latuszewski
Gary 124

Laudenbach
Jane 411

Laudenslager
Bradley 258
Carol 311
Charles Elwood (1918-1993) 367, 370
Charles I. (1849-1936) 266
Dallas Eugene 428
Dora Kathryn (1916-2005) 266
Evelyn Louise 428
Fred (1915-1992) 180
Gary (1950-) 180
Gary Lee 429
Gary Lee (1975-1998) 180
Harry Victor 367
Haven (-2014) 336
Helen Marie (1921-1994) 267
Henry (1920-1968) 311
Herman Sylvester (1913-1915) 266
Irene I. (1931-2000) 148
Jay W. (1917-1999) 258
John Adam 428
John Harrison (1889-1973) 266
John W. (1937-2008) 258
Joseph Daniel 311
Joseph Daniel (1888-1969) 187
Judy L. 367
Kevin 258
Lawrence 311
Lenore May (1923-2004) 268
Marian E. 439
Marie H. (1921-1994) 267
Mary H. (1922-) 187
Mary Jean (1917-2014) 266
Penny (1946-) 336
Robert 258
Robert Leon (1943-) 367
Rochelle 311
Roger 311
Sula C. 55
Terry George (1941-) 367, 370
Tiffany Ann (1974-) 367, 370
Todd 258
Wilbur Witmer (1920-2000) 428

Laudenslayer
Jay 365
Joyce 365

Lauderbach
Tammy (1967-) 164

Lauer
Pamela Ann (1951-) 285

Laughlin
John 400

Laundau
Charles B. 467

Launders
William (1881-1948) 310

Laurence
Lynne 262

Lauver
Adam B. (1856-1918) 387
Austin 387
Charles E. (1918-1972) 387
Charles Ronald (1939-1961) 387
Chrystal 387
Clyde (1931-) 387
Fredereick L. (1924-1977) 387
Jean Louise (1938-1998) 387
Jullian 387
Robert (Dr.) III 387
Robert III Dr. 387
Robert M. (1893-1945) 387
Robert O. Jr. 387
Robert O. Sr. (1922-2013) 387
Tammy 387

Lavey
Caitlin Elizabeth (1994-) 164
Gregory George (1959-) 164
Robert Thomas (1996-) 164

Law
(--?--) 207

Lawley
- Adam L. (1903-1982) 56
- Anne Mabel (1885-1941) 55
- Arthur Wellington (1888-1939) 56
- Carl David (1921-) 55
- Dorothy (1928-) 55
- Heather Ann 322
- Irene V. (1902-) 55
- Joseph (1852-1919) 54
- Lucy Rosia (1891-1950) 56
- Nancy (1935-) 55
- Oscar E. Jr. (1911-1957) 55
- Oscar Edward (1883-1953) 55
- Roland (1905-1970) 55
- Shirley Viola R. (1910-1995) 55
- Thomas Edward (1947-) 55
- William Charles (1882-1951) 54

Lawrence
- Joan (1949-) 463
- Paul (-1988) 281
- Thomas (-2015) 90

Leach
- Joel M. (1953-) 105, 106
- Raymond 105, 106

Leader
- Richard 326

Leblanc
- (--?--) 226

LeBlanc
- Adelaide 426

Lebo
- April Louise (1962-) 326
- Arnie (1929-1979) 325
- Arnold Klinger (1929-1979) 325
- Barbara Ann 117, 416
- Bertha (1905-) 390
- Burma Mae (1936-1940) 326
- Deborah Ann (1940-) 437
- Doris 246
- Emmaline (1844-1929) 407
- Faune (1960-) 326
- Frank 246
- George 246
- Harvey W. 405
- Homer Arthur (1905-1956) 325
- Homer Arthur (1924-1924) 325
- Howard (1916-) 437
- Ira M. 325
- Isabel 395
- James Donald (1933-2014) 326
- James Earl 268
- James Earl Jr. (1921-1993) 268
- James Robert 268
- James Robert (1965-) 326
- Jason Michael 325
- Jennie (1893-1986) 255
- Jennifer 246
- Jonathan 407
- Joseph 429
- Kari Marie 325
- Kathryn L. 268
- Kelly Lynne 325
- Kim Louise (1957-) 326
- Kimberly Ann 325
- Kristen Michelle (1950-) 325
- Lamar 246
- Linda I. 268
- Marvine 471
- Melvin 405
- Melvin Robert (1909-1959) 405
- Michael 405
- Michelle 246
- Pamela Gail (1954-) 326
- Penelope Ann (1953-) 325
- Ralph Edwin 416
- Ralph Edwin Jr. 117, 416
- Richard (1947-) 437
- Robert (1954-) 437
- Robert Arthur (1928-1995) 325
- Robert Arthur (1950-) 325
- Ted (1926-1998) 325
- Theisen James 268
- Theodore Milton (1926-1998) 325
- William (Dr.) 390
- William Dr. 390

Lechlenleiter
- Harvey 132
- Naomi (1935-) 132

Lee
- Robert E. Jr. (1950-) 300

Leffler
- Brian Paul (1969-) 171
- Craig D. (1940-) 341
- Guy 335
- Jean (1938-) 335
- Lincoln (1900-1978) 171, 335
- Lori Ann (1958-) 171
- Paul (1937-) 171

LeFrancois
- Irene M. (1935-2005) 215
- William 215

Lehman
- (--?--) 393
- Charles (1864-) 119
- Charles W. (1902-) 119
- Debra Jean (1966-) 418
- Esther A. 219
- George 87
- Kathleen Christina (1958-) 418
- Maggie E. (1891-) 119
- Robert W. (1949-) 418
- Robin Mary (1962-) 418

Lehner
- Ronald 316

Lehr
- Daniel L. 497
- Helen (1928-2012) 75
- Jennie M. (1886-1980) 497
- Jordan 233
- Ryan 233
- Savilla Jane (1872-1942) 57, 112

Leibert
- Diane Marie (1950-) 267
- Kathryn I. (1957-) 268
- Patricia Ann (1952-) 268

Leidigh
- Lester G. (-1959) 295

Leinbeck
Jay 279
Leininger
Amber Marilyn (1987-) 285
Andrew R. (1974-) 285
Corey Jay (1972-) 285
Douglas James (1993-) 285
Douglas Wayne (1968-) 285
Henry A. 284
Jade Lynn (1990-) 285
Johnathan Michael (1995-) 285
Kenneth Randall (1992-) 285
Nevin Jerroll (1966-) 285
Norman Ray (1943-) 285
William H. Jr. (1942-) 284
William Henry (1921-1996) 284
Leiser
Holly Marie (1963-) 188
Ron 430
Leitzel
(--?--) 130
Aaron Lynn (1963-) 420
Albert 103
Allen LaRue (1956-) 420
Amanda 335, 351, 419, 444
Amy Sue (1969-) 419
Anna Lorraine (1929-) 185
Anna Mae (1928-) 419
Annette Angela (1960-) 335, 351, 419, 444
Barbara Ann (1941-) 418
Bessie J. (1895-) 209
Betty Marie (1941-) 418
Bonnie 452
Brenda (1958-) 69
Brenda Joyce (1950-) 185
Brenda Kay (1953-) 419
Burlington Lee (1922-1959) 142
Candith Yvonne (1958-) 158
Carol (1951-) 334, 351, 419, 444
Carol J. (1935-) 196
Carol Ruth (1945-) 452
Charles Naldy (1932-) 420
Christine E. (1959-) 420
Christine Elizabeth (1949-) 185
Clair Ernest (1921-2007) 334, 419
Clarence Elmer (1903-1969) 69
Cyrus T. (1870-1944) 209
Daisy D. (1916-) 142
Daisy V. (1916-) 142
David Byerly (1839-1921) 143
Dennis C. (1956-) 420
Deresa Stella (1893-1986) 205
Diane Elaine (1957-) 103
Elaine 451
Forrest (1922-) 142
Fred (1906-1988) 325
George Adam Troutman (1869-1947) 158, 184, 418
Glenda (1955-) 69
Glenn (1952-) 148
Glenn Eldon (1953-) 335, 351, 419, 444
Glenn Hubert (1935-2008) 69
Gloria Jean (1949-) 184
Guy Monroe (1918-2003) 184
James Clifford (1922-) 158
James E. (1957-) 420
James M. (1943-) 420
Jason (1975-) 419
Jennifer Ann (1969-) 420
John 453
John Adam (1924-1995) 419
John P. 130, 184
Kody Michael (1988-) 103
Lawrence Kenneth (1930-1979) 420
Lawrence S. (1895-1945) 334, 418
Lee Melvin (1923-) 185
Leonard (1918-) 142
Lottie Irene (1910-1992) 416
Lydia (1834-1868) 158
Mabel Hannah (1884-1971) 107
Mark Allen 419
Mark Edgar (1920-1992) 418
Mary 364
Mary J. (1926-) 419
Mary Jane (1871-1954) 143
Mary L. (1897-1970) 158
Michael E. 130, 184
Michael Robert (1961-) 103
Michael W. (1965-) 420
Moses Richard (1887-1959) 451
Naldy (1894-1953) 184
Nikki Ann (1992-) 419
Paul 166, 451, 452
Rahn 335, 351, 419, 444
Ralph D. (1920-1967) 142
Robert (1958-) 419
Robert L. (1930-1994) 103
Robert Lee (1966-) 419
Robert Mark (1947-) 419
Rodney D. (1954-2015) 69
Roy Richard (1916-1999) 451
Ruth Ann (1946-) 184
Ryan 69
Samuel 205
Samuel Ammon (1880-1963) 142
Sandra Lee (1959-) 103
Sarah A. 130, 184
Seth M. 130, 184
Shannon (1970-) 420
Shappell Leona (1969-) 420
Sharon Lou (1958-) 420
Shauntell Louise (1966-) 420
Shirley Sue (1928-) 325
Stephen (1978-) 148
Susan R. (1955-) 420
Terry Allen (1958-) 419
Thomas C. 452
Thomas Lee (1952-) 185
Timothy Paul (1958-) 185
Violet B. (1903-) 133
Virginia 451
Wayne Alton (1923-1998) 419
Wayne Robert (1949-) 419
Wayne Robert Jr (1969-) 419
William Ford (1918-1996) 452
William Oscar (1866-1938) 451
Lekutis
Thomas J. (1955-) 488
Lemon
Amber Dawn (1960-) 206
Connie Lou (1954-) 206

Helen Lorene (1896-1973) 461
Marcus Dean (1904-1937) 206
Richard Grant (1928-) 206
Simon Grant (1866-1930) 461

Lengle
Alice 285

Lenhart
Charles J. (1923-2007) 456
Charles J. Jr. 456
Eric M. 456
Evelyn M. 456
Paul L. (-2007) 456

Lenig
Carol 50
Mabel Virginia (1930-1989) 471
Marlin George 50
Michael E. 50
Ralph Clair 471
Walter D. 50

Lenker
(--?--) 126, 127
Adam Spencer (1964-) 106
Albert Ray (1920-2002) 105
Allen Franklin (1926-1975) 106, 403
Alverta Mae (1918-1983) 104
Angela Dawn 429
Annie M. (1872-) 430
Annie M. (1897-) 429
April Dawn (1961-) 115
Arlene Loraine (1953-) 106
Arlene M. (1934-) 326
Ashley Lynn (1983-) 185
Bernice June (1937-2017) 107
Boyd L. (1903-) 430
Brian Scott (1981-) 185
Bruce L. 107
Charles Allen III (1950-) 106
Charles Allen Jr. (1929-1978) 106
Charles Allen Sr. (1891-1949) 104, 403
Charles D. (1928-2000) 406
Charles David (1928-2000) 429
Charles Nicholas (1971-) 106
Chris Harold (1969-) 194
Christopher 429
Clarence Andrew (1940-) 429
Clarence I. (1909-2007) 206, 321
Clayton Johnathan (1862-1944) 104
Clayton Philip (1935-2012) 107
Curt David (1973-) 194
Curtis Lee (1963-) 107
Danielle 107
David Allen (1950-) 106, 403
David Luther (1868-1924) 428
Debra Roberta (1956-1988) 207, 321
Dolores 430
Donald Eugene (1934-2012) 429
Donald R. (1938-) 436
Dorothea 429
Dorothy (-2008) 430
Dorothy Virginia (1924-) 106
Edward (1840-1920) 428
Edward Dean 429
Erin Lorraine (1982-) 185
Evangelina 107
Evelyn (-2008) 430
Floyd Luther (1930-) 429
Floyd Luther Jr. 429
Franklin L. (1928-) 430
Gerald Robert (1927-1991) 207, 321
Gregory Abe (1951-1967) 105
Harold Jerome (1948-) 194
Harvey James (1935-2006) 104
Hattie R. (1896-1958) 428
Herbert Charles (1913-1996) 104
Isaac Newton 417
Jaclyn F. 107
James Allen (1956-) 185
James Henry (1927-) 185
Janet 207
Janice Elaine (1948-) 105
Jason Edward 429
Jeffrey 436
Jeremiah W. (1868-1943) 206
Joan Marie (1954-) 106, 403
John William Jr. (1941-) 409
June A. (1932-2007) 207
Katie Julian (1902-) 138, 417
Lee Earlington 194
Linette 106, 403
Lloyd W. Jr. (1958-2010) 429
Lloyd William (1936-2014) 429
LuAnn Marie 429
Marion Edward (1902-) 415
Marlene 429
Mary A. (1847-1900) 119
Mary A. (1872-) 430
Melissa Ann (1970-) 115
Meredith 436
Michael 429, 436
Michael L. (1853-1925) 206
Mildred Marie (1916-1999) 104
Mindy Marie (1983-) 194
Morris E. (1867-) 415
Nathaniel 106, 403
Nicholas D. 429
Paul Edward (1939-1991) 429
Paul Luther (1900-1962) 429
Pauline Elizabeth (1915-1952) 104
Pearl Marie (1937-2007) 104
Philip 428
Phyllis Mae (1953-) 105, 106
Randy Lee (1954-2010) 107
Raymond Frederick (1922-1994) 105
Richard E. (1923-2008) 430
Richard Eugene (1952-) 185
Robert 430
Robert (1864-) 428
Robert (1927-1991) 207
Robert J. 429
Roy 326
Ruby Irene (1966-) 107
Russell L. (1913-1972) 436
Sallie M. (1909-) 430
Sally (1860-1928) 436
Sandra Kathleen (1948-) 207, 321
Sarah 106, 403
Sarah Elizabeth (1902-2000) 206
Shirley J. (1935-2013) 430
Steve 429
Steven Craig (1949-) 104

Teddy 430
　　Thomas 115
　　Thomas Edward 115
　　Tony Lee (1959-1999) 107
　　Tyler Lee (2003-　) 194
　　Verna Jane (1934-　) 106
　　William Clarence Jr. (1966-　) 115
　　William Clarence Sr. (1938-2010) 115
　　William Robert (1940-　) 104

Lentz
　　(--?--) 195
　　Elmer (1875-　) 376
　　Galen 54
　　Glen 54
　　James (　-1930) 53
　　Magdalena Amelia (1873-1903) 358
　　Pearl I. (1914-2011) 53
　　Rosie J. (1924-　) 142
　　Ryan 54
　　Savada (1897-　) 376
　　Virginia E. (1912-　) 53

Leon
　　Michael Irvin (2005-　) 381
　　Sergio Michael 381
　　Sophia Mae (2007-　) 381

Leon Guerrero
　　Adam Vincent (1978-　) 71
　　Christopher Jason Barto (1976-　) 71
　　Evan Michael Squino (1994-　) 71
　　Joy Christine (1974-　) 71
　　Timothy James Barto (1987-　) 70
　　Vicente (1970-　) 71
　　Vicente Cruz (1949-　) 70

Leonard
　　Andy 293
　　Beth 293
　　Dene 88
　　Elaine 293
　　Erin 64
　　Joy 293
　　Matthew 64
　　Peter 293
　　Randy 64
　　Richard 293
　　Ruth Maxine (1923-2009) 272
　　Walter C. 272

Leopold
　　Wilhelmine 221

Lepley
　　Emma (1925-2010) 378
　　Frederick E. (1921-1987) 378
　　Frederick T. (1897-1970) 378
　　Thomas 378

Leppert
　　Carlea M. 106

Lerch
　　Phyllis L. 300

Lerman
　　Ethan 281
　　Roy 281

Lesher
　　Anna Lois (1933-　) 181
　　Glennon E. (1916-　) 432
　　Henry (1843-　) 432
　　Henry H. (1888-1961) 432
　　Isabella S. (1854-1934) 147, 209
　　Jean (1925-　) 432
　　Jeff 377
　　Joy Lynne 194
　　Junior (1929-　) 432
　　Kathryn Lovina (1899-1952) 138
　　Margaret I. (1914-　) 432
　　Marlin L. (1910-　) 432
　　Minnie (1908-　) 432
　　Pauline E. (1918-　) 432
　　Ruth (1927-　) 432
　　Terry 377
　　Vernon (1924-　) 432

Leshko
　　Sharyn Anne 106

Lessard
　　Horace J. (1873-1926) 426
　　Isadore 426

Letterman
　　George 385

Lettich
　　Anna Savilla 428
　　Connie Ann (1943-　) 477
　　Earl Henry (1920-1998) 477
　　Ellen Sevilla (1877-1962) 482
　　Helen 88
　　Norman 204
　　Travis (1999-　) 282

Lettig
　　Amanda (1840-1890) 132

Leuschner
　　Erin 117

Levan
　　Abram 260
　　Adelaide Katherine 260
　　Niki Lee (1970-　) 353
　　Terry Lee 353

Levonick
　　Julia 370

Levy
　　(--?--) 452

Lewis
　　Arthur David (1886-　) 393
　　Audrey 393
　　Audrey (1918-　) 394
　　Charles Alfred (1883-1968) 393
　　Eleanor 496
　　Elizabeth 210
　　Elizabeth Louise (1921-2006) 394
　　Ella G. (1897-1993) 394
　　Elsie (1907-　) 393
　　Elva R. (1910-　) 393
　　Emma Jane (1931-2007) 394
　　Emma M. (1899-1995) 394
　　Florence L. (1894-1979) 394
　　Garfield J. (1889-1973) 393
　　Hannah 125
　　Helen (1895-1967) 166
　　Ivan C. (1922-　) 393
　　James 393
　　James (1856-1917) 393
　　James G. (1915-2011) 393
　　James Garfield (1889-1973) 393

Jamie (1958-2000) 393
  Jean (1912-2003) 393
  John Llewellyn (1925-1998) 394
  M. Maude (1886-1918) 221
  Mary Janes (1891-1897) 394
  May E. (1907-) 393
  Rhoda Harriet (1924-2000) 394
  Ruth Delphine (1928-2011) 394
  Thomas Morgan 221
  William Henry (1881-1966) 393
Liebert
  Lewis 267
  Lewis Jr. (1915-1981) 267
Light
  Emma 60
Lileck
  Anna (1914-2001) 230
  Peter 230
Limric
  Sean 250
Lindemuth
  Connie 376
  Donna 376
  Gerald M. (-1988) 376
  Robert 376
Lindgren
  (--?--) 124
  Logan 124
  Tyler 124
Lindo
  Garret 467
Lingelbach
  Andrew Zachary (1992-) 145, 315
  Jacob Ryan (2000-) 145, 315
  Leroy Ernest Jr. 145
  Troy Douglas (1963-) 145
Lingle
  Betty J. 146
Lipphardt
  Christina (1950-) 463
Lisk
  (--?--) 271
Litchfield
  John 128
Little
  (--?--) 61
  Dorothy (1905-1977) 228
  Rachel 61
Littlefield
  (--?--) 234
  Christopher 234
  Melissa 234
Livelsberger
  (--?--) 359
Lively
  Deborah Ann 325
Livingston
  Peggi 294
Llewellen
  Nelson R. 250
Llewellyn
  David 400
  Katherine 400

Loan
  Nguyen thi bach (1942-) 411
Lobaugh
  Edith 62
Logan
  (--?--) 65
  Amy (1966-) 413
  Heather 298
  Thomas 298
Lohr
  Brittany M. 485
  George (1925-2007) 484, 485
  Georgetta D. 485
  Georgette 485
  John 484
  Larry Nevin 107
  Steven S. 485
Lomano
  Nicole (1969-) 160
Lombardi
  Alan 199
Long
  (--?--) 76, 246, 381
  Adam (1862-1932) 73
  Alan 156
  Alison J. (1978-) 196
  Almira 277
  Barbara 319
  Bessie 480
  Brian E. (1967-) 331
  Corey 276
  Dona 276
  Ethel Mary 278
  Eva M. (1906-) 73
  Hannah 227
  Ida May (1879-1959) 229
  Irene 252
  Jerald 382
  John Adam (1864-1945) 87
  John C. (1910-1992) 65
  Kasey Marie (1994-) 331
  Kyle Ernest (1991-) 331
  Larry 276
  Lena Alice 471
  Mabel Adelia (1903-1973) 73
  Marion Thurston (1925-2016) 462
  Mark 196
  Mary (1897-1915) 386
  Mary Ellen (1890-1977) 73
  Max Adam (1900-1962) 462
  Myrtle Viola (1930-) 325
  Roy 325, 480
  Sarah E. (1893-) 73
  Vesta (1890-1989) 87
Longenecker
  Dolly Michelle (1973-) 483
  Glenn James 483
  James Glenn (1970-) 483
Lontz
  Cathy A. 429
  LaVerne Jean 117
  Paul J. 429
Loose
  Mabel L. (1887-1947) 77

Marietta L. (1912-1997) 211
Max C. 211

Loranger
Christopher Robert (1976-   ) 162
Heidi Dawn (1977-   ) 162
James Edmund (1922-   ) 162
Jeffry Allen (1959-   ) 163
Michele Ann (1954-   ) 162
Paula Renee (1953-   ) 162
Robert James (1955-   ) 162

Lotz
Roy James Jr. (1923-1997) 76

Love
Dale 274
Gillian 153, 435, 450
Gregory 274
James 231
Jeffrey 153
Thomas 274
Vickie 231

Low
Mary E. (1866-1913) 332, 363

Lowes
Eva 344

Lubold
Arthur 69
Audrey Louise (1951-   ) 475
Carl W. (1912-1986) 242
Carl William Jr. (1940-   ) 243
Catherine Elizabeth (1900-2000) 481
Charles 474
Clinton 242
Eva M. (1919-1997) 474
George James (1897-   ) 474
Harvey (1921-   ) 475
Harvey Charles Jr. (1942-2009) 475
Helen Irene (1917-1965) 474
Linda Marie (1948-   ) 475
Lucille Mary (1928-   ) 218, 475
Marie Annis (1925-1926) 475
Melvin James (1923-   ) 475
Olive M. 52
Riley (1869-1961) 51
Ruby V. (1905-1997) 51
Stephanie 475
Vicki 475
William Klinger (1970-   ) 243
William Roger (1940-   ) 476

Lucas
(--?--) 255, 411
Bonnie Lou (1950-   ) 284
Bryce 411
Christine 263
Elwood E. (1926-1998) 196
Matilda 474

Luce
Barbara (1930-   ) 293
Eric 293
Jean M. (1927-1999) 293
Michelle 293
Nancy J. 293
Robert W. (1894-   ) 293
Robert W. Jr. 293
Steven D. (-1984) 293

Virginia L. (1929-   ) 293

Ludwig
Alice Kay (1966-   ) 476
Amanda Kay (1983-   ) 476
Arthur (1894-   ) 134
Bethany Nicole (1987-   ) 476
Bonnie (1956-   ) 265
Bryon (1992-   ) 475
Carrie (1882-   ) 134
Cathy Marilyn (1960-   ) 476
Charles (-1940) 133
Chrystal Dawn (1980-   ) 476
Donald James (1955-1971) 476
Flossie (1898-   ) 134
Herbert William (1905-1987) 475
Jane G. (1924-   ) 393
Jeffrey William (1970-   ) 475
John (1901-   ) 134
Judith Ann (1993-   ) 476
Kenneth Glen (1964-   ) 476
LaVerne K. (1925-   ) 393
Lester Herbert (1927-   ) 218, 475
Mabel (1891-   ) 134
Marie (1904-   ) 134
Marie Ann (1951-   ) 218, 475
Robert 265
Robert (1892-   ) 393
Sarah (1897-   ) 134
Steven Lester (1946-   ) 475
Susan Diana (1975-   ) 475
Thomas (1885-1940) 134
Thomas Herbert (1954-   ) 476
Timothy Steven (1967-   ) 475
Walton (1897-   ) 134
William 133

Luisi
Laura (1924-   ) 486

Lukens
Jan 178

Lund
Brian 179

Lunn
Dollie Mabel 465

Lupold
Amy 485
Chris P (Dr.) 485
Chris P. Dr. 485
Effie M. (1902-1955) 408
Harvey E. 408
June S. (1922-   ) 387
Lanny 485

Luring
James Paul 220
Kevin James 220

Luu
Katia P. 146, 182
Kevin Q. 146

Lyman
Richard 146

Lynch
George Parker 207
Harry 198
Julius 350

Lyons
    David (1905-) 316
    Gloria 486
Lytle
    Blanche Lulu (1887-1953) 381
MacDonald
    Carole Jeanne (1968-) 297
    Thomas Edward (1966-) 297
    William C. 297
    William Charles (1963-) 297
Mace
    Allen Woodworth (1909-) 255
    Eugene Harry (1938-2014) 128
    Florence 422
    Harry 128
    James 476
    Kathryn Eleanore (1930-1989) 255
    Lillian (-1996) 476
    Mark 147
Machamer
    (--?--) 216
    Florence (1884-) 312
    John A. (1855-) 362
    Kathryn Eileen (1964-) 483
    Robert Jr. 156, 451
    Robert M. (1939-2012) 156
    Roland 156
    Roy Ambrose (1902-1988) 362
Mack
    Barbara (1940-2011) 276
    Carl Allen 276
Mackay
    Annie 421
MacKenbee
    (--?--) 334
Mackey
    Robert (-2013) 201
Mackiewicz
    Eva 170
Macon
    Terrance 130
MacPherson
    Nancy Lee (1949-) 172
Madenford
    (--?--) 353
Madeo
    Robert A. 163
    Samantha Christine (1988-) 163
Mady
    Carol 247
Magaro
    Feliciana 400
Magilton
    Michael Alan 207
Mahar
    Edward 249
    Jerrold 249
    Louis 249
    Michael 249
    Stephen 249
Maiden
    Virginia (1944-) 481

Maidenford
    Amanda 427
Makinson
    (--?--) (-1922) 220
Malarkey
    Amelia 303
    Charles J. (1917-1992) 303
    Dennis 303
    Dennis C. (1940-) 304
    Thomas 304
    William 304
    William J. 303
Malehorn
    Jade Olivia 327
    Janna Michelle 327
    Joel Mark 327
Malick
    Garrett 148
    Garrett (1981-) 148
    Morgan (1983-) 148
    Ronald 148
    Ronald Craig (1956-) 148
    Shannon 148
    Shannon Marie (1977-) 148
Malinowski
    Albert 282
    Maureen Marie 282
Malloy
    Violet 62
Malnick
    Jonathan 454
    Joseph P. (1885-1958) 454
    Richard (1917-1981) 454
    Richard S. 454
    Sharon A. 454
    Sheri A. 454
Malone
    Lamar 369
    Lulu 238
Mangueira
    Alexandra Grace (1993-) 95
    Flora Santos (1935-) 95
    Hunter Hamlin (1995-) 95
Mangueira-Warner
    Benton Marcos (1966-) 95
Mangus
    Dorothy L. (1925-2010) 383
    Orville (-2010) 383
Manhart
    Berdine 349
Manley
    James E. 91
    James Ernest 91
    Stephen (1972-) 347
    Thomas 347
    Thomas II (1970-) 347
Mann
    Christiana C. 102, 352
    Harry William (1878-1957) 81
Manthone
    (--?--) 219
    Margo (1937-) 219

Marberger
    Wanda (1958-)..188
March
    Edgar T. Jr. 117
Marcheskie
    Frances Marlene (1937-) 144
Marconnier
    Emma Mai 210
Margerum
    Anthony 282
    Mandy 282
Marino
    Antonio 341
    Carol L. 241
    Eustacio Richard Jr. 342
    Eustacio Sr. (1923-2017) 341
    Pamela 341
    Ralph 240
    Ralph J. 240
    Susan Mae 76
    Vincent J. 241
Markel
    Alice B. (1893-1968) 401
Marks
    Cyrus Ephraim (1894-1961) 54
    Evelyn G. (1915-2006) 77
    George 54
    Helen M. (1903-) 384
    Mildred C. (1923-1997) 54
    Patricia Ann (1950-) 309
Marple
    Bruce 223
    Clinton 223
    Daniel Kirk (1970-) 486
    David Scott (1965-1979) 486
    Don 486
    Douglas 223
    Douglas Gene (1962-) 486
    Eric 223
    Russell 223
Marr
    Doug 426
    Greg 426
    Ivan G. (1936-) 426
    Larry 426
    Terry 426
Marrocco
    Carissa Walela (2001-) 331
Marshall
    James 77
    Louise Diane (1929-) 316
    Mary Florence 466
    Ronn 366
    Samuel B. (1900-1977) 316
    Virginia 303
Martin
    Cheryl L. 125
    Corinne 437
    Doris Alma (1942-) 57
    George E. 125
    George E. (-2005) 125
    James 233
    Mae Beatrice 473
    Marlene Elaine (1950-2001) 125
    Martha 383
    Valen Tinia 369
    Wendy 290
Marty
    Eaves (1962-) 324
    Marvin Lee (1962-) 324
Martz
    Alana Marie (1982-) 331
    Allison Heather (1990-) 331
    Alyssa Luellan (1994-) 331
    Andrew D. (1983-) 472
    Blanche Jean (1931-) 472
    Bradford C. (1979-) 472
    Carl Gurney (1933-2012) 472
    Carole A. 258
    Carolyn Jean (1952-) 471
    David William (1960-) 472
    Dennis Samuel (1963-) 472
    Donna Virginia (1949-) 471
    Doris Edith (-1993) 494
    Douglas 257
    Gary Lee (1960-) 471
    Gurney George (1902-1966) 471
    Harlan Oscar (1926-1985) 471
    Harry (-2002) 257
    James H. 257
    Janelle Elizabeth (1984-) 331
    Jaspar Allen (1987-) 331
    Jeffrey Allen (1961-) 331
    Kimbra 257
    Kimbra Yvonne 326
    Larry Harlan (1954-) 471
    Mae Arlene (1927-) 471
    Mary Irene (1921-) 155
    Melissa Ann 245
    Natasha L. (1982-) 472
    Randy Carl (1956-) 472
    Samuel Oscar (1875-1954) 471
    Steven Albert (1955-) 472
    Tina E. (1958-) 472
    William G. Jr. 245
    William G. Sr. 245
Marzolf
    Alice E. 293
    Irene 293
    John 293
    Mary L. 294
    Robert J. (1904-1995) 293
    Tom 293
Maslin
    Don 361
Mason
    Marcia Ann (1954-) 412
Masser
    (--?--) 478
    Chloe Elizabeth (2005-) 288
    Elias (1836-) 66
    Gine (1834-1834) 66
    Heinrich (1846-1847) 67
    Henry (1846-1847) 67
    Joan Elizabeth (1952-) 154
    Johann (1844-1845) 67
    Johannes (1773-1813) 66
    John 66

John (1844-1845) 67
Joshua Lamont (2001-) 288
Lamont Mark 288
Manassas 66
Mark (1929-) 288
Moses 66
Rebecca Catherine (1998-) 288
Sharon Louise (1946-) 186

Masteller
Amy (1978-) 293
Barbara L. 293
John R. 293
Michael John (1979-) 293
Robert J. (-1997) 293

Matalonas
Alphononso 348
Diane 349
Gerald 348
Rosemary 348

Matlock
Mary Louise (1937-) 452

Matott
Grace Dortha 373
Henry 373

Matsko
Margaret 206

Matter
Catharine (1823-) 404
Daniel Alexander (1985-) 412
David 456
David LeRoy (1950-) 412
Dewayne L. (1968-1968) 442
Earl Leroy (1942-) 412
Eugene Jr. 442
Eugene P. 441
Frederick (1967-) 412
Glenn Edward (1914-2005) 408
Grant Drew (1992-) 412
Harold E. (1925-) 408
Harvey Jeremiah (1894-1970) 411
Harvey Leroy (1915-1983) 412
Hickory (1915-1983) 412
Ida Selena (1865-1925) 360
Ira A. 402
James Lee (1956-) 412
Janet Louise (1956-) 412
Jared 456
Jon William (1937-) 408
Kally N. (1970-) 412
Katie Ellen (1886-1973) 106, 402
Kim Lamarr (1955-) 412
Kirby Douglas (1943-) 411
Kristen A. (1992-) 412
Lauren E. (1983-) 412
Loretta Louise (1947-) 412
Marilyn Arlene (1948-) 412
Mark Kevin (1952-) 412
Mark Klinger (1914-1985) 411
Marlin Eugene (1920-1983) 412
Mary Elizabeth (1928-1999) 412
Michael 155
Morgan 456
Nancy 412
Paul Eugene (1942-) 408
Peter Adam (1862-1943) 411
Red (1920-1983) 412
Richard Eugene (1940-1980) 412
Ruth N. (1926-) 412
Susannah (1798-1861) 448
Teresa (1969-) 412
Tina 442
William Edward (1890-1958) 408
Winifred M. (1934-) 413

Mattern
Dale (-2006) 365
Dawn Linda (1953-) 197
Dennis Lee (1950-) 471
Dorene M. 365
Hanna (1851-1908) 249
Hilda S. (1914-2000) 192, 339
Jennie E. (1900-2008) 129
John Franklin 395
Leon (1912-1986) 365
Linda Charmaine (1952-) 472
Lloyd Edward 471
Mae Sarah 482
Romaine E. 365
Rosa Sevilla (1885-1933) 193
Samuel H. 339
Sara Ellen (1916-1967) 395
Wellington 424
William Herman (1930-) 471

Matternas
Anna Margaret (1899-1963) 81
Ella V. (1897-1976) 81
Harry (1879-) 81
John (1903-1974) 81
Mary (1901-) 81
Sallie C. (1906-) 81

Matterness
Susan 225

Mattis
Bailey Elisabeth (1997-) 414
Blair 323
Brian (1966-) 413
Bright 323
Bright Byrley (WW-II) (1919-1994) 323
Heather (1987-) 413
Kara (1991-) 414
Lacey (1998-) 414

Mattucci
Daniel (1981-) 302
Janine (1984-) 302
Joseph 302
Joseph (1979-) 302

Maulfair
Laura C. 284

Maurer
(--?--) 425, 455
(--?--) (1996-) 242, 253
Abraham (1853-1913) 167
Agnes M. (1871-1951) 220
Amelia (1853-1937) 485
Archie 168
Arlene 109
Arthur S. (1887-1960) 221
Brian Roger (1970-) 308
Brielle Isabella (2013-) 242, 253

Bruce Elwood 189
Bryan Roger (1970-) 308
Chase Avery (1996-) 242, 253
Chelsea Mae-Lynn (2000-) 242, 253
Clarence O. (1910-1989) 307
Clark Snyder (1899-1961) 253
Colin Perthemore (1993-) 307
Collin Ray (1996-) 253
Darlee 106
David Walter (1901-) 158
Dorothy M. (1912-) 202
Emma (1897-) 167
Emma (1918-2002) 150
Ernest (1898-) 167
Esther J. (1906-1958) 456
Evan Garret (1992-) 242, 253
Francis Herb (1882-1950) 150
Frederick 168
Grace Gertrude (1887-1922) 220
Gurney V. (1883-1969) 202
Hal 167
Harry (1878-) 168
Helen Viola (1880-1959) 220
Ida Celara (1875-1941) 167
Jeffry Allen 320
Jeraldine 347
Joel Richard (1877-1959) 157, 203
John Richard (1965-) 307
John W. 221
Joseph 167
Loren 253
Lydia H. (1903-) 435
Mamie (-2006) 349
Manassas (1826-1882) 167
Mary 497
Mary (1854-1899) 221
Matilda 239
Maude May (1897-1971) 157, 203
Morris (1872-) 167
Norman L 320
Peter 157
Ralph Emerson (1885-1916) 220
Randall Allen (1963-) 307
Ray 415
Rebecca Cate (1995-) 308
Roger Gene (1939-) 307
Sadie Alvena (1898-1968) 157
Samuel K 220
Seth William (1990-) 242, 253
Sharon Louise (1962-) 307
Shirley 245
Steven (1985-) 189
Tammy (1969-) 253
Terrance William (1947-) 241, 253
Theodore William (1925-) 253
Thomas Ambrose (1950-) 253
Timothy Lee (1960-) 189
Todd (1964-) 253
Tricia (1972-) 253
Troy (1967-) 241, 253
Vernon Clark (1953-) 253
William V. (1917-) 202
Maus
Lorie Ann 189

Mauser
Mary E. (1947-) 189
William 244
William H. (1893-1947) 244
Mausser
Alexis (1992-) 335, 444
Alisa (1985-) 335, 444
Amanda (1987-) 335, 444
Ashley (1984-) 335, 444
Darlette 254
Debbie (1968-) 335, 444
Doris Virginia (1929-) 185
Edna 366
Edna Elizabeth (1893-1993) 366
Harry (1964-) 335, 444
Harry M. (1942-) 335
Jacob (1868-1938) 356, 366
Marian Marie (1938-1998) 469
Raymond (1907-1971) 469
Verdie Minnie (1895-1980) 356
Maxwell
Claude G. 98
Thelma Mae (1917-1996) 98
May
(--?--) 496
Aaron 264
Earl Edward 284
Julie E. (1962-) 284
Madeleine 496
Sam 496
Mayer
Bradley 226
Edward H. (1930-2013) 226
Harry W. 226
Jennifer 226
Luke I. (1903-1939) 226
Sue 226
Thomas (1931-) 226
Maynard
Mary Dorothy (1923-) 253
Mazzo
Joseph III 238
Joseph Jr. 238
Kathleen 238
Mazzone
Albert Arron 354
Daniel Westley Brandon (1985-) 354
David Whitney Burton (1983-) 354
McAndrew
Ida Marie (1945-2001) 347
Joseph L. (-2001) 347
McCabe
Bridget 321
McCain
Albert 199
McCarthy
Ann Louise 191
Ann Marie (1929-2008) 212
Dennis 212
Elizabeth Carolyn (1966-) 314
Jay 495
Joe 253
John Thomas III (1964-) 314
John Thomas Jr. 314

John W. 191
Marty 263
Mary (1926-) 212
Michael Joseph (Dr.) (1892-1952) 212
Michael Joseph Dr. (1892-1952) 212
Nancy 191
Paul Franklin (1947-) 253
Terry 191

McClain
Cecile 325
Sarah Roberta (1901-1998) 329

McClaren
(--?--) 167
Richard 167

McClaskey
Paul Edward 124

McCleellan
(--?--) 99

McClintock
(--?--) 200

McCloy
Bruce M. 281
Sandra 281
William 281

McClure
Allen Lee (1959-) 98
Amy Lynn (1982-) 488
Arthur (1908-) 98
Debra Sue (1957-) 98
Donald L. (1930-) 98
Donna Jo (1961-) 98
Kenneth (1935-) 98
Marcia Ann (1960-) 98
Rex Arnold (1956-) 488
Ryan Matthew (1985-) 488

McCombe
Catherine 230

McConnell
Bud (1917-) 227
Carol 227
Cathy 227
Colleen 227
Edward 227
Elwood (1920-) 227
Mary Ellen 227
Patricia 227
Pearl (1923-) 227
Raymond W. 227
Robert R. (1917-) 227
Sharon 227

McCormick
(--?--) 157
Kelly 296
Patricia 113
Tom 296
Wes 296

McCorriston
David 380

McCrackin
Robert 484
Shirley A. (1938-2014) 484

McCready
Florence Elnora 174
Joan C. 457

McCreary
(--?--) 384
Michael Paul (1977-) 115
Sarah Jo Ann (1976-) 115

McCrone
Agis A. 280
Elizabeth E. (1905-1989) 280

McCullough
Joseph R. 226
Marie C. 226

McCurley
Joan Mace 292

McDermott
Grace L. (1894-1991) 122
James (1925-1990) 66
Marsha (1949-1975) 66
Richard Arthur (1996-) 306
William III 306
William IV (1994-) 306

McDonald
Ambrose J. (1922-1997) 437
Ann 232
Vera E. 110
William P. (1892-) 437
William P. (1950-2013) 437

McDonough
Alice Marie 218

McElroy
William 367

McFadden
Marisa A (1978-) 487
Patrick G. Jr (1976-) 487
Patrick G. Sr (1952-) 487

McFann
William Albert 380
William Albert (1905-) 380

McFarren
Ernest Earl (1889-1935) 94

McGaughey
Bob 273

McGee
Richard T. 114

McGehee
James 276

McGinley
Alice 199
Lisa 199
Regina 199
Thomas P. (1918-1974) 199

McGough
Rose (-2010) 383

McGovern
Helen G. (1913-2006) 212

McGrath
Winifred 212

McGready
Rose 247

McGuire
Mary Kay (1958-) 94

McHenry
Chris 296
Ella 296

McKee
    Sandra...262
McKelvey
    Janice G...263
McKenzie
    Margaret (1886-1941) 166
McKinney
    Annora (1872-) 459
    Anora and Nora (1872-) 459
    Bobbie Jean (1943-) 57
    Catherine (1908-) 459
    Charles A. (1912-) 459
    Charles Oliver (1886-1913)..................................459
    Cordelia (1877-1897) 459
    Daniel Arthur (1881-1940) 459
    Daniel R. (1893-) 459
    Guy (1909-) 459
    Harrie G. (1907-) 459
    Kattie M. (1905-) 459
    Louisa (1868-) 459
    Margaret..59
    Mary Elizabeth (1883-) 459
    Pearl L. (1900-) 459
    Philip (-1846) 459
    Philip (1845-1906) 459
    Sallie (1874-1876) 459
    Samuel E. Jr. (1874-1961)....................................122
    Theodore Henry (1869-) 459
McLain
    Aleese (1926-1997) 264
    John Wesley 264
McManus
    Andrew W. 422
    Bill..265
    Bruce L..422
    Dorothy 422
    John H. 422
McMichael
    Frances 287
McNalis
    (--?--) 140
McNalley
    Opal Charlene (1915-1958) 162
McNaughton
    Dean (1969-) 412
McNeal
    Donna (1929-) 343
McNeeley
    Betty (1946-) 328
McPherson
    Blaine...470
    Blaine (1953-) 470
    Cynthia Colleen (1957-) 470
    David Earl (1980-) 470
    Jennifer Leigh (1981-) 470
    John (1880-) 99
    Joseph Paul (1981-) 470
    Karen Ann (1966-) 470
    Sharon Marie (1954-) 470
    Susan Carol (1959-) 470
McSheehy
    Andrea 254
    Kelly Kathleen (1968-) 254
    Kevin Wayne (1961-) 254

    Sean Dale (1962-) 254
    Wayne E. 254
Meadows
    Evelyn (1920-) 436
Mease
    Earl S. (1905-1987)..79
    Elizabeth 50
    Marvin E. (1927-2002) 79
    Rodney E. 79
    Roger E. 79
Meckley
    Sarah E. 194
Medd
    Frank Davis..362
Medina
    Nicole Edelia (1980-) 86
Meetz
    Donna..233
Mehrwein
    (--?--) 209
Meinhardt
    Catharine Louise (1890-1956) 221
    Gustav 221
Melideo
    Sophia Rose (1999-) 477
    Thomas (1998-) 477
Mellefont
    Alice Catherine (1885-) 283
Melli
    Margaret..246
Melville
    Brooke 397
    Dennis 397
Mendelson
    Richard Herbert (1945-).....................................222
Menendez
    Henry L. 474
    Louis R. 474
Mengle
    Henry 384
Mentzer
    Alexis Nicole (1993-)................................. 174, 441
    Edward George (1972-) 174
    Harry M. 247
    Lanston 247
Mercer
    Lee 82
Meredith
    John...387
Meriano
    Charles Francis Sr. (1946-2016) 265
Merkel
    Catharine (1793-1858)...310
Merold
    Harry (1911-) 221
    Lawrence Eugene (1907-1943) 221
    Patrick (1873-1934) 221
    Rufus Mark (1915-1998) 221
Mertz
    Heinrich 99
    Nicolaus (1822-) 99
Mervine
    Carolyn K. (1941-) 337

Guy 198
Merwine
    Elsie Marie (1994-   ) 252
    Kelly M. 252
    Kris W. 252
    Rodger 252
Messersmith
    Angeline (1861-1920) 221, 453
    Eleanor (1918-   ) 451
    Sidney Ann (1876-1954) 343
Messick
    Cory L. 344
Messimer
    Melissa 280
Messner
    Alice 132
    Brandon James (1985-2014) 336, 444
    Brent Allen 336, 444
    Cameron A. 336, 444
    Feye 361
    Jerry 361
    Maude P. 56
    Nancy (1946-1978) 114
    Robert A. (1944-2006) 336
    Rodney Allen 336
Mettler
    Robert 297
Metz
    Flora (1853-1905) 374
    Marguerite Elizabeth (1866-1942) 251
    Mary Celesta (1894-1981) 358
    William Henry (1866-1914) 358
Metzgar
    Susanne (1945-   ) 348
Meyer
    Ashley 277
    Roy 277
    Salome 118
Meyers
    Pauline 368
    Sylvia 293
Micallef
    Jane Frances deChantal (1969-   ) 86
Michael
    Elizabeth (1817-1885) 83
Michaels
    Edna 442
    Helen 250
Michetti
    Angelina Mae (1981-   ) 154, 435, 450
    Antonio David (1979-   ) 154, 435, 450
    Joseph C. Jr. 154
    Maria Malina (1983-   ) 154
    Maria Melinda (1983-   ) 154, 435, 450
    Rosalynda Mary (1980-   ) 154, 435, 450
    Yolanda Marion (1984-   ) 154, 435, 451
Michijalia
    Mary (1909-1974) 424
Micka
    Darlee 189
Mickanis
    Judith Ann 76

Mickelbart
    Francis (1887-1940) 488
    Theresa Agnes (1933-2009) 488
Mielke
    Linda 187
Mihailoff
    (--?--) 491
Mikel
    Betty (1937-   ) 92
Millar
    Albert 397
    Minerva E. 397
Millard
    Anne S. (1928-   ) 301
    Benjamin J. (Dr.) (1870-1946) 301
    Benjamin J. Dr. (1870-1946) 301
    Brooke Amanda (1999-   ) 336, 444
    Burton M. (1903-1970) 301
    Mary Alice (1924-   ) 301
    Troy Eugene (1969-   ) 336
Miller
    (--?--) 170, 190, 261, 292
    (--?--) (1915-1915) 173
    Abraham 75, 222
    Ada 236
    Adam Lawson 317
    Addison Noelle (2010-   ) 458
    Alice 147, 277
    Allison Kay (1977-   ) 287
    Amanda 431
    Amanda (1850-1913) 55, 356
    Amelia Estella (1880-1923) 454
    Amos S. 273
    Amy M. (1889-1930) 99
    Andrew J. 317
    Angelica Nicole (1986-   ) 105
    Anna B. 89
    Anna Mae 385
    Anna Maria (1814-1896) 186
    April 104
    Arlene Susan (1916-2007) 216
    Arlene Suzanne (1916-2007) 216
    Barbara Amanda (1863-1913) 290
    Barbara Ann (1939-   ) 192
    Barbara I. (1942-   ) 147
    Bertha M. (1881-   ) 358
    Betty E. (1920-   ) 248
    Betty R. 117, 416
    Brent (1975-   ) 192
    Brian (1975-   ) 192
    Brooke (1977-   ) 192
    Byron Richard (1968-   ) 306
    Carl James (1937-   ) 104
    Carl Stephen (1975-   ) 162
    Carol Ann Elizabeth (1998-   ) 306
    Carrie E. (1908-1966) 212
    Carrie Manerva (1898-1989) 399
    Carrie S. (1902-1966) 78
    Cathie Mae (1959-   ) 174
    Charity 301
    Charles F. (1919-2011) 363
    Charles M. (1865-1902) 247, 257
    Charles R. 247
    Charles Victor (1915-1991) 247

Chase Landon (2004-)	332
Chris	458
Christine Mae (1958-)	308
Cindy Ann (1970-)	309
Clara J.	408
Clarence (1948-)	309
Clarence E. (1898-1952)	390
Clark C. (1891-1988)	54
Clayton R. (1886-1939)	99
Cletus	276
Clyde	340
Clyde Jacob	416
Clyde L. (1907-)	216
Clyde L. Jr. (1933-)	216
Colton Robert (1993-)	283
Corrina Marie (1974-)	105
Corrine Eileen	58
Craig (1948-)	192
Craig Arthur (1963-)	306
Curtin Ray (1895-1974)	247
Cynthia	247
Daisy (1904-1987)	204
Dale L.	105
Dalton Richard (1994-)	284
Daniel	50
Daniel (-2011)	363
Daniel D.	478
Darlene Kay	109
Darwin Eugene (1922-1975)	192
David L.	105
Dawn Louise (1957-)	104
Dean L.	105
Debbie A.	105
Deborah (1963-)	412
Dennis	118
Dennis Eugene (1943-)	159
Dennis Eugene Jr. (1961-)	159
Dennis Marlin (1946-)	283
Diane L.	247, 257
Dollie (1876-1931)	93
Dolores (1930-)	81
Dorothy Maria (1939-)	309
Dustin Dennis (1995-)	283
Dwayne L.	105
E. Guy (1916-2007)	216
Earle F. (1907-1985)	294
Eddie L.	423
Edith Levina (1885-1960)	423
Edna L. (1881-)	99
Edna Violet (1911-2009)	204
Edward	212, 352
Edward J.	60
Elias C. (1851-1924)	99
Elijah (1996-)	306
Elizabeth	271
Emory	255
Enola	281
Esta J. (1897-1960)	248
Esther	382
Esther (1897-1960)	248
Esther Marie (1921-)	276
Esther May (1913-2003)	344
Eva (1923-2014)	75
Everett	273
Florence (1919-1919)	191
Floyd Allen (1913-1972)	104
Fox	205
Frances (1933-1990)	217
Frank	452
Frank J. Jr.	452
Franklin B. (1863-1934)	309
Fred William (1891-1948)	247
Frieda Louise (1907-2011)	273
Gabriel (1859-1910)	358
Gary Floyd (1950-)	105
Gary Ray (1965-)	332
George	118
George (1934-)	81
George E. (1899-1940)	81
Gina	105
Gloria P.	471, 479
Gloria Renee (1938-)	173
Guerney Edward (1890-1972)	309
Guy	390
Guy A. (-2012)	390
Guy II	390
Hailey	292
Hannah Elizabeth (1910-1986)	173
Harold Leroy (1925-1945)	174
Harold Stephen (1954-)	162
Harrison (1870-1942)	416
Harry Abraham (1884-1957)	173
Harry E. (1884-)	99
Harry R. (1896-)	358
Heidi Lynn (1977-)	110
Helen	278
Henry	389
Henry A.	54
Hilda	416
Inez M. (1919-)	217
Ira Oliver	399
J. Curtis and Curtis R. (1895-1974)	247
Jacob	344
James	191
James (1920-)	390
James A. (1885-)	358
James D. (1912-)	137
James E. (1894-1986)	247, 257
James E. Jr. (1918-)	247, 257
James M. (1899-1971)	191
Janet Marie (1941-)	105
Jay Guy (1910-1998)	163
Jeffrey	247, 317
Jennie M. (1877-)	99
Jennifer J. (1982-)	291
Jestine Elnora (1908-1971)	173
Joan M. (1936-)	216
John	147, 247
John Harry Abraham (1920-1990)	174
Josh	478
Josiah	274
Juanita Sue (1952-)	105
Judith	247
Judith L.	247, 257
Judy A.	363
Karen	104, 118
Katharine	118
Kathleen	62
Kathleen M. (1926-)	54
Kathryn Ann (1940-)	255

Kathryn H.	137
Katie	484
Katie Ann	474
Katie T. (1866-1914)	222
Kayla	478
Kelly M. (1987-)	291
Kenneth (-2008)	118
Kim	452
Kimberly Ann (1971-)	309
Landon	306
Larry	186, 266, 383
Larry Richard	291
Lauretta E. (1919-)	248
Leon	371
Leroy C.	247
Leslie Jo (1944-)	163
Lewis Franklin	291
Lidia (1819-1896)	90
Lillian C. (1872-1945)	50
Linda Jean (1943-1979)	105
Lorene K. (1917-1989)	54
Lorie	401
Lorrie Lynn	318
Lucinda	478
Lulu Ellen (1916-)	173, 441
Lydia Mc Clade (1870-)	360
Lyle C. (1925-2016)	478
Mabel	167
Mabel Alice	113
Madeline R. (1927-)	60
Manavilla	52
Marci Louise (1965-)	306
Margaret (-2006)	248
Margaret Irene (1920-1985)	115
Margaret Magrarita (1924-)	54
Marlin Monroe	283
Mary (1879-)	99
Mary (1922-)	390
Mary Alice (1914-1979)	173
Mary Ellen (1945-)	256
Mary Elva (1919-)	247, 257
Mary L.	411
Matthew David (1984-)	287
Maud Mabel	389
Michael	247, 273
Michael David	287
Michael Lee (1959-)	104
Michael Lee Jr.	104
Mitch	273
Morris W. (1874-)	99
Nancy K.	247, 257
Ned E. (1923-1999)	247, 257
Newton Williams (1888-)	358
Nolen E. (1892-1938)	137
Nolen Edward (1891-1938)	358
Olivia Grace (1992-)	284
Paige Elizabeth (2005-)	170
Pamela	275
Pamela Ann (1973-)	162
Patricia Ann (1958-)	185
Peggy (-2006)	248
Peggy (1954-)	192
Penny	273, 390
Phyllis P. (1927-)	152
Ralph Leroy (1949-1996)	105
Rathmus (1877-)	204
Ray H. (1892-)	216
Rhonda	105
Richard (1937-)	305
Richard Scott (1968-)	284
Ricky Allen (1956-)	104
Robert	306
Robert (1919-)	390
Robert Dennis (1964-)	283
Robert W.	275
Ronald	108
Ronald Lee (1946-2012)	105, 106
Rose Jane (1906-2008)	204
Rosie and Rosa (1906-2008)	204
Ruth	364
Ryan	390
Sadie	308
Sallie	217
Sandra	248
Sandra Ann (1942-2012)	105
Scott Leroy	108
Sevilla	205
Shane	266
Sharon E. (1951-)	159
Sonya	105, 106
Stanley (1917-1968)	255
Stella (1876-)	99
Steven C.	340, 446
Stuart (1965-)	306
Susan	236, 390
Susan (1959-)	487
Susanna	404
Susie (1887-1975)	274
Tammy Jo (1961-)	105
Teresa Ann (1960-)	104
Thomas	318
Timothy David (1979-)	309
Todd	273
Todd Anthony (1965-)	159
Todd Michael (1980-)	287
Todd Wesley	275
Tracy Ann (1963-)	332
Travis	266
Trey	292
Valerie	452
Verna Elizabeth	287
Victoria Ann (1857-)	389
Vincent C. (1927-)	81
Wilbur	287
William (1857-)	204
William D.	478
William Edward	216
William F. (1905-)	70
William R. (1901-2009)	204

Mills

J. Robert (1970-)	58
Robert J.	58
Robert J. (1937-)	58
Robert J. Jr. (1962-)	58
Sharon Marie (1968-)	58
Susan	398
Susan (1896-)	304

Milne

Gerald	269
Jeffrey	269

Kenzie Marie (2001-) 269, 479
Milot
   (--?--) 260
Minarich
   Scott E. 181
Miner
   Alon D. (1895-1898) 93
   Cyrus (1866-) 93
   Dewey (1898-1983) 93
Mingus
   Donald (1927-2006) 466
   Howard 466
Minnich
   (--?--) 75
   Ada Matilda (1914-2004) 73
   Arthur F. 141
   Clarence Richard (1911-1988) 73
   Clinton W. (1890-1974) 73
   Debra Louise (1958-) 141
   Donna Mae (1934-2013) 263
   Ellen 73
   Frank 73
   George D. 263
   Grace (1918-1920) 73
   Guy William (1916-1917) 73
   Holly 366
   John 317
   John Arthur (1937-2005) 141
   Justine L. (1962-) 366
   Kristina Kay 155
   Lamar (1927-) 366
   Laura May (1898-1967) 437
   Lori Jean (1960-) 141
   Robert W. (1911-1965) 263
   Roxanne R. (1966-) 366
   Tina (1962-) 366
   William 366
   William Henry (1865-1941) 437
Minnick
   David 349
Mirillo
   Richard 201
   Robert 201
Miscka
   Ernestine 145
Misiak
   John 394
Mitchele
   William 375
Mitchell
   Allison Jaye 355
   Leona Mae (1902-1991) 155
Miyata
   (--?--) 306
Mock
   (--?--) 439
   James (1922-) 377
   Jessica 439
   Mildred (1919-) 377
   Rhodes James (1895-) 377
Modesto
   Angelina 341

Moffet
   Alex Edwarde 268
   David Aaron 268
   Edward 268
   Eric Adam 268
   Jennie Louisa (1907-1965) 113
   Robert Jr. 113
Moffett
   Mary A. 388
Mohamed
   Hasan 124
Mohar
   Edward 249
   Gerald 249
   Michael 249
   Steven 249
Molko
   Mary E. 141
Mollica
   Christine A. (1957-) 488
   Falon Inez (2011-) 488
   Janine Marie (1975-) 488
   Michael Anthony (1981-) 488
   Orlando J. (1924-1992) 488
   Ronald R (1951-) 488
Molliter
   Maryann 246
Moltz
   Catherine 133
Moneyheffer
   Deborah 274
   Donald 274
   Jacob 274
   Kimberly 274
   Margaret 274
   Wayne (1915-1998) 274
Mongold
   David Calvin 158
   John Calvin (1889-1982) 107
   Violet Elizabeth (1928-1958) 107
Montoya
   Rick Lee (1963-) 230
   Ryan Lee (1991-) 230
   Samantha Ann (1988-) 230
Moody
   Milton (2000-) 71
Moore
   Carolyn 146
   Debbie (1972-) 419
   Dorie A. (1881-1964) 422
   Edna (1906-1990) 238
   Elizabeth Caroline (1910-2004) 422
   Emilie (1893-1966) 72
   Emma Jean (1953-) 108
   James A. (1928-) 423
   John 199
   Joseph 142
   Joseph Jr. (1922-) 142
   Melvin H. (1912-1989) 422
   Melvin H. Jr. (1937-) 422
   Rae (1919-) 142
   Ray 60
   Ruth (1924-) 142
   Ruth Naomi (1919-1998) 422

Stephanie R. (1939-1950) 422
Wanda Marie (1930-2010) 60
Morgan
  Allison 478
  Amanda 264, 478
  Anna Mae (1996-) 475
  Arlene (1915-1973) 288
  Ashley Nicole (1999-) 263
  Bessie 281
  Bessie Susan (1895-1936) 489
  Betty J. (1923-) 475
  Bobbie Jo 263
  Bryan (1969-) 475
  Bryan Keith (1969-) 475
  Carolyn 263
  Chester 255
  Christopher Charles (1970-) 476
  Craig Eugene (1953-) 255
  Curtis 218
  David O. 56
  Debra Louise (1952-) 255
  Denise (1956-) 255
  Donna Jean (1960-) 255
  Edgar T. (1905-1964) 216
  Edith Elda (1921-1996) 56
  Elvin Daryl 475
  Emerson 263
  Harvey Daniel (1905-1935) 218
  Heather Geist (1992-) 263
  Irvin 485
  Ivan 196
  Jachary (1995-) 475
  James Burton (1987-) 85
  James C. 478
  James C. Jr. 478
  James Edward (1960-) 85
  Janet A. (1951-1999) 264
  Jared Michael (1993-) 476
  Jayme 478
  Jeffrey Miller (1965-) 147
  Jennifer 264
  Joan Mae (1954-) 340
  John 216
  John D. Jr. 147
  John D. Sr. 147
  John L. 264
  Joseph I. 288
  Joshua Ryan (1997-) 475
  Justin (1990-) 476
  Katelyn C. (1997-) 476
  Kenneth M. 263
  Kenneth Michael Jr. (1998-) 263
  Lena Luella (1906-1959) 102
  Lisa Ann (1994-) 475
  Mark Daniel (1929-2002) 218
  Matt 255
  Melissa Ann (1981-) 471
  Nancy 306
  Nicholas Bryce (1998-) 476
  Rachel Elizabeth (1990-) 85
  Ralph 310
  Sarah 422
  Shirley L. 286
  Tamie Sevilla (1869-1947) 309
  Thelma E. (1918-1988) 243

  Thomas D. 263
  Thomas D. Jr. 264
  Thomas Leroy (1914-2001) 263
  Tiffani Geist (1996-) 263
  Timothy Emerson 471
  Todd 112
  Tonya 112
  Woodrow G. 112
Morgans
  Alice (1903-) 422
  George Raymond 422
  Mabel (1906-) 422
  William 422
  William (1908-) 422
Morris
  (--?--) 175
  Amos (1893-) 177, 447
  Beatrice (1896-) 177, 447
  Cody 121
  David H. 54
  Edna C. (1918-1986) 362
  Eman (1893-) 177
  Emans (1893-) 177
  John S. 121
  Louis (1898-) 177, 447
  Marcia Mildred (1936-) 68, 329
  Michael (1965-) 322
  Robert (1929-2013) 54
  William 175
  William J. 177
Morrison
  Sara Hanna 53
Mort
  Lizzie E. (1886-1974) 375
Morton
  Henry Edward (1832-1878) 295
  Ida (1874-1920) 296
Moseley
  Jewel 217
Moser
  Archibald A. 219
  Carrie Viola (1907-1994) 219
  Jacob 159
  Matthew 159
  Mitchell 159
  Nathan 159
Motter
  (--?--) 193
Mowan
  Lori 273
Mower
  Hazel Marie (1913-1999) 246
  Peter 246
Mowery
  Anna 243
  Archie 168
  Catherine Arine (1935-2003) 321
  Emma (1897-) 167
  Ernest (1898-) 167
  Frederick 168
  John 321
  Roy 353
Moyer
  (--?--) 90, 438

Abbey	454
Alane	88
Alane Virginia	368
Alma Mary Edna (1902-1992)	334, 418
Annie R. (1875-)	418
Catherine	100
Darwin D.	116
Donald	309
Elisabeth (1837-1911)	435, 481, 485
Ethel Laura (1909-1911)	407
Flo-Ella C. (1932-2016)	216
Grace Emmaline (1921-1995)	407
Harold	216
Hilda Margaret (1922-1942)	475
Irv	454
Irvin P. (1952-)	196
John Edgar (1878-1956)	418
Katie Mae (1897-)	305
Lindsey	454
Lottie M.	217
Luke Mandan (1912-1912)	407
Lynne Errol	424
Mabel Elizabeth (1887-1972)	70
Maggie (1872-)	418
Mandan	407
Mark S. (1904-)	407
Martha E. (1907-)	407
Mary L. (1925-1993)	115
Paul C. (1911-1921)	407
Salem C. (1880-1959)	407
Salem Clair (1918-1966)	407
Samuel Stanford	475
Thomas B. (1847-1921)	418
Tina	290
Wanda	155

Mucher
John	65
Sarah Ann (1858-1944)	65

Muckel
(--?--)	80
Cory	80

Muench
Jacob DeWald	118
Margaret Anna (1842-1913)	68, 118

Mull
(--?--)	379, 384
Craig Alan	305
Steven	305

Mullenhour
James Ora (1930-2001)	59
John Corbin (1902-1962)	59

Muller
Heidi	491
Ronald Herbert (1947-)	412

Mulvaney
Matthew (1863-)	296
Nellie Helen (1888-1961)	296

Mumma
Dylan	64
Mary A.	157
Mick	64
Travis	64

Mumper
George R. (1911-1980)	63
Patricia A. (1939-1992)	63

Mundorf
Jane	320

Munk
Barbara (1931-)	178
John	178

Munroe
William F.	341

Munson
Josephine	373

Muntzing
Mary M.	221

Murphy
Thomas	325
Virginia Mae (1930-)	325
Wendy Ann	255

Murray
Paul S.	402

Musgrove
Jan (1959-)	163

Musolino
Brian	335
Mykenna Adell (2002-)	335, 351, 419, 444
Vince	335

Musser
Edith (1860-1922)	206
Henry	206

Mussleman
Shirley A. (1939-)	219

Mutchler
Beatrice E. (1899-1968)	374
Eileen A. (1908-1977)	375
Harry E. (1881-)	374
Harry E. Jr. (1913-)	375
Helen C. (1906-)	375
Howard J. (1901-1945)	375
Irene (1908-1977)	375
Jean (1930-)	375
Roland E. (1903-1959)	375
Rolland (1903-1959)	375

Muth
Charles	68, 122
Charles E. (1918-1985)	68, 122, 135
Donna	68, 122, 135
Henry D. (1866-1943)	68
Mary Louisa (1922-2009)	68, 122
Reuben Harris (1896-1961)	68

Myers
(--?--)	394
A. Ralph (1903-1942)	222
Aldus J.	222
Anna Kathryn (1905-2006)	223
Carolyn Ann	223
Carrie W.	247
Charles F. (1910-)	223
Charles Gaul (1884-1925)	222
David	318
Dennis (1952-)	318
Doris (1936-)	223
Dorothea C.	223
Edward Klinger (1913-1994)	223
Edward S.	223
Evelyn (1918-1965)	318
Harry Edward (1894-1969)	388

Ida Jane (-2007) 54
Jane (1946-) 318
Janet R. (1919-2012) 262
Joyce Marie (1924-1999) 389
Marlin Theodore (1921-1968) 318
Michelle (1972-) 350
Mike 318
Ray W. (1891-1955) 318
Robert B. 223
Robert Matthew (1915-1989) 223
Stella Keeley 236

Naber
Brenda 296

Nace
Bertha 387
Cora Louise (1890-1953) 413
Maria E (1867-1955) 442
Sharon Lynn 483

Nagle
Deborah 281
Kimberly 281
Robert 281

Nahodil
Diane (-2015) 381
Franz (1884-1959) 381
Jane 381
Richard (Rev.) 381
Richard Rev. 381
Roslyn 381
Russell Frederick Sr. (1907-1986) 381
Russell Jr. 381

Namoro
Jean Mc 345

Narlock
Brandon (1982-) 102
Jared (1980-) 102
Jerry (1952-) 102

Natale
Carmen 493
Lucile 493

Naugle
Jannette 383

Neal
Calvin Richard (1903-1968) 83
Ella (1903-) 80
Ellen (1903-) 80
Rosanna E. (1927-) 83

Neff
Nettie 274

Neibauer
Edward (-1949) 375
Mary B. (1909-1962) 375

Neidig
(--?--) (-1910) 378
Connie Mae (1942-) 473
David A. (1907-) 379
George Freeman 473
Helen M. (1908-) 379

Neidlinger
Sandy 79

Neiman
Charles N. (1882-) 411
Delton Wilbur (1907-1966) 411
Evelyn Mae (1934-) 411

Mary Hilda (1909-) 411
Melvin Arlington (1911-1993) 411

Neiswender
David 335
Michael 335, 444
Ottmer 174

Neiter
(--?--) 359
Debra F. 360
Fred 326
Jean Mae (1936-) 326
Kathy L. 360
Thomas H. 360
Timothy A. 360

Neitz
Shannon Lee (1972-) 183

Nelson
Alverta 127
Gary Jonathan (1984-) 57
Graham Forrest (1998-) 85
Jeffrey David (1963-) 85
Joseph Kenneth (1997-) 85
Kenneth Richard (1937-) 85
Matthew Jonathan 57
Norma Agnes (1891-1933) 414
Patricia Sue (1968-) 85
Philip 296
Rachel Anne (1999-) 85
Rebecca Anne (2004-) 85
Tim 396
Timothy Scott (1965-) 85
William J. 414

Nesvold
Gerald 299

Nettles
Craig (1944-) 165
Reginald (1925-) 165

Neugard
Brady (1966-) 372
Brittney Lynne (1992-) 372
Brockton Paul (1998-) 372
Helen Jennie (1913-1991) 485

Neumeister
Cora (1886-) 352, 474

Neuner
(--?--) 246

Nevadomsky
John 264

Nevil
Annamae Marie 427
Joseph Montgomery 427

Newberry
Annabelle 143
Darlene (1937-2007) 384
Stephen 384

Newcomer
Cynthia 74
Elizabeth (-2012) 131
Morris (1919-) 73
Oma 274
Ray (1920-) 73
Reuben T. (1895-1978) 73
Theodore 73
Wilbert (1925-1996) 74

Newitt
    Amy E. 305
Newman
    Charles Matthew (1963-) 484
    Jennifer 409
    Julie 409
    Marvin 409
Newton
    Amy Lynn (1972-) 350
    Lowell Allen (1931-) 350
Ney
    (--?--) 128
    Andrew Allen (1970-) 171
    Ashley 128
    Benjamin F. (1909-1984) 214
    Benjamin F. Jr. (1934-) 214
    Catherine (1942-1942) 214
    Clair 171
    Deloris Mable (1938-1997) 214
    Dennis (1937-) 171
    Donny 128
    Earl 290
    Elsie Mae (1903-1995) 271
    Harvey 214
    Jeremiah J. 128
    Linda (1951-) 357
    Margaret (1921-1992) 290
    Martha 293
    Rufus 293
    Shirley J. (1932-) 214
    William 271
Nguyen
    M. Thank 336
Nice
    Arthur 333
    Diane Marie 321
    Ruthanna May (1938-) 333
Nicholaus
    Linda L. (1948-1998) 123
Nichols
    (--?--) 436
Nickels
    Christian III 478
    Christian Jr. 478
    Jill Kristin 478
    Jonathan Michael 478
Nickerson
    Lois (1937-1999) 190
Nicklo
    Julia 359
Nicksic
    James 292
    Lisa 292
    Stacy 292
Nilsson
    Gunner (1908-) 168
    Lisa Britt (1957-) 168
Noblet
    Anetta 206
Noblit
    Edward Jr. 108
    Jennifer Marie (1992-) 108
    Jessica Mae (1991-) 108

Nolan
    Marie 479
Nolen
    Belinda Suzanne (1952-) 115
    Bradley Lee (1955-) 115
    John Leroy (1928-1971) 115
    John Rodney (1954-) 115
Noll
    David 210
    Esther Irene (1916-1988) 210
    Pierce Elmer (1887-1918) 210
    Ruth Elizabeth (1918-1998) 211
Nolte
    Donna Jo 321
Noneckere
    Rose (1955-) 412
Nonnecke
    Brian 153
    Eric 153, 435, 450
Norbeth
    Agnes C. 394
Norbuntas
    Dominikas 394
Norris
    Betty Jean (1933-) 94
    Clarence Albert (1909-1985) 94
    Earl Edwin (1911-1992) 94
    Helen Bernice (1914-1991) 95
    John (1887-1971) 94
    Mary Catherine (1921-1966) 96
    Nellie (1917-1926) 95
    Ruth Maxine (1919-) 95
Northrup
    Erie (1845-) 97
    Maud Alice (1879-) 97
Novinger
    (--?--) 364, 416
    Earl M. (1902-1970) 430
    Franklin B. (1873-) 430
    James (1960-) 330
    Kenneth L. 419
    Laura (1993-) 330
    Natalie Nicole (1987-1987) 330
    Paul Deibler (1899-1965) 401
    Rose Marie (1989-) 330
    Ruth Pauline (1895-) 430
    Tricia (1984-) 330
Noyes
    Maxine 275
Nunley
    Pamela Y. (1936-1999) 212
Nusbaum
    Billy W. 278
    Dean 278
    Jane Ann (1944-1944) 278
    Jean Ellen (1944-1944) 278
    Kelly 278
    Lamar 278
    Lisa 278
    Rodney 278
    Russell 278
    Shiela 278
    Wayne 278

Nuss
  Lewis T. (1906-1976) 375
Nutt
  Marilyn 458
Nuttall
  Frank L. (1874-1954) 426
  Goldie Marie (1912-1982) 426
  Hazel M. (1901-1980) 426
Nye
  (--?--) 366
  Daisy C. 417
  Lucy 217
  Michael 108
  Paul (1894-1958) 76
  Paul Harvey (1923-2006) 76
Oakes
  Delbert 398
  H. Eugene (1910-1985) 398
  Helen 54
Ober
  Alice 76
Ochs
  Alberta 170
  Alberta M. (1920-2012) 195
  Arland A. (1899-1957) 224
  Ida Gottschall (1885-1954) 150
Ochsenrider
  Michael Henry 161
O'Donell
  Garrett 276
  Mark 276
Ogden
  Margaret Blanche (1883-) 83
  Tolbert D. (1856-) 83
Oglesbee
  Rachael (1953-) 94
Ohmacht
  Adam 104
  Christopher 104
  Dana 104
  Ralph 104
O'Kane
  Kristin 232
  Samuel 232
O'Keefe
  Katie (1986-) 408
  Michael 408
Oldham
  Thomas Edison (1948-2005) 252
  Wylie A. 252
Oldt
  Edna V. 59
  Elanora (1882-1952) 78
Olinick
  Andrew (1920-1985) 248
  Ariana 248
  Cassandra 248
  Michael 248
  Patricia 248
  Paul 248
  Stephen 248
Olsen
  Donald Jr. 118
  Donald Sr. 118
  Larry 118
  Loraine 118
Olt
  Edwin 74
  Ivy Minerva (1902-2003) 74
Omholtz
  Mary A. (1884-) 135
Omlor
  Mary 349
O'Neill
  Anna M. (1905-) 407
  Bertha Bulah (1886-) 406
  Ethel Irene (1900-1903) 407
  Jean M. (1933-2012) 359
  Joseph 359
  Laura Etta (1887-1956) 407
  Mona Helen (1892-1904) 407
  William Oscar (1890-1891) 407
  Willis (1859-1928) 406
O'Niell
  Lydia (1885-1955) 381
Orner
  June Delaine (1923-) 105
  Roxanne Catherine (1972-) 332
Orr
  Anna 113
  Anna Laura 218
  Margaret (-2008) 457
Ortega
  Franc 275
Orth
  Sandra 223
  Victoria 223
  William A. 223
Osman
  Elmer 349
  Irene E. (1919-2015) 349
Ossman
  Amelia A. (1859-1928) 205
  Benneville 205
  Fronie (1887-) 389
  Helen Mabel (-2007) 289
  John H. (1859-1948) 389
  Lyllian (1909-) 427
  Mae 480
Ostling
  Axel H. (1896-) 424
  Harold Olaf (1909-) 424
  Nancy 424
Oswald
  Mary Elsie 124
Ott
  Michael Lee 159
Ottengier
  Karen 103
Otto
  Aaron Henry (1915-) 137
  Anna (1829-1882) 295
  Annetta P. 290
  Clarence (1923-) 137
  Harry E. (1887-) 137
  Janice 475

Page 604

Janice D. (1928-)..352
Jonathan (1805-1887)....................................295
Mary S..234
Norma R. (1910-)...352
Overhiser
Janet Louise (1938-2000)..............................426
John Lawrence (1914-2004)..........................426
Karl J..426
Marjorie Ann (1939-1999).............................426
Overlingas
Petronella...488
Owens
Bertha M...61
Caroline Catherine (1888-1945)....................297
Carrie...73
Kate..210
Mary...211
Oxendine
Marc A. (1984-)..109
Matthew A. (1988-).......................................109
Michael A...109
Oxenreider
Mary Ann (1849-1894)..................................161
Oxenrider
Arlene (1927-)..470
Bernice Arlene (1927-)................................470
Billie Earl (1961-)...............................129, 470
Carrie Irene (1903-1934)......................129, 153
Christopher Lee..187
Dean Harold (1938-).....................................471
Dean Herald (1938-).....................................471
Debra Ann (1955-)..............................129, 470
Earl Monroe (1906-1998).....................129, 470
Florence Irene (1941-)..................................187
Francis Gordon (1887-1964)..........................186
Henry Archie (1881-1950).............................470
James..496
Jason Earl (1981-)...............................129, 470
Jennifer (1979-)..496
John Elias (1916-2001)..................................186
Johnny Lynn...187
Linda Lou (1947-)...471
Lucy (1981-)...496
Lynnette Ann (1979-)..........................129, 470
Marie Irene (1931-2012)................................470
Mary Irene (1931-2012).................................470
Ray H. (1933-2012)..470
Rita Mae (1940-)...471
Teresa Ann (1960-).......................................471
Willard Earl (1929-)............................129, 470
William A. (1938-)..187
William E. Jr..187
William Russell (1938-)................................187
Oyster
Ethel...167
Pace
Jim..282
Kim Fran (1969-)..282
Paczkowski
Dennis...199
Padalion
Eva...52
Padelford
Leman...421

Paffenberger
Adam R. (1852-)...167
Page
Gary..254
Melissa Jolene..254
Palatinus
Mary Ann (1937-)...98
Palityea
Dolores...302
Palm
Mary Magdalena..259
Palmer
Adaha Dorothy (1903-1972)................. 143, 315
Adam..421
Andrew Michael (1992-)..............................348
Delores...244
Jennie May (1877-1908)................................421
Minnie (1879-)..167
Richard Alan..348
Palumbis
Mary...301
Pang
Baw Ki...429
Pangelinan
Thomas..70
Panhorst
Scott (1994-)...235
Paponetti
Lisa R.. 146, 182
Paul G. (1934-2008).......................................146
Parker
Claudia Mae (2002-)....................................478
Edith Charlotte (1927-2013)..........................299
Isaiah..299
John..128
Myah Eliza (1996-)......................................478
Pryce...477
Parks
Jean Ellen (1949-)..272
Norman..168
Parry
Agnes M. (1888-1960)...................................210
Anna Pearl (1886-)...72
G. Thomas..211
George T. (1906-1992)...................................211
Helen I. (1895-1981)......................................211
Herman Harry (1901-1917)...........................211
Jennie Esther (1890-1964).............................211
Marilow..211
Morgan L...72
Pearl Josephine (1897-1976).........................211
Sue (1930-)...211
Thomas J. (1864-1934)..................................210
William...210
William Roy (1893-1982)..............................211
Parsons
Albert (1915-)...359
August..374
Dorothy (1939-)..360
Evelyn Fay (1937-2015).................................359
Ronald (1933-2015).......................................359
Partrick
J.D..166

Partridge
- Dorothy Elle (1906-1933) 422
- John W. 422
- Judy 96
- Michael 97
- Robert 96

Paschley
- Cathleen J. 265
- Christine 265
- Jan Marie 265
- John 265

Pasirba
- (--?--) 292

Paterson
- Sharon 436

Patrick
- Kathleen Jane (1919-) 215
- Oliver 215
- Susan 472

Patterson
- Elizabeth 295

Patton
- Christine A. 107
- Dea Denelle 57
- Elwood 110
- Paul 110
- Richard 110
- Roy Thomas Mitchell (1929-2006) 107
- Tony 110
- Vicki Lee (1958-) 160

Paul
- (--?--) 311, 334
- Abbie 306
- Alex 306
- Amanda (1873-1943) 356, 366
- Amy S. (1888-1918) 175
- Anita (1918-) 174
- Annette 254
- Barbara 114
- Bertha (1882-1949) 174
- Betty Renee (1925-2012) 306
- Beulah Elizabeth 417
- Daniel S. 493
- Debbra (1960-) 194
- Deborah 220, 230
- Delbert 220
- Dorothy Ellen (1906-1907) 404
- Edna M. (1916-1995) 433
- Eleanor Marie (1946-) 194
- Eli 174
- Elizabeth (1889-1972) 175
- Ellen 441
- Elmira (1853-1935) 165
- Festus (1887-1915) 174
- Francis I. (1917-1976) 440
- Frank W. (1881-) 404
- Gabriel 168
- George A. (1917-) 185
- George E. (1887-) 185
- Glenn Fertig Jr. (1962-) 306
- Glenn Fertig Sr. (1922-2014) 306
- Grace Helen (1930-) 111
- Grady 220, 230
- Harlan F. (1922-) 185
- Henry W. 306
- Infant (1950-1950) 442
- Jennie May (1890-1955) 493
- Jeremiah Kleckner 174
- John 404
- John Adam (1890-1951) 194
- John Alfred (1892-) 120
- Joseph Lewis (1897-1965) 306
- Katie (1872-1954) 303
- Kay Ann (1946-2009) 441
- Martin Luther (1908-) 404
- Meda Mabel 452
- Milton J. (1868-1958) 356
- Pamela Renee (1955-) 306
- Pearl E. (1889-1957) 356
- Phyllis Eva Mae (1929-) 181, 476
- Rose Marie (1929-) 134
- Roy D. (1938-) 194
- Russel D. (1918-1995) 194
- Ruth 214
- Stella 103
- Stiles Kleckner (1884-1935) 174
- Susan Gregory (1951-) 306
- Viola May (1914-1998) 120

Paulus
- Arthur Lamar (1911-2008) 276
- Byron 276
- Carl Frederick (1936-) 276
- Caroline 276
- Dawn Marie (1948-1948) 276
- Dennis 276
- Donald 276
- Heidi E. 276
- Marilyn Elaine (1946-1946) 276
- Ralph Leroy 276
- Robert Duane (1944-1969) 276
- Tamra 276
- Tara L. 276
- Tracy L. 276
- Trena M. 276
- Trevor L. 276

Payton
- Florence 287

Pearson
- Dora 189

Peay
- (--?--) 160

Peffley
- Anna L. 258

Peifer
- Arthur (1950-) 420
- Catherine (1953-) 420
- Dwayne (1967-) 420
- Emery E. 437
- Karen Ann (1965-) 438
- Leonard D. (1954-) 438
- Ned Joseph (1924-1996) 225
- Ray C. (1923-) 419
- Rebecca I. (1963-) 225
- Shelley Ann (1958-) 225
- Truman (1947-) 419
- William H. (1933-2000) 437

Peiffer
- Dorothy 320

Kate 133
Lizzie Alice (1877-1952) 200
Pelayo
Susana Alatorre 355
Pellerite
Camelia 227, 228
Peltz
Jeff 265
Pendal
(--?--) 151
Katelynn 151, 449
Pensyl
Arthur (1913-1967) 201
Gary Lee (1954-2013) 201
Pentz
Gladys E. (1914-1998) 393
Pepe
Albert Joseph 354
Perhach
Gladys V. 216
Perry
(--?--) 120
Jonathan 120, 181
Judy (1943-) 151
Shawn 120, 181
Persing
(--?--) 375
William 191
Pesarchick
Helen 282
Peters
Barry 88
Doris Mary (1880-) 168
Doshia 272
Jay Russell (1910-1983) 381
Michelle 238
Stephanie 238
Walter 238
William Daniel 381
Peterson
Jay 296
Louie 296
Steven 296
Tena 296
Petrino
Michael 215
Sebastian 215
Traci 215
Petrowsky
Andrew 199
Pfeifer
Jesse Melvin (1904-1951) 93
Pfeil
Ruth Ann 317
Phelan
Heather 107
Lawrence 107
Philips
Dorothy Marie (1922-) 277
Effie (1914-1985) 498
Elizabeth (1887-) 375
George W. (1893-1989) 277
Lewis F. 277
Vannie (1912-) 498
William E. (1884-1963) 498
Phillippy
Angela 79
Craig James 79
David 79
Diane 79
Hillery 79
Isaac G. 79
Jeffrey Lee (1954-2013) 79
Jeffrey Lee Jr. 79
Kandice 79
Ralph Aaron (1927-2006) 79
Phillips
Alice E. (1895-1975) 88, 440
Alma A. 79
Alta 68, 135
Betty Lou (1945-) 331
Brad Eugene (1956-) 94
Charles Jay (1889-1984) 179
Christina Michelle (1982-) 94
Christopher Ryan (1981-) 94
David Cameron (1985-) 94
Edwin 393
Elizabeth Renae (1979-) 94
James Edward (1931-) 94
John Jacob (1861-1943) 88
Julia Ann (1983-) 94
Maude A. (1879-1964) 393
Oscar 68
Sarah (1855-1946) 288
Sarah Elizabeth (1985-) 94
Stephen Allen (1953-) 94
Piccolo
Elizabeth 267
Pickup
Amanda 113
Amber 113
Anne T. (1944-) 112
Betty E. (1926-2001) 112
Blanche (1924-1945) 112
Cathy 113
Charlene Caroline (1951-) 112
Charles J. (1932-2002) 113
Debra Sue 113
Jennifer 112
Jerry 113
Lucinda 113
Michael J. (1947-) 112
Michael Richard (1954-) 113
Robert B. (1919-1965) 112
Ruth Marie (1928-1992) 112
Thomas Eugene (1929-1997) 112
Thomas Eugene III 112
Thomas Eugene Jr. (1948-) 112
Thomas Lester (1898-1981) 111
William (1858-) 111
William P. (1922-1985) 112
William P. Jr. (1946-) 112
Picola
Cheryl Ann 419
Pierce
(--?--) 82
Annette 51

  Emily (-2013) 237
Pinkerton
  Charles 320
  George 141
Pinotti
  Daniel 296
  Floyd 296
  Joseph C. 296
  Michael Albert 296
Piper
  Charles Scott 165
Pitcock
  Viola Catherine 285
Pitman
  Sally R. 298
Pittelli
  Joseph 315
Pittello
  Patricia 302
Pletcher
  Abram 279
  Brian 279
  Donald Eugene (1915-2006) 279
  Harold Edgar (1910-2000) 279
  Harvey E. (1879-) 279
  Henry Edgar (1939-1961) 279
  Howard R. 279
  Howard W. (1918-1999) 279
  Jean 279
  Kathleen 279
  Larry 279
  Molly 279
  Nora 279
  Pamela 279
  Philip 279
  Rebecca 279
  Stanley K. (1947-2016) 279
  Stephen 279
  Treva Victoria 276
Plummer
  Cora 98
Poffenberger
  Alvin Joseph Adam (1872-1931) 167
  Flora Jennie May (1895-1918) 167
  Hattie 167
  June Madeline (1925-) 168
  Roby Earl (1896-1971) 168
  Roy Alvin (1893-) 167
Pohner
  Richard 437
Poletti
  Ava Grace (2007-) 267
  Michael 267
Polm
  Kate 325
Poore
  Mary Elizabeth (1928-) 110
Porter
  Clifford 117
Portzline
  Wanda Lou (1952-) 483
Posey
  Naomi 259
  Vollie 259
Poteiger
  (--?--) (-1930) 407
Potteiger
  Roberta 248
Pottiger
  Warren D. 104
Potts
  Donald 74
  Katie 74
  Ryan 74
Powell
  Eleanore 362
  Frances 168
  Francis (1871-) 168
  George 237
  Karen Marie (1980-) 237
  Mary A. 125
  Mary Ann 394
  Sevilla 168
  Susan 237
  Theresa 237
  Timothy 168
Powers
  Keri Nichole (1977-) 59
Powley
  Mary Catherine (1861-1925) 50
  Michael 50
Presher
  Doris Helen (1912-2003) 465
  Herbert Leroy 465
Price
  Cody 215
  Deborah 273
  Deborah Ann 284
  Doris R. (1941-) 366
  Richard 199
  Robert 366
  Shawn 215
  William Byers (1906-1982) 386
  William Klinger (1951-1951) 386
Pritz
  Frances Mae (1924-) 76
  Frank Joseph 76
Propst
  Christopher D. 281
  Christopher L. 281
  Franklin 281
  Kirsten M. 281
  William Andrew 281
Pry
  Harry Thomas 380
  Ruth Ersilla (1907-1984) 380
Pulley
  John 82
  Nicole 82
  Scott A. 82
Punch
  (--?--) 401
  Larry D. 401
  Nancy 401
Putt
  Charles B. 393

Harry Bender 393
Quartz
    Jennie E. (1896-1982) 376
    Wilbert 376
Quick
    Marshall 384
Quidachay
    Julia (1928-) 70
Quillian
    Brendan 212
    Colin 212
    Halley 212
    Joseph 212
Rabbitt
    Carol A. (1949-) 237
Rabuck
    Annie Laura (1866-1914) 68
    Bertha M. (1930-2008) 480
    Eva Kathryn 441
    Gurney E. (1899-2008) 479
    Hannah (1847-1849) 158
    Jackie (-2008) 480
    James E. (1935-2009) 480
    Jason T. 480
    Mark L. 480
    Melinda J. 480
    Rodney L. 480
    Rose M. 480
    William H. (1928-2008) 480
Radel
    Carl (1921-) 427
    Carlynne (1951-) 427
    Clayton C. (1891-) 427
    Eleanor (1916-) 474
    Elizabeth Mae (1934-) 254
    Esther Miralda Mae (1899-1985) 494
    Frank 254
    Guy Frederick (1895-1955) 254
    Jana Lea (1976-) 254
    Joy Ann (1948-) 427
    Juliana 427
    Katharine (1908-) 100
    Khris Elaine (1958-) 254
    Lincoln Carl (1921-) 427
    Lovina (1849-1931) 83
    Mary S. (1914-) 474
    Michael (1807-1864) 83
    Paul Herman (1918-1941) 427
    Paul Herman (1954-) 427
    Robert R. (1920-) 474
    Ruth O. (1912-) 474
    Sylvia Laura (1907-) 187
    Tammy 254
    Thomas (1890-1948) 474
    Thomas R. (1937-) 254
Radell
    Grace A. (1898-1965) 371
Ragan
    Eldon 57
Rager
    James Samuel 81
Rahm
    Daniel Patrick (1982-) 91
    Kirsten Alicia (1989-) 91
    Patrick Michael (1952-) 91
Rahn
    Harry Francis (1897-1982) 239
    Infant Daughter Janet Isobel (1924-1924) 239
Raho
    Albert Eugene (1935-) 115
    Albert F. Jr. (1911-1993) 114
    Janine Marie 115
    Jit (1935-) 115
    Mitchell Lester Jr. 115
    Mitchell Lester Sr. (1944-) 115
Rahr
    Richard 324
    Veronica Marrite (1963-) 324
Ramberger
    Charles 318
    Daniel Edgar (1871-1960) 130, 472
    Kathryn 159
    Katie Irene (1907-1999) 130
    Keith (1964-2011) 434
    Laura Alverta (1912-2006) 472
    Paul William (1934-) 434
    Susan P. (1924-) 318
    William Clarence (1900-1965) 434
Ramer
    Corrine Dorcas (1910-1982) 397
    Edward Luther (1874-1956) 397
    Jean Eleanor (1917-1978) 397
    Rhoda Lucille (1913-1977) 397
Ramos
    Jeremias 159
    Julian 159
Ramsey
    Deanna Lynn (1957-) 185
    Roy 205
Randell
    Carrie Van Dorn 229
Rank
    Allen W. (1901-1974) 240
    Darrell Shaffer (1926-2005) 240
    Harry William (1880-1973) 240
    J.L. 240
    Kevin 240
Rankin
    Joanne (1934-) 315
    Robert 123
Rapoli
    Rosemary 348
Rasbatch
    Jennie 422
Rau
    Ed 208
Rauchut
    (--?--) 248
    Douglas C. 248
    Glenn A. 248
    Shawn M. 248
Raudabauch
    Stephanie Ann 352
Raudenbach
    Elizabeth (1836-1924) 454
Rauenzahn
    Joel Llewellyn 407

Minerva Rebecca (1888-1956) 407
Rautzahn
    John 338
    Joseph 338, 445
Raver
    Shirley Barton 145
Rawls
    Albert Dupree 381
    Virginia Louise (1919-2008) 381
Reagen
    Margaret (1943-) 315
Ream
    Marie Rebecca (1902-1997) 81
Reber
    Betty Mae 287
    David 284
    Dewey I. 287
    Minnie (1899-1985) 284
    Pearl 451
Rebock
    Johannes Conrad (1788-1857) 156
Rebuck
    Alfis E. (1856-1923) 161
    Allen A. (1906-) 480
    Alma Margaret (1926-2007) 195
    Annie (1904-) 480
    Arthur (1901-) 480
    Catherine (1813-) 377
    Catherine (1843-1914) 157
    Cecelia (1859-1923) 206
    Charles 459
    Charles E. (1919-) 481
    Charles E. Jr. (1929-) 195
    Charles Elias (1890-1971) 194
    Donald 479
    Doris 480
    Earnest G. (1921-) 195
    Edith 480
    Elias F. (1842-1921) 194
    Eliza 157
    Emanuel (1849-1918) 343, 479
    Erma M. (1918-) 481
    Ernest F. (1912-) 480
    Esther Miriam (1937-1991) 195
    Eve Elizabeth (1858-) 161
    Frankling (1854-1865) 161
    Goldie A. 179
    Gurney 480
    Gurney (1899-2008) 479
    Hannah (1847-1849) 158
    Harriet (1850-1929) 158
    Harry E. 334
    Henry (1909-) 480
    Ida Minerva (1900-1941) 130, 495
    Ira (1891-1991) 161
    Iva (-2010) 404
    Jacob W. (1853-1909) 161
    John Robert (1849-1859) 158
    Joyce 479
    Katherine (1843-1914) 157
    Lewis E. (1918-1918) 161
    Lloyd G. (1926-1992) 480
    Mabel 161
    Mabel M. (1896-1962) 442
    Mark L. (1916-) 480
    Marlene 194
    Marlin Harvey (1926-1995) 334
    Mary (1844-1909) 157
    Mary Sarah (1910-2006) 154
    Peter (-1938) 161
    Peter S. (1818-1858) 156
    Polly (1844-1909) 157
    Russell (-2010) 194
    Sallie Agnes (1885-1947) 343
    Samuel (1840-) 157
    Shawn (1988-) 334, 351, 444
    Theodore (1910-) 480
    Theodore E. (1874-1939) 479
    Todd B. (1961-2013) 334, 351, 444
    Tonya L. (1969-) 334, 351, 444
    Walter (1897-) 479
Redfield
    Alfred 256
    Debra 256
    Scott 256
Reed
    (--?--) 338
    (--?--) (1996-) 443
    (--?--) (1999-) 443
    Adam 133
    Alfred Harold (1863-1941) 281
    Alice E. (1894-1895) 284
    Alice Marian (1947-) 283
    Aliza Jacqueline (1988-) 284
    Allen Daniel Adam (1922-1978) 483
    Alverta Eva (1900-1936) 284
    Amy Lynne 233
    Brad 478
    Brett 478
    Brittany Lee (1991-) 283
    Bruce Allen (1951-) 483
    Bruce Lamar (1942-) 282
    Carol Ann (1959-) 282
    Chelsea Lynn (1992-) 283
    Chester Harvey (1913-2003) 283
    Clair E. 474
    Clay Michael 442
    Connor Lee (1993-) 442
    Courtney Lyn (1978-) 282
    D. Randall 367
    David Alan (1964-) 282
    David Alexander (1985-) 284
    David Michael (1979-) 483
    Dennis Dale (1958-) 483
    Donald Chester (1936-) 283
    Donald Chester Jr. (1960-) 283
    Douglas Warren (1957-) 284
    Drucilla Marjorie 169
    Edith G. (1915-) 346
    Eric Rand (1954-) 284
    Estella May (1889-1890) 284
    Ethel Kathleen (1918-1995) 212
    Eva M. (1910-1966) 132
    Frederic David (1937-) 282
    Fremont H. (1891-1893) 284
    Harvey Alfred (1887-1944) 281
    Helen Irene (1909-1995) 458
    Herman D. 474
    Irene Katherine (1911-1990) 192, 339

James 233
Janet Elaine (1961-   ) 282
Jeffrey Peter (1971-   ) 282
Joel 247
John S. (1881-1969) 192
John W. Sr. 442
Lamar Nelson (1930-   ) 284
Lee E. (1946-1993) 442
Leighton B. (1914-1997) 382
Levi 281
Makenzie Fran (1994-   ) 282
Margaret (1904-1912) 288
Margaretta I. (1904-1912) 288
Mary (1803-1846) 307
Mary Ada 397
Meredith E. 474
Michael 338, 445
Mildred Torell (1910-1998) 282
Nelson (1896-1932) 284
Palmer Harold (1911-1991) 282
Palmer Harold Jr. (1935-   ) 282
Pamela Wilson (1961-   ) 283
Paul Daniel 441
Paul Raymond 169
Rebecca 474
Robert 474
Rose Ann (1964-   ) 483
Rufus 282
Sarah A. (1846-1906) 122
Scott 441
Shannon Elizabeth (1988-   ) 283
Sharon Louise (1962-   ) 282
Shawn 349
Steven Dale (1972-   ) 483
Steven P. 441
Suzanne Karoline (1989-   ) 284
Taryn 443
Tiffany Natasha (1996-   ) 282
Tina Ellen (1962-   ) 483
Todd 442
Ty 443
Violet Elizabeth (1919-   ) 158
Vivian (1919-2003) 284
Warren Daniel (1908-1974) 215
William 132
William Garfield 169, 483
William Henry 458
William R. 478

Reeder
(--?--) 339
Carl James (1982-   ) 86
Charles Edgar (1962-   ) 86
Daniel Thomas (1987-   ) 86
Faith Elizabeth (2009-   ) 86
Josiah Phillip (2007-   ) 86
Mandy Marie (1984-   ) 86
Mary C. (1895-   ) 87

Reedinger
August M. (1884-   ) 358
Fredoline (1820-   ) 358
James L. (1886-   ) 358
Julia K. (1890-   ) 358
Julia Katharine (1889-1976) 361
Laura M. (1897-   ) 358
Leo (1856-   ) 358

Samuel M. (1887-   ) 358

Reedy
Bessie Fietta (1886-1930) 204, 280
Franklin M. 240
Helen Grace (1902-1978) 204
Matilda S. (1911-1990) 240

Reese
(--?--) 125, 493
Franklin John 231
James F. (1949-   ) 231
John Franklin (1983-   ) 231
Kaili Sarah (2014-   ) 231
Leah Irene (1983-   ) 231
Newton (-1963) 172
Samuel Ira (1983-   ) 231
Sarah Curry (1980-1980) 231

Rehm
Kimberly 138
Stephanie 138
Steven 138

Rehrer
Catharine (1833-   ) 69
Phaon (1891-1951) 390
Rebecca (1823-1897) 207

Reibold
(--?--) 75

Reibsane
Diane Ruth (1948-   ) 116

Reich
Mary (1910-1970) 224

Reichard
(--?--) 82
Andrew 82
Florence 380
Richard 82

Reichenbach
Esther Mae (-2013) 387
Margaret H. 87

Reid
Ashley (1989-   ) 305
Victor 305

Reider
Benjamin F. 269
Russel Conwell (1897-1980) 269

Reidinger
Barbara 187
Chloe 375
John 375

Reif
Evelyn C. 256

Reifschneider
John 49

Reifsnyder
Daniel 49
Jacob 49

Reightler
Mark Louis (1922-1985) 204
Warren Thomas (1951-2002) 204, 241

Reigle
Joane Loretta 59
Mary (1904-1991) 410
Nathan 191

Reilly
Kathleen 303
Rein
Daniel Edward (1960-) 85
Jeffrey Michael (1988-) 85
Katherine Ross (1992-) 85
Reiner
Carl 196
Cathy 196
Grace Mamie (1912-1978) 212
James Lamar Jr. (1957-) 115
James Lamar Sr. (1930-2003) 111, 115
Jean Marie (1955-) 111, 115
John Joseph (1958-1970) 115
Lizzie S. 339
Mabel Hanna (1923-) 186
Pauline 365
William Frank 212
Willy 196
Reinert
(--?--) 176
Dora 137
Reinfeld
Darrell Emory (1969-) 492
Darryl Lee 492
Grant Marcus Frederick 492
Kymberly Lee (1968-) 492
Mychelle Christine (1967-) 492
Reinhard
Jayna Katie (1993-) 334, 351, 444
Patricia (1953-) 172
Thomas 334
Reinhart
Annie E. (1905-2005) 78
Reininger
Katherine (1900-1983) 438
Reinoehl
George 218
George Charles (1920-1988) 218, 468, 475
Lynn George (1953-) 218, 468
Robert Roy (1924-1997) 218
Roy Henry (1898-1924) 218, 468
Ted John (1947-) 218, 468, 475
Reis
James Martin (1972-) 419
Martin (1948-) 419
Tammy Sue (1970-) 419
Reisch
Helen Mae 370
Reish
Marie Eleanor 357
Reissinger
William (1860-) 205
Reist
Carolyn Diane 123
Reitinger
Eva 400
Reitz
(--?--) 130
Dennis 195
Eileen 195
Emerson 383
Irvin E. (1924-2002) 195
Janet 195
Julianna (1792-1857) 156
Lewis E. (-2002) 195
Remley
Gerald 386
Renn
Flora 383
Renner
Daniel (1927-) 142
Frank 142
Kathy 249
Matthew 249
Myraline (1925-) 142
Renninger
Dale 438
Earl W. (1924-2009) 438
Elsie E. (1927-) 438
Kay 438
Leroy 438
Sarah E. (1928-) 438
William 438
William M. (1899-2009) 438
Reppe
Norman 285
Patricia Ann (1952-) 285
Reppert
(--?--) 137
Resser
Lane 206
Ressler
(--?--) 366
Courtney Marie 288
Dondi Elvis (1956-) 117
Eugene 288
Frank J. 234
George 455
Gerald M. Jr. (1966-2004) 118
Gerald M. Sr. 118
Heath (1969-) 288
James 288
James Henry 288
Kevin 118
Kimberly 118
Kristian (1968-) 288
Kristin and Kirsten (1968-) 288
Lamar Raymond Jr. (1948-) 117
Larissa Elizabeth 288
Linda Lou (1946-1947) 117
Louella Jane (1939-) 117
Maddie 118
Mandy 118
Morris 366
Oscar 287
Peggy Ann (1942-) 117
Raymond Lamar Sr. (1916-1984) 117
Sadie 118
Sandra Gayle (1938-) 287
Shane Hugh (1958-) 117
Spenser Eugene 288
Tanar 118
Terry Lee (1950-) 117
Valissa Chantel (1972-) 288
Vincent Roland (1922-1972) 234
Wayne Delmar (1944-) 117

William E. (1901-1959) 234
Retek
   Ernie 99
Rettinger
   Claude Henry Matthias (1897-1920) 423
   Edgar Solomon (1876-1956) 421
   Ellen Carolyn (1911-2001) 421
   Henry (1852-1910) 421
   Jennie Edna (1884-1962) 422
   Mabel I. (1887-1962) 422
   Mary Elizabeth (1904-1956) 421
   Myrtle (1915-1978) 421
   Nina (1898-) 390
   Raymond Clarence (1888-1947) 423
   Rebecca (1880-) 421
   Susan May (1882-) 422
   Susie (1882-) 422
Revotskie
   Alisha (1984-) 303
   Jill (1956-) 303
   Martin (1890-) 303
   Melissa (1987-) 303
   Michael (1953-) 303
   Mischa (1976-) 303
   Nicholas (1919-1996) 303
   Peter (1944-) 303
   Shaleen (1986-) 303
   Shanti (1976-) 303
   Susan (1948-) 303
Reyes
   Karl Tudela (1941-) 71
   Karl Tudela (1972-) 71
   Reinhold Reid (1978-) 71
   Rheta Inez Barto (1975-) 71
   Sean Spencer (1980-) 71
Reynolds
   Gertrude (1921-) 71
   Keith Andrew (1976-) 331
Rhen
   Edna (1903-1989) 173
Rhenn
   Thomas 219
Rhoad
   Jacob L. (1886-1964) 77
   Lester T. (1911-2006) 77
Rhoades
   Ida Marie 347
Rhoads
   Elwood 395
   Fay B. (1931-2007) 395
   Harriet Mae (1883-1948) 84
   Henry Landis 84
Rhodes
   Kathryn 215
Rhody
   Linda Maria (1954-) 361
Rice
   Drinda 415
   Edwin 415
   Jucinda 415
   Kirk 415
   Linda 415
   May Elizabeth 275
   Michelle 415

   Virgie Mae 467
   William A. (1912-1991) 415
   William Arthur (1937-) 415
Richards
   Chad 392
   Crystal 392
   Kerry 392
   Martha 66
   Olive 266
Richardson
   Ron 265
Richie
   (--?--) 405
Richmond
   A.C. (1907-) 97
   Gladys (1910-) 97
   Harry C. (1905-) 97
   Hazel L. (1934-) 97
   James Elmer (1866-) 97
   Karen 487
   Marie (1902-) 97
   Merle (1913-) 97
   Myrle (1913-) 97
   Patricia Ann (1929-) 97
   Verna (1899-) 97
Richter
   William Henry 160
Rickard
   David Lee (1956-) 346
   Mark (1960-) 346
   Matthew (1992-) 346
   Michael (1987-) 346
   Russell (1933-) 346
Rickel
   (--?--) 371
   Alec 371
   Anthony 371
Rickels
   Jack 249
Rickert
   (--?--) 255
   Dorothea (1923-2002) 256
   Harry Melvin (1899-1987) 256
   James Leroy (1918-1999) 280
   John Emerson (1877-1941) 256
   Joyce W. 256
   Mary Ann (1932-) 346
   Ramona Marie (1948-) 280, 458
Rider
   Brigit 269
   Hillary 269
   James F. (1933-) 269
   Jamie 269
   Jill 270
   John L. (1937-) 269
   Judith 269
   Kimberly 269
   Lillian 269
   Michael 269
   Patricia 269
   Randall 269
   Russell 269
   Russell C. (1932-) 269
   Samuel 269

  Tracey 269
  Tyrus 269
  William L. (1935-) 269
Ridge
  Russel (1905-) 177
Riegel
  Avis (1916-2010) 455
  Brenda 455
  Evelyn 456
  Hannah (1925-) 455
  Harry G. (1882-) 455
  Lee A. (1923-2010) 455
  Mary (1927-2010) 455
  Mary Jane 381
  Pap (1923-2010) 455
  Paul (1917-2010) 455
  Yvonne 189
Riegle
  Annie Rebecca 432
Riethof
  Henry 273
  Thomas Robert (1927-) 273
Rife
  Kelly 135
Righter
  John M. 422
  Mary B. 422
Riland
  Dean 207
  Frank 326
  Matthew 207
  Myron E. 207
  Patty Lou (1934-) 326
  Rena 207
  Todd 207
Rinden
  Thor W. 240
Rindfleisch
  Albert (1900-1946) 296
  Albert E. (1928-) 296
  Allen 296
  Audrey 296
  Carol Ann (1932-1987) 296
  Donna F. 296
  Matthew 296
  Rita Kay (1935-) 297
  Roger 296
Ring
  Dennis (1952-) 412
  Diane 303
  Lula 64
Ringer
  Minnie 229
Ringo
  Patricia 348
Rink
  (--?--) 274
Rinkenberg
  Shirley Ann (1938-) 230
Rios
  David V. 260
Rische
  Corrine H. (1893-1893) 397

  Dorothy M. (1902-1929) 397
  Henry 396
  Mark Nelson (1904-1985) 397
  Maude I. (1891-1960) 396
  Nelson (1868-1944) 396
Risser
  Nancy Ethel 426
Rissinger
  James 399
  Mary (1878-1937) 323
  William 205
Rist
  Dorothy (1910-1996) 230
Ritter
  (--?--) 201
  Allen Earl (-1970) 219
Rittle
  Delmar V. 226
  Paul 226
Rittner
  David E. (1916-2001) 404
  Jan H. 404
  Myrl V. 404
  Patricia D. 404
Ritz
  (--?--) 88
Ritzman
  Bradley 190
  Charles 190
  Esther 260
  Grayce I. (1891-1953) 390
  Judith I. (-2012) 127
  Kathryn 289
  Mary (1819-1861) 423
  Myrtle Amy (1896-1973) 216
  William 216
Roach
  Brandon Tyler 441
  James 441
  Trent Garrick (1992-) 441
Roadcap
  Carl (1963-) 134
  Carol Ann 131
  David Eugene (1949-) 108
  Dawn (1965-) 134
  Heather Marie (1977-) 108
  Kevin R. (1967-) 134
  Ward 131
Robb
  Edward 72
Robebacker
  Sophia B. 403
Roberti
  Angela M (1928-) 487
Roberts
  Edward Allen (1950-) 253
  Eileen C. 274
  Elizabeth Ann (1937-) 299
  Julia 274
  Leslie Nichole 306
  Lindsey Michelle 306
  Michael Lynn 306
  Patricia S. 436
  Rex Anthony (1953-) 299

  Robin 274
  Susan Mary (1947-   ) 299
  William Allen 253
  William J. (1907-1986) 298
  William Kenneth (1947-1970) 253
Robertson
  Kathleen 346
  Nancy Helen 421
Robinski
  Daniel Joseph 288
  Jacob Reed (1992-   ) 288
  Joseph 288
Robinson
  (--?--) 135
  Arthur J. (1911-   ) 99
  Betty (1925-   ) 294
  Clarence (1886-1927) 99
  Curtis Joel (1951-   ) 99
  Dorothy M. (1910-   ) 178
  Elizabeth (1925-   ) 294
  Howard W. (1909-   ) 99
  John C. Jr. (1932-   ) 294
  John Clark III (1968-   ) 294
  John Clark Sr. (1884-1979) 294
  Kenneth C. (1938-   ) 178
  Kenneth J. (1910-   ) 178
  Nancy K. (1942-   ) 179
  Pamela 244
  Rebecca (1974-   ) 294
  Robert (1865-   ) 394
  Thomas (1971-   ) 294
Robinstine
  Catherine 62
Roche
  Henry T. 178
  Laura A. (1957-   ) 178
  Susan L. (1954-   ) 178
  Teresa (1952-   ) 178
  Timothy J. (1962-   ) 178
Rock
  James Lee (1943-   ) 322
  Kimberly (1970-   ) 322
  Scott Lee (1968-   ) 322
Rodichok
  Anna 436
  Barbara 117
  Bernard Leo (1938-1969) 116
  Chad Michael (1967-   ) 117
  David Michael (1966-   ) 116
  Gary David (1954-   ) 117
  Gwendolyn 117
  Ian Michael (1989-   ) 117
  Jodi 117
  Joseph 117
  Leo Joseph (1914-1964) 116
  Madison Margaret (1992-   ) 117
  Michael George (1943-2015) 116
  Steven 117
  Thomas C. (1969-   ) 116
  Walter Terry (1945-1991) 117
Roe
  Harold 426
  Kim (1957-   ) 426
  Stephen (-1972) 426

Roeder
  Mildred (1922-2013) 74
  Rufus 74
Rogers
  Dana (1970-   ) 57
Rohrer
  Clement (1940-   ) 305
Romanczyk
  Ann Marie (1961-   ) 85
Romberger
  Alexa Dianne (1999-   ) 271
  Alice (1869-   ) 418
  Alice I. (1936-2002) 255
  Alice Lorraine (1934-   ) 155, 365, 451
  Allan (1909-1992) 155
  Allen Clark (1909-1992) 155, 364, 451
  Allen Isaiah (1927-1983) 155, 364, 451
  Alma Jean (1930-1950) 152, 449
  Alvin Nathan 396
  Amy Marie (1981-   ) 150, 449
  Angela Renae (1976-   ) 400
  Ann Irene (1955-   ) 454
  Anna Irene (1905-1984) 453
  Anna Irene (1930-   ) 453
  Arland Seth (1900-1967) 254
  Arland Stephen (1949-   ) 254
  Barbara Lee (1938-   ) 155
  Barbara Marie (1941-   ) 155, 435, 451
  Bernice Alverta (1926-   ) 253
  Bertha Viola (1885-1931) 150, 449
  Betty Jane (1932-2006) 454
  Betty Jean (1925-   ) 253
  Beverly Verna (1950-   ) 153, 435, 450
  Brian (1975-   ) 153, 434, 450
  Brian Adam (1983-   ) 150, 449
  Carl 372
  Carl Francis (1937-   ) 151, 449
  Carol (1944-   ) 253
  Catharine Amanda (1854-1936) 266
  Charles 489
  Charles (1894-1895) 152, 449
  Charles Daniel (1866-1895) 93, 451
  Charles Isaac (1881-1968) 363
  Charles Raymond (1904-1987) 255
  Clarence (1888-   ) 56
  Clark Allen (1966-   ) 155, 365, 451
  Colleen Ann (1960-   ) 151, 449
  Curtis Ray (1922-1923) 151, 449
  Dale Lee (1952-1994) 154, 435, 451
  Daniel (1816-1882) 418
  Daniel Davis (1956-   ) 454
  Daniel James (1991-   ) 271
  David 155
  Diane M. 151, 449
  Dianne Lea (1947-   ) 153, 434, 450
  Donald 112
  Donna Lee (1953-   ) 153, 434, 450
  Dutch (1927-1983) 155
  Earl Thomas (1926-1981) 152, 449
  Edna F. (1896-   ) 252
  Edward (1841-1907) 418
  Edward Vernon (1898-1980) 253
  Ellen Mary (1902-1976) 254
  Elmer W. (1872-1942) 418
  Elvin Philip (1911-1998) 363

Erma Elmira (1920-   ) 253
Estella (1906-1929) 155
Etta 317
Flora Eva (1895-1895) 452
Frederick Gottshall (1914-1969) 396
Gail Ann (1953-   ) 153, 435, 450
Gary Gene (1959-   ) 150, 449
Gary Michael (1955-   ) 152, 449
Gene Thomas (1935-   ) 309
Gene Thomas (1935-2005) 150, 449
George 112, 116
Gertrude (1892-1935) 93, 451
Gertrude Catherine (1896-1989) 452
Gladys B. (1917-2010) 489
Hannah Agatha (1906-2001) 255
Harold C. (1920-1987) 271, 335
Harold Paul (1954-   ) 271
Harry Clark (1897-1953) 152, 354, 450
Harry Klinger (1873-1939) 453
Heinrich (1773-1822) 49
Helen Mae (1922-   ) 152, 354, 450
Helen Susannah (1911-1972) 156, 451
Isaiah Klinger (1864-1919) 150, 364, 434, 448
Jane Marie (1954-   ) 155, 435, 451
Jean Elizabeth (1924-2011) 454
Jennie Irene (1894-1960) 453
Jody Ann (1964-   ) 151, 449
Johann Christian (1797-1874) 448
John (1802-1891) 210
John Albert (1925-   ) 454
John George 252
John George Jr. (1874-1931) 252
John Isaiah (1912-1989) 150, 449
John Klinger (1876-1954) 453
John Ralph (1960-   ) 150, 449
John Seth (1975-   ) 254
John Silliman (1945-   ) 254
Joyce Elizabeth (1948-   ) 153, 435, 450
Karen A. 151, 449
Kelly Yvonne (1975-   ) 335, 351, 419, 444
Keneth M. (1947-1954) 212
Kenneth W. (1910-1981) 212
Kristene Lea (1953-   ) 155, 364, 451
Kristie Ann (1977-   ) 335, 351, 419, 444
Kristine (1953-   ) 155
Kyle L. (1985-   ) 187
Larry E. 151, 449
Laurie Alice (1982-   ) 255
Lawrence John (1920-1980) 264
Lee Lamar (1932-   ) 154, 435, 451
LeeAnn 151, 449
Leona May (1914-2004) 255
Lillian Alice (1891-1974) 451
Lori Ann (1962-   ) 151, 449
Lulu (1888-1960) 93, 451
Mabel Amelia (1903-1903) 453
Mabel Laura (1920-1982) 116
Mae Elmira (1914-1978) 151, 449
Marie A. 264
Marie Leona (1922-   ) 454
Marie Louise (1922-   ) 454
Marion Anna (1929-2005) 154, 435, 450
Marion Marie (1936-   ) 152, 449
Mark Marlin (1939-   ) 155
Mark Martin (1939-   ) 155, 435, 451
Mary A. (1908-1981) 364
Mary Ann (1868-   ) 451
Mary Edna 418
Mary Hazel (1899-1977) 452
Mary Jean (1934-   ) 255
Mary Lou (1933-   ) 152, 449
Michael Allen (1954-   ) 155, 364, 451
Michael Irvin (1968-   ) 155, 435, 451
Michael Roger (1953-   ) 255
Paul Franklin (1897-1975) 252
Paul W. (1900-   ) 418
Quentin Stanley (1920-1991) 153, 434, 450
Ralph Troutman (1900-1974) 454
Randy Lee (1965-   ) 151, 449
Renee Mary (1959-   ) 154, 435, 450
Richard Lee (1958-   ) 255
Robert Edward (1946-   ) 253
Robert Lamar (1939-   ) 151, 449
Robert Roland (1923-1974) 253
Robert W. (1946-1970) 151, 449
Robin Lee (1959-   ) 155, 435, 451
Rodney Roy (1958-   ) 187
Roger Lamar (1931-2013) 255
Roland James (1946-   ) 153, 435, 450
Roland Russel (1923-2009) 153, 435, 450
Ronald 399
Ronald T. 151, 449
Roy Albert (1934-   ) 155, 435, 451
Roy Elwood (1920-2003) 151, 449
Roy Robert (1934-   ) 155
Russell Roland (1928-   ) 152, 449
Ryan R. (1983-   ) 187
Sadie 318, 325
Samuel Walter (1888-1895) 150, 449
Sarah A. (1853-1919) 217
Sophie 194
Stanley Clark (1901-1957) 152, 434, 450
Stella Joanna (1906-1929) 155, 451
Stuart Allen (1951-   ) 334
Susannah (1815-1891) 49
Terry Lee (1942-2008) 151, 449
Thomas Clark (1891-1945) 150, 449
Thomas Stace (1951-   ) 152, 449
Tina (1967-   ) 151, 449
Verna 366
Vernon Edward (1898-1980) 253
William (1837-1876) 93, 150, 448
William Austin (1870-1928) 451
William Ray Wiest (1907-1973) 453
Zane David (1997-   ) 155, 435, 451

Rombyer
Candice 61
Charles H. (1902-   ) 60
Daniel Wesley (1945-2004) 61
Frederick 60
Frederick II 61
Gary 61
Hazel May (1893-1960) 60
Herbert (1869-1949) 60
Jessie (1899-1942) 60
Patrick 61
Robert J. 60
Thomas Charles (1926-2003) 60
Thomas G. (1947-2010) 61
Wilford W. (1905-1992) 61

Romlyer
    Bert (1869-1949) 60
Rooney
    Roseanne (1963-) 308
Rose
    Ersal Agnes (1915-) 243
Rosen
    Anissa 393
    Jan L. 393
    Joel 393
Rosenberger
    (--?--) 264
Rosenbluth
    David (1904-1967) 263
    Morris 263
    Wanda M. (1936-) 263
Rosenstael
    Sandra (1946-) 193
Ross
    Andrew Barto 72
    Charles E. 383
    Elizabeth Marie (1991-) 307
    Ella Josephine (1880-1962) 84
    Melissa Gray (1989-) 307
    Paul 72
    Raymond M. 54
    Robert Milton (1921-1989) 54
    Sarah Elizabeth (1898-1972) 383
    William Gray (1960-) 307
Rossi
    Constantino 215
    Margaret Marie (1924-1994) 215
Rosti
    Georgine M. (1928-2012) 199
Roth
    Wilfred 376
Rothermal
    Jennie Sarah (1888-1978) 170
Rothermel
    (--?--) 431
    Abraham M. (1777-1861) 168
    Abraham W. (1864-1950) 185
    Alice Elizabeth (1885-1970) 178
    Allen Samuel (1895-1966) 184
    Alma Mae (1925-2014) 129, 184
    Alyssa Lian (1990-) 183
    Amos Robert (1899-1944) 120, 181
    Amos W. (1850-1907) 176, 447
    Andrew (-1923) 168
    Andrew Todd (1992-) 183
    Annie B. (1868-1952) 168
    Arlene (1926-) 120, 181
    Arlie May (1889-) 169
    Austin D. (1894-1969) 169
    Blanche Anna (1914-) 179
    Bryant 179
    Carl Raymond (1942-2003) 179
    Carlina (1853-1854) 178
    Carrie Myrl (1906-1997) 373
    Catharine (1853-1854) 178
    Catherine G. (1959-) 180
    Charles (1905-1905) 177, 447
    Charles A. (1853-) 177
    Charles A. (1886-1953) 241, 288
    Charles Edwin (1887-1957) 129, 182
    Charles Ellsworth (1869-) 169
    Charles Henry (1887-1889) 179
    Charles K. (1876-) 177, 447
    Claude F. (1883-1958) 177
    Claude L. (1883-) 177, 447
    David L. 236
    Dennis Nevin (1942-) 183
    Dick (1929-2011) 180
    Dorothy Hannah (1917-1991) 241, 288
    Dorothy Pearl (1913-) 177, 447
    Dorthea (1913-) 177
    Dwight (1982-) 184
    Earom (1860-1933) 182
    Edwin (1874-) 177, 447
    Edwin E. (1928-) 182
    Edwin Francis (1906-) 177, 447
    Eleanor Elizabeth (1939-1941) 183
    Elizabeth 177
    Elizabeth (-2006) 153
    Elma Ethel (1905-1978) 180
    Elwood Lester (1915-1999) 331
    Emma (1867-) 169
    Emma Bertha 440
    Emma Bertha (1894-1966) 179
    Eva M. (1897-1963) 180, 494
    Eve Elizabeth (1850-1852) 177
    Ezram E. (1860-1933) 182
    Florence May (1904-1997) 169
    Gail I. (1956-) 180
    Gena Eleanor (1976-) 183
    George Linton (1863-) 168
    Gladys Margaret (1908-) 177, 447
    Gloria (1923-) 177, 447
    Guy W. Jr. (1965-) 184
    Guy William (1930-2014) 184
    Hannah (1866-1929) 185
    Hannah Jane (1899-1973) 184
    Harry Burton (1920-) 177, 447
    Harry Norman (1899-1983) 180
    Helen 178
    Helen (1921-) 177, 447
    Herbert Milton (1916-) 177, 447
    Ida M. (1889-1984) 179
    Infant daughter (1885-1885) 181
    Infant daughter (1888-) 185
    Infant son (1880-1880) 181
    Infant son (1884-1884) 181
    Infant son (1888-) 185
    Infant son (1892-) 181
    Infant son (1892-1892) 185
    Isaac Monro (1862-1923) 182
    Isaac Monroe (1820-1896) 168, 447
    Isaac Monroe (1874-) 186
    James (-2009) 405
    James (1879-1883) 177, 447
    James (1879-1954) 373
    Jane (1882-1892) 178
    Jay William (1892-1949) 185
    Jean M. (1929-) 182
    Jennie and Janie (1882-1892) 178
    Jestie B. (1884-1959) 178
    Jestina (1847-1925) 171
    Joan 179
    John E. (1907-1974) 182

John E. (1940-) 182
John L. (1891-1979) 179
Joseph W. (1892-1949) 185
Kathryn S. (1911-2009) 405
Kathy 184
Kenneth D. (1953-) 180
Kristine 120, 181
Larry 179
Lazarus W. (1855-1934) 178, 494
Lillie Ida (1865-) 168
Lloyd K. (1921-1959) 179
Lucy (1881-) 177, 447
Lucy Ann (1849-1928) 174
Mabel G. (1904-1954) 146, 182
MacLada (1871-) 177, 447
Mae H. E. (1901-1966) 185
Manasses (1909-1958) 182
Manasses S. (1870-1929) 169
Manasses W. (1857-1929) 120, 146, 181
Margaret (1915-) 177
Margaret Jones 178
Marie Terese (1890-1961) 236
Marlin James (1947-) 183
Martha (1915-) 177, 447
Mary (1907-) 177, 447
Mary Olive (-1953) 177
Mazie M. (1901-) 180
Michael J. (1961-) 180
Mildred E. (1914-1992) 182
Mildred Marie (1929-) 120, 181
Milton (1873-) 177, 447
Minnie (1892-) 171
Minnie E. (1903-) 180
Monroe (1880-) 170
Monroe W. (1862-1923) 182
Nevin Charles (1916-2006) 183
Norman Lester (1910-) 177, 447
Norman Richard (1929-2011) 180
Paul Raymond (1915-1968) 179
Polly (1874-) 170
Randall Charles (1949-1949) 120, 181
Randy C. (1954-) 180
Rhonda 120, 181
Richard S. (1952-) 180
Robert Amos (1899-1944) 181
Roxey A. (1924-2014) 179
Roy (1919-1926) 184
Russell H. (1920-) 177, 447
Ruth B. (1900-1965) 181
Ruth Ella (1948-) 331
Sadie Edna (1889-1986) 403
Samuel Edgar (1895-1971) 179
Shirley (1929-2014) 180
Solomon 403
Stanley (1925-2015) 120, 181
Steve 179
Susan 120, 181
Suzanne Elizabeth (1949-) 183
Tara Lynn (1971-) 183
Timothy L. (1966-) 180
Todd Dennis (1963-) 183
Ty Marlin (1974-) 183
William Wilson (1842-1922) 169

Rothermol
  (--?--) 469

Alma 405
Amos (1850-1907) 176
Anna Kathryn 468
Blanche Marie 169
Cora May (1876-1968) 322
Edwin (1874-) 177
Elwin (1866-) 177, 447
Infant (1880-) 177, 447
John (1876-) 177, 447
Lazareth (1855-1934) 178
Lucy (1881-) 177
Meclada (1871-) 177
Milton (1873-) 177
Monroe (1874-) 186
Theodore (1868-) 177, 447

Rotz
  Gene D. (1935-1962) 77
  Horace (1909-1970) 77

Rouleau
  (--?--) 92

Roush
  (--?--) 104
  Clarence (1905-1989) 104

Row
  Adaline 240
  Albert Theodore 52
  Daniel Adam 416
  Rebecca 421

Rowe
  (--?--) 312
  Annie Sarah (1886-1952) 52
  Bernice 384
  Paul 384
  Raymond Henry (1919-) 88, 170
  Raymond John (1944-) 88
  Sadie Eleanor (1898-1957) 342
  Susanne Louise (1947-) 88, 170

Rowland
  Esther (1901-) 93
  James T. Rowland Sr. (1929-2013) 495
  Renae 495

Rubendall
  Agnes (1864-1934) 356
  Catherine (1836-1919) 119
  Sarah Ann (1838-1911) 186, 460

Rubinger
  Shelley Lynn 234
  Zachary (2003-) 234

Ruch
  (--?--) 260
  Christopher 260
  Clara (1888-1939) 99
  Emanuel (1854-1929) 99
  Infant (1930-1930) 146, 203
  Linda 241, 253
  Matthew 260
  Merrill E. (1903-1958) 145
  Myrtle (1881-1939) 99

Rudahl
  Julius (1901-1978) 296
  Marlene June (1933-) 296
  Paulene Olive (1937-) 296

Rudenauer
  Carl 237

Sabina (1926-2007) 237
Rudisill
    Albert M. 55
    Lena 65
    Shirley Sylvia (1923-2015) 55
Rudy
    Leona (1938-   ) 70
Ruhle
    William 51
Rumberger
    Amos (1834-1892) 210
    Anne Justine (1931-2000) 212
    Charles Edward (1929-1999) 212
    Charles F. (1875-1944) 211
    Clarence A. (1933-1991) 212
    Clarence C. (1907-1983) 212
    Daniel (1873-1935) 211
    Elizabeth Anna (1867-1940) 210
    George M. (1865-1932) 210
    Harry Ezra (1880-1943) 212
    Harry Kimmel (1902-1970) 212
    Helen I. (1899-1921) 212
    Jennie C. (1884-1956) 213
    Kenneth M. (1947-1954) 212
    Kenneth W. (1910-1981) 212
    Mabel (1900-1987) 212
    Mary Elizabeth 53
    Mary Jane C. (1884-1956) 213
    Mary Louise (1950-   ) 372
    Philip (1840-1918) 59
    Robert D. (1938-   ) 212
    William Francis (1877-1954) 212
Runk
    Harry V. 205
    Myrtle 205
Runkle
    Byron 290
    Charles L. (-2009) 252
    Chester 290
    Chester Guy (1904-   ) 178
    Clara L. 415
    Clarence Lamar 264
    Cynthia A. 290
    Franklin C. 211
    Gail 290
    Gary L. 290
    James 178
    James L. (1926-2009) 290
    Joanne Marie 264
    Jordan James (1991-   ) 290
    Karyn S. 290
    Lester A. 264
    Linda C. 290
    Lyman Elias (2008-   ) 264
    Michael 264
    Minnie Ellen 471
    Moxley Benjamin (2005-   ) 264
    Raymond Lewis (1892-1976) 211
    Robert D. 290
    Sharon Sue (1952-1964) 290
    Wendy 252
Rupert
    Maude M. 273

Rupp
    Barbara (1955-1971) 110
    Carl David (1952-   ) 110
    Edna (1885-1924) 300
    Gloria Jean (1948-   ) 110
    Jeremiah Snyder Jr. (1923-1983) 110
    John 73
Rushon
    Mary Amanda 59
Russell
    (--?--) 417
    Bert 60
    Everett Dewey (1898-1963) 60
    Everett Harvey (1930-1998) 60
    Frank S. (1962-   ) 412
    Isabelle 126
    La Jane (1922-   ) 60
    Max Dean (1923-2000) 60
Rusty
    Herbert Russell (1979-   ) 467
    Kilby (1979-   ) 467
Ruth
    Betsy Ann 491
    Franklin William Jr. 491
Rutherford
    Charles 51
    Florence Mae (1894-1974) 51
Rutter
    Anna 53
Ryan
    John P. 471
    John Patrick (1963-   ) 471
    Patricia Marie (1964-   ) 471
Rydbom
    Adora Delight (1931-2010) 123
    Audrey Dale (1940-   ) 123
    Calvin Bernard (1935-   ) 123
    Charles Andrew (1944-   ) 123
    Ellen Ruth (1937-   ) 123
    Julie 123
    Kim 123
    Larry Blain (1941-1942) 123
    Loretta Marie (1942-   ) 123
    Rea Naomi (1930-   ) 123
    Richard Clair Jr. (1928-   ) 123
    Richard Clair Sr. (1903-1972) 123
    Robert James (1936-2013) 123
Ryland
    Anna M. (1891-1966) 266
Sablotny
    Hildegard 265
Sadoski
    Bernard Jr. 232
Salada
    Arlene Florence (1924-1974) 344
    Barbara 244
    Fayne Lama (1957-   ) 344
    Fayne Lamas (1927-   ) 344
    Gary Joseph (1943-   ) 344
    Joseph (1900-1953) 344
    Leroy Irwin (1926-1997) 344
    Renee JoAnna (1937-   ) 344
    Robert Allen (1963-   ) 344
    Sandra Elaine (1947-   ) 344

Sallada
- David Harold (1937-2011) 56
- Dean 56
- Florence Henrietta (1917-1992) 56
- Harold V. (1913-1983) 56
- Harry (1911-) 56
- Henry 56
- Lori 56
- Nancy (1939-) 56
- Nancylee (1939-) 56
- Ronald E. 344
- Velma Alverta (1907-1958) 56
- Walter Logan (1885-1943) 56

Saltzer
- Ada Dianna 263
- Annie 447
- Buell 447
- C. A. 224
- Catherine A. (1864-1934) 241
- Clara 447
- Colonel (1877-) 448
- Edwin Blaine (1892-) 448
- Elias Warrer (1886-) 448
- Ellen 448
- Emma Salera Isabella (1870-1922) 288
- Ethel (1896-) 239
- Frances (1874-) 448
- Fremont (1868-) 448
- Gabriel 448
- Harry Herbert (1877-) 448
- James 239
- Jennie Edna 341
- Jeroma 447
- John 169
- John Adam 67
- John W. 241
- Josiah D. (1845-1898) 447
- Katie Eva (1890-) 448
- Lincoln 447
- Maggie (1869-1873) 448
- Melvina (1879-) 448
- Molly 417
- Orson (1878-) 448
- William 288
- William (1876-) 448

Sampson
- Darlena D. (1975-) 324

Samuels
- Howard E. (1928-) 257
- Jennifer Susan (1956-) 257

San Nicolas
- Christian Michael Leon Guerrero (2002-) 71
- Michael Scott (1974-) 71
- Mikayla Liann Leon Guerrero (1994-) 71

Sanchez
- Argimiro 352
- Gino Anthony (1995-) 352
- Otto 251

Sanders
- Jill 259
- Walter S. (1883-1943) 378

Sands
- Connie 104
- Harry Ellsworth (1868-1940) 213

Santak
- William Leck (1934-) 152

Sapiano
- James 475

Saputo
- Andrew A. (1915-2004) 304
- Christopher 304
- James 304
- Randy 304
- Susanne C. 304

Sarcinello
- Andrew Patrick (1992-) 307
- Dana Michelle (1995-) 307
- Michael Vincent (1961-) 307

Sarfine
- (--?--) 433

Sattazahn
- (--?--) 387
- Darya 387
- Esther A. (1921-2002) 219
- Warren I. 219

Sauers
- Sarah E. 89

Sausser
- Estella Laura (1899-1992) 481

Savage
- Donald 294
- George 294
- George E. (1939-1998) 294

Savas
- Constantine 469
- Elizabeth (1991-) 469
- Halley (1999-) 469
- Hannah (1994-) 469
- Madison (1997-) 469
- Perry (1992-) 469
- Peter G. (1948-) 469
- Tess (1995-) 469

Savidge
- (--?--) 425
- Alice Sevilla (1870-1948) 310
- Carrie E. (1925-) 309
- Catherine (1918-) 308
- Catherine M. (1903-1971) 309
- Charles (1922-) 55
- Charles D. (1910-) 310
- Clair M. (1925-) 308
- Clayton Richard (1900-) 55
- Daniel 307
- Daniel K. (1873-1873) 310
- Elias (1864-1865) 307
- Frank F. (1905-1988) 309
- Fremont K. (1868-1908) 310
- George Washington (1897-) 309
- Harrison (1894-1978) 308
- Harry M. (1894-1978) 308
- Helen S. (1921-) 309
- Howard M. (1920-) 309
- Infant (1876-1876) 310
- James E. (1902-1976) 309
- Jennie A. (1899-) 309
- John E. (1901-1905) 309
- Jonas (-1991) 252
- Katherine (1903-1971) 309

Katie Annie (1877-1934) 310
Laura E. (1907-1967) 309
Lizzie (1874-1956) 310
Mae I. (1927-   ) 309
Mark E. (1917-   ) 309
Mary Alice (1890-1972) 307
Mary Elizabeth (1863-1863) 307
Maude (1913-   ) 310
Mildred (-1991) 252
Morrison (1861-   ) 307
Oliver K. (1859-1944) 307
Paul Lester (1916-1993) 308
Robert E. (1924-1928) 55
Samuel K. (1866-1942) 307
Sarah Lorraine (1926-1997) 55
Sevilla (1870-1948) 310
Susanna H. (1896-   ) 308
Thomas C. (1921-1922) 55
Valentine (1800-1877) 307
Valentine (1835-1920) 307
William Isaac (1920-1920) 55
William K. (1888-1946) 310
William V. (1892-1978) 308

Sawyer
(--?--) 168

Scanlan
Catherine L. (1924-2011) 78
Joseph 78

Schach
Howard G. (1880-   ) 259
Joan M. 260
John Howard (1922-2008) 260
John Howard Jr. 260
Jonathan A. 260
Katherine 260
Martha Mae (1904-1985) 259
Mary (1899-1998) 259
Naomi Kathryn (1911-1913) 260
Nicole M. 260
Paul (1915-1998) 260
Paula R. 260
Verna (1902-1989) 259

Schade
Betty 245
Betty Joan (1932-1970) 197, 245
Cathy 245
David 244
David L 245
Deborah J. 245
Don B. 208
Donald 245
Harry Edwin (1890-1939) 244
Infant (1914-1914) 244
Infant (1925-1925) 245
James A. 245
James M. Jr. 208
James M. Sr. 208
Leah 245
Leroy J. (1918-1987) 244
Linda 243
Luke Harry (1940-2012) 245
Mae A. (1916-1996) 244
Mary Ellen 245
Nancy 245
Phyllis 244

Warren Monroe (1922-1982) 245

Schadel
(--?--) 201, 400
Adam 201
Brenda (1965-   ) 336, 444
Christiana (1855-1936) 180, 474
Eva 476
George H. (1827-1899) 474
Guy Ambrose (1917-1996) 179
Harold (1937-   ) 336
Harvey 476
Harvey J. 476
James 179
Justin 201
Kate (1831-1888) 356
Maggie McClata (1863-1942) 410
Margaret 489
Maria (1829-1895) 150, 178, 442
Mazie C. (1912-2001) 189
Miriana 476
Ray Woodrow Wilson (1917-1941) 179
Sarah (1829-1897) 134
Susannah (1854-1926) 242, 327

Schadle
James Charles (1940-2005) 174, 441
Leon Mark (1936-2006) 243, 441
Lynn Charles (1961-   ) 174
Megan 244
Ray Dale (1942-   ) 441
Rebecca Sue (1970-   ) 174
Roy Dale (1942-   ) 441
Russell Rue (1934-2010) 89, 440
Steven James (1962-   ) 174
Steven Reid (1992-   ) 174
Violet Jane (1932-2006) 440

Schaefer
Dan 478

Schaeffer
Annabelle (1928-   ) 133
Ellen Rebecca (1885-1943) 404
Erma (1921-   ) 133
Fern (1916-   ) 133
Frank 133, 239
Grace Alice (1912-1971) 239
Levi 404
Lucinda 206
Mabel (1919-   ) 133
Mildred (1926-   ) 133
Ray (1924-   ) 133
Wilson (1890-1929) 239

Schaeffler
David R. 345
Ruth Delores 345

Schaffer
(--?--) 410
Catharine 376
Catherine 244
Charles Daniel (1889-1970) 452
Emma J. (1861-1937) 312
Ida (1870-   ) 161
Maria Sarah (1799-1878) 372
Martha Elaine (1942-   ) 173
Pauline 126
Susan Amelia (1889-1929) 401

Schaffler
 Shirley Mae 344
Schaffner
 (--?--) 160
 Anna Louise 242
 Brock (1950-) 409
 Colleen (1948-) 408
 Jason 409
 Jill 409
 Leslie (1952-) 409
 Mark Lee (1965-) 409
 Melva Pauline (1920-1984) 484
 Ray 242
 Rock Christian (1954-1971) 409
 Russell R. 408
 Russell Rose Jr. (1926-1984) 408
Schartel
 Mary (1854-) 209
 Polly (1854-) 209
Schauer
 Donald M. 123
Scheck
 Herbert B. 229
 James J. (1900-1984) 219
Scheib
 (--?--) 200
 Albert Earl (1906-1969) 219
 Albert Oscar (-1937) 481
 Allen E. (1914-1986) 127
 Alvena Marie (1910-1999) 220
 Alvin Ralph (1943-) 485
 Amelia C. (1895-1990) 455
 Amelia G. and Millie C. (1895-1990) 455
 Ammon Ellerslie (1906-1961) 482
 Angela Jean (1960-) 484
 Annie J. (1884-1974) 454
 Annie M. (1918-) 481
 Bertha Vesta (1891-1959) 455
 Bessie Edna (1921-) 481
 Betty L. (1925-1985) 477
 Bonita 456
 Carlos Raymond (1907-1995) 103
 Carlos Rufus (1903-1934) 482
 Carol 456
 Catherine (1911-1975) 484
 Cathryn Edna (1911-1975) 484
 Charles Monroe (1861-1931) 454
 Crystal Ann (1963-) 484
 Dale Lamar (1933-1936) 482
 Daniel Ronald (2000-) 476
 Dean Irvin (1942-1999) 484
 Donald 475
 Donald (-2003) 252
 Donald E. (1937-1998) 233
 Donna 233
 Eddie 233
 Edna Pauline (1929-) 483
 Elizabeth (1872-1956) 435
 Elmer F. (1896-1939) 489
 Elsie Lavina (1919-2005) 183
 Elwood 481
 Emma Jane (1884-1974) 454
 Ethel (1920-) 482
 Eva Viola (1904-1987) 219
 Florence (1914-) 220, 229
 Francis Washington (1883-1967) 103
 Franklin (1833-1885) 435, 481, 485
 Franklin Ellsworth 219, 229
 Franklin Markel (1867-1946) 485
 Gary (1950-) 482
 Gary Lee 416
 Gerald 220
 Gloria (1934-2010) 457
 Harry Franklin (1922-1987) 482
 Harry H. (1905-1984) 456
 Harry H. (1931-2012) 457
 Hilda 251
 Hilda Marie (1945-) 484
 Homer William (1900-1941) 116, 344
 Ira G. (1888-) 455
 Irvan Monroe (1908-1984) 484
 Irvin Monroe (1908-1984) 484
 Jade Aimee-Louise (1996-) 233
 James Isaac (1876-1944) 481
 Janet Helen (1952-) 485
 Jean M. (1936-2003) 116
 Jean Renee (1933-) 152
 Jeannette 456
 Jennifer Ann (1981-) 181
 John 233
 Johnny Allen Oscar (1947-) 127, 342
 Joshua (1831-1891) 454
 Joy 233
 June Rose (1926-2010) 481
 Kelly 482
 Kevin Ronald (1965-) 476
 Kieth Donald 475
 Lauren 457
 Lester L. (1909-1984) 233
 Lewis Andrew (1895-1948) 183
 Linda 456
 Luke Alfred (1930-) 484
 Mabel Irene (1926-) 482
 Maddison Susan-Marie (1998-) 233
 Mae (1938-) 485
 Margaret (1927-) 482
 Margaret Marie (1954-) 197
 Mark 457
 Mark Roy (1933-) 484
 Mary Eleanor (1929-) 344
 Mary Elizabeth (1943-) 484
 Mary May (1902-) 455
 Megan 482
 Michael A. 252
 Michael B. (1986-) 181
 Mildred Marie (1935-) 127, 342
 Natalie 457
 Nathan Tyler (1994-) 476
 Nettie E. (1902-1975) 357
 Nevin O. (1916-) 416
 Oleda 242
 Oscar E. (1873-1937) 127
 Patricia Lou (1937-) 103
 Phyllis 439
 Ralph Alvin (1914-1992) 485
 Richard G. 457
 Robert Benjamin (1926-1995) 181, 476
 Roger G. (1928-2010) 456
 Ronald Elwood (1935-) 103

Ruby 481
Samuel James (1994-   ) 476
Stanley (1928-   ) 482
Steven Dennis (1956-   ) 181
Tillie Arlene (1923-1978).. 489
Tracy 443
Verna Mae (1946-   ) 484
Vernon Arthur (1901-1971)... 481
Vickie (1960-   ) 103
Wendy (1964-   ) 103
Zachary Robert (1991-   ) 476

Scheidler
Dean Marlin (1946-2000)... 493
Debra L. 492
George Franklin (1883-1976)... 492
Riland George 492
Sheila Marie (1949-1999)... 493

Schell
Robbie Sr. 89

Schemberg
Freda Catherine (1946-   ) 85

Schepp
Mary R. 210

Scherdel
Elizabeth (1837-1855).. 67

Schieb
Elva Arlene (1927-2010)... 483
William H. (1866-1922)... 357

Schiliro
Peter 266

Schinkel
June (1925-   ) 328
Walter Daniel (1902-1924).. 328

Schive
Ezra Percival (1872-1936)... 385

Schlarb
Earl E. (1893-   ) 74
Mary Elizabeth (1915-1990) 75

Schlegal
Allen Ray (1894-1987)... 160

Schlegel
Anna (1905-   ) 133
Anna C. (1928-   ) 437
Annie Cordella (1928-   ).. 308
Beulah Maud (1886-1938).. 213
Brenda Eileen (1955-   ) 308
Carrie (-2010) 439
Chad (1979-   ) 308
Charles Daniel (1868-1943) 371
Charles W. (1910-1976) 307
Daniel Eugene (1958-1990).. 308
Debra Susan (1962-   ) 307
Devon 371
Dora I. (1919-1958)... 371
Doris Elaine (1949-   ) 308
Edward (1866-1932).. 312
Elmer L. (1894-1929) 213
Elsie... 497
Emma (1873-   ) 138
Guy.. 249
Harlan Edgar (1916-1990).. 307
Hattie (1900-1983) 101
Ira Daniel (1894-1973) 371
Irvin (1885-   ) 213
Irvin John (1920-1996).. 307
Irwin Francis (1890-1964) 307
James D. (1870-1954) 200
Jean E. (1932-1954) 371
Josephine Hardesty (1921-   ) 104
Krista 371
Lanier Harold (1939-   ) 307
Lillian (1891-   ) 213
Marian (1928-   ) 133
Matthew 371
May A. (1892-1970) 312
Michael 371
Miriam (1922-   ) 308
Neil 208
Oscar (1880-   ) 133
Perdie Minerva (1892-1950) 213
Richard D. (1934-2014) 371
Stella (1898-   ) 200
Vera Edna (1941-2004)... 307
Willard (1927-   ) 371
William 213
William (1902-   ) 133
William Wallace (1904-1945).. 371

Schleif
Grace Iona (1901-1990)... 314

Schmeltz
Aaron Michael (1989-   ).. 483
Alexander James (1964-   ) 466
Andreas (1751-1834)... 398
Ann Margaret (1970-   ) 466
Bruce Lamar (1954-   ) 197
Byron Robert (1953-1976)... 483
Catherine (1794-1872) 374
Catherine (1845-1918) 186
Christopher John (1980-   ) 483
Daniel (1807-1873) 186
David Lee (1971-   ) 467
David Monroe (1955-   ) 483
Dawn... 466
Debra Ann (1957-   ) 197
Diane Marie (1959-   ) 197, 245
Donna Marie (1955-2008) 466
Elizabeth (1800-1874) 316
Elizabeth (1866-1956) 182
Frank Gideon (1898-1962)... 466
Glenn Ira (1943-2003) 467
Gurney Webster (1894-1994) 194
Henry Ammon (1955-   ) 483
Ida 326
Joyce 485
Kate 67
Katie Alice (1885-1934) 68
Lee Darwin (1929-2016).. 466
Leroy... 485
Lester 197, 245
Lillie Alberta (1901-1982).. 257
Lois Grace (1946-   ) 467
Mae Kathryn (1932-2000) 466
Magdalena (1805-1878)... 398
Marilyn Mae (1946-   ).. 483
Monroe (1870-1954) 257
Nicole Leigh (2005-   ) 467
Patricia Ann (1968-   ) 466
Rebecca (1988-   ) 467
Reuben (1862-1903) 466

Riley Oscar (1880-1980) 474
Robert Bryan (1923-1982) 483
Roy 356
Ryan Matthew (1986-) 483
Sabrina Maria (1984-) 483
Samuel A. (1862-1933) 194
Sharon Eileen (1950-) 483
Sheila Marie (1951-) 483
Stella Catherine 169, 483
Stephen Michael (1976-) 483
Susannah (1836-1863) 168
Tiffany Rae (1992-) 467
William Francis (1953-2012) 466
William Henry (1897-1961) 483
William Roy 197

Schmick
Leo Donald 117

Schmidt
(--?--) 239, 475
Anna 237
John Anderson (1983-) 305
Joseph (1928-) 239
Joseph J. 239
Nellie E. 397
Sarah Elizabeth (1985-) 305
William 305

Schminky
Carol (1934-) 469
Joseph Nevin (1913-1978) 469

Schmitt
Jeffrey (1959-) 149
Laura (1986-) 149

Schmucker
Arlene Janette (1932-) 277
Daniel M. 277

Schneck
Bertha E. 82
Clarence (-2000) 257
Esther Marie 438
Mary Sophia (1884-1952) 81

Schneider
Alice (1920-2005) 302
Anna Margaret (1906-1986) 301
Anne (1906-1986) 301
Carolyn E. (1967-2007) 79
Clem Joseph Jr. (1934-1972) 302
Clement (1871-1956) 301
Clement John (1909-1991) 301
Eleanor (1919-) 205
John 205
Lester (1921-) 205
Mary Magdalena 210
Mildred (1901-1986) 301
Mildred L. (1922-) 206
Patricia Ann (1940-) 301
Paul (1903-1981) 301
Paul Christian (1934-1981) 301
Ramona (1901-1968) 301
Valerie Anne (1940-) 302

Schnell
Savilla 218

Schnoor
Craig 406
Jacquelyn 406
Melvin D. (1921-1995) 406

Schnorr
Martha 271

Schoffstall
Adam (1853-1922) 67, 122
Albert 68
Alberta E. (1934-) 69
Amanda (1849-1925) 67
Ann Elizabeth (1847-1918) 67
Anna 54
Annie (1862-1919) 69
Bud (1924-2009) 69
Catherine (1844-) 67
Charles A. (1907-) 69
Charles H. 68
Edna (1920-2004) 69
Elias (1857-1912) 69
Elizabeth (1843-) 67
Emma E. (1881-1934) 68, 122
Eva S. (1915-1951) 68
Gerald 69
Hannah D. (1913-1977) 68
Harry 67
John (1771-1840) 67, 448
John A. Jr. (1917-2007) 69
John Adam (1890-1958) 68
Leroy (1910-) 69
Linda 69
Lydia Ann (1862-1919) 69
Mary A. (1877-1928) 67
Mary Ann (1821-1884) 448
Maudie E. (1908-) 69
Pauline 208
Samuel (1805-1886) 316
Samuel (1810-1891) 67
Sara Jane (1938-) 69
Stanley H. (1924-2009) 69
Susannah (1841-) 67
William 67

Schofstahl
Allen 137
Jean (1920-) 137

Scholl
Betty 289
Deirdre 105
Derwin 105
Derwin L. 105
Dierdre 105
Henry L. 107
Ralph Leroy (1939-2005) 105
Shirley Fae (1936-2010) 107

Schomper
(--?--) 207
Kylie 207
Timothy 207
Tyler 207

Schornman
Margared Magdalena 420

Schorr
Denise 114
Gloria-Dean Elizabeth (1931-) 115
John Frederick Jr. (1930-1986) 114
John Marlin (1912-1975) 114
Kevin Eugene 114

Schott
Kim John 114
Melanie 114
Randy Lee 114
Todd 114

Schott
Henry O. 371

Schovin
Marlin 305
Sharon Lee (1946-) 305

Schrader
Jacob 229
Laura Jane (1869-1957) 220, 229

Schrawder
Cora (1882-1945) 104
Elmer 242
Rosa 107
William T. (1920-1999) 242

Schreck
Dean 453

Schreffler
Anthony L. 405
Ashley Nicole 187
Austin 187
Curtis 187
Ernie 373
Faye Renee (1943-) 475
Infant (1956-) 405
Janice (1943-) 187
Jason F. 187
Jeremiah 373
Jo Ellen (1949-) 405
Joan Marie (1942-) 402
John 66
Julie 187
Justin 187
Larry Steven (1945-2013) 187
Leah 187
Leslie 187
Linda Jane 291
Marlin Jefferson (1914-1997) 187
Marlin Leroy (1921-2014) 130
Marlin Randy (1952-) 187
Martin 475
Mary J. (1906-) 304
Maude (1890-1953) 66
Maynard E. (1939-) 187
Merl 291
Michael 130
Nevin (-1944) 402
Nolan 373
Richard 130
Russell 263
Samuel (1881-1965) 130, 405
Shyla 187
Susan 130
Timothy H. (1915-1979) 405
Timothy T. 405
William Freeman 185

Schreiber
Benjamin O. 109
Bill (1918-1980) 109
Brenda Jean (1972-) 111, 115
Calvin Carlos (1940-) 111
Candace Marie (1971-) 111, 115
Carol Jean 111
Charles E. (1922-1968) 110
Chow (1922-1968) 110
Chutt (1927-) 110
Cora Jane (1929-) 110
Debra 109
Dope (1931-) 111
Dorothy Mae (1919-2008) 109
Eddie Wayne (1967-) 111
Edith Ann (1927-) 110
Ernest Leroy (1954-) 111, 115
Ethel Irene (1923-1996) 110
Etz (1923-1996) 110
Hailee Joelle 111
Harvey Mark (1948-) 110
John Albert (1924-1952) 110
John Albert Jr. (1946-) 110
Kathrine Louise (1979-) 111
Keith Carlos (1966-) 111
Kenneth M. (1943-) 110
Kim (1951-) 111
Landy (1921-1986) 110
Loretta Marie (1934-2008) 111
Louis C. (1947-2008) 123
Louis J. (1923-1996) 123
Lynn 111
Mark 111
Mark Otis (1921-1986) 110
Mark Umeholtz (1899-1964) 109
Marshall Irving (1967-) 110
Mary E. 110
Myrt (1936-1987) 111
Myrtle Irene 110
Myrtle Jean (1936-1987) 111, 115
Ray Melvin (1931-) 111
Ray Melvin Jr. (1981-) 111
Retz (1934-2008) 111
Robert Frederick (1942-) 111
Robert J. (1965-2004) 111
Tabitha Amanda (1996-) 111
Terry D. (1950-2005) 124
Terry Lee (1950-) 110
Troy Allen (1985-) 111
William (1952-) 110
William H. (1918-1980) 109
William Jr. 109

Schreiner
Fronie T. (1876-1958) 126
Katherine M. 392

Schriever
Bert David (1919-1979) 91
Debelt David (1890-1918) 91

Schrock
Harold 275

Schroeder
Bessie 133

Schrope
Catherine Ann (1859-1913) 256
Dale Otto 290
Elizabeth A. 270
Eric Brad (1973-) 290
Irvin H. (1883-) 283
Kirby (1966-) 290
Marian Elizabeth (1915-1993) 283
Mary Jane (1029-2012) 349

Ned Wallace 290
Paul Simon Sr. 270
Schroy
Emma R. 54
Schuchman
Greg 387
Kendyl 387
Schuck
Augustus (1892-) 97
Schucker
(--?--) 120
Catherine 212
Emma 349
Eva (1902-) 335
Schuerkamp
Mary 107
Schuh
Anna Kathryn 73
Schuler
Dee 106
John 167
Schultz
Crystale Michelle 322
Douglas Harvey (1968-) 149
Harold Eugene (1921-2002) 60
Norma F. 225
Ruby Arlene (1923-1974) 198
Schureman
Jean (1922-1952) 463
Schutt
Caroline 235
Schutz
Michael 251
Schwalm
(--?--) (-1915) 247
(--?--) (1901-1901) 281
Aaron Franklin (1958-) 265
Ada (1885-) 135
Adam (1984-) 265
Agatha Barbara (1851-1929) 249
Agatha V. (1851-1929) 249
Agnes Virginia (1925-) 280, 458
Albert Ellsworth (1904-1985) 293
Albert F. 293
Albert Peter (1871-1929) 182, 476
Alice Marie (1871-1953) 294
Allen M. (1910-1974) 247
Alma May (1891-) 290
Alma Meda (1900-1926) 476
Amanda Jean 234
Amelia Jane (1857-) 493
Andrea L. 262
Andrew Edward (1957-) 232, 366
Andrew J. 184
Angela 182
Ann (1947-) 235
Anna Irene (1903-1988) 234
Annice (1927-1979) 477
Arielle Lynn (1989-) 262
Arlene 281
Arthur Harrison (1896-1980) 277
Ashton 292
Aubrey Noel (1990-) 232, 366
Aziza Rashuan Annette (2007-) 234

Barbara Ann Elizabeth (1930-2008) 232
Beatrice Isabella (1902-1986) 293
Bernice Amelia Hannah (1898-1899) 236
Bertha Esther (1907-1997) 263
Bessie Eva (1899-1991) 474
Beth Jan 262
Betty (1920-) 277
Beulah Este (1888-1966) 242
Beulah Louise (1922-1999) 277
Bradley (-2002) 246
Bradley Jack 262
Bruce D. 476
Bruce Elvin (1925-) 265
Bruce Franklin (1896-) 281
Bruce J. 262
Bruce Jr. 281
Burt J. (1955-) 262
Calvin Franklin (1901-1938) 260, 353
Cameron A. (1999-) 266
Carol 240, 281, 292
Carolina (1825-1891) 210
Caroline (1883-1943) 280
Carolyn (1936-) 220, 230
Carolyn Rojean (1928-) 478
Carrie E. (1879-) 136
Carrie Estella (1883-1943) 280
Catherine (1849-1873) 238
Catherine Isabelle (1915-2011) 289
Chad R. (1977-2007) 246
Charles Albert (1909-1993) 235
Charles Henry (1862-1918) 135, 459
Charles Lee (1904-1906) 232
Clair Millard (1926-2011) 291
Claire Louise (1946-) 292
Clara Alice (1877-1953) 271
Clarence William (1884-1948) 266
Clayton Allen (1901-1967) 232
Clifford Kenneth (1905-1974) 478
Cynthia Louise (1951-) 280, 458
Dale Eugene (1930-) 277
Daniel A. (1871-1949) 478
Daniel Calvin (1954-) 265
Daniel S. (1840-1916) 135
David Henry (1945-) 477
Dawson Paul (2000-) 183
Dean Lamar (1929-2014) 273, 275
Deborah 292
Debra 477, 478
Dennis (1960-) 102
Dennis I. 183
Diane 288
Donald Duane (1960-) 477
Donald Edward (1936-) 479
Donna Jean (1927-) 275
Dora Mae (1936-) 292
Dorothy E. (1925-) 291
Earl Morris (1925-1996) 74
Eda May (1879-1955) 234
Eda May (1915-1916) 235
Edith (1879-1955) 234
Edith I. (1905-1995) 263
Edmund P. (1929-1988) 230
Edna I. (1920-2007) 242
Edna Katie (1897-1899) 245
Edward (1844-) 474

Edward (1915-1969)	479
Edwin and Eldin (1908-)	135
Elda Matilda (1911-1976)	478
Eleanor May (1922-1926)	477
Elizabeth M.	246
Ellen Barbara Justina (1870-1958)	247, 257
Ellen Marie (1949-)	246
Elsie (1887-)	136
Elva C. (1913-1996)	241
Elvin R. (1908-)	135
Elvin Ray (1881-1968)	234
Emily Beth (1998-)	183
Emily Dawn (1976-)	264
Emma A. (1890-)	137
Emma Sarah (1921-2002)	290
Emma Vesta (1877-)	186
Erma A. (1916-1989)	242
Ernest L.	247
Esther Elnora (1918-2015)	278
Ezra Norman (1872-1932)	220, 229
Fietta (1847-1917)	228
Florence D. (1916-2000)	263
Florence May (1900-1992)	184
Frances (1916-1917)	280
Frances Saloma Elizabeth (1874-1950)	247, 257
Francis (1875-1880)	294
Frank E.	266
Frank Henry (1924-2007)	290
Franklin Henry (1853-1935)	257
Fred F. (1899-1981)	231, 366
Fred Junior (1921-)	265
Frederick (1796-1872)	210, 228, 248
Frederick Stein (1831-1902)	67, 186, 460
Fremont Edward (1924-1985)	279
Fremont Harrison (1882-1948)	279, 458
Fyetta (1847-1917)	228
George Harrison (1919-2009)	289
George Washington (1853-1856)	239
Geraldine A. (1939-)	235
Gertrude (1893-1972)	277
Gladys Naomi (1908-1991)	294
Glen H. (1966-)	189
Glen Henry (1945-2000)	189
Gleta Bernice (1903-1987)	274
Grace Katharine (1902-)	237
Gurney Harrison (1890-1972)	288
H. Allen (1906-1972)	232
Halden (1884-1934)	135
Hannah (1851-1926)	238
Harrison Monroe (1855-1922)	271
Harry A. (1906-1972)	232
Harry Alfred (1916-1991)	281
Harry Ray (1894-1963)	281
Harry Ray (1899-1964)	246
Harvey Edward (1872-1948)	268, 474
Harvey Russell (1898-1948)	291
Harvey W. (1882-1922)	274
Hattie Estella (1893-1974)	290
Hattie Pruella (1895-1961)	244
Heather	477
Helen M. (1920-1980)	477
Henry A. (1949-2014)	266
Henry E. (1862-1933)	241
Henry Lester (1910-1910)	263
Henry Ray (1899-1964)	246
Hilda M. (1910-1978)	232, 434
Hilda M. (1917-)	479
Holden E. (1884-1934)	135
Homer C. (1907-)	135
Homer Raymond (1911-1975)	241
Hugh Samuel (1928-)	280, 458
Ida Esta (1898-1936)	137, 417
Infant (1915-1915)	247
Infant Daughter (1879-1879)	279
Infant Son (1870-1870)	294
Ira Clayton (1877-1947)	230
Ira I. (1909-1983)	182
Irene Mae (1917-2016)	290
Iva Irene (1898-1971)	231
Jacob (1823-1896)	228
Jacob Nathaniel (1857-1938)	240
James (1987-)	265
James A. (1884-1905)	235
James Andrew (1979-)	247
Jane Iris (1932-)	275
Janet E. (1936-)	281
Jason M.	182
Jean Iris (1926-2011)	262
Jeffrey	290
Jennie E.	266
Jennie M. (1895-)	137
Jennifer Dale (1974-)	264
Jennifer Sue (1978-)	289
Jenny Rebecca (1894-1900)	474
Jeremiah F. (1992-)	262
Jerred Franklin (1927-)	262
Joan	281
JoAnn Gertrude (1934-)	220, 229
Joanne	235
Jodi	292
John	478
John Alfred (1907-1961)	189
John Jacob (1899-1983)	271
Joseph S.	264
Joseph Samuel (1953-)	265
Joyce Betty (1922-2005)	261, 353
June Helen (1924-2004)	265
Justina E. (1855-1926)	239
Karen Ruth (1960-1961)	262
Karl E. (1948-)	235
Katie Ella Nora (1879-1945)	259
Keith Edward (1960)	230
Kelsey Rae (1996-)	189
Kenneth	247
Kermit Kenneth (1921-1923)	260
Kevin	292
Kimberly Elise (1992-)	230
Kristen L. (1994-)	266
Larry Gordon (1938-)	479
Lawrence Henry (1927-1992)	189
Lee Wayne (1898-1964)	281
Leon H. (1918-1986)	476
Leon Lamar (1927-1980)	246
Leon Linscott (1884-1945)	241
Leslie J. (1905-1981)	281
Lillian Irene (1905-1991)	293
Lilly Agnes (1886-1893)	266
Linda Ann (1963-)	230
Linda Lou (1951-)	246
Lisa Ann	241

Lizzie and Mary Elizabeth (1865-1939) 281
Lizzie May (1884-1966) 275
Lois (1934-) 278
Lois Marie (1928-) 230
Lorraine (-2003) 476
Lou (1928-) 281
Lucille Odene (1925-) 231
Lucinda Ann 273, 275
Lyle Reuben (1924-2013) 262
Lynn Edward (1942-1965) 477
Mabel E. (1918-1989) 246
Mabel Grace (1914-2001) 268, 478
Mabel L. (1886-1958) 236
Mabel V. (1893-) 137
Mabelle (1886-1958) 236
Madyson Michelle (2006-) 182
Margaret A. (1919-2014) 278
Marian Isabel (1917-2004) 264
Marie Bernice (1916-2011) 277
Marie Elizabeth (1921-2005) 236
Marietta Maude (1887-1906) 236
Marion Elanore (1927-) 232
Mark 182
Mark Alton (1918-2013) 235
Mark David (1983-) 290
Mark Milliard (1917-2003) 289
Martha Ann 246
Mary 246
Mary A. (1859-1920) 204, 241
Mary Alice (1891-1966) 266
Mary E. 281
Mary E. (1866-1880) 247
Mary Elizabeth (1865-1939) 281
Mary Elizabeth (1881-1955) 280
Mary Elizabeth (1931-2011) 262
Mary Ellen (1900-1972) 236
Mary Ellen (1928-1978) 238
Mary Jane (1926-1997) 290
Maryellen (1928-1978) 238
Mason R. (1891-1962) 243
Matthew (1978-) 265
Meda Mae (1899-1986) 476
Merle Lamar (1909-2000) 275
Michael A. 246
Michael B. (1977-) 265
Michael Johannes (1982-) 235
Michael Kenneth (1980-) 230
Michael Neil (1970-) 289
Millard Stanley (1900-1944) 291
Minnie 469
Minnie A. Schwalm (1896-1962) 474
Minnie Elda (1896-1962) 474
Minnie M. (1889-) 136, 459
Monroe Ellsworth Peter (1864-1937) 244
Nan Elizabeth (1954-) 232, 366
Nathaniel (1980-) 265
Nathaniel J. (1857-1938) 240
Nora C. (1879-1961) 240
Nora Myrtle (1899-1978) 279
Norman Edward (1910-1938) 230
Norman Elias (1934-) 230
Orpah Naomi (1919-2012) 271, 335
Patricia Diane (1944-) 234
Paul I. (1935-2016) 182
Paul Jacob (1908-2000) 230

Pauline Nora 290
Peter Monroe (1926-1989) 246
Polly (1854-1914) 67, 122
Polly (1866-1880) 247
Randall Wesley William (1985-) 478
Ray (1900-1987) 74
Ray Allen (1920-) 241
Ray Alvin (1918-1987) 234
Raymond Theodore (1906-1991) 238
Rebecca 266
Rebecca J. (1943-2005) 189
Reilley A. (1861-1925) 280
Reilly (1861-1925) 280
Reno Palmer (1929-1995) 232, 366
Richard G. 478
Richard G. Jr. 478
Robert 246
Robert Joseph (1986-) 232, 366
Roger Lee (1943-) 247
Roger Raymond Jr. 234
Roger Raymond Sr. 234
Roger Sherwood (1943-) 234
Ronald Wayne (1960-1960) 477
Roswell Jacob (1891-1961) 236
Roy 182
Roy Ezra (1905-1975) 220, 229
Roy S. (1904-1955) 246
Rufus M. (1883-1955) 120
Russell J. 246
Russell Lee (1922-1985) 246
Ruth (1903-1963) 229
Ryan 275
Sadie Mabel (1895-1977) 244
Sallie (1915-2007) 120
Sam (1945-) 264
Samuel (1827-1903) 248
Samuel E. (1959-) 265
Samuel Ellsworth (1881-1967) 260
Samuel Emanuel (1848-1913) 229
Samuel Fremont (1879-1940) 274
Samuel Klinger (1904-1949) 280, 458
Samuel Peter (1858-1927) 279, 458
Sandra 476
Sandra Lee (1950-) 265
Sandra M. 246
Sarah Elizabeth (1993-) 183
Sarah Ellen (1874-1947) 460
Scott 477
Scott Berry 234
Scott Paul (1957-) 183
Shirley A. 281
Shirley Belle (1932-) 235
Sonja 189
Stanford W. (1888-1943) 240
Stephen (1949-) 280, 458
Stephen L. 246
Steven 476
Steven E. (1952-2005) 278
Steven T. (1957-) 292
Stu (1978-) 265
Synary Ellsworth (1868-1923) 288
Tammy Lynn 278
Tania Lee (1965-) 189
Terry 183
Tessie M. (1894-1968) 243

  Theodore R. (1906-1991) 238
  Tillie I. (1894-1970) 268, 478
  Timothy 275
  Timothy A. 266
  Torrie (1873-1873) 248
  Tracy M. 278
  Travis Ryan (1994-) 189
  Vera Irene (1921-) 291
  Verna Christiana (1909-1992) 478
  Vernon Frances (1910-1911) 280, 459
  Vernon Franklin (1887-1972) 277
  Vincent 476
  Wallace A. (1922-1923) 235
  Walter Wilson (1952-) 288
  Wanda 278
  Wayne 246
  Wayne Samuel (1918-2009) 264
  Wayne Samuel Jr. (1945-) 264
  Wendy 478
  William Arthur (1906-1976) 234
  William D. (1902-1980) 476
  William Harvey (1902-1980) 476
  William R. (1929-2003) 478
  William R. Jr. 478
  Wilson Ellsworth (1912-1993) 288
  Wilson F. (1912-1993) 288
  Winston 275
  Wynn 275

Schwan
  Herman 302
  Rosemary (1897-1982) 302

Schwanke
  Amy Ann (1977-2014) 235
  Arlynn 235
  Erica Ann (1984-) 235
  Mark Walter (1980-) 235
  Todd Daniel (1972-) 235

Schwartz
  Bonita Lee (1954-) 352
  Brian (1969-) 292
  Catherine 229
  Charles 73
  Dale E. (1952-) 410
  Edna Viola (1920-) 307
  Elsie 82
  Eric Andrew (1977-) 352
  Floyd (1938-) 73
  Frederick Samuel (1906-1975) 73
  Irvin E. 292
  Jacob 292
  Jill (1971-) 292
  Lloyd Francis 352
  Lloyd Francis Jr. (1951-) 352
  Nathan Scott (1974-) 352
  Nora Alice (1897-1929) 308
  Rena Marie (1962-) 352
  Tobi (1976-) 410
  William 292
  William E. 292

Schwenk
  Aaron (1844-) 210
  Abraham K. (1847-) 210
  Abraham S. (1816-1885) 209
  Almira K. (1850-) 210
  Daniel 210
  Daniel K. (1848-1850) 210
  Frederick K. 209
  George (1856-1859) 210
  Jacob (1858-1859) 210
  Jeannette 210
  John E. K. (1854-) 210
  Lillian 209
  Mary E. 209
  Peter III 210
  Peter N. K. (1854-1934) 210
  Peter N. K. Jr. 210
  Samuel K. (1842-1915) 210

Scicchitano
  Carmen D. 233
  Carmen D. Jr. (1972-1997) 233
  Lisa 233
  Melissa 233

Scott
  Edna E. 285
  Geri Hopper (1950-) 328
  Sharon 87
  Tony L. (1962-) 230
  Virginia R. 93
  Walter H. 285

Scudder
  Darin 306

Seachrist
  Susan (1838-1920) 83

Seaholtz
  Paul 265
  Robin 265

Seals
  Connie M. 298

Seaman
  (--?--) 89
  Ida Elizabeth (1889-1954) 77
  Jeffrey 67
  Jeremy J. 67
  Zachary C. 67

Seamon
  Cora 481

Searer
  Audrey Bernice (1921-2013) 272
  Audrey Elizabeth (1921-2013) 272
  Caroline K. 272
  David 272
  Evaline 271
  Frank 271
  Gary 272
  George W. 271
  Herman (-2005) 272
  James 272
  John 272
  Karen 272
  Kathy 272
  Keith (1923-2005) 272
  Lori Ann 272
  Max Newell (1928-) 272
  Michelle 271
  Noble (1896-1991) 271
  Noble Jr. 271
  Norman J. 271
  Norman J. Jr. 271
  Richard Owen (1925-2014) 272

Richard Owen Jr. 272
Robert 272
Robert Carlisle (1930-) 272
Robert E. 272

Seebold
Ann Elizabeth (1955-) 305
Daniel Jacob (1996-) 304
Nelson (1901-) 304
Robert J. (1924-2012) 304
Robert Joseph (1994-) 304
Robert Nelson (1952-) 304

Seeger
James 454

Seel
Albert 124
Marlene R. (1943-2010) 124

Seeler
Cinthia (1954-) 323

Seese
Georgia 277

Seibel
Carlee Lynn (1988-) 151, 449
Gregory Allen (1955-) 151
Heather Ann (1982-) 151, 449

Seibert
Brian 54
Harry 54
Keith 54

Seiders
Eric Thomas (1989-) 399
Thomas Edward 399

Seiger
Arlene M. (1924-2013) 338, 445

Seiler
Barry (1960-) 486
Christina 486
Clyde (1929-) 485
Diane (1954-) 486
Ernest (1905-1946) 485
Franklin (1935-) 486
George (1963-) 486
George Harvey (1906-1908) 486
Harvey Franklin (1878-1908) 485
Lillian (1949-) 485
Lou Ann (1963-) 173
Mary (1937-) 486
Mary (1962-) 486
Rebecca 51
Richard Troutman (1859-1937) 485
Sarah Ruth Fern (1908-1999) 486
Steven (1989-) 486

Seip
Irene 458

Seitz
Catharine (1829-1907) 198
Charles Elvin (1894-1989) 259
Elmira (1865-1888) 297
Helen E (1922-2008) 259
Helen G. 370
Jacob (1824-1904) 297

Selinsky
Joseph 200

Sell
Daniel 96
Jennifer 96
Matthew 96
Michael 96
Olive Angeline (1911-1979) 256

Seman
Eloise Stephanie Barto Leon Guerrero (1967-) 70

Semerod
(--?--) 425

Sepavich
(--?--) 390
Victoria 390

Serra
Jose Antonio (1956-) 86
Matthew James (1989-) 86
Michael Joseph (1986-) 86
Rebecca Ann (1982-) 86

Server
Arthur (Dr.) 298
Arthur Dr. 298
Gary Sanford (1950-) 298
Jon Alan (1956-) 298

Servern
George 123
Georgia 123

Seward
Dale G. (1957-) 286

Sfaxi
Muhammed 111

Sgrignoli
Albert Salvator (1921-1994) 400
Gayle Ann (1943-2015) 400
Jeffrey William (1975-) 400
Keith Eugene (1948-) 400
Mauro 400
Robert 88

Shaak
(--?--) 328

Shade
Albert Leroy 129
Amelia Jane (1855-) 452
Annie 263
Arthur P. Jr. 403
Arthur P. Sr. (1911-1983) 403
Chris (1970-) 102
Christine E. 183
Daniel Andrew (1869-1877) 203
Edna Stella May (1885-) 204
Ellen S. 403
Elmer 138
Ernest E. 403
Fern 340
Gary (-1994) 183
Gary Lee (1944-1991) 102
Hannah Elizabeth (1878-1961) 203, 241
Jack Eugene Sr. (1929-2002) 357
Jeff A. 412
Jeffrey 129
John (1808-1869) 203, 372
Jonathan Monroe (1871-1888) 203
Juliana (1851-1919) 344, 479
Julie Marie 129
Kiley 254
Lawrence Elvin (1902-1980) 102
Leroy Arthur 129

Lulu May (1895-   ) 146, 203
Lura May (1895-   ) 146
Margaretha (1803-1829) 372
Marlin R. (1908-2000) 453
Martha Francis (1928-2013) 267
Matthew Rodney (1977-   ) 357
Minnie (1893-1981) 145, 203
Miriam (-1999) 455
Nathaniel A. (1869-1877) 203
Oscar M. (1873-1954) 203
Reuben H. (1846-1916) 203, 241
Rodney Lee (1953-2007) 357
Samuel G. (1885-1921) 453
Sevilla Promelia (1888-1976) 205
Tamie Caroline (1898-   ) 170
Tara Jane (1976-   ) 357
Victoria (1861-1911) 244
William Franklin 403

Shadel
(?)341
Fietta (1847-1908) 280
Jennie (1914-1991) 309

Shadle
Alice Mae (1960-   ) 89, 440
Alice May (1960-   ) 89
Alyssa 244, 441
Caleb Richard (2015-   ) 289
Chloe (1987-   ) 328
Corey Matthew (1978-   ) 289
Dan (1965-   ) 328
Daniel (1990-   ) 328
Emma (1992-   ) 328
Emma Marie (2006-   ) 289
Gabrielle (2005-   ) 328
Gina L. 441
Hattie Perstella (1877-1913) 409
James Phillips 440
Joanne Patricia (1953-   ) 288
John Russell (1963-   ) 89, 440
John Russell Rue (1963-   ) 89
L. Mark (1968-   ) 244, 441
Lori (1960-   ) 244, 441
Lynn Charles (1961-   ) 174, 441
Lynnette 441
Marie 116
Mary A. (1929-   ) 88
Mary A. (1931-   ) 336
Mary Sevilla (1899-1950) 288
Megan 244, 441
Monroe Joel (1929-2006) 288
Ray Woodrow Wilson (1913-1941) 89, 174, 243, 440
Rebecca Sue (1970-   ) 174, 441
Richard 289
Robert Wilson (1857-1940) 288
Sarah M. 290
Steven James (1962-   ) 174, 441
Steven Reid (1992-   ) 174, 441
Yvonne Lee (1958-   ) 244, 441

Shafer
May 61

Shaffer
Amanda Marie (1990-   ) 144
Brian Edward (1975-   ) 145
Brittney 411
Brooke 411

Cheryl Anne (1986-   ) 144
Christine Lisa (1993-   ) 144
Christopher Lawton (1978-   ) 145
Clifford 479
Dakota 411
Daniel Morris (1871-   ) 145
Daniel W. (1827-1905) 143, 169, 459
David Kimber (1971-   ) 145
Dorothy Mary (1934-   ) 321
Elias Zerbe (1862-1941) 182
Emma 241
Francis (1803-1871) 99
Francis (1879-1939) 146
Francis Palmer (1922-1986) 143
Gary 160
Helen B. (1904-   ) 240
Herman E. (-2011) 411
Ida Clara 391
Jane Anne (1930-   ) 144
John F. Jr. (1923-1966) 160
Joseph 321
Judith A. 289
Kimber Cleaver (1901-1972) 143, 315
Kimber Cleaver (1943-1981) 145
Linda I. (1967-   ) 144
Lisa 160
Lois J. (1968-   ) 144
Margaret Ruth (1959-   ) 144
Mark 333
Mark William (1962-   ) 144
Martin Anthony (1989-   ) 144
Mary (1830-1912) 99
Mary Cardella (1892-1988) 129, 182
Mary Justina (1903-1989) 116, 344
Melissa 180
Michael (1789-1837) 143
Michael Francis (1964-   ) 144
Mindy 333, 351, 443
Patricia Ann (1932-   ) 323
Philip E. 411
Phrene Elmira (1875-1956) 145, 203
Richard Kimber (1961-   ) 144
Rick 160
Robert 323
Robert M. 289
Sadie I. (1892-1896) 143
Sara A. (1849-1913) 169
Sevilla (1857-1923) 459
Susan 161
Thomas Lee 333, 351, 443
Timothy (-2013) 333, 351, 443
Todd 411
Wendy 160
William Albert (1936-   ) 144
William Elsworth (1869-1950) 143
William R. (1936-1977) 314
Winnie Alva (1894-1972) 143
Winnie Elizabeth (1943-   ) 144, 314

Shaffner
Julia E. Fidler (1878-   ) 70

Shambaugh
Anna Barbara 64

Shamrock
Wilma 320

Shank
    Florence Edna (1910-) 275
    John 275

Shannon
    Anna M. (1891-) 423
    Annie (1891-) 423
    Bessie (1888-) 423
    Carrie (1886-) 423
    Frederick J. (1885-) 423
    Harvey E. (1883-) 423
    Hervey E. (1883-) 423
    James (1863-1920) 423
    Maxine (1913-) 423
    Merle (1911-) 423
    Neil (1914-) 423
    Robert A. (1893-) 423
    Robin A. (1893-) 423
    Selma B. (1895-) 423
    Steven (1958-) 481
    Thelma B. (1895-) 423

Sharp
    Henry Franklin 362

Shawver
    Jeff 191

Shearer
    Dennis (1944-2005) 193
    Dennis Jr. (1971-) 193
    Mark D. 217
    Teena (1966-) 193

Sheehan
    Peter William (1919-1975) 395

Sheely
    Barbara Ann (1968-) 159
    Derek Thomson (1989-) 159
    Kenneth Brian (1966-) 159
    Keyton Sierra (1993-) 159
    Roy Jay (1943-1993) 159
    Timothy Andrew (1970-) 159

Sheesley
    Tim 494

Sheets
    Clinton Skelly 468
    Vera (1908-) 468

Sheetz
    Jimmy 432

Shefflet
    Paula 472

Sheffley
    Rosa 50

Shelly
    Catherine D. (1869-1939) 57

Shenk
    Edith 231
    Robert 439
    Rose 439

Shepherd
    (--?--) 95

Shepley
    (--?--) 127

Sheridan
    (--?--) 389
    James 389

Sheriff
    Clarence E. (1899-) 374
    Harry E. (1880-1917) 374
    Margaret E. (1907-) 374
    Ralph (1909-) 374

Sherman
    Elizabeth 281
    Marie E. 486
    Nellie (1885-1969) 168
    Nettie (1887-1973) 166

Sherry
    John 481

Shertel
    Amelia (1856-) 209
    Casse (1861-1862) 209
    Elizabeth (1859-) 209
    Eve 209
    George 209
    Mary (1854-) 209
    William (1835-1874) 209

Sherwood
    Jeffrey Scott (1962-) 466
    Mark Richard (1959-) 466
    Milena Brieanne (1983-) 466
    Richard (-1992) 465

Shetterly
    Fred 411
    Frederick Jason 411
    Nicole 411
    Sharon 411
    Shawna 411

Shield
    Mary 385

Shields
    Martha E. 65

Shiffer
    John 68

Shiko
    John S. 180

Shiley
    Dora (1886-1965) 361
    Oscar 403
    Ruth Ellen (1918-2006) 403
    Verna 480

Shindler
    Blanche Josephine (1905-1976) 392
    Clarence (1907-1981) 116
    John William 392

Shingara
    Margaret Irene 130

Shipe
    Abbie 372

Shipley
    (--?--) 109

Shipman
    Dorothy Arlene 127

Shippy
    Cora (1897-1983) 415
    Perry 415

Shiro
    Allen Eston (1938-) 330
    Annie Marie 188
    Audrey Carol (1967-) 330

    Bryan Allen (1989-) 330
    Dolores Elaine (1969-) 331
    Heidi Arlene (1971-) 331
    Kelly 292
    Kelly Marie (1964-) 330
    Ricky Allen (1960-) 330
    Shelly Kay (1966-) 330
    Steven Michael (1983-) 330
    Tina Ann (1962-) 330
    Valerie Marie (1986-) 330
    Vicki Sue (1974-) 331

Shive
    Susan 174

Shivley
    Richard 277

Shoffler
    Brenda (1959-) 363

Shoffstall
    Adam (1853-1922) 67
    Angeline (1831-1880) 316
    Charles (1874-) 67
    Minnie 67

Sholly
    Mary (1825-) 73

Shomper
    Charles Monroe (1876-1956) 422
    Clyde Albert (1913-1980) 422
    Daneca M (1978-) 322
    David Lester (1952-) 322
    Donna Louise (1962-) 484
    Dora T. (1921-2007) 358
    Dorothy (1940-2006) 422
    Elsie Arlene (1904-1969) 422
    Felicia (1990-) 323
    Harold Eugene (1905-1993) 422
    Henry E. (1921-2006) 322
    James Lamar (1964-) 484
    Jessica C. (1983-) 323
    John Edward Jr. (1983-) 323
    John Edward Sr. (1953-) 323
    Lamar Eugene (1936-) 484
    Landon David (1986-) 322
    Ralph Edward (1907-1929) 422
    Richard Leroy (1946-) 322
    Robin (1980-) 322
    Ruth Miriam (1916-2012) 297
    Shirley Jean (1948-) 322
    Thomas Edward (1972-) 484

Shoop
    Alexis 108
    C. James (1968-) 171
    Clair L. (1947-) 105
    Clarence J. (1948-2010) 171
    Emma 108
    Felicia 108
    James W. 491
    Karl Dean (1923-1993) 52
    Katie 403
    Kimberlee Ann (1969-) 171
    Lena Elizabeth (1922-2001) 52
    Louretta 51
    Mark Curtin (1899-1991) 52
    Michael 108
    Miriam Ruth (1934-2011) 491
    Patrick Todd (1971-) 171
    Rebecca Jane 114
    Robert William 114
    William J. 171

Short
    Diana Lee 466

Shott
    Sally Kathryn 145

Showers
    Elizabeth M. (1891-1964) 143
    Eugene W. 217
    Pearle 491
    Robert W. (1925-) 217

Shrawder
    Jacqualine 257

Shuey
    (--?--) (1913-) 359
    Daniel Milton 489
    Leroy 291
    Mark (1977-) 291
    Mary Augusta (1915-1978) 489
    Michael (1977-) 291
    Randy 326
    Sharon (1976-) 291

Shugars
    George 285
    Virginia Charlotte (1927-) 285

Shultz
    Fred 374
    J. Frank 236
    John Merl (1896-1929) 236
    John W. (1867-) 457
    Michael Lee (1977-) 59
    Myrl R. (1895-) 457
    Nancy Ruth (1928-1961) 236
    Ronald L. 59
    Sherwood Lee 59
    Tony Lee (1974-) 59

Shumaker
    Christine Elizabeth 159

Shuman
    Courtney 464
    Richard 464
    Steven 464

Shumate
    (--?--) 64

Shur
    (--?--) 184

Shutt
    (--?--) 344

Sibert
    Bruce (1915-) 97
    Calvin E. (1874-) 97
    Charles B. (1915-) 97
    Charles F. (1878-) 97
    Earie (1907-) 97
    Elizabeth Anne (1920-) 97
    Emerson C. (1901-) 97
    Frederick A. (1845-1927) 97
    Frederick A. (1893-) 98
    Gladys (1904-) 97
    Henrietta (1851-1871) 93
    Ida May (1872-1878) 97
    Irving (1921-) 98

    Jean M. (1917-)...97
    John (1926-)..98
    Lucille F. (1913-)..97
    Lula (1888-)..97
    Lulu (1888-)..97
    Orey H. (1913-)..97
    Rena (1882-)...97
    Roy F. (1908-)..97

Sieger
    Myrle Elbert..71

Siegfried
    Doris..294

Siemanski
    Jere...254

Sierer
    Walter..206
    Walter Jr..206

Sigafoos
    Frantz Reed (1930-)......................................173

Sigmundsen
    Karen...249

Siler
    Earnest W. (1905-1946)..................................485

Silks
    Bessie (-2009)...127
    George O. Jr...471
    Leonard Lee...471

Silliman
    Ethel Charlotte (1914-1991).............................254
    Harry F..254

Silveira
    Susan (1965-)...463

Simmendinger
    John Jr. (1858-1931).......................................314
    Rosanna Christina (1884-1945)......................314

Simmons
    Agnes Janetha..221

Simpson
    (--?--)...421

Sims
    Alan...131
    Brian...131
    Carolyn Sue (1962-)......................................131
    Doreen...131
    Erica..250, 258
    Henry (-2012)..131
    Loretta (1948-1997).......................................109
    Mark Richard (1934-2012).............................131
    Ryan..250
    Sydney..250, 258

Sines
    Minnie Jane...221

Sinkey
    Emery B..65
    Evelyn (1919-2006)..65

Siperko
    Michael...191
    Michelle...191
    Phil..191

Siren
    Pamela (1951-)..329
    Richard Lloyd (1929-1980).............................329
    Susan Michele (Dr.) (1955-).........................329

    Susan Michele Dr. (1955-)............................329

Sitlinger
    Catherine Irene (1888-1961)....................329, 368
    Emory Isaiah (1903-1991)..............................147
    George Edward (1862-1925)..........................329
    Janet L. (1951-)..336
    Russell Benjamin (1929-)..............................336
    Wayne LeMar (1941-)...................................147

Sivriling
    Florence...222

Skelton
    Tammy...472

Sleighter
    James...246
    James Jr..246

Slotterback
    Daniel...199

Slotterbuck
    Verna L...245

Slough
    (--?--)...344

Smeck
    (--?--)...415
    Joe...415
    Joseph..415
    Julie...415

Smeltz
    (--?--)...200
    Anna M. (1941-2003)......................................105
    Arnie...138
    Betty Jean (1941-)..474
    Brad...442
    Carl..442
    Heather...442
    James Riley (1944-)......................................474
    Jason Lamar (1976-)....................................197
    Jay (1918-1971)..442
    Jeremy Lester (1979-1993).............................197
    Joyce...357
    June Marie..104
    LeRoy C. (1927-2013)....................................356
    Mary..234
    Matthew..442
    Nancy..357
    Nancy (-1950)..442
    Palmer D. (1916-1987)...................................474
    Palmer Daniel (1938-)...................................474

Smeltzer
    Agnes S. (1876-1946).....................................406
    Jonas (-1900)..406

Smiddy
    Virginia Lee (1937-)...57
    William J. (1909-)..57

Smiley
    Rose Mary..221

Smink
    H. Charles (1930-2011)..................................192
    Henry..192

Smith
    (--?--).......................................65, 123, 353, 486
    Alma I. (1920-)..226
    Amelia..326
    Annie F...422
    Asa..374

Barry Arthur (1948-) 298
Brayden 353
Brian 318
Brielle 353
Brody 353
Carolyn 92
Carroll Lee (1952-) 300
Charles (-2010) 129, 153
Charlotte 223
Chet 318
Cindy L 286
Clinton James (1990-) 305
Courtney 349
Daniel (1990-) 96
David (1960-) 96
Dawn 349
Donna Rae 476
Dorothy (1916-1960) 469
Dorothy Clara (1926-2010) 129
Esther S. (1906-) 226
Florence Elizabeth 281
Franklin 374
Glenn Arthur 298
Glenn Blaine (1921-2007) 300
Gwendolyn Irene 286
Halbert (1934-) 92
Harry G. (1883-1957) 225
Harvey 171
Helen 63
Howard 349
J. Warren (1881-1944) 300
Jack Woodrow (1997-) 305
Jacque Lamar 184
James 305
James D. 264
James Vernon 281
Jamie (1983-) 350
Jean Elizabeth (1924-2013) 153
Jennifer 92
Jesse 304
John B. 225
Johnson F. 310
Joleen 69
Justin Benner (1994-) 305
Kathryn 184
Kimber David (1948-) 300
Lindsay (1985-) 350
Lynne Elizabeth (1969-) 174
Margaret M. 250
Mary (1871-1936) 371
Melba 70
Patricia 220
Perry Owens (1954-) 298
Rachel Catherine (1987-) 96
Robin 350
Sarah Elizabeth (1860-1943) 63
Scott 324
Shirley A. (1939-2000) 77
Sidney 298
Son 1 486
Son 2 486
Son 3 486
Stephanie (-2006) 350
Stephen 231
Stewart 82

William (1931-1989) 52
Smucker
Arlen (1955-) 197
Smyre
Matthew George (1984-) 330
Rob (1957-) 329
Smyth
Patricia (1925-) 165
Robert G. (1895-1957) 165
Snead
John 281
Karen 281
Larry 281
Sneck
Diana 493
Snell
(--?--) 224
Snep
Douglas 96
Gregory 96
Janet Sue 96
Janice Marie 96
Larry 96
Pamela 96
Phillip 96
Robert H. (1919-2001) 96
Suzie 96
William 96
Snody
Beulah Mae (1916-1994) 104
James (1871-1951) 104
Mary Virginia (1906-1987) 69
Snoke
Arlene (1924-) 418
Snowe
(--?--) 101
Snyder
(--?--) 464
(--?--) (-1892) 149
(--?--) (1892-1892) 149
Alexandra Grace (2005-) 193, 339, 446
Alexis Lamar 193, 339, 446
Alexis Victoria 327
Alma Gertrude (1901-1969) 252
Alverta Hilda (1895-1991) 270
Amy Beth (1973-) 491
Angelia Lynn (1978-) 410
Annie (1881-) 118
Arthur 472
Ashley James 193, 339, 446
Audrey 370
Barbara (1850-1920) 146
Ben C. (1876-1951) 206
Bernice N. (1922-2012) 331
Carl Leroy (1954-) 383
Carrie Minerva (1898-1980) 329, 495
Catherine 373
Catherine A. 415
Catherine Alice (1872-1935) 158, 184, 418
Cathy 419
Chadwick Bowman 327
Charles 118, 340, 391
Charles E. 256
Charles H. 60

Name	Page
Clara Elizabeth (1883-1883)	119
Clayton (1896-)	170, 405
Clayton Malcom (1922-1987)	405
Cody	472
Cora	206
Dale Eugene (1945-)	327
Daniel	206
Daniel (1887-)	119
Daniel B. (1816-1873)	132, 156
Daniel Wiest (1848-1908)	146
Darlene Lillian (1945-)	491
David Guy (1957-)	491
Dennis Eugene (1952-)	106
Derle Marlin (1943-)	491
Diane	405
Douglas	476
Edgar L.	252
Edna (1889-)	119
Ellen Jane (1850-1920)	146
Ellen Jane (1867-1967)	358
Emma Jane (1869-1960)	453
Emory Woodrow (1912-2001)	490
Etna (1889-)	119
Floyd Emory (1934-2011)	491
Franny (1845-1906)	143, 156
Gary Lee (1947-)	183
George Alvin (1930-)	106
George E.	181
Glenn William (1937-)	491
Gregory (-2012)	433
Guy Alvin (1931-2015)	491
Guy Jefferson (-1995)	473
Hanna Matilda	240
Harriette (1868-1950)	260, 432
Harry (1884-)	119
Harvey Clarence (1886-1975)	193
Helen	250, 439
Helen I. (1917-1991)	63
Helen Mae (1935-2013)	215
Henry Albert (1910-1989)	193
Henry Edward (1883-1883)	119
Hilda (1919-)	391
Hunter Mark (1996-)	253
James	193
Jeffrey	405
Jeffrey Alvin (1956-)	106
Jennie Nora (1884-1967)	260
Jennifer (1969-)	194
Jennifer Mae (1970-)	491
Jennifer Rebecca (1971-)	327
Jill (1957-)	193
Jim	179
Jo Ann	405
Joanine	405
John	206, 247, 260
John (1860-1937)	118
John (1895-)	119
John A.	63
John Wiest (1855-1913)	149
Joyce Christia (1947-)	492
Joyce Christiana (1947-)	492
Judy	383
Julie Christianna (1965-)	491
Karen Ruth (1977-)	491
Kenneth	89
Lee Samuel (1904-1980)	327
Lena Melinda	473
Leonard D. (1940-)	194
Leroy (1927-)	383
Lillie (1870-)	60
Lisa Mae (1968-)	491
Lois Ann (1953-)	383
Loren	439
Lori (1960-)	193
Lorraine B. (1938-2014)	194
Mabel E. (1884-1957)	90, 356
Mae	318
Maggie Verdilla (1873-1952)	461
Margaret	215, 227
Marguerite Arlene (1926-1995)	107
Maria (1843-)	142
Marian Geraldine (1924-2016)	340
Marjorie (1966-)	194
Mark	253
Martha	384
Martha Amelia (1906-1971)	256
Mary E. (1882-1960)	226
Mary Elizabeth (1865-1928)	122
Mary Eva (1877-1919)	130, 472
Mary Jane	388
Michael	476
Millard	215
Moses (1891-)	107
Nathan (1970-)	194
Nathan D.	472
Nicole	253
Nicole Jill (1972-)	183
Nora Margaret (1871-1943)	478
Oliva A. (1882-)	208
Orpha M. (1916-2001)	252
Patricia Jane (1960-)	106
Patricia Jean (1957-)	383
Paul	405
Pauline M.	394
Peggy (1952-)	188
Phyllis	116
Ralph L. (1933-)	193
Randolph	89
Richard	105, 455
Robert (1955-)	197
Robert L. (1946-)	183
Ruth A.	319
Ruth Alvereta (1911-1997)	247
Ruth Arlene (1943-)	96
Sadie Alverta (1899-1989)	437
Samuel	383
Samuel Wiest (1853-1904)	149
Sarah (1849-1932)	194
Sarah Jennie (1880-)	180
Sonya Marie (1961-)	491
Spence Rodney (1969-)	183
Stella M.	217
Stephen James (1953-)	491
Sylvia	476
Thomas H.	170
Timothy George (1954-)	106
Tracy (1961-)	193
Victor C.	252
Wanda Mae (1956-)	491
Washtell (1890-1892)	149

- Wilhelm (1838-) 142
- William 122
- William (1873-) 327
- William Henry (1869-1954) 437, 490
- Winifred 405
- Yvonne M. 428
- Zebrilla (1962-) 111

Sock
- Mary 316

Sockel
- John 262

Sommers
- Natalie 243

Sones
- Allan (Rev.) 195
- Allan Rev. 195
- Andrea (-1987) 195
- Kaitlin 195
- Kristin 195
- Nicole 195

Sonnen
- Cheyenne Caitlin (1998-) 233
- William 233

Sorrell
- (--?--) 135

Sostar
- Jeffrey Michael (1973-) 110
- Roger Lee 110
- Roger Lee Jr. (1972-) 110

Sowatsky
- (--?--) 92

Soyster
- Anna Lynn 225
- Jack Walter 225
- Scott 225

Spade
- Dolores W. 201

Spaeth
- (--?--) 211
- Barbara Ann 325

Spangler
- Clair 385
- Lewis Edward (1907-1978) 52
- Mishon 248
- Ronald 248

Spanotius
- Winifred 256

Specht
- (--?--) 160
- Charles Theodore (1923-1993) 382
- Clifton Rearick (1919-1982) 382
- Crayton Homer (1890-) 382
- Crayton Homer (1925-1928) 382
- Edwin Clair (1933-1995) 383
- Ellen Endora (1920-2010) 382
- Hattie Marie (1927-1927) 382
- Hilda T. (1922-2010) 382
- Jack 477
- Laura 410
- Miriam Elizabeth (1933-) 383
- Ruth Iris (1929-) 382
- Shane 477
- Shannon Lee 477
- Somer Anne 477
- Wanda May (1927-) 382
- Wilda Pauline (1922-2010) 382

Speck
- (--?--) 195

Speicher
- Dean 274
- Donelle Sue (1967-) 274

Spencer
- (--?--) 390
- Carl 390
- Samuel 390

Spiess
- Donald R.C. 296

Spirko
- Peter N. (1926-) 152

Spohn
- Margaret (1853-) 271
- Peter 271

Sporhase
- Emma E. (1920-2005) 295
- John 295

Spotts
- (--?--) 121
- Cadey 292
- Carl 357
- Dianne M. 121
- Donna 121
- Eva Jane (1871-1945) 206
- Gloria 357
- Gloria (1927-) 357
- Grace V. (1909-1961) 232
- James 292
- Linda Mae 192
- Sydney 292
- Terry 121

Sprauer
- Mark 411
- Shari 411

Spring
- Carolyn 436

Spya
- John 370
- Michael (1944-) 370
- Michael (1970-) 370
- Stephen James (1972-) 370

Srewaet
- Darla Layne 261

Srnka
- Christopher 237
- John 237
- Scott 237

St. Jacques
- Lisa Marie 144

Staats
- Denise 276
- Doug 276
- Nathan 276
- Neil 276
- Paul E. 276

Stackhouse
- Dale 254
- Dale L. Jr. 254
- James 94

Maci Radel (2005-) 254
Mary Belle (1913-2011) 94
Myah Rose (2002-) 254

Stadler
Christopher Scott (1989-) 300
Emily Paige (1993-) 300
H. Scott 300
Jonathon Michael (1995-) 300

Stahl
(--?--) 389
Arletta G. (1911-1992) 94
Frances 389
Kathleen (1928-1974) 111

Stahley
LaVonda 277

Staily
Horace B. 398
J. Warren (1881-1956) 398

Stall
Ida M. 56

Staller
June 475

Stamm
Lester 77

Standifer
Gwendolyn Sue (1935-) 163

Standish
Patricia Jane 220

Stanley
Les 324
Sandra 277

Stantzenberger
Amelia 60

Staple
Annie 238

Staples
Art (1898-1978) 426
Herbert G. (1930-1931) 426

Stapleton
Beth Ann (1960-) 164
Daniel Benton (1963-) 165
John Thomas (1962-) 165
Thomas Gardner (1927-) 164

Stark
Bonnie 293

Starkey
Bonnie Juanita 254

Starkman
(--?--) 424

Starr
(--?--) 489
Alma Marie (1920-) 187
Alpha F. (1897-1971) 432
Beverly N. (1938-1979) 186
Blanche Irene (1918-1972) 186
Brandi Marie (1969-) 188
Carol (1942-) 187
Carolyn Louise (1942-) 187
Christine (1961-) 186
Christopher (1971-) 188
Darlene Kay (1949-1997) 188
Debra Denise (1952-) 134
Dennis E. (1945-) 186
Earl Wellington (1922-2002) 187
Elura Grace (1894-1976) 337
Gary Franklin (1949-) 188
Gurney Arthur (1891-1962) 186
Lee Percy (1914-1964) 134
Lillie Alvertta (1868-1940) 425
Marie (1941-1979) 186
Mary J. 439
Morganne 186
Nevin Willard (1926-1995) 188
Oscar Adam (1868-1956) 186, 432
Rebecca J. (1943-2005) 189
Ruby Edna (1928-) 189
Russell Woodrow (1915-1994) 186
Sally A. 284
Shirley Irene (1950-1990) 188
Troy 186
Tyler 186
Violet (-1940) 137

Statton
George Raymond 92
Norma Jo (1928-2016) 92

Stauffer
Georgina Marie (1966-) 186
Thomas Ray (1939-) 186

Stavrianeas
Amaleah Olega (2000-) 163
Leah (2000-) 163
Stasinos (1966-) 163

Steel
Barbara Jean (1962-) 330
John 226
Miriam (1909-1973) 226

Steely
Helen Irene (1912-1991) 341
William D. 341

Steffen
Helen Rachael (1919-) 382

Steffie
Daniel 353
Daniel Howard (1979-) 353

Stehling
Virginia 324

Stehr
Alvin H. (1922-2007) 180
Craig R. 180, 494
Susan K. 180, 494
Terry L. 180, 494

Steich
Kayla Ann Wenhold (1989-) 483
Kenneth (1964-) 483

Steily
Grace (1914-1982) 282

Stein
(--?--) 200
Anna E. 240
Catharina (1801-1850) 210, 228, 248
Christopher 164
Elizabeth (1805-1885) 310
Isaac F. 240
Jay Merton (1964-) 164
Jennie Lee (1968-) 164
John 218
Nicholas 164

Patton 164
Peter (1768-1827) 310
Ronald Merton 164

Steinbrecher
Adam 49

Steinbruch
Catharina (1774-1845) 49

Steinbrunn
Katie 74

Steinhoff
Alvin W. (1910-1994) 296
Henry D. (1883-1967) 296
Kenneth D. (1935-) 296
Richard A. (1939-) 296

Stellwagen
Elberta M. (1929-) 396

Stence
Amanda Jean (1947-) 111
Freeda Mae (1926-2014) 138
John 138
John Charles (1924-2003) 111

Stender
Janice 462

Stephens
Charles E. Jr. (1926-) 61
Charles Edgar (1898-2013) 61
Jesse K. 61
Paul A. (1928-2013) 61
Robert 386
Robert Q. (1936-) 61
Roger L. 61
Vernon E. (1930-) 61
William A. (1933-) 61

Stepp
Catherine 202

Sternberger
Douglas A. 113
Homer D. (1919-1987) 113
James E. 113
Kim 113
Lori J. 113
Michael D. 113

Sterrett
Mary E. (1890-1943) 64

Stevens
Drew 88

Stevenson
Margaret 177

Stewart
Annabelle 397
Aspen Dawn (1982-) 328
Cynthia Ellen (1960-) 328
Dennis Marshall (1948-) 328
Marshall Shane (1978-) 328
Martin Van Buren (1923-2005) 328
Martin Van Buren Jr. (1944-) 328
Mitchell Wayne (1955-) 328

Stickel
Connie Sue (1953-2010) 278

Stickler
Anna Belle L. (1932-) 76
John 76

Stiely
Alpha 433
Amy 183
Angela Diane (1972-) 345, 369
Anne Louise (1957-) 258
Ben William (2001-) 233, 434
Betty E. (1924-2014) 250, 258
Beverly Grace (1938-2014) 433
Bobby 432
Clair (1953-) 346
Dona Mary (1937-1980) 433
Donald 433
Donna (1937-1980) 433
Donnie 263
Eric Christopher (1969-) 345, 369
Evelyn Esther (1932-) 433
Fred (1901-1981) 250, 258
George Earl (1934-) 433
Glenn David (1952-1954) 434
Guy Leroy (1933-1936) 433
Hannah Elizabeth (1884-1934) 470
Harry 433
Harry Allen (1911-1987) 233, 432
Ida Sophia (1904-1994) 260, 353
Ivan Roger (1951-) 434
Jerry L. (1944-2009) 233, 434
Jesse L. (1940-2015) 434
Jimmy 432
John 270
John Kirby (1915-1980) 345, 369
John Michael (1999-) 233, 434
John Roger (1950-) 345, 369
Kris L. 233, 434
Marvin (1939-1939) 433
Nancy Jeannette (1935-2012) 433
Paul Isaac (1949-) 434
Perry Albert (1931-1941) 433
Perry Alvin (1931-1941) 433
Perry M. (1868-1958) 260, 432
Terri J. 233, 434
Tina E. (1956-) 258
Tina Nicole 263
Warren Fred (1920-1985) 258

Stiles
(--?--) 488
Bethany 488
Brandon 489
Jane C. (1933-) 414

Stillson
Sandy 95
Susan 95
William 95

Stillwell
Harold William 144
Richard William (1951-) 144

Stine
Amy Marie 452
Ashley Carol 452
Jeff 245
Jeffrey Robert 452
John W. 453
Mark Edgar (1896-1967) 402
Mary Elizabeth (1910-2006) 453
Matthew 245
Peter I. 452

Robert Peter (1944-) 452
Stinson
  (--?--) 194
Stites
  Robert 278
Stitzer
  Laurel 229
Stitzman
  Shirley 282
Stoffer
  Debra May (1967-) 462
  Neal 462
Stokes
  Donald T. (-1970) 290
  Eugene 290
Stone
  Barry L. Sr. 106
  Barry Lee Jr. (1969-) 106
  Melissa Lee (1971-) 106
Stoneroad
  Florence (1920-) 429
  John Leroy (1921-1973) 52
  Lewis L. 52
  Minnie A. 455
Stong
  Edith F. 226
Storck
  William 76
Stork
  (--?--) (2006-) 283
  Hunter Thomas (2009-) 283
  Richard Charles (1970-) 282
  Thomas William 282
Storm
  Kelly 477
Stoudt
  Alfred H. 380
  Donald H. (1929-) 380
  Raymond C. (1903-2004) 380
  Raymond C. Jr. (1938-) 380
  Robert R. (1927-1937) 380
Stouffer
  Maude Irene 220
Stout
  (--?--) 125
  Chester Melton (1928-1973) 123
  Rhea 287
Stover
  Gerald 117
Stowell
  Judith A. 285
Stratton
  Cindy J. 163
Straub
  (--?--) 201, 410
  (--?--) (-1910) 371
  (--?--) (1893-1893) 371
  Ailene M. (1919-) 368
  Albert William (1888-1947) 352
  Alma (1891-) 365
  Alma Winifred (1926-) 366
  Alvena Mae (1908-1981) 155, 364
  Amelia Viola (1894-1894) 367

  Amy Lynn (1984-) 332, 368
  Annie (1899-) 364
  Annie Tema (1918-2010) 367, 370
  Arabel C. (1925-) 337, 369
  Arthur Harrison (1892-1960) 366
  Barbara 364
  Barbara (1948-) 419
  Beatrice May (1907-1907) 352
  Bertha Hannah (1903-1973) 371
  Beulah M. (1890-1959) 365
  Bradley J. (1964-) 370
  Brady G. (1863-1949) 364
  Carolyn 368
  Carolyn Mary (1940-) 151, 372
  Carrie R. (1893-) 364
  Charles Alvin (1914-2013) 363
  Charles Austin (1926-) 367, 369
  Charles W. (1890-) 364
  Cheryl 253
  Clair S. (1930-) 371
  Clarence Guy (1903-1971) 371
  Datie 366
  David (1925-2007) 368
  David Michael 370
  Dean 368
  Debra Sue (1953-) 369
  Delbert 368
  Delroy F. (1962-) 370
  Delroy Fayne Sr. (1940-2001) 370
  Diann Elizabeth (1954-) 370
  Dora E. (1919-) 365
  Dorothy Jean (1926-) 371
  Dorothy K. (1922-1989) 366
  Drinda Yvonne (1951-) 367, 370
  Duane Charles (1948-) 370
  Edgar W. (1888-) 155, 364
  Elvin Wilson (1915-1988) 367
  Elvina May (1908-1981) 364
  Emina Ellen (1899-) 364
  Emma E. (1900-1986) 246
  Eric 480
  Eric Eugene (1970-) 419
  Ernest (-2012) 364
  Ernest E. (1947-1996) 419
  Ernest R. (1947-1996) 419
  Esten Homer (1889-1939) 364
  Esther 368
  Eston (1889-1939) 364
  Fred Samuel (1885-1968) 352
  Garman A., Geirman A., and German A. (1886-1970) .. 363
  Geirmon (-2012) 419
  Geirmon Andrew (1886-1970) 363
  George Brady (1863-1949) 364
  George H. (1908-) 352
  Gertrude (1912-) 232, 366
  Glenn Allen (1948-) 370
  Hannah Bertha (1903-1973) 371
  Harry Austin (1899-1996) 337, 368
  Harry Dean (1929-2013) 369
  Harry S. (1881-1963) 363
  Harvey T. (1911-) 332, 363
  Helen (-1981) 493
  Helen M. (1917-2007) 368
  Helen Marie (1920-) 371
  Homer Samuel (1895-1944) 367

Howard Edward (1913-) 365
Iva 363
Janet L 363
Jean (1928-) 371
Jeremy Martin (1985-) 369
Jessica K. (1990-) 332, 368
John (1861-) 364
John S. (1861-) 351
Judy (-2007) 368
Katie 255
Katie A. (1892-1966) 152, 261, 352
Katie Angeline (1892-1966) 352
Katie Hannah (1892-) 364
Keith Wayne (1963-) 332, 368
Kevin L 189
Larry Lamar (1942-) 370
Lawrence (1923-2007) 368
Lee (1928-) 364
Leo George (1928-1974) 345, 369
Leon Samuel (1921-2002) 332, 368
Lester (-2007) 368
Lori Ann (1961-) 370
Lottie Alma (1913-) 371
Luma Fay (1906-) 371
Lynn Leo (1957-) 369
Mahlon William (1919-1999) 352
Mamie Alice (1898-) 368
Marian A. (1926-2012) 364
Marion (1926-2012) 364
Mark R. (1921-2007) 368
Marlin N. (1937-2007) 189
Mary Arlena (1909-) 365
Mary Elizabeth (1864-) 371
Mary Ellen (1945-) 370
Mary P. (1914-) 352
Mary S. (1919-1987) 363
Mason (-2012) 367
Maude H 309
Maudy Hannah (1897-) 356
Meda E. (1921-2013) 363
Michael David (1965-2010) 370
Miles Venus (1923-1944) 368
Minerva C. (1915-) 365
Minnie Helen (1917-1995) 367
Minnie Mildred (1910-) 352
Minnie Viola (1911-) 365
Moses Homer (1895-) 355
Naomi Elizabeth (1916-1951) 366
Nelson T. (1924-2012) 419
Nelson T. (1925-2012) 364
Nicholas C. (1999-) 189
Nolan Clark (1993-) 189
Oscar W. (1869-1930) 371
Paul Arthur (1918-) 366
Peggy 345
Peggy Diane (1951-) 345, 369
Penny L. (1968-) 369
Phyllis J 363
Ralph Edwin (1901-1941) 370
Raymond (1896-2007) 368
Raymond Tobias (1897-1971) 371
Richard 480
Robert B. (1927-) 365
Ronald Eugene (1934-2005) 370
Ronald L 363
Ronald M. Sr. (-2007) 368
Roy Edwin (1906-1907) 372
Roy Irvin (1908-) 371
Ruby (1917-) 481
Ruby Alvena (1915-) 352
Russell E. (1917-) 365
Ruth 171
Samuel (1836-1899) 363
Samuel Frederick (1885-1968) 352
Samuel Harry (1881-1963) 332, 363
Samuel Homer (1895-1944) 332, 367
Sarah Elizabeth (1856-1888) 229
Sean Arthur (1985-) 370
Stanley L. (1917-2003) 363
Stephen Michael 370
Tammie (1918-2010) 367
Terry E 363
Terry Gordon (1946-1967) 171
Tobias Albert (1857-1934) 332, 363
Tobias O. (1857-1934) 363
Violet May (1930-) 366
Vivian Elda (1919-2012) 367
Walter C. (1890-) 364
Wendy M. (1951-) 171
William Albert (1888-1947) 352
William D. (1920-1994) 171
William Oscar (1869-1930) 371

Strayer
Florence 55
Margaret E 68

Strmiska
(--?--) 233
Jaelyn Marie (1998-) 233
Joelyn Marie (1998-) 233
Joscelyn 233

Strohecker
Agnes Lavena (1866-1943) 306
Albert Tobias (1906-1980) 337
Annette Renee (1967-) 492
Bertha Elizabeth 179
Cassie (1872-) 166
Catie (1872-) 166
Charles 477
Chrystal Ann (1964-) 492
Crystal (1964-) 492
Dane Lee 121
Debra 477
Delroy 364
Doris 364
Ella Mae (1930-2016) 478
Emma 253
Estella L 155, 364
Flossie May (1888-1904) 468
Fred Raymond (1911-1975) 433
George Emory 478
Gerald Mark (1969-) 492
Grace 166
Hannah (1883-1958) 100
Hannah Wiest (1863-1940) 100
Jacob Weist (1850-1931) 166
Joel Ray 491
John Weist (1870-1915) 166
Leonard L. Jr 129
Lucilla Mae (1929-) 338, 445
Mabel Savilla (1927-) 338, 445

Page 641

Margaret Fay (1926-)	338, 445
Mark Eugene	491
Mark Eugene Jr.	492
Mary	166
Randy (1967-)	433
Robert Neal (1928-2013)	338, 445
Sula	166
Susan	477
Terry G. (1944-)	433
Walter	364
William (1811-1889)	166
William P. (1866-1947)	337

Stroup
Amanda	107
Cynthia Marie (1952-)	188
Karen	117
Martha E. (1901-)	456
Mary Esther (1937-1997)	108
Ricky	107

Strovinsky
Alex J. (1931-1986)	262
Mary A.	262
Michael J.	262

Strubhar
Nellie M. (1897-1971)	75

Strycker
Annette Renee (1963-)	278
Max	278

Stryker
Clayton	272
Virginia Rae (1929-1984)	272, 275

Studebaker
Florence	277

Stump
Geraldine (1949-)	59
John	59

Stuppy
Patricia A. (1934-2011)	326
Walter	326

Stutzman
Albert	366
Alyssa Lynn (2000-)	269, 479
Arthur W. (1968-)	366
Augusta	282
Barbara A.	270
Carrie	435
Daniel J. (1988-)	269, 479
Debra K.	270
Edward (1977-)	269, 479
Edward Keith (1947-2013)	269, 479
Elizabeth	230
Elke Briggitta (1960-)	268, 478
Eric L.	270
Frances E. (1928-2006)	366
Frank J. (1918-1993)	270
Gary	270
Helen (1933-)	89
Helen D. (1933-)	232, 366
Ingrid A.	270
James (1891-1920)	268, 478
James Leroy (1938-)	268, 478
James Scott (1964-)	269, 479
Joel	268
Joel Andrew (1975-)	269, 479
Joel Ethan (2008-)	269, 479
Joel Fred (1941-)	268, 479
Julie Ann (1970-)	269, 479
Lamar L.	270
Leroy J. (1914-1995)	268, 478
Lillian I. (1915-2007)	269
Lloyd Monroe (1916-1998)	270
Mabel M.	224
Marian Alice	271
Marian Rice	269
Mary Alice	371
Melissa J. (1969-)	269, 479
Raymond R. (1906-)	232, 366
Ruth	115
Ruth Anna (1970-)	366
Stefanie (1974-)	268
Stefanie Sue (1974-)	268, 479
Steven Joel (1960-2016)	269, 479
Susan Elizabeth (1966-)	366
Timothy Edward (1974-)	269, 479
William L. (1942-)	366

Subick
Lisa	288

Suder
(--?--)	193

Sullivan
Cathy	182
Mary (1945-)	485

Sultzbach
Earl	327
Joan D. (1933-)	327

Sultzbaugh
Emma	53
Henry Isaac	113
Marion V. (1913-1991)	113
Mildred Irene	458

Summers
Pearl	272

Summerson
Francis Ann	84

Summy
Elmer Keener	52
Kathryn E. (1921-2015)	52

Sunday
Amos	481
Scott (-1989)	333

Sung
Lawrence (1931-1984)	105

Susanna
Klinger (1817-1885)	67
Susannah (1817-1885)	67

Sutcliffe
Annie Elizabeth (1979-)	482
John Allen (1982-)	482
Mark Andrew (1983-)	482
Thomas Jr. (1947-)	482

Suter
(--?--)	214

Sutton
Alan	385
Pearl	382

Swab
Alex	345

Bronwen Elaine (1977-)..........................68
Jeff..345
Lora..345
Mary Ann (1838-1908)..........................398
Peggy Lou (1931-)................................188
Swalm
Allen Robert (1930-1994)........................74
Anna Mae (1931-)...................................74
Darrell Warren (1941-1998)..................241
George...73
George (1898-).......................................74
Katie (1903-1973)....................................74
Luella (1896-1996)..................................73
Minerva (1908-1986)...............................74
Morris (1872-1947).................................73
Paul J. (1908-2000)...............................230
Ray (1900-1987)......................................74
Warren Stanford (1914-2000) 240
Swanepoel
Bianca (1993-)...58
Charles Fredrick (1958-)........................58
Swangler
(--?--)...134
Ruth (1906-)..134
Swartz
Bill..498
Swavely
Beth..249
Sweeney
Paul Edward...282
Susan Gay...282
Sweigart
Alvin...205
Kelten B..205
Melvin R...73
Sweitzer
Charles (1889-)......................................207
Swinehart
(--?--)...78
Rhea...291
Swope
Mary M. (1901-)......................................76
Swoyer
Christina E...289
Theresa..495
Sykes
Margaret (1911-)...................................328
Szilage
(--?--)...417
Tallman
George A...289
George W..289
Tamburelli
(--?--)...253
Tamburello
Alice Mae (2005-)..................................487
Jackson Charles (2013-).......................488
Julia Rose (2009-)..................................487
Lily Grace (2007-)..................................487
Michael (1977-)......................................487
Phoebe Elizabeth (2011-).....................488
Tarbutton
Judy (1945-)..359

Tarman
Norman D...82
Tasker
Nellie A. (1885-1978).............................314
Tatarunas
Aleksa Roma (2001-).............................488
Olivija Theresa (2001-)..........................488
Tadas Andrius (1999-)...........................488
Vidas (1959-)..488
Tate
Joanne M..273
Taylor
Rodney Lee (1963-)...............................331
Teeter
Erma Irene (1923-)................................105
Mary...246
Telesca
(--?--)...193
Tennant
Bobbie Jo..284
Tentromano
Louise (1940-).......................................190
Teter
Andrew Philip (1986-)...........................352
Bryan Curtis (1984-)..............................352
Bryan Wayne..352
Rachel Elina (1988-)..............................352
Thareesut
Arom..107
Theobald
Amy..274
Mark...274
Peter...274
Wayne..274
Thibeault
Marie..175
Thoma
Sherri...319
Warren E..319
Thomas
(--?--)...66
Barbara..304
Betty Jane..125
Charles E..125
Charles M. (1864-)..................................69
Ellen...374
Grace..379
Jeffrey..304
Jennifer Lynn...467
Joseph George Jr....................................125
Joseph George Sr. (1925-1982)..............125
Kathalene Ann (1952-2000)...................125
Minnie M. (1882-1929)...........................314
Rhonda...488
Samuel Raymond (1893-1945).................56
William J..304
William Powell (1923-1985)...................304
Thomason
Donald..466
Donald Jr..466
Thompson
Adam Kerry (1985-)..............................353
Carrie N..298

Charles R. (1914-1981) 220
Charles Ralph (1932-1997) 220
Dale 477
Darryl 289
Eric Malcolm (1987-) 353
Eunice Wiest (1913-1976) 163
Gary J. (1936-2004) 289
Jean C. (1933-1992) 113
John H. 113
Joseph 289
June Ora (1919-1998) 164
Katherine R. 298
Kerry Arthur 353
Laura Mae (1911-1987) 163
Lindsey M. 298
Lyndon 477
Mark T. 298
Martha (1922-1984) 376
Mary Belle (1927-) 164
Pamela Ann (1955-) 283
Randall 477
Ronnie 76
Ruth Elizabeth (1910-2000) 70
Terri A. 289
Theona Evelyn (1906-1943) 49
Thomas Jr. (1881-1943) 163
Violet Charlotte (1904-1910) 163
William 283
William A. 298

Thomson
Kristen Lynn 159

Thornbush
Annette 319

Thornton
James 79

Thurston
Rhoda Alaura (1901-1985) 462

Thygeson
Dorothy 294

Tibbins
James 404

Tibbitts
Lela (1890-) 97

Tice
Grace M. 217

Ticer
Casaundra Jolene (1987-) 164
Joseph (1955-) 163
Megan (1985-) 163

Tietsworth
Ruthanne Natalie 476

Timko
Aleck 218
Christa Ann (1968-2003) 218

Tobias
Alta Miriam (1934-) 219
Amy R. 52
Angeline (1852-1927) 142, 490
Emma C. 73
George 219
Ida Sevilla (1887-1963) 471
Marvin Ira (1945-1986) 495
Michael (1972-) 495
Roma L. (1924-1980) 82

Walter Vincent (1874-1945) 219
William 471

Tocket
Cynthia Ann (1948-) 159
Danielle Nadine (1976-) 159
Gregory Von (1947-2011) 159
Heather O'Neal (1978-) 159
Jeffrey Earl (1954-) 160
Neilo Joseph (1920-2011) 159
Susan Lynn (1950-) 160
Van 159

Tolbert
Aamani Jade (2008-) 305
Arianna Mariah 305
Webster 305

Tomacyk
Nancy 70

Tomlinson
Mary Octavia 323

Tonini
Ada T. (1925-) 52
John 52

Tophoney
Virginia (1927-2010) 198

Torres
(--?--) 190

Transue
Eleanora 229
Harry 229

Trautman
Frank (1891-1937) 211
Franklin Junior (1921-1998) 211
William 211

Trautwein
Brooke 253
Robert 253
Taylor Laken (1994-) 253

Travitz
Mary 171

Trea
Richard Atwood (1930-) 314
Richard Edward (1953-) 314
Ricky (1953-) 314

Treas
Francis Xavier (1889-) 453

Treesh
Viola E. (1882-1967) 91

Trefsger
Daniel 224
Delmer E. (1921-2009) 224
Delmer Jr. 224
William Millard 224

Treon
Eva M. (1888-1961) 65
John Henry (1859-1923) 65

Trexler
Blaine Joseph (-1982) 463
Paul Howard (1947-) 463

Triplett
Christopher 474
Gary E. 474

Troisi
(--?--) 212

Trojan
- Randy 247

Troop
- Margaret 222

Trout
- Jean 63

Troutman
- (--?--) 343
- (--?--) (-1916) 158
- (--?--) (1918-1918) 158
- Abraham (1773-1852) 83
- Alice Amelia (1880-1920) 453
- Alice Bertie (1878-1961) 142
- Allen Ray (1908-) 365
- Alma (1915-) 365
- Amelia 451
- Ammon J. (1894-) 160
- Anna (1927-) 137
- Benneville R. (1859-1931) 365
- Betty L. (1927-) 160
- Beulah Minerva (1897-1967) 344
- Brenda Rae (1944-) 159
- Bruce Herman (1914-1998) 252
- Carl L. 252
- Carol Ann 249
- Catherine A. (1864-1915) 134
- Charles (-2008) 453
- Charles Lloyd (1911-) 365
- Charlotte (1926-) 137
- Christopher R. 252
- Clair (1913-) 142
- Clara Mary (1894-1943) 222
- Clarence R. (1889-1944) 158
- Cora Mae (1901-1993) 187
- Craig 249
- Daisy 257
- Daisy (1910-) 141
- Daisy Ardella (1916-) 369
- Dale (1948-) 102
- Daniel (1817-1880) 398
- Darvin Elmer 131
- Debora 252
- Deborah Ann (1957-1957) 158
- Dennis Lamar (1952-) 345
- Donald 453
- Donald (1934-) 142
- Donna Lee (1942-) 159
- Donna Rae (1945-) 350
- Doris Shirley (1933-) 160
- Dorothy E. (1913-1999) 341
- Douglas 252
- Douglas (1964-) 158
- Earl Eugene (1891-1949) 158
- Earl George (1928-2016) 154
- Edna (1919-) 142
- Edna Elizabeth (1901-1989) 251
- Edwin (-2006) 349
- Elaine Carrie (1938-) 159
- Elaine Marie (1959-) 102
- Eleanor E. (1930-1997) 160
- Elizabeth 207
- Elizabeth (1825-1881) 186
- Elizabeth (1856-1916) 134, 141
- Elizabeth (1865-1952) 202
- Elizabeth A. 459
- Elsie (1931-) 365
- Elsie V. (1898-1952) 102
- Elvin K. (1912-1991) 252
- Emma Jane (1866-1931) 87
- Eva Alvesta (1905-1995) 322
- Eva Amilia (1899-1980) 251
- Eva G. (1896-) 160
- Eva J. (1896-) 160
- Eva Maria (1802-1897) 99
- Ferne Isabel 249
- Florence Beulah (1903-1964) 463
- Florence Emma (1903-1914) 251
- Frances Loretta (1864-1931) 346
- Gene 249
- George L. (1858-1934) 453
- George Monroe (1907-1976) 154
- Gertrude Mabel (1897-1969) 249, 258, 317
- Gilbert Eugene (1921-2008) 102
- Glenn 249, 340
- Glenn Lamar (1954-) 154, 435, 450
- Grace M. (1922-2012) 160
- Grant L. (1888-1973) 158
- Guy Clifford (1930-) 345
- Harriet (1851-1934) 170, 317, 364, 459, 468
- Harriet (1881-) 142
- Harry (1891-) 141
- Harry N. (-2005) 157
- Harvey E. 131
- Heather Lynne (1978-) 154, 435, 450
- Helen 249
- Henry Lesher (1847-1897) 142, 490
- Hillary April (1985-) 154, 435, 450
- Howard W. (1910-1954) 252
- Isaac L. (1849-1919) 459
- James 249, 252
- James Allen (1943-) 102
- Jason 249
- Joan (1935-) 160
- Joanna Joyce (1943-) 469
- John 249
- John David (1911-2003) 345
- John E. 341
- John Henry (1877-1929) 322
- Johnny (1930-) 345
- Joy Abraham (1893-1952) 102
- Judith Ann (1944-) 350
- Judith Ann (1946-) 102
- Judy (1944-) 350
- June V. 456
- Karen Lee (1951-) 350
- Kathy 249
- Kay (1951-) 102
- Kaye Louise (1951-) 102
- Keith Allen 132
- Kenneth C. 252
- Kevin 249
- Kevin Jeffrey 327
- Kevin Jeffrey (1958-) 158
- Kristopher Douglas 327, 454
- Kyra Ann (2005-) 252
- Laura Mae (1906-1985) 251
- Laura May (1906-1985) 484
- Lear Elwyn (1916-1970) 158
- Leroy E. (1923-2006) 349
- Lillian Oneda (1894-1982) 195, 490

Linda Lou (1947-) 350
Linda Sue (1950-) 345
Lloyd Ervin (1881-1961) 365
Louisianna (1819-1857) 83
Margaret E. (1913-1989) 233
Margaret Viola (1912-2006) 365
Maria Anna (1842-1912) 143
Maria Elizabeth (1858-1928) 398
Mark 249
Mark Kent (1927-1929) 160
Mary Ellen (1923-2005) 157
Mary K. (1927-1929) 160
Matthew James (1982-) 154, 435, 450
Michael (1978-) 154, 435, 450
Michelle 249
Mush (-1989) 489
Nancy (1946-) 194
Nardelle Elizabeth (1938-) 158
Nettie T. (1898-1915) 160
Noble (1931-) 365
Owen Donald (1919-1977) 159
Paul Leo (1906-1935) 160
Pauline Catherine (1922-2009) 159
Peter (1790-1854) 186
Phyliss 252
Phyllis 252
Polly 407
Ray A. 249
Ray A. (1896-1984) 249
Ray Clayton (1912-1989) 332
Rebecca (1829-1909) 474
Richard 453
Robert A. 249
Robert Jr. 453
Robert Ray (1931-) 453
Rodney 252
Ronald V. (1937-2013) 252
Roscoe Roy (1900-1977) 160
Roy 292
Roy K. (1923-1929) 160
Ruby Mary (1955-) 154, 435, 450
Ruth Faye (1902-1985) 160
Scott 249
Sheila Jean (1950-) 102
Sheri Lynn (1960-) 158
Simon (1840-1898) 134
Steve 130
Steven Earl (1952-) 154, 435, 450
Susan (1955-) 350
Tanya 249
Terry 453
Terry Lear (1940-) 158
Thomas E. (1920-1953) 365
Valerie (1980-) 154, 435, 450
Vickie (1954-) 102
Victor William (1882-1947) 332, 345
Wendy Lee 89
Wendy Lynn (1961-) 158
William (1915-) 142
William Ellsworth (1864-1941) 158
William F. (1892-) 160
William H. 249
William H. (1874-1929) 249
William Howard 249
William Jr. (1931-) 137

William K. (1831-1897) 158
William P. (1903-1969) 137
Wilma R. (1933-1987) 292
Troxel
   Lorna Jean 277
Troxell
   Roy Emmanuel (1929-2006) 111
Truitt
   Feneta R. 99
Trulinger
   Julia 374
Trumbo
   Amy 77
   James Irvin (1896-1977) 77
   Mae (1928-) 77
   Mayanna M. (1928-) 77
   Milton 77
Trunzo
   Linda (1946-2003) 456
   Theodore 456
Tschopp
   Absalom (1844-) 103
   Ann Marie (1966-) 243
   Barry Lynn 243
   Barry Lynn Jr. (1969-) 243
   Elizabeth Ida (1883-1963) 103
   Elizabeth Regina (1780-1844) 83
   Elva M. 440
   James 100
   Mary Diana (1871-) 103
   Russell 243
Tucker
   Brenda Darlene 123
Tudela
   (--?--) 71
   Christopher James Coward 71
Tullgren
   Ashley Inez (1984-) 488
Turner
   Alina R. (1982-) 58
   Lee 306
Twigg
   Jennifer 294
   John 294
   Michael 294
   Wendy 294
Tyler
   (--?--) 306
   Stephen 258
   Tabatha 258
   Toban 258
Uhler
   Elizabeth 54
   Harry Clarence 227
   Henry M. (1915-1981) 227
   Hettie (1847-1932) 418
   Jay Henry (1939-) 227
   Mary 227
   Michael 418
Ulfeng
   Jonathan 251
Ulmer
   Christopher Philip (1977-) 324

Wilbur 178

Ulsh
Adam R. (1994-   ) 225
Greg 225
Madison 218
Matthew P. (1991-   ) 225
Nathaniel 218
Stephen E. 218

Umbenhaur
Andrew (1857-   ) 72
Harry (1885-   ) 72
Mabel (1888-   ) 72

Umberger
(--?--) (1909-   ) 359

Umholtz
Aaron A. (1855-1897) 389
Anetta Salome Mae (1893-1955) 353
Annetta Salome Mae 292
Barbara 385
Caroline Corinda (1874-1945) 389
Carrie (1874-1945) 389
Carrie May (1895-1950) 119
Christine 120
Cora S. 109
Dale 120
E. Ray (1890-1894) 389
Elizabeth 390
Eric 120
George F. (1885-1947) 389
Herman Harper (1876-1929) 389
Kirby 120
Laura 319
Mary Ellen (1848-1908) 418
Mary Marie 452
Michael 120
Nora (-2008) 136
Samuel (1814-1883) 418
Sarah Jane (1886-1961) 104
Vergie 389

Umstead
Tracy 383

Underkoffler
Aaron Milton (1906-1990) 226
Alma J. (1916-1977) 227
Alvin Wilson (1908-1975) 256
Andrew J. 343
Arland A. Jr. 224
Arland Albert (1899-1957) 224
Barbara 227
Bertha M. (1918-   ) 227
Beulah Mae (1904-1942) 280
Bryan K. 343
Carol Ann (1949-2010) 228
Catherine Marie (1929-2004) 226
Catherine N. (1930-   ) 226
Charles Monroe (1884-1958) 256
Christine J. (1923-   ) 227
Christopher Alan (1973-   ) 106
Clair E. (1923-1979) 227
David 399
David (1827-1895) 223
Donna Lee (1947-   ) 106
Doris (1924-   ) 228
Douglas (1968-   ) 400
Douglas Scott (1968-   ) 361
Edward 224
Eileen 343
Elias (1852-1899) 256
Elvin Lawrence (1881-   ) 204, 280
Esther J. (1893-1953) 227
Floyd Harper (1921-2004) 106
Gayle Jean (1962-   ) 256
Gene Russell (1930-   ) 256
Gregory 226
Gregory Jr. 227
Harold (1920-1995) 224
Harold Jr. 224
Harry J. (1886-1966) 226
Helen (1884-1940) 225
Henry Mark (1921-1939) 227
Herman A. (1890-1938) 227
Herman W. (1890-1938) 227
James Jr. 228
James M.A. (1928-   ) 228
Joseph Thomas (1928-1991) 226
Karl Leo (1937-1937) 204, 241
Kathryn June (1929-2010) 228
Kenneth W. (1954-2005) 343
Kitty (1929-2010) 228
Kitty Ann (1934-   ) 257
Kristine Antinette (1959-   ) 256
Lamar L. (1963-2011) 343
Larry 228
Leo Elvin (1906-   ) 204
Lillian J. 394
Lisa Marie (1962-   ) 256
Lloyd 222
Lori 343
Marie Catherine (1929-2004) 226
Mark W. (1959-2010) 343
Mark W. III 343
Mark William (1919-1999) 343
Marlin (1919-1978) 224
Mary 392
Mellie M. (1896-1962) 227
Mick (1959-2010) 343
Mildred J. (1925-   ) 228
Milton D. (1856-1933) 223
Minnie P. (1879-1947) 223
Nellie May (1896-1962) 227
Patricia 228
Patty Jo (1956-   ) 106
Ralph Stephen (1905-   ) 226
Ralph Stephen Jr. (1925-1986) 226
Rebecca Lynn (1986-   ) 361
Rebecka Lynn 400
Red (1963-2011) 343
Robert 343
Robert Charles (1934-2000) 256
Rodney Floyd (1952-   ) 106
Ronald Lee (1940-2005) 228
Russell Gene (1958-   ) 256
Russell Vernon (1906-1972) 256
Ruth Jeannette (1928-   ) 256
Shannon Rodney (1977-   ) 106
Sharyn D. 343
Talbert H. (1898-1981) 227
Terry 228
Tolbert Henry (1898-1981) 227

U

Underkoffler (continued)
- Tolbert Jr. (1927-) 228
- Vincent K. (1902-1962) 228
- Vincent M. Jr. (1925-) 228
- Vincent M. Underkoffler (1902-1962) 228
- William Charles (1937-1984) 226
- William Howard Taft (1908-1933) 227

Underwood
- Eri 59
- Mary M. (1848-1913) 59

Unger
- Bertha (1895-1977) 247
- Jerry Lynn 116
- Nancy L. 117
- Sarah Emma 466

Updegrave
- (--?--) 264
- Edward 268
- Frances Isabel (1931-2012) 270
- Harrison (1884-1941) 268
- Jeannette Marie 184
- Lucille Marie (1934-2009) 271

Updegrove
- (--?--) 127, 212
- Hilda Viola (1913-1991) 214
- Ira 214
- Terri 243

Updike
- Alfred 60
- Alfred Owen (1885-1947) 60
- Christine 75
- Debra 75
- Earle Eugene (1918-1998) 60
- Joseph 75
- Mary Louise (1922-2002) 60

Urban
- Adele A. (1908-1991) 299
- Arthur 227
- Erma Elizabeth (1924-2014) 227

Urich
- Daniel B. 417
- Dave J. 417
- John E. Jr. 417
- John Edward (1923-1995) 417
- Kandace L. 417
- Renee E. 417

Urmston
- Lillian 496

Urvan
- Alyssa Rena (1993-) 399
- Anthony James (1964-) 399
- Carl M. (1994-1994) 399
- Marc A. (1994-1994) 399
- Robert M. (1994-1994) 399

Usfaszewski
- David Mathew 231

Van Aken
- Robert 248
- Shawn 248

Vanaulen
- Barry Lee 354
- Jered Lee Broderick (1992-) 354

Vance
- Charles Glenn 217
- Donald Leon (1936-1966) 217
- Elisabeth 273
- Hubert (1896-) 273
- Mary Louise (1925-2010) 273
- Owen E. 273

VanDamme
- Louis 272
- Louise Alfonsine (1917-2009) 272

Vandergrift
- Charlene 237
- Kyra J. 269

Vandeventer
- (--?--) 233
- Abigayle 233
- Khylei 233
- Rhea 233

Varvel
- Mart Dean (1953-) 348

Vaughn
- Naomi (1906-) 424
- Raymond L. (1883-) 424

Vera
- Gabriel 116

Verbish
- (--?--) 335

Vestal
- Jennifer (1958-) 414

Vetovich
- (--?--) 125

Viers
- Ernest 94
- James 94

Vigliotti
- Beth Ann (1981-) 172
- Laura Marie (1984-) 172
- Mark A. (1950-) 172
- Rachel Lynn (1988-) 173
- Sarah Louise (1987-) 172

Violin
- Dorothy 304

Vogel
- Catherine Mary 76

Vogelsong
- Helen G. (1928-1999) 404

Volberding
- Lisel Zane (1979-) 287
- Louis Earl Jr. (1954-) 287
- Louis Earl Sr. 287
- Tabor Brianne (1986-) 287
- Tegan Corrine (1991-) 287
- Toben Le (1992-) 287
- Tzeitel A. (1983-) 287

VonDurant
- Aletha 279

Vottero
- Alicia (1969-) 302
- Francis 302
- Janelle (1976-) 302
- Mark (1973-) 302
- Scott (1971-) 302

Vuolo
- (--?--) 114

Waddell
- Angela (1966-) 486

    Annette (1968-) 486
    Christina Leigh (1989-2013) 486
    Donald 485
    Elenor (1897-1969) 162
    Scott 486

Wagaman
    Laura 226
    M. Grace 386

Wagenhals
    Anna Kathleen (1986-) 162
    Eric Sayers (1985-) 162
    Owen Hunter (1984-) 162
    Stan (1956-) 162

Wagner
    (--?--) 280, 368
    Allen 136
    Ariel Grace (1993-) 292
    Benjamin Luke (1989-) 292
    Carl 428
    Catharine 425
    Charissa (1985-) 292
    Dale 292
    Dale Millard (1963-) 330
    Danelle Charlene (1986-) 292, 330
    Daniel 292
    David (Rev.) 292
    David Rev. 292
    Dorothy 470
    Elizabeth 60
    Grace Mildred (1911-1959) 469
    Jane 313
    Julie Danielle (1993-) 292
    Kyle Daniel (1988-) 292
    May 136, 459
    Nellie 428
    Ryan Andrew (1989-) 292
    Stephanie Ann (1988-) 292, 330
    Tom 428
    Verna 356
    Verna May 197
    William 292

Walborn
    Marie A. 170
    Terry L. (1948-1982) 361

Waldridge
    Emily Renay (1999-) 487
    Lawrence Webster Jr (1964-) 487

Waldrin
    Larry 167

Walker
    Charlotte Mary 283
    Joshua 466
    Lavina (1920-2007) 466
    Scott 466
    William Clark 466

Wallace
    Meridith Sue (1938-) 164

Waller
    Anna Maria (1768-1846) 398

Walsh
    Timothy 343

Walt
    Amy J. 187

Walter
    Jacob (-1972) 123
    Katie 384
    Russell 405
    Stacey Jae (1965-) 183

Walters
    Chad 405
    Madeline 226
    Mary 179
    Paul Keim (1908-1991) 219

Waltman
    Charles 123

Walton
    June Ann (1950-) 286

Waltz
    (--?--) 227
    Donna 168

Walz
    Clara Nathalia (1856-1915) 380
    Jacob R. Jr. (1932-1961) 190
    Jean (1954-) 190
    Peggy (1958-) 190

Wanamaker
    Delano 261
    Jason Allen (1982-1999) 261, 354
    Lacie Alice (1991-) 261, 354
    Lacreanne (1991-) 261
    Ricky Allen 261

Ward
    Alan J. (1979-) 178
    Brian J. (1982-) 178
    Diane 138
    Eric J. (1977-) 178
    John Jr. (-2008) 138
    Larry (-2008) 404
    Leslieann 138
    Michael 178
    Robert 404
    Shirley 404

Wardford
    Vincent 327

Warfel
    Amanda Alice 416
    Anita Nichole (1978-) 174
    Arthur C. 52
    Mahlon Jr. (1940-) 174
    Mary Marguerite Ellen (1926-) 52
    Milton S. 222
    Ruth Naomi (1917-2006) 222

Warfield
    Allen G. (1901-1979) 180
    Alton M. (1926-) 181
    Carol A. 289
    Darwin (1923-) 181
    Ellen 289
    Ernie 289
    Eva M. (1907-1984) 246
    Kenneth 289
    Lee Jacob (1914-2003) 289
    Nancy (1937-) 289
    Rudy C. (1876-) 180

Warg
    Shawn 191

Warner
- Angela Marie (1970-) 96
- Bonita Jo (1963-) 96
- Brian Carlos Mangueira (1968-) 95
- Dean Paul (1944-) 96
- Debra (1965-) 96
- Elisabeth Louise (1996-) 96
- Elissa Wade (1999-) 96
- Emma (1854-1931) 72
- Erin Katherine (1996-) 96
- Jack Eugene (1940-) 95
- Jean Marie (1931-2011) 79
- Jeanette 324
- John 72
- Juan Marcos (1989-) 95
- Kevin Lee (1969-) 96
- Lisa (1996-) 96
- Lorraine Verling (1920-) 95
- Marsail Carlos (1991-) 95
- Rex Jay (1942-) 96
- Samuel 79
- Timothy Alan (1972-) 96

Warren
- Elliot Robert (2008-) 112
- Liam Clark (2007-) 112
- Robert Jr. 112

Wary
- Jeanne 201
- Stanley 201

Wascavage
- Alison (1981-) 302
- Brian (1966-) 302
- Gerald 302
- Kevin (1979-) 302
- Krisa (1978-) 302
- Michailyn (1968-) 302

Wasson
- Daniel Webster (1983-) 172
- Diane Louise (1955-) 172
- Donald William (1951-) 172
- Erika Lee (1974-) 172
- Heather Marie (1976-) 172
- Jeffrey Scott (1981-) 172
- Julie Meredith (1984-) 172
- Karen Marie (1953-) 172
- Terry Lee (1947-) 172
- William Harold (1899-1984) 172
- William Harold Jr. (1924-1983) 172

Waters
- Gladys 380
- Olive Ann Elizabeth (1900-1953) 359

Watkins
- Ivan Clyde (1892-1954) 394

Watson
- Brenda Ann 355

Watts
- Guy M. (1901-) 456
- Helen R. (1927-2006) 456

Weahy
- Grace 132

Weary
- Hannah 125

Weaver
- Adeline (1860-) 207
- Angela 120
- Brenda 419
- Brenda J. 480
- Bruce 194
- Chester W. 105
- Chrisianna 325
- Dale 325
- Deirdra J. 480
- Edna Irene 429
- Elizabeth 279
- Fred 120
- George 246, 480
- Jennifer (1974-) 325
- Linda J. 105
- Lovina 273
- Marie Elaine (1939-) 343
- Marlene 120
- Oscar M. (1935-1964) 105
- Phyllis R. (1930-2002) 246
- Rudolf (-1972) 480
- Sadie L. 406
- Shelva 494
- Shelva J. 480
- Tara J. 480

Webb
- Antoinetta 275
- Mary M. 284
- Stanley 386

Weber
- Jennilyn Nichole (1991-) 353
- Juliann 353
- Susan 271
- William 353

Webry
- Theresa F. (1929-) 192

Webster
- David Larry (1955-) 323
- Jennifer Marie (1977-) 323
- Joshua Caleb (1979-) 323

Wedde
- Beverly Sue (1959-) 186
- Boyd L. 186
- Brandon 338, 369, 445
- Gary 338
- Peggy Ann (1965-) 186
- Randal Allen (1957-) 186

Wehry
- (--?--) 443
- Betty Ellen (1976-) 193
- Dertha (1897-1975) 227
- Joseph 227
- Lloyd E. 193
- Sarah Jane (1879-1935) 54
- Washington 54

Weida
- Robert 273

Weidensaul
- Bernadette 477

Weidman
- Sadie I. (1911-1965) 419

Weigel
- Daniel Thomas (1992-) 152, 355, 450
- John Michael 152
- Leah Marie Genevieve (1995-) 152, 355, 450

Weik
- Ann M. (1932-) 259
- Harry W. 259
- Jean L. (1936-) 260
- Luther Amos (1904-1977) 259

Weikel
- Arlin 194
- Ellsworth 304
- Helen E. (1903-1982) 304
- Maude Irene (1889-1918) 66
- William 194

Weinreich
- Arleda M. (-1995) 485
- Ashley 472
- Paul 472

Weir
- Agnes (1861-1945) 298

Weiser
- (--?--) (1868-1868) 172
- Hannah Jennie (1885-1957) 173
- Jacob Monroe (1877-1951) 172
- John (1842-1905) 171
- John Albert (1905-1996) 173
- John Jacob (1784-1846) 171
- Martha (1902-1990) 172
- Mary E. (1872-1946) 172
- William Isaac (1875-1881) 172
- Wilson Monroe (1912-) 173

Weiske
- Brian Herriot 230
- Charles 230
- Jane 230
- Kermit 230
- Laura 230
- Mary 230
- Michael 230
- Stephanie 230
- Stephen 230

Weiss
- Benjamin Franklin (1866-1947) 119, 416
- Daniel K. (1899-) 417
- Erma 476
- Henrietta (1905-1982) 147

Weist
- (--?--) 311
- Betty 311
- Edward (1886-1937) 312
- Edward H. (1888-) 311
- Elizabeth 311
- Ernest J. (1917-2013) 313
- George Franklin (1866-1947) 311
- Jean 311
- Katie J. (1891-) 311
- Kenneth (1925-1976) 313
- Lena 311
- Ralph 311
- Walter 311

Welcomer
- Sherry 110
- William W. 110

Weldy
- Sarah Jane 277

Welker
- Adam Sr. (1869-) 303
- Andrew Michael (1987-) 413
- Debra Marie (1965-) 189
- Esther 107
- Harriet Agatha (1926-2001) 304
- Harry Clayton (1893-1970) 199, 303
- Jennie Louisa (1883-1952) 148
- Larry 148
- Larry C. Jr. (1976-) 148
- Larry C. Sr. (1951-) 148
- Larry Jr. 148
- Marion Caroline (1919-2010) 303
- Nettie E. (1920-1968) 304
- Sallie E. (1885-1947) 345, 439
- Salome Ellen (1904-1976) 103
- Susan Alverta (1898-1962) 414
- Tracy 148
- Tracy (1978-) 148
- Virginia M. (1918-2013) 199, 303

Wells
- (--?--) 456
- Betty J. 272

Welsh
- George A. (1921-2007) 222

Wendt
- Donald (1938-) 164
- Franz 268
- Hilldegard (1937-) 268

Wenrich
- (--?--) 69
- Amanda J. 197
- Anna Mae 216
- Annie Jane (2004-) 291
- Becky 196
- Charles 368
- Claude 384
- David E. Jr. 197
- David Ellis (1952-2006) 197
- Dawn R. 197
- Derron (1993-) 254
- Ellis Clarence (1903-1946) 197
- Hilary M. 197
- Hilda E. (1906-1993) 337, 368
- Jennifer Rose (1978-) 197, 332
- Jessica Ann (1981-) 197, 332
- Joanne 259
- Linn 254
- Lori A. 197
- Lynn L. 197
- Michael (1989-) 254
- Randy E. Jr. 197
- Randy Ernest (1954-2012) 197
- Richard Lee (1955-) 197, 332
- Tammy S. 197
- Whelan Ellis (1932-) 197, 332
- Whelan Ellis (1956-) 197

Wentzel
- Amelia (-2006) 259
- Eva Elizabeth (1856-1898) 181
- Katie (1857-1905) 133

Wert
- Anna Virginia (1918-2008) 432
- Beatrice E. (1924-) 457
- Carol 105
- Earl (-2008) 457

Elizabeth (1794-1864) 143
Jennie 179
Jennie M. 63
Jeremiah Franklin 432
John J. (1901-1962) 143
Mary Louise (1856-1925) 453

Wertz
Albert Clarence 458
Allison Nikol (1993-) 362
Avery Jean (2009-) 270
Brody Michael (2009-) 270
Charles Joseph (2000-) 362
Charles Mervin (1946-) 362
Charles Samuel (1969-) 362
Devin Ray (2003-) 270
Ernest 270
Jacqueline Marie (1990-) 362
Jeanne Alice (1932-) 458
Jeffrey 270
Jillian Mikayla (2005-) 270
Kay 270
Mary 52
Mary A. (1862-1926) 393
Michael 270
Paula Marie 483
Riley 393
Shirley 170

Wesner
Katie 245

Wessner
Carole (1943-) 453

West
Rachel L. 280

Westenberger
Stella 215

Wetherell
Alfonso 61
Ella (1908-2009) 61

Wetzel
(--?--) 438
Alice 101
Andrew 240
Anna Viola (1913-1991) 484
Brenda 199, 303
Carl 480
Carlos Ira (1918-1987) 199, 303
Carol Ann 198
Charles 378
Charles H. (1853-1932) 378
Cheryl 199, 303
Cindy 199, 303
Clayton Allen (1878-1951) 399
David L. Jr. 200
David Lawrence (1939-1999) 200
Dawn 199, 303
Debbie 199, 303
Deborah 200
Della B. (1877-) 378
Denise 200
Dominic F. 198
Donald G. (1940-) 199, 303
E. 157
Emma J. (1879-1894) 378
Gail 199, 303
Gerald C. (1937-1989) 199, 303
Gerald C. III 199, 303
Gerald C. Jr. (1964-2006) 199, 303
Henry E Jr. (1915-1982) 198
Henry III 199
Henry Irvin (1892-1964) 198, 303
Henry Irvin Jr. (1915-1982) 198
Hettie 418
Janet (1927-) 199
Jean R. (1923-1973) 199
Josephine Retta (1912-) 198
Kaden Alan (2003-) 270
Kameron Alan (2005-) 270
Kris Alan 270
Krista 199, 303
Kristy 199
Lillie M. (1878-) 378
Lydia A. (1842-1917) 210
Mary Jane (1933-1998) 200
Matthew 199
Mazie M. (1884-) 379
Micah G. 198
Micah G. II 198
Minnie May (1881-1939) 207
Misti 270
Nelson O. 270
Paul (1920-) 199
Peter 210
Ralph S. (1928-1997) 199
Ralph S. Jr. 199
Raymond W. Jr. 198
Raymond William (1951-2004) 198
Regina 198
Richard (1934-) 198
Richard L. 240
Roger 270
Ronald (1932-1975) 198
Ronald E. (1932-1975) 199, 303
Rose (1922-2009) 199
Rosella M. (1922-2009) 199
Sadie Isabella (1894-1979) 379
Samuel 198
Sandra 199
Sidney S. (1882-) 378
Tamie A. (1875-1915) 378
Wendy 199, 303
William (1934-) 200

Wetzler
Charlotte Fannie (1885-1957) 380
Johyn Nicholas (1853-1942) 380

Weyrauch
Charles R. III 299

Whalen
Frederick 50
George (1865-1945) 50
Helen Mae (1903-1953) 50
Walter Luther (1906-1906) 50
Williard (1912-) 50

Wharton
Michael B. 102
Nancy Darlene 424

Whary
Barry K. 104

Wheary
    Mary Ann (1845-1888) 135
Wheatcroft
    George Thomas III (1960-2002) 360
    George Thomas Jr. (1912-2003) 360
Wheeler
    John 326
    Shawn 439
    Shelby 439
    Stanley 326
    Taylor 439
Whelan
    Willard L. (1912-) 50
Whetstone
    Gary Lyn 58
    Jacqueline Florence (1969-) 58
Whetstone DuClos
    Jacqueline Florence (1969-) 58
Whinney
    Beatrice Mae (1895-1970) 212
Whipple
    (--?--) 209
    Peter 209
Whistler
    Edna M. (1915-) 208
Whitaker
    (--?--) 486
    Brian 486
    Carrie 272
    Meriel Lois (1913-2000) 66
    Stephanie 486
Whitcomb
    (--?--) 56
    Clair Edward (1919-1979) 222
    George 222
Whitcraft
    (--?--) 227
White
    (?)341
    (--?--) 64
    (--?--) 493
    Fannie 227
    Freda 281
    Ivy I. (1908-1973) 82
    Phyllis 251
Whltehead
    Camora D. 274
    Cecil Marie (1897-1986) 272
    Doris Evelyn (1938-) 274
    George A. 274
    Hillary 274
    Janell Marie 274
    John Galen (1901-1983) 274
    Samuel E. 272
    Spencer 274
    Stephen W. 274
    Thomas M. 274
    Tyler 274
    Wayne Schwalm (1926-) 274
    William Dean (1925-2008) 274
Whiteman
    Masry Ellen 222

Whitenight
    (--?--) 474
    Susan 474
Whitesel
    Ron 233
    Vicki 233
Whitman
    Emogene (1936-) 286
    Jarvis Cooper 286
Whitmore
    (--?--) 140
Whitney
    Marion Anna 175
Whittaker
    Raymond 216
Widdows
    Timothy 223
Wider
    Bette Lou 490
Wiedman
    M. 281
Wiegand
    (--?--) 224
Wieman
    Alexandra Clara (1998-) 305
    Benner Matthew (2003-) 305
    David 305
Wiest
    (--?--) 82, 141
    (--?--) (1843-1843) 311
    (--?--) (1940-1940) 68
    Albert Jacob (1908-1994) 178
    Albert Klinger (1849-) 312
    Alice Clara (1896-) 198, 303
    Allan A. (1907-1980) 316
    Allen A. (1907-1980) 316
    Almon L. (1901-1980) 209
    Alta Mollie (1912-) 178
    Amelia (1854-1919) 168
    Amelia Jane Troutman (1849-1918) 203, 241
    Andrew (1965-) 190
    Andy B. (1958-) 178
    Anna Irene (1912-1977) 193
    Annetta Mae (1937-1953) 190
    Anthony (1962-) 191
    Arlee Ila (1919-1954) 162
    Arthur Boyd (1908-1909) 200
    Augustus (1877-1883) 168
    Augustus Monrovia 166
    Barbara (1814-1886) 132, 156
    Barbara Ann (1946-1946) 69
    Barbara Carolyn (1937-1971) 314
    Barbara E. 368
    Barbara Merkel (1832-1894) 146, 457
    Bernita Jane (1939-2000) 191
    Bessie Mildred (1905-1921) 316
    Betty Jane (1956-) 181
    Betty Margretta (1924-) 162
    Beulah (1891-) 100
    Beulah (1906-) 271
    Beulah A. (1889-1890) 208
    Billy Lamar (1932-) 147
    Blair A. (1914-) 68
    Bonnie 201

Name	Page
Bonnie (1946-)	241, 253
Bradley F. (1960-)	68
Brenda (1957-)	336
Brian David (1960-)	190
Brient Arden (1938-)	190
Bryant Harry (1926-2006)	201
Butch (1946-)	162
Carley L. (1927-2014)	208
Carlos Howard (1932-)	190
Carlos Ray (1897-1918)	200
Carol	147
Carol (1962-)	190
Carolyn M. (1946-2010)	191
Carrie (1889-1903)	202
Carrie M. (1898-1962)	194
Carrie S. (1878-1923)	205
Catharina (1816-1868)	150
Catharine (1799-1863)	209
Catharine (1852-1919)	167
Catherine (1816-1868)	143, 150
Catherine Elizabeth (1874-1957)	157, 202
Catherine Trautman (1861-1940)	207
Catherine V. (1886-1921)	201
Charles (1873-)	206
Charles (1882-1943)	168
Charles Leroy (1919-1978)	147
Charles Monroe (1870-1958)	194
Child (1925-)	314
Clara Catherine	166
Clara Katie Elizabeth	208
Clare Elizabeth (1914-)	179
Clarence Austin (1904-1960)	209
Clarence Edwin (1907-1992)	192, 339
Clarence F. (1897-)	313
Claus Maynarc (1939-)	469
Clifford (1903-1922)	165
Clippy (1907-1992)	192
Clyde (1901-1963)	165
Corbin	313
Cynthia (1955-)	190
Cyrus (1883-1964)	166
Daisy Marie (1915-)	147
Daniel (1848-1927)	166
Daniel Jr. (1846-1846)	311
Daniel Merkel (1822-1901)	310
Daniel Merkel (1846-1846)	311
Daniel Oscar (1902-1903)	195
Daniel Schadel (1862-1903)	442
Daniel William (1906-)	314
Darlene (1956-)	190
Darlene Adeline (1929-2006)	189
Darwin Clair (1923-)	181
Daughter	165
David (1964-)	190
David Lynn (1962-)	181
David Richard (1879-)	209
Dawn (1966-)	190
Dawn E.	208
Deborah Elaine (1955-)	163
Deborah Kay	117
Della Jennie (1911-1984)	255
Denise Renee (1965-)	431
Dennis (1957-)	190
Diamond Jack (1876-1963)	166
Dora Bella (1905-1979)	165
Dora Belle (1888-1917)	167
Edward H. (1889-)	206
Edward J. (1889-)	206
Edward Troutman (1854-1927)	206
Edward Witmer (1886-1937)	312
Elizabeth	167, 312, 313
Elizabeth (1849-1924)	166
Elizabeth (1881-)	206
Ella Amanda (1853-1888)	167
Ellen Reba (1958-)	135
Elsie May (1916-)	200
Emma (1871-1945)	198
Emma Catherine (1873-1930)	451
Emma D. (1912-1951)	313
Emma J. (1883-)	205
Emma Jane (1938-)	200
Emma Mary (1861-1927)	489
Emma Ottilla (1901-1960)	316
Emma Schadel (1867-1896)	451
Ennette M. (1937-1953)	190
Erma M. and May E. U. (1903-2014)	208
Ernest J. (1917-2013)	313
Estella Alice (1903-)	178
Eston Edward (1907-1910)	200
Ethel A. (1898-1898)	206
Etta Traphina	208
Eugene (1918-)	208
Eugene Allen	431
Eva Beatrice (1922-1995)	194
Evelyn (1907-)	209
Evelyn L. (1918-)	205
Fairy (1882-1914)	165
Fayette or Feyetta (1859-1862)	168
Felix Klinger (1854-1909)	314
Florence (1888-)	206
Florence Winifred (1907-1980)	316
Flossie T. (1888-)	206
Francis (-1917)	312
Francis (1874-1922)	165
Frank (1866-1947)	311
Frank L. (1897-)	206
Frank Troutman (1851-1925)	205
Frank Troutman Jr. (1897-)	206
Franklin	417
Frantz K. and Francis (1847-)	311
Franz Klinger (1847-)	311
Gabriella (1899-1972)	194
George (1882-1956)	207
George Daniel (1878-1951)	316
George Orin (1879-)	167
Gertrude M. (1908-1908)	206
Gertrude Sophia (1907-1981)	195, 492
Glen Gordon (1946-)	162
Gloria Jean (1945-)	191
Gordon Grant (1885-1953)	162
Gordon Grant (1918-1957)	162
Gordon Grant (1978-)	162
Grace Iona (1932-)	314
Grace Mervine	68
Gregory (1962-)	190
Grovene	366
Guerney (1884-1945)	205
Guy W. (1910-1990)	198
Hallie Marie (1910-)	178
Hannah (1823-1887)	168, 447

Hannah B. (1824-1885)	454
Harper H. (1894-)	313
Harry A. (1893-)	313
Harry Alvin (1922-)	147
Harry George (1906-1962)	314
Harry Jay (1897-1948)	200
Harry Troutman (1844-1917)	186
Harvey E. (1901-)	313
Heidi	201
Heiram Klinger (1846-1864)	313
Helen Louise	316
Helen M. (1921-2006)	200
Helen Myrtle (1908-1914)	315
Henry	312
Henry F. (1923-2011)	200
Henry Morris (1874-1948)	198
Homer (1900-1973)	180
Ida (1873-1943)	166
Ida Carrie	219
Infant Son (1902-1902)	192
Ira Victor (1899-1918)	200
Isaac Timber (1875-1946)	314
Isabella (1857-1938)	168
Jacob	161
Jacob (1775-1811)	132, 209
Jacob A. (1881-1947)	205
Jacob Beisel (1844-1919)	161
Jacob Beisel (1926-1990)	163
Jacob Klinger (1826-1878)	186
Jacob Merkel (1835-1915)	168
Jacob Schadel (1870-1947)	178
Jacob Trautman (1857-)	207
Jacqueline Kay (1956-)	316
James	201
James Allen (1934-)	148
James Kenneth (1954-)	163
Janes (1954-)	163
Jeffrey (1954-)	190
Jemima Amelia (1900-1984)	194
Jennie E. (1886-1888)	208
Jennie Lynn (1950-)	162
Jennie Mae (1886-1975)	163
Jennifer (1968-)	190
Jestina (1828-1872)	209
Johanna (1847-1896)	150, 448
Johannes (1794-1881)	310
Johannes (1851-1851)	313
John	165
John (-2006)	200
John (1878-1964)	200
John A. (1876-1963)	166
John Adam (1903-1921)	200
John Alvin (1904-1924)	195
John Baum (1863-1935)	100
John Baum (1873-1945)	166
John Beisel (1850-1897)	166
John Edward (1882-1883)	203
John Francis	165
John Hokenson (1943-1991)	316
John Jacob (1924-1924)	147
John Klinger (1821-1877)	161
John Robert (1913-1981)	315
John Troutman (1846-1919)	201
Julianna (1848-1922)	311
June	320
June Emma (1930-1977)	201
Katherine (1925-2011)	200
Kathryn Mae (1905-1980)	192
Kathy Jean (1955-)	68
Katie (1888-1888)	311
Katie (1905-1980)	192
Kenneth (Rev.)	316
Kenneth Clyde (1925-1976)	313
Kenneth Rev.	316
Kerry Lynn	320
Kevin (1971-)	190
Kyle (1987-)	68, 330
Laer Jean (1856-1941)	168
Larona A. (1936-)	192, 339
Larry	451
Laura Alvena	311
Laura Alverna (1892-1963)	187
Laura M. (1899-)	208
Laura Mae (1880-1898)	206
Leona (1936-)	192
Lindsey Alene (1984-)	162
Linwood Nevin (1931-1991)	190
Lisa Ann (1963-)	159
Lori Jane (1962-)	163
Lottie (1899-)	313
Luther A. (1906-1975)	159
M. Dillie (1879-1922)	205
Mabel C. (1894-1972)	203
Mabel Edith	208
Mabel M. (1887-1887)	206
Mabel Sevilla (1914-1999)	193
Madelyn Rose (1949-)	316
Maisie Jemima (1900-1974)	191
Maizie (1900-1974)	191
Mamie G. (1901-)	313
Mardell S. (1934-2001)	190
Margaret	207
Maria (1818-1888)	156
Maria (1845-1851)	165
Marie A. (1930-2014)	417
Marlin E. (1936-)	68, 329
Marlin E. Jr. (1958-)	68, 329
Martha	309
Mary (1806-1884)	357
Mary and Polly (1818-1888)	156
Mary Baum (1851-1908)	166
Mary Florence	208
Mary Jane	165
Mary Jane (1875-)	198
Mason N. (1935-)	190
Mattie Elizabeth (1906-)	314
Maude M. (1888-1944)	202
Maurice William (1901-1921)	200
May E. (1906-1958)	202
Maybelle Agnes (1905-1979)	165
Maye (1903-2014)	208
Melanie (1963-)	191
Milton Monroe (1911-2001)	208
Milton Monroe Jr.	208
Minnie Edna (1896-1966)	186
Monroe (1886-)	208
Monroe Trautman (1863-)	207
Moses Merkel (1826-1902)	150, 178, 442
Nathaniel Andrew (1868-1941)	186
Nevin Andrew (1897-1982)	189

Nevin Andrew Jr. (1943-2002) 191
Nicholas Jacob (1979-) 163
Nolan 201
Nolan Heim (1870-1950) 202
Nora 202, 207
Norman Jay (1936-1998) 200
Park Gene (1933-) 159
Patricia Louise (1954-) 181
Philip Penrose (1882-1963) 316
Phoebe J. (1954-) 178
Preston Troutman (1865-1916) 208
Ralph (1898-) 208
Randy 320
Randy Eugene 320
Ray 166
Ray C. (-1995) 253
Raymond 168
Raymond W. (1906-) 208
Rhonda L. (1955-) 178
Richard (1875-) 314
Richard Daniel (1904-1937) 200
Ricky Gene (1958-) 159
Ritschart (1852-1852) 313
Robert L. (1921-2005) 206
Roger Hamilton (1958-) 163
Rojean 147
Roland Allen Jr. (1974-) 163
Ronald Allen (1957-) 163
Ronald E. (1932-) 178
Rose Anna (1913-1976) 315
Roy 209
Roy (1900-1918) 202
Rufus Leon (1888-1972) 68
Ruth (1926-) 206
Ruth C. (1897-1908) 202
Ruth Ethel (1915-1974) 316
Sallie Ann Minerva (1876-) 496
Sallie Baum (1882-1972) 332, 345
Samuel (1795-1867) 132
Samuel (1875-1883) 168
Samuel Baum (1857-1877) 496
Samuel Baum (1878-1957) 180
Samuel Beisel (1845-1922) 165
Samuel Elmer (1912-) 200
Samuel Maurice (1874-1920) 167
Samuel Merkel (1819-1866) 166, 496
Samuel Trautman (1857-1928) 206
Sara Leah (1905-1981) 144, 314
Sarah (1816-1865) 166
Sarah Alice 166
Schartel Klinger (1853-1905) 313
Schertel and Shardel (1853-1905) 313
Sevilla (1859-1862) 168
Sevilla (1878-1945) 166
Shanna M. (1961-) 178
Sheila 201
Sheila Ann (1965-) 68
Shirley 209
Shirley Arlene (1930-1931) 147
Shirley Catharine 200
Son 200
Stella 120
Stella (1911-2007) 206, 321
Stella May (1886-) 206
Sylvester Schadel (1858-1941) 147, 209
Tammy (1968-) 190
Thomas E. (1907-) 314
Tillie 312
Tillie Irene (1916-2002) 147
Tim or Timothy (1875-1946) 314
Tobias Baum (1844-1912) 166
Tucker Adam (1982-) 163
Velma Beatrice (1910-1984) 313
Vernon Francis (1909-1935) 165
Vicky Kay (1959-) 159
Victor Baum (1856-1924) 451
Violet 205
Violet (1932-2012) 200
Violet M. (1924-) 200
Violet May (1908-) 314
Vivian (1916-) 166
Walter (1884-1886) 168
Walter M. (1880-1937) 314
Wendy (1959-) 190
Wendy Kay (1961-) 469
William A. (1895-1975) 147
William Beisel (1848-1929) 165
William Irvin Heim (1868-1938) 202
William Irvine (1903-1968) 314
William James (1876-1959) 314
William Morris (1870-1904) 166
William Oscar (1882-) 208
William Oscar Troutman (1859-1887) 207
William V. Jr. 313
William Victor (1873-1906) 313
Wilma Maxine (1922-1993) 162

Wikel
   Edna 79

Wilbert
   Amanda E. (1862-1942) 404
   George E. 438
   James 438
   James E. (1956-) 438
   Monica Lou (1963-) 438
   Philip (1821-) 404
   Rodney C. (1960-) 438

Wilbur
   Betty Jo (1943-1995) 162
   Marla Rae (1948-) 162
   Winthrop Ray (1922-) 162

Wilden
   Sue 276

Wilfong
   Ryan David (1962-) 173

Wilhelm
   Charles 53
   J. Amson 227
   Mildred E. (1917-1982) 227
   Regena Elizabeth (1922-1986) 53

Wilkins
   Frederick M. (Dr.) (1928-) 149
   Frederick M. Dr. (1928-) 149
   Kimberly Anne (1955-) 149

Wilkinson
   Denise 104
   Steven Lamar (1960-) 174
   Tiffany Ann (1988-) 174
   Timothy Jacob (1988-) 174

Will
    Ed208

Willard
    Allen H. (1910-1991) 146, 182
    Ashton Alan 146, 182
    Daniel C. 50
    Daniel R. (1970-) 170
    Delores Vera (1939-) 146, 182
    Frederick Warren 170
    Jennifer (1976-) 170
    John E. 180
    Lori Ann (1962-1991) 146, 182
    Marshall Wynn 146, 182
    Milton Clair (1882-1932) 50
    Pearl N. (1928-1929) 146, 182
    Samuel M. (1930-2016) 146, 182
    Sheridan Samuel 146, 182
    Shirley Mae (1937-2009) 146, 182
    Warren W. 170
    Wynn Alan 146, 182

Williams
    Andrew Jackson (1830-1879) 49
    Andrew L. (1861-1935) 51
    Anthony 346
    Bertha C. (1930-) 150, 449
    Bessie Ann (1881-1931) 50
    Brian Griffith 441
    Carrie (-2011) 363
    Carrie Ellen (1889-1931) 50
    Donald Eugene (1950-1950) 325
    Donna Jean 324
    Dorothy L. (1904-1976) 422
    Edwin S. 297
    Elsie 136
    Ervin John 471
    Fred E. (1908-) 150
    Gary Ramon (1950-1969) 441
    Genevieve 275
    George Howard (1886-1956) 50
    George W. (1858-1932) 50
    Glenn P. Jr. 441
    Glenn P. Sr. (-2005) 440
    Helen C. (1904-1995) 327
    Holly M. 441
    James 441, 471
    Jamie Wayne 325
    Janet Marie 86
    Jarad Andrew (1982-) 308
    John 255
    John Wesley (1857-1912) 49
    Kathryn 384
    Kenneth O. (1917-) 308
    Kenneth Wayne 325
    Lavina May (1884-1938) 50
    Lee (1918-1972) 324
    Lovina Mae (1884-1938) 50
    Luther C. (1927-) 150, 449
    Mallory Michelle 325
    Mary Elizabeth (1880-1941) 49
    Michael John (1970-) 308
    Morgan Reid (1993-) 346
    Raymond George 440
    Ruth A. (1893-1953) 50
    Ryan Todd (1975-) 308
    Sandra Lee 324
    Sheila J. 441
    Steve (1949-) 308
    Susan 294
    Thomas 404
    Thomas L. 422
    Walter Stanley (1901-1926) 297
    Zachry 325

Williamson
    Alfred A. (1921-1992) 67
    C. Leonard (1928-2003) 67
    Camille (1983-) 308
    Denise 67
    Elvin (1912-1988) 67
    Erik Paul (1945-) 167
    Estes J. 167
    George Oliver 166
    Harvey (1950-) 167
    Hedwig (1943-) 167
    J. Raymond 167
    James 67
    James A. 67
    Janice 67
    Jessica (1981-) 308
    Jimmy 67
    John (1956-) 308
    Lester Sherlock 166
    Lou Elsie Geraldine 166
    Melanie Brook (1978-) 308
    Nancy (1927-) 167
    Oliver (1954-1972) 167
    Pete (1928-2003) 67
    Richard H. 67
    Samuel 314
    Sara (1854-1890) 314
    Virginia 167
    William 150
    William H. (1858-1947) 166
    William Jr. (-1968) 166

Williard
    (--?--) 425
    (--?--) (-1900) 221
    Alice R. (1940-) 370
    Alvin Ray (1912-1976) 68, 197, 329
    Andy 147
    Ann Marie (1953-) 155, 365, 451
    Anna (1916-) 221
    Annie L. (1891-1959) 332, 363
    Arlene M. 147
    Barbara Sedora (1877-1948) 146
    Brenda Sue 89
    Brooke (1989-) 472
    Carrie A. (1914-1993) 391
    Catherine (1836-1915) 357
    Catherine Elizabeth (1876-1957) 316
    Cheryl Darlene (1948-1985) 495
    Cindy 147
    Clarence R. (1916-1975) 147
    Dale Melvin (1951-2004) 495
    Daniel Franklin 391
    Daniel H. (1888-) 290
    Darwin Randolf (1910-1963) 155
    David Allen (1964-) 337, 445, 495
    Debra Sue (1958-) 68, 329
    Donald R. 370
    Dorothy Evangeline (1881-) 327

Dorsey Angeline (1881-) 327
Douglas Eric (1969-) 433
Edna (1885-1945) 234
Edna Mamie 170
Eli Theodore (1879-1882) 327
Elias (1879-1882) 327
Ellwood Sr. 472
Emma Jane (1884-1973) 329
Ertha 222
Eva M. (1897-) 221
Flora 290
George D. (1844-1902) 55, 356
Geraldine Mae (1945-) 495
Glenn Lincoln (1955-1965) 433
Gurney Edward (1892-) 221
Gurney Israel (1883-1934) 55
Harrison (1850-1917) 146
Harvey McKinley (1897-1934) 329, 495
Helen 482
Henry Oscar (1863-1939) 290
Howard W. (1907-1978) 433
Ivan 494
Jack Russell (1930-2012) 155
Jack Russell Jr. (1955-2016) 155, 365, 451
James L. (1935-2004) 147
Jeffrey Allen (1957-) 156, 365, 451
Jerry 147
John (1910-) 221
John Carl (1940-) 109
John L. (1805-1880) 357
Jonathan 316
Jonathan C. (1848-1929) 316, 363
June Annabelle (1930-) 329
Karen 496
Karl 472
Karly (1998-) 472
Kerry Lamar (1963-) 337, 445, 495
Larry Lamar (1943-) 337, 495
Lauretta E. (1917-) 367
Lee L. (1947-2008) 147
Leroy James (1904-1911) 56
Luke (1980-) 156, 365, 451
Mabel 289
Madison (2000-) 472
Martha Irene (1914-2004) 332, 368
Mary A. (1899-) 221
Mary E. (1872-1954) 471
Mary Elizabeth (1869-1946) 90, 356
Mary McClata (1877-1942) 317
Melissa (1968-) 337, 445, 495
Melvin Harvey (1919-2000) 337, 495
Mitchell 105
Moses Alvin (1889-1953) 329, 368
Patricia Delores (1941-) 330
Patsy (1941-) 330
Perry 482
Perry Harrison (-1986) 494
Ray A. 147
Richard M. (1977-) 495
Robert Leroy 429
Ronald Alvin (1944-) 331
Samuel Morris (1876-1953) 146, 182
Sarah Arlene (1922-2005) 68, 197, 329
Sharon 441
Shelley Roxanne 429

Sherri Ann (1967-) 331
Tammy Jane (1960-) 197, 332
Terry 147
Trudy Darlene (1947-) 332
Wendy Lou (1965-) 331
William 146
William H. (1933-2002) 433
Zach Hershel (1985-1987) 156, 365, 451
Zachary (2000-) 472

Willier
(--?--) 291
Albert F. 269
Arlene Mae (1938-) 288
Bill 291
Carol Ann (1941-) 269
Dud 452
Karen 291
Lillie Ann (1893-1968) 68
Rufus F. (1865-1933) 68
Russell 291
Susan 253

Willow
Sandra (-2014) 336

Wilson
(--?--) 246
Claude Kellogg Jr. 283
Clyde 112
Elinore 427
James Jr. (1960-) 173
John A. 217
Mary J. (1925-2002) 217
Matthew James (1982-) 173
Megan Renee (1985-) 173
Patricia Ann (1938-) 283
Thomas Bryant (1940-) 71

Wingard
Larry Lee 103

Winkelman
H. S. (1880-) 161

Winter
Leanne (1982-) 144
Matthew William (1980-) 144
Timothy Charles (1955-) 144

Wire
Stewart A. Jr. 88

Wirt
James Edwin (1881-1969) 87
Luther C. (1904-1979) 87
Tolbert G. (1907-1997) 87
Violet L. E. (1909-1997) 87
William (1854-) 87

Wise
Charles M. (1903-1971) 417
Charles Marlin (1903-1971) 138, 417
Chester 364
Cindy Mae (1949-2005) 417
D. Richard (1929-) 417
Daniel (1831-) 416
Daniel K. (1899-) 417
Faye P. (1926-) 417
Hattie Naomi (1897-1985) 416
Infant Son (1938-1938) 417
June E. (1925-) 417
Maggie (1872-1948) 416

Mark Franklin (1905-2002) 119, 417
Matilda 73
Neal Franklin (1928-1963) 417
Randy 364
Romain N. (1926-1993) 138, 417
Shelly 364
Shirley E. (1923-) 417
Truman William (1908-1992) 417
William T. (1908-1992) 417

Wisman
    Rae Ann 63

Wisniewski
    Diann 272

Witham
    Donald 178

Witmer
    (--?--) (-1900) 207
    Anna Jane (1932-) 185
    Betty J. (1936-2009) 140
    Cardie A. (1897-1967) 455
    Carol A. 289
    Carrie 175
    Carrie E. (1892-) 207
    Clyde Marvin (1923-) 318
    Daniel (1821-1899) 207
    Edwin 318
    Elizabeth (1849-) 103
    Emma Ruth 414
    Florence 345
    Gary Todd (1962-) 318
    George Edwin (1859-1949) 207
    Harry Ephraim 140
    Ida 312
    Jacob Daniel (1881-1964) 207
    Jeffrey 370
    Jennie A. (1890-) 207
    Larry Clyde (1957-) 318
    Lilly Adeline 428
    Lizzie S. (1883-) 207
    Louisa (1843-1922) 84
    Magdalena 88
    Mary Florence 140
    Morris R. (1887-1955) 207
    Randy Lee (1960-) 318
    Tonya A. (1970-) 370
    Violet (1940-) 158

Wolf
    Catherine 207
    Clara Milissa (1863-1929) 379
    David 440
    Edward R. (1913-1956) 312
    Ella (1867-1896) 93, 451
    Eva (1872-1906) 93
    Gladlis (1925-) 312
    Harvey E. (1891-1960) 312
    Henry H. (1838-1896) 379
    John C. (1843-1921) 93, 451
    Lawrence D. (1919-1963) 312
    Mary A. (1867-1943) 208
    Melvin S. (1910-) 312
    Nevin L. (1911-1969) 312
    Oscar W. (1889-1953) 312
    Sara 182
    Sarah E. (1910-) 182
    Virgie R. (1891-1972) 340

William Oscar (1889-1953) 312

Wolfe
    (--?--) (1894-1894) 312
    Adam H. 51
    Alfred Jacob (1874-1956) 78
    Alice Estella (1932-1981) 52
    Alison 259
    Allen C. (1919-2013) 78
    Allen Henry (1907-1944) 170
    Amy Jean (1979-) 414
    Barbara 78
    Billy Elias (1932-1995) 170
    Brenda Lee (1962-) 170
    Bruce Allen (1945-) 170
    Carol Elaine (1942-) 171
    Chase Every (2005-) 170
    Clarence Elias (1899-1945) 78
    Dale R. (1927-2010) 52
    Denise S. 421
    Dewey (1940-) 52
    Donald Edgar (1925-2003) 421
    Donald T. (-2009) 421
    Doris M. (1926-2013) 51
    Ellen 249
    Emily Christine (1986-) 414
    Frederick Wayne (1937-1995) 421
    Gally (1919-2013) 78
    George 421
    George (-2006) 259
    George Stanley (1928-1992) 421
    George W. 421
    Glen Alan (1965-) 171
    Glenda L. 52
    Henry (1823-1896) 311
    Henry A. (1852-1915) 311
    Hilda I. (1921-1976) 151
    Jacob Milton (1880-1950) 170
    Jean 78
    June (1950-) 170
    Larry Errol (1946-1973) 170
    Laurie Ellen (1983-) 414
    Lottie M. (1884-1981) 81
    Maria (1838-1913) 126
    Marian J. (1922-2013) 78
    Mark Elmer (1971-) 171
    Mary (1886-) 312
    Michael 259
    Millie Marie (1940-) 171
    Nathan Thomas (1981-) 414
    Nora S. (1901-) 312
    Norman Henry (1900-1960) 51
    Ralph Eugene (1896-1963) 421
    Ralph Eugene (1924-1971) 421
    Robert Albert (1949-) 88, 170
    Robert Allen (1925-) 88, 170
    Sandra Lee (1947-) 170
    Sarah A. 372
    Simon Larry (1971-) 170
    Thomas Franklin 414
    Thomas Samuel (1946-) 414
    Tom 421
    Twila Naomi (1933-) 171
    Violet (1926-) 78
    Violet Ismay (1930-) 170
    W. Clarence (1899-1945) 78

Walter W. (1903-1984) 51
William L. (1877-1904) 51
William Walter (1925-1998) 51
Wojtek Mackiewicz (1973-) 170

Wolfgang
   Adam L. (1980-) 198, 245
   Alfred (1928-) 197, 245
   Allen Stanley (1935-) 339, 446
   Amelia Elizabeth (1876-1943) 252
   Anna Irene (-1976) 434
   Bella (1874-1950) 249
   Carrie and Flora E. (1887-1951) 256
   Cartie 181
   Catherine A. (1856-1917) 257
   Charles Edward (1907-1976) 52
   Charles Monroe (1878-1938) 52
   Clara Estella (1887-1951) 256
   David (-2010) 439
   Deborah K. (1953-) 245
   Earl Alfred (1937-) 339, 446
   Fronie E. (1898-1941) 169
   Gail 472
   George 52
   George (-2006) 153
   Glenn D. 339, 446
   Helen Mae (1903-1965) 52
   Jacob (1826-1908) 257
   Jared Michael (1992-) 271
   John Garret 271
   John R. 271
   Lovina 309
   Mae Irene (1934-) 339, 446
   Maria 257
   Mary 344
   Mary E. (1880-1964) 256
   Mary Kathryn (1925-2006) 153
   Paul (1852-1919) 249
   Randy (1958-) 197, 245
   Rebekah Sue (1987-) 198, 245
   Stanley A. (-1991) 339
   Tory Isabelle (1874-1950) 249
   Ursula H. (1895-1993) 482
   Violet Gladys (1913-2006) 52
   Warren Carl (1921-1977) 52
   Wayne Lester (1926-2010) 439
   William Earl 245

Wollum
   Carla Justine (1985-) 286
   Henry Marshall (1988-) 286
   Henry Marvin 286
   Henry Michael (1950-) 286

Wood
   Charles 189
   Louis E. (1921-2009) 189

Woodall
   Bryan K. 421
   Earl Leroy (1917-2000) 421
   Ellen L. 421

Woodbridge
   Addie Rebecca 380

Woodbury
   Laurie 297

Woodridge
   Ada E. (1894-1968) 281
   William A. 281

Woodring
   Emily (1988-) 193, 339, 446
   Homer E. Jr. (1954-) 192
   Homer E. Sr. (1926-2001) 192
   Marion E. (1925-2002) 192
   Mary E. (1933-) 124
   Sarah Elizabeth (1986-) 193, 339, 446

Woodruff
   Dean 464
   Debra 464
   Lee 464
   Michael 464
   Richard Lee (1942-2009) 464

Woods
   Elisa Donee (1989-) 235
   Francis Joseph III (1952-) 256
   Francis Joseph Jr. 256
   Frank (1965-) 235
   Joan Ellen (1956-) 256
   Richard Russell (1954-) 256

Workman
   Columbus Jay 275
   Danny 275
   David 276
   Dean 275
   Donna M. (1932-2013) 276
   Michael 276
   Nancy 276
   Nina G. 276
   Ronald (1935-) 276
   Ronald Floyd (1904-1995) 275
   Sarah 211

Wormer
   Florence 214

Worrell
   Harriet (1904-) 377
   Hazel C. (1896-) 377
   Helen (1903-) 377
   Henry C. (1877-) 377
   Jennie M. (1899-) 377
   Mary G. (1898-1930) 377

Wren
   Emma Catherine (1915-1990) 56
   Ira A. 56

Wright
   Charles C. (1915-) 86
   Clayton (1815-) 98
   Colleen (1960-) 98
   Grace Elizabeth (1999-) 299
   Jeannette 304
   Joyce (1952-) 413
   Lorraine 163
   Mary Cosette (1898-1988) 92
   Mary Ellen (1855-1934) 93
   Nancy Kay (1934-) 86
   Raymond 98
   Timothy 299
   Tina Marie (1962-) 98

Wrightstone
   Edwin Underwood (1874-1957) 62
   Irene Mary (1905-1988) 62

Wrubel
   Carol Ann 113

David Alan 113
James Andrew 113
John Joseph III 113
John Joseph Jr. 113
Michael Anthony 113
Michelle Maria 113
William Thomas 113

Wydra
Adrienne 376
Prisethane (-2012) 376
William Jr. 376
William Sr. 376

Wyland
(--?--) 212
Christopher M. 212
Patricia A. 212
William C. 212

Wynn
Carl (1933-) 384
Clifford Calvin (1924-) 384
David (1906-1947) 314
Dorothy Arline (1916-2007) 382
Elaine L. (1936-) 314
Gayle J. (1935-) 314
George W. 383
George Warden (1902-1968) 383
George Warden Jr. (1922-1988) 383
Geraldine Flora (1931-2008) 384
Grover C. (1892-) 382
Grover Irvin (1914-1974) 382
Ivan (1951-) 434
Karl David (1933-) 384
Katherine Marie (1937-) 382
Keith Larue (1929-) 384
Luke Thomas (1995-) 289
Robert Charles (1919-1945) 382
Samuel David Jr. 289
Samuel Jacob 289

Wyshner
Peter 497
Rose (1909-) 497

Yates
Richard 140
Richard Jr. 140

Yeager
Anna M. (1861-1899) 385
Brandon 107
Brian 74
Carissa 74
Catharine 51
Catharine (1778-1872) 168
Catharine (1800-1865) 49
Crystal Ann 322
Eleanor 117
Elizabeth 404
Elizabeth Amanda (1915-2011) 316
Eugene (-2011) 316
Jennifer 107
Kevin 107
Kevin Jr. 107
Krista 74
Madison 74
Rachelle 107
Wayne 74

Yeakley
Annie F. 341

Yeich
Ray 335

Yeick
Helen (1906-) 139

Yeiter
Blanche 93

Yerger
(--?--) 84
Andrew 84
Cindy 84
Donald 84
Philip 84
Wyatt 84

Yerges
Sallie 327

Yesalavage
Albert A. (1902-1975) 299
Jerome (1935-1978) 299
Kerry Jerome (1961-) 299
Lisa Jane (1967-) 299
Max Adam (1973-) 299
Nicole Marie (1987-) 299

Yingst
(--?--) 80
Margaret 238

Yockey
Glady 272

Yoder
Estella (1889-1979) 281
Franklin Reed 281
Jane 272
John Lawrence 428
Kyle 104
Ruth (-2014) 336

Yohe
Hannah Mayme 212

Yohn
Ruth 260

Yordy
Hannah E. (1842-1904) 379

Young
Ann E. (1949-2014) 125
April 124
Barbara Bowman 327
Benjamin Todd (1987-) 144
Connor 124
Elizabeth D. 240
Emily Margaret (1985-) 144
Homer Joseph (1901-1963) 124
Homer Joseph Jr. (1927-1928) 125
Ida Rebecca (1902-1970) 454
Mary M. 240
Peggy (1949-) 419
Richard Allen (1922-2010) 124
Rodger 128
Ronald R. 124
Susan 293
Todd 124
Todd Alan (1960-) 144

Yourgal
Joseph J. 313

Youse
  Lori 126
Yunginger
  Adam Michael (1992-) 283
  Alexander Reed (1998-1998) 283
  Amy Patricia (2000-) 283
  Michael Edward (1961-) 283
  Ronald Eugene 283
Yurick
  Barbara Ann 282
  Peter 282
Yurkonis
  Adam George (1905-1958) 486
  Julie 488
  Robert (1944-) 488
  Robert Jr. 489
  Scott Louis 489
Yuslum
  Ashley Khristen (1984-) 254
  McKenzie Addison (2007-) 254
  Stephen B. (1957-2016) 254
  Stephen E. 254
  Stephen Tyler (2001-) 254
  Steven Thomas (1982-) 254
Zagnojny
  Joseph Walter (1922-) 66
  Theodore 66
Zanette
  Johanna 159
Zapcic
  (--?--) 401
Zartman
  Alice May (1883-) 380
  Sarah 168
Zdiera
  Eugene 347
  Michael Thomas (1992-) 347
Zechman
  James 455
Zeiders
  Bertha Viola (1896-1967) 373
  Mary 321
  Richard 213
Zemitis
  (--?--) 265
Zerbe
  Allen (1900-2008) 204
  Amanda 268
  Bill 244
  Charles R. (1899-1966) 455
  Corey 244
  David (1844-1926) 100
  Elise (1929-2008) 204
  Elsie E. (1929-2008) 204
  Frank (1862-1945) 168
  Irvin (1926-) 204
  John I. (1926-) 204
  Lola Alberta (1898-1966) 134
  May A. (1922-) 455
Zerby
  Angela (1962-) 319
  James 319
  Karen L. (1958-) 322
  Trisha (1969-) 319
Zhablocki
  Lorraine (1931-) 365
Ziegler
  Chad 138
  Chase (-2016) 138
  John Norris 94
Zimmerman
  (--?--) (1921-1921) 464
  Amanda R. (1886-1960) 52
  Bertie (1882-1882) 52
  Beulah M. (1896-1934) 53
  Catherine E. (1903-1937) 54
  Clair R. (1913-2008) 54
  Craig 256
  Cynthia Ann (1952-) 464
  David Frank 353
  Dianne Jayne (1951-) 464
  Harriet C. (1900-1988) 78
  Henry Franklin (1880-1906) 52
  Ida Sevilla (1884-1959) 52
  Infant (1895-1895) 53
  Jan 256
  Jennie G. (1893-1975) 53
  Jill Denise (1969-) 353
  Joe D. (1969-) 353
  John F. (1860-1934) 51
  Joseph Philip (1985-) 469
  Kate Rebecca (1986-) 469
  Katie (1903-1937) 54
  Kent 256
  Lewis B. 469
  Lewis Samuel (1953-) 469
  Marilyn M. 54
  Nathan Samuel (1891-1945) 53
  Paul Franklin (1917-1977) 53
  Pearl I. (1899-1955) 54
  Raymond P. 54
  Richard 256
  Robert Grant (1919-1981) 463
  Robert Grant (1947-) 463
  Sadie M. (1879-1934) 51
  Samuel 51
  Sandra A. 54
  Sarah (1851-1921) 80
  Sarah Sevilla (1922-1972) 464
  Solly (1889-1890) 53
  Verna M. (1914-2002) 53
  William D. (1871-1960) 463
  William Daniel (1917-1989) 463
  William Grant (1894-1933) 463
Zipf
  Mary E. 334
Zohn
  Edward W. 245
Zon
  (--?--) 292
  Audrianna 292
Zu
  Ming 78
Zunker
  Lawrence 274
  Steven Lawrence 274

Zurawski
    Alan 293
Zurn
    Stephanie 237

Zwiebel
    Aaron Batson (1991-   ) 316
    Colin Batson (1989-   ) 316
    William John 316

www.ingramcontent.com/pod-product-compliance
Lightning Source LLC
Chambersburg PA
CBHW060332010526
44117CB00017B/2805